6th edition

SOCIAL PSYCHOLOGY

David O. Sears
University of California, Los Angeles

Letitia Anne Peplau
University of California, Los Angeles

Jonathan L. Freedman
University of Toronto

Shelley E. Taylor
University of California, Los Angeles

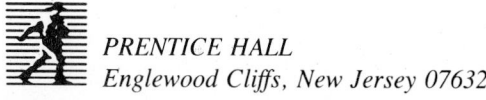

PRENTICE HALL
Englewood Cliffs, New Jersey 07632

Library of Congress Cataloging-in-Publication Data

Social psychology.

   Rev. ed. of: Social psychology / David O. Sears,
Jonathan L. Freedman, Letitia Anne Peplau. 5th ed.
© 1985.
   Bibliography: p.
   Includes indexes.
   1. Social psychology. I. Sears, David O. [DNLM:
1. Psychology, Social. HM 251 S6788]
HM251.F68 1988   302   87–32865
ISBN 0–13–817669–8

Editorial/production supervision: **Hilda Tauber**
Interior and cover design: **Linda Conway**
Manufacturing buyer: **Ray Keating**
Photo research: **Page Poore**

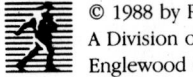

Printed in the United States of America
10 9 8 7 6 5 4 3 2 1

ISBN 0-13-817669-8   01

Prentice-Hall International (UK) Limited, *London*
Prentice-Hall of Australia Pty. Limited, *Sydney*
Prentice-Hall Canada Inc., *Toronto*
Prentice-Hall Hispanoamericano, S.A., *Mexico*
Prentice-Hall of India Private Limited, *New Delhi*
Prentice-Hall of Japan, Inc., *Tokyo*
Simon & Schuster Asia Pte. Ltd., *Singapore*
Editora Prentice-Hall do Brasil, Ltda., *Rio de Janeiro*

CONTENTS

18 POLITICAL PSYCHOLOGY 535

PREFACE

When we wrote the first edition of this book nearly twenty years ago, our task was a much simpler one. The field of social psychology then was relatively new and relatively small. In the intervening decades it has changed dramatically.

There has been an explosion of research and theory, and a corresponding proliferation of journals meeting the specialized needs of social psychologists. There has been a renewed interest in the practical applications of social psychology for understanding urgent social issues. Women and ethnic minorities have been attracted to the field and have enriched it with new perspectives and new research questions. The students who take social psychology courses today are also a more diverse group: Minority students are better represented that ever before; women are now over half the students in American colleges; and more and more older students are taking our courses.

Our book has grown and changed with the times. This sixth edition incorporates the major new topics of research, the outstanding new studies, and the most contemporary examples. But all is not focused on newness; certain basic principles and goals have guided us in the development of this edition.

We believe that social psychology, like any science, is cumulative. As researchers push toward exciting new frontiers, they build on the accumulated knowledge of the field. The new findings of today are best understood as adding to this body of knowledge. Our primary goal in this edition, as in each prior edition, has been to present the "basics" of the field—the core theories and findings that form the shared heritage of our discipline. We believe this has been one of the distinctive merits of the book through its several editions.

We have also been sensitive to the important changes taking place in contemporary social psychology. Over time, the core of the field has gradually shifted. There is less emphasis today on group dynamics, and more on intimate relationships, less interest in attitude change and more in social cognition, and so on. This changing core is reflected in this new edition. We have made every effort to include the most recent new research and the most advanced theories in social psychology.

A third goal has been to offer an integrated presentation of the field. As we discuss different topics, we have tried to keep the main theoretical ideas and traditions of social psychology firmly in view, so that students can see the underlying conceptual continuities in the field. For example, we initially introduce social cognition and attribution theory in our discussion of social perception, and then show how they have been used to understand such topics as attitude change, aggression, prejudice, and bias against women.

The application of research methods and theories to understanding social issues has been a major theme in social psychology. Throughout the text, we highlight ways in which social psychology sheds light on everyday experiences and social problems. We conclude with a section on applied social psychology that explores the most recent research and theory on prejudice, gender roles, environmental psychology, health psychology, and political psychology.

The success of any text depends ultimately on its ability to communicate clearly to student readers and to spark interest in the field. Our goal has been to present materials simply, without oversimplifying. The text is comprehensive, but not encyclopedic. We have written a textbook for undergraduate students, not a handbook of social psychology for professionals. We have paid special attention to selecting examples that illustrate basic principles in a lively way and to sharing our own personal enthusiasm for the field.

Special Features of the Sixth Edition

This book has been successful throughout its life. Although our basic philosophy about the text remains the same, much has changed in the sixth edition. We think that the old book was good, but we have not left well enough alone. Here are some of the main features of the sixth edition.

SHELLEY TAYLOR JOINS THE AUTHOR TEAM   A strong team can often benefit from the addition of new talent, particularly as the directions and emphases of a field change. We are fortunate to have Shelley Taylor bring her impressive expertise to this new edition. Shelley is the author of a bestselling book on *Social Cognition* (with Susan T. Fiske) and a leading textbook in *Health Psychology*. Her contributions are particularly evident in the completely revised chapter on social cognition and in the new chapter on health psychology.

ORGANIZATION   The book is organized to provide a systematic presentation of the material. Two beginning chapters on theory and methods are followed by five major sections that progress from individual-level topics to dyads and groups, and then to specific applications of social psychology.

Part One on social perception includes expanded coverage of new work on social cognition and attribution. Part Two presents work on attitude theory, attitudes and behavior, and attitude change. Part Three discusses interpersonal attraction, personal relationships, aggression, and prosocial behavior. Part Four on groups incorporates work on conformity and compliance as well as group behavior. Part Five on applied social psychology has chapters on prejudice, gender, environmental psychology, health psychology, and political psychology. We think that this sequence will fit well with the teaching preferences of many instructors. However, each chapter is self-contained and so the chapters can be used in any order.

STYLE   We have made a major effort to keep the clarity and interest level of the text high. As in previous editions, we have kept the level of writing non-technical, and geared for the beginning student of social psychology. We have scrutinized every line of text, every table and figure, and every photograph. We enlisted the aid of undergraduates in our classes to help make the book readable. We have included many concrete examples. For instance, the book begins with several vignettes about social behavior for students to ponder. These illustrations raise questions about such topics as conformity, bystander intervention, and TV violence. In Chapter 2, we use specific studies that address the topics in these vignettes to illustrate different research methods.

LEARNING AIDS   Various teaching aids further increase the effectiveness of the text. Each chapter begins with an outline. At the end of each chapter is a comprehensive summary of major concepts and findings. Key terms, which are shown in boldface in the text, are listed at the end of each chapter and are defined in the glossary. Each chapter includes suggestions for further reading. The bibliography at the end of the book is extensive and up-to-date.

HIGHLIGHTS OF NEW CONTENT   This edition provides a comprehensive survey of the mainstream of contemporary social psychology. In every chapter we present both classic early studies that shaped the field and the best of very recent work. The new additions to this edition reflect two major trends in social psychology today: greater interest in the cognitive side of social psychology and greater attention to the application of social psychology to practical problems. Some of the highlights of new material in the sixth edition are:

- A completely revised chapter on social cognition presents the most active research areas in social psychology such as cognitive heuristics, categorization, salience, schemas, and person memory.

- The latest work on attribution processes is presented, including new material on the role of attributions in emotion, self-handicapping, false consensus, and learned helplessness.

- An updated discussion of attitudes gives major coverage to the elaboration-likelihood model of attitude change, especially research on peripheral cues, argument strength, repetition, and forewarning.

- Two chapters on interpersonal attraction and personal relationships include the latest research on loneliness, physical attractiveness, and social exchange theory, as well as a new "triangular" theory of romantic love.

- A completely revised chapter on prejudice presents major theories of prejudice, and includes the latest work on cognitive processes in stereotyping, social identity theory, and contact theory.

- A new chapter on health psychology discusses when and why people practice good health behaviors, how people know when they are sick and need treatment, how stress affects illness and how effective coping can mute the effects of stress, and how people adjust to long-term disability and disease.

- A new chapter on political psychology has sections on personality and politics, voting behavior, racial and gender conflict in politics, political socialization, mass media and politics, and international conflict and peace research.

- A chapter on gender in social life supplements the extensive coverage of gender throughout the book and provides in-depth coverage of gender stereotypes, androgyny and gender differences in social behavior, including new methods of meta-analysis that have challenged our views about sex differences in several areas.

Instructor's Manual and Study Guide

The text is accompanied by a comprehensive *Instructor's Manual with Tests* prepared by Gary T. Long. The manual outlines learning objectives for each chapter and provides detailed suggestions for lectures. Also included are numerous ideas for classroom discussions, student projects, paper topics, and other activities. There is a complete listing of films, references, and other materials to enrich the course. An extensive testbank of multiple-choice questions test students' recall of material as well as their ability to comprehend and apply the concepts presented in the text. Essay questions are also provided.

An important new feature of this edition is a student *Study Guide* prepared by Albert T. Smith and Deborah Prentice. For each chapter, the guide includes a detailed outline, a set of learning objectives to highlight the most important material, and a section on key terms and concepts. Multiple-choice questions permit students to test their own mastery of each chapter and aid in effective studying. Suggestions for student activities are included to enhance the learning of materials in the text.

ACKNOWLEDGMENTS

Special thanks go to Carolyn Drago, Julie Verette, Monique Watson, and Leigh Anne Locke for their invaluable help in researching and preparing this manuscript. We are grateful to Prentice Hall for continuing support, and especially to our Psychology Editor, Susan Finnemore, and to Hilda Tauber, production editor. We appreciate also the useful feedback we have received from students who have used this book. Finally, this text has benefited greatly from the thoughtful reviews of the manuscript by Professors Howard Friedman, University of California, Riverside; Tom Gilovich, Cornell University; and Richard Reardon, University of Oklahoma.

ABOUT THE AUTHORS

David O. Sears

Letitia Anne Peplau

Jonathan L. Freedman

Shelley E. Taylor

David O. Sears is Professor of Psychology and Political Science, and Dean of Social Sciences, at the University of California, Los Angeles. David received his B.A. in History from Stanford University, and his Ph.D. in Psychology from Yale University in 1962, and has taught at UCLA since then. He has been a visiting professor at Harvard University and the University of California, Berkeley, and a Guest Scholar at the Brookings Institution. He has served on the review panel on social psychology for the National Science Foundation, on the Council of Representatives for the American Psychological Association, and on the Board of Overseers of the National Election Studies. His duties at UCLA have included service as Chair of the Social Psychology program and of the Human Subject Protection Committee. His other books include *Public Opinion* (with Robert E. Lane), *The Politics of Violence: The New Urban Blacks and the Watts Riot* (with John B. McConahay), *Tax Revolt: Something for Nothing in California* (with Jack Citrin), and *Political Cognition: The 19th Annual Carnegie Symposium on Cognition* (edited with Richard R. Lau). He has published articles and book chapters on a wide variety of topics in social and political psychology, including attitude change, mass communications, ghetto riots, political socialization, voting behavior, and racism.

Letitia Anne Peplau is Professor of Psychology and Director of the Graduate Program in Social Psychology at the University of California, Los Angeles. Anne received her B.A. in Psychology from Brown University and her Ph.D. in Social Psychology from Harvard University. Since 1973, she has taught at UCLA, where she helped to found the campus Women's Studies Program and has developed popular undergraduate courses in the psychology of gender and close relationships. Her other books include *Loneliness: A Sourcebook of Current Theory, Research and Therapy* (with Daniel Perlman) and *Close Relationships* (with Harold H. Kelley et al.) She has published numerous articles and book chapters in social psychology on such topics as loneliness and social support, friendship, heterosexual dating, homosexual relationships, and social power.

Jonathan L. Freedman is Professor of Psychology at the University of Toronto. He received his B.A. from Harvard University and his M.A. and Ph.D. from Yale

University. Jonathan taught at Stanford University where he was assistant and associate professor, and at Columbia University as full professor. He was associate editor of the *Journal of Experimental Social Psychology* and has served on the boards of many other journals. His early work was on various topics in social influence, compliance, and deviancy, resulting in his book *Deviancy* (with Anthony Doob). He has studied the effects of crowding, and his book *Crowding and Behavior* won the American Psychological Association Gold Medal Award. The effects of time pressure, psychology and law, and the effects of incentives are his current research topics.

SHELLEY E. TAYLOR is Professor of Psychology and Chair of the Health Psychology program at the University of California, Los Angeles. Shelley received her A.B. in Psychology from Connecticut College and her Ph.D. in Social Psychology from Yale University. She taught at Harvard University until 1979 when she joined the faculty at UCLA. She has won a number of awards for her work including the American Psychological Association's Distinguished Scientist Award for an Early Career Contribution, and a Research Scientist Development Award from the National Institute of Mental Health. She is currently an Associate Editor of *Health Psychology* and has served on the editorial boards of many other journals. Her other books include *Social Cognition* (with Susan T. Fiske) and *Health Psychology*. She has published numerous articles and book chapters in social cognition and health psychology.

1 INTRODUCTION

■ WHAT DO SOCIAL PSYCHOLOGISTS STUDY?
    First Impressions and Lasting Relationships
    Conformity and Attitude Change
    Violence on Television and in the Streets
    Woman in Distress: No One Came to Help
    The Eichmann Defense: Just Obeying Orders

■ THE SOCIAL PSYCHOLOGICAL APPROACH

■ THEORIES IN SOCIAL PSYCHOLOGY

■ LEARNING THEORIES
    Learning Mechanisms
    Distinctive Features

■ COGNITIVE THEORIES
    Basic Principles
    Causal Attribution
    Social Cognition
    Distinctive Features

■ MOTIVATIONAL THEORIES
    Need Satisfaction
    Rational Decision Making
    Social Exchange
    Distinctive Features

■ SOCIOLOGICAL THEORIES
    Symbolic Interaction
    Social Roles

■ BIOLOGICAL THEORIES
    Instinct
    Sociobiology
    Individual Differences

■ SOCIAL PSYCHOLOGY TODAY

WHAT DO SOCIAL PSYCHOLOGISTS STUDY?

Social psychology is the systematic study of social behavior. It deals with how we perceive other people and social situations, how we respond to others and they to us, and in general how we are affected by social situations. To start with, let us take a look at the kinds of things social psychologists are interested in understanding. Here are five vignettes, each illustrating a somewhat different area of interest in social psychology.

First Impressions and Lasting Relationships

While you are driving to class, listening to some music on the radio, you are suddenly jolted out of your dreamlike state by a young woman who cuts in front of you. She is driving a bright red sports car considerably faster than the speed limit. She speeds on, finally squealing around a corner and disappears into the distance. You are a little startled, but then you reflect on the experience. You are surprised to find how quickly you came to have a strongly negative feeling toward her, even though you had only the briefest encounter. You quickly categorized her as a spoiled rich kid, probably from the wealthy neighborhood up in the hills near the campus. You also find that you came to a quick judgment about the causes of her behavior—you concluded that she cut in front of you because she is a generally reckless driver, not because she was avoiding a pothole or another driver or because she was getting ready to turn. When you think about it, you are a little surprised to realize that you have such a clear impression of a person with whom you have had only the briefest and most fleeting contact.

Then your mind drifts to the mixer you went to last Friday afternoon. You start to think about Mark, the student you met and talked to for about three-quarters of an hour. He seemed quite attrac-tive and had a good sense of humor. Your room-mate's brother went to high school with him and said he was a good student and people liked him. But you wonder. You noticed that he was wearing a religious medallion, and it is not your religion. He talked about going to religious services earlier in the week, so he seems to be fairly religious himself, and you are not. You had been telling him about the beautiful house your mother had just put on the market with her real estate firm, and Mark had asked how your father felt about that because he wasn't sure *he* wanted his wife to have a full-time job. You were certainly interested in Mark, but you have begun to wonder. How impor-tant is attractiveness over the long haul? What about differences in values? Are those issues that can iron themselves out over time, or be negotiated to mutu-ally satisfactory agreements? Or do they just get more important over time, causing increasing amounts of conflict? What kinds of problems might they create? How could those problems be dealt with?

Social relationships always involve elements such as these. They raise many questions about how we form impressions, what is important in a relationship, how relationships change over time, and so on. The study of interpersonal relationships is central to social psychology.

Conformity and Attitude Change

In your modern history class, you see a documen-tary on student protest on your campus in the 1960s. All the students have long hair and wear jeans and various kinds of old clothes. The males all seem to have beards or mustaches. They are passing mari-juana cigarettes around, and they are constantly coming together in crowds, carrying signs and pos-ters, and listening to speakers argue politics. There

A couple celebrates their 40th wedding anniversary. What factors have kept this marriage together for so many years, while other marriages end in divorce?

mentary? How can everything be so different? Why are students today so much less interested in protest? Why did students in the 1960s seem so upset and angry about everything? Where did their attitudes come from? Have their attitudes changed? Are they now driving imported cars and living in the suburbs and wearing coats and ties or dresses to work every day? What about the overt behavior the students were exhibiting? Is everyone just an incredible conformist, so that whatever clothing or hair style is in fashion is adopted by everyone?

You do not feel much like a blind conformist yourself, yet you notice that you are dressed much like everyone else. What makes people behave so similarly? And what about those large groups and crowds the 1960s students got into? What makes people join such groups? How are people different when they are in groups? Does a group make people do extreme things? Hostile things? Out of the corner of your eye, just as you are lost in these thoughts, you see two students walking along in punk rock outfits, and you see that one of them was your straight roommate's best friend in junior high school. What *is* going on?

Violence on Television and in the Streets

is an atmosphere of rebelliousness, of great activity in large crowds, and certainly a feeling of general carelessness, sloppiness, and untidiness about personal appearance.

After the film, you walk out onto your late 1980s campus. The students all are quite nicely dressed, and some of the clothes look quite expensive. Everyone is neat, clean, and tidy. The men all have fairly short hair. The students occasionally see someone they know and call out a greeting to them. No one seems to be angry or rebellious; on the contrary, almost everyone is smiling and friendly. There are no crowds, just groups of two or three or four friends walking along or talking. There are no signs or posters in evidence, or anything political at all. War and protest seem a million light years away.

Why have things changed so much? Can this be the same campus that was shown in the docu-

Violent crime is a major problem in America. All over the country, people have become afraid to leave their homes at night because of the danger of being assaulted. For example, 47 percent of those surveyed in 1982 (National Opinion Research Center) said there were areas within a mile of their homes where they would be afraid to walk alone at night. Many observers have noted that the rate of violent crime has increased during the same period that television has become the dominant entertainment medium in America. Almost all Americans seem to watch huge amounts of television—virtually every household has a set, and the average set is on about seven hours a day. Young people are exposed to enormous amounts of television: By the age of 18, the average American child has spent 20,000 hours watching television, more time than they spent in classrooms, churches, and all other educational and cultural activities put together.

Much television programming depicts violent physical force. By the early 1980s, prime-time television exposed viewers to almost five acts of violence involving physical force per hour, involving more than half of all the leading characters in prime-time shows. And almost three-fourths of all the shows contained violence (Comstock, 1982).

Many have linked these two developments and concluded that such widespread crime must stem at least in part from violent television. Sometimes they offer vivid anecdotes to support this view. For example, in San Francisco, an 11-year-old girl was raped with a soda bottle shortly after a television movie had depicted an assault with a similar weapon. In Miami, the lawyer for a boy who had killed someone pleaded that the boy was not responsible for the death because he was just imitating what he had seen on television. The belief that television violence causes crime is widely held. In the mid-1970s, the national PTA began a campaign to monitor television content. The American Medical Association adopted a resolution calling on broadcasters to reduce television violence as a menace to the nation's health. An advisory committee to the U.S. Surgeon General said there was reasonable evidence of a link between television violence and aggressive behavior.

The origin of violent crime, or of aggressive behavior in general, is a central topic for social psychology. That violent television breeds violent crime is a popular theory. But is it true? And if so, under what conditions does media violence have such an effect? Does it occur for all kinds of people? Of all ages? What about the effects of going to a boxing match, or watching a football game? In asking whether or not viewing television violence increases aggression, we may really be raising a more general question: Namely, what are the effects of watching *any* kind of violence, be it on television or anywhere else? These are among the many questions social psychologists have raised about violence.

Woman in Distress: No One Came to Help

At about 9 P.M. on Sunday, March 6, 1983, a 21-year-old woman walked into a bar in a blue-collar

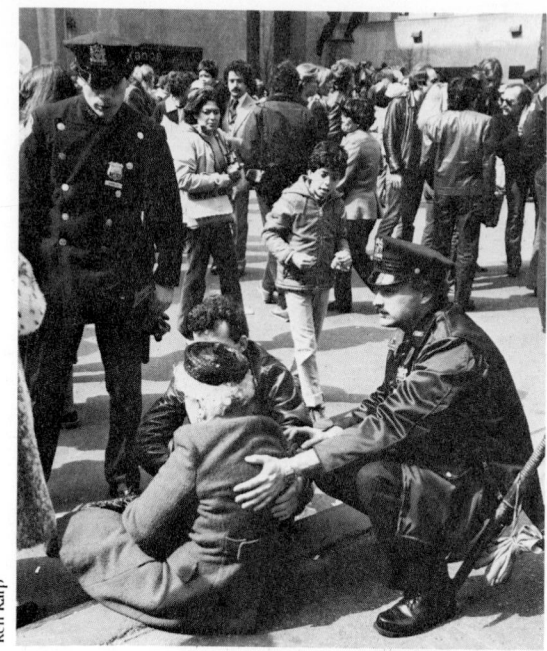

Ken Karp

Why does this woman get help, unlike those in the text? Why is it only police officers who seem to be helping?

neighborhood of New Bedford, Massachusetts, and stopped to have a drink. She later stated that when she tried to leave, a man blocked the door, tackled her, stripped off her clothes except for a sweater, and attacked her. Two other men held her down and tried to force her to perform oral sex acts. As she struggled, screaming and pleading for help from the other customers at the bar, she was lifted onto the pool table and raped. In the words of the police, "She cried for help, she asked for help, she begged for help—but no one helped her." The bartender told police he gave a customer a dime to call the police, but that the customer dialed a wrong number. No one went to the woman's aid, the bartender said, because one of the attackers brandished a butter knife.

The woman finally broke free and ran out of the tavern, naked from the waist down. She flagged down a car, and the driver took her to a telephone. She was treated at a hospital and released. Police later arrested six men between the ages of 23 and 26, though the men who witnessed the incident did not come forward. Under public pressure, the bar owner handed in his liquor license two days later, and the bar was closed for good. Ultimately, four men were convicted of aggravated rape, and given long prison sentences.

There have been other highly publicized cases of refusal to help, notably that of another young woman, Kitty Genovese. On March 13, 1964, as she was coming home from work late at night, she was attacked and repeatedly stabbed in front of her apartment building in Kew Gardens, New York. During her half-hour struggle with the attacker, she repeatedly screamed that she was being stabbed and begged for help. Thirty-eight people living in adjacent houses and apartments later said they had heard her screams. But no one came to her aid or even called the police. They said they did not want to get involved. The police were not called until twenty minutes after she died; then they arrived in two minutes. Even then, none of her neighbors would come out onto the street until an ambulance arrived to take her body away.

Why did no one help? How did the bystanders perceive these two victims? How did they perceive their own responsibility and the morality of what they and others were doing? Furthermore, how can we explain the fact that in other situations, bystanders often do volunteer assistance. We know of instances where volunteers work tirelessly for long hours to save the lives of people trapped by earthquakes, floods, or accidents. Or cases where passers-by risk their own lives to help someone being mugged on the street. At times, people act helpfully, even heroically toward total strangers. Under what conditions do people step forward to help others, and when do they just passively permit suffering to continue? Social psychologists are concerned with uncovering the answers to these questions.

The Eichmann Defense: Just Obeying Orders

Before World War II, nearly 9 million Jews lived in Europe. The European Jewish community had had a long and brilliant tradition of culture, artistic and intellectual achievement, and religious devotion. Adolf Hitler and the Nazi party came to power

Nazi official Adoph Eichmann testifies from a bullet-proof booth. An Israeli court found him guilty of sending Jews to their death, thus rejecting his claim that he was innocent because he merely obeyed orders.

in Germany in 1933, contending that the Aryan race was superior to such "mongrel races" as the Jews and gypsies, and that Europe needed to be racially purified. Within a few years, the Nazi regime had begun to arrest and imprison Jews in Germany. By 1939, when Germany invaded Poland, hundreds of thousands were already in concentration camps.

Soon thereafter, Nazi officials began secretly exchanging memos on "a final solution to the Jewish problem." Under the effective management of Adolph Eichmann, a dedicated career bureaucrat, Jews throughout Europe were systematically rounded up and shipped to concentration camps such as Dachau and Auschwitz, where they were starved, gassed, shot, cremated, and buried in mass graves. By 1945, when World War II ended, about 6 million European Jews had died. Of those Jews who had lived before the war in the 21 countries fully occupied by the Germans, three out of every four were dead. Atomic bombs would have had to have been dropped on a hundred cities to have killed as many Japanese.

Eichmann fled to Argentina after the end of the war, where he was ultimately captured by Israeli investigators in 1961. He was taken to Israel and tried for murder. His defense was that he was not personally responsible for the deaths of the Jews, because he had simply been following orders. The argument was rejected, and he was held accountable for his crimes and put to death. The "Eichmann defense" has come to stand for the claim that a person is justified in committing terrible actions because he or she is "just following orders."

There can be no question that the virtual annihilation of the European Jewish community could have been carried out only with the conscious cooperation of thousands of ordinary Germans—bureaucrats, soldiers, janitors, doctors, railroad workers, carpenters. Did these behaviors emerge from pathological characteristics of the German people? More frighteningly, did they arise out of the normal operation of everyday social processes, such as simple obedience to authority? Under what conditions will people commit terrible acts when ordered to? For social psychologists, such events raise fundamental questions about obedience to authority and the conditions under which people will comply with or resist directives that violate their own standards of morality.

THE SOCIAL PSYCHOLOGICAL APPROACH

Social psychology begins with the study of perceptions and attitudes: how people perceive each other, how they interpret other people's behavior, and how their attitudes form and change. It includes all forms of interaction between people—attachment and affiliation, liking and close relationships, aggression, altruism, and conformity and influence. It is concerned with how people act in groups and how groups affect their members. The ideas and methods of social psychology have been applied to such topics as prejudice, political behavior, sex roles, the effects of the environment, and social factors in physical health. The discipline of social psychology tries to answer any and all questions about how people affect one another and how they behave in social situations. Not all of these questions have been answered fully. The job of social psychologists is to ask the important questions and then to look for answers.

Of course, many other fields also deal with these matters. Sociologists, urban geographers, anthropologists, economists, political scientists, and other types of psychologists are all concerned with social behavior. What is distinctive about the social psychologist's approach? At the simplest level, scholars from the other social sciences tend to use the *societal* level of analysis—they use broad societal factors to explain social behavior. People behave as they do because of economic, historical, or social forces, such as class conflicts, clashes between competing ethnic groups, the crops a particular area can produce, the governmental institutions of the nation, or technological changes in the economy. At the other extreme, clinical and personality psychologists use an *individual* level of analysis—they use the person's individual characteristics to explain behavior. In particular they use each person's unique personality traits and conflicts to explain why we all behave somewhat differently in any given situation.

Social psychologists adopt a level of analysis somewhere in between—what we might call the *interpersonal* level. They mainly explain behavior in terms of a person's current social or interpersonal situation. That social situation would include the other people in the environment, their attributes and their behaviors, the context within which they are acting, and so on. For example, what aspects of other people determine whether we will like them or not? Is physical attractiveness or intelli-

These marchers are protesting the South African government's policy of racial apartheid. What individual, interpersonal, and societal factors might explain this march and the growing opposition to apartheid?

gence more important? What aspects of another person, and a particular situation, will make us more likely to obey? Must the person have an official role? act in an authoritative way? issue commands from an official place, like an office or a laboratory? threaten us with punishment if we disobey? In all these cases, social psychologists seek to identify those aspects of the immediate social situation that determine human behavior.

Let us compare these three levels of explanation in terms of a specific example. Suppose we are interested in analyzing the origins of violent crime. The societal level approach, typical of economists, political scientists, and sociologists, looks for broad social explanations. These social scientists might point out that high rates of violent crime tend to be associated with poverty, rapid urbanization, and the industrialization of a society. To provide evidence for such a conclusion, they might point to certain facts: Poor people commit many more violent crimes than wealthy people do; violent crime is much more common in slum areas than it is in wealthy neighborhoods; crime rates go up in eco-

nomic recessions and drop when the economy recovers. Such explanations simply relate the large social forces on the extreme left of Figure 1–1 with the outcomes shown at the extreme right. They do not concern themselves with individual persons at all, or with their immediate situations.

The individual approach of other disciplines within psychology would tend to look for explanations for crime in the unique histories and characteristics of the criminal individual. Developmental, personality, and clinical psychologists would ask what individual differences lead some people to commit crime when others in seemingly identical situations (city dwellers with the same income, age, race, and so on) do not. To understand the individual differences that lead to crime, they focus on the person's background. How was the person raised? What kind of discipline did the parents employ? Were they abusive or alcoholic or not affectionate to the child? Perhaps abusive parents tend to produce children who do not learn to behave properly, who become angry at the world, or who do not learn the usual cultural values and morals.

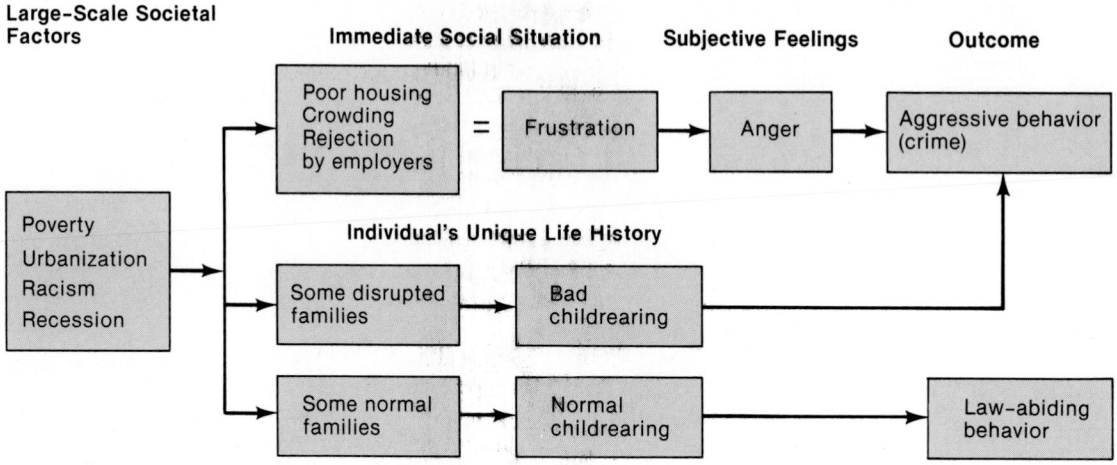

Large-Scale Societal Factors   **Immediate Social Situation**   **Subjective Feelings**   **Outcome**

FIGURE 1–1   **How three different approaches might explain aggressive crime.**

One line of research might compare the incidence of criminal behavior among children who were abused by their parents with that of children whose parents were not abusive. Or it might compare the family backgrounds of delinquent and nondelinquent children, or follow a large group of children over many years and relate their criminal or noncriminal behavior to their family backgrounds. The bottom of Figure 1–1 shows that such analyses focus on how people in the same situation may behave differently because of unique past experiences.

In contrast, the special focus of social psychology is to understand how people respond to immediate social situations. It considers what subjective feelings are generally produced in a particular kind of social situation, and how those in turn affect overt behavior. What kinds of interpersonal situations lead to feelings of anger, and increase or decrease aggressive behavior?

For example, one basic principle of social psychology is that frustrating situations make people angry, and they become more likely to engage in aggressive behavior. This effect of frustrating situations is one explanation for crime. It has been tested in laboratories and in the outside world. This particular relationship can explain not only why aggression occurs in a certain situation, but also why

certain economic and societal factors lead to crime. For instance, people who are poor and crowded into urban slums are frustrated: They cannot buy what they want, cannot get good jobs, cannot live in the way they would like. This frustration may in turn be the direct cause of much criminal behavior. The social psychological approach also usually involves some subjective feelings produced by the interpersonal situation, which in turn influence the individual's overt behavior. In this example, the frustrating situation produces anger, which in turn produces aggressive behavior. Thus the frustration-aggression hypothesis explains criminal behavior at quite a different level from either the societal or individual explanations. It focuses on the immediate social situation and on the subjective feelings such situations produce in people of many different backgrounds.

Each of these approaches is worthwhile and indeed essential if we are to understand complex social problems. And there is, of course, considerable overlap among disciplines in the kinds of studies that are done. The point is that a single question—Why does crime occur?—can be asked and answered in many different ways. The focus can shift from general to specific explanations, and from sociological to psychological processes.

THEORIES IN SOCIAL PSYCHOLOGY

Just as a problem can be studied from different viewpoints by several disciplines, it can be approached within a single discipline from different theoretical orientations. In psychology, students are often introduced to the major comprehensive theories of human behavior popular in the early twentieth century. Almost all psychology students have heard of **psychoanalytic theory** and Sigmund Freud; of **behaviorism** and John B. Watson and B. F. Skinner; of **gestalt** theory and the European psychologists Wolfgang Köhler, Kurt Koffka, and Kurt Lewin. Each of these theories arose from the work of a few charismatic individuals who inspired a fierce sense of loyalty to their own ideas and equally fierce attacks on the supposedly grievous errors of other schools of thought. These pioneers modeled their theories on those of the physical sciences. Their goal was to explain and predict all human behavior, and they wanted theories as detailed, universal, and complete as, for example, atomic theory in physics.

Many of these theories were applied to the analysis of social behavior and to research in social psychology. The idea of developing general theories is useful and important—but in the long run, the problems studied by social psychologists have turned out to be too complex to fit any one general theory. Even so, social psychologists' approaches to a wide variety of different problems have been guided by a few basic ideas easily traced back to the general theories of yesteryear. Present-day controversies are often modern versions of old feuds. We think today's research in social psychology can be understood better if we understand its roots in the large, general theories, developed nearly a century ago.

In the next sections, we present a few of these basic and often rather simple ideas. We do not intend to be comprehensive or detailed; rather, we want to convey their essence and particularly the contrasts between them, so that we can refer to them in explaining controversies in later chapters. To emphasize the contrasts, we will apply each approach to the specific problem of understanding crime.

Consider this situation: At 3 A.M. one morning, a police officer catches a high school dropout, Claude, coming out of the rear door of a liquor store with a bag full of money. The store, like everything else in the neighborhood, has long since been closed for the night. The officer shouts at Claude to stop and put his hands up. Claude turns, pulls a pistol from his pocket, and shoots the officer, wounding him in the leg. Claude is later apprehended and ultimately sent to jail. The statistics predict that Claude's stay in jail will not be productive or happy; it will be costly for society, and the chances of his committing further crimes are fairly high.

Let us consider how researchers using different theoretical approaches would view this event and explain it. We begin with the three major approaches in social psychology—learning theories, cognitive theories, and motivational theories. We also consider two other perspectives from sociology and from biology.

LEARNING THEORIES

For many years, learning theory was the dominant approach in psychology. The central idea in this approach is that a person's behavior is determined by prior learning. Current behavior is shaped by past experiences. In any given situation, a person learns certain behaviors which, over time, may become habits. When presented again with the same situation, the person tends to behave in the same, habitual way. When a hand is extended to us, we shake it, because that is how we learned to respond to an extended hand. When someone says something nasty to us, we may be nasty back or we may try to make the other person like us, depending on what we have learned to do in the past. Learning theory became popular in the late 1920s, spurred by work on association, or "classical" conditioning, by the Russian psychologist Ivan Pavlov and the American John B. Watson. Later, Clark Hull and B. F. Skinner explored principles of reinforcement as they affected learning. As applied to social behavior by Albert Bandura an others, this approach has been called **social learning theory.**

Learning Mechanisms

There are three general mechanisms by which learning occurs. One is **association,** or classical conditioning. Pavlov's dogs learned to salivate at the sound of a bell because they were presented with meat every time the bell was rung. After a while they would salivate to the sound of the bell even in the absence of the meat because they associated the bell with meat. We can learn attitudes by association. For example, the word "Nazi" is generally associated with horrible crimes. We learn that Nazis are bad because we have learned to associate them with terrible things.

A second learning mechanism is **reinforcement.** People learn to perform a particular behavior because it is followed by something pleasurable

One of the most powerful mechanisms of learning is imitation. Children often imitate adults, especially their parents and others they like and respect.

UPI/Bettmann Newsphotos

and need-satisfying (or they learn to avoid behavior that is followed by unpleasant consequences). A boy may learn to retaliate against insults in school by fighting with a tormentor because his father praises him for sticking up for his rights when he does it. Or a student may learn not to contradict the professor in class because each time he does, she frowns and looks angry, and snaps back at him.

A third major mechanism is **observational learning** or imitation. People often learn social attitudes and behaviors simply by observing the attitudes and behaviors of models. A little boy may learn how to light fires in the fireplace by watching his mother do it. Children and adolescents may acquire their political attitudes simply by listening to their parents' conversations during election campaigns. Imitation may occur without any external reinforcement at all, through simple observation of the model.

Distinctive Features

The learning approach has three distinctive features that set it off from the other core ideas in social psychology. First, the causes of behavior are supposed to lie mainly in the past learning history of the individual. Perhaps in Claude's previous encounters with the police, they had been rough, rude, antagonistic, suspicious, and unsympathetic. Perhaps he had been reinforced in the past for responding violently to situations involving conflict with authority, and nonviolent responses had not brought him satisfaction as often. Or perhaps his father often acted in a violent way himself, so Claude had learned to imitate a violent model. The learning theorist is especially concerned with past experience and somewhat less with the details of the current situation.

Second, the learning approach tends to locate the causes of behavior mainly in the external environment and not in the individual's subjective interpretation of what is happening. It emphasizes the external events previously associated with a stimulus, or the past reinforcement contingencies operating on a response, or the role models to which a person has been exposed. All these are external to the individual. Learning approaches would not emphasize, as causes of behavior, such subjective states as perceptions of the situation (for example, whether or not Claude expected the police officer to attack or shoot him), or emotions (for example, whether Claude was fearful or angry).

Third, the learning approach usually aims to explain overt behavior instead of psychological or subjective states. It would try to explain Claude's overt act—shooting the police officer—not his perceptions or thoughts or such emotional states as fear, anger, or guilt. The learning approach would try to explain why Claude's behavior in this situation was violent: He could have argued, run away, frozen in place, or obeyed the officer. Instead, he shot him.

COGNITIVE THEORIES

The main idea in the cognitive approach to social psychology is that a person's behavior depends on the way he or she perceives the social situation. People spontaneously organize their perceptions, thoughts, and beliefs about a social situation into simple, meaningful form, just as they do with objects. No matter how chaotic or arbitrary the situation, people will impose some order on it. And this organization, this perception and interpretation of the world, affects how we behave in social situations.

Basic Principles

This approach to social psychology has been strongly influenced by the ideas of Koffka, Köhler, and other psychologists working in Germany in the 1930s. In their view, people do not perceive situations or events as made up of many discrete elements, but rather as "dynamic wholes." Think about your favorite pop song. When you last heard it, did you perceive the song as a series of individual notes and separate words? Probably not. More likely, you perceived the song as a total unit integrating the relationships among the notes and the meaning of the words. This emphasis on perceiving the environment as a whole that is more than the sum of its parts is known as **gestalt** psychology, from the German word for shape or form. Kurt Lewin applied these gestalt ideas to social psychology, emphasizing the importance of the social environment as perceived by the individual—what Lewin called the person's "psychological field."

A core idea in this perspective is that people tend spontaneously to *group* and *categorize* objects. Put this book down and look around you. Instead of seeing objects individually, you see them as parts of larger groupings. You see a row of books on a shelf as a unit, not as so many individual books. You probably perceive other people in the library in groups—perhaps as students and librarians, or as the line of people at the checkout desk, or as a couple going off for coffee. You experience the pile of dirty dishes by the kitchen sink as an oppressive heap, not as individual dishes. We tend to group objects according to some very simple principles, such as similarity (dishes look more like each other than the stove and refrigerator do, so we group the dishes together), proximity (books stacked in a pile go together; the isolated books strewn all over the library table do not), or past experience (tables and chairs go together; so do David and Goliath or Dick and Jane; but a stove and chair do not, nor do Woody Allen and a B-52 bomber).

Second, you will notice that you immediately perceive some things as standing out (*figure*) and

What do you think is going on in this social situation? Are the police being kind and understanding, or are they causing trouble for an innocent person?

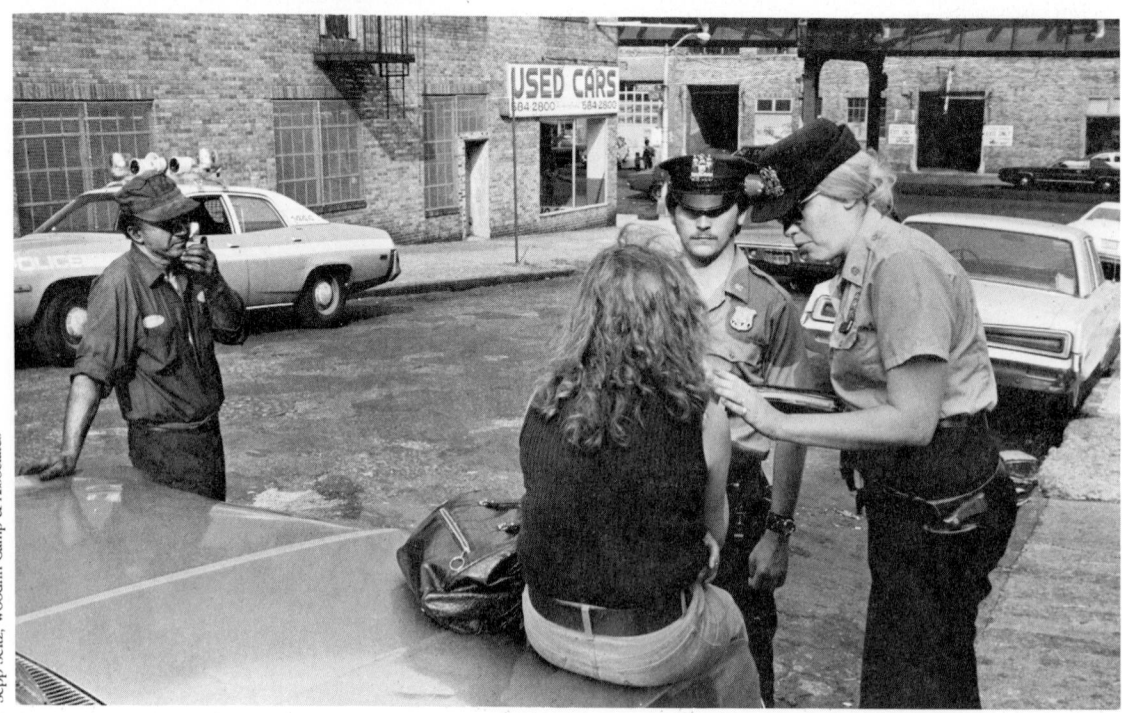

some things as just being in the background (*ground*). Usually we perceive colorful, moving, noisy, unique, nearby stimuli as figure, whereas bland, drab, stationary, quiet, common, faraway stimuli are ground. Our attention is drawn to cheerleaders at a football game not because they are so numerous—there may be only a dozen in a crowd of nearly 100,000 people—but because they move a lot, yell, wave their arms, and wear colorful uniforms. In contrast, we experience the crowd as just that—a crowd—not as a collection of thousands of distinctive, fascinating individuals.

These two principles—that we spontaneously group or categorize the things we perceive, and that we focus attention particularly on the most prominent (figural) stimuli—are central not only to our perception of physical objects, but to our perception of the social world as well. These cognitive principles are important for our interpretations of the intangible aspects of people—the things we cannot see, hear, touch, or smell—such as intentions, motives, attitudes, or personality traits. As social thinkers, we try to arrive at meaningful interpretations of how people feel, what they want, what kinds of people they are, and so forth.

Causal Attribution

One important direction for research has been the study of causal **attributions,** the ways in which people use information to determine the causes of social behavior. For example, how do we decide whether a salesperson's ingratiating behavior is caused by a genuine desire to be helpful as opposed to a desire to butter up a customer for a big sale? Why do you think someone turned you down for a date? Why did one rape victim fight off her attacker successfully, and another make no effort to defend herself? Why did the audience at your music recital give such a loud and enthusiastic response to your performance? The answers to these questions about causes can have a strong influence on our feelings and behavior. Deciding that the recital audience applauded because you gave a flawless performance may lead you to feel proud and to redouble your efforts to become a professional musician. In contrast, deciding that they applauded because they were friends and family who always overlook your faults may not enhance your self-esteem or professional aspirations.

Social Cognition

More recently, the cognitive perspective in social psychology has been fueled by developments in cognitive psychology. Cognitive psychologists study how people process information. As applied to social psychology, research on **social cognition** focuses on how we process social information about people, social situations, and groups. Social cognition researchers examine the flow of information from the environment to the person. Three research areas have been emphasized:

1. *Social perception* research examines the ways people perceive and encode social stimuli. For example, why do we pay attention to some actions that people perform and ignore others? Why do we overlook a person scratching his head, but pay attention if he shouts?

2. *Social memory* research examines how individuals store information about people and social events. The representations that people have in their heads about people and events are called *schemas*. Schemas represent the integrated knowledge we have about our social environment, including the people and events we frequently encounter. Research on social memory has focused on how people retrieve information when they need it. For example, how does an eyewitness to a murder store information about the crime? How can the prosecutor best help this witness to remember specific details of the event?

3. *Social judgment* research examines the ways people integrate or put information together to arrive at inferences and conclusions about the social world. For example, when students visit colleges to decide which one to attend, how do they sort the information they have gathered and put it together to arrive at the conclusion that one school is a warm and friendly place, and that another school is much too impersonal?

Distinctive Features

Cognitive approaches differ from learning approaches in two major ways. First, cognitive approaches focus on the present, not the past. Second, they emphasize the importance of the individual's perception or interpretation of a situation, not the "reality" of the situation as it might be viewed by a neutral observer. To return to Claude's run-in with the law, cognitive approaches would emphasize the importance of the way Claude interpreted the present situation. How did Claude perceive his actions in taking the money? When the police officer shouted at Claude to stop, how did Claude interpret the situation? He probably perceived this person as a police officer whose job is to arrest criminals, or perhaps as someone who is prejudiced against people like Claude. He may have seen the officer as threatening, biased, or perhaps even cruel. He perhaps assumed that this police officer would act like other police officers Claude had encountered. Ultimately, it was Claude's interpretation of the situation that led him to shoot the police officer.

MOTIVATIONAL THEORIES

A third general approach focuses on the motivational factors that drive and guide human behavior. The Freudian or psychoanalytic view of human nature was that behavior is motivated from within by powerful internal drives, impulses, or needs. Thus, psychoanalytic theorists have sought to understand the inner forces—sometimes unconscious—that energize and direct behavior. A very different approach to understanding motivation comes from the work of economists and others who view people as making rational choices among available alternatives, based on the costs and benefits associated with each option. Within social psychology, we can distinguish three versions of the motivational approach emphasizing need satisfaction, rational decision making, and processes of social exchange.

Need Satisfaction

One motivational approach emphasizes the satisfaction of important human needs. It views the individual as having certain specific needs or motives and as behaving in ways that satisfy those needs. Consider, for example, how we might explain which of two women a particular man falls in love with. He might be a person with a great need to have his self-esteem built up, and also a strong need for peace and quiet in his life. One woman might constantly boost his ego by telling him how smart and handsome he is. The other might want to give parties all the time. According to the needs satisfaction approach, we should look at the needs that the man has (for esteem and quiet), and at the need satisfaction offered by the two women (an esteem booster and a destroyer of peace and quiet, respectively) in order to predict which woman he would choose. Similarly, we might explain Claude's actions in terms of the tremendous amounts of pent-up frustration and anger stored up in him. His shooting of the police officer could be understood as a way of satisfying his need to express anger.

Rational Decision Making

A contrasting view assumes that people are fairly rational decision-makers. People calculate the costs and benefits of various actions and pick the best alternative in a fairly logical, reasoned way. They choose the alternative that gives them the greatest benefit at the least cost. Numerous such theories have been developed, of which **expectancy-value theory** is perhaps the most typical (Edwards, 1954). This holds that decisions are made on the basis of the product of two factors: (1) the value of the various possible outcomes of the decision and (2) the probability or likelihood that each outcome will actually result from the decision.

Suppose you are trying to decide between two new cars, a racy sports car and a solid family-type car. In comparing the two cars, you feel almost certain (high expectation) that the sports car will give you more fun (high positive value). There is also some possibility (low expectation) that the sports car will cost you more in repair bills, but since your brother-in-law owns a repair shop, you feel those bills will not be very expensive (low negative value). A definite high positive value outstrips an uncertain low negative value, so you buy the sports car. Such rational models generate clear predictions about how decisions *ought* to be made, so they are useful normative models. They are also widely used by economists as descriptive models to predict the economic choices made by individuals, firms, and governments. Social psychologists, however, are more likely to emphasize departures from rationality than adherence to rationality, as we will see.

To return to Claude's situation, let's suppose that he has the choices of fleeing, surrendering, or shooting. He expects that if he flees, he will be chased and probably shot, which adds up to a considerable cost. If he surrenders, he is sure to go to jail, another major cost. However, he may think that by shooting the police officer, he is likely to get away—and with the money, too.

Social Exchange

As two people interact with each other, they exchange rewards and costs. In some instances, they may do this very deliberately. You may agree to help your roommate learn French in return for help with your advanced statistics course. In the heat of an argument, you and a friend may "trade" insults. But even when we are not aware of it, the process of interaction creates rewards (information, smiles of approval, money, feelings of being loved, etc.) and costs (boredom, disapproval, feelings of being misunderstood, wasted time, etc.) for the people involved. **Social exchange theory** analyzes interpersonal interaction on the basis of the costs and benefits to each person of possible ways of interacting.

For example, the interaction between Claude and the police officer might be analyzed as turning hostile because of their conflicting interests. Claude would benefit from escaping, while the police officer would benefit from arresting him. In contrast, an exchange theory analysis of the interaction between a nurse and a patient might focus on the benefits to the patient from cooperating with the nurse (the patient gets the right medication and is helped toward recovery) and the benefits to the nurse of being friendly (the patient cooperates, and the nurse gets a reputation for doing a good job.) In this case, the interests of both parties converge on sharing a cooperative and friendly interaction. Social exchange theory is particularly useful for analyzing bargaining situations in which two parties must come to a common agreement despite their separate interests. It has also been elaborated by Harold Kelley and others to apply to close relationships between friends or lovers.

Distinctive Features

Motivational approaches emphasize that people act on the basis of what they have to gain or lose by any given behavior. Sometimes a cost/benefit analysis is expanded to deal with conflicts people may experience between two possible behaviors. In this case, we would consider whether the consequences of each behavior are positive or negative, and how positive or negative they are. *Approach-approach* conflicts involve behaviors, each of which has only benefits. For example, if two people ask you out for dinner on the same evening, and you like them both and would enjoy spending the evening with either, you will experience an approach-approach conflict. *Avoidance-avoidance* conflicts involve two negative alternatives. For example, if you have to decide between going to the dentist and spending hundreds of dollars for new fillings—or letting your teeth gradually rot away, you face an avoidance-avoidance conflict. An *approach-avoidance* conflict concerns a single behavior that has both positive and negative aspects. For example, going to visit a senile relative in a nursing home is a kind and affectionate act, but it may also prove embarrassing and boring.

Motivational approaches differ among themselves in the image they present of human nature. At one extreme, the need-satisfaction version describes a rather impulsive person driven primarily by internal forces. At the other extreme, rational choice models depict the individual as a rather calculating, almost scientific chooser. But all three versions emphasize the forces that motivate behavior and that lead a person to opt for one course of action rather than another.

These approaches differ from learning approaches in two main ways. First, they deal with the relative advantages and disadvantages of possible responses to the current situation, not with habits learned long ago. The causes of behavior, then, are assumed to lie in the immediate situation surrounding a person. Second, like cognitive approaches, motivational analyses are very much concerned with internal states and not just the external environment. Our perceptions of the situation, our positive and negative feelings about it, our expectations about the consequences of alternative acts, our hopes and fears, are all central to this perspective.

SOCIOLOGICAL THEORIES

Social psychology is rooted not only in psychology, but also in sociology. Indeed, some view social psychology as the field that bridges between the disciplines of psychology and sociology. Courses titled social psychology are often taught in both psychology departments and sociology departments. Although these "two social psychologies" have much in common, they also have somewhat distinctive characteristics (Stryker & Statham, 1985). We will consider the sociological approach to social psychology by looking at analyses of symbolic interaction and social roles.

Symbolic Interaction

The symbolic interactionist perspective begins with the observation that what distinguishes humans from other animals is our vast capacity to create and use symbols. We are able to think about abstract ideas, to consider and choose among several alternative courses of action, to reflect on our own character, and so on. A social situation or object has no meaning in and of itself; rather, people create meaning through their actions and interpretations. Our young burglar, Claude, may see a liquor store as a convenient place to get some fast cash. For

the owner, it means a way to earn an honest living. For the family living next door, the store may be a public nuisance that attracts "undesirables" to the neighborhood.

Social interaction is fundamentally a process in which people communicate meaning to each other. We communicate not only with words, but also with facial gestures, voice tones, and "body language." We can usually "read" the meaning of another's smile of welcome or frown of disapproval. Our ability to function in social situations requires that we be able to "take the role of the other"— to put ourselves in the other person's place and anticipate how they are likely to act. In social situations, people do not merely react and respond automatically to events and other people. Rather, the social actor works actively to define, interpret, and construct social patterns.

An important concept from symbolic interactionism is the *definition of the situation*. The idea here is that when people interact, they arrive at a shared understanding of the meaning of their behaviors— implicit agreements about who they are and what they are doing. For example, when a group of neighborhood kids get together after school, they may agree that they are the "Maple Street Rangers," that the old shed in the backyard is their "clubhouse," that the neighbor's pet is their "watch dog," and that the grove of trees is their "secret campsite." Their activities may center around finding and punishing "bad guys" who "threaten" their town. Old clothes and toys may be used as props. For symbolic interactionists the shared beliefs, perceptions, and understandings that emerge in interaction are more important than the actual facts of the situation as seen by observers. The children respond to each other and to their environment as they interpret it—not as outsiders might understand it. In the case of the children at play, it is easy to recognize the active way in which group members create their own social reality. Symbolic interactionists believe, however, that similar processes affect all our social interactions in daily life.

Another important idea from symbolic interactionism is that the *self*—our concept of who we are and what we are like—is created from our interactions with others. Charles Cooley used the term "looking glass self" to capture the idea that we see ourselves through the mirror of how others behave towards us. We come to know ourselves through the eyes of others and from the ways in which others react to us. To return to Claude, a symbolic interactionist might investigate Claude's self-concept. Perhaps a series of failures in school have led Claude to see himself as poorly equipped for academics. In contrast, he may have learned about stealing from peers, enjoyed the easy money and peer approval he could get from stealing, and come to take pride in seeing himself as a "clever, successful burglar."

The symbolic interactionist perspective shares common elements with other cognitive approaches in social psychology, most notably an emphasis on the way people perceive and interpret social situations. However, a distinctive feature of symbolic interactionism is a focus on the interactive creation of meaning—the ways in which people communicate and negotiate to arrive at shared meanings about their interactions. Thus, teen gang members may develop a shared and positive interpretation of robbing stores that differs dramatically from the way robbery is interpreted by the police or local merchants. Symbolic interactionists see social interaction as a dynamic process by which social life is continuously created and recreated.

Social Roles

The term "role" is frequently used in everyday speech to describe the different parts that we play in social interaction. You have probably been in the role of student, or employee, or friend, or customer. In attempting to analyze social roles systematically, sociologists have taken two approaches, one that emphasizes social structure and a second that focuses on interaction processes.

The social structural approach to roles uses imagery borrowed from the theatre. The individual acting in society is like an actor in a play. In the theatre, the script sets the stage, defines the roles that actors will enact, and dictates what actors say and do. Similarly, sociologists argue, society existed long before we as individuals arrived on the scene and presents us with many preestablished social roles. In technical terms, a **social role** refers to the specific norms or rights and responsibilities that apply to a particular position in a social system. Let's consider each element in this definition.

A *social system* is any interacting group or social organization—such as a family, a baseball team, a girl scout troop, or a university. From the structuralist perspective, we can analyze a social system in terms of the various positions involved. In a college, for instance, the positions would include students, professors, administrators and staff. Typically, positions vary in their *status*—with more prestige and value accompanying some positions than others. Teachers, for example, are usually accorded greater status than students; seniors often enjoy greater prestige than first-year students. Social systems also entail shared **social norms,** which are rules and expectations about what members of the group should do or be like. A few norms may apply to all members of the system. On campus, everyone is expected to obey traffic signs and put litter in wastebaskets. But frequently, the norms that apply depend on your position in the social system. For example, professors are supposed to come to class on time, prepare lectures and lead class discussions, write and grade tests, serve on college committees, and so on. In return, professors are entitled to a regular paycheck, to the services of support staff, and other benefits of their position. Rather different norms apply to students, who are expected to take notes in class, study for tests, write term papers, pay tuition, etc. A role refers to the set of norms that apply to each position in a social system.

People may adhere to social norms in part because they are conformists who fear disapproval, but also because they want to live up to standards that they themselves value. From this perspective, roles are a major determinant of how an individual behaves in social situations. For instance, knowing that a person is a college professor, wife, mother, and amateur tennis player may tell us a good deal about her daily activities and social behaviors. The structuralist perspective emphasizes that individuals, like actors, play out preexisting scripts. This perspective is especially useful in understanding behavior in formal settings such as a college classroom, military unit, or religious service—where role definitions are fairly clear and detailed.

Whereas the social structuralist approach views people as actors reading fixed social scripts, the contrasting interactionist perspective views people as characters improvising and constructing their own social scripts. Drawing on ideas from symbolic interactionism, this perspective emphasizes the processes of *role-making* through which individuals create, modify, and redefine roles during the course of social interaction. For example, although most people learn general expectations for roles in marriage, newlyweds usually find that they need to negotiate with each other about the specific details of their relationships to arrive at their own understandings of who will do what, when, and how. During the lifetime of a marriage, roles may be reshaped as circumstances change—for instance, when children are born, when one partner becomes ill, when a spouse decides to return to school or retires. Another idea is that when we learn roles, we learn not only our own part, but also many aspects of the complementary role. Being a wife requires considerable knowledge of the role of husband, since the norms and expectations for both roles are closely interrelated. Whereas the structuralist view tends to depict people as relatively passive players on the stage of social life, the role-making view depicts us as active creators who, in large measure, write or at least revise our own scripts and define our own characters.

From the interactionist approach, a criminal act, like any social act, involves a sequence of choices and behaviors. For example, Claude had to decide which store to rob, how to break in, what time was best for the burglary, what to take from the store, whether to carry a weapon, and so on. His choices were guided to some degree by his knowledge of what burglars typically do—that they work at night, try to pick unguarded stores, and so on. But Claude had considerable freedom to shape the course of his own actions and to create his own personal script for burglary.

BIOLOGICAL THEORIES

Human beings are born with many biological characteristics that distinguish them from other animals and from each other. There is no question that biological characteristics play a role in determining behavior. At the simplest level, they limit what humans can do and the stimuli they respond to. Humans cannot fly, they can eat meat, they are quite strong and physically skilled compared to many other animals, and so on. Humans are also intelligent, have language (or the capacity to develop it), have good memories, and live long lives. They have excellent hearing and vision, but respond to only a limited range of sounds and light. Humans mature slowly, being quite helpless as babies; and until they have lived at least 6 years or so, they are unable to fend for themselves. Goats, in contrast, can walk almost at birth and can manage by themselves soon after. The list of important innate human characteristics could be much longer, but clearly all these qualities affect the kind of animal we are and our social behavior.

Instinct

The question is not whether any of these innate characteristics affect our social behavior, but rather how big a role they play and just what difference they make. For instance, it has been suggested that humans have an *instinct* to be aggressive. Konrad Lorenz and others have argued that built into the human organism, present at birth and unalterable, is an aggressive impulse. In slightly different terms, Freud's psychoanalytic theory also proposes an innate drive toward destructiveness (though Freud thought it could be channeled into nondestructive behavior such as sports). The notion that aggression is instinctive does not help us much in understanding why Claude robbed the store or shot the police officer, except to say that the potential for aggressiveness is part of human nature. It does not tell us why Claude fired the gun whereas other people would not have; nor why Claude is a criminal and the police officer is not.

Sociobiology

The newest and most controversial analysis of the relationship betwen biology and social behavior is found in **sociobiology.** This approach uses evolutionary theory to explain social behavior in animals. In this view, behavior is at least in part genetically determined, and behavior patterns have evolved over time by the natural selection of particular genes. Darwin proposed that any genetically determined trait that has high survival value (that helps the individual survive) will be passed on. This occurs because an individual with the trait is more likely to survive than one without the trait, and so produces more offspring, each of whom will tend to have the trait and will in turn be more likely to survive and reproduce, and so on. Obviously, if an animal is healthier and lives longer, it will produce more healthy young and its genes will be carried on to the next generation. Eventually, individuals with genes that carry this trait will grow

more numerous than those without these genes and will come to dominate the species.

Harvard entomologist Edward Wilson (1975) and other sociobiologists believe that evolutionary processes of genetic selection apply not only to physical characteristics, but also to behavioral dispositions.

> Sociobiology has emerged from the recognition that behavior, even complex social behavior, has evolved and is adaptive. Its excitement derives from the further recognition that evolution has a great deal to say about behavior; it is the underlying thread that unifies all living things. (Barash, 1977, p. 8)

Sociobiology has been used to analyze a wide range of human social behavior, including sexual behavior and mate selection, parents' attachment to their children, homosexuality, and altruism (Cunningham, 1981). A sociobiological perspective on aggression emphasizes that aggressive behavior can have considerable survival value. However, like the earlier instinct theories, sociobiology does not provide a good explanation for the aggressive behavior of specific individuals, such as Claude.

Sociobiology has generated a growing body of empirical research, almost entirely with birds, insects, and animals other than humans. The theory has attracted a group of enthusiastic supporters, mainly in the biological sciences. At present, the applicability of sociobiology to human social behavior is a controversial matter that has evoked much debate. Critics of sociobiology see it as reminiscent of the "social Darwinism" of the nineteenth century that used the language of natural selection to justify racism and sexism as "natural" and appropriate. Extreme critics have argued that sociobiology is really a political stance more than a scientific theory; they worry that it can be used to justify prevailing social inequalities. It remains to be seen how useful sociobiology will ultimately prove to be in predicting and explaining human social behavior.

Individual Differences

Another biological approach focuses on how biological differences between people might produce individual differences in behavior. Some people grow up to be much bigger and stronger than others; some are smarter than others; some have better vision and finer coordination than others. Some of us are females and can give birth to young; others are males and cannot give birth. Similarly, some individuals may be more prone to aggression than others. It has been argued, for example, that people who have a particular type of genetic structure (specifically XYY chromosomes instead of the more usual XY or XX) are more likely to become criminals. Although there is as yet little evidence to support this idea, it would obviously be a partial explanation of criminal behavior. Perhaps Claude has an extra Y chromosome (all XYY people are males), and that is why he is so violent. Others have stressed individual differences in hormones or in brain functioning to explain aggressiveness. It is known, for instance, that certain parts of the brain, especially the hypothalamus, can produce uncontrolled aggressiveness in animals. Research derived from this approach would seek to identify the biologically based characteristics that distinguish individuals who are highly aggressive from those who are not. Finally, it appears that men are more likely to behave aggressively than women (Eagly, 1987), although we do not know whether this sex difference is caused by biological factors or social factors or both.

The common element in these and other biological approaches is the idea that the causes of behavior, including human social behavior, can be found in the biological nature of the individual. Specific biological approaches differ from each other in the emphasis they give to innate characteristics, the evolutionary history of the species, genetic factors, physical characteristics that develop after birth, or more temporary physiological states of arousal that might be produced by hormones or brain stimulation. Social psychologists acknowledge the importance of biological approaches to understanding the human animal, just as they also acknowledge the importance of economic, historical, and sociological approaches. But, as we have seen, the field of social psychology emphasizes a more interpersonal approach and focuses on the ways in which human experiences are influenced by the more immediate social environment.

SOCIAL PSYCHOLOGY TODAY

Over the years, social psychologists have found that the complex topics we study cannot be fully understood by any one of the "grand" theories of yesteryear. Instead, social psychologists have developed more specific **middle-range theories.** These theories attempt to account for a certain limited range of phenomena, such as attitude change, aggression, or interpersonal attraction. In this book, you will be introduced to many of these more focused theories. But as you will see, these specific theories and models continue to reflect the influence of our basic theoretical traditions.

Another trend in recent years has been for social psychologists to try to combine and integrate ideas from different theoretical traditions. Instead of focusing solely on overt behavior or exclusively on thoughts and cognitions, newer theorists seek to understand the interrelationships among behavior, thoughts, and feelings. As you read about research on specific topics in social psychology, such as helping behavior or conformity, consider how current social psychological analyses try to encompass all facets of human experience including behavior, cognition, and motivation. And, as you learn more about social psychology from reading this book, look for ways in which the "grand" theoretical traditions of the past continue to influence social psychology today.

KEY TERMS IN CHAPTER 1

association	gestalt	reinforcement	social norms
attribution	middle-range theories	social cognition	social role
behaviorism	observational learning	social exchange theory	sociobiology
expectancy-value theory	psychoanalytic theory	social learning theory	

SUMMARY

1. Social psychology has a unique vantage point on social behavior. It emphasizes factors in immediate social situations that induce the same general response from most people. It is less concerned with large social forces than are the other social sciences. And it is less concerned with unique individual responses and individual differences than are personality or clinical psychology.

2. There are three general theoretical approaches to social psychology, including learning theories, cognitive theories, and motivational theories. These are not necessarily contradictory. Rather, each emphasizes one aspect of the causes of behavior without necessarily claiming that the others are unimportant or irrelevant.

3. Learning theorists stress a person's life history and past experience. They analyze current behavior in terms of what a person learned in the past through the mechanisms of association, reinforcement, and observational learning. Since learning theories emphasize the impact of the external environment on a person's overt behavior, they have often understated the importance of thought processes. Early learning theorists ignored people's expectations, beliefs, and feelings, tending instead to view people as responding rather automatically to any current stimulus. In recent years, most learning theorists have begun to incorporate cognitive processes into their models.

4. Cognitive theorists emphasize that behavior is determined mainly by people's perceptions and interpretations of current social situations. People group and categorize objects and events, and tend to focus on the most prominent (figural) aspects of a situation. As social thinkers, people try to arrive at meaningful interpretations of social events. Attribution theory examines the way that people infer the causes of behavior, either their own or that of others. Social cognition research focuses on such important topics as social perception, social memory, and social judgment.

5. Motivational theorists focus on the internal needs, goals, and values that drive and direct human behavior. One approach, deriving in part from the ideas of Sigmund Freud, has emphasized the importance of powerful internal drives and impulses. In contrast, a rational decision-making approach, deriving in part from work in economics, views people as rather rational decision-makers who weigh the costs and benefits of various alternatives. A third approach emphasizes the social exchanges that occur during interaction as two people provide rewards and costs for each other.

6. Sociological approaches in social psychology have included the analysis of symbolic interaction and

of social roles. For symbolic interactionists, social interaction is fundamentally a process in which people communicate meaning to each other. A social role refers to the set of norms that apply to a particular position in a social system. A structuralist analysis of roles views people as actors reading fixed social scripts. In contrast, an interactionist analysis of roles views people as characters improvising and constructing their own social scripts during the course of interaction.

7. Biological approaches look for causes in innate characteristics or physiological mechanisms. Sociobiology uses evolutionary theory to explain social behavior, arguing that during the course of human history, predispositions for social behaviors that have a high survival behavior have become part of our genetic heritage.

8. Today, most social psychologists are working to develop middle-range theories or models to explain specific aspects of human behavior, such as attitude change, aggression, or interpersonal attraction. Another recent trend is for social psychological theories to try to combine and integrate ideas from the "grand" theoretical traditions of the past.

SUGGESTED READINGS

ARON, A., & ARON, E. (1986). *The heart of social psychology*. Lexington, MA: D. C. Heath. A delightful insider's view of the field, filled with fascinating stories about important people and research in social psychology.

BANDURA, A. (1977). *Social learning theory*. Englewood Cliffs, NJ: Prentice-Hall. An excellent review of social learning theory, illustrating some of its adjustments to a more cognitive approach.

DEUTSCH, M., & KRAUSS, R. M. (1965). *Theories in social psychology*. New York: Basic Books. Still the best coverage of the classic theories.

FISKE, S. T., & TAYLOR, S. E. (1984). *Social cognition*. Reading, MA: Addison-Wesley. An excellent textbook that presents the cognitive approach to social psychology.

LINDZEY, G., & ARONSON, E. (eds.). (1985). *The handbook of social psychology*, 3rd ed., 2 volumes. New York: Random House. A comprehensive survey of the major topics and theories in social psychology, written by leading experts in the field.

WILSON, E. O. (1980). *Sociobiology*, abridged edition. Cambridge, MA: Harvard University Press. The most influential recent effort to apply a biological approach to social behavior.

2 RESEARCH METHODS

One of the most fascinating aspects of social psychology is that we all know a lot about social behavior without having studied it systematically. We live our lives surrounded by other people and we are constantly observing them. We have some idea of what people do in many social contexts. Most other scientific disciplines are very different. We know little about nuclear physics, high-pressure chemistry, or laser technology before studying them. We come to physics or chemistry in almost total ignorance; but we come to social psychology with a great deal of relevant experience.

Much of what is taught in social psychology will fit in with what you already know from your own experience and should be relatively easy to relate to and to learn. One of the exciting aspects of social psychology, therefore, is that you can become familiar with and discuss the very latest findings almost from the beginning. The disadvantage is that you may often believe that you already know much of the material, that research is not needed because the facts are obvious, or that a particular finding is wrong because it is not consistent with your own experience.

But personal experience is not always a very good indicator of how people generally behave. Our observations are usually quite casual. We are not systematic; we do not write down each incident and describe it in an objective, unbiased way. We form *impressions* of how people behave that are sometimes correct and sometimes incorrect. For example, consider the following statements:

- When we are anxious, we like to be with other people.

- Advertisements that try to make people afraid backfire and are less effective than ads that do not arouse fear.

- People in groups will cooperate rather than compete if it is in their own self-interest, and raising the stakes increases the amount of cooperation.

- The more you pay people to make speeches against their own beliefs, the more they will change their minds to agree with the speech they make.

- In choosing friends and lovers, the most important principle is that opposites attract.

- People who live in cities have higher rates of mental illness than people in small towns.

You may not agree with some of these statements, but it is fair to say that they all sound plausible. Yet research has demonstrated that all of them are either false or oversimplifications.

Why do our casual observations lead us to wrong conclusions? Sometimes we are biased and misinterpret what happens. Sometimes we see correctly but remember wrong. Sometimes what we see is a very unusual group of people or situations. Systematic research collects data in such a way as to rule out any sources of bias, to make sure the people observed are representative, and to keep track of the "numbers" so we do not rely on memory or general impressions. Casual observations, even by very careful people, cannot replace systematic research in any field.

The main task of social psychology is to conduct scientific research on social behavior. Our research has several goals. One is to provide careful and systematic descriptions of social behavior that permit us to make reliable generalizations about how people act in various social settings. Another goal is to develop theories about social behavior that help us to understand why people behave the way they do. As we learn more about general principles and the specifics of particular types of behavior, we become better able to control behavior. The application of social psychology may help people learn to control their own aggressive impulses or to develop more satisfying personal relationships. It may also help social planners to design interventions that can help many people—by reducing smoking, by creating more cooperation in the workplace, and so on. The possibilities are exciting—but they must be based on a firm research foundation.

AT THE BEGINNING: THE QUESTION

In this chapter we will describe the research process from start to finish, from generating an idea to the completed empirical test of that idea. All research begins with a question. We then design a study to answer the question as directly as possible. Of course, this is not always easy. In fact, the main difficulty is taking a problem that may be extremely complex and finding a way to get an answer. As we will see, this often involves ingenuity and patience—and even then any one study or series of studies may not give us a firm conclusion. This is why psychologists do many studies on the same problem. Each is designed to answer one part of the question or to narrow down the possible answers.

The Goal: Causal Explanation

Almost all research in social psychology has the basic goal of establishing causal relationships between two variables. A *variable* is the basic ingredient in any analysis. It is any general factor that is either the cause or effect in the analysis. For example, we might want to know if "likes attract." Translated into more technical language, we would be asking if one variable—degree of similarity to a potential partner—affects another variable—liking for that partner. Put another way, we ask whether the degree of similarity causes the amount of liking. In commonsense language we would think of these as cause and effect—the cause, similarity, produces the effect, liking. More formally, we would describe the cause as an **independent variable,** because it is free to take any value; the level of similarity does not depend on the level of liking. But the effect is described as the **dependent variable,** because its value is dependent on the independent variable: If the two people are very similar, liking will be great, while if they are very dissimilar, they may not like each other very much.

Theoretical vs. Nontheoretical Questions

The next step is to identify what kind of question we have. There are two basic kinds of questions: those that are directly related to a theory and those that are not.

A **theoretical question** starts with a theory we want to test. A theory can be any abstract generalization that tells us what to expect in more specific, concrete cases. A good example is Darley and Latané's theory of the diffusion of responsibility in helping situations. In Chapter 1 we described two cases in which women were attacked in front of a number of witnesses, yet no one helped stop the attack or even called the police. One woman was repeatedly raped, and the other was ultimately killed. What makes people help or not help others in such situations? Darley and Latané (1968) hypothesized that people are least likely to help when they think there are other witnesses to the emergency, so that they do not feel directly and personally responsible.

This hypothesis follows from their more general theory of diffusion of responsibility: Anything that diminishes an individual's sense of responsibility for solving a problem makes that person less likely to help others with it. This general theory leads to many more specific, concrete, and detailed *hypotheses*, such as that people will help out less in an emergency when there are other witnesses (as in their experiment; see Box 2–1), that they will work less hard to solve a common problem when in a large group, or that they will pay less attention to instructions when co-workers are also listening. From that one theoretical statement, we can deduce what to expect in numerous more specific situations. Put another way, a general theory generates hypotheses or predictions about how people will behave in a number of more specific situations.

As we saw in Chapter 1, social psychology has

BOX 2–1

Diffusing Responsibility in an Emergency

To test this "diffusion of responsibility" idea, Darley and Latané conducted a laboratory experiment in which every subject overheard an apparent emergency. Some subjects thought they were the only witnesses. Others were told that other people were waiting with them and therefore thought that others overheard the emergency as well. The hypothesis was that the subjects would be more likely to try to help when they thought they were the only witnesses to the emergency because they would feel more personal responsibility for the victim's fate. In the study itself, all subjects were placed in separate rooms and communicated only over intercoms. Some were told there were just two subjects; others, that there were six subjects. A confederate of the experimenters, who acted as if he were one of the real subjects, said initially that he was prone to seizures. Later he said, "I think I need a little help . . . I've got one of these things coming on and I could really use some help . . . (choking sounds) . . . I'm gonna die . . . (chokes, then he was quiet)."

Consistent with the hypothesis, helping was reduced with more witnesses. When the subjects thought no one else had heard the cries for help, 85 percent reported the incident to the experimenters before the confederate fell silent. Of the subjects who thought they were in six-person groups, only 31 percent reported the incident. Bystanders were indeed less likely to intervene to help a stranger in distress when they thought other bystanders were present.

Source: Darley & Latané (1968).

moved slowly toward middle-range theories and away from the all-encompassing general theories popular earlier in the century. Diffusion of responsibility is a good example of a middle-range theory because it deals with a moderate range of phenomena—situations in which individuals are trying to solve problems and their responsibility for the solution varies. It does not attempt to deal with all social behavior. But whether the theory is a grand general theory or a middle-range theory, theoretical research is based on the specific hypotheses derived from theory.

Theoretical research begins with a specific prediction or hypothesis from a theory. The major goal of the research is to evaluate the theory. If the hypothesis is confirmed, the theory is supported. If the hypothesis is disconfirmed, it might suggest that the theory is at least partially wrong. We could then go back and discard the theory or alter it to make it consistent with the new finding. On the other hand, no matter how the research came out, we would want to evaluate the accuracy of the study very carefully. The study might support the hypothesis, but we might conclude that the study was so flawed it should not be taken as support at all. Or it might disconfirm the hypothesis, but we might reject the study as so poorly done it should not count.

Often, however, research is not concerned with a theory at all. Researchers may simply be interested in discovering more about a particular behavior. Research motivated by **nontheoretical questions** is not designed to test predictions from a more general theory and provide a test of the general theory. It is simply designed to gather information about the specific phenomenon in question. We might be interested in what differentiates divorced couples from those who have been married for many years. We might find out how similar the members of the couple are in political and religious values, whether or not they both come from similar ethnic groups and social classes, whether or not they have children, and how many; whether they differ in age a great deal; how overtly they argue and fight when they have conflicts; whether or not they are financially well off; whether both members of the couple work; and so on. There might be a great many variables we would take into consideration not to test any particular theory, but just to describe the differences between successful and unsuccessful marriages.

The ultimate goal of psychology, indeed of any science, is to have simplifying theories that explain known facts in a particular realm. Theories help us understand, appreciate, and cope with the world. Data without a theory are difficult to understand and to fit into the rest of our knowledge. On the other hand, sometimes we just need to begin collecting exploratory data because we do not yet have a good theory. So there is great value in both kinds of research—research that focuses on testing particular hypotheses that have been generated from clear theories, and research that simply collects interesting facts about an important phenomenon.

Basic vs. Applied Questions

Another major distinction is whether the researcher is interested in building up knowledge for knowledge's sake, and is therefore doing **basic research,** or is trying to gain knowledge in order to solve some practical problem, which is called **applied research.** Research on the effects of televised violence, for example, can be motivated by either goal. Its aim might be to understand how people respond to any kind of observed violence just because it is an interesting scientific problem. Or its aim might be to measure the effects of specific television programs that might be thought to be harmful.

Does observing violence produce imitation, so that the viewers become more violent themselves? Or does it more often produce empathy with the victim, and so reduce violence? What determines which reaction the viewer will have? The answers to these very general questions may tell us a little about the effects of any given program now being shown on prime-time television and, in that sense, may have application, but that is not the main goal.

In contrast, the research may start with a specific, real world problem. One practical question is whether watching the crime shows currently being shown on prime-time television actually causes people to commit violent acts themselves. If the research shows that it does, there could be a practical consequence: Reduce the violence on television in order to reduce crime. Unlike basic research, here the emphasis is on a particular problem. It may be that the effects of television are quite different from the effects of any other form of communication and that the research has no general value except for what it tells us about TV and crime.

How is watching violence on television likely to affect the viewer's aggressive behavior? How would you isolate the effects of programs from other factors?

Charles Gatewood

But someone doing applied research is relatively unconcerned about the broader issues. At least for the moment, the emphasis is on the immediate problem and how to solve it.

Clearly, both basic and applied research are important. In fact, the distinction is really a continuum: Much research is really a blend of basic and applied research. If we conducted a study on the effects of a popular crime show, it might tell us about prime-time television, but it also tells us something more general about the effects of observed violence. Moreover, basic research almost always grows out of a concern with real problems and must necessarily be related to them, even if indirectly; and applied research has to start somewhere and relies on principles derived from basic research. The ideal arrangement is for each type of work to take ideas from the other.

Basic research is most often also theoretical research, and applied work is usually nontheoretical. However, the other two possible combinations also exist. For example, the learning theory idea that watching violence produces imitative behavior might be conveniently tested in an applied research project designed to discover the effects of prime-time television viewing. The applied situation may simply be a convenient place to test a general theory. Similarly, nontheoretical but basic research is common in the early stages of studying a particular area; research may be quite exploratory and guided by little more than hunch. Research on helping, for example, began with some hunches developed from cases like the Kitty Genovese killing and then tried to test the effects of some of those factors, such as the presence of other people. Theory came later.

CORRELATIONAL VERSUS EXPERIMENTAL DESIGNS

After an investigator has decided what research question to ask, the most difficult decision still remains: how to do the study. Although variations are virtually unlimited, there are two basic types of research designs: correlational and experimental. Each has advantages and disadvantages. As we will see, the type chosen depends largely on the problem being studied and the goals of the research.

A **correlational research design** consists of passively observing the relationship between two or more variables. It asks this question: When variable A is high, is variable B also high (a positive correlation), low (a negative correlation), or is B's value unrelated (no correlation)? Height and weight are positively correlated, because tall people tend to weigh more than short people; the temperature on a given day and the amount of clothing worn tend to be negatively correlated—that is, people usually wear less clothing on hot days. However, height and amount of clothing worn are probably uncorrelated; tall people and short people probably

wear about the same number of pieces of clothing, in general.

A good example of correlational research comes from studies of whether or not watching violence on television is a cause of increased aggressive behavior. Correlational studies have simply measured how much a child watches violent programs on television and the amount of aggressive behavior he or she engages in, and have tested for the level of correlation between the two. Are the children who watch the most violence on television also the most aggressive in their daily behavior? Huesmann (1982) found that those elementary school children who watched violent programs the most were also described by their peers as the most aggressive. So we would say that viewing violent programs on television was positively correlated with aggressive behavior among those children.

In an **experimental design,** we arrange two (or more) conditions that differ in exactly specified ways, randomly assign people to experience these different conditions, and then measure the behavior we are interested in. In experiments on media violence, one group of children might be shown a violent film, while another group is shown a nonviolent film. All the children might then be placed in a test situation in which their aggressive behavior can be measured. If those shown the violent film behave more aggressively, filmed violence is concluded to be a cause of aggressive behavior. A good example is a study by Hartmann (1969). He had one group of teenage boys view a 2-minute film showing two boys shooting baskets and then getting into an argument and finally a fistfight. A second group was shown another 2-minute film depicting an active but cooperative basketball game. After watching the film, each boy was asked to help out in what was described as a study of the effects of performance feedback on learning. The subject was supposed to be a "teacher," and to administer shock to a "learner" every time that "learner" made a mistake in the learning task. The "teacher" could deliver as strong a shock as he wanted, within certain limits. It turned out that the subjects who had seen the violent film delivered more shock than those who had seen the nonviolent one. In this situation, at least, observed violence caused an increase in aggressive behavior.

Causal Ambiguity in Correlational Studies

Most correlational studies, and all experimental studies, aim first to establish a cause-and-effect relationship between the independent variable and the dependent variable. In the Huesmann and Hartmann studies, the intent was to assess the causal role of observed violence in producing later aggressive behavior. The point of correlating elementary school children's viewing preferences with their aggressive behavior is to understand the causal role of viewing television violence (the independent variable) in producing aggressive behavior (the dependent variable). The point of experimentally comparing the effects of a violent with a nonviolent film is to determine whether or not observed violence affects aggressive behavior.

The major weakness of correlational studies is that they leave the cause and effect relationship

ambiguous in two ways. One is that the direction of causality is ambiguous. This is the **reverse causality problem.** If viewing violent television is correlated with high levels of aggressive behavior, maybe the viewing does indeed cause more aggression. But the correlation could also reflect causality in the reverse direction: Maybe children who are very aggressive in their daily lives, getting into fights and yelling and screaming all the time, especially like to watch other people fighting. Maybe engaging in the aggressive behavior causes the viewing of violence. In other words, a correlation between two variables does not, by itself, tell you which variable is the cause and which is the effect. This reverse-causality problem occurs whenever two variables are correlated with each other, and each one can just as plausibly be the cause as the effect of the other.

The other serious ambiguity in correlational research is the possibility that neither variable is directly affecting the other. Some other unspecified factor may influence both of them. This is called the **third-variable problem.** For example, aggression is much more common in the homes of lower-class disadvantaged people, where there are typically high levels of unemployment and marital instability, not much money, and a great deal of frustration and anger. In such households, family members may prefer violent television because it seems more realistic and familiar to them. And children in those households may grow up being unusually aggressive themselves because of the high levels of anger and frustration surrounding them. In contrast, children who grow up in more comfortable middle-class homes may enjoy family comedies more and may be much less aggressive themselves. If all this were true, viewing television violence would be correlated with aggressive behavior—but the correlation would be due to a third variable that caused both of them: the level of frustration and anger in the child's family. The correlation between viewing televised violence and aggressive behavior would be called "spurious" because it was artificially created by a third variable that was not considered. Television would have no causal role itself.

These two ambiguities are often a problem in correlational studies. But sometimes we can be sure that reverse causality could not be operating. Many studies have found a correlation between gender and aggressive behavior—boys are more aggressive than girls. But we can be confident that it is their "boyness" that causes their aggressiveness and not the other way around. Children do not begin sexually neutral and then become physiologically male or female depending on whether or not they fight on the playground.

Nor is the "third-variable" problem always a fatal difficulty, since we can check to see whether or not the most plausible third variable is really responsible for the correlation we have observed. For example, we could add measures of frustration and anger in the child's family to Huesmann's (1982) correlational study of elementary school children. Then we could check to see whether or not the correlation of television viewing with aggressive behavior was in fact due to home life. The strategy would be to see if the original correlation between television viewing and aggression holds with the third variable held constant; that is, for people at all levels of that third variable. Does it hold both in angry, aggressive families and in happy, peaceful families? If so, we can conclude that the third variable (home life) was not responsible for the original correlation.

Of course, this procedure does not completely eliminate the third-variable problem. There still could be some other "third variable" (now actually a fourth, of course) that we still had not measured, such as intelligence. Perhaps the less intelligent children like to watch crude, brute force rather than the subtleties of more verbal drama, and maybe they are more aggressive in school because of their frustration from constantly doing poorly. Again the solution would be to measure this new "third variable," intelligence, and then see if the original correlation held up for both highly intelligent children and those below average in intelligence.

This sounds as if it could go on and on. But at some point the process ends, because we can no longer think of any more plausible "third variables." That does not mean there are none, but it at least means that for the moment, we will accept the correlation as reflecting a cause-and-effect relationship until someone else thinks of some further possible variable and it is examined.

Causality in Experiments

The great strength of the experimental method is that it avoids these ambiguities about causality. In social psychology, experiments consist of randomly assigning people to different conditions and seeing if there is any difference in their responses. If the experiment has been done properly, any difference in responses between the two conditions must be due to the difference in the conditions. To put it in more formal terms, the causal variable (the independent variable) must have caused the difference in the outcome (the dependent variable). In the example of media violence, the amount of violence in the film, the independent variable, must have caused the amount of aggressive behavior, the dependent variable.

There are two crucial elements in an experiment. First, the independent variable is controlled by the experimenter. This is called "varying" or "manipulating" that particular factor. For example, the experimenter might vary or manipulate the amount of violence shown in a particular film by randomly assigning some subjects to view a violent film, and others to view a nonviolent film. If the experimenter is attempting to manipulate only the amount of violence in a film, the violent and nonviolent films should not differ in other ways, such as being cartoon vs. realistic, or black and white vs. color, or old-fashioned vs. modern. The experimenter's control over the independent variable is crucial because it later allows us to pinpoint the exact cause of any differences that emerge between the two groups of people. Hartmann (1969) treated the two groups of adolescent boys identically in every respect with just one exception: One group watched basketball game. Any differences between the two groups in their later behavior (the dependent variable) must be attributed to this one difference in how they were treated.

The second crucial element is that subjects must be randomly assigned to conditions. **Random assignment** is crucial because we must assume that the two groups of subjects did not differ before they were placed into the two different conditions. If they differed in some way before we introduced the experimental conditions, we cannot interpret any later differences in behavior as being solely due to those conditions. The differences in behavior could be due to those prior factors and not to the independent variable.

We could try to rule out such previous differences by measuring all the boys' aggressiveness before the experiment began, and then deliberately ensuring that the boys in the two groups did not differ to begin with. This procedure risks not catching some real differences on dimensions we did not think to measure. As a result, more often, we ensure the initial equality of the two groups by leaving it up to chance. We make the assignments by deciding by chance which condition to put each subject in. This can be done by flipping a coin, cutting a deck of cards, or more commonly and more precisely by using a set of random numbers.

Perhaps the most dangerous departure from random assignment lies in allowing the subjects themselves to select their experimental condition, directly or indirectly. Suppose you asked subjects whether they preferred to watch violent or nonviolent television programs and assigned them according to their choices. Then, after having subjects watch either violent or nonviolent TV for some period of time, you might find that those who watched violent programs were more aggressive. But you could not conclude that the programs made them more violent, because they might have been more aggressive in the first place. It would be no surprise to find that more aggressive people liked more violent programs. The "experiment" would be meaningless.

Advantages of the Correlational Method

Correlational techniques sometimes let us study problems to which experimental methods may not be applicable. Many real world problems do not allow us to control the situation. For example, the experimental method generally cannot be used to study the effects of natural disasters or many of the most important events in people's lives. We cannot assign people to air raids, floods, and surgery entirely at random. It is not chance alone that leads some people to be poor, to live in cities, or to get divorced. It is difficult for both practical and ethical reasons to expose people to such extreme conditions in an experiment. We could not actually conduct an experiment in which a person was given an order to kill another person, and given the opportunity to do so. So any research on such variables must be correlational rather than experimental. We must settle for doing experiments that operate within a range of rather mild and inoffensive human experiences.

A second advantage of a correlational study is that it allows us to collect more information and test more relationships than we can in most experiments. If we wanted to explore what caused some children to be more aggressive than others, we could collect information on a great many potential causal factors, including television viewing, family lives, intelligence and personality, relationships with other children, and so on. Moreover, we could measure aggressive behavior in a number of different ways—in terms of teachers' impressions, observing children in school, their reputations for aggressiveness among other children, parents' reports, and so on. The experimental method is inefficient for collecting large amounts of data on many variables. Since experimenters must produce each independent variable, they are usually limited to studying one or two at a time. They could not test 20 variables at once, as is often done in correlational studies. It would take a tremendous number of experimental studies to investigate the effect of each of these factors on each behavior. So correlational studies are often used in nontheoretical or exploratory research because they make possible the efficient collection of large amounts of data.

Correlational and experimental work complement each other. There are many cases in which both methods are useful. Still, each has its relative advantages and disadvantages. These are shown in Table 2–1. In general, correlational studies are particularly effective in the collection of large amounts of data; they provide us with ideas and hypotheses that can then be studied in more detail experimentally. They do have the disadvantage of causal ambiguity, which can never be completely overcome, so it is always helpful for experimental research to supplement correlational studies.

TABLE 2–1

Characteristics of Correlational and Experimental Research

	Correlational	Experimental
Advantages of Experiments		
Independent variable	Varies naturally	Controlled by researcher
Random assignment	No	Yes
Unambiguous causality	No	Yes
Theory testing	Often	Usually
Advantages of Correlational Studies		
Exploratory	Often	Usually not
Real world problems	Often	Usually not
Tests many relationships	Usually	Usually not

FIELD VERSUS LABORATORY SETTINGS

The next step is to decide where research should be done: in a field setting or in a laboratory. Research done in a field setting means that we study the kind of behavior the person normally engages in as it occurs in its natural habitat. We might study factory workers' productivity or morale right in the factory itself, people's television viewing in their own living rooms, commuters' responses to an emergency on the subway train they normally ride home from work, third-graders' aggressive behavior toward schoolmates on the school playground, or college students' relationships with their roommates in a college dormitory. Laboratory research, in contrast, is done in an artificial situation, one the person normally does not inhabit. Usually laboratory research is conducted in some specially outfitted room in a psychology building at a university or research institute. It may have all kinds of special equipment, such as video equipment to show stimuli to subjects, audio equipment to record interaction between subjects, one-way mirrors to permit observation of group interactions, physiological recording equipment, or intercoms to limit interaction between people to audio channels only. Or it may simply have tables and chairs at which people fill out questionnaires. The point is that the researcher brings the subject to an artificial environment.

Although most research in social psychology during the last 30 years has been conducted in the laboratory, some has always been conducted in the field. Both experimental and correlational research can be done in either the laboratory or the field, and each setting has advantages and disadvantages.

Advantage of the Laboratory

The major advantage of work in the laboratory is the control it permits over the situation. Researchers can be quite certain about what is happening to each subject. If they are doing experimental work, they can randomly assign the subjects, expose them to the exact experiences necessary to study the problem, minimize extraneous factors, and go a long way toward eliminating unwanted variations in the procedure. Laboratory researchers have great control over the dependent variable and can measure it in considerably more detail and in a more uniform manner than in the field. Therefore, the

AGGRESSIVE ADOLESCENT BOYS IN THEIR NATURAL

HABITAT

Some field experiments have arranged for some subjects to be shown violent television programs, while others are shown nonviolent programs (such as situation comedies), in their natural living environments. Then all are observed for a few days to determine which ones act most aggressively toward the people they normally interact with. Studies conducted in the subject's natural habitat ("in the field") rather than in the artificial environment of a laboratory are presumably more realistic. In one study, Feshbach and Singer (1971) had adolescent boys who lived in boarding schools watch either primarily violent programming or nonviolent TV programs. They found that the boys who had watched violent programs did not become more aggressive in their relations with friends and teachers compared to those who watched nonviolent programs. They concluded that viewing violent television does not increase aggressive behavior in normal day-to-day environments, regardless of its effects in a laboratory situation.

laboratory is the ideal place in which to study the exact effects of one variable on another. All of these advantages fall under the heading of **internal validity:** We can be fairly confident that the results are valid in the confines of this context, so that if others try to do exactly the same study, they will probably get similar results.

In contrast, in field settings, it is generally extremely difficult to assign subjects to conditions randomly, to be certain they are all experiencing the same thing, to get accurate measures on the dependent variable, and so on. A great many extraneous events and conditions enter into a field study and often obscure the effects of the variables in which the researcher is interested.

In particular, it is difficult to find pure manipulations of the independent variable and pure measures of the dependent variable. The experimenter must find or arrange circumstances that produce specific differences—and no others—between con-

ditions. For example, Feshbach and Singer (1971; see Box 2–2) were able to assign some boys to a constant diet of violent television in their boarding schools, and other boys to a diet of nonviolent television. And the boys shown the violent diet were actually somewhat lower in aggressiveness than boys shown the nonviolent diet. So far so good: Observed violence seems to reduce aggressive behavior. But most of the boys preferred the more violent programs, so those assigned to nonviolent television may have been more frustrated than the other group because they were not allowed to watch their favorite programs. As a result, it is not clear whether the observed lack of effect of the violent diet is due to its real lack of effect, or due to the frustrations brought on by the assignment itself. This would not be such a problem in a laboratory study, because the researchers would not have had to interfere with the subjects' normal television viewing practices, and therefore would not have induced frustration in one group and not in the other.

Another advantage of the laboratory is convenience and cost. It is usually much easier and cheaper to set up research in a room down the hall from your office than it is to set it up at a site where people are living their daily lives. With sufficient ingenuity, it is sometimes possible to find field situations that are easy to conduct research in.

For example, one team of researchers was interested in whether or not people tended to choose dating or marital partners of the same level of physical attractiveness as themselves. They observed couples in the lobbies of movie theaters, and indeed found the couples matched each other very closely (Silverman, 1971). However these tailor-made situations for research tend to be few and far between in the field. The world is generally not set up to facilitate the study of a specific problem that psychologists want to study.

Advantages of the Field

The most obvious advantage of field settings is that they are more realistic, and therefore allow the results to be generalized more readily to real life situations. This is called **external validity** to reflect the fact that the results are more likely to be valid in situations outside (external to) the research situation itself (Campbell & Stanley, 1963). This can be seen if we compare the Hartmann (1969) laboratory experiment on observed violence described earlier in this chapter with the Feshbach and Singer

field experiment on the same topic (see Box 2–2).

In Hartmann's laboratory study, the independent variable, observed violence, was artificial—a brief film on a fistfight especially prepared for the study itself. In Feshbach's and Singer's field study, it was the violence shown on prime-time television shows all over the country. The dependent variable, aggressive behavior, was artificial in the laboratory study—the amount of shock delivered in the "teacher-learner" situation constructed especially for the study. In the field study, the dependent variable consisted of observers' ratings of how much physical and verbal aggression the boys engaged in in their normal interactions with peers and teachers. Suppose we want to generalize from these studies to the effects of prime-time television on teenage boys' aggression in their everyday lives. In the field study we are already dealing with exactly the kinds of observed violence, aggressive behavior, and situation to which we want to generalize. So it would be more appropriate to generalize from the field study.

Another advantage of work in the field is that we are sometimes able to deal with extremely powerful variables and situations that could not be studied in the laboratory. This is particularly true of correlational work. We can observe people in extreme situations—when they are waiting for open-heart surgery in a hospital or huddled together under artillery bombardment.

But the field also sometimes allows us to study such powerful, real-life variable in experiments, as well. In these cases the independent variable

TABLE 2–2

Characteristics of Field and Laboratory Research

	Field	Laboratory
Advantages of Laboratory		
Control over variables	Low	High
Random assignment	Rarely	Almost always
Convenience and economy	Low	High
Advantages of Field		
Realism	High	Low
Impact of independent variables	Tends to be higher	Tends to be lower
Minimizes suspicion and bias	Yes	No
External validity	High	Low

may be manipulated by nature rather than by the experimenter. This depends on the occurrence of some natural event that just happens to affect people randomly and therefore fits the criteria for an experiment. Researchers wanting to investigate the effects of heat on violence could take advantage of the fact that the hottest days occur at random through the summer. If ghetto riots occurred on the hottest days of the summer, then heat must be one causal factor (Carlsmith & Anderson, 1979).

Because research in the field deals with everyday life, it tends to minimize suspicion by the subjects. Their responses are more spontaneous and less susceptible to the kinds of bias suspicion produces. Whenever college students know they are subjects in an experiment, there is always the possibility that they are not behaving naturally or spontaneously. They may be trying to please or displease the experimenter, may be behaving in the way they think they should, may not accept the experimental manipulation because they are distrustful, and so on. Any of these effects could produce bias in the results or obscure actual relationships and effects.

Although field and laboratory research do differ in the ways we have described, these differences are easily exaggerated. It is possible to obtain considerable control of variables outside the laboratory, and it is possible to make laboratory situations extremely realistic. Research in both types of settings is necessary to avoid the pitfalls of either.

DATA COLLECTION

The next step is to decide on a technique of data collection. Basically, we have three options. (1) We can observe behavior directly. (2) We can get the subjects to report on their own behaviors, perceptions, or attitudes. (3) We can go to an archive and use data originally collected for other purposes.

Observational Research

Direct observation is a widely used research technique. In studying group behavior, you can observe the interactions and note what everyone says, how often they talk, and how often they look at or touch one another. With children, you might observe the number of fights, sharing, talking, and playing with toys. This is the same technique ethologists (people who study animals in their natural habitat) use to study the behavior of animals. We obviously cannot ask lions how often they fight or chimps whether they use tools. Of necessity, ethologists have had to observe what the animals *do*.

Observational research in natural situations is usually quite difficult and time-consuming. The first task is to decide what actions to record. In doing this, the researcher must face the fact that one cannot observe and record everything. For example, even a brief conversation is enormously complex. It is easy to record how often each person talks and what he or she says; but each act of speaking also involves the pitch, amplitude, and speed of the utterance, the tone used, the number of pauses between words, and so on. As a result, people who study speech can spend hours analyzing a 2-minute conversation. Moreover, people use complicated facial and body gestures when they are talking. To make the project manageable, we would need to decide what aspects of the conversation we were most interested in.

Next, a simple method of recording the observed behaviors must be devised. It is essential that observers agree on what happened. For example, a category called "acted friendly" might not be useful because it is often difficult to decide whether or not an act is friendly. Instead, observers use more specific categories, such as "smiled at other person," "offered to share toy," or "helped up from ground," which they can agree on. It can be decided later whether or not all these are indications of friendliness. Much of the difficulty with observation

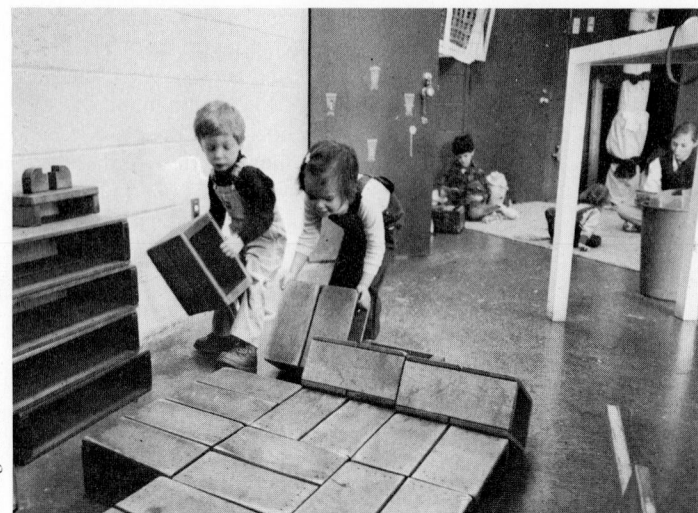

Our coding categories depend on what we want to know. How would you code this behavior? Piling up boxes? Cooperation? Interaction with opposite sex?

Teri Leigh Stratford

in research and in the real world is that we disagree on what a particular behavior means. Interpreting behavior tends to be fairly difficult and produces disagreements among observers, while simple descriptions of behavior do not to the same degree.

Observational research can be conducted either in natural field situations or in the laboratory. As indicated earlier, Feshbach and Singer (1971) had supervisors in boarding homes rate teenage boys' levels of aggressiveness in normal interactions with friends and teachers after the boys had seen either violent or nonviolent television. Observational research can also be done in artificial, controlled situations such as in the Darley-Latané (1968) study of bystander intervention. These researchers created an artificial emergency in the laboratory, and observed the subject's response.

The advantage of observing behavior in a field situation is its external validity. If the independent variable influences people's behavior in their everyday worlds, it must be important. Also, the meaning of behavior in natural settings is often easier to interpret. When children fight in a schoolyard, we can conclude with some certainty that aggression is being expressed. When someone in the laboratory is told to give electric shock to another subject and does it, it is not so clear that only aggression is involved. Giving the shock may simply indicate

obedience to authority, with no ill-will intended toward the victim.

On the other hand, one disadvantage of naturalistic observation is that the behavior of interest may not occur frequently enough to make the study useful—children in fact do not come to blows in a schoolyard very often. So we could wait a long time before such a spontaneous aggressive act occurred. The advantage of the controlled situation is that it is constructed to induce the behavior being studied. The Hartmann and Darley-Latané studies were set up so that aggressive and helping behavior were very likely to be quite frequent.

Self-Report

Perhaps the most common technique of data collection in social psychology uses people's self-reports of their own perceptions, attitudes, or behaviors. A person can be asked for her preference between two presidential candidates, as in Gallup polls done before each election. Children can be asked to report on their perceptions of their classmates' aggressiveness, or on their own actual television viewing behavior, as in Huesmann's study. In all these cases, the basic data are the individuals' own reports about their thoughts, feelings, and actions.

Self-reports are obtained in a wide number of different settings. The Huesmann study collected information from children in a classroom, and questionnaire studies are often done in a laboratory, especially as part of a controlled experiment.

Survey research is another common method of collecting self-report data. In most surveys, people are interviewed by a professional interviewer. Surveys are done about almost every conceivable topic, ranging from product preferences to politics to sexual relations. Until recently, surveys were most often done face-to-face in the home. Now this is increasingly expensive and difficult. People have become more suspicious of strangers coming to the door; the increasing number of working women has made it harder to find people at home; and rising labor costs have made it inefficient for interviewers to be driving all over town, only to find that no one is at home. So survey researchers have turned to telephone or mail surveys.

Telephone surveys yield data that are similar to those from home interviews, except that they usually must be somewhat shorter and are much less expensive to do. When telephone surveys were first used, in the 1930s, only people with some money had telephones, so they tended to give quite biased results. But almost everyone has a telephone now so telephone surveys no longer yield such biased samples of respondents. On the other hand, mail surveys are not usually very reliable, because relatively few people will return mail questionnaires, and the ones who do are not usually representative of the general population.

The big advantage of self-report questionnaire or interview techniques is that they allow the investigator to measure subjective states such as perceptions, attitudes, or emotions. These can only be inferred indirectly from observational studies, and as we will see in Chapter 3, observers' inferences of such internal states from overt behavior are not very reliable. Any study that requires us to have information about internal states must almost always use self-report techniques. For example, it would be very difficult for observers to tell how lonely another person feels without getting that person's self-report.

The principal disadvantage of self-report techniques is that we must rely on the people to give honest reports of their own internal feelings. But

Ken Karp

How might the answers of these respondents to this marketing survey be affected by their answering together?

people sometimes disguise socially unacceptable feelings (such as racial prejudices), and sometimes they are not fully aware of their own feelings. These are precisely the reasons that led behaviorists like Watson and Skinner to reject introspectionist techniques years ago. However, social psychology has come a long way toward learning the conditions under which such self-reports can be trusted, and they have become the dominant data-gathering technique.

Archival Research

A final kind of study is **archival research,** in which the investigator uses data that had previously been collected in earlier research projects. An example of the use of archives is the study described in

The U.S. Census is a major source of archival data. Such massive data collection efforts must be carried out by large research teams with large funding resources.

Chapter 10 on the relationship between cotton prices and lynchings of blacks in the South. The investigators (Hovland & Sears, 1940) started with the general theory that frustration leads to aggression. They then reasoned that drops in cotton prices produced frustration that would in turn produce an increase in aggression in the form of lynchings. The data on cotton prices and on the number of lynchings were readily available in statistics collected by the United States government and others. The investigators simply looked up these data and ran correlations between the two variables. The years with low cotton prices had the most lynchings, supporting the hypothesis.

Almost all major universities now have their own data archives. They usually include data on a wide variety of topics. Perhaps the best-known archival data come from the U.S. Census that has been collected every 10 years for two centuries. The government also collects and archives vast quantities of economic statistics. Another important source is the Interuniversity Consortium for Political and Social Research (ICPSR). This is an organization headquartered at the University of Michigan which has stored and distributed the data from most of the major survey studies done in the social sciences

in the past 30 years. Among many other things, it has the major studies of presidential elections done by the National Election Studies, the General Social Survey done at the University of Chicago, and the New York Times/CBS News polls, all of which provide survey data on the American people over many years. Many colleges and universities subscribe to the Consortium, which means that all these data are available to any researcher at those institutions.

There are many advantages of using archival data. Most obvious is that it is very cheap to use data that may have been enormously expensive to collect. The U.S. Census costs millions of dollars to collect, but the data can be used for next to nothing. Archival data also allow us to test hypotheses at various time points, or even trends over time, rather than being limited to one historical moment. We might want to know how many people say they would vote for a woman for president, and the availability of archival data on that question over many years can give us a rich historical context for our findings. On the other hand, archival data almost always were collected with some research question in mind other than the one we wish now to use them for. As a result, the questions are usually not exactly the ones we would ask, or they may be worded the wrong way for our purposes, or the persons in the study may not be exactly the group we would prefer. As a result, the uses of data archives are limited in some ways. Neverthe- less, as they continue to expand in the years ahead, they will prove of increasing importance to social psychology.

DEVELOPING AND CONDUCTING THE STUDY

Once the questions and the method have been chosen, the investigator must design and conduct a study. Let us take as an example the design and execution of a laboratory experiment. An investigator has gotten interested in the effects of fear on attitude change. Sometimes advertisers or politicians claim dire consequences will follow if people do not use a product or vote for them. People will be stranded with a flat tire at midnight in a rainstorm on a deserted highway, or their taxes will go up. Does making people fearful make them more susceptible to a propaganda message? Or does it just frighten them so much they don't want to think about anything at all?

Suppose the researchers hypothesize that fear arousal produces attitude change, and have decided to do an experimental study. They must set up a situation in which the independent variable (fear) is experimentally manipulated; the subjects are randomly assigned to groups; and the high and low fear groups differ only in terms of fear arousal, the independent variable. Then the experimenter must measure the dependent variable, attitude change, in order to see what effect the independent variable, fear arousal, has had.

The Independent Variable

The first step in the process generally is to decide on the specific way to manipulate the independent variable. The psychologists start with a *conceptual definition*. Let us say they defined fear as the internal feeling produced by the anticipation of pain or harm from a known source. This conceptual definition may sound impressive, but it is very general.

The experimenters' big problem is deciding on the particular way in which they are going to arouse fear; that is, to decide on an *operational definition* of fear. An operational definition is the specific procedure, or operation, that is used to implement, in a particular study, the much more general conceptual variable we are interested in. According to the conceptual definition, they must set up a situation in which the person anticipates harm from a known source. The operational definition provides the specific procedure by which this is done; for example, showing the subject a terrifying film depicting the horrible rot and pain that can occur if people do not follow good dental hygiene practices.

There are several criteria for a good manipulation. One is that it should work in a similar manner on all subjects. If a manipulation uniformly creates the same experience for all individuals, its effects are more likely to be significant. Therefore, the psychologist wants to use something everyone or almost everyone is afraid of.

Another is that it provide several levels of a particular variable rather than simply its presence or absence. Without any fear at all, people simply may not pay attention to the propagandist. With too much fear, they may get too frightened and tune out. With moderate fear, they may be maximally responsive. So we want to think of the independent variable as a continuum, ranging from low to high levels of fear, and the experimental conditions as falling at various points on that continuum. So in this example we might show three films: a high fear film, that shows a mouth with rotting teeth that are falling out; a medium fear film, that shows the person in some pain and requiring some treatment; and a low fear film, that shows the person with some discoloration of back teeth.

How can we be certain that the manipulation really created differences in the independent variable we have conceptually defined? There are two main ways of pinning down the meaning of the experimental manipulation. One is to check directly on the manipulation by the use of self-reports or by some other variable that we know from previous research to be highly correlated with fear. For example, we could ask people how fearful or nervous they felt. Or we could take measures of blood pressure and pulse rate. Although physiological measures are generally poor indicators of the presence of fear, they do tend to be correlated with it. The greater the fear, the higher should be the blood pressure and pulse rate.

The other way is to use many different kinds of fear manipulations, all derived from our conceptual definition. If all these different manipulations produce the same effect on the dependent measure (for example, if in all cases the high-fear group was more persuaded than the low-fear group), we can be quite confident that fear is producing the effect.

Unfortunately, neither approach is particularly easy in most instances. A great deal of care is required to be certain of our interpretation of the manipulation, and much controversy often revolves around different interpretations of the same experimental manipulation.

The Dependent Variable

We must now decide how to measure the dependent variable, attitude change. Again we must go from a conceptual to an operational definition with a minimum of ambiguity because we would like to be absolutely sure it is attitude change we are measuring. In this case, the researcher might operationally define attitude change as a change in the subject's desire to buy a particular brand of flashlight battery from before to after viewing a fear-arousing commercial or magazine advertisement about it.

Often researchers cannot find a perfect measure of the variable they are interested in. One solution to this problem is to use many different measures of the same variable. If the measures all produce the same results and are all designed to tap the same variable, we can have increased confidence in the meaning of the findings. Any one measure might be interpreted in a variety of ways, but if ten different measures produce the same result, it is more likely that the intended variable has been measured.

BIASES

Before actually running the experiment, however, the wise researcher must anticipate the various kinds of biases that might arise and take steps to minimize their effects. All scientists are concerned about bias, and social psychologists are no exceptions. Three kinds of bias are particularly troublesome in social psychology: the selection of a subject population, the experimenter's behavior, and bias associated with a subject's feelings about being in an experiment.

Subject Population

How do we decide what people to study? One obvious starting point might be that we want to study the people about whom we later want to generalize. If we want to generalize about women who work full time, we should study working women. But clearly we will never be able to afford to study all the people we want to generalize to.

So instead we study some smaller number of them, but chosen in such a way that they are representative of the larger group. We cannot study the television habits of all fourth-grade boys in the United States, but we can study some smaller group of them, and if they are representative of fourth-grade boys in general, we will have some confidence that our conclusions will hold for the population as a whole. This is known as a *representative sample*.

The best way to ensure this general representativeness is to study a random sample of the larger population to which we want to generalize. In formal terms, a **random sample** means that each person in the larger population has an equal chance of being included in the study. If we selected a sample of telephone numbers from the phone directory at random (using a table of random numbers, for example), we could be assured that ours was a random sample of all listed phone numbers in the area covered by that telephone book. The laws of probability assure us that a large and truly random sample will almost always be representative of the population within a certain margin of error. It will include approximately the same proportion of women, minorities, unemployed, elderly, and so forth as the population from which we have sampled.

Most of the time social psychologists want to generalize to people in general, not just some subgroup like elementary school children in Austin, Texas, or people who use laundromats in Nashville, Tennessee. Yet it is extremely expensive to study random samples of people in general, as you can readily imagine. It would be especially unrealistic to try to get a random sample of people in general into an experiment in your laboratory at your university. Even Supersaver airfares are not that cheap. So social psychologists try to make realistic compromises between the goal of collecting valid data that can be generalized beyond the few people they test, on the one hand, and practicality on the other.

One very common compromise is to use college students as subjects. It has often been said that American social psychology is based on college sophomores, because they are the ones who are most available for experiments in laboratories. About 75 percent of all published articles in social psychology use undergraduate subjects, and about two-thirds use undergraduates in the laboratory

(Sears, 1986). Another compromise is to use volunteer subjects, such as those who might leave their names and phone numbers in response to a plea for subjects left on our church bulletin board. Clearly neither college students nor such volunteers are representative samples of the general population, and social psychologists usually do not make any pretense that they are. How dissatisfied should we be with such unrepresentative samples?

Our need for a representative sample depends on the question we are asking. For the most descriptive, applied research, when we are trying to describe the characteristics of a given population, plainly we need a representative sample. If, for example, we are trying to determine how many hours a day fourth-grade boys normally watch television, we need a representative sample. It would not do to interview boys on the local playground or our friends' sons; soccer players and college professors' sons may not watch as much television as other boys. Suppose we are commissioned to do a study to find out how to introduce automated office equipment into offices where the workers have worked together for decades, are almost all women, and never went past high school. We would not be confident of understanding what techniques would work with them if we did our study on college students who had never met each other before the study and who had no experience with any kind of office machinery or work.

On the other hand, in basic research the representativeness of the sample is sometimes less crucial. The basic researcher is not interested in describing specific groups but in laws that apply to all people. For example, either Ivy League college students or passers-by on Fifth Avenue should help less in the presence of other people than when alone, according to Darley and Latané's diffusion of responsibility theory. The assumption is that all people work in about the same way. So, just as chemicals form the same compounds in about the same way no matter what laboratory you are working in or what company produced the chemicals, almost any subject population is regarded as appropriate for basic research in social psychology.

Moreover, college students may be especially appropriate for studying some phenomena. Suppose we were studying loneliness. National samples indicate that loneliness is greatest among young adults, and that the transition to college induces even more loneliness. So it may be that freshmen college students would be an optimal subject population for that purpose.

However, there are probably some areas in which college students may actually be somewhat misleading as a source of data (Sears, 1986). College students are much younger, in a higher social class, and superior in cognitive skills, especially in test situations, than the general population. For problems in which these are central factors, college students may be misleading. For example, studies of friendship and social influence would need to take into account the fact that college students' relationships with their friends have generally been rather brief compared to the most important friendships of older people. Similarly, studies of personality should take into account the fact that most college sophomores are still rather young, and their personalities have not developed as fully as have those of mature adults. The same is likely to be true of their political and social attitudes. If we did research only on college students, we might be misled into concluding that long-term social ties are not very important in influencing people's attitudes, values, or physical health, or that their personalities have little impact on their behavior.

The use of volunteers is also subject to some fairly predictable biases (Rosenthal & Rosnow, 1975). For example, what kind of people volunteer for a study called "Responses to Erotica"? They are, not surprisingly, people who are relatively relaxed about their own sexuality, are more sexually experienced, and show less negative emotion when they are shown erotic films (Saunders et al., 1985).

The best advice to give about these problems is that they should be anticipated before beginning the study. Usually it is possible to anticipate the particular kinds of biases that nonrepresentative samples will introduce into the study. Then we can predict whether or not those biases will threaten the conclusions of the study. Thinking carefully about these potential biases before doing the study saves a lot of grief later on.

Experimenter Bias

One problem that is particularly troublesome in social psychology is **experimenter bias.** Subjects in an experiment are extremely susceptible to influence by the experimenter. They will do virtually anything the experimenter asks. The social psychologist Martin Orne tells of asking several students to sit in a room and add 2000 pages of random numbers. He told them: "Continue to work, I will return eventually." Five and one-half hours later, he returned; the students were still adding. Finally, the *experimenter* gave up!

Subjects tend to be compliant even when the experimenter does not make any direct requests. If the experimenter implies, consciously or otherwise, that he or she would like subjects to respond in a certain way, there is a tendency for them to respond in that way. Subtle cues tend to be picked up by subjects and to influence their behavior. For example, consider the studies of media violence that have subjects shock another person after the subject has viewed a violent or a nonviolent movie. A well-intentioned but perhaps overly eager experimenter, knowing that the subjects who had seen the violent movie were supposed to be the most aggressive, might subtly encourage these subjects to give more shock. She might smile, giggle, make eye contact, or act encouraging in a wide variety of subtle ways. For the subjects who had seen the nonviolent movie, she might frown or act cold when they give the shock, because they are violating the hypothesis.

There are two solutions to this problem. One is to keep the experimenters ignorant as to the experimental condition of the subject. This is usually referred to as keeping experimenters *blind.* If they do not know which experimental conditions they are dealing with, there is no way for them to affect the conditions. In this case, we could have one experimenter show the movies and a second one administer the shock task, and arrange it so that the second experimenter did not know which movie the subject had seen.

A second solution is to standardize the situation in every way possible. If everything is standardized and there are no differences between conditions other than those that are deliberate, there can be no bias. In the extreme case, the subjects might appear for an experiment, find a written instruction on the door telling them to enter, have all instructions presented on tape, and complete the experiment before they meet a live experimenter. In this way, every factor in the situation would be absolutely standardized, and experimenter bias would be eliminated.

In actual practice, the solution to the problem of bias is usually a combination of the two procedures we have described. As much as possible, the experimenter is kept blind as to the subjects' experimental conditions; also as much as possible, instructions are standardized by the use of tapes or written materials.

The Subject Role

An even subtler source of bias in a social psychology experiment stems from the subject's motives and goals when serving in the role of a research subject. One major potential problem concerns most subjects' desires to give the "correct" response in the situation, in part because they want to impress the experimenter. This *social desirability bias* occurs when a person's desire to give the "right" answer leads the person to give biased responses.

For example, an experimenter might be interested in the effects of frustration on whites' aggression toward blacks. She might frustrate white subjects and then give them the choice of aggressing against either a white or a black. If this were done in a straightforward manner, many subjects might suspect that the experimenter was interested in whether whites or blacks were the targets of aggression. Most white college students think it is wrong

BOX 2–3

THE BOGUS PIPELINE

Jones and Sigall (1971) devised an ingenious procedure for minimizing social desirability biases. The general idea was to construct a situation in which subjects would give their true opinions, feelings, and attitudes regardless of what the experimenters wanted or might think of them. In other words, the situation was constructed to make the subjects ignore any concerns they might have had about being nice to the experimenters, impressing them, or even looking good to themselves. To the extent that the subjects were able to respond honestly, the situation was designed to elicit their real opinions.

The method was to tell the subjects that they were hooked up to what was essentially a fancy lie detector that could tell their true opinions from a variety of physiological measurements. Electrodes were attached to the subjects' arms and legs. A very impressive-looking piece of machinery with moving dials stood in the room emitting all sorts of whirring noises. The machine actually measured nothing. The subjects were then asked to respond to a few questions just to check on the machine's accuracy. These questions were selected to make it appear as if the subjects' true feelings could be known, but actually the experimenters knew them from a questionnaire they gave the subjects earlier. Thus the subjects discovered that the machine did, in fact, give the right answers. Then the subjects were asked to respond to other questions, including the ones the experimenters were really interested in. Under these circumstances, the subjects had no reason to lie and so gave honest answers, even if the answers were unpleasant or uncomfortably revealing.

to be prejudiced against blacks. So the "correct" response would be to aggress equally against whites and blacks, or even to bend over backward and aggress more against whites. However, in a real-life situation many whites do feel considerable prejudice against blacks and may have a tendency to aggress more against them than against other whites. In this example, then, social desirability biases may interfere with the subjects' natural behavior and distort their responses.

A related problem concerns the **demand characteristics** of the experimental situation. Some experiments are constructed so that they readily tip subjects off to what they "should" be doing if they are acting as good subjects. The problem is that what the experiment "demands" them to do may turn out to be exactly what confirms the experimenter's hypothesis! Then the hypothesis is supported not because it is a correct description of social behavior, but because the experiment has been constructed to get the "right" answer from the subjects.

Weber and Cook (1972) have carried out perhaps the most careful analysis of the roles subjects adopt in laboratory experiments. They distinguish several different roles: the "good subject," who tries to help the researchers by confirming the hypotheses; the "negativistic subject," who tries to sabotage the experiment; the "faithful subject," who scrupulously follows instructions and tries to avoid acting on the basis of any suspicions about the nature of the study (either to help, or to hurt, the research); and the "apprehensive subject," who is mainly anxious about his own performance.

Such biases are almost impossible to eliminate entirely, but they can be minimized in a variety of ways. The goal is to produce a situation in which the subjects respond spontaneously without worrying about the correctness of the response. This feeling can be minimized somewhat by having the subject respond anonymously so that the experimenter will not know how she behaved in the situation. Unfortunately, this does not solve the problem. Most subjects want to impress not only the experimenter, but also themselves. They want to think of themselves as good people and therefore do what they can to behave in the right way. As long as a subject is thinking about these considerations, it is virtually impossible to eliminate this kind of bias.

Another tactic is not to tell subjects they are being observed. We could observe how white salespeople in a store treat black and white customers on a particularly busy, hard day compared to an easy day. If frustration leads to aggression, the salespeople should be nastier on the hard day, and even more so to blacks than to whites if that aggression is directed at people of the two races differentially. Or experiments can be set up so that the crucial measure is taken after the subject thinks the experiment is over.

Yet another tactic is to use unobtrusive or so-called nonreactive measures, in which the subject does not know that a measure is being taken. As a measure of hostility, we could observe how near to a black or white person the subject sits when entering the room.

Perhaps the most obvious and common tactic is simply not to let the subject know what our hypothesis is. The study must be designed carefully so that it is difficult for the subject to figure out what our intention is. We do not inform the subject about our hypotheses until the study is complete. We embed our crucial measures in the midst of others that deal with other topics. All these techniques reduce the possibility that the dependent measure reflects the subject's view of what is socially desirable more than his or her natural inclination.

RESEARCH ETHICS

During the late 1950s and early 1960s, many people became concerned about the ethics of research on human subjects. Some of the concern stemmed from the discoveries of Nazi atrocities during World War II, such as the dangerous and often fatal experiments carried out by doctors in concentration camps on unwilling camp inmates. Some of it stemmed from the discovery of medical experimentation of dubious ethicality in this country, such as the notorious Tuskegee case. In 1932, the United States Public Health Service began a 40-year experiment on 399 poor and semiliterate blacks in Alabama who had syphilis. The goal was to trace the effects of syphilis on untreated males over many years. The men were told they were being treated, but in fact they never were, despite the fact that penicillin had become available in the 1940s and was highly effective against the disease. Even by 1972, treatment was still withheld from the survivors as the study continued.

Some of the concern also focused on experiments that involved deception or potential psychological harm to subjects. The Milgram experiment on obedience described in Box 2–4 received much criticism because of its deception. His subjects genuinely thought they were hurting another person, just as the Tuskegee patients thought they were being treated. The ethical issue is that the subjects were induced to commit seemingly dangerous acts toward another person without being informed about the real nature of the experiment. The study violated **informed consent:** The subject did not agree to participate in the study on the basis of adequate information about the procedure.

Such studies raise a number of issues. When are researchers justified in deceiving subjects about the research they are participating in? When is it legitimate to do harmful things to subjects? How far does the right to privacy go when one is a subject of research? Was it ethical for Milgram to deceive subjects into thinking they were really delivering harmful shocks to other people? Can exposing subjects to such risks be justified if the research has great scientific value, as perhaps the Milgram study did? Such questions, and others, are raised not only by concerned researchers but by the subjects themselves (e.g., Forsyth & Pope, 1984).

These questions led to efforts within professional associations to define ethical behavior. The American Psychological Association, the American Sociological Association, and the American Association of Public Opinion Research all drew up codes of ethics for their researchers. However, the standards were of necessity rather general and therefore ambiguous, and compliance was voluntary, so they did not really provide effective protection against abuse.

By the 1960s, the federal government was funding much of the research on human subjects done in the United States. Not surprisingly, many people felt the government should take responsibility for the ethical standards of the research. This raised a number of rather touchy issues. Who should make those judgments? Should government bureaucrats dictate the procedures to be used by every researcher all over the country, setting up an authoritarian and cumbersome system that might stifle free inquiry? Or should the foxes be guarding the henhouses—should the researchers themselves be allowed to make their own judgments, at the risk of permitting some unscrupulous investigators to harm subjects? The solution finally agreed upon in the late 1960s was to have a committee of researchers at each research institution review all proposed research using human subjects. This institutional review board would be responsible for ensuring that all research using human subjects would be conducted according to a set of general principles laid down by the federal government's Department of Health and Human Services.

BOX 2–4

THE TENDENCY TO OBEY

When thousands of Germans obeyed orders to send Jews to the gas chambers, were they simply acting in the way people normally act? Or was this behavior an example of some pathology in their own individual personalities, or in the German people as a whole? Stanley Milgram (1963) believed that their actions reflected a normal human tendency to obey the orders of legitimate authorities, even when it means hurting innocent people. He conducted an experiment to try to demonstrate this. The study was described to the subjects as a study of the effects of punishment on memory. Two subjects (one was actually a confederate of the experimenter) participated at a time. The real subject was told he would be the "teacher," and the other subject (the confederate) would be the "learner." Whenever the "learner" made an error, the subject was to punish him by shocking him. The subject was given a "shock generator," with 30 clearly marked levels ranging from 15 to 450 volts. The label "Danger: Severe shock" appeared at the 375-volt level; even higher levels of shock were marked "XXX."

As the experiment proceeded, the "learner" would make occasional mistakes, and each time the experimenter would instruct the "teacher" (the real subject) to administer the next highest level of shock. At 300 volts, the learner (who was in a separate room) pounded on the wall. At 315 volts, more pounding was heard. After that, no more was heard. Nevertheless, the "teacher" was told to keep on shocking the learner as though a failure to respond was the same as an error. When the subject finally refused to give any more shock, the experiment ended.

In Milgram's basic experiment, all subjects administered at least 300 volts. And 65 percent (26 of 40 subjects) gave the maximum possible shock: 450 volts. A comparable group of college students, given a full description of the experiment, had estimated that on the average subjects would go no further than 150 volts. So Milgram's intuition was correct, and theirs was wrong: Ordinary people would indeed administer very dangerous shocks to perfect strangers, simply on command from a legitimate authority.

This does not mean the anti-semitism of the Nazi party, or of many other Germans and East Europeans, had no role in the Holocaust. Plainly it did. But it suggests ordinary people will do extraordinarily harmful things to innocent strangers, out of a desire to obey.

These general principles include three requirements for each research project. First, it must obtain the subject's informed consent to participate in the research. The subject must voluntarily agree to participate, without any coercion. And the subject must understand what the participation involves.

Second, there must be **minimal risk;** that is, the research procedures must "not unnecessarily expose subjects to risk." And third, there must be a **risk-benefit analysis,** such that the *risks* to the subjects are *balanced* by the expected *benefits* of the research, either to the subjects themselves or

The Milgram obedience study. (Copyright 1965 by Stanley Milgram. From the film *Obedience*, distributed by the New York University Film Library.)

to society at large. In social psychology, of course, unlike medical research, there are usually no great benefits to the subjects themselves. The justification for the research is usually in terms of the benefits obtained by enlarging knowledge about human behavior.

Informed Consent

"Participation by subjects should be voluntary and based on informed consent to the extent that it is consistent with the objectives of the research." Ordinarily, individuals should not be subjected to research unless they have agreed to it. Whenever possible, this agreement should be given after they have heard exactly what is going to take place during the course of the study. The researcher has an obligation to tell potential subjects as much as possible about the study before asking them to participate. The federal regulations are quite specific about the exact nature of this informed consent. It must

be written out, and the subject must sign an informed consent form. The form must describe the research procedures, identify any risks and/or benefits of the research, specify that refusal to participate or withdrawal during the research can be done without penalty, and indicate to whom inquiries or complaints can be addressed.

These requirements sound quite reasonable, but many create some problems for social psychologists. As we have just seen, it may be important not to tell subjects the true purpose of the study, to avoid biasing their responses. Even in the simplest research, subjects are rarely told the specific hypotheses that are being tested.

Several of the studies we discussed in this chapter did not provide fully informed consent, and it is hard to see how they could have. Darley and Latané did not tell their subjects in advance that a confederate would feign a seizure in order to determine whether or not the subject would rush to help. Milgram did not tell his subjects that the learner was really a confederate, and that they were not really shocking him. Knowing that the confederate was not really having a seizure in the Darley-Latané study or that he was not in fact being shocked for making a "mistake" in Milgram study would certainly influence how much the subject helped or obeyed orders. It is hard to imagine either study being valid if the subjects had really given full "informed consent." Imagine what would have happened if Darley and Latané had told their subjects the study concerned bystander intervention, and they were testing to see if the subject would help in an emergency!

Some people believe that deception of any kind is unethical in psychological research. They feel it demeans the subjects and should never be used. A more moderate position endorsed by most research psychologists is that deception should not be used if at all possible, or used only after considering its possible harmful effects. Subjects, however, should always have *volunteered* to be in the study. Perhaps they need not necessarily be told everything that will happen, but they should know that they are in an experiment and should have freely given their permission. In other words, only someone who has given informed consent or consent based on trust should be exposed to potentially distressing conditions.

And subjects should always be *debriefed*; that is, the purposes and procedures of the experiment should always be explained to them afterward. They should be given an opportunity to ask questions, express their feelings, and generally recover from any upset the experiment has caused. After his debriefings, Milgram found that 84 percent of his subjects were glad to have participated.

Minimal Risk

Another key research guideline is to minimize potential risks to the subjects. Minimal risk means that the risks anticipated in the research are no greater "than those ordinarily encountered in daily life." What are the kinds of risk sociopsychological research can pose?

One of the most important is the invasion of *privacy*. An individual's right to privacy must be respected and cherished. As a president's panel on privacy and behavior research stated, every individual must be allowed to "decide for himself how much he will share with others his thoughts, his feelings, and the facts of his personal life." Although privacy is a complex matter, certain guidelines can be observed.

Clearly some areas are more sensitive than others. The most sensitive are matters that could affect one's legal status or one's job, such as information about illegal behavior, sexual behavior, alcohol or drug use, or health-related matters. People are generally private about their income, partly because the Internal Revenue Service has strong feelings about that income, and some legal clout. Religious and political feelings are considered private by many people, though many others have no hesitation about expressing them to one and all. How people behave when they are angry, frustrated, or scared can also be quite personal. Research designed to obtain such information must carefully observe the guidelines on privacy.

On the other hand, public behavior, or events on the public record, do not have to be protected as carefully. Births, marriages, and deaths are all on the public record. Anyone can go to the local courthouse and look up who, when, and how in all those cases. In contrast, surgical or other medical procedures are private. A woman's giving birth is public, whereas her having an abortion is private. Whether someone crosses the street when the light is red or smokes cigarettes is relatively public information. Almost anyone can obtain it merely by watching the individual's behavior in public.

Threats to privacy, like all the risks involved in social psychological research, can change over time as the society itself changes. For example, people are much more willing to discuss details of their sexual relationships now than they were a generation ago. Similarly, a generation ago cancer was a disease to be kept private at all costs. Obituaries would describe someone as having died from "a long illness" or "a lingering illness," but never from "cancer." The subject's privacy must be protected, but we must also remember that standards of privacy must be adjusted as people's needs for privacy change with time.

One of the most important ways of protecting privacy is through maintaining the confidentiality of the data. Perhaps we are conducting a study of status relationships within an organization, and we wish to obtain a secretary's candid perceptions of her relationship with her boss. It is vital that we guarantee her the boss will not have access to those perceptions. If we conduct studies like Milgram's on obedience or the Darley-Latané experiment on bystander intervention, we must guarantee subjects that their responses will be confidential. It would be a gross violation of privacy to publicize which subjects obeyed or failed to help, because of the embarrassment that could result. Responsible researchers today protect confidentiality carefully, usually by having the person participate in the study anonymously, by replacing the subject's name with a code number on all records, and by keeping all data in a secure place, such as a locked file cabinet.

The other main category of risk in social psychology experiments comes from stresses of various kinds. Some are fairly obvious. Fear can be created in the laboratory, and at times can build up to fairly high levels. A classic case is the study by French (1944). Groups of subjects were put in a room at the top of an old building at Harvard, ostensibly to discuss a problem. Soon after the experimenter left, smoke began coming under a door in the room. The subjects soon discovered that all the doors were locked, and at this point most presumably became quite frightened. However, they did not take this kind of situation lying down. Several groups included varsity football players, and they broke down the door, terminating the experiment. Other groups managed to break into the closet from which the smoke was pouring and discovered the smoke machine. Still others convinced themselves it was an experiment and calmly went about discussing the problem, ignoring the smoke that was beginning to fill the room.

Other stresses may be less obvious. Some studies may threaten the individual's self-respect. As we will see in Chapter 5, many studies in recent years have been focused on the causal explanations, or attributions, that people make for their own successes and failures. To do such studies frequently requires that success or failure be experimentally manipulated. A gratuitous failure experience in a psychology experiment is no fun. Similarly, neither the Milgram obedience study nor the Darley-Latané bystander intervention study threatened the subject physically. But the person who later finds that he willingly obeyed orders that might have killed an innocent person, or who is confronted with the fact that he was unwilling to go to the aid of a person who was having a life-threatening seizure, may well lose some self-respect. It would not be surprising if some subjects became resentful about having been deceived into participating in studies that confronted them with unpleasant truths about themselves.

Being deceived is itself an unpleasant experience for some people. Smith and Richardson (1983), for example, did a survey of students who had participated in psychology experiments at the University of Georgia. Of them, 20 percent reported experiencing some harmful consequence, such as being deceived, humiliated, experiencing physical discomfort, or being angered. Such reports were almost twice as common among students who had participated in deception experiments as among those who had not. Most students reported no harm, of course, but a substantial minority did.

How much risk should a subject be exposed to? The first and most important principle is once again informed consent. If at all possible, the subjects must be allowed to make that decision for themselves, based on adequate information. The situation is like the decision people face about what surgical procedure to undergo: Ultimately, the decision must be in the hands of the patient, but it must be as informed a decision as possible.

But if it is not always possible to fully inform a subject in a social psychology experiment about the exact nature of the study, the investigator or the institutional review board must make a decision about how much risk is allowable. Then a second rule of thumb comes into play: The risks faced in the research should be no more severe than those the person is likely to encounter in normal life. Being threatened with an injection may be frightening, but it is a usual occurrence—we all get injections. In contrast, being threatened with isolation for 5 hours is also frightening, but it is not a usual occurrence—most people never face this threat. So we would be more hesitant about deceiving a person about isolation than about a harmless injection.

Finally, another general rule many researchers and review boards use in evaluating risk is that the subjects should leave the study in essentially the same state of mind and body in which they entered. That is, participation in the study should have no substantial effect of any kind that carries over once the subject has finished. Another way of stating this is that the study may be pleasant, interesting, and enjoyable, or mildly unpleasant, boring, or tedious—but the subjects' state of mind, knowledge of themselves, and general attitudes should not be altered by the experience. This guideline, if followed closely, would ensure that subjects would not have been exposed to excessive risk.

KEY TERMS IN CHAPTER 2

applied research	experimental design	informed consent	random sample
archival research	experimenter bias	internal validity	reverse-causality problem
basic research	external validity	minimal risk	risk-benefit analysis
correlational design	field experiment	nontheoretical question	theoretical question
demand characteristics	independent variable	random assignment	third-variable problem
dependent variable			

SUMMARY

1. Although we all know a great deal about social behavior from our daily observations and experience, some of our impressions are incorrect. Systematic research is necessary to be certain which of our intuitions are right and which are wrong.

2. Theoretical research is designed to test a theory, to compare two theories, or to assess the limits and exceptions to a theory. Nontheoretical research starts with a general question that is not directly related to a theory and tries to discover new relationships or test a hunch or intuition.

3. Basic research deals with fundamental questions, general principles, or theories. Applied research is directed toward answering a question related to a specific problem in the world—such as how to reduce prejudice, sell toothpaste, or design housing.

4. Correlational research asks whether two or more variables are related, without trying to manipulate either. Correlational research can deal with a great many variables at once, and can investigate factors that cannot usually be manipulated in the laboratory, such as very high fear, poverty, or social class. But correlational research usually does not allow strong causal inferences.

5. In experimental research, subjects are randomly assigned to situations that differ only in specific deliberately varied ways. If there is any difference in behavior, it is due to that variable. This provides control over the situation and allows unambiguous causal statements.

6. Research in the laboratory provides more control, but research in field settings is closer to the real world and often permits a greater range of intensity in the variables studied.

7. The most common sources of data are systematic observations of behavior, self-report, and data archives.

8. In designing an experiment, the key questions are how to manipulate the independent variable and how to measure the dependent variable.

9. Great care must be taken to avoid the effects of bias. The experimenter can affect the results, even unintentionally, or subjects can give results they think are "correct" but are not what they would have done spontaneously.

10. Social psychologists face many ethical problems in doing research. They must be careful to guard the safety of subjects, to respect their privacy, and to ensure that their research produces no harmful effects on anyone involved. Current guidelines emphasize obtaining informed consent to whatever extent possible, and exposing subjects to no more than minimal risk.

SUGGESTED READINGS

ARONSON, E., BREWER, M., & CARLSMITH, J. M. (1985). Experimentation in social psychology. In G. Lindzey & E. Aronson (eds.), *The Handbook of Social Psychology*, 3rd ed. Vol. 1. Reading, MA: Addison-Wesley. The generally accepted mainstream treatment of experimentation in social psychology.

COOK, T. D. & CAMPBELL, D. T. (1979). *Quasi-experimentation: Design and analysis issues for field settings*. Chicago: Rand McNally. The use of nonexperimental techniques in field situations is becoming increasingly important. This presents the state-of-the art thinking about how to design and interpret such studies.

HYMAN, H. H. (1972). *Secondary analysis of sample surveys: Principles, procedures, and potentialities*. New York: John Wiley & Sons. A clear and straightforward explanation of how to use archival data, with many interesting examples.

JONES, J. H. (1981). *Bad blood*. New York: Free Press. A fascinating historical account of the "Tuskegee case" that revolutionized protection of human subjects.

SEARS, D. O. (1986). College sophomores in the laboratory: Influences of a narrow database on social psychology's view of human nature. *Journal of Personality and Social Psychology, 51*, 515–520. An analysis of the possible dangers of relying too heavily on college sophomores in laboratory experiments.

WEBB, E. J., CAMPBELL, D. T., SCHWARTZ, R. D., & SECHREST, L. (1966). *Unobtrusive measures: Nonreactive research in the social sciences*. Chicago: Rand McNally. An engaging description of many clever techniques for collecting data without letting people know you are doing it. Often not very ethical, but they minimize subject bias!

WEBER, S. J., & COOK, T. D. (1972). Subject effects in laboratory research: An examination of subject roles, demand characteristics, and valid inferences. *Psychological Bulletin, 77*, 273–295. An intriguing analysis of the various roles that subjects may play in psychology experiments.

3 PERSON PERCEPTION

A murder trial hinges on the testimony of one key witness. The jury members' belief in this witness will determine their decisions. The impression they form of her in her brief appearance in the courtroom will determine whether the defendant goes to jail or stays free. They examine her face, her features, her clothes, the quality of her voice, and her answers, trying to decide what kind of person she is.

Two freshmen destined to be roommates arrive at college and meet for the first time. Each one's personality—how easy each one is to get along with, how nice each is—will have an important effect on the other's life. In the first few minutes of their meeting, each tries to form an impression of the other, because they know they will be spending a great deal of time together during the year. How late does each one stay up studying at night? What kind of music does the other like? How loud? How does each feel about parties in the room? They try to find out as much about each other as they can.

Our knowledge of and expectations about others are determined first of all by the impressions we form of them. A glance at someone's picture or at an individual passing on the street gives us ideas about the kind of person he or she is; even hearing a name tends to conjure up images of what its owner is like. When two people meet, if only for an instant, they form impressions of each other. With more contact, they form fuller and richer impressions that determine how they behave toward each other, how much they like each other, whether they will associate often, and so on.

People use whatever information is available to form these impressions of others—to make judgments about their personalities or hypotheses about the kinds of persons they are. In this chapter we deal with this process, which is called **person perception:** how we make first impressions, what biases affect them, what kinds of information we use in arriving at them, and how accurate our impressions are.

FORMING IMPRESSIONS

People tend to form extensive impressions of others on the basis of very limited information. Having seen a person or even a photograph for only a few minutes, people will tell us how much they like him and how much they think they will like the person if they can get to know him better. They will also make judgments about a large number of that person's specific characteristics. They are generally willing to estimate another's intelligence, age, background, race, religion, educational level, honesty, warmth, and so on. Although ordinarily individuals are not overly confident of opinions formed in this way, they generally are willing to make such judgments.

Evaluation

The most important and powerful aspect of first impressions is **evaluation.** Do we like or dislike this person? How much do we like or dislike him? Our immediate impression may be composed of other dimensions; he may seem friendly, talkative, and helpful. But all these specific traits are fundamentally tied to the question of whether we like or don't like him.

Put more formally, the evaluative dimension is the most important of a small number of basic dimensions that organize these unified impressions of people. This was shown in work by Osgood,

Suci, and Tannenbaum (1957) on the so-called *semantic differential*. In their study, subjects were given a list of trait pairs and asked to indicate which trait particular persons and objects fell closest to. The list consisted of such trait pairs as happy-sad, good-bad, strong-weak, and warm-cold, and the items the subjects had to place ranged from mothers to boulders. For example, the subject had to rate whether "mothers" fell closest to "happy" or "sad," and so on. Osgood and his associates then analyzed the responses for any basic dimensions on which all things had been described.

Three underlying dimensions accounted for most of the ratings: *evaluation* (good-bad), *potency* (strong-weak), and *activity* (active-passive). Once a particular person or object was placed on these three dimensions, little additional information could be gotten from getting additional ratings of it. In other words, once we know that someone rates "mother" as very good, moderately strong, and somewhat passive, we learn little more about these perceptions of "mother" by asking for additional ratings.

Of the three, evaluation was the main dimension underlying such perceptions, with potency and activity also playing some lesser role. Once we place someone on this dimension, much of the rest of our perception of him or her falls into place. A favorable or unfavorable impression in one context, at one meeting, extends to all other situations and to other seemingly unrelated characteristics.

Much other research has supported the hypothesis that evaluation is the most important underlying dimension of person perception. It has also led to the identification of two distinct dimensions of evaluation in common use. Rosenberg, Nelson, and Vivekananthan (1968), for example, found that people evaluated others in terms of their separate task-related or *intellectual* qualities, and their interpersonal or *social* qualities, at least some of the time. However, this distinction does not alter the basic point: People think primarily in terms of liking and disliking when they perceive other people.

The Averaging Principle

Suppose you've just met someone, and you notice that she is neat, tall, dark-haired, attractive, flirtatious, and "preppy" in dress. Or you meet someone else who is a premed, deeply religious, a tennis expert, an extrovert, and engaged to be married. How do we put such separate pieces of information together into simple overall impressions?

How confident is this couple likely to be about their impression of the woman? What aspects of her life and personality would they feel confident about?

Psychologists have two main views on this matter, one emphasizing learning and the other cognitive factors. The learning approach, in its simplest form, suggests that people combine information in a rather mechanical, simple-minded fashion, without thinking about it much. Just as a pigeon or a rat develops a habit rather mechanically, without seeming to interpret or give the experience meaning, so a person forms an impression without reinterpreting or analyzing available information very much. If we receive mainly favorable ideas about a person, we develop a favorable impression of that person. If we hear mainly unfavorable or lukewarm things, we develop that kind of impression instead.

As applied to impression formation, this learning approach has evolved into an **averaging principle** (Anderson, 1965). Here is how it works: Suppose Susan has just met her blind date, John. She quickly perceives that he is witty, intelligent, and courteous—but very short and poorly dressed. She processes this information in terms of how positive or negative she thinks those traits are. Suppose that she were asked to indicate her degree of favorable or unfavorable evaluation of those traits on a scale from +10 (very positive) to −10 (very negative). She might feel that being witty or intelligent are extremely favorable qualities and assign them the maximum value each (+10); that being courteous is quite favorable (+4); that being very short is somewhat unfavorable (−5); and that being poorly dressed is very unfavorable (−9). Now she combines these traits to form an overall evaluation of John. The averaging model suggests the person would receive an overall evaluation that was approximately an average of the five traits—that is, he would be considered moderately positive (+2). This is shown in Table 3–1.

A variant of the averaging idea is an *additive principle*. It hold that people integrate separate pieces of information by adding scale values rather than averaging them. The major difference occurs when the person is confronted with two pieces of information on the same side of zero, one more extreme than the other. Supposing Susan had liked John very much (+6), but then she learned something new about him that was only mildly favorable, such as that he is "cautious" (+1). According to the averaging principle, she should like him a little

TABLE 3–1

Susan Sizes Up Her Blind Date, John

Individual Traits	Susan's Evaluation
Witty	+10
Intelligent	+10
Courteous	+4
Very short	−5
Poorly dressed	−9
Overall impression	+10/5 = +2.00

less as a result, because the average (+3.5) is lower than the original evaluation (+6). According to the additive principle, however, she should like him more, because adding any additional positive information to an already positive impression should make it even more favorable.

Norman Anderson, in a series of careful and precise experiments (1959, 1965), produced strong evidence in favor of an averaging rather than an additive principle. He found that when a piece of information that is only moderately favorable was combined with a previous very favorable impression, the overall evaluation did not increase and could even decrease. Similarly, two strongly negative traits produced a more negative evaluation than two strongly negative plus two moderately negative traits.

As a result of further research, Anderson proposed a refinement that predicts impression formation even more accurately—the weighted averaging model (1968a). According to this model, people form an overall impression by averaging all traits but giving more weight to those they feel are most important. For example, an administrator interviewing scientists as candidates for a laboratory job would probably weigh "intelligent" more heavily than "attractive"; but someone hiring an actor for a television commercial might reverse that priority. An administrator interviewing candidates for a job as a counselor in a rape crisis center might give "warmth" more weight than either intelligence or attractiveness. This body of research as a whole indicates quite convincingly that the best way to account for impression formation is the weighted average principle, though it is probably not the only principle at work.

Consistency

Evaluation also introduces distortions and inaccuracies in several different ways. One is that people tend to form evaluatively consistent characterizations of others, even when they have only a few pieces of information. We have a tendency to view others in a way that is internally consistent. Since evaluation is the most important dimension in person perception, it is not surprising that we tend to categorize people as good or bad, not as both.

Following from this basic evaluation, we may go on to perceive other traits as consistent with it. If a person is likable, she should also be attractive, intelligent, generous, and so on. If she is bad, she should be sneaky, ugly, and inept. The other person is not seen as both honest and dishonest, warm and frightening, considerate and sadistic. Even when there is contradictory information about someone, he or she usually will be perceived as consistently good or bad, likable or dislikable. The perceiver distorts or rearranges the information to minimize or eliminate the inconsistency. This may also happen when people perceive objects, but it is particularly strong in person perception.

HALO EFFECT   This tendency toward consistency is called the **halo effect.** The stimulus person is seen as likable or not very likable, and all other qualities are perceived as consistent with this decision. This is called the halo effect because one who is labeled "good" is surrounded with a positive aura, and all good qualities are attributed to him or her. The converse (what should be called a "negative halo" or a "forked-tail" effect) is that one who is labeled "bad" is seen as having all bad qualities.

A good illustration of these effects is provided in a study by Dion, Berscheid, and Walster (1972). In this study, subjects were given pictures of people who were physically attractive, unattractive, or average. The subjects then rated each on a number of characteristics that had nothing to do with attractiveness. As you can see in Table 3–2, the attractive people were rated highest and the unattractive people lowest on almost all characteristics. Just because someone looked good and therefore had one positive trait, that person was perceived as having other positive traits; conversely, those who looked bad were perceived as having other bad traits.

An interesting question is just how far this halo effect goes. A number of studies have explored its boundaries with respect to physical attractiveness. It is one thing to expect a beautiful woman to be warm (who wouldn't be, if everyone were always reacting to you as if you were wonderful?), but quite another to expect her to be highly intelligent, innocent of any crime she might be accused of, or especially qualified for high political office.

In fact, the halo effect for physical attractiveness has been shown to generalize into a number of

TABLE 3–2

The Halo and Forked-Tail Effects Illustrated by Ratings of Attractive, Average, and Unattractive Stimulus Persons

Trait Ascription[a]	Attractive Stimulus Person	Average Stimulus Person	Unattractive Stimulus Person
Social desirability of personality	65.39	62.42	56.31
Occupational status	2.25	2.02	1.70
Marital competence	1.70	.71	.37
Parental competence	3.54	4.55	3.91
Social and professional happiness	6.37	6.34	5.28
Total happiness	11.60	11.60	8.83
Likelihood of marriage	2.17	1.82	1.52

[a] The higher the number, the more socially desirable a personality, the more prestigious an occupation, and so on, the stimulus person is expected to possess.
Source: Dion et al. (1972).

areas that are quite irrelevant to physical beauty. For example, Landy and Sigall (1974) presented male subjects with essays on the role and effects of television on society. The essays were supposedly written by the women whose pictures were attached to them. The women were either attractive or unattractive. Some essays were written well (clear, grammatical, organized) and some poorly (ungrammatical, spelling errors, clichés). The subjects were instructed to rate the quality of each essay. The essay written by the more attractive woman was rated better than the essay written by the unattractive woman, regardless of whether the essays were objectively good or bad.

Other studies have found that attractive people are treated more leniently when they do something wrong. Dion (1972) found that transgressions committed by attractive children were viewed less harshly by adults than the same acts committed by unattractive children. Similarly, Landy and Aronson (1969) found that members of a mock jury sentenced an unattractive defendant to more years in prison than they did an attractive defendant, given a crime described in exactly the same terms. Moreover, in two different studies they found that killing an attractive victim brought a longer sentence than killing an unattractive victim.

But, as with all things, the attractiveness-based halo effect has its limits. Sigall and Ostrove (1975) hypothesized that jurors would actually be *more* punitive toward a beautiful defendant if her offense were somehow directly related to her attractiveness. So they gave mock jurors the details of a case, along with a picture of the defendant. The charge was one of burglary, which could have almost nothing to do with the defendant's beauty, or swindling, which is something a beautiful woman might use her looks to get away with. Attractiveness did reduce the burglar's sentence, as in the studies cited above. But the beautiful swindler was given a somewhat harsher sentence than the unattractive one. The results are shown in Table 3–3. And verifying this hunch about connecting crime to attractiveness, a control group, not shown the photographs but given the case materials, did in fact rate the swindler as probably more attractive than the burglar.

In some cases, the halo effect is based on some irrational need to have a consistent impression, with such irrational results as punishing unattractive

TABLE 3–3

Mean Sentence Assigned, in Years

Offense	DEFENDANT'S ATTRACTIVENESS		
	Attractive	Unattractive	Control
Swindle	5.45	4.35	4.35
Burglary	2.80	5.20	5.10

Source: Sigall and Ostrove (1975).

children more than attractive children for minor misbehavior. But at other times it may have a more realistic basis. Attractive people may in fact develop more pleasing personalities over time, because their self-esteem is constantly being enhanced and their self-confidence built up. Attractive people are likely to go further occupationally, because they do in fact get promoted faster, and so on. Indeed, Goldman and Lewis (1977) showed that more attractive people have more social skills. In their study, college men phoned a woman student they had never met. The two students chatted for 5 minutes, and then they each rated their phone partners for social skills. The more attractive students were rated as having greater social skills, even by partners who had never met them and had only talked with them on the phone, and therefore had no direct way of knowing whether they were physically attractive or not.

In these examples, we have described halo effects that result from physical attractiveness. But halo effects can result from anything that produces a positive impression. A person can be regarded favorably because of being an outstanding athlete, a great scholar, a powerful business executive, or a warm family member. There will be a tendency to misperceive all that person's characteristics as favorable to make them consistent with the overall impression. Similarly, there is an unfortunate tendency to see a person with some shortcomings as negative in other areas as well. It is common to perceive an overweight person, or one with a physical handicap, or one who comes from an unpopular nationality as having many other negative characteristics as well. These are all examples of a general tendency to develp impressions that are evaluatively consistent.

MAINTAINING CONSISTENCY How do perceivers maintain such consistent impressions? Certainly it is not because the people they perceive are themselves so consistent. In fact, everyone we know is sometimes kind and sometimes selfish, and sometimes smart or sometimes foolish (even if some people are kinder or smarter than others). So it seems more likely that there is a psychological bias toward consistent impressions.

People work hard to maintain consistent impressions of other people. We tend to think in terms of people we like and people we don't like. This tendency toward consistency is particularly strong when we are thinking about a particular person as a whole, as opposed to thinking about more specific aspects of the person or situation. Focusing attention on the whole person has been called a "person focus" (though it might be equally well termed a "whole person focus").

The role of a "person focus" in maintaining consistency can be illustrated in a study using a mock jury situation (Devine & Ostrom, 1985). Subjects read a detailed transcript of a murder case concerning a hit-and-run fatality. The evidence from three of the four witnesses pointed to one verdict, but the fourth witness contradicted the others. There was reason to reject this inconsistent witness's evidence, since she was described as having a "special relationship" to the defendant (such as being his embittered ex-wife who claimed he was a bad driver).

The hypothesis tested in the authors' study was that a "person focus" would lead subjects to reject this inconsistent evidence. If focusing on whole persons indeed leads to more consistent impressions, subjects should accept the testimony from the first three witnesses, and reject the whole testimony from the inconsistent fourth witness. To test this, the authors manipulated the degree of person focus. In the "high person focus" condition, attention was focused on the witnesses as whole persons, by presenting first the full testimony from one witness, then the full testimony of another witness, and so on. In the "low person focus" condition, attention was focused on the details of the testimony rather than on witnesses as individual persons, by presenting the testimony on a particular point from all the witnesses, then the testimony on another point from all witnesses, and so on. They found

the high person focus produced the greatest rejection of the inconsistent witness' testimony. This illustrates quite nicely both how we organize person perception in terms of evaluatively consistent impressions of whole individuals, and how focusing attention on individual persons increases that tendency toward consistency.

One way to maintain consistency is simply to avoid inconsistent information. Erber and Fiske (1984) make the reassuring suggestion, however, that we are more likely to take inconsistent information seriously when the information is important to us—that is, when the stakes are high. In their experiment, students were assigned to work on a task with a confederate, and a prize was to be given for the best work. In the high stakes condition, the prize would go to the pair that produced the best work, so it was important for the subject to know whether their partner (the confederate) was competent or not. In the low stakes condition, the prize went to the best individual, so it did not matter how competent the confederate was. This confederate's level of competence had been described at the beginning of the experiment, but later the subject was given various kinds of further information about the confederate, some of which was inconsistent with that original description. Attention to this inconsistent information was greater in the high stakes condition—that is, when the prize went to the best pair, so that the subject needed to know about the confederate's strengths and weaknesses.

In short, people have a strong tendency toward forming evaluatively consistent impressions of others. They like some and dislike others, and their perceptions of the other person's characteristics tend to follow along. This tendency seems to be linked to a need to form a coherent impression of a whole individual. It can be overridden to some extent when the stakes are high enough, and we really need to have an accurate impression of the other. But even then, consistency pressures have significant effect.

Positivity Bias

A second general evaluative bias in person perception is toward positive evaluations of other persons.

They are much more common than negative ones. This tendency for positive evaluations of other people to outnumber negative evaluations has been called the **positivity bias** (Sears, 1983).

For example, in one study students rated 97 percent of their professors in college favorably (that is, above "average" on a rating scale), despite all the mixed experiences students have in their college classes (Sears, 1983). Similarly, public opinion polls show that individual political leaders are consistently approved of more often than they are disapproved of (Sears, 1982). In Gallup polls done in the United States since the mid-1930s, about three-fourths of the specific persons asked about were liked by more people than disliked them. As you might expect, then, when an impression changes, it generally tends to become more favorable rather than more unfavorable, everything else being equal (Sears & Whitney, 1973).

There are some plausible hypotheses about why people are evaluated so leniently. One stems from what Boucher and Osgood (1969) have called the "Pollyanna Principle." They, and later Matlin and Stang (1978), have suggested that people feel better if they are surrounded by good things, pleasant experiences, nice people, good weather, and so on. Even when their houses are falling down, they are sick, neighbors are terrible to them, and the weather is dismal, they will evaluate their situation favorably. The result: Most events are evaluated "above average" most of the time; pleasant events are thought more common than unpleasant ones; good news is communicated more frequently than bad news; and pleasant words are recalled more accurately and recognized more quickly than unpleasant ones. As a result, positive words are more common than negative words, in a wide variety of cultures and contexts.

Sears (1983), on the other hand, contends there is a special positivity bias in our evaluations of other human beings which he describes as the *person-positivity bias*. People feel more similarity to any other person they evaluate than they do to more impersonal objects, and therefore extend them a more generous evaluation. According to this view, the person-positivity bias operates most in evaluations of individual people, and it should not show up as strongly when impersonal objects are being evaluated.

In testing this idea, Sears confronted the problem that people and objects are so different it is hard to compare them. You could compare evaluations of one's mother with evaluations of a rock, but they differ in so many other ways it would be hard to attribute any difference in evaluation just to the fact that one is a person and the other an impersonal object. To try to make this person versus object comparison in a fair way, Sears turned to evaluations of professors. At UCLA, students routinely fill out a standard form for evaluating their classes that includes comparable items for the evaluation of the instructor (a person) and for the evaluation of the course (an impersonal object): What is your overall rating of the instructor, and, What is your overall rating of the course? Presumably, both ratings concern approximately the same experience—a specific course. But the course rating concerns mostly impersonal aspects of the class, such as books, exams, and class meetings. The instructor ratings concern only individual teachers.

Confirming the person-positivity bias, the personal stimulus, the professor, was rated higher than the impersonal object, the course, in 74 percent of the cases (in 7 percent they were equal, and 19 percent of the time the course was rated higher). So when we evaluate specific, concrete human beings with whom we can identify and empathize, we usually give them a special break.

One implication is that when incumbent elected officials run for re-election, they have a strikingly good chance of being returned to office (Sears & Whitney, 1973). Presumably if most Americans assumed all elected officials were scoundrels unless they heard something good about them, they would constantly be voting them out. But incumbents are usually returned to office, presumably because voters assume they must be doing a good job unless they hear otherwise.

THE COGNITIVE APPROACH

Up to this point, we have described person perception as dominated by two assumptions: (1) The process of impression formation rather mechanically reflects the nature of the stimulus person, and (2) is dominated by evaluation rather than cognition. Both assumptions have their roots in a learning theory approach. That impression formation mechanically reflects available information resembles a simple learning theory analysis of how a white rat learns to turn right rather than left in a T maze. If the rat is given food pellets on the right side and is shocked on the left side, it will learn to turn right without great analysis or distortion of the realities of the situation.

A simple averaging theory also assumes that the process of impression formation is primarily evaluative. All information is immediately reduced to some evaluation. "Friendly" is just a +5, "strong," just a +3, and "dull," just a −3. This, too, resembles a simple learning theory in that the environment is treated as consisting mainly of rewards and punishments. We learn to like and approach good things and dislike and avoid bad things.

Although there is much value in these two assumptions, they do oversimplify the process. We do not just take in a literal copy of the environment. We do not perceive people as disconnected bits of flesh and clothing and movement and sound, though that is literally what they consist of. We are active, organizing perceivers. The focus on evaluation, though central to impression formation, is also incomplete. It ignores cognitive processing mechanisms.

The cognitive approach to impression formation emphasizes somewhat different features of the process. First of all, although human beings clearly have a greater capacity for processing information than other animals, it is not infinite. We can absorb only a limited amount of the stimulation we are bombarded with every minute; and when we need

to retrieve it from our memory, we cannot get it all back in a flash. So any analysis of person perception must start out by acknowledging our limited processing abilities.

We might be described as lazy perceivers (McGuire, 1969), or somewhat more charitably as **cognitive misers** (Taylor, 1981a). When we perceive other people, we try to cut corners and save effort. We do not try to perceive or remember all possible bits of information; we do only what is necessary to get a clear impression of what is going on.

Second, while we take in information selectively, we then organize it into a meaningful **gestalt** that makes sense out of the full input. Each piece of information is taken as an aspect of a coherent whole, rather than as simply another isolated trait to be averaged into the overall impression. The major implication for impression formation is that processing is not mechanical, but involves an attempt to perceive some coherent *meaning* in the stimulus object.

The cognitive approach, therefore, views people as trying to develop meaningful impressions out of the information they have about another person (or event, or whatever), rather than just averaging in each separate element separately. This is what lies behind the old saying that "the whole is greater than the sum of its parts." The perceiver does not just consider each separate piece of information in isolation, but tries to come to an impression about the person as a whole.

This emphasis on cognitive process is one of the main approaches to social psychology. At its core is the view that person perception is a cognitive process: People are actively organizing perceivers, not passive receptacles; they are motivated by the need to develop coherent and meaningful impressions, not just likes and dislikes. And our limited processing capacities lead to the use of a series of cognitive shortcuts. These can produce efficiencies in processing, but they also can produce biases and errors. The cognitive approach is a supplement to the simpler, more mechanical processes described earlier. It asks what else is going on besides the simple judgment of liking or disliking.

Here we will discuss four of the general ideas that have been developed from the cognitive approach, beginning with the simplest:

(1) Processing of information about people involves perceiving some coherent *meaning* in the stimulus object. Here the central thrust has been to find exceptions to a simple averaging principle, reflecting more complex cognitive processing.

(2) Perceivers tend to pay special attention to the most *salient* features of the perceptual field rather than giving equal attention to everything. That is, figural people, or figural aspects of a particular person, get more attention than does the background. On a rainy day, our attention is drawn to the police officer in the middle of a crowded intersection, because he or she is wearing a bright orange raincoat and all the other colors in the intersection are drab.

(3) We organize the perceptual field by *categorizing* or grouping stimuli. Of course everything we see, hear, smell, or feel is a little different from everything else, but we do not perceive them that way. Rather, we tend to see each separate stimulus as part of a category or group; a Porsche as a car, a person wearing a white lab coat as a doctor, and a motion with the foot as a kick, even though each of these may have features that make them quite different from other cars, doctors, or kicks.

(4) We perceive stimuli as part of some kind of *structure*. Each separate stimulus tends to be related to others in time, space, and a causal flow. We see a downhill skier as part of a broader context: She is in a ski race, so she begins skiing when the starter gives the order; she skis between the flags down the hill; and she stops when she crosses the finish line. All we literally see is a young woman in motion, but that is part of a much more complex cognitive structure which includes our knowledge of the rules of slalom racing and our impression of her grace, agility, and power. In other words, we spontaneously embed the individual stimulus in a broader structure of knowledge.

Seeking Meaning

CONTEXT Assume perceivers are trying to arrive at a meaningful impression of whole persons, rather than just to absorb each new piece of information separately. Their understanding of any new piece of information will depend in part on the context. The meaning of "intelligent" in the context of knowing that a person is a "warm, caring therapist" will probably be quite positive. But the meaning of "intelligent" when the person is otherwise a "cold, ruthless Russian spy" will probably be more negative; it makes the person seem even more dangerous. To predict the impact of new information, we need to know the context, because that influences its meaning.

Considerable research has shown that context does indeed influence the impact new information has on an existing impression. But the effects of context are a matter of some debate. Anderson (1966), consistent with his averaging approach, suggests that the influence of the context on the value of the new attribute can be predicted by just averaging in its value along with the value of the new information. In this example, suppose "intelligent" is a +2 when it is considered all by itself. And suppose the value of the "cold, ruthless, Russian spy" context is −4. In this case, the contribution of "intelligent" to the overall impression would be influenced by the context, and so would be an average of its own value and that of its context, or −1. On the other hand, if the value of "warm, caring" context is +4, including "intelligent" would produce an overall impression of +3 in that context. Anderson describes this effect of context as a *generalized halo effect*. As you can see, he does not assume much deliberate thought; the new attribute merely mechanically absorbs some of the good or bad feelings associated with the context.

For Asch (1946), on the other hand, working mainly out of the cognitive approach, the whole is more than a mechanical average of its parts. Perceivers create a meaningful whole out of whatever information is given, and the whole will change with different information. So any given attribute will have different meaning if it is placed in a different context. Wearing only a bikini has quite a different meaning in a symphony concert hall than it does on a summer beach, and would be evaluated quite differently, even though it, and both contexts, may all be quite pleasant.

Asch says a new attribute undergoes a **shift of meaning** when placed in a new context. "Intelligence" in a cold, ruthless person could be threatening, potentially hostile, and destructive. In a warm, caring person, "intelligence" might be expected to contribute to empathy, to insight, and to the ability to give to another person.

A good bit of research has been done on these two explanations for context effects. One way to approach the controversy is to determine whether in fact a given trait has a different meaning in different contexts. Hamilton and Zanna (1974; Zanna & Hamilton, 1977) found that the connotations of a particular trait changed when placed in different contexts. For example, in a positive context the word "proud" bore the connotation of "confident." In a negative context, it connoted "conceited." Further, Wyer (1974) found that the evaluations of these connotations also reflected the context. To use this example, the connotation ("conceited") of the original trait ("proud") implied by a negative context itself bore a negative evaluation. Such studies show that contextual effects are partly determined by a shift-of-meaning phenomenon.

CENTRAL TRAITS   A second point at which the evaluative and cognitive approaches potentially differ concerns whether or not certain traits imply more about an individual than others. The averaging approach simply assumes that all traits are plugged into the process at whatever value they have; for example, "cold" is always a −5, "warm" is always a +7. The cognitive approach, instead, assumes that some traits are inherently more meaningful than others. For example, the pair of traits "warm-cold" appears to be associated with a great number of other characteristics, whereas the pair "polite-blunt," under most circumstances, is associated with fewer. Traits that are highly associated with many other characteristics have been called **central traits.**

In a classic demonstration of their importance, Asch (1946) gave subjects a description of an individual that contained seven traits—intelligent, skillful, industrious, warm, determined, practical, and cautious. Other subjects were given exactly the same list except that "cold" was substituted for "warm." Both groups were then asked to describe the individual and to indicate which of various pairs of traits he or she would be most likely to possess. The portraits that resulted were very different: Substituting "cold" for "warm" made a substantial change in subjects' impressions of the other person. In another condition, instead of the "warm-cold" pair, Asch used "polite-blunt." He found that substituting "polite" for "blunt" made considerably less difference in the overall picture formed by the subjects.

A later study by Kelley (1950) replicated this result in a more realistic setting. Students in psychology courses were given descriptions of a guest lecturer before he spoke. The descriptions included seven adjectives similar to those Asch used; half the students received a description containing the word "warm," and the other half were told the speaker was "cold"; in all other respects the lists were identical. The lecturer then came into the class and led a discussion for about 20 minutes, after which the students were asked to give their impressions of him. The results are shown in Table 3–4. As in the Asch study, there were great differences between the impressions formed by students who were told he was warm and those who were told he was cold. In addition, those students who expected the speaker to be warm tended to interact with him more freely and to initiate more conversa-

TABLE 3–4

Effect of "Warm" and "Cold" Descriptions on Ratings of Other Qualities

Quality	INSTRUCTIONS[a]	
	Warm	Cold
Self-centered	6.3	9.6
Unsociable	5.6	10.4
Unpopular	4.0	7.4
Formal	6.3	9.6
Irritable	9.4	12.0
Humorless	8.3	11.7
Ruthless	8.6	11.0

[a] The higher the rating, the more the person was perceived as having the quality.
Source: Adapted from Kelley (1950).

tions with him. The different descriptions affected not only the students' impressions of the other person, but also their behavior toward him.

The averaging model has been adapted to handle such phenomena. Its weighted-averaged version assumes that some traits are more important than others, and therefore are weighed more heavily. Presumably warmth is one of these. Most of the time, it is very important to us whether someone is warm or cold, and perhaps not very important whether they are good jumpers or not. So we weigh very heavily any information about warmth or coldness in coming to an overall impression and give little weight to information about jumping ability. This example also illustrates Asch's point about how context influences meaning. In the context of a party, "warm-cold" is probably quite a central trait, because it is so important to whether we enjoy the person or not. But in the context of a basketball game or Olympic tryouts, "warm-cold" may not be very central, and jumping ability may be weighed much more heavily.

Salience

People are sensitive to many cues in others, and use these cues to form impressions. But clearly people do not use all the cues available to them. A major relevant principle of perception is the **figure-ground principle.** According to this, people direct their attention to those aspects of the perceptual field that stand out—the figure—rather than to the background or setting—the ground. In the case of impression formation, the main implication is that the most salient cues will be utilized most heavily. If a student appears in a wheelchair the first day of class, everyone else in the room is likely to form an impression that is most heavily influenced by the fact of the person's physical handicap. Clothing, hair style, and perhaps even age, race and sex will all be secondary.

What determines the **salience** of one cue as opposed to another? A number of clearly specifiable objective conditions make cues stand out. *Brightness, noisiness, motion,* or *novelty* are the most powerful conditions, according to gestalt principles of object perception (McArthur & Post, 1977). A man in a bright red sweater stands out in a crowded classroom, and the sweater is his most salient feature. The student who gets up shouting in the middle of a lecture and leaves the room draws our attention because she is noisy and moving, and almost everything else in the classroom is quiet and stationary. A student in white robes and a turban is a novel stimulus, and we may notice few of the other people in a classroom.

So, anything that makes a cue objectively *unusual* in its context makes it subjectively more salient, more likely to be attended to, and more heavily utilized. A novel cue is unusual in the time dimension; it is unlike anything that preceded it and so attracts our attention. Openly gay men and lesbians were novel in the early 1970s, and so were punk rockers in the early 1980s. Impressions of them were heavily influenced by their sexual preference and colored hair, respectively. Loud noises are unusual in sound, and their distinctiveness attracts attention; we probably notice very little else about a waiter who drops a tray in a restaurant. Red hair is more unusual than brown, so we are more likely to describe a redhead in terms of hair color than we would a brunette.

Another way to make the same point is to think of the *extremity* of a cue in is normal distribution in the population. The wheelchair, exciting behavior, white robes, red sweater, and red hair are all extreme in the normal distribution of paraphernalia, classroom behavior, clothing, and hair color.

EFFECTS OF SALIENCE Salience has a number of consequences for person perception. If you think about people as "cognitive misers," you will see that they are always trying to get the most accurate and meaningful impressions of people and events around them by expending the least cognitive effort. One of their most valuable shortcuts is to respond to the most salient stimuli without trying to process all the information they could possibly obtain. So, salient behaviors draw more attention than do subtler, less obvious ones (McArthur, 1981). Second, salience influences perceptions of causality in that more salient people are seen as having more influence over their social context. The student who sits in front of the class and asks an occasional question is more likely to be perceived as dominating the discussion than the student who sits in the back and talks just as much.

What stimuli are most salient in this picture of the U.S. Supreme Court? What makes them salient? Do the "solo" black and woman justices stand out? (Thurgood Marshall is at the bottom left; Sandra Day O'Connor is at the top right.)

Third, evaluations of salient people are more extreme than evaluations of less salient people. Taylor et al. (1977) ran a series of experiments in which they varied the "solo" status of black group members; some groups had an even mixture of white and black members, other groups had only one black member. The "solo" black was clearly more salient than blacks in the evenly divided groups. A pleasant black group member was evaluated more favorably when "solo" than when in an evenly divided group, and an unpleasant one was evaluated more negatively.

Last, salience increases the coherence of an impression (Taylor, 1981b). If the salient person is a member of a stereotyped group, such as "drug addict," he or she will be seen as possessing all the stereotyped attributes of that group, such as having criminal tendencies, weak moral character, slovenly manner and dress, a lack of honesty, and so forth.

Salient stimuli draw the most attention; they are seen as the most causally powerful; they produce the most extreme evaluative judgments; and they produce more consistency of judgment. These effects of salience have been described as "top of the head" by Taylor and Fiske (1978) because they seem to occur at the relatively superficial level of simply directing our attention. That is, they occur because they focus the perceiver's attention one way or another, not because they involve any very deep changes in thinking. As might be expected, therefore, they seem to be strongest when the stimuli are sufficiently interesting and exciting to attract the perceiver's real attention. The salience of different stimuli matters more when the perceiver is responding to exciting conversations, such as humorous debates, than when he or she is responding to stiffer, more formal and boring situations (McArthur, 1981). But salience effects appear to be rather general, occurring on important issues as well as unimportant ones (Taylor et al., 1979; Borgida & Howard-Pitney, 1983).

VIVIDNESS So far we have been considering salience in terms of the perceptual unusualness or extremity of a stimulus. Some researchers have extended the idea of salience to include the notion of *vividness*: "Information may be described as vivid, that is, as likely to attract and hold our attention and to excite the imagination to the extent that it is (a) emotionally interesting, (b) concrete and imagery-provoking, and (c) proximate in a sensory, temporal, or spatial way" (Nisbett & Ross, 1980, p. 45). Vivid stimuli might be especially influential for a variety of reasons: They might be more readily noticed, easier to remember, easier to visualize, and/or their greater emotional impact might make them particularly important. For example, opposition to the Vietnam war in its later stages is often ascribed to its vivid presentation. It was "the television war": People could watch all the horrors in living color in their living rooms. This more vivid presentation of the Vietnam experience, compared to the blander reporting of past wars in the printed press, is said to have created a greater public reaction.

But there is little evidence that vividness in fact has any special power in impression formation. Many studies of its effects have been done, but only rarely have vivid messages been more powerful (Taylor & Thompson, 1982). Why salience should have such reliable effects while vividness does not remains something of a puzzle. Salience is usually defined more clearly and precisely, in terms of such objective characteristics of the stimulus as novelty, intensity, and change; vividness has a looser definition, which could lead to less clear results.

THE NEGATIVITY EFFECT Another exception to the averaging principle is that people weigh negative information more heavily than positive information in arriving at a complete impression. That is, a negative trait affects an impression more than a positive trait, everything else being equal (Fiske, 1980). This has been called the **negativity effect.** It follows that a positive impression is easier to change than a negative one (Hodges, 1974). People are more confident of evaluations based on negative traits than of those based on positive traits (Hamilton & Zanna, 1972). And it also follows that the averaging principle does not hold for negative traits quite as well as it does for positive traits.

This difference is particularly noticeable with the more extreme negative traits. They seem to have a "blackball" effect: One extremely negative trait produces an extremely negative impression, no matter what other traits the person possesses (Anderson, 1965). For example, Lau (1982) found that voters' evaluations of presidential and congressional candidates in the period from 1968 to 1980 were more strongly shaped by negative information about the candidate than by positive information. When we are told that a prominent public leader is "a crook," our evaluation of him becomes quite negative, regardless of what else we know about him. If we are told he is "patient," we will just average that mildly positive quality in with whatever else we know about him.

The main explanation for this negativity effect is based on the figure-ground principle. As we noted in the discussion of the person-positivity bias, positive evaluations of other people are much more common than negative evaluations. Negative traits, being more unusual, are therefore more distinctive. In a simple perceptual sense, then, a negative trait is *figural*; it stands out the way an unusual deformity or bright clothing or something of great size stands out. People may simply pay more attention to those negative qualities and give them more weight. For example, Lau (1985) found that negative information had most impact upon evaluations of presidential candidates among those voters who were most trusting of government. That is, the negativity effect was strongest among those who generally respect political leaders, for whom negative information would be most figural.

Remember not to confuse these two. They are quite different, and in fact the negativity effect is probably due mainly to the positivity bias. The positivity bias suggests that positive evaluations outnumber negative evaluations. The negativity effect suggests that because negative evaluations are therefore more unusual, they then have more impact on impressions when they are present.

Categorization

Perceivers do not respond to salient stimuli in isolation; they immediately and spontaneously perceive them as part of some group or category. We do not see that unshaven, dirty, disheveled man in the park with worn-out shoes and a couple of old shopping bags as just another human being; we immediately categorize him as a derelict. When we go to a basketball game, we usually categorize people right away into members of one or another of five social groups: players on one team or the other, referees, cheerleaders, and spectators. The **categorization** or grouping process is immediate, spontaneous, and does not take any time or thought, any more than you need to think about what category of objects your pencil belongs to.

CATEGORIZING PEOPLE   At the crudest level, we categorize on the basis of natural similarities in appearance. We tend to assign people to the category of "men" or "women" on the basis of their physical characteristics, usually their secondary sex charac-

BOX 3–1

WHERE DOES LIZE FIT?

The Union of South Africa categorizes all people into one of three groups: White, Colored, or Black. All persons of mixed blood are included in the Colored category. This categorization determines much of the pattern of the person's life due to the practice of apartheid. Blacks are forbidden to vote; they must go to all-black schools; they generally must leave their families in the countryside if they go to the cities to work; they cannot marry or have romantic or sexual relationships with persons in the other categories, and so on.

Lize Venter was a 2-week-old infant found in a field, and her parents were unknown. The authorities were unable to decide which category to place her in, since she was light-skinned and her face showed no definable racial characteristics: "She's cute, that's all I can say," one nurse was quoted as saying. The problem arose because the hospital wished to put her out for adoption. But what kind of a family should she go to? If she were Colored, she could not be adopted by a white family, would have to live in a nonwhite area, and would be forbidden to marry or have sexual relations with a white. If she were determined to be white, the same prohibitions would hold in reverse. As an orphan, she was entitled to public assistance from the government. But since the public assistance services were also segregated by category, no agency would handle her case until a decision had been made about her category. Ultimately a decision would be made by the Department of Internal Affairs, and that decision would determine much of Lize's future life.

Source: Los Angeles *Times*, July 27, 1983.

teristics, and culturally defined differences in appearance (hair length, makeup, type of clothing). The same is true of assigning people to other social groupings such as racial categories, as illustrated by the story of Lize Venter (see Box 3–1).

Recent research suggests a more precise answer, however. The crucial similarity is between the object being categorized and a typical or ideal example of the category, called a **prototype** (Cantor & Mischel, 1977). For example, a dog would be a more prototypical mammal than would be a whale, because most species of mammals have body hair, move on four legs, and live on land. So most people would probably decide whether or not an unfamiliar animal was a mammal by comparing it to a dog, not to a whale.

What are the consequences of categorization? It speeds information-processing time, as the "cognitive miser" idea suggests. For example, Brewer and associates (1981) presented subjects with photos of people in three different categories, "grandmother," "young woman," and "senior citizen," along with verbal labels clearly identifying their category. Then they presented the subjects with additional information about each target person, and measured how long the subjects took to incorporate the information into their impressions. Information consistent with the prototype of the category ("kindly" for "grandmother") was processed faster than information inconsistent with it (such as "aggressive" for grandmother).

Categorizing simplifies and makes processing easier, of course. The other side of the coin is that it can lead to misperception. Oversimplification can hide some of the person's unique characteristics. For example, Taylor and her colleagues (1978) had college students listen to a tape of a small group discussion and simultaneously observe slides that purportedly pictured the group members. The tape-slide show depicted six men discussing a publicity campaign for a play. Three of the men were white, and three were black. At the end, the students were given a list of the suggestions made during the discussion and asked to identify which discussant had made each suggestion.

Categorization led to misperception. They mistakenly credited discussants with the suggestions made by others of the same race, but not with those made by discussants of the opposite race.

That is, the observers made more mistakes within a race than between races. Apparently, as they watched the show, they categorized the suggestions as being made by a black or by a white discussant, rather than remembering which individual made the remark. Such categorizations certainly are unfair when they lead us to overlook the unique characteristics of a particular person.

Schemas

A still more complex organization of cognition is called a **schema.** This refers to an organized, structured set of cognitions, including some knowledge about the object, some relationships among the various cognitions about it, and some specific examples (Taylor & Crocker, 1981). We might, for example, have a schema of a "preppie," a WASP college student who wears alligator shirts and khaki pants, buys clothes from L. L. Bean, is partial to pink and kelly green, sports Oxford cloth button-down shirts with madras ties, and likes to sail and jog and play tennis. This "preppie" schema would probably not include going bowling, wearing Caterpillar tractor caps, driving a 1979 Chrysler Imperial, or having a beer belly.

What all schemas have in common is not their content, but their structural characteristics and the effects these have on processing. Schemas help us process complex bodies of information by simplifying and organizing them. They can help us remember and organize details, speed up processing time, fill in gaps in our knowledge, and help us interpret and evaluate new information. As we will see, such preexisting cognitive structures organize the processing of new information. Our perceptions of new information are biased to make them consistent with what we already know. If we think someone is "warm," for example, we are more likely to talk to him and interpret his behavior as reflecting that warmth.

Schemas can be about different things. There are *person schemas*, which are structures about people. They can focus on particular people. For instance, you may have a schema about Abraham Lincoln. It might include such elements as his being deliberate, honest, serious about his duties, and concerned for oppressed people. This would be a schema if in your view these qualities were all related to one another in President Lincoln, in the sense that you perceive them all as aspects of his basically decent and conscientious personality, not unrelated traits he just happened to display from time to time.

Another version of a person schema is a schema you have about yourself, or a *self-schema*. A self-schema describes the dimensions along which you think about yourself. For example, Markus (1977) investigated the extent to which people had schemas of themselves as independent or dependent by determining whether or not they would apply to themselves such adjectives as "individualistic," "unconventional," "assertive," "cooperative," "timid," or "moderate."

You may be very concerned about maintaining and displaying your own independence by refusing to take money from your parents for college, doing your own laundry, not asking your roommate for help with your math, and so on. Or you may be more interested in dependent relationships and think a lot about ensuring security for yourself by surrounding yourself with people you can depend on, like your brother, girlfriend, doctor, minister, and so on. You could do both, perhaps with some conflict and ambivalence. In any of these cases, you would have a strong self-schema concerning the independence-dependence dimension. On the other hand, you may just not think of yourself very much in connection with that dimension, in which case you would not be thinking schematically in these terms. You would be described as *aschematic* on the dimension of independence-dependence.

Person schemas can also focus on particular types of people. For example, our schema of an "extrovert" might include such elements as "spirited," "outgoing," "enthusiastic," and "self-assured." Sometimes this type of schema is described as a prototype (Cantor & Mischel, 1977) because it describes the features of a particular type of person (see Figure 3–1). A related concept is an **implicit personality theory** (Schneider, 1973) because it seems to be a theory about what traits go with what other traits, and which ones do not go together. On overhearing someone say that Suzi is "spirited" the person would infer that she was probably outgoing and self-confident even in the absence of any other information about her. An

A.T.&T.

Many stereotypes have been broken in recent years.

implicit personality theory, then, is this web of presumed relationships among traits.

Other schemas focus on groups. The most familiar is the group **stereotype,** which attributes specific traits to a particular group of people. An early study by Katz and Braly (1933) found white college students checking "superstitious," "lazy," and "happy-go-lucky" as the most common traits of blacks, and "scientifically minded," "industrious," and "stolid" as most common for Germans. Such stereotypes would be schematic if each perceived trait was part of a coherent underlying structure about the group.

You might expect a student who is in the Beta fraternity to act like other Betas, or a black football player to act like other black football players, or people from Boston or Texas or Iran to resemble one another. All these involve having a particular schema for the personality and behavior of mem-

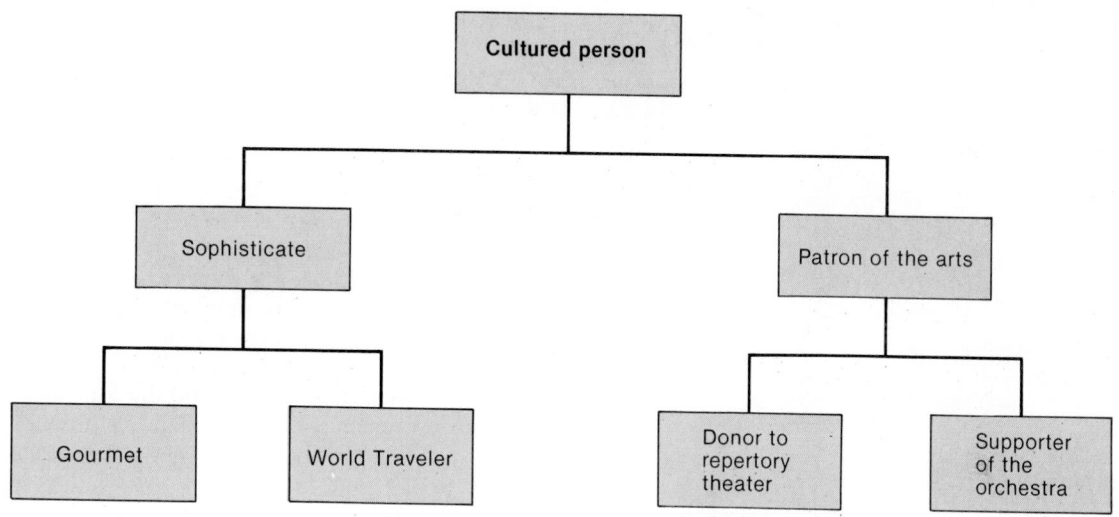

FIGURE 3–1   A schema for "cultured person." (After Cantor & Mischel, 1979.)

bers of a group. We will take up stereotypes in some detail in Chapter 14.

Then there are *role schemas*. These represent the organized, abstract pictures we have of people in a particular role, such as cowboy, professor, receptionist, or devoted lover. Sometimes these schemas are unrealistic. If our schema for "devoted lover" includes elements such as always understanding, always supportive, never angry, never childish, and always concerned first with the other person's happiness, we could be in trouble. Not too many people will live up to that schema.

Similar problems sometimes arise between college students and faculty when each has an unrealistic schema for the other's role. A faculty member's schema about the student role might include constant interest and attention to the course, while the student's schema for professor might include endless patience and consideration. But students sometimes are sick or distracted by other problems in their lives and unable to pay attention in class. Faculty members may have arguments with their spouses and therefore behave irritably toward innocent students.

People also have schemas for events, or standard series of events. Sometimes such schemas are called *scripts* (Abelson, 1976). A script is a standard sequence of behavior over a period of time. One script might be called "ordering for a group in a Chinese restaurant." Everyone sits down, and the waiter brings the menus. Several people talk at once, giving their favorite dishes, while others say they never know what to have and would someone else just please decide. Then people go through the menu section by section, haggling over which soup to have, bargaining away their favorite beef dish (which no one else wants) for sweet and sour pork (which at least one ally does), and finally appointing the most self-confident and brash person to communicate the whole negotiated package to the waiter.

We could generate similar scripts for other ritualized series of events, such as having a baby, taking a shower, taking a final exam, or playing a basketball game. The essence of a script is in its boundedness in time, its causal flow (early events cause later ones), and in its being a simple, coherent, perceptual unit.

The Self

So far this cognitive approach could be applied to perceiving almost anything, not just perceiving people. When we are perceiving objects in a zoo or in a forest or in an art gallery, the context deter-

Even in a crowd, a person can feel alone and preoccupied with the self.

mines the meaning of the things we see, salient objects attract our attention, we divide objects up into categories, and we have schemas that help us interpret and understand what we see.

But people are different in an important respect: They are part of our own species. So they are more like us than other objects. It would not be surprising, therefore, if our perceptions of other people are strongly influenced by our perceptions of our own selves. After all, our self is probably the most salient object in our world for most of us, most of the time. We know more about our self than about anything else, because we have had the richest and most extended experience with it, so we

are most likely to have a schematic view of the self.

As a result, researchers have recently pursued the provocative hypothesis that the self operates as our main point of reference in perceiving other people: "The self acts as a background or setting against which incoming data are interpreted or coded" (Rogers, Kuiper, & Kirker, 1977, p. 678). Take for example Karen, who perceives herself as unusually shy. She regularly comes to lectures, but she is so shy that she is afraid to say anything, even to the person who usually sits next to her, and so she never gets to know anyone in the class. She thinks about this shyness, and the loneliness it produces, much of the time. In fact, she thinks about it more than she thinks about most other things. So it would be easy to understand how she might use this perception of her own shyness as a lens to understand other people she sees. She might perceive some as shy, and other as bold and outgoing, but either way her perceptions of them would be colored by her perception of her own shyness.

To put this point in the language we have just been using, people perceive others in terms of their own self-schemas. It is likely that Karen has quite an elaborate, schematic view of her shyness, including many experiences in the past of being rebuffed and hurt by other people, experiences of being afraid to talk to or interact with others, lonely Saturday nights in her dorm room alone while other students are out on dates or at parties, and so on. Her perceptions of others would be much enriched by the connections to her own experiences if they were to be embedded in this familiar schema about the shyness of her own self.

One implication is that memory for others' characteristics should be improved when they are linked to the self, because that enriches their meaning. Karen is more likely to remember hearing her roommate say that Jeff "has overcome his terrible shyness" than that he is an excellent auto mechanic (Karen does not even have a car, much less one that is breaking down all the time!). A number of experiments have tested for this **self-reference effect;** that is, improved memory for others' characteristics when they are linked to one's self. Rogers and his colleagues (1977) presented trait adjectives such as "shy" or "outgoing" to subjects in several different conditions. In the "self-reference" condition, the subjects were asked "whether the word describes you." In the "other-reference" condition, the subjects were asked "whether the word describes the experimenter" (another person). The other conditions asked subjects to rate the word in simple mechanical terms, such as whether it was short or long or whether it was specific or general. Later the subjects were asked to recall all the adjectives with which they had been presented. Indeed those words presented in the self-reference context were much better recalled than those placed in more neutral contexts, and the person found the task less difficult, and had more confidence in his or her ratings. These findings are shown in Table 3–5.

Later experiments obtained similar findings, using perhaps still a tougher comparison, by using well-known public figures in the other-reference conditions, such as Johnny Carson or the noted TV newsman Walter Cronkite. Essentially the same findings emerged: Adjectives were remembered better with self-reference than with the other-person reference (Lord, 1980; Brown, Keenan, & Potts, 1986; Kuiper & Rogers, 1979; Bower & Gilligan, 1979). However, it should be noted that self-reference does not always improve memory relative to the other-person context when the other people are personally well known to the subject, such as a lab instructor who has been teaching the person all term (Kuiper & Rogers, 1979; Bower & Gilligan, 1979).

In short, when people think about a trait or utterance in connection with their own self, it is more likely to be remembered than if it is thought about in connection with another person or something impersonal. This is the so-called self-reference effect: Later recall of traits is improved when people must first think about whether or not the trait applies to them personally.

Why does this happen? The explanation most favored by researchers is that self-reference produces "deeper processing" (Craik & Tulving, 1975), because the self-reference gets the person to consider a wider and deeper range of associations to the trait (Rogers et al., 1977). Consistent with this view, the self-reference effect seems to be dependent on getting people to think about traits in connection with their own personal experiences, not just the self. To illustrate this, Bellezza (1984) presented subjects with traits and had them either relate the trait to some real incident from their lives or to some personal body part. For example, the subject might have related the trait "hostile" to an experience of getting into an argument with

TABLE 3–5

Self-Reference Produces Better Recall, Less Difficulty, More Confidence

Experimental Condition	Question	Recall	Mean Difficulty Rating	Mean Confidence Rating
Structural	Rate whether you feel the word is long or short.	.18	3.08	3.83
Semantic	Rate whether you feel the word has a specific meaning or relates to a specific situation.	.15	4.25	3.83
Other-reference	Rate whether you feel the word describes the experimenter.	.18	5.00	2.75
Self-reference	Rate whether you feel the word describes you.	.31	2.00	6.00

Note: Recall values can range from 0 to 1.00, where 1.00 indicates that all were recalled. Difficulty and confidence ratings were made on a 7-point scale, with 7 as extremely difficult or extremely confident.
Source: Adapted from Kuiper & Rogers, 1979.

someone, or, alternatively, to the body part "fist." Thinking about the trait in connection with the personal experience made it more memorable than did thinking about it in connection with the body part. The extra meaningfulness provided by reference to the self seems, therefore, to stem specifically from the rich array of experiences it brings to mind from our past lives, which form a self-schema to which we can relate information about others.

ACCURACY OF JUDGMENTS

How accurately do people usually perceive others? One implication of these various evaluative and cognitive biases is that person perception must not be very accurate. On the other hand, people must be reasonably accurate in order for society to function as smoothly as it does. After all, we interact with other people a great many times every day, and these interactions usually require fairly accurate judgments of them. Since most interactions proceed without serious difficulties or mistakes, person perception must be fairly accurate.

People seem to perceive external, visible attributes fairly accurately. It is generally no more difficult to judge the height of a person than it is to judge the height of a bookcase, a car, or a camel. The same is true of weight, skin color, or style of clothing. We make these kinds of judgments about the external attributes of all objects, and we make them fairly accurately. And it is fairly easy to make judgments about somebody's social role, as long as the appropriate cues are provided. The man in the blue suit with the gun strapped to his side is a police officer, and we treat him accordingly. The woman in a business suit with a briefcase rushing down a platform toward a train is obviously a commuter in a hurry to get to work, and we get out of her way to make it easier for her to catch the train. The contexts in which we see the people enable us to make accurate assumptions about their roles.

But person perception becomes more difficult when we try to infer *internal states*—traits, feelings, emotions, and personalities. The bookcase obviously has none of these; the car had them only in advertisements and fantasies; perhaps the camel has them, but we usually do not worry about camels. However, we do attempt to judge the internal states of human beings. We look at people and perceive them as angry, happy, sad, or frightened. We form an impression of another person and think of her as warm, honest, and sincere. We also make judgments about such internal characteristics as the person's attitudes toward various issues. We guess whether she is a Republican or a Democrat, religious or nonreligious, an environmentalist or not.

Judgments of such internal states as emotions, personality traits, and attitudes are often extremely difficult. The person's internal state cannot be observed directly—it must be inferred from whatever cues are available. Therefore, the question of accuracy focuses primarily on the judgments individuals can make of internal states, and on the cues used to make these judgments.

The Eye of the Beholder

One possibility raised by the tendency toward consistency is that perceivers may just impose their own perspectives on the target person, rather than reflecting the real qualities of that target. For example, beauty may truly be in "the eye of the beholder" rather than being in the person being evaluated. This would lead to considerable inaccuracy in person perception, because everyone would have a different perception of the same person.

It does seem to be true that different people organize their perceptions of others along different dimensions. For example, one person might always describe others in terms of their sense of humor,

What emotions would you infer this couple is feeling if you only paid attention to their facial expressions, and not the context?

Ken Karp

another person in terms of their honesty, and still another their intelligence. Someone else might consider these characteristics to be relatively unimportant and instead would emphasize the individual's religiosity or athletic prowess. This variety of perspectives was illustrated in a study by Dornbusch and colleagues (1965), in which all the children at a camp was asked to describe, in their own words, every other child. The children were provided with no scales or specific questions but were simply asked to give free descriptions of the others. These descriptions were then analyzed in two ways—in terms of the characteristics each child used in making descriptions, and in terms of the characteristics used in describing each child. The experimenters could then examine the characteristics either in terms of those used by each child perceiver or in terms of those used about each child as a stimulus object.

When the data were examined in this way, a clear pattern emerged. It might have been thought that some children would have a particularly outstanding characteristic, such as a sense of humor or aggressiveness, and that everyone would describe them in these terms. This was not the case. There was no agreement about which dimensions described any given child. But the situation was entirely different for the children writing the descriptions. Here great consistency emerged. Each child tended to use the same characteristics no matter who was being described. The children differed among themselves as to which characteristics they used, but they all had their favorites which they used for virtually all their descriptions. So perceptions of other children depended more on who was *perceiving* than on who was *being perceived*. The major implication of this phenomenon is that people do not see the world in the same way; they emphasize different aspects of other people, notice and focus on different qualities. People do differ on the personality qualities they consider important and their impressions of others are based on their own standards.

Perceivers do arrive at more consensus on the

BOX 3–2

IS BEAUTY IN THE EYE OF THE BEHOLDER

OR IN THE BEAUTY?

The old saying, "Beauty is in the eye of the beholder," clearly is true to some extent. There are some culturally defined aspects of beauty that not everyone over the globe shares; for example, great body weight is prized in parts of Africa but not on the beach at St. Tropez. But many observers, including Charles Darwin, have been struck by certain constancies in ideas of beauty. Within our own culture, there is considerable consensus on what characteristics mark beautiful women. Cunningham (1986) had male students rate for beauty pictures of finalists in the Miss Universe beauty contest and pictures of seniors from a women's college. Then he measured the exact characteristics of those faces along 24 different dimensions. The most beautiful women differed from ordinary women in three general ways, they had: (1) the features normally associated with "child cuteness", that is, large and widely spaced eyes, small nose areas, and small chin; (2) two features of more mature faces—wide cheekbones and narrow cheeks; and (3) expressive features of highly set eyebrows, wide pupils, and a large smile. As the "halo effect" would lead you to expect, these features were also associated with such positive characteristics as being "bright," "sociable," "assertive," "fertile," and having few medical problems. And when it came to attractiveness for romantic, sexual, and family liaisons, the "child-cuteness" characteristics, rather than the mature or expressive features, proved most important. Interestingly, some of these same features—large round eyes, high eyebrows, and narrow chin—are associated with perceptions of "baby-facedness" in male stimulus persons, which in turn is strongly associated with attractiveness, warmth, and kindness (Berry & McArthur, 1985).

These features seem particularly to be those associated with youthful, childlike features, along with a critical few features that definitely mark a woman as postpubescent. Features associated with expressiveness, particularly joy and happiness, are also important. As you might expect, then, these features do provide one little exception to the halo effect. Such attractive women were expected to be the least "modest" and the least likely to avoid having extramarital affairs. And "baby-faced" men were thought to be lowest in perceived responsibility! The perceptions of youthfulness in such features seem to carry some of the liabilities of youth as well as their benefits.

likeability of specific target persons than they do on their traits or other attributes, however. When one person talks about another's warmth and sense of humor and someone else talks about his kindness and good-naturedness, the only disagreement may be one of semantics. We generally agree more on how likeable other people are than on why they are likeable—whether it is their sense of humor, considerateness, intellectual ability, or whatever. Put more formally, perceivers will characteristically use their own dimensions to describe another person and may not agree much with each other on which dimensions to use—but they will generally agree more on an evaluation of the person.

Park (1986) demonstrated this in a study of her seminar students. These seven students, who did not know each other well before the class, agreed to write out impressions of each other each week through the school term. This provided an opportunity to determine whether their impressions were due to the "eye-of-the-beholder" effect—did each perceiver use their own favorite dimensions to describe all the various target persons, but different dimensions from those used by the other perceivers? Or were their impressions due to the real qualities of each target person—did the perceivers generally agree on which dimensions applied to each target person?

She found a considerably stronger "eye-of-the-beholder" effect on the specific dimensions used to describe other people than on evaluations of those people. That is, two different judges tended to evaluate a given target person in about the same way, but each perceiver tended to use their own particular dimensions to describe the person, such as "yuppie," "the sunny, California beach type," "kind," "aware of her faults," or "loud and boisterous." This again emphasizes the importance of evaluations in the person perception process.

Recognition of Emotions

Much of the work on the accuracy of person perception has focused on the recognition of emotions, on whether a person is happy or afraid, horrified or disgusted. The basic procedure is to present a subject with a stimulus representing another person and ask the subject to identify the other's emotion. For some studies, trained actors portrayed a number of different emotions, and pictures were taken of their expressions. One picture was chosen for each emotion. These were then shown to subjects, who were asked to indicate what emotion was depicted. Some of these pictures are shown in Figure 3–2. Other studies have used real people or disembodied voices.

Given this wide range of techniques, it is perhaps not surprising that the results have also been varied.

FIGURE 3–2 Examples of stimuli used in the study of the perception of emotions. The photographs illustrate expressions posed to portray the emotions listed. (You might try to identify them before looking at the following key.) *Top* (left to right): glee, passive adoration, complacency. *Middle*: amazement, optimistic determination, dismay. *Bottom*: rage, mild repugnance, puzzlement.

Early studies seemed to indicate that people could not judge emotions in facial expressions at better than a chance level. Later studies have shown that people can discriminate among the major groups of emotions, even if they cannot discriminate very well between each individual emotion. Woodworth (1938) suggested that emotions can be arranged on a six-point continuum, with the ease of distinguishing between any two emotions being related to the distance between them on this continuum. This generated a number of such studies. They generally agree on finding people expressing seven categories of emotions. The seven groups are:

1. Happiness, joy
2. Surprise, amazement
3. Fear
4. Sadness
5. Anger
6. Disgust, contempt
7. Interest, attentiveness

People seem to be quite good at distinguishing emotions in categories that are three, four, or five points apart—they rarely confuse happiness with disgust or surprise with contempt. People have a particularly easy time distinguishing pleasant from unpleasant emotions in others' faces (again indicating the importance of the evaluative dimension

BOX 3–3

EYEWITNESS TESTIMONY

Criminal charges often rest quite heavily on reports of eyewitness identification. A cashier who has been held up at a 7–11 store must pick the robber out of a lineup and testify to his or her identity in court. A rape victim may have to do the same in more difficult circumstances if the crime happened at night, by surprise, if the victim's life was threatened, if the rapist was partially disguised, and so on. A number of studies have found eyewitness identification not to be very accurate (see Penrod, Loftus, & Winkler, 1982). To be sure, eyewitnesses tend to be highly confident that they are successfully picking out the true perpetrator. But their level of certainty bears almost no relationship to their accuracy level: Highly confident eyewitnesses are no more accurate than those who are uncertain (Wells & Murray, 1984). This is especially distressing because the general public (and thus most jurors, presumably) believes that eyewitness self-confidence is a valid sign of credibility, and it is one of the standards the U.S. Supreme Court has set for admissibility of eyewitness testimony (Kassin, 1985).

There are techniques for enhancing the accuracy of eyewitness testimony, such as reinstating the original context. Krafka and Penrod (1985) had store clerks identify a previously encountered customer from an array of photographs. When the photograph was accompanied by some physical cues from the original encounter situation, such as a photocopy of identification the customer had shown, and a check like the one the customer had cashed, accuracy was improved. But even so, by 24 hours later, only half the clerks correctly identified the customer (against about one-third in the no-reinstatement condition). Even though the reinstatement manipulation increased accuracy, it had no effect at all on the witness's confidence. Eyewitness confidence continued to bear little relationship to accuracy.

in person perception). But they find it almost impossible to discriminate emotions in the same category or only one group away.

Still more recent studies using the same kind of approach find a simpler structure with two basic underlying dimensions: pleasantness and arousal (Russell & Bullock, 1985). Positive emotions such as excitement and happiness were distinguished from negative ones such as fear, anger, and disgust. But among the positive emotions, arousing ones such as excitement are distinguished from nonarousing ones such as contentment; similarly, negative arousing emotions such as fear and anger are distinguished from nonarousing ones such as sadness.

One artificial aspect of these studies has been that they involve static, posed faces, frequently using just one model. Later studies have used videotaped presentations, such as of ordinary people viewing a variety of emotionally evocative situations (Wagner, MacDonald, & Manstead, 1986). Others have used several different actors portraying different emotions in videotaped scenes (for example, Wallbott & Scherer, 1986). Again, though, the typical finding has been that expressions can be differentiated fairly well into those that express positive emotions (such as happiness) or negative emotions (disgust, sadness, or anger). To some extent high arousal can be distinguished from low arousal. But beyond that, accuracy is not very great.

Universal Emotional Expressions

People are at least crudely accurate in judging others' emotions, then. One reason might be that all people use the same facial expression for expressing a given underlying emotion. Perhaps we all smile when we feel happy, frown when we are worried, and so on. To illustrate this, Craig and Patrick (1985) induced pain by immersing subjects' hands and wrists into icy water just at freezing temperature. They found such consistent responses as raising cheeks with tight eyelids, raising the upper eyelid, parting the lips, and closing eyes or blinking.

In 1872, on the basis of his evolutionary theory, Charles Darwin proposed that facial expressions convey the same emotional states in all cultures.

His argument was that universal expressions have evolved because they have great survival value for Homo sapiens: They allow us to communicate our emotions and thereby control others' behavior. For example, if one animal shows an angry or threatening face, others may behave more submissively, which allows the first animal to win the encounter without risking an actual fight.

In fact, virtually all species of Old World monkeys and apes have been found to use facial gestures to signal dominance or submissiveness. Differing eyebrow positions seem to be crucial: Typically, the brows are lowered on dominant or threatening individuals and raised on submissive or receptive individuals (Keating et al., 1981). The evolutionary argument is that there may be a link between the facial expressions used by subhuman primates to communicate with, and control, other species members, and those used by humans for the same purpose. If so, presumably the same link between emotion and facial expression would exist among humans across all (or most) cultures.

Are there such universals in humans? Do we have particular facial expressions or body postures for each emotion? Does everyone who is feeling a particular emotion have the same facial expression? Or is it possible that one person's expression of disgust is another person's expression of contentment? The link between lowered-brow expressions and dominance in nonhuman primates suggests a possible similar link in human beings. To test for this, Keating et al. (1981) had people from each of a number of countries in Europe, Africa, North and South American, and Asia pose with brows lowered, and then again with brows raised. The researchers also tested for a link between perceptions of smiling and happiness because a number of studies had suggested a link between primates' grins (or grimaces) and communicating submissiveness. On the other hand, there was some evidence that among humans, smiling was related to happiness. So they had people pose with a smile or with mouth relaxed. The only differences between poses were brow or mouth position. The subjects were presented with pictures of the model from their own country and asked, in their native language, to judge the pose for dominance and happiness. Keating found that nonsmiling and lowered-brow poses were generally associated with dominance, especially among the most Westernized peoples. Smiles were identified with happiness.

These findings parallel those from other studies in the West in which lowered brows are identified with anger, assertive behavior, working on competitive tasks, and dominance. Raised brows are associated with social deference in a number of ways: with children's fleeing during disputes, with perceptions of fear or surprise, and as a signal inviting social contact. Smiles (see Box 3–4) are generally associated with greeting, approval-seeking behavior, and happiness or joy (Keating et al., 1981). It

is possible, then, that the analog to the human smile is the primate submissive grin. When an ape grins it means submission. Perhaps there is an evolutionary link to the human tendency to express sociability and submissiveness in the same manner.

An even tougher test of the universality of particular emotional expressions was a study conducted with people from a remote part of New Guinea who had never lived in any Western settlement or government towns, had seen no movies, understood neither English nor Pidgin, and had never worked for a Caucasian. Presumably these people

BOX 3–4

WHAT'S IN A SMILE?

Smiling might be thought always to reflect the underlying emotion of happiness or joy. Anything that makes people happy ought to make them smile. Smiling might also be a communicative act—it might have little to do with the person's underlying emotion, but might instead be a gesture of friendliness. Kraut and Johnston (1979) observed a large number of people in ordinary interaction to test this contrast. They found that bowlers smiled when engaging in social contact, such as looking at their friends, but not when avoiding social contact, such as looking at the ground. However, their smiling was only weakly related to happiness; they smiled 30 percent of the time after a spare or a strike, and 23 percent of the time otherwise. In another set of observations, the researchers checked whether the smiling of pedestrians is caused by being with friends, and therefore by engaging in social interaction, or by the happiness caused by good weather. As this table shows, the weather had very little effect. Being with friends, however, had a strong effect. So it would seem that smiling is part of social interaction—a technique of communication—more than an intrinsic sign of happy emotions.

	PERCENTAGE OF PEDESTRIANS SMILING	
	Good Weather	Bad Weather
Social interaction	61%	57%
No interaction	12	5

Source: Kraut & Johnston (1979).

had had no visual contact with conventional Western facial expression of emotions. Each was given a brief story depicting an emotion, such as for "sadness," "His child has died, and he feels very sad." Then the participant was given one photograph Western observers overwhelmingly agreed depicted that emotion, and two pictures depicting other emotions. On the average, both children and adults chose the "correct" picture more than 80 percent of the time (Ekman & Friesen, 1971). This does not prove there are no cultural differences in the facial expression of emotion, but it does provide evidence of universals that transcend cultural boundaries.

In particular, happiness, sadness, anger, and disgust can be detected with high levels of agreement both within and across cultures. Fear and surprise were often confused with each other (Ekman, 1982).

There are some qualifications, however. Cultures do differ substantially in *amount* of emotional expression that is customary. Swedes tend to be relatively impassive; Italians are quite expressive. Sometimes social norms forbid honest expression—we are supposed to conceal disgusted reactions to someone with a terrible deformity, or anger at being belittled by our superior at work. Still, the level of consensus on the meaning of facial expressions is impressive, given the fact that most of these studies have used photographs and hence provide no information about context.

Judging Personality

Considerable research has been done on judging more permanent personality traits, such as dominance-submission or need for affiliation. This work is more discouraging, for a number of reasons. First, a wide variety of biases often influence observers. Second, it is very difficult to measure personality traits, so there is a problem in identifying the proper criteria for accuracy. A third problem is that, according to some influential psychologists (such as Mischel, 1979), any given personality trait may only influence behavior consistently in a fairly limited range of situations. That is, we may have unique,

How would you react if asked to imagine finding a dead animal that had been lying in the sun for several days or to imagine that a friend has come to visit? Research shows that the facial expressions of this New Guinea tribesman are remarkably similar to those of American college students given the same instructions. Can you tell which photos show anger, happiness, sadness, or disgust?

From P. Ekman and W. V. Friesen. *Unmasking the face.* Englewood Cliffs, NJ: Prentice-Hall, 1975, p. 27. (Answers in numerical order are happiness, sadness, anger, and disgust.)

idiosyncratic dispositions that make us regularly react in our own distinctive way to any given situation, but these may not be very constant from one set of situations to another. It may therefore be more useful to think of personality traits as holding in some fairly limited set of situations, rather than to think of traits as holding in all situations.

For example, it used to be that psychologists would talk about a *general* trait of honesty or dishonesty and thus describe a person as "honest" or "dishonest." The implication of Mischel's work, however, is that we are better advised to generalize about the person's honesty only within more limited classes of situations. We know a man who frequently cheats at pool or when he is playing golf; he often seems to replay poor shots without giving himself a penalty. But he is scrupulously honest in his dealings with co-workers and subordinates.

Should we describe him as generally a "somewhat dishonest person"? Or are we better off saying that he is honest in professional situations and cheats at competitive games?

The problem this raises for the accuracy of person perception is that if personality traits are limited to certain classes of situations, they become more difficult for observers to judge accurately. The observers would need to perceive both the person's tendencies and the situation accurately. But people tend not to do this. As we will see in Chapter 5, observers have a tendency to ascribe general personality traits to people, ignoring the fact that people may behave quite differently in different classes of situations.

For all these reasons, social psychologists believe that people are not very accurate in judging other people's personality dispositions.

NONVERBAL COMMUNICATION

If you think about it, you will realize that you make judgments about another person's emotional state on the basis of more than facial expression. If studies show that perceivers are not perfectly accurate in detecting emotions from facial expressions, what other cues do they use? And if they use a wider range of cues, do they become more accurate? What about other internal states, such as attitudes or intentions, or personality traits or lies? What are the ways in which people communicate internal states in general, and what cues do observers use in detecting them?

Generally speaking, people communicate information about themselves through three main channels. The most obvious is *verbal communication*, the content of what a person says. The other channels are nonverbal and provide a whole set of much subtler cues. *Nonverbal communication* is the sum of the ways in which we transmit information without using language. This communication comes to us through a *visible channel*, which includes such expressive behaviors as facial expression, gesture,

posture, and appearance, and a *paralinguistic channel*, what is left in the speech signal when the content has been removed, such as the pitch, amplitude, rate, voice quality, and contour of speech.

The visible and paralinguistic channels have generated a good bit of enthusiasm among researchers and they do prove informative to perceivers. As research has progressed, a wide variety of different nonverbal cues have been identified, and observers seem to get quite different kinds of information from them. However, as helpful as they can be, nonverbal communications provide no magic clues to another person's internal states. Perceivers usually require other information about a person.

The Visible Channel

Some of the main nonverbal cues of the visible channel are expressed through distance, gesture, and eye contact.

DISTANCE In general, the more friendly and intimate a person feels toward another, the closer he or she will stand. Friends stand closer than strangers (Aiello & Cooper, 1972); people who want to seem friendly choose smaller distances (Patterson & Sechrest, 1970); and people who are sexually attracted to each other stand close (Allgeier & Byrne, 1973). Although most people do not think much about personal space, we are all aware that standing close is usually a sign of friendship or interest. It may be one of the most important and easiest ways of telling someone you have just met that you like him or her. The other person is immediately aware of your interest, and if he or she is not interested, will generally move away to make that clear.

GESTURES In recent years many popular books have been published on the subject of **body language.** These books suggest that you can tell exactly what someone is thinking or perfectly interpret what they say merely by observing their bodily movements and posture. An open palm is an invitation, crossed legs are defensive, and so on. Clearly bodily gestures and posture carry information. There are straightforward, direct gestures and very subtle ones. Many bodily movements are generally accepted and convey specific information or direc-

tions—the gestures for "stop" and "come" are examples, as are pointing and gestures for "sit down," "yes," "no," "go away," "goodby." Various obscene gestures have well-known meanings. In a sense, all these gestures are a sign language.

But gestures have meaning mainly when observers and participants understand the context, and especially when they understand the culture. An open palm is not always an invitation: Putting a hand up with palm out means "stop," not "go"; the reverse gesture, with the palm in and the fingers moving toward the body, means "come" or "enter." No one has constructed a reliable dictionary of gestures. Popular books on body language are usually not based on scientific research and should be read with healthy skepticism. The meaning of gestures depends on the context, or the person doing the action, on the culture, and probably on other factors also.

EYE CONTACT Eye contact is an especially interesting form of nonverbal communication. As with other forms, the meaning of eye contact varies greatly and depends on the context. But in nearly all social interactions eye contact does communicate information.

At the minimum, eye contact indicates interest

People are able to interpret each other's gestures quite easily when they are familiar and in a known context.

Ken Karp

or lack of it. Hollywood movies often have a couple staring into each other's eyes to portray love, affection, or great concern. Certainly we are all familiar with eye contact held for a long time as a means of demonstrating attraction for someone. An otherwise casual conversation can become an expression of romantic interest if one of the speakers maintains eye contact. Conversely, avoiding or breaking the contact is usually a sign that the person is not interested. Indeed, when someone does not make eye contact during a conversation, we tend to interpret this as an indication that he or she is not really involved in the interaction. No matter how attentively someone answers questions, nods at appropriate times, and carries on the conversation, lack of eye contact means he or she is not interested in what we are saying.

But there are obvious exceptions to this general principle. Someone who is conveying bad news or saying something painful may avoid eye contact. Lack of eye contact can sometimes mean the person is shy or frightened. When people have feelings they are embarrassed about, they do not like to be the focus of a direct gaze. In a study by Ellsworth and colleagues (1978), female college students were told they would have to discuss questions "about rather intimate personal areas of your life, things that college students usually do not like to talk about." Each student then had to wait with a confederate who stared directly at her 75 percent of the time, or just glanced at her once. By far, most subjects preferred the gaze-averting confederate. Other subjects who were not expecting an embarrassing conversation did not. The direct gaze apparently threatened the embarrassed women.

Moreover, eye contact can be used more actively, to threaten. In another experiment, someone stared at a subject who was in a position to act aggressively

Eye contact leads to quite accurate inferences in contexts people understand well. We would be surprised if this man were not in love, or at least, very fond of the person facing him.

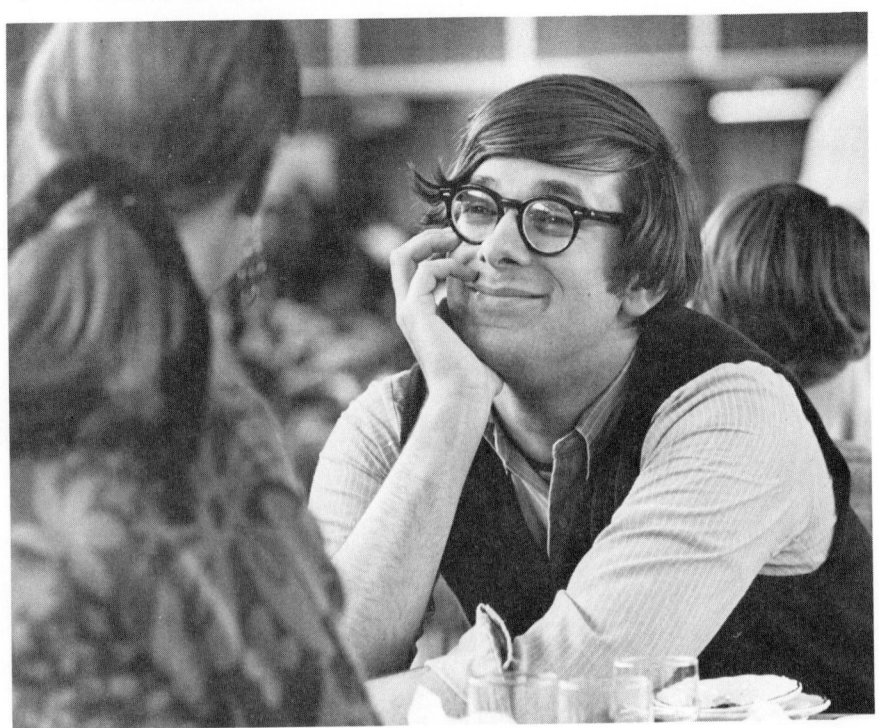

toward the starer. Subjects who were stared at were less aggressive than when there was no staring (Ellsworth & Carlsmith, 1973). Apparently prolonged eye contact can be interpreted as a threat and causes people to escape or act in a conciliatory manner. We all can probably remember teachers who have used this technique very effectively on us.

It is perhaps not surprising that eye contact can have two seemingly contradictory meanings—friendship or threat. In both cases, eye contact indicates greater involvement and higher emotional content. Whether the emotion is positive or negative depends on the context; the nonverbal cues themselves have no fixed meaning.

FACIAL EXPRESSIONS   Facial expressions also can be intended to communicate to others. One interesting case of this is mimicry. It has often been observed that people (and chimpanzees) physically mimic the responses of others. Darwin noted that in particular people mimic distress when others are feeling it. It is possible that this mimicry is an expression of sympathy for the victim; the mimic may want the other person to know that distress about the painful experience is shared. To test this idea, Bavelas and her colleagues (1986) had undergraduate women individually view a person accidentally drop a heavy TV monitor on an already injured finger, one with a heavily taped splint on it. In some cases the victim, a confederate (badly bruised!) then looked directly at the observer; in other cases no eye contact was made. Most of the observers in turn displayed an expression of pain, but it quickly faded in the absence of eye contact. Moreover, the observers were considerably more likely to smile when eye contact was made, probably in an effort to be reassuring. The facial expressions of the observers were in fact rated as more "knowing" and "caring" in the eye contact condition than without, suggesting that they were successfully communicating feelings of empathy and sympathy.

Paralanguage

Variations in speech other than the actual verbal contact, called **paralanguage,** carry a great deal of meaning. Pitch of the voice, loudness, rhythm, inflection, and hesitations convey information. Parents can often tell whether their baby is hungry, angry, or just mildly cranky by how it cries. Dogs bark in different ways, and each means something different to someone familiar with the animal. And, of course, the significance and meaning of adult speech depend in part on these paralinguistic factors.

A simple statement such as "You want to move to Japan" can mean entirely different things depending on emphasis and inflection. Say it aloud as a flat statement with no emphasis, and it sounds like a mere statement of fact. Say it with an inflection (rising voice) at the end, and it questions the wisdom of going to Japan; you are expressing doubt that it is a good place to move to. Say it with added emphasis on the first word and it turns into a question as to whether or not the person addressed is qualified; you are raising doubts about whether or not the person is capable of getting along in such a foreign country. The short phrase "I like you" may indicate almost anything from mild feeling to intense passion, depending on its paralinguistic characteristics.

These variations are often crucial in conveying emotion. In fact, they are so important that they often must be added to written language. To show that someone thought Japan was an unlikely choice, the sentence might read, " 'You want to move to Japan?' he said with disbelief." To describe the feeling behind a statement of liking, one might write, " 'I like you,' she murmured passionately." Without these paralinguistic clues, the statements are hard to interpret.

One of the difficulties in studying paralanguage (and most other kinds of nonverbal behavior) is that the cues have no fixed meaning. We all agree on the meaning of words. We all know what "Japan" refers to, and with some variations we know that when someone says he "likes" you, he is making a statement of positive feelings. But people differ considerably in the meanings they attach to paralinguistic cues. For some people, a pause may be for emphasis; for others, it may mean uncertainty. Higher pitch may mean excitement or lying; loudness can be anger, emphasis, or excitement. The particular meaning depends on the context. It is hard to interpret what is communicated when a speaker talks louder at you: If the person makes a fist, it is anger; if the person hugs you, it is affection.

It also depends on individual habits and characteristics.

Multiple Channels

Which of these three channels of communication—verbal, visible, and paralinguistic—provides the most information about a person's real emotions? Many writers in recent years have speculated that observers weigh nonverbal cues most heavily and tend almost to disregard verbal communication. For example, Birdwhistell (1970) says that no more than 30 to 35 percent of the social meaning of a conversation is carried by the words. Mehrabian (1972) estimated that only 7 percent of the communication of emotion was accomplished by the verbal channel, 55 percent was accomplished by the visible channel, and 38 percent by the paralinguistic channel. Other writers have gone even further, arguing that the visible channel dominates in the communication of emotion; that is, "video" information is more important than "audio" (De Paulo et al., 1978).

The question of which channels are taken most seriously becomes particularly important when the observer is receiving conflicting cues from different channels. How do you interpret your girlfirend's feelings when she says she loves you but moves away from you and won't look at you? The verbal and visible channels of her communication seem to conflict. What if your roommate shouts at you at the top of her lungs that she is really *not* mad at you, *at all*, for breaking her favorite coffee cup? Shakespeare said, "Methinks she doth protest too much." Conflicts across channels ought to be particularly important in interpreting apparently deceptive communications. In such cases, is nonverbal, and especially visible, communication truly relied on most heavily, as some of these researchers suggest?

Only recently have such claims been subjected to rigorous tests. In one of the clearest of such studies, Krauss et al. (1981) presented subjects with videotapes of the 1976 televised debate between the two candidates for vice-president, Walter Mondale and Robert Dole. The debate started pleasantly, but turned rather heated and rancorous. The researchers selected twelve passages for each speaker, half of which seemed to display positive emotions

and half negative. Then each subject was presented these passages in one of four conditions: (1) audiovisual—the standard videotaped version; (2) verbal only—a written transcript as published in the *New York Times*; (3) video only—with the audio channel turned off; and (4) paralinguistic—the audio track only, but with content filtered out so that speech was unintelligible, while nonverbal features such as pitch, loudness, rate, and so on were preserved.

The full audiovisual condition provided all three channels of communication; the other three provided, respectively, only verbal, visible, and paralinguistic information. The basic question was which of the latter three yielded responses most similar to those obtained from the full, audiovisual version. Presumably that would show which individual channel communicated the most information about the speakers' true emotions.

The written transcript turned out to be critical for detecting whether positive or negative emotions were being expressed; that is, verbal information was most important, contrary to speculations about the importance of nonverbal communications. The data from this study are shown in Table 3–6.

To see if the same finding would hold with communication more typical of students' daily lives, Krauss and associates did a second experiment presenting subjects with undergraduates' responses to affectively loaded questions ("Who is the person in your life you like most? Describe what he/she is like and your reaction to that person") under the same four conditions as in the debate study just described. The results were very similar: The actual written transcript of the person's comments carried the most weight in determining perceptions of the person's feelings.

In both studies, the visible channel made little contribution to observers' judgments. Paralinguistic information did contribute to judgments of the potency and activity levels of the speakers' presentations. That is, observers who were given only the unintelligible soundtrack gave the same kinds of judgments about energy levels as did those given full audiovisual information. The implication is that paralinguistic information, like eye contact, can be sufficient to detect energy and involvement, even if it is not sufficient to detect the particular kind of emotion expressed.

A follow-up study by Apple and Hecht (1982)

TABLE 3–6

Importance of Various Channels of Information in Judgments about Vice-presidential Debaters

	Verbal Only	Video Only	Audio Filtered
Dimension of judgment			
Evaluation	51.8[a]	2.2	8.8
Potency	3.4	29.6	45.1[a]
Activity	0.1	36.8	5.2

[a] $p < .05$.
Note: The entry is the percentage of variance in judgments of full audiovisual communication that was accounted for by each individual channel. Rows do not sum to 100 percent because factors other than these three channels account for some of the full-channel judgment process.
Source: Adapted from Krauss et al. (1981), pp. 316–317.

found that paralinguistic information could be particularly useful in detecting sadness. They had speakers deliver sentences that varied in the kind of emotion they presented: happiness, sadness, anger, or surprise. No visual cues were provided, and the verbal content of the sentence was screened out from the recording. Listeners were able to identify the sadness sentences quite readily, but they could identify the others at only slightly better than chance levels. The authors speculate that sadness is expressed through distinctive paralinguistic cues (slow, soft, low-pitched speech), whereas the other emotions are expressed with more energetic cues that easily confuse the listener.

In general, then, nonverbal cues—paralinguistic or visible—are not very precise guides, by themselves, to emotional feelings in others. There is nothing magically or unambiguously communicative about nonverbal cues. Most can communicate a variety of messages depending on the context. A touch on the arm by an attractive acquaintance means something quite different from the same touch made by a derelict in a subway station. Being tapped on the shoulder by your boss may mean something still different. A smile on the face of a bully as he moves in on a helpless prey means something quite different from the smile on a friend's face when he or she sees you walking across the campus. Nonverbal cues can be informative, but only when they are solidly embedded in a familiar context, when we know the role of the other person, have some notion of his or her general goals, know the norms for the situation, and so on. When we do not have a known or familiar context, as in a first visit to a foreign country, we frequently feel lost and can make little sense of nonverbal cues.

THE PROBLEM OF DECEPTION

A particularly important area of conflict between verbal and nonverbal cues is judging when people are lying or otherwise trying to deceive observers. Police, judges, and jurors are constantly trying to learn the truth from people who try to mislead them.

Nonverbal Leakage

As might be expected from our discussion of nonverbal communication, one important theory is that people will give away deception through nonverbal cues even when they are successful in lying verbally.

Ekman and Friesen (1974) argue that people attend more to what they are saying than to what they are doing with their bodies. If they are trying to deceive someone, for example, they may lie verbally in a calm way, but reveal their true emotions through nonverbal cues. In Ekman's terms, there is **nonverbal leakage.** True emotions "leak out" even if the person tries to conceal them. A student may say she is not nervous about a test, but will bite her lower lip and blink more than usual, actions that often indicate nervousness. A young man waiting for a job interview may attempt to appear calm and casual, but will cross and uncross his legs continually, straighten his tie, touch his face, play with his hair. As a result, he will in fact come across as a nervous wreck.

Liars often betray themselves through paralinguistic expressions of anxiety, tension, and nervousness. It sometimes is possible to tell when someone is lying by noting the pitch of the voice. Several studies (Ekman et al., 1976; Krauss et al., 1976) indicate that the average (or more technically, fundamental) pitch of the voice is higher when someone is lying than when he or she is telling the truth. The difference is small, and one cannot tell just by listening. But electronic vocal analysis reveals lying with considerable accuracy. In addition, shorter answers, longer delays in responding, more speech errors, and more nervous, less serious answers all are characteristic of people perceived as liars or of people instructed to tell lies (Apple, Streeter, & Krauss, 1979; Kraut, 1978; Zuckerman, DePaulo, & Rosenthal, 1981).

The concept of "leakage" implies that some nonverbal channels "leak" more than others because they are less controllable. Several studies (Zuckerman, DePaulo, & Rosenthal, 1981) have found that the body is more likely to reveal deception than the face. Paralinguistic cues can also "leak" because, like the body, tone of voice is less controllable than facial expression. Zuckerman, Larrance, Spiegel, and Klorman (1981) have found that senders were better able to modify (suppress and exaggerate) facial expressions than tone of voice. The "leakage" hypothesis proposes, then, that when people are trying to conceal something, they may be able to control their verbal content and facial expressions fairly well, but their deception may "leak" out in bodily gestures and paralinguistic cues.

Accuracy of Detection

Perceivers do quite consistently perceive deceptive messages as somewhat less truthful than truthful messages. Across dozens of studies, deception accuracy usually exceeds chance, but rarely by an impressive margin (DePaulo et al., 1982). Not surprisingly, people can detect the fact of lying better than they can figure out the nature of the liar's true feelings.

For one thing, people have trouble distinguishing deception from genuine ambivalence. This was illustrated in a study by DePaulo and co-workers (1982). They had senders record messages that either (1) truthfully described their positive (or negative, as the case may be) feelings about another person, (2) untruthfully described their positive (or negative) feelings, or (3) truthfully described their genuinely mixed feelings about another person. These messages were presented to observers through different channels. They found that observers were not able to distinguish truthful messages about mixed feelings from deceptive messages about positive *or* negative feelings. Perhaps people are able to distinguish true expressions of positive or negative feelings from everything else, but are not able to isolate deception itself without any further information—all they know is that the person does not sound wholeheartedly positive or negative.

On the other hand, people usually do have other information about the person's motives. They usually know whether or not the person has reason to want to lie. It may be that we are better at detecting deception when we know the person has such reasons. To test this, DePaulo and her colleagues (1985) had "senders" describe their opinions on four issues to their "partners." They manipulated lying by instructing the "senders" to honestly agree or disagree on two issues, and to pretend to agree or disagree on two others. Then they varied the incentive for senders to lie in several ways. In the high incentive conditions, the "partner" was of the opposite sex, the partner was attractive, and the sender was instructed to feign agreement. Presumably all these would give the sender reason to be most ingratiating. In the other conditions, the sender would have less apparent incentive to lie: the "partner" was unattractive, or of the same sex,

BOX 3–5

DETECTING SMUGGLERS AT THE CUSTOMS GATE

How good are ordinary people at detecting lying? What cues do they use in detecting it? One of the most realistic studies was conducted by Kraut and Poe (1980). They induced airline travelers to try to smuggle some "contraband" past an interview with a real U.S. Customs inspector. The participants were people who happened to be waiting for an airline departure in Syracuse, New York. Some were randomly selected to serve in the "smuggler" condition and were given contraband, such as small pouches of white powder or miniature cameras, and told to hide them on their persons. They were offered a prize of up to $100 for being able to smuggle the contraband successfully past the customs inspector. Others were randomly selected to be in the "innocent" condition and were given no contraband. The whole interaction of passenger and inspector was videotaped. To determine what special nonverbal behaviors were displayed by people actually engaged in deception, each passenger's behavior with the inspector was coded by other judges for many of the visible and paralinguistic variables of nonverbal communication we have been discussing: grooming, postural shifts, relaxed posture, smiling, gaze avoidance, speech errors, response latency, response length, evasiveness, nervousness, and difficulty in answering. Each interaction was also played back to observers who attempted to identify which of the passengers were "smugglers" and which were not.

There were no discernible systematic differences in behavior between the innocent and smuggling passengers. If the "smugglers" were "leaking" their deceptiveness, they were not doing so consistently via the nonverbal behaviors coded. Not surprisingly, then, neither the real customs inspectors nor the observers who later viewed the videotapes were successful in picking out the "smugglers" from the "innocent" passengers. This finding suggests that observers have limited ability to detect deception in a real life situation, when they only have nonverbal cues to go on.

Despite this lack of accuracy, there was strong consensus among observers on who the actual smugglers were. They also showed considerable consensus on the specific cues associated with "smuggling": the person's apparent nervousness, taking a long time to answer a question, giving short answers, shifting the body more, and avoiding eye contact with the inspector.

In short, neither professional nor untrained observers could accurately determine whether or not a traveler was lying. And in fact the lying and honest travelers did not differ in any way that could be coded in terms of verbal and nonverbal behavior. Yet observers came to a striking level of consensus about who was smuggling, and what cues supposedly revealed it. All this is consistent with the notion that the observers shared a clear but inaccurate schema about how smugglers behave. As in controlled laboratory situations, observers are not terribly accurate detectors of deception on the basis of nonverbal cues, though they are often quite confident about being able to detect it, and have many ready explanations for this "skill."

or the sender was instructed to feign disagreement. These communications were videotaped and later played back to neutral judges, varying which channels were available. The judges rated the communications on a scale of sincerity-insincerity.

The main finding is that lies were easiest to detect when they were apparently motivated by ingratiation, that is, when the sender had the greatest motivation to lie—communicating agreement to an attractive partner of the opposite sex. Deception was harder to detect without any specific information about reasons to lie—that is, when the sender was communicating disagreement to an unattractive member of one's own sex.

Does it help to be warned explicitly that the target person may be lying? One would think so, because perceivers then should attend more closely to "leaky" channels, such as the face and tone of voice. However, it seems not to help very much. In a study by Toris and DePaulo (1984), subjects participated in simulated job interviews. The applicants were told to be honest in some cases and dishonest in others, while the interviewers were told to expect the applicant to try to convey a false impression in some cases and were given no warning in others. However, this warning of deceptiveness just made the interviewers suspicious about everyone, perceiving all applicants as more deceptive; they were no more accurate in singling out the dishonest ones. Not only that, but they were less confident of their own judgments.

The Giveaways

What cues do observers use to discover deception? Is the leakage hypothesis correct? Is the body less controllable than the face, and do people catch deception primarily through nonverbal bodily cues? Or is the voice an even leakier channel than the body? It may be that the tone of voice—pitch, loudness, speed, and so forth—is even more difficult to control than the body, even when the person can control the content of verbal communication.

Most of the research shows that all these cues help a little to trap a potentially deceptive communicator. But they are really useful only when the observer also has access to the content of the person's speech. A typical study is one done by Zuckerman,

Amidon, Bishop, and Pomerantz (1982). They had "senders" describe either a target person they liked (a "liked target") or someone they disliked (a "disliked target"), and they did so in one of three modes: "truth," in which they conveyed their true feelings; "concealment," in which they tried to conceal their true feelings; and "deception," in which they tried to communicate feelings opposite to those they really had. The "receivers" did not know the senders' true feelings, or which mode the sender was instructed to use.

The crucial comparison is between the channels in which receivers were then given these communications: full audiovisual (face plus verbal content), full audio only (verbal content, no face), visual plus filtered speech (face, no verbal content), or filtered speech only (no verbal content, no face). The question was how access to the face, to verbal content, and to paralinguistic cues affected observers' ability to detect whether the sender really liked or disliked the target.

The results showed that either face or tone of voice added significantly to ability to detect deception. This can be seen in Table 3–7. The receivers were significantly able to distinguish a liked from a disliked target when given only filtered speech, without being able to see the face or hear any verbal content (as indicated by the fact that they perceived the truly liked target as liked + .31 more, on the average, than the truly disliked target). Second, adding access to the face significantly increased detection of the sender's true feelings, as indicated by the fact that face plus filtered speech is higher (+.74) than filtered speech only (+.31), even when

TABLE 3–7

Accuracy of Perception of Communicators' True Feelings about Target Person

| | VERBAL CONTENT | |
	Available	Not Available
Face present	+.85	+.74
Face absent	+.84	+.31

Note: The entry is the perception of communicator's true feeling about the liked target minus the perception of communicator's true feeling about the disliked target, each rated on a nine-point scale.
Source: Adapted from Zuckerman et al. (1982), p. 353.

verbal content was not available. Both channels are somewhat "leaky," then, in the sense that both communicated significantly to the receiver about a possibly deceptive sender's true feelings, even when the receiver could not understand the content of the communication.

The main finding, however, is that accuracy is greatest when verbal content is available. The table shows the highest accuracy in the left-hand column, with verbal content available. Moreover, adding visual nonverbal cues helps the perceiver very little when verbal content is available (+.85 is almost identical to +.84).

Again, however, observers do better, with less, when they have other information about the senders' motives. Earlier we described the DePaulo and associates (1985) study in which incentive for lying was varied—communicating agreement to an attractive member of the opposite sex (high incentive to lie) versus communicating disagreement to an unattractive member of one's own sex (low incentive to lie). Consistent with the "leakage" hypothesis, the nonverbal channels became more important in detecting lies as senders became more motivated to lie successfully. Their interpretation was that "as senders become more motivated to

lie successfully, they will try harder to control all their verbal and nonverbal behaviors . . . [but] nonverbal behaviors may be less readily and effectively controlled than verbal behaviors" (p. 1200).

We have discussed a number of studies, then, which have tried to determine what cues help detect lying in another person. For the most part, nonverbal cues do not seem to be sufficient. Rather, people infer lying from other kinds of information they receive about the person: whether the supposed liar seems to have something to gain from lying, or fits the stereotype of a liar, or from verbal communication from the person. Nonverbal cues add something when this other information is available, but are not sufficient by themselves.

Nevertheless, there is some evidence for the "leakage" hypothesis: People can detect deception significantly through nonverbal cues, such as the face, filtered speech, or the body. We have little reason yet to say that the face is a great deal less leaky than tone of voice or body. But it is quite clear that the best guide to deception is hearing what a person has to say—which includes both the content and paralinguistic cues—and from knowing something about the person's motives.

KEY TERMS IN CHAPTER 3

averaging principle	figure-ground principle	nonverbal leakage	salience
body language	gestalt	paralanguage	schema
categorization	halo effect	person perception	self-reference effect
central traits	implicit personality theory	positivity bias	shift of meaning
cognitive miser	negativity effect	prototype	stereotype
evaluation			

SUMMARY

1. People tend to form highly consistent impressions of others, even with very little information.

2. The evaluative dimension is the most important organizing principle behind first impressions. People seem to decide first how much they like or dislike another person, then ascribe characteristics to them that fit this pleasant or unpleasant portrait.

3. Various identifiable perceptual biases distort our judgments of others, such as the halo effect (we tend to think a person we like is good on every dimension), and the positivity bias (we tend to like most people, even some who are not so likeable).

4. There are two rival points of view about how people process information about other people: The learning approach, which has people essentially averaging information in a quite mechanical manner; and the Gestalt approach, which has people forming more coherent and meaningful impressions.

5. Our judgments of other people are not always very accurate. In particular, we have a hard time judging people's emotions from their facial expressions. We can tell fairly easily if the emotion is a positive or a negative one, but we have diffi-

culty telling which positive or negative emotion is being experienced. Nevertheless, there do seem to be some universal connections across cultures between certain emotions and certain facial expressions.

6. We use a wide variety of cues in arriving at impressions of people, including physical appearance, verbal behavior, and nonverbal cues. Nonverbal communication includes cues from both the visible channel (such as facial expressions, gestures, and posture) and the paralinguistic channel (cues in speech when the content has been removed, such as the pitch, rate, and delays of speech).

7. A person's verbal communication is probably the single most important source of information about them. However, visible and paralinguistic information make an important additional contribution, particularly when the content helps us to interpret their meaning.

8. Deception "leaks" out in numerous nonverbal ways, such as nervous gestures or high-pitched and rapid speech. Observers can usually detect deception at slightly better than chance levels, but they need all three channels of communication to do so effectively.

SUGGESTED READINGS

ANDERSON, N. H. (1965). Averaging vs. adding as a stimulus-combination rule in impression formation. *Journal of Experimental Psychology*, 70, 394–400. This gives the flavor of averaging research, using trait adjectives about hypothetical stimulus persons.

ASCH, S. E. (1946). Forming impressions of personality. *Journal of Abnormal and Social Psychology*, 41, 258–90. This is the classic statement of the Gestalt approach to impression formation, and indeed to social perception in general.

EKMAN, PAUL (Ed.). (1982). *Emotion in the human face*. (2nd ed.). New York: Cambridge University Press. The best treatment of how people judge emotions from facial expressions.

HALL, EDWARD T. (1966). *The hidden dimension*. Garden City, N.Y.: Doubleday. An original statement by one of the pioneers in the study of nonverbal communication.

KRAUSS, R. M., APPLE, W., MORENCY, N., WENZEL, C., & WINTON, W. (1981). Verbal, vocal, and visible factors in judgments of another's affect. *Journal of Personality and Social Psychology, 40,* 312–320. An interesting and careful analysis of how people combine cues from different channels to arrive at impressions.

MEHRABIAN, A. (1972). *Nonverbal communication*. Chicago: Aldine. A useful summary of research on nonverbal communication.

SCHNEIDER, D. J., HASTORF, A. H., & ELLSWORTH, P. C. (1979). *Person perception* (2nd ed.). Reading, Mass.: Addison-Wesley. A paperback that pursues the material in this chapter in more detail.

4 Social Cognition

I magine that you have completed college and are interviewing at a company for your first job. You have met the personnel director, the executive who would be your boss, and several of your prospective co-workers. You also have toured the facilities, seen where your office would be if you were to join the firm, and learned a great deal about the work the company does and your responsibilities to the company. How do you put all of this information together? How do you decide if this is indeed the kind of company you want to work for, if you would like the work itself or the people you would work with? Answering these questions involves processes called social cognition.

Social cognition is the study of how people form inferences from social information in the environment (Fiske & Taylor, 1984). It explores how people make social judgments about other individuals or social groups, about social roles, and about their own experiences in social settings. The process of making social judgments is more difficult than we might imagine. Often, the information available to us is incomplete, ambiguous, or downright contradictory. We may be confronted with many complex details. How do we use all this information to arrive at a coherent judgment? This is the core question in research on social cognition.

Much of the early work on social cognition compared the social judgments actually made by people to those we would expect from a **rational model of inference.** By rational model, we mean that there are logical and correct ways to put information together to reach a judgment. Presumably, to make correct decisions and wise judgments, people should try to use social information as logically and carefully as possible (Einhorn & Hogarth, 1981). In the interests of making accurate inferences, people should try hard to avoid logical errors and subjective biases. Consequently, rational models of inference were considered to be appropriate standards against which to evaluate people's everyday processes for forming judgments and making decisions.

Studies comparing actual social judgments to the rational model have taught us much about the processes of social cognition. Contrary to what the rational model predicts, however, people's everyday methods of gathering and combining social information are often illogical. In the next section, we discuss some of the typical errors and biases that affect the social perceiver. Then we turn to newer research that explains some of the good reasons why the social perceiver is not completely rational.

SOCIAL INFERENCE

Any social inference is composed of several steps: gathering information, deciding what information to use to reach a judgment, and integrating the information into a judgment. For example, as you are learning about your possible new employer, you are gathering information about the people, products, and general feel of the organization, and you are gathering information from people around

you through the questions you ask and the types of facilities or people that you request to see. When you return home and mull over your visit, you must then decide which of the multitude of information you received will be most relevant to your decision, and then integrate that information into an overall impression or judgment concerning whether or not this company is the right one for you. Each of these steps in the social inference process appears to be subject to particular kinds of errors and biases.

Gathering Information

When people gather information that is relevant to some inference they will ultimately form, they might plan to do so in an even-handed and unbiased manner. However, research suggests that actual information gathering is often colored by peoples' *prior expectations*. For example, suppose you learn that a college acquaintance of yours, an uptight, serious, humorless fellow, works for the company you are considering, and finds it very much to his liking. If he likes the company so much, you might suspect that it is because he has found people there who are like he is. Consequently, you might infer that everyone at the company must be stiff and uptight. Accordingly, as you learn about the company with this suspicion in mind, you might selec-tively gather information consistent with this prior expectation. You might note that prospective co-workers seem a little stiff or formal when you meet them, and conclude that indeed your classmate is typical of the people at this firm. But in doing so, you might fail to remember that most people are a little stiff or formal when they are meeting someone for the first time. Their formality might simply be due to the fact that you are a stranger to them. They might actually turn out to be very friendly people. But with your prior expectations in mind, you might dismiss them as stiff and formal people without giving them a chance. This is how prior expectations can bias the process of gathering information.

Of course, prior expectations are often very helpful in sifting through a lot of information that may otherwise be uninterpretable. They can provide structure and meaning for information that would otherwise be hard to interpret. However, sometimes prior expectations can cause us to draw inaccurate inferences. Three conditions are especially

Social information is often ambiguous and subject to multiple interpretations. Therefore, social inference processes are important for giving social interactions structure and meaning.

Ken Karp

problematic (Nisbett & Ross, 1980). The first is if the expectations are faulty. For example, your belief that the company is stiff and stodgy merely because it attracted one such individual to its ranks is likely to be incorrect. Therefore, letting this expectation guide your collection of information will probably lead you to incorrect answers. A second condition under which prior expectations can be problematic occurs when the social perceiver fails to recognize how prior expectations bias the collection of information. For example, you may be unaware that your impressions of your stodgy college classmate are actually guiding your judgments of your prospective co-workers. This lack of awareness means that later on you will be unable to correct the biasing effect of your prior impression. Your judgments concerning your prospective co-workers will stray on the stodgy and serious side without your realizing that your own biases contributed to this inference. Third, prior expectations can create problems when they overrule consideration of information altogether. If you decide on the basis of your college classmate's attributes not to meet your potential co-workers at all, you would be guilty of this error.

Once the social perceiver has decided what information is relevant to an inference, information must actually be collected. The individual must determine which bits of information from the wealth that is potentially available should be examined. For example, obviously you cannot meet everybody during your job interview visit, and so the people you do meet will help give you an impression of the qualities of your co-workers. But forming judgments on the basis of limited information can be thrown off when there are *biases in the information*. For example, if you are introduced to a particularly outgoing and friendly co-worker, your impression of the attributes of the workers in the company may be falsely influenced toward the outgoing and friendly side.

One study that illustrates this point was conducted by Rothbart, Fulero, Jensen, Howard, and Birrell (1978). Subjects were given information about members of two groups, including the fact that some of the members had committed crimes. For one group, only moderate crimes were listed. In the second group, the same number of crimes was listed, but the list included several particularly severe ones such as rape and murder. Although

the actual number of crimes was the same in the two groups, when asked to recall which crimes had been committed by members of which group, subjects misremembered that more individuals had committed crimes in the second group, that is, the group in which a few members had committed highly serious crimes. Presumably, the extreme examples of crimes had led to a strong association between that group and crime in general, leading to the incorrect inference that the second group had actually committed more crimes.

Inferences are also problematic when they are based on very little information. People are often unaware that a *small sample* of information can actually produce a very biased picture. For example, if you are introduced to only two of your prospective co-workers who seem pleasant enough but you will actually be working with twenty individuals, there is the possibility that these two are not typical of the larger group. The other eighteen may not be quite as pleasant. But often people forget that they are dealing with very little information and make confident inferences nonetheless.

Even when people are warned that information may be biased, they sometimes fail to understand the full implications of that bias. For example, in one study (Hamill, Wilson, & Nisbett, 1980), researchers told subjects that they would be viewing a videotape of an interview with a prison guard. Some subjects were told that this prison guard was typical of most prison guards, whereas others were told that he was very different from most prison guards. In the third condition, subjects were not given information about how typical the guard was. Half the subjects then saw a tape in which the prison guard appeared as a highly compassionate, concerned individual. The other half saw a tape portraying him as an inhumane, macho, cruel person. Subjects were later asked a set of questions about the criminal justice system that included questions about what kinds of people become prison guards. The results showed that subjects exposed to the interview of the humane guard were more favorable in their attitudes toward prison guards than were subjects who saw the interview with the inhumane prison guard. More important, subjects' inferences about prison guards were unaffected by whether or not they had been told that the interview with the prison guard was typical or not typical.

Consider an analogous situation in your hypothetical job interview. Suppose you wanted to meet some of your co-workers but were told that they were away at a seminar this week and unable to meet with you. But so that you could form some impressions of the workers of the company, you might be introduced to one or two of the company's employees from a neighboring office but with whom you would not be working directly. You might find that your judgments about your prospective co-workers would be influenced by the one or two individuals you do meet. You might fail to correct for the fact that these individuals actually have a different job and would not be in your work group at all. Therefore, your impressions of them might have little if anything to do with the attributes of your actual co-workers.

Another distinction that is important in understanding how people use information is between *statistical information and case history information*. Statistical information involves information about a large number of individuals, whereas case history information involves information about only a few specific individuals. It turns out that when people are exposed to both statistical information and a colorful case history, the case history often has more influence on their judgments. This occurs even when the statistical information is objectively better. For example, one type of information you might want to gather during your job interview is knowledge about how quickly people advance in the company. Clearly, the most appropriate information to look at is the statistical information about promotion rates for all the employees and for those in your division particularly. However, suppose you are told about Mark Comet, a particularly dynamic fellow who managed to go from clerk to associate vice-president in three short years. It is very likely that the case history of Mark Comet's dramatic rise to fame and fortune within the company will bias your impression of how quickly people advance. It may lead you to ignore the more appropriate statistical information that would suggest that most people advance fairly slowly within the company.

Most of us seem to know that we really should use broadly based statistical information in making our judgments. People draw on statistics all the time when they are trying to make a persuasive argument, and a person can often be quite persuasive if he or she has statistical information available. However, generally speaking, when more engaging anecdotal case history evidence is present, people often ignore relevant statistical evidence and are instead overly persuaded by the case histories (Bar-Hillel & Fischhoff, 1981; Manis, Avis, & Cardoze, 1981).

Integrating Information

The next task in the inference process involves bringing information together and combining it into a social judgment. When people's integrative capabilities are compared against rational models, it appears that the human judgment process is rather haphazard and does not closely follow the principles of a rational model.

Consider the example of college admissions. When there are many applicants and only a few openings, one must develop criteria for deciding which people to admit and which to reject. Most college admissions departments have a formula for admitting students which dictates how heavily they weigh SAT scores, high school grades, letters of recommendation, the personal essay, and other sources of information. With such clear standards available, one would assume that the college admissions decision-makers do a good job of using this formula to determine who will be admitted and who will not. However, it turns out that when there are clear standards for combining information into a judgment, a computer typically outperforms a human decision-maker (Meehl, 1954; Sawyer, 1966).

Why is this the case? Human decision-makers have great faith in their abilities to make decisions. When asked what procedures they use to make decisions, they typically report being more consistent, using more pieces of information, and making more complex judgments than is actually the case. The reason that computers typically outperform human judges is that the computer consistently uses criteria established by people, weights information in a standard way, combines the information according to the formula, and reaches a judgment. The human decision-maker, in contrast, may be swayed by pet theories or stereotypes that influence the information selected. Two extensive studies have pitted human judges against the computer or other mechanical aids, and both have yielded the same conclusion (Meehl, 1954; J. Sawyer, 1966): When people can specify the rules of inference they want to use to combine information into an overall decision or judgment, computers and other mechanical aids always do a better job of following these rules than human judges do.

Imagine how this process might work after your job interview. A small group of individuals who had met you during your visit would be assigned the task of deciding whether or not to hire you. Each person would have only a modest amount of information about you. One person might point out that you seemed nervous under pressure as evidenced by the fact that you dropped your roll on the floor during lunch. Another, however, might argue that you may be a potential Mark Comet, given that you both have competitive tennis in your background. Another might point out that your transcript shows you have high grades in virtually every subject, suggesting great ability. The next person, however, might complain that if you did well in everything, you have not shown any special talents. In short, then, each evaluator may have certain idiosyncratic ways of viewing the information derived from your brief visit which he or she considers relevant to the overall judgment of whether or not you should be hired. It is indeed unnerving to realize one's fate often depends upon this type of decision-making process.

Judgments of Covariation

In addition to putting information together to form coherent impressions of people and events, we are also concerned with figuring out "what goes with what" in social life. Many of our beliefs involve statements about the relationship between things. For example, the adage "All work and no play makes Jack a dull boy" implies that working too hard and being dull are related and that playing and not being dull go together. Similarly, the statement "Blondes have more fun" implies a relationship

between being blonde and having fun and between not being blonde and having less fun. Technically, such ideas about the associations between things are called judgments of **covariation.**

In making judgments about covariation, people are prone to certain errors. Consider the statement, "Blondes have more fun." As Figure 4–1 illustrates, the first step in assessing covariation is deciding what information is relevant. In order to determine if blondes actually have more fun, one needs to look at both blondes and nonblondes and examine the frequency with which they have fun and do not have fun. However, most people believe that cell A (fun-loving blondes) is the relevant information from which to determine whether blondes have more fun. They fail to recognize that the number of brunettes and redheads who have fun and do not have fun are just as relevant as the number of blondes who have fun or do not. After all, to know if blondes have more fun, one needs to know that there are brunettes and redheads who are having less fun.

The second step in assessing covariation is gathering instances of blonde, brunette, and redheaded men and women to see if they are having fun or not. As we already noted, people are very poor at gathering information. They tend to draw on their own acquaintances, which may represent a biased sample. Most people assessing whether or not blondes have more fun would think about a few blonde friends and leave the information gathering task at that.

The third step in the covariation process is classifying instances as to the type of evidence they represent, and again, the social perceiver's expectations can get in the way. Cases that contradict the proposed relationship may be mislabeled as supportive instances if they are ambiguous, or they may be dismissed as due to error or faulty information gathering if they are not ambiguous. Positive instances are more quickly or easily identified and incorporated into the inference task (see, for example, Owens, Bower, & Black, 1979). Thus, for example, happy blondes will quickly be seen as relevant. Happy brunettes may be judged to be happy "dirty blondes" and happy redheads labeled as "strawberry blondes." Unhappy blondes might be judged to have dyed their hair blonde—and thus be irrele-

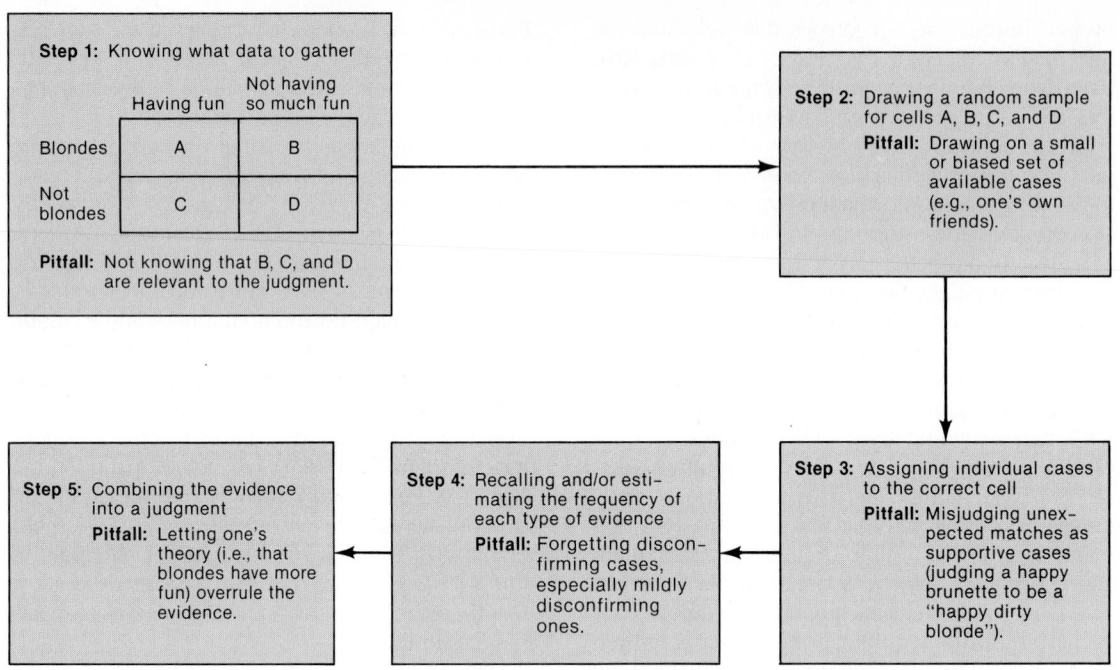

FIGURE 4–1 The assessment of covariation and its pitfalls. Do blondes have more fun?

vant to assessing whether or not blondes have more fun.

Information must next be put together, which requires recalling the frequency of each type of evidence. Unfortunately, the social perceiver remembers confirming cases well but tends to forget cases that contradict the relationship, especially those that are mildly disconfirming (Hastie & Kumar, 1979). For example, the ecstatic raven-haired woman might be remembered, but the contented brown-haired individual might be forgotten.

In short, then, when people are making judgments of covariation, they rarely follow the rational model for so doing. Instead, prior expectations lead them to focus primarily on positive instances (such as fun-loving blondes) and to pay relatively less attention to other evidence. Thus, when a relationship between two variables is expected (for example, if the perceiver believes that blondes have more fun), a person is likely to overestimate the degree of relationship that exists between the two factors or impose a relationship when none exists. This

intriguing phenomenon has been called illusory correlation.

ILLUSORY CORRELATION   We were introduced briefly to the concept of **illusory correlation** in the preceding chapter. It will be recalled that at least two factors can produce an illusory correlation: associative meaning in which two items are seen as belonging together because they "ought" to on the basis of prior expectations, and paired distinctiveness, in which two items are thought to go together because they share some unusual feature. Thus, as we saw in the previous chapter, members of minority groups are often seen as having attributes stereotypically associated with their group because of their membership when, in fact, any given individual in the group may not exhibit the stereotypic behavior or may contradict it altogether (Hamilton & Gifford, 1976; McArthur & Friedman, 1980; Spears, Van der Pligt, & Eiser, 1985). Similarly, we noted that individuals who are salient by virtue of an irrelevant factor such as appearance or seating position are thought to have a more potent role in the conversation in which they participate. Illusory correlations, then, often substitute for real correlations when people have prior expectations or theories about whether or not two factors go together.

Inference: A Summing Up

Overall, how well does the social perceiver fare on tasks of social inference? The evidence we just considered suggests that, when evaluated against rational models, social inference suffers from predictable errors and biases (Einhorn, 1980; Hogarth, 1980: Nisbett & Ross, 1980; Shweder, 1980). This evaluation prompts at least two reactions. The first is concern over disconcerting ways in which social perceivers let their prior expectations override and ignore relevant information. The second reaction is puzzlement. How do people manage in their social lives as well as they seem to if their social judgments are biased?

Some researchers are now coming to the opinion that rational models may often be inappropriate bases for evaluating social inference (Einhorn & Hogarth, 1981; Kahneman & Tversky, 1982, Nisbett, Krantz, Jepson, & Fong, 1982; Nisbett et al., 1983). One reason is that the conditions of the real world are often such as to make use of a rational model nearly impossible. Much of the time social information is unreliable, biased, and incomplete. Even reliable, unbiased, and complete information may not be presented to the average social perceiver in a clear or usable fashion, and sometimes information that is needed is not available.

Consider, again, the use of the rational model in the judgment, Do blondes have more fun? Is it

FIGURE 4–2   Social inference and its pitfalls.

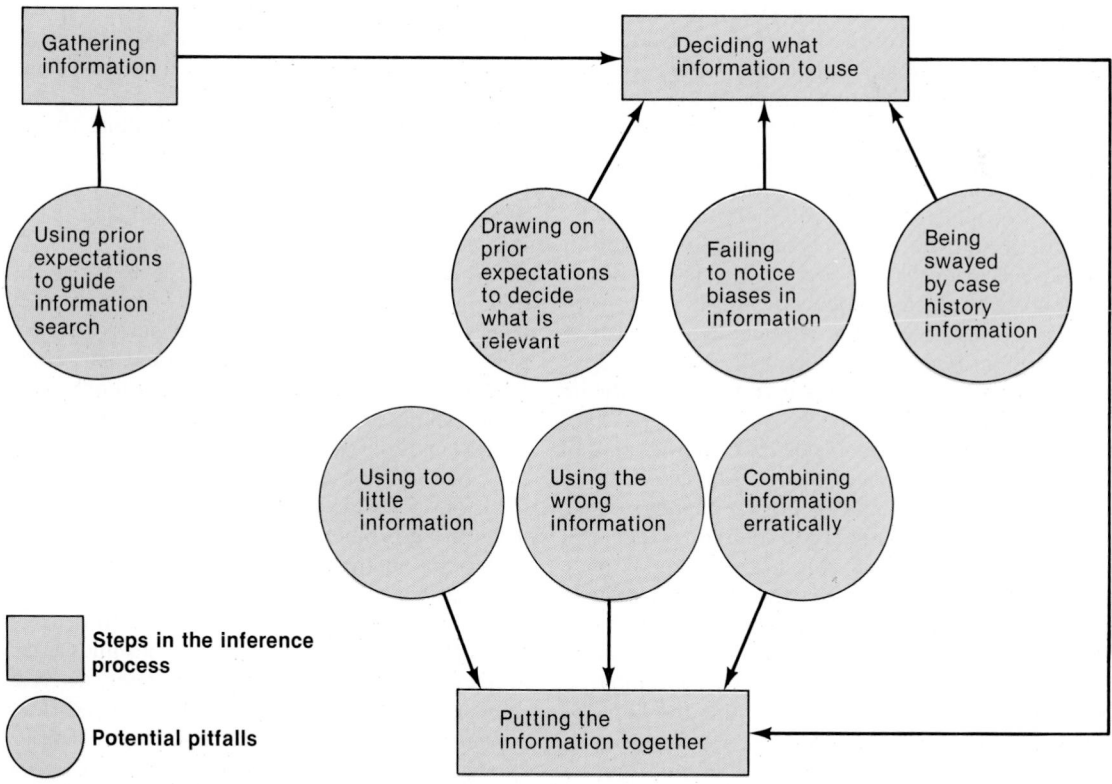

really worth it to you to get a sample of blondes, observe whether or not they have fun, get a sample of brunettes and redheads, see whether or not they have fun, and calculate a statistical relationship? How many people would you need to survey? How long should you wait before you decide that any given person is not having fun? The conditions that maximize accuracy seldom occur in real life, and accordingly in many situations, social perceivers could not apply a rational model even if they were so inclined (see Crocker, 1981; Nisbett et al., 1982).

Rational models describe ideal inferential processes under conditions in which time and environment are frozen. Yet people make inferences in environments that are constantly changing and that provide feedback. Inferences are made in a world filled with consequences. Once ventured, an inaccurate inference may be corrected by the environment because other people or new information show it to be wrong. One can then change the inference. For example, if you believe a particular acquaintance is overly serious and say so to a friend, the friend may inform you about the acquaintance's silly side, forcing you to change your belief.

Many of the errors produced by faulty inferential procedures do not truly matter. For example, suppose you pick a particular group of friends on the basis of their flashy fun-filled lives rather than their personal qualities. Suppose you then find out that they are into drugs, fast cars, and hard rock, and these are activities you do not want to participate in. You can gradually withdraw from the circle of friends and make new ones without any long-term repercussions. Spending time with a particular group of people does not force you to spend the rest of your life with them.

Perhaps most important is the fact that the tasks facing the social perceiver may be fundamentally different from the tasks defined by rational models of inference. Rational models of inference place a premium on *accuracy* of inference. For the social perceiver, *efficiency*, that is, processing information quickly, may be at least as important. Consider the sheer volume of information that an individual encounters in a particular day. Even an act as simple as crossing the street requires watching the lights and signs, the flow of the traffic, and the pedestrians on one's own side and the other side of the street.

If people truly had to make all their inferences using rational models of inference, they might still be plotting a course to follow across the street when the light changed back to "Don't Walk." In other words, rational models of inference assume that a person has time to do inferential work, and given the blooming, buzzing confusion of the real world, time is a very expensive commodity.

Consequently, people draw on their preexisting conceptions of people and situations and use inferential shortcuts to make social judgments quickly and efficiently. This is not to say that the errors we have just documented in the social inference process are inconsequential. Indeed, they can often have problematic consequences in that people clearly make what are objectively wrong decisions and inferences. Improving the inference process, therefore, is an important priority for social cognition researchers. But it must be done in the context of understanding the processes people typically use, rather than the rational models of inference developed by statisticians (see Lord, Lepper, & Preston, 1984).

To begin to understand how the social perceiver actually forms inferences and why those inferences do not correspond to the assumptions of rational models requires an important observation. The act of bringing information together and solving a problem, as we have noted, can be an extremely time-consuming task involving substantial processing capabilities. When one's attention is absorbed in forming a particular inference, there is relatively little attention that is available to perform other tasks such as monitoring the environment successfully, solving other problems, and the like. However, memory seems to have almost a limitless capacity. Think, for example, of the number of rock songs for which you know all the lyrics. The number may total in the hundreds or even thousands. Or think of all the friends you have and everything that you know about each of them. These simple tasks point out the astonishing amount of information that we are able to carry in our heads and retrieve from memory when we need it. Thus, problem solving is very costly in that it consumes attention and drains resources for other tasks, whereas memory appears to be nearly limitless and does not drain resources for other tasks. For example, knowing a great deal about one friend does not preclude learning a great deal about another friend. This important difference is fundamental to how people actually make inferences. Rather than engaging in elaborate and often time-consuming problem solving for each individual task that the environment presents, instead people often draw on the knowledge that they have stored in memory to interpret the environment that confronts them.

SCHEMAS

What we have so far been referring to as prior expectations goes under the general term *schemas*. As we saw in Chapter 3, a schema is an organized, structured set of cognitions about some concept or stimulus which includes knowledge about the concept or stimulus, some relations among the various cognitions about it, and some specific examples (Fiske & Taylor, 1984). As Chapter 3 made clear, schemas can be about particular people, social roles, the self, attitudes about particular objects, stereotypes about groups, or perceptions of common events.

Schemas are important generally to social cognition because people draw on them substantially to interpret the environment. That is, each time we are confronted with a new situation, we don't try to understand it afresh. Instead we draw on our knowledge of past similar situations for making interpretations, and this is the way in which schemas help us to process information. They help us recognize what aspects of a situation or stimulus are important. They add structure and organization to information. Schemas enable us to remember information better, to organize details, and to process information relevant to the schema very quickly. As we have already seen, schemas can sometimes fill in gaps and knowledge, as well as help people interpret and evaluate new information.

Hierarchical Organization of Schemas

An important feature of schemas is that they often have some hierarchical organization. They may have some abstract and general elements, and some more concrete, specific ones. Suppose we had a schema of "cocktail party." We know that cocktail parties usually are held in the later afternoon or evening, usually in someone's home. They have a number of guests and usually a host and a hostess; they have some food and a lot of alcoholic drinks (all of which are more likely to be prepared and served by the host and hostess than by the guests). Normally the people interact by standing and talking to each other rather than by watching some common event (like a singer) or sleeping or running in circles. In short, we have a clear, well-developed, somewhat abstract picture in our minds about a "cocktail party." It has a standard sequence, a number of elements, and clear causal interrelationships among them.

At a more specific level, the schema might well have different categories of cocktail parties, all of which would be clearly distinct. For example, a wine-and-cheese party held at the opening of an art gallery would be clearly different from the weekly Saturday night bashes at the country club, where all the local businesspeople and their spouses get together and drink too much and get loud and sloppy, or from a formal diplomatic reception at a foreign embassy. At a still more specific level, our schema might include several specific parties we have attended. All told, we might have a hierarchical schema of "a cocktail party" that would include a general, abstract concept covering all kinds of cocktail parties we have gone to.

Individual Differences in Schemas

To some extent, we all share the same schemas. Most of us have schemas about teachers, extroverts, and check cashing. However, many schemas are personal and reflect individual interests and values. For example, a person who loves the out-of-doors may have schemas for hiking, volleyball, and sailing, whereas the stay-at-home television watcher will not. Having a schema for a particular domain will, in turn, greatly modify how one processes information. For example, a veteran baseball coach will have a richer and more detailed set of baseball schemas and will impute more meaning to an out-fielder's play than will a foreigner attending his first baseball game (Lurigio & Carroll, 1985; Markus, Smith, & Moreland, 1985). A person to whom honesty is important will be more likely to judge other people according to whether they are dishonest or not than will someone who is not as concerned with the trait of honesty (Markus & Smith, 1981). To summarize, then, some schemas may be widely shared within a given culture, whereas others may be quite idiosyncratic.

SCHEMATIC PROCESSING

Advantages

Schemas are important because they help us process an enormous amount of information swiftly and economically. Indeed, schemas make processing more efficient in several different ways. They help us remember information, interpret new information, draw inferences from it, and evaluate whether or not we agree with it. They help us fill in gaps in our knowledge by suggesting what is likely to be true. And they help us prepare for the future by structuring our expectations about what is likely to happen. These advantages of schematic processing have been demonstrated in a wide variety of studies (see Fiske & Taylor, 1984; Taylor & Crocker, 1981; Markus & Zajonc, 1986, for reviews).

A schema can aid recall. Memory often works best when we can bring back some schematic representation of past events or people, because the schema will bring many details along with it. For example, Cohen (1981) presented subjects with a videotape of a woman and her husband sitting in their home. Half were told that the woman was a librarian, and half that she was a waitress. Some of the features of the woman fit the schema of a librarian (as measured separately), such as wearing glasses, eating salad, drinking wine, and playing the piano. Others fit the schema of a waitress, such as having a bowling ball in the room and no book-shelves, and eating a chocolate birthday cake. Later the subjects were asked to recall the details of the videotape. They remembered the schema-consistent details better, no matter whether recall was assessed immediately or a week later.

Schematic processing can be triggered simply by the attempt to form an impression of another person. Hamilton (1981) conducted a study that demonstrates this point. Half the subjects were instructed to form an impression of a stimulus person, and so they were operating under an impression-set. The other half of the subjects were told to memorize the attributes of the person, and thus were operating under a memory-set. All subjects were then given a list of attributes of the person such as warm, friendly, or dignified. Hamilton found that the subjects who had been instructed to form an impression of the stimulus person recalled more information about him than did the memory-set subjects. Presumably, the impression-set induced the subjects to use various person-relevant schemas that helped them to organize and recall the material better than was true for the memory-set subjects.

But schema-inconsistent material is not always recalled poorly. Both schema-consistent and schema-inconsistent material are remembered much better than things that are simply irrelevant to the schema (Hastie & Kumar, 1979; Brewer, Dull, & Lui, 1981); this may be because it is difficult to learn material that is irrelevant to a schema. Sometimes information that contradicts a schema is better recalled than information that is consistent with the schema. This is especially likely if a person has a well-established schema. People who are familiar with a domain may more easily recognize inconsistencies, whereas people who are just forming a schema may be more attentive to consistent information because it helps them to learn the domain (Higgins & Bargh, 1987). So, for example, if you have just met an individual who seems somewhat cold to you, you may especially notice his formal style with others or the fact that he doesn't hug his children. You may overlook acts of warmth such as picking up a lost kitten or greeting an old friend in an especially warm way. However, if you have a well-established belief that this person is chilly, these warm events may seem quite surprisingly and you may notice and recall them better.

Speed of processing information is affected by schemas. Markus (1977) contrasted subjects with self-schemas of being independent, self-schemas of being dependent, and neither self-schema. She read them sentences about certain independent or dependent behaviors. People with self-schemas were able to indicate more quickly than those without self-schemas whether or not the behavior was typical of them. Processing time was much longer for schema-inconsistent than consistent information. But not all research finds that schemas speed processing up. In some cases, evoking a schema slows things down by introducing a more complex mass of information that must be processed (Taylor & Crocker, 1981). So, for example, if you are strongly ambivalent about your dependency needs, you might take more time to decide if a dependent behavior is typical of you than would someone who is aschematic with respect to dependency.

Another important attribute of schematic processing is that some schema-related inferences appear to occur automatically without any conscious effort on an individual's part. For example, if a particular person you meet seems to be especially friendly, you may automatically attribute other attributes associated with friendliness to him such as kindness and warmth, and be completely unaware that you have done so. These automatic effects are most likely to occur if the information in the environment strongly suggests a particular schema, or if there is some kind of affective or emotional rela-

tionship between the perceiver and the information (Bargh, 1984; Smith & Lerner, 1986; Fazio et al., 1986).

A schema can help us fill in missing information when there are gaps in our knowledge. If we read about a policeman but have no information about his clothing, we imagine him to be wearing a blue uniform. We assume a nurse will be warm and caring, and a queen to be rather aloof and haughty. Missing information is filled in by adding schema-consistent details, even when we must invent them.

Schemas also help us interpret new information. For example, when a pediatrician diagnoses a child as having mumps, it enables her to make a whole series of other inferences with confidence: how the child got the disease, what symptoms should be present, what the course of the disease will be, what treatment is best, and so on. To a person with no schema for mumps, none of this would be possible. The problem would just seem mysterious. Schemas allow confident inferences about matters that would otherwise not be clear.

Schemas also contain expectations for what should happen. These expectations in turn can determine how pleasant or unpleasant we find a particular situation. When experience matches expectations, the result may be pleasant, whereas violations of expectations are often experienced as unpleasant. Suppose a black student who had worked to educate himself was nonetheless unable to find a job at his level of expertise. This experience might violate his expectations and would be likely to make him quite angry. A sense of deprivation relative to expectation has been cited as one of the causes of ghetto riots and other forms of social rebellion (Sears & McConahay, 1973).

Schemas can also include affect, that is, the feelings we have about the domain. Consequently, use of a particular schema can produce an emotional response. For example, most of us have a fairly well-developed schema for a "politician." It may include information about what the politician does in his or her job, and what kinds of people are attracted to being a politician. The schema will also include any affective responses we have to the concept of politician. For example, some of us will feel positively about politicians, thinking of them as helpful statesmen, whereas others may feel negatively about politicians, thinking of them as sly, self-serving, power-hungry individuals. When information in the environment fits a particular schema, then it will trigger the affect attached to that schema (S. T. Fiske, 1981, 1982). The affect that is triggered by a schema is an efficient affective processing device: One can say "I know that type and I know how I feel about him or her."

Under some circumstances, bringing a schema to bear on information in the environment can actually change the feelings one has toward the environment. A series of studies by Tesser (see Tesser & Conlee, 1975; Millar & Tesser, 1986) suggests that simply thinking about something with a schema in mind can intensify the affect one feels for that object. If, for example, you feel that a professor belittled the comments you made in class, the longer you think about it, the more upset you are likely to become. Under other circumstances, however, schemas may make affect simply more complex, not more extreme (Linville & Jones, 1980; Linville, 1982). For example, if a good friend of yours snaps at you one day, this behavior may produce a fairly complex evaluation. You have so much information about your friend and about yourself that coming up with an explanation for this behavior may be difficult. Your evaluation of the incident may be complex.

Liabilities of Schemas

All these advantages of schematic processing have their accompanying disadvantages, and many of them are precisely the errors and biases that we discussed at the beginning of this chapter. The tendencies to be overly accepting of information that fits a schema or theory, to fill in gaps in thinking by adding elements that are schema-consistent, to apply schemas even when they do not fit very well, and to be unwilling to change schemas can all be *liabilities*. We can easily be misled by oversimplifications.

There are so many familiar examples of the dangers of this kind of stereotyping that it hardly seems necessary to labor the point. Everyone knows that people frequently behave in ways contrary to the stereotype generally held about their groups, so schematic processing can lead the perceiver to some dangerously false inferences about individual members of the group. (We will discuss these issues in somewhat more detail in Chapters 12 and 13).

Implicit personality theories can also lead to errors, since there is a strong tendency for people to infer from the presence of one trait the presence of others. Knowing someone is intelligent causes most people to expect the person also to be imaginative, clever, active, conscientious, deliberate, and reliable. Knowing someone is inconsiderate leads most people to expect him or her also to be irritable, boastful, cold, hypercritical, and so on. These inferences are not derived logically from the given trait; they are based on assumptions about personality. Intelligence does not necessarily denote activity, nor does inconsiderateness denote irritability. The tendency to make these assumptions is sometimes called the *logical error*, because people see certain traits as going together and assume that someone who has one of them also has the others.

The examples given of "learning from the past" (see Box 4–1) illustrate some of the deficiencies of schematic processing. Applying "the lessons of Munich" may be quite inappropriate in Third World countries such as Lebanon, El Salvador, and Vietnam, where wars are caused by ancient tribal, religious, and class conflicts, and anticolonial nationalism. This "lesson of Munich" was that dictators are always trying to expand their territories, so free nations must stand up to them and not permit any expansion. This theory had, by the early 1960s, evolved into the very similar "domino theory" of Communist expansion, which held that communism was advancing around the globe, and every time one nation fell to communism, its neighbor became endangered. According to this theory, it was dangerous for us to allow even one nation to fall under Communist domination. As the conflict in Vietnam wore on, however, it became clearer and clearer that the war there was not a pure conflict between the free world and Communist expansionism. It also involved the ancient desire of the Vietnamese to be free of any foreign domination, whether Chinese, French, or American. And it involved considerable hostility toward the corrupt political regime with which we had allied ourselves in South Vietnam.

In more recent conflicts, the "lesson of Munich" has also prevented foreign policy decision-makers from seeing clearly the strength of longstanding

BOX 4–1

LEARNING FROM HISTORY

A number of writers have observed how political leaders often apply "the lessons of history" when arriving at decisions about foreign policy. The "lessons" they apply frequently turn out to be analogies from events that occurred in their formative years (Jervis, 1976). John F. Kennedy was very impressd during his years in college, in the late 1930s, by the British blunder of appeasing Hitler at Munich.

In 1938, British and French leaders held a highly publicized meeting with Adolf Hitler at Munich, Germany, to discuss his desire to expand the borders of Germany. They arranged a compromise with him that allowed the Germans to take over the Sudetenland, the region of Czechoslovakia closest to Germany. The British prime minister returned to London, triumphantly announcing that they had ensured "peace in our time." In just a few short months, of course, Hitler invaded Poland and Belgium, not in the least bit satisfied by the territory he had been given at Munich.

The "lesson of Munich" was that dictators need to be confronted and stopped or they will continue to make inroads. Kennedy applied this "Munich schema" to the civil wars in Southeast Asia in the early 1960s, and came to the conclusion that America needed to stand up militarily to the Communists there, or other "dominos" would fall, just as they had in Europe after Munich. In contrast, a "Vietnam schema" has become common since the end of that war. It describes the dangers to the United States of becoming involved in faraway civil wars and nationalist, anti-imperialist revolutions in the Third World.

The power of such schemas to dictate preferences about current foreign policy is illustrated in an experiment by Gilovich (1981). He presented two hypothetical case studies of a small democratic country threatened by an aggressive, totalitarian neighbor. They differed only in having salient Munich-like, pre-World War II symbols as opposed to those associated with Vietnam. The first case study mentioned in passing Winston Churchill Hall, "blitzkrieg," boxcars, and FDR; the second case study mentioned Dean Rusk Hall, chinook helicopters, small boats, and LBJ. Otherwise the two cases were the same, and clearly hypothetical. Subjects given the irrelevant allusions to pre-World War II events were more likely to support intervention than were those given the Vietnam allusions. Exactly the same facts could be interpreted in two quite different ways, with very different implications, depending on whether the irrelevant cues had induced them to apply their Munich or their Vietnam schemas.

religious rivalries in Lebanon, which made Russian-American conflicts almost incidental to the tremendous violence of the Lebanese civil war. In Central America, the "lesson of Munich" similarly blinds many Americans to the terrible inequality and corruption in some Central American nations, which has led to strongly supported local revolutionary movements. Whether or not the Russians and Americans were involved, those revolutions would have much local support.

So schematic processing has the advantage of speed and efficiency and of making events compre-hensible and predictable. It has the disadvantage of leading to wrong interpretations, inaccurate ex-pectations, and inflexible modes of response.

MENTAL SHORTCUTS: USING COGNITIVE HEURISTICS

Because problem-solving activity typically con-sumes so much time and attention, people often resort to mental shortcuts that reduce seemingly complex problem solving to more simple judg-ments. These shortcuts help people invoke their schemas to process information in the environment. These shortcuts have been called **heuristics** (Tver-sky & Kahneman, 1974).

The Representativeness Heuristic

Is John, the new guy in your math class, really the incurable romantic he seems to be, or is he a cad who moves on every woman he meets? Is Linda a dependable person who can be counted on to do her share of a joint project or not? The act of identifying people or events as examples of particu-lar schemas is fundamental to all social inference and behavior. That is, the question, "What is it?" must be answered before any other cognitive task can be performed. A mental shortcut called the *representativeness heuristic* provides a rapid method for accomplishing this task.

Basically, the representativeness heuristic matches information in the environment against schemas to determine the likelihood that the match is appropriate. Consider the following description: "Steve is very shy and withdrawn, invariably helpful, but with little interest in people or the world of reality. A meek and tidy soul, he has a need for order and structure and a passion for detail" (Tver-sky & Kahneman, 1974). Suppose you are now asked to guess Steve's occupation. Is he a farmer, a circus clown, a librarian, a con artist, or a pediatrician?

With adequate information about the number and characteristics of the people in these different occupations, one could conceivably estimate the likelihood of a meek clown, a shy con artist, and so on. This task, however, would likely take a long time, and good information on which to form these judgments would undoubtedly be lacking. In such cases, the representativeness heuristic provides a quick solution. One decides whether Steve is repre-sentative of (or similar to) the average person in each of the occupational categories and makes one's judgment about his occupation accordingly. Stu-dents given this task usually guessed that Steve is a librarian because the description of Steve is *repre-sentative* of attributes that are stereotypically associ-ated with librarians (Tversky & Kahneman, 1974).

The representativeness heuristic, then, helps one decide if a particular person or event is an example of a particular schema. Basically, one matches the attributes of the information in the environment to the schema, and if there is a match, the schema is invoked. However, this quite rapid method of identifying people and events is occasionally fallible because people sometimes fail to take in other important qualifying information. For example, if Steve lives in a town with lots of farmers and only one librarian, the likelihood that he is a farmer and not a librarian is very high. The representative-ness heuristic would not incorporate this qualifying information. As we noted earlier, people often ig-nore relevant statistical information that they ought to incorporate into their inferences. Under these kinds of circumstances then, use of the representa-tiveness heuristic would probably produce an in-correct answer.

The Availability Heuristic

Sometimes we try to answer such questions as "How often does a person break a leg skiing?" or "How many college students are psychology majors?" These are questions about the frequency of events or the likelihood that a particular event will happen. A common way that people answer such questions is to use examples that come to mind. If you can think of lots of college students who are psychology majors among your friends or acquaintances, you may assume that there are many psychology majors on campus. Or if you can think of several people who broke their legs skiing, you may assume that the chances of breaking your leg skiing are rather high. Using the ease of remembering examples or the amount of information you can quickly remember as a guide to making an inference is called using the *availability heuristic*.

As is the case with the representativeness heuristic, little cognitive work need be performed to accomplish this task. If you have no trouble thinking of psychology majors among your acquaintances, you will probably assume that a great many people in college are psychology majors, whereas if you have trouble bringing to mind examples of psychology majors, you may conclude that relatively few individuals are psychology majors.

Under many circumstances, use of the availability heuristic produces correct answers. After all, when examples of something can be easily brought to mind, it is usually because there are lots of them. Therefore, availability is usually a good estimate of frequency. However, there are also biasing factors that can increase or decrease the availability of some kinds of phenomena or events without altering their actual overall frequency. For example, if you are a psychology major, many of your friends and acquaintances are likely to be psychology majors as well, and consequently you will have relatively little difficulty bringing examples of psychology majors to mind. Because of this bias among your friends, you are likely to overestimate the frequency of psychology majors. In contrast, another student who is a chemistry major and who spends most of his time hanging out with chemists or physicists would probably underestimate the number of psychology majors on campus, because

he cannot bring examples of many psychology majors to mind.

The availability heuristic, then, enables you to answer questions like "how many are there" or "how often does something happen" on the basis of how quickly or easily examples can be retrieved from memory. The ease with which the process can be accomplished, or the volume of information that can be retrieved quickly, determines the answer.

The Anchoring Heuristic

Imagine that someone asks you to guess how many people attended the UCLA-USC football game last night in the Los Angeles Coliseum. You have absolutely no idea, but you do know that last week's game in the Coliseum drew a crowd of 55,000. Assuming that the UCLA-USC contest drew a much bigger crowd, you might guess that 70,000 people attended. In this case, you have no information about the specific event in question, but you use information about a similar event as a reference point or "anchor." You then adjust reference information to reach a final conclusion (Tversky & Kahneman, 1974).

In fact, when people are attempting to form judgments from ambiguous information, they will often reduce ambiguity by starting with the beginning reference point or anchor and then adjusting it. Social judgments are no exception. Information about other people is often ambiguous, and therefore anchors can be helpful when one is trying to interpret the meaning of ambiguous behavior (see, for example, Wyer, 1976; Cervone & Peake, 1986).

A common anchor that is used in social perception is the self. For example, suppose someone asks you whether Ellen, a classmate of yours, is smart. It may be easiest for you to answer this question by trying to decide if Ellen is smarter than you or not. If she seems to be smarter than you are, you may decide that she is very smart. But if she seems to be not as quick as you are, you may decide that she is not very bright. Your judgment about Ellen's intelligence, then, is based, not on her absolute standing on an I.Q. test or some other objective information, but rather on

TABLE 4–1

Some Heuristic Strategies for Making Judgments under Uncertainty

Heuristic	Some Types of Judgments Heuristic Is Used for	Description	Example
Representativeness	Probability judgment	Representativeness is a judgment of how relevant A is to B; high relevance yields high estimates that A originates from B.	Deciding that George (A) must be an engineer because he looks and acts like your stereotype of engineers (B)
Availability	Frequency or probability judgments	Availability is the estimate of how frequent or likely a given instance or occurrence is, based on how easily or quickly an association or examples come to mind.	Estimating the divorce rate on the basis of how quickly one can think of examples of divorced friends
Anchoring and adjustment	Estimates of position on a dimension	Anchoring and adjustment is the process of estimating some value by starting with some initial value and then adjusting it to the new instance.	Judging another person's productivity based on one's own level of productivity

whether or not she seems brighter or less bright than yourself (see Markus & Smith, 1981; Markus, Smith, & Moreland, in press). The anchoring heuristic, then, provides people with a departure point for a judgment task that might otherwise be ambiguous. In social judgment tasks, the self seems to be a common anchor. For a description of the various heuristic strategies, see Table 4–1.

WHICH SCHEMAS ARE USED?

Suppose you observed two people feverishly searching a room. How do you decide what they are doing? In other words, how do you select which schemas to apply to the situation? As we implied in our earlier discussion, sometimes appropriate schemas are suggested by the nature of the information itself. For example, if you know the two people in question are roommates who keep gerbils and you see an empty cage, you may guess that they are trying to find their missing gerbils. Under other circumstances, information in the environment may not immediately suggest which schemas to invoke. Are the two searchers looking for something that they have lost? Are they burglars? Are they undercover policemen conducting a drug bust? In this section, we consider the factors that influence which schemas people use to interpret information.

Natural Contours

The most obvious and probably also the most powerful determinant of which schema is brought to bear on information in the environment is the structure of the information itself. That is, schemas follow the *natural contours* of the information we receive. If you are watching a football game, you will employ your schemas for football games, football players, cheerleaders, and the like for interpreting what is going on in the field. The information in the environment makes it obvious which schemas to use, and you would not invoke your schemas for cocktail parties, tennis games, or final examinations to interpret what is going on.

But people cannot absorb everything in their environment at once. They tend to perceive behavior in coherent, meaningful chunks of action that are marked off by **breakpoints** (Newtson, 1976). For example, imagine watching an outfielder break into a run at the sound of the bat hitting the ball; he dashes to the outfield wall, leaps up, catches the ball, lands on his feet, sets for a throw, and then throws the ball to the third baseman to stop the baserunner. Newtson argues that we perceive such a flow of activity as a sequence of separate behaviors, not as one continuous act. Breakpoints occur between the separate actions and mark where one ends and another begins.

Breakpoints are inherent in any stream of behavior; they are not imposed on it by the perceiver. In this sense, they follow the natural contours of the information we receive. To identify these breakpoints, Newtson had subjects watch a film and push a button to indicate when they thought one segment had ended and another had begun. This method is quite reliable: Perceivers agree on where certain breakpoints occur in films of someone in action, and they perceive the same breakpoints again when shown the film five weeks later. It also seems quite easy and comfortable for subjects to do. All this argues that the breakpoints occur naturally within the flow of behavior in a given scene.

When do breakpoints occur? Some ingenious research has tied them to changes in behavior, specifically to changes in the movement of different parts of the body (Newtson, Engquist, & Bois, 1977). Breakpoints also occur when the state of objects associated with the person changes. For example, breakpoints would be perceived when a baseball's trajectory is suddenly interrupted by the outfielder's glove, when it disappears from view, or when it suddenly flies through the air back toward the infield. Breakpoints convey the most information about a sequence of behavior. When the breakpoint moments of a film are shown to subjects as still photos in order, they convey the story almost as well as the full movie itself. People also seem to remember the breakpoints better than any other moments during the sequence.

The more general point, then, is that we do not simply take in environmental information whole when forming an inference. Rather, we absorb meaningful, structured chunks of it. The chunking process is partly imposed on the flow of behavior by the perceiver's own experiences, expectations, and needs. And partly the chunks reflect real changes within the behavioral sequence.

Salience

Environmental salience is also a factor that influences which schemas people use to interpret information. As we saw in Chapter 3, sometimes our interpretation of other people's behavior is influenced by what information about them is made salient by the environment. For example, if Linda is the only woman in a group that is otherwise composed of men, her sex will be particularly salient, and therefore her behavior may be interpreted according to a gender schema for women. For example, her request for help from a newcomer to the group might be interpreted as a sign of dependence, a trait often associated with women. However, if Linda is in a group composed of several men and several women, her behavior toward the newcomer might not be interpreted in gender-related terms. Instead, a schema for "newcomers" might be invoked and her gesture might simply be interpreted as an effort to make the newcomer feel at home. Salience, then, can influence the processing of information in the environment by determining which schemas will be invoked to interpret information that may be subject to multiple interpretations.

Priming

When a schema has been recently used, it is likely to be used again to interpret new information. Suppose you have just come from a classroom discussion in which the professor castigated the class for its lack of commitment to intellectual pursuits. Walking across campus, you meet Stan who enthusiastically tells you that he has just been appointed to the cheering squad. How do you interpret his enthusiasm? In the context of the prior lecture, you may regard his behavior as shallow and anti-intellectual. In contrast, if you had just come from a discussion of the importance of being a well-rounded college student, you might interpret the behavior as a sign of extracurricular interests. This tendency for recently used schemas to be employed in unrelated subsequent situations is called the **priming effect.**

A study that demonstrates this point was conducted by Higgins, Rholes, and Jones (1977). Subjects were first exposed to trait words designed to invoke either the positive schema of adventurousness (such as brave) or the negative schema of recklessness (such as foolish, careless). In a second study ostensibly unrelated to the first task, they read about Donald who shot rapids, drove in a demolition derby, and planned to learn skydiving. People who had previously been exposed to the positive schema of "adventurousness" evaluated Donald more positively than people who had been primed with the negative schema of "recklessness." This priming effect did not occur when the primed schemas were not applicable to the description of Donald (such as neat or sly).

Essentially, then, activating a schema puts it at the top of the mental heap, making it easily accessible for interpreting new information (Srull & Wyer, 1979; Wyer & Srull, 1980, 1981). However, an important qualification is that previously activated schemas are only invoked to explain new information when the schema is relevant to the new information. When new information is irrelevant to the primed schemas, those schemas are not used to interpret it (Higgins & Bargh, 1987).

Importance

Which schemas are used to interpret information by the environment and how many schemas are called up can also be influenced by the importance of the information being processed. When the circumstances for making inferences are relatively trivial, people may make schematic inferences relatively quickly with little thought. They may, for example, invoke a schema on the basis of which information is most salient. However, in circumstances when the outcome of an inference is important, a person may spend more time studying the

situation and invoke more schemas, yielding more complex inferences (Chaiken, 1980; Borgida & Howard-Pitney, 1983). For example, if asked your impression of a fellow classmate, you may answer relatively quickly that he or she seems nice, if your judgment of the person has no particular importance for you. However, if you are trying to decide whether or not to ask this classmate out on a date, you would probably spend more time thinking through what you know about the person to decide whether or not he or she is fun, attractive, nice, and attracted to you. Your inferences might consequently be more complex, based on more than one schema.

Individual Differences

Not everyone interprets the same information the same way. One reason is that different people have different schemas. For example, one person might describe other people primarily in terms of their sense of humor or warmth, whereas someone else might consider these characteristics to be relatively unimportant and instead be concerned with another person's diligence and religiosity.

Groups of people may differ in their schemas. One interesting case concerns the theories people hold about intelligence. College students have schemas for intelligence that relate it closely to academic performance, whereas nonstudents (people interviewed in supermarkets and at a railroad station) viewed intelligence as more closely related to every day problem solving, social competence, and the like (Sternberg et al., 1981).

Goals

Which schemas are brought to bear on information in the environment is also based on the goals a social perceiver has in a particular situation. As we have seen, schemas are not just passive reflections of the information in the environment. The person must actively organize the information into a more abstract, cognitive structure. One way in which this organizing cognitive activity is triggered is through an individual's goals. For example, goals have been manipulated experimentally by telling

TABLE 4–2

The Impression Set Leads People to Organize Impressions in Terms
of the Objective Contours of a Stimulus Person's Personality

	Match of Impressions to Built-in Trait Categories[a]	Percent of Categories Labeled with Built-in Traits
Impression set	28.17	65%
Recall set	7.17	17

[a] Range 0–50, hi = greater match.
Source: Hoffman, Mischel, & Mazze (1981), pp. 216, 218.

subjects either to form a coherent impression of a person (impression formation goal) or to try to remember the separate bits of information they may be exposed to (remembering goal). We would expect that under impression goal conditions people would form organized impressions that reflect the underlying structure of the input information.

Hoffman, Mischel, and Mazze (1981) demonstrated this by experimentally varying the traits presented in descriptions of stimulus persons. Each subject was presented with 25 short behavioral episodes (about three sentences each) concerning a particular target person. Each episode was chosen to illustrate one of five traits (such as dishonesty or generosity), so over the set of 25 episodes, each trait was emphasized in 5 episodes. One episode which was intended to illustrate the trait of dishonesty had the target person looking through her friend's purse and stealing some amphetamine pills. Subjects were told either that they would have to present an impression of the target person (impression set) or recite the details of the episodes they

had read (recall set). Finally, they were asked to organize the episodes into clusters.

The impression set subjects tended to organize the episodes along the lines of the underlying traits and gave labels to the clusters that corresponded to those underlying traits. For example, the impression-set subjects clustered the information around the trait of dishonesty and labeled the cluster accordingly. In short, when the subjects tried to organize information about a stimulus person into a coherent impression, they began to think schematically about the target person and therefore to organize their thinking along the lines of dimension actually underlying the target's personality. As shown in Table 4–2, the impression set led subjects to organize their impressions around the traits built into the episodes, and to label the categories in their impressions according to these built-in traits. In contrast, people with a recall set did not organize their impressions nearly as tightly around these built-in traits (see also Trzebinski et al., 1985).

SCHEMAS IN ACTION

The use of schemas for processing information in the environment is important not only because it helps people to form judgments and make decisions, but because it provides guidelines for interac-

tions with others. We learn about other people in many ways. Sometimes we hear about them before meeting them, or we may have hints about the kind of people they are like on the basis of their initial behavior. Regardless of how we form an impression of another person, we may relatively quickly develop ideas concerning what the person is like. As we are interacting with the person, how do these ideas (or schemas) influence one's behavior? Considerable research suggests that people behave toward others in ways that tend to confirm the beliefs they hold about those others. Perceivers employ interaction strategies for eliciting information from others that preferentially support these schemas.

How does this process work? Suppose you learned that Susan, an attractive young woman in your psychology class, is with the cheering squad for the school, and you quickly form an image of her as an outgoing, athletic, and enthusiastic person. In talking with her, you might ask her about the various sports she has played, the parties she has been to this year, what she thinks of the games she has attended, and so on. All of this information tends to confirm your view of her as an extroverted, athletic, fun-loving person. However, after seeing her for several weeks, you might discover that she is actually rather shy and introverted, she's fairly klutzy at sports, and she is not a cheerleader at all, but rather coordinates uniform purchases and bus transportation to out-of-town games. You might wonder how you came to be so deceived. Looking back on the situation, however, reveals that Susan may have done nothing at all to deceive you. Rather, you deceived yourself by selectively seeking information that supported your beliefs. There aren't many college students who didn't play some kind of sport in high school or attend at least a couple of parties. Because you asked Susan about these kinds of activities, this is the information she gave you, which augmented your image of her as a fun-loving, athletic party girl.

This process has been called *confirmatory hypothesis testing*, and it has been demonstrated under a broad range of circumstances (see Higgins & Bargh, 1987, for a review). For example, M. Snyder and Swann (1978) told college student subjects that they would be interviewing another student. Half were told to find out if the other was an extrovert (that is, outgoing and sociable), and half were told to find if the other was an introvert (that is, shy and retiring). All subjects were then given a set of questions assessing introversion and extrover-

sion, and they were told to pick out a set of questions to ask the other student. Students who were told to find out if the person was an extrovert preferentially selected extroversion questions (such as, What would you do if you wanted to liven things up at a party?), and those who were told to find out if the person was an introvert picked introversion questions (such as, What factors make it really hard for you to open up to people?). These questions, in turn, made the target students appear especially extroverted or introverted respectively simply because they answered the questions they were asked (see also Curtis & Miller, 1986).

Sometimes, a prior schema you have about an individual will influence not only the kind of information you ask or seek from the person and the subsequent inferences you draw, but will also affect the other person's actual behaviors and self-impressions. When a perceiver's false expectations about another person lead that person to adopt those expected attributes and behavior, this is called a **self-fulfilling prophecy** (see Figure 4–3).

For example, Snyder, Tanke, and Bercheid (1977) gave college student men a folder of information about a woman on campus that included a picture, representing the woman as either highly attractive or as unattractive. In actuality, the photos were fake and were randomly assigned to women regardless of their true looks. Each student was then asked to phone the woman whose folder he had read and chat for ten minutes. Tape recordings were made of the conversations. The men who believed they were talking to attractive women behaved more warmly on the phone than did the men with unattractive women. Even more remarkable, the women who had been miscast as highly attractive were perceived by other students judging the tapes to be more friendly, likable, and sociable in their interactions with the men than those miscast as unattractive. These kinds of *self-fulfilling prophecies* have been widely demonstrated (for example, Curtis & Miller, 1986; see Darley and Fazio, 1980, for a review).

The implication of the discussion thus far is that schemas are so powerful that they can not only influence how information in the environment is interpreted, but also help push the environment to become consistent with the schema. Obviously, this is not always the case. For example, sometimes

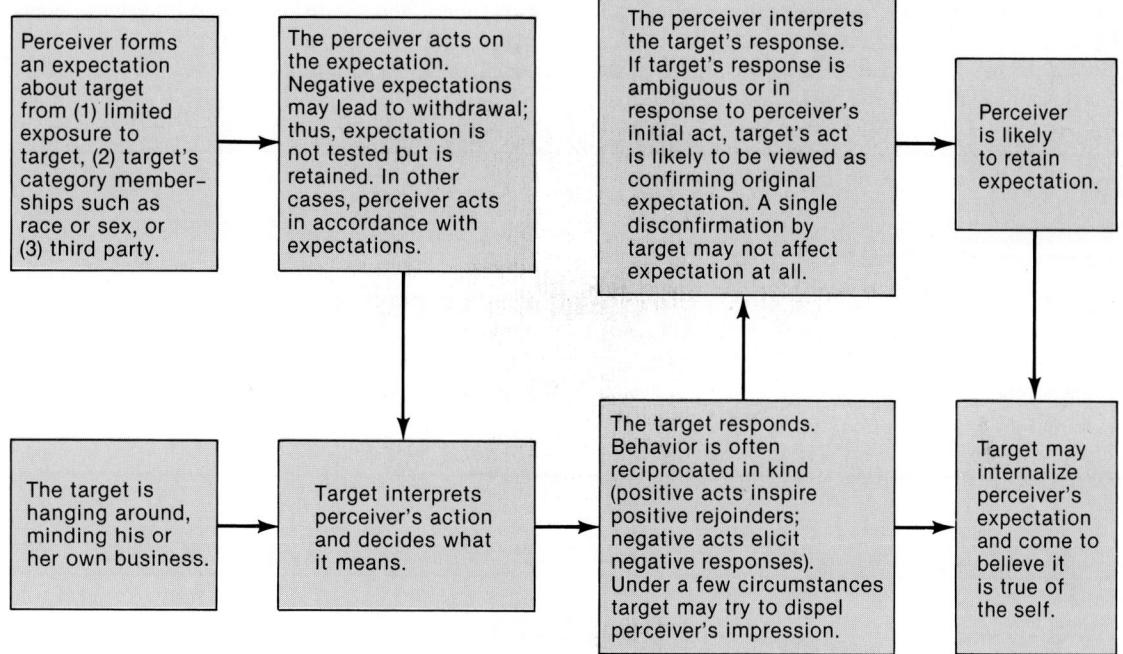

```
┌──────────────────┐   ┌──────────────────┐   ┌──────────────────┐   ┌──────────────────┐
│ Perceiver forms  │   │ The perceiver    │   │ The perceiver    │   │ Perceiver        │
│ an expectation   │   │ acts on the      │   │ interprets       │   │ is likely        │
│ about target     │→  │ expectation.     │   │ the target's     │→  │ to retain        │
│ from (1) limited │   │ Negative         │   │ response.        │   │ expectation.     │
│ exposure to      │   │ expectations     │   │ If target's      │   │                  │
│ target, (2)      │   │ may lead to      │   │ response is      │   └──────────────────┘
│ target's         │   │ withdrawal;      │   │ ambiguous or in  │
│ category member- │   │ thus, expectation│   │ response to      │
│ ships such as    │   │ is not tested    │   │ perceiver's      │
│ race or sex, or  │   │ but is retained. │   │ initial act,     │
│ (3) third party. │   │ In other cases,  │   │ target's act     │
└──────────────────┘   │ perceiver acts   │   │ is likely to be  │
                       │ in accordance    │   │ viewed as        │
                       │ with             │   │ confirming       │
                       │ expectations.    │   │ original         │
                       └──────────────────┘   │ expectation. A   │
                                              │ single           │
                                              │ disconfirmation  │
                                              │ by target may    │
                                              │ not affect       │
                                              │ expectation at   │
                                              │ all.             │
                                              └──────────────────┘
```

FIGURE 4–3   The development of a self-fulfilling prophecy. (Based on Darley & Fazio, 1980.)

people hold beliefs about others that those others feel are untrue about themselves. Consequently, those others may be motivated to disconfirm what they feel is an incorrect belief. For example, if a professor whose opinion you value saw you commit a foolish prank with some of your friends, you might be highly motivated to correct the professor's low opinion of you.

Under these circumstances whose viewpoint will triumph? The perceiver's misconceptions or the target's beliefs about the self? Research by Swann and Ely (1984) attempted to address this question by considering the certainty of perceiver's expectations and target's self-conceptions. Perceivers first formed relatively certain or uncertain expectations about targets that were inconsistent with the target's self-conceptions. Thus, for example, some perceivers were lead to believe that the target was extroverted (when the target actually perceived the self to be introverted), whereas other perceivers were led to believe the target was introverted (when the target considered herself extroverted). The perceivers then interacted with targets who either possessed relatively certain or relatively uncertain self-conceptions about their introversion or extroversion. The results indicated that the target's self-concept was a stronger determinant than the perceiver's expectancy of the perceiver's ultimate opinion of the target. That is, the perceivers' impressions of the targets after they had interacted together were more in line with the targets' self-concepts than with the perceivers' initial expectations. Only when targets were uncertain about their introversion or extroversion and perceivers were certain about their expectations did behavioral confirmation occur. That is, when perceivers were certain and targets were uncertain about their attributes, the perceivers' expectations tended to win out. The general point, then, is that perceivers' expectations may have some effect on a target's behavior. But they do not lead targets to act in ways that are counter to their self-concepts (Swann & Ely, 1984; Hilton & Darley, 1985; Miller & Turnbull, 1986; Higgins & Bargh, 1987).

Overall, then, schemas and schematic processing are important for several reasons. They help people to organize their past experiences in ways that can be useful in new situations. They help in the processing of new information by determining what is relevant, by filling in gaps, by influencing what is recalled, and by making some inferences automatic. And they can act as effective guidelines for behavior in social interaction.

KEY TERMS IN CHAPTER 4

breakpoints

covariation

heuristic

implicit personality theory

illusory correlation

priming effect

rational model of inference

self-fulfilling prophecy

SUMMARY

1. Social cognition is the branch of social psychology that examines how people form inferences from social information in the environment.

2. When we examine how people make impressions and form inferences and compare those processes against rational methods for accomplishing these tasks, we find that social perceivers are prone to certain errors and biases in their judgments. In particular, prior expectations and theories weigh heavily into the judgment process.

3. These predictable errors and biases appear to stem from the fact that people need to make judgments relatively quickly and efficiently in order to process the multitude of information they encounter.

4. Cognitive structures called schemas help us organize information about the world. Schemas make information processing more efficient and speedy, aid recall, fill in missing information,

and provide expectations. However, they sometimes fill in erroneous information or may lead us to reject good but inconsistent evidence.

5. Heuristics are shortcuts that help relate information in the environment to schemas. Heuristics reduce complex or ambiguous problems to more simple, judgmental operations.

6. The schemas that are most likely to be used to interpret information are those that match the natural contours of that information. In addition, which schemas a social perceiver uses is influenced by salience, goals, priming, and individual differences.

7. Schemas not only help people form judgments and make decisions but provide guidelines for interactions with others. In some cases, schemas may be so powerful that they bring about self-fulfilling prophecies.

SUGGESTED READINGS

FISKE, S. T., & TAYLOR, S. E. (1984). *Social cognition*. New York: Random House. A readable introduction to the field of social cognition for college students; available in paperback.

HASTORF, A., & A. M. ISEN (1982). *Cognitive social psychology*. New York: Elsevier North Holland, Inc. An edited collection that emphasizes applications of social cognition to such areas as emotion, stereotyping, legal psychology, organizational psychology, and health psychology.

HIGGINS, E. T., RUBLE, D. N., & HARTUP, W. W. (1983). *Social cognition and social development*. Cambridge University Press. An edited collection that examines how social cognition research elucidates social development and close relationships in children and adults.

KAHNEMAN, D., SLOVIC, P., & TVERSKY, A. (1982). *Judgment under uncertainty: Heuristics and biases*. Cambridge University Press. An edited collection of research on shortcuts, errors, and biases in social inference processes.

MARKUS, H., & ZAJONC, R. B. (1985). The cognitive perspective in social psychology. In G. Lindzey & E. Aronson (Eds.), *Handbook of social psychology*. New York: Random House. A thoughtful analysis of the historical development of social cognition with an emphasis on current trends in the field.

5 ATTRIBUTION

I magine you are standing on a curb on a rainy day and a car whips past you, splashing dirty water from the gutter all over you. You might explain the driver's behavior in one of two ways. He could have been driving in the lane close to the curb because traffic was heavy and he had no choice. If so, you might feel forgiving and do nothing. Or he might have been doing it beccause he gets a kick out of splashing pedestrians. Then you would be likely to feel angry and want to retaliate against the driver. You might shout or wave a fist.

How do we form judgments about internal states in other people that we might need to know about, such as motives, personality, emotions, and attitudes? We do not have direct information about such internal states. We only have access to limited external cues such as facial expressions, gestures, what the person says about his or her internal state, what we remember about his or her behavior in the past, and so forth. So we must make such inferences on the basis of the indirect information given by external cues.

Making inferences about internal states is part of a more general process of explaining the behavior of other people and of ourselves, which is called making causal **attributions.** This is the process by which people arrive at causal explanations for events in the social world, particularly for actions they and other people perform. When someone says something that hurts our feelings, we ask ourselves why it happened. Sometimes we conclude it was caused by some relatively permanent internal state, such as the person's having a long-standing grudge against us. We might decide it was due to temporary internal states, such as having a stomach ache or being in a bad mood. Or perhaps it was due to external pressures, such as trying to show off in front of fraternity brothers. But whatever our explanation for the behavior, we must infer it from a few external cues; we do not have direct access to the true cause.

Causal attributions in turn determine our own feelings, attitudes, and behavior. According to Weiner (1982), for example, anger usually results when something negative happens to us, and we perceive it as being under someone else's control.

That is the case if we assume the driver could have been driving further from the gutter. We feel angry if the driver could have avoided splashing us, but not if it was the only lane and there was no choice.

Pity arises when a negative event happens to someone else and no one could have controlled it. You feel pity for a cerebral palsy victim; no one could have prevented the handicap. Pride results from perceiving one's own efforts as the cause for a success. You feel pride when you work on a term paper and get an A. But if the professor gives an A to every paper, even some poor ones, you will no longer feel that pride; the A was caused by the professor's lax grading, not your good work.

Our expectations about the future are influenced by our attributions for past events. We are likely

Expectations about the future are often very important and are influenced by our attributions about past events.

Ken Karp

to expect future successes if we attribute our past successes to ability (Weiner, 1979). If we attribute our A's in high school English to a natural talent for literary analysis, we will be more optimistic about similar successes in our college career. But if we attribute these past A's to teachers who were easy graders, we are not likely to expect such high grades later on. Dweck (1975) has shown that training children to make internal attributions for their behavior—training them, for example, to explain successes and failures as resulting from the amount of effort they put forth—can make them work harder in the future.

Our attributions for events in the political arena can also influence our political attitudes. Feldman (1983) has shown that blaming blacks' poverty on discrimination and other failures of environment is associated with support for special government aid to blacks. Blaming their poverty on laziness and unwillingness to get appropriate job training is associated with opposition to government aid.

In these and numerous other ways, our understanding of the causes of behavior are crucial mediators of our reactions to the social world. Our reactions to other people—liking, aggression, helping, conformity, and so on—frequently depend on our interpretation of their behavior. So causal attributions have become a major focus of research.

BASIC PRINCIPLES

Although there are different approaches to the attribution process, they rest on a common set of basic principles called **attribution theory**. These concern the entire process of making causal attributions: what motivates people to generate causal explanations, how they decide which particular cause is most important, and the biases in attributional processes that prevent people from arriving at accurate causal explanations. Let us start by considering the most basic of these attributional principles.

Heider's Naive Psychology

Theorizing about attributions began with Fritz Heider (1958). He was interested in how people in everyday life figure out what causes what. Like most in the cognitive tradition in social psychology, he proposed two strong motives in all human beings: the need to form a coherent understanding of the world, and the need to control the environment.

One of the essentials for satisfying these motives is the ability to predict how people are going to behave. If we cannot predict how others will behave, we will view the world as random, surprising, and incoherent. We would not know whether to expect reward or punishment for our work performance, a kiss or punch in the jaw from a friend.

Similarly, to have a satisfactory level of control of our environment, we must be able to predict others' behavior. To avoid an accident, we need to be able to predict that the big truck will not suddenly make a U turn into our front bumper. To control our diet, we need to be able to count on getting a club sandwich when we order it in a restaurant, rather than suddenly being presented with an entire roast pig.

To be able to predict how others are going to behave, we need some elementary theory of human behavior. Heider proposed that everyone, not just psychologists, searches for explanations for other people's behavior. He called the result a **naive psychology**—that is, a general theory of human behavior held by each ordinary person.

Dimensions of Causality

LOCUS OF CAUSALITY   The central issue in most perceptions of causality is whether to attribute a given act to *internal* states or to *external* forces. That is, what is the "locus of causality"? You have asked the young woman who sits next to you in lecture to go out to a movie this weekend, but she has said she is busy. What is the "real" cause of her refusal? It could be due to some internal state, such as her lack of attraction to you or her interest in doing something else. Or it could be due to some external factor, such as that she really does have some other obligation. **Internal attributions** include all causes internal to the person, such as moods, attitudes, personality traits, abilities, health, preferences, or wishes. **External attributions** would include all causes external to the person, such as pressure from others, money, the nature of the social situation, the weather, and so on. So is this young woman really busy (an external attribution), or has she just decided that she is not interested in dating you (an internal attribution)?

A student who is failing a course wants to know whether it is because she is not smart enough or doesn't work hard enough (internal causality), or because the professor's lectures are ambiguous, the text is too difficult, or the tests are unfair (external causality). Debates rage in school board meetings, academic conventions, courtrooms, and legislative halls about whether black children do less well in school than white children because of inferior native endowment or low motivation (internal causality) or because of racial discrimination, insensitive middle-class white teachers, inferior facilities, and unstimulating peer groups (external causality).

So the major question is whether to make an external or an internal attribution for the stimulus person's behavior. External attributions ascribe causality to anything external to that person, such as the general environment, some other person being interacted with, role constraints, possible rewards or punishments, luck, the specific nature of the task, and so on. Internal causes include personality traits, motives, emotions, moods, attitudes, abilities, and effort.

STABILITY OR INSTABILITY   A second dimension of causality is whether the cause is *stable* or *unstable*. That is, we need to know whether or not the cause is a relatively permanent feature of that external environment or of the internal dispositions of the person. Some external causes are quite stable, such as rules and laws (the prohibition against running

a red light, or against breaking the throwing arm of an overly successful opposing quarterback), occupational roles (professors are called upon to give lectures year in and year out), or the difficulty level of certain tasks (it is always hard to hit a curveball, and always easy to get our daughter to laugh by tickling her).

Some external causes are quite unstable: The weather has a lot of influence over whether we spend Saturday out shopping or at home reading, but the weather varies a lot. Sometimes Fernando Valenzuela gets every pitch where he wants it, and sometimes his control is not so good and his pitches go where they are easier to hit. So the batters' success is controlled by an unstable, external cause. Certain jobs vary a good bit in the external demands they place on the jobholder. Being a general places quite different external forces on a person in wartime than in peacetime, and even quite different demands depending on the sector of combat.

Internal causes can also be stable or unstable. Woody Allen almost always has a genius for making funny remarks; his talent for humor is quite stable. On the other hand, Hamlet is famous for his lack of stable resolve about what to do with his stepfather. Some baseball players are legendary for going on hot streaks and then becoming enmired in terrible slumps; on the average they are quite talented, but the talent seems quite unstable.

In other words, causes can consist of any combination of these two dimensions. An illustration is Weiner's typology for simple achievement tasks, shown in Table 5–1. A student's success or failure at a particular task could be attributed to one or more of four possible causes: ability, effort, luck, and task difficulty. And these causes fall quite neatly into the four categories, as the table shows.

TABLE 5–1

Classification Scheme for the Perceived Causes of Achievement Behavior

	LOCUS OF CONTROL	
Stability	**Internal**	**External**
Stable	Ability	Task difficulty
Unstable	Effort	Luck

Source: Weiner (1974), p. 6.

CONTROLLABILITY A third general dimension of attributions is *controllability*, according to Weiner (1982). We perceive some causes as within the individual's control and others as beyond their control. Perceived controllability or uncontrollability can coexist with any combination of locus of control and stability. For example, an unstable internal cause like effort is generally seen as controllable; a student can try to work hard, or can decide not to. A stable internal cause like ability is less often perceived as within the person's control. A "born genius" or someone who is "gifted" with "native talent" is assumed not to control that ability. Sometimes, though, ability is perceived as controllable. Some highly successful people are perceived as having developed their abilities through long and patient hard work. Similarly, luck is sometimes seen as controllable—"she makes her breaks"—though more often as uncontrollable. In short, it is easy to think of virtually any combination of the three basic dimensions of causal attribution.

These three are the most logical dimensions of causal attribution. They also seem to be the ones people use most frequently in explaining outcomes. Studies asking college students to account for others' exam performances, or for their own high school achievement experiences, show that causal explanations tend to rest on these underlying dimensions (according to factor analyses conducted by Meyer, 1980, and Meyer & Koebl, 1982).

When Are Attributions Made?

When do people engage in this process of asking "why?" Though human beings are supposedly a curious species, they do not go around asking why about everything that happens. They do not wake up in the morning and ask why the sun comes up, why the boxer on TV is wearing gloves, or why the bus they are riding in has started moving as the red light has changed to green. Most natural events and human acts probably do not inspire much cognitive effort to search out the correct causal attribution. As we saw in the last chapter, human beings tend to be miserly with their cognitive resources; they take many shortcuts and avoid cognitive work in a wide and creative variety of ways. What are the conditions under which we do undertake the search for causes?

Ken Karp

What would be the most common explanations for the differences between the two men in the center of the picture?

People tend to be especially curious about causality when something unexpected or unusual happens. Unexpected events create a need for greater predictability, both to prevent nasty surprises, and because a simple, predictable world permits automatic processing, as we saw in the last chapter. As a result, explanations for the sun's and moon's movements are sought more around the time of an eclipse than normally. Newspaper readers, government officials, and social scientists want answers when there is a sudden, unexpected outburst of racial violence or student unrest than when things are humming along as usual. Lau and Russell (1980) found that unexpected outcomes of World Series and college and professional football games relative to pregame gambling odds generated considerably more causal explanation per inch of newsprint in the sports columns than did expected outcomes. Journalists focused on attributions most when a big favorite was upset or won only narrowly.

Bad, painful, unpleasant events also inspire a search for causal attributions. To illustrate this point, a recent study considered distressed couples who had come to a clinic for marital therapy. All were asked to list a variety of positive or negative events that happened in their marriages and how frequently they occurred. Then they were asked for their thoughts about these events, which were coded for the presence of causal attributions. They found that the most attributional thoughts were made about the most distressing events: their partners' frequent negative behaviors, or their infrequent positive behaviors (Holtzworth-Munroe & Jacobson, 1985). For example, the frequent event "he's always late for dinner" might elicit the additional thought "because he is just not a punctual person," which would attribute his lateness to his personality. In intimate relationships, conflict frequently triggers both partners to search for the causes of the problem and often even to exchange competing explanations (see Orvis, Kelley, & Butler, 1976).

Not surprisingly, the most extremely distressing events in life stimulate the greatest search for causal explanation. Taylor found (1982) that 95 percent of her sample of cancer victims made attributions about the cause of the disease. Among their family members, for whom the disease was presumably less painful, only 70 percent did so. Bulman and Wortman (1977) poignantly document the efforts of paraplegics crippled by spinal cord injuries to analyze why it happened to them. Most of the injuries were the result of unavoidable accidents, but still the victims wanted some more definite explanation. The assassination of John F. Kennedy inspired not only the Warren Commission's official explanatory effort, but a number of amateur investigations.

Two Simple Principles

How do we arrive at attributions? Attribution theory begins with two simple principles: the principle of covariation and the discounting principle. According to Heider, the principle of **covariation** means that we tend to look for an association between a particular effect and a particular cause across a number of different conditions. If a given cause is always associated with a particular effect in many different situations, *and* if the effect does not occur in the absence of that cause, we attribute the effect to that cause. The cause always covaries with the effect; whenever the cause is present, so is the effect; and whenever the cause is absent, so is the effect. Suppose your roommate gets grouchy and complains about everything right before exams, but is quite pleasant the rest of the time. Do you conclude that she is a grouch in general—that is, that she has a generally grouchy personality? Probably not. Instead, you would attribute her complaints to the tensions associated with exams, rather than to her being generally a short-tempered person. Her grouchiness is almost always associated with exams and does not occur in the absence of exams, so you attribute it to exams, not to her personality.

This principle of covariation is, of course, exactly the same as the scientific method scientists use. A scientist also arrives at a judgment of causality by seeing that a particular factor is associated with a particular effect across a number of different conditions. If scientists find, for example, that objects invariably fall from higher elevations to lower elevations, no matter whether they are feathers or cannonballs, no matter whether they dropped from the top of a building or waist height, they conclude there is a general causal factor—namely, gravity. As naive psychologists, ordinary people observe the behavior of others and look for regular, invariant effects that follow a particular stimulus. In that way, they arrive at an attribution.

The other main principle in making causal attributions is what Kelley calls the **discounting principle:** "the role of a given cause in producing a given effect is discounted if other plausible causes are also present" (1972, p. 8). That is, we are less likely to attribute the effect to any particular cause, and make less confident attributions, if more than one cause is likely. An insurance salesperson is very nice to us and offers us coffee, but we may not be able to make a confident attribution about why he or she is so friendly. We could attribute the behavior to a real liking for us. More likely, we may discount that possible cause and attribute the behavior partly to the salesperson's wanting

our business. On the other hand, if the person knows we have no money to buy insurance we may not do any such discounting, because the desire for business is no longer a plausible cause.

The Naive Scientist

By and large, research findings do seem to follow the pattern described by the covariation and discounting principles. People do seem to review what information they have about their own behavior, or the behavior of others, and attribute it to internal or external causes, depending on the information available. If there is strong evidence of internal dispositions, an internal attribution is made. If there is evidence of no internal causes or just weak ones, with evidence of strong external forces, an external attribution is made.

Harold Kelley has generated the most formal and comprehensive analysis of attribution, which he calls the *covariation model*. As indicated earlier, the principle of covariation states that "The effect is attributed to that condition which is present when the effect is present and which is absent when the effect is absent" (1967, p. 194). But Kelley goes beyond that to specify that people use three specific types of information to arrive at causal attribution. They check to see whether or not the same effect occurs across: (1) *stimulus objects*, (2) *actors* (persons), and (3) *contexts*. This is perhaps easiest to grasp with a simple example. Suppose our friend Mary shows up at work one day and tells us that she went to a local nightclub the night before. She tells us the show featured a comedian. She laughed hysterically at his jokes, and in fact thought he was the funniest thing she had heard in years. We should definitely go see him.

We want a causal attribution for her hysterical laughter. If the cause was that the comedian really is very funny, we should follow her advice. But if it was just something unusual about Mary, or about the situation that night, we would not be so likely to go. That is, we try to decide whether her behavior is caused by something specific to the stimulus object (the comedian), to the actor (Mary), or to the context (the people she was with, the drinks, etc.).

Kelley suggests that we would search for an attribution by checking each dimension in turn. This involves answering three questions for ourselves: (1) Is the behavior specific to a particular stimulus object? Does Mary always laugh at *any* comedian, or did she really laugh unusually hard only at this one? (2) Is the behavior specific to a particular actor? Have we heard the same report from others, or is Mary the only one who laughed at this particular comedian? (3) Is the behavior specific to a particular context or occasion? Did she laugh each night she went to see this comedian, or did she only laugh the night there was a packed house and she was with her best friend and had one more drink than usual?

Kelley's theory suggests that people use all three of these kinds of information in trying to arrive at a causal attribution: (1) *Distinctiveness* information. Does the person act in this manner only in regard to this stimulus object, and not in regard to other objects? Is Mary's reaction distinctive to this particular object? (2) *Consensus* information. Do other people act in the same way in this situation? Did other people like this comedian as well? (3) *Consistency* information. Does this person consistently react the same way at other times or in other situations? Did Mary react this way to this comedian on only this one occasion?

Kelley hypothesizes this process occurs when we attribute a given effect to a given cause. We quickly review our store of information along these three dimensions. The review may be implicit and automatic rather than deliberate and conscious, but still we review what we know.

For an external attribution to be made—that is, for the comedian's comic ability to be the true cause of Mary's laughter—all three tests have to be passed in the appropriate manner: high distinctiveness, high consensus, and high consistency. Her reaction has to be distinctive to this comedian and not to others; other people have to like the comedian; and she has to like the comedian consistently in this and other situations.

For an internal attribution to be made—that is, for her laughter to be attributed to her general disposition to laugh at anything—low distinctiveness, low consensus, and high consistency must hold. She laughs at all comedians, no one else does, and she laughs in all places and at all times.

McArthur (1972) made the first systematic study of Kelley's predictions. She gave subjects a simple hypothetical event, varied the kind of consensus, distinctiveness, and consistency information available to them, and then measured their attributions. The three main predictions and the results are shown in Table 5–2, using this same example. The first condition is the same and promotes an attribution to the object itself, since it passes all three tests. Everyone else was also laughing, Mary didn't laugh at any of the other performers, but she always laughed at this one. So he must be a funny comedian. Mostly, the subjects saw it that way too; given this pattern of information, 61 percent attributed her reaction to the comedian (the other 39 percent made other attributions).

The second condition leads the observer to make

TABLE 5–2

Why Did Mary Laugh at the Comedian?

Condition	AVAILABLE INFORMATION			Most Common Attribution
	Distinctiveness	Consensus	Consistency	
1	High—she didn't laugh at anyone else.	High—everyone else laughed too.	High—she always laughs at him.	Stimulus object: The comedian (61%)
2	Low—she always laughs at comedians.	Low—hardly anyone else laughed.	High—she always laughs at him.	Person: Mary (86%)
3	High—she didn't laugh at anyone else.	Low—hardly anyone else laughed.	Low—she has almost never laughed at him.	Context: (72%)

Source: Adapted from McArthur (1972).

a person attribution: Mary laughs at any comedian and always laughed at this one—but hardly anyone else did. Mary must be a laugher (86 percent). The third condition leads us to think there is something special about the context: She didn't laugh at anyone else, she has almost never laughed at him before, and hardly anyone else laughed. Something unique must have happened. And 72 percent did attribute her laughter to the particular circumstances.

Does this indicate that people do in fact behave like "naive scientists?" In this study they did tend to arrive at the attributions that we would expect from Kelley's rational decision-making model. At the same time it is obvious that not everyone did so. When the situation genuinely matters, people tend to process information in a more rational manner. Harkness and colleagues (1985) presented a similar task to college women, this time having to do with "Tom's" decisions about dating women with various characteristics. In a high involvement condition, they were told they would themselves date "Tom" later on in the month, while in a low involvement condition no mention of dating was made. Their attributions fit the covariation model more accurately when they expected to date him; that is, when the situation had some real stakes for them.

ATTRIBUTIONS ABOUT OTHERS

These theoretical principles are usually applied to attributions about the behavior of other people. The most important question is this: When do we infer that others' actions reflect real dispositions, such as traits, attitudes, moods, or other internal states? When do we assume that others are simply responding to the external situation? Or, using the terms we will use through most of this chapter, when do we make a **dispositional** as opposed to a **situational attribution?**

We know that people do not always say or do what they really believe. A prisoner of war may say things contrary to his real attitudes. Or a boy may try to act cheerful and happy in school the morning after his girlfriend has jilted him. On the other hand, sometimes a POW expresses real, heartfelt criticism of his own nation's war effort. This certainly happened in Vietnam with some American soldiers and airmen. And the boy may have some genuine sense of relief if the affair had been depressing him for a long time. So how can we tell when a person's actions are a true reflection of their internal attitudes or other dispositions?

The discounting principle suggests that we would first consider whether or not any plausible external forces might have led the person to misstate his or her true attitude. For example, was someone holding a gun to the person's head? If so, an external attribution might be made. In the absence of such plausible external forces, however, external causes would be discounted, and an internal attribution would be made: The person must really hold the attitude he says he does.

A number of studies have shown that the discounting principle operates when perceivers are trying to determine another person's true attitude. Jones and Harris (1967) presented subjects with essays written by other students, in four conditions: The essays supported Fidel Castro or opposed him and were supposedly written on an assigned side or with free choice of position.

With the free choice conditions, observers readily inferred that the writer's expressed opinion was the same as his or her true underlying attitude. The pro-Castro and anti-Castro speeches were seen as reflecting underlying pro- and anti-Castro attitudes, respectively. The subjects discounted the possibility of external causality, given the presence of free choice. Data from their two very similar experiments are shown in Table 5–3.

On the other hand, when the writer was described as having no choice of position (strong external forces), observers still generally felt the written position reflected the underlying attitude, but they were less sure that this was so.

In other words, the discounting principle suggests that we typically give some weight to external forces when they are evident. In this Jones and Harris study, observers were more likely to make an external attribution for attitudes toward Fidel Castro expressed in an essay when the writer had no choice about what position to write. Observers apparently partially discounted the possibility of an internal attribution (that the writer actually believed the position taken in the essay), given clear external pressure.

A second factor is our *expectancy* about the individual's true underlying attitudes, based on any information we might have about the person. Usually we know more about the person than just this one statement of attitude. We might have heard the person speaking about this issue before, or we might have heard him or her speaking about other related issues. Either kind of additional information might give us some expectations that help us make a confident attribution in the current case. We know our friend has long been a supporter of black liberation movements in South Africa. So when we have dinner with her parents and see her nodding agreeably at her parents' conservative statements, we nevertheless infer that she is a strong supporter of the movement and make an external attribution for her nodding. We have past information about her attitudes on this issue that gives us an expectancy about what she really believes. We use that information, along with our perception of her current overt behavior (which seems to be somewhat antimovement) and the external forces (she does not want to get into an argument with her parents), to give us a confident attribution.

In general, as this example suggests, we are likely to make more of an external attribution when people depart from a customary pattern of behavior. Kulik (1983), for example, had subjects watch videotapes of male students in conversation in two different settings. The students behaved in a consistently extroverted, consistently introverted, or inconsistent manner in the two episodes. The subjects were most likely to make a situational attribution for the second episode when it was inconsistent with the first episode.

Kulik calls this a "confirmatory attribution": Peo-

TABLE 5–3

Attitude Attributed to Writer

Condition	Pro-Castro	Anti-Castro
Experiment 1		
Choice	59.6[a]	17.4
No choice	44.1	22.9
Experiment 2		
Choice	55.7	22.9
No choice	41.3	23.7

[a] A high score indicates a pro-Castro position attributed to the writer.
Source: Jones & Harris (1967), pp, 6, 10.

ple adopt attributions that confirm whatever prior expectation or schema they have about others. If people act in a way consistent with our prior schemas about them, we believe the behavior is dispositionally caused. If they behave in a new and different way, we believe it is situationally caused. This need to confirm a prior schema is strong enough that it occurred even in this study, when the schema was based on nothing more than a very brief videotaped exposure to the person (see also Crocker et al., 1983).

A second general source of expectancies about others' attitudes comes from our knowledge of their attitudes on other issues. Even if we had never heard our friend talk about black liberation movements in South Africa, we might have a pretty clear expectation about how she feels based on conversations about other topics, such as revolutions in Central America, special admissions for minorities, and so on.

To test this, Jones and associates (1971) did an experiment much like the earlier Jones-Harris study, but this time directly varying additional information about attitudes on other issues held by the essay writer. The writer again either had or did not have free choice about the position taken in the essay. As in the Jones and Harris study, choice led to more confident internal attributions. When the position taken in the essay was expected from the writer's other attitudes, the observers made confident internal attributions, even when the writer had had no choice of position. Put another way, observers felt that overt behavior corresponded to a true underlying attitude (1) when there were no obvious external forces (the free choice condition), or (2) when the overt position was consistent with expectancies about the writer's overall sociopolitical attitudes, even given strong external forces.

In general, then, observers do attribute overt behavior to internal dispositions in the absence of clear external forces, or when they have other information about past behavior that allows them to discount the role of the external forces.

ATTRIBUTIONS ABOUT THE SELF

One of the most interesting hypotheses in attribution theory is that people arrive at perceptions of their own internal states in the same way as they arrive at perceptions of others' states. This idea derives from the general assumption that our own emotions, attitudes, traits, and abilities are often unclear and ambiguous to us. We have to *infer* them from our own overt behavior and from our perceptions of the environmental forces surrounding us.

The approach suggests that in self-perception, just as in the perception of others, we search for invariant associations of causes and effects and use the discounting principle to divide up responsibility about various plausible causes. If we perceive strong external forces pushing us in the direction of our own behavior, we are more likely to come to a situational attribution. In the absence of clear external forces, we assume that a dispositional attribution is more correct. This approach has generated a good deal of research on the self-perception of attitudes, motivation, and emotion.

Attitudes

Psychologists have long assumed that people figure out their own attitudes by *introspection*, by reviewing the various cognitions and feelings in their consciousness. Bem (1967) argued instead that we receive only minimal and ambiguous internal cues to our attitudes, just as we have no direct access to the internal cues in others. If so, we must infer our own attitudes by observing our own overt behavior. When we observe our own behavior in a situation with no strong external forces, we assume we are simply expressing our own true attitudes and make an internal attribution. In contrast, when there are strong external pressures on us to do something (such as having been assigned a particular position in a debate), we perceive our statements to be externally caused.

In other words, we learn about our own attitudes by observing how we behave in environments with different external pressures in them, not by introspecting to see how we feel. Bem does not hold that people never use internal evidence, just that to a surprising degree people rely on the external evidence of their overt behavior, and the conditions under which it occurs, to infer their own true attitudes.

To test Bem's self-perception theory, we would need to manipulate an individual's perception of his behavior while holding other factors constant (such as the actual behavior and the pressure of the environment). Then we could determine whether the person's perception of his own behavior determined his perception of his own attitudes. To test this, Salancik and Conway (1975) cleverly manipulated subjects' descriptions of their own religious behavior: Some were asked if they "occasionally" read a religious newspaper or magazine, attended a church or synagogue, or consulted a minister about personal problems. Many students had engaged in at least these minimal religious acts, so students in this condition reported lots of religious behavior. Others were asked if they "frequently" did each of these things. Since most college students do not do them "frequently," students in this condition reported very little religious behavior.

Since the two groups were randomly selected, they were presumably in fact almost exactly the same in actual behavior. But because of these differences in the wording of the questions, the first group of subjects described themselves as engaging in quite a variety of religious behaviors, while the second group described few religious acts. And sure enough, when later asked about their own overall religious attitudes in the form of the question "How religious are you?" the first group, which had been subtly induced to describe themselves as engaging in more religious behaviors, said they were more religious in general.

Motivation

A similar idea has been applied to the self-perception of motivation. The idea is that performing a task for high rewards will lead to an external attribution—I did it because I was paid so well for it. Performing the same task for minimal reward will lead to an internal attribution—I couldn't have done it for that small amount of money I got, so I must have done it because I really enjoyed it. This leads to the paradoxical prediction that minimal rewards will lead to the greatest intrinsic interest in a task because the person attributes performance to intrinsic interest, not to extrinsic reward. Put another way, *overjustification* for engaging in an activity undermines intrinsic interest in the activity.

The earliest demonstration of overjustification varied whether or not nursery school children were given awards for engaging in a task (playing with felt-tip pens) which they enjoyed doing anyway (Lepper, Greene, & Nisbett, 1973). Some children were told they would get a "Good Player Award" with a gold star and ribbon if they would draw pictures with a felt-tip pen for a few minutes. Other children were not told about any award. All the children then did the drawing, and the first group was given their awards. A few days later, all the children were observed in a free-play situation with felt-tip pens provided. The children who had been given the awards spent half as much time drawing as the no-award children did. Their intrinsic interest in drawing had been undermined by the extrinsic reward.

This finding has been repeated in many contexts since then (see Deci & Ryan, 1985). Kunda and Schwartz (1983), for example, asked subjects to help record material for a blind student for payment or without payment. Later they were asked how morally obligated they would feel to help others in a number of ways, including reading school work to a blind student. Those given no money felt significantly more obligated.

An interesting consequence of overjustification is that it can even undermine not just the productivity of people's work on a task, but their creativity as well. Amabile and associates (1986) found that the creativity of children's storytelling was significantly reduced when they were offered an explicit reward for telling the story. In the reward condition, they were told that if they told a story, they would be able to take two photographs with an instant camera—an important reward. In the no-reward condition, they were asked to do the storytelling with no mention of a reward. Coders, working "blind" (not knowing which condition the child was in), rated the stories as significantly more creative in the no-reward condition.

If extrinsic rewards for engaging in pleasurable tasks reduce intrinsic interest, then external threats that prevent engaging in specific behaviors ought to increase interest. For example, the stricter the penalty for using an illegal drug, the more attractive the drug should seem to be. Here people attribute their avoidance of the activity to the threat, not the unpleasantness of the activity itself. Wilson and Lassiter (1982) found some evidence for this hypothesis, when they varied threatened punishment for cheating.

The same reasoning would also suggest that the overjustification effect would be increased when external rewards are made more salient (Ross, 1975) and decreased when the real initial interest in the activity is made more salient. In an experiment to test this latter point, Fazio (1981) had children play with magic markers, and then later varied whether or not they were shown photos of themselves engaging in this highly pleasurable task on the earlier occasion. Otherwise the experiment closely resembled the Lepper et al. (1973) study described earlier. For the children shown those photos of their earlier play, initial intrinsic interest in playing with the magic markers was highly salient, so extrinsic rewards had little undermining effect. They knew they had really enjoyed the magic markers, so they attributed their later play to their own pleasure, not to the reward.

The implications of this research are important. Rewards can sometimes backfire: Instead of encour-

Being overpaid for one's work can undermine intrinsic interest in it. Relative to other professionals, classical musicians are usually paid poorly and even research scientists are usually not paid lavishly. How do you think their payment affects their interest in their work?

Laimute E. Druskis

Ken Karp, Sirovich Senior Center

aging people, they can actually turn them away from activities they would otherwise enjoy. And punishments may make a forbidden activity seem all the more attractive, though there is less evidence on this point.

Labeling Emotions

Traditional theorists of emotion proposed that we recognize what we feel by considering our physiological state, our mental state, and the external stimulus causing these states. But recent evidence indicates that many emotional reactions are biochemically similar. We can distinguish high arousal from low arousal, but not various types of emotion. For example, it is hard to tell the difference between intense jealousy and intense love. So we need other information to identify our own emotions.

Stanley Schachter (1964) has taken a self-perception approach to emotion. He suggests that perceptions of our emotions depend on (1) the degree of physiological arousal we experience and (2) the cognitive label that we apply, such as "angry" or "happy." To arrive at a cognitive label, we review our own behavior and the situation. If we feel physiologically aroused and are laughing at a comedy show on television, we might infer that we are happy. If we are snarling at someone for shoving us on a crowded street, we might infer that we are angry. In each case, our behavior and our interpretation of the situation provide us with the cognitive label that allows us to interpret our internal experience of emotional arousal. Like Bem's theory of self-perception, this point of view again emphasizes the ambiguity of internal states, and therefore that self-perception is highly dependent on perceptions of overt behavior and of the external environment.

LABELING AROUSAL Schachter and his colleagues conducted a number of studies based on the idea that high degrees of physiological arousal give rise to a search for an appropriate attribution. If a plausible attribution exists for the arousal, it will be accepted. If no such attribution exists, the person will search the environment for something that could have caused the arousal. Whatever the environment provides as an explanation will also provide the label for the emotion.

If you suddenly felt yourself to be very physiologically excited but did not know why, you would do a quick search to try to discover the cause. If you suddenly remembered that someone had just insulted you, you might label your arousal as anger at that person and explain it that way. Although this sounds very conscious and deliberate, it all probably happens in a flash, so that we may not even be aware of going through this process. The key ideas, then, are that arousal is undifferentiated and leads to a search for explanation, that we frequently adopt whatever explanation the environment offers most readily, and that we use that explanation to provide a specific label for our emotion.

In the first of these experiments, Schachter and Singer (1962) gave subjects an arousing drug, epinephrine, which produces physiological arousal generally associated with emotions. Some of these subjects were told that the drug would produce a noticeable physiological arousal, such as more rapid heartbeats, and others were not. Some of the aroused people could thus attribute their internal state to the drug, whereas others had no ready explanation. All subjects were then placed in a situation in which a confederate of the experimenter pretended to be experiencing a particular emotion. Half the subjects were exposed to someone behaving in a euphoric, elated way; he made paper planes and flew them around; started a small game of basketball using crumpled papers and an old wastebasket; sang, danced, hopped around, and in general presented a zany, lightheaded attitude. The other half were exposed to an angry confederate who made nasty remarks, had an unpleasant expression on his face, muttered to himself, and generally presented a disgruntled, annoyed impression.

Those who had been aroused by the drug and had not been informed of this (the "no-explanation" condition in Table 5–4) became more euphoric in the euphoria condition and more angry in the anger condition than the other subjects. When they were aroused without any plausible cause, the subjects presumably interpreted their arousal as being caused by the situation. What was the nature of that situation? Perhaps the clearest clues to that lay in the confederate's behavior. If he behaved in a euphoric manner, it must be a situation generat-

TABLE 5–4

The Schachter-Singer Experiment

| | SEQUENCE | | | | |
Condition	Step 1 Given Arousing Drug	Step 2 Told it Would Be Arousing	Step 3 Confederate's Behavior	Step 4 Presumed Attribution for Own Arousal (Unmeasured)	Step 5 Own Behavior (Measured)
No explanation	Yes	No	⎧ Euphoric or angry ⎫ ⎨ in all cases ⎬ ⎩ ⎭	Situational	Euphoric or angry
Informed	Yes	Yes		Drug	Calm
No arousal	No	No		None	Calm

Source: Adapted from Schachter & Singer (1962).

ing euphoria. If he behaved angrily, it must be one generating anger. Consistent with this logic, the "no-explanation" subjects tend to act happy when the confederate was euphoric, and angry when he was angry.

But when aroused subjects could attribute their arousal to the drug (in the "informed" condition), they were relatively unaffected by the other person's behavior. They knew their physiological state was due to the drug and therefore did not interpret it as emotional arousal. The procedure and results of this experiment are shown in Table 5–4.

The key element here is that when subjects were both aroused and placed in a situation with no other attribution (the "no-explanation" condition), they "caught" the salient emotion from the external situation. That is, in the absence of any alternative, they attributed their arousal to the situation's capacity for producing either euphoria or anger and they acted in a more euphoric or angry way. In the "informed" condition, where arousal was explicitly attributed to the drug, no such emotion was experienced. Nor was it in a control condition with no arousing drug provided.

What was important for the experience of emotion was first of all the *arousal*, and second the *cognitive label* or the attribution made for the arousal. When the experimenter provided a label attributing the arousal to the drug, the subjects acted as if they experienced no particular emotion. When they did not know the drug was responsible for their arousal, they took their cues about the emotions from the external environment.

One implication of this reasoning is that internal arousal states are so ambiguous that they can be attributed to any plausible stimulus. Whichever emotion is experienced therefore depends more on available plausible causes than it does on the nature of the actual internal sensations. Even fake internal sensations should be sufficient, given an external cause that can supply a plausible label.

Valins (1966) tested this idea by giving random false feedback to subjects about their own arousal. He presented heterosexual male subjects with slides of nude females. After each slide he provided them faked feedback through earphones about their own heart rates. After some slides, subjects heard increased heartbeats, which they thought were their own; after others, they heard decreased heartbeats; and after still others, they heard what they thought were irrelevant sounds. Valins found that subjects rated the nudes accompanied by the supposedly changed heartbeat as the most attractive.

After the experiment was over, subjects were allowed to take some slides home. They mostly chose slides that had been associated with the fake feedback about changed heartbeat. Presumably they had searched the environment for a plausible cause for the change in their heartbeats, found the slides of the nude females to be a reasonable cause, and therefore labeled their arousal as sexual. This was evidence that people infer their own emotions from the perception of arousal (in this case, faked changes in heartbeat) and a plausible external cause (in this case, pictures of nudes).

Another example illustrates how readily people

ignore real internal cues when there is a plausible external cause. Cantor, Zillman, and Bryant (1975) had heterosexual male subjects ride an exercycle vigorously enough to reach a high level of physiological arousal. Physiological arousal based on this kind of exercise tends to last longer than the person realizes. A few minutes later, the subjects no longer felt aroused, but objective indicators of arousal showed they were. Female nudes shown at this point were rated as more attractive than those rated immediately after the exercise (when they presumably attributed their arousal to the exercise) or at a still later point (when there was no remaining arousal to be wrongly attributed to the nudes).

MISATTRIBUTION   Nisbett & Schachter (1966) proposed that if people could be induced to attribute arousal to a drug that had really caused it, perhaps they could also be persuaded to misattribute to a neutral pill arousal caused by the environment. To do this, they gave all subjects an ordinary sugar pill. Experimental subjects were told the pill would produce physiological symptoms, such as hand tremors and palpitations; control subjects were told

---

BOX 5–2

A PRETTY DAY CAN MAKE FOR A HAPPY LIFE

People can base self-perceptions about enduring internal states on temporary moods. Schwarz and Clore (1983) showed that people evaluated their lives as a whole as more happy and satisfying on sunny days than on rainy days. Using telephone interviews, they asked people: "What we are interested in is people's moods . . . could you just answer four brief questions? First, on a scale of 1 to 10, with 10 being the happiest, how do you feel about your life as a whole? . . . All things considered, how satisfied or dissatisfied are you with your life as a whole these days? And, how happy do you feel at this moment?" Half the respondents were called on sunny spring days, and half on rainy spring days. The higher the number, the happier they said they were. As the table shows, they were happier at the moment on sunny days, and evaluated their "lives as a whole" as happier and more satisfying. Their momentary mood, induced by the chance event of the day's weather, influenced their self-perception of stable internal states.

	WEATHER	
	Sunny	Rainy
Happiness of mood at moment	7.5	5.4
Happiness of life as a whole	7.4	5.0
Satisfaction with life as a whole	6.6	4.9

Source: Adapted from Schwarz & Clore (1983), pp. 519–520.

it would produce only nonphysiological symptoms. Finally, all subjects were administered painful electric shock. The hypothesis was that the experimental subjects would attribute their physiological reactions after the shock to the pill rather than to the shock itself, and so would perceive the shock as hurting less. The control subjects, having no basis for an attribution to the pill, would blame their reactions on the shock itself. And indeed it was found that these control subjects found the shock more painful than did the experimental subjects. A number of these **misattribution** studies have been done, and they generally share the same basic idea: If people can be persuaded to misattribute their negative emotional states from the real external causes to some other, more neutral cause, the level of emotional distress associated with the real external cause will diminish.

SOME LIMITATIONS   The most extreme forms of this self-perception viewpoint would seem to argue that we get almost no information about our own attitudes and emotions by introspection; outside observers know as much about our own internal feelings as we do. This is almost surely too extreme.

First of all, this self-perception process works mainly when there is a good bit of ambiguity or uncertainty about our internal states. People do have attitudes that endure and are not based entirely on current behavior. They do not decide about whether or not they like steak on the basis of whether or not they have recently eaten steak. They have real feelings toward steak and it is those feelings that determine their responses. Israelis have certain attitudes about Nazis, and bigots have certain attitudes about minorities, which they are quite clear about regardless of their most recent behavior. When we are slapped in the face, we do not have to wait to see if we strike back to know if we are angry. When our boyfriend says he no longer loves us, we know we feel hurt no matter whether tears come or not.

If a male subject is shown a whole series of beautiful nude females, it may be fairly easy to alter his preferences among them based on false feedback. But it strikes us as unlikely that the same subject, shown a nude Miss July and a nude hippopotamus and given false feedback that his heartbeat had accelerated more for the hippo, will seriously think he desires the hippo and will want to take her slide home.

A second limitation is that this self-perception process seems to work best when people do not care very much about what response they make. When it really matters, people seem to monitor their own attitudes and emotions more carefully and are less influenced by external cues. To test this idea, Taylor (1975) ran an experiment like the Valins nude-slides study—except that this time *female* college students were presented with pictures of full-face color photographs of clothed *male* graduate students. She first had each of the women rate these pictures for attractiveness. Then the subject was given false feedback about her physiological reactions to one of the slides by overhearing a confederate saying that she (the subject) had reacted more strongly to that slide than to any other slide. Half the time this false feedback concerned a slide the subject had already rated as highly attractive, and half the time it concerned a slide of a man the subject had rated as only medium in attractiveness. According to the self-perception idea, this false high-arousal feedback ought to boost ratings of the attractiveness of the slides linked to false feedback.

Taylor's hypothesis was, however, that people would be influenced by false feedback mainly when nothing was at stake. So she told half the women they would later meet this man, and half did not expect to meet him. False feedback changed initial attitudes significantly only when no future meeting was expected; that is, when the ratings were not very important. In general, people probably use external cues to determine their own attitudes most often under conditions of low involvement. When the subjects actually expected they might meet the stimulus person, they evidently paid closer attention to their own true feelings and were not much influenced by the false feedback.

When these "misattribution" or "reattribution" studies were first done, they gave some promise of providing a new therapeutic tool for dealing with disruptive anxieties, fears, depressions, low self-esteem, and other seemingly neurotic emotions. A variety of other studies have tried to apply reattribution therapies to public speaking anxiety, test anxiety, depression, and other unwanted emotions (Storms & Nisbett, 1970, Valins & Ray, 1967).

The general technique was to try to get the person to reattribute anxieties to less threatening sources. However, the effects have been short-lived, unreliable, limited to weak anxieties, or so slight as to be unimportant (see Slivken & Buss, 1984; Fiske & Taylor, 1984; Harvey, Weary, & Harris, 1981). So the technique is probably not powerful enough for therapeutic purposes.

Specific Affects

Some attributions generate specific emotions. Weiner's theory, shown in Figure 5–1, is that successes produce very general positive feelings (like happiness) and failure produces generally negative feelings (like sadness). Under some conditions, such as when the outcome is different from what was expected or when the outcome is extremely important, people try to figure out why they succeeded or failed. The attribution they make stimulates specific kinds of emotions. For example, you may feel bad if you get a "D" on the midterm, but *which* bad emotion you feel will depend on how you explain the low grade. If you think the

test was unfair and you blame the teacher, you will feel angry; if you think you did poorly because you are not smart enough to do better, you may feel depressed; but if you feel you didn't study hard enough, you may feel guilty.

Weiner (1982, 1986) has shown that which emotion people experience depends on their attribution. Different attributions produce different emotions. The locus of control dimension determines whether a person will feel pride, shame, or gratitude. When a person is successful, internal attributions (ability, effort) produce pride, while external attributions (easy test, a helpful roommate) produce gratitude. Failures explained by internal causes (lack of effort, low ability) breed feelings of shame, while failures explained externally (test harder than expected or unfair) produce surprise or anger (Weiner et al., 1979).

The controllability of perceived causes is also important. Internal attributions for negative outcomes, such as a poor grade on a midterm, can produce quite different emotions, depending on the controllability of the cause. "Guilt" comes from controllable internal causes, such as effort (I could have studied, and I just wasted the whole evening),

FIGURE 5–1   Attributional analysis of emotion. (Adapted from B. Weiner, 1986, p. 122.)

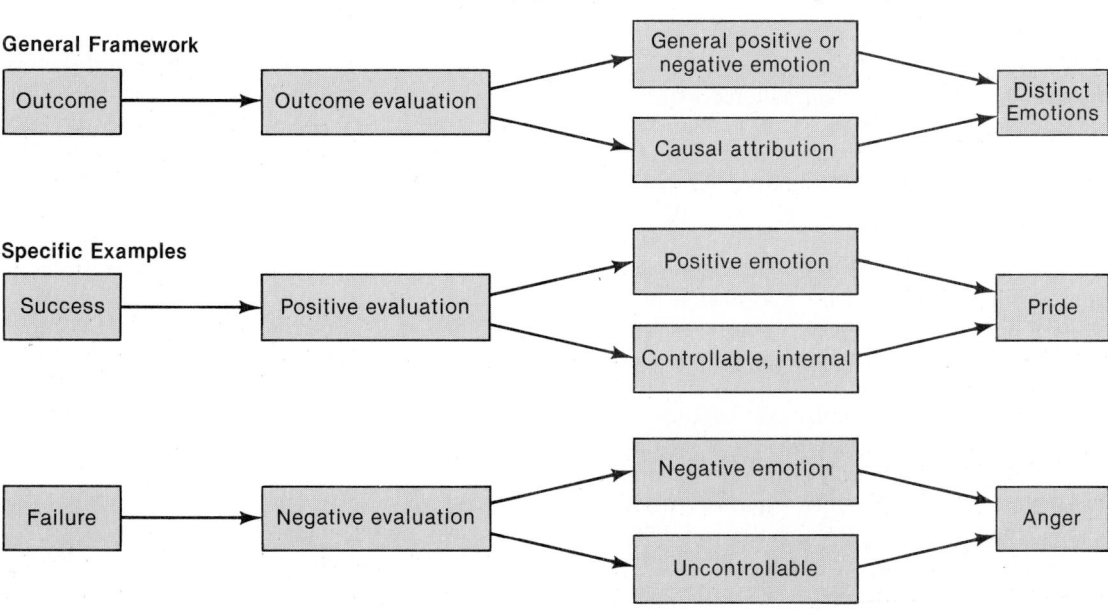

while "depression" comes from causes that cannot be controlled very well, such as lack of ability (I'm just not smart enough for this) or personality characteristics (I'm not self-disciplined enough to be in college) (Weiner et al., 1979; Weiner, 1986). "Anger" is associated with controllable causes. One example Weiner gives is: "My roommate brought her dog into our no-pets apartment without asking me first. When I got home she wasn't there, but the barking dog was. . . . As well, the dog had relieved itself in the entry" (1986, p. 137). The person was angry at the roommate, because she could have controlled whether the dog was there or not. A chronically lying boyfriend or husband, a woman who is on welfare for years but who could be working, a foreign country that deliberately shoots down one of our domestic airliners—all attract anger, because these actions are interpreted as controllable.

"Pity" or "sympathy," on the other hand, is aroused by behavior interpreted as uncontrollable.

A handicapped child who accidentally knocks over a vase may elicit sympathy (she couldn't help it); a drunk who does it elicits anger (he should have controlled himself; if he hadn't gone out and gotten drunk, he wouldn't have done it). To show this, Weiner (1980) described to college students either a person who apparently was drunk and fell down in a subway: "He is carrying a liquor bottle wrapped in a brown paper bag and smells of liquor," or a person who was ill and fell down. The college students said that they would have negative affects such as anger toward the drunk, but not toward the ill person. Poor people who are old or handicapped tend to evoke sympathy from most others. Even crime caused by a factory's closing, or by an economic depression that eliminates jobs, elicits some sympathy because the criminals are not considered totally responsible for their behavior. But poverty perceived as caused by the laziness of unemployed able-bodied people evokes anger.

COGNITIVE BIASES

Attribution theory as described up to this point tends to describe an essentially rational, logical process. In fact, Kelley's "naive scientist" model draws an analogy between the person in the street who tries to arrive at causal attributions for everyday events and the systematic scientist who applies the scientific method to achieve causal explanations for natural events. In this form, attribution theory assumes that people process information in a rational way, and that they are fairly objective in assessing information and in combining it to produce a conclusion.

However, as we saw in the last chapter, people tend to be intellectually lazy (or at least cognitively miserly). It is unlikely that they spend most of their waking moments diligently trying to ferret out the causes of things. Moreover, since psychologists themselves have such a struggle unraveling the causes of human behavior, ordinary people can

hardly be expected to do much better. Furthermore, people are far from being logical and rational. Indeed, most of this book, and most of psychology, is devoted to studying the irrational aspects of human behavior. For that reason, we now turn to several biases that have been identified in attributional processes. We begin with a consideration of various cognitive biases that derive from the tendencies to respond more to salient or figural stimuli than to background stimuli, and to simplify perception by developing meaningfully structured impressions.

Salience

One way we simplify cognitive processing is to overreact to *salient* stimuli. This bias leads us to perceive the most salient stimuli as the most influential ones. If something is in motion, or colorful, or loud, or novel, we are likely to see it as the main cause of whatever else is changing in the environment. The person who is running down the street is seen as causing the bank alarm system to go off. The loud thunderclap is perceived as causing people to scurry for cover. The woman in the red dress is thought to cause people's head to turn.

Sometimes the most salient stimuli are in fact the strongest causes of people's behavior, so such attributions would then be accurate. Bias arises because the most perceptually salient stimuli often dominate causal explanations even when they are not actually the most powerful causes.

In a most elegant way, Taylor and Fiske (1975) tested this idea, that whatever is perceptually salient will be seen as the dominant cause. Two confederates served as "actors." They engaged in a conversation, facing each other. The ordinary subjects were "observers" sitting behind the confederates or next to them. Each actor thus had observers sitting behind him and facing him. Clearly, the actor and his behavior would be more salient for those who faced him than for those who sat behind him. But both actors ought to be equally salient for the observers sitting to the side, equidistant from the two actors.

This arrangement is illustrated in Figure 5–2. The confederates held a standardized 5-minute conversation, chatting as if they had just met. They exchanged information about majors, common job plans, home towns, family, extracurricular activities, and the like. The conversation was carefully monitored to make sure that roughly the same conversation occurred in all experimental groups.

Then the subjects were asked for their causal perceptions: How much had each confederate set the tone of the conversation, determined the kind of information exchanged, and caused the other actor to behave as he did? The results are shown in Table 5–5. It shows that the more perceptually salient actor (the confederate the subject faced) was given the dominant causal role, and that the less salient actor (the one the confederate sat behind) was seen as less influential. Subjects sitting equidistant from both confederates saw both as about equally potent. Thus actor A was seen as most powerful by those facing him (observers 1

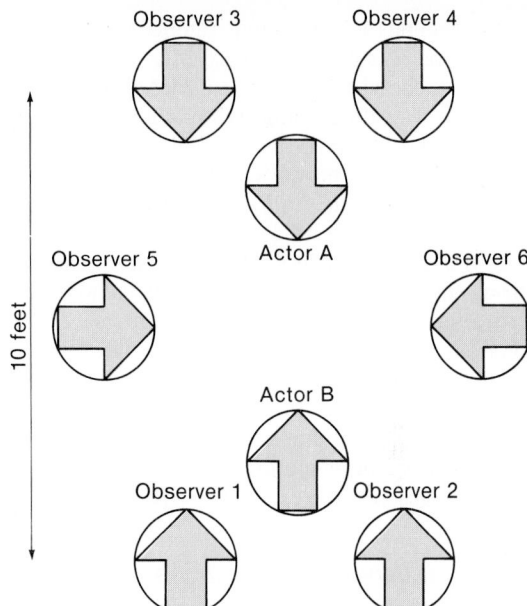

FIGURE 5–2 Seating arrangements for actors and observers, with arrows indicating visual orientation. (Adapted from Taylor & Fiske, 1975, p. 441.)

and 2), while actor B was seen as most powerful by those facing *him* (observers 3 and 4)—even though all subjects in reality were observing exactly the same interaction (and one in which both actors contributed about equally, according to unbiased observers 5 and 6 in the center).

TABLE 5–5

Mean Ratings of Causal Role Attributed by Observers to Each Actor as a Function of the Observer's Seating Position

Observer's Position	ACTOR	
	A	B
Facing actor A (observers 1 & 2)	20.25	15.54
Center (observers 5 & 6)	17.51	16.75
Facing actor B (observers 3 & 4)	12.00	20.75

Source: Taylor & Fiske (1975), p. 441.

The finding that perceptual salience induces exaggerations of a person's causal role turns out to be quite general. Robinson and McArthur (1982) found the same thing using audio rather than visual salience: The louder of two unseen speakers was perceived as the most causally dominant, even though the difference in loudness was only 75 to 70 decibels.

And indeed this effect of perceptual salience is strong enough to overcome some quite unfavorable circumstances. Taylor and her colleagues (1979) found the same thing even under conditions they thought would reduce the importance of salience: when the perceiver was distracted, when impressions were assessed after a delay, when the conversation itself was very interesting, and when the perceivers themselves were involved in the discussion.

Overattributing to Dispositions

One consequence of this effect of salience is that we are too likely to explain others' behavior as resulting from such dispositions as their general personality traits or their attitudes, while we tend to overlook the importance of the situation they are in. When we ask for information from a clerk at a window in the college administration building and he seems impersonal, brusque, and unhelpful, we think he is a cold, unfriendly person. We tend to ignore the fact that he must have scores of such brief encounters with anonymous complaining students each day. It probably is his particular job situation, rather than his personality, that is most likely to make him act brusquely. Overattribution to dispositions, and underestimation to situations, is so common that Ross (1977) has called it the **fundamental attribution error.**

We have already seen one example of this fundamental error in the Jones and Harris (1967) study of attributions about the attitudes of people writing essays on Fidel Castro. We already discussed the fact that essay writers who freely chose to take a pro-Castro position were regarded as truly much more pro-Castro than were writers taking an anti-Castro position. But internal attributions were made even when the writer had no choice about which position to take in the essay. Even when the writer had no choice about which position to take, observ-

ers much overestimated the role of internal dispositions (the writer's true position on Castro), and much underestimated the strength of the external situation (that is, the lack of choice about what position to take) in trying to explain the position taken in the essay. This can be seen in Table 5–3.

This finding, that observers make internal attributions even when actors have no choice, is an important one. It illustrates the principle that causal attributions for the behavior of others are biased in the direction of overemphasizing dispositions and underemphasizing the environment. Quite a number of later studies have been done to determine whether this Jones and Harris result is typical, and almost all have found substantially the same thing. The phenomenon seems to hold up even when the subjects have themselves actually and knowingly induced the speaker's behavior (Gilbert & Jones, 1986). And the phenomenon holds up even when the observers themselves have been through the same procedure and know that no choice is involved. For example, Miller, Jones, and Hinkle (1981) repeated the same general study, this time assigning subjects to write either an essay designed to convince a reader that they were introverted or a more extroverted essay. Because each of the subjects also wrote one of the essays, they knew no choice was involved. They *still* overestimated the role of dispositions: They still thought the "introverted" essays were written by people who were more introverted.

All in all, it appears that the tendency to take speakers' positions as their true attitudes seems amazingly resilient, even in conditions when it should be easy to make an external attribution: when speakers have no choice, are unenthusiastic, give weak arguments, and are simply reading somebody else's speech. Only under the most extreme situational constraints, and with very weak arguments delivered in drab, written form, does the phenomenon disappear, and do observers finally see the full causal role of external forces (see Snyder & Jones, 1974; Schneider & Miller, 1975; Miller, 1976; Watson, 1982).

Why do we do this? Why do we resist information about external constraints? Salience is the most likely explanation for this attributional bias. According to Heider, "Behavior . . . has such salient properties that it tends to engulf the field"; that is, we pay so much attention to the person's behavior that we tend to ignore the situation in which it occurs. The behavior becomes figure and stands out against the surrounding ground of the situation. And as we have seen in the previous section, such salience leads to the perception of causality. Thus the essay writer, rather than the situation, is seen as the primary causal factor.

The second key link is that behavior is perceived as emerging from the person's stable characteristics. Jones (1979), following Heider, contends that people and their actions form a natural perceptual and cognitive unit. They are in a "unit relation." We think of the two as indivisible. It is *the person's* action," not an independent event that temporarily seems to be in the same physical space as the actor. It is very hard to break a unit relation by detaching the two perceptually. So we naturally connect people to their acts and perceive the people as the main cause of their own behavior.

Increased salience of the actor, then, should lead to still more dispositional attributions. To show this, McArthur and Post (1977) presented subjects with videotapes of getting-acquainted conversations, manipulating the visual salience of the actors in various ways. In one study, the salient actor was seated in a bright light, while the nonsalient actor was seated in a dim light. In another, the salient actor was seated in a rocking chair, while the other sat still. In the other studies, the salient actor wore a brightly patterned shirt rather than a solid gray one, or was of a different sex than the other in the conversation. In all these cases, the salient actor's behavior was attributed more to dispositional causes than was the nonsalient actor's behavior.

This bias toward interpreting others' behavior as stemming from their dispositions may not be just an irrational blunder. On the contrary, it may be quite functional. As Hoffman and associates (1984) have pointed out, when we are required to communicate verbally to other people or about them, we need to simplify a rich and detailed store of information about them into brief and meaningful form. Traits (or other dispositions) are very convenient summaries for all that information. It is easier to say, "She's a little immature," than to list all the events that lead us to say that. And indeed these authors have shown that expecting to communicate with another person increases the tendency to attribute global traits to that person, presumably because then it becomes more important to be able to think and talk in economical terms.

Actors versus Observers

One of the most interesting aspects of the fundamental attributional error is that it holds for observers, but apparently not for actors perceiving their own behavior. Actors instead seem to overemphasize the role of external factors. For example, some parents set fairly restrictive rules for their adolescent children, such as that they can go out on dates during weekends only; they have to be home at a certain hour; they can watch television only during certain hours; and so on. How is this rule making interpreted? The "observers," the adolescents, frequently perceive these rules as dispositionally caused: The parents are mean, authoritarian, arbitrary, and old-fashioned. The "actors" themselves, the parents, are often more likely to explain their behavior in terms of the situation: They are just doing what is best for their children, living up to the role of the parent, or responding to the rebelliousness and irresponsibility of the children themselves.

How do both sides interpret it if the adolescents repeatedly violate the rules? The "observers," this time the parents, interpret it dispositionally: The adolescents are rebellious, bad, irresponsible, and so on. The "actors," this time the adolescents, interpret their own behavior as situationally caused: The party was fun so they didn't want to leave, the parents' rules are unreasonably strict, the parents misunderstand them, and so on. In short, observers overestimate dispositional causes, actors overestimate situational ones. Both groups are causally explaining the same behavior, but with quite different attributions.

This **actor-observer bias** (Jones & Nisbett, 1972) has proved to be one of the most widely researched of the various attributional biases. In one of its earliest demonstrations, Nisbett and colleagues (1973) asked male students to write a paragraph on why they liked the woman they dated most, and why they had chosen their major. Then they were asked to answer the same questions as if they were their best friend. Responses were

HOW TO SEEM SMART

One ingenious use of this fundamental attribution error made observers considerably overestimate other students' general knowledge. Ross, Amabile, and Steinmetz (1977) set up pairs of Stanford students in a quiz situation. One was a "questioner," and the other a "contestant." In the experimental condition, each questioner was allowed to make up ten "challenging but not impossible" questions on any subject he or she wanted and then pose them to the contestant. Both then rated themselves and their partner for general knowledge.

The questions that were made up were indeed fairly difficult (such as, on the order of "What is the capital of New Mexico?"), and contestants only got four of ten right, on the average. But the important finding was that contestants vastly overestimated the questioners' knowledge. Contestants rated the questioners as extremely well informed by comparison to themselves, while questioners rated both as about equal, as shown below.

The fundamental attribution error occurs when observers take overt behavior too seriously and ignore the situation. These contestants apparently thought the questioners were really well informed since they had known the answers to seemingly hard questions. They ignored the artificiality of the situation—that is, the questioners were able to make up any question they liked and were obviously likely to make up questions they knew the answers to.

| Rating Made by | RATING[a] OF: | |
	Questioner's Knowledge	Contestant's Knowledge
Questioner	53.5	50.6
Contestant	66.8	41.3

[a] High = more knowledgeable on a 100-point scale.
Source: Ross, Amabile, & Steinmetz (1977).

scored for the extent to which the behavior was attributed to the actor's disposition (such as, I need someone I can relax with, or I want to make a lot of money) or externally, to aspects of the woman or major (such as, chemistry is a high-paying field). The subjects gave external reasons for their own behavior much more than for another person's be-havior. And there was some tendency, though it was not as strong, to give more dispositional reasons for a friend's behavior. This difference between actors and observers in causal attributions has, in subsequent research, proved to be an unusually robust phenomenon (Watson, 1982).

Jones and Nisbett offered two explanations for

this difference in attributions. One was that the participants have access to *different information* and therefore naturally come to different conclusions. Actors have access to much more historical information about their own behavior in different situations than the usual observer. With all this inside information about how their own behavior has varied across situations, actors should be more likely to attribute it to the unique characteristics of each particular situation, rather than perceiving themselves as behaving uniformly due to some general predisposition. This would be the covariation model explanation.

The other explanation, and the one pursued by most researchers, is that the difference is due mainly to *different perspectives*, with the key factor again being differences in salience. The observer is naturally focused on the actor. This special salience of the actor leads the observer to overattribute the actor's behavior to dispositions, as we have already seen. This is "the fundamental attributional error." But the actor is not looking at her own behavior. She is looking at the situation—the place, the other people, their expectations, and so on. The actor's own behavior is not as salient to herself as it is to an observer who is watching her. For this reason, the actor will see the situation as more salient and therefore more causally potent. In short, for the observer, the actor's behavior engulfs the field, and so it becomes perceived as the major causal force. For the actor, the environment rather than behavior is most salient, and *it* engulfs the field and becomes the main causal explanation.

Storms (1973) succeeded in showing that this differential perspectives idea could explain the actor-observer difference. He reasoned that if the actor-observer difference in attributions was simply due to a difference in perspective, it could be reversed by giving each person the other's point of view. If the actor's own behavior was videotaped and played back to him, he ought to perceive himself as the most salient object in the field and ascribe causality to his own dispositions. If the observers see a videotape from the actor's perspective, they will see more of the situation to which the actor is responding, rather than just focusing on the actor, and so they ought to ascribe more causality to the situation rather than simply seeing the actor's dispositions as the major cause.

To test this hypothesis, Storms again set up a situation in which two strangers (the actors) meet to get acquainted. Sitting at the other end of the table from them were two observers watching their conversation, each assigned to watch a different actor. Both actors were videotaped. Then the interaction was played back on videotape for all four participants. One actor's behavior was shown and the other's was not (the experimenter said one camera had not worked). One actor saw himself, which should have increased his dispositional attributions for his own actions. The other actor saw the same thing that he had seen during the conversation, the other actor, so he should have given the same situational attributions he had given earlier for his own behavior. Similarly, one observer saw a videotape of the actor to whom *his* actor had been responding, and therefore should have been more attuned to the situational forces operating on his actor. The other observer saw a repeat of the same thing he had seen earlier, so he should also respond as he had earlier.

The results of this experiment are shown in Table 5–6. The first column shows that perceptions of the conversation itself, without any videotape replay, yielded the standard actor-observer difference: Observers were more likely to give dispositional attributions (4.80) than the actors were (2.25). The second column shows what happened when eveyone saw a videotape of the interaction, but from exactly the same perspective as the one in which they had viewed the original interaction. Again the standard actor-observer difference emerged: Observers made more dispositional attributions (4.90) than the actors (0.15) did, as expected, because neither had changed perspective. The crucial condition was the one in which the videotaped replay reversed the perspectives. This is shown in the right-hand column of Table 5–6. When the actors saw their own behavior played back, their attributions became much more dispositional (6.80). And when the observers watched a videotape replay of the situation to which their actor had been responding, they generated much more situational attributions for their own actor's behavior (1.60).

This experiment confirms the basic prediction of Jones and Nisbett, that under normal circumstances actors make more situational attributions

TABLE 5–6

Tendency to Give Dispositional Rather than Situational Attributions[a]

Attribution	No Videotape	Videotape— Same Orientation	Videotape— New Orientation
Actors' attributions for own behavior	2.25	0.15	6.80
Observers' attributions for actor's behavior	4.80	4.90	1.60

[a] The higher the number, the more dispositional relative to situational attributions.
Source: Adapted from Storms (1973), p. 169.

and observers make more dispositional attributions. But it also suggests that this difference occurs because of different perceptual orientations or points of view. That is, they are receiving different current information from their respective perceptual fields. When this perceptual orientation is reversed, so are the causal attributions.

Regan and Totten (1975) added another wrinkle to this same idea. They found that if the observer adopted a more empathic attitude and tried to think or see things the way the actor did, the observer would see the world the same way the actor does. That is, when the observers had the normal observer set, they were inclined to give more dispositional than situational attributions. However, under instructions to empathize with the actor, this reversed slightly. The surrounding situation became more prominent, presumably just as it would have been for the actor herself. Similarly, observers who merely anticipate engaging in the same actions start giving actorlike attributions—that is, they start to use the situation to explain the actor's behavior, just as the actor does (Wolfson & Salancik, 1977). Presumably they are empathizing and identifying with the actor and are already starting to see things from the other perspective.

These studies give good evidence that the actor-observer effect can be produced merely by the different points of view actors and observers have. Does this invalidate the differential-information hypothesis? Probably not. It is more likely that each is most important under different conditions. In general, when historical factors or internal states are crucial determinants of behavior, actors will have better information and will probably be more accurate attributors. But when the behavior itself or the external situation is salient, the differential-perspective theory will account better for differences between actors' and observers' attributions (Monson & Snyder, 1977).

Underusing Consensus Information

One safeguard against the fundamental attributional error ought to be consensus information. With high consensus, we should make a situational attribution. If we know that almost everyone responds the same way to a given entity in a given context, a dispositional attribution ought to be quite unlikely. For example, if we know that almost everyone thinks calculus is difficult, we should not attribute Kenneth's trouble with calculus to low ability or effort. We should attribute it to a difficult situation.

But people tend to underuse consensus information. Kelley's covariation model assumes that consensus, distinctiveness, and consistency information will all be used about equally. None of these three is regarded as inherently more informative than any other. Yet experiments comparing them have found that people do not use consensus information as much. For example, in trying to explain why Mary laughed at the comedian, it makes little difference to most observers whether other people laughed at him or not. Instead, they respond mainly in terms of Mary's own past history—whether she always laughs at this comedian or not, and whether she laughs at all comedians or not. Consistency and distinctiveness information get used, but people tend not to pay much attention to consensus information (McArthur, 1972; Nisbett & Borgida,

1975; Ruble & Feldman, 1976; Wells & Harvey, 1977).

When are people most likely to ignore information about others in forming causal attributions? That is, when are they most likely to ignore consensus information? When people have direct sensory experience with the object in question, they seem more likely to trust their own experience than reports of how others feel. Feldman and co-workers (1976) showed subjects videotapes of a person choosing their favorite of several pictured items. Immediately after this choice, four other people visible within camera range were asked whether or not they liked that object best too. They all responded positively that they did (high consensus) or negatively (low consensus). Then the subjects were asked to explain the original person's choice.

From Kelley's model, high consensus should lead to an attribution to the stimulus object: If everyone likes Apple computers, they must be excellent computers. Low consensus should lead to a person attribution: If only one person likes anchovy pizzas, it must be a special quirk. So Feldman et al. also varied whether the subjects were also shown the same pictures of the objects as shown to the actor, or not. The results showed that consensus information had little effect when the subjects had direct information about the object in question.

People also tend to ignore new consensus information when they already have plenty of experience about how others feel and behave. They may depend on their own sense of others' feelings, rather than use some new information about social consensus. Higgins and his colleagues (1982) showed children videotapes of other children choosing among pictures of animals, cars, cartoon characters, and colors. This provided consensus information about others' choices. But this consensus information was much less influential in children's attributions when it came from their own agemates than when it came from children of other ages. Presumably the reason is that the children had a pretty good sense already of how their own agemates would react to these objects, so they tended to ignore the skimpy consensus information given in the videotape. But they were less likely to have a good sense of how children of other ages would react, so they used the videotape to help them with that.

Finally, in some situations everyone is likely to do the same thing, because idiosyncratic personal values are not very relevant. Almost everyone would prefer a new Mercedes-Benz 450SL to a 10-year-old Ford Pinto. But in other situations, idiosyncratic values are more important. Whether you would prefer to go to an all-Beethoven orchestra concert or to a boxing match probably will depend more on your own taste than it will on the fame of the conductor or the expertise of the boxers. And not surprisingly, consensus information proves to have less effect when choices are made so strongly on the basis of personal taste.

In a study by Gilovich and colleagues (1983), students ignored consensus information on the question of whether they would prefer to watch gymnastics or a track and field meet because they assumed such choices are quite personal and idiosyncratic. They took consensus more seriously on a choice between buying stock in IBM or Exxon, since the objective characteristics of which stock was the better investment presumably would determine most people's decisions.

Are people being "irrational" in ignoring consensus information in these situations? It does seem they are throwing away good information when they ignore consensus just because they too happen to have seen a picture of the object in question, as in the Feldman et al. (1976) study. Perhaps the salience of the object placed the other judges in the background. But it would have been informative to know how everyone else looking at the object felt about it.

It would seem irrational if we disregarded the reports of all our friends who have seen a particular movie and instead decided about it on the basis of a short preview. On the other hand, it seems quite reasonable that 4-year-olds would have a pretty good sense of what 4-year-olds would like and would therefore disregard a videotape of a few of them. And it would seem reasonable to disregard consensus on matters of personal taste. So, as we suggested earlier, the Kelley covariation model is a good starting point for determining whether people are arriving at reasonable attributions or not. But, as Kelley (1967) himself originally expected, there are important cognitive biases in addition to the rational processes described in the pure covariation model.

MOTIVATIONAL BIASES

A second general class of biases arises from people's efforts to satisfy their own needs and motives. The cognitive biases we have just discussed were analyzed as if people had only one kind of need—the need to have a coherent, clear understanding of their environments. This is a characteristic operating assumption of the cognitive viewpoint, as we indicated in Chapter 1. But in reality people have many other needs—for love, revenge, self-esteem, prestige, material goods, and so on. Quite a lot would be left out of our account if these factors were ignored. And they prove to play a substantial role in biasing causal attributions. Most of the motivational biases that have been researched fall into two categories: self-serving biases, that enhance one's own self-esteem, and biases toward internal control, that enhance our sense that people can control their own lives.

Self-Serving Biases

Perhaps the most common motivational bias in the attribution process is the **self-serving bias.** This term describes attributions that glorify the ego or defend self-esteem. Perhaps the simplest example is that we tend to attribute our successes to internal causes such as our own ability, hard work, or general goodness. We tend to blame our failures on external factors like bad luck, an oppressive political structure, a nagging wife or sexist husband, bad weather, and so on. For example, in one study college students attributed A and B grades in the examinations in their course to internal factors such as ability and effort, whereas they attributed C, D, and F grades to external factors such as test difficulty and bad luck (Bernstein et al., 1979).

In numerous experimental studies, subjects have been given a success or a failure experience and then asked to explain the outcome. Others have had subjects try to teach a student something while

manipulating the "learner's" success or failure. Either way, most subjects attribute their successes to internal causes and their failures to external ones (see Bradley, 1978; and Zuckerman, 1979, for careful reviews). In a more applied setting, Riess and Taylor (1984) tested over two hundred competitors in slalom and giant-slalom races at American skiing resorts. They found that the skiers attributed their wins to internal factors, such as ability and effort, significantly more than they did their losses.

The same self-serving bias emerges from an analysis of players' and coaches' postgame explanations for the outcomes of World Series and college and professional football games, as coded from their statements in newspaper articles (Lau & Russell, 1980). Internal attributions (as opposed to external) were made by 80 percent of the winners and 53 percent of the losers. The winning manager of one World Series game made an internal attribution, saying that his star player "had done it all." A losing player explained the same outcome externally: "I think we've hit the ball all right. But I think we're unlucky." Even the home town sportswriters have some tendency to provide these rationalizations for their team's performance. As shown in Figure 5–3, they too tend to provide more internal explanations for their home team's wins than they do for their losses.

These self-serving attributional biases have proven to be extremely common in the interactions of married couples, especially those displaying a lot of marital conflict. In a typical study we mentioned earlier, Holtzworth-Munroe and Jacobson (1985) compared "distressed" couples with those who were well adjusted. Each member of a couple first described positive and negative events in their relationships, then were asked the reasons why they occurred. The attributions tended to fit our definition of self-serving biases. Distressed spouses tended more than well-adjusted couples to discredit their partners' positive behavior by attributing it

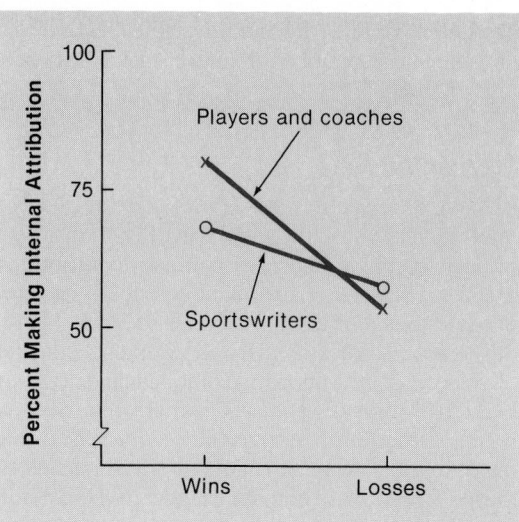

FIGURE 5–3   Self-serving attributions for wins and losses in professional sports. The entry is the percent making an internal, as opposed to external, attribution for their major league baseball or football team's wins and losses. Sportswriters' attributions were for home team's performance. (Adapted from Lau & Russell, 1980, p. 33.)

to outside circumstances, or by saying it had occurred unintentionally or involuntarily. For example, they would tell their therapist that the spouse had done something nice only because the therapist had "told him to." On the other hand, they attributed their spouse's negative behaviors to global, stable personality traits, and intentional and voluntary actions. The spouse never picks up his clothes because he is a permanent and total slob, and stays out too late at night because he is mean and wants to make his wife miserable. Not surprisingly, these authors conclude that such biased attributions simply perpetuate marital conflict in these couples and sabotage whatever efforts either party might make at improving the situation.

Self-handicapping

A related but more desperate strategy for dealing with failure has been called **self-handicapping** (Berglas & Jones, 1978; Jones & Berglas, 1978). People sometimes engage in actions that produce insurmountable obstacles to success so that later, when they experience the resulting inevitable failure, they can attribute it to the obstacle, not to their own lack of ability. The student who stays up all night before the calculus exam can attribute her low grade to fatigue, not to her complete lack of ability to comprehend math; the golfer who rarely practices can attribute his afternoon in the woods and sandtraps to lack of practice, not lack of ability; the alcoholic can attribute the loss of his job to his drinking, not to poor performance. In Kelley's language used earlier, the ability attribution is discounted because another plausible cause is present: the handicap.

In an early experiment testing for this self-handicapping phenomenon, Berglas and Jones (1978) gave male students either soluble or insoluble problems, and then either success feedback (they had solved 16 of 20 problems) or no feedback about their performance. Then the students were told to expect another set of similar problems. The actual solutions to the problems were sufficiently ambiguous that the false feedback on success or failure was quite plausible. Still, the insoluble problems were recognized as difficult: The students had much less confidence in their ability to solve them than did those given soluble problems, and were more likely to attribute their success to luck.

The students given insoluble problems and success feedback were expected to engage in self-handicapping, because they knew success was very unlikely to come their way again. So the experimenters offered the students a choice between two drugs, one that supposedly would enhance their performance, another which would disrupt it. As Figure 5–4 shows, half of the students given insoluble problems and success feedback picked the disruptive drug, while in the other groups fewer than 20 percent chose it. Presumably the students who had experienced success, but were guaranteed failure in the future, wanted a handicap to which they could attribute that expected failure, to preserve their positive feelings about their previous success (even though those feelings were really undeserved). The authors suggest that experiences of success without a real sense of internal control could promote such strategies as substance abuse that protect one's self-image.

People also protect their images of their own competence by *claiming* to have handicaps that prevent success, even when those handicaps do

FIGURE 5-4 Self-handicapping: Choosing a disruptive drug after success feedback. Entry is percent choosing the supposedly disruptive drug rather than the supposedly facilitative drug. (Adapted from Berglas & Jones, 1978, p. 414.)

not necessarily exist. Snyder and others have shown that in evaluative situations threatening failure, people are particularly likely to claim such symptoms as test anxiety, social anxiety, shyness, depression, or a history of traumatic incidents (DeGree & Snyder, 1985; Snyder et al., 1985). Reporting such symptoms also can protect people from having to make ability attributions for their own failures: The cool response you get from that beautiful girl that just moved onto your dorm floor is just because you are shy, not because you are ugly. As you might expect, when people claim such excuses, it does tend to reduce their negative affect about failure, at least as long as no one else knows the real truth about the situation (Mehlman & Snyder, 1985).

There are two versions of the self-handicapping strategy, then: *behavioral* self-handicapping, in which people actively construct genuine handicaps, such as fatigue, alcohol, drugs, lack of punctuality, inattention, etc., and *self-reported* handicaps, in which people simply claim to be ill, anxious, shy, or the victim of traumatic incidents, when such states might excuse poor performance (Leary & Shepperd, 1986; Arkin & Baumgardner, 1985). In both cases, as with self-serving attributional biases in general, the key motive is the self-protective or

ego-defensive one of avoiding a stable, uncontrollable, internal attribution for failure, such as inherent lack of ability.

Egocentric Bias

Another version of the self-serving bias is that people consistently exaggerate their own contribution to shared activities. This might be called the **egocentric bias.** For example, Ross and Sicoly (1979) did several studies of married couples' estimates of relative contributions to joint activities, college basketball players' estimates of their own roles in recent games, and recent college graduates' estimates of their own contribution to their bachelors' theses. In each case, people exaggerated their own contributions. Sande, Ellard, and Ross (1986) repeated this finding in an experiment in which students were assigned to be supervisor, or worker, or observer in a personnel selection task. Students tended to rate themselves as having more responsibility than the other group members for the group's decisions, no matter which role they were in.

Thompson and Kelley (1981) found the same thing: Each member of a couple consistently claimed he or she took more than half the responsibility for such joint activities as carrying the conversation when the two of them were alone, waiting for the other person, resolving conflicts, or being sensitive to the other's needs. It should be noted that this overestimate of one's own role was not limited to socially desirable activities. Each member of the couples also overestimated his or her role in causing arguments. In these cases, people seem simply to exaggerate their own importance in activities shared with others.

False Consensus

People also tend to imagine that everyone responds the way they do. They tend to see their own behavior as typical. This tendency to exaggerate how common one's own opinions or behavior are is called the **false consensus** effect. In an early demonstration of this effect, students were asked if they would walk around their college campus for 30 minutes wearing a large sandwich board with the message "Eat at Joe's." Some students agreed, others refused. But both groups estimated that about two-thirds of the other students on the campus would make the same choice they did. Both groups clearly could not be right (Ross, Greene, & House, 1977).

This false consensus effect has been shown to occur in a number of different situations (Sherman, Chassin, Presson, & Agostinelli, 1984; Nisbett & Kunda, 1985). For example, smokers in junior high and high school are likely to estimate much higher levels of smoking, both among youths in school and in the general population, than are nonsmokers (Sherman et al., 1983). It begins early: Even school-age children demonstrate the effect (Wetzel & Walton, 1985). It can be shown to occur in the adult population on political issues. For example, Fields and Schuman (1976) report on surveys done in the Detroit area that asked people for their own opinions and for their perceptions of the opinions of "most people in the Detroit area." They were asked such questions as the proper U.S. response to a Russian attack on Western Europe, or to a Communist revolution in Latin America: Should the U.S.A. "send troops" or "not interfere"? Over 75 percent of those taking each position themselves thought most other Detroiters agreed with them. Even when their own position was in fact held by only a minority—such as "attack Russia immediately" (only 25 percent agreed with that)—people thought there was a strong consensus on their side.

Motivational Interpretations

Self-serving biases have been interpreted in several ways. Perhaps the simplest is the motivational interpretation. Such self-serving attributions make people feel better and give them more self-esteem. We feel better about ourselves if we think we are responsible for our successes and blameless in our failures. Several kinds of evidence indicate that esteem maintenance is indeed an important factor.

When people have success experiences, internal attributions give them a more positive feeling both in terms of a more positive mood and higher self-esteem than do external attributions such as task ease or chance. So it is to the subject's advantage, in terms of self-esteem, to claim the credit for suc-

cess internally rather than sharing it (McFarland & Ross, 1982).

Self-serving biases are even stronger on tasks with heightened ego involvement. As a task becomes more personally important, people are more motivated to bias their attributions to protect bruised egos (Miller, 1975). Furthermore, self-serving biases are stronger for actors than for observers, presumably because the emotional stakes are greater for the actor (Snyder, Stephan, & Rosenfield, 1976). As would be expected, therefore, observers instructed to empathize with the actor also show the self-serving bias. Gould and Sigall (1977), for example, asked subjects to empathize with the target person: "While you are watching him, picture to yourself how he feels. . . . try to forget yourself." Then they learned the target person had succeeded or failed at a task. With empathy, subjects attributed the target person's success to internal factors and his failure to external factors.

All these findings indicate that self-serving biases are enhanced as the emotional stakes of the task outcome increase, that is, as success or failure becomes more important to the individual. So there is substantial evidence that the needs to bolster self-esteem, and to protect oneself from losses in self-esteem, are at least partially responsible for self-serving biases in attribution.

Similarly, the most likely explanation for the false consensus effect is motivational: People who feel threatened, because they are actually in the minority or are deviant, or have been told their belief is incorrect, are the most likely to exaggerate support for their position, presumably as a way of propping up their self-confidence. For example, children in two studies who were in the minority showed a greater false consensus effect than did those who were in the majority. Campers who liked the least popular camp activities showed more exaggeration of support for their preferences than did campers who liked the most popular activities. In like vein, that minority of junior high school students who smoked showed a greater false consensus effect than did the majority of nonsmokers (Wetzel & Walton, 1985; Sherman et al., 1983). Similarly, students who thought they would be personally harmed by a new tuition surcharge plan, and who were therefore personally threatened by it, estimated greater support for their position than did students who felt they would not be affected (Crano, 1983). And in another set of studies, students who had just been told their answers were incorrect on an experimental task tended to exaggerate how many other students would have made the same answer (Sherman, Presson, & Chassin, 1984). In all these cases, then, the false consensus effect—people exaggerating how many others share their own preference—tends to increase when people are personally threatened or feel insecure about their preferences.

Cognitive Interpretations

Some authors (Miller & M. Ross, 1975; Nisbett & L. Ross, 1980) suggest there might be cognitive instead of motivational reasons for the self-serving bias. For instance, perhaps subjects in experiments who experience failure and blame it externally have been much more used to success than to failure experiences (high school and college students receive few Fs) and therefore failure comes as a surprise to them. Experiences consistent with past experience should lead to an internal attribution: If I always perform this way, then my latest performance must be due to something about me; therefore my success must be internally caused. On the other hand, if my performance departs from what I expect from past experience, it must be due to this new situation; therefore my failure must be situationally caused. In Kelley's terms, a success would be high consistency information and would provoke an internal attribution. Failure, being low consistency information, would provoke an external attribution. People might show a pattern of attributions that would appear to be self-serving, but for cognitive reasons, without ego enhancement being a factor at all.

One problem with this argument is that most people do not have universally successful experiences. Their judgment of their success is normally determined by some subjective level of aspiration, not by some absolute standard. For example, most college students do not regard getting a C or D as a success experience, even though it is a passing grade. Some even feel disappointed by a B. Most people have had many experiences they regard

as failures, and it is doubtful that their past history leads them to expect success most of the time.

But the question is an empirical one: Do self-serving biases in fact disappear with such expectancies for success or failure held constant, as this cognitive interpretation would suggest? An experiment by Ross and Sicoly (1979) tested that in a clever way. First they put subjects through a task that supposedly measured their "social perceptiveness." The subjects were led to believe they had either succeeded or failed at the task. Since this was a novel task, the experience determined their expectancies for further success or failure. A critical variation was therefore introduced at this point: The subject was told that the outcome was more internally caused, or more externally caused, than the subject had claimed.

No matter which it was, this new information was equally unexpected, since it departed by the same amount from the subject's judgment as already expressed. So expectancy was held constant. Finally, the subject was asked how accurate this new feedback was. Ego-enhancing feedback (internal attributions for successes, and external for failures) was judged to be considerably more accurate than ego-deflating feedback. Self-serving biases, therefore, are present even when expectancies are held constant.

Impression Management

Yet a third possibility is that self-serving biases may simply serve a self-presentation or impression-management function. That is, we may not really misperceive the causes of our outcomes at all. But when asked, we try to persuade other people we are responsible for our successes and blameless in our failures, because then they will have a higher opinion for us.

Bradley (1978) has argued that many of the studies showing self-serving biases can be reinterpreted in this vein. In partial support of this view, Orvis (1977) found that people in intimate relationships argued publicly for more self-serving explanations of their conflicts than they thought were probably true. In discussions with their partner, they would frequently blame the partner for their conflicts more than they privately thought was justified.

But this tendency to be especially self-serving in public pronouncements does not explain away all instances of self-serving biases in attributions. People really believe their own self-serving propaganda. A number of studies have shown that people exhibit self-serving biases even under very private conditions, when it is unlikely they are trying to impress other people. For example, Greenberg et al. (1982) and Schlenker et al. (1983) found self-serving biases even when subjects thought the experimenter did not know how they performed. Riess et al. (1981) found them whether or not subjects were hooked into the "bogus pipeline" (see Box 2–3, p. 43), an apparatus that supposedly would detect any lies.

In general, self-serving biases are not merely "fronts" for impression management, though they probably serve that function on occasion. There seems to be quite a strong tendency for attributions to be biased by self-esteem needs, especially in the case of taking credit for good events and avoiding blame for bad ones. But the confirmation or disconfirmation of expectancies is also an important factor in our attributions for success or failure. When something surprising happens, we need a new explanation. At this point, the motivational interpretation is probably most often accurate. But all three interpretations probably have some validity.

THE ILLUSION OF CONTROL

We have seen how people tend to distort the social world perceptually into a more orderly, organized, predictable, and sensible thing than it really is. They do it in many ingenious ways, using first impressions, schemas, scripts, attributional biases, and a wide variety of other cognitive mechanisms. But people do not only perceive the world as more orderly than it really is. They distort it in more *controllable* directions as well. They systematically overestimate their own control over events, and underestimate the role of chance or uncontrollable factors.

Langer (1975) has called this the **illusion of control.** Calling it an illusion may be a little strong; it is more like a systematic bias of modest magnitude than a total lack of contact with reality. But such a bias has been demonstrated in some interesting ways.

The typical experiment has led subjects to exaggerate their control over chance outcomes. For example, Wortman (1975) put two different marbles in a can and told subjects that each marble stood for a different prize. Some subjects were told which marble stood for the prize they wanted, and some were not. Then subjects either chose a marble or

were given one, without being allowed to see which marble was which. There was no conceivable way they could actually control the outcome. Nevertheless, when they knew in advance which marble stood for the prize they wanted and were allowed to choose a marble, they thought they were more responsible for the outcome than when they were just given a marble. They had the illusion of control.

A Just World

The illusion of control implies that people have more control over their fates than they in fact do. One consequence of this illusion is the tendency to blame the victim. A person who is involved in a traffic accident must have been driving carelessly. Victims of theft are perceived as having brought it on themselves by not taking adequate security precautions (Tyler & Devinitz, 1981). A woman who is raped must have been acting in a provocative manner and brought it on herself. Even the victims blame themselves. For example, many rape victims blame themselves for being raped; they see themselves as having behaved in the wrong way, such as hitchhiking or leaving their apartment window unlocked (Janoff-Bulman, 1979). Other people also tend to blame the victims of attacks. Women's characters seem particularly to be blamed for such attacks as robbery or rape: They are too passive, or careless, or trusting (Howard, 1984). Minorities who are discriminated against are often seen as being too pushy, unmotivated, or passive and are believed to alienate people with their demands; they therefore are seen as deserving their fates. Earthquake, tornado, hurricane, and flood victims are believed to have shown insufficient preparedness.

There are many accounts of the guilt experienced by survivors of disasters and accidents, or by bereaved family members. They frequently dwell on the period before the incident, thinking of some way they could have averted the tragedy. They desperately imagine ways they could have controlled what is usually uncontrollable (Wortman, 1976). In short, people are presumed to control their environments and are seen as getting what they deserve and deserving what they get.

To explain such observations, Lerner (1965) has offered the notion that we believe in a **just world:**

Good people get good outcomes, and bad things happen to bad people. The key idea is that observers attribute chance events to the victims' moral dispositions. That is, instead of making the seemingly obvious attribution to luck, the fates, or some other aspect of the situation, people make an attribution to the victim's moral character. Thus, I blame you for being a lousy driver because someone ran a red light and hit you at an intersection on the way to campus. To test this notion, Lerner ran several laboratory experiments in which victims were picked at random to be given electric shock. Even so, the subjects tended to denigrate them, as if the victims were morally responsible for their chance misfortunes.

Lerner interprets these indications of a belief in a just world as reflecting a need to believe we can control events, much like the illusion of control. To protect this sense of control, we blame people for the bad things that happen to them. If people in general are responsible for any disaster that befalls them, presumably we ourselves can avoid personal disaster by acting properly. One unfortunate consequence of the tendency to see the world as

There is increasing controversy about the homeless. Much of it revolves around disagreements about the causes of their fate: laziness, lack of jobs, mental illness, as well as others.

a just place, as Lerner (1980), Ryan (1971), and others have pointed out, is that it provides a justification for the oppression of society's victims. If people themselves are responsible for the fact that they are sick, poor, or disabled, there is no need for the rest of us to help them.

Control: an Adaptive Illusion?

What happens when this sense of control is threatened? Suppose a woman student is followed by a strange man one night on the way home back to her dormitory from the library. She has always felt safe in this well-lit part of the campus, but suddenly she feels alone and very vulnerable. He finally comes close to her and grabs her arm and tries to pull her off the path. She breaks away and runs to the dormitory, panic-stricken. She arrives there safely. But after this episode, she no longer feels safe walking at night alone on that path. She has lost her sense of control; something bad can happen to her at any moment, no matter what she does. How do people who have lost the illusion of control respond?

Reactions vary all the way from seeking information (Swann & Stephenson, 1981), to pain, increased reactivity to stress, and declines in performance (Glass & Singer, 1972), anger or hostility (Brehm & Brehm, 1981), or hopelessness and apathy (Abramson et al., 1978). But a major response is the attempt to restore control. Even when people get cancer, a disease that is among the most difficult to control and whose causes are very poorly understood, they try to regain a sense of mastery in a variety of ways. Taylor (1983, p. 1164) reports these efforts to restore control among women afflicted with breast cancer:

> [Where the cancer came from] was an important question to me at first. The doctor's answer was that it was a multifaceted illness. I looked over the known causes of cancer, like viruses, radiation, genetic mutation, environmental carcinogens, and the one I focused on very strongly was diet. I know now why I focused on it. It was the only one that was simple enough for me to understand and change. You eat something that's bad for you, you get sick.

Another woman said:

> I felt that I had lost control of my body somehow, and the way for me to get back some control was to find out as much as I could. It really became almost an obsession.

And one spouse described his wife:

> She got books, she got pamphlets, she studied, she talked to cancer patients, she found out everything that was happening to her, and she fought it. She went to war with it. She calls it taking in her covered wagons and surrounding it.

Indeed, a number of psychologists feel that a strong sense of control over oneself and one's life is extremely adaptive—even if it is based in part on illusion: "Far from impeding adjustment, illusion may be essential for adequate coping" (Taylor, 1983, p. 29).

For example, Bulman and Wortman (1977) interviewed twenty-nine paraplegics in a rehabilitation institute who had been disabled in accidents ranging from being shot to being tackled in a football game. They were each rated by a nurse and a social worker on how well they were coping with the accident, in terms of accepting the reality of the accident and attempting to deal positively with the paralysis. The more they blamed another person and the less they blamed themselves for the accident, the worse they coped. The authors suggest that "the ability to perceive an orderly relationship between one's behaviors and one's outcomes is important for effective coping" (p. 362).

Learned Helplessness

A similar phenomenon is what Seligman (1975) has called **learned helplessness.** When people feel a lack of control over the environment, hopelessness results and they begin to lose motivation and performance deteriorates. Seligman contends it can lead to depression and even to death.

The learned helplessness model of depression led to a great deal of research. It soon turned out, however, that depression was more closely associated with negative internal attributions than it was to uncontrollable external events. Depressed people had a tendency to blame themselves for their misfortunes. This led to a revised model of learned helplessness based more centrally on attributions.

The basic idea is that attributing negative events

to internal, stable, and global factors—that is, to large, internal, uncontrollable factors—leads to depression (Abramson, Seligman, & Teasdale, 1978). I got a C rather than an A on that math midterm because I am terrible at math and always will be. The young man I went out with last week never called me back because I am just not attractive to men and never will be. Once we being making such attributions, we go on to avoid exerting control in situations where we might in fact be effective. I decide not to go to the post-midterm review session run by the math TA because I think my situation is hopeless. In reality, I might learn from my mistakes and do better the next time. When my neighbor in French class asks me out for coffee, I say I'm busy because I'm convinced he won't like me when he gets to know me. In reality, he might be pretty interested and could be quite receptive.

An example of how such internal, stable, global attributions for negative events produce depressive affect comes from a study by Metalsky et al. (1982). They found students who were biased initially toward making such attributions showed bigger jumps in depressive affect after getting a poor grade on a midterm than did students who normally made external or less global attributions. In another example, Peterson et al. (1981) found that blaming one's enduring *character* rather than one's own *behavior* (that is, making more global attributions) was associated with more depressive symptoms in female college freshmen.

Such findings have proven quite general. Sweeney and associates (1986) conducted a meta-analysis of 104 studies on learned helplessness to determine how general the support for this theory is. They found indeed that depression is systematically associated with internal, stable, and global attributions for failure, while such attributions for success are associated with nondepressed states. These links have been found among children, as well. Nolen-Hoeksma and colleagues (1986) found that in grade-school-aged children, such attributions were significantly associated both with depression and with poor achievement. It is likely, therefore, that the pattern begins early.

However, such associations produce the same ambiguities in interpretation that most correlational studies pose. In fact, the direction of causality may actually be the opposite from what is claimed by the learned helplessness theory. Such attributions may be symptoms rather than causes of such serious clinical depressions. When you feel depressed (for whatever reason, even perhaps just because you are hungry), you may begin to interpret everything in a gloomy way: Your failures may seem permanent and nothing can be done about them, and your successes, flukes that will never be repeated. There is some evidence for this reverse-causality interpretation (Cochran & Hammen, 1985). Nevertheless, the learned helplessness model is a provocative one, and it has generated much intriguing research.

So there are two different perspectives on the adaptability of this sense of internal control. One is that a belief in personal control over one's outcomes is adaptive, as indicated in Taylor et al.'s work on cancer patients. The other, the learned helplessness perspective, is that self-blame for negative events that could not be controlled is maladaptive—it just leads to depression and poor performance. One possible reconciliation is that blaming one's *character* is maladaptive—this is the global, stable, internal attribution emphasized in the learned helplessness model. However, blaming one's bad *behavior* may be adaptive, because that can be controlled in the future (Janoff-Bulman, 1979). There is certainly evidence that characterological self-blame is associated with poor coping with bad life events. In one study, women who blamed their unwanted pregnancies on their characters (I'm not strong enough, I'm not responsible enough) did cope worse with having an abortion (Major et al., 1985).

However, it is premature to conclude that this simple resolution explains all the data. Sometimes it is true that behavioral self-blame is associated with better coping. In one study, when mothers of children with prenatal medical problems blamed their own behavior for the problems, this attitude tended to be related to their belief that they could prevent similar occurrences in the future (Tennen et al., 1986). On the other hand, sometimes both kinds of self-blame are associated with poorer coping, as in a recent study of rape victims (Meyer & Taylor, 1986). More research is required to determine the conditions under which a sense of internal control over bad outcomes is adaptive as opposed to leading to depression and other maladaptive responses.

Valuing Internal Control

A number of phenomena described in this chapter have been seen to reveal a pervasive bias toward perceiving internal or dispositional control of behavior. The fundamental attribution error overestimates internal control. Work on the illusion of control, the just world, and learned helplessness all documents how people prefer to believe in internal control, and in fact are often disrupted psychologically when they are forced to face their own helplessness and the randomness of much that affects their lives. Why does this pervasive sense of internal control exist?

One possibility has been considered in the preceding discussions. Perhaps, at a simple perceptual level, actors and observers alike tend to see an act as so thoroughly connected to the actor (in what Heider called a "unit relation") that they cannot easily attribute it to some external cause (Jones, 1979).

Another possibility is that all human beings share a strong emotional commitment to the feeling of free will, and to feeling that they are free to act any way they choose. The illusion of choice or of control may be crucial to our motivational systems and feelings of well-being, for some adaptive reasons deriving from natural selection (Brehm, 1966; Monson & Snyder, 1977). Perhaps it is only the belief in internal control that keeps us actively trying to manipulate our environment, which in turn is crucial for survival.

There seems little question about the fact that we value a strong sense of internal control. In one study, Jellison and Green (1981) had students rate their relative liking for four stimulus persons who differed in their beliefs about whether human behavior is caused by internal or external factors. The stimulus persons who most believed in internal control were liked by far the most. In a second study, the same authors found that students rated themselves as believing more in internal control than does the average undergraduate, suggesting that all the best people (that is, "me") believe in internal control. In yet a third study, students were asked either to try to create a positive impression or to try to create a negative impression, and then filled out the same questionnaire. Those trying to make a positive impression indicated greater belief

Henry Ford had a remarkable success. Looking back on his career, how would you decide what caused such great success?

Ford Motor Company

in internal control of human behavior. When people fail, they are liked better if they express an internal attribution for the failure (Carlston & Shovar, 1983; Weary, Jordan, & Hill, 1985). In short, there seems to be a general tendency to emphasize internal causative factors, and people who display that tendency most are the most liked and approved of.

Belief in internal control seems therefore to be a strong and persuasive cultural norm.

But a third possibility is that this bias toward internal attribution is a cultural norm particularly characteristic of Americans. Many observers have noted how dedicated Americans are to individualistic values, to the beliefs that individual people can

BOX 5–4

AMERICANS ARE MORE INTERNAL

An interesting recent study tested directly for such cultural differences in internal attributions. Miller (1984) asked Americans and Hindus from India of different ages to explain some common events. She found that American adults were more likely to use internal, dispositional attributions, while Hindu adults were more likely to invoke the external context. For example, an American who was asked to explain her neighbor's cheating on taxes said, "That's just the type of person she is. She's very competitive." Or a colleague who stole someone else's idea and presented it as his own was described by an American as "just a very self-absorbed person. He was interested only in himself." In both cases, dispositions were invoked to explain the behavior. What about someone who was cheated of 1500 rupees by a man who was supposed to do some construction work and didn't, and kept the advance? A Hindu said "The man is unemployed. He is not in a position to give that money [back]." Another, explaining why someone put his name as first author on a paper from his student's thesis, said "She was his student. She would not have the power to . . . publish it by herself" (pp. 967–968). The situation explains behavior, according to these Hindu respondents. Further evidence for the cultural explanation of these findings is that the difference is not present among young children; it only shows up with age, as would be the case if it needed to be learned over time.

	DISPOSITIONS		SITUATION	
	U.S.	India	U.S.	India
Adult	40%	18%	18%	40%
15 years	20	12	30	31
11 years	14	11	20	28
8 years	10	10	24	23

Source: Miller (1984), p. 967

control their own destinies, are responsible for their outcomes, and so on. The Horatio Alger myth is one of our hardiest: Poverty is due to the laziness and stupidity of the poor, while wealth is due to the genius and hard work of the successful. Inkeles (1983), for example, reports that when Americans are asked to explain why one person has succeeded and another failed, despite having the same skill and training, 1 percent invoke fate or God's will. But in six developing countries he found luck or fate was the explanation of about 30 percent. Another example of the same finding is shown in Box 5–4.

This individualism has been traced back to America's Protestant heritage (see, for example, McClelland, 1976; Sears & McConahay, 1973; Sniderman & Brody, 1977). More interdependent cultures emphasize the collective and interpersonal causes of events, and not so much the free acts of individuals (Sampson, 1977). The tradition in the United States, on the other hand, is that individuals stand on their own two feet. Most Americans do not think of themselves as part of a larger social whole, such as an extended family or church or community. For example, in the United States, the decision to marry is supposed to be the free choice of the persons involved and is based on romantic love. In many other cultures, such decisions are made collectively by family or kinship groups because marriages are thought to affect the whole community. Nevertheless, it remains for further research in other cultures to determine how much this emphasis on dispositions, free will and choice, and personal control is limited to our culture, with its strong tradition of Protestant individualism, and how much it is a more general human characteristic.

KEY TERMS IN CHAPTER 5

actor-observer bias	dispositional attribution	illusion of control	naive psychology
attribution	egocentric bias	internal attributions	overjustification
attribution theory	external attributions	just world	self-handicapping
covariation	false consensus	learned helplessness	self-serving bias
discounting principle	fundamental attribution error	misattribution	situational attribution

SUMMARY

1. Attribution theory is concerned with how ordinary people explain social events. The most common causal attributions explain behaviors as internal or external to the person, stable or unstable, and controllable or uncontrollable.

2. Theorists begin from the assumption that people are motivated to explain the events around them. They do so by looking for invariance; that is, which causes are regularly associated with which effects. And they use a discounting principle; that is, to the extent that several causes are plausible, they will spread their explanations among them.

3. Kelley's theory suggests that people base their attributions on three kinds of information: distinctiveness (is this the only situation in which the person does this), consensus (would other people

do the same thing in that situation), and consistency (does the person always do this in this situation).

4. Other people's personality traits and attitudes are normally inferred from their overt behaviors by considering the external forces operating on them at the time. If these forces are strong, attributions are shared between external and internal causes. If these forces are weak, internal attributions are made.

5. Attribution theory can be applied to self-perception as well as to the perception of others. That is, the same principles may account for how we infer the causes for our own acts and how we infer the causes for others' acts.

6. To some extent, we infer our own attitudes from our own behavior, particularly when we are not especially involved in our attitudes and when they have little consequence for our future lives.

7. The internal cues we receive from our own emotional arousal states are more ambiguous and undifferentiated than has commonly been assumed in the past. Consequently, we infer both the nature and degree of our own emotional arousal by an attributional process that relies on evidence about our own behavior, external indications of our arousal states, and environmental conditions.

8. In its purest form, attribution theory describes a logical, rationalistic mechanism for arriving at causal explanations. But several systematic biases have been discovered.

9. In general, people ascribe more causality to internal dispositions than they should and less to external forces. This has been called the fundamental attribution error. It is particularly true for observations of other people's behavior. Self-perceptions may indeed be biased in the opposite direction and overattribute causality to external forces. Together, these form the actor-observer bias, seemingly due mainly to the relative salience of the behavior and of the situation.

10. People are quite heavily influenced by the need to give explanations that support or protect their own self-esteem. This leads to self-serving biases, self-handicapping, egocentric biases, and false consensus.

11. People seem to need the illusion of control over their environments. Their perceptions exaggerate their own level of control, and they become emotionally disturbed when they feel they have no control. They believe in a just world in which people get what they deserve, seemingly based on the assumption that people can control their own outcomes.

SUGGESTED READINGS

FRIEZE, I. H., BAR-TEL, D., & CARROLL, J. S. (Eds.). (1979). *New approaches to social problems.* San Francisco: Jossey-Bass. Applications of attribution theory to a wide variety of social problems.

KELLEY, H. H. (1967). Attribution theory in social psychology. In David Levine (Ed.), *Nebraska symposium on motivation.* Lincoln: University of Nebraska Press. Still the best and most coherent basic statement of attribution theory.

JONES, E. E., KANOUSE, D. E., KELLEY, H. H., NISBETT, R. E., VALINS, S., & Weiner, B. (1972). *Attribution: Perceiving the causes of behavior.* Morristown, NJ:

General Learning Press. An influential early collection of theoretical statements on attribution theory. Includes excellent chapters on the actor-observer effect, self-perception, negativity, and others.

HARVEY, J. H., & WEARY, G. (Eds.). (1985). *Attribution: Basic issues and applications.* Orlando, FL: Academic Press. A good contemporary collection of work on attribution.

WEINER, B. (1986). *An attributional theory of motivation and emotion.* New York: Springer Verlag. A comprehensive account of Weiner's attributional theory, emphasizing achievement and affect.

6 ATTITUDES

What makes someone a Republican or a Democrat, a conservative or a liberal, a Protestant or a Catholic? Why are some people anti-Semitic, others antiblack, and still others not prejudiced at all? Why do people decide that one toothpaste is best or that cigarette smoking is dangerous? What determines whether or not someone will change her mind about toothpastes or cigarettes? How can we convince Republicans to vote for a Democrat? How can we prepare our own supporters to resist the propaganda put out by the other party's candidates? If our friend decides smoking is bad, what will make her actually quit doing it? These questions form the basis for the extensive work on attitude formation and change, which has been a central core of social psychology in the United States for many years.

DEFINING ATTITUDES

Each of the traditional definitions of **attitudes** contains a slightly different conception of what an attitude is or emphasizes a somewhat different aspect of it. G. W. Allport (1935) proposed that "an attitude is a mental and neural state of readiness, organized through experience, exerting a directive or dynamic influence upon the individual's response to all objects and situations with which it is related" (p. 810). Because this definition was much influenced by the learning tradition, it also emphasized how past experience forms attitudes. For the same reason, it viewed an attitude primarily as a set to respond in a particular way, and thus emphasized its behavioral implications.

In contrast, Krech and Crutchfield (1948, p. 152), who were strongly committed to a cognitive perspective, defined an attitude as "an enduring organization of motivational, emotional, perceptual, and cognitive processes with respect to some aspect of the individual's world." Notice that they omit any reference to the origins of the attitude and instead are concerned with current subjective experience. Note also that they emphasize organization; they view the person as a thoughtful and actively structuring organism. And finally, note there is no mention of overt behavior. The cognitive tradition emphasizes the person's subjective experience.

The Three Components

Today, the most common definition combines elements from both approaches. An attitude toward any given object, idea, or person is an enduring orientation with cognitive, affective, and behavioral components. The **cognitive component** consists of all the cognitions the person has about that particular attitude object—the facts, knowledge, and beliefs concerning the object. The **affective** (or **evaluative**) **component** consists of all the person's affects or emotions toward the object, especially evaluations. The **behavioral component** consists of the person's readiness to respond or tendency to act regarding the object.

Consider a student's attitude toward nuclear weapons. The cognitive component might include some information about their size, mode of delivery, the number of warheads on a missile, and some beliefs about which countries probably have them, their destructive potential, and the likelihood of their being used. The affective component would include the person's feelings, which in this case might be dominated by a strong negative evaluation, mixed perhaps with some fear or even dread of nuclear destruction. The behavioral component refers to the student's tendencies to act with respect to nuclear weapons, such as a tendency to sign petitions and march in protest against the deployment of nuclear missiles, to vote against candidates supporting missiles, and so on.

This is the definition of attitudes that most social psychologists share today and the one we will use here. The thing to remember is that any attitude toward a particular attitude object has these three different components or aspects. The components are distinguished for analytic convenience because they follow somewhat different principles. They are not always consistent with each other; indeed, questions about that consistency have led to some of the most interesting research in the area.

Consider another example of an attitude, shown diagrammatically in Figure 6–1. The figure shows our friend's attitude toward smoking cigarettes. The focus of the whole attitude is on the attitude object, in this case smoking cigarettes. Surrounding the object are the various elements perceived as relevant. Some of these are people, such as parents or roommates; others are personal states such as

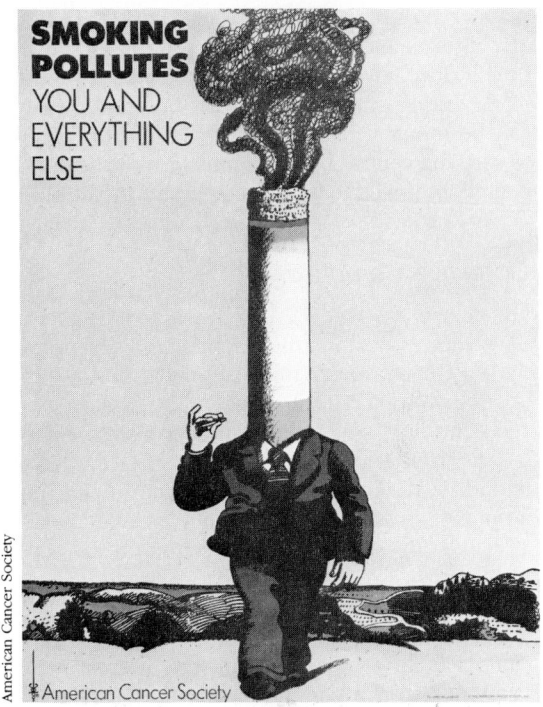

This strongly affective ad should also evoke a number of cognitions in most people.

FIGURE 6–1   One person's attitude toward smoking cigarettes. The core object is related to several other cognitions. The signs refer to the affective component of her overall attitude toward smoking and her affects toward the separate cognitions she associates with smoking. A positive sign (+) refers to a favorable affect and a negative (−) to an unfavorable affect.

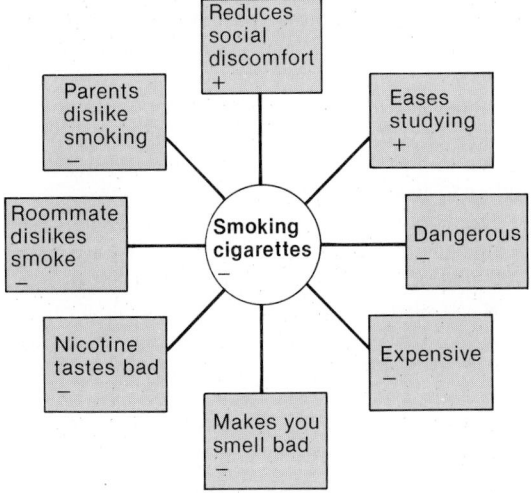

one's own smell; and others are simple attributes of the object itself, such as its price or taste. This whole cluster of cognitions and their link to the main attitude object, then, constitute the cognitive component of an attitude.

Next there is the affective component. The separate cognitive elements themselves have positive or negative feelings connected to them, and the central attitude object does too. In Figure 6–1 positive and negative evaluations of the elements and central object are indicated by plus and minus signs, respectively. The evaluations of the related objects are shown in the boxes. Her negative feelings about smoking come from the dislike her roommate and parents have for smoking, its bad taste and smell, and her feelings that smoking is dangerous and too expensive. To be sure, she likes studying to go easier, and to be relieved of some social discomfort. Still, the affective component of her attitude toward the central object, smoking, combines evaluations of all these separate cognitions. And she plainly has a strong negative evaluation of cigarettes. She dislikes and is afraid of them. This is shown in the diagram by the minus sign in the central circle. The affective component of the attitude, then, can be thought of as consisting of all the affects toward the central object and toward the separate cognitions linked to the attitude object in question.

Cognitive Complexity

One feature of many attitudes is congitive complexity. We have a great many thoughts and beliefs about the object. They may not all be factually correct, but the cognitions are numerous. In Figure 6–1 we have shown only a few of the cognitions an individual could have regarding cigarettes. And a number of other factors are not included in the structure. For example, each cognition can vary in importance (e.g., the fact that cigarettes are expensive is probably less important than the fact that they are linked to lung cancer). The attitude can get quite complex and include a great many cognitions that vary in the nature of their relationship to the core and in their evaluative component. This figure is an oversimplification of many attitudes in real life.

Just think of the Pandora's box opened up by the fact that these cognitions are related to one another and to many others, rather than existing in a vacuum. The thought that cigarettes help studying is meaningful only when an attitude toward studying is considered. And then attitudes toward studying can bring in attitudes toward parents, teachers, a future career, and so on. The full cluster would contain all the person's thoughts in connection with cigarettes.

Evaluative Simplicity

Most attitudes tend to be as evaluatively simple as they are congitively complex. Even though our friend has many cognitions about smoking, her evaluation of it is relatively simple: Smoking alienates her roommate and parents, tastes bad, smells bad, is expensive, runs the risk of lung cancer—even though it would help her study late at night. Almost all the attributes or consequences of smoking are

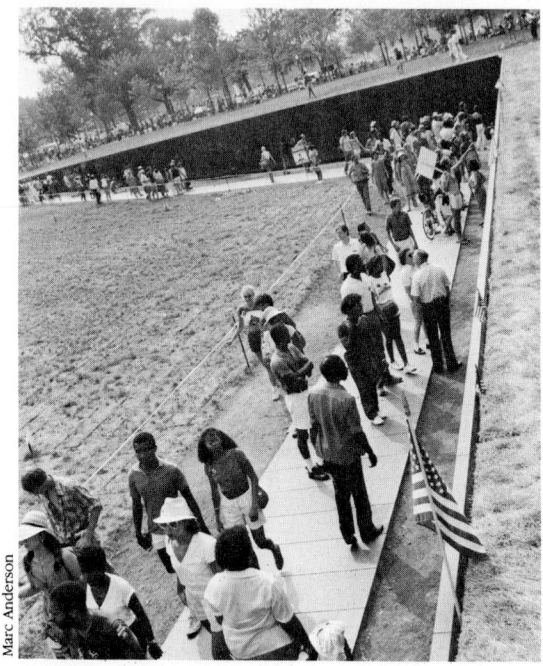

The memorial for Vietnam veterans on the Mall in Washington, D.C. generates many complex thoughts and emotions. What cognitions do these people have, do you think, as they read name after name of the Americans who died in Vietnam?

negative, and so is her overall attitude. This pattern is quite common: A multitude of cognitions may exist in people's minds, but by and large, the evaluative components of their attitudes are much simpler.

There have been many demonstrations of the evaluative simplicity of most attitudes. As noted in Chapter 3, our impressions of other people quickly tend to become evaluatively consistent. No matter how much we know about them, we tend generally either to like them or to dislike them.

Even at the more remote level of attitudes about public affairs, where peole often do not have much information, their attitudes are quite consistent, at least on such important issues as evaluations of the president of our country, race relations, abortion, use of drugs, and so on (Kinder & Sears, 1985). On racial issues, white Americans tend to have highly interrelated attitudes. Whites who tend to support civil rights in general tend also to be most supportive of affirmative action for blacks, busing of schoolchildren for racial integration, and so on (Sears, Hensler, & Speer, 1979).

Cognition vs. Affect

Much research concerns itself with the different implications of the cognitive and affective components of attitudes. As we have seen in earlier chapters, the cognitive versus affective contrast runs through much of social psychology, such as the bases for contextual effects in impression formation or for attributional biases. These are manifestations of fundamental theoretical differences in perspective, between those who view affect as a primitive, spontaneous, immediate response (Zajonc, 1980) and those who view it as controlled by perceptions and cognitions (Lazarus, 1984; Weiner, 1986).

One general difference on which most would probably agree is that the affective component of an attitude is more difficult to change than the cognitive component, everything else being equal. This is perhaps easiest to illustrate if we think of the commonsense distinction between "attitudes"—which include an affective component along with a cognitive component—and beliefs in "facts," which have only a cognitive component.

A scientist believes that it is 252,710 miles to the moon or that human beings have 46 chromosomes. She also has a complex collection of other beliefs about the moon and chromosomes. But under most circumstances, she does not have any emotional feelings toward either—she does not think the moon is good or bad. She does not like or dislike chromosomes. In contrast, she has a collection of "facts" about Ronald Reagan or poison gas, but she also *does* have emotional feelings about these.

As a result, facts and attitudes function differently. Attitudes, once established, are much more resistant to change than beliefs in "facts." The scientist who believes that humans have 46 chromosomes in most cases has no strong commitment to that belief or strong feelings about it one way or the other. Not so many years ago, scientists were convinced that humans had 24 chromosomes. Then somebody discovered that there were 46. Those who originally believed we had 24 probably changed their belief quite readily when they saw the evidence. Certainly

high school and college biology students, who were in no way involved in the controversy, changed their "knowledge" almost instantaneously.

This is different from the way people react when their attitudes are concerned. Attitudes are more complicated in this respect than facts. People do not change their attitudes without putting up a fight and being exposed to a considerable amount of pressure. The presence of the affective component seems to change the dynamics considerably; it makes the attitude-change process much more difficult.

One reason why the affective component is so resistant to change is that the evaluation of an attitude object can persist long after the content that produced it is forgotten, as Anderson and Hubert (1963), among others, have shown. The affective component is more durable and central than the cognitive component.

This leads to a second general difference between the two components. The affective component tends to have more influence over attitudes and behavior than does the cognitive component. We have earlier seen one example of this in the "halo effect." Positive or negative evaluations control impressions of a person regardless of the details of that person's characteristics.

Similarly, the evaluative component of the attitude is the major determinant of behavior. Although the details of users' and police officers' behavior toward drugs is influenced by the knowledge they have, the general direction of their behavior is influenced primarily by their overall evaluation—whether they consider drugs to be positive or negative.

Attitudes and Behavior

The third component of an attitude concerns behavioral tendencies. Suppose we have persuaded our friend that smoking contributes to lung cancer and heart disease, so the cognitive component is in place. She now feels that smoking is bad, so the affective component is in place. But will she stop smoking? That is, will her behavioral component fall into line? Much research in social psychology suggests that actual behavior is often inconsistent with attitudes, and that people seem to be able to

THREE COMPONENTS OF ATTITUDES TOWARD SNAKES

Attitudes toward snakes present a good example of this three-component model of attitudes. The cognitive component consists of beliefs in such factual matters as "snakes are soft and smooth" or "snakes control the rodent population." The affective component consists of the person's feelings toward snakes (e.g., "I feel anxious" or "tense" or "affectionate"). The behavioral component consists of relevant behavioral tendencies, describing past behavior (e.g., "I like to handle snakes") or current behavior (e.g., refusing an experimenter's request to handle a live snake). A recent analysis of items measuring these three components of attitudes toward snakes revealed, as most such analyses do, that they are distinctive but related dimensions (Breckler, 1984). That is, it is sensible to describe these three as separate components of an attitude, but there is a good deal of consistency among them as well. In this study, the correlations among the three components ranged from +.38 to +.70. This consistency will be one of the main themes of the rest of the chapter.

live quite comfortably with the inconsistency. Many smokers do believe smoking is bad for your health, and many do not like the taste of nicotine. But it is hard for them to give up. Their smoking behavior is not controlled by their negative evaluations and cognitions about smoking. So the behavioral component of an attitude is not always consistent with the affective and cognitive components.

The opposite causal link between attitudes and behavior is of interest. Overt behavior can control the evaluative and cognitive components of attitudes. People can behave in a certain way, and their attitudes may fall into line. Perhaps our friend gets pregnant and gives up smoking because her doctor says it would be bad for the unborn baby, her husband is worried about the baby, and her

friends criticize her for jeopardizing the baby's health. For 9 months, she stops smoking. She may gradually become convinced that smoking is bad not just for baby but for Mama, she may learn to dislike the smell and taste of nicotine, and she may learn new facts about the dangers of smoking. By the time her baby is born, she may have a repertoire of antismoking cognitions and negative evaluations of smoking.

So the causal relationships between the cognitive and affective components of an attitude, on the one hand, and overt behavior, on the other, can go in either direction. In the last half of this chapter we will discuss both: ways in which attitudes control behavior, and ways in which behavior controls attitudes.

THEORIES OF ATTITUDES

Now that we have a general view of an attitude, we can consider the theoretical frameworks within which attitudes have been studied. The main theoretical approaches outlined in Chapter 1 have been applied in one form or another to research on attitudes just as with other areas of social psychology. The learning approach sees attitudes as habits, like anything else that is learned; principles that apply to other forms of learning also determine the formation of attitudes. Motivational theories, of which the relevant version is incentive theory, holds that a person adopts the attitude that maximizes his or her gains. Each side of an issue has its costs and benefits, and the individual will adopt the side on which the net gains are greater. Finally, the cognitive consistency approach asserts that people seek harmony in their attitudes, and between attitudes and behavior. It particularly emphasizes acceptance of attitudes that fit into the person's overall cognitive structure. These approaches are not necessarily contradictory or inconsistent. They represent different theoretical orientations and differ primarily in the factors they emphasize when explaining attitudes.

Learning

The learning approach is most closely associated with Carl Hovland and others at Yale University (1953). The basic assumption behind this approach is that attitudes are learned in much the same way as other habits. People acquire information and facts; they also learn the feelings and values associated with these facts. Children learn that a certain animal is a dog, that dogs are friends, that they are good; finally, they learn to like dogs. They learn both the cognitions and affects of an attitude. And they learn them through the same processes and mechanisms that control other kinds of learning.

This means that the basic processes by which learning occurs should apply to the formation of attitudes. The individual can acquire information and feelings by the process of *association*. Associations are formed when stimuli appear at the same time and in the same place. If a history teacher, a parent, or a television reporter shows us a mean-looking military man in a storm-trooper uniform and says the word *Nazi* in a hostile tone, we form an association between negative feelings and the word Nazi. Conversely, we may be exposed to positive things that can become associated with the U.S. Marines: A friend says they are good, or we see a movie in which they are doing something heroic.

Many of the studies described in the chapter on person perception illustrate this association process. For example, Norman Anderson (1965) conducted experiments in which he listed a number of attributes of a person and then asked subjects to state their impression of that person. As you

A portion of the nearly 300,000 participants at a Nazi party convention march before Adolf Hitler in 1936. What is your affective response?

Wide World Photos

will remember from Chapter 3, the subject's final attitude was roughly an average of the listed characteristics (warm, friendly, intelligent, ambitious, courageous, and so on). The subject learned to associate those characteristics with the stimulus person. By doing so, the subject also associated their values with the person. The subject likes the stimulus person with whom the very positive values of "warm" or "friendly" are associated. The subject learned an attitude toward the stimulus person by a process of association, acquiring both a cognitive component (the specific characteristics of the stimulus person) and an affective component (the resulting evaluation of the person).

This process of association leads to attitudes toward things as well as toward people. Individuals learn the characteristics of a house, a country, an idea, a bill pending in Congress, or anything else. An attitude consists of that knowledge plus the associated evaluative component.

Learning can also occur through *reinforcement*. If you take a class in psychology, and get an A in it and enjoy it, the act of taking psychology classes is reinforced and you will be likely to take more in the future. Similarly, if you say that psychology is really interesting and your friends all agree with you and support you, positive attitudes toward psychology are reinforced.

Finally, attitudes can be learned through *imitation*. People imitate others, particularly if those others are strong, important people. One of the most important sources of basic political and social attitudes in early life is the family. Children are likely to imitate their parents' attitudes. In adolescence, they are more likely to imitate peers' attitudes on many matters. Later, many students find that friends, teachers, and books in college confront them with ideas and values different from those they had previously learned. They find they have learned contradictory attitudes and are under great stress to resolve the conflicts.

Association, reinforcement, and imitation are the major mechanisms in the learning of attitudes. As a result, learning theories have dominated the research on the *formation* of attitudes. The learning approach to attitudes is relatively simply: It views people as primarily passive. They are exposed to stimuli, they learn by means of one learning process or another, and this learning determines the person's attitude. The final attitude contains all the associations, values, and other bits of information the individual has accumulated. A person's ultimate evaluation of a person, object, or idea depends on the number and strength of the positive and negative elements learned.

Contemporary research and theory stemming from the learning approach has been turning more to an emphasis on information processing—that is, on how people deal with incoming information. Here, a helpful concept is *automatic processing*. When an individual encounters the attitude object, the person's attitude is activated spontaneously and without any conscious effort on his or her part. This is to be distinguished from "controlled processing," a more reflective process in which the person actively considers his or her attitude (Fazio et al., 1983; Shiffrin & Schneider, 1977). Automatic processing occurs when the person has a very well-learned response and is presented with a strong stimulus—or "prime," in the language used earlier in the social cognition chapter.

As a result, strongly learned evaluative associations can be evoked quickly and automatically; weak associations cannot be. The idea is that when positive evaluations are made salient, through a positively evaluated prime, people more speedily process positive information, whereas when negative evaluations are made salient, through a negatively evaluated prime, then people will more speedily process negative information. Fazio and colleagues (1986) demonstrated this activation of automatic processing in a simple way. First they identified a series of emotionally loaded primes by determining which words (drawn from animals, social groups, names, or activities, among others) the subject most speedily identified as "good" or "bad." Some of the most common good ones were *party*, *music*, *gift*, or *cake*; bad ones included *death*, *hell*, *guns*, or *crime*. Then, in the experiment itself, the subject was presented first with one of these primes, and then a target adjective such as *delightful* or *repulsive*. The question was how quickly the subject could identify whether the target adjective was positive or negative. The experiment tested the subject's speed at pressing the "good" or the "bad" button in response to the target adjective. So, for example, the subject might see a positive prime, such as *cake*, and then the target adjective, *delightful*. How

BOX 6–2

THINGS GO BETTER WITH COKE

(OR MAYBE IT'S PEPSI . . .)

In one study supporting the transfer-of-affect process in attitude change, college students were given peanuts and Pepsi-Cola while they read a series of four persuasive communications on different topics; others read the same communications but were given nothing to eat or drink (Janis et al., 1965). The students who had received food and drink while reading were more positively influenced on all four topics than were those who had not received them, as shown in the table below. The positive associations to the peanuts and Pepsi-Cola apparently transferred to the persuasive communications being read.

| | EXPERIMENTAL CONDITION | |
Topic	With Food and Drink	Without Food or Drink
Cure for cancer	81%	62%
Size of armed forces	67	43
Moon shot	55	30
Three-D movies	67	60

Source: Adapted from Janis et al., 1965, p. 184. Entry is percent of subjects' changing attitudes in advocated direction minus percent changing in opposite direction.

quickly would the subject press the "good" button for *delightful*?

The researchers' basic hypothesis was that automatic processing would be activated when the target word was consistent with the prime *and* the prime was strongly evaluative (such as *death*) rather than weakly evaluative (such as *recession*). And indeed the data showed that reaction times were fastest when both the prime and target word were evaluatively consistent (both positive or both negative) and the prime was strong rather than weak. This idea of automatic processing, then, portrays the person as responding emotionally, quickly, and without reflective thought.

Incentives

In Chapter 1 we described motivational theories as those that view people as responding in terms of the costs and benefits associated with each possible choice, or in terms of the needs that a particular response might satisfy. Basically, the question is, what has the person got to gain or lose with each response?

The version of these motivational theories that is most relevant for the study of attitudes is *incentive theory*. This views attitude formation as a process of weighing the pros and cons of various possible positions and then adopting the best alternative. It describes a more thoughtful and reflective consideration of the alternative than does the learning approach. A student might feel partying is fun, and exciting, and her friends like to do it. These considerations give her a positive attitude. But she knows her parents don't want her just to party while she's in college, and it interferes with her studying, and she wants to go to law school. These considerations give her a negative attitude toward partying. According to incentive theory, the relative strengths of these incentives determine her attitude.

One common version of the incentive theory is the **expectancy-value approach** (Edwards, 1954). People adopt positions that would lead to the most probable good effects, and reject positions that are likely to lead to bad effects or unlikely to lead to good effects. Put more formally, this approach assumes that in adopting attitudes, people try to maximize the subjective utility of the various expected outcomes. The subjective utility of any given position is the product of (1) the *value* of a particular outcome, and (2) the *expectancy* that this position will produce that outcome.

Suppose you are trying to decide whether to go to your friend's party tonight. You would try to think of the various possible outcomes (dance, drink beer, not study for your midterm tomorrow, meet someone interesting), the values of those outcomes (somewhat enjoy the dancing and drinking beer and meeting someone interesting, might be somewhat hungover, and will get a very bad grade on the midterm), and the expectancy of those outcomes (certain to dance and to get a terrible grade, but unlikely to meet anyone new at a small party). Taking both expectancy and value into consideration, it's time to start studying: A certain terrible grade is not balanced by a little fun dancing and drinking beer.

Another important version of the incentive approach to attitudes is **cognitive response theory** (Greenwald, 1968; Petty, Ostrom, & Brock, 1981). This theory assumes that people respond to a communication with some positive or negative thoughts (or "cognitive responses"), and that these thoughts

in turn determine whether or not the people change their attitudes as a result of the communication. Suppose you listen to a televised speech by a senator in which she advocates cutting government medicare payments to the elderly. If you say to yourself, "But what about retired people on small pensions, or people who can't support themselves, like the handicapped, or the poor? Somebody has to support those people, and government programs are about the only way to do it." These negative cognitive responses would mean you are unlikely to be persuaded by the speech.

But if you said to yourself, "That's right! Taxes are too high and those programs are probably just paying for extravagant hospital costs for people who could be paying their own medical bills anyway!" you are likely to come to the speaker's support. The key assumption of the cognitive response viewpoint is that people are active processors of information who generate cognitive responses to messages, rather than being mere passive recipients of whatever messages they happen to be exposed to.

Both versions of the incentive approach are similar to the learning approach in that the attitude is determined more or less by a sum of the positive and negative elements. One difference is that incentive theories ignore the origins of the attitude, and consider only the current balance of incentives. Another difference is that the incentive theories emphasize what people have to gain or lose by taking a particular position. Whether or not their friends would like them, how enjoyable the experience is, and so forth are the critical considerations. When there are conflicting goals, people adopt the position that maximizes their gains. The result is that it treats people more as deliberate, calculating, active decision-makers. In contrast, the learning approach treats people as more emotional, as more passively controlled by the environment and as less rational and deliberate.

Finally, yet a third theory suggests that people can respond either in the thoughtful, cognitive, deliberate way the incentive theories suggest *or* in the more automatic, emotional way the learning theories suggest, depending on the circumstances. Petty and Cacioppo's (1986) **elaboration-likelihood model** of persuasion proposes that, under some conditions, people are motivated and able to engage in issue-relevant thinking; under others, they are not. When conditions are right, people are more likely to attend to the appeal, access relevant memories, scrutinize the arguments in the communication, and draw inferences and evaluations from the communication on the basis of this scrutiny. Under other conditions, people are likely to draw their conclusions from more peripheral cues irrelevant to the merits of the arguments, such as the attractiveness and prestige of the source, the pleasantness of the context (e.g., a pretty girl or handsome man smoking the advertised brand of cigarette), and so on. This provocative theory is perhaps more realistic than the others, in that it recognizes that people are capable of processing information in very different ways, depending on the circumstances. The challenge is to identify those conditions that produce one response rather than another. We will return to this in the next chapter.

Cognitive Consistency

Another major framework for studying attitudes emphasizes **cognitive consistency**. The cognitive consistency approach grows out of the cognitive tradition; it depicts people as striving for coherence and meaning in their cognitive structures. This approach includes a number of somewhat similar theories. They differ in some important respects, but the basic notion behind them is the same: They all assume that people seek consistency among their cognitions.

People who have several beliefs or values that are inconsistent with one another strive to make them more consistent. Similarly, if their cognitions are consistent and they are faced with a new cognition that would produce inconsistency, they strive to minimize the inconsistency. Trying to maintain or restore cognitive consistency is the primary motive.

BALANCE THEORY There are three main variants on the cognitive consistency idea. The first is **balance theory**, which involves consistency pressures among the affects within a simple cognitive system (Heider, 1958). Such a system consists of two objects (one of which is often another person), the relationships between them, and an individual's evaluations of them.

There are three evaluations: the individual's evaluation of each of the objects and of the relationship of the objects to each other. That is, one person's (P, for person) feelings about another person (O, for other), and both their feelings about an object (X, for some thing). For example, consider a student's attitude toward a teacher and both their feelings about abortion. If we limit ourselves to simple positive-negative feelings, there is a limited number of combinations of these elements. They are diagrammed in Figure 6–2 with the symbols P, O, and X standing for the student (person), teacher

FIGURE 6–2 The balance model of liking. There are eight possible configurations of two people and an object. According to the model, the imbalanced structures tend to become balanced by a change in one or more elements.

(other), and abortion (attitude object), respectively. The arrows indicate the targets of the feelings. A plus sign means a positive affect, and a minus sign means a negative one. The first diagram shows that the student likes the teacher and that they both support abortion.

The notion of balancing forces comes originally from Gestalt theories of perceptual organization. As we have noted, people try to achieve "good form" in their perceptions of others, just as they try to achieve "good form" or "good figures" in their perceptions of inanimate objects. Balanced relations between people "fit"; they "go together"; they make a sensible, coherent, meaningful picture. The main motive pushing people toward balance is trying to achieve a harmonious, simple, coherent, and meaningful view of social relationships. So a balanced system is one in which you agree with a liked person or disagree with a disliked person. Imbalance exists when you disagree with a liked person or agree with a disliked person. That is, the system is balanced only when either one or three of these relationships is positive.

On the left side of Figure 6–2 are four possible balanced situations—situations in which the relations among the elements are consistent with each other. When the student likes the teacher and both support abortion, the system is balanced. It is certainly consistent when two people who like each other like the same things; their relationship is harmonious because they both agree. If the student likes the teacher and both dislike abortion, balance (harmony) also exists. Neither likes abortion, and they are united in opposition to it. Finally, if student and teacher disagree about abortion, but the student dislikes and would not want to have much to do with the teacher anyway, there is no conflict.

The imbalanced systems have an odd number of negative relations. These occur when the student and the teacher like each other but disagree about abortion, or dislike each other and agree about it. The inconsistency lies in the fact that we expect those we like to have similar likes and dislikes to ours and those we dislike to have different likes and dislikes.

The second assumption of the balance model is that imbalanced configurations tend to change toward balanced ones. It is this assumption that gives the model its importance. Imbalanced systems produce pressures toward attitude change and con-

tinue this pressure until they are balanced. That is, the systems on the right side of the figure will change toward becoming like those on the left.

The change can occur in many ways. Balance theory uses a *least effort principle* to predict the direction of change. People will change as few affective relations as they can and still produce a balanced system. Any of the relations may be altered to produce balance. For example, if the student likes abortion but the teacher does not, and the student likes the teacher, balance could be produced in several ways. The student could decide that she really does dislike the teacher, or that she actually dislikes abortion. Alternatively, she might distort reality by misperceiving that the teacher really supports abortion. Which mechanism is chosen depends on the ease of using it and on the individual doing the changing. The important point is that various possibilities exist.

Research on balance theory has generally supported these predictions: People do adjust imbalanced systems toward balance, and in ways that minimize the number of changes that must be made (Abelson et al., 1968). But balance pressures seem to be weaker when you dislike the other person than when you like him or her. Newcomb (1968) calls such situations "nonbalanced" rather than "imbalanced." His idea is that we simply do not care very much whether we agree or disagree with someone we dislike; we just cut off the relationship and forget about the whole thing.

Aside from this, perhaps the main value of this research is that it describes the notion of cognitive consistency in extremely simple terms and provides a convenient way of conceptualizing attitudes. The balance model makes it clear that in a given situation there are many ways to resolve an inconsistency. It focuses our attention on one of the most important aspects of attitude change—the factors that determine which of the various modes of resolution are adopted.

COGNITIVE-AFFECTIVE CONSISTENCY A second version of the consistency approach is that people also try to make their cognitions consistent with their affects. That is, our beliefs, our "knowledge," our convictions about the facts of the matter are determined in part by our affective preferences, and vice-versa.

The idea that information determines our feelings is pretty obvious. If we know that a dictator has imprisoned and murdered most of his opponents, we don't like him. The more interesting version of cognitive-affective consistency is that our evaluations influence our beliefs. Suppose a voter develops a strong negative affect toward the new governor because all his friends at work voted against him, but doesn't really know anything about him. Consistency theory suggests he will then acquire the cognitions necessary to support that negative evaluation. In other words, people will alter their beliefs and sense of the facts to fit their evaluative preferences, even if they do not have any good, new information that would justify doing so.

Rosenberg (1960) provided a striking demonstration of the cognitive changes created by a change in affect toward an attitude object. He obtained from white subjects a comprehensive description of their attitudes toward blacks, racial integration, and the whole question of relations between blacks and whites. He then hypnotized the subjects and told them that their attitude toward blacks moving into their community was the opposite of what it had previously been. If the subject had previously been strongly against integrated housing, he was told he now was in favor of it (or vice-versa). That is, Rosenberg reversed the subject's affect toward integrated housing.

The important point is that he changed their affects without supplying any new cognitions or changing any old ones, since he did it by hypnotic induction. The subjects were then awakened from their hypnotic trance and questioned about their current attitudes about blacks and integration.

Rosenberg found that the change in this one affect he had produced under hypnosis was followed by many dramatic reversals in the subjects' cognitions relevant to integration. For example, the subjects who had originally been opposed to integrated housing came to believe integration was necessary to remove racial inequality, that it was necessary to maintain racial harmony, that it was the only fair thing to do, and so on. These ramifying changes tended to reduce the imbalance that had resulted from the induced change. As the theories of cognitive consistency would predict, the pressures toward reducing inconsistency resulted in a variety of cognitive changes once affect had been changed.

This process is important because many attitudes are acquired as strong affects without many supporting cognitions. Children who grow up as Democrats because their parents vote Democratic need to rationalize that favorable affect later on by acquiring pro-Democratic cognitions. Citizens are supposed to grow up patriotically supporting their own country, even though they love it mainly by virtue of having been born in it; they must come up with most of the supporting cognitions later on.

DISSONANCE THEORY A third variant of the cognitive consistency approach is that attitudes will change in order to maintain consistency with overt behavior. Its main expression is cognitive dissonance theory, first proposed by Leon Festinger (1957). As originally proposed, dissonance theory focused on two principal sources of attitude-behavior inconsistency: the effects of making decisions, and the effects of engaging in counterattitudinal behavior.

A decision usually creates some inconsistency, because the behavior of deciding means you have to give up something desirable (all the things you decided not to do) and accept something partially undesirable (even the best choice usually has some flaws). When you engage in counterattitudinal behavior, such as working at a boring job (maybe because you need the money) or taking an uninteresting class (maybe because it is required), inconsistency is produced between your attitudes and your behavior. Such inconsistencies are described as producing cognitive dissonance, which may be reduced in a number of different ways. The most interesting way is to change attitudes so they are no longer inconsistent with behavior. We will discuss this theory in a later section of this chapter, spelling out its predictions and describing some of the ingenious research it has led to.

ATTRIBUTION THEORY Attribution theory has also been applied to attitude-behavior inconsistencies. Psychologists usually assume that people figure out their own attitudes by reviewing the various cognitions and affects in their consciousness. However, as we saw in the last chapter, Bem (1967) has argued that people know their own attitudes not by inspecting their insides, but by inferring them from their own behavior and their perceptions of the situation.

The implication is that when people change their behavior, they may then infer that their attitudes have changed as well. If I suddenly find myself

These young Moslem boys are participating proudly in Algeria's independence day parade. What is their likely understanding of this patriotic event?

studying biochemistry every night, I infer I must really like it. We will discuss research related to this idea in a later section.

Social psychologists' research on attitudes has focused on two general areas. One is the link between attitudes and behavior. As we have seen, the causal flow between attitude and behavior may well go in both directions, which has given rise to much provocative research. The remainder of this chapter is concerned with such issues. The other area of psychologists' research is what changes attitudes; the next chapter is concerned with that topic.

ATTITUDES AND BEHAVIOR

Originally it was simply assumed that people's attitudes determined their behavior. People who favor a certain political party are likely to vote for its candidates; those who like cocaine are likely to snort it; people who are prejudiced against blacks are unlikely to send their child to a school with mostly black students. Much of the interest in attitudes comes from the assumption that they do affect behavior.

And yet we know of many instances in which behavior does not follow from attitudes. How many times have you seen people smile and say how pleased they are to meet someone when, indeed, you know they are bored stiff or hate them? The Watergate tapes revealed just how far President Nixon's public behavior departed from his private attitudes. To what extent do attitudes in fact control behavior?

The degree of influence of attitudes over behavior has become one of the important controversies in attitude research. In a classic study, LaPiere (1934), a white professor, toured the United States with a young Chinese student and his wife. They stopped at 66 hotels and motels and at 184 restaurants. Although at the time there was rather strong prejudice against Orientals in the United States, all but one of the hotels and motels gave them space, and they were never refused service at a restaurant. Sometime later, a letter was sent to the same establishments asking whether they would accept Chinese as guests. Of the 128 replying, 92 percent said they would not. That is, the Chinese couple received nearly perfect service in person, but nearly universal discrimination in the subsequent letters.

LaPiere, and many after him, interpreted these findings as reflecting a major inconsistency between behavior and attitudes. Almost all the proprietors behaved in a tolerant fashion, but they expressed an intolerant attitude when questioned by letter. A similar inconsistency between intolerant verbal attitudes and tolerant overt behaviors was found by Kutner, Wilkins, and Yarrow (1952). A group of two white women and one black woman was seated in all eleven restaurants they entered. But later they telephoned for reservations for a group that included blacks and were refused by six of the restaurants.

Part of the controversy centers on how typical these early studies were. Wicker (1969) conducted one widely cited review. He looked at studies testing for consistency between attitudes and behavior in the areas of race relations, job satisfaction, and classroom cheating. Summarizing 31 separate investigations, Wicker concluded: "It is considerably more likely that attitudes will be unrelated or only slightly related to overt behavior than that attitudes will be closely related to actions."

Yet this conclusion has been widely criticized as underestimating attitude-behavior consistency. Indeed, later studies show much higher degrees of consistency than Wicker reported. In one study, a large sample of Taiwanese married women was asked "Do you want any more children?" In the subsequent three years, 64 percent who had said "Yes" had a live birth, whereas only 19 percent who had said "No" had a child.

Another example is voting behavior. Kelley and Mirer (1974) analyzed large-scale surveys conducted during the four presidential election campaigns from 1952 to 1964. Voters' partisan attitudes, as revealed in preelection interviews, were highly related to actual voting behavior: 85 percent of the respondents showed a correspondence between attitude and behavior, despite the fact that the interviews took place over a two-month span prior to election day. Moreover, most (84 percent) of the inconsistencies occurred for persons whose attitudes showed only weak preferences for either candidate or party.

Such studies led a later careful review to the following conclusion: "Most attitude-behavior studies yield positive results. The correlations that do occur are large enough to indicate that important causal forces are involved, whatever one's model of the underlying causal process may be" (Schuman & Johnson, 1976, p. 199). But everyone acknowledges there is substantial variation across different situations in just how consistent attitudes and behavior are. In recent years, the major research effort has gone into trying to determine the conditions that yield greater or lesser degrees of consistency.

Strength of the Attitude

One set of important conditions affecting consistency is whether the attitude is a *strong* and *clear* one. Inconsistencies can come from weak or ambivalent attitudes. As mentioned, Kelley and Mirer (1974) found that most attitude-vote inconsistencies came from voters with conflicted or weak attitudinal preferences to start with. Similarly, consistent be-

Ken Karp

havior may not follow when the affective and cognitive components of the attitude conflict (Norman, 1975).

Anything that contributes to a strong attitude should increase attitude-behavior consistency. One factor contributing to strong attitudes is information about the attitude object. Davidson and others (1985) tested this with two studies on undergraduates' voting in local elections. They found that the students who were most informed about the candidates and the election issues were the most likely actually to vote (behavior) for the candidate they said they preferred before the election (attitude). Similarly, Kallgren and Wood (1986) found that students' environmental behaviors (agreeing to a home visit to hear about a recycling project, agreeing to participate in the project, or signing petitions to protect the environment) were most consistent with their environmental attitudes among those who knew the most about preservation of the environment.

Another factor that strengthens attitudes is being forced to rehearse and practice them. Fazio and

colleagues (1982) showed that when people have to think about and express their attitudes, their behavior became more consistent with the attitude, presumably because this helped to strengthen the attitude.

Having direct personal experience with an issue gets us to think and talk about it more than if it is remote to us. So one hypothesis has been that we will have firmer attitudes about an attitude object when we have direct experience with it than when we only hear about it from someone else, or read about it. If we have firmer attitudes about it, they should also be especially consistent with relevant behaviors.

Regan and Fazio (1977) showed this with students at Cornell University during a severe housing shortage. Many freshmen had to spend the first few weeks of the fall semester in temporary housing, usually a cot in a dormitory lounge. Unlike students assigned immediately to permanent housing, they had direct personal experience with the shortage. While all this was going on, the researchers measured both sets of students' attitudes toward the crisis and their interest in possible behavioral actions, such as signing and distributing petitions, or joining committees to study the crisis. These attitudes and behavior were much more closely related for the students with direct personal experience with the crisis ($r = .42$) than they were for students with only second-hand experience, such as talking to friends or reading about it in the student paper ($r = .04$).

There are numerous other examples of the strong relationship of behavior with attitudes based on direct, current experiences. The effects of direct experience with smoking have been studied among nonsmoking junior high and high school students, in terms of how often they were around adults or other students who smoke. Attitudes about smoking were more closely related to behavioral intentions (would they start smoking in the near future) among those with more of such direct experience with smoking (Sherman et al., 1982). Similarly, adults' intentions about getting a flu shot were more likely to be realized, behaviorally, if they had experience with flu shots in the past (Davidson et al., 1985). And Manstead et al. (1983) studied predictors of whether mothers would breast-feed or bottle-feed their babies. They found mothers' own attitudes were a better predictor of their choices if they had already had children and had personal experience with feeding an infant. First mothers' behavior depended relatively more on other people's judgments, and less on their own attitudes.

Another source of attitude strength presumably comes from having some vested or selfish interest in the issue. Sivacek and Crano (1982) found support for this notion using the issue of the minimum drinking age. A ballot proposition in Michigan in 1978 would have raised the legal age from 18 to 21. Presumably students under 21 had more of a selfish interest in the issue than did older students. Indeed, attitudes toward the proposal were considerably more tightly correlated with behavior (volunteering to call voters) among these with a vested interest than among the disinterested.

There are of course other reasons why attitudes are strong. But these examples illustrate the general point: Any substantial attitude-behavior relationship depends in part on the attitude itself being a strong one.

Stability of the Attitude

Another critical point is that attitudes may change over time. The attitude held by a person some months or years ago will certainly not affect behavior as much as the person's current attitude. One would not expect to find a close relationship between a college girl's attraction to a boy and her dating behavior with him if her attraction is measured when she is a freshman, and her behavior when she is a senior. Therefore, consistency between attitudes and behavior ought to be maximum when they are measured at about the same time. Kelley and Mirer (1974) found that errors in predicting the vote declined quite rapidly as the preelection interviews got closer to election day.

Partly these longer time intervals diminish the attitude-behavior correlation because attitudes change. But the person and the situation change in other ways as well. We might find that a woman's attitude about having children at age 25 does not predict her behavior at age 30. But in fact the woman might continue not to want to have a child, but her husband may threaten her with divorce if she does not agree to have children.

The longer the interval between measuring the attitude and measuring the behavior, the more such unforeseen contingencies might have arisen. So, when assessing whether or not people "do what they say," make sure you don't try to hold them to something they said two years ago! Things may have changed.

Relevance of Attitudes to Behavior

Another obvious, but often ignored, point is that the more relevant attitudes are to behavior, the more they will be correlated. Attitudes vary quite a bit in how relevant they are to the act in question. LaPiere's asking proprietors about their feelings about Orientals in general is plainly not as relevant as asking about their attitudes toward this particular Chinese couple (who happened to be quite well-dressed and dignified). In general, behavior tends to be more consistent with attitudes specifically relevant to it than with very general attitudes that apply to a much larger class of potential behaviors.

DOES THE INDIVIDUAL FIT THE STEREOTYPE?

As we indicated earlier, the question of inconsistency between attitudes and behavior began with the problem of prejudice and discrimination against minority groups. Did people behave toward an individual member of a group consistently with their attitudes toward the group as a whole? But the individual member may or may not be perceived as representative of the group as a whole, and thus may draw behavior inconsistent with general attitudes toward the group; a female Nobel Prize–winning biological scientist may not be perceived as fitting the stereotypes of women in general, whereas a warmly humanitarian person such as Sister Theresa may be.

Attitude-behavior consistency should be greatest when the individual fits (that is, is most relevant to) the prototype of the group as a whole. Lord et al. (1984) tested this hypothesis using male Princeton students' orientations toward homosexuals. First they measured the students' prototypes of homosexuals, in terms of their typical traits. Then they were presented with a description of a specific individual, "John B.," who was thinking of transferring to Princeton, and who either fit that prototype closely or was somewhat uncharacteristic of it. Then they tested for consistency of attitudes toward homosexuals in general with behavioral orientations toward this individual (would they be willing to show him around campus, introduce him to their friends, host a weekend visit). Other students' willingness to interact with him was much more consistent with their attitudes toward homosexuals in general when he fit their prototype of homosexuals ($r = .38$) than when he did not ($r = .02$). Again, attitude-behavior consistency depends on relevance of the behavior to the attitude; here, a close cognitive fit between the individual and prototype.

Several studies have asked people whether they believe in God or consider themselves religious, and then noted whether they in fact attended church. Typically there was only a weak relationship between those two attitudes and church attendance (e.g. Wicker, 1971). But attending church is not necessarily perfectly relevant to a belief in God or even to being religious. Many people who believe in God and even consider themselves religious do not attend church. They may not like organized religions or just wish to practice their religious beliefs privately. Other people may only be moderately religious and attend church for a variety of other reasons as well as religion. That may be their one social outing of the week.

Thus, it is not surprising that these two attitudes do not relate directly to church attendance. On the other hand, if people were asked whether they thought attending church was a good idea, presumably the relationship to actual church attendance would be much stronger because that attitude would be more directly related to the behavior.

This point is clear in a study of the predictors of oral contraceptive use (Davidson & Jaccard, 1979). Attitudes toward using "the pill" in the next two years correlated .57 with actual behavior, but

TABLE 6–1

Correlations of Attitude Measures Varying in Specificity with Behavior (Use of Birth Control Pills during a 2-Year Period)

Attitude Measure	Correlation with Behavior
1. Attitude toward birth control	.083
2. Attitude toward birth control pills	.323
3. Attitude toward using birth control pills	.525
4. Attitude toward using birth control pills during the next 2 years	.572

Source: Davidson & Jaccard (1979).

attitudes toward birth control *in general* correlated only .08 with the use of oral contraceptives in the next two years. This is shown in Table 6–1. Schwartz (1978) found the same to be true with regard to volunteering to tutor blind children: Attitudes toward the specific behavior predicted it very well, even over several months' or years' time, but attitudes toward altruistic acts in general did not. Similarly, Weigel, Vernon, and Tognacci (1974) found that very general environmental attitudes were not significantly related to willingness to engage in various actions on behalf of the Sierra Club, but attitudes specifically toward the Sierra Club were (a correlation of .68).

Salience of Attitude

In most situations, several different attitudes may be relevant to behavior. Cheating on college examinations might be determined by lax attitudes about honesty or by a strong desire to get into law school. "White flight" behavior, putting one's child in a private school to avoid integrated schools, might be determined by attitudes about racial equality or by perceptions of the quality of education in integrated schools. A school superintendent's decision about letting a gay rights sympathizer address a high school assembly might be dictated by his favorable attitude toward the general principle of free speech or by his distaste for gays.

So one important determinant of attitude-behavior consistency should be the salience of the attitude in question. The consistency between intolerant attitudes and discriminatory behavior will probably

be fairly low if people have other attitudes in mind at the time. Perhaps the restaurant has so little business the proprietor cannot afford to turn anyone away. Serving a Chinese couple may be consistent with the attitude most salient at the moment, which is making some money, even though it is inconsistent with the attitude the proprietor is not even thinking about, such as ethnic prejudice.

As a general matter, then, when a specifically relevant attitude is made particularly salient, it is more likely to be related to behavior. Snyder and Swann (1976) assigned subjects to a mock jury situation and gave them a sex discrimination case. In the "salient" condition, subjects' attitudes about affirmative action were made salient by instructing them to take a few minutes before the case to organize their thoughts on affirmative action. In the "not salient" condition, subjects were not given any warning that affirmative action was involved. When attitudes were made salient, they were highly related to jurors' verdicts in the case. But attitudes about affirmative action were not closely related to verdicts when they had not been made salient. Actively thinking about a salient attitude improves attitude-behavior consistency still further (Miller & Tesser, 1986).

As you might expect, salience is particularly crucial when the attitude is not a very strong one. When the attitude is very strong, presumably it does not have to be brought very forcefully to the person's attention to be strongly related to behavior. Borgida and Campbell (1982) studied students during a campus parking shortage at the University of Minnesota. Some students were more directly affected by the shortage than others, because they usually drove to campus and either spent a long time looking for a parking place, or got a lot of parking tickets. The researchers exposed some students in each group to a conversation that included complaints about the parking situation, in order to make attitudes about parking more salient. Others heard a conversation on summer job plans and the merits of racquetball. It turned out that the conversation including the parking issue enhanced the consistency of attitude and behavior (willingness to sign a full-page ad in the campus newspaper) only for students with little real interest in or experience with the issue, for whom the attitude was presumably not very strong.

Situational Pressures

Whenever people engage in overt behavior, they can be influenced both by their attitudes and by the situation. When situational pressures are very strong, attitudes are not generally likely to determine behavior as strongly as when such pressures are relatively weak. This is easy to see in the LaPiere study. Well-dressed, respectable-looking people asking for rooms are hard to refuse, despite feelings of prejudice against their ethnic group. The external pressures are even stronger when the law requires giving rooms to anyone who wants one and can pay for them.

A similar dramatic impact of situational pressures on attitudes can be seen in a study of teenage marijuana smoking (Andrews & Kandel, 1979). Attitudes toward marijuana (whether or not it should be legalized, whether use causes physical harm) correlated fairly strongly with actual marijuana use. But situational forces, in this case peer pressure (as indexed by the number of friends using marijuana), had an effect several times greater.

The relative effects of attitude strength and situation change from one setting to another. In another study, teenagers' attitudes toward drinking beer, hard liquor, and wine were the best predictors of frequency of actual drinking of them, but only at

parties. At home, actual drinking behavior was better predicted by perceptions of their parents' positions toward drinking, a situational force (Schlegel et al., 1977).

The Reasoned Action Model

These findings suggest that the theory that attitudes determine behavior is too simple. Sometimes they do and sometimes they do not. The question is, when do they? We have described some factors that are important. Perhaps the most influential effort to generate and test a general model of attitude-behavior links is Fishbein and Azjen's "theory of reasoned action" (1975; Azjen & Fishbein, 1980). It is an attempt to specify what factors determine attitude-behavior consistency, starting with the assumption that people behave fairly rationally. The model is diagrammed in Figure 6–3.

The Azjen-Fishbein model has three steps:

1. It predicts that a person's behavior can be predicted from intention. If a woman says she intends to use birth control to avoid getting pregnant, she is more likely to do so than is someone who does not intend to.

2. Behavioral intentions can be predicted from two main variables: the person's attitude toward the

FIGURE 6–3 The reasoned action model of factors determining a person's behavior. (From Azjen & Fishbein, 1980, p. 8.)

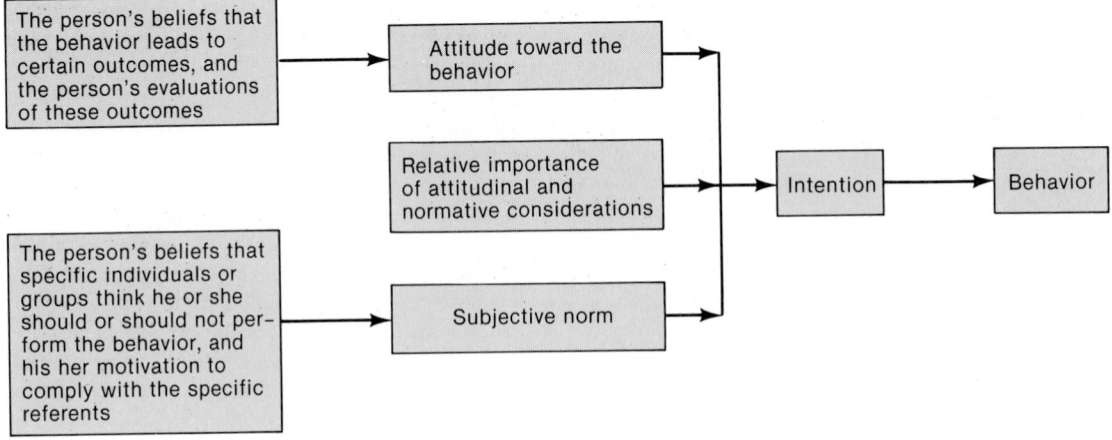

behavior (does she think birth control is a good and desirable step for her?) and the "subjective norm," her perception of what others think she should do (does her husband want her to? what about her church, and her mother?).

3. Attitudes toward the behavior are predicted using the expectancy-value framework. Attitude is a function of how good the outcomes of the behavior will be, considering how likely each outcome is. The predictors of the "subjective norm" are the person's beliefs about others' preferences and his or her motivation to comply with them.

This model has been widely used. A simple example is the study by Manstead and colleagues (1983) mentioned earlier predicting whether pregnant women would wind up breast-feeding or bottle-feeding their babies. From prenatal questionnaires the researchers measured behavioral intentions (did the woman intend to breast-feed?), attitude toward the behavior (for example, did she believe that breast-feeding establishes a closer mother-baby bond, and how important is that bond?), and subjective norm (what did the woman's husband, mother, closest female friend, and doctor prefer, and how motivated was the woman to follow their wishes?). The researchers found the model was very successful in predicting later behavior. The correlation of these various attitudes with actual postbirth breast-feeding was .77, which is quite high.

Bentler and Speckart (1981) also used the model quite successfully to predict college students' exercise, dating, and studying behavior over a two-week period. It has been shown to apply well to college women's behavioral intentions about the use of contraceptive techniques (Pagel & Davidson, 1984). Similar findings have been reported by Ajzen and Fishbein (1980) and their numerous collaborators on a wide variety of other behaviors, such as weight loss, consumer choices, voting behavior, women's occupational choices, and so on.

The model appeals to many social psychologists because it makes people seem reasonable and restores attitudes to a central place in determining behavior. Of course no model is perfect. What are some of the difficulties with this one? The role of behavioral intention is one source of problems. Sometimes "behavioral intention" is not, as measured, very different from "attitude toward the behavior," so it does not add very much to our understanding to bring it in as a separate factor. Asking a pregnant woman whether she intends to breast-feed her baby or not may be almost the same thing as asking her whether she thinks it is a good idea or not. And the model is a good bit more successful in predicting behavioral intentions than it is actual behavior, as you might expect (e.g., Azjen & Madden, 1986).

In some studies, the model does pretty well without referring to behavioral intention at all (Bentler & Speckart, 1981). Sometimes attitudes have effects on behavior apart from their effects on behavioral intention (Manstead et al., 1983). A number of factors we mentioned earlier but that are not in the model determine the closeness of the link between behavioral intention and behavior, such as the time interval between the two, their relevance to each other and so on. Prior behavior also influences future behavior, above and beyond attitudes. How a woman fed her first child influences how she will in fact feed her second, no matter what she or all her friends and family members think is right (Manstead et al., 1983). People are to some extent creatures of habit.

Finally, you will remember from our discussion of attribution (Chapter 4) that perceived control is a crucial variable in maintaining people's motivation to do something. There is now some evidence the same is true for carrying out behavior consistent with attitudes. In a study of female students about their weight, Schifter & Ajzen (1985) found that intentions to lose weight were more likely to result in genuine weight loss among those who felt they had control over their weight, and who felt that they could be successful in losing weight if they tried. Attitudes about the desirability of weight loss had little effect on behavior for those who felt helpless about the whole thing.

With these reservations, this theory clearly has value in helping to understand the role attitudes play in determining behavior. In general we believe a great deal of evidence now supports the idea that attitudes affect behavior. But clearly there are numerous other factors that play a major role in determining the degree of attitude-behavior consistency.

COGNITIVE DISSONANCE THEORY

We have been discussing attitude-behavior consistency in terms of the conditions under which attitudes determine behavior. But under other conditions, our behavior influences our attitudes. Put another way, our attitudes are often rationalizations for the things we have already done. The person who has given up smoking through a long and agonized process becomes the most obnoxious critic of anyone else who smokes. The newlywed couple expecting the birth of an unplanned baby abandon their ambivalence about having children and broadcast their great delight at the prospect. The military commander who commits his troops to a chancy mission that turns out to be a disaster, costing thousands of casualties, now resolutely declares he was certain he was right all along, and would not change his tactics in any way if he had it to do all over again.

All these examples depict a process in which a person's behavior is followed by substantial attitude change. It also assumes pressure toward consistency between attitudes and behavior, but in a far less flattering manner than the theory of reasoned action. It says that people's behavior controls their attitudes no matter how unthinking the behavior was, rather than that people deliberately and reasonably act on the basis of their thinking.

Most of the research on this problem was originally inspired by the theory of **cognitive dissonance** (Festinger, 1957). Like several other theories we have discussed, cognitive dissonance theory assumes there is a pressure toward consistency. Although it can be applied to inconsistencies between any cognitions, dissonance theory has dealt most creatively with inconsistencies between behavior and attitudes. It has dealt with two particular kinds of behavior-attitude inconsistencies, those produced by making decisions, and those produced by engaging in behavior contrary to our attitudes, called attitude-discrepant behavior.

Dissonance creates psychological tension, and people feel pressured to reduce or remove it. Dissonance operates much like any other drive: If we are hungry, we do something to reduce our hunger; if we are afraid, we do something to reduce our fear; and if we feel dissonance, we do something to reduce it also. We want to restore consistency, or *consonance*. The main way of reducing dissonance, if the behavior cannot be revoked or changed in some way, is to change one's attitude.

Postdecision Dissonance

One behavior that almost always arouses dissonance is making a decision. Whenever we must decide between two or more alternatives, the final choice is to some extent inconsistent with some of our beliefs. After we decide, all the good aspects of the unchosen alternative and all the bad aspects of the chosen alternative are dissonant with the decision. If we decide to buy a Mercedes-Benz instead of a Civic, the Mercedes' speed and stylishness, and the Civic's relative crampedness and homeliness, are consonant with the decision. But the Mercedes' price and its expensive repairs, and the inexpensiveness of the Civic, are dissonant with it.

This dissonance can be reduced by improving our evaluation of the chosen alternative, because everything positive about it is consonant with the decision. Dissonance can also be reduced by lowering the evaluation of the unchosen alternative. The less attractive it is, the less dissonance is aroused by rejecting it. Therefore, after people make decisions, there is a tendency for them to increase their liking for what they chose and to decrease their liking for what they did not choose.

A study by Brehm (1956) demonstrated this effect. College women were shown eight products, such as a toaster, a stopwatch, and a radio, and were asked to indicate how much they would like to have each of them. They were then shown two of the eight products and told they would be given whichever they chose. After the objects were chosen and the subjects received the one they selected, they were asked to rate all the objects again. As shown in Table 6–2, on the second rating there was a strong tendency for the women in the high-dissonance condition to increase their evaluation of the item they had picked and to decrease their evaluation of the other item.

A no-dissonance control group (shown on the bottom line in the table) shows that the effect was due primarily to dissonance reduction. These women made the first rating but, instead of next choosing between two items and receiving their preference, they were simply given one of the products they had rated favorably. When they rerated all the products, they showed no tendency to improve the evaluation of the object they owned. This demonstrated that the reevaluation in the high-dissonance condition was not simply due to pride of ownership—making the decision was the critical factor.

The tendency toward reevaluation is particularly strong when the two alternatives are initially rated close in attractiveness. Suppose you are trying to choose between a Ford and a Honda, and you initially much prefer the Honda. You would have little difficulty deciding and little dissonance afterward. There are few reasons why you should have made the opposite choice and therefore little dissonance. Since there is little dissonance, there should be relatively little change in your evaluations of the two alternatives. On the other hand, if the Ford and the Honda were close in your estimation before the decision, it should arouse a great deal of dissonance. The more reason you had for choosing the Honda, the more dissonance is aroused by picking the Ford. Thus, when two alternatives are close in attractiveness, a great deal of dissonance is aroused. After the decision is made, there should be greater reevaluation of the two alternatives.

Brehm tested this notion also. In the high-dissonance condition he gave the women a choice between a product they had ranked high and one they had ranked next best. In the low-dissonance condition the women were given a choice between a high-ranked product and one they ranked as much inferior. As shown in Table 6–2, the high-dissonance condition generated considerably more dissonance reduction. As the theory predicts, the closer the alternatives to begin with, the more dissonance is aroused by the decision and the more attitudes change after the decision is made.

In this case, dissonance was created by choosing between two almost evenly matched alternatives. But postdecisional dissonance can also be produced when we commit ourselves to a course of action that later turns out badly. This happened to a group who predicted that the world was going to end on a particular day, and that they would be saved by a spaceship from outer space (Festinger, Riecken, & Schachter, 1956). In the days and weeks after

TABLE 6–2

Dissonance Reduction Following a Decision

Condition	Rating of Chosen Object	Rating of Unchosen Object	Total Dissonance Reduction
High dissonance (objects initially rated close)	+.32	−.53	+.85
Low dissonance (objects initially rated far apart)	+.25	−.12	+.37
No dissonance (gift with no choice)	.00	na	.00

Note: The entries in the first two columns are the mean changes in evaluation of the chosen and unchosen objects from before to after the decision. The difference between the two is the total amount of dissonance reduction, shown in the third column.
Source: Brehm (1956).

making this prediction, the group kept to itself, avoided publicity, and in general was quiet about its beliefs.

When the fateful day arrived and passed without the world being destroyed, they were initially greatly shaken. Their response, however, was not to give up their beliefs and return to normal life. This would not have reduced the dissonance caused by knowing that nothing had come of all the effort they had put into their plans. Instead, they decided that the day was put off but that the end of the world was still coming soon. In addition, they changed their style considerably. Instead of being quiet and avoiding publicity, they argued that their efforts had postponed the end of the world. And they became much more active in trying to get new supporters. Presumably, this helped reduce their dissonance by showing that their original beliefs were basically correct and that, in fact, more and more people were accepting these ideas.

Part of the appeal of cognitive dissonance theory is that it often makes counterintuitive predictions. In this case, common sense might suggest that the group would give up after its prediction failed so miserably. But dissonance theory predicts that this disproof would lead them not to abandon the theory, but to argue it even more forcefully. And that was just what happened.

Attitude-Discrepant Behavior

The other situation to which the theory of cognitive dissonance has been most often applied is that of

---

BOX 6–4

POSTDECISION DISSONANCE AT POSTTIME

According to dissonance theory, making a decision produces dissonance and also produces attitude change that will help justify that decision. Knox and Inkster (1968) reasoned that bettors at a horse track ought to be susceptible to this process. After they have irreversibly put their money down on a horse at the betting window, they ought to be in a state of dissonance. To justify the bet, they should overestimate their horse's chances. So they interviewed one sample of bettors just before they reached the window, and another sample just after they had completed their bets.

They found the postbet group was considerably more certain their horse would win than was the prebet group, as dissonance theory would predict. A control group was interviewed before making a bet and then again afterwards, to determine whether last-minute switches to the favorite might have explained the difference, but none had changed horses in the short time span between interviews.

The authors conclude with a quote from one of the prebet subjects, who approached the postbet interviewer and volunteered this: "Are you working with that other fellow there?" (indicating the prebet experimenter who was by then engaged in another interview). "Well, I just told him that my horse had a fair chance of winning. Will you have him change that to a good chance? No, by God, make that an excellent chance."

attitude-discrepant behavior. When an individual holds a belief and performs an act inconsistent with it, dissonance is produced. The person has, in fact, performed the act and would find it difficult to convince himself that he did not. Most of the pressure must be relieved by changing the attitude.

For example, many people when they are in high school or college rebel against the routinized, conformist ways of the ordinary adult working world. They swear they will never let themselves get trapped in a 9 to 5 routine, wearing suits and ties or tailored dresses. Whether they describe themselves as bohemians, beatniks, hippies, or punks, they dress differently, stay up late at night, drink, smoke, or take drugs, and generally do not behave in a conventional, suburban middle-class manner. Yet these same people often wind up a few years later wearing suits and ties, working 9 to 5, worrying about the crabgrass or the mortgage or the next raise, and so on. Not only that, but they believe it is right, and that people who do not conform should not be hired or should be fired. Why the change?

Dissonance theory would argue that they began engaging in attitude-dissonant behavior when they first got a job, because that was the condition of the job. To get paid, they had to dress well, and so on. But this created dissonance: Their behavior was inconsistent with their attitudes. So with time, they adjusted their attitudes to become more consistent with their behavior.

But dissonance is not always generated by engaging in attitude-discrepant behavior. Thus, much of the research on this topic has tried to identify the conditions under which it produces dissonance-reducing attitude change.

BARELY SUFFICIENT INCENTIVES   The most interesting prediction from dissonance theory concerns the level of incentive required to produce attitude

BOX 6–5

ROLE-PLAYING AND ATTITUDE CHANGE

An impressive example of the attitude-changing effects of engaging in discrepant behavior was provided by Irving Janis. In his work on convincing people not to smoke (Janis & Mann, 1965), cigarette smokers playacted the role of someone who has lung cancer. The subjects became extremely involved in their roles—they looked at x-rays, pretended they were talking to the doctor, playacted their response to the news that they had cancer, imagined themselves waiting for the operation and finally undergoing it, and so on. It was an intense, emotionally arousing experience for them. Janis reported that subjects who went through this experience were more likely to be successful in giving up cigarette smoking than were people who did not participate in such intense role-playing.

In a follow-up survey 6 months later (Mann & Janis, 1968), a large percentage of the people in this condition were still not smoking cigarettes. The subjects who had engaged in less intensive playacting were considerably less successful in giving up smoking. Apparently the intensive role-playing was an unusually effective persuasive device. This study is just one of a number that show active playacting, or role-playing, to be highly effective in producing attitude change.

change. On the one hand, there has to be enough incentive to make the person commit the counterattitudinal act. People normally do not act in a way contrary to their attitudes unless there is some reason to do so. Something has to get that new alum to put on a tie in the morning. So imagine the person as being subjected to a certain level of pressure to perform the attitude-discrepant act. The pressure had to be enough to produce the act.

But if there is great pressure on the individual to perform the discrepant act, it is consistent with the decision and does not produce much dissonance. If the new alum is told explicitly that he must wear a tie or be fired, and if he had been unemployed for a year and this was the only job he could get, he will experience little dissonance about wearing it. He may even joke about it with his friends to show he does not really believe in it.

In short, there has to be enough pressure on the person to produce the counterattitudinal act. Yet beyond that level, the more pressure is exerted, the less the dissonance, and thus the less the attitude change. The optimal level of pressure is thus a *barely sufficient* amount—enough to produce the behavior, but not enough to prevent dissonance arousal.

POSITIVE INCENTIVES The most obvious incentive for performing attitude-discrepant behavior is money. Some minimum payment is necessary to get the person to perform it. But beyond that minimal positive incentive, the more money someone is paid for performing an attitude-discrepant act, the less dissonance should be produced by performing it. So paradoxically, after a certain point, the *more* money the person is paid, *the less* he will change his attitude to justify having done it.

Suppose you are offered a menial summer job but the pay is extremely good, such as day labor on a construction site. There is no dissonance and so there is no pressure to reevaluate the job; it is a crummy job but at least you earn good money. But suppose you are working at a volunteer job in the local hospital. Then dissonance is created, which you might reduce by reevaluating the job. Perhaps you start to think that it is an educational experience, or that you meet very interesting peo-

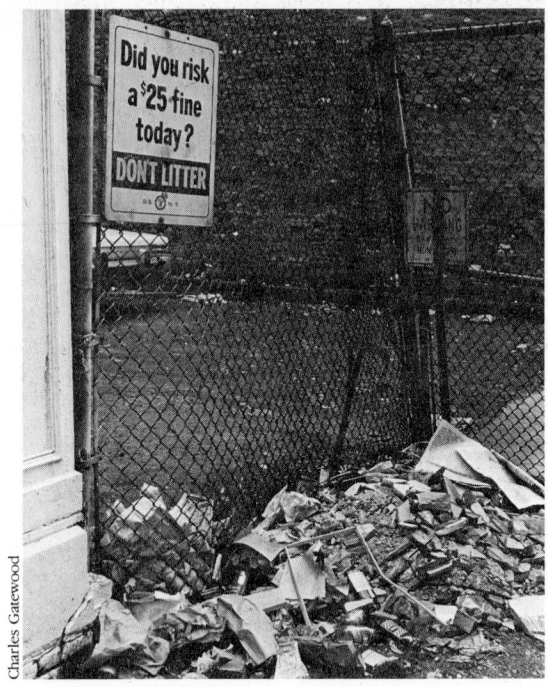

Charles Gatewood

Well, the incentive *does* have to be sufficient to produce the attitude-discrepant behavior!

ple, or that you have plenty of freedom to do other things.

The idea is that the *more* original pressure to perform the act (that is, the more consonant cognitions), the *less* the pressure to change your attitudes to make them consistent with the action. The best early example of this point is found in a study by Festinger and Carlsmith (1959). Volunteers for an experiment worked on an exceedingly dull task. After they had completed it, the experimenter said he needed their help because his usual assistant could not be there that day. He said he was studying the effect of preconceptions on people's performance on a task. He was studying several groups of subjects who were told good things about the task ahead of time, bad things, or nothing.

The next subject was supposed to receive favorable information about the task before performing it. The experimenter asked the subject whether he would be willing to do this for him. All he would have to do is stop the next subject as he was coming into the room, talk to him briefly about the experiment, and tell him that the task was an exceedingly enjoyable one. In other words, he was supposed to pretend to be a regular subject who was just completing the experiment and to lie to the next subject about the dull task by saying that he had found it enjoyable.

At this point, the key experimental manipulation was introduced. Some subjects were told the experimenter would pay them $1 for helping, and others were told they would be paid $20. Virtually all the subjects agreed to the arrangement and proceeded to describe the task to the next subject as very enjoyable. There was also a control group, the members of which were not asked to lie. Soon afterward, the experimenter had all the subjects indicate how much they had actually enjoyed the task. Dissonance about telling the lie could be reduced by changing attitudes about the task—that is, by deciding that the task was quite enjoyable.

The key comparison was between the $1 and $20 conditions (Table 6–3). Those who were paid $1 rated the task more positively than those who were paid $20. This is what dissonance theory would predict. The larger amount of money served as an additional reason for performing the task; therefore it was a consonant element in the situation and reduced the overall amount of dissonance. The less dissonance, the less attitude change.

This was an extremely influential experiment. It supported the surprising prediction that liking

TABLE 6–3

Positive Attitudes Resulting from Attitude-Discrepant Behavior

	DEPENDENT VARIABLE	
Condition	Enjoyment of Task	Willing to Participate in Similar Experiments
$1 reward	+1.35	+1.20
$20 reward	− .05	− .25

Note: A positive number indicates greater enjoyment of the task or greater willingness to participate in similar experiments.
Source: Adapted from Festinger & Carlsmith (1959).

for a disagreeable task would actually be greatest when the person was paid least to do it. Many similar experiments have been conducted. Some have also used money. Others have used other kinds of positive incentives, such as the amount of justification for performing a boring task (Freedman, 1963; Rosenfeld et al., 1984), and have gotten similar results.

THREATS In principle, negative incentives ought to work exactly the same way as positive incentives. One way to try to get people to perform disliked acts is to threaten them with punishment. If they do not wear a tie to work or pay their income taxes or do their homework, they are penalized. Threats are also used to prevent people from doing things. If people drive too fast, steal cookies from the cookie jar, play with a forbidden toy, or sell cocaine, they may be punished. The severity of the possible punishments varies enormously. They may get a mild reprimand, miss dessert, be fined $100, spend 5 years in jail, or even face execution. But, as with positive incentives, greater threat should produce less attitude change, assuming the threat of punishment is strong enough to produce the desired behavior or suppress the wrong behavior.

In experiments by Aronson and Carlsmith (1963) and Freedman (1965), children were shown a group of toys and then forbidden to play with one of them. They were threatened either with mild or with severe punishment if they played with that particular toy. Under these circumstances, if they obeyed and did not play with the toy, dissonance was aroused. The attitude "I would like to play with that toy" is dissonant with the behavior of not playing with it. On the other hand, the behavior of not playing with the toy is consonant with the perceived threat of punishment. Therefore, the *less* severe the threat, the more dissonance it provided.

If the children did not play with the toy, we would expect the dissonance to produce some change in their attitude toward it. A convenient way to reduce the dissonance would be to decide that the toy was not attractive. This would make their attitude less dissonant with their behavior. The greater the dissonance aroused, the more changes of this sort should occur. And because

BOX 6-6

COLD COOK, GREAT GRASSHOPPERS

Another positive incentive we might have for engaging in a discrepant act is how much we like the person who is trying to get us to do it. If your best friends ask you to do something—lend them ten dollars, drive them to the airport, help them cheat on an exam—there is a considerable amount of pressure to agree. If someone you dislike asks you, you are under considerably less pressure. Under most circumstances, it is more difficult to refuse a friend. Thus, if you do something for someone, there should be more dissonance if you dislike the other person than if you like the person. This, in turn, means that performing a discrepant act for somebody you dislike should produce more attitude change than performing the same act for someone you like.

This effect was demonstrated in a study in which subjects were persuaded by two different kinds of experimenters to eat grasshoppers (Zimbardo et al., 1965). In one condition, the experimenter was pleasant, casual, relaxed, and friendly. He presented his arguments in an offhand manner and did his best to be as attractive as possible. In the other condition, the experimenter was cold, formal, somewhat aggressive, and rather forbidding. In general, he did everything he could to be unpleasant. After the subjects who had chosen to eat the grasshoppers had done so, they indicated how much they liked them.

The analysis in terms of dissonance is straightforward. Everyone disliked eating grasshoppers, so choosing to eat them produced dissonance. This dissonance could be reduced by making evaluations of the grasshoppers more positive. To the extent that the subjects liked the experimenter and were eating the grasshoppers as a favor to him, they had additional justification for performing the discrepant behavior. Therefore, the more they liked the experimenter, the less dissonance would exist and the less need they would have to decide that they really liked the grasshoppers.

The results were consistent with this analysis. Subjects who ate the grasshoppers when there was a nasty experimenter liked the grasshoppers more than those who ate the grasshoppers when there was a pleasant experimenter. The pleasant experimenter provided justification, which reduced the dissonance and therefore made it less necessary to reevaluate the grasshoppers.

---

the greater the threat, the less the dissonance, there should be more attitude change with lower threats. Thus, the children would experience more attitude change when the mild threat was used to prevent them from playing with the toy than when the severe threat was used.

In these experiments, none of the children played with the toy, regardless of whether they were threatened with mild or severe punishment, because both threats were strong enough to prevent them. In the two studies, the children either rerated the toys at this point, or were given another oppor-

TABLE 6–4

Effect of Severity of Threat on Forbidden Behavior

Condition	Percentage Devaluing Forbidden Toy[a]	Percentage Not Playing with Forbidden Toy[b]
Mild threat	36	71
Severe threat	0	33

Note: The entry shows the percentage of subjects in each condition showing dissonance-reducing attitudes or behavior.
Source: [a] Aronson & Carlsmith (1963); [b] Freedman (1965).

tunity to play with the toy several weeks later. The results of the two experiments are shown in Table 6–4. It can be seen that the children reduced their evaluation of the forbidden toy more and were less likely to play with it later on under mild threat than under severe threat. The greater dissonance in the mild-threat condition was reduced by devaluing the toy or deciding it was wrong to play with it.

Other Conditions for Dissonance

We have identified two general situations in which our behavior may change our attitudes: making decisions and engaging in attitude-discrepant behavior. Attitude change depends on the magnitude of dissonance, and dissonance theory specifies the conditions under which more or less dissonance will be created. Two of these conditions are minimal positive incentives or minimal threats. What are some of the other factors necessary for dissonance-reducing attitude change to occur?

IRREVOCABLE COMMITMENT   An interesting aspect of the effect of decisions is that the reevaluation appears only when the result of the decision is certain. If you have taken the Mercedes on a lease-purchase agreement and can get most of your money back if it breaks down, the threat of expensive repairs will not create as much dissonance as if there was no turning back. One key, therefore, to attitude change as a dissonance-reducing mechanism is maintaining the person's commitment to the deci-

sion or behavior. As long as the person feels irreversibly committed to that course of action, dissonance promotes attitude change. But if the person feels she can get out of the decision if it works out badly, or she can do it half-heartedly, or she may not have to go through with it at all, dissonance will not be present, and no attitude change may occur. Little dissonance will be created by paying $4,000 tuition if you know you can drop your classes anytime before finals and get all of it refunded.

FORESEEABLE CONSEQUENCES   A related point is that people must feel they could have anticipated the consequences of their behavior. There should be nothing dissonant about making a choice or performing an act that turned out badly as long as there was no way for the individual to foresee this negative outcome.

If someone decides to walk to class on the left side of the street rather than the right side, and as she walks along a brick suddenly falls off a roof and hits her on the head, this is a terrible misfortune. But (if she lives), she should not experience dissonance. "I chose to walk on the left side of the street" is not dissonant with "a brick hit me on the head." For all intents and purposes, the two cognitions are not relevant to each other. On the other hand, if she knew that there was some chance that she would get hit on the head, perhaps because in the last week three other people had been hit on the head by bricks, dissonance probably would be aroused.

Goethals, Cooper, and Naficy (1979) predicted that *foreseeable* consequences, even if unforeseen, would produce dissonance and attitude change; only unforeseeable consequences would not. They had students at Princeton record speeches favoring the doubling of the size of the freshman class. That was a disagreeable possibility to the subjects, given Princeton's reputation as a relatively small, elite college. The possible negative consequence was that the speech might help bring about that undesirable change. Some (foreseen consequences) were told the speech might be given to the board of admissions, which was considering such an increase; others (foreseeable consequences) that it would be given to some other groups, but they were not named. Still others (unforeseeable consequences) were not told of any further use of the speech. After the speech was recorded, all were told of the negative consequences: their counterattitudinal speech would be given to the board of admissions.

Under what circumstances did the subjects change their attitudes in the dissonance-reducing direction of their speech? It turned out that either foreseen or foreseeable consequences promoted attitude change, in line with the notion that either can produce dissonance.

These Vietnam veterans did not support the war in which they fought. What conditions prevented pro-war dissonance reduction resulting from their service?

UPI/Bettmann Newsphotos

CHOICE Another major contributor to dissonance is the feeling of choice about the behavior. If you feel you freely and of sound mind chose the Mercedes, you will have dissonance to reduce afterward. But often we do not feel much sense of choice about what we do. Maybe the salesperson talked us into signing a contract and writing a check before we knew what was happening. Or maybe our old car had been wrecked and this was the only new one available. Without the feeling of choice, there is no dissonance.

Similarly, attitude-discrepant behavior creates dissonance only when the behavior is freely chosen (or at least the person feels it is freely chosen). This is shown quite clearly in two experiments by Linder, Cooper, and Jones (1967). Students wrote an essay that disagreed with their opinions. Some subjects were made to feel they had a choice about whether or not they wrote the essay; others were given no choice. Half the subjects in each condition were paid $2.50, and half were paid $0.50. The amount of attitude change in the four conditions for the two experiments is shown in Table 6–5.

With free choice, the typical dissonance effect appeared. There was more change with less reward. With no choice, the dissonance effect did not obtain. There was more change with greater reward.

RESPONSIBILITY FOR CONSEQUENCES The importance of perceived choice is that it brings with it perceived responsibility for all consequences, whether or not it is "logical" to feel responsible for them. As we saw in the last chapter, people tend to make internal

TABLE 6–5

The Effects of Incentive and Choice on Attitude Change

Condition	Free Choice	No Choice
Experiment 1:		
$0.50 incentive	2.96	1.66
$2.50 incentive	1.64	2.34
Experiment 2:		
$0.50 incentive	3.64	2.68
$2.50 incentive	2.72	3.46

Note: The figures are ratings on a scale from 1 to 7. The higher the figure, the greater the attitude change.
Source: Adapted from Linder, Cooper, & Jones (1967).

attributions whenever behavior is committed under free choice, and assign moral responsibility for behavior that is internally caused. A series of studies has shown the crucial role of this feeling of responsibility for dissonance arousal.

Even unforeseen negative consequences provoke dissonance, as long as decision-makers feel responsible for the consequences. If they feel no responsibility for the outcome, there is no dissonance regardless of how disastrous the result. If they do feel responsible, then dissonance occurs whether the consequence could reasonably have been foreseen or not. Pallak and his colleagues designed a series of studies to illustrate this point. In the first one (Pallak, Sogin, & Van Zante, 1974) a boring task was reevaluated in a more favorable direction, consistent with dissonance reduction, even when the negative consequences (learning that the task was just wasted time) were not known until after the task was completed—as long as the subject completed it under high perceived choice. In later work (Sogin & Pallak, 1976), they pinpointed the dissonance effect as depending on an internal attribution. If the negative consequences came about because of something the subject felt responsible for, a dissonance reevaluation would take place whether the effects were foreseen or unforeseen.

So the critical question regarding unforeseen negative consequences is whether or not people *feel* their own prior behavior was responsible for them. That is why perceived choice is so important. When people choose something that works out badly, they feel responsible for the outcome, and it creates dissonance.

These, then, are the main preconditions for cognitive dissonance, and for the attitude change that results from taking decisive action: minimum incentives, irrevocable commitment and foreseeable consequences, perceived choice, and personal responsibility for the consequences. This is a somewhat narrower set of conditions than originally proposed by dissonance theorists. Both postdecisional dissonance and dissonance produced by attitude-discrepant behavior are not as common as had been believed in the earliest versions of dissonance theory. But they do occur fairly reliably, given this restricted set of circumstances.

SELF-PERCEPTION THEORY

Cognitive dissonance theory originally inspired this research on the effects of behavior on attitude change, and for a number of years provided the only theoretical interpretation of these findings. However, Bem (1967) has offered another interpretation in terms of self-perception theory. As we saw in the last chapter, he argued that many of our attitudes are based simply on our perceptions of our own behavior and/or the circumstances in which this behavior occurs.

If we eat oranges and somebody asks us how we feel about oranges, we say to ourselves, "I just ate oranges; nobody forced me to eat them; therefore I must like oranges." Accordingly, we tell the person we like oranges. Similarly if we vote for a Republican in a free election, we assume that we have Republican attitudes; if we go to church, we assume that we are religious; and so on.

It is easy to see how this might apply to attitude-discrepant behavior. A subject is paid $1 to tell someone that a particular task was very enjoyable. When the subject is subsequently asked how enjoyable he himself thought the task was, he says to himself, "I said that the task was enjoyable and I was paid only one dollar. One dollar is not enough to make me lie, so I must really think that the task is enjoyable." On the other hand $20 perhaps is a sufficient amount to tell a lie. So the subject then might say to himself, "The reason I said it was enjoyable was just to get the $20; I didn't really believe it."

Thus this self-perception explanation makes the

same predictions as dissonance theory: The more the subject is paid to make the discrepant statement, the less he will believe it. The major difference is not in the prediction, but in the interpretation. The two theories offer radically different views of attitudes and of the way in which behavior influences attitudes. The more traditional view of attitudes reflected in dissonance theory is that they are enduring, learned predispositions. When people engage in counterattitudinal behavior, they suffer from unpleasant tensions that can be relieved only by giving up their attitudes. Dissonance theory describes people as stubbornly resisting change. They have to be lured and cajoled into a very particular set of circumstances in which they finally feel so involved and committed they must change. Bem's self-perception theory suggests that people's expressions of attitude are "top of the head" phenomena, rather casual verbal statements. People have no great stake in their attitudes; rather, they seem simply to be trying to cooperate with a curious questioner by giving a plausible answer, without strong conviction or feelings. So they readily change these superficial answers.

Conditions for Self-Perception

Dissonance theorists at first reacted with horror to Bem's reinterpretation. The very original, painstakingly created, and ingenious experiments they had done were now being seriously misinterpreted as reflecting some alien process. Their initial response was to try to design experiments that would disprove Bem's interpretations. This proved to be surprisingly difficult. Today, social psychologists assume that both processes occur on some occasions. The real question is this: Under what conditions is one more likely to occur than the other?

The self-perception process should be most likely to occur when people's own attitudes are vague and ambiguous. It would not be surprising if we should arrive at an attitude about a new and unfamiliar laboratory task on the basis of our perceptions of our behavior in the experimental situation. It would be more surprising if we were to use self-perception to figure out our attitude about our favorite foods, like beer or pizza or broiled lobster. We do not need to feel ourselves salivate

or watch ourselves devour every last morsel to know that we love those things; we know that when we think about them.

Chaiken and Baldwin (1981) tested the hypothesis that self-perception theory works only when people do not possess well-defined prior attitudes. They first separated subjects with strong, consistent attitudes toward ecology and the environment from those with relatively inconsistent attitudes. Then they put all subjects through the procedures developed by Salancik and Conway (1975) and described in the last chapter. Briefly, this involved manipulating subjects' perceptions of their own behavior by asking some subjects whether or not they do something "on occasion," and others whether or not they do it "frequently." Those asked about doing something "on occasion" are more likely to say they engage in the behavior, and so are more likely to perceive themselves as having attitudes consistent with the behavior.

If the self-perception process works, the variation in labeling of one's own behavior should result in parallel differences in self-perceived attitudes. People who say they "litter on occasion" should perceive themselves as being weak in environmental attitudes. However, those who firmly reject the idea that they "litter frequently" should perceive themselves as having more pro-environmental attitudes. These attitudes were measured on items concerning nuclear power, solar energy, outlawing nonreturnable soft drink bottles, aerosol cans, and so on.

The hypothesis, that the self-perception process would work only for those without strong and well-defined prior attitudes, was quite strongly supported. This can be seen in Table 6–6. Among the subjects whose prior attitudes were highly consistent, the manipulation of self-reported environmentalist behaviors had no significant effect on attitudes, as shown in the top row. However, among those with relatively inconsistent attitudes, the manipulation had the large effect predicted by Bem's self-perception theory: People who had been induced to describe their behavior as pro-environment perceived themselves as being more pro-environmental in their attitudes than did those induced to describe their behavior as more anti-environment.

The conclusion (Chaiken & Baldwin, 1981, p. 8) was that "the self-perception account of attitude

TABLE 6–6

Self-Perceived Environmentalism

	INDUCED REPORTS OF OWN BEHAVIOR AS:	
	Pro-Environment	Anti-Environment
Initially strong environmentalists	9.00	9.68
Initially weak environmentalists	11.33	8.25

Note: The entry is mean score on a pro-environmental scale.
Source: Adapted from Chaiken & Baldwin (1981), p. 6.

expression holds primarily for individuals who do not possess well-defined prior attitudes toward the target attitude object. . . ." Later research has developed this conclusion. Well-defined prior attitudes might not be available because the individual has relatively few prior beliefs, or has had relatively few prior experiences with regard to the issue (Wood, 1982). Or it might be because the person has no immediate sensory data relevant to the issue—as, for example, never having tasted the food products one is trying to decide between (Tybout & Scott, 1983). Under the opposite conditions, in which people do have well-defined prior attitudes, we might expect the dissonance process rather than the self-perception process to operate.

Is Dissonance a Drive?

Another approach to this controversy between these theoretical positions involves the contention that dissonance is uncomfortable, that it acts as a drive much like hunger, and that people do what they can to reduce this discomfort. Bem's analysis would not expect attitude-discrepant behavior to arouse discomfort or drive. Fortunately, this difference between the theories is directly testable.

One implication is that dissonance should result in physiological arousal. Elkin and Leippe (1986) had students write counterattitudinal essays, varying choice and effort. The high-choice, high-effort condition should have produced the most dissonance. These authors did find both choice and effort produced greater physiological arousal, in terms of galvanic skin response.

A second implication comes from the misattribution studies discussed in the last chapter. Subjective arousal states can be reduced to the extent that the person attributes them to other stimuli, such as a pill. If dissonance is a subjective arousal state, it could be reduced in this manner.

The dissonance-as-drive idea holds that no attitude change should occur if arousal can be attributed to some cause other than inconsistency. To test this, Zanna and Cooper (1974) gave subjects a pill; in one condition they were told the pill would make them feel tense, in the other, that it would make them feel relaxed. Subjects were then induced to write counterattitudinal essays under either high- or low-choice conditions.

Subjects who were told they would feel tense because of the pill showed no dissonance effect—that is, high choice produced no more attitude change than low choice. Presumably when the subject could attribute arousal to the pill, there was no dissonance, and therefore no dissonance-produced difference in attitude change. However, when they were told the pill would just make them feel relaxed, the high-choice condition produced more attitude change in the direction of the essay than did the low-choice condition, in line with the usual dissonance effect. Presumably the subject could not attribute arousal to the pill, because it was supposedly a relaxation pill. This gives additional evidence for supposing that dissonance effects do depend on some kind of physiological arousal mechanism, which can be eliminated or reduced if the subject can attribute arousal to some extraneous stimulus.

In short, situations involving commitments or counterattitudinal acts create tension under the conditions we have described: choice, foreseeable negative consequences, minimal external pressure, and so on. Attitude change as a response depends on not being able to reduce the tension in some other way, such as blaming it on external pressure, a drug-induced state (especially if unpleasant; see Higgins et al., 1979), or revoking the behavior. And the two processes probably work best in different arenas: dissonance theory with more controversial, involving issues; and self-perception theory with more vague, uninvolving, minor, novel issues.

KEY TERMS IN CHAPTER 6

affective (evaluative) component

attitude-discrepant behavior

attitudes

balance theory

behavioral component

cognitive component

cognitive consistency

cognitive dissonance

cognitive response theory

elaboration-likelihood model

expectancy-value approach

incentive theory

SUMMARY

1. Attitudes have a cognitive (thought) component, an affective (feeling) component, and a behavioral component.

2. People often have cognitively complex attitudes. However, like personality impressions, attitudes tend to be organized around the affective (or evaluative) dimension and to be evaluatively simple.

3. The learning approach views attitudes as learned by association, reinforcement, and imitation. The incentive approach views attitudes as the products of cost-benefit calculations by the individual. Cognitive consistency theories view people as attempting to maintain consistency among their various attitudes, between their affects and cognitions toward a given object, and between their attitudes and behavior.

4. It is usually assumed that behavior arises from attitudes, but considerable research questions how consistent the two are with each other. Now it appears that attitudes influence behavior most under certain conditions: strong, clear, specific

attitudes, and with no conflicting situational pressures.

5. Dissonance is most commonly created by the individual's behavior. Dissonance arises following decisions and following behavioral acts contrary to the individual's attitudes.

6. Dissonance can be reduced in a variety of ways. If the behavior itself cannot be revoked, the most important alternative is attitude change to reduce attitude-behavior discrepancies.

7. Postdecisional dissonance is greatest when people remain committed to their decisions for a long time, if they have free choice in their decisions, if the consequences of the decisions are known in advance and are certain, and if they feel responsible for the consequences.

8. Dissonance following attitude-discrepant behavior depends upon barely sufficient incentives to commit the behavior. These incentives can be either minimal threat or minimal promised reward. The maximum dissonance following attitude-discrepant behavior occurs with minimum

incentive, negative consequences of the act, and clear personal responsibility for the consequence.

9. Alternative explanations for these dissonance effects have been generated by attribution theorists. When people have rather vague, undefined attitudes, behavioral acts may lead to fresh self-perceptions of attitudes, thus leading to attitude-behavior consistency through an attribution rather than a dissonance-reduction process.

SUGGESTED READINGS

ABELSON, R. P., ARONSON, E., McGUIRE, W. J., NEWCOMB, T. M., ROSENBERG, M. J., & TANNENBAUM, P. E. (1968). *Theories of cognitive consistency: A sourcebook.* Chicago: Rand McNally. An extensive compilation of papers on almost every version of consistency theory, by almost everyone who ever wrote about it. Its nickname is TOCCAS.

AJZEN, I. & FISHBEIN, M. (1980). *Understanding attitudes and predicting social behavior.* Englewood Cliffs, N.J.: Prentice-Hall. A succinct treatment of the "theory of reasoned action," applying it to such social problems as obesity and weight loss, family planning, career choices, and voting behavior.

BEM, D. J., (1972). Self-perception theory. In L. Berkowitz (Ed.), *Advances in experimental social psychology,* Vol. 6. New York: Academic Press. The clearest and best statement of the self-perception approach to attitudes.

COOPER, J. & FAZIO, R. H. (1984). A new look at dissonance theory. In L. Berkowitz (Ed.), *Advances in experimental social psychology,* Vol. 17. New York: Academic Press. A recent update of research on cognitive dissonance theory.

DAVIDSON, A. R., & JACCARD, J. J. (1979). Variables that moderate the attitude-behavior relation: Results of a longitudinal survey. *Journal of Personality and Social Psychology, 37,* 1364–76. A sophisticated state-of-the-art study of attitudes and behavior.

FESTINGER, L., (1957). *A theory of cognitive dissonance.* Stanford, CA: Stanford University Press. The original statement of cognitive dissonance theory. It is elegant in its simplicity, and offers plausible speculations about a broad range of psychological phenomena.

KIESLER, C. A., COLLINS, B. E., & MILLER, N. (1969). *Attitude change: A critical analysis of theoretical approaches.* New York: Wiley. A good overview of the several different approaches to attitude theory covered in this chapter.

7 ATTITUDE CHANGE

What makes a person vote for a Democartic candidate in one election and switch to his Republican opponent in the next election? Why did so many Americans change their anti-German and anti-Japanese attitudes during World War II to support for these new allies a few years later? Why do people change their attitudes toward long hair, or crew cuts, or pink hair, or miniskirts, or neckties, in such short periods of time?

A major answer is that our attitudes are influenced by other people. Corporations pour millions of dollars into advertising aimed at convincing us that last year's skirts are too long or too short, that our old cars are passé and should be replaced at once, and so on. Political candidates spend sizable fractions of their campaign budgets to buy TV time and put much energy into figuring out how to get additional free exposure. Although we may not think of it in the same way as advertising, the government, schools, and other social institutions also seek to shape and change attitudes. Public debates over the content of school textbooks and school prayer suggest that many people are concerned about the messages being presented by our public institutions. Our family and friends and co-workers are constantly trying to change our attitudes, about getting good grades, about our new boyfriend, and about our work habits. This chapter analyzes the attitude change that results from such persuasive communication.

A MODEL OF PERSUASION

Much of the research on communication and attitude change began with a program organized by Carl Hovland at Yale University after World War II. Figure 7–1 presents a model based largely on Hovland's work but simplified and changed to bring it more in line with recent work in this area.

There must be a communicator who holds a particular position on some issue and is trying to convince others to hold this position. To do so, this person produces a communication designed to persuade people that the position is correct and to induce them to change their own positions in the direction of this one. Such a communication is presented in a given situation. These constitute the external stimuli—the source, the message, and the surroundings. Similarly, the target individual is no blank slate. Each person comes to a situation with prior attitudes and predispositions that will influence his or her openness to the message.

Part of the story, then, is knowing the independent variables that affect persuasion. But to fully understand the effects of persuasive communica-tions, we must also understand the underlying social-psychological processes. In Chapter 6 we touched on the best-known theories of attitude change, which have grown out of the general learning, incentive, and cognitive approaches. So another goal of this chapter is to describe the underlying processes that determine how these communicator, communication, situation, and target factors affect attitude change. Finally, there are many possible effects of a persuasion attempt other than attitude change. The viewer may wind up thinking the communicator is a fool rather than believing the message. The viewer may miss the message altogether; he or she may think the beer commercial was trying to sell flashlights. So we need to consider other outcomes as well.

The External Stimuli

The *communicator* is one of the first things we notice in communication situations. Some commu-

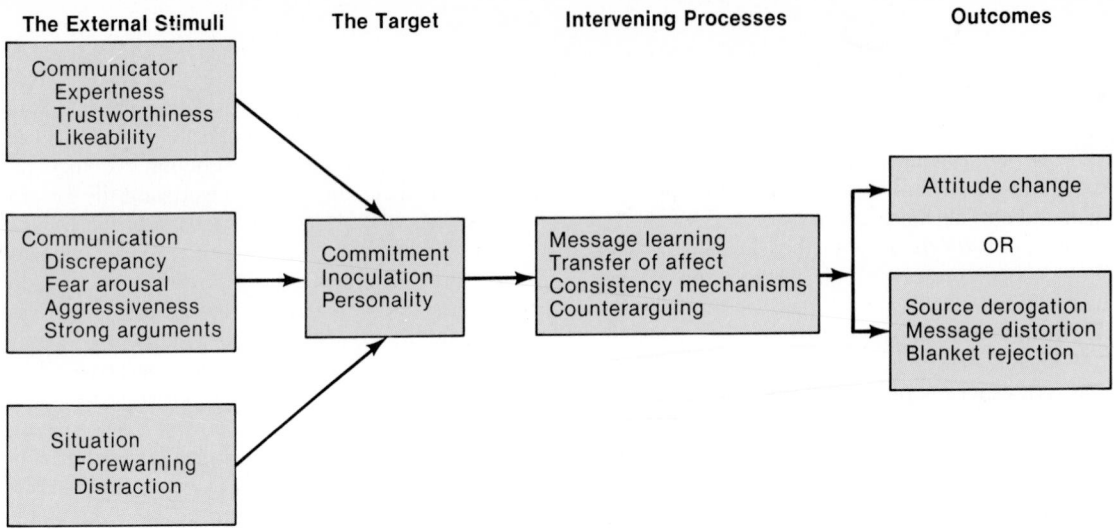

FIGURE 7–1   Model of the persuasion situation.

nicators are authoritative, like our strict high school geometry teacher or a scientist being interviewed on public television about her research on African apes. Others may be more humorous, like the weekend touch football players who urge us to buy a particular beer from their sweat-stained vantage points in a crowded bar. Others may not seem like communicators at all, like the friend we ask for advice about where to buy a formal skirt and sweater for an upcoming job interview. Whatever the nature of the person delivering the message, he or she is a crucial ingredient in its persuasive success.

In the typical attitude change situation, individuals are confronted with a *communication* in favor of a position different from the one they hold. They may have a negative attitude toward capital punishment and someone tells them that it really deters crime; they may be Democrats listening to a Republican campaign speech; they may be gays hearing the Surgeon General link AIDS to unsafe sex practices. The discrepancy between the individual's attitude and the attitude expressed in the communication places some pressure on the person to resolve the discrepancy.

But mass communications always reach the individual in a context. Part of that context involves the external *situation* around the person, such as

whether he or she has been forewarned of what the communicator will say or how distracted the person is at the moment. Someone watching a football game briefly interrupted by a beer commercial may be dazzled by a horde of joking retired professional athletes, some flirting with attractive women. But this person is in quite a different situation from the one who has deliberately tuned in to watch a hated political candidate argue for some disagreeable position; this latter person is ready and waiting, forewarned and undistracted.

The Target

Target individuals vary in a number of respects that affect persuasion. They may have a predisposition to agree with the message, or a predisposition to disagree with it altogether. A strong liberal Democrat who watches a news conference by a conservative Republican president, such as Ronald Reagan, is predisposed to find flaws and disagree with most of what he says. The viewer may not be very intelligent, or have had one too many glasses of wine, and so not be able to attend closely to the message. A television viewer may hate all beer, or drink a different brand, or distrust all television commercials, and so be unresponsive to persuasion. Or

Dan Rather is one of the best-known communicators on American television. What characteristics does he have that help make him a credible and persuasive source of information?

the person may be a heavy beer drinker with no strong brand preference and be quite amused by the ad. So the target individual is a major factor in the outcome of the persuasion attempt.

The Response

Usually the communicator intends to produce attitude change in the members of the audience. This means that affects, cognitions, and behaviors regarding the attitude object would all change. The used car salesman on late-night television wants us to feel that his cars are the best; to believe that they are the cheapest and most reliable used cars in town; and he wants us to come out and buy one the next day. All three components of an attitude would change, if attitude change were complete.

The particular insight of the consistency theory approach, and of Hovland's model of attitude change, is that attitude change is only one of several alternate responses to communication (see Hovland & Janis, 1959; Abelson, 1959). There are other modes of resolving the tension produced by a discrepant communication. The major problem for the communicator is to maximize the likelihood that attitude change will be chosen as the mode of resolution and to minimize or eliminate the use of other modes. Therefore, one of the critical factors in any attitude-change situation is whether or not other modes of resolution are present and, if they are, the extent to which they are used. We need to consider how the person can resist persuasion and still reduce the pressure created by a discrepant communication. Therefore, before discussing attitude change in detail, we will describe briefly the most important alternative responses the individual can make.

DEROGATING THE SOURCE Someone who is faced with a discrepant communication can reduce the inconsistency by deciding that the source of the communication is unreliable or negative in some other way. This is called **source derogation.** If we look at the balance model described earlier, we see there is nothing inconsistent about disagreeing with a negative source. In fact, people expect to disagree with a negative source.

Such an attack on the source of a communication is common in politics, informal debates, courtroom trials, and practically every kind of adversary proceeding. The defense attorney in a trial tries to discredit the witness whose testimony is damaging. The politician calls his opponent a communist or a liar or some other name when he finds it difficult to argue on the issues themselves.

Attacking the source of the communication is an effective way of reducing the pressure produced by a discrepant communication. It has the additional benefit of making all future arguments from the opponent much less powerful. When an opponent has been discredited, anything he or she later says carries less weight.

DISTORTING THE MESSAGE Another type of resolution is distorting or misperceiving the communication to reduce the discrepancy between it and one's own position. The Surgeon General says it is extremely dangerous to smoke because smoking has been shown to be a significant cause of lung cancer. The confirmed smoker reads this message and decides that the Surgeon General is recommending a decrease in smoking but that the evidence on lung cancer is not yet conclusive.

Smokers can do this by grossly misperceiving the article when they read it, by distorting the article in memory, or perhaps by reading only part of the article and reconstructing the rest of it in their minds. However they accomplish it, the result is the same—the message becomes considerably less discrepant.

Alternatively, the person may exaggerate the communication to make it ridiculous. Many environmentalists want to slow down the development of undeveloped lands and restrict the building of pollution-causing plants and buildings. Developers and many other businesspeople naturally oppose these restrictions. It is fairly common for them to distort the positions taken by environmentalists to make those positions appear so unreasonable no thinking person would ever support them. They might argue that environmentalists want such extreme restrictions that no factories could operate in the area at all.

Hovland has suggested that message distortion follows certain rules. When a discrepant position is quite close to that of the audience, they perceive it as closer than it actually is. This is called **assimilation.** This reduces tension by eliminating the discrepancy between message and target. When it is quite far away, they perceive it as farther away than

it is. This process is called **contrast.** This can reduce tension if the communicator's position is then perceived as so extreme as to be ridiculous, which makes it easy to discredit the communicator (Hovland, Harvey, & Sherif, 1957). We will discuss the conditions for these misperceptions later; for now it is enough to note that either could reduce the inconsistency in an attitude change situation.

BLANKET REJECTION   A discrepant communication is inconsistent with one's prior attitude, so the most primitive (and perhaps most common) mode of resolution is simply to reject the communication altogether. Rather than refuting the arguments on logical grounds or weakening them by attacking their source, individuals simply reject arguments for no apparent reason.

A typical response by a smoker to a well-reasoned, logical attack on cigarette smoking is to say that the arguments are not good enough to make her stop. She does not answer them; she just does not accept them. When someone who believes in capital punishment is shown overwhelming evidence that it does not deter homicide, he tends to be unconvinced. He shrugs off the evidence, says he does not believe it, and continues to maintain his position. So it often takes more than a good argument to convince people of something.

PROCESSES OF ATTITUDE CHANGE

It would be impossible to keep track of all the factors that can affect attitude change if they were not organized in some way. The theories described at the beginning of the last chapter are the most commonly cited efforts to account for processes that concern attitudes. But not all of them have been useful in explaining research results. Here we will emphasize four somewhat more specific versions of those theories that have proved helpful in understanding the results of studies on attitude change. These are message learning and transfer

of affect, which follow from learning theories; consistency mechanisms, which follow from consistency theories; and counterarguing, which follows from incentive theories.

Learning the Message

Perhaps the most obvious idea is that learning the message is crucial in attitude change. If the person learns the message, change will follow. If this were true, the key question would be what increases or decreases learning. For example, expert communicators might be very effective because people want to remember what they have said, and complex messages would be ineffective because they are difficult to learn.

Surprisingly, however, actually learning the message is much less important than we might expect. Most studies have shown only weak relationships between the learning of the content of a persuasive communication, or later memory for the information in it, on the one hand, and attitude change on the other (Greenwald, 1968; Lichtenstein & Srull, 1985; McGuire, 1985, pp. 251, 268). Similarly, recall of television commercials is usually not closely related to change in brands purchased (Beattie & Mitchell, 1985).

To be sure, it is vital that the listener know what position is being advocated. If the president is advocating military aid to a Central American nation, the listener must learn that and not think the president wants to send toys to Norway. But beyond this learning of the communicator's basic position, additional learning of the details of the message seems not to affect attitude change very much one way or the other. In other words, beyond some necessary minimum, message learning has turned out to be relatively unimportant in determining the success of persuasion. It seems to be enough for people to get the general conclusion of the message. Whether or not they get the details is not terribly important, since at that point other processes seem to matter more.

Transfer of Affect

People may simply transfer an affect from one object to another that is associated with it. Imagine a television commercial for an automobile. To persuade you to have a positive attitude toward it, the automobile is associated with many other positive objects. We are not simply shown a sleek car and told how powerful, quiet, and comfortable it is. While the message is being delivered, we are shown beautiful women, handsome men, and lovely children, with perhaps some graceful horses or cute dogs in the background. Or the car may be endorsed by a famous athlete or movie star. Presumably, all this

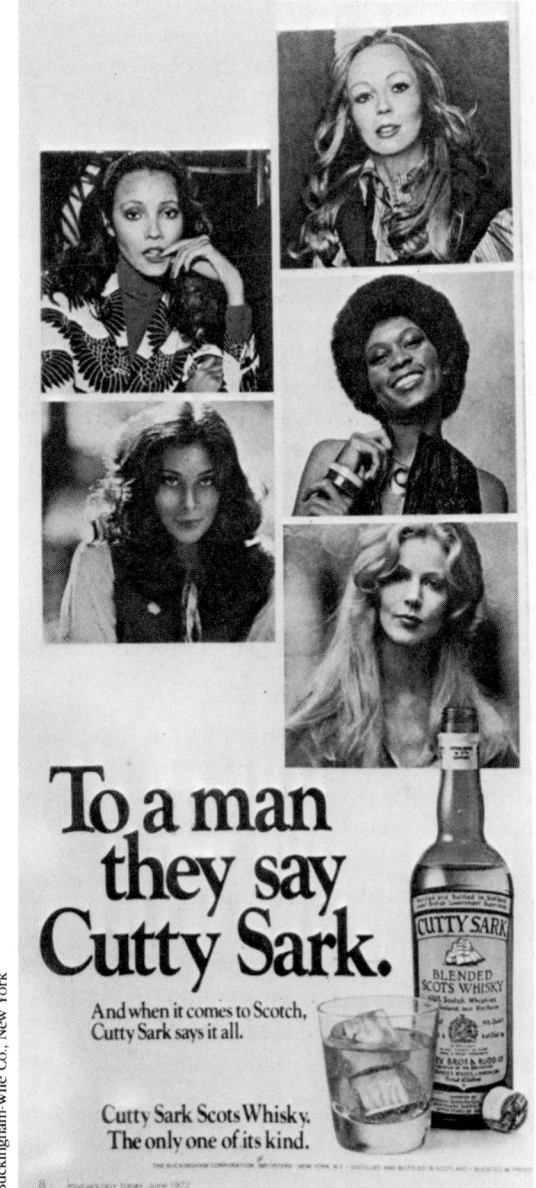

Buckingham-Wile Co., New York

A classic case of transfer of affect.

beauty, fame, and popularity will become associated with the car, thus increasing our positive feelings toward the car and the likelihood that we will buy it. In other words, people simply transfer their feelings about one object (beautiful people) to another (the car). This idea comes from the association version of learning theory discussed earlier.

To test this **transfer of affect** notion, Lorge (1936) presented American students with the following message: "I hold that a little rebellion, now and then, is a good thing, and as necessary in the political world as storms are in the physical." He found that students agreed with the message when it was attributed to Thomas Jefferson, but disagreed with it when it was attributed to Lenin. Lorge argued that the positive affect associated with Jefferson transferred to the message, and made it more positive when it was attributed to Jefferson, while the negative affect associated with Lenin—when he was described as the author—transferred to the message with opposite effect. Later research has supported this transfer-of-affect idea in a wide variety of contexts.

Consistency Mechanisms

A third approach derives from consistency theories and emphasizes that inconsistency produces psychological tension.

Suppose you have just voted for your state's new governor, and she comes out in favor of some changes you really do not like, such as increased tuition and reduced student aid for the state universities. You are faced with an inconsistency between your support for the governor and her endorsement of positions you oppose. According to the consistency theories, this inconsistency should be uncomfortable for you and lead you to change. You may change your attitudes about tuition and student aid, or you may change your attitude about the governor, but some change is required if consistency is to be restored.

In general, a communication causes some pressure toward change when it is discrepant from the recipient's original position. Consistency theories suggest the pressure can be reduced in a variety of ways. If the recipients change their attitudes, reducing the discrepancy, then this pressure ought to be reduced. Most research on attitudes has concentrated on this mechanism for restoring consistency. The emphasis on so-called alternative modes of resolution is one of the important contributions of Carl Hovland's model of attitude change and of the cognitive consistency models, as we have seen in discussing alternative responses to the communication.

Counterarguing

You read a story in the student newspaper about a proposal to ban all students from driving their cars to campus because of severe parking and traffic problems surrounding the campus. You think this is a bad idea. Right off the bat you can think of some serious problems the proposal would create. You know students who live in a town 30 miles from campus; how could they get to school? The local bus service goes to some neighborhoods where students live but not to others, and it is too far for those students to walk or bike. Some women students have labs or work in the library until very late at night, and it might be risky for them to walk or hitchhike home at that hour. You have friends who work off campus, and you cannot see how they could make their classes and get to their jobs on time if they used the bus. All in all, you see a lot of arguments against the ban.

Sometimes the recipients can resist by considering and actively attempting to refute the arguments. They can engage in a debate and attempt to demonstrate to themselves that their own position has more merit than the other one. This debate can be implicit or explicit, verbal or nonverbal, perhaps even conscious or unconscious. They can argue against the discrepant communication, produce evidence to support their own positions, show how the other side is illogical or inconsistent, and in general do anything they can to weaken the impact of the communication. To the extent that they are able to do this, the pressure to change should be reduced. This counterarguing mechanism differs from the consistency mechanisms, which describe a person who resists persuasion but who does not deal with the merits of the arguments.

Cognitive response theory is one statement of this counterarguing view (Petty, Ostrom, & Brock, 1981). As described in the last chapter, it depicts the recipient as responding to the communication with a series of thoughts about it. These cognitive

This man quite plainly has not accepted the communication. Which one or more responses has he probably had instead of attitude change?

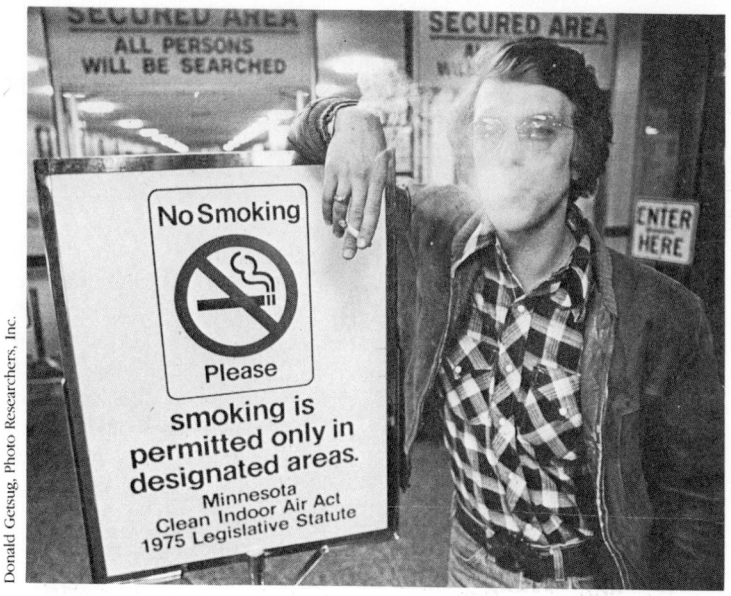

Donald Getsug, Photo Researchers, Inc.

responses determine the person's overall response to the message. But attitude change will depend on how much and what kind of counterarguing the message triggers. Conversely, persuasion can be produced by interfering with the counterarguing process. If the person cannot think of any good counterarguments, or can be distracted from thinking of them while listening to the message, the communicator has a better chance.

This process describes the recipient as actively relating the new arguments to prior attitudes and beliefs. In so doing, people rehearse their own attitudes and consider the details of the communication. The problem with this mode of resolution is twofold: Usually recipients are rather lazy, and communicators are more motivated. Most people, most of the time, are not very motivated to analyze the pros and cons of complex arguments.

Moreover, persuasive messages are usually designed to be difficult to reject on purely logical grounds. The authors of the communication naturally present as strong a case as they can and are generally better informed on the topic than the recipients. Therefore, although arguing against the

discrepant communication is a rational mode of resolution, it is often difficult to employ.

To take account of these grim realities, Petty and Cacioppo (1986) developed their **elaboration-likelihood model** of persuasion, which we discussed in Chapter 6. This distinguishes conditions under which people actively engage the arguments in a communication—and counterargue if they are discrepant—from conditions in which people act in a more lazy manner, and simply judge a communication on the basis of some superficial cues, such as who the source is, or whether the product is surrounded by attractive men and women, and so on. We will return to this more realistic version of a counterarguing theory later.

These, then, are four simple ideas to keep in mind about why attitude change occurs: message learning, transfer of affect, the consistency mechanisms, and counterarguing. With these in mind, we can turn to a consideration of the independent variables that increase or decrease the amount of attitude change produced by a persuasive communication, following the model in Figure 7–1.

THE COMMUNICATOR

You strike up a conversation with the secretary in the Psychology Department office. She tells you that the word processing machines the department has been using for a year or two are always breaking down, and are out of service as often as they are in service. Your mechanic tells you you are lucky to have bought your car when you did, because the same model from the previous year was a real lemon; it had a lot of bugs that were not worked out until the next year. The campus policeman advises you not to walk down a particular poorly lit walkway late at night; there have been reports of harassment of women students in that area. In all these cases, you are inclined to go along with these observations, because you are confident all these people are knowledgeable about these matters.

One of the most straightforward and reliable findings in attitude change is that the more favorably people evaluate the communicator, the more they are apt to change their attitudes. This follows from any of the cognitive consistency models. If the teacher says abortion is immoral but the student thinks it is a basic women's right, the system is unbalanced. The student can reduce the imbalance by changing her attitude toward abortion and agreeing with her teacher. In contrast, if she dislikes the teacher anyway because he is a sexist conservative, his discrepant position creates no imbalance and no pressure to change.

Thus, the more favorably people evaluate the source of a discrepant communication, the more likely they will be to change their attitude. But there are several ways in which a communicator can be evaluated favorably, and not all of them yield exactly the same results.

Research on this phenomenon began with "the prestige effect." This was illustrated in the work of Lorge on transfer of affect. It simply compared the effectiveness of favorably evaluated authorities like Jefferson with that of unfavorably evaluated

authorities like Lenin without attempting to specify the exact characteristics making up "prestige." Later work narrowed this concept to **credibility,** which in turn consisted primarily of two factors: expertness and trustworthiness (Hovland & Weiss, 1952). However, the mechanisms by which these two factors influenced attitude change turn out to be somewhat different, so it subsequently became important to make that distinction.

Expertness

The effect of expertness (though described more generally by the researchers as credibility) was demonstrated in a study by Hovland and Weiss (1952). Subjects heard communications concerned with four issues: the advisability of selling antihistamines without a prescription, whether the steel industry was to blame for the steel shortage, the future of the movie industry in the context of the growing popularity of television, and the practicality of building an atomic-powered submarine.

Each communication came from either a high- or low-credibility source. For example, the communication on anti-histamines was supposedly from the *New England Journal of Medicine,* or from a monthly mass-circulation pictorial magazine. The results indicated that communications attributed to high-credibility sources produced more change than those from low-credibility sources.

In another study (Aronson, Turner, & Carlsmith, 1963), subjects were told they were in an experiment on esthetics and were asked to evaluate nine stanzas from obscure modern poems. They then read someone else's evaluation of one of the stanzas they had not liked very much. The communication argued that the poem was better than the subject had indicated.

The crucial variable was that the communication was supposedly from T. S. Eliot, the famous poet, or Agnes Stearns, who was described as a student at Mississippi State Teachers College. After reading the communication, the subjects reevaluated the poems. There was more change with the high-credibility communicator than with the low-credibility one.

These effects of expertness are fairly straightforward and reasonably noncontroversial. An interesting question, not yet fully answered, is how far experts in one field can transfer the influence of their expertise to other fields. If T. S. Eliot, who was respected in the field of poetry, had taken a stand on politics or education, would his opinion have carried more weight and produced more attitude change than that of someone less well known? The question of the transferability of prestige is an open one and should be more fully investigated in the future.

Trustworthiness

Regardless of the expertise of the communicator, it is extremely important for the listener to believe the communicator is unbiased. Someone may be the world's greatest expert on poetry, but we would not be influenced by her writing reviews of her own poetry or of poetry written by a friend of hers. We would not be concerned about her ability to write accurately; we would be concerned about her objectivity and therefore her trustworthiness. If she is perceived as having something to gain from the position she is advocating or if she is taking that position for personal reasons, she would be less persuasive than someone perceived as advocating the position for entirely objective reasons.

One way for communicators to appear trustworthy is to argue for positions contrary to their self-interest. Consider a situation in which a district attorney and a criminal are each making statements about whether or not law enforcement agencies should be strengthened. Normally the district attorney should be seen as much better informed and more prestigious, and therefore be more persuasive. And in a study by Walster, Aronson, and Abrahams (1966), that is exactly what happened—as

FIGURE 7–2 Effectiveness of communicators when advocating positions for and against their own self-interest. (Walster, Aronson, & Abrahams, 1966, p. 333.)

long as the speaker was advocating less power for law enforcement agencies.

With that position, the district attorney was much more persuasive than the convicted criminal, as shown in Figure 7–2. But what if the criminal takes a position against his own self-interest, and argues in favor of strengthened law enforcement? As shown, the criminal becomes quite persuasive, and indeed even matches the persuasive power of the district attorney.

So one way to become more trustworthy, and therefore have more influence, is to argue against your own interest. The criminal may really be repentant and feel that society needs stricter law enforcement so that people like him cannot get away with crimes. The head of the state taxpayers' association may really believe that taxes need to be raised, or else the schools will deteriorate so badly that people in the state will be worse off. A union leader may feel that an immediate wage increase is a bad idea because it would damage the financial standing of the company. People often argue against their own self-interest, for a variety of reasons, and it usually makes them more persuasive when they do.

ATTRIBUTIONS How does a recipient decide whether or not the communicator is trustworthy? The audience's judgments must be based on the attributions about the causes of the speaker's statements: Is she taking that position because she knows the facts of the matter, or because she hopes to get something out of it? Or is it because the position fits her own prejudices and biases? For example, when an American president says the Soviet Union is responsible for the latest guerrilla movement in Central America, we try to figure out whether he is saying that because his strong anticommunist biases lead him to see Russian subversion behind every rebellion anywhere in the world, or because he is just cynically trying to use the Communist menace as a way to distract voters from his failures in other areas, or because he has information that points specifically to dangerous levels of Russian involvement in this case.

Three attributions are possible. The communicator's statement may simply be perceived as reflecting the truth, its causes lying in reality. Or, the statement may be perceived as biased, in two different ways.

His statement may be biased even though he is reporting his attitudes honestly and faithfully. He may not have enough information to know the real facts, or he may have been misinformed by others, or his own prejudices may have blinded him to the truth. In short, he may be reporting his own attitudes quite truthfully, but they do not square with the realities of the subject matter. This is called *knowledge bias* (Eagly, Wood, & Chaiken, 1978).

Third, he may have really accurate and truthful underlying beliefs, but he may not communicate them to other people in an accurate and honest way. This is called *reporting bias*. Reporting bias could happen for any number of reasons, since people frequently have strong incentives to take a public position they do not really hold. A politician running for reelection, an applicant at a job interview, or a person on a first date all have strong incentives to engage in some reporting bias. But whichever of these three attributions is made, the cause attributed to a communicator's statement should make an important difference in judgments of trustworthiness, and thus in the audience's willingness to agree with his or her position.

So a key factor in trustworthiness is making attributions to reality rather than to the communicator's biases or other dispositions. When do we make attributions to an individual's dispositions? As we saw in Chapter 5, observers are especially likely to make dispositional attributions when the actor's behavior is consistent with expectations based on past behavior. So we are more likely to attribute a conservative president's statements about Central America to his dispositions when his statements fit those biases than when they do not. If he claims the Russians are behind some guerrilla action, that is consistent with our expectations about him, so we tend to attribute it partially to his dispositions. On the other hand, if he says the rebellion is a genuine nationalistic movement with no Soviet involvement, we are likely to attribute it to some evidence he has.

EXPECTATIONS The implication is that when a communicator says something contrary to expectations, the audience is more likely to make an attribution to evidence rather than disposition. The communicator is perceived as more trustworthy and should produce more attitude change. This sequence has been examined in several recent studies, such as that by Wood and Eagly (1981). They had a male communicator give communications supporting or opposing pornography. To set up prior expectations about his general political philosophy, subjects had earlier been given a short autobiographical statement by the speaker that described his general attitudes about freedom of speech, abortion, and religion. His later communication about pornography could then be seen as consistent or inconsistent with his general political views.

As Table 7–1 shows, when his message confirmed expectations about him, it was more likely to be attributed to his background and less likely to be attributed to factual evidence; he was perceived as more biased; and he produced less opinion change. Note that expectancy confirmation had no effect on message comprehension: The mechanism responsible for the trustworthiness effect on attitude change here is the attribution, not message learning.

TABLE 7–1

Effects that Follow When a Communicator Confirms or Disconfirms Expectations about the Communicator's Position

| | EXPECTATIONS | |
Effects	Confirmed	Disconfirmed
Attributions		
To source's background	11.81	6.40
To factual evidence	10.39	11.84
Communicator bias	9.35	7.43
Message comprehension	2.36	2.08
Opinion change	1.56	2.51

Note: A high score indicates more of the effect; e.g., more attribution to the source's background.
Source: Adapted from Wood & Eagly (1981), p. 254.

Liking

As consistency theories suggest, people change their attitudes to agree with those of the people they like. Anything that increases liking ought also to increase attitude change. For example, physical attractiveness increases liking; Chaiken (1979) has shown that students rated by other students as physically attractive were also more persuasive communicators.

Similarity is another important basis of liking, so people tend to be influenced more by those who are similar to them than by those who are different. For example, Brock (1965) conducted an experiment in the paint department of a retail store. Salesmen were taught to vary how similar they said their own paint use was to that of a customer. The more similar salesman was more effective than the dissimilar salesman in getting buyers to change their minds about the brand of the paint they wanted to purchase.

Similarity also increases influence because we assume people with backgrounds like our own share our general values and perspective about things. Suppose someone is similar to us in terms of national, economic, racial, and religious background. If he then says that he doesn't like a particular new movie, we would probably assume he made this judgment on the same bases we would. Accordingly, his judgment tends to carry considerable weight. Thus, in terms of both increased liking and

shared perspectives, the greater the similarity between the source and recipient of a discrepant communication, the more attitude change.

Many of the communicator effects cited earlier are no doubt due to a simple transfer-of-affect process; any conclusion that is associated with a favorably evaluated source itself becomes more favorably evaluated. But it is not enough to leave it at that. Sometimes a source's conclusion will be accepted simply because an expert or otherwise favorably evaluated source stated it, regardless of the arguments. On other occasions the arguments themselves are important. What is the difference between these situations? Several factors seem to be important.

One is whether the favorable evaluation of the source stems from the source's expertness or likability. Good arguments are critical to an expert's persuasiveness, but may not be terribly important for a liked nonexpert. Norman (1976) tested this idea by using two sources: an unattractive expert and an attractive nonexpert. Since the topic was the number of hours of sleep required per night by the average person, the expert was a professor of physiological psychology who had just coauthored a book on sleep; the nonexpert was a 20-year-old college student.

Their pictures and other personal information were also presented. The student was an attractive, athletic young man recently elected to the student government, whereas the professor was middle-aged and not very attractive. In each case, half the subjects received extensive arguments on why people should cut down on their sleep, while the other half received the simple statement that they should cut down. The addition of arguments significantly increased the expert's persuasiveness, but it did not affect the amount of attitude change produced by the attractive nonexpert.

Reference Groups

One of the strongest sources of persuasive pressure is a group with which an individual identifies. The group can be as large and inclusive as all American citizens or the middle class or a labor union. It can also be a much smaller, more specialized group, such as a college fraternity, the Elks Club, a group of friends, or an extended family.

Note that there is an important distinction between a **reference group** and a **membership group.** The key factor here is whether people feel identified with the group, and refer to it for guidance, rather than whether they are actually members of it or not. A person does not have to be a dues-paying member of the Democratic party to regularly prefer its candidates for state assembly and state treasurer. Similarly, a person can be quite influenced by middle-class norms of behavior, dress, and morality even though living, objectively, in poverty; that is, actually being a member of the lower class.

The opinion of a reference group can be an extremely persuasive force. If the Young Republicans endorse a particular candidate, there is a tendency for all the members of the club to feel she is a good candidate. If our friends tell us they are in favor of anti-apartheid student activism or like the latest Sylvester Stallone movie, we probably are convinced by them. If most of the members of a fraternity think initiations are a good idea, the others will probably agree with them.

A second key factor in group influence is clear **group norms.** The group's position on the issue must be a clear one for it to influence its followers. Converse and Campbell (1960) showed that labor unions influenced voters only when the union made a clear endorsement and the voter was strongly identified with the union.

Another way of demonstrating the effect of group norms is to show how changes in the norms can pull people away from their own old positions. Kelley and Woodruff (1956) played subjects a tape recording of a speech arguing against their group's norm—they were education students, and the speech argued against "progressive education." The speech was interrupted periodically by applause which the experimenters attributed to faculty members and recent graduates of the college in one experimental condition ("members' applause"), or to an audience of college-trained people in a neighboring city, interested in community problems related to education ("outsiders' applause"). Attitude change toward the speech was much greater in the "members' applause" condition. This gives additional evidence of the power of groups in producing

or blocking attitude change; in this case, subjects confronted with an apparent change in their group's norm were likely to change their own attitudes to fit the group's new position.

Attachment to the group can also serve to prevent somebody from being influenced by a communication from an outside source. If the group agrees with the individual's opinion, they provide that person with strong support. Consider a member whose fraternity believes strongly in initiations. He may occasionally be exposed to an attack on initiations from someone outside the fraternity. Whenever this happens, knowing that his group agrees with him makes it easier for him to resist persuasion.

This dual effect of groups—changing a member's opinion to make it coincide with the group's opinion and supporting a member's opinion so he or she can resist persuasion from outside—depends to some extent on how strong the individual's ties are to the group. The more people want to be a member of it and the more highly they value it, the more they will be influenced by the group's beliefs.

Kelley and Volkart (1952) demonstrated the effect of attachment to the group on members' resistance to outside influence. A communicator attempted to change some Boy Scouts' opinions on various issues away from their troop's norms. The more the Scouts valued their membership in the troop, the less effect the communicator had on their opinions.

The reasons why reference groups are so effective in producing attitude change are those we have just discussed: *liking* and *similarity*. If people like a group, it is a highly credible, highly esteemed source of communication. When the group says something, each member tends to trust it and believe the message.

If they like the group, they want to be similar to the other members. When the other members express a particular opinion, each member thinks his or her own opinion wrong if it is different. Only when the opinion is the same as the group's is it correct or "normal." Therefore, they tend to change their opinion to make it agree.

This assumption of similarity to other group members, and its importance in strengthening one's own attitudes, is nicely illustrated in a study by Holtz and Miller (1985). They had students from two groups—fraternity residents and commuters—estimate the attitude positions of other group members on a variety of issues. They found people assumed much greater attitudinal similarity with members of their own group than with members of the other group. More important, they found that simply estimating the opinions of their fellow group members significantly increased their certainty in their own opinions about these issues. Reviewing their own perceptions of agreement with fellow group members presumably reminded them of this support for their own attitudes, and thus made them more confident of their views.

Consistency mechanisms are critical to communicator effects, no matter whether the communica-

tor is a group or an individual. In general, any characteristic of communicators which implies they know what they are talking about (are experts), are being honest (have no ulterior motive), or are likable increases the effectiveness of the communication. Since derogation of the communication source is a major way of avoiding attitude change, these variables relating to the communicator are extremely important.

Any disliking of the communicator or lack of trust in his or her competence or credibility makes it relatively easy to reject the message by attacking the source. In this way, targets free themselves from the pressure of worrying about the complex details of the message itself.

THE COMMUNICATION

But what about the actual content of the message? Advertisers try to sell a particular product; is it any good or not? Politicians try to get elected; are they actually qualified for the job or not? Your friend tries to get you to go to a particular party with her; will it actually be a good party or not?

Of course, it is easier to sell something good. Crest became the best-selling toothpaste in part because it really did offer protection against cavities; the automobile became popular because it was a useful product; and some political candidates are more qualified than others. Given a particular product or opinion to sell, however, a number of variables in the communication itself have important effects on the amount of attitude change produced.

Discrepancy

As noted earlier, a major source of pressure for attitude change comes from the **discrepancy** between the target's initial position and the position advocated by the communication. The greater the discrepancy, the greater potential pressure to

change. If the typical person needing eight hours of sleep per night hears a distinguished health scientist say that only six hours are necessary, the individual's attitude is under some pressure; if the communication argues that only four hours are really necessary, there is much more pressure.

With more discrepancy, more change is required if the pressure is to be reduced. As might be expected, therefore, within a wide range, there is more attitude change with greater discrepancy (Hovland & Pritzker, 1957).

However, the effect of discrepancy on pressure and amount of change is not always this simple. There is more pressure with greater discrepancy, but it does not always produce more change. There are two complicating factors. First, as discrepancy becomes quite great, the members of the audience find it increasingly difficult to change their attitudes enough to eliminate the discrepancy. Moreover, an extremely discrepant statement tends to make individuals doubt the credibility of the source. So at high levels of discrepancy, the pressure tends to be reduced more by source derogation than by attitude change. In other words, source derogation rather than attitude change is chosen as the mechanism for restoring consistency.

Suppose a person hears the scientist say that eight hours of sleep are not really required. If the scientist's message is at low discrepancy, and says that six hours are adequate, the person is likely to be somewhat influenced. There would be some pressure on her to change her opinion in the direction of the scientist's, and if the scientist presented a fairly persuasive argument, the person would probably do so. In this situation, it is difficult to reject a credible communicator but easy to change one's opinion the little bit required to reduce the discrepancy.

As the discrepancy becomes greater, however, it becomes much harder for individuals to reduce the pressure by changing their opinion. It is extremely difficult for the person who thinks eight hours are required to decide that only four hours will do. The person then starts to doubt the communicator's credibility. She begins to think that the scientist does not know much about real human beings. The result is that attitude change generally increases with greater discrepancy up to a point, and then declines if discrepancy increases still further (e.g., Freedman, 1964; Eagly & Telaak, 1972). At high discrepancy, source derogation starts to occur instead.

Greater credibility, therefore, should allow communicators to advocate more discrepant positions with success, because they will not be rejected as easily. If one deeply respects the scientist who says that four hours of sleep is enough, it is harder to decide he does not know what he is talking about. Therefore, the greater the credibility of the communicator, the higher the level of discrepancy at which the maximum change occurs. Similarly, a lower-credibility source makes rejection relatively easy and the maximum point occurs at lower levels of discrepancy.

These effects of discrepancy and credibility are nicely illustrated in a study by Bochner and Insko (1966), as shown in Figure 7–3. They had a Nobel Prize winner (high credibility) and a YMCA instructor (low credibility) give messages regarding the number of hours of sleep the average person requires per night. Each subject received one message from one source. Some subjects received a message saying eight hours were required, others a message saying seven hours were required, and so on. Since the great majority of subjects initially thought eight hours was correct, these messages varied in discrepancy accordingly; zero discrepancy for the eight-hour message, one-hour discrepancy for the seven-hour message, and so on.

As you can see, there was more change at moderate levels of discrepancy than at higher levels. In addition, as expected, the optimal level of discrepancy was greater for the high-credibility source. The YMCA instructor did best by advocating three hours of sleep, but the high-credibility source got the maximum attitude change by arguing that only one hour was really necessary. Even so, the high-credibility source still could at best reduce the subjects' attitudes only from an average of eight hours per night to an average of about six.

Thus, the level of credibility does not change the basic inverted-U relationship between discrepancy and attitude change, but it does change the point at which maximum change occurs. The more difficult it is to reject the communicator, the greater the discrepancy at which maximum change occurs. This example illustrates both how an interplay of forces determines which mode of resolution is adopted in a given situation, and how the use of one mode implies less use of another.

Another example of alternative modes of resolution concerns how discrepancy affects misperception of the message. Discrepant positions that are close to the individual's are often seen as closer than they actually are (assimilation), whereas those that are far away are seen as farther away than they are (contrast). Exaggerating the closeness of a discrepant position makes it easy to change enough to reduce the small discrepancy, or it may eliminate the need for change by making the two positions essentially identical. Exaggerating the remoteness of a position makes it easier to attack the credibility of the person advocating it (Hovland, Harvey, & Sherif, 1957).

The same misperceptions occur when people estimate the attitudes of social groups. They tend to overestimate the extent to which members of their own group agree with them; that is, they tend to assimilate fellow group members' attitudes. For example, whites think that other whites agree more with them about racial integration and segregation than is in fact the case (Granberg, 1984).

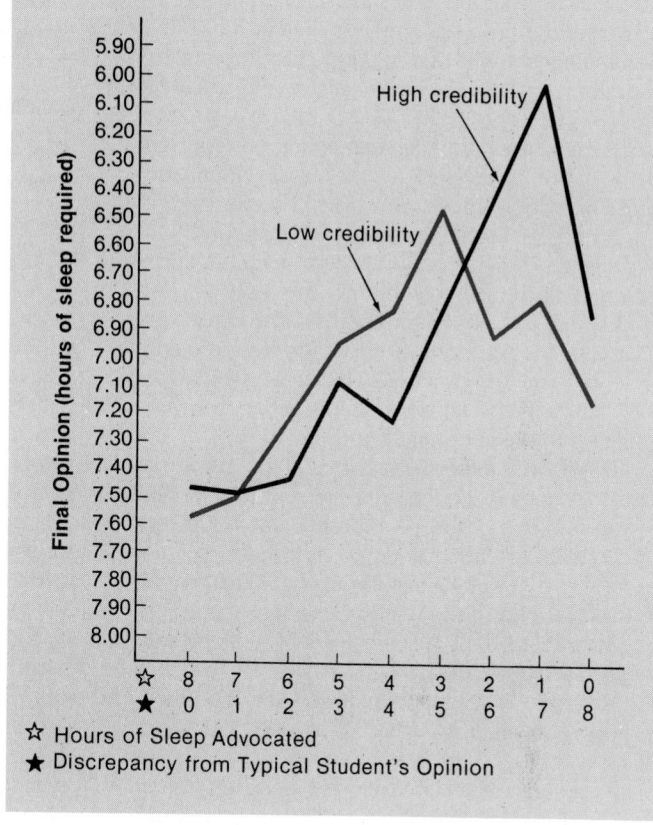

FIGURE 7–3. Opinion change produced by high- and low-credibility communicators at various levels of discrepancy. (Bochner & Insko, 1966.)

Fear Arousal

Arousing fear is one of the most natural ways of trying to convince someone to do something. A mother tells her young son he will be run over if he crosses the street without her. Religious leaders frighten their followers with threats of eternal damnation and suffering. Political candidates warn that if their opponents are elected, the economy will be ruined, people will starve, or war will break out. Environmentalists warn of chemicals in our vital organs, dying fish in polluted lakes and streams, and mass deaths from cancer. Opponents of environmental improvement warn of rising unemployment.

All these arguments could be made on a nonemotional basis, but they often are based on the arousal of great fear. Given a particular argument in favor of a position, how does the amount of fear aroused affect the success of the argument?

The learning approach suggests that motive arousals would lead to attitude change only when accepting the message will reduce the arousal. If fear is aroused by seeing gruesome pictures of lung cancer victims and we accept the communicator's position and stop smoking, our fear should be reduced. Attitude change depends on reducing arousal.

The original study in this area was conducted by Janis and Feshbach in 1953. They showed high school students a film that emphasized the importance of brushing one's teeth three times a day, after every meal. The film described the dangers of not doing this and explained the advantages of good dental care. High fear was aroused by showing pictures of badly decayed teeth and gums, closeups of diseased teeth, mouths in which the gums had pulled away from the teeth, and so on. In the mild-fear condition, subjects saw less dramatic and less frightening pictures. And in the no-fear, or control, condition, the subjects saw no pictures of diseased teeth.

The subjects in the high-fear condition reported being more impressed by the presentation and agreeing with it more. However, a week later it was found that the subjects in the no-fear condition had changed their behavior more than had subjects in either of the fear conditions. The authors concluded that the maximum effect was produced by the persusive arguments without the fear-arousing slides. Too much fear aroused defensive avoidance, they felt, and the subjects simply refused to pay attention to the communication.

Many of the experiments done after that early study have produced the opposite result, however. For example, a series of experiments conducted by Howard Leventhal and his colleagues at Yale University have shown that the arousal of fear tends to facilitate both attitude and behavior change. In one study (Dabbs & Leventhal, 1966), college students were urged to get inoculations for tetanus. The disease was described in detail—it was pointed out how serious it was, that it was often fatal, and that it was easy to catch.

In the high-fear condition, the descriptions of the disease were extremely vivid, the symptoms were made very explicit, and everything was done to make the situation as frightening as possible. In the second condition, a moderate amount of fear was aroused; and in the third, very little. In addition, the students were told that the inoculation was extremely effective and that it gave almost complete protection against the disease. Students were then asked how important they thought it was to get the inoculation and whether or not they intended to get one. The university health service, which was nearby, recorded how many of the students went for inoculations during the next month.

The findings (Table 7–2) are straightforward and impressive. The greater the fear aroused, the more the subjects intended to get shots. Perhaps more important, higher fear induced more subjects to go to the health service and receive inoculations. Thus, fear arousal not only produced more attitude change, but also had a greater effect on the relevant behavior.

TABLE 7–2

Effects of Fear Arousal on Attitudes and Behavior

Condition	Intention to Take Shots[a]	Percentage Taking Shots
High fear	5.17	22
Low fear	4.73	13
Control	4.12	6

[a] The figures are ratings on a scale from 1 (lowest) to 7 (highest).
Source: Adapted from Dabbs & Leventhal (1966).

Various other studies have used such issues as automotive safety, atom bomb testing, fallout shelters, and dental hygiene to study the effects of fear. Under most circumstances, fear arousal seems to increase the effectiveness of a persuasive communication (Higbee, 1969; Leventhal, 1970).

On the other hand, Janis (1967) argues that the relationship between fear and attitude change depends on the level of fear involved. He holds that at low levels greater fear produces more attitude change, but that at some point the fear becomes too intense, arouses defensive mechanisms, and thereby produces less change. This would explain some seemingly contradictory results from studies that involved different amounts of fear.

For example, high fear normally has had its strongest effects in experiments on tetanus, which is a simply prevented disease and rarely scares people much. However, high fear arousal is less often successful on lung cancer and smoking, probably because lung cancer causes too much fear and is too difficult for a lifelong smoker to prevent. Janis (1967) has reanalyzed a number of experiments in these terms, and although not all the data fit this model, most of the results appear to be consistent with it.

Even more specific theories about the conditions under which fear is effective have been developed by Leventhal (1970) and others (Rogers & Mewborn, 1976). These rest generally on an expectancy-value approach and view the individual as somewhat more cognitive and rational than does the Janis model. These theories take into consideration the character of the feared event, the person's perceived vulnerability to the feared event, and the effectiveness of the recommended measures. They try to predict the special conditions under which fear will influence attitude change.

For example, fear should increase attitude change if highly effective measures are recommended, but not if there is little or no remedy. These theories can also account for some of the data, though it seems clear that people do not always calculate the most rational response in these situations.

To sum up, the evidence indicates that under most circumstances arousing fear increases the effectiveness of persuasive communications. But arousing too much fear may be disruptive. Causing people to be too frightened can make them either so paralyzed that they are unable to act or so threatened that they tend to deny the danger and reject the communication. At moderate levels, however, it appears that fear-arousing arguments are more effective in producing attitude change than arguments which arouse little or no fear.

Aggression

The learning approach argued that motive arousals can produce attitude change if accepting the communicator's position satisfies the motive. A fear-arousing message should be accepted if it is accompanied by a fear-reducing recommendation the listener can carry out. And the same should be true of other motives, such as **aggression.**

Arousal of aggression should lead to attitude change when the listeners can reduce their aggression by accepting the recommended new attitude. Political leaders would be able to produce attitude change by stirring up their followers' aggression—but only if they provide their followers with something to hate, like a convenient enemy or scapegoat, so the listeners can express their aggression.

A study by Weiss and Fine (1956) tested this hypothesis, that aggression arousal produces attitude change only when the communication urges an aggressive position. Some subjects were put through an annoying, frustrating experience designed to make them feel aggressive. Other subjects had the opposite experience—they had a pleasant, satisfying experience. Then both groups were exposed to a persuasive communication that took a lenient attitude toward juvenile delinquency, or one that took a punitive position. The experimenters hypothesized that the subjects who had been made

to feel aggressive would be more likely to accept the punitive communication, because the punitive message would provide aggressive subjects with a way of expressing their aggression. The lenient message would be more likely to satisfy the relatively nonaggressive needs of the nonaggressive subjects.

The results were in line with these expectations—the aggressive subjects were more influenced by the punitive communication, and the nonaggressive subjects were more influenced by the lenient one. So personal frustrations might make a person more vulnerable to persuasive communications advocating military action, attacks on minorities, or harsh treatment of dissidents, but probably they would not increase susceptibility to such nonaggressive appeals as charity campaigns.

Strong Arguments

Sometimes the arguments in a communication are strong and compelling, and sometimes they are weak and specious. The evidence for a causal role of smoking in lung cancer, or for unsafe sexual practices in producing AIDS, is very compelling. The evidence that Caucasians were intended by God to be a superior race, or that the Nazis never slaughtered millions of Jews in World War II, is very weak.

One would think that strong arguments would always be better than weak ones. But that is not always the case. Earlier we discussed the *elaboration-likelihood model* proposed by Petty and Cacioppo (1986). This focused particularly on the conditions under which people are motivated and able to think carefully about the arguments in a persuasive communication, and generate either supportive or contrary arguments on the issue. When they do scrutinize the communication closely, strong arguments are indeed better than weak ones. But under many other circumstances, people do not give the message very detailed or careful thought. Then such peripheral cues as source attractiveness or the sheer volume of argument are the main determinants of attitude change. Research by Petty and Cacioppo and others has succeeded in identifying a number of variables that differentiate these two situations, and thus determine when the strength of arguments is a crucial factor.

FIGURE 7–4 Post message attitudes are affected by argument quality, source expertise, and personal relevance of the issue. The top panel shows that any argument quality matters with high issue relevance, but only source expertise matters with low issue relevance. (Adapted from Petty & Cacioppo, 1986, p. 144, based on research by Petty et al., 1981.)

PERSONAL RELEVANCE One implication is that the strength of arguments should be most important in determining attitude change when the issue is highly relevant and important to the person. In contrast, superficial communicator characteristics, such as likeability, should be more important when the issue is not relevant to the person, who is therefore not very motivated to process the information. Petty and colleagues (1981) demonstrated this

in a marketing study. In the high-relevance groups, subjects were asked to review magazine ads for a new razor and were told that they would get a free razor in return. In the low-relevance groups they were provided no razor (they got toothpaste instead). As Figure 7–4 shows, with high relevance, the strength of arguments was the key factor; with low relevance, source expertise was. In a later study (Petty et al., 1983) they repeated the same finding about source characteristics, this time comparing famous sports celebrities endorsing the product with endorsements by ordinary citizens.

In short, when the outcome mattered to the subject, the arguments were carefully processed. When it did not, the subject was content to rely on the superficial attributes of the communicator.

MEDIUM The communication medium also affects whether or not the subject processes the arguments carefully, and therefore whether or not strong arguments matter. A visual or even an audio communication provides many nonverbal cues to the recipient. As we saw in Chapter 3, these nonverbal cues can be very important in determining impressions of a person. So, not surprisingly, they also turn out to be quite important in determining a communicator's persuasiveness. Chaiken and Eagly (1983) have shown that communicator likeability is much more important in visual or audio communications, where such nonverbal information about the communicator is available. In written communication, however, where only verbal information is available, the arguments are processed more carefully, so the message content is relatively more important.

They varied likeability by having the communicator praise or derogate the students, faculty, and overall institutional quality of the university the students were attending (the University of Toronto). Then he delivered a persuasive communication supporting a change to the trimester system on videotape, audiotape, or via a written transcript. As shown in Table 7–3, the communicator's likeability contributed to opinion change only in the video or audio versions, where nonverbal cues about him were available.

Additional evidence pointed to the conclusion that communicator attributes are central in video and audio, and message factors relatively more im-

TABLE 7–3

Opinion Change as a Function of Source and Medium

	COMMUNICATOR	
	Likeable	**Unlikeable**
Videotape	4.87	0.48
Audiotape	4.82	1.47
Written	3.66	3.43

Note: The entry is the mean amount of attitude change on a 15-point scale.
Source: Adapted from Chaiken & Eagly (1983), p. 246.

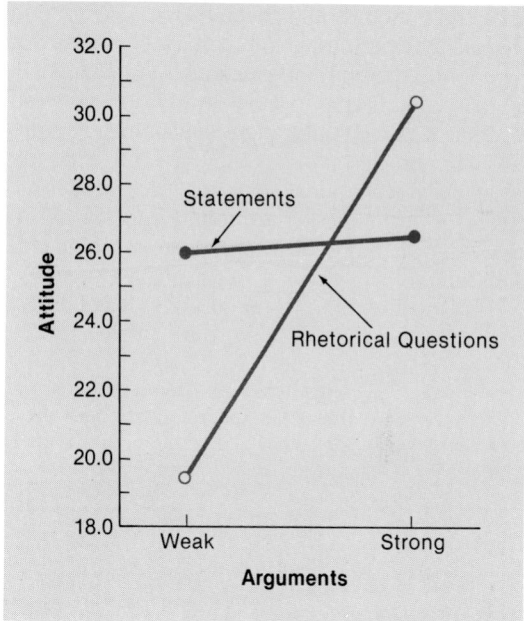

FIGURE 7–5 Effects on attitude of grammatical form and argument quality. (Burnkrant & Howard, 1984.)

portant in written communications. The students' cognitive responses were also measured after the communication. In the video and audio conditions, opinion change was related to the favorability of communicator-oriented thoughts. In the written condition, opinion change was related to the favorability of message-oriented thoughts.

The implication is that simple transfer of affect processes were most important in the video (and to a lesser extent audio) situations, whereas the message-oriented counterarguing process was crucial in written communication. In other research, these investigators have shown that written communications have a greater advantage over video or audio communication as the arguments get more complex, presumably because the written medium does induce a message-oriented mentality (Chaiken & Eagly, 1976).

RHETORICAL QUESTIONS The asking of rhetorical questions also should stimulate thought. In one such study, the persuasive arguments were introduced either by rhetorical questions or by simple assertions of the conclusions. Since the issue concerned a new requirement of comprehensive exams for all undergraduates, the rhetorical questions included ones such as, "Will passing a comprehensive exam be an aid to those who seek admission to graduate and professional schools? Would it add to the prestige of the degree, help students get jobs, increase learning, improve teaching, etc.?" (Burnkrant & Howard, 1984). The researchers predicted, consistent with Petty and Cacioppo's model, that introducing such an unpopular proposal with rhetorical questions would stimulate more thinking. Again, thinking more about the communication

would enhance the advantage of strong arguments. And indeed, that was the result. The rhetorical questions motivated more thinking, more favorable thoughts about the strong arguments, and gave a considerable advantage to strong arguments. These data are shown in Figure 7–5. Similar results have been obtained in other studies (see Petty & Cacioppo, 1986, pp. 198–203).

REPETITION Consider your reaction to seeing the same potato-faced athletes in a TV commercial downing the same brand of beer at the same bar week after week. Does the repetition reinforce your association between that brand of beer and the athletes? Perhaps, if the message is complex enough, repetition helps you understand it, and decide whether the arguments are strong or weak. Or do you just get sick of the commercial and tune it out?

Much research by Zajonc (1968) and others shows that familiarity based on repetition increases liking, as we will see in Chapter 8. This would imply repetition should generally increase attitude change. With persuasive communications, however, repetition apparently increases attitude change only up to a point. Cacioppo and Petty (1979) presented students with communications containing eight different arguments on increasing university expenditures. Each communication was presented one, three, or five times. They found agreement increased with more exposure up to a point and then fell off.

This inverted-U function occurred whether the communication advocated a position that was "desirable" and low discrepancy for students, arguing for an increase in the luxury tax, or an "undesirable" high-discrepancy one arguing for an increase in tuition. Similarly, Gorn and Goldberg (1980) found that children viewing an ice cream commercial during the television program "The Flintstones" preferred the product more when they saw the commercial a moderate (three) rather than low (one) or high (five) number of times.

Why might repetition have these effects? Theoret-

This poster by Brooke Shields, National Youth Chairman for the American Lung Association, challenges the idea that smoking is glamorous, and proclaims "Smoking Spoils Your Looks." Are her beauty and glamorous career truly "peripheral cues"?

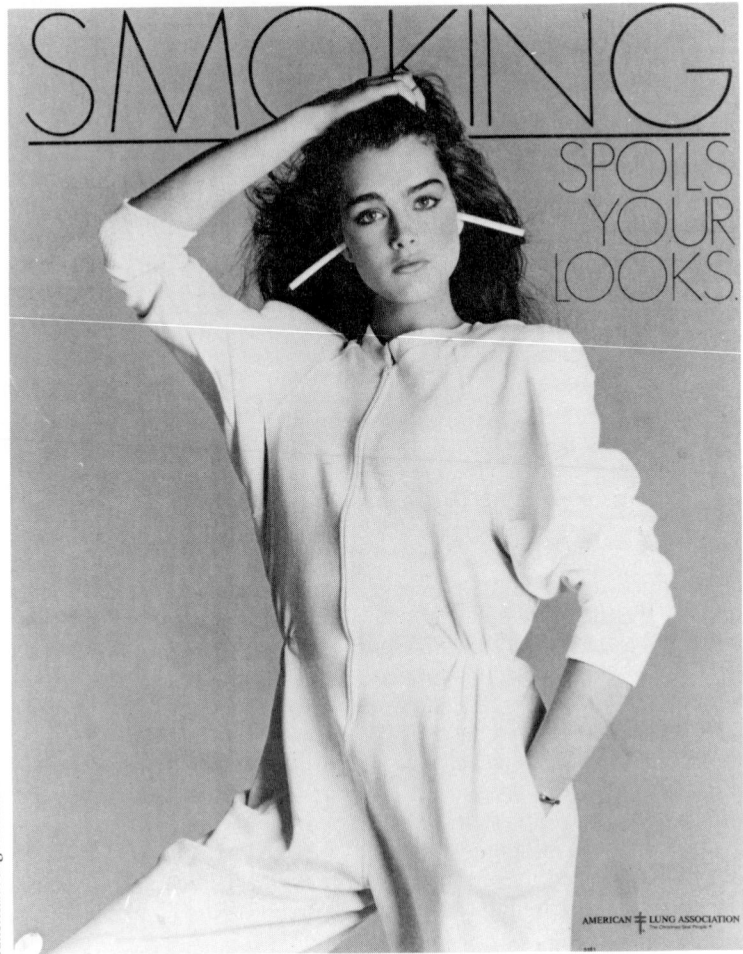

American Lung Association

ically, it is easy to imagine that repetition might have two separate effects: It increases the opportunity to consider the content of a persuasive communication (enhanced processing), and it also increases the chances of tedium and therefore a negative reaction (Cacioppo & Petty, 1985). For example, in the just-mentioned example of the children viewing ice cream commercials, the children commonly said, "Oh, not again" or "Not another one" in the high-exposure condition.

The implication of enhanced processing is that repetition will help strong arguments, because it allows them to be processed better, but will hurt weak ones, because it exposes their flaws. Cacioppo and Petty (1985) found that three exposures to strong arguments for senior comprehensive exams increased their impact, but three exposures decreased the impact of weak arguments. How can tedium be dealt with? Presumably by varying the content a little. Hence the same authors report evidence that repetition of commercials for a particular product achieves increased effectiveness if the commercials are varied somewhat, but not if exactly the same commercial is used each time.

PERIPHERAL CUES   When a person is poorly motivated to think about the arguments (e.g., when the issue has little importance to the person) or when the person is unable to process them well (e.g., when uninformed or distracted, etc.), then more peripheral cues become more important in determining attitude change. We have already mentioned a number of simple peripheral cues that allow a person to respond to a communication without thinking very much about its arguments. The credibility or likeability of the source and the discrepancy of the communicator's position are two good examples.

The number of arguments in a message and the length of the arguments are two more such factors. Petty and Cacioppo (1984) have shown that simply presenting more arguments in a message increases attitude change when the issue is not very relevant to the person and therefore provides little motivation to think about it. Presenting more arguments increases attitude change for strong and weak arguments alike, indicating little processing is going on. Similarly, longer messages are more influential than short messages—but only among the uninformed, who presumably give them little thought. Among the better informed, strength of agruments is the more important factor (Wood et al., 1985).

Surrounding a commercial message with pleasant music enhances its effect—but only when the person has no incentive to think about the commercial message. When there is some incentive to think about it—in terms of providing advice to an ad agency on the best commercials, and getting a gift in return—information rather than pleasant music has been decisive (Gorn, 1982).

A variety of factors increase attentive processing of the communication, therefore, giving an advantage to strong arguments: personal relevance, lack of audiovisual cues, rhetorical questions, and repetition. In their absence, more peripheral cues have greater impact, such as source characteristics or the volume of argument.

THE TARGET

Even after a message from a particular source has reached the target, the problems of attitude change are not over. The effects of an ad for environmental protection may be quite different for the owner of a strip coal mine than for a suburban university professor. Characteristics of the target and the target's experience also affect reactions to the message.

Commitment

The ultimate impact of a persuasive message depends in great part on the strength of targets' **commitment** to their prior attitudes. Several factors affect strength of commitment. One is *behavior* engaged in on the basis of attitudes, as we saw in

Such public religious commitments are among the most binding. What are the crucial ingredients in this one that will help keep the young man committed in the years to come?

Laimute E. Druskis

Chapter 6. Someone who has just bought a car is more committed to the belief that it is a fine car than before buying it. And new car owners are generally not very open to hearing that the car they have selected is not a very good one.

Second, *public statements* of the attitude produce more commitment. Someone who has just told all his friends that he thinks smoking is bad for health and is an evil, dirty habit is more committed to this attitude than if he had kept his thoughts to himself. Changing his attitude is harder if he expressed it publicly because then the change would involve admitting to his friends he was wrong. Whenever changing an attitude would cause the individual to give up more, suffer more, or change more of his other attitudes or behaviors, his commitment to his initial attitude increases and makes it more difficult for him to change it.

Third, free *choice* of a position produces a greater feeling of commitment than being forced. In one study (Freedman & Steinbruner, 1964), sub-jects were given information about a candidate for graduate school and asked to rate him, under circumstances of either high or low choice. The subjects were either made to feel that they had made up their own minds and freely selected the particular rating, or that they had virtually nothing to do with the decision and had been forced to select the rating. The subjects were then exposed to information that strongly contradicted their initial rating and were allowed to change the rating if they desired. Those who had made the first rating with a feeling of free choice changed less than those in the low-choice condition.

In general, then, strong commitment reduces the amount of attitude change produced by a discrepant persuasive communication. Greater commitment makes it harder for people to change an attitude and means that they are more likely to use other modes of resolution instead.

The exact mechanism by which commitment increases resistance is still not very clear. Greater commitment makes people give more counterarguments when they are confronted with discrepant information (Petty & Cacioppo, 1979), but it is not clear whether they are necessary to produce this added resistance to change.

The joint effects of commitment and discrepancy on attitude change are similar to those of credibility and discrepancy. Commitment to an initial position also shifts the amount of discrepancy at which maximum attitude change occurs, but in the opposite direction. The greater the commitment to one's initial attitude, the lower the discrepancy at which rejection of the source starts to substitute for attitude change. Therefore, the greater the commitment, the lower the discrepancy at which maximum attitude change occurs (Freedman, 1964; Rhine & Severance, 1970).

Inoculation

In the aftermath of the Korean war, William McGuire and others became very interested in reports of "brainwashing" of American prisoners of war by Chinese Communists. A number of POWs had given public speeches denouncing the American government, and several said publicly that they wished to remain in China when the war was over, rather than return to the United States. McGuire speculated that some soldiers might have been vulnerable to influence because they were being attacked on matters they were quite inexperienced and ignorant about—many soldiers, especially the less educated ones, had never been forced to defend the United States against the sophisticated Marxist arguments used against them by the Chinese.

McGuire hypothesized that an important source of resistance to change in the target comes from past experience with the issue. He and his associates conducted a series of experiments on the effects of giving people experiences designed to increase their ability to resist persuasion. He pictured the individual faced with a discrepant communication as being like somebody attacked by a virus or a disease. The stronger the persuasive message (virus), the more damage it would do; the stronger the person's defenses, the better able he or she is to resist persuasion (disease).

There are two different ways of strengthening people's defenses against a disease. We can strengthen their bodies generally, by giving them vitamins, exercise, and so on; or we can strengthen their defenses against that particular disease by building up antibodies. McGuire argued that these two approaches are also applicable to the influence situation.

To begin with, he identified a number of *cultural truisms*—opinions so universally held in our society that they are almost never subjected to any kind of attack. One example is the belief that it is good to brush one's teeth after every meal. Probably almost everybody in the United States believes that this is basically a good idea in terms of dental health. And most people have never heard anything to the contrary. Thus, someone holding this opinion is like people who have never been exposed to the smallpox germ. They have never been forced to defend themselves from attack so they have never built up any defense against attack.

One procedure that strengthens resistance is to build up the person's opinion directly by providing additional arguments supporting the original position. McGuire called this a **supportive defense.** If people believe it is good to brush their teeth three times a day, they are shown a study by the United States Public Health Service which shows that people who do so have fewer cavities than those who brush their teeth less often or not at all. Giving individuals this kind of support for their position does, in fact, somewhat increase their resistance to subsequent persuasive communications.

A different approach is to strengthen the individual's defenses against persuasion. McGuire argued that, as with diseases, the most effective way of increasing resistance is to build up defenses. If people are given mild cases of smallpox that they are able to fight off, their bodies produce antibodies which in the future provide an effective and strong defense against more powerful attacks. Similarly, if a particular opinion has never been attacked, it is extremely vulnerable because no defenses have been built up around it. When such an opinion is suddenly subjected to persuasive pressure, the individual does not have a set of defenses, and the opinion tends to be relatively easy to change. However, someone whose opinion has been attacked, and successfully defended, should be able to resist later attacks because a relatively strong defensive system will have been built up.

In other words, McGuire argued that it is possible to inoculate individuals against persuasive attacks just as we can inoculate them against diseases. **Inoculation** is accomplished by weakly attacking the individual's attitude. The attack must be weak, or it would change the attitude and the battle would be lost. To be certain this does not occur, the target is helped to defend against the mild attack by also being given an argument directed specifically at the attack or by being told that the attack is not very good and should be easy to refute.

The key study by McGuire and Papageorgis (1961) used both the supportive and inoculation methods to build up defenses. There were three groups of subjects: One group received support for their position; one group had their position attacked weakly and the attack refuted (the inoculation condition); and the third group received neither procedure. Afterward, all groups were subjected to a strong attack on their initial position. Table 7–4 shows how much each group changed as a result of this final attack. The supportive method helped subjects resist persuasion a little—the group receiving support changed a little less than the group that had no preparation. But the inoculation method helped a great deal; subjects receiving this preparation changed much less than the other subjects.

One implication would be that supportive defenses are best when the target simply needs to be taught specific arguments. The inoculation defense would be better when the targets must be stimulated to think up their own defensive arguments. Consistent with this view, later research has shown that support tends to be particularly effective

TABLE 7–4

The Effects of Supportive or Inoculation Defenses on Resistance to Persuasion

Condition	Amount of Attitude Change
Supportive defense	5.87
Inoculation defense	2.94
Neither	6.62

Source: Adapted from McGuire & Papageorgis (1961).

when the subsequent attack contains arguments similar to the content of the supporting arguments, but it is relatively ineffective when new arguments are used. In contrast, inoculation is effective even when the attack includes new arguments (McGuire, 1964).

The specific mechanism by which inoculation operates is not yet clear. Cognitive response theory is perhaps most often used to explain these results. It suggests that in refuting the mild attack, people use and therefore exercise all their defenses. They prepare arguments supporting their own positions, construct counterarguments against the opposing position, derogate the possible sources of opposing views, and so on. This would make each of the defensive mechanisms stronger and would provide the individual with a more effective position.

Personality Factors

Some people are generally more persuasible than others, regardless of the issue involved or the type of influence being attempted. Experiments have been conducted (Hovland & Janis, 1959) in which subjects were exposed to persuasive communications on a variety of issues with different types of appeals and arguments and in different persuasion situations. They indicated that subjects who were highly persuasible under one set of conditions tended also to be more persuasible under others.

The effect is not very strong; it explains only a small percentage of the total variance. But considering the diversity of the situations and issues studied, the consistency found offers convincing support for the existence of the trait of general persuasibility.

One fairly consistent finding has been that subjects with low self-esteem tend to be more persuasible than those with high self-esteem. The standard explanation is that low self-esteem people place a low value on their opinions, just as they do on everything else about themselves. Since they do not value their own opinions, they are less reluctant to give them up and are more likely to change them when they are attacked.

As indicated earlier, Petty and Cacioppo's (1986) elaboration-likelihood model focuses on factors that make people give careful attention to the communication. One such factor is "need for cognition." This refers to the level of enjoyment people get from engaging in effortful information processing. It is measured by agreement with such items as "I find satisfaction in deliberating hard and for long hours." In one study, they presented students of either high or low need for cognition with arguments for increasing the tuition substantially at their university at some point in the distant future (Cacioppo et al., 1986). Some students got strong arguments, and others weak arguments. The study's prediction was that higher need for cognition would inspire people to greater thoughtfulness about the proposal, and therefore greater acceptance of strong arguments, and greater rejection of weak arguments. These were the results obtained.

It also might seem that individuals with high intelligence would be less persuasible than those with lower intelligence, because of greater critical ability. Research has not generally supported this assumption. On the average, people of high intelligence are persuaded just as much as people of low intelligence. However, there is reason to believe that intelligence does have some effect on the kinds of persuasive appeals that are most effective. People of high intelligence are influenced less by inconsistent and illogical arguments than are people of lower intelligence, and the latter may be influenced less by complex, difficult arguments (Eagly & Warren, 1976). It is important to note that the lack of an overall correlation between intelligence and persuasibility does not necessarily mean that intelligence is entirely unrelated to the influence process. Rather, it indicates that the relationship is complex.

Other than these few factors, there is little to support hypotheses about how personality affects persuasibility. There have been many suggestions (authoritarianism, richness of fantasy), but the evidence is rather weak at the moment.

THE SITUATION

The factors described thus far have concerned the communicator, the message, and the target. Yet mass communications usually are delivered within a broader context in which other things are happening, and these also often prove to have decisive effects on the success of persuasion attempts.

When we watch a political candidate's television commercial in an election campaign, we know that she is running for election; her statement is not a dispassionate, academic one. Most people watch television news in the midst of all the hubbub of family members returning home from work, talking to each other, making dinner, children shouting and screaming, and so forth. We watch commercials for new cars during the halftime of football games, in the midst of getting up to get another beer, going to the bathroom, and making sarcastic comments about the commercials with our friends. These situations all are likely to influence the success of attempts at persuasion. Let us now consider some of the most important situational variables in attitude change.

Forewarning of Position

If someone is told ahead of time that she is going to be exposed to a discrepant communication on an issue she cares strongly about, she is better able to resist persuasion by that message. In a study by Freedman and Sears (1965), teenagers were told ten minutes beforehand that they were going to hear a talk titled "Why Teenagers Should Not Be Allowed to Drive." Other teenagers were not told about the talk until just before the speaker began. Under these circumstances, those who had the warning were less influenced by the talk than were the others. This **forewarning** enabled them to resist this very unpalatable message.

This is certainly a plausible finding, and it seems

to be believed by many people in the business of persuasion. For example, we often hear an advertisement on radio or television with no warning that this is going to be an advertisement. Instead, the station sneaks in the ad before we are fully aware of what it is. A similar although more altruistic example is the dentist who warns us that something is going to hurt. He seems to feel that we will be better able to withstand the pain if we are warned. In fact, there is some experimental evidence that subjects who are warned ahead of time that they are going to receive an electric shock report it hurts less than do subjects who are not warned.

All this sounds plausible and reasonable, but why does it occur? Why does a ten-minute warning help people resist persuasion? It is important to keep in mind that all the subjects know the speaker disagrees with them—the only difference is that some people know it ten minutes ahead of time and others know it only just before the speech. The greater resistance shown by those with the longer warning is due to some mechanism that operates during those minutes between the warning and the speech.

Most likely, as with the inoculation procedure, the individual's defenses are in some way exercised and therefore strengthened. Although there is little evidence to demonstrate directly how these defenses are strengthened, the individual probably uses all the maneuvers and tactics we discussed previously. She may anticipate the arguments that will come from the opponent and try to make up counterarguments. Indeed Petty and Cacioppo (1977) have shown the delay period between warning and exposure to the communication allows subjects to generate more counterarguments, though they had no way of being certain that anticipatory counterarguing was responsible for the increased resistance.

Listeners also probably use derogation of the discrepant source. The person who has been through the inoculation procedure has plenty of opportunity to derogate the opponent. Similarly, the forewarned person has ten minutes to convince himself that the communicator is unreliable, prejudiced, and misinformed.

In other words, the individual who is warned (or who has just experienced a mild attack) is like

Forewarned is forearmed (except when you like fast cars anyway): She surely was forewarned of the position he would advocate. Does that help her resist persuasion? Or was her position not very discrepant from his to begin with?

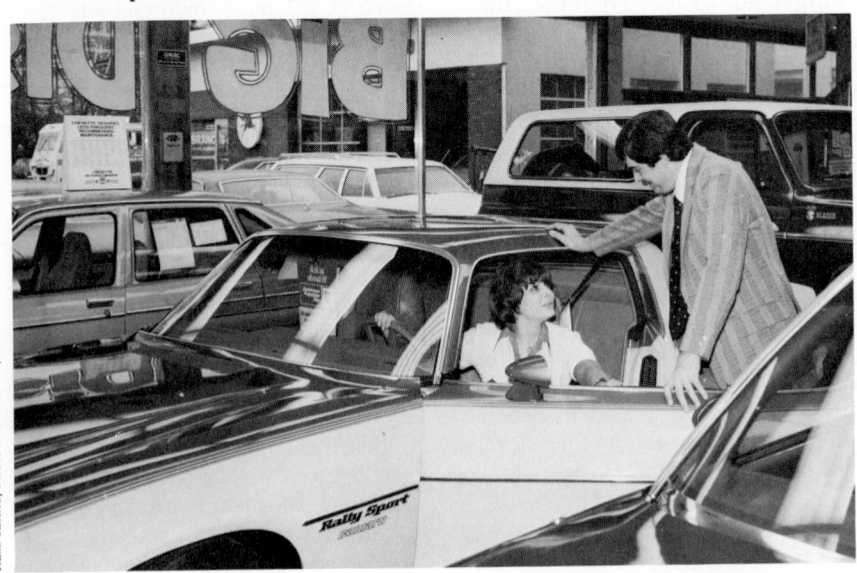

Russ Kinne, Photo Researchers, Inc.

a fighter who has prepared for a match. He has been through training, so when the fight comes, he is in better shape and able to meet his opponent. He also spends time convincing himself that his opponent is not very good and that he, himself, is great. This makes him more confident and better able to do his best.

All this work has been done on situations in which the recipient was strongly committed to a position discrepant from the communicator's. When the listener is not very committed to a position, though, warning turns out to have the opposite effect—it actually facilitates attitude change. When the person is unlikely from the start to cling very tightly to the original attitude, the warning seems to operate as a cue to propel her along the road she was destined for sooner or later anyhow.

For example, Apsler and Sears (1968) hypothesized that warning would actually facilitate attitude change among subjects who were not personally involved in the topic, whereas it would have the usual effect of blocking change among highly involved subjects. They gave subjects a persuasive communication advocating replacement of professors by teaching assistants in many upper-division courses, a change opposed by almost all subjects. Some subjects were told the change would come quickly, in time to affect their own education (high involvement); others were told it was several years off and would not affect them (low involvement).

Forewarning helped block change among the highly involved subjects, just as it had among the teenagers who were highly involved in the issue of teenage driving in the Freedman and Sears experiment. However, it facilitated change in the low-involvement condition. This is shown in Figure 7–6.

These two effects of warning frequently can be detected even before the subject receives the communication. The highly committed person seems to begin to resist even before she is exposed to the communication, while the uncommitted person seems to moderate his stand. In one experiment, subjects highly committed to their initial position became more extreme (and presumably more resistant to change) when warned of a debate, while weakly committed subjects became more moderate (and presumably more receptive to change) (Sears, Freedman, & O'Connor, 1964).

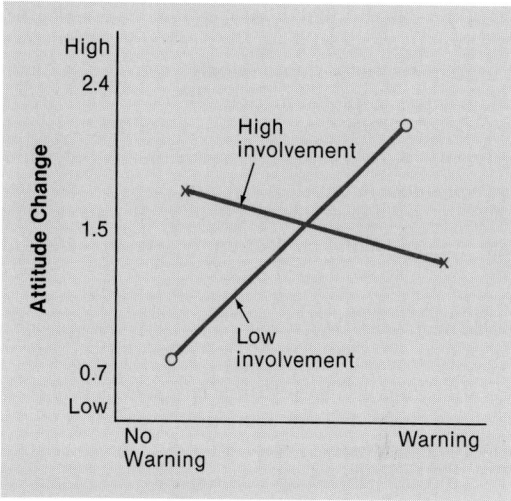

FIGURE 7–6   Effects of forewarning and involvement on persuasiveness of a discrepant message. N = 20 in each cell. The larger the score, the greater the amount of change in the advocated direction on a 16-point scale. (Adapted from Apsler & Sears, 1968, p. 164.)

Cooper and Jones (1970) have shown that these anticipatory changes are due to the subjects' expectations of exposure to the communications and their likely effects, rather than just to the knowledge of their existence. Weakly committed subjects changed when warned of forthcoming exposure to the communication, but not when told that such a communication existed without any implication of forthcoming exposure.

There are still some controversies surrounding the exact nature of these responses to warning. The elaboration-likelihood and cognitive response theories contend that forewarning produces more thought, and therefore counterarguing. But at this point we do not know whether the increased resistance of highly committed persons is based on real thought and anticipation of arguments, increased blanket rejection of the communication, or source derogation. Forewarning does inspire more counterarguing, but that could just be a byproduct of a stubborn refusal to give in.

And some researchers suggest that the anticipatory attitude change among the uncommitted may be more apparent than real. That is, it may just be done to avoid looking like a compliant person, and may not be genuine. Finally, we do not mean to give the impression that all these maneuvers are done deliberately. Rather, people tend to think about the issue a little, go over some of the points in their minds, and in this way prepare for exposure. As far as we know, the process is all quite casual and almost accidental. But the effects are clear.

Forewarning of Intent

Another kind of forewarning is that which signals the intent to persuade. Sometimes we know in advance that a communicator intends to try to change our attitude. Almost all commercials and political speeches take that form. Other times we may be exposed to a persuasive message without realizing persuasion is intended. For example, sometimes a teacher or a friend seems simply to be trying to inform us about something, but in reality is trying to persuade us of a particular position.

Forewarning of intent to persuade generally motivates more thinking about the arguments, if the issue is one of relevance and importance to the recipient. To show this, Petty and Cacioppo (1979) told subjects either that the message was "designed specifically to try to persuade you and other college students" or that it was prepared as part of a class project. Then the message argued for comprehensive exams for all seniors. In the high-relevance condition, the exam would be instituted at that college the coming year. In the low-relevance condition it would be far in the future or at another university. They found that the most counterarguing against this unpopular proposal, and the least attitude change, occurred with forewarning and high personal relevance.

Distraction

In parts of our discussion, we have described the individual as actively fighting the persuasive message. People whose opinions are attacked usually try to resist changing, especially when they are committed to their attitudes. They counterargue, derogate the communicator, and generally marshal all

their forces to defend their own positions. One important implication of this is that the ability to resist persuasion is weakened by anything that makes it harder to fight the discrepant communication. In particular, distracting attention from the battle may enable the persuasive message to get through.

A study by Festinger and Maccoby (1964) demonstrated this effect of **distraction.** Subjects listened to a speech against fraternities while watching a film. For some of the subjects, the film showed the person making the speech. For others, the film was "The Day of the Painter," a funny, somewhat zany satire on modern art. Presumably, those watching the irrelevant film were more distracted from the antifraternity speech than those watching the person speak. Subjects who initially disagreed with the speech (who were in favor of fraternities) were more influenced in the distraction than the nondistraction condition. Taking the subjects' minds off the speech increased its effectiveness.

Enhanced persuasion with mild amounts of distraction appears to be a reliable finding. Petty and Brock (1981) reviewed 22 separate studies on the topic and found some increased persuasion with distraction in all but two of them. Much of this work has been guided by a cognitive response approach. As might be expected, therefore, distraction does not facilitate attitude change under all conditions. Distraction should increase persuasion only when it interferes with an otherwise effective counterarguing process. Petty, Wells, and Brock (1976) have shown that distraction fosters attitude change more when the message otherwise easily generates many counterarguments.

So distraction would help persuasion much better on a familiar issue on which we know our own arguments, such as against a person advocating racially segregated schools, than on an issue we do not have ready arguments about. It seems to work best when the communications are highly discrepant and on very involving topics, presumably because these inspire the most vigorous counterarguing. And it works best with high-credibility sources, because they are the most threatening and therefore trigger the most counterarguing (Petty & Brock, 1981). These results are consistent with Petty and Cacioppo's (1986) elaboration-likelihood theory about the effects of distraction on motivation and ability to process the arguments of a communication.

In any case, the effect must depend on the right amount of distraction. As usual, there is a conflict between getting the message through and getting it accepted. Obviously, too much distraction prevents the persuasive message from being heard at all and reduces its effectiveness to zero. If the person is totally focused on something else, none of the message can get through. The idea is to get the position through but inhibit counterarguing.

Advertisers may want to distract television viewers from the main point of commercials by irrelevant pictures and action. They do not, however, want to have the irrelevancies so fascinating that the message is lost. Having a beautiful woman in the background during a soap commercial may help sell soap; having her in the foreground may help; but having her in the foreground singing so loudly that the commercial can barely be heard would certainly reduce the effectiveness of the ad. Distraction may work under some conditions, but it is important that the distraction not be too great, or the effect will be reversed.

ATTITUDE CHANGE OVER TIME

So far we have focused on immediate responses to one-shot communications—that is, under what conditions does a televised speech, radio ad, or conversation with a friend *immediately* produce attitude change? In many cases, however, we want to know how attitudes change over time. We especially want to know the effects of repeated exposure to a message and what effects are likely to last when the exposure ends.

Spontaneous Attitude Change

Attitudes apparently get stronger the longer people hold them. Tesser (1978) has done a series of studies that find thinking about an attitude object tends to make the attitude more extreme. According to Tesser, people review and rehearse their cognitions, and consistency pressures move them toward more evaluatively consistent clusters. So if you spend more than the usual amount of time thinking about your best friend, you will probably like her better, whereas if you think about your enemy more often, you will probably dislike her even more.

In thinking about your best friend, you might remember additional good qualities or enjoyable experiences you shared. And you might reinterpret some of your less pleasant memories to excuse your friend's behavior. The same could happen with your enemy: You would lengthen your list of offenses and find seamy motives for her apparently good and generous acts.

Basically, Tesser's hypothesis is that thinking about an issue produces more polarized attitudes because thinking allows people to generate more consistent attitudes: They can generate new beliefs consistent with their previous attitudes, reinterpret old beliefs, and suppress inconsistent beliefs. But all this cognitive activity requires that the individual already have a knowledge structure, or schema, about the issue. Without some schematic understanding of the issue, it would be difficult to generate new beliefs, or know how to reinterpret old ones, and so on.

This hypothesis therefore predicts that thought will polarize attitudes only if the person already has a schema about the issue, and if the thought is specifically focused on that issue rather than on some other, irrelevant question. To test this, Chaiken and Yates (1985) tested two groups of people, some who already had a highly consistent knowledge structure about the issue (capital punishment), and others who did not. Then every person wrote an essay either about that issue or about a different, irrelevant issue (censorship). The dependent variable was whether their attitudes became more extreme, or less extreme, following the essay writing. Indeed, the highest polarization occurred after the highly consistent subjects wrote an essay on the topic in question—capital punishment. No significant polarization occurred in any of the other conditions. To polarize attitudes, then, the thought must be relevant to the issue, and the person must have sufficient cognitive resources.

Attitudes also spontaneously move toward logical consistency over time, even in the absence of explicit pressure to think about them. McGuire (1960, 1981) has investigated the so-called *Socratic effect*, by which people arrive at logical conclusions simply from being asked about a set of premises. You will recall that Socrates was able to lure his students into very sophisticated and correct conclusions just by asking them leading questions, even when they were sure they did not know the ultimate answer he was driving at.

McGuire shows that the same process occurs spontaneously with ordinary people. He has shown that asking questions about the premises and conclusions of logical syllogisms makes them become more consistent over time. For example, if you believe that the number of automobiles in your area is likely to increase and that people are not likely to allow more freeways to be built, then over time you are likely to come to expect increased traffic congestion, even in the absence of any direct evidence of it. In McGuire's research the increased consistency of the conclusions occurred no matter whether the subjects had been asked about the premises ten minutes or seven days ahead of time.

Persistence of Attitude Change

A last question concerns the persistence of attitude change over time, once it has been induced by a communication. It seems clear that, in general, memory for the details of an argument decays with time in a way resembling an Ebbinghaus forgetting curve—that is, decreases are rapid at first, then diminish later on. In general, though, the persistence of attitude changes is not necessarily dependent on retention of the details of arguments. As indicated earlier, a good bit of research finds memory for arguments of only secondary importance

(McGuire, 1985). Other events that occur after the communication are of much greater significance.

One important factor may be whether or not the recipient is later reminded of important cues other than the arguments themselves, such as the credibility of the source. Kelman and Hovland (1953), for example, manipulated source credibility and found the usual difference on an immediate posttest: The high-credibility source had produced more attitude change. Three weeks afterward, the credibility difference was gone. The low-credibility source's message was, by then, just as effective. The original credibility difference could be reinstated, however, if the subject was reminded of the original source of the message.

This study led to some controversy and considerable research. If attitude change increased because the association of message with low-credibility source was forgotten, the **discounting cue** hypothesis would suggest that reinstating this degrading association would kill off that gradual increase in attitude change. The idea is that various cues surrounding a message indicate to the recipients whether or not they should disregard the message. Low credibility of the source may be one such cue, as would be any other indication that the arguments are misinformed or biased. If these cues are forgotten over time, attitude change may actually increase, a phenomenon known as the **sleeper effect**.

Cook and Flay (1978) and others (see Petty & Cacioppo, 1981, p. 92) have concluded that such sleeper effects are likely to happen primarily when discounting cues originally followed the message. When the discounting cue follows the message, the recipients will have already listened to the arguments and taken them seriously. If they hear the discounting cue before the message, the recipients will probably not even pay attention to the message and there will be no memory of the arguments to take over when they have forgotten the low-credibility source.

This has come to be known as the "differential decay" hypothesis (Pratkanis et al., 1987). It suggests that the sleeper effect occurs when the impact of a discounting cue (such as a low-credibility source) dissipates more quickly than the impact of the message itself. The person may remember hearing

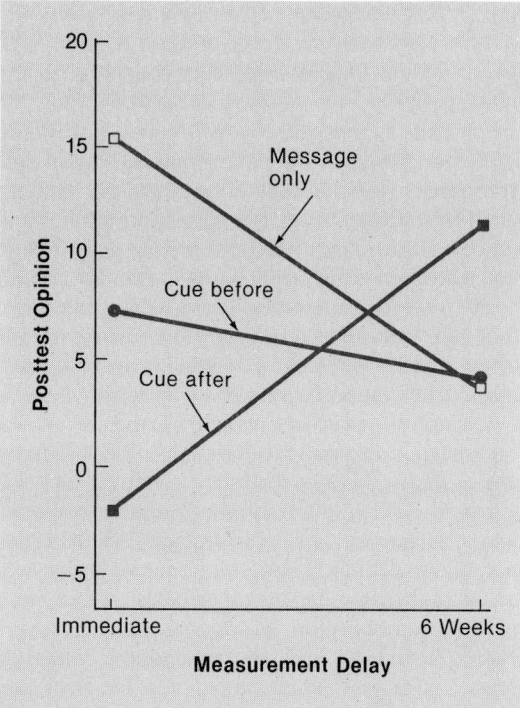

FIGURE 7–7 A sleeper effect occurs when the cue is given after the message, but not before. (From Pratkanis, Greenwald, Leippe, & Baumgardner, 1987.)

some very powerful arguments but not whom they were made by. Immediately after hearing the message, both the discounting cue and the message are accessible in memory, so there is little immediate apparent attitude change. But a few days later, the impact of the discounting cue may be lost, while that of the message is retained, producing the surge in attitude change described as the "sleeper effect."

Pratkanis and colleagues (1987) report a study demonstrating this effect. Subjects were presented a 1000-word message arguing against a 4-day work week, and a powerful discounting cue—a note from the editor stating the message conclusion was wrong. Again, if the discounting cue is given before the message, it will prevent substantial message impact right off the bat, so little attitude change

will occur, either immediate or delayed. But if the cue is given immediately afterwards, the sleeper effect should occur. Figure 7–7 shows the results.

When subjects were given the message only, initial impact was substantial, but it dissipated over time. When the discounting cue was given before the message, the immediate persuasive effect was understandably diminished—the subjects had just been told to expect a wrong conclusion. Its impact remained fairly modest six weeks later. And when the discounting cue was given right after the message, it substantially reduced the initial impact of the message. However, consistent with the differential decay hypothesis, attitude change surged forward when measured again 6 weeks later. Presumably the discounting cue no longer had any effect, whereas the impact of the message persisted.

Low credibility is not the only discounting cue. Attitude change may also be artificially suppressed by warning the recipient about the communicator's intent. People tend to become stubborn when they feel the source is trying to persuade them. But over time, such people seem to show increased attitude change, presumably as the discounting cue (persuasive intent) is forgotten (Watts & Holt, 1979).

Another determinant of persistence, and probably the most important, is the kind of social support given the person after exposure to the communication. The best example is Newcomb's (1963) study of the long-term changes in political attitudes of young women attending Bennington College in the 1930s. Most became considerably more liberal while they were in college. Persistence depended on the environment they established after graduating. Those surrounded by liberals stayed liberal; those surrounded by conservatives "regressed" to their precollege conservatism. We will discuss this study in more detail in Chapter 18.

If there is a lesson in all this, it may be that there is no such thing as a free lunch in the day of a persuader. A low-credibility source may get a message through, but the message is always vulnerable to its weak auspices' becoming salient again. Or, one may momentarily trick a person into changing by failing to warn her, but with time the persuasive impact will be lost. And a message can temporarily change people's attitudes, but it needs to be consistent with their long-standing values, and

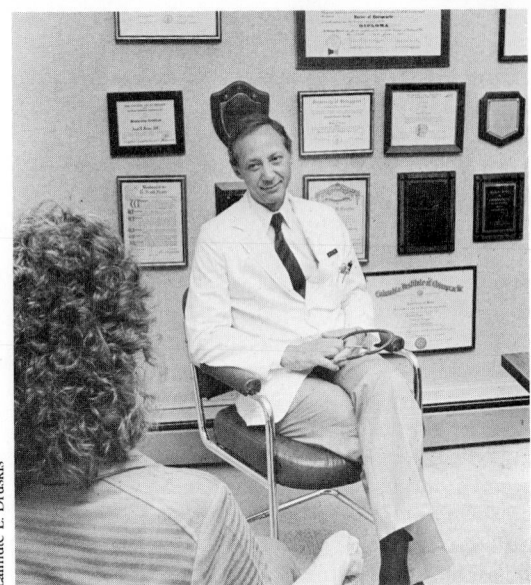

What special efforts has this man made to enhance his credibility?

with those of their friends, if it is going to endure. So it is a good idea to be skeptical of reports of sudden, dramatic changes. Unless they are supported by evidence, friends, and basic values, such changes are likely to be short-lived.

Concluding Comment

Many factors affect attitude change. Some act by appealing to a person's reason, by increasing the trust in the communication, strengthening the persuasive message, and, in general, determining how much the individual believes what is being said. An attempt to influence someone's opinion need not, however, be done in an entirely logical, unemotional, cognitive situation. The situation may, and often does, involve strong motivations, appeals to deep-seated needs, and a great many factors extraneous to the logical arguments contained in the message itself.

An entirely rational, cognitive person would be influenced only to the extent that the arguments presented were logically sound. But since there are few entirely rational beings, motivational and emotional factors are also important in determining the effectiveness of a persuasive communication.

As research on attitude change has developed, there has been some change in theoretical emphasis along these lines. Much of the early research was guided by some version of a transfer-of-affect or rote-learning approach, which treated people as rather emotional and reflexive. More popular now are cognitive theories that place relatively less emphasis on affect and emotion. Cognitive response theory suggests that people change their attitudes not in some unthinking, emotional way, but as a result of the thoughts they have about the content of the communication. We vote against the conservative incumbent because we disagree with her positions on the issues, and when we hear her speak we make up arguments against her underneath our breath. The theory of reasoned action suggests that people act on their beliefs in quite a reasonable way: If people believe they should do something, and think it is the socially approved thing to do, they will do it. The elaboration-likelihood model expects that people will often give diligent attention to the merits of the arguments.

Of course the study of attitude change will always produce a variety of views of human beings, because people are quite various and no one simplified theory will always be correct. But the trend in studying attitude change, like the trend in the study of social perception, has been away from models based on emotion and rote learning and toward models stressing cognitive processes and rational thinking.

KEY TERMS IN CHAPTER 7

aggression	credibility	forewarning	sleeper effect
assimilation	discounting cue	group norms	source derogation
cognitive response theory	discrepancy	inoculation	supportive defense
commitment (to an attitude)	distraction	membership group	transfer of affect
contrast	elaboration-likelihood model	reference group	

SUMMARY

1. A useful model of the attitude change situation classifies possible influences on the target in terms of communicator, communication, and situational and target variables.

2. The major mechanisms by which people resist persuasion include refutation of the communicator's arguments, simple blanket rejection of the message, derogating the communicator, and distorting the message.

3. The target's evaluation of the source of the communication is one of the most critical factors in the success of a persuasion attempt. More attitude change is likely if the source is viewed as credible, trustworthy, and is generally liked by the target. A reference group with which the target identifies is another potent source of influence.

4. The most important aspect of the communication is how far its position differs from that already held by the target—that is, its discrepancy. The more discrepant the communication is, the more influence it has—up to a point, when it starts to fall off again. With high source credibility and/or low commitment, this fall-off point occurs at higher levels of discrepancy.

5. Generally speaking, attitude change increases with greater fear arousal. But at very high levels of fear, when the message becomes too threaten-

ing or disruptive for the person, fear-arousing communications may become ineffective.

6. Strong arguments are more effective than weak ones when the target can be induced to think more about them, such as when the issue is personally relevant or when no audiovisual cues are present.

7. The degree of commitment to an opinion is a critical determinant of persuasion. With higher commitment, there is less persuasion.

8. A person can become inoculated against persuasion by being exposed to weak versions of the forthcoming persuasive arguments, and learning to combat them.

9. Forewarning of the position to be advocated tends to increase resistance to change when the listener is highly committed to a very discrepant position.

10. Distraction can help create persuasion by reducing the listener's defenses against very discrepant messages.

11. Repetition of a message is important if attitude change is to be maintained. Too much repetition leads to boredom and lessened support for it, however. Similarly, reinstatement of helpful cues associated with the message, such as high credibility of the communicator, will help attitude change to persist.

SUGGESTED READINGS

Alwitt, L. F., & Mitchell, A. A. (Eds.). (1985). *Psychological processes and advertising effects: Theory, research, and application*. Hillsdale, NJ: Erlbaum. A useful and current collection of applications of research on attitude change to advertising.

Hovland, C. I., Janis, I. L., & Kelley, H. H. (1953). *Communication and persuasion*. New Haven, CT: Yale University Press. The original presentation of the best program in experimental studies of attitude change. Much of the rest of the work described in this chapter springs from work originally presented here.

Leventhal, H., & Niles, P. (1964). A field experiment on fear arousal with data on the validity of questionnaire responses. *Journal of Personality, 32,* 459–479. An ingeniously designed, realistic field experiment conducted at the New York City Health Exposition, on the effects of fear arousal regarding smoking and lung cancer.

McGuire, W. J. (1985). The nature of attitudes and attitude change. In G. Lindzey & E. Aronson (Eds.), *Handbook of social psychology*, 3rd ed., Vol. 2. Reading, MA: Addison-Wesley. The most complete review of attitude research and theory.

Petty, R. E., & Cacioppo, J. T. (1986). *Communication and persuasion: Central and peripheral routes to attitude change*. New York: Springer-Verlag. The most complete presentation of the elaboration-likelihood model of attitude change.

Petty, R. E., Ostrom, T. M., & Brock, T. C. (Eds.). (1981). *Cognitive responses in persuasion*. Hillsdale, NJ: Erlbaum Associates. A useful and complete application of the cognitive response approach to many of the problems in attitude change presented in this chapter.

8 INTERPERSONAL ATTRACTION

umans are basically social animals. Think for a minute about how you spent your time yesterday. What were you doing at 9 A.M.? at noon? at 4 P.M.? at 8 P.M.? Chances are that you spent much of your day in the company of other people, whether at home, at school, or at work. In one carefully controlled study of time use, Larson and his colleagues (1982) asked a sample of adults and a sample of teenagers to carry electronic pagers for a week. At random times from early morning to late evening, the researchers activated the pager, sounding a beep that signaled participants to fill out a short questionnaire describing what they were doing and whether they were alone or with others.

As shown in Table 8–1, teenagers spent 74 percent of their waking hours with someone else; for adults, the average was 71 percent. People were most likely to be with others when they were at school or work. They were most likely to be alone when they were doing household tasks, taking a bath, listening to music, or studying at home.

For most of us, the tendency to affiliate—the desire to be with other people—is quite strong. What are the origins of human affiliation? The earliest roots are to be found in infancy, when infants form strong attachments to one or more adults. This attachment relationship has been described as the child's first love affair.

TABLE 8–1

How People Spend Their Time

Activity	ADOLESCENTS		ADULTS	
	Alone	With Others	Alone	With Others
At Home				
Housework	6.7%	5.6%	5.4%	8.6%
Self-care (bathing, etc.)	2.1	0.5	2.2	1.2
Studying (adolescents only)	3.5	1.4	—	—
Eating	0.6	3.1	0.7	2.4
Socializing (includes by phone)	2.6	5.4	—	3.8
Watching television	2.0	3.9	2.2	5.1
Personal reading	2.0	1.4	1.5	1.4
Doing hobbies and art	0.7	0.5	0.3	0.2
Idling, listening to music	1.8	2.5	2.4	3.3
All at home activities	20.0	24.3	14.7	26.0
At Work or School				
Working at work	1.6	2.2	5.9	20.9
In class (adolescents only)	—	15.6	—	—
Other activities at work or school	1.2	13.5	3.6	11.5
All at work or school activities	2.8	31.3	9.5	32.4
In Public				
In transit (on bus, etc.)	1.3	3.3	2.9	3.6
Other practical activities	1.2	6.2	0.8	1.1
Leisure	0.6	9.0	1.2	7.9
All public activities	3.1	18.6	4.9	12.6
TOTAL TIME (Alone + With Others = 100 percent)	25.9	74.1	29.1	70.9

Note: The table shows what percentage of the time people reported that they were alone or with others doing each specific type of activity. For instance, adolescents reported spending 6.7 percent of their time doing housework alone.
Source: Adapted from Larson et al. (1982).

ATTACHMENT IN CHILDHOOD

Infants become attached to the person with whom they interact most often and most lovingly. This is usually the mother, although it could be anyone with whom the infant has regular contact. By **attachment** we mean that an infant responds positively to specific people, wants to spend time with them, feels better when they are close, seeks them out when frightened, and so on. Attachment is typically a two-way process, so parents usually become attached to their children.

Infant attachment develops in steps (Ainsworth, 1973). Initially, newborns respond indiscriminately to people. Within a few weeks or months, however, they become able to distinguish between familiar people and unfamiliar ones, and begin to respond accordingly. With familiar people, infants smile and vocalize more, are more easily comforted, and show more concern about the person's leaving. At about

six months, clear-cut attachment develops. Now infants actively seek to stay close to the attachment person and protest if the person leaves. As the infant's physical capacities mature, the child calls to the attachment person, crawls after him or her, or climbs on the person's lap. So from a very early age, infants tend to affiliate and express preferences about whom they want to be with.

Attachment serves two major functions for children (Shaver & Klinnert, 1982). First, children derive a sense of security from being with the attachment person. When children are frightened or confronted with unfamiliar situations, they turn to this person for comfort and reassurance. Infants show less distress when a stranger approaches if they are being held by their mothers than if they are several feet away from the mother. A second function of attachment is to provide information

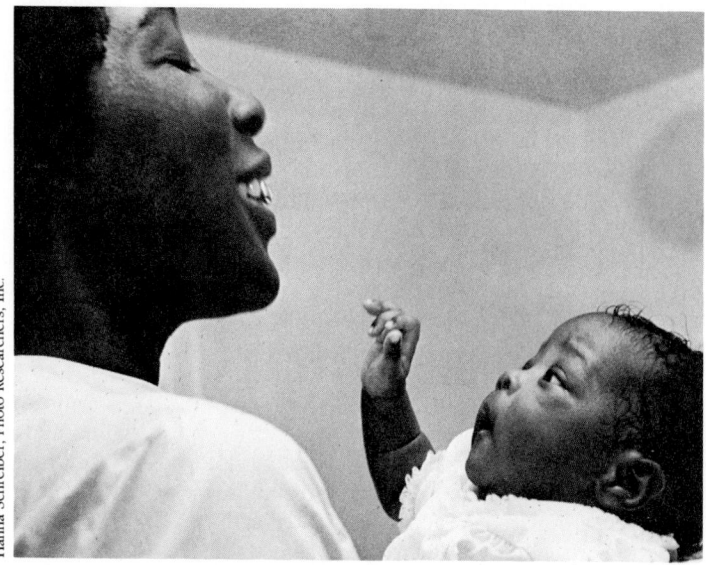

An infant's intense gaze shows her fascination with her mother. At just a few weeks of age, babies begin to form strong attachments to their parents.

Hanna Schreiber, Photo Researchers, Inc.

about the environment. When children are uncertain about how to respond to a novel situation, they look to their attachment person for guidance.

In one study (Klinnert, 1981), for instance, infants aged 12 to 18 months were put in a play room with their mothers and presented with such novel stimuli as a large remote-controlled spider, a remote-controlled dinosaur, and a life-size model of the incredible Hulk's head. When one of these strange objects first appeared, most children looked questioningly at their mothers. If the mother (following instructions from the researcher) showed fear, the child usually moved toward the mother. If the mother showed pleasure and smiled, the child moved toward the new toy. Nonverbal cues from the mother guided the child's response.

All children develop an attachment to their primary caretaker. However, the nature of this attachment between infant and parent may vary. Mary Ainsworth and her associates (1978) have identified three major styles of attachment between infants and parents. *Secure attachment* occurs when the parent is generally available and responsive to the child's needs. *Avoidant attachment* occurs when the parent is generally unresponsive or even rejecting. Infants may initially "protest" this lack of attention, but ultimately become "detached" from the caretaker. *Anxious/ambivalent attachment* occurs when the primary caretaker is anxious and does not respond consistently to the infant's needs. The caretaker may sometimes be available and responsive, but at other times be unavailable or intrusive.

Children's attachment has been explained both by innate biological factors and by learning. The biological view (see Bowlby, 1969) emphasizes the survival value of attachment for the child. Human infants are helpless creatures who need to be taken care of, protected, fed, and kept warm. When children are old enough to move around, it is important that they not wander too far from their parents because they might get into dangerous situations or simply get lost. Attachment was adaptive in human evolution because it ensured that children got the attention they needed to survive.

The biological explanation of attachment holds that certain behaviors and responses of the infant and parent are "wired in" genetically, and that these cause the attachment to form. The infant's ability to suck and the mother's ability to provide breast milk are one example of biologically based responses. Further, all infants cry, and almost all parents tend to come when their babies cry. Crying is a distress signal parents find difficult to ignore. If babies did not cry, it would be extremely hard for parents to know when help is needed, and so parents would not appear as regularly. Similarly, infants are genetically disposed to smile and tend, once they can distinguish among people, to greet their parents with a smile. The parents respond with pleasure to this greeting. Thus, the parent is drawn to the baby by the smiles, while the baby becomes attached because the parent comes in response to crying and in order to receive those smiles.

According to the biological view, the development of attachment is a two-way process. Both parent and child play a role. Clearly, if the parent seldom responded to the child's cries or smiles, then the child might not become attached. In addition, some children do not elicit attachment. They do not cry normally or do not stop crying when held; they do not smile; they do not react to the presence of the adult. This behavior makes it much harder for the parent to become attached to the child (Bell, 1968).

A second explanation is that attachment is due to learning and follows all the usual rules that govern the learning of any behavior. The child becomes attached to the parent because the parent feeds and comforts the child; the parent becomes attached to the child because the child rewards the parent. Many of the behaviors described above may be involved. For example, when the child cries, the parent comes because he or she knows that crying usually means the child needs something. The parent arrives, gives the child food or changes a diaper. The child stops crying.

Both have been reinforced by the interaction: The child feels better because it is no longer hungry or uncomfortable; the parent feels good because the child has stopped crying. Similarly, the parent is reinforced by the child's smile. As we all know, almost nothing is more rewarding than having a baby smile at us, especially if the baby favors us with more smiles than it gives to others. So the child learns to love its parent if the parent provides the attention and care it needs. And the parent learns to love the child if the child responds to this care with positive reinforcements in the form of smiles, hugs, lack of crying, and so on.

Both the biological and learning approaches probably contain much truth. Clearly, many innate behaviors of the child contribute to the formation of attachment. The child does not have to learn to cry, to smile, or feel good when comforted; all these inborn responses are important for producing an attachment bond between parent and child. On the other hand, there is no question that seeing a child smile or hearing it stop crying in response to your presence is reinforcing, and that without this reinforcement you might not develop a strong attachment to a child. Indeed, in unusual cases where a child does not respond to a parent's pres-ence, attachment may not develop. So one could say that certain innate behavior patterns help produce attachment, and that the mechanism by which they operate is through mutual reinforcement of parent and child.

Work on attachment raises the possibility that the tendency to affiliate is, at least in part, biologically based. As a species, humans may be disposed to form emotional attachments to those with whom they interact regularly and to feel more comfortable and secure in the presence of these people. It seems likely that the capacity for emotional attachment that first appears in infancy continues throughout life, as we form bonds to close friends, lovers, and children.

OUR DIVERSE SOCIAL NEEDS

As we grow up, our social needs become more complex and diverse. We affiliate to have fun, to get help, to share sexual intimacies, to feel powerful, to get approval, and so on. Researchers have tried to identify the broad range of social needs that relationships can satisfy.

Laboratory Studies of Affiliation

One of the earliest research approaches to under-standing affiliation used controlled laboratory ex-periments to test specific hypotheses about factors that increase or decrease the tendency to affiliate. The model for much of this research came from an influential series of studies conducted in the 1950s by Stanley Schachter (1959). He began with the plausible hypothesis that adults, like infants, affiliate to reduce fear. Thus, if we randomly assign adults to a condition where they will experience either high or low fear, we should observe signifi-cant differences in their desire for human company.

To test this idea, Schachter recruited women undergraduates. When subjects arrived for the study, they were greeted by an experimenter in a white laboratory coat, surrounded by electrical equipment of various sorts. The experimenter intro-duced himself as Dr. Gregor Zilstein of the Depart-ment of Neurology and Psychiatry, and he explained that the experiment concerned the effects of electric shocks. To make some subjects more afraid than others, the experimenter used two different de-scriptions of the electric shock.

In the high-fear condition, instructions de-scribed the shocks in ominous tones. Subjects were told: "These shocks will hurt. . . . In research of this sort, if we're to learn anything at all that will really help humanity, it is necessary that our shocks be intense. . . . These shocks will be quite painful but, of course, they will do no permanent damage." By continuing at some length in this vein, Dr. Zil-stein clearly suggested that the subject was in for a very frightening and painful experience.

In the low-fear condition, by contrast, every at-tempt was made to make the subject feel relaxed and to minimize the severity of the shocks. For example, the subjects were told: "I assure you that what you will feel (electric shock) will not in any way be painful. It will resemble a tickle or a tingle more than anything unpleasant." Thus, although both groups of subjects were told that the experiment would concern electric shock, one group expected a painful and frightening experience, whereas the other group expected a mild and unthreatening experience. When questioned, women in the high-fear condition were indeed more afraid.

Following the arousal and measurement of fear, Dr. Zilstein told the subjects there would be a 10-minute delay while he prepared the equipment. He explained that there were a number of other rooms in which the subjects might wait—comfortable rooms with armchairs and magazines. The experimenter then said it had occurred to him that perhaps some people would prefer to wait alone; others might prefer to wait with other subjects in the experiment, and for these there was a classroom available. Each was asked to indicate whether she preferred to wait with others, alone, or had no preference. She was also asked to indicate the strength of her choice. In this and most subsequent experiments on the topic, the choice and rating of the intensity of subjects' desire to affiliate were the basic measures of affiliation.

The results of Schachter's study are shown in Table 8–2. The answer to the question of whether highly fearful subjects want to affiliate more than subjects with low fear is "yes." The greater the fear, the greater the tendency to affiliate. Subsequent studies have confirmed this finding. Research has also shown that fear must be distinguished from other stressful situations that may actually decrease affiliative tendencies. For instance, if we are confronted with a situation that is not only stressful but also embarrassing, we may prefer to avoid other people.

This point was demonstrated by Sarnoff and Zimbardo (1961). Their study included high- and low-fear conditions plus a new condition designed to arouse "oral anxiety." In the high oral anxiety condition, men were asked to perform a series of embarrassing tasks, such as sucking on baby bottles and rubber nipples. The results were that men in the high-fear condition were eager to affiliate, but men in the embarrassing high oral anxiety condition preferred to wait alone.

Given that fearful people usually want company, just what is it that they expect to get from being with others? What is the psychological process involved? Two possibilities have been investigated. The first is the mere presence or distraction hypothesis: Fearful people affiliate to take their minds off their problems. In this case, it should not matter very much who they affiliate with—almost anyone will do. In contrast, **social comparison theory** suggests that people affiliate to compare their own feelings with those of others in the same situation. When we are in a new or unusual situation and are uncertain about how to react, we turn to others as a source of information. In this case we should be interested in affiliating only with people who are confronted with the same situation.

Several studies have tested these two possibilities, and results consistently support the social comparison hypothesis. In one study (Schachter, 1959), for example, women subjects were exposed to a high-fear condition. Some subjects were given a choice of waiting alone or waiting with women taking part in the same study. Other subjects were given a choice of waiting alone or with women students who were waiting to see their faculty advisor. As social comparison theory would predict, the fearful women in this study preferred to wait

TABLE 8–2

Effect of Fear on Affiliation

| Condition | WAITING PREFERENCE | | | | Mean Strength of Affiliation Tendency (Scale from −2 to +2) |
	Together	Don't Care	Alone	Total	
High fear	62.5%	28.1%	9.4%	100.0%	.88
Low fear	33.0	60.0	7.0	100.0	.35

Source: Adapted from Schachter (1959).

with others in the same situation, but not with others in a different situation. As Schachter has concluded: "Misery doesn't love just any company, it loves only miserable company."

Social comparison theory is helpful in understanding why fearful people want to affiliate. But the theory is actually much broader in scope. As described by Leon Festinger (1954), the theory has two basic ideas:

1. People have a drive to evaluate themselves.
2. In the absence of objective nonsocial criteria, we evaluate ourselves by comparison with other people.

All of us want to know how good we are at the things we care about. Am I a good tennis player, a talented writer, a graceful dancer, a loyal friend? Sometimes we can evaluate ourselves on objective criteria. If we get a perfect score on an exam, we know we are doing very well. But most of the time there is no convenient standard, so we turn to other people to help us evaluate ourselves. This is especially true when feelings and emotions are involved. Should I enjoy eating chocolate-covered grasshoppers, or laugh at the comedian's dirty jokes, or be afraid of the huge but harmless snake? Knowing how others are responding helps us to clarify and evaluate our own thoughts and feelings.

Thus, both Schachter's laboratory experiments on affiliation between strangers and studies of parent-child attachment emphasize that affiliation is linked to fear and to uncertainty. At any age, affiliation is likely to be most beneficial if we can associate with someone who is both sympathetic and knowledgeable.

Satisfying Our Needs

Theorists have attempted to classify the major types of benefits people receive in relationships. One analysis of affiliative needs has been proposed by Robert Weiss (1974). He identified what he called six basic "provisions of social relations"—important things relationships provide for individuals:

- *Attachment* is the sense of security and comfort provided by our closest relationships. As children we are usually strongly attached to our parents; as adults we may experience this intimacy with dating partners, spouses, or other close friends.
- *Social integration* is the sense of having shared interests and attitudes that is often provided by relationships with friends, co-workers, or teammates. Such relationships offer companionship and give a sense of belonging to a community.
- *Reassurance of worth* is provided when people support our sense of being a competent and valued person.
- A *sense of reliable alliance* involves knowing that there are people who will assist us in times of need. When emergencies arise, we often turn to our families for help.
- *The obtaining of guidance* is provided by counselors, teachers, doctors, friends, and others to whom we turn for advice and information.
- *The opportunity for nurturance* occurs when we are responsible for the well-being of another person. Taking care of someone provides us with a sense of being needed and important.

This analysis of specific social needs highlights two major points about human affiliation. First, the rewards of companionship are numerous and diverse. We could undoubtedly add many other social needs to Weiss's list. Second, this approach emphasizes that no single relationship can fulfill all our affiliative needs. A love relationship may provide a sense of attachment, but not a sense of belonging to a community. Our neighbor may water our plants while we're out of town, but not provide the sympathetic ear we want in a close confidante. A rich and healthy social life requires a network of social relations capable of satisfying all these varied needs (Cutrona & Russell, in press). Those whose relationships fail to satisfy essential social needs suffer the pain of loneliness.

LONELINESS

Few people escape the misery of loneliness. As a child, you may have felt lonely when you started in a new school, moved to a new town, or went away to summer camp. As a young adult, you may have suffered the loneliness that follows breaking up with someone you once loved. Life is filled with social transitions that disrupt personal relationships and set the stage for loneliness. For many people, the social challenges of going to college create feelings of loneliness, as noted in Box 8–1.

Loneliness versus Aloneness

Loneliness and aloneness are not the same. **Loneliness** refers to the subjective discomfort we feel when our social relations lack some important fea-ture. This deficit may be quantitative: We may have no friends, or fewer friends than we want. Or the deficit can be qualitative: We may feel our relation-ships are superficial, or less satisfying than we would like. Loneliness goes on inside a person and cannot be detected simply by looking at some-one.

In contrast to subjective feelings of loneliness, aloneness is the objective state of being apart from other people. Aloneness can be pleasant or unpleas-ant. If you're stranded on a dark street with a stalled car, being by yourself may be distressing. But soli-tude can also offer many rewards (Suedfeld, 1982). Religious leaders go off on solitary quests to seek spiritual inspiration. Writers and musicians fre-quently do their best work alone, away from the distractions of social interaction. In daily life, we may crave time alone to study for an important

The misery of time alone is seen in this young man's sense of loneliness and rejection. The pleasures of time alone are seen in this young woman's romp at the beach.

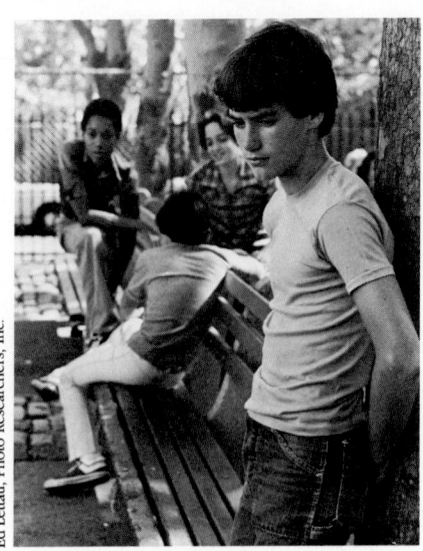

Ed Lettau, Photo Researchers, Inc.

Bill Bachman, Photo Researchers, Inc.

BOX 8-1

LONELINESS ON CAMPUS

For many students, the excitement of beginning college is mixed with the temporary loneliness of leaving friends and family, and anxiety over building a new social life. One student commented:

> Coming to a large university such as this was a big change for me. After being voted in high school "Best Personality" and "Most Popular," I had to start over. Seeing nothing but strangers was rather difficult at first, but I find myself getting used to it.

To learn about the social transition of going to college, Carolyn Cutrona, Daniel Russell, and Anne Peplau conducted a study of entering students at UCLA. Participants in the study were contacted during their first few weeks on campus and then seven months later in the spring (Cutrona, 1982).

At the start of the school year, 75 percent of new students had experienced at least occasional loneliness since their arrival on campus. More than 40 percent reported that their loneliness had been moderate to severe in intensity. Fortunately, most students were able to cope successfully with the adjustment to college. By spring, only 25 percent were still lonely.

How did students who overcame their loneliness differ from those who remained lonely throughout their first year of college? The most striking difference was found in their attitudes. Students were more likely to recover from loneliness if they began the school year with positive expectations that they would be successful in making friends and if they felt good about themselves and their personality. In other words, optimism and high self-esteem were significant ingredients in creating a satisfying social life at college.

Students living at home with parents were no more lonely than students living in a dorm on campus. Successful and unsuccessful students reported about the same frequency of such activities as joining clubs, playing intramural sports, going to parties, or talking to strangers in classes. Both groups were also equally likely to report efforts to improve their appearance and social skills or to find new ways to meet people.

But there may be more subtle differences in the behavior of students who do and do not recover from loneliness. Jones (1982) observed that lonely college students interacted in a more self-focused way than did the nonlonely. For instance, in a conversation with a new acquaintance, lonely students asked fewer questions about the other person, made fewer statements focusing on the other, and responded more slowly to comments by the partner. Lonely people tended to be more negativistic and self-absorbed and were less responsive to others. Other research (Solano, Batten, & Parish, 1982) suggests that lonely college students may be atypical in their patterns of self-disclosure, either pouring out their heart to someone they've just met or revealing unusually little about themselves. The researchers suggest that these inappropriate disclosure levels may interfere with the development of close relationships.

test, read a good book, or think over a problem. Even living alone can be a positive experience that provides a sense of accomplishment and independence.

There is no inevitable link between aloneness and loneliness: We can be happy alone or lonely in a crowd. Nonetheless, people are somewhat more likely to feel lonely when they are alone. For example, in the time use study by Larson described earlier, people felt lonelier when they were alone than when they were with others. A closer look at the data revealed, however, that this pattern resulted primarily from being alone on Friday or Saturday night. People did not feel particularly lonely if they were alone during the week while shopping or studying. But being alone on a weekend evening when personal preference and social norms suggest you should be out with friends was a major impetus to loneliness.

The Experience of Loneliness

In national surveys (such as Bradburn, 1969), roughly one American in four says he or she has felt "very lonely or remote from other people" in the past 2 weeks. Loneliness can range from fleeting twinges of discomfort to severe and persistent feelings of intense misery (Peplau & Perlman, 1982).

DURATION OF LONELINESS   Sometimes loneliness is caused by a life change that takes us away from friends and intimate relationships. So-called *situational loneliness* occurs when a person has had satisfying relationships until some specific change takes place in his or her life. Situations that commonly cause loneliness include moving to a new town, going away to school, starting a new job, being separated from friends and loved ones while on a trip or in the hospital, or ending an important relationship through death, divorce, or breaking up. People usually recover from situational loneliness and reestablish a satisfying social life, although this is obviously more difficult in some situations than in others. We may make friends at our new job in a few months, but take a year or more to get over the ending of a love relationship.

Some people suffer from loneliness for many years, more or less independent of changes in their lives. They are experiencing *chronic loneliness*. Such individuals might describe themselves as a "lonely person," rather than someone who is in a lonely period of life. Perhaps 10 percent of American adults suffer from severe and persistent loneliness.

TYPES OF LONELINESS   Robert Weiss (1973) has distinguished two types of loneliness, based on the specific social provision that a person lacks. **Emotional loneliness** results from the absence of an intimate attachment figure, such as might be provided for children by their parents or for adults by a spouse or intimate friend. **Social loneliness** occurs when a person lacks a sense of social integration or community that might be provided by a network of friends or co-workers.

It is possible to experience one type of loneliness without the other. A young couple who get married and move to Alaska to seek adventure may not feel emotional loneliness—they have each other. But they are likely to experience social loneliness until they make friends and start feeling a part of their new community. A widow may feel intense emotional loneliness after the death of her husband, but continue to have many social ties to family and friends.

Who Is at Risk for Loneliness?

No segment of society is immune to loneliness, but some people are at greater risk than others (Peplau & Perlman, 1982). Certain childhood experiences may predispose individuals to loneliness. Phillip Shaver (1986) has used infant-parent attachment theory to predict that adults will be less vulnerable to loneliness if they were securely attached to their parents during childhood. Two recent studies by Shaver have provided preliminary support for this idea. Other research, presented in Box 8–2, suggests that children who lose a parental attachment relationship because of death or divorce may be at greater risk for loneliness as adults than are children from intact families.

Taking a slightly different approach to this issue, Lobdell and Perlman (1986) gave questionnaires to college-aged women and also to their mothers and fathers. One of their most striking findings

BOX 8–2

CHILDREN OF DIVORCE

Divorce, once an unusual event, is now common, and most divorces today involve families with children. Divorce affected less than 15 percent of children born in 1955. Today, that percentage has doubled. It has been estimated that a third of the children born in the 1980s will experience a parental divorce before they reach age 18 (Bane, 1976). Researchers are only beginning to understand the many ways that divorce can affect children (Guidubaldi, Perry, & Nastasi, 1987). One possibility is that children of divorce may be more vulnerable to loneliness as they become adults.

In a large survey of Americans, Rubenstein and Shaver (1982) found that adults whose parents had divorced were more likely to be lonely, especially if the divorce occurred before the person was 6 years old. Perhaps surprisingly, the death of a parent during childhood was not related to adult loneliness. To explain these findings, Shaver and Rubenstein (1980) turned to the work on parent-child attachment discussed earlier in this chapter. They suggested that the loss of a parental attachment relationship through divorce influences children in two major ways.

First, children often blame themselves for the divorce. Although it is an irrational belief, many children believe that they have in some way caused their parents' marriage to end. This tendency seems especially strong among preschool children, whose cognitive development is immature and self-focused (Wallerstein & Kelly, 1975). If children are older at the time of the divorce, they are usually better able to understand that the divorce was not their fault. The legacy of this self-blame can be persistent low self-esteem—an enduring belief that one is unlovable and unworthy of affection. Studies of adults (Peplau & Perlman, 1982) show a clear link between low self-esteem and loneliness. The person who lacks self-confidence may be less willing to take risks in social situations and may subtly communicate a sense of unworthiness to others. This, in turn, may set the stage for poor social relationships and for loneliness.

Rubenstein and Shaver also speculate that children of divorce may come to see other people as rejecting and unreliable. If a child perceives a parent as unresponsive or frustrating, the child may develop a more generalized view of people as untrustworthy and of relationships as undependable. Such a "model" or image of relationships established in childhood may persist into adulthood, making it harder for the individual to form rewarding relationships. Consistent with this idea are data showing that children of divorce have more negative and less trusting views of other people (Shaver & Rubenstein, 1980). This problem may be greater for children of divorce than for children whose parents die. In divorce, children usually continue to see the noncustodial parent, and may regard each visit as an opportunity to entice the parent to return. When the parent leaves at the end of the visit, the child may perceive that he or she has been rejected still again.

The possibility that childhood experiences in the family influence loneliness in adulthood is intriguing, and an important topic for additional research. We should be cautious, however, not to overstate the impact of childhood events on later loneliness. Many children of divorce have gone on to create close and satisfying relationships as adults. Further, greater awareness about the potential effects of divorce may enable divorcing parents to help their children cope more effectively with this major life transition.

Beauty is often an advantage in social relations. Other things being equal, attractive people tend to be liked more than people considered less physically attractive.

was that lonely parents tended to have lonely daughters: There was a significant correlation between the grown daughter's current level of loneliness and the current loneliness of her mother and father. In addition, the daughter's *perception* of her parents' childrearing practices was also linked to her loneliness. Women who were least lonely described their parents as having been positively involved during their childhood, as being reliable and trustworthy, and as having a happy marriage. These results are consistent with the notion that childhood experiences predispose adults to loneliness. However, as Lobdell and Perlman are quick to point out, the direction of causality cannot be determined from their correlational data. It may also be that people who are currently lonely are prone to remember and reinterpret their childhood experiences in negative ways.

Other factors also affect the risk of loneliness. Married people are less likely to be lonely than others. It is interesting to note, however, that some married people—18 percent in one large study—do feel lonely. Married people might be lonely because they lack friends or because their marriage is not personally satisfying. Loneliness is more common among the poor than the affluent. Good relationships may be easier to maintain when people have the time and money for leisure activities and entertaining.

Loneliness is related to age. Popular stereotypes depict old age as a time of great loneliness. But research shows that loneliness is highest among teenagers and young adults, and lowest among older people. In one large survey (Parlee, 1979), 79 percent of people under age 18 said they were sometimes or often lonely, compared to only 53 percent of those 45 to 54, and 37 percent of those 55 and over. Researchers have not yet determined the reasons for this age pattern. In part, there may be a "generation gap," with young people being more willing to talk about their feelings and acknowledge loneliness than are older adults. It is also true, however, that young people face a great many social transitions, such as leaving home, living on their own, going to college, or taking a first full-time job—all of which can cause loneliness. As people get older, their social lives may become more stable. Age may also bring greater social skills and more realistic expectations about social relations.

Several personality factors have been linked to loneliness (Peplau & Perlman, 1982). Lonely people tend to be more introverted and shy, more self-conscious, and less assertive (Jones, Briggs, & Smith, 1986). Lonely people often have low self-esteem and, in some cases, have poor social skills (Jones, Carpenter, & Quitana, 1985). Loneliness is also associated with anxiety and depression. Several of these personality factors can be both a cause and a consequence of loneliness. For example, people with low self-esteem may be less willing to take risks in social settings. This could make it harder for them to form friendships and thereby increase their chances of loneliness. On the other hand, the experience of being lonely for a long time may lead a person to see him or herself as a social failure and so cause a drop in the person's self-esteem.

Having examined some of the many reasons why people affiliate, we now turn to a new question. Why are we attracted to some individuals and not to others?

BASIC PRINCIPLES OF INTERPERSONAL ATTRACTION

You're sitting in the first meeting of a seminar on English literature, listening to the discussion with one ear and sizing up your new classmates. You've taken an instant dislike to one rather pompous man who seems bent on dominating the conversation. Whenever he opens his mouth, you and the woman sitting across the table exchange knowing glances and smiles. She seems to be friendly, and you decide to talk to her during the coffee break. As your eyes travel around the seminar table, you think about each student, making mental notes about who you like and who you don't like.

We saw in Chapter 3 that the major dimension of first impressions is evaluation. Why is it that we like some people and not others? What determines who will become our friends? Perhaps the most general answer is that we like people who reward us and who help us to satisfy our needs. Learning theories and motivational theories both offer explanations of the specific mechanisms through which rewards influence liking.

ASSOCIATION   A useful principle from classical conditioning is *association*. As applied to interpersonal attraction, the core idea is that we come to like people who are associated with good experiences and dislike people who are associated with bad experiences. More detailed analyses are provided in the "reinforcement-affect" model proposed by Clore and Byrne (1974) and the newer "reinforcement-context" model proposed by Cramer et al. (1985).

A demonstration of the association principle applied to liking comes from a study by May and Hamilton (1980). They were interested in the impact of pleasant versus unpleasant background music on interpersonal attraction. They first determined which type of music college women liked most (rock music) and least (avant-garde classical music). They then had other women students rate photographs of male strangers. While the women made their ratings, they heard rock music, avant-garde classical music, or no music. The results were clear-cut. Women rated the men least favorably when their photos were associated with disliked music and most favorably when they were associated with enjoyable music. The idea is that liking for someone can be influenced by a conditioned emotional response to events arbitrarily associated with that person.

This association notion is important. Yet, as with so much that occurs with people, its very truth and simplicity should not blind us to other processes that may reverse it on occasion. For instance, someone with whom you spend a very painful or stressful time may wind up a close friend, even though by association the person should make you think of pure misery. For example, Kenrick and Johnson (1979) put subjects in a situation that involved very noxious, unpredictable bursts of loud noise. Subjects' liking for each other increased even though they hated the experience. Sometimes shared misery creates a sense of solidarity that forms the basis for friendship.

REINFORCEMENT   A basic principle from learning theory is *reinforcement*. We like people who reward us in one way or another. One important type of reward is social approval, and many studies have shown that we tend to like people who evaluate us positively. In one experiment (Aronson & Linder, 1965), subjects went though a series of brief interactions with a confederate who was posing as another subject. After each interaction, the subject overheard an interview between the confederate and the experimenter in which the confederate gave his impressions of the subject.

In one condition, the confederate was quite flattering and said at the beginning that he liked the subject; he continued to make positive statements about the subject after each interview. In another condition, the confederate was critical. He said he was not sure that he liked the subject much and gave fairly negative descriptions of him. He continued being negative throughout the study. Afterward, the subjects were asked how much they liked the confederate. The results are shown in Table 8–3. As expected, subjects liked the confederate significantly more if he said positive things about them than if he was negative in his evaluations.

SOCIAL EXCHANGE   This perspective proposes that our liking for another person is based on our assessment of the costs and benefits the person provides us. According to *social exchange theory*, we like people when we perceive our interactions with them to be profitable—that is, when the rewards we get from the relationship outweigh the costs. Thus, we may like Allen because he's interesting and funny, and overlook the fact that he is perpetually late. Social exchange theory also emphasizes that we make comparative judgments, assessing the

TABLE 8–3

Liking in Response to Another's Evaluation

Condition	Liking
Positive evaluation by confederate	6.4
Negative evaluation by confederate	2.5

Numbers are ratings on a scale from −10 to +10.
Source: Adapted from Aronson and Linder (1965).

profits we get from one person against the profits we get from another.

With these general principles in mind, we now turn to research on more specific factors that influence interpersonal attraction. Four powerful determinants of liking are: personal qualities of the other individual, similarity, familiarity, and proximity. As we discuss each of these important factors, we will also note occasional exceptions—special cases that differ from the general pattern.

PERSONAL CHARACTERISTICS

Just what is it that makes us like one person more than another? There is no single answer to this question. Some people find red hair and freckles irresistible; others may dislike them intensely. Some of us prize compassion in our friends; others value intelligence. Individuals vary in the things they find most rewarding in other people. There are also large cultural differences in those personal qualities considered socially desirable. Many Americans equate feminine beauty with being thin, but other societies consider plump women the most attractive. Researchers have sought to identify some of the general characteristics associated with liking in our society.

Some years ago, Norman Anderson (1968b) compiled a list of 555 adjectives that are used to describe people. He then asked college students to indicate how much they would like a person who had each of these characteristics. A sample

of these adjectives is given in Table 8–4. There seemed to be general agreement among the students in this study on which characteristics were desirable and undesirable. One of the most striking results was that for students in the 1960s, sincerity was the most valued trait. Of the eight top adjectives, six—*sincere, honest, loyal, truthful, trustworthy*, and *dependable*—related to sincerity in one way or another. Similarly, the adjectives rated lowest included *liar* and *phony*.

Two other themes that emerged in the list of highly likeable traits were personal warmth and competence. These correspond to the two fundamental dimensions of liking proposed by Zick Rubin (1973). According to Rubin, the key components of liking are affection and respect. Affection stems from the way another person treats us, and is experienced as emotional warmth and closeness. Respect is based on admiration for a person's desirable

TABLE 8–4

Likeableness of Personality Traits

Highly Likeable	Slightly Positive to Slightly Negative	Highly Unlikeable
Sincere	Persistent	Ill-mannered
Honest	Conventional	Unfriendly
Understanding	Bold	Hostile
Loyal	Cautious	Loud-mouthed
Truthful	Perfectionistic	Selfish
Trustworthy	Excitable	Narrow-minded
Intelligent	Quiet	Rude
Dependable	Impulsive	Conceited
Thoughtful	Aggressive	Greedy
Considerate	Shy	Insincere
Reliable	Unpredictable	Unkind
Warm	Emotional	Untrustworthy
Kind	Bashful	Malicious
Friendly	Naïve	Obnoxious
Happy	Restless	Untruthful
Unselfish	Daydreamer	Dishonest
Humorous	Materialistic	Cruel
Responsible	Rebellious	Mean
Cheerful	Lonely	Phony
Trustful	Dependent	Liar

Source: Adapted from Anderson (1968b).

characteristics and competence. Both warmth and competence have been the topic of psychological research.

Warmth

In Chapter 3 we described research showing that warmth is a central trait affecting our first impressions of another person. What is it that makes one person seem warm and friendly, while another comes across as cold and unfriendly? One clue comes from a series of experiments by Folkes and Sears (1977). These researchers suggested that people appear warm when they like things, praise them, and approve of them—in other words, when they have a positive attitude toward people and things. In contrast, people seem cold when they dislike things, disparage them, say they are awful, and are generally critical.

In this research, subjects read or listened to interviews in which the interviewee was asked to evaluate a long list of things such as political leaders, cities, movies, or freshman courses. Sometimes the interviewees expressed predominantly positive atti-

tudes—they liked most of the politicians, cities, movies, or courses. In other cases, the interviewees expressed mainly negative attitudes. As predicted, subjects liked the interviewees more if they were positive rather than negative in their attitudes. Folkes and Sears concluded that the explanation lay in the greater warmth communicated by the positive attitude, because other analyses showed that the liking effect was not due to any greater perceived intelligence, knowledge, or similarity of attitudes on the part of the positive interviewees.

Competence

In general, we like people who are socially skilled, intelligent, and competent. The particular type of competence that matters most depends on the nature of our relationships with the person: We are attracted to friends who are good conversationalists, to mechanics who are good at fixing cars, to professors who are interesting lecturers, and so on. Competent people are usually more rewarding to be with than inept people.

A recent study (Leary, Rogers, Canfield, & Coe, 1986) investigated one aspect of interpersonal competence—the ability to be an interesting rather than boring conversationalist. In a first study, they found that college students reported being bored by speakers who talked too much about themselves or about trivial, banal topics. Students also reported being bored with people who were overly passive, tedious, and serious in their interactions. In a second study, students listened to taped conversations designed so that the target speaker was either boring or interesting. Students evaluated the boring speakers quite negatively. Boring speakers were liked less, and rated as less friendly, enthusiastic, popular, and more impersonal. In contrast, being a good conversationalist enhanced a person's likeability.

An interesting exception to the competence-leads-to-liking principle is the case of someone who is a little "too perfect" for comfort. A study by Aronson, Willerman, and Floyd (1966) demonstrated this effect. Participants listened to a tape recording of a student who was trying out for a College Quiz Bowl team. In one condition, the candidate gave an outstanding performance and answered nearly every question correctly. In the second condition, the candidate gave a mediocre performance. As an added twist to the experiment, after the tryout was over, the candidate was sometimes heard to spill coffee on his suit.

The results showed the usual competence-leads-to-liking effect: The outstanding candidate was liked better than the mediocre one. However, the outstanding candidate was liked even better when he made a minor blunder or "pratfall" than when his performance was flawless. Apparently, spilling coffee served to "humanize" the brainy student and so made him more likable. In contrast, the blunder only detracted from the evaluations of the mediocre applicant. He was liked less when he spilled coffee than when he didn't.

Physical Attractiveness

One of the first things we notice about a person is appearance. Other things being equal, people considered attractive are liked more than people considered unattractive (Hatfield & Sprecher, 1986). In a classic study, Walster and associates

(1966) conducted a "computer dance" in which college students were randomly assigned to each other as dates for the evening. The researchers secretly made ratings of the physical attractiveness of each participant. At the end of the evening, students were asked to rate how much they liked their assigned partner. Liking was closely related to the person's physical attractiveness. Both men and women who were considered attractive were liked more.

In a more recent study, researchers (Green, Buchanan, & Heuer, 1984) investigated interpersonal attraction at a commercial dating service. Clients of this dating service were predominantly white, middle class, and in their 30s. They screened prospective partners on the basis of detailed files containing a photograph, background information, and answers to open-ended questions about interests, hobbies, ideals, and relationship goals. As part of the dating service's regular procedures, each client selected five partners they would like to date, and also indicated five people they would definitely not be interested in dating. For both male and female clients, physical attractiveness (as measured by raters' evaluations of the photos) was a major factor in partner selection: Both sexes chose better-looking people and rejected less attractive people. In addition, age was also a factor. Most women selected men who were older than themselves; most men preferred women who were younger. An independent study of a California video-dating service (Woll, 1986) replicated these results, finding that both men and women relied strongly on looks and age in their initial screening of prospective dates.

Other research has investigated the specific physical features that contribute to a person being perceived as attractive. For example, Michael Cunningham (1986) predicted that men would give highest attractiveness ratings to women whose faces had certain "cute" features usually associated with children such as relatively large eyes, small nose, or small chin, and to certain "expressive" features associated with the communication of emotion such as larger smiles and higher eyebrows. In this study, college men rated photographs of women who varied in their facial features. Independent raters also took physiognomic measurements of various features of the women's faces. Results generally supported the predictions: Women who were rated as more attractive tended to have large eyes, small noses, small chins, and wide smiles. In another study, Alicke, Smith, and Klotz (1986) showed that both facial features and body build have significant and independent effects on the ratings of women's physical attractiveness.

Finally, a recent study by Snyder, Berscheid, and Glick (1985) examined individual differences in the importance people give to physical attractiveness as a basis for selecting dating partners. The assumption was that some individuals are more attuned to the "exterior" appearance of prospective partners, while others pay more attention to the "interior" personality characteristics of potential partners. In this research, college men were first classified as high or low on "self-monitoring." Individuals high in self-monitoring seem to monitor the impression they make on others in social situations and try to control the image that they convey. It was hypothesized that high self-monitoring men would be particularly concerned about the public image a potential girlfriend conveys, consistent with the folk-saying, "A man is judged by the company he keeps." In constrast, it was hypothesized that men low on self-monitoring would pay more attention to "interior" personal qualities of potential partners. The results of two studies supported this hypothesis. In gathering informaion about prospective partners and in the actual choice of whom to date, low self-monitoring men gave greater weight to personality whereas high self-monitoring men gave greater weight to physical attractiveness.

One reason for the strong influence of appearance is the halo effect discussed in Chapter 3. We tend to assume that people who are physically attractive also have other desirable characteristics, such as being warm or having a pleasant personality. A second factor is the so-called radiating effect of beauty. People may find it rewarding to be seen with a particularly attractive friend or date because they think it will enhance their own public image. Indeed, studies have shown that both men and women *are* rated more favorably when they are accompanied by an attractive romantic partner or friend than when they have an unattractive companion (see Geiselman, Haight, & Kimata, 1984; Kernis & Wheeler, 1981). For an interesting exception to the radiating effects of beauty, see Box 8–3.

BOX 8–3

PEOPLE WATCHING: ARE BEAUTIFUL FRIENDS A SOCIAL ASSET?

Television presents a world largely populated by beautiful people—adorable children, sexy young women, men with rugged good looks, and so on. Even TV news reporters are coached to improve their clothes and physical appearance. Social critics argue that these idealized images create unrealistic standards that few of us can attain. Critics note that even the actors and actresses we see on the screen do not look nearly as attractive in real life, without the help of makeup artists, wardrobe experts, flattering lights, and other props. Do these media beauty standards actually influence how we react to people in everyday life?

To find out, Douglas Kenrick and Sara Gutierres (1980) designed a clever field study. College men were contacted in their dorm either before or after they had watched "Charlie's Angels," a popular TV show starring three very beautiful young women. To reduce response bias, the men were not told they were in an experiment. Two college students (confederates of the researchers) approached groups of men sitting in a dorm lounge and asked them to help settle a personal debate about how pretty a particular young woman was. The men were shown a photo of the woman and were asked to write their ratings of her beauty secretly, so they wouldn't be influenced by each other. The woman had previously been rated by other college men as being of average attractiveness, about 4 on a 7-point scale.

As predicted, men who had just watched three lovely actresses for an hour rated this typical woman as less attractive than did men who had not seen the TV show. The same researchers replicated this effect in two more laboratory studies. In both, exposure to a photo of a highly attractive woman led to lower attractiveness ratings of an average-looking woman by both male and female subjects. All three studies found a "contrast effect": The average-looking person was seen as less attractive because of the extreme beauty of the recent comparison stimulus.

Michael Kernis and Ladd Wheeler (1981) took this research one step further by asking when the contrast effect occurs and when, as noted in the text, an opposite "radiating effect" occurs. They hypothesized that the relationship between the average-looking person and the beautiful person makes a difference. They designed a laboratory experiment so that subjects saw two people, a target person of average attractiveness and a comparison person of either above-average or below-average looks. As a further variation, these people were sometimes presented as being strangers and sometimes as being friends.

The two relationship conditions (stranger and friend) produced opposite results. When the two people were thought to be strangers, a contrast effect occurred. The average-looking target person was rated less favorably when paired with a very attractive stranger. But when the two people were believed to be friends, a radiating effect occurred. The target person was rated more favorably when seen with a very attractive friend, and less favorably when seen with a very unattractive friend. The contrast effect was apparently offset by other influences leading subjects to assume that someone with a beautiful friend was somehow more attractive. Gender did not affect these patterns: The same results were found regardless of whether the subject and the people being evaluated were male or female.

We need to be cautious in applying these findings to real-life situations. These studies involved ratings of strangers. As people learn more about each other, the effects of physical attractiveness may change. Just when contrast and radiating effects occur in interactions with friends and lovers is an important question for future research.

SIMILARITY

Another basic factor in interpersonal attraction is similarity. We tend to like people who are similar to us in attitudes, values, interests, background, and personality. This similarity effect applies to friendships, dating, and marriage. There is much truth in the old adage that "birds of a feather flock together."

Research Findings

One of the first demonstrations that similarity leads to friendship was done by Theodore Newcomb (1961). He took over a large house at the University of Michigan and offered male undergraduates free housing in return for taking part in his research. Before the students arrived, they filled out various questionnaires about their attitudes and values. Newcomb controlled the assignment of roommates so that some had very similar attitudes and others had very dissimilar attitudes. He then intervened very little during the semester. The results showed that roommates with similar preacquaintance attitudes generally liked each other and ended up as friends; dissimilar roommates tended to dislike each other and did not become friends.

Attraction through similarity has been the focus of much research. In a series of experiments, Donn Byrne (1971) and his associates carefully examined attitude similarity. To rule out other factors such as appearance or personality that might influence liking, Byrne developed the *phantom-other technique*. In these studies, participants fill out questionnaires describing their own attitudes. They then read questionnaires allegedly filled out by a stranger.

In actuality, there is no other person (hence, the term "phantom-other"). Experimenters deliberately select the answers to be either very similar, moderately similar, or dissimilar to the person's own answers. Subjects are then asked how much they think they would like this other person. The results of these studies have shown that attitude similarity strongly determines liking. The more similar the attitudes, the greater the anticipated liking. This effect has been demonstrated with very diverse groups including children, college students, medical patients, job trainees, and alcoholics.

The importance of similarity extends well beyond attitudes. Similarity in ethnic background, religion, politics, social class, education, and age all influence attraction. Kandel's (1978) study of the friendships of 2,000 high school students illustrates this point. Each student identified his or her "best friend in school" and completed questionnaires about his or her own background and attitudes. Most best friends were similar in gender, year in school, age, and race. Best friends also tended to

A shared family background is often an important basis for interpersonal attraction. Here, a family reunion brings together three generations to celebrate their shared ancestry.

Christa Armstrong, Photo Researchers, Inc.

be similar in their school grades and their attitudes toward drug use.

In dating and marriage, the tendency to choose similar partners is called the **matching principle.** It is unusual for an ardent feminist to date a sex-role traditionalist, or for an orthodox Jew to date a fundamentalist Christian. Dating partners and spouses tend to be relatively matched in their physical and social characteristics. For example, one study of dating couples (Hill, Rubin & Peplau, 1976) found that partners tended to resemble each other in age, intelligence, educational plans, religion, physical attractiveness, and even height. They were also matched in their attitudes about sexual behavior and sex roles. Furthermore, couples who were most similar in background at the beginning of the study were most likely to be together a year later.

Explaining the Similarity Effect

Why should similarity be so important in interpersonal attraction? There are several explanations (Rubin, 1973). First, similarity is usually rewarding. People similar to us will tend to agree with our ideas and bolster our confidence in the rightness of our views. In contrast, it is unpleasant to have someone disagree with us, criticize our beliefs, and challenge our taste and judgment. Similar values and interests provide the basis for sharing activities with another person, whether this be picketing a nuclear power plant or going to a prayer meeting. Conversely, differences in values and interests can lead to dislike and avoidance (Rosenbaum, 1986; Byrne, Clore, & Smeaton, 1986).

A second explanation for the similarity-liking connection comes from the theory of cognitive dissonance, described in Chapter 6. According to this theory, people strive to maintain harmony or consistency among their attitudes, to organize their likes and dislikes in a balanced, consistent way. To like someone and at the same time to disagree with that person about fundamental issues is psychologically uncomfortable. We maximize cognitive consistency by liking those who support our views; we minimize cognitive dissonance by disliking those who disagree with us.

Another explanation of the matching phenomenon is that people deliberately select partners who are similar to themselves in social desirability. We might all like to date someone who is beautiful, rich, and famous! But most of us wind up with partners who resemble ourselves. Our abstract ideals are brought down to reality by the constraints of social life. This is consistent with the expectancy-value theory of decision-making discussed in Chapter 1. The theory proposes that people consider not only the reward value of a particular choice (here, a potential date's attractiveness), but also the expectancy of being successful with this choice (here, actually going out with the person). The implication is that people will pursue the most attractive possible partner only if the probability of being rejected is fairly low.

In real life, however, the most socially desirable people are most in demand, and so the chance of rejection is usually high. Expectancy-value theory argues that people will go for the most desirable person they can realistically expect to get. People therefore tend to select someone roughly similar to themselves in attractiveness.

Research on physical attractiveness illustrates this process. We saw earlier that people usually like handsome men and beautiful women more than less attractive persons. But actual dating partners tend to be matched in physical appeal, with beautiful women dating handsome men, while average-looking men date average-looking women (Hill et al., 1976; White, 1980). For instance, Folkes (1982) studied members of a video-dating service. As part of the service, members watch videotaped interviews of potential dates, and then decide about asking the other person out. Folkes rated members on physical attractiveness and interviewed them about whom they had contacted for a date. She found that both men and women were most likely to pursue a relationship with someone similar to themselves in physical attractiveness. Only the most attractive people sought dates with the most attractive partners.

Limits to the Similarity Effect

Although similarity usually leads to liking, there are exceptions to this general pattern. Sometimes similarity is threatening. If someone similar to us has a heart attack or suffers from some other unfortunate fate, we may worry that we are also vulnerable and so we may prefer to avoid that person. This point was demonstrated by Novak and Lerner (1968). In a variation of the Byrne "phantom-other" study, subjects read a questionnaire supposedly completed by another student whose attitudes were either very similar or dissimilar to their own. The researchers also led students to believe that this other person was either emotionally disturbed or normal.

In the "disturbed" condition, the other person had written at the end of the questionnaire: "I don't know if this is relevant or not, but last fall I had a kind of nervous breakdown and I had to be hospitalized for a while. I've been seeing a psychiatrist ever since. As you probably noticed, I'm pretty shaky right now." In the "normal" condition, no such information was added. For subjects confronted with a normal person, attitude similarity increased liking as usual. For subjects confronted with an emotionally disturbed person, attitude similarity *decreased* liking; people were more eager to avoid the other person if he was similar than if he was different.

Another point is that differences between people are sometimes very rewarding. Few of us want to associate with clones, people who are identical to us in virtually every respect. The joys of friendship include stimulation and novelty—learning about new ideas and coming to appreciate the rich variety of human experience. Research suggests that we may be most open to the rewards of difference when we feel that another person accepts us. In one study, Walster and Walster (1963) hypothesized that college students would be more willing to associate with dissimilar strangers if they knew in advance that the strangers would like them. Subjects could choose to participate in a discussion group with people who were very similar to themselves (introductory psychology students) or with people who were very dissimilar (psychologists, factory workers).

Before making their choice, some students were told that people in all groups were disposed to like them; others were told that group members were disposed to dislike them. When students were assured of being liked, they greatly preferred to be with dissimilar people. When students thought they might be disliked, they wanted to talk to similar others. A feeling of acceptance may be a prerequisite for appreciating differences.

Another advantage of dissimilarity is that it enables us to divide tasks according to people's distinctive skills and interests. In planning a group camping trip, it is convenient to have one person who knows about tents and equipment, someone else who can plan for meals, and a third person who knows the area and can pick a good campsite. In a traditional marriage, where the wife is the "homemaking expert" and the husband is the "breadwinning expert," the spouses' roles are different but complementary. When we say that "opposites attract," we are often referring to role relationships such as these, where people with different skills and knowledge contribute to a shared enterprise. However, most cases of complementarity require that partners have *similar* values and goals—such as a desire to spend a weekend camping in the wilderness or shared beliefs about how to organize married life.

FAMILIARITY

A third factor in liking is familiarity. Consider, for example, Parisians' reactions to the Eiffel Tower. When it was first constructed, they were outraged and thought it was hideous, a blot on the landscape of their beautiful city. Today it is a beloved monument, and has even come to symbolize Paris. Familiarity can induce liking not only for buildings, but more significantly, for people.

The Mere Exposure Effect

Familiarity is an important factor in interpersonal attraction. Simply being exposed frequently to a person can increase our liking for that person. This **mere exposure effect** has been demonstrated by Robert Zajonc and his associates (Moreland & Zajonc, 1982; Zajonc, 1968). In one study, Zajonc showed college students pictures of faces. Some of the faces were shown as many as 25 times, others only once or twice. Afterward, subjects indicated how much they liked each face and how much they thought they would like the person pictured.

The results are presented in Figure 8–1. The more often the subjects had seen a face, the more they said they liked it and thought they would like the person. The same result has been found for repeated exposure to actual people (Saegert, Swap, & Zajonc, 1973).

Another ingenious demonstration of the familiarity effect involves people's reactions to their own faces. Faces are not perfectly symmetrical; maybe our left eye is a little higher than the right, our smile is a little crooked, our hair is parted on the right instead of the left, and so on. Our friends see our face as it looks to an outside observer. But we see a different face—the mirror image of the one our friends see. Here the right eye is higher, the part is on the left, and so on.

According to the mere exposure hypothesis, our friends should prefer our face from the perspective they are used to, and we should prefer our mirror image. Mita, Dermer, and Knight (1977) showed just that. They photographed college women and showed these pictures to the women and their friends. Some pictures were true prints and others were made from reverse negatives (what we would see in the mirror). The women themselves preferred the mirror image (by 68 to 32 percent). Their friends, however, preferred the true prints (by 61 to 39 percent). Each liked best the face that he or she had seen the most.

LIMITS ON EXPOSURE   There are some limits on the mere exposure effect. Exposure is most effective in enhancing liking for a person or object that is initially perceived as pleasant or at least neutral, but not as strongly negative. To make this point, Zajonc uses the example of repeatedly seeing a particular man in handcuffs. After a while, we become convinced he really is a criminal. Perlman and Oskamp (1971) tested this idea by presenting subjects with pictures of people presented positively (as scientists), neutrally (dressed in a sports shirt), or negatively (in a police lineup). They found that repeated exposure to positive and neutral pictures increased liking, but had no effect on negative pictures. The results are shown in Figure 8–2.

Another exception to the familiarity-liking connection occurs when two people have conflicting interests, needs, or personalities. As long as they see little of each other, the conflicts are minimized. They may not particularly like each other, but they have little reason to dislike each other. When contact is increased, however, the conflicts are exagger-

FIGURE 8–1   The relationship between frequency of exposure and liking. Subjects were shown photographs of different faces and the number of times each face was shown was varied. The more often the subjects saw a particular face, the more they said they liked the person pictured. (Adapted from Zajonc, 1968.)

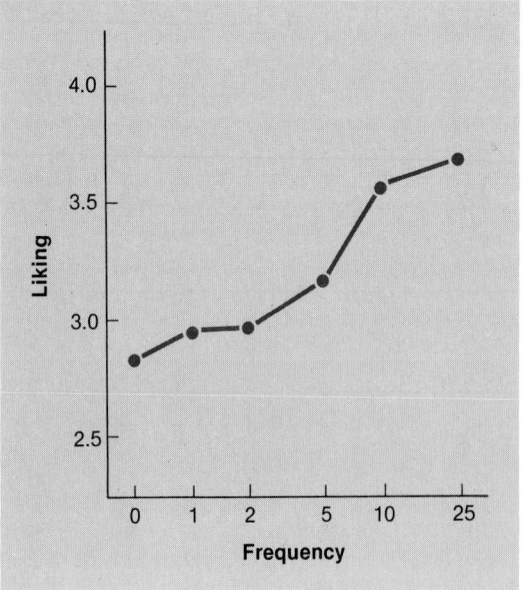

Because the human face is not perfectly symmetrical, the way we see our own face in the mirror differs subtly from the way other people see us during interaction. The left photo shows a woman as her friends view her. The right photo is a "reverse image" that shows the woman as she appears to herself. Research finds that people like best the face they have seen most often.

Laimute E. Druskis

ated and aggravated. Under these circumstances, they may dislike each other even more as a result of frequent contact.

A third limitation is that a lot of repetition causes boredom and satiation. There is probably some

FIGURE 8–2   Mean change in evaluation of stimulus persons, as a function of frequency of exposure and picture content (positive, neutral, or negative). Positive scores indicate a positive shift in evaluations. (Adapted from Perlman and Oskamp, 1971.)

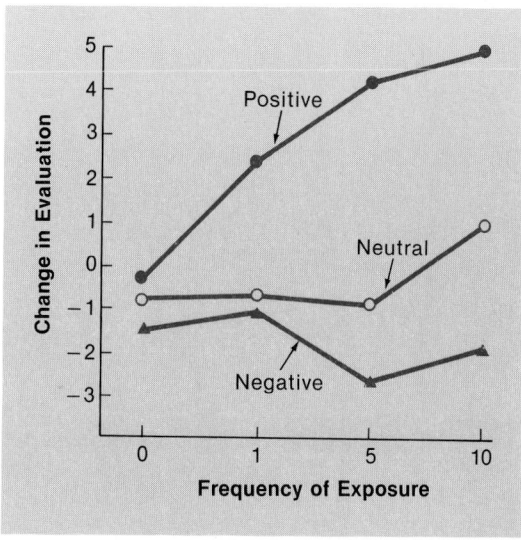

optimal level of exposure to maximize liking, depending on the people and the situation. For an application of this to politics, see Box 8–4.

How Familiarity Works

Why does familiarity increase liking? Repeated exposure undoubtedly improves our recognition of someone, and this may be a helpful first step in coming to like them. As people become more familiar, they also become more predictable. The more we see the new neighbor in our apartment building, the more we learn about her and the better we can predict how she will behave in the elevator and the laundry room. As a result, we feel more comfortable in her presence.

As people become more familiar, we may also assume them to be more similar to ourselves. Moreland and Zajonc (1982) showed college students a photo of a male college student once a week for four weeks. Some people saw the same man each week; others saw a different photo each week. Subjects were also asked to indicate their own attitudes on a variety of issues, and to guess the attitudes of the person in the photo. With repeated exposure, subjects came to rate the person in the photo as more similar to themselves and also as more likeable than before.

BOX 8–4

POLITICAL ADVERTISING: DOES MERE EXPOSURE WORK?

One application of the mere exposure principle is in political advertising. Millions of dollars are spent annually on campaigns designed to influence voters. Candidates with more money can clearly buy more ads, but does this increased exposure actually attract more voters?

Grush, McKeough, and Ahlering (1978) proposed that political ads work *only* under limited conditions—namely, when there are many candidates (so voters would have difficulty identifying any one candidate without ads), when there is generally high exposure (all candidates have many ads), and when candidates are previously unknown (so candidates are not overexposed). Under other conditions, the researchers predicted that voting would be influenced by how well known candidates were before the campaign even began, with the advantage going to officeholders who are already familiar to voters.

To test these predictions, they investigated the 1972 primary elections for the U.S. Senate and House of Representatives. All their predictions were confirmed. The amount of money spent by candidates on advertising was the best predictor of success *only* in races with unknown candidates who did not currently hold a major state office and when all candidates spent a good deal on advertising. Otherwise, the best predictor of success was the winner's precampaign visibility, based on being an incumbent, holding a highly visible public office, or having a famous name. Interestingly, advertising was the best predictor of victory in only 19 percent of the races studied. There appear to be fairly severe limits on when the mere exposure effect works in real-life politics.

PROXIMITY

Probably the best single predictor of whether two people are friends is how far apart they live. If one of them lives in Brazil and the other in China, it is almost certain they are not friends. If one lives in Chicago and the other in Phoenix, or even if they live on opposite sides of the same city, it is unlikely they are friends. In fact, if two people live only 10 blocks apart, it is much less likely that they are friends than if they live next door to each other.

Proximity Studies

Some years ago, W. H. Whyte (1956) studied friendship patterns in Park Forest, a newly built suburban town. Almost everyone moved to this community at about the same time. Because all the houses were similar, residents had chosen their homes and neighborhoods pretty much by chance. There were no "better" areas, no cheap houses. It was almost as though a large group had been randomly assigned to houses.

Whyte tracked the social activities of residents by reading the social column in the local newspaper. Almost everyone at a baby shower lived within a few blocks of one another, and almost everyone

who lived in the area was there. The same was true on the other side of town at a weekend barbecue. In the whole town, there were practically no friends who did not live near one another. Similarly, most people who lived close together became friends.

The same proximity effect occurs on a smaller scale in apartment buildings and dormitories. A study by Festinger, Schachter, and Back (1950) investigated friendship patterns in Westgate West, a large apartment complex. Westgate West had 17 separate two-story buildings, each containing 10 apartments (5 on a floor). The layout is shown in Figure 8–3.

The apartments were almost identical. More important, residents did not choose where they were to live; they were given apartments as the apartments became vacant. In other words, like Park Forest, Westgate came close to being a field experiment with residents randomly assigned to a condition.

All residents were asked, "Which three people in Westgate West do you see socially most often?" Results clearly showed that residents were most friendly with those who lived near them.

People on the same floor mentioned their next-

FIGURE 8–3 Floor plan of Westgate West. All the buildings in the housing development had the same layout. In the study, functional distance was defined as the number of doors apart two people lived. (Adapted from Festinger, Schachter, & Back, 1950.)

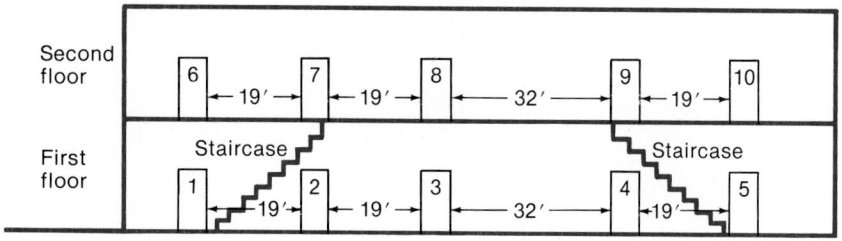

door neighbor more often than their neighbor two doors away, and their neighbor two doors away more often than their neighbor at the other end of the hall. Of next-door neighbors, 41 percent were chosen, whereas only 22 percent of those two doors away and 10 percent of those at the end of the hall were chosen. In actuality, the physical distances involved were very small. People who lived next door were 19 feet apart (in the case of the two middle apartments, 32 feet apart), and the maximum distance between two apartments on one floor was only 88 feet. But these distances, only a few extra seconds in walking time, were important factors in determining friendships.

In addition, people who lived on different floors (the bottom line of the graph) became friends much less often than those on the same floors even when the physical distance between them was roughly the same. This was probably because it takes more effort to go up or down stairs than to walk down a hall. Thus, people on different floors were in a sense farther way than those on the same floor. The investigators referred to this as *functional dis-*

tance, meaning that the probability people would meet was determined by the design of the apartment house plus actual distance. The closer people lived, as measured by either physical or functional distance, the more likely they were to be friends.

Another demonstration of the proximity effect comes from a study done at the Training Academy of the Maryland State Police (Segal, 1974). Trainees were assigned seats in classrooms and to dormitory rooms by name in alphabetical order. Thus, the closer their last names were alphabetically, the more likely trainees were to spend time in close proximity, both in and out of the classrooms.

After six months, each trainee was asked to name his closest three friends on the force. To an astonishing degree, the trainees' friends turned out to be those with names near theirs in the alphabet. On the average, each person chosen as a friend was only 4.5 letters away from his chooser in the alphabet. So the mere fact of being assigned to a room and sitting close dictated friendship choice, despite an intensive training period in which all trainees became well acquainted.

The social life on these dormitory balconies shows the importance of functional distance. Although the entrances to these rooms may be quite far apart, the balconies bring people together and allow the formation of friendships.

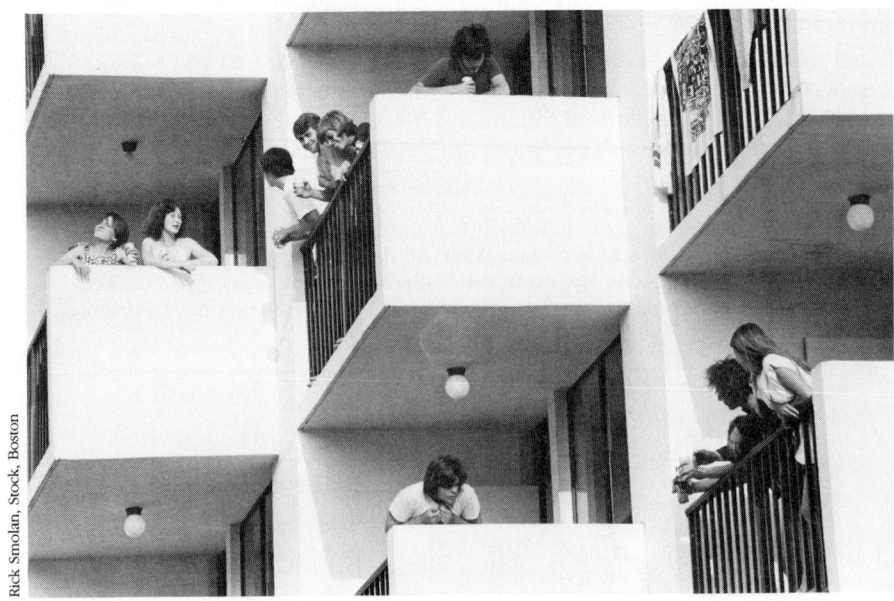

Rick Smolan, Stock, Boston

Why Proximity Causes Liking

The proximity effect incorporates many of the factors we have already seen are important in interpersonal attraction. First, proximity usually increases familiarity. We see our next-door neighbor more often than the person down the street. This repeated exposure, in and of itself, can enhance liking. Second, proximity is often linked to similarity. Although the citizens of Park Forest did not select their neighbors, people who decided to live in that community tended to start out with things in common. They all had enough money to afford nice homes, they wanted to live in suburbia, and so on. Over time, Park Forest neighbors developed other points of shared interest, as they gossiped about the noisy teenagers down the block or complained about the pothole in their street. In other words, we often choose to live and work with people who resemble us, and our geographical closeness further enhances our similarities.

A third factor is that people who are physically close are more *available* than those who are distant. Obviously, we cannot like or be friends with someone we do not know! We choose our friends from people we know. The ready availability of people close by also affects the balance of rewards and costs of interacting, a point emphasized by social exchange theory. It takes little effort to chat with a neighbor or to ask about bus service to the airport. Even if a neighbor's company is only moderately pleasant, we come by it "cheaply"—and so may find it profitable. In contrast, long-distance relationships require time, planning, and money. When good friends move apart, they often vow to keep in touch regularly. But many find that their contacts dwindle to an occasional birthday card or phone call.

A fourth explanation of the proximity effect is based on cognitive consistency. It is psychologically distressing to live or work side-by-side with someone we dislike, and so we experience cognitive pressure to like those with whom we must associate. One formulation of this theory was proposed by Fritz Heider (1958). He distinguished between *unit relations* and *sentiment relations*. People or objects that "belong together" comprise a unit. Most people would perceive me as having a unit relationship with my cat, with my car, with my sister, and with my roommate. Proximity is a common basis for unit relationships. Sentiment relations involve feelings—liking or disliking between the person and the other. Do I like my sister or my roommate? The basic idea of Heider's **balance theory** is that we strive to maintain balance between our sentiment and unit relations. More specifically, we are motivated to like those we are connected to, and to seek proximity with those we like.

When does the desire to balance unit relations with sentiment relations affect liking? The most obvious case is when we are in a unit relation with someone we dislike. Then our positive unit relation is unbalanced by our negative sentiment relation. Suppose you arrive at college to meet your assigned roommate and instantly dislike him or her. To try to balance your unit relation with your sentiment relation, you have two options. You can avoid the roommate as much as possible and try to move to another room. Or you can reevaluate the roommate, trying to see some good qualities, to avoid conflicts, to make the best of the situation.

The issue comes down to which of these relations, unit or sentiment, you are able to change. Often it is nearly impossible to break off the unit relation. Your dorm counselor may insist that you cannot change roommates until the term ends. Therefore you experience pressure to increase your liking.

Tyler and Sears (1977) demonstrated this effect experimentally. Women in this study first met a person who was quite obnoxious. This person (secretly a confederate of the experimenter) forgot the subject's name, snapped gum, blew smoke in her face, claimed the subject was saying silly things, and did not look at the subject when she talked. This was done to establish a negative sentiment relation. Next, the experimenter told the subject that she would spend another 40 minutes talking to the obnoxious person (creating a unit relation with the unpleasant person), or she would spend 40 minutes talking to someone else. Finally, the subject was taken into a separate room to fill out a questionnaire which, among other things, asked how much she liked the confederate. As predicted, liking for the obnoxious person increased significantly with anticipated interaction.

Other studies have also shown that the anticipation of interaction increases liking. In one study (Berscheid et al., 1976), college students agreed to let the experimenters organize their dating life for a period of five weeks. Then the subjects saw videotapes of various people, separated at random into those described as future dates and those described as people they would not date. The prospective dates were liked significantly better. More generally, if we know we are going to interact with someone in the future, we tend to play up the person's positive traits and ignore or minimize the negative ones. A desire for cognitive balance motivates us to like our neighbors, roommates, and others in close proximity.

There are, of course, exceptions to the proximity-liking connection. Sometimes no amount of cognitive reevaluation will convince us that the rude secretary in our office is really nice or that our bratty kid sister is really a little angel. Proximity is most likely to foster attraction when the people involved have similar attitudes and goals. Indeed, when there are initial antagonisms or conflicts be-

tween people, increased proximity and contact may actually intensify negative feelings.

Research has shown that similarity, familiarity, and proximity are powerful forces in interpersonal attraction. To give a complete account of the processes of interpersonal attraction, we have noted various exceptions to these patterns. But these minor exceptions should not obscure the importance of the general principles involved.

These factors are not only causes of liking, but consequences as well. Proximity causes liking, but once we like someone, we often take steps to ensure that we will be close to them in the future. First-year roommates may be thrown together by chance. But if their proximity leads to friendship, they will probably ask to live together the following year. Similarity can work in the same way. Similarity may bring two people together in the first place, but as their friendship continues and they share ideas and experiences, they tend to become even more similar because of their association. Similarity is both a cause and a consequence of liking.

KEY TERMS IN CHAPTER 8

attachment	emotional loneliness	matching principle	social comparison theory
balance theory	loneliness	mere exposure effect	social loneliness

SUMMARY

1. Most people spend most of their waking hours in the company of others. This tendency to affiliate begins in childhood, when infants form strong attachments to the significant adults in their lives. The attachment process is affected by both biology and learning.

2. Adults have diverse social needs. Laboratory experiments have shown that affiliative tendencies are strongest when people are afraid or uncertain. Weiss and others have attempted to classify specific social needs, such as a need for attachment, for social integration, or for guidance.

3. Loneliness is the subjective discomfort we feel when our social relations are lacking in some important way. Loneliness can range from a temporary state resulting from a change in our social life to a chronic and enduring condition. Weiss has distinguished emotional loneliness, caused by the lack of an attachment relationship, from social loneliness, caused by the lack of social integration.

4. We like people who reward us and who help us to satisfy our needs. Three important principles affecting interpersonal attraction are association, reinforcement, and social exchange.

5. People differ in the qualities they most value in others. In general, we tend to like people who are sincere, warm, competent, and physically attractive. Being seen with a beautiful date or friend may have a "radiating effect," causing others to evaluate us more favorably. Sometimes, however, being associated with a very attractive stranger leads to a "contrast effect": A person of average attractiveness suffers by comparison with a particularly beautiful other.

6. We tend to like people who are similar to us in attitudes, values, interests, background, and personality. In dating and marriage, the tendency to select similar partners is called the "matching principle." The importance of similarity can be explained in terms of rewards, cognitive consistency, and the expectancy-value theory of decision making.

7. Familiarity also enhances liking. If a person or object is initially evaluated as neutral or mildly positive, repeated exposure usually increases liking.

8. A final factor in attraction is proximity. People who are physically close to us tend to be more familiar and are often, coincidentally, similar to us in background or interests. Social exchange theory suggests that people close by are more available for interaction, and so the costs of a relationship are usually less. According to cognitive balance theory, we may experience psychological pressure to like those with whom we must interact.

SUGGESTED READINGS

AINSWORTH, M. D. S., BELHAR, M. C., WATERS, E., & WALL, S. (1978). *Patterns of attachment*. Hillsdale, NJ: Erlbaum. Presents research and theory on human attachment behavior.

BERSCHEID, E. (1985). Interpersonal attraction. In G. Lindzey & E. Aronson (Eds.), *Handbook of social psychology*, 3rd ed., Vol. 2. New York: Random House, pp. 413–484. A leading expert provides a comprehensive review of research and theory on interpersonal attraction.

BREHM, S. S. (1985). *Intimate relationships*. New York: Random House. A well-written textbook that provides an excellent introduction to the field. Included are chapters on love, sexuality, communication, power, jealousy, and other important issues.

BURNS, D. D. (1985). *Intimate connections*. New York: Morrow. A detailed and very readable presentation of a cognitive-behavioral approach to helping lonely individuals.

HATFIELD, E., & SPRECHER, S. (1986). *Mirror, mirror . . . The importance of looks in everyday life*. Albany, NY: State University of New York Press. A very readable paperback that expores the many ways in which physical attractiveness influences us from childhood through old age.

PEPLAU, L. A., & PERLMAN, D. (Eds.). (1982). *Loneliness: A sourcebook of current theory, research, and therapy*. New York: Wiley Interscience. A survey of research findings and theories.

9 PERSONAL RELATIONSHIPS

The tender attachment of parent and infant, the good-humored rivalry of tennis partners, the finely-tuned cooperation of astronauts on a space mission, the passion of a love affair—the variety of human relationships is immense. We experience our strongest emotions in relationships: the pleasures of love, the pain of rejection, the anger of conflict. Some relationships are freely chosen; we usually pick our friends and lovers. Other relationships are thrust upon us by fate, when we are assigned to a particular first-grade teacher, a college roommate, or a therapist at the counseling center. But from birth to death, relationships are at the core of human experience.

Social psychologists try to see beneath the great variation in human relationships to discover general principles. This chapter presents concepts and theories about personal relationships and explores such key issues as power, self-disclosure, and love.

DEFINING A RELATIONSHIP

When two people are in a relationship, their lives are intertwined: What each does influences the other. The specific ways people can influence each other are very diverse. Another person can make us feel happy or sad, tell us the latest gossip or criticize our opinions, help us to get something done or get in our way, make us laugh or keep us awake at night worrying, give us advice or tell us off, bring us presents or make us spend money. As these examples illustrate, influence in relationships involves feelings, beliefs, and behavior. The defining feature of a relationship is that two people have mutual influence on each other, that they are interdependent (Kelley et al., 1983).

A model of pair **interdependence** developed by Levinger and Snoek (1972) is shown in Figure 9–1 (see p. 257). The model shows two people, P and O, in increasing stages of interdependence. At one extreme, the two people are completely unaware of each other and are unrelated in any way. They are at the point of *zero contact*.

The stage of *awareness* exists when one person notices or learns something about another, but no direct contact has taken place. We often form impressions of people from observing their appearance and behavior. We may form an impression of a new co-worker from watching the person in meetings, even before we are introduced. Sometimes we learn about another person from a third party, as when a friend arranges a blind date and tells us about the date before we actually go out. Awareness can be unilateral (as shown in Figure 9–1 by the one-way arrow from P to O), or bilateral, as when two strangers glance at each other across a room. The awareness stage can be quite important. If we form a favorable impression of another person, we often take the initiative to interact with that person. Indeed, people sometimes have very intense experiences in the awareness stage, as when fans develop passionate feelings for rock singers and movie stars they have never met.

The next level of relatedness is *surface contact*. Here, two people begin to interact, perhaps by talking or exchanging letters. Surface contact is the beginning of interdependence, and hence the beginning of a relationship. When we exchange small talk with a friendly supermarket checker or chat with the passenger next to us on an airplane, we are engaging in surface contact. These interactions are usually brief; the topics of conversation are superficial; the impact people have on each other is limited; and the contact is often defined by specific social roles. Many relationships never develop beyond this stage of minimal interdependence.

Neil Goldstein

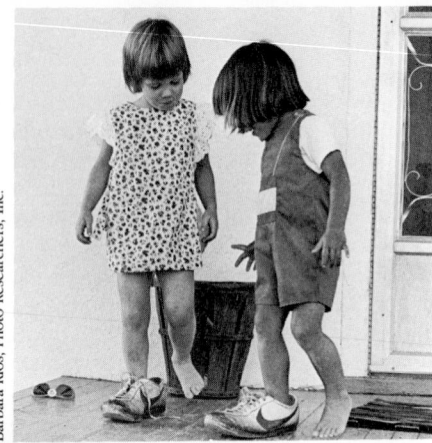

Barbara Rios, Photo Researchers, Inc.

Irene Springer

From childhood to old age, close relationships with loved ones, friends, and colleagues are at the core of human experience.

Laimute E. Druskis

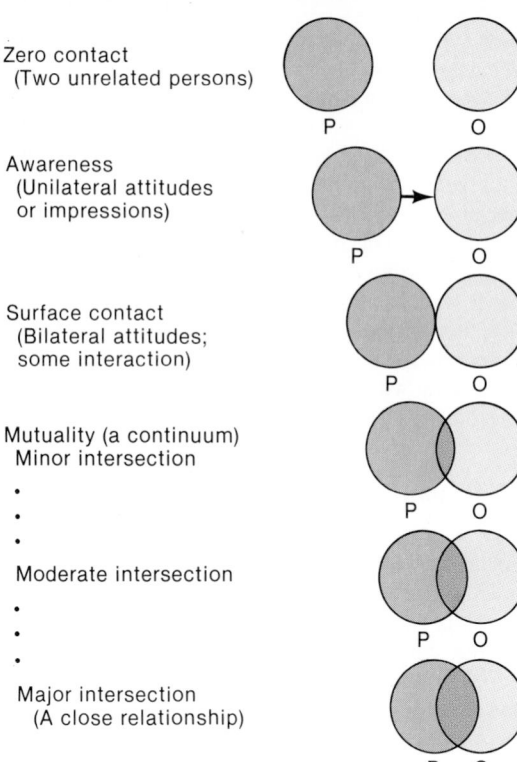

Zero contact
(Two unrelated persons)

P   O

Awareness
(Unilateral attitudes
or impressions)

P   O

Surface contact
(Bilateral attitudes;
some interaction)

P   O

Mutuality (a continuum)
Minor intersection

•
•

P   O

Moderate intersection

•
•

P   O

Major intersection
(A close relationship)

P   O

FIGURE 9–1   A model of pair interdependence.
(Adapted from Levinger & Snoek, 1972, p. 5.)

As the degree of interdependence increases, the pair moves to the stage of *mutuality*. Levinger and Snoek conceptualize mutuality as a continuum from lesser interdependence (shown by little overlap in the circles in Figure 9–1) to extensive interdependence (shown by much overlap). An example would be the increasing mutuality experienced by people who go from being casual acquaintances to becoming best friends.

Social psychologists use the term **close relationship** to refer to relationships that involve much interdependence (Kelley et al., 1983). These can be relationships with parents, a best friend, a teacher, a spouse, a co-worker, or even an important rival or competitor. All close relationships share several basic characteristics. First, they usually involve frequent interaction that continues over a relatively long period of time. Second, close relationships include many different kinds of activities or events. In a friendship, for example, people discuss many different topics, and generally share a wide range of activities and interests. This contrasts with superficial relationships focused around a single activity or topic.

Third, in close relationships, the influence between people is strong. We may quickly forget a snide remark from a salesclerk, but agonize for weeks about a comment made by our best friend. We may be momentarily grateful for the help offered by a bus driver, but benefit daily from the cooperativeness of our roommate. Further, when two people are highly interdependent, they have the potential for arousing strong emotions in each other. We like to think of our close relationships as a source of positive feelings of love, caring, and concern. But it is also true that our strongest emotions of anger, jealousy, and despair are likely to occur in our closest relationships.

A SOCIAL EXCHANGE PERSPECTIVE

The most influential perspective on social relationships is social exchange theory (Blau, 1964; Burgess & Huston, 1979; Kelley & Thibaut, 1978). This perspective analyzes the rewards and costs partners give and receive in relationships. The theory proposes that we select those partners we think are best able to reward us, a point that was emphasized in Chapter 8. The theory also states that we try to arrange our interactions to maximize our own rewards.

In order to receive rewards, however, we must also give them. For instance, as children we learn a general rule or **norm of reciprocity:** We are expected to reward those who reward us. If people help us, we feel obligated to help them (Gouldner, 1960). If we invite someone to dinner, we expect that person to return the invitation in the future. Social interaction can thus be viewed as a process of exchange between partners.

Rewards and Costs

A *reward* is anything a person gains from a relationship, such as feeling loved or getting financial assistance. What is rewarding for one person may be of little value for someone else. A useful analysis of the rewards of relationships was proposed by Foa and Foa (1974), and is shown in Figure 9–2.

They identify six basic types of rewards: love, money, status, information, goods, and services. These can be classified along two dimensions. The dimension of *particularism* concerns how much the value of a reward depends upon who provides it. The value of love, or more specifically of such things as hugs and kisses, depends very much upon who they come from. Thus love is a particularistic reward. In contrast, money is useful regardless of who it comes from; money is a nonparticularistic or universal reward. When we say that a relationship is very special to us, we often mean that it provides us with unique or particularistic rewards that we cannot get elsewhere. The dimension of *concrete-*

ness captures the distinction between tangible rewards—things you can see, smell, and touch—and nonconcrete or symbolic rewards, such as advice or social approval.

Costs are the negative consequences that occur in a relationship. A relationship might be costly because it requires a great deal of time and energy, because it entails much conflict, because other people disapprove of the relationship and criticize us for it, and so on. A further cost of relationships is that they may deprive us of the opportunity to do other rewarding activities: If you spend the weekend skiing with a friend, you do not have the time to study or visit your family.

Evaluating Outcomes

Social exchange theory assumes that people keep track of the rewards and costs of a particular relationship. People seldom do this very explicitly; we do not typically make lists of the good and bad things about a relationship. Nonetheless, we are aware of the costs and rewards involved. In particular, we focus on the overall *outcome* we get in a relationship—that is, whether on balance the relationship is profitable for us (rewards outweigh costs), or whether we are experiencing an overall loss (costs outweigh rewards). People do not necessarily evaluate relationship outcomes very consciously or systematically, but the basic process is reflected in such statements as "I'm really getting a lot out of this relationship" or "I don't think our relationship is worth it anymore."

People use several standards for evaluating relationship outcomes. The simplest standard is whether the relationship is profitable or costly. Also important are comparisons we make between relationships, assessing how one relationship compares to others we have been in or that we know about. Thibaut and Kelley (1959) have emphasized two main comparison standards.

The **comparison level** reflects the quality of outcomes a person believes he or she deserves. This baseline standard undoubtedly differs from one type of relationship to another: We have different standards for a platonic friendship than for a love relationship. Our comparison level reflects our past experiences in relationships. For example,

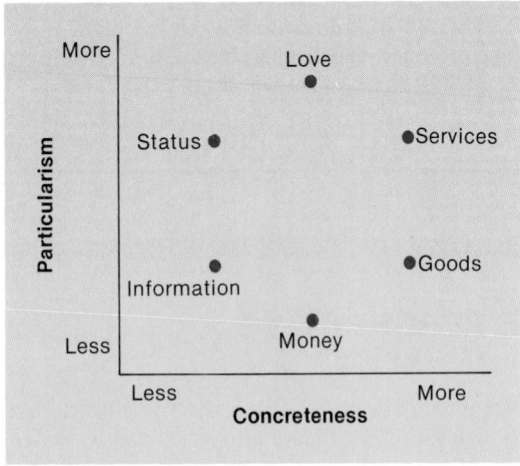

FIGURE 9–2 Rewards people exchange. (Adapted from Foa, 1971, p. 347.)

we may consider whether a current dating relationship is as good as those we have had in the past. Or we may compare our new boss at work to our general experiences with other supervisors in the past. We may also compare a current relationship to those we have seen in movies, heard about from friends, or read about in pop psychology books. The comparison level is our personal belief about what constitutes an acceptable relationship. Our comparison level may change as we have new experiences.

A second major standard is the **comparison level for alternatives.** This involves assessing how one relationship stacks up against other relationships that are currently available. Is our current dating partner better or worse than the other people we could readily be going out with right now? Is our current boss better or worse than other people we might realistically work for at this point in our lives? Even if a relationship is profitable in absolute terms, we may leave it if a *more* profitable alternative becomes available. In contrast, if our relationship is the best we think possible, we may stay in it, even if the gains are small. Our dependence on a relationship is based on our perceptions of the relationship as a unique source of rewards not available elsewhere.

Coordination of Outcomes

A key fact about relationships is that one person's outcomes are interlinked with the outcomes of the partner. Consider a young married couple deciding how to spend the income tax refund they just received. The wife would like to spend the money for a new sofa; the husband would like to buy a video recorder. Since the couple has a limited amount of money available and cannot afford both the sofa and the VCR, they must coordinate their use of the funds and resolve their conflicting interests.

They might solve the problem in one of several ways. They might decide to spend the money on a trip—neither person's first choice, but an alternative that is attractive to both. Or, they might decide to take turns, buying the sofa this year and the VCR next year. Coordinating outcomes is a basic issue in relationships (Thibaut & Kelley, 1959).

How easy or difficult it is to coordinate outcomes in a relationship depends on how much the two people share the same interests and goals. When partners like to do many of the same things and value the same activities, they will have relatively few coordination problems. In such cases, they are said to have *correspondent outcomes*, because what is good for one is good for the other, and what is bad for one is bad for both (Thibaut & Kelley, 1959).

When partners have different preferences and values, they have *noncorrespondent outcomes*, and are therefore more prone to conflicts of interest and coordination problems. One reason similiarity is such a powerful factor in relationships is that similar people usually have fewer problems of coordination, and so may find it easier to develop a mutually rewarding relationship.

Of course, even well-matched partners experience conflicts of interest from time to time. When this occurs, the partners must negotiate a settlement. Common solutions are to select a less preferred alternative that is acceptable to both or to take turns. Another possibility is to make an explicit exchange of some sort: "I'll watch you play soccer if you'll come with me to the ballet."

Settling conflicts of interest by negotiation is at best a time-consuming activity and at worst, a source of arguments and bad feelings. Over time, partners often develop rules or **norms** about coordinating their behavior. Neither spouse may like to take out the garbage or pay the bills, but they may agree that he will do one if she will do the other. Shared norms reduce the need for continual negotiation to arrive at coordinated behavior patterns.

In many types of relationships, cultural rules prescribe certain coordinated patterns. At work, there are usually fairly clear understandings about what the employer and employee will do, and how they will interact. Lawyers and their secretaries seldom need to negotiate to decide who will draft legal briefs and who will type them, or who will answer the phone and who will make court appearances. Traditional marriage provides another example of a relationship in which roles are predetermined. The traditional pattern is clearly for wives to do the housekeeping tasks and for husbands to have paying jobs.

In Chapter 1, we defined **social roles** as clusters

of rules about how people should behave in a particular type of relationship. Roles provide solutions for some of the problems of coordination that participants are likely to encounter. In some relationships, such as traditional marriage or lawyer–secretary interactions, social roles offer fairly specific guidelines for action. In other relationships, such as between same-sex friends, cultural rules are much less explicit.

When social guidelines are vague or in the process of change, individuals have greater freedom of action, but must put more effort into coordinating interaction successfully. Today, traditional sex roles are being questioned. As a result, dating and married couples may be uncertain about who should do what. For example, a couple out on a first date may hesitate as they approach a doorway, trying to decide if the man should open the door for the woman or not. They may pause uncomfortably after a dinner out, waiting to decide whether to split the bill or have the man pay for both.

We can contrast the process of *role-taking*, in which people act out conventional cultural roles, and the process of *role-making*, in which people develop their own shared norms for social interaction (Turner, 1962). In personal relationships, both processes operate. People adopt conventional guidelines about how to behave with classmates, co-workers, friends and family, but they also improvise and create their own solutions to problems of interdependence.

Barbara Rios, Photo Researchers, Inc.

Learning to share with friends is an important step in understanding principles of fairness in social relations.

Fair Exchange

People are most content when their social relations are fair. We don't like to feel exploited by others, nor do we usually like to take advantage of others. Equity theory, an offshoot of social exchange theory, focuses on fairness in relationships (Greenberg & Cohen, 1982; Walster, Walster & Berscheid, 1978).

People use various rules for determining whether or not a relationship is fair. Consider the case of two teenage boys trying to decide how to divide a chocolate cake. They might decide to "share and share alike," using the *equality* rule that everyone should receive equal profits. Research suggests that people are more likely to use the equality principle when they are friends rather than strangers (Austin, 1980). Children are more likely than adults to use the equality rule, perhaps because it is the simplest principle (Hook & Cook, 1979).

The boys might instead use the principle of "to each according to need," the idea that the *relative needs* of the people should be taken into account. By this rule, one boy might get a larger piece of cake if he was especially hungry, or if he hadn't had cake in a long time. This principle is illustrated by a family that spends most of its income to care for a seriously ill child who needs expensive medical treatment.

A third fairness rule is *equity* or distributive justice. The key idea is that a person's profits should be proportional to their contributions (Deutsch, 1985). Here, the boy who contributed more to the cost of buying the cake, or who had exerted greater effort by baking the cake himself, should be entitled to a larger portion. In this view, equity exists when:

$$\frac{\text{outcomes of person P}}{\text{contributions of person P}} = \frac{\text{outcomes of person O}}{\text{contributions of person O}}$$

Both people receive the same ratio of outcomes to contributions. This is the fairness rule that has been the focus of equity research.

Equity theory has three basic assumptions:

1. People in relationships try to maximize their outcomes.

2. Dyads and groups can maximize their collective rewards by evolving rules or norms about how to apportion rewards fairly to everyone concerned.

3. When individuals perceive that a relationship is inequitable, they feel distressed and take steps to restore equity.

Research has supported several specific predictions from equity theory (Greenberg & Cohen, 1982; Walster, Walster, & Berscheid, 1978). It has been shown, for example, that when relationships are not equitable, the partners feel distressed. It makes sense that the underbenefited (exploited) person feels distress. But research shows that the overbenefited person who receives more than he or she deserves also feels distress, perhaps because they feel guilty or uncomfortable about the imbalance.

There is also evidence that people will try to restore equity when they perceive a relationship to be unfair. A person can do this by restoring *actual equity*: For example, a husband might agree that he hasn't been doing his share of the housework and do extra work to compensate. Sometimes, however, individuals use cognitive strategies to alter their perception of the relationship, thus restoring *psychological equity*. The husband might distort reality and argue that he really has done a fair share of the work.

Whether people restore actual or psychological equity depends on the costs and benefits associated with each particular alternative. Much of the re-search on equity has come from laboratory studies of strangers interacting for short periods of time. More recently, however, studies are beginning to show that equity considerations also influence close relationships (see Kidder, Fagan, & Cohn, 1981; Lloyd, Cate, & Henton, 1982; Walster, Walster & Traupmann, 1978).

The Balance of Power

In any personal relationship, people often have different preferences for their activities and try to influence each other in order to accomplish their own goals. **Social power** refers to a person's ability to influence deliberately the behavior, thoughts, or feelings of another person (Huston, 1983). In some relationships, both individuals are equally influential. In other relationships, there is an imbalance of power with one person making more of the decisions, controlling more of the joint activities, winning more of the disagreements, and generally being in a position of dominance. What factors determine whether or not a relationship is equal in power? Three important factors are social norms, relative resources, and the principle of least interest.

SOCIAL NORMS Patterns of influence in relationships are often dictated by social norms. When teenagers take a part-time job at a fast-food restaurant, they expect to take orders from the boss and to follow company regulations. It is generally understood that subordinates follow instructions from their superiors—at least in job-related matters.

In heterosexual dating and marriage, social convention has traditionally conferred greater authority on men. Until recently, for example, state laws gave husbands legal control over all family property and permitted husbands, as the "head of the household," to decide where the family should live. More informally, women were taught to "look up to" the man they married and to defer to his wishes (Bernard, 1972).

Today, some people are rejecting these traditional power norms as outdated and unfair. Instead, they believe that dating and marriage relationships should ideally be equal in power (egalitarian). In one study (Peplau, 1984), 87 percent of college men and 95 percent of college women said that ideally both partners in a dating relationship should have "exactly equal" influence in the relationship.

RELATIVE RESOURCES Norms are not the only determinant of the balance of power. Social exchange theory (see Blau, 1964) proposes that the relative resources of the two partners also affect their relative power. A resource is anything that "can be used to satisfy or frustrate needs or move persons further from or closer to their goals" (Huston, 1983, p. 206). Rewards, coercion, information, and expertise are all personal resources.

The prediction from exchange theory is that when partners are imbalanced in their resources, the person who has more resources will have more power. In dating or marriage, the partner who earns more money, has more education, has a more prestigious job, is more physically attractive or socially desirable, and so on has a power advantage. To the extent that it is men who pay the bills, have the "more important job," and are believed to be more knowledgeable about life decisions, equality in male-female relations may be hard to achieve. As women gain greater resources, however, we may expect to see more equal-power relationships (Scanzoni & Scanzoni, 1981).

THE PRINCIPLE OF LEAST INTEREST Exchange theory proposes that another determinant of power is the relative dependency of the two partners on the relationship, based on their comparison level for alternatives. In some relationships, both partners are equally attracted and committed, and this tends to build power equality. In other relationships, one partner is more dependent on the relationship (Molm, 1985) or cares more about continuing the relationship. This sets the stage for an imbalance of power.

Sociologist Willard Waller (1938) called this the **principle of least interest:** The less interested partner in a relationship has greater power. An implicit bargain is struck in which the more interested and dependent person defers to the other's wishes in order to ensure that the relationship will continue. An illustration of this principle is provided by Margaret, an unpopular young woman who had an affair with an older man:

I accepted his structuring of our relationship. When he chose to deal in wit rather than in real information, I followed suit. When he acted casual about sex, so did I. I wanted something real from him. . . . Even when I knew this was impossible on my terms, I went ahead with it in his way. . . . I didn't back off, because I thought the potential was there, and a dateless summer had taught me that opportunities didn't come up all that often. (Cited in Goethals & Klos, 1970, p. 283)

Ultimately, relationships based on lopsided dependencies usually prove unsatisfactory to both partners. We would expect such relationships to change toward more equal involvement or to end.

A study of college-age dating couples found that the balance of involvement was a strong predictor of power (Hill, Rubin & Peplau, 1976; Peplau, 1984). There was a significant link between perceiving an imbalance of involvement and an imbalance of power, with the less interested partner being seen as having greater power. Further, in a one-year follow-up, couples who initially reported an imbalance of involvement were significantly more likely to have broken up than couples who were equally involved. In sum, equal power is most likely in relationships if social norms favor equality, if partners have comparable personal resources, and if partners are equally dependent on the relationship for valued rewards.

In traditional marriages, all three of these factors tipped the balance of power in favor of male dominance. Women were supposed to defer to their husband's authority, controlled fewer resources, and were relatively more dependent on marriage for financial support. Today, however, marriages in which the husband is the undisputed head, with near-total control of decision-making, are rare (Huston, 1983). But are most male-female partnerships totally equal in power? This question is surprisingly hard to answer.

In long-term relationships, power is difficult to assess precisely, and partners frequently disagree in their assessments of the balance of power (Huston, 1983; Peplau, 1984). For instance, one partner might say that the relationship is egalitarian because both partners share fully in day-to-day decisions about their joint activities. The other partner might agree that daily decisions are shared, but give more

Teri Leigh Stratford

Conflict and arguments are common in many close relationships.

weight to a few major decisions in which one person was especially influential.

Power in close relationships is, to some extent, in the eye of the beholder. Precise statistics about the proportions of equal-power, male-dominant, and female-dominant relationships are not available. A common pattern in research on dating and marriage is for many people to say that their relationship is equal, a large minority to say it is male-dominant, and a small percentage to say it is female-dominant (Scanzoni & Scanzoni, 1981).

Conflict

Conflict is the process that occurs when the actions of one person interfere with the actions of another (Peterson, 1983). Conflict is common in personal relationships. In one national survey (Gurin, Veroff, & Feld, 1960), 45 percent of married people said they had had "problems getting along with each other." In a classic study of 1000 engaged couples, Burgess and Wallin (1953) found that about 80 percent had had disagreements. Indeed, conflict occurs even in couples who are very satisfied with their relationship. Gurin et al. found that 32 percent of people who rated their marriage as "very happy" nonetheless reported having had conflict. Of course, conflict is not limited to married couples. It also occurs in relationships with friends and roommates, co-workers and supervisors, family and neighbors.

The potential for conflict increases as two people become more interdependent. As interactions become more frequent and cover a more diverse range of activities and issues, there are more opportunities for disagreement. Braiker and Kelley (1979) found that conflict was usually quite low during casual dating, but increased significantly for serious dating relationships. Couples can apparently fight about almost anything, from politics and religion to work and money, from how to spend their time to how to divide household chores. Gottman (1979) found 85 different kinds of conflict among young married couples!

Braiker and Kelley (1979) have suggested that specific conflict problems can be grouped into three general categories:

PERSONAL RELATIONSHIPS **263**

- *Specific behaviors.* Some conflicts focus on specific behaviors of a partner, such as getting drunk at a party or forgetting to pick up milk at the grocery store. One partner's actions are costly to the other, such as one roommate playing loud music that interferes with another's studying. Or a partner fails to provide rewards desired by the other, perhaps by refusing to do something that the other wants.

- *Norms and roles.* Some conflicts focus on more general issues about the rights and responsibilities of partners in a relationship. Conflicts of this sort might concern a failure to live up to promises, a lack of reciprocity, or neglect of some agreed-upon task. Thus one roommate might complain that the partner is not doing a fair share of the cleaning. Or a worker and supervisor might disagree about the worker's job responsibilities.

- *Personal dispositions.* People frequently go beyond specific behaviors to make attributions about the intentions and attitudes of a partner. One person might complain that the partner is lazy, inconsiderate, or lacks self-discipline.

According to Braiker and Kelley, these three types of conflict reflect the fact that people are interdependent at three levels. At the behavioral level, partners have problems of coordinating specific activities. At the normative level, they have problems negotiating rules and roles for their relationship. At the dispositional level, they disagree about each other's personality and intentions.

This last type of interdependence arises because partners are important sources of validation for our self-image. Conflicts can easily arise if a person thinks of him or herself as kind and considerate, but has a partner who insists he or she is really self-centered and rude. Conflicts may escalate as partners use specific problem behaviors to make more general attributions about each other's character.

In close relationships, events are often open to different interpretations (Kelley, 1979). Consider a husband who does not give his wife a present on their wedding anniversary. The wife may consider this an insult and complain about it to her husband. The husband may see his actions differently and try to justify them to his wife. In such situations, people tend to explain their own and their partner's behaviors differently, consistent with the actor-observer attributional bias discussed in

Chapter 4 (Kelley, 1979; Orvis, Kelley & Butler, 1976).

The complaining person tends to attribute the event to the partner's negative characteristics. The wife might insist, "You forgot our anniversary because you don't really love me anymore." Her motivation may be to punish the husband's misconduct or to challenge him to show he really does care. In contrast, the person who performed the act tends to excuse the behavior ("I meant to buy you something, but I was preoccupied with a big deadline at work"), or to justify the action ("I thought we agreed not to spend money on each other"). The husband's explanations are an attempt to avoid blame and to keep the event from disrupting the relationship.

Conflict can help or harm the development of a relationship, depending on how it is resolved. Conflict can provide an opportunity for clarifying and changing expectations about the relationship and conceptions of the self and the partner. Lovers' quarrels allow lovers to test their own and their partners' dependence on the relationship, to discover the depth of their feelings for each other, and to renew their efforts to create a satisfying relationship. On the other hand, because conflicts arouse strong emotions, they may not provide the best setting for constructive problem-solving. The escalation of conflict and the trading of personal insults is unlikely to benefit a relationship.

Caryl Rusbult (1987) and her colleagues have identified four common approaches people take to problem solving in romantic relationships. These are:

- *Voice*: A person voices the problems, tries to compromise, seeks help from a counselor, tries to change the self or the partner, or more generally works to improve the relationship.

- *Loyalty*: A person responds more passively by waiting, hoping, or praying that things will improve with time or by supporting the partner in the face of criticism.

- *Neglect*: A person reacts by spending less time with the partner, ignoring the partner, refusing to discuss problems, treating the partner badly, or "just letting things fall apart."

- *Exit*: A person moves out of a joint residence, actively physically abuses the partner, or ends the relationship by leaving or getting a divorce.

From the perspective of continuing the relationship, loyalty and voice are constructive, relationship-promoting responses; neglect and exit are destructive to the relationship. Of course, for the individuals involved, ending the relationship may be a personally helpful and appropriate action.

Rusbult has shown that social exchange factors influence the type of problem solving used. In one study (Rusbult, Zembrodt & Gunn, 1982), college students were more likely to use relationship-promoting responses of voice and loyalty when they had been satisfied with the relationship before problems arose, when they had made substantial investments in the relationship, and when they had poor alternatives. In contrast, students were more likely to end the relationship when their pre-problem satisfaction was relatively low, their investments were low, and they had good alternatives. A more recent study of college dating couples (Rusbult, Johnson & Morrow, 1986a) reported that the use of destructive approaches was significantly associated with greater distress in couples. Another interesting finding was that girlfriends were significantly more likely than boyfriends to use constructive approaches of voicing problems and showing loyalty, and girlfriends were somewhat less likely to engage in neglect.

Satisfaction and Commitment

When a young couple falls in love, the partners often wonder how to make their relationship "good" and how to make sure it will "last." In the world of work, employers are concerned about how to keep their workers "happy" and how to increase workers' sense of loyalty to the company. For their part, the employees are usually concerned with pleasing their boss and keeping their jobs. In more technical terms, two important aspects of relationships are personal satisfaction and commitment to continuing the relationship.

Conceptually, there are important differences between satisfaction and commitment (Berscheid & Walster, 1978; Kelley, 1983). For example, in an "empty-shell marriage," spouses feel little love for each other but stay together because of religious principles, concern for the welfare of their children, or fear of loneliness. They are committed, despite low satisfaction. Or consider the case of a college woman who loves a man intensely, but recognizes that he does not return her passion. Despite her love, she may realize that continuing her commitment is not in her own best interests, and so she may end the relationship to seek a more compatible mate. In business, a worker may continue in an unhappy job because there are no better alternatives, or leave a very satisfying work environment if a better opportunity comes along. Satisfaction and commitment are not the same.

Satisfaction refers to an individual's subjective evaluation of the quality of a relationship. Satisfaction depends on two factors: the outcomes we receive from the relationship and our general comparison level. We are satisfied if a relationship is profitable and if it compares favorably to our hopes and expectations. Perceptions of fairness also affect satisfaction: Even if a relationship provides many benefits, we will not be fully satisfied if we perceive that we are being treated unfairly. In love and friendship, lopsided relationships in which one person gives much more—or gets much more—than the other are usually not as satisfying as balanced exchanges. In business, partners are usually dissatisfied if they perceive the relationship to be inequitable.

Commitment refers to all the forces, positive and negative, acting to keep an individual in a relationship. People who are strongly committed to a relationship are likely to stay together "through thick and thin," "for better or for worse." Positive forces of attraction are one determinant of commitment. If we like another person, enjoy that person's company, and find it easy to get along, we will be positively motivated to continue the relationship. Social exchange theory emphasizes, however, that commitment is also based on negative forces or constraints that make it costly for a person to leave a relationship.

One barrier to leaving a relationship is a lack of alternatives. We may dislike our boss and regret having to interact daily, but continue the relationship because we need the salary and can't find another job. We may date someone who falls below our comparison level because he or she is the only eligible person we know. If we are dependent on a relationship to provide things we value and cannot obtain elsewhere, we are unlikely to leave.

In more technical terms, commitment is closely related to our comparison level for alternatives.

The investments we have made in a relationship are another factor influencing commitment (Rusbult, 1980; 1983). *Investments* can include time, energy, money, emotional involvement, shared experiences, sacrifices for a partner, and so on. To invest much in a relationship and then find it unrewarding can arouse cognitive dissonance, and so we may feel psychological pressures to see the relationship in a positive light and downplay its drawbacks (Rubin, 1973). The more we have put into a relationship, the more costly it would be for us to leave. One of the many costs of divorce is dividing the joint property a couple has accumu-

lated together. The greater our investment, the more committed we are to a relationship.

Empirical research has demonstrated the importance of exchange considerations for satisfaction and commitment in relationships (Levinger, 1979; Michaels, Acock & Edwards, 1986; Rusbult, 1983; Rusbult, Johnson & Morrow, 1986b). For example, in a study of dating relationships, Caryl Rusbult (1980) explicitly tested an exchange model. College students completed detailed questionnaires assessing the rewards they got from their dating relationship (such as the partner's attractiveness and intelligence, the couple's ability to coordinate activities) and the costs (such as conflict or the partner's embarrassing behaviors). Participants also described during this period, they continued to invest as much in the relationship as did the stayers. Rusbult suggests that the abandoned experienced entrapment. Because of their poor alternatives, they remained committed to (and trapped in) a relatively unsatisfactory relationship until the partner ended it.

Further evidence for the importance of exchange factors comes from a longitudinal study of college dating couples by Hill, Rubin and Peplau (1976). They found that relationships with an imbalance of involvement were significantly more likely to end than were relationships in which both partners were equally involved. It was most common for the less involved partner to end the relationship. But in a minority of cases, it was actually the more involved person who, sensing that the partner did not reciprocate the strong attraction, ended the relationship.

There are two sides to every breakup, a point emphasized by Hill, Rubin and Peplau. They found that very few breakups were truly mutual, with both partners deciding at the same time to end the relationship. Over 85 percent of students reported that one partner wanted to end the relationship at least somewhat more than the other. However, partners did not always agree about who was the leaver and who was the rejected lover. Each partner tended to say that he or she was the one who wanted to end the relationship. This self-bias may make it easier to accept and cope with the breakup. Both women and men felt freer, happier, less depressed, less lonely, but more guilty when they perceived that they were the one to initiate the breakup.

One other interesting finding in the Hill, Rubin, and Peplau study was that breakups were not randomly distributed throughout the academic year. Instead, breakups peaked in September, December–January, and June. Factors external to the relationship such as graduation may have contributed to some breakups. In other cases, vacations may have made it easier to call off a relationship that was already in trouble. It is probably easier to say "Let's date others during the summer," rather than to say, "I'm bored with you and want to end our relationship."

the quality of the best available alternative to their current relationship, and indicated how much they had invested or "put things into" the relationship.

Finally, they completed several measures of satisfaction and commitment. Consistent with exchange theory, the strongest predictors of satisfaction were rewards and costs; investments and alternatives did not affect satisfaction. The most satisfied people reported many rewards and few costs. In contrast, commitment was affected by satisfaction, investments, and alternatives. People felt most committed when they were satisfied with the relationship, had invested a lot, and had relatively less desirable alternatives.

In many relationships, satisfaction and commit-ment go hand in hand. As a young couple discovers the special rewards of their developing relationship, they take steps to build commitment. They may stop dating other people, exchange presents, and forego other activities to be with each other. As their affection blossoms into love, they may take public actions to demonstrate their feelings and to build a future together.

A wedding ceremony, buying a home together, having children—these investments in the relationship are usually based on love, and further serve to build commitment. If the couple encounters difficult times of conflict and disagreement, their commitment may provide the motivation to "work to improve the relationship" and to rekindle their love. But satisfaction and commitment are not inseparable. We sometimes find ourselves stuck in unsatisfying relationships, and we sometimes avoid commitment despite strong attraction.

Beyond Exchange

Social exchange principles help us understand many kinds of relationships, ranging from interactions among co-workers to lifelong marriages. Most people recognize that exchange influences casual relationships, but may resist the idea that exchange factors also govern our most intimate relationships. It is certainly unromantic to suggest, as did sociologist Erving Goffman (1952), that "A proposal of marriage in our society tends to be a way in which a man sums up his social attributes and suggests that hers are not so much better as to preclude a merger or a partnership in these matters" (p. 456).

Social psychologist Zick Rubin (1973) voiced the common concern about exchange theory:

The notions that people are "commodities" and social relationships are "transactions" will surely make many readers squirm. Exchange theory postulates that human relationships are based first and foremost on self-interest. As such, it often seems to portray friendship as motivated only by what one person can get from another and to redefine love as a devious power game. . . . But although we might prefer to believe otherwise, we must face up to the fact that our attitudes toward other people *are* determined to a large extent by our assessments of the rewards they hold for us. (p. 82)

It may be helpful to remember that although exchange theory borrows terminology from economics, the rewards and costs involved are often very personal and unique: An adorable smile and shared secrets are as much a part of exchange theory as money and fur coats.

You may have noticed that in some of your relationships, exchange issues seem to be much more important than in others. For example, you may be willing to trade work shifts with a co-worker this week, but clearly expect that he'll do the same for you next week. In contrast, you and your best friend may do many favors for each other and help each other in times of need without consciously keeping mental records of what you give and receive. Clark and Mills (1979) have distinguished between what they call *exchange relationships* and *communal relationships*. In both types of relationships, exchange processes operate, but the rules governing the giving and receiving of benefits differ significantly.

Clark and Mills propose that in exchange relationships, people give benefits with the expectation of receiving comparable benefits in return soon afterwards. Exchange relationships occur most often with strangers or casual acquaintances and in business relations. In exchange relationships, people feel no special responsibility for the welfare of the other person. In contrast, in communal relationships, people feel a special responsibility for the needs of the other. Communal relationships usually occur with family, friends, and romantic partners. In these relationships, people provide benefits to the partner to show concern and to respond to the other's needs, with no expectation of receiving similar benefits in the near future. Clark and Mills have conducted a program of research to identify the differences between these two orientations towards relationships. For example, one study (Clark, 1984) found that partners in an exchange relationship are much more likely to keep track of their individual contributions to a joint task for which they will be rewarded than are partners in communal relationships. Another study (Clark, Mills & Powell, 1986) found that people pay more attention to the needs of a partner in a communal relationship than in an exchange relationship.

In long-term relationships, patterns of reciprocity and rules of exchange become complex. In our most intimate relationships, we may develop a sense of unity or "we-ness" so that we perceive benefitting a loved one as a way of benefitting ourselves. Exchange principles may not tell the whole story of personal relationships, but they do play an important part.

SELF-DISCLOSURE

Self-disclosure is the sharing of intimate feelings and information with another person. Many people consider self-disclosure to be a key aspect of intimacy in close relationships.

Self-disclosure can be both descriptive and evaluative (Morton, 1978). In descriptive disclosures, we reveal facts about ourselves that might otherwise be unavailable to a listener—the kind of work we do, where we live, how we voted in the recent election. In evaluative disclosures, we reveal our personal opinions and feelings—that we like the other person, that we feel guilty about being overweight, that we hate getting up early in the morning. Self-disclosure can serve many different functions (Derlega & Grzelak, 1979). Some of these are summarized in Table 9–1.

Altman and Taylor (1973) proposed a model of relationship development that gives a central role to self-disclosure. They call the process of attaining interpersonal intimacy **social penetration.** As shown in Figure 9–3, social penetration occurs along two major dimensions of breadth and depth.

As relationships develop from superficial to intimate, people disclose increasingly more personal things about themselves. We might willingly talk with a stranger about our preferences in food and music, talk with a casual acquaintance about our attitudes on politics and religion, but reserve for close friends discussions of our personal relationships or fears in life. Relationships also develop from narrow to broad, as over time people discuss a wider range of topics and share more diverse activities. These phases of relationship development are shown in Figure 9–3 as "wedges" that one person makes into the personality and life experiences of another.

We have seen that self-disclosure is an important way in which we begin new relationships and increase the intimacy of established relationships. But along with the benefits of self-disclosure go potential risks. Revealing personal information can make us vulnerable. A leading expert on self-disclosure, Valerian Derlega (1984), has suggested some of the many possible risks individuals may incur when they self-disclose:

1. *Indifference*: We may share information with another person in a bid to begin a new relationship. Sometimes, our disclosure is reciprocated by the other person, and a relationship develops. At other times, however, we may find that the other

TABLE 9–1

Five Main Reasons for Self-Disclosure

1. *Expression*: Sometimes we talk about our feelings to "get them off our chest." After a hard day at work, we may eagerly tell a friend just how angry we are at our boss and how underappreciated we feel. Simply being able to express our feelings is one reason for disclosure.
2. *Self-clarification*: In the process of sharing our feelings or experiences with others, we may gain greater understanding and self-awareness. Talking to a friend about a problem can help us to clarify our thoughts about the situation.
3. *Social validation*: By seeing how a listener reacts to our self-disclosures, we get information about the correctness and appropriateness of our views. Other people may reassure us that our reactions "seem perfectly normal"—or that we're "blowing things out of proportion." In either case, listeners provide useful information about social reality.
4. *Social control*: We may reveal—or conceal—information about ourselves as a means of social control. For instance, we may deliberately refrain from telling things about ourselves to protect our privacy. We may emphasize things we think will make a favorable impression on our listener. In extreme cases, people may deliberately lie to exploit others, as when an imposter claims to be a lawyer but has actually had no legal training.
5. *Relationship development*: The sharing of personal information and confidences is an important way to begin a relationship and move toward increasing levels of intimacy. For young lovers, self-disclosure may have moved from initial exchanges of background information to the discovery of shared interests to the first expression of "I love you."

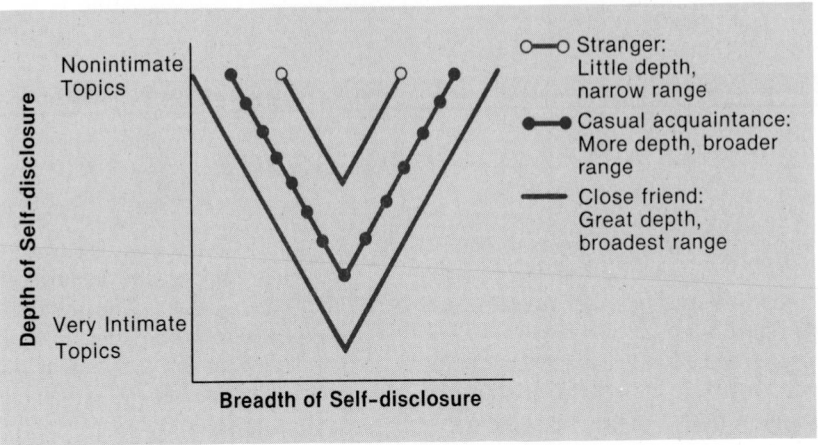

FIGURE 9–3   The breadth and depth of self-disclosure are represented as "wedges" into the personality and experience of the person. For strangers, the wedge is narrow and superficial. For a close friend, the wedge is deeper (more intimate) and broader in the range of topics disclosed. (Adapted from Altman & Haythorn, 1965, p. 422.)

person is indifferent to our disclosures and not at all interested in getting to know us.

2. *Rejection*: Information we reveal about ourselves may lead to social rejection. For example, a college student may not tell her roommate that she has epilepsy, out of a concern that misinformation and fear will lead the roommate to reject her.

3. *Loss of Control*: There is some truth to the old adage that "knowledge is power." Sometimes, others try to use information we share to hurt us or to control our behavior. Derlega suggests, for instance, that a teenage boy may tell a friend some little-known but potentially embarrassing information about his fear of women. In an angry moment, the friend may remind the young man of his weaknesses to try to establish dominance in the relationship.

4. *Betrayal*: When we reveal personal information to someone we often assume—or even explicitly request—that the knowledge be treated confidentially. Unfortunately, such confidences are sometimes betrayed.

Self-Disclosure and Liking

Liking is an important cause of self-disclosure. People reveal much more to spouses and best friends than to co-workers and casual friends. The more interesting question is how the act of self-disclosing affects liking. One view might be that self-disclosure is inherently rewarding, and "the more the better." Research generally supports a different view, however, that we like people most whose self-disclosure is appropriate to the situation (Derlega & Chaikin, 1975).

Altman and Taylor (1973) argued that self-disclosure leads to liking only if it is carefully paced. It must be slow enough that it does not become threatening to either person. If it races ahead prematurely into areas of great personal intimacy, it will arouse anxiety and defensiveness. Someone who "comes on too strong, too fast" will be disliked.

An illustration of this effect comes from a study by Kaplan and colleagues (1974). They varied both the formality of the interaction setting and the intimacy of the subject's own self-disclosure. College men came to a laboratory to be interviewed in one of three contexts. One was highly formal: The paneled and carpeted room was decorated with management and business journals, and the interviewer was supposedly a business student. In the medium-formality condition, the room was stocked with psychotherapy literature and the interviewer was supposed to be a student in clinical psychology. In the low-formality condition, the room contained marital counseling and sexology literature, and the interviewer was a "human relations" student learning how to do sexual counseling.

The interviewer asked the subject questions that

Self-disclosure ranges from a casual chat with strangers to the shared intimacies of long-time friends.

were highly intimate ("How often do you masturbate?" and "Would you describe anything you dislike about your mother?") or nonintimate ("What are the kinds of movies that you like to see?" and "How many hours of sleep do you need to feel your best?"). Ratings of attraction to the interviewer were obtained in an unusual way: After every question, the subject pressed a button indicating liking, ostensibly to give an ongoing measure of the "interviewer's" performance. The results are shown in Figure 9–4.

Liking for the interviewer was highest in the informal setting with nonintimate questions—that is, for a quite modest level of social penetration between these two complete strangers. Liking was least for the formal-context interviewer asking inti-

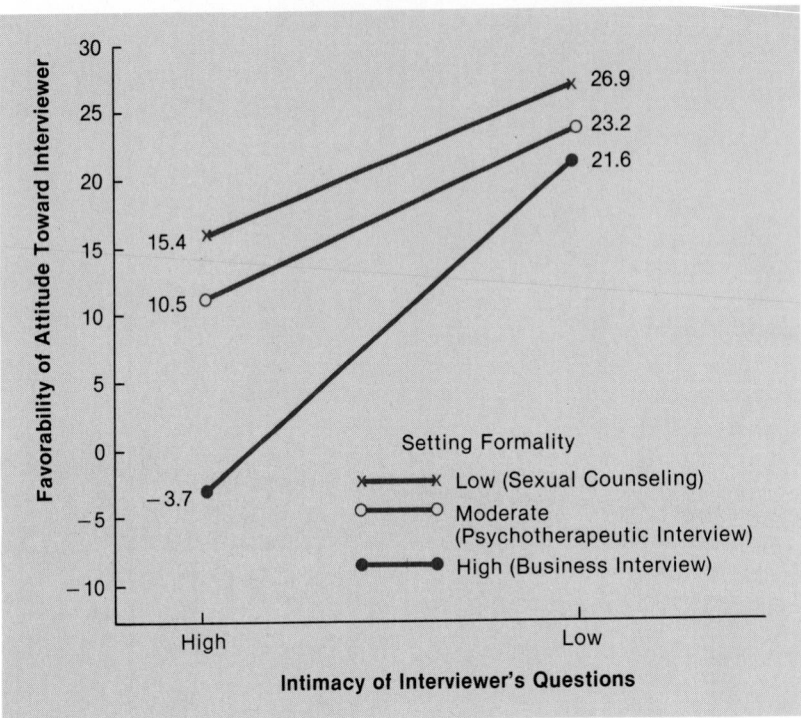

FIGURE 9–4 Interview setting formality and liking. (Adapted from Kaplan, Firestone, Degnore, & Morre, 1974.)

mate questions. Clearly, this person was probing at too deep a level too fast. His demands for intimate self-disclosure were especially inappropriate given his own formality. In sum, we are most apt to like someone whose own disclosures and requests for us to disclose are appropriate to the situation and the nature of the relationship.

Reciprocity

Consistent with social exchange theory, there appears to be a norm of reciprocity for self-disclosure (Ludwig, Franco & Malloy, 1986; Miller & Kenny, 1986). If someone tells us something personal, we usually feel obligated to respond with a comparable revelation. A gradual process of mutual self-disclosure, paced over time, spurs the growth of a relationship.

Altman and Taylor proposed that we like best people who disclose at about the same level of intimacy as we do. Someone who discloses more

intimate personal details than we do threatens us with a premature rush into intimate territory, and we may want to put on the brakes. If we are disclosing at a more intimate level than the other person, we are left feeling vulnerable or foolish.

There is much evidence that reciprocity in self-disclosure is a key factor in liking. In the Kaplan study, the formal interviewer asked for extremely intimate self-disclosure, but provided none in return. And he was not liked. A more direct test of the reciprocity idea would involve experimentally manipulating the intimacy level of both persons' self-disclosures.

Chaikin and Derlega (1974) videotaped two actresses improvising a first-acquaintance encounter in a school cafeteria. Each actress did this in two ways: at a high and at a low level of self-disclosure. Then the experimenters presented the performances to subjects in each of the four combinations of self-disclosure: both women high in self-disclosure, both low, high-low, or low-high.

In the high self-disclosure case, one woman told immediately of her relationship with her boyfriend "Bill," who was her first sexual partner, and of her parents' reactions; the other woman's high-intimacy disclosures concerned her mother's nervous breakdown and hospitalization, her fighting with her mother, and the possible divorce of her parents. In the low self-disclosure cases, the women talked about the problems of commuting to school, where they went to high school, the courses they were taking, and so on.

The main finding is that liking for both women was higher when they disclosed at the same level of intimacy than when they were at different levels. Breaking the reciprocity norm led to less liking, but for different reasons. The woman who disclosed too little (relative to the other) was thought cold, whereas the more intimate norm breaker was thought maladjusted.

Demands for reciprocal intimacy of self-disclosure seem to be especially strong in two circumstances. Early in a relationship, we expect reciprocity for *nonintimate* disclosures. If you tell the stranger next to you in the lecture hall that you like this course, she is supposed to reciprocate with her reactions to it. In this opening stage of a relationship, there is no norm for reciprocity about intimate matters. If she suddenly changes the subject and tells you about her parents' rancorous divorce, you do not feel obligated at all to tell her anything intimate about your life. Indeed, her revelation may seem inappropriately intimate, since she is a complete stranger.

Later in the development of a relationship, reciprocity about *intimate* details becomes important. Suppose you sit next to her for several weeks, then go to the campus coffeehouse after the first midterm. If you start telling her about your doubts about your ability in school, and your worry that maybe you should have gone to an easier college, you are putting yourself out on a limb. It is important that she make some reciprocal gesture, to show that she is interested in having a closer relationship too. If, in the midst of your disclosures about your secret fears, she suddenly starts talking about the weather, you may feel hurt and want to pull back to a less intimate level. Reciprocity is important for supporting tentative moves toward a closer relationship.

People generally do not reciprocate sudden intimate disclosures by strangers. For example, Rubin (1975) found that people waiting in an airport responsed *less* intimately to a student who provided intimate disclosures and then asked for reciprocation than to a student who provided more impersonal material. Their reluctance is partly due to feeling pressured into reciprocity, or "reactance" against loss of freedom. Archer and Berg (1978) found telling recipients it was perfectly all right to say anything they wanted—and thereby removing the pressure to reciprocate—made them feel much freer to reciprocate with intimate disclosures.

A more gradual approach to self-disclosure is more conducive to reciprocity. For example, Davis (1976) set up an acquaintance exercise in which two people took turns disclosing to each other. He found that the average intimacy level increased throughout the exercise, as might be expected from our discussion of social penetration. More important for the reciprocity norm, he found that both the average level of intimacy and the rate of increase of intimacy were closely matched between partners. As one person became more intimate, or slowed down, so did the other.

In a later study, Davis (1977) allowed the two discussion partners to talk more explicitly between turns about their feelings about the interaction itself. The intimacy of each partner's disclosures was still matched over the entire discussion, but the reciprocity norm was relaxed a little. Apparently they did not feel that both sides of every exchange had to be equally self-disclosing; instead, they came to a rough overall agreement that allowed an exchange to be unbalanced temporarily.

Also, with more explicit discussion of the disclosure process itself, the two partners became more equal in taking the initiative. There was less tendency for one person to take the lead, with the other following. Finally, because of the explicit attention to the process, they reached a more intimate level of disclosure more rapidly.

Sex Differences in Self-Disclosure

Stereotypes depict men as "silent types" who keep their feelings to themselves, and women as "talkers" who freely share confidences. As one wife complained about her husband, "He doesn't ever think there's anything to talk about. I'm the one who has to nag him to talk" (cited in L. Rubin, 1976, p. 124). How accurate is this traditional stereotype about gender differences in self-disclosure?

In *same-sex* relationships, women do indeed disclose more than men, on average (Dosser, Balswick, & Halverson, 1986; Reis, Senchak, & Solomon, 1985). Throughout adult life, women are more likely than men to have an intimate, same-sex confidant, and to emphasize the sharing of personal information. In a study of college students (Caldwell & Peplau, 1982), for example, women were more likely than men to say that they enjoy "just talking" to their best woman friend, and to indicate that talking helped form the basis of their relationship. In contrast, college men emphasized sharing activities with their best male friend.

In *opposite-sex* relationships, however, gender differences are much less clear-cut. In general, heterosexuals disclose more to spouses than to anyone else. The most common pattern is for both spouses to reveal at equal levels, with some couples sharing a lot and others disclosing relatively little (see Komarovsky, 1967). The norm of reciprocity encourages partners to disclose at comparable levels.

It seems that young Americans today expect more self-disclosure in their intimate relationships than did earlier generations. Rands and Levinger (1979) asked college students and senior citizens to describe relationships characteristic of 22-year-olds of their own generations. They found that today's young people expect pairs to be more expressive, to do more things together, and to disclose both positive and negative feelings more openly than the young people of two generations ago. Studies also find that younger dating couples today usu-

ally do disclose at quite high and equal levels (see Rubin, Hill, Peplau, & Dunkel-Schetter, 1980). It should be noted, however, that when exceptions to this equal-disclosure pattern occur, it is usually the man who discloses less.

The fact that men and women often disclose at equal levels of intimacy does not mean that they necessarily reveal the same kinds of personal information. One study (Hacker, 1981) of college students found that in male-female relationships, women were more likely to reveal their weaknesses and to conceal their strengths; men showed a reverse pattern of disclosing their strengths and concealing their weaknesses. Another study (Derlega, Durham, Gockel, & Sholis, 1981) found that men disclosed more on "masculine" topics such as when they had been aggressive or had taken risks; women disclosed more on "feminine" topics such as when they felt childlike or were sensitive about their appearance.

Rosenfeld (1979) investigated why people sometimes avoid disclosure. For both sexes, the most important reason was concern about "projecting an image I do not want to project." However, men also expressed concerns about losing control over another person; women expressed concerns about providing information that might be used against them and about hurting the relationship.

In general, research does not support the stereotype that all men are inexpressive. In heterosexual dating and marriage, men and women usually disclose at similar levels. Sex differences are most pronounced in same-sex relationships, with women friends showing a strong preference for talking, and men friends showing a greater interest in sharing activities.

LOVE

Personal relationships are often highly colored by strong emotions. Passionate desire for a new lover, anger at an insult from a co-worker, grief at the loss of a grandparent, the joy of playing with a baby—emotions such as these are basic elements of social life.

TABLE 9.2

Would You Marry Without Love?

How college students answered the question "If a man (woman) had all the other qualities you desired, would you marry this person if you were not in love with him (her)?" (Numbers are percentages.)

	1967		1976		1984	
	Men	**Women**	**Men**	**Women**	**Men**	**Women**
Yes	11.7	4.0	1.7	4.6	1.7	3.6
Undecided	23.7	71.7	12.1	15.4	12.7	11.5
No	64.6	24.3	86.2	80.0	85.6	84.9

In all years, data are questionnaire responses from college men and women. The earliest data were collected by Kephart (1967); his question was worded identically to that above except that he used "boy(girl)" instead of "man(woman)."
Source: Based on data from Simpson, Campbell & Berscheid, 1986. Used by permission of Sage Publications, Inc.

In recent years, the study of emotion has become a "hot" topic in psychology. New work is underway to develop theories about the nature of emotions, and to understand the biological and social origins of human emotions. Social psychologists have emphasized the importance of the social context of emotional experiences (e.g., Berscheid, 1983; Gordon, 1981).

In a recent series of studies, Phillip Shaver, Judith Schwartz, and their co-workers have investigated the way that young adults think about emotions (Shaver, et al., in press; Schwartz & Shaver, in press). Their research has shown that people conceptualize emotional experiences as falling into five basic categories or prototypes: love, joy, anger, sadness, and fear. In one study, they asked college students to write a detailed description of a real incident in which they felt each of these five basic emotions. For instance, "Think of a real incident in which you felt particularly IN LOVE or LOVING." Systematic analyses showed that most of these descriptions of emotional experiences referred to close relationships. Not surprisingly, all the love descriptions focused on a personal relationship. But so did 91 percent of the anger episodes, 90 percent of the sadness episodes, 47 percent of the fear episodes, and 44 percent of the joy episodes. For example, most of the sadness accounts concerned the loss of a close relationship through death, illness or separation. A majority of the anger accounts were directed toward family members, romantic partners or friends. Reports of fears included social anxieties, as well as threats to life or limb, often intensified

by being alone. Experiences of joy were divided between happiness based on social relations and individual achievements. As these data suggest, emotions are closely linked to social relationships.

In this section, we will focus on love and romance. Long a favored subject for poets and songwriters, love is now a popular topic for scientific research as well. Most Americans consider love to be essential to a successful marriage. In the 1960s, Kephart first asked young adults about the love–marriage connection. The question he posed to over 1,000 college students was: "If a boy (girl) had all the qualities you desired, would you marry this person if you were not in love with him (her)?" The results are shown in Table 9–2. Twenty years ago, the majority of men said no, they wouldn't marry a woman they didn't love. However, the majority of women said they were undecided; only one woman in four clearly answered no. In the intervening years, both sexes—but especially women—have become more romantic in their approach to marriage. In 1976 and again in 1984, Simpson, Campbell and Berscheid (1986) asked new generations of college students the same question. In 1976, 86 percent of men and 80 percent of women said they would not marry without love; by 1984, the proportion of men who said no was the same, but women had increased to 85 percent. Today, the vast majority of young people appear to view love as a prerequisite for marriage.

Before turning to other research findings on love, we might set the stage by considering this newspaper story of young love:

On Monday, Cpl. Floyd Johnson, 23, and the then Ellen Skinner, 19, total strangers, boarded a train at San Francisco and sat down across the aisle from each other. Johnson didn't cross the aisle until Wednesday, but his bride said, "I'd already made up my mind to say yes if he asked me to marry him." "We did most of the talking with our eyes," Johnson explained. Thursday the couple got off the train in Omaha with plans to be married. Because they would need to have the consent of the bride's parents if they were married in Nebraska, they crossed the river to Council Bluffs, Iowa, where they were married Friday.

This account may remind you of such star-struck lovers from literature as Romeo and Juliet. But have you personally ever experienced this rather magical love at first sight?

When Averill and Boothroyd (1977) asked university students how closely their own most intense love experience corresponded to this romantic model, only 40 percent said there was a strong resemblance. Another 40 percent said they had never experienced anything at all like this story, and the rest thought their most intense love relationship bore only a partial similarity to this one. This range of answers highlights one of the dilemmas of love researchers—how to capture the essential features of love, and at the same time depict the diverse experiences of people in love.

Love versus Liking

One of the first researchers to study romantic love was Zick Rubin (1970, 1973). He was interested in the connection between love and liking. One view is that love is merely a very intense form of liking. According to this unidimensional view, our positive feelings of attraction range along a continuum from mild liking to strong liking to mild love

Drawing by Handelsman; © 1987 The New Yorker Magazine, Inc.

"I suppose I should have let a few minutes elapse between declaring my love for you and announcing that I also loved lobster."

to strong love. A contrasting view, and the one Rubin favored, is that liking and love are qualitatively distinct and represent two different dimensions. This view seems consistent with folk wisdom that we can like someone a great deal, but not be in love with him or her—and that we can feel passionate love for someone we do not totally like or respect.

To study this issue, Rubin first compiled various statements that people thought reflected liking and other statements that people thought reflected love. These included such things as idealization, trust, sharing emotions, believing someone is intelligent, and tolerating the other's faults. Next Rubin asked several hundred college students to rate how characteristic each of these statements was of their feelings toward their boyfriend or girlfriend and toward a nonromantic friend of the other sex. Rubin believed that if love and liking are distinct, some statements would characterize a romantic partner but not a friend. The results of this first study supported the idea that love and liking are distinct.

Based on these findings, Rubin constructed two separate paper and pencil tests, a Love Scale and a Liking Scale. Each scale consists of nine statements. A sample liking statement is "I have great confidence in _____'s good judgment." Respondents rate each statement on a nine-point scale from strongly disagree to strongly agree.

To collect further evidence that these scales were measuring somewhat different attitudes, Rubin recruited 182 dating couples at the University of Michigan. Both members of each couple filled out detailed questionnaires about their relationship and also participated in lab experiments. Rubin's results supported the distinction between love and liking. For example, he found that although students rated their dating partner and best friend equally on the Liking Scale, they rated their boyfriend or girlfriend much higher on the Love Scale.

In an experimental session, Rubin found that couples who scored high on the Love Scale spent more time making eye contact than did low scorers, confirming the idea that lovers often gaze into each other's eyes. Those with high love scores were more likely to say that they and their partner were in love. Strong lovers also gave a higher estimate of the probability of eventually marrying the partner.

In a follow-up study six months later, Rubin examined whether love scores were related to staying together versus breaking up. Strong lovers were more likely to stay together, but only if they were also high in "romanticism," the belief that true love conquers all. Taken together, these and more recent data suggest that although love and liking are related experiences, there are important qualitative differences between the two.

The Experience of Romantic Love

Research has begun to identify the various thoughts, feelings, and behaviors that are associated with romantic love (Kelley, 1983). Most of the information we have about love comes from studies of young adults in our society. The experience of love is quite different in other cultures and at other historical times (Hunt, 1959). We need to be cautious about generalizing from current findings to "all lovers."

THOUGHTS OF LOVE   Rubin's Love Scale conceptualizes love as an attitude we have toward another person, as a distinctive cluster of thoughts about the loved person. Rubin identified three main themes reflected in his scale items. One theme, which Rubin called attachment, is a sense of need and urgency. A sample statement is "It would be hard for me to get along without _____." These statements reflect a person's awareness of their dependence on the other to provide valued rewards.

A second theme concerns caring for the other person, as illustrated in this item: "I would do almost anything for _____." A desire to promote the other person's welfare and to be responsive to his or her needs is a central idea. The third theme emphasized trust and self-disclosure. These ideas of love contrast with the Liking Scale, which concerns beliefs that the other person is likable, intelligent, well-adjusted, and has good judgment.

A study by Steck, Levitan, McLane and Kelley (1982) investigated the relative importance of various components of the Love Scale to people's perceptions of how much someone is in love. College students read several Love Scale questionnaires, each with a different pattern of responses. Students indicated how much love the person who completed each questionnaire felt for the partner. By manipulating responses to specific questions, the researchers created different versions of the scale that had the same total score, but differed in the importance given to needing, caring, and trust.

Results showed that perceptions of how much a person loved a partner were more strongly influenced by the degree of caring than by needing. In other words, if two men both scored moderately on the Love Scale but one emphasized how much he cared for his girlfriend and the other indicated how much he needed his girlfriend, the caring person was seen as loving more. The person who showed great need but not great care was rated as showing "attraction" but not "love." In judgments of love, trust was given much less importance than either caring or needing. In ratings of friendship, however, trust was the most important factor.

BEHAVIORS OF LOVE   In assessing whether someone loves us, we usually depend not only on their words, but also on their actions. If someone professes love but forgets our birthday, goes out with other people, criticizes our appearance, and never confides in us, we may doubt their sincerity. Swensen (1972) asked people of different ages what behaviors they thought were most closely associated with love for a romantic partner or spouse. The answers fell into seven categories or types of love behaviors:

1. Verbal statements of affection, such as saying "I love you."

2. Self-disclosure.

3. Nonmaterial signs of love, such as showing interest in the person's activities, respecting his or her opinions, or giving encouragement.

4. Communicating nonverbally such feelings as happiness and relaxation when the other is present.

5. Material signs of love, such as giving presents or doing tasks to help the other person.

6. Physical expressions of love, such as hugging or kissing.

7. Showing a willingness to tolerate the other and to make sacrifices to maintain the relationship.

Swensen found that many of these romantic love behaviors were also seen as signs of love for parents, siblings, or same-sex friends.

In a more recent study, King and Christensen (1983) identified specific events that indicated how far a heterosexual dating couple had progressed toward marriage. In most cases, the college couples in their research went through a predictable sequence of events moving toward greater commitment. Events that usually occurred early in the development of a relationship included spending a

Irene Springer

whole day together and calling the partner by an affectionate name. At a later stage, partners started referring to each other as "boyfriend" and "girlfriend," and received invitations to do things together as a couple. A further development was to say "I love you" and to date each other exclusively. A common next step was to discuss living together or marriage, and to take a vacation together. Events indicating greatest progress included living together or becoming engaged. Although couples varied in how far their relationship had developed and in the speed with which they moved toward permanence, most couples followed a similar sequence of key events.

FEELINGS OF LOVE   One feature that often distinguishes romantic love from friendship is the experience of physical symptoms. According to popular songs, a lover's heart skips a beat now and then, the lover loses sleep and has trouble concentrating. To investigate this matter, Kanin, Davidson, and Scheck (1970) asked 679 university students to rate the intensity of various feelings they had had during their current or most recent love experience.

The most common reactions were a strong feeling of well-being (reported by 79 percent of students) and great difficulty concentrating (reported by 37 percent of students). Other reactions included "floating on a cloud" (29 percent), "wanted to run, jump, scream" (22 percent), feeling "nervous before dates" (22 percent), and feeling "giddy and carefree" (20 percent). Strong physical sensations such as cold hands, butterflies in the stomach, or a tingling spine were reported by 20 percent and insomnia by 12 percent of students.

Researchers also found differences between the love experiences of women and men, with women being more likely to report strong emotional reactions. Dion and Dion (1973) found a similar sex difference: Women more often reported feelings of euphoria associated with love. Whether these results reflect actual sex differences in the experience of love or women's greater willingness to disclose such feelings is not known.

Research has identified some of the thoughts, feelings, and behaviors Americans commonly associate with love. But studies also find that individuals differ in their specific love experiences. This suggests that there are distinct types of love. In the next section, we examine two major models of love. For a more detailed look at ways people define love, see Box 9–2.

Passionate Love and Companionate Love

Passionate love has been described by Berscheid and Walster as "a wildly emotional state: tender and sexual feelings, elation and pain, anxiety and relief, altriusm and jealousy coexist in a confusion of feelings" (1978, p. 177). Emotions play a central role in passionate love. People are swept off their feet by uncontrollable passions that draw them irresistibly toward the loved person.

The physiological arousal that fuels the passion of this type of love can have many sources. Sexual desire, the anxiety of possible rejection, the excitement of getting to know someone, the frustration of outside interference, the anger of a lover's quarrel—all may contribute to the strong emotions experienced in passionate love. Berscheid (1983) has suggested that the uncontrollable quality of passionate love provides a convenient justification for lovers to engage in behaviors they might otherwise

We feel companionate love for that special person with whom our lives are deeply intertwined.

Laimute E. Druskis

BOX 9–2

DEFINITIONS OF LOVE

When people say "I love you," they can mean very different things. How would you personally define love?

Researchers have identified six different ways in which people commonly define love (Lasswell & Lobsenz, 1980; Lee, 1973). These love styles are idealized types; each individual may define love in a way that combines more than one style:

- *Romantic love.* Love is an all-consuming emotional experience. Love at first sight is typical. Physical attraction is essential to love. A romantic lover might agree that, "At the first touch of his/her hand, I knew that love was a real possibility."

- *Possessive love.* The possessive lover is emotionally intense, jealous, obsessed with the beloved. The possessive lover is highly dependent on the beloved, and therefore fears rejection. Preoccupation with the loved one swings quickly from peaks of joy to valleys of despair. The possessive lover might agree, "When my lover doesn't pay attention to me I feel sick all over."

- *Best friends love.* Love is a comfortable intimacy that grows slowly from companionship, mutual sharing, and gradual self-disclosure. A best friends lover is thoughtful, warm, and companionate. He or she might agree that "The best kind of love grows out of a long friendship."

- *Pragmatic love.* According to Lee, this is "the love that goes shopping for a suitable mate, and all it asks is that the relationship work well, that the two partners be compatible and satisfy each other's basic or practical needs" (1973, p. 124). The pragmatic lover is logical and thoughtful in selecting a suitable partner, and seeks contentment rather than excitement. The pragmatic lover might agree that "It makes good sense to plan your life carefully before you choose a lover."

- *Altruistic love.* This style of love is unconditionally caring, giving, and forgiving. Love means a duty to give to the loved one with no strings attached, with no expectations of reciprocity. Altruistic love is expressed through self-sacrifice, patience, and faith in the beloved. An altruistic lover might agree that "I try to use my own strength to help my lover through difficult times, even when he/she is behaving foolishly."

- *Game-playing love.* This person plays at love as others play games: to enjoy the "love game" and to win it. In game-playing love, strategy is important, and commitment is to be avoided. The game-player may have several relationships going at once. No relationship lasts for long, usually ending when the love partner becomes boring or too serious. A game player might agree that "Part of the fun of being in love is testing one's skill at keeping it going and getting what one wants from it at the same time."

The two general models of love discussed in the text can be seen as combinations of several specific love styles. Passionate love is often a mix of romantic and possessive love. Companionate love combines being best friends and being pragmatic.

To study these love styles empirically, Lee (1973, 1977) and other researchers have developed techniques to assess how individuals rate on each of the six types. The statements given above are from a love questionnaire developed by Lasswell and Lasswell (1976). Research has found at least preliminary support for the idea of distinct love styles. Individuals are rarely a "pure" type, but instead may score high on two or three styles, or may be moderate in some styles and low in others.

Gender differences in love styles have emerged in several studies (Hatkoff & Lasswell, 1979; Hendrick et al., 1984). In general, men are more likely to be romantics who believe in love at first sight or game players who enjoy the thrill of the chase. Women are more likely to adopt a best friends or pragmatic approach to love.

Intrigued by these findings, researchers have freely speculated about the possible reasons for sex differences in love styles (Rubin, Peplau & Hill, 1981). The most common explanation concerns the social and economic context of mate selection. As sociologist Willard Waller (1938) explained, "A man, when he marries, chooses a companion and perhaps a helpmate, but a woman chooses a companion and at the same time a standard of living. It is necessary for a woman to be mercenary" (p. 243). Men, it is argued, can afford to be more frivolous and romantic in love.

consider unacceptable—such as an extramarital affair. The lovers' defense is that they "couldn't stop" themselves.

Another element of passionate love is preoccupation with the other person. The lover is obsessed with thoughts of the new love. There is a tendency to idealize the loved person, to see the person as wonderful and perfect in every way. Passionate love is often said to strike suddenly and fade quickly. This type of love is intense, but fragile.

Companionate love has been defined as "the affection we feel for those with whom our lives are deeply intertwined" (Berscheid & Walster, 1978, p. 177). This is a more practical type of love that emphasizes trust, caring, and tolerance of the partner's flaws and idiosyncrasies. The emotional tone of companionate love is more moderate; warmth and affection are more common than extreme passions.

Kelley (1983) suggests that companionate love develops slowly as two people build a satisfying relationship. He also speculates that companionate love is more common in equitable relationships where partners perceive that they are benefitting

in equal measure from the partnership. Companionate love is believed to provide an enduring basis for long-term relationships.

The models of passionate and companionate love represent different images of the experience of love. People differ in their beliefs about which type of love is the better or truer form. The contrast between passionate and companionate love raises interesting questions about the experience of emotions in close relationships.

Why might it be that the early stages of a romantic relationship are usually characterized by extreme emotions, whereas the later stages are marked by emotional tranquility and moderation? Berscheid (1983) has suggested that over time, the novelty and surprise of the relationship wear off. Idealization of the partner confronts the reality of human imperfection. The couple develops routine ways of interaction, and life together becomes more settled.

However, Berscheid also suggests that as a relationship continues over time and interdependence grows, the *potential* for strong emotion actually increases. The greater our dependence on another person, the greater the possible influence of the partner in our lives. But, paradoxically, because long-term couples learn to coordinate their activities successfully, the actual frequency of strong emotions is usually fairly low.

The latent potential for strong emotion may emerge occasionally, however. When partners are separated because of travel or illness, they often have intense feelings of loneliness and desire. Another situation that can arouse strong emotions in a long-term relationship is the threat posed by a partner's involvement with another person.

Jealousy occurs when a person perceives a real or potential attraction between the partner and a rival (White, 1981). Jealousy is a reaction to a perceived threat by a rival to the continuity or quality of a valued relationship. A husband's discovery that his wife is having a sexual affair with someone else would be an example. Jealousy involves two types of threats—threats to the relationship from the possible loss of the partner and threats to the person's self-esteem from being rejected by the partner or losing to the rival (Mathes, Adams & Davies, 1985). Feelings of anger, anxiety, and depression are common.

According to Berscheid (1983), jealousy should be greatest when the person is highly dependent on the partner and when the person perceives that the threat is a serious one. Although empirical research on jealousy is still quite new, there is some evidence linking jealousy with both dependence and insecurity (Buunk & Bringle, 1987; Pines & Aronson, 1983; White, 1976). For example, Hansen (1985) found that married people who believed they would have few alternatives if their current spouse left them appeared more vulnerable to jealousy.

New Perspectives on Love

In the past 20 years, social-psychological research on love has provided much information about this fascinating topic. Two very recent theoretical analyses of love suggest important new directions for future research.

A TRIANGULAR THEORY OF LOVE   In an effort to provide a comprehensive theory about love in different types of relationships, Robert Sternberg (1986) suggests that all love experiences have three components, which are shown as the points of a triangle in Figure 9–5.

The *intimacy component* refers to feelings of closeness, connectedness, and bondedness in a relationship. This component includes admiring and wanting to take care of the loved one. Self-disclosure and intimate communication are important. Sternberg believes that this component is essentially the same in love for a romantic partner, a child, or a best friend. Intimacy is a common core in each of these loving relationships.

The *passion component* refers to the drives that lead to intense emotions in love relationships. In a romantic relationship, physical attraction and sexuality may be prominent. However, other motives such as needs to give or receive nurturance, needs for self-esteem, or needs for dominance can also be involved.

The *decision/commitment component* refers in the short term to the decision that one loves someone else, and in the long term to a commitment to maintain that love. This is the most cognitive component of love.

An analysis of these three components leads Sternberg to identify eight kinds of love, depending on the presence or absence of each component.

FIGURE 9–5   In Sternberg's triangle theory (1986), love has three main components, each represented by one end of the triangle.

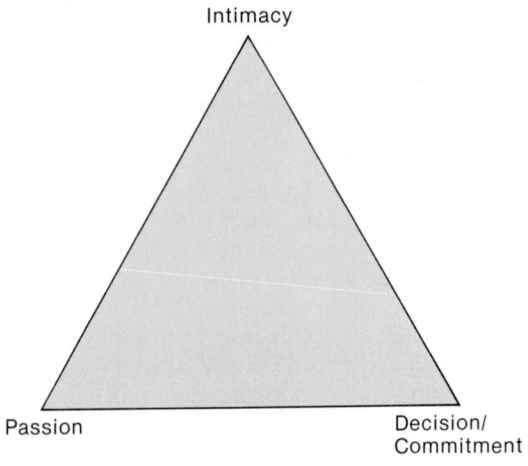

TABLE 9–3

Sternberg's Taxonomy of Kinds of Love

| | COMPONENT | | |
Kind of Love	Intimacy	Passion	Decision/ Commitment
Nonlove	−	−	−
Liking	+	−	−
Infatuated love	−	+	−
Empty love	−	−	+
Romantic love	+	+	−
Companionate love	+	−	+
Fatuous love	−	+	+
Consummate love	+	+	+

Note: A plus (+) indicates that a component is present; a minus (−) indicates that the component is absent. These eight kinds of love represent the limiting cases or "extreme" types based on the triangular theory. However, since each component is actually a range rather than a point, most loving relationships will fall between these extreme categories.
Adapted from Sternberg (1986), p. 123.

These are shown in Table 9–3. For instance, a relationship that involves commitment and intimacy, but no passion is described as "companionate love." A relationship that involves commitment but neither intimacy nor passion is described as "empty love." A relationship that has all three is called "consummate love," and might be found not only in some adult love relationships but also in some relations between parents and children.

Sternberg's theory is an interesting new attempt to pull together many previous findings and concepts. As with any new theory, more research will be needed to assess the usefulness of this perspective.

LOVE AND EMOTIONAL ATTACHMENT Cindy Hazan and Phillip Shaver (1987; Shaver, Hazan & Bradshaw, in press) have recently analyzed romantic love from the perspective of attachment theory. In Chapter 8, we discussed the attachment bonds that develop between infants and their parents. We saw that infants develop strong emotional ties to their caretakers—bonds that provide an important sense of security. Although all children become attached to their primary caretaker, this attachment can take three forms: secure attachment, avoidant attachment, and anxious/ambivalent attachment.

Hazan and Shaver propose that adult love relationships are similar to infant attachments in several

ways. First, infant attachment and adult romantic love share common features such as intense fascination with the other, distress at separation, and efforts to maintain proximity and to spend time together. Second, Hazan and Shaver propose that romantic attachments are similar in form to the three types of infant attachment. That is, adults' styles of romantic involvement can be secure, avoidant, or ambivalent/anxious. Third, like infant attachments, adult romantic bonds are believed to have a biological origin. "Romantic love is a biological process designed by evolution to facilitate attachment between adult sexual partners who, at the time love evolved, were likely to become parents of an infant who would need reliable care." (Hazan & Shaver, 1987, p. 423). Finally, Hazan and Shaver propose that our earliest love relationships with our parents influence the way we approach romantic involvements as adults.

Hazan and Shaver (1987) have conducted two studies to examine these ideas. They have found that adults' romantic experiences can be categorized into the same three types described for attachment in infancy. In fact, the proportion of adults classified into each of the three attachment types was remarkably similar to the proportion of infants typically found in each group. Although most of the adults studied had had at least one important love relationship, their experiences of adult love differed.

- *Secure adults*: Adults were said to have "secure" romantic attachments if they described themselves as finding it relatively easy to get close to others and said they seldom worry about being abandoned. About 56 percent of the adults tested were in the secure group. Secure adults tended to describe their most important actual love relationship as especially happy, friendly, and trusting. Secure adults were more likely than others to describe their parents in positive terms—as caring, fair, affectionate, and having a good marriage.

- *Avoidant adults*: In contrast, "avoidant" adults (roughly 24 percent of those tested) reported being somewhat uncomfortable getting close to others or trusting a romantic partner completely. In describing their most important love relationship, avoidant lovers reported fear of intimacy, emotional highs and lows, and jealousy. Compared to secure adults, avoidant adults tended to describe their parents as more demanding, critical, and uncaring.

- *Anxious/ambivalent adults*: Finally, those adults (20%) who seek intimacy, but worry that others won't reciprocate their love and won't stay with them were called "anxious/ambivalent." The anxious/ambivalent respondents described their most important love relationship as involving obsession, desire for reciprocation and union, emotional highs and lows, and extreme sexual attraction and jealousy. Compared to secure adults, anxious/ambivalent respondents tended to describe their parents as more intrusive and demanding, and their parents' marriage as unhappy.

At present, these findings must be viewed as very tentative. But they do raise the fascinating possibility that there are continuities between the emotional bonds we experience in childhood and the attachments we form in adult love relationships.

The study of personal relationships is a field of growing interest in social psychology. Researchers in this area hope to gain a better understanding of how relationships actually work. Ultimately, greater knowledge may help people to create more satisfying relationships.

KEY TERMS IN CHAPTER 9

close relationship	comparison level for alternatives	norm of reciprocity	social penetration
commitment	equity theory	passionate love	social power
companionate love	interdependence	principle of least interest	social roles
comparison level	norm	satisfaction	

SUMMARY

1. A relationship exists when two people are interdependent—that is, when each person influences the other. We call a relationship close if there is frequent interaction involving many different kinds of interaction and strong mutual influence.

2. The most influential analysis of relationships comes from social exchange theory. In this view, people are concerned with the outcomes (rewards and costs) they receive in a relationship. People use several standards to evaluate their relationship outcomes including a general "comparison level" and a "comparison level for alternatives." When two people are in a relationship, their individual outcomes are in some measure interdependent, and so partners try to coordinate their activities to maximize their joint profits.

3. People care whether their relationships are fair. Three major rules of fairness are equality, relative needs, and equity. Equity exists when each person's outcomes are proportional to their contributions to the relationship. According to equity theory, when individuals perceive inequity in a relationship, they feel distress and take steps to restore equity.

4. Social power refers to a person's ability to influence deliberately the behavior, thoughts, or feelings of another person. The balance of power describes whether partners have equal power or whether one person is dominant. Three determinants of the balance of power are norms, the relative resources of the partners, and the "principle of least interest."

5. Conflict occurs when the actions of one person interfere with the actions of another. Conflicts can be about specific behaviors, norms and roles, or personal dispositions. Rusbult has identified four approaches people take to problem solving in relationships, called voice, loyalty, neglect and exit.

6. Commitment refers to all the forces, positive and negative, that keep a person in a relationship. Positive factors include satisfaction, liking, and love. Negative factors are barriers that make it costly for someone to leave a relationship. Two important barriers are the lack of alternatives and the investments a person has already made in a relationship.

7. Self-disclosure is the sharing of intimate feelings and information with another person. There is a norm of reciprocity for self-disclosure, so part-

ners tend to disclose at similar levels of intimacy. In the formation of a relationship, we are most apt to like someone whose disclosures are appropriate to the situation.

8. Psychological research on romantic love is relatively new. Rubin has shown that liking and love are qualitatively distinct. Although the two often go together, it is possible to like someone a lot without loving them, and to love a person without fully liking them. Theorists have distinguished between passionate love (the exciting and emotionally-charged experience some people have early in a love relationship) and companionate love (the deep affection, trust, and caring a person feels for a long term partner.) Two new perspectives on love are Sternberg's triangular theory of love and Shaver and Hazan's analysis of love as an attachment process.

SUGGESTED READINGS

ALTMAN, I., & TAYLOR, D. A. (1973). *Social penetration: The development of interpersonal relationships*. New York: Holt, Rinehart & Winston. A thoughtful analysis of the development of intimate relationships, with emphasis on self-disclosure.

BREHM, S. S. (1985). *Intimate relationships*. New York: Random House. A very readable and comprehensive textbook for college students, available in paperback.

BURGESS, R. L., & HUSTON, T. L. (Eds.). (1979). *Social exchange in developing relationships*. New York: Academic Press. Leading experts use exchange theory to discuss such topics as the initiation of relationships, conflict, and breakups.

DUCK, S. (1986). *Human relationships: An introduction to social psychology*. Beverly Hills: Sage. This recent paperback examines such topics as social emotions, communication skills, and interaction patterns in long-term relationships.

HENDRICK, C., & HENDRICK, S. (1983). *Liking, loving, and relating*. Monterey, CA: Brooks/Cole. A basic introduction to the field written for undergraduates.

KELLEY, H. H., et al. (1983). *Close relationships*. New York: W. H. Freeman. A team of psychologists provide a professional-level analysis of the nature of close relationships, including such topics as interaction, development, emotion, power, roles, conflict, and commitment.

PERLMAN, D., & DUCK, S. (Eds.). (1987). *Intimate relationships: Development, dynamics and deterioration*. Beverly Hills, CA: Sage. An edited collection of new research on many relationship topics including mate selection, jealousy, and nonverbal communication in marriage.

RUBIN, Z. (1980). *Children's friendships*. Cambridge, MA: Harvard University Press. A delightful paperback about how young children learn to be friends.

STERNBERG, R. J., & BARNES, M. (Eds.). (In press). *Anatomy of love*. New Haven, CT: Yale University Press. Leading experts present the latest research and theories about love.

WALSTER, E., WALSTER, G. W., & BERSCHEID, E. (1978). *Equity: Theory and research*. Boston: Allyn and Bacon. A clear presentation of equity theory and how it applies to various types of relationships.

10 AGGRESSION

When we think of aggression and violence, most of us probably think first of crimes committed by one individual against another. As the 1980s began, the United States was experiencing over 20,000 murders per year, over 75,000 rapes, and over 600,000 assaults—in reported crimes alone. The murder rate in the United States far exceeded that in most other civilized countries. New York City had 22 murders per 100,000 population and Los Angeles 18, but London had less than 2, and New Delhi only 0.1. The murder rate was 10 times as high in New York City and Los Angeles as it was in London, and 200 times as high as it was in New Delhi. The murder rate was over double in 1980 what it had been in 1960, and the assault rate was four times as high.

We probably also think of war. There were over 50 wars in the 1970s, almost all in Third World countries—those most oppressed by poverty, disease, and all manner of other problems. Each year, the nations of the world spend over $500 billion on military forces, or about $170 for every man, woman, and child on the globe.

But the greatest threat to humankind comes from the threat of nuclear war. By the early 1980s, the United States had over 1000 intercontinental ballistic missiles (ICBMs). The nuclear warhead on each Titan II missile has the explosive power of 9 million tons of TNT—the equivalent of 700 Hiroshima bombs. If the United States or the Soviet Union were to launch an ICBM, it would take about 30 minutes to reach the other nation. Experts estimate that of those 30 minutes, about 10 would be required to communicate word of the attack throughout the entire command structure of the targeted nation, including getting word to the chief of state. The American president or the Soviet premier would thus have about 20 minutes to decide whether or not to retaliate—and in any event, at least one nation would be devastated.

This is violence and aggression on a global scale, but in fact most violence is committed against people closest to us—against those in our own families, our spouses, children, and brothers and sisters.

According to a recent national survey (Straus, Gelles, & Steinmetz, 1981), each year 16 percent of all married persons engage in some act of physical violence against their mate, ranging from throwing something to using a knife or a gun on them. Straus et al. estimate that about 2 million Americans have at one time or another beaten up their spouses (and husbands and wives do so with about equal frequency), and another 1.7 million have used a knife or gun on their mates.

A great many parents commit surprising levels of violence against their own children. The same study showed that 13 percent of the parents had hit their child with an object in the previous year, 58 percent had slapped or spanked their child, and 3 percent had threatened their child with a gun or knife sometime in the child's life. The authors estimate that about 1.5 million children are

A surprising number of small children are subjected to real brutality, even from their parents and often even in quite affluent, comfortable life circumstances.

UPI/Bettmann

physically injured by their parents each year. The most violence in families occurs between siblings. In a given year, 40 percent of all children hit their own siblings with an object, and 16 percent beat up their sibling.

Because people frequently treat one another so badly, even destructively, social psychologists have done a great deal of research to try to understand the violence people do to each other, usually under the general heading of research on aggression.

DEFINING AGGRESSION: THREE DISTINCTIONS

Although it might seem that everybody understands what aggression is, there is considerable disagreement about how to define it. Let us make three important distinctions here. The first is whether we should define aggression simply in terms of *hurtful behavior*, or whether we need to take into consideration whether the person has *hurtful intentions*. The simplest definition of aggression, and the one favored by those with a learning or behaviorist approach, is that aggression is any behavior that hurts others. The advantage of this definition is that the behavior itself determines whether or not an act is aggressive.

Unfortunately, this definition ignores the intention of the person who does the act—and this factor is critical. If we ignored intent, some actions intended to hurt others would not be labeled aggressive because they turned out to be harmless. Suppose an enraged man fires a gun at a business rival, but the gun turns out to be unloaded. The act is harmless because firing an unloaded gun is not dangerous. Despite the fact that the man was enraged and was trying to kill someone, he was not being aggressive because no actual harm was done.

Ignoring intention can also produce the opposite error—calling some acts aggressive that are not, by the usual meaning of the term. If a golfer's ball accidentally hits a spectator, has the golfer committed an aggressive act? She has in fact caused somebody a great deal of pain, but surely no one would believe the golfer was being aggressive. Similarly, criminal law provides exceptions for acts that are painful but intended to help the victim, such as surgery performed by physicians.

Intentions have a central role in our judgments about aggression in another way. People are particularly motivated to make causal attributions when others' actions are painful to them. People should therefore be especially likely to search for an attribution when they are the victims of aggressive acts.

One of the first attributions people make about aggression is of the person's intent. If a person tries to hurt someone, we ordinarily consider her to be aggressive; if she is not trying to cause harm, she is not being aggressive.

Thus, we will define **aggression** as any action that is *intended* to hurt others. This conception is more difficult to apply, because it does not depend solely on observable behavior. Often it is difficult to know someone's intention. But we will accept this limitation because we can define aggression meaningfully only by including intent.

A second major distinction is also needed, between **antisocial** and **prosocial** aggression. Normally we think of aggression as bad. After all, if an aggressive act results from an intent to hurt another person, it must be bad. But some aggressive acts are good. We applaud the police officer who shoots a terrorist who has killed innocent victims and is holding others hostage. The question is whether the aggressive act violates commonly accepted social norms, or supports them.

Unprovoked criminal acts that hurt people, such as assault and battery, murder, and gang beatings clearly violate social norms, so they are described as antisocial. But many aggressive acts are actually dictated by social norms, and therefore are described as prosocial. Acts of law enforcement, appropriate parental discipline, or obeying the orders of commanders in wartime are regarded as necessary.

Some aggressive acts fall somewhere between prosocial and antisocial, and we might label them **sanctioned aggression.** This includes aggressive acts that are not required by social norms, but that are well within their bounds. They do not violate accepted moral standards. A coach who disciplines a disobedient player by benching him or her is usually thought to be well within his rights. So is a shopkeeper who in self-defense hits someone who is criminally assaulting him, or a woman who strikes back at a rapist. None of these acts is required of the person, but they fall within the bounds of what is permitted by social norms.

A third distinction is between aggressive *behav-*

BOX 10–1

WHO ARE THE WORST AGGRESSORS?

Because prosocial aggression obeys the law, and antisocial aggression does not, we usually think antisocial aggression is worse. But which is in fact the most destructive?

Something you might give some thought to: How common are these various types of aggression? Most of the terrible atrocities seem to have been committed as official acts of government. The murder of 6 million European Jews by the Nazis in World War II was by official order of the German government. The murder of more than 3 million Cambodians in the mid-1970s by the Pol Pot regime was by government order. Widespread torture of and violence against dissidents, such as that uncovered by Amnesty International in repressive regimes in Argentina, Chile, El Salvador, Iran, and the USSR, has all been by government order. The mass suicides at Jonestown in Guyana in 1979 occurred by order of the cult's leader, Jim Jones, and the norms of the cult were that everyone had to obey the leader.

The irony is that all these atrocities are examples of *prosocial* aggression. Each was committed by the legitimate leadership of the nation or group, and supposedly for the broader social good. The Nazis claimed the noble goal of "purifying" the German race, leaders in Argentina and other nations wanted to restore "law and order," and so on.

Sanctioned aggression too can open the doors to much cruelty and barbarism. Consider the near extinction of the American bison; although it was not caused by government order, it was certainly legal and was encouraged by the economic system.

In contrast, there are, relative to these mass atrocities, few individual murders in any society at any given time. How much antisocial aggression do you see in everyday life? Is the most serious problem of civilized societies prosocial aggression or antisocial aggression? Crime is a major problem in the United States today. Yet the Founding Fathers felt in some respects that unrestrained governments as well as unrestrained private citizens could be extremely dangerous. The Bill of Rights is a partial response to that fear. What do you think?

ior and aggressive *feelings*, such as **anger.** Our overt behavior does not always reflect our internal feelings. Someone may be quite angry inside, but make no overt effort to hurt another person. Society discourages and condemns most forms of aggressive behavior, and indeed can exist only if people control their aggressive feelings most of the time. We cannot have people hitting other people, breaking windows, or acting violently whenever they feel like it. Society places strong restraints on such expression; and most people, even those who feel angry much of the time, rarely act aggressively.

We need to consider both the factors that increase anger and the restraints that may prevent it from being translated into aggressive action. We thus have two separate questions—what produces angry feelings and what produces aggressive behavior?

SOURCES OF ANGER

An aggressive feeling is an internal state that cannot be observed directly. We all experience anger, and virtually everyone at one time or another would like to hurt someone else. Indeed, most people report they feel at least mildly or moderately angry anywhere from several times a day to several times a week (Averill, 1983, p. 1146).

But these feelings are not necessarily expressed openly. Aggressive impulses must be studied largely by asking individuals how they are feeling or by inferring the existence of their internal state from physiological measures or behavior, neither of which is a reliable indicator. Nevertheless, there has been a considerable amount of research on the factors that arouse anger.

One of the most common sources of anger is being attacked or bothered by another person. Imagine that you are waiting at a red light, and the driver of the car behind you blows the horn just as the light turns green. Or imagine that you are reading a newspaper, and someone unexpectedly pours a glass of water down your neck. Or, finally, imagine a student's reaction when he expresses an opinion in class and someone else disagrees with him and says he is stupid to hold such an opinion. In all these cases, someone has done something unpleasant to someone else. Depending on how the injured person takes it, he or she has been annoyed or attacked. It is extremely likely that the person will become angry and feel aggressive toward the source of the attack. Similarly, aversive stimulation of a wide variety of other kinds produces aggression. For example, people exposed to foul odors, irritating cigarette smoke, and disgusting scenes show increased aggressive feelings (Berkowitz, 1983).

People often respond to attack with retaliation, in an "eye for an eye" fashion (Baron, 1977). This was shown clearly in an experiment by Greenwell and Dengerink (1973). Male college students were placed in a competitive task with a fictitious opponent. Each was allowed to shock the other. They received information, supposedly from this person, indicating that (1) their opponent was intentionally raising the level of his shock settings over trials or that (2) he was deliberately maintaining those shocks at a constant, moderate level. For half the subjects within each of these groups, the strength of the shocks received actually *did* increase; for the others, it remained constant.

The results indicated that the opponent's intentions were more important in determining the subjects' own shock settings than was the strength of the actual shocks they received from this person. The apparent motives or intentions behind another person's actions—especially when these are potentially provocative—may often be far more important in influencing our tendency to aggress against him or her than the nature of these actions themselves.

This can produce an escalation of aggression. Gang warfare often starts out with a few insults and ends up in murder, as depicted so clearly in Shakespeare's *Romeo and Juliet* or the musical *West Side Story*. One of the consequences of this retaliatory tendency is that domestic violence breeds more domestic violence. Many cases of family violence involve not one aggressor and one victim, but a pattern of mutual violence within a married couple or between parents and children (Straus et al., 1981, chap. 5).

Frustration

A second major source of anger is **frustration.** Frustration is the interference with or blocking of the attainment of a goal. If one wants to go somewhere, perform some act, or obtain something and is prevented, we say that person is frustrated. One of the basic tenets in psychology is that frustration tends to arouse aggressive feelings.

The behavioral effects of frustration were demonstrated in a classic study by Barker, Dembo, and Lewin (1941). Children were shown a room full of attractive toys but were not allowed to enter it. They stood outside looking at the toys, wanting to play with them, but were unable to reach them. After they had waited for some time, they were allowed to play with them. Other children were given the toys without first being prevented from playing with them. The children who had been frustrated smashed the toys on the floor, threw them against the wall, and generally behaved very destructively. The children who had not been frustrated were much quieter and less destructive.

This effect of frustration may also be seen in broader perspective in society at large. Economic depressions produce frustration that affects almost everyone. People cannot get jobs or buy things they need and are greatly restricted in all phases of their lives. The consequence is that various forms of aggression become more common.

Evidence of this was presented by Hovland and Sears (1940) and confirmed by Mintz (1946). They found a strong relationship between the price of cotton and the number of blacks lynched in the South during the years 1882 to 1930. When cotton prices were high, there were few lynchings; when

Neil Goldstein

A common source of frustration occurs when someone tries to take something away from you. Sometimes our anger is so intense that we are oblivious to our surroundings.

prices were low, the number of lynchings was relatively high. A drop in the price of cotton signified a depressed period economically. This depression produced frustration, which in turn led to more aggression. An extreme manifestation of the increased aggression was the increase in lynchings.

The survey of family violence we referred to before (Straus et al., 1981) found that the most commonly reported source of conflict in American families is housekeeping. Families argue and fight endlessly about what and how much to clean, about the quality of food served, about taking the trash out, mowing the lawn, and fixing things. These authors report that one-third of all American couples say that *always* disagree about housekeeping. Close behind are conflicts about sex, social activities, money, and children, in that order (p. 157).

Some families have higher levels of frustration than others, for reasons that are easy to understand. There is more family conflict and more domestic violence in working-class than in middle-class families. There is also more in families with unemployed breadwinners or with especially large numbers of children (Straus et al., 1981). Of course, many working-class families with large numbers of children and marginal economic situations are loving, relatively conflict-free, and free of domestic violence. But on the average, these life stresses lead naturally to greater frustration, and ultimately to more violent incidents.

These examples illustrate the typical effect of frustration, but the original statement of the relationship between frustration and aggression was in more absolute terms. Dollard, Doob, and others at Yale began the work on this problem. They asserted that *"aggression is always a consequence of frustration.* . . . the occurrence of aggressive behavior always presupposes the existence of frustration and, contrariwise, . . . the existence of frustration always leads to some form of aggression" (Dollard et al., 1939, p. 1). It appears now that neither *always* in these assumptions is correct. Although frustration usually arouses anger, there are circumstances when it does not; increased anger may not always lead to more aggressive behavior. And, as we will see below, factors other than frustration can also produce aggressive behavior.

The Role of Attributions

For an event to produce anger and aggressive behavior, the key is that the victim must perceive the attack or frustration as intended to harm. This is easily understood in terms of attribution theory. If the victim attributes the frustration to unavoidable circumstances, then it will not create so much anger. But if there are no such justifying external forces and an internal attribution is made, the anger is much greater.

In Weiner's (1982) terms, anger is most likely when the attack or frustration is perceived as under the personal, *internal* control of the other person. This theory was discussed in the chapter on attribution. For example, we would expect more anger among newly unemployed workers if they have been fired by a boss who said she did not like them than if they were laid off because a recession forced the entire plant to shut down.

Averill (1983) did a survey of occasions on which people felt angry. In 59 percent of the episodes, anger was a response to an act perceived as voluntary and unjustified; 28 percent of the time, to a potentially avoidable accident or event; and only 2 percent of the time to an unavoidable accident or event.

The result is that arbitrary or unjustified frustrations produce more anger and aggressive behavior than nonarbitrary ones. If the frustration is perceived as being unintended, justified, mitigated by extenuating circumstances, or accidental, apparently it does not make people as angry, and they are less likely to be aggressive. A teacher who prevents the class from taking a trip to the zoo is frustrating their wishes. If she explains that the trip is a bad idea because rain is expected, less anger will be aroused than if she says she just doesn't feel like going. A good reason for frustration minimizes aggressive feelings. Thus retaliation following an attack is most likely when the attack is perceived as unjustified (Dyck & Rule, 1978).

The timing of information about intention or mitigation is also important. If people already understand the mitigating reasons before they are frustrated, they are considerably less likely to get angry and become aggressive. Explaining all the good reasons afterwards, while the person is already steaming, is not so likely to reduce the anger! To show this, Johnson and Rule (1986) had a confederate anger male undergraduates by giving them bursts of loud noise while insultingly evaluating an essay they had written, describing them as uncreative, poor students. Then the subject could administer loud noise in return to the confederate, under the guise of evaluating the confederate's essay. Mitigating information about the confederate that would explain his behavior was provided to the subject: The confederate had just gotten a poor grade in an important midterm, which would prevent him from entering medical school. This mitigating information was more effective in reducing physiological arousal and aggression when it was given prior to the insults than when it was given afterwards.

A good example of aggressive behavior concerns the effects of heat. Common sense certainly tells us we are more irritable and susceptible to becoming aggressive when it is too hot. Folk wisdom tells us that it is the heat of ghetto summers ("a long hot summer") that is partly responsible for riots and crime. Indeed, violent episodes such as assaults and household disturbances are more likely to occur on warm, mild days than on cold ones

BOX 10-2

INSTINCT THEORIES OF AGGRESSION

It has been proposed by Freud, McDougall, Lorenz, and others that humans have an innate drive or instinct to fight. Just as they experience physiologically based feelings of hunger, thirst, or sexual arousal, so too it is argued that they have an innate need to behave aggressively. Although there are no known physiological mechanisms connected with aggressive feelings as there are for the other drives, they argue that aggression is a basic drive.

It is true that many subhuman animals respond aggressively to certain stimuli whenever they appear and that these responses appear to be instinctive. If two male Siamese fighting fish are put in the same tank, they immediately attack and fight until one is badly mauled or dead. The presence of another male is sufficient to produce this aggressive behavior in each one. The aggression seems to be triggered automatically by the other's presence and was obviously not learned.

There are countless other examples of similar reactions. Animals certainly do a great deal of fighting. They fight for food, to protect their territory, to defend their young, and so on.

But our definition of aggression as requiring the intent to harm may not be appropriate to much of this behavior. A lion that chases and kills a buffalo obviously intends to harm the buffalo. On the other hand, as far as we know, the killing is not done in response to anger or with intent to cause suffering. The lion must hunt for food and the buffalo happens to be its natural prey. The lion kills to satisfy hunger, not to satisfy some aggressive drive. Fighting for mates and for territory also seems to be motivated by sexual drives or the need for food.

The work by ethologists on animal behavior is fascinating. It indicates that many species respond instinctively to specific cues and have many instinctive drives. It does not, however, provide evidence concerning humans. Although some ethologists continue to be convinced that all animals have instinctive aggressive drives, most psychologists now dispute this. Among animals relatively low on the phylogenetic scale, instinct plays an important role in producing aggression, but there seems little reason to believe that humans have instinctive impulses toward aggressiveness.

(Rotton & Frey, 1985). But high heat is normally not something we perceive as resulting from an intent to harm us.

And a series of rather careful experiments has shown that heat, by itself, does not increase hostility or aggressive behavior. Nor does it make angry people any more likely to aggress. In fact, the opposite tended to happen: heat (averaging 94° vs. averaging 73°) tended to diminish the aggressive behavior of subjects angered by a confederate (Baron & Bell, 1975, 1976). Presumably, under oppressive heat an angry person attributes the anger to the environment, rather than to an annoying confederate. And the person may attribute the anger-arousing behavior by the confederate to the heat, and for that reason react less angrily to the confederate's apparently justified annoyance.

Attribution theory also suggests that other kinds of emotional arousal can sometimes be misperceived as anger. The notion follows from Schachter's two-factor theory of the self-perception of emotions discussed in the chapter on attribution. Arousal stemming from any number of sources might promote aggressive behavior, as long as it is labeled as anger. For example, vigorous exercise seems to increase aggressivness when it occurs in a situation that seems to call for anger.

Zillmann and Bryant (1974) did a study that varied nonspecific arousal by having the subject pedal a bicycle ergometer for one minute (high arousal) or thread nickel-size disks with off-center holes onto a plastic-coated wire (low arousal). Verbal attack by a confederate was also varied, on the assumption that such verbal attacks would help the high-arousal subjects mislabel arousal stemming from their energetic exercising as anger. Finally, the subject was allowed to deliver loud, painful noises to the confederate.

As is shown in Table 10–1, the highest aggression was delivered in the high-arousal attack condition. The subjects who were attacked and exercised subsequently behaved more aggressively than when the exercise was not included. But the *least* amount of aggression occurred with exercise and no attack, presumably because the aroused subject then had no basis for labeling the arousal as anger. Similar findings have been obtained from arousals due to loud noises (Green & O'Neal, 1969) or competitive behavior (Rocha & Rogers, 1976).

TABLE 10–1

Painful Noises Delivered to Confederate

	Attack	No Attack
High arousal (exercise)	126.5	58.0
Low arousal (no exercise)	90.1	75.0

Note: The entry is the mean level of painful noise delivered by the subject to the confederate in each condition.
Source: Adapted from Zillmann & Bryant (1974), p. 789.

So even arousal that is apparently irrelevant to aggressiveness or anger can increase aggressive behavior, provided it occurs in a situation where arousal may plausibly be labeled as "anger." Arousing any kind of drive or emotion may produce aggression if the person somehow misattributes the arousal as stemming from anger, rather than from exercise, the game, the film, or whatever else is in fact arousing that individual. With aggression, then, as in so many other contexts discussed in Chapter 5, the person's attribution is a key to response to frustration.

A lot of annoying things happen to us all the time, of course, and only some of them come attached with "intent-to-annoy" attributions. This is not to say that we *never* feel angry unless there is some intent to annoy. Inanimate objects can create a great deal of anger: flat tires, snowdrifts, leaky faucets, burnt scrambled eggs, and rocks on which one stubs one's toe are not usually ascribed the human property of trying to harm us (though there are exceptions to everything). What it does suggest is that many frustrations and annoyances will make us much less angry when no intent to harm is present.

LEARNING AGGRESSION

Attack and frustration tend to make people feel angry, and these angry feelings constitute one important determinant of aggressive behavior. But people often feel angry and behave peacefully, or at least are not overtly aggressive. In one survey, people reported engaging in overt physical aggression on only 10 percent of the occasions when they felt angry, expressed verbal aggression 49 percent of the time, and engaged in various kinds of nonaggressive calming activities 60 percent of the time (Averill, 1983). Indeed, people typically did *not* behave aggressively when they felt angry, though they usually felt some urge to do so. This is shown in Table 10–2.

It is also possible for people to act aggressively without *feeling* angry. So the factors that control aggressive behavior are as important as those that arouse anger in the first place. The problem is like the attitude-behavior problem discussed in the chapter on attitudes. Attitudes control behavior to some extent, but other factors play a role as well.

The main mechanism determining human aggressive behavior is *past learning*. A newborn infant expresses aggressive feelings quite impulsively. Whenever it is the least bit frustrated, whenever it is denied anything it wants, it cries in outrage, flails its arms, and strikes out at anything within range. In the earliest days of life, an infant does not realize that other people exist and therefore cannot be deliberately trying to harm it. When the infant does discover the existence of others, it continues to vent its rage and probably directs much of it toward these people.

But by the time the individual is an adult, this once savage, uncontrolled animal has his or her aggressive impulses under firm control and aggresses only under certain circumstances, if at all. This development is primarily due to learning. We learn habits of behaving aggressively in some situations and suppressing anger in others, to aggress against some kinds of people (like siblings) and not others (like police), and in response to some kinds of frustration and not others. These habits are crucial to our control of our own aggressive behavior.

TABLE 10–2

How People Respond When They Feel Angry

Response Type	Felt the Impulse to Act Aggressively	Actually Acted Aggressively
Direct aggression		
Verbal or symbolic aggression	82%	49%
Denial or removal of some benefit	59	41
Physical aggression or punishment	40	10
Indirect aggression		
Telling a third party in order to get back at the instigator (malediction)	42	34
Harming something important to the instigator	25	9
Displaced aggression		
Against a nonhuman object	32	28
Against a person	24	25
Nonaggressive responses		
Engaging in calming activities	60	60
Talking the incident over with a neutral party; no intent to harm the offender	59	59
Talking the incident over with the offender without exhibiting hostility	52	39
Engaging in activities opposite to the instigation of anger	14	19

Note: Entry is the percent of episodes during which the person felt angry (*n* = 160), when the person felt like or actually engaged in the behavior indicated or the specific times they felt angry. For example, out of all times the respondents felt angry, 82% of the time they felt like engaging in verbal aggression, and 49% of the time they actually did so.
Source: Adapted from Averill (1983), p. 1148.

Reinforcement

One major mechanism by which this learning occurs is reinforcement. When a particular behavior is rewarded, an individual is more likely to repeat that behavior in the future; when it is punished, he or she is less likely to repeat it. Just as a child learns not to track mud onto a rug, so he learns not to express aggression. He is punished when he punches his brother, throws stones at the girl next door, or bites his mother, and he learns not to do these things. He is rewarded when he restrains himself despite frustrations, and he learns this also.

For example, in one study (Geen & Pigg, 1970) subjects were verbally reinforced ("that's good," "you're doing fine") for shocking a confederate. Other subjects in a control group shocked the confederate but were not rewarded. The reinforced subjects gave considerably more intense shocks than did nonreinforced subjects. We could give many other examples making the same point: Aggressive acts are, to a major extent, learned responses, and reinforcement is a major facilitator of aggression.

Imitation

Imitation is another mechanism that shapes a child's behavior. All people, and children in particular, have a strong tendency to imitate others. A child watches people eat with a fork or listens to them talking and tries to do the same. After a while, the child also uses a fork and talks. This imitation extends to virtually every kind of behavior, including aggression. A child observes other people being aggressive or controlling their aggression, and copies them. The child learns to aggress verbally—to shout at people, to curse, and to criticize—and not to resort to violence—not to punch people or throw stones or blow up buildings.

The child also learns when, if ever, each of these behaviors is permissible. At certain times one should not aggress even verbally (such as when one disagrees with one's parents), but at others, any kind of aggression is not only allowable but even necessary (such as when one is being attacked). Thus the child's own aggressive behavior is shaped and determined by what he or she observes others doing.

An experiment by Albert Bandura and his co-workers (Bandura, Ross, & Ross, 1961) illustrated this imitative learning of specific, aggressive behaviors. Children watched an adult play with tinker toys and a Bobo doll (a 5-foot, inflated plastic doll). In one condition, the adult began by assembling the tinker toys for about a minute and then turned his attention to the doll. He approached the doll, punched it, sat on it, hit it with a mallet, tossed it in the air, and kicked it about the room, all the while shouting such things as "Sock him in the nose," "Hit him down," "Pow." He continued in this way for nine minutes, with the child watching. In the other condition, the adult worked quietly with the tinker toys and ignored the doll.

Some time later, each child was frustrated mildly and then left alone for twenty minutes with a number of toys, including a 3-foot Bobo doll. The children's behavior was rated as shown in Table 10–3. They tended to imitate many of the actions of the adult. Those who had seen the adult act aggressively were much more aggressive toward the doll than those who had witnessed the adult working quietly on the tinker toys. The first group punched, kicked, and hammered the doll and uttered aggressive comments similar to those expressed by the aggressive adult.

The key theoretical notion in these experiments is that children learn specific aggressive responses by observing others perform them. It therefore follows that such vicarious learning should be increased when the adult's behavior is reinforced, and when the situation promotes identification with

TABLE 10–3

Aggression by Children Witnessing Violent or Neutral Model

Condition	AMOUNT OF AGGRESSION	
	Physical	Verbal
Violent model	12.73	8.18
Neutral model	1.05	0.35

Note: The entry is the mean amount of physical or verbal aggression children administered to the Bobo Doll after watching the type of model indicated.
Source: Based on Bandura, Ross, & Ross (1961).

the adult model. So in these Bandura experiments, there was more imitative aggression (1) when the model was rewarded, (2) with a model of the same sex as the child, and (3) when the child had had a previous nurturant relationship with the model (when the model was a friend or teacher of the child; Bandura et al., 1963).

The children in this situation learned to attack a certain type of doll. They might also attack the same kind of doll in a different situation, and perhaps a different kind of doll, as well. Just how far this would extend—whether or not they would also punch their siblings—is not clear; but it is clear that they would be somewhat more likely to attack some things than they were before. Through the process of imitation, these children showed more aggressive behavior.

Children do not imitate indiscriminately—they imitate some people more than others. The more important, powerful, successful, and liked the other people are, the more a child will imitate them. Also, the people they see most often are the ones they imitate most. Parents fit all these criteria, and they are the primary models for a child during the early years. Since parents are both the major source of reinforcement and the chief object of imitation, a child's future aggressive behavior depends greatly on how parents treat the child and on how they themselves behave.

This joint dependence on the parents for reinforcement and imitation produces an interesting consequence. Punishing a child for acting aggressively might be considered an effective method of teaching the child not to be aggressive, but it often produces the opposite effect. Punishment should make the aggressive behavior less likely in the future. The child learns that she will be punished if she hits her sister, so she avoids the punishment by not hitting her. More generally, she will not be aggressive whenever she expects to suffer for it. She will not ordinarily start a fight with someone who is certain to beat her; she will not start a fight, even if she can win it, if she expects to be severely punished for it afterward. Parents are aware of this simple relationship and employ it to stop children from fighting.

As far as the parents are concerned, this tends to have the desired effect. A child who is punished for fighting does tend to be less aggressive—at

home. Home is where the risk of punishment is greatest and therefore where the threat of punishment has the strongest inhibiting effect. Unfortunately, the situation is quite different when this child is out of the home. A child who is punished severely for being aggressive at home tends to be more aggressive outside (Sears, Whiting, Nowlis, & Sears, 1953).

The explanation for this effect is that the child imitates the parents' aggressive behavior. When she is in a situation in which she has the upper hand, she acts the way her parents do toward her. They are aggressive and so is she. The punishment teaches her not to be aggressive at home, but it also teaches her that aggression is acceptable if she can get away with it. Regardless of what parents hope, children will continue to do what their parents do as well as what they say.

One form of imitative aggression that is important in crime and in crowd behavior is **contagious violence.** The French sociologist Tarde introduced the idea of contagious violence when he noted that news of a spectacular crime in one community produced imitative crimes. He pointed out that lurid news stories about the Jack the Ripper murders inspired a series of female mutilation cases in the English provinces (Tarde, 1903). Police in this country have at times offered similar observations. In 1966, Richard Speck murdered 8 nurses in Chicago in July, and Charles Whitman shot 45 people from the University of Texas Tower in August. In November, Robert Smith, an 18-year-old high school senior, walked into an Arizona beauty school and shot 4 women and a child. He told police he had gotten the idea for a mass killing from the news stories of the Speck and Whitman outbursts.

Many other illustrations of apparently contagious violence can also be cited. Berkowitz (1970) found evidence for an increase in violent crimes (murder, rape, aggravated assault, and robbery) following the 1963 assassination of President John F. Kennedy. Phillips (see 1986) found that highly publicized suicides (suicides presented on the front page of the newspaper) provoke suicidal acts, such as fatal single-vehicle auto accidents or noncommercial airplane crashes. Similarly, heavyweight championship prize fights are followed by a rise in the homicide rate, whereas Super Bowl games are not. Stories about executions, on the other hand, seem temporarily to depress homicide rates, but only temporarily (Phillips, 1986). Presumably the publicity given these suicides, prize fights, and executions induces imitative acts in a contagious manner.

It should be noted that there is considerable controversy about the reliability of these findings by Phillips. At the moment the issues are not really resolved (see Freedman, 1984; Baron & Reiss, 1985; Phillips, 1986; Turner et al., 1986). But the ideas are provocative.

Social Norms

A third aspect of the learning approach is that we learn the general norms of our society that regulate when and how it is appropriate for any of us to aggress. It is all right to yell at a child who hits you on the playground, but not to yell at a teacher who marks your spelling as incorrect. People learn whether or not to aggress as a habitual response to certain cues. If such aggression-eliciting cues as being hit are present in the situation, anger is more likely to be converted into aggression (Berkowitz, 1965). But if aggressive-suppressing cues are present, anger is not likely to produce aggressive behavior.

Which cues are associated with expressing aggression, and which are associated with suppressing

it, is regulated in a very fine-tuned manner by the **social norms** we are all taught for specific situations. We learn that it is all right to honk at someone stopped at a green light but not a red light. An American soldier will shoot a German in March 1945, while World War II was on, but not in December, after the war was over. An argument will lead to a brawl in a bar or on a playing field but rarely in an office building. A schoolboy will get into a fight with another boy but rarely with a girl or with a crippled child. Of course, some aggressive behavior is impulsive, and some is inappropriate to the situation. But the most impressive thing is how much aggressive *behavior* is controlled by the very complex, and often subtle, social norms developed by every human culture or subculture. Therefore it must also be controlled by cues that inform us about the norms for the situation we are in.

What we learn are the social norms concerning the expression of aggression. Sometimes these norms apply to the whole society; for example, we all generally share the view that it is wrong to kill another person, except under fairly extreme conditions (self-defense, executions).

We learn norms about *prosocial* aggression, where aggression is the appropriate behavior. In one national survey, 77 percent regarded slapping or spanking a disobedient 12-year-old as "normal," and 71 percent as "good" and 70 percent as "neces-

Ken Karp

Complex social norms regulate aggression: The norms that regulate aggression in a civil disobedience protest are very complex indeed, but they have become quite predictable and everyone seems to share them and understand them. The protestors must be passive and nonviolent, while the police are supposed to be firm, make arrests, but not physically harm nor verbally abuse the protestors. When either side breaks these rules, they tend to get into trouble.

sary" (Straus et al., 1981). Similarly, 71 percent supported the use of capital punishment in cases of murder (Blumenthal et al., 1972, p. 108).

We also share norms about *sanctioned* aggression, which are situations that permit but do not require aggression. For example, 60 percent "strongly agreed" that "a man has a right to kill another man in a case of self-defense," and 58 percent agreed that "a man has the right to kill a person to defend his house" (Blumenthal et al., 1972).

Most of the time we also agree on what is antisocial aggression. There is broad agreement about what is meant by such terms as "murder" or "assault," reflecting consensus about when violence is antisocial. But occasionally we do not agree. In the 1960s, many blacks rioting in protest of discrimination and deprivation felt quite justified in their aggression, whereas most whites felt quite the opposite (Sears & McConahay, 1973). Members of youth gangs may feel retaliatory killings are justified,

BOX 10–3

THE ANGER OF THE "NEW URBAN BLACKS"

The 1960s witnessed an outbreak of violence by black people that had no real precedent in American history. Yet blacks were in most ways better off than they had been since being forcibly brought to this country as slaves two centuries earlier.

Sears and McConahay (1973) analyzed this change as being due to changes in blacks' learning concerning expressed aggression. They identified a new generation of blacks, brought up in northern cities in the post-World War II era, as having been socialized to a new set of norms. They called them the "new urban blacks," to compare them with the previous generation of blacks, who had mainly been brought up in the rural and small town South of pre-World War II days.

The "new urban blacks" had grown up in the urban North, an environment whose formal norms were racially egalitarian, unlike the earlier generation, which had grown up in the formally racially segregated old South. Moreover, the postwar era saw the desegregation of many major institutions, such as the armed services, educational institutions, and professional sports. Finally, the era of civil rights protest, in the late 1950s and early 1960s, provided models of aggressive blacks demanding their rights.

The "new urban blacks" were better educated, more politically sophisticated, took more pride in being black, and were more politically disaffected. Most important, they had more aggressive feelings about racial issues by the time of the ghetto riots. They were more sympathetic to the use of violence in achieving political aims, and more demanding of their rights.

As a result, they themselves showed higher rates of active participation in ghetto riots than did older, southern-reared blacks. Sears and McConahay concluded that the new ghetto norms promoted both more angry impulses and more overt aggression on the part of the "new urban blacks."

whereas most other people would disagree. Members of the Johnson and Nixon administrations felt the mass killings of North Vietnamese in bombing raids were justified because of the threat of communism, whereas antiwar protestors called them war crimes.

But such dramatic instances of disagreement should not obscure the consensus almost all humans share about the vast majority of aggressive acts. Unprovoked aggression against an innocent victim is wrong. Killing is wrong except in certain very clearly specified cases. Aggressive acts in the service of social control, by duly authorized authorities, are permissible within certain boundaries. All over the world, and in all cultures, there is broad agreement on such general principles.

Understanding the differences among antisocial, sanctioned, and prosocial aggression depends on knowing what the relevant social norms are. The distinctions are sometimes quite subtle. But individuals must learn them in order to function effectively in society. Those who never control their aggression will not be allowed to remain free; those who never use aggression are probably worse off than those who use it at appropriate times. The critical problem in socialization is not how to teach children never to aggress, but how to teach them when aggression is appropriate and when it is not. The impressive thing is how well almost all people do learn these complex norms. Almost everyone can tell us when aggression is all right and when it is not. The few who cannot make at least the broad distinction

BOX 10–4

THE TYPE A PERSONALITY

One personality dimension that has received much attention is the contrast between Type A and Type B personalities. Type A "behavior is characterized by extremes of competitive achievement striving, time urgency, and aggressiveness" (Carver & Glass, 1978, p. 361). Type B is the absence of these qualities. In a number of studies, the Type A personality has been found to be associated with about twice the prevalence of coronary heart disease as Type B (Glass, 1977). In studies investigating their psychological characteristics, Glass and his colleagues (see Carver & Glass, 1978, p. 361) have found that Type A's work "at near maximum capacity, irrespective of the presence or absence of a time deadline. The hard-driving character of the Type A individual is also manifest in a tendency to suppress subjective fatigue. . . ."

Type A's also respond more aggressively to frustration than do Type B's. In a pair of studies, Carver and Glass (1978) frustrated and insulted some male undergraduates by having a confederate tell them the puzzles they were supposed to solve were simple and obvious, trying to hurry them up, and so on. Others were not insulted. The subjects were then given the opportunity to shock the confederate. Type A's delivered more shock than did Type B's, but only when frustrated. Later research has suggested that Type A's are especially prone to hostile aggression such as occurs in child abuse, rather than instrumental aggression (Strube et al., 1984).

are thought insane and are not held responsible for their actions.

Individual Differences

Social psychologists tend to focus more on situational determinants of behavior than on personality, as we indicated in the first chapter. As a result they focus particularly on independent variables that have the same effect on everyone, rather than on the idiosyncracies of particular individuals. That is, they tend to be less interested in *individual differences*.

Nevertheless, there are special reasons to consider individual differences when it comes to aggression. Some individuals plainly are much more aggressive than others. Some are bullies and violent criminals, while others are gentle and law-abiding. Similarly, some types of people are more aggressive than others. Men are generally more aggressive than women, by a variety of indicators, such as hitting, fighting, violent criminal behavior, and even fantasy aggression (though the data are less clear on verbal aggression; see Reinish & Sanders, 1986). People with a lower class background tend to be more aggressive than middle class people. Because of the special importance of individuals who are especially aggressive, it is appropriate for us to make an exception in this chapter, and spend a little time on the question of individual differences.

Some people do regularly get angry more often than other people do (Siegel, 1986), no matter what situation they are in. These individual differences may be quite stable over time. Huesman and his colleagues (1987) conducted a longitudinal study in which they measured aggression at age 8 (as judged by the child's peers), and then investigated a variety of indicators of aggression at age 30: spouse abuse, criminal convictions, drunk driving, and self-rated aggressiveness. There was a significant relationship: The most aggressive children were most likely to be the most aggressive adults later on.

AGGRESSIVE BEHAVIOR

Deindividuation

Normally people's behavior is fairly tightly regulated by social norms. An interesting exception occurs in mob behavior. The sociologist LeBon (1896) observed that people in crowds often feel free to gratify "savage, destructive" instincts. He felt that the reasons lay in two general feelings that people have when they are in large crowds: invincibility and anonymity. "The individual forming part of a crowd acquires . . . a sentiment of invincible power which allows him to yield to instincts." Moreover, "a crowd being anonymous, and in consequence irresponsible, the sentiment of responsibility which always controls individuals disappears entirely" (p. 30). More recently, Zimbardo (1970) described this phenomenon as **deindividuation,** and suggested it leads to unrestrained behavior. A number of factors associated with being in a crowd have been hypothesized to produce deindividuation: anonymity, diffused responsibility, size, activity, a novel unstructured situation, arousal due to noise, and fatigue.

Deindividuation will be discussed in more detail later in the chapter on groups. But it is important for aggression as well. A good example is Watson's (1973) analysis of the factors associated with extreme forms of aggression in warfare carried out by primitive peoples. The most extreme violence was carried out by peoples who used such deindividuating devices as masks, face and body paint, and special garments. Similarly, Mullen (1986) analyzed deindividuation in the lynching of blacks by white lynch mobs in the United States in the first half of the twentieth century. He found that larger crowds relative to the number of victims, engaged

BOX 10–5

THE BAITING CROWD

Leon Mann (1981) applied the notion of deindividuation to a well-known phenomenon called "the baiting crowd," in which a crowd has gathered at the base of a tall building where a person is threatening to commit suicide by jumping from a ledge or window. Frequently members of the crowd begin to yell at the person to jump, which is the reason for calling it "the baiting crowd." Mann analyzed a number of such incidents, one being the night in New York in 1938 when thousands of persons waited, some for eleven hours, until a man jumped from a seventeenth-floor hotel ledge. From newspaper listings of suicides and suicide attempts in the 1960s and 1970s, Mann found 21 cases in which crowds had gathered to observe someone threatening to or succeeding in committing suicide by jumping from a building, bridge, tower, or cliff. In 10 cases, the crowd had taunted and urged the victim to jump.

What had produced a baiting rather than a nonbaiting crowd? The main factors were those that might be expected to produce deindividuation. Baiting was more common when people were more anonymous, being in larger crowds (over 300 people), involved in episodes that occurred at night, or in crowds at some distance from the victim (not on the same level or on adjoining roofs or windows). They were also more likely to bait the victim in longer episodes, when the crowd became larger, more irritable, and developed some crowd intensity.

in more atrocities such as burning, lacerating, or dismembering the victim. Although there was some tendency for the biggest crowds and the most atrocities to occur when the black victim had allegedly committed a rape-murder, this did not account for the greater number of atrocities with large crowds; presumably deindividuation was responsible.

Closer to home, Prentice-Dunn and Rogers (1980; Rogers & Prentice-Dunn, 1981; Prentice-Dunn & Spivey, 1986) have done several experiments to test whether these deindividuating factors do in fact lead to more aggressive behavior. They used a modification of the sham-learning situation described in Chapter 2. Students were told they were to shock another student in a learning experiment. The subject became the "teacher" and a confederate became the "learner." Then the "teacher"

was supposed to punish the "learner" for errors with electric shock.

In a "deindividuating cues" condition, subjects were not addressed by name; they were told the experimenter would not know what shock intensities they chose; they were told they would not meet or see the victim. The experimenter took full responsibility for the victim's well-being, and the room was dimly lit.

In contrast, in an "individuating cues" condition, the subjects wore name tags, were addressed by their first names, and the experimenter took keen interest in the shock intensities selected. Subjects were told that they would meet the victim after the experiment and that the victim's well-being was the subjects' responsibility. The room was well-lit.

As expected, this manipulation created significant differences in a number of subjective dimensions of deindividuation, such as a lack of feeling of inhibition, and lack of concern for the victim's, experimenter's, and other group members' reactions. In these experiments, deindividuation led to significantly greater shock being administered.

Instrumental Aggression

Instrumental aggression occurs when a person uses aggression to attain some practical goal by hurting others. Some people are paid killers or paid assassins; they kill for money, not because of anger. Sometimes young thugs mug people in big cities not because they are angry, but to steal money. Slave-trading Europeans committed many acts of violence against eighteenth- and nineteenth-century Africans not out of anger, but for commercial motives. National leaders often take their countries to war with their neighbors not out of anger, but because they want to acquire territory, raw materials, or a better defensive position. In all these cases, aggressive behavior is committed simply as a way to attain other valued goods, and not because of angry feelings.

One particularly important form of instrumental aggression stems from what LeVine and Campbell (1972) have called **realistic group conflict.** Sometimes two groups are in a situation in which they are competing for the same scarce resources. The two groups may aggress against each other as a way of trying to get those resources. For example, one quite common analysis of antiblack prejudice in the South in the earlier part of this century blames it on realistic group conflict. At that time, the South was relatively impoverished, depending heavily on cotton and tobacco farming, and with relatively little industry. Jobs were few and far between. As a result, working-class whites were in direct competition for these scarce jobs with blacks, most of whom were unskilled laborers and poorly educated. According to this theory, the conflicts between these two groups helped perpetuate racial prejudice, and contributed to discrimination against blacks in employment, since whites had much greater economic and political power. In short, sometimes anger is the main motive, and sometimes it is not.

REDUCING AGGRESSIVE BEHAVIOR

Aggressive behavior is a major problem for human societies. Individual crimes and large-scale social violence are extremely damaging and harmful both to individual well-being and to the general social fabric. Freud viewed aggressive instincts as central dilemmas for social control in every society. Human beings have the capacity for great anger and for very destructive behavior. All societies expend much energy simply to control this tendency toward violence. So it is vital to understand how to reduce aggressiveness.

Whether or not somebody aggresses in a particular situation is determined by three variables: (1) the strength of the person's angry feelings, which in turn is determined partly by the degree of frustration or attack that produced them, and partly by the extent to which the individual's interpretation of this frustration produces feelings of anger; and (2) the tendency to express the anger, which in turn is determined by what the person has learned about aggressiveness in general, and by the nature of this situation in particular; and sometimes (3) violence is committed for other, more instrumental reasons.

This analysis suggests some of the ways in which aggressive behavior can be reduced: (1) Frustration can be reduced. (2) People can be taught not to aggress in a particular situation, or can be taught to restrain aggressiveness in general. For example, children are taught not to fight in the classroom, and indeed are taught to be careful about really hurting each other in general. But any solution

One of the dangers of aggressing when you are angered by others in traffic is that they will retaliate.

has its own risks and unintended consequences. So let us look systematically at the possible techniques for reducing aggressive behavior.

Punishment and Retaliation

It seems obvious that the fear of punishment or retaliation should suppress aggressive behavior. The kind of rational people described earlier by incentive theories would certainly include such future consequences in their calculations about aggression, and avoid behaving aggressively if punishment seemed likely. Indeed, Bond and Dutton (1975) and Wilson and Rogers (1975), both using the shock-learning technique (see Chapter 2), found reduced aggression when the subject was told that the roles would later be reversed, so he (or she) would be in the position of being shocked.

Consistent with these findings, younger children are consistently more likely to be victims of domestic violence than older children because they are weaker and less likely to retaliate (Straus et al., 1981, p. 69). But as a general matter it turns out not to be so simple. For one thing, children who are frequently punished for being aggressive turn out themselves to be more aggressive than normal (Sears, Maccoby, & Levin, 1957). Perhaps it is be-

cause they model themselves on an aggressive parent. Perhaps it is because frequent punishment, like any attack, generates a lot of anger itself. In any case, punishment of children's aggressiveness does not result in a simple inhibition of their aggressive behavior.

A second problem is that fear of punishment or retaliation seems to spark *counteraggression*. People who are attacked have a tendency to retaliate against their attackers, even when retaliation is sure to provoke more attacks. One series of studies set up a situation in which subjects could avoid further attacks by responding to a first attack with nonaggression. But they did not; they continued to counteraggress following the first attack, even if it brought more attacks on them (Dengerink, Schnedler, & Covey, 1978). It seemed that the subjects just wanted to get back at their tormentors, even when this deepened their own trouble. Many lives have been lost on battlefields (and in presidential and royal palaces) because national leaders have felt that "national honor" demanded counteraggression, even though it almost guaranteed further retaliation and bloodshed.

The effects of anticipated punishment or retaliation are not simple. Sometimes they simply suppress aggression, as the person quite rationally wants to avoid future pain. But sometimes the threats are simply interpreted as attacks, and inspire

BOX 10–6

THE SOCIAL HEREDITY OF DOMESTIC VIOLENCE

This tendency for punishment to make the target even more aggressive—whether it occurs because of modeling or because of increased anger—passes aggressiveness down from one generation to the next, as well. The best data come from the national survey of domestic violence cited earlier (Straus et al., 1981). Of the married men who had seen their parents attack each other, 35 percent had hit their own wives in the past year; of those who had not seen any such violence between their parents, only 11 percent had hit their own wives. The same held for wives: 27 and 9 percent, respectively, had hit their own husbands (p. 100). Men and women who had been physically punished as children were much more likely to be violent themselves toward their families in adulthood. Violent parents pass their own violent tendencies on to the next generation—and conversely, nonviolent parents pass their own more peaceful tendencies on. This relationship between family violence experienced in growing up, and marital violence engaged in as an adult, is shown quite clearly in the following figure.

Marital violence in survey year by amount of family violence experienced as a teenager. (Straus et al., 1981, p. 112.)

even more aggression. Even if punishment, or threat of retaliation, were usually temporarily effective in suppressing direct aggression, it is too expensive to be a general solution to the problem. There are too many people in too many places for all to be monitored constantly. As it is, many people who commit serious crimes, such as murder, are never caught and punished. It is simply impossible to depend on external controls to minimize violence, and anyway we would not want a society with such repressive control of individual citizens' behavior. So the threat of punishment or retaliation cannot be a general solution to the problem of violence.

Reducing Frustration

A better technique may be to reduce the potential for attack and frustration. All societies, to one degree or another, try to ensure some level of equality of access to the necessities of life, such as food, clothing, shelter, and family life. A major reason is to avoid large-scale violent disruptions of daily life from especially frustrated groups. For example, after the ghetto riots of the 1960s, the Kerner Commission recommended a sweeping set of social changes to improve the treatment of blacks in America, on the assumption that reducing their frustration would reduce the chance of further rioting.

Similarly, most societies make some provision for collective police protection so that ordinary people are not continually subject to attack from bandits or otherwise violent persons. This helps to reduce the chances for widespread violence in two ways: People are protected, and they are not themselves goaded into retaliation. In the nineteenth century, life on the frontier in the United States was often lived without benefit of such tight community control over attack. The result was that people were quite vulnerable to attack and sometimes responded with retaliatory vigilantism.

Efforts to reduce instrumental aggression must focus on the underlying causes of the aggression as well as on the overt behavior itself. We avoid war not only by training political leaders to inhibit their aggressive impulses, by trying to make them less angry, or by threatening them with retaliation. We also avoid war through patient diplomatic efforts to reduce real conflicts.

Some societies, particularly those organized around socialist philosophies, make a particular effort to minimize the frustration of their citizens. Capitalist societies, on the other hand, tend to accept some frustration as part of the price of freedom. The evidence is that socialist societies generally do provide more economic equality. There is, of course, much debate about other costs of that equality in terms of overall productivity, individual freedom, and so on.

But even the nations most conscientiously dedicated to the public's well-being cannot eliminate all individual frustration. There always will be conflict between parents and children, or between co-workers or schoolmates; no one ever will have exactly what and as much as he or she wants to eat when he or she wants it; some people will never be able to achieve what they would like; some people will always be dissatisfied with the things their mates do, and so on. That is the nature of life. So while forward-looking societies are wise to try to minimize as much large-scale frustration as they can, they can never completely eliminate frustration, or probably even come close. So other techniques for minimizing violence are necessary.

Learned Inhibitions

Another technique to reduce aggression is for people to learn to control their own aggressive behavior, whether or not they are in danger of being punished. Just as people learn when aggression is desirable or permissible, so too they must learn when aggressive behavior must be suppressed. There are two general lessons people learn: to suppress their aggressive behavior in general, and to suppress it in specific situations.

The general learned inhibition of aggression can be called **aggression anxiety** (or *aggression guilt*). The person feels anxiety when nearing an aggressive response. Like a burnt child approaching a stove, the person then backs off and suppresses the urge to aggress. Not everyone has equal amounts of aggression anxiety, of course. Women have more than men do. Children reared in middle-class homes tend to have more than children raised in lower-class homes. Parents who use reasoning and withdrawal of affection as disciplinary techniques produce children with more aggression anxiety than parents who use high degrees of physical punishment (Feshbach, 1970).

We also learn anxiety about expressing aggression in certain very specific situations. All through our lives we are learning and relearning "the ropes," the norms of our social environments. Students learn not to curse their professors to their faces, and professors learn not to throw things at their students. We learn that it is all right to yell and scream at our children, but that it is not all right to beat them up. We can kill animals for sport or food, but we cannot kill each other or someone's pet animal. We all possess a great many finely graded distinctions about what is and what is not permissible aggression. These learned inhibitions represent the most potent controls of human violent behavior we have; no police force could ever be numerous enough, far-sighted enough, or quick enough even to catch them.

These learned inhibitions are triggered by cues that tell us what kind of a situation we are in—one that calls for expression, or one that calls for suppression, of aggression. Do pain cues trigger these inhibitions? What about a potential victim's reaction? Signs of a victim's distress sometimes do arouse, vicariously, a similar negative emotional state in the aggressor: He or she identifies with the victim, has empathy for the person's suffering, and inhibits further attack. Still, since the intent of aggression is to hurt, the signs of pain in another person might simply reinforce the aggression, and increase it still further.

To test these possibilities, a number of studies have been done varying the pain cues transmitted by victim to aggressor. Baron (1971a), using the shock-learning technique, transmitted the supposed physiological reactions of the shock victim to the subject in the form of a "pain meter." This registered either high or mild levels of pain. The subject was angered in two ways: by having his own initial efforts at solving a problem criticized by the confederate, and by having the confederate shock him. But pain cues reduced further aggression, whether the subject had been angered or not. Then Baron (1971b) varied attitude similarity of subject and victim, on the assumption that the subject would not feel much empathy with a very

dissimilar person. Even here pain cues led only to decreased aggression.

Finally, Baron (1974) suggested that pain cues might increase aggression if higher levels of anger were used. This time, instead of just giving the confederate instructions to shock the subject to induce anger, the experimenter told the confederate he could shock the subject or deliver light flashes. The confederate then shocked the subject, totally incensing the person and arousing high levels of anger, as planned. This time pain cues did increase further aggression, at least in the angry condition. In general, then, signs of a victim's suffering inhibit further aggression, except in cases of extreme anger, when they are taken as signs of successful hurting.

For such reasons, the phenomenon of *dehumanization* is thought to increase aggression against victims who are far away or anonymous to their attackers. For example, it was thought that it was easier to bomb North Vietnamese from the great heights of a B-52, or to order troops into battle from the distance of Washington, D.C., than to attack at closer, more personal range. Having the victim distant or anonymous supposedly makes aggression easier, because the pain cues are absent. Conversely, making the victim more human, so that the attacker empathizes with the person's suffering, should reduce aggression.

ALCOHOL AND DRUGS   It is sometimes said that "the conscience is soluble in alcohol." Among the aspects of conscience that can be ignored when drinking, learned inhibitions against expressing aggression would seem to be prime candidates. Barroom brawls and murders by drunken husbands are legendary, and not just in Hollywood movies. Intoxicated offenders commit as much as 60 percent of the murders in the United States and comparably high proportions of other violent crimes such as rape, robbery, assault, domestic violence, and child abuse (Steele & Southwick, 1985). Such statistics raise the question of whether or not alcohol generally has a disinhibiting effect on aggression.

To test the effects of alcohol on inhibitions against aggression, Taylor and Gammon (1975) put each subject in a competitive reaction-time task against a confederate. Whichever one was faster was supposed to shock the other. Before they began, however, they were given either a high dose of alcohol (1.5 oz. per 40 pounds of body weight, which would be about three or four stiff drinks for the average subject), or a low dose (0.5 oz. per 40 pounds). As can be seen in Figure 10–1, the subject delivered more shock if he had drunk more alcohol (regardless of whether it was vodka or bourbon).

Why does alcohol usually produce more violence? When sober people are provoked to aggression, they are responsive to such inhibiting cues as the instigator's intent and potential retaliation, whereas intoxicated subjects tend to plunge ahead with retaliatory aggression, oblivious to the potential consequences of their behavior (Zeichner & Pihl, 1979). In short, alcohol produces a loss of inhibitory control, because of a loss of self-awareness.

By this argument, alcohol should have its strongest effects on behaviors normally under strong inhibitory *conflict*—when the instigation is very strong (high frustration, high sexual arousal, etc.) *and* the inhibition is normally strong as well (when the behavior is criminal, like rape or assault or vandalism). Steele and Southwick (1985) tested this hypothesis and found it to be true; i.e., alcohol particularly increased aggression under high con-

flict, such as when the person was strongly provoked *and* immediate physical retaliation was likely. It did not have such effects in low conflict conditions, such as those with no provocation or when no retaliation was likely.

Another disinhibiting drug, marijuana, has the reputation of not increasing aggression. For example, in a recent study (Myerscough & Taylor, 1985) male undergraduates were given varying doses of THC, the primary psychoactive agent in marijuana, and then were engaged in a competitive task with a supposed opponent whom they could shock. The subject lost on many of the first few trials, and received shock himself, provoking much aggression in response. But the subjects' own aggression increased over time only with low doses of THC, not with high doses. In other research, marijuana has been shown actually to reduce aggression, quite contrary to the enhancing effects of alcohol on aggression (see Taylor et al., 1976).

Similarly, a careful review of the extensive clinical and field research on marijuana concludes that marijuana does not precipitate violence in the majority of those people who use it chronically or periodically. It does leave open the possibility that some people might have such weak inhibitions against aggression that marijuana would trigger their aggressiveness, but the research evidence on this point is too skimpy to draw a firm conclusion now (Abel, 1977). Other drugs, such as PCP ("angel dust"), often trigger extremely violent reactions.

Displacement

What happens to aggressive feelings when, for one reason or another, they cannot be expressed against the cause of the anger? People are often frustrated or annoyed by someone but unable to retaliate against that person—the person may be too powerful, not available, or they may be too anxious and inhibited to do it. In such a situation, they are likely to express aggression in some other way, one of which is called **displacement**—that is, expressing aggression against a substitute target.

When a man forbids his son to go to the movies on a school night, the boy feels angry and aggressive. He cannot attack his father because his father is too strong and because there are social inhibi-

FIGURE 10–1 Mean shock settings as a function of type of alcohol and dose. (Taylor & Gammon, 1975, p. 171.)

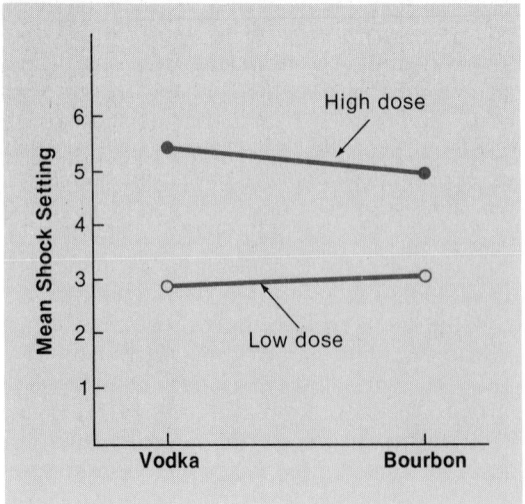

tions against it. Also, doing so would probably make it less likely that he would be permitted to go to the movies in the future. So he vents his rage on someone else. He has a wide range of people available. There is his mother, his older brother, his older sister, his younger brother, and a boy his own age who lives next door. The question is, what determines which of these people he will select and how much aggression he will express?

The basic principle of displacement is that the more similar a target is to the original source of frustration, the stronger will be the individual's aggressive impulses toward that target. In this case, the boy's aggressive impulse is strongest toward his father and gets weaker as the target toward whom it is directed becomes less similar to his father. It is not very strong toward his dog, for example. But the boy's anxiety operates in much the same way as his anger. Just as his impulse to hurt the source of frustration generalizes to other people, so does his anxiety about attacking the source. The more similar the person is to this source, the stronger the anxiety felt toward him or her.

An important characteristic of displaced aggression is that, as the targets become increasingly dissimilar, anxiety declines faster than does the aggressive impulse. This is shown in Figure 10–2. As long

as the anxiety is stronger than the aggressive impulse, the individual will restrain him or herself; when the tendency to aggress becomes stronger than the anxiety, the individual will express aggression. As a result, aggressive behavior is most likely to occur against a person moderately dissimilar from the original target—someone similar enough to draw some anger, but dissimilar enough to be associated with relatively little anxiety.

In this case, the boy's younger brother may be just dissimilar enough to the father that the boy is not afraid of him and similar enough that the aggressive impulse is still quite strong. So because the boy is unwilling to hit his father, he makes a nasty comment to his brother.

In general, therefore, displaced aggression is most likely to be directed toward targets who are perceived as weaker and less powerful. One example comes from a learning situation in which women were insulted and angered by a co-worker and then were instructed to punish a child for errors (Berkowitz & Frodi, 1979). They tended to give the most punishment to children who were physically unattractive or who stuttered. These children were more likely to be the targets of displaced aggression than more attractive children or those who spoke normally.

The dimension along which similarity is determined need not be as simple as the one in our example. For example, many adolescents tend to have feelings of anger against their parents. Parents are the source of power in the family, they are the authority, and they must inevitably frustrate their children's wishes to some extent. In some cases, this anger is expressed directly against the parents. In many cases, however, it is displaced to other people who represent authority. School administrators, trustees, teachers, the government, and so on fit the criterion and become likely objects for aggression.

Or, displacement may occur along a dimension of response similarity as well as along a dimension of target similarity. The adolescent boy may become surly and uncooperative rather than overtly belligerent. It creates less anxiety, but also expresses less anger. This kind of response is not a direct act of aggression in response to frustration; rather, it is displaced to subtler, more covert forms. In fact, there is a term for people who habitually resort

FIGURE 10–2 Displaced aggression.

When children are punished by their parents, they sometimes take out their feelings of aggression on dolls or other surrogate objects.

to such indirect forms of aggression: the *passive-aggressive personality*.

Catharsis

One final idea is that angry feelings can be reduced simply by expressing the aggression. Freud called this process **catharsis.** In common-sense language, it involves "letting off steam" or "getting it out of your system." The core of the catharsis notion is that when people feel aggressive, committing aggressive acts should reduce the intensity of their feelings. This, in turn, should make them less likely to act aggressively afterward. If someone annoys us by honking a horn at us, we feel angry. If, at the next traffic light, we find ourselves behind that car and honk at it, this should reduce the anger.

Freud's version of the catharsis theory presupposed that we always have a reservoir of instinctual aggressive energy within us. No matter what the situation is, we have a certain amount of aggressiveness that we need to "get off our chest." The problem with this view is that it predicts aggressive behavior will always reduce anger, because that reservoir is always with us. Some empirical evidence contradicts this: Aggressive behavior increases aggressiveness in nonangry people; they have built up steam instead of letting it off (Doob & Wood, 1972; Konecni, 1975).

A later version came from the frustration-aggression hypothesis which assumed that aggressive drives are not instinctual, but are instigated by situational factors like frustrations and attacks. The implication was that aggressive behavior would produce catharsis only for those people who were angry to start with. Since there is no permanent reservoir of aggressive energy in this theory, catharsis would reduce aggressiveness only for those people in whom it had been built up through frustration or attack.

Some early research on physiological arousal supported this view. Two studies (Hokanson, 1961; Hokanson & Burgess, 1962) found that aggressive behavior decreased angry feelings, as indexed by physiological arousal. In these studies, subjects were insulted by a low-status person, which increased their blood pressure, indicating increased physiological tension. Presumably they were angry. Some of the subjects were then given an opportunity to deliver shocks to the experimenter who had annoyed them; some were not given this opportunity. Being allowed to express aggression resulted in lower blood pressure among those who were angry.

DIRECT AGGRESSION   Later research has found, however, that catharsis is successful in reducing aggression only when an angry person has expressed that anger directly against his or her frustrator. A typical demonstration is in an experiment by Konecni and Ebbesen (1976). First, the subject was insulted. She did an anagram task with the confederate, who finished her own problems quickly and then proceeded to insult the subject, criticize her for being so slow, and express doubts about her intellectual ability. Then some subjects were given the opportunity to aggress against the confederate, while others were not.

Using a variant on the standard sham-learning situation, the subjects were required to deliver loud blasts of noise to the confederate each time she made an error. Control subjects did not send any noise to the confederate. The dependent variable involved a "creativity test" in which all subjects were given a two-button box, one labeled "good" and the other "noise." The subject could administer either reward or punishment, depending on her feelings.

The results clearly showed that delivering blasts of noise at the confederate reduced a subsequent tendency to do so. A similar study by Doob and Wood (1972), using shock rather than noise, found essentially the same thing: When the subjects were angered by a confederate, catharsis resulted from giving shocks to the confederate.

However, relying on this kind of direct retaliatory catharsis as a way of reducing aggression is risky because it may have a number of undesirable side effects. There is the possibility of **disinhibition.** We all control our anger fairly tightly most of the time. But if it is once released, particularly when it seems to be socially approved, we may relax our inhibitions about further hostilities. So expressing aggression may lead to even more aggression. Geen and Quanty (1977) cite the reaction of a man who killed four people: "He said . . . he had a funny feeling in his stomach but after the first [killing] . . . it was easy" (p. 29). Aggression may

be reinforced if it relieves emotional tension (as it appears to). Then reinforced behaviors would tend to recur more frequently. And aggressive behavior also may provide practice and cues for further aggression that would not have been present without it.

Another risk is that within any given sequence of behavior, aggression seems to escalate rather than to decline, as we indicated earlier in discussing the effects of retaliation. That is, catharsis seems to reduce aggression only when there is some break in the action, a change in the victim, or some change in the mode of expression of aggression. This has been a common finding with the Buss aggression machine, which has been used in so many experiments. As the experiment goes on, the "teacher" almost always gives increasingly strong shocks to the "learner," no matter what conditions they are in.

Goldstein, Davis, and Herman (1975) found the same thing with verbal responses, using the same teacher-learner situation. The subject was given a list of standard verbal responses from which to choose, depending on whether the "learner" had made an error or not. The subject tended to give more and more intense punishments for errors. For example, if the subject first responded to an error with "That's no good," he later would escalate with "You're a jerk," through "I never met anyone as dumb as you," to "Stupid son of a bitch." So if you get into a fight, it is likely that the fighting will increase your aggression toward your opponent rather than decrease it. The authors suggest this *escalation phenomenon* may be the same thing that happens in the "battered child" syndrome, in which the level of violence just seems to keep increasing.

INDIRECT AGGRESSION   Given the hazards of directly expressing aggression against a frustrator or attacker, what about the possibility that more indirect expressions of aggression might produce catharsis? Aristotle felt that watching tragedy could produce catharsis, because the audience could vicariously experience the actors' emotions. Freud developed the same idea by hypothesizing that people could reduce their aggressive impulses through aggressive fantasy, such as in violent daydreams, cruel jokes, or writing stories. If such indirectly expressed aggression truly did cathart aggressive energy, aggressive behavior might be reduced without all the negative side effects we have enumerated.

An early study of the possible effects of **fantasy aggression** was conducted by Seymour Feshbach (1955). First, most of the subjects were angered by being insulted in class by their instructor. Then half the subjects were allowed to express aggression on a fantasy task—responding to four cards from a projective test that showed ambiguous pictures for which the subjects were to make up stories. The other half of this group did not respond to the cards. Afterward, their aggressiveness toward the instructor was measured. The insulted subjects who were given the opportunity to express aggression on the fantasy task were somewhat less aggressive on the final measure than the insulted subjects who did not do the fantasy task.

However, fantasy aggression may not be an especially reliable way to reduce aggressiveness either. Freud felt that hostile humor could serve as an indirect mechanism for releasing aggressive energy. When we are angry and hear someone tell a hostile joke (like a hostile ethnic joke), we vicariously engage in the expression of hostility and should no longer feel so angry ourselves. To test this idea, a number of studies have aroused various degrees of anger, presented hostile (or unhostile) jokes to the subjects, and then measured their subsequent aggressiveness.

The catharsis theory predicts that the angered subjects will show less aggression after being shown hostile jokes than after being shown nonhostile jokes, because the hostile jokes help to siphon off their anger. Research testing this hypothesis has produced generally inconsistent results, though humor does seem to distract people from their frustrations and annoyances (Mueller & Donnerstein, 1977), and generates responses incompatible with aggressive behavior, such as laughter (Baron & Ball, 1974).

The question of fantasy aggression is also relevant to the hot political issue of whether violence on television or in the movies affects aggressive behavior. If watching a crime movie actually reduced our aggressiveness, it would be quite an important matter, so we will discuss this issue in some detail in the next section. But from the above findings our suspicion must be that vicariously experienced aggression against some neutral person is generally not especially cathartic. Watching a boxing match may not really do much about the fact that your girlfriend is going out with your rival at that very moment, and it apparently would not be likely to do much to relieve your anger either.

Evidence that modes of expressing aggression other than physical acts produce catharsis have also been sought. One is *displaced aggression*; that is, aggression against someone other than your tormentor. Another is *vicarious aggression* against your tormentor; that is, aggression actually committed by someone else. A third is *verbal* rather than physical aggression. In these cases, there are some studies that find cathartic effects (e.g., Konecni and Doob, 1972; Bramel, Taub, & Blum, 1968), but other studies that do not (see Geen & Quanty, 1977). In fact, the rates of various kinds of aggression turn out to be relatively highly correlated.

For example, couples that were in the highest quarter of the population in verbal aggression had extremely high levels of physical violence against each other: 56 percent had engaged in at least one violent episode within the past year. Couples in the lowest quarter on verbal aggression very rarely were physically violent—only 0.5 percent had had a violent incident in a year (Straus et al., 1981). So in married couples, verbally "getting it off your chest" is not associated with peace and harmony, but with later outbreaks of even more serious violence.

At the moment, social psychologists simply do not know whether or not such alternative modes of expressing anger produce a cathartic reduction in aggressive behavior, and if they do, what additional conditions would be necessary for them to do so regularly. In any event, catharsis does seem to reduce the expression of aggression fairly reliably only when (1) the person is angry, and (2) is able to express aggression in a fairly direct manner, and (3) is able to express aggression against the person who he or she perceives as responsible for the anger—the attacker, annoyer, or frustrator. These are fairly stringent limitations on the catharsis effect.

MEDIA VIOLENCE

It is an understatement to say that in recent years movies have begun to portray a great deal of violence. Fighting, beating, killing, and murder have always been common in Westerns and gangster movies. But the level of violence has risen over time. Content analyses show a long-term trend dating from the early 1930s of increasing violence in films shown in theaters (Comstock, 1982). And more recent movies have escalated the amount of carnage as well as its vividness. People did not just die at a distance or clutch their stomachs and fall slowly to the ground. In these movies they actually bled and suffered; the bullet wounds gaped; blood pumped rhythmically from victims' bodies, rather than slowly staining their clothes. Rambo takes on the communists, Charles Bronson takes on criminals, and Clint Eastwood, as Dirty Harry, dares a criminal to shoot, saying, "Make my day."

Television has also used quite a bit of violence in its programming. With the exception of talk, variety, doctor, and comedy shows, virtually all original programming for prime time television, as well as shows designed specifically for children, involve violence in one form or another. Westerns, police, gangster, and spy shows, and most television movies include a full complement of fighting, shooting, and killing. Saturday morning cartoons feature more of the same. Although the violence on television is much less explicit and vivid than that in the movies, it is remarkably pervasive.

It is certainly widely assumed that such media violence stimulates people to aggressive behavior. For example, a few years ago, a television drama, *Born Innocent*, portrayed an artificial rape scene. A few days later, some adolescent boys carried out a similar artificial rape blamed on the movie (Linz et al., 1986). In 1983 the chief of the California state prisons adopted a policy of preventing "any movie that glorifies sick violence" after he discovered that the movie *The Texas Chainsaw Massacre* had been shown at the men's prison in Chino.

But as we have seen, aggression is a very complex behavior. Mere exposure to films may not have much effect on it one way or the other. The catharsis theory would even predict that violent films might reduce aggression. So we explore this question in some detail, especially since this has become one of the more controversial areas of the application of social psychological research.

The Surgeon General's Report

The politics of media violence have become very important. Indeed complete books have been written on that subject alone (Rowland, 1983; Cater & Strickland, 1975). Congressional concern about violence on television began to be expressed in hearings as early as 1952. As a result of congressional action, an enormous amount of money was made available for research on media violence in the late 1960s. A report was finally prepared for the Surgeon General of the United States Public Health Service, which had administered the research grants. This report concluded, rather cautiously, that:

> [There is] a preliminary and tentative indication of a causal relation between viewing violence on television and aggressive behavior; an indication that any such causal relation operates only on some children (who are predisposed to be aggressive); and an indication that it operates only in some environmental contexts (Surgeon General's Scientific Advisory Committee on Television and Social Behavior, 1972, p. 11).

This report immediately came under harsh attack, partly because some of the members of the committee that prepared it had been representatives of the television networks, and it was felt (quite understandably, but not necessarily accurately) that they therefore could not be disinterested scientific observers (Cater & Strickland, 1975).

This 1963 Birmingham scene was repeated over and over in the civil rights demonstrations of the early 1960s. Television coverage of these confrontations was thought by some to be partly responsible for the ghetto riots of the late 1960s.

Most of the criticism held that the commission had underestimated the effects of media violence. The report led to the preparation of a number of briefer reviews, which arrived at widely differing conclusions (contrast Comstock, 1975, with Kaplan & Singer, 1976, for example). Nevertheless, the mid-1970s saw considerable further political action on this question. By 1975, the American Medical Association had passed a resolution against television violence, and the National Parents and Teachers Association had mounted an active campaign to reduce it. The Coalition for Better Television sponsored a boycott of NBC. The National Coalition on Television Violence claimed to have 100,000 supporters behind a campaign to put pressure on companies that advertise on violent television programs, which its research director, a psychiatrist, estimated was the cause of "25% to 50% of everyday family anger and aggression."

One of the responses to this Surgeon General's report was that the Federal Communications Commission persuaded the networks to adopt a "family viewing hour" in the early evening as the first prime time hour, and the hour preceding would exclude programming "inappropriate for viewing by a general family audience." However, the courts later held that this constituted excessive government intervention, and ruled that it could not be enforced (Linz et al., 1986).

Ten years later, the National Institute of Mental Health asked the behavioral science community to evaluate the effects of televised violence once again. This time the reviewing committee was dominated by academic researchers active in the effort to assess the effects of televised violence. They came up with two findings in particular. One was that there had been no reduction in violence on television since the late 1960s, despite all the controversy. Indeed, among the most violent programs on television were weekend shows aimed at children. Second, "the consensus among most of the research community is that violence on television does lead to aggressive behavior by children and teenagers who watch the programs. . . . A causal link between televised violence and aggressive behavior now seems obvious" (National Institutes of Mental Health, 1982, p. 6). A similar report was issued in seven volumes by the Canadian Royal Commission, which concluded that there was a definite connection between violence in the media and violent crime in Canadian society.

These reports met with much approval from many researchers in the field, who had long since become persuaded of the success of this conclusion. For example, the Society for the Psychological Study of Social Issues, comprised mainly of liberal activists, brought out an issue of its journal composed entirely of articles promoting this view (Huesmann & Malamuth, 1986).

The networks issued more skeptical reports. For example, ABC said the conclusions were "unsubstantiated when subjected to scientific analysis" (Walsh, 1983). We might be tempted to dismiss such statements because the networks have a financial stake in having free rein over their own programming. But self-interest does not necessarily mean their statements are unjustified. Nor can we safely assume that social scientists who do research in the area are necessarily unbiased; they may have quite strong preconceptions about the dangers of media violence. So telling the good guys from the bad guys may not be as simple as it might seem.

What is the evidence on the effects of media violence? Basically three types of studies have been done: laboratory experiments, correlational surveys, and field experiments. It is perhaps useful to look at all three, both because all can help us understand this particular research question, and because they provide good examples of how different kinds of research get applied to a practical problem.

Laboratory Experiments

Various social psychological theories would argue that violence on television or in the movies increases aggression among those who watch it. Bandura's imitation theory, for example, suggests that it would lead the viewers to engage in imitative aggression. Other learning theories would suggest that media violence presents cues that trigger habitual aggressive responses among viewers. Yet the catharsis theory makes exactly the opposite prediction; it predicts that watching aggression or violence done by others will actually reduce anger among those who are feeling angry. Which is correct?

The strongest early proponent of the catharsis theory in situations involving observed aggression was Seymour Feshbach. He did a pioneering experiment (1961) in which angered and nonangered subjects were shown either a violent boxing film or a neutral film. Measures of aggression taken after the film showed that watching the boxing film lowered the aggressiveness of angered subjects, supporting the catharsis prediction. Observing others involved in aggression seemed to be a way of working through angry feelings, thereby reducing anger and aggressive behavior. But this one demonstration of catharsis stands as an exception in the large body of laboratory studies done on aggression. Practically all the other laboratory studies have shown that watching others' violence actually increases subsequent aggressive behavior. These studies have typically followed one of two procedures.

The imitation experiments done by Bandura us-ing a Bobo doll, as described earlier, represent one type. The point of these experiments was to demonstrate that young children can learn aggressive behavior by imitating the aggressive behavior of adults. Preschool-age children were mildly frustrated, and then they observed an adult batting a Bobo doll around. When the children themselves were placed in the room with the doll, they repeated many of the aggressive behaviors performed by the adult.

A second common type of laboratory experiment has involved showing a brief film embodying violent physical aggression to college students who had either been angered (typically by insult) or not angered. The dependent variable has usually been shock supposedly administered to a confederate, in the standard sham-learning situation. One of the films often used was a seven-minute clip from a boxing film starring Kirk Douglas called *The Champion* (e.g., Berkowitz, 1965). Viewing the violent film generally produced more attacks on a confederate whether or not the subject himself had previously been attacked (e.g., Geen & O'Neal, 1969).

Anything that linked the subject to the film aggressor, or the confederate to the film victim, tended to increase aggression. For example, when subjects were told to identify with the winner of the boxing match, they displayed more aggression than did subjects who were told to identify with the judge or were not given any instructions about how to watch. Similarly, in another study the confederate was described as a boxer or as a speech major, and the boxer received more shock. A confederate named "Kirk" got more shocks than one named "Bob" after seeing Kirk Douglas play the boxer who got beaten up in the film (Berkowitz & Geen, 1966). When the film presented justified aggression, by presenting the loser of the boxing match in an unfavorable light, more aggression was displayed (see Berkowitz & Rawlings, 1963; Berkowitz & Geen, 1967). In other similar research, greater aggression has occurred when fellow observers approve of the media violence, when available victims are most similar to the target of media violence, when the viewers believe in the realism of the media violence, and when the subject is angry at the time of exposure (Linz, Penrod, & Donnerstein, 1986).

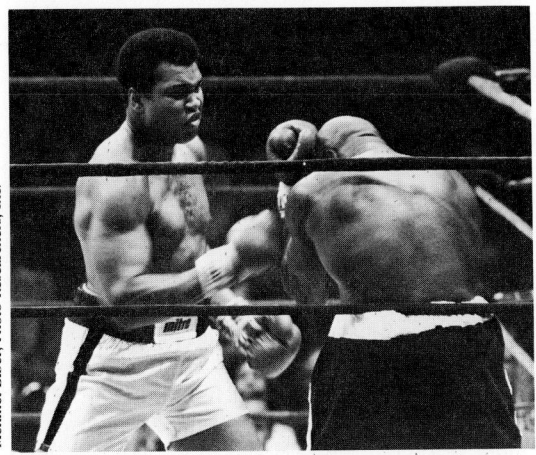

Relative to other kinds of violence on television, boxing matches are short, mostly composed of sanctioned violence, and depict little that is not violent. However, Muhammed Ali was renowned for his humor, especially his humorous poems, and for a well-publicized protest against the Vietnam War which cost him his world heavyweight championship.

In short, the more similar the subject to the filmed aggressor, or the confederate to the film victim, or the more justified the film violence, the more behavioral aggression shown by the subject. The vast majority of these laboratory experiments have shown that observing aggression provokes greater aggressive behavior, not less. The catharsis effect rarely occurs. Whether one describes the effect as imitating, stimulating, activating, or triggering aggression, the result is the same: In these laboratory experiments, observing aggression produces heightened aggressive behavior.

External Validity

Nevertheless, it is quite a long step from such typical laboratory studies to the real-life situations to which we might want to generalize. These laboratory experiments must be judged, therefore, in terms of their **external validity** (Campbell & Stanley, 1963). External validity asks the question of *generalizability*. Do these laboratory findings hold up in other situations, with other populations, other measures, and other ways of manipulating the same variables?

Most important, do they hold up in the real-life situations we are most concerned about?

One way to approach the question of external validity is to see how closely the real-life situation to which we most want to generalize matches the experimental situations we have been studying. The concern about media violence has been expressed most about television, since it is piped free into the home and exposure is virtually uncontrolled (and nearly uncontrollable). Mostly the concern is that young males, who are most responsible for violent crimes, will watch a great deal of violent television, then go out and commit violent crimes.

But these laboratory experiments differ in some important ways from this real-life situation. Consider the independent variables. The segments presented to subjects are normally brief, and they are almost entirely composed of a single violent episode, like a few rounds from a boxing match, or an adult beating up a Bobo doll.

In contrast, the normal child in real life spends up to four hours a night watching television and sees a number of different programs. Each program contains quite a mixture of romantic stories, humor, altruistic behavior, heroism, ordinary conversation, and all sorts of other human acts having nothing to do with violence. Even violent cops-and-robbers programs have humor, romantic entanglements, loyalty between cops, scenery, and other nonviolent matters. So instead of the brief, concentrated dose of exposure to violent models typical of experiments, television in real life presents children with a varied diet of all manner of possible behaviors to imitate.

Laboratory experiments differ even more from real life in the dependent variable. In virtually all experiments, the subject engages in aggression that is fully sanctioned, and often even prosocial. The Bobo doll experiments involve sanctioned aggression. Children know it is perfectly all right to hit the Bobo doll; nobody will disapprove of them or think they are bad for doing it. Indeed, experiments that show the model being punished for hitting Bobo have produced markedly reduced imitative aggression. Other experiments have used a variant of the sham shock-learning machine. The subject is told she is in a learning experiment and is supposed to punish the victim for errors. This is prosocial aggression. The subject has been instructed to shock the confederate to help increase scientific knowledge.

The concern about aggression in real life, in contrast, focuses exclusively on antisocial aggression. We are worried about unprovoked assaults, armed robbery, assault and battery, rape, and murder. The concern is about the media causing too much antisocial aggression, not too much sanctioned or prosocial aggression.

Laboratory measures of aggression differ from real-life violence in several other ways. There is normally no possibility of retaliation; indeed, where there is, aggression is reduced. Often the aggressive task is fun, novel, and a game; one writer has described Bobo-beating as "solitary aggressive play." A 5-year-old playing with what is obviously a new toy is a far cry from a gang of teenagers holding up a gas station and shooting the manager.

Finally, in these experiments the aggression measure is taken immediately after exposure to the film because any delay would obviously reduce the effect of the film. In fact, it is hard to imagine a seven-minute film clip having an effect that would last more than a couple of hours. Several studies have shown that the effects can wear off within a matter of minutes. But in real life, the boy does not rush out of his living room with a knife and attack the first person he sees. Most crime is committed quite a long time after the person has watched television. People who are roaming the streets are not home watching television; in fact, we might all be safer if they were.

So the external validity of these experiments is open to some question: (1) The film itself tends to be brief and to be composed of pure violence, rather than containing the broad mixture of themes customary in most drama; (2) the viewing situation is controlled and socially isolated, providing few distractions from the violence; (3) the subject's response is measured immediately after the film; (4) the "aggressive" behavior measured is usually prosocial or sanctioned aggression, with the subject knowing he or she is doing no harm to anyone or at least being directly told by the experimenter to perform the "aggressive" response; and (5) there is no likelihood of retaliation. The important point is that all these special conditions of laboratory experiments have themselves been shown to increase aggression. They are likely to present an

exaggerated portrait of the aggression inspired by violent films. So to generalize more confidently to real-life situations, we probably need to turn to studies done under conditions that more nearly resemble real life.

Correlational Surveys

One solution to the problem of external validity is to conduct **correlational surveys** to determine whether the children who watch the most violent television are also the ones who are the most aggressive. If they were, the causal interpretation might still be open to question; personal aggressiveness might lead children to watch more violent television, rather than vice versa, or some third variable might produce both a preference for watching violent television and higher levels of personal aggressiveness. But if the correlation between the two was zero, it would be much harder to make a case for the causal role of media violence. So the results from correlational surveys would be valuable, even if not decisive.

Many studies have used children's self-reported television preferences to measure their actual television viewing. Aggressive behavior has been assessed using ratings by peers about how aggressively the children behave. In most cases, it is the most aggressive children who watch the most violent television. But the strength of the correlations between the two vary quite widely. In some studies (Eron et al., 1972; Eron, 1982; Singer et al., 1984; Huesmann, 1982), there are modest but significant correlations, even when viewing preferences are measured some years earlier than the aggression. In a cross-national study of children in five nations, early exposure to television violence was associated with significantly greater later levels of aggression in half the comparisons, though the correlations were not significant in the other half (Huesmann & Eron, 1986; Turner, Hesse, & Peterson-Lewis, 1986). In other studies, using very similar measures, the correlations are weaker, and generally nonsignificant (Milavsky et al., 1982).

On the average, the correlations tend to be rather weak but usually positive. Nonetheless, it is possible to argue that even very weak correlations reflect socially significant effects (Rosenthal, 1986). And it is also argued that quite small effects due to media exposure over relatively short periods of time, such as three years, become considerably larger when cumulated over an entire childhood and adolescence; this view is consistent with at least some interpretations of available studies (Turner et al., 1986). All that said, it remains true that the correlations are, on the average, not very strong.

Moreover, like all correlations, even these relatively weak ones lend themselves to a variety of causal interpretations. So the correlational studies do not provide strong evidence for a causal role of media violence in producing aggressive behavior in real life.

Field Experiments

A third approach to studying the media-aggression link uses experiments that come closer to matching real-life conditions. To clarify the causal role of viewing violence, we would want to maintain the experimental variation of exposure to violent, as opposed to neutral or nonviolent, films. But we would want to do it in the context of something more closely resembling the normal media diet of adolescents, and then observe their aggressive behavior in ordinary, day-to-day situations. Such studies are called **field experiments,** because they are done in the individual's natural situation, or in "the field." Only a few major field experiments have been done. The first was conducted by Feshbach and Singer (1971).

Boys in private boarding or state residential schools were randomly assigned to two groups: One group watched largely aggressive television programs such as "Gunsmoke" and "The FBI," while the other group was limited to nonaggressive programs such as the "Ed Sullivan Variety Show" and "Bachelor Father." The boys watched only shows on the designated lists and could watch as much as they wanted as long as they spent at least six hours a week watching television. Various measures of aggressiveness were given before and after the six-week viewing period, and both peers and adult supervisors also rated the boys' aggressiveness.

The results showed that boys in the state schools who watched aggressive programs actually became less aggressive. They engaged in fewer fights and argued less with their peers. The effect was the same but somewhat weaker for the boys in the private schools. This study thus indicates that, at least under some conditions, observing television violence under ordinary conditions might actually decrease aggressive behavior. The explanation offered for this effect follows from the catharsis notion. The children identified with both the heroes and the villains in the programs, and vicariously expressed some of their aggressive feelings.

On the other hand, it must be noted that the effect could be due to the fact that boys who were limited to the nonaggressive programs might have been annoyed because they were not allowed to watch their favorite television shows. A very similar study by Wells (1973) found that violent versus nonviolent television diets made very little difference. Despite these complications, these studies do attempt to test how ordinary television affects aggressiveness, and they do suggest that the effect may not be to increase it.

Three other studies were done in minimum-security penal institutions for juvenile offenders in the United States and Belgium (Leyens et al., 1975; Parke et al., 1977). After a week of observation, the boys in some living cottages were shown violent movies (*Iwo Jima, Bonnie and Clyde*), while boys in other cottages were shown neutral films (*Lily, Daddy's Fiancée*). In the Belgian study, two cottages saw an aggressive film every night for a week, and two saw a neutral film every night. In the first U.S. study, one cottage watched a violent film every night for a week, and another saw a neutral film. In the second U.S. study, one cottage saw a violent film each night for five nights, and another saw a neutral film; a third cottage saw one violent film one night, and the last cottage saw just one neutral film on one occasion. Then the boys' behavior was observed for an additional week.

These studies found little evidence that violent films increased aggressiveness. The Belgian study found an increase in overall aggressiveness immediately after the film for one cottage but not the other, though even this increase had disappeared by the next day. The first American study also found a greater increase in aggressiveness immediately after violent than nonviolent films, but the second found little difference, and neither found any cumulative or lasting effects of exposure.

Friedrich and Stein (1973) put nursery school children on a diet of twelve violent cartoons (*Batman*, *Superman*), or prosocial entertainment (*Mister Rogers*) or neutral films (e.g., about nature) for a period of four weeks. They were carefully observed by trained observers. They had three measures of aggression, and five others of good classroom behavior (rule obedience, delay tolerance, task persistence, cooperation, and prosocial behavior). The groups differed significantly on at most two of these eight measures, so the effect of the filmed violence cannot have been very great.

A somewhat different set of studies was done by Milgram and Shotland (1973). They prepared special versions of a prime-time television show—"Medical Center"—that included illegal (but nonviolent) acts. Three different versions of the episode were prepared. For example, in one, the protagonist smashes several charity-drive collection boxes, steals the money, and escapes to Mexico. Subjects viewed the program in a theater, and then were offered a free radio if they would show up at a downtown office a week later. At the office, there was a sign saying there were no more radios, and there was a charity donation box containing some money, including a $1 bill sticking partway out. Concealed TV cameras coded whether or not the subject took the dollar. Viewers of different versions did not differ. Seven experiments were done in this general style, and none showed any effect of viewing illegal acts.

There are also certain "natural experiments," such as have occurred when television has been newly introduced into areas where there had been no television. Hennigan and her colleagues (1982) studied the relationship between the introduction of television to various areas of the U.S. and changes in the crime rate. They found no increase in violent crimes, burglary, or auto theft—the crimes usually portrayed on television. The only change was an increase in larceny—a crime rarely shown on television.

Each of these studies has its flaws. As was pointed out before, in the Feshbach-Singer and the Wells studies, the adolescent boys in the nonviolent conditions were deprived of their normal favorite programs. This frustration could by itself have in-

creased their aggressiveness, thus eliminating any possible differences between the violent and nonviolent conditions.

The Leyens, Parke and associates studies used group-viewing situations in dormitories where boys in prison had been living together for some time. This was perhaps a little like watching movies in a fraternity (except with juvenile delinquents instead of college boys), and it evidently stimulated a good bit of rowdiness during and right after the movies. But this rowdy-group context is not the usual one for TV viewing in the home. The Milgram-Shotland studies were at the mercy of the idiosyncrasies of their specific versions of "Medical Center," and in most cases so little stealing emerged that it would have been hard for anything at all to influence it enough to be detectable.

But all studies in social science are flawed. It is a myth that a perfect study can be devised. The minute we patch up one problem, another emerges (often created by the patch, in fact). The way to come to a conclusion about an important area of research is to look at the pattern of the data. The effects of these violent versus nonviolent TV field experiments are not very dramatic. Feshbach and Singer get diminished aggression from the violent diet, but only in one set of schools. The studies by Wells, Friedrich, and Stein, and Milgram and Shotland show no strong results. Parke and colleagues find increased aggression in some cottages, but it does not last and may be an effect more of group contagion than individual arousal. Milgram and Shotland get no differences in seven experiments. So it is difficult to see a very powerful effect of movie or TV violence on aggressive behavior leaping out at us from these field studies. Rather, observed violence in movies or television seems not to affect aggressive behavior much in these real-life situations, one way or the other.

Other Possible Effects of Media Violence

The potential role of media violence is not limited to imitative aggression, however. A number of other questions can readily be raised. Why is there so much violence in movies and television? Is it because of some compelling interest viewers have in violent content? Furthermore, watching violence may have effects other than allegedly stimulating violent behavior. We may become so accustomed to the sight of violence that it no longer offends or shocks us. On the other hand, being confronted at close range with the vicious things that people do to each other may make us more resolved than ever to turn this into a peaceful world.

It was argued that the comprehensive television coverage of the Vietnam war (the "first televised war") hastened public condemnation of the war and ultimately helped remove our armed forces from it. Some observers fear that even nonviolent erotic literature, pictorial magazines, and movies provide yet another stimulant to violence, especially against women. In all these cases, research is so preliminary as only to be suggestive. But it is perhaps worth seeing what can be said at the moment about these other possibilities.

PUBLIC INTEREST IN VIOLENCE   Is violence especially interesting and exciting to people? Apparently not for its own sake. Violent programs do not get markedly higher ratings than nonviolent programs (Comstock, 1982, p. 109). Diener and De Four (1978) did content analysis ratings of television programs for violence, drama, humor, and action. Then they correlated these qualities with the relative popularity of various programs. They found humor and action were crucial determinants of popularity, but violence was not.

Angry, aggressive people may prefer more violence in their films, however. Fenigstein (1979) induced subjects to have aggressive fantasies or to behave aggressively using the sham teacher-learner procedure, and found they were more likely to want to watch film clips that featured violence, such as rioting at a rock concert, fist fights, and so on.

DESENSITIZATION TO VIOLENCE   Media violence is also thought by some observers to desensitize viewers to any later real-life violence. The argument is that when you watch people being killed and maimed and beaten up on television, you become accustomed to the sight of violence, and it therefore no longer upsets you as much. Ultimately, it is argued, you yourself will be more willing to hurt other people, or at least you will be less likely to

step in to prevent violence in real life (Linz, Penrod, & Donnerstein, 1986).

The argument implies a two-stage sequence. It first suggests that the constant sight of media violence reduces our emotional response to it later in the real world. Then, second, this lower emotional responsivity should reduce our tendency to stop aggression in real life. There is a little evidence of at least short-term reductions in emotional arousal. Physiological arousal during violent films was reduced by exposure to a prior eleven-minute excerpt from a television police series (Thomas et al., 1977), or among children who are especially heavy television viewers (Cline, Croft, and Courrier, 1973). But it is not yet clear that such exposure reduces the tendency to help stop aggression.

SPORTS EVENTS   Some people argue that sports events help spectators relieve their everyday frustrations by allowing them to yell, cheer, boo, and root for their favorite teams. Sports events, they say, are cathartic because they allow people to reduce their tensions in a vicarious, playful manner that hurts no one. Others argue that the moblike atmosphere of sports events reduces people's inhibitions to aggression or leads them to imitate aggressive behavior (particularly in violent sports like hockey, boxing, and football).

Sometimes terrible violence occurs after sports events. In Guatemala in 1977, for example, soccer fans of the losing team attacked the fans of the winning team with machetes and hacked five persons to death (Arms, Russell, & Sandilands, 1979).

There is some association between participation in aggressive sports and other forms of violence. Keefer and colleagues (1983) have shown that nations with the greatest Olympic games participation—particularly in body contact events—are also the most likely to have been involved in wars (holding constant their population size and density). In another study, undergraduates who participated in aggressive video games became more hostile as a result, in terms of mood (Anderson & Ford, 1986).

To test whether sports events increase aggression in spectators, Goldstein and Arms (1971) and Arms and associates (1979) gave spectators paper-and-pencil tests of hostility before and after a football game, a hockey match, a professional wrestling match (all having a high degree of physical aggres-

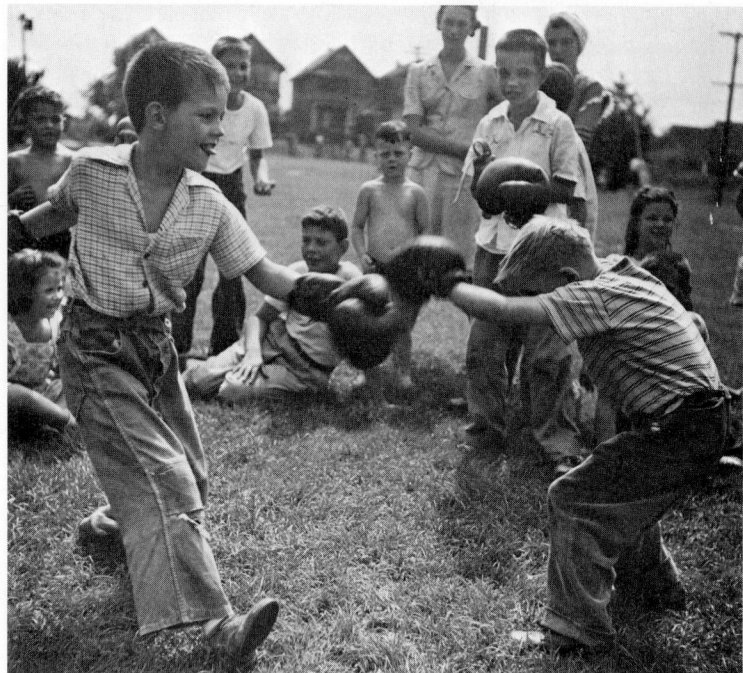

What effect is this boxing match likely to have on its spectators?

sion), and a gymnastics meet and a swimming meet (neither of which present much aggression). On some tests, watching violent sports seemed to increase irritability and hostility more than did watching the nonviolent ones. However, the effects were not very strong.

SEXUAL VIOLENCE

So far, our discussion of the effects of media violence has focused on films that show murders, beatings, and other gruesome forms of aggression. A related area of interest concerns the effects of sexually explicit materials on aggressive behavior. According to recent studies, about one-quarter of North American women have been raped or sexually assaulted at some point in their lives (Malamuth & Briere, 1986, p. 75). Does pornography, and perhaps especially violent erotica, increase sex crimes, antisocial behavior, or aggression more generally? The interest in this question derives partly from a concern that sexual content in films, books, and magazines makes men more violent toward women. But as a theoretical question it bears on the same underlying processes as the effects of witnessed aggression: the stimulation of aggressive behavior by witnessing others' behavior.

Political Background

In the late 1960s, President Lyndon Johnson appointed a Commission on Obscenity and Pornography. After a careful review of the research evidence, the committee reported (1970) that it could document no antisocial effects of pornography. The growing availability of pornography in the United States and Europe was not associated with a rise in sex crimes (relative to other crimes). Juvenile delinquents seemed to have no more experience with pornography than did their peers. The early background of sex offenders was generally sexually repressive and restrictive, not permissive. Antisocial aggression among young men is more heavily influenced by peers than by the media. This report therefore suggested that early socialization and peer influence, rather than pornography, were the key factors in antisocial sexual aggression.

As might be expected, the matter did not rest there. Politically conservative and religious groups immediately attacked the commission's conclusions. Later, feminists too criticized these conclusions, arguing that some types of pornography degrade women and do encourage sexual violence (see Diamond, 1980; Lederer, 1980).

Feminists emphasized a distinction between acceptable erotica and violent or coercive pornography. For example, Gloria Steinem, the feminist editor of *Ms. Magazine*, said: "Look at any photo or film of people . . . really making love . . . there is usually a sensuality and touch and warmth. . . . a sense of shared pleasure. [But] look at any depiction of sex in which there is clear force, or an unequal power that spells coercion. It may be very blatant, with weapons of torture or bondage, wounds and bruises, some clear humiliation. . . . there is no sense of equal choice or equal power" (1980, p. 37). Feminists argued that aggressive pornography, and pornography that degraded women generally, had increased sharply during the 1970s. This opened the possibility that the commission's findings were limited to the effects of "soft core" pornography, and were not applicable to "hard core" or violent pornography.

By the mid 1980s, the American public generally felt that showing sexual violence was inappropriate and should be banned, but that showing nudity and even sexual relations should not be. A 1985 poll showed that 63 percent felt video cassettes featuring sexual violence should be banned, while only 21 percent felt that magazines showing nudity should be, and 32 percent, X-rated video cassettes for home viewing (Commission, 1986, p. 927). It

is the violence, not the sex, that is most troubling to most people.

At the same time, Attorney General Meese appointed another commission to investigate pornography. The report of this commission (1986) generated a storm of public debate because its conclusions were very different from those of the earlier commission. It contended that sexually violent material had become much more common, and that depictions of violence in a sexually explicit manner are likely to increase the incidence of sexual violence, sexual coercion, and unwanted sexual aggression (Attorney General's Commission on Pornography, 1986). It recommended stricter anti-obscenity legislation and prosecution.

Field Research

What does the new evidence show? The availability of pornography has been increasing greatly in recent years, especially violent pornography, just as the crime rate (including sex crimes) has increased. Some argue for a causal link between the two. However, careful research in other countries suggests neither any such consistent pattern nor causal link (Commission, 1986, pp. 939–952).

Although media sexual aggression appears to have increased markedly in the period between the two reports, it remains considerably lower than nonsexual violence in the media. Content analyses have found considerable variability in the amount of violence in sexually explicit magazines, movies, and books. Magazines portray the least (in about 5 percent of the content), movies an intermediate amount (in about 15 percent), and "adult" books portray the most (in about 30 percent) (Malamuth & Briere, 1986, p. 76).

The nature of the violence also differs when it occurs in a sexual context. Victims usually are portrayed as abhoring nonsexual violence, and try to avoid it. With sexual violence, on the other hand, victims are often shown as initially resisting, but later come secretly to derive pleasure from it. There rarely are negative consequences: The perpetrator rarely gets punished, and the victim has little lasting trauma.

Finally, there remains little evidence that sex offenders are particularly likely to be consumers of pornography, and indeed the basic causes of criminal sexual deviancy still seem remarkably unclear (ibid, p. 975).

Laboratory Research

VIOLENT PORNOGRAPHY   Simultaneously there has been a surge of research on the possible effects of violent pornography on aggressive behavior (see Malamuth & Donnerstein, 1982). The central question is whether or not aggressive pornography produces more behavioral aggression than either nonaggressive erotica or nonsexual violence alone. That is, is there something special about the *mixture* of violence and sexual themes that triggers unusual levels of aggression against women? There is particular concern about pornography that depicts violent or coercive sex and that shows the female victim as enjoying the experience, since this is thought to be one stereotype which may incite men to rape.

The best studies have used films and some variant of the sham teacher-learner aggression procedure. A confederate makes the subject angry (or does not), the subject is exposed to some erotic pictures, literature, or films, and then is assigned to the teacher role with instructions to shock that confederate. Donnerstein's aggressive-erotic (1980) film contained black and white scenes in which a man with a gun forces himself into a woman's home and coerces her into having sexual intercourse with him. The Donnerstein-Berkowitz (1981) version depicts a young woman who comes into view, apparently to study with two men. They have been drinking, and she is forced to sit between them and drink. They then tie her up, strip her clothes off, slap her around, and rape her.

A number of such studies have shown that violent

BOX 10–8

LEGISLATING AGAINST PORNOGRAPHY: THE ISSUES

Feminist activists argue that if pornography is harmful, the victims must have some legal recourse. A city ordinance passed by the city council in Minneapolis in early 1984 was based on just this legal theory. Its supporters believed that pornography is central to "creating and maintaining the inequality of the sexes . . . just being a woman means you are injured by pornography." They defined pornography as "the sexually explicit subordination of women" in one or more of nine specific ways, such as presenting women who "experience sexual pleasure in being raped or mutilated." The ordinance would have allowed any woman who was the victim of sexual violence to sue magazine publishers or movie theater operators, and indeed it would have been possible for any woman to sue those involved in distributing and selling pornography. The ordinance was finally vetoed by the mayor, a man with a long history of commitment to liberal causes, partly because of his concern about the violation of free speech. Such a proposal raises a number of issues that are worth thinking about. How clear is the evidence that pornography does harm to women in general? What are the permissible limits on free speech? Should men who contribute indirectly to sexual violence be held responsible for it?

pornography produces more such aggression than does nonviolent pornography (see Malamuth & Donnerstein, 1982; Donnerstein, 1980; Donnerstein & Berkowitz, 1981). However, this comparison of violent and nonviolent pornography adds little to the laboratory experiments on media violence discussed above. It shows that viewing violent films produces more aggression than viewing nonviolent films, in laboratory experiments. It does not deal with the possibly unique effects of witnessing *sexual* violence.

More relevant to this point is a study comparing males viewing this aggressive pornographic film with males who viewed an aggressive but *non*pornographic film (Donnerstein, 1983). In the latter film, the woman is tied up and slapped around, but there is no nudity or even simulated sexual activity. The two films were perceived as similar in aggressiveness, but quite different in sexuality. When subjects were angered by a female and then viewed the aggressive pornography film, they gave more intense shocks to a confederate than in any other condition.

ATTITUDES   In extrapolating from such data to violent sexual crimes, one must again be cautious. Sexual violence may take many forms: sexual harrassment, "acquaintance" or "date" rape, condoning or supporting violence by others against women, etc. (Malamuth, 1986a, p. 4). Even rape itself has multiple causes; e.g., sexual aggression can be caused by sexual arousal in response to aggression, need for sexual dominance, hostility toward women, and approval of violence toward women. All of these have been shown to be correlated with males' reports of sexual aggression against women (primarily acquaintances) (Malamuth, 1986b).

Some social psychologists have been skeptical that this new commission report had established a direct causal link between most sexually explicit material and any act of sexual violence. They were more concerned that pornography might lead to demeaning or callous attitudes toward women than that it would directly produce rape or other acts of violence (Malamuth, 1986a).

The media may therefore have indirect rather than direct effects upon rape, by influencing men's attitudes toward women. Then normally censured acts become intellectually and emotionally acceptable. In other words, such pornography may change social norms about sexual violence.

It is perhaps worth noting that use of force is not a common theme in the usual sexual fantasies of either men or women. For men, they are much less common than purely heterosexual or voyeuristic fantasies; similarly, for women, dominance and suffering are much less common sexual fantasies than romantic or exhibitionistic fantasies (Arndt et al., 1985). Rapists have aggressive sexual fantasies more often than ordinary people do, but no one knows what role pornography plays in that (Commission, 1986, p. 980). Indeed, there is evidence that the most sexually arousing written stories, to men, are those that are sexually explicit and *non*aggressive (Malamuth et al., 1986, p. 332); i.e., depiction of aggressiveness reduces the arousal potential of sexually explicit materials. However, as might be expected, depictions of rape produce more aggressive fantasies than do mutually consenting versions of a sexual encounter (Malamuth, 1981). And men become more sexually aroused when women are depicted as consenting in a sex scene than when they are shown as abhorring the experience.

Numerous studies have also shown that viewing violent sexuality produces more accepting attitudes about violence against women. It also leads to accepting such myths as that women often enjoy being raped or being forced to perform various sexual acts. For example, Malamuth and Check (1981) compared the effects of viewing the films *Swept Away* and *The Getaway*, both showing women as victims of erotic and noneortic aggression, with those of viewing more neutral films. The more aggressive films increased males', but not females', acceptance of violence against women. This study was particularly useful because the films were viewed in regular theaters, while the viewers' attitudes were measured in regular class sessions, so they were not aware of being subjects in an experiment. In these several ways, then, viewing violent erotica seems to induce more sexually aggressive fantasies and attitudes.

Greater sexual arousal, and attitudes condoning sexual violence toward women, are in turn correlated with more aggressive behavioral tendencies. Greater sexual arousal from depictions of forceful sexual encounters is correlated with such variables as greater acceptance of rape myths, belief in male dominance over women, acceptance of aggression against women, attraction to coercive acts (Malamuth et al., 1986), laboratory aggression, and aggression in dating situations (Malamuth, 1983). There is also evidence that attitudes condoning sexual violence against women are, among men, associated with men's self-reported likelihood of engaging in violence against women and laboratory aggression against women. Rapists also endorse such attitudes more than do ordinary male citizens (Malamuth & Briere, 1986, pp. 83–87). However, it must be remembered that such correlations can always be interpreted in various ways; e.g., such attitudes may be rationalizations of, and thus determined by, aggressive behavior, or both variables may be influenced by some third variable.

NONVIOLENT EROTICA Exposure to nonviolent erotica turns out to increase violent behavior, at least under one set of limited conditions: when subjects are angry to start with; the erotic materials are extremely explicit, realistic, "hardcore" pornography; and the predominant affect experienced by the subject is negative (disgust or distaste).

For example, Donnerstein (and Barrett, 1978; Donnerstein and Hallam, 1978) had his confederates shock male subjects. Then he showed them some hard-core black-and-white stag films depicting oral and anal intercourse and female homosexuality. Such subjects shocked the offending confederate more than did nonangered subjects, or subjects shown no film or a neutral wildlife documentary. Similar findings were reported by Jaffe et al. (1974), who used highly explicit literary passages (though their subjects were not first angered).

However, almost any form of erotica less explicit than "hard-core" or "blue movies" seems not to increase aggression, and indeed often actually *reduces* aggression below normal levels (that is, below the levels of no-film or neutral-film control groups). For example, viewing still colored pictures of nude women or of sexual intercourse tended to reduce aggression below normal levels (Baron & Bell, 1977; Donnerstein et al., 1975). In at least one case, this reduction was greatest for previously angered subjects (Zillmann & Sapolsky, 1977).

There is some debate about why nonviolent erotica has such different effects. One possibility is that the "hard-core" material may itself be rather frustrating, because it is too arousing for the etiquette of the psychological experiment situation. Or, the more common, milder "soft core" material may be distracting from the original anger-arousing provocation by the confederate. Most likely, though, the more "hard core" material is inherently not very pleasant to most subjects. Indeed White (1979) has shown that college students find pictures of same-sex masturbation or mutual oral-genital contact much less pleasant than more common forms of pictorial erotica, such as conventional intercourse and lovemaking.

So he concludes, rather persuasively, that erotica decreases aggression when it produces positive feelings, though it may increase aggression somewhat when it produces a negative effect. So presumably any erotic materials that depict sex in an ugly, disgusting way would be more likely to inspire aggression than would materials that are more artistic, and/or present acts the subjects themselves feel comfortable looking at. Indeed, he suggests that any such pleasurable experience, whether or not it concerns sex, would have the same aggression-suppressing effect.

THE ROLE OF PEERS Indeed it may be that in real life, peer influence rather than the media is the most powerful factor in producing sexual aggression, as suggested by the original commission report. Ageton (1983) and Alder (1985) found that in two separate samples of adolescent boys and adult males, the strongest predictors of sexual aggression were, in the first case, involvement with delinquent peers, and second, having sexually aggressive friends. It seems likely that most actual acts of sexual violence involve a wide variety of converging factors, of which the media may at best be only one: attitudes, personality, arousal, disinhibition due to alcohol, social pressure, acute frustrations (like insults, etc.) (Malamuth & Briere, 1986, p. 78).

Conclusions

The effects of media violence have become one of the most passionate and most political of research topics in social psychology. Some researchers work for the television networks, and their conclusions are suspected (rightly or wrongly) of being influenced by the networks' interests in absolving themselves of any blame for violence in our society. On the other hand, many academic researchers approach the topic with a passionate desire to expose what they regard as a serious social ill, and it is hard to imagine that their research is any more disinterested. But the real question is not what biases the researchers approach the topic with, because few scientists are ever completely free of some preconception or another. The major question is how the evidence really stacks up.

We have discussed three different methods of researching the effects of media violence. Laboratory studies seem quite generally to show that observed violence increases aggressive behavior. But these studies have been conducted in such a way that they may not be especially applicable to real-life instances of antisocial violence. For the reasons given earlier, we do not have much confidence in generalizing from these laboratory studies to crime in the streets.

Most correlational surveys find a modest positive association between children's liking for violent television programs and various indicators of their behavioral aggression. However, these relationships are never very strong, and in some of the best studies are not even statistically significant.

The field experiments we have described come much closer to realistic replicas of real life. They have presented the typical movie and television fare of the day to male adolescents living in their normal life situations (though most of these have been in boarding schools, rather than living at home with their parents). They have measured genuine interpersonal aggression in a free, unconstrained atmosphere. However, these studies have generally shown that media violence has little or no systematic effect on interpersonal aggression. Some show a modest, temporary increase in aggression. Others show a debatable decrease in it. But on balance

there is no major impact one way or the other. Therefore, it seems correct to say that at the moment the field experiments also show media violence having little impact.

From a policy point of view, the question is whether the evidence is strong enough to urge the suppression of certain kinds of entertainment programs in order to reduce crime and violence. There are social conditions we all know are important in producing violence, such as unemployment, racial prejudice, poor housing, poor medical care (especially for people with mental health problems), the widespread availability of guns and alcohol and illegal drugs, a highly mobile population that does not settle into tight little self-policing communities, and parental indifference to the welfare of their children, among many other things. It seems to us that, at most, television and the movies could contribute only a small amount above and beyond such large social factors.

And we must be very careful about censorship of any kind. Today the government might decide that it is illegal to depict a knifing on television; tomorrow some censor may decide that it is illegal to depict an adulterous act, because people might imitate that; and the next day a censor may decide that it is illegal to depict protest demonstrations. Once the principle of censorship is accepted, it becomes harder and harder to draw the line.

So it is no idle academic matter, this business of the effects of media violence on interpersonal aggressiveness. We should recognize that no matter how passionately we feel about the issue, we must be cautious about taking a stand before we have sufficient evidence. It is fair to say that most psychologists today believe TV violence does generally increase aggressiveness. In our opinion, however, the actual empirical evidence is weak and has not shown a role of media violence in increasing crime. At this time there would seem not to be sufficient positive evidence to justify imposing restrictions on entertainment programs.

KEY TERMS IN CHAPTER 10

aggression	contagious violence	external validity	prosocial aggression
aggression anxiety	correlational survey	fantasy aggression	realistic group conflict
anger	deindividuation	field experiment	sanctioned aggression
antisocial aggression	disinhibition	frustration	social norms
catharsis	displacement	instrumental aggression	

SUMMARY

1. Aggression is defined as an action that hurts another person, and that is perceived as intended to do so.

2. Aggressive acts can be antisocial, prosocial, or merely sanctioned, depending on whether they violate or conform with social norms.

3. Aggressive feelings, or anger, need to be distinguished from aggressive behavior.

4. The major determinants of anger seem to be attack and frustration.

5. Frustrations that are not attributed to intent on the part of the frustrator do not create as much anger. Generalized, nonspecific arousal states can result in experienced anger if they are accompanied by the appropriate cognitive labels.

6. Aggressive behavior has as its major determinants angry feelings and the learning of aggressive responses. This learning can take place through direct reinforcement of aggressive responses or through imitation.

7. Social norms are crucial in determining what aggressive habits are learned.

8. Fear of punishment or retaliation can reduce aggressive behavior. However it may sometimes result instead in covert aggression, or actually increase aggression over the longer run.

9. Learned inhibitions of aggression are the most important control over it. Anxiety can be associated with the expression of aggression in general, or with its expression in quite specific contexts. Most people reduce their aggression when they see signs of pain in others. Such inhibitions can also result in the displacement of aggression to other innocent parties, and to the scapegoating of members of minority groups.

10. Observed aggression generally increases aggression in laboratory studies, whether they are done with small children, adolescents, or adults. It is especially potent in increasing aggression when the model is rewarded or when the observed victim is similar to the target of the subject's own aggression.

11. Field experiments of televised or movie violence, on the other hand, have not generally shown that it increases aggressive behavior in real-life settings. Therefore the laboratory studies of observed aggression may not generalize to real-life situations. The evidence that media violence contributes to violence and crime in our society is still rather indirect.

12. Laboratory studies indicate that observing violence produces more aggressive behavior than nonviolent erotica does. However, peer influence may be more powerful than pornography.

SUGGESTED READINGS

BANDURA, A. (1973). *Aggression: A social learning analysis*. Englewood Cliffs, N.J.: Prentice-Hall. The definitive statement by the most influential spokesman for the social learning and imitation approach to aggression.

BARON, R. A. (1977). *Human aggression*. New York: Plenum Press. A thorough, readable, comprehensive treatment of aggression from a social-psychological perspective.

COMSTOCK, G., CHAFFEE, S., DATZMAN, N., McCOMBS, M., & ROBERTS, D. (1978). *Television and human behavior*. New York: Columbia University Press. A conscientious review of research on the effects of television, concerning aggression, politics, advertising, and other areas.

DOLLARD, J., DOOB, L., MILLER, N. E., MOWRER, O. H., & SEARS, R. R. (1939). *Frustration and aggression*. New Haven: Yale University Press. The original statement of the theory that frustration breeds aggression. As well as discussing their laboratory experiments, it ranges far into the larger social manifestations of aggression, such as criminality, war, and fascism.

FREUD, S. (1955). *Civilization and its discontents*. London: Hogarth Press, first published 1930. The classic exposition of how civilization must deal with aggressive instincts. One of Freud's most brilliant and influential critiques of society.

NATIONAL INSTITUTE OF MENTAL HEALTH. (1982). *Television and behavior: Ten years of scientific progress and implications for the eighties*. Rockville, Md. This is the follow-up report on the effects of television, following all the research done in the ten years since the Surgeon General's original report. It is a useful summary, though influenced by the authors' own perspectives.

SEARS, D. O., & McCONAHAY, J. B. (1973). *The politics of violence: The new urban blacks and the Watts riot*. Boston: Houghton-Mifflin. A social-psychological analysis of the causes of ghetto riots.

SURGEON GENERAL'S SCIENTIFIC ADVISORY COMMITTEE ON TELEVISION AND SOCIAL BEHAVIOR. (1972). *Television and growing up: The impact of televised violence* (Report to the Surgeon General, U.S. Public Health Service, U.S. Department of Health, Education, and Welfare, Publication NHSM 72-9090). Rockville, Md.: National Insitute of Mental Health. This was the report that created such furor.

11 PROSOCIAL BEHAVIOR

On January 21, 1984, 11-year-old Timothy Diakis ran to the burning apartment next door to rescue his 83-year-old neighbor. Awakened from sleep and clad only in his underwear, the young boy crawled on his hands and knees through the smoke-filled apartment to reach the bedroom where the woman he called "Grandma" was trapped. He pulled her to the floor where a few pockets of air remained, and then tried desperately to lead her to safety. As they made their way toward the exit, they faced flames creeping down the hallway. Overcome by smoke at last, Timothy and Sarah

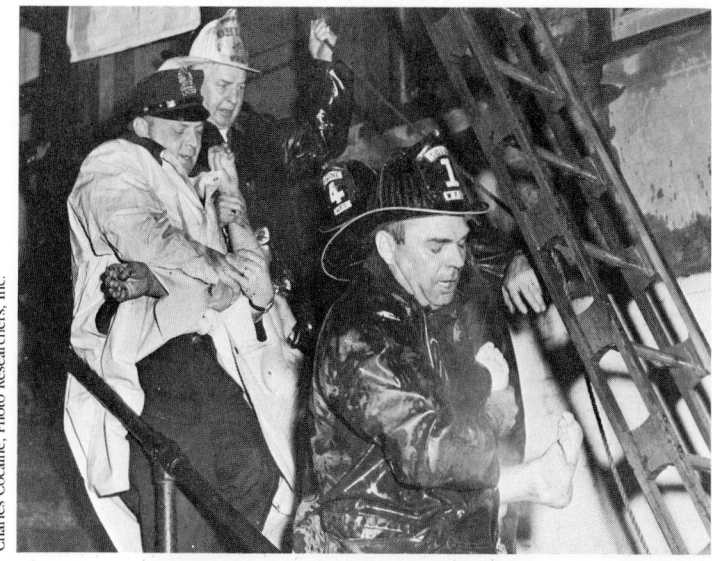

Charles Cocaine, Photo Researchers, Inc.

The bravery of firefighters risking their lives to save others contrasts vividly with scenes of people ignoring the plight of those in need of help.

Jan Lukas, Photo Researchers, Inc.

Sherman lapsed into unconsciousness just as fire engines arrived. Firefighters wearing protective masks and clothing ultimately rescued both and rushed them to a nearby hospital. Sarah suffered minor injuries, but Timothy spent months in the hospital undergoing skin grafts for severe burns. Firefighters say Sarah would have died had the youngster not rushed in and dragged her at least part way to safety. When newspaper accounts of the story reported that the family had no medical insurance, readers moved by the boy's altruism sent more than $50,000 in donations to help pay his expensive medical bills.

Acts of altruism and public generosity such as this stand in stark contrast to stories of public apathy to the plight of victims. In Chapter 1 we recounted the tragic story of Kitty Genovese, a young woman stabbed to death on a city street while at least 38 people watched and did nothing. There are countless stories of this sort. People are beaten, raped, robbed, and killed while those who could give assistance stand by. Clearly, humans are capable of helping or ignoring others in distress. Why do people sometimes help another? And why, sometimes, do they fail to give badly needed assistance?

BASIC DEFINITIONS

Before trying to answer these questions, we should be clear about the meaning of altruism and prosocial behavior. **Altruism** refers to an act performed voluntarily to help someone else when there is no expectation of receiving a reward in any form (except perhaps a feeling of having done a good deed). By this definition, whether or not an act is altruistic depends on the intentions of the helper. The stranger who risks his life to pull a victim from a burning car and then vanishes anonymously into the night has performed an altruistic act.

Prosocial behavior is a much broader category. It includes any act that helps or is designed to help others, regardless of the helper's motives. Many types of prosocial behavior are not altruistic. For example, if you give a hefty contribution to your boss's favorite charity in the hope of making a good impression and getting a raise, you are not acting altruistically in the pure sense. Prosocial behavior ranges over a continuum from the most selfless acts of altruism to helpful acts motivated entirely by self-interest (Rushton, 1980).

Our everyday experiences provide many examples of prosocial behavior. As infants, we all benefit from the help and nurturance of adult caretakers. Throughout the lifecycle, families and friends are important sources of help and support. Research has documented that people often help each other in a wide variety of ways. For example, helping activities can be seen even in young children. One

Friends and family help each other in many ways both small and large. Here a woman accompanies her elderly neighbor on a shopping trip and helps her to cross a busy intersection.

Stephen Capra

study observed children ages 3 to 5 at play in a university preschool (Strayer, Wareing, & Rushton, 1979). On average, each child engaged in 15 helpful acts per hour, ranging from giving a toy to another child to comforting an upset friend, or helping a teacher.

Prosocial behavior is affected by the type of relationship between people, as everyday experience clearly shows. Whether because of liking, social obligation, self-interest, or empathy, we are more helpful to intimates than to strangers (Schoenrade, et al., 1986).

One study (Bar-Tal et al., 1977) examined college students' expectations about receiving help from parents, siblings, close friends, acquaintances, or strangers. Results indicated that the closer the relationship, the stronger the expectation that help should be given, the less gratitude expressed when help is given, and the more resentment felt if help is refused.

Although we are most helpful to those we know and care about, people often also show a willingness to help total strangers. Research conducted in a midwestern American city found that over half of women shoppers were willing to give 40 cents for bus fare to a university student who explained that his wallet had "disappeared" (Berkowitz, 1972). In New York City, most pedestrians responded positively to requests for help by a passerby. Eighty-five percent of New Yorkers gave the time of day, 85 percent gave directions, and 73 percent gave change for a quarter (Latané & Darley, 1970). In another study on the streets of New York, 50 percent of people who found a wallet that had been "lost" mailed it back to its owner (Hornstein, Fisch, & Holmes, 1968). Prosocial behavior even occurs on city subways. When a passenger (actually a researcher) fell down with an apparent knee injury, 83 percent of those in the subway offered assistance (Latané & Darley, 1970). In another subway study, a researcher pretending to be physically disabled repeatedly fell down and always received help (Piliavin, Rodin, & Piliavin, 1969).

Social psychological research on prosocial behavior has focused on behaviors at the altruistic end of the helping continuum, where the immediate rewards for helping are minimal. More specifically, researchers have often examined **bystander intervention,** situations in which a person comes to the aid of a stranger in distress. In the next section, we review and analyze these studies.

BYSTANDER INTERVENTION: HELPING A STRANGER IN DISTRESS

On your way home one evening, your car breaks down by the side of the road. You open the hood and stand beside the car, hoping that someone will stop to offer assistance or a ride into town. What factors determine whether you get help and which of the possible passing motorists is most likely to stop? Social psychological studies have found that bystander intervention is affected by characteristics of the situation (is the evening pleasant or freezing cold?), characteristics of the potential helper (is the passing motorist late for an appointment?), and characteristics of the person in need (are you male or female?).

The Situation

Even the most dedicated altruist is less likely to offer aid in some situations than in others. Research has documented the importance of several situational factors, including the presence of other people, the nature of the physical environment, and the pressures of limited time.

THE PRESENCE OF OTHERS One of the shocking things about the Kitty Genovese murder is that so many people heard the young woman's screams and yet did not even call the police. Many social commentators interpreted this as a sign of widespread moral decay and alienation in society. Another hypothesis was offered by social psychologists Bibb Latané and John Darley (1970). They proposed that the very presence of so many onlookers may have been a reason for the lack of helping. Those who witnessed the murder may have assumed that others had already called the police, and so may have felt little personal responsibility to intervene.

To test this idea that the number of witnesses affects helping, Darley and Latané (1968) designed the laboratory study described in Chapter 2. College students who overheard an "emergency" were much more likely to respond if they were alone than if they thought others also knew about the situation. The more people present, the less likely it was that any one individual actually offered help, and the longer the average delay before help was given. Darley and Latané called this the **bystander effect.**

Many studies have replicated this finding in different settings (Latané & Nida, 1981). For example, Latané and Darley (1970) conducted a field study in the Nu-Way Beverage Center in Suffern, New York. The researchers staged a series of robberies. When the salesclerk went to the back of the store to check on something, two husky young men muttering, "They'll never miss this," walked off with a case of beer. The robberies were staged when either one or two customers were in the store. As expected, people who witnessed the crime alone were significantly more likely to report the theft to the clerk than people who were in the store with another customer.

Why does the presence of others sometimes inhibit helpfulness? A cost-benefit or decision-making analysis of prosocial behavior suggests several explanations. One is the *diffusion of responsibility* created by the presence of other people. If only one person witnesses a victim in distress, then he or she is totally responsible for responding to the situation and will bear all the guilt or blame for nonintervention. When others are present, help can come from several people. The responsibility for helping and the possible costs of failing to offer aid are shared. Further, if a person knows that others are present but cannot actually talk to them or see their behavior, as in the Kitty Genovese case,

the person may assume that others have already done something to help, such as calling the police. Experiments (Korte, 1971; Ross, 1971) have supported this idea—that it is not the number of people present that is crucial, but the lessened feelings of personal responsibility that can result from being in a group.

A second explanation for the bystander effect concerns *ambiguity* in the interpretation of the situation. Potential helpers are sometimes uncertain whether a particular situation is actually an emergency. The behavior of other bystanders can influence how we ourselves define a situation and react to it. If others ignore a situation or act as if nothing is happening, we too may assume that no emergency exists. The impact of bystanders on interpreting a situation was demonstrated by Latané and Darley (1970).

In this experiment, college men sat filling out a questionnaire. After a few minutes, smoke began to enter the room through a vent. Soon the smoke was so thick it was difficult to see and to breathe normally. When subjects were alone, they usually walked around the room to investigate the smoke, and 75 percent reported the smoke to the researcher within four minutes. In a condition where the real subject was in a room with two confederates who deliberately ignored the smoke, only 10 percent reported the smoke. This result is all the more dramatic because the smoke was very noticeable and unpleasant. Apparently the calmness of the other people led subjects to define the situation as not dangerous.

A third factor in the strength of the bystander effect is *evaluation apprehension*. If we know that other people are watching our behavior, we may try to do what we think others expect of us and to present ourselves in a favorable light (Baumeister, 1982). In some situations, such as the smoke-filled room, subjects may have feared they would look foolish or cowardly by showing concern about the smoke when others were apparently calm. The desire to avoid the cost of social disapproval inhibited action. In other situations, however, such as witnessing a person become seriously ill, we may assume that intervention is called for; here, the knowledge that others are aware of our actions may facilitate helping (Schwartz & Gottlieb, 1980).

ENVIRONMENTAL CONDITIONS   The physical setting also influences willingness to help. Think for a moment about whether you are more likely to stop to help a stranded motorist on a pleasant, sunny day or a cold, rainy one? On a dark street in a poor section of town, or in a well-lighted affluent area? On a country lane, or in a big city? Much research has documented the impact of environmental conditions such as weather, city size, and noise level on helping.

The effects of weather on helping were investigated in two field studies by Cunningham (1979). In one study, pedestrians were approached outdoors and asked to help the researcher by completing a questionnaire. People were significantly more likely to help when the day was sunny and when the temperature was comfortable (relatively warm in winter and relatively cool in summer). In a second study conducted in a climate-controlled restaurant, Cunningham found that customers left more generous tips when the sun was shining. Other research suggests that people are more likely to help a stranded motorist in sunny rather than rainy weather (Ahmed, 1979) and during the day rather

than at night (Skolnick, 1977). In short, weather does make a difference in helping, although psychologists are still debating the exact reasons for this effect.

A common stereotype is that city dwellers are unfriendly and unhelpful, whereas small-town people are cooperative and helpful. Several studies indicate that when it comes to helping strangers in distress, *city size* does make a difference (see House & Wolf, 1978; Korte, 1981). Amato (1983) investigated helping in 55 Australian communities ranging from small villages to major cities. To ensure a diverse sample of prosocial behaviors, five different types of helping were studied. These included a student asking pedestrians to write down their favorite color as part of a school project, a pedestrian inadvertently dropping an envelope on the sidewalk, a request to donate money to the Multiple Sclerosis Society, overhearing a salesclerk give obviously wrong directions to someone, and witnessing a man with a bandaged leg fall to the ground and cry out in pain.

The results of this study are presented in Figure 11–1. On four of the five helping measures, the

FIGURE 11–1   Percentage of people helping, by community size. (Adapted from Amato, 1983, p. 579.)

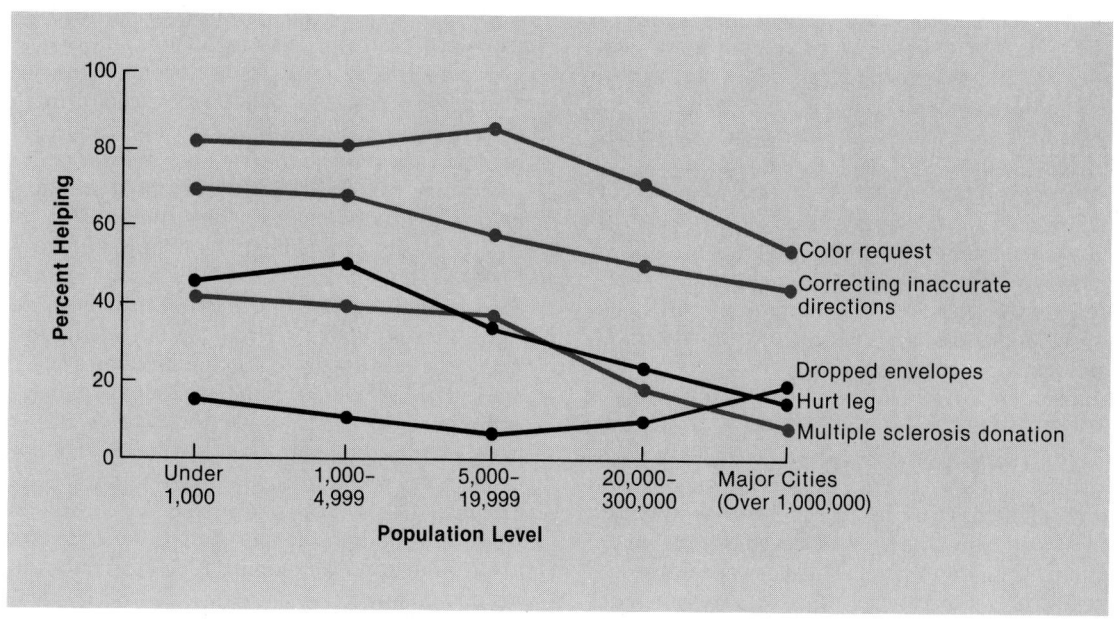

percentage of people who helped was significantly greater in small towns than in larger cities. The one exception to this pattern was the lost envelope. It generally brought little helping, and seemed to get more in the largest cities. What should also be kept in mind, of course, is that these studies dealt only with help offered to strangers: There is no reason to believe that city dwellers are any less helpful than small-town people when it comes to helping friends and relatives.

Many explanations for the lesser helpfulness of city dwellers have been offered. These include the anonymity of urban life, the sensory overload experienced by city dwellers who are constantly bombarded by other people, and possible feelings of helplessness from dealing with unresponsive urban bureaucracies and governments. We don't yet know which explanation is most important.

Another environmental factor that can affect prosocial behavior is noise. Starting with the general idea that noise can reduce people's responsiveness to all events in the environment, several researchers have investigated whether noisy conditions reduce the likelihood of helping a stranger in distress (see Sherrod & Downs, 1974). In one lab study (Mathews & Canon, 1975), for example, it was found that noise decreased the likelihood that students would help a person who had dropped some papers on the floor. When only regular room noise was present, 72 percent of subjects helped, compared to only 37 percent when very loud noise was present. In a field study, the same investigators arranged to have a man wearing a cast on his arm drop some of the books he was carrying from his car. When only typical street noises were present, 80 percent of passersby helped; when a noisy lawn mower was going, only 15 percent helped. The researchers suggested that loud noise causes people to ignore others in their environment and motivates them to leave the situation quickly, thus creating less helpful bystanders.

TIME PRESSURES   Imagine that you're walking across campus when a student stops you to ask for help with a fund drive for needy children. Are you more likely to help if you're out for a stroll or if you're late for a midterm exam? Both common sense and research evidence suggest that we are sometimes in too much of a hurry to help.

A clear demonstration of this effect comes from an experiment by Darley and Batson (1973). As part of this study, individual students were asked to walk to another building where they were to give a short talk. Some were told to take their time, that the talk wouldn't begin for several minutes. Others were told to hurry because they were already late and the researcher was waiting. As the subject went from building to building, he encountered a shabbily dressed man slumped in a doorway, coughing and groaning. The question of interest was whether or not the subject would offer assistance.

A further twist to the study was that all participants were theological students. For some, the assigned topic for their talk was the Bible story of the Good Samaritan, about a person who came to the aid of a man who lay injured on the roadside, the victim of robbers. Other students were to talk about a topic not relevant to helping—the sorts of jobs seminary students might pursue after graduation. The results of the study showed that time pressure had a strong impact on helping. In a post-experiment interview all students recalled seeing the victim. But only 10 percent of those in a hurry helped, compared to 63 percent of those who were not in a hurry.

Perhaps surprisingly, the speech topic made no difference. Students about to talk on the Good Samaritan were no more likely to offer assistance than those preparing to talk on jobs. The researchers suggested that time pressure caused some students to overlook the needs of the victim. Another factor may have been a conflict about whom to help—the experimenter or the victim.

The possibility that conflict rather than callousness was at work is supported by a second study (Batson et al., 1978) using a somewhat similar design. When students arrived for this study, they were sent individually to another building to interact with a computer. Some were told to hurry, and others were not. In addition, some were led to believe that their participation was of vital importance to the researcher, whereas others were told that their data were not essential. As the student went from building to building, he encountered a male undergraduate slumped on the stairs, coughing and groaning.

Would the subject help this victim? Results (see

TABLE 11–1

Percentage of Subjects Who Offered to Help

Time Pressure	IMPORTANCE TO THE EXPERIMENTER		
	Low	High	Average
Low	80%	50%	65%
High	70	10	40
Average	75%	30%	52.5%

Source: Adapted from Batson et al. (1978), p. 99.

Table 11–1) showed that students in a hurry were less likely to help (40 percent) than those with no time pressures (65 percent), but that this was primarily true for subjects who thought their research participation was essential. When subjects thought the researcher was not counting on them, those in a hurry were just about as likely to help (70 percent) as those not in a hurry (80 percent). These results are consistent with the cost-benefit model discussed earlier. Apparently subjects weighed the costs and benefits to both experimenter and victim before arriving at a final course of action.

The Helper

Situational factors can greatly increase or decrease the likelihood that people will act in a prosocial way. What these studies also show, however, is that some people offer aid even when situational forces discourage helping, and others fail to help even under the most favorable conditions. Individual differences do exist. In an effort to understand why some people help more than others, researchers have investigated both relatively enduring personality characteristics and more fleeting moods and psychological states.

PERSONALITY FACTORS Efforts to identify a single personality profile of the "helpful person" have not been very successful. Rather, it appears that specific personality traits dispose people to help in some types of situations, but not in others (Romer, Gruder, & Lizzadro, 1986). For instance, Satow (1975) found that people with a high need for approval were more likely to donate money to a charity than those low in need for social approval, but *only* when others were watching them. Presumably, people high in need for approval were motivated by a desire to win praise from others

Mother Theresa has devoted her life to helping the homeless children of India. She was awarded the Nobel Peace Prize for her humanitarian works.

Calogero Cascio, Photo Researchers, Inc.

and so acted more prosocially only when their good deeds would be noticed (Deutsch & Lamberti, 1986).

In another study, people high in the need to be nurturant were most likely to volunteer to give advice about personal problems to a same-sex high school student (Gergen, Gergen, & Meter, 1972). But nurturance was not related to willingness to counsel someone of the other sex, or to volunteer to help in a research project, or to assist in preparing course materials. In other words, the link between personality and helping depends on the specific trait in question and on the specific type of assistance needed.

Further insights about the people most likely to help come from studies of people who have

BOX 11–1

GOOD SAMARITANS IN ACTION

As the young man drove by a dance hall, he noticed a man assaulting a young woman. This is how he described it:

> I went over there and I grabbed the dude and I shoved him over and I said lay off the chick. So me and him started going at it. I told him to get out of here, man, look at her, man, the girl's mouth's all bleeding, she got her teeth knocked out, she got a handful of hair pulled out. Everybody was just standing around. (Quoted in Huston, Ruggiero, Conner, & Geis, 1981, p. 17)

Before the police arrived, the men exchanged more blows, one of which broke the intervener's jaw. What motivates this man and other "Good Samaritans" to endanger their own welfare to help a stranger?

Huston, Ruggiero, Conner, and Geis (1981) conducted in-depth interviews with 32 people who had intervened in dangerous crime episodes, such as bank holdups, armed robberies, and street muggings. The responses of these Good Samaritans were compared with a group of noninterveners matched for age, sex, education, and ethnic background. Given the dangerous situations involved, it is perhaps not surprising that the Good Samaritans were significantly taller, heavier, and better trained to cope with emergencies than the noninterveners. All but one of the interveners were men, the exception being an older woman who rescued her 83-year-old neighbor from a knife-wielding attacker. The Good Samaritans were more likely than the noninterveners to describe themselves as strong, aggressive, and principled. And they had more life-saving, medical, and police training.

The results suggested that the interveners were not primarily motivated by humanitarian concern for the victim, but rather acted from a sense of their own ability and responsibility, based on their training and physical strength. The personal qualities that lead someone to stop a crime or mugging may be quite different from those that lead someone to donate money to charity or to help a stranger who collapses from a heart attack. Whether a potential helper intervenes depends on the match between the person's competence, values, and motives, and the requirements of the particular situation.

helped in extreme real-life situations. In one study, London (1970) interviewed Christians who lived in Europe during World War II and had risked their lives, often repeatedly, to save Jews from Nazi death camps. All these rescuers had a very strong personal sense of morality, and a close identification with a parent who served as a model of moral conduct. One man recalled his mother teaching him that "regardless of what you do with your life, be honest. When it comes the day you have to make a decision, make the right one" (p. 247). Another characteristic of these people was a sense of adventurousness, a willingness to take risks. Finally, many of the rescuers had also felt somewhat apart from others in their community because of their background or values.

MOOD   There is considerable evidence that people are more willing to help when they are in a good mood. For example, people are more likely to help if they have found a dime in a phone booth (Isen & Simmonds, 1978), been given a free cookie at the college library (Isen & Levin, 1972), succeeded on some experimental tasks (Isen, 1970), or listened to soothing music (Fried & Berkowitz, 1979) than if these mood-enhancing events have not occurred. Apparently a warm glow of positive feeling increases the willingness to act prosocially.

There are important limitations to the "feel good" effect, however. First, the effects of positive moods can be quite short-lived—only 20 minutes in one study (Isen, Clark, & Schwartz, 1976). Second, a good mood may actually decrease helpfulness when giving assistance would detract from the person's good mood (Isen & Simmonds, 1978). People in a good mood apparently want to maintain their positive feelings.

The effects of bad moods such as sadness or depression are more complicated, and research results have not been entirely consistent (Cialdini, Baumann, & Kenrick, 1981). If a bad mood causes us to focus on ourself and our own needs, it may lessen the likelihood of our helping someone else (Thompson, Cowan, & Rosenhan, 1980). On the other hand, if we think helping someone else might make us feel better and so relieve our bad mood, we may actually be more likely to offer assistance (Cialdini, et al., 1987). A further complication is that the link between feeling bad and helping others

is clearer in adults than in children (Cialdini et al., 1981). One reason for this may be that children have to learn, as part of growing up, that helping others is a gratifying act that can improve their own feelings.

ALTRUISTIC VERSUS SELF-SERVING MOTIVES   We noted earlier that true altruism is defined by the person's intentions; we act altruistically only when we help with no expectation of receiving a personal benefit. This reasoning has led researchers to study the *motives* that lead people to help, and to contrast helping based on personal distress versus empathic concern.

To understand this distinction, picture for a moment the sight of people in serious distress: the mangled bodies of victims in a train crash, a starving child in ragged clothes, an anguished father whose child has disappeared. Witnessing people in need often evokes powerful emotions.

Personal distress refers to our own personal reactions to the suffering of others—our feelings of shock, horror, alarm, concern, sadness, helplessness, or whatever. In contrast, **empathic concern** refers to feelings of sympathy and caring for others, in particular to sharing vicariously or indirectly in the suffering of others. The key difference is that personal distress focuses on the self, whereas empathic concern focuses on the victim.

Personal distress motivates us to reduce our own discomfort. We might do this by helping a person in need, but we can also do it by escaping from the situation or ignoring the suffering around us. In contrast, empathic concern can be reduced only by actually helping the person in need. Since the goal of empathic concern is enhancing the welfare of someone else, it would clearly be an altruistic motive for helping. In contrast, helping motivated by a desire to reduce our own personal distress is not truly altruistic.

Several studies have shown that empathy increases prosocial behavior (Hoffman, 1981). For example, in one study (Toi & Batson, 1982), college students learned of the plight of Carol, another student who had broken both legs in a car accident and was seriously behind in her school work. After listening to a tape-recorded interview with Carol, each subject was asked if she would be willing to help Carol. Empathy was manipulated by varying the listening instructions given to subjects. In a high-empathy condition, subjects were told: "Try to take the perspective of the person who is being interviewed, imagining how she feels about what has happened and how it has affected her life." In a low-empathy condition, subjects were told: "Try to be as objective as possible, carefully attending to all the information presented. . . . Try not to concern yourself with how the person being interviewed feels about what happened."

As expected, subjects in the high-empathy condition experienced significantly greater empathy, as reflected in self-ratings of feeling sympathetic, compassionate, and "moved" by Carol's story. Also as predicted, subjects in the high-empathy condition were significantly more likely to volunteer to help Carol than those in the low-empathy condition, even when it would have been easy to avoid helping (71 vs. 33 percent offered to help). Taking the perspective of someone in distress and sharing his or her suffering can be important factors in prosocial behavior.

A controversy currently exists, however, about how to interpret studies showing this empathy-helping link (Fultz, et al. 1986). One view is that instructions emphasizing empathy increase an altruistic motivation to help. In contrast, it has been suggested that when experimenters give instructions designed to enhance empathy, they may actually increase not only the subject's concern for the victim, but also increase the subject's own personal feeling of sadness or distress (Cialdini, et al, 1987). According to the second interpretation, helping based on empathy would not be entirely altruistic.

The Person in Need

As you near the Student Union, someone approaches you and asks to borrow a quarter to make a phone call. Are you more likely to help if the person is a clean-cut preppie type or a punk rocker? Would it matter if the person explained that his or her wallet had been stolen or that he or she had forgotten to bring any change to school? Although the true altruist may be blind to everything but the needs of a person in distress, everyday prosocial behavior is often influenced by characteristics of the person in need.

For example, people on a college campus were more likely to give money to the March of Dimes if they were asked for a donation by a paraplegic woman in a wheelchair than if asked by a nonhandicapped woman (Slochower et al., 1980). In another study (Piliavin, Piliavin, & Rodin, 1975), subway riders in New York City saw a man carrying a cane stumble and fall to the floor. Sometimes the victim had a large red birthmark on his face; sometimes he did not. In this situation, the victim was more likely to receive aid if his face was unblemished (86 percent) than if he had an unattractive birthmark (61 percent). In understanding these and other research findings, two themes seem most important: We are more likely to help people we like and people we think deserve assistance.

HELPING THOSE WE LIKE   In Chapter 8 we saw that our initial liking for another person is affected by such factors as physical attractiveness and similarity. Research on prosocial behavior finds that the same characteristics also influence helping. In at least some situations, those who are physically attractive are more likely to receive aid. For example, in a field study (Benson, Karabenick, & Lerner, 1976), researchers placed a completed application to graduate school in a telephone booth at the airport. The application was stamped and ready to be mailed, but had apparently been "lost." To manipulate appearance, the photo attached to the application was sometimes of a very good-looking person and sometimes of a less attractive person. The measure of helping was whether the individual who found the envelope actually mailed it or not. Results showed that people were much more likely to send in the application if the person in the photo, whether male or female, was attractive.

The degree of similarity between the potential helper and the person in need is also important. Some years ago, researchers (Emswiller, Deaux, & Willits, 1971) had confederates dressed as a "hippie" or as a "straight" person approach students and ask to borrow a dime. The researchers also used appearance to categorize the potential helpers as "hippie" or "straight." Results clearly showed that people were most likely to help those similar to themselves. For example, hippie men helped a fellow hippie about 77 percent of the time, but helped a straight person only about 32 percent of the time. There is also evidence that helpfulness is greater toward someone who is from the same country rather than a foreigner (Feldman, 1968), and toward someone with similar attitudes (Tucker et al., 1977).

HELPING THOSE WHO DESERVE HELP   Whether a person receives help depends in part on the "merits" of the case. For example, people in a supermarket were more likely to give someone money so they could buy milk rather than cookie dough (Bickman & Kamzan, 1973), presumably because milk is more essential for health than cookies. Passengers on a New York subway were more likely to help a man who fell to the ground if he appeared to be sick rather than drunk (Piliavin, Rodin, & Piliavin, 1969). In both cases, the legitimacy or appropriateness of the request or problem made a difference. Of course, judgments about the importance of a particular need may be strongly influenced by values.

In addition to evaluating the deservingness of the need itself, potential helpers may also make inferences about the causes of the person's need, following the principles of causal attribution outlined in Chapter 5. A teacher might, for example, spend more time helping a student who missed classes because of a death in the family rather than because of a trip to the Caribbean. Several studies indicate that the key causal factor is *personal con-*

trol: We are more likely to help someone if we believe the cause of the problem was outside the person's control. For instance, in one study (Meyer & Mulherin, 1980), college students said they would be more willing to lend rent money to an acquaintance if the need arose due to illness (an uncontrollable cause) rather than laziness (a controllable cause).

In another study (Weiner, 1980), students said they would be more likely to lend their lecture notes to a classmate who needed them because of something uncontrollable, such as the professor's being a poor lecturer, rather than something controllable, such as the classmate's not trying to take good notes. If a person could have prevented the predicament by his or her own actions, we are less likely to help. Attributions may also influence how we feel about a person in need. We may feel sympathy and concern for those who suffer through no fault of their own; we may feel anger and disgust toward those who are responsible for their own problems (Meyer & Mulherin, 1980; Weiner, 1980).

Our focus up to now has been on factors that affect one type of prosocial behavior, specifically our willingness to help a stranger in distress. In the next section, we broaden our perspective by considering three theoretical approaches to understanding prosocial behavior.

THEORETICAL PERSPECTIVES ON HELPING

Our understanding of prosocial behavior has benefitted from three broad theoretical perspectives. Some theorists have emphasized the historical roots of helping. Sociobiologists, for example, propose that a predisposition to help has become part of our genetic, evolutionary heritage. A contrasting historical view is that rules about helping others in need have developed as part of the history of human civilization. A second approach proposes that helping is learned, following basic principles of reinforcement and modeling. The third perspec-

tive, decision-making, focuses on the processes that influence our judgments about when help is needed. It also emphasizes the weighing of costs and benefits in the decision to give help.

Historical Roots

Prosocial behavior is not an invention of the twentieth century. Two contrasting analyses of historical forces that may have encouraged altruism are offered by sociobiology and social evolution.

SOCIOBIOLOGY Scientists have long observed pro-social behavior among animal species. Charles Darwin (1871) noted that rabbits will make noise with their hind feet to warn other rabbits of predators. In termite hives, the soldier termites will defend a nest against an intruder by putting themselves in front of the other termites and exposing themselves to danger (Wilson, 1971). Many soldiers die so that others may live and the nest survive. Some varieties of baboon have a characteristic pattern of responding to threats (Hall, 1960). The dominant males take the most exposed positions, and may even rush at an intruder. As the tribe moves away from the threat, the males risk their own safety by remaining to protect the rest of the group.

Dolphins show a fascinating pattern of rescuing injured peers. Since dolphins are mammals, they must breathe air to survive. If an injured animal sinks below the surface, it will die. Several observers have reported that dolphins will aid an injured companion. In one case (Siebenaler & Caldwell, 1956), a dolphin was stunned by an explosion in the water. Two other adults came to its aid by holding the animal afloat until it recovered and was able to care for itself.

Humans are not the only animals that help each other. Here, one monkey is grooming another, perhaps because it expects to be groomed in return.

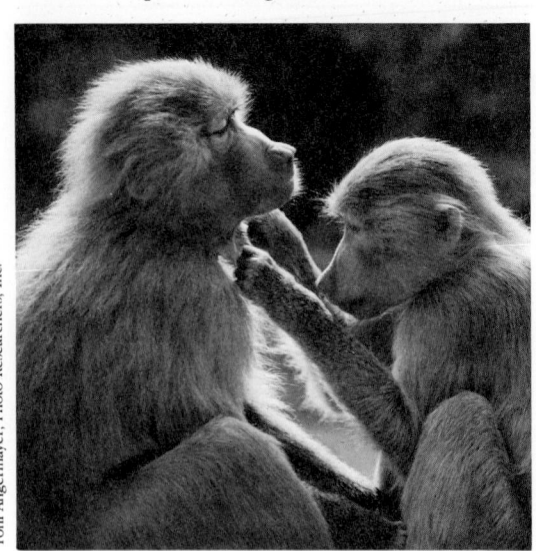

Among many animals, parents will sacrifice themselves when their young are threatened. An impressive example is the female nighthawk, which responds to a potential attack on her young by flying from the nest as if she had a broken wing, fluttering around at a low level, and finally landing on the ground right in front of the intruder but away from the nest (Armstrong, 1965; Gramza, 1967).

This portrait of animals helping and sacrificing for each other runs counter to the dog-eat-dog, survival of the fittest image that some people have of the animal kingdom. Indeed, the existence of altruism has posed a problem for evolutionary theorists: if the most helpful members of an animal species sacrifice themselves for others, they will be less likely to survive and pass along their genes to the next generation by having offspring. How then does a biological predisposition to act altruistically persist among animals or humans (Hoffman, 1981)?

Sociobiology, a theoretical perspective introduced in Chapter 1, has tried to resolve this paradox (Krebs & Miller, 1985; Wilson, 1975). Remember that according to sociobiology, any genetically determined trait that has a high survival value (that helps the individual survive) will tend to be passed on. In the case of altruism, the tendency to help others may have high survival value for the individual's genes, but not necessarily for the individual. Imagine a bird that has fathered six chicks. Half of the genes in each chick come from the father. Together, the six chicks have three times as many of the father's genes as he does himself. If the father sacrifices himself to save the chicks, his particular gene pool is still ahead of the game. Similar analyses can be done for other relatives who have varying percentages of the individual's genes. From the sociobiological viewpoint, helping close relatives contributes to the survival of an individual's genes in future generations, and hence can be understood by the basic principles of evolutionary biology.

Sociobiologist Robert Trivers (1971) has argued that only mutual or *reciprocal altruism* is biologically based. In his view, the potential costs of altruism to the individual are offset by the possibility of receiving help from others. But such a system of mutual help giving is threatened by potential "cheaters" who accept help but offer none in return. To minimize cheating, natural selection may have favored a disposition to feel guilt and a tendency to enforce mutual helping through social means such as punishing those who do not follow group rules.

One good feature of the sociobiological approach is that it leads to testable predictions. For example, animals should be most altruistic to those who are genetically most closely linked to themselves. They should be more helpful to immediate family than to distant relatives or strangers. The theory also predicts that parents will behave more altruistically to healthy offspring than to unhealthy ones who are less likely to survive. A further prediction is that mothers will usually be more altruistic to their offspring than will fathers. The reasoning here is that males have the biological potential to sire a great many offspring and so can perpetuate their genes without investing much in any one infant. Females can produce only a relatively small number of offspring, and so must help each of these young to thrive to ensure the survival of the mother's genes.

The idea that altruism is a genetically determined part of "human nature" is quite controversial. To date, research has largely been conducted with animals other than humans. Just how well the theory applies to people is still an open question (see Rushton, et al., 1986). What this perspective suggests, however, is that self-preservation may not be the overwhelming motive that we sometimes think. Biological dispositions to aggression may coexist with biological dispositions to altruism.

SOCIAL EVOLUTION   Critics of sociobiology argue that social factors are much more important than biology in determining prosocial behavior. Donald Campbell (1975) suggests that genetic evolution may help explain a few basic prosocial behaviors such as parents' caring for their young, but that it does not apply to more extreme instances of helping a stranger in distress. Such cases are better explained by what Campbell calls *social evolution*—the historical development of human culture or civilization. In this view, human societies have gradually and selectively evolved skills, beliefs, and technologies that promote the welfare of the group. Because prosocial behavior is generally beneficial to society, it has become part of the social rules or norms. Three norms in particular may be most important for prosocial behavior: social responsibility, reciprocity, and social justice.

A **norm of social responsibility** prescribes that we should help others who depend on us. Parents are expected to care for their children, and social agencies may intervene if parents fail to live up to this obligation. Teachers are supposed to help their students, coaches to look after team members, and co-workers to assist each other. The religious and moral codes of many societies emphasize the duty to help others. Sometimes this obligation is even written into the law.

The state of Minnesota recently enacted a statute requiring that "Any person at the scene of an emergency who knows that another person is exposed to or has suffered grave physical harm shall, to the extent that he can do so without danger or peril to himself or others, give reasonable assistance to the exposed person." Laws are one way of emphasizing to people that they have a responsibility to help. Later in this chapter we will review studies documenting the fact that an increased sense of personal responsibility does indeed increase the likelihood of an individual's giving assistance.

The **norm of reciprocity** says that we should help those who help us. Several studies (Berkowitz, 1968; Wilke & Lanzetta, 1970) have shown that people are more likely to help someone from whom they have already received aid. A study by Regan (1968) illustrated this idea that favors are reciprocated. College students were tested in pairs, one partner actually being a confederate of the experimenter. The study was described as dealing with perceptual and esthetic judgment. The subjects were put in separate rooms, shown a series of pictures, and asked to rate how much they liked each picture. After they had rated one series of pictures, there was a short break. The subjects were told they could do what they wanted as long as they did not talk about the experiment.

At this point, the confederate got up, left the building, and returned several minutes later carrying two bottles of Coke. He handed one to the subject, saying "I asked him [the experimenter] if I could get myself a Coke and he said it was okay, so I brought one for you, too." The subject took the Coke, and the experimenter gave them a second series of pictures to rate. In another condition, the experimenter went out, returned with two Cokes, and handed one to the confederate and one to the subject, saying: "I brought you guys a Coke." In the third condition, no Coke was given to the subject.

After the second series of pictures was rated, there was another short break, during which the confederate asked the experimenter (loud enough for the subject to hear) whether he could send a note to the subject. The experimenter said that he could as long as it did not concern the experiment. The confederate then wrote the following note:

> Would you do me a favor? I'm selling raffle tickets for my high school back home to build a new gym. The tickets cost 25 cents each and the prize is a new Corvette. The thing is, if I sell the most tickets I get 50 bucks and I could use it. If you'd buy any, would you just write the number on this note and give it back to me right away so I can make out the tickets? Any would help, the more the better. Thanks. (Regan, 1968, p. 19)

The measure of helping was how many tickets the subject agreed to buy. The results are shown in Table 11–2. When the confederate gave the subject a Coke and then asked him to do a favor, there was considerably more helping than when the experimenter gave the subject a Coke or when no Coke was given. Helping in the latter two conditions did not differ appreciably.

The reciprocity norm seems to be quite strong and has been shown to operate in many cultures (Gergen et al., 1975). The strength of feelings of obligation is influenced by factors in the situation. For example, Greenberg and Frisch (1972) found that a larger favor was reciprocated more often

TABLE 11–2

Effect of Doing a Favor on Helping

Condition	Mean Number of Tickets Bought
Confederate gave a Coke	1.73
Experimenter gave a Coke	1.08
No Coke	.92

Source: Adapted from Regan (1968).

than a smaller one. People's attributions about the motives of the helper also matter. Returning a favor is more likely when the original help was perceived to be given intentionally and voluntarily. Goranson and Berkowitz (1966) found that subjects who had been helped by someone tended to repay that specific person, but were not especially likely to offer aid to someone else.

Human groups also develop **norms of social justice,** rules about fairness and the just distribution of resources. One common fairness principle is equity. According to this principle, two people who make equal contributions to a task should receive equal rewards. If one receives more than the other, the people will feel pressure to try to restore equity by redistributing the rewards. The short-changed person obviously feels aggrieved. The more interesting fact is that even the person who receives more than a fair share may give some to the person who got too little. And a third person, observing the unfair situation, might be tempted to give to the one who suffered. Everyday acts of "helping the less fortunate" such as donating to a charity seem to be motivated by a desire to create a more equitable situation.

Numerous studies have demonstrated that over-benefitted people will act to restore equity when they can (Walster, Walster, & Berscheid, 1978). In several experiments (Berscheid & Walster, 1967), subjects played a game in which one person, through no fault of her own, lost a lot of money or trading stamps while the partner won a good deal. At the end of the game, the winner (the real subject) was given an opportunity to give some of the money to the partner who lost. There was a strong tendency to give some of the winnings to the loser, even though they had been won legitimately. In contrast, in a condition where both partners had equal winnings, there was little tendency for the subject to give any winnings to the other player.

In another study (Schmitt & Marwell, 1972), one member of a team, given more than his partner, tended to give some of the money to the partner in order to make their rewards more equitable. In addition, the overrewarded partner often chose to play a different game when assured that this would result in a more equal division of the rewards. In other words, not only did he give away some of his own money to produce a more equitable division, but he also changed the situation to avoid producing more inequity.

These three norms—social responsibility, reciprocity, and social justice—are common in human societies. They provide a cultural basis for prosocial behavior. Through the process of socialization, individuals learn these rules and come to behave in accord with these guidelines for prosocial behavior.

Learning to Help

A second perspective on prosocial behavior emphasizes the importance of learning. In growing up, children learn their society's norms about helping. At home, at school, and in the community, adults teach children that they should help other people. You can probably remember times when you were praised for being helpful, or chided for forgetting

When dad helps his son get dressed, he offers a model of helpfulness that the child may learn to copy. Modeling is one major way that children acquire prosocial behavior.

Alice Kandell, Photo Researchers, Inc.

to help when you should have. Two general learning principles discussed in earlier chapters are again important here. People learn to help through *reinforcement*, the effects of rewards and punishment for helping, and *modeling*, observing others who help.

Studies show clearly that children will help and share more when they are rewarded for their prosocial behavior. For example, 4-year-olds were more likely to share marbles with another child when they were rewarded with bubblegum for their generosity (Fischer, 1963). A study of sixth-grade girls (Midlarsky, Bryan, & Brickman, 1973) showed the impact of seeing a helpful model. Girls played a special pinball machine to win chips that could be exchanged for candy and toys. Before her own turn came, each girl watched an adult model play the game.

In one condition, a selfish model put all the chips she won into a jar labeled "my money." In another condition, a charitable model put some of her chips into a jar labeled "money for poor children." Regardless of condition, the model then urged the girl to think about the poor children who would "love to receive the prizes these chips can buy." Results showed a clear effect of modeling. Girls who had seen a charitable model donated an average of 19 tokens to the poor, compared to only 10 tokens given by girls who saw the selfish model.

Another study (Rushton & Teachman, 1978) combined both modeling and reinforcement. First, a helpful adult model was used to get boys to behave altruistically by giving some of the tokens they won at bowling to an orphan named Bobby. Then the model rewarded the child for his generosity ("Good for you." "That's really nice of you.") or punished him ("That's kind of silly for you to give to Bobby."). There was also a no-reinforcement condition in which the adult said nothing. As Figure 11–2 shows, children who were rewarded gave more to Bobby on later trials than did children who were punished. Two weeks later, when children again played the same game and were reminded about Bobby, the effects of the earlier reward or punishment still influenced how much they gave to Bobby.

Modeling is also a strong promoter of prosocial behavior in adults, as a study of adult blood donors clearly showed. In this clever experiment (Rushton

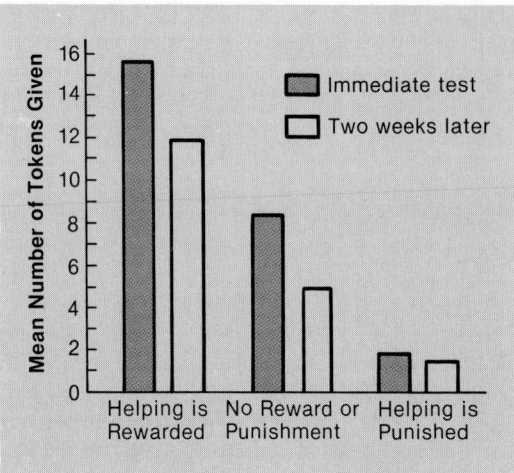

FIGURE 11–2 Effects of reward and punishment on giving tokens to an orphan. (Based on Rushton & Teachman, 1978, p. 324.)

& Campbell, 1977), female college students first talked to a friendly woman (actually a confederate of the researchers) as part of a study of social interaction. The researchers arranged things so that as the two women left the interaction study, they passed a table set up in the corridor, staffed by people asking for blood donations. Half the time, the confederate immediately volunteered, modeling prosocial behavior. In another condition, the confederate stepped aside to talk to someone else.

The effects of the model's behavior were striking. A helpful model led 67 percent of subjects to pledge to donate blood, compared to only 25 percent of subjects who saw no model. More impressive were data on whether the women actually followed through on their pledges to give blood. None of the women in the no-model condition actually gave blood, but 33 percent of those who saw the altruistic model did. Similar evidence of modeling effects has been found in a variety of situations, such as donating money to a Salvation Army kettle at Christmas or helping a stranded motorist fix a flat tire (Bryan & Test, 1967).

Experiments have also shown that adult helping is influenced by reinforcement. In one study (Moss & Page, 1972), individuals walking along the main street in Dayton, Ohio, were approached by an attractive woman who asked how to get to a local department store. After getting instructions, she either rewarded the helper (by saying, "Thank you

very much, I really appreciate this") or punished the helper ("I can't understand what you're saying, never mind, I'll ask someone else"). When the naive subject continued walking down the street, he or she encountered another woman who accidentally dropped a small bag and continued walking as if she didn't know she had lost it. The question of interest was whether the subject would help the woman by returning the bag to her. In the reward condition, 90 percent of people helped; in the punishment condition, only 40 percent helped.

Taken together, these and other studies provide convincing evidence of the power of reinforcement and modeling to shape prosocial behavior. Over time, people learn norms about who they should help when, and develop habits of helping. The childhood origins of prosocial behavior depend largely on external rewards and social approval. For adults, helping can become an internalized value, not dependent on external supports. It can be enough to know that you've lived up to your own standards and to feel the warm glow of having done a good deed.

Deciding to Help

So far, we have discussed general ways in which biological dispositions, social norms, and previous learning experiences can influence helping. But even the most motivated altruist does not offer aid all the time. In any particular situation, the decision to help involves complex processes of social cognition and rational decision-making (see Latané & Darley, 1970; Schwartz, 1977). A person must first notice that something is happening and decide whether or not help is required. If help is needed, the person may consider the extent of his or her own personal responsibility to act. Third, the person may evaluate the rewards and costs of helping or not helping. Finally, the person must decide what type of help is needed, and just how to provide it.

PERCEIVING A NEED It's 2 A.M. and a piercing shriek fills the night air. Some people sleep on, oblivious to all but their private dreams. You wake up with a start. A woman shouts, "Stop it! Leave me alone!" You hear an angry male voice, but you can't quite make out what he's saying. Quickly you ask yourself what is going on—is it merely a noisy lovers' quar-

BOX 11–2

LASSIE TO THE RESCUE

Can children's television shows influence prosocial behavior? Research suggests that they can. In one study, 3- to 5-year old children were exposed to one of three television diets for a four-week period (Stein & Friedrich, 1972). In an aggressive condition, children watched Batman and Superman cartoons. In a prosocial condition, they watched episodes from "Mister Roger's Neighborhood." In a neutral condition, they watched scenes such as children working on a farm. At the end of the testing, children who had seen prosocial programs showed an increase in helping relative to children in the other two conditions. A problem with this study, however, was that the programs varied in many ways, such as format, interest level, and educational goals.

To correct these problems, another study (Sprafkin, Liebert, & Poulos, 1975) exposed children to different episodes from the popular children's TV show "Lassie." Half the first-graders in the study watched an episode that focused on Lassie's efforts to keep her puppy from being given away. At the story's climax, the puppy falls into a mining shaft. Unable to rescue the puppy herself, Lassie brings her owner Jeff and his grandfather to the scene. Jeff risks his life by hanging over the edge of the shaft to save the puppy. In the neutral condition, children watched an episode of Lassie that dramatized Jeff's attempt to avoid taking violin lessons. It contained no examples of humans helping a dog, although Lassie was obviously featured in a positive light.

Children watched the TV program individually, and were then given an opportunity to help some puppies, but only at the cost of foregoing personal benefits. A female researcher took the child to another room and showed the child how to play a game to earn points. The more points scored, the better the prize the child would receive. The woman also explained that she had to leave the room briefly, and asked the child to do something for her while she was gone. She said that she was using earphones to listen to some dogs who were in a nearby kennel to make sure they were safe. The child was asked to wear the earphones while playing the game.

If the child heard barking, he or she could help the puppies by pressing a button marked "Help." The researcher left the room and shortly turned on a tape recording in which the dogs began to bark frantically. Would the children give up playing their point game in order to help the dogs? During the 3-minute testing period, most children pressed the Help button at least briefly. But children who had watched the prosocial TV show were significantly more helpful: They helped for 93 seconds compared to 52 seconds for children who had watched the neutral show. This and other studies (Ahammer & Murray, 1979) show that watching helpful models on TV can indeed increase children's prosocial behavior.

rel, or a serious physical attack? Is this an emergency requiring outside intervention?

The crucial first step in any prosocial act is noticing that something is happening and deciding help is required. In some situations, the need is clear: Flood waters are rising in the river in your town and all able-bodied people are needed to fill sandbags to hold back the water; your child has gashed her head playing soccer and needs medical attention. But in many situations, such as hearing screams in the night, it can be difficult to decide. Uncertainty about a situation is a major reason why people sometimes fail to offer assistance (see Clark & Word, 1974; Solomon, Solomon, & Stone, 1978). For example, one study (Clark & Word, 1972) found that when students heard an unmistakable emergency— a maintenance man falling off a ladder and crying out in agony—all of them went to the man's aid. In another condition, where students heard an ambiguous emergency—the sounds of an identical fall but without verbal cues that the victim was injured—help was offered only about 30 percent of the time.

What cues do people use in deciding whether there is an emergency requiring intervention? Research by Shotland and Huston (1979) identified five important characteristics which lead to the perception that an event is an emergency:

1. Something happens suddenly and unexpectedly.
2. There is a clear threat of harm to a victim.
3. The harm to the victim is likely to increase over time unless someone intervenes.
4. The victim is helpless and needs outside assistance.
5. Some sort of effective intervention is possible.

For example, most people considered a drug overdose, a heart attack, a rape in progress, and a car accident with the driver motionless on the ground to be emergencies. People were less certain about whether an emergency existed if there was a power blackout, if a friend said he was miserable and depressed, or if there was a disabled car on the side of a road.

Our interpretation or definition of a situation is a vital factor in whether or not we offer aid. Shotland and Straw (1976) showed that people respond quite differently to an identical fight scene, depending on whether they perceive it as a lovers' quarrel or a fight between strangers. In this study,

students came to the psychology department individually in the evening to fill out an attitude questionnaire. While working on the task, the student heard a loud fight break out in the corridor (actually staged by drama students). A woman screamed and pleaded with a man to "get away from me." In a "marriage" condition, where the victim yelled "I don't know why I ever married you," only 19 percent of students intervened. But in a "stranger" condition, where the woman yelled, "I don't know you," 65 percent of subjects intervened either directly or by calling the police. Even though the fights were identical in all respects, subjects perceived the situation as more serious and the woman as more eager for help in the stranger condition.

In a real-life fight where the relationship between people is unclear, onlookers may assume it to be a lovers' quarrel and so decide not to intrude. Perhaps this is unfortunate, but it means that the lack of help is often due to misinterpretation of the situation, not to unwillingness to help.

TAKING PERSONAL RESPONSIBILITY You're at the beach, lying in the sun. A woman spreads her blanket near yours and turns on her portable radio to a local rock station. After a few minutes she goes for a swim, leaving her radio on the blanket. A bit later a man comes along, notices the radio, snatches it up quickly, and walks off. What do you do? Chances are that you do not try to stop the theft—reminding yourself, perhaps, that it's not your responsibility.

In an experiment re-creating the scene just described (Moriarity, 1975), only 20 percent of people intervened by going up to the thief and demanding an explanation. In a second condition, however, the owner of the radio first approached the person next to her on the beach and asked if they would "watch my things." Once such a commitment had been established, 95 percent of people intervened to stop the thief. When individuals feel personal responsibility, they are significantly more likely to act in a prosocial way.

Another demonstration of the importance of taking personal responsibility comes from a recent field study (Maruyama, Fraser, & Miller, 1982). Groups of children who came to a certain house while trick-or-treating for Halloween were asked to donate candies for hospitalized children. There were three experimental conditions, designed to manipulate the children's perceptions of responsi-

BOX 11-3

AVOIDING HELPING

A request for aid often arouses mixed feelings. On the one hand, people would like to help because it is a nice thing to do. On the other hand, they realize that costs are involved, costs that they would perhaps rather not assume. Indeed, one study (Pancer et al., 1979) demonstrated that people sometimes actively avoid a situation in which they will be asked for help. A table was set up in a passageway. In some conditions it held a box for donations to charity; in others it did not. People tended to walk farther away from the table when donations were requested than when no donations were requested. Similarly, when someone was sitting at the table collecting donations, people avoided it more than when no one was there. And finally, when a handicapped person was sitting at the table, people steered farther away than when the person was not handicapped.

In each case, the stronger the request for aid, the more people avoided the situation. Clearly, helping situations can create conflict, and people tend to minimize this conflict by keeping away. Presumably, it is easier not to donate money when you are far away than when you are close.

George Malave, Stock, Boston

bility. In one condition, the woman who greeted the kids made each child responsible for donating candies by putting the child's name on a bag for the candies. In another condition, she made one child responsible for the entire group. In the third condition, no one was given responsibility.

The variations in responsibility had clear effects on the number of candies donated by the children. When each child was individually responsible, the average donation was 5 candies; when one child was responsible for the group, this dropped to 3.3; when no one was responsible, an average of only 2.2 candies per child was given.

Another factor influencing perceived responsibility is competence (Bickman, 1971). We apparently feel a greater sense of obligation to intervene in a situation where we have the skills to help effectively. In one study, for instance (Clark & Word, 1974), participants witnessed a person (actually a confederate) pass out from an electrical shock from malfunctioning equipment. Of participants who had formal training or experience in working with electrical equipment, 90 percent intervened to help; among those with no electrical skills, only 58 percent intervened. In a more recent study, Shotland and Heinold (1985) showed that training can also influence the type of help given, in particular whether a person tries to intervene directly or helps indirectly by calling for assistance.

WEIGHING THE COSTS AND BENEFITS   According to the decision-making perspective described in Chapter 1, people consider the potential gains and losses that will result from a particular action, including helping another person (see Lynch & Cohen, 1978; Piliavin et al., 1981). So a person will act prosocially when the perceived profits (rewards − costs) for helping outweigh the profits from not helping.

Sometimes it is relatively easy to help; at other times, helping may involve considerable costs in time, energy, and complications. If someone asks you for directions, it is easy to stop for a moment and help out if you can. But if you are driving along a highway and see someone stuck at the side of the road, it is much more time-consuming to stop to help. In both situations, the costs will depend in part on whether you perceive any possible threat to your own safety. Does the person needing help look respectable, or is there some chance that you will be robbed? The greater the perceived costs, the less likely you are to help.

We are more likely to intervene in an emergency if we know how to help effectively. By taking a course in cardiopulmonary resuscitation (CPR), these people will have the knowledge to help heart attack victims.

There is also some cost to not giving assistance. You may feel guilty about not helping. Other people may see that you have not been helpful, and you will feel badly because they may have a poor opinion of you. You may have a general moral value that says you should help if you can, and not helping will make you feel that you have not been a good person. Thoughts such as these influence whether or not you offer help.

On the other hand, there are benefits to helping which provide positive incentives. The greater the good you perceive you will do, the more likely you are to help. The more the person deserves to be helped, and the more help you are able to give, the better you may feel about offering assistance. For example, Gruder, Romer, and Korth (1978) had a female confederate telephone people and request aid. The woman's story was that her car had broken down and she needed to reach a service station. She had gotten a wrong number, and asked the person to call the station for her. In some cases, she was in great need; in others less. In some cases, her problem was largely her fault because she said she had forgotten to take the car in for service even though she knew it needed repairs; in others, it was not her fault—the car had broken down with no warning. People helped more when her need was greater and when she was not at fault, and therefore presumably was more deserving of help.

Several researchers (see Lynch & Cohen, 1978; Morgan, 1978; Morgan & Leik, 1979) have tested this model of helping and have found generally supportive results. It seems likely that cost-benefit considerations do influence helping, at least in some situations. On the other hand, they do not fully explain all helping decisions. The person who instantly rushes into a burning building to save a child is unlikely to have weighed carefully the expected utility of the action. Rather, such acts may be motivated by basic emotions and values having to do with human life, courage, and so on.

DECIDING HOW TO HELP AND TAKING ACTION A final element in the decision to help is figuring out what type of assistance to offer, and then taking action.

Should you intervene directly in the fight outside your door, or act indirectly by calling the police? Should you try to administer CPR to the accident victim, or call the paramedics? Whether a person takes direct action or seeks further assistance from someone else depends on many factors, such as the type of aid needed and the expertise or physical size of the potential helper. In emergencies, decisions are often made under great stress, urgency, and sometimes even personal danger. Unfortunately, sometimes well-intentioned helpers are not able to give assistance or may even mistakenly do the wrong thing.

Our analysis of different elements in the decision to help highlights the many reasons why people may fail to give needed assistance. They may not notice that a problem exists, or may misperceive the situation as a trivial problem. They may recognize a need, but not feel personally responsible for helping. They may believe the costs of helping are too great. They may want to help, but be unable to. Or they may hesitate, caught in a state of indecision.

THE EXPERIENCE OF RECEIVING HELP

Sometimes we react to getting help with happiness and gratitude. The novice swimmer saved from drowning by an alert lifeguard is thankful to be alive and grateful for getting help when it was needed. The student who gets a ride to the airport from a friend is genuinely thankful for the favor. A soldier may come to like and respect a platoon buddy who voluntarily offers help (Cook & Pelfrey, 1985). But there are also instances when people react negatively to receiving help. When Dad offers to help his five-year-old get dressed, she may indignantly insist she'd rather do it herself. Welfare recipients may react toward social workers with veiled hostility rather than warmth. Countries receiving millions in U.S. foreign aid complain about American policies and "exploitation" of developing nations. What these examples point out is that receiving help can be a mixed blessing. Several social psychological theories help explain these reactions.

REACTANCE THEORY: LOSS OF FREEDOM According to reactance theory (Brehm, 1966), people want to maximize their personal freedom of choice. Perceived threats to this freedom are experienced negatively, and may lead to efforts to reassert one's independence. So when foreign aid recipients criticize U.S. policies, they may be symbolically proving their independence and reducing feelings of reactance.

Evidence that those who receive aid perceive a substantial loss of freedom comes from a study of welfare recipients (Briar, 1966). Nearly 70 percent of the welfare families surveyed believed they should not complain if a social worker made a surprise visit in the middle of the night, even though they knew this was probably not legal. Most families (67 percent) also said they would feel obligated to get marriage counseling if asked to do so, whether or not they thought it necessary. Intrusions on privacy and personal freedom can easily lead to feelings of hostility toward those providing aid (Gross, Wallston, & Piliavin, 1979).

EXCHANGE THEORY: COSTS OF INDEBTEDNESS   Providing help involves an exchange of resources from one person to another. When the exchange of help in a relationship is largely one way, it leads to indebtedness and can create an imbalance of power in the relationship (Worchel, 1984). Young adults who receive financial support from their parents may appreciate the assistance, but may also feel that accepting aid gives their parents greater rights to influence their lives.

The exchange perspective suggests that help may be most appreciated when it can be reciprocated, hence maintaining a balance of equity and power in the relationship. Research shows that people are less likely to ask for help when they think they will be unable to repay the aid in some form (Fisher, Nadler, Whitcher-Alagna, 1982). There is also evidence that people like a benefactor more if they are able to make some return for the aid they receive (see Gross & Latané, 1974). In short, lopsided help giving can threaten equity in a relationship, foster power imbalances, and increase negative feelings on the part of the recipient.

ATTRIBUTION THEORY: THREATS TO SELF-ESTEEM   Accepting help can have important implications for our self-esteem. If we perceive that people are helping us because they genuinely care about us and our welfare, we may get an ego boost. If accepting aid implies that we are incompetent, unsuccessful, and dependent, help may threaten our self-esteem (Fisher et al., 1982). For instance, people are sometimes reluctant to seek aid from social agencies because they fear humiliation and embarrassment (Williamson, 1974).

According to attribution theory, people are motivated to understand why they need help and why others are offering to give them help. If people can attribute their need to external or uncontrollable forces rather than to personal inadequacies, they will be able to maintain positive self-esteem. Several studies (Fisher et al., 1982; Tessler & Schwartz, 1972) have found that people are more likely to seek help when they can attribute their problem to a difficult situation, rather than to a personal deficiency. It has also been found that help may be easier to accept when the person in need does not have to ask for it explicitly. A year-long study of welfare recipients (Gross, Wallston, & Piliavin, 1979) found that people used more of the social services available if their caseworker initiated contacts than if the family had to initiate contacts. The researchers suggest that people avoid asking for help to protect their sense of pride and self-worth.

We have seen that the experience of receiving help is not always positive. There are times when accepting aid can limit our freedom, diminish our power, and lower our self-esteem. An understanding of these processes helps to explain why people sometimes react negatively or ambivalently toward help givers and why people may prefer not to ask for help even when they badly need it. Social-psychological factors may also explain the popularity of self-help groups, in which people with a common problem work together to help one another. Because self-help groups are run by the people in need, offer opportunities for reciprocal helping, and foster the knowledge that others have the same problem, they may minimize the costs of receiving help.

KEY TERMS IN CHAPTER 11

altruism	empathic concern	norm of social responsibility
bystander effect	norm of reciprocity	personal distress
bystander intervention	norm of social justice	prosocial behavior

SUMMARY

1. Altruism is helping someone with no expectation of reward or personal benefit. Prosocial behavior includes any act that helps or is designed to help, regardless of the helper's motives.

2. Bystander intervention means coming to the aid of a stranger in distress. Research shows that people are less likely to intervene when others are present. This so-called bystander effect may result from a diffusion of responsibility, from other people influencing how an individual interprets the situation, and from evaluation apprehension. Other situational factors that influence helping are weather, city size, noise, and time pressures.

3. People are more likely to help when they are in a good mood and feel empathy for the plight of the victim. People are also more helpful to those they like and to those they believe deserve help.

4. A historical perspective on helping is provided by sociobiologists who believe that a tendency to help is part of our human evolutionary heritage. In contrast, the social evolution view is that society creates rules about helping which include norms of social responsibility, reciprocity, and social justice.

5. A social learning perspective emphasizes that children learn prosocial behaviors and norms by reinforcement and modeling.

6. A decision-making perspective emphasizes that the cognitive processes leading to prosocial behavior are complex. The potential helper must perceive that help is needed, take personal responsibility, weigh the costs and benefits, and decide how to intervene.

7. People sometimes react to receiving help with a mixture of gratitude and discomfort. Receiving help may threaten our sense of freedom, make us feel indebted to others, and threaten our self-esteem.

SUGGESTED READINGS

DePaulo, B. M., Nadler, A., & Fisher, J. D. (1983). *New directions in helping: Help-seeking*. New York: Academic Press. An analysis of factors that lead people to seek help and factors that determine how people respond to receiving help.

Eisenberg, N. (1986). *Altruistic emotion, cognition, and behavior*. Hillsdale, NJ: Erlbaum. A recent discussion of how prosocial behavior is affected by empathy, causal attributions, self-perceptions, and moral reasoning.

Krebs, D. L., & Miller, D. T. (1985). Altruism and aggression. In G. Lindzey & E. Aronson (Eds.), *Handbook of social psychology*, 3rd ed, Vol. 2. New York: Random House, pp. 1–71. A comprehensive overview that links research and theory on prosocial behavior to work on aggression.

Latané, B., & Darley, J. M. (1970). *The unresponsive bystander: Why doesn't he help?* New York: Appleton-Century-Crofts. Reviews the classic studies of bystander intervention conducted by these authors.

Piliavin, J. A., Dovidio, J. F., Gaertner, S. L., & Clark, R. D. (1981). *Emergency intervention*. New York: Academic Press. Reviews research and theory on bystander intervention with an emphasis on cost-benefit factors.

Staub, E., Bar-Tal, D., Karylowski, J., & Reykowski, J. (Eds). (1984). *Development and maintenance of prosocial behavior*. New York: Plenum. An excellent collection of theoretical and research reviews written by leading experts.

12 CONFORMITY AND COMPLIANCE

onsider these three examples of social influence: In the 1950s, American college men were virtually all clean-shaven, with short hair. Only farmers wore blue jeans as everyday clothing. College women almost invariably had short hair, and dressed in blouses and skirts, with hemlines well below the knee. By the late 1960s, college students of both sexes grew their hair long and wore blue jeans regularly. Why do students tend to dress so similarly? How would you describe fashion trends at your college today?

As you hurry into the local supermarket, a young woman stops you and asks you to sign a petition urging the city to build a new shelter for homeless families. You somewhat reluctantly read and sign the petition. Next the woman asks you to donate $5 to a campaign to help the homeless. You give her a dollar and duck into the market. Why did you comply, at least partially, with her requests?

In Nazi Germany during the second World War, Adolf Hitler commanded his troops into battle—a common practice for heads of state during wartime. But he also ordered the construction of concentration camps where millions of civilians were put to death. Why did so many people obey Hitler's extraordinary orders to kill children and unarmed civilians?

Social psychologists have long been interested in questions such as these about the ways in which our behavior is influenced by other people and groups. Indeed, Elliot Aronson (1984, p. 6) has defined the core topic of social psychology as "the influences that people have upon the beliefs or behaviors of others." Earlier chapters in this book have already explored several facets of social influence, for instance, in our analysis of the processes of attitude change (Chapter 7) and our discussion of power in personal relationships (Chapter 9). This chapter examines three types of social influence that are of special importance in groups and organizations: conformity, compliance, and obedience to authority.

When someone voluntarily performs an act because others are doing it, we call it **conformity**. College students are presumably free to pick their own clothes and hairstyles. But students often prefer to dress like others in their social group, thus conforming to current standards of fashion on campus. What factors affect conformity to group pressures?

When people do what they are asked to do,

These college couples from earlier eras conformed to the norms of their peer group in hairstyles, dress, interests, and values. How would you describe a "typical" college couple on your campus today?

even though they might prefer not to, we call it **compliance**. The distinguishing feature of compliance is that we are responding to a request from another individual or group. Compliance might occur in many settings—when a friend asks us for a ride to the airport, or a group of Halloween trick-or-treaters ask for candy, or a volunteer organization asks for donations.

In some social situations, we perceive one person or group as having the *legitimate authority* to influence our behavior. The government has a right to ask us to pay taxes; parents have a right to ask their children to wash the dishes after dinner; and medical personnel have the right to ask us to take off our clothes for a physical exam. In these cases, social norms permit those in authority to make requests. Although authorities often make reasonable and appropriate requests, this is not always the case. During the Nazi war crime trials after the war, many individuals accused of murdering civilians tried to excuse their behavior because they were "just following orders" from those in command.

CONFORMITY

Because conformity is such a powerful phenomenon, it has proved relatively easy to study in the laboratory. We'll begin our discussion with two classic studies that illustrate how conformity works.

A Guess in the Dark: The Sherif Study

The task in this classic study by Muzafer Sherif (1935) seemed straightforward: A college student sat in a darkened room and was shown a single point of light. He was told that the light was moving, and that his job was to estimate how far it moved. Most subjects found it extremely difficult to estimate how far the light moved, since it often appeared to move at varying speeds and in different directions. Actually, the study used a perceptual illusion known as the *autokinetic effect*: a single point of light seen in the dark appears to move, even though it is really stationary.

Given the ambiguity of this situation, subjects could not be sure of their judgments, and their initial estimates varied enormously. Several people thought the light moved only 1 or 2 inches, whereas one person thought it moved as much as 800 feet. (Apparently, this person thought he was in a gymnasium, although actually he was in a small room.) After the subject had made several estimates, a second person was brought into the situation, also supposedly a subject who was judging how far the light was moving. This other person was in fact a confederate who had been told to make his estimates consistently lower or higher than those of the real subject. The same procedure was repeated for a number of trials.

Under these conditions, the subject soon began to make his estimates more and more similar to those of the confederate. For instance, if the subject began by estimating that the light moved between 10 and 14 inches and the confederate said it moved only 2 inches, on the next trial the subject tended to lower his estimate, and on the following trial he would lower it even more. By the end of the series, the subject's estimates were very similar to those of the confederate.

As Plain as Day: The Asch Study

Perhaps conformity occurs only in rather ambiguous situations, then, when people are quite uncertain about what the correct standard of behavior is. This was the way Solomon Asch (1951) reasoned. He thought that if the stimulus situation was clear, there would be little or no conformity. When people consider a clear reality, they will trust their own

"Well heck! If all you smart cookies agree, who am I to dissent?"

perceptions and remain independent even when every member of a group disagrees with them. Asch therefore designed an experiment to test this expectation (Asch, 1951).

Five students arrived to take part in a study on perception. They sat around a table and were told they would be judging the lengths of lines. They were shown a white card on which three black lines of varying lengths had been drawn and a second card containing one line. Their task was to choose the line on the first card that was most similar in length to the line on the second card. As shown in Figure 12–1, it was an easy task. One of the lines was exactly the same length as the standard, whereas the other two were quite different from it.

When the lines were shown, the subjects answered aloud in the order in which they were seated. The first subject gave his choice and then each of the others responded in turn. Since the judgment was so easy, there were no disagreements. When all had responded, a second set of lines were shown, responses were given, and a third set was produced.

At this point, the experiment seems dull and pointless. On the third trial, however, the first subject looked carefully at the lines as before and then gave what was obviously the wrong answer. In the example in Figure 12–1, he might have said A rather than B. The next subject gave the same wrong answer, as did the third and fourth subjects. When it was time for the fifth subject to respond, he was quite disturbed. It was clear to him that the others were giving wrong answers. He knew that B was the line most similar to X. Yet everyone else said it was A.

Under these circumstances many people sitting fifth gave the wrong answer—they agreed with the others even though they knew it was incorrect. In fact, among these college students with good eye-

FIGURE 12–1   A representative stimulus in the Asch conformity study. Subjects were shown the four lines simultaneously and asked which line was most similar in length to line X. When a number of confederates unanimously gave the incorrect answer (e.g., C), subjects conformed about 35 percent of the time. (Adapted from Asch, 1951.)

sight and presumably sharp minds, the incorrect answer was given about 35 percent of the time. Some subjects never gave the wrong answer, some did all the time; but overall they averaged about one wrong response in three. Of course, in this classic study by Solomon Asch, the situation was staged. The first four "subjects" were confederates of the experimenter and were responding according to a script. But the real subject did not know this and gave the wrong answer rather than disagree with the others.

It is important to keep the unambiguousness of this situation in mind if we are to understand the phenomenon. There is a tendency to think that the conforming subjects are uncertain of the correct choice and therefore are swayed by the majority. This is not the case. The subjects were quite certain of the correct choice and, in control groups with no group pressure, chose correctly 100 percent of the time. When they conform, they are conforming despite the fact that they know the correct answer.

Later studies have found conformity using other physical stimuli, opinion statements, statements of fact, and logical syllogisms. Subjects have agreed that there is no population problem in the United States because 6,000 miles of continent separates San Francisco from New York; that men are 8 to 9 inches taller than women on the average; and that male babies have a life expectancy of only 25 years. In other words, regardless of the type of stimulus and of how clear the correct choice is, when individuals are faced with a unanimous group opinion, the pressure exerted by the majority is often strong enough to produce conformity.

These results are very clear. People do conform—even when doing so means contradicting their own perceptions of the world. They do not always accept what the others are saying; in many cases, they continue to believe that their private judgments are correct. Nevertheless, when asked to respond publicly, they give the same incorrect response the others give. This is what we mean by conformity.

Why Do People Conform?

Basically, people conform for two major reasons—to be right and to be liked.

INFORMATIONAL INFLUENCE: THE DESIRE TO BE RIGHT

One reason for conformity is that the behavior of other people often provides useful information. A thirsty traveler at an oasis in the Sahara Desert who sees Arabs drinking from one well and avoiding another well would be smart to copy their behavior. By drinking from the popular well, the traveler may avoid drinking contaminated water. Our tendency to conform based on informational influence depends on two aspects of the situation: how well-informed we believe the group is and how confident we are in our own independent judgment.

The more we trust the group's information and value their opinions in a situation, the more likely we are to go along with the group. If our thirsty traveler in the desert sees that the Arabs drinking at the oasis are city dwellers on their first tourist trip to the desert, he or she might be inclined to wonder how much they know about wells and so may not conform to their example. If they are clearly desert nomads traveling on their usual route, the person would be far more likely to trust them and follow their example. Anything that increases confidence in the correctness of the group should increase conformity and, conversely, anything that leads us to doubt the group's knowledge or trustworthiness should decrease conformity.

Balanced against the individual's confidence in the group is the individual's confidence in his or her own views. Early studies found that the more ambiguous or difficult the task, the more likely people were to conform (Coleman, Blake & Mouton, 1958), presumably because they were less certain of their own judgment. For example, the Sherif task was more difficult than the Asch task, and so produced more conformity. Other research has found that the more competent and knowledgeable we feel about a topic, the less likely we are to conform (Wiesenthal, et al., 1976). Recently, Campbell, Tesser and Fairey (1986) experimentally manipulated subjects' level of self-confidence in their ability to do an embedded figures test, and found that high self-doubt individuals conformed significantly more than those with low self-doubt.

NORMATIVE INFLUENCE: THE DESIRE TO BE LIKED

A second major reason for conformity is to gain the approval, or avoid the disapproval, of the group. We often want the group to accept us, like us, and

"I fear we must have misread the invitation."

treat us well. In deciding how to dress for a job interview or senior prom, we may try to wear the "right" clothes so that we will fit in, give a good impression, and avoid disapproval. In growing up, people often learn that one way to get along with a group is to go along with group standards.

This fear of being deviant is justified by the group's response to deviance. When someone does not go along with a group, that person becomes the target of efforts to bring them in line, and ultimately risks rejection. This was shown in an early study by Stanley Schachter (1951), in which three confederates were included in a larger discussion group. One confederate (the deviant) consistently took a position different from that of the group; one confederate (the "slider") started deviant and then changed toward the group; and the third took the same position as the group. The rest of the group spent a great deal of time trying to change the position of the two confederates who held deviant positions. They argued with them, presented reasons to support the group position, cajoled, and did whatever they could to change the deviates' stand to agree with the group's. Being the object of such an intense campaign is not pleasant. In

this situation, the "slider" who changed toward conformity was ultimately accepted and treated like any other member of the group. But the confederate who maintained a deviant position was eventually ignored and overlooked for leadership positions.

A group can also apply punishment directly, as shown in a study done at the Hawthorne plant of the Western Electric Company (Homans, 1965). Observations were made of the behavior of a number of workers whose wages depended on their productivity. By working harder and accomplishing more, each worker could receive higher pay. However, the employees had developed their own standards as to the right amount of work to do in a day. Every day, after they did this amount of work, they slacked off. By working just this much, they earned a reasonable sum of money and didn't have to work too hard. Anyone who worked harder would make the others look bad and might cause management to increase its expectation of output.

The group exerted intense pressure on its members to conform to the group standard for productivity. People who worked too much risked being called "rate busters," and those who worked too little were called "chiselers." In addition, the

The Hawthrone study: Some physical environments make it easy for the group to enforce conformity. How could management have organized this workplace to prevent "binging" or other productivity-reducing types of conformity?

group devised a novel way to enforce the productivity rule. Anyone who worked too fast or too slow could be "binged." Binging consisted of giving the deviate a sharp blow on the upper arm. Not only did this hurt, but it was a symbolic punishment for going against the group. Any group member could deliver the punishment, and the person who was binged could not fight back. The punishment had to be accepted and with it, the disapproval it indicated. Binging is a dramatic example of the kinds of pressure present in all groups that cause members to conform to accepted opinions, values, and behavior. In many cases, just being aware of the potential costs of nonconformity and the benefits of conformity leads people to follow group standards. When this fails, groups use persuasion, threats of ostracism, direct punishment, and offers of rewards to pressure individuals to conform.

In summary, the motivation to conform stems from a desire to be right and a desire to be liked by the group. The strength of these two motives varies considerably depending on the situation.

When Do People Conform?

Research has identified several important features of the group situation that can affect conformity including commitment to the group, group size, and unanimity.

COMMITMENT TO THE GROUP Conformity is affected by the strength of the bonds between individuals and the group (Forsyth, 1983). In Chapter 9, we defined **commitment** as all the forces, positive and negative, that act to keep an individual in a relationship. This concept also applies to group membership. Positive forces attracting an individual to a group might include liking other group members, believing the group accomplishes important goals, feeling that the group works well together, expecting to gain from belonging to the group, and identifying with group values, etc. Negative forces keeping an individual from leaving a group include such barriers as having few alternatives or having made large investments in the group that would be costly to give up. The more committed a person is to a group, the greater the pressures for conformity.

We use the term **cohesiveness** to describe the extent to which group members as a whole are strongly or weakly committed to the group. In general, the more highly cohesive a group, the greater the potential pressures toward conformity. Groups with high morale, where members enjoy working together and believe they function well as a team are more vulnerable to conformity pressures than less cohesive groups.

GROUP SIZE Suppose there were two people in a room and one of them said it was very warm. If the room was in fact quite cold, the second person would be unlikely to agree with the first. She would feel cold and would assume that the other was mistaken or feverish. If forced to make a public statement on the temperature of the room, she would probably say she thought it was rather cold.

If the room contained five people and four of them said it was warm, the situation would change. Even if one person felt cold, she would be likely to doubt her own perceptions. After all, it is unlikely that all four of the others were feverish or mistaken. If the person were asked how she felt, she might be uncertain enough to agree with the rest. She might say the room was warm and then wonder what was wrong with her. When one person disagrees with you, he or she is feverish; when four others do, you must be sick yourself. Four people tend to be more trustworthy than one, in terms of both honesty and the reliability of their opinions; it is harder to mistrust a group than one person (Insko et al., 1985).

A series of experiments has demonstrated that conformity does increase as the size of the unanimous majority increases, at least up to a point (Tanford & Penrod, 1984). In some of his early experiments, Asch (1951) varied the size of the majority from two to sixteen. As shown in Figure 12–2, he found that two people produced more pressure than one, three a lot more than two, and four about the same as three. Somewhat surprisingly, he found that increasing the size of the group past four did not increase the amount of conformity, at least up to sixteen. He concluded that to produce the most conformity, the optimal group size was three or four.

Using quite a different procedure and a different measure, Milgram and associates (1969) produced quite different results. The situation was very simple. On a crowded street in New York City, a number of people played the old game of looking up to see whether anyone else would look up also. This time it was done as a deliberate experiment, and careful observations were made of passers-by.

The confederates stood and looked up at the sixth-floor window of an office building across the street. Either one, two, three, five, ten, or fifteen confederates stood around looking up at the window. The chief measure is what percentage of those who passed by actually stopped and looked up at

the window also. When one person was looking up, only 4 percent of the passers-by also looked up; with five confederates, it went up to 16 percent; with ten, it was 22 percent; and with fifteen, it was 40 percent.

A similar increase in conformity as group size increased was found by Mann (1977) in a study of getting in line for the bus in Jerusalem, Israel. When two or four people lined up, there was little tendency for others to join the line. But when six or more were on line, newcomers usually also went on line. The more people there were on line, the more likely it was that other people would join it.

However, research by Wilder (1977) makes it clear that it is not simply the number of people that makes the difference. In this study, subjects heard the opinions of varying numbers of other people. The important difference between this and previous work was that these other people were sometimes expressing their opinions independently and sometimes as members of groups. Some subjects heard the opinions of four people who belonged to one group, some heard the opinions of four people who were members of two different groups, and others heard the opinions of four independent people.

FIGURE 12–2 Group size and conformity. (Adapted from Asch, 1951.)

People usually enforce social norms about waiting in line very vociferously. What would be the conformists' reactions here if one person broke the line? Two people? How much would it depend on the total number of people in the line?

Wilder found that group size had little effect on amount of conformity. But the number of independent opinions, from separate groups or from individuals, had a major effect. This may explain why increasing the size of a group above three or four adds little to conformity. Once the group is seen to be acting as a unit, the number of additional individuals within the group does not matter. But adding independent judgments from people outside the group might increase conformity.

GROUP UNANIMITY   An extremely important factor in producing conformity is the unanimity of the group opinion. A person faced with a unanimous group decision is under great pressure to conform. If, however, a group is not united, there is a striking decrease in the amount of conformity. When even one other person does not go along with the rest of the group, conformity drops to about one-fourth the usual level. This is true when the group is small, and it also appears to hold with up to 15 people. One of the most impressive things about this phenomenon is that it does not seem to matter who the nonconforming person is. Regardless of whether this is a high-prestige, expert figure or someone of low prestige who is not at all expert, conformity tends to drop to low levels (Asch, 1951; Morris & Miller, 1975).

This reduction in conformity is found even when the other disagreer gives the wrong answer. If the majority says A, another person says C, and the correct answer is B, the subject is less likely to conform than if everyone agreed on one incorrect answer. Simply having some disagreement within the group makes it easier for one person to remain independent despite the fact that no one agrees with him.

In a study by Allen and Levin (1971), subjects in five-person groups were presented with a unanimous majority, or a three-person majority and a dissenter. The dissenter gave the correct answer or gave an answer that was even more incorrect than that of the majority. The subjects were given three different types of judgment tasks—perceptual evaluations such as those used by Asch, information questions such as whether Hawaii was a state, and opinion items for which there was no correct answer but some popular ones. The results are shown in Table 12–1. For all three items, the presence of a dissenter reduced conformity, even when the dissenter was more incorrect than the majority. The effect was strongest for the perceptual items and weakest for the opinion items.

Morris and Miller (1975) showed that the timing of dissent made a difference. When one person dissented *after* the majority had expressed its opin-

TABLE 12–1

Conformity Produced by Unanimous Majorities, and by Majorities with One Dissenter Who Gives the Correct or an Even More Incorrect Choice

	TYPE OF JUDGMENT		
	Perception	Information	Opinion
Unanimous	.97	.78	.89
Dissenter correct	.40	.43	.59
Dissenter more incorrect than majority	.47	.42	.72

Higher numbers indicate more conformity.
Source: Adapted from Allen & Levin (1971).

ion, conformity decreased. But when the dissenter answered *before* the majority, conformity decreased even more. Apparently, when the subjects heard the correct response at the beginning, the majority's incorrect position carried less weight.

The dramatic decrease in conformity when unanimity is broken seems to be due to several of the factors we have already discussed. First, the amount of trust or confidence in the correctness of the majority decreases whenever there is disagreement, even when the person who disagrees is less expert or less reliable than those who make up the majority. Of course, this is in a situation in which the real subject is also disagreeing with the majority. That is, the subject initially holds an opinion different from theirs, and discovers that someone else does also. The mere fact that someone else also disagrees with the group indicates that there is room for doubt, that the issue is not perfectly clear, and that the majority might be wrong. This reduces the individual's reliance on the majority opinion as a source of information and accordingly reduces conformity.

Second, if another group member takes the position the individual favors, it serves to strengthen self-confidence about that judgment. As we have seen, greater confidence reduces conformity. A third consideration involves reluctance to appear deviant. When one person disagrees with everyone else, that person stands out and is deviant in both his or her own and the others' eyes. When someone else also disagrees, neither is as deviant as he or she would be alone.

This last result should probably be taken as en-

couragement to speak one's mind. In the story "The Emperor's New Clothes," for example, the whole crowd watched the naked emperor in his supposedly beautiful new clothes. However, when only one child had the strength to say that the emperor was naked, everyone else found strength to defy the majority.

Certainly, this is a strong argument for freedom of speech, because it suggests that even one deviant voice can have an important effect as long as there are other people who inwardly disagree with the majority but are afraid to speak up. It may also explain why in totalitarian states and some orthodox religions no dissent is allowed. Even one small voice disagreeing could encourage others to do likewise. After a while, the regime itself might be endangered. The finding that any dissent substantially reduces conformity stands out as one of the most striking aspects of conformity.

Minority Influence: Innovation in Groups

Conformity to majority patterns is a basic aspect of social life. But our emphasis on the power of the majority should not blind us to the importance of **minority influence**. Sometimes a forceful minority with a new idea or unique perspective can effectively change the position of the majority.

Early studies showing that dissent reduces conformity began to raise questions about the existence of an "all-powerful" majority. In the past 15 years, the major new developments in conformity research have been attempts to understand the influence of minorities (Maass & Clark, 1984). Pioneering work by the French psychologist Serge Moscovici (1985) has been especially important.

In an early experiment, Moscovici, Lage and Naffrechoux (1969) used an Asch-type conformity paradigm and showed subjects an unambiguous physical stimulus, namely slides of colors. In this study, members of 6-person groups were asked to rate the color of the slides. In actuality, all slides were blue but varied in their luminance. In control groups of 6 naive subjects, virtually all slides were described as blue. In the experimental group, however, two confederates consistently labeled the blue slides as "green." Subjects had previously been told that all group members had normal vision, so these "green" responses could not be attributed to color blindness. With this minority pressure, about a third of the subjects reported seeing at least one "green" slide, and 8 percent of all judgments were that slides were "green." Clearly, the minority view had a noticeable effect on the naive majority.

Moscovici has proposed that the *behavioral style* of a minority is important. To be effective, a minority must be consistent, coherent and forceful. This behavioral style is interpreted by the majority as a sign of the minority's confidence and certainty in their position (Maass & Clark, 1984). As a minority persists in their position over time, the majority may start to question the correctness of their views. Ultimately, some majority members may "convert" by changing their own position in the direction of the minority. If enough members change their views, the minority may be transformed into a new majority.

Recent research has identified other factors that also determine the influence of minorities (Maass & Clark, 1984). First, minorities are most effective when their behavioral style is logically consistent but not "rigid," that is, when they are seen as having a well-defined position but a flexible style of presentation. Second, the general social climate also makes a difference. A minority will be more effective if it argues for a position in line with current social trends. For example, in an era of increasing sexual conservatism, a minority arguing for sexual permissiveness will be less effective than a minority arguing for sexual restraint.

Minorities are also more likely to succeed when they are similar to the majority in most respects except for the behavior or attitude in question. These *single minorities* can be contrasted with *double minorities* who differ not only on the relevant issue, but also in other social characteristics. An example of a double minority would be a homosexual advocating gay rights to heterosexuals; the gay person differs from the majority of Americans not only in beliefs but also in sexual orientation. A study by Maass and Clark (1984) found that an ostensibly gay minority arguing for gay rights was less influential than a heterosexual minority arguing for gay rights, in part because the gay minority was seen as having more self-interest in the topic. Another study (Maass et al., 1984) showed that conservative male subjects were more strongly influenced by a man arguing for a liberal position on abortion than by a woman taking the same liberal position. When a minority group can be perceived as having a personal stake in their position, their views can more easily be discounted as reflecting self-interest. More generally, minorities have more influence when their position is taken seriously and seen as reflecting certainty and competence. Minorities are less influential when they can be discounted as bizarre, dogmatic, or self-interested.

A current controversy in this area is whether the processes of majority influence (conformity) and minority influence (innovation) are fundamentally the same or different. There is evidence on both sides of this debate, and it is too soon to decide definitively between the single process versus dual-process perspectives. A brief look at each will highlight the issues in question.

Several theorists (Latané & Wolf, 1981; Tanford & Penrod, 1984) have made the case that the impact of majorities and minorities reflect a single underlying influence process. Majority and minority influence differ in quantity, not quality; majorities usually have more influence because they are more numerous. Results from several studies are consistent with this single-process view (e.g., Wolf, 1985).

On the other hand, Moscovici and other researchers (Maass & Clark, 1984; Nemeth, 1986) argue that there are important qualitative differences between minority and majority influence. For example, there is evidence that majority influence most often leads to changes in overt behavior but not necessarily to changes in private attitudes. In contrast, the influence of minorities is more likely to result in changed attitudes. In addition, Charlan Nemeth (1986) has shown that minorities can cause other group members to think more carefully about an issue or situation and to consider a wider variety of possible explanations or novel solutions. Nemeth's results suggest that minorities can sometimes improve group functioning, and can have a beneficial impact out of proportion to their small numbers.

COMPLIANCE

One of the most basic ways we influence other people is to ask them directly to do something. Think of some of the requests you might make of a friend—to water your plants while you are on vacation, to borrow some money for a few days, to refrain from smoking in your car, to tell you what they really think of your new haircut, to join the volunteer group you organized, and so on. How might you present these requests to increase the chances that your friend will comply? Research on compliance has attempted to understand some of the processes that lead people to comply (or refuse to comply) with requests.

Sometimes we seem to comply with requests for no reason at all. In one study, researchers approached people using a photocopying machine and asked to go first in line because "I have to make copies" (Langer, Blank, & Chanowitz, 1978). This so-called explanation actually gave no real justification for going out of turn. But many subjects went along with the request, apparently not paying much attention to the content of the explanation. Ellen Langer refers to this behavior as *mindlessness* because people respond without thinking seriously about their behavior. Perhaps out of habit, we have learned that when someone asks for something, especially something trivial, and gives a reason (even a contentless reason), we should go along. We spare ourselves the mental effort of thinking about the situation and simply comply with the request. Mindlessness may not explain most instances of compliance, but it is a fascinating aspect of human behavior.

Six Bases of Social Power

When David Kipnis (1984, p. 186) asked managers in business organizations how they try to influence their co-workers to do something, they said things like: "I simply order him to do what I ask," "I act very humble while making my request," or "I explain the reasons for my request." In contrast, when he asked dating couples how they influence their partners, they said things like: "I get angry and demand he give in," "I act so nice that she cannot refuse when I ask," or "We talk about why we don't agree." Social psychologists have tried to understand the diverse ways people try to get others to comply with their wishes. For an analysis of how young lovers try to influence each other in the sexual arena, see Box 12–1.

A useful way to classify influence strategies is provided in a model developed by Bertram Raven and his colleagues (French & Raven, 1959; Raven & Rubin, 1983). They identify six distinct major bases of power, each reflecting a different type of resource a person might use to influence someone.

REWARDS   One basis for power is the ability to provide positive outcomes for another person—to help that person accomplish a desired goal or to offer a valued reward. Sometimes people make explicit bargains: A father might promise to take his daughter to the zoo if she cleans up her room. Sometimes there is no explicit contract, but rather a general awareness that rewards are often recipro-

BOX 12-1

COME-ONS AND PUT-OFFS: POWER IN SEXUAL ENCOUNTERS

How do young lovers try to influence each other to have or to avoid sexual intercourse? To find out, Naomi McCormick (1979) asked college students to imagine that they were alone with an attractive dating partner whom they had known for a few weeks. They had "necked," but had not yet had sexual intercourse. In one question, students were asked to describe in their own words how they might influence this partner to have sexual intercourse. In a later question, they were asked to indicate how they would avoid having sex with a "turned on" date. These essays were then coded for the particular power tactics used.

When their goal was to have sex with the partner, both men and women said they were most likely to use indirect strategies of seduction. One student wrote: "First of all I would put on some soft music and offer some wine, then I would start kissing gently and caressing [the person's] body, then I would give a massage with oil" (p. 199). The use of body language (sitting closer, touching the partner) and of changing the environment (putting on music, dimming the lights) were common. Some students said they would emphasize the nature of their relationship: "I would tell my date that we have a very strong, close relationship and that it is time to express it through sexual intercourse."

Tactics for *avoiding* sex were usually more direct. The favored approach by both men and women was to emphasize that it was too early to have sex. Others proposed using logic or information—for example, telling the partner that they were concerned about pregnancy or that they weren't in the mood for sex. Some suggested using body language (moving farther away) or manipulating the interaction by changing the conversation. A few would invoke moral principles.

McCormick was interested in whether men and women report using different power tactics in sexual encounters (McCormick & Jesser, 1983). In the study described above, where students were asked to imagine how they might hypothetically try to seduce or reject a partner, few gender differences were found. Both men and women approached seduction similarly, and both proposed similar ways to reject a sexual advance. In actual dating, however, the situation is rather different.

A consistent finding from this and other studies is that men and women usually have different sexual goals in a dating situation. It is more often men who are the sexual initiators trying to seduce their partner, and women who are the limit setters trying to avoid sex. Despite changing sexual attitudes and the women's movement, this traditional role-playing persists in the early stages of dating.

Thus when people are asked what strategies they have actually used in sexual encounters, women usually report tactics for avoiding sex, and men report tactics for having sex. Similarly, when people are asked how others have typically tried to influence them, women report being the targets of attempted seductions, and men report having been turned down.

cated in the relationship: If I do what you want now, you'll be more likely to do what I want later.

COERCION Coercion can range from actual physical force to threats of punishment or subtle signs of disapproval. After trying futilely to convince a young child to take a nap, a parent may simply place the struggling child in the crib, walk out, and close the door. A spouse may threaten divorce if a mate refuses to begin marriage counseling. A supervisor may threaten disciplinary action if an employee continues to arrive late for work.

Rewards and coercion are not exact opposites. To obtain rewards, people are motivated to make their "good" behavior known. In contrast, the target of coercion may do what the influencer wants, but only so long as he or she is being watched. Coercion may lead to secrecy rather than actual compliance.

EXPERTISE Special knowledge, training, and skill are sources of power. We defer to experts and follow their advice because we believe their knowledge will help us to achieve our personal goals. If a trusted physician advises us to take three little green pills daily for an allergy, we are likely to comply whether or not we know what the pills are or understand what the pills will do. We may unquestioningly accept a friend's suggestion about a new recipe for homemade ice cream because we know that the friend is a gourmet cook with specialized knowledge. A group of mountain climbers will follow the advice of their experienced guide, even though the route suggested for scaling the mountain looks hazardous.

INFORMATION We often try to influence people by giving them information we think will suggest the right course of action to them. A child might get her mother to serve dinner later than usual by telling her there will be a special educational program on TV during the regular dinner time. A friend might convince us to go to a concert by informing us that our favorite rock group is performing. In these cases, the influencer is not an expert. Rather, it is the content of the message that produces the desired effect. If roommates try to settle a conflict using information power, their discussion might appear somewhat like a rational debate over specific information and details of the situation.

REFERENT POWER A basis of influence with special relevance to personal relationships and groups is referent power. This exists when we admire or identify with a person or group, and want to be like them. In such cases, we may voluntarily copy their behavior or do what they ask, because we want to become similar to them. In everyday life we may not think of identification as a type of influence, but it can be very effective. A young child who looks up to an older brother, tries to imitate

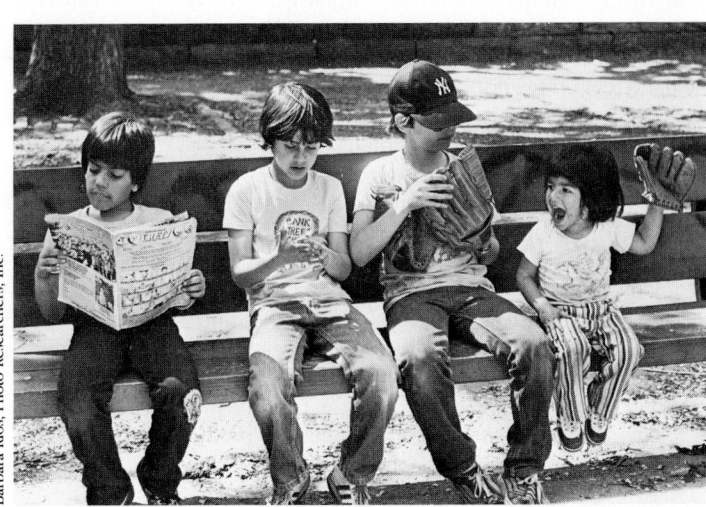

A three-year-old copies the gestures of his brother and friends. In Raven's model, social influence based on identification is called referent power.

Barbara Rios, Photo Researchers, Inc.

Children can be induced to do quite unusual things in doctors' and dentists' offices, usually without much reward offered or punishment threatened. The power of a simple request from "the doctor" is based on both expertise and legitimate authority.

Ken Karp

his mannerisms, and adopts his interests is one illustration. A young man who drinks a particular brand of beer because he identifies with the "macho" image of the sportsmen promoting the product in TV commercials is also being influenced by referent power.

LEGITIMATE AUTHORITY   Sometimes one person has the right or authority to ask another person to act a certain way. The manager who "simply orders" a subordinate to do what she wants or the general who orders his troops into battle are likely to be exercising legitimate authority. Similarly, in most families, parents feel they have the right to tell young children when to go to bed, and children usually feel obligated to comply. Children may try to renegotiate bedtime rules or ask to make an exception for a special occasion, but they usually accept the parents' authority to make rules.

Social roles such as parent–child, teacher–student, or supervisor–employee often dictate the legitimate rights and responsibilities of people in a relationship. Even quite young children seem to sense that the requests of physicians and dentists should be obeyed. When someone deviates from agreed-upon rules, we feel we have the right to remind them of their obligations. A prerequisite for effective legitimate authority is that all parties agree about the norms in their relationship.

A special case of legitimate power is what Raven has called the "power of helplessness." Consider these requests: a small child asks his mother for help in taking off his snow boots; a well-dressed foreign tourist asks in broken English for directions to the bus stop; a partially-blind grocery shopper asks for help in reading the price marked on a can of soup. In each case, the person asking for help is in a powerless or helpless condition. And, in each case, others are likely to comply with their requests. Our culture has a clear **norm of social responsibility** (discussed in Chapter 11 on Pro-social Behavior.) We expect people to help those who are less fortunate, and this social obligation makes it legitimate for those in need to ask for help. However, Raven suggests that the legitimate power of helplessness is sometimes costly for those who use it. People who constantly rely on helplessness may come to see themselves as incompetent (and so suffer from lowered self-esteem) and may actually perpetuate their powerless situation.

Specific Compliance Techniques

One line of research has investigated the techniques people use deliberately to gain compliance. Robert Cialdini (1985) has studied car salesmen, con artists, and other professionals who earn a living by getting

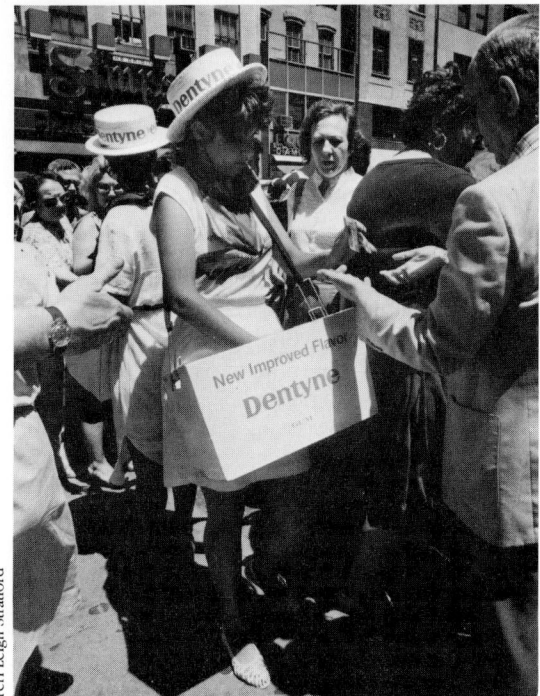

By giving out free samples of their chewing gum, the manufacturer hopes to encourage people to buy the product. What social-psychological principles are used in this approach?

people to buy their products or go along with their schemes. He and other social psychology researchers have identified several important compliance techniques.

THE FOOT-IN-THE-DOOR TECHNIQUE   One way of increasing compliance is to induce a person to agree first to a small request. Once someone has agreed to the small action, he or she is more likely to agree to a larger request. This is the so-called **foot-in-the-door technique.** It is used explicitly or implicitly by many advertising campaigns. Advertisers often concentrate on getting consumers to do something connected with the product—even sending back a card saying that they do not want it. The advertisers apparently think that any act connected with the product increases the likelihood that the consumer will buy it in the future.

A classic study by Freedman and Fraser (1966) demonstrated this effect. Experimenters went from door to door and told homemakers they were working for the Committee for Safe Driving. They said they wanted the women's support for this campaign and asked them to sign a petition which was to be sent to the state's senators. The petition requested the senators to work for legislation to encourage safe driving. Almost all the women agreed to sign. Several weeks later, different experimenters contacted the same women and other women who had not been approached before. At this time, all the women were asked to put in their front yards a large, unattractive sign that read "Drive Carefully."

The results were striking. Over 55 percent of the women who had previously endorsed the petition (a small request) also agreed to post the sign (a relatively large request). In contrast, less than 17 percent of the other women agreed to post the sign. Getting the women to agree to the initial small request more than tripled the amount of compliance to the large request. This effect has been replicated in several studies (e.g., Seligman, Bush & Kirsch, 1975).

Why this technique works is not entirely clear. One explanation is that people who agree to a small request get involved and committed to the issue itself, to the behavior they perform, or perhaps simply to the idea of taking some kind of action. Any of these factors would probably make someone more likely to comply with future requests.

Another explanation is based on self-perception theory which was introduced in Chapter 6. The idea here is that in some ways the individual's self-image changes as a result of the initial act of compliance. In the safe-driving experiment, for example, a woman may have thought of herself as the kind of person who does not take social action, who does not sign petitions, who does not post signs, or, perhaps, who does not even agree to things that are asked of her by someone at the door. Once she has agreed to the small request—which was actually difficult to refuse—she may have changed her perception of herself slightly. Since she agreed to sign a petition, perhaps she is the kind of person who does this sort of thing. Then, when the second request was made, she was more likely to comply than she would have been otherwise.

THE DOOR-IN-THE-FACE TECHNIQUE Sometimes the opposite technique of the foot-in-the-door also works. First asking for a very large request and then making a smaller request can increase compliance to the small request. This is sometimes called the **door-in-the-face technique,** since the first request is typically so outrageously large that people might be tempted to shut the door in the requester's face. In one study (Cialdini et al., 1975), subjects were asked to contribute time to a good cause. Some were asked first to give a huge amount of time. When they refused, as almost all did, the experimenter immediately said then perhaps they might agree to a much smaller commitment of time. Other subjects were asked only the smaller request, while a third group was given a choice between the two. The results were striking. In the single small-request condition, only 17 percent of subjects agreed. In the choice condition, 25 percent of subjects complied with the request. But in the condition where subjects had first turned down a big request, 50 percent agreed to the smaller request.

This effect is familiar to anyone who has engaged in bargaining with a used car dealer, a union, or management. The tactic is to ask for the moon and settle for less. The more you ask for at first, the more you expect to end up with eventually. The idea is that when you reduce your demands, the other person thinks you are compromising and the amount seems smaller. In a compliance situation, such as asking for charity, the same might apply—a dollar doesn't seem like much when the organization initially asked for a hundred dollars.

Clearly, both the foot-in-the door and the reverse tactic work at times, but we do not yet know when each of them will operate (Dillard, Hunter, & Burgoon, 1984). Both seem to work best when the behavior involved is prosocial, that is, when the request is to give money or help a worthwhile cause. One difference seems to be that the door-in-the-face technique works when the smaller request follows the larger request immediately and is obviously connected. The foot-in-the-door technique works even when the two requests are seemingly unconnected, and may work best when there is no obvious incentive such as money to perform the small request.

THE LOW-BALL TECHNIQUE Consider how likely you would be to agree to the following requests. In one case, a researcher calls you on the phone and asks you to participate in an experiment scheduled for 7:00 in the morning. In a second case, a researcher calls and asks you to participate in a study. Only after you initially agree to participate does the researcher inform you that the study will be scheduled at 7:00 AM. When Robert Cialdini and others (1978) actually compared these two procedures, they found that the second approach was much more effective. When students were told from the outset that an experiment would be conducted early in the morning, only 25 percent agreed to participate and showed up on time. In contrast, using the second approach of concealing the time of the study, 55 percent of students agreed to the initial request and almost all of them actually showed up for the early morning appointment. Once having agreed to participate, few people backed out of their agreement when they were informed about the time of day.

This tactic, in which a person is asked to agree to something on the basis of incomplete information and is later told the full story, is called the **low-ball technique.** Essentially, the person is tricked into agreeing to an attractive proposition, only to discover after they've agreed to the deal that the terms are actually different than they expected. This technique appears to work because once an individual has made an initial commitment to a course of action, he or she is reluctant to withdraw, even when the groundrules are changed. Although this technique can be effective (Burger & Petty, 1981), it is clearly deceptive. To protect consumers from unscrupulous salespersons, laws have been enacted to make low-balling illegal for several industries such as automobile dealers.

Our discussion of the foot-in-the-door, door-in-the-face, and low-ball techniques by no means exhausts the possible tactics people use to gain compliance. Recent research by Jerry Burger (1986) has begun to explore another strategy that he calls the "*that's-not-all*" technique. Consider this situation. A salesperson describes a new microwave oven to a potential customer and quotes a price. Then, while the customer is mulling over the decision, the salesperson adds, "But that's not all. Today only, we're having a special deal. If you buy the microwave now, we'll give you a 5-piece set of microwave dishes at no additional cost." In actuality, the salesclerk intended to include the dishes with the oven all along, but by presenting the dishes as a "special deal" or something "just for you," hopes to make the purchase even more attractive. The essence of this technique is to present a product at a high price, allow the customer to think about the price, and then improve the deal by either adding an additional product or by lowering the price.

In a series of seven experiments, Burger (1986) has demonstrated the potential effectiveness of this approach. In one illustrative study, experimenters held a psychology club bake sale on campus. At random, half the people who stopped at the table and asked about the cupcakes were told that they could buy a prepackaged set including one cupcake and two cookies for 75 cents. In this control condition, 40 percent of those who inquired actually purchased a cupcake. In the "that's not all condition," people who inquired were first told that the cupcakes were 75 cents each. A moment later, they were told that actually, they would get not only the cupcake but also 2 cookies for the 75 cent price. In this "that's not all" condition, 73 percent of people bought a cupcake, a substantially higher proportion than in the control condition.

Limits to External Pressure

We have seen that external pressure can often increase compliance. But we should also be aware of the limits of these approaches. The heroic soldier refuses to divulge the secret information even though cruelly tortured; the typical nonheroic smoker refuses to give up cigarettes despite the best efforts of family members; the letter writer refuses to use zip codes despite a variety of threats and persuasion from the Postal Service.

Social psychological research has investigated some of the many reasons why efforts to gain compliance fail. In some cases, people simply do not control the resources—rewards, punishments, expertise, etc.—that would be needed to induce compliance. In other cases, psychological processes may reduce the effectiveness of influence attempts.

REACTANCE Sometimes, too much pressure may actually cause a person to do the opposite of what the influencer desires. Brehm (1966) describes this phenomenon as **reactance**. The basic idea behind Brehm's research is that people attempt to maintain their personal freedom of action. When this freedom is threatened, they do whatever they can to reinstate it. If an individual perceives an influence attempt as a threat to freedom of action, the person protects it by refusing to comply or by doing the opposite of what is requested. We are all familiar with the child who, when asked to do something, says, "I won't." But when her parents say, "All right, then, don't," the child goes ahead and does what was initially requested. This behavior also occurs in adults!

OVERJUSTIFICATION Another limit on external pressure concerns **overjustification**, a concept we introduced in Chapter 5. It is not always true that the larger the reward, the more effective it will be in getting someone to do something. Sometimes a large external reward can undermine a person's intrinsic interest in an activity. It is probably true that greater rewards will be more effective, as long as we continue the rewards indefinitely. However, we often use rewards to get someone to comply in the first place, and then withdraw the rewards in hopes that they will continue the behavior. For example, we might give a child an extra cookie for making his bed, or give a third grade class a prize for mastering a list of spelling words. Advertisers often provide small rewards in the form of prizes or coupons for trying new products. In all these instances, those giving the rewards do not want to continue to offer them forever.

The implication of overjustification for compliance is that rewards may sometimes backfire. If an activity is basically uninteresting or even unpleasant, rewards will probably be helpful because they will increase the likelihood of compliance in the first place. And since the task is not enjoyable, there is no basic interest to undermine. But when the activity is inherently enjoyable or satisfying, giving rewards may reduce future compliance. If you think that children can learn to get satisfaction from cleaning their rooms, rewarding them too much may reduce the chance of this occurring.

OBEDIENCE TO AUTHORITY: THE MILGRAM STUDIES

In this final section we take a closer look at one of the six bases of power identified by Raven: obedience to legitimate authority. In any social group, organization, or society, it is important that people obey orders from those who have legitimate authority. In wartime, generals expect soldiers to obey orders, and punish disobedience seriously. Most people believe that public health officials have the right to require that school children get vaccinations against polio and other communicable diseases. We expect drivers to follow the orders of police directing traffic. Obedience is based on the belief that authorities have the right to make requests. In many cases, we agree with the policies of those in charge, and obey orders willingly. But what about

Most people obey without question the orders of a police officer directing traffic.

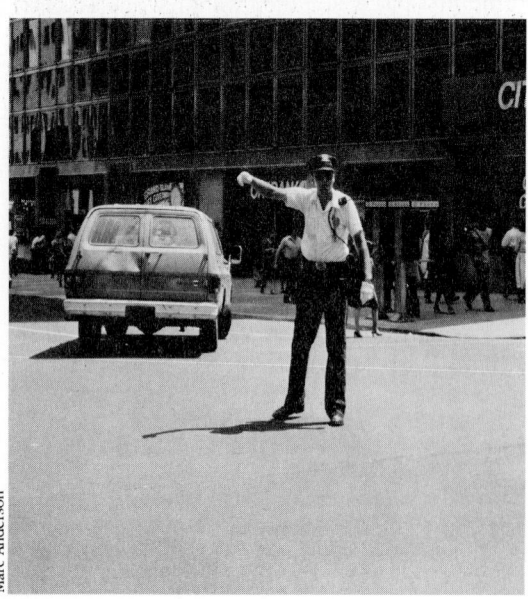

Marc Anderson

situations in which the demands of the authorities conflict with our own beliefs and values? How do parents respond if they believe that a new vaccination required for public schools is potentially hazardous to their children? How do soldiers and citizens react if they believe their government is pursuing a misguided or immoral policy? In the 1960s, an important series of laboratory experiments by Stanley Milgram (1963, 1974) sought to understand these issues.

As first described in Chapter 2, Milgram began his research by placing newspaper ads asking for men to participate in a psychology study. The volunteers were scheduled in pairs and were told that the purpose of the study was to investigate the effects of punishment on learning. One of them was selected by chance as the "learner" and the other as the "teacher." The teacher's job was to read aloud pairs of words that the learner was supposed to memorize. Each time the learner made a mistake, the teacher was to administer a punishment.

The teacher sat in front of a large, impressive "shock machine" containing a number of levers, each of which was labeled with the amount of shock it would deliver. The range was from 15 volts to 450 volts. Above the numbers representing voltage were labels describing the severity of the shock: "Slight," "Extreme Intensity Shock," and "Danger: Severe Shock."

The learner was put in a chair in another room. His arm was strapped down to the chair, and electrodes were taped to it. He could not be seen by the teacher or anyone else; they communicated entirely by intercom. Before the testing began, the learner mentioned that he had a slightly weak heart. He was assured by the experimenter that the shocks were not dangerous. Then the experimenter gave the teacher a sample shock, to give him some idea of what the shocks he would be delivering felt like. It was actually fairly severe and hurt considerably, but the teacher was told it was a mild shock.

During the testing, the learner made a number of errors. The teacher told him he was wrong and delivered a shock. Whenever a shock was given, the learner grunted. As the level of shock increased, the learner's reactions became increasingly dramatic. He yelled, begged the teacher to stop shocking him, pounded the table, and kicked the wall. Toward the end, he simply stopped answering and made no response at all. Through all this, the experimenter urged the teacher to continue. "Please continue." "The experiment must go on." "It is necessary for you to continue." The experimenter also assured the teacher that the responsibility was his, not the teacher's.

Under these circumstances, a large number of subjects dutifully delivered supposedly severe electric shocks. All 40 subjects delivered the 300-volt shock, and 65 percent continued to the final 450-volt level. They did this even though the person they were shocking screamed for mercy, had a heart condition, and was apparently experiencing great pain. In reality, of course, the "learner" was a confederate of the experimenter and did not receive any shocks. All responses, including errors, grunts, and groans, were carefully rehearsed and then tape-recorded to make them identical for all subjects. The "teacher," however, had no way of knowing that the situation was staged.

In a series of 18 studies, Milgram (1965, 1974) sought to identify conditions that increased obedience. Situational changes that made individuals feel more responsible for their actions or that emphasized the negative aspect of what they were doing reduced the amount of obedience. Milgram found, for example, that bringing the victim closer to the subject substantially reduced obedience. In the extreme case, when the victim was seated right next to the subject, obedience decreased dramatically. Tilker (1970) supported this finding, and demonstrated that reminding subjects of their own total responsibility for their actions made them much less likely to administer shocks.

Subjects in the Milgram studies often experienced considerable stress and conflict. On the one hand, they felt enormous pressures from the situation and the experimenter to continue. On the other hand, they were concerned about the welfare of the victim and about their personal responsibility for inflicting pain. As long as subjects could shift responsibility to the experimenter and minimize in their own minds the pain the victim was enduring, obedience was high. To the extent that they felt responsible and were aware of the victim's pain, they were less obedient.

Milgram interpreted his findings as showing that "normal" people can be led to perform destructive acts when exposed to strong situational pressure from a legitimate authority. Miller (1986) has called this the "normality thesis"—the idea that evil acts are not necessarily performed by abnormal or "crazy" people. Rather, average individuals who see themselves as mere agents in an organization, carrying out the orders of those in command, can behave in destructive ways.

Although the pressures to obey legitimate authorities are strong, individuals do not inevitably obey. Several factors seem to make a difference. First, obedience is reduced when the suffering of the victims is highly salient. Second, obedience is reduced when an individual is made to feel personally responsible for his or her actions (Hamilton, 1978). Third, people are more likely to resist authorities when others in the situation model disobedience. Fourth, encouraging individuals to question the motives, expertise, or judgment of authorities can reduce obedience. Finally, sensitizing people to the potential impact of authorities may make a difference. What personal lessons do you draw from the social psychological research on conformity and compliance presented in this chapter?

KEY TERMS IN CHAPTER 12

cohesiveness	conformity	low-ball technique	overjustification
commitment	door-in-the-face technique	minority influence	reactance
compliance	foot-in-the-door technique	norm of social responsibility	

SUMMARY

1. Three important types of social influence are conformity, compliance, and obedience to authority. Conformity occurs when someone voluntarily performs an act because others are doing it. Compliance occurs when people do what they are asked to do, whether they want to do it or not. Obedience to authority is a particular kind of compliance; it occurs when we believe that the requester has a legitimate right to ask us to do something.

2. Classic studies by Sherif on the autokinetic effect and by Asch on line judgments showed that individuals will often conform to group norms in making both ambiguous and clearcut perceptual judgments. Basically, people conform for two reasons—to be right (informational influence) and to be liked (normative influence).

3. People are most likely to conform when they feel strong commitment to a group, when the group has about three or four members (or subunits), and when the majority view is unanimous.

4. Recently, Moscovici and others have shown that a forceful minority can change the position of the majority in a group. Minorities are most effective when they are persistent, and when their behavior is logically consistent, but not "rigid." Single minorities (who differ from the group in only one important way) may be more effective than double minorities (who differ in two ways), because single minorities are less likely to be seen as acting out of self-interest.

5. We may comply with a request for many different reasons. Raven and his colleagues have identified six bases of power that can produce compliance: rewards, coercion, expertise, information, referent power, and legitimate authority. A special case of legitimate power is the "power of helplessness"; a strong cultural norm of social responsibility dictates that we should help those who are less fortunate and less powerful than we are.

6. Researchers have identified several specific compliance strategies, including the foot-in-the-door technique, the door-in-the-face technique, the low-ball technique and the that's-not-all technique.

7. In everyday life, obedience to legitimate authority is adaptive and contributes to smooth social functioning. But sometimes, people obey orders that are harmful to other people and that violate their own personal beliefs and values. In one of the best known studies in social psychology, Milgram investigated this phenomenon. He found that a majority of "normal" adults would administer severe electric shocks to a helpless victim if ordered to do so by a researcher.

8. Obedience to legitimate authority is lessened when individuals are made aware of the suffering they cause, feel personally responsible for their actions, observe others who disobey the authority, and are encouraged to question the motives and judgment of the authority.

SUGGESTED READINGS

CIALDINI, R. B. (1985). *Influence: Science and practice*. New York: Random House. A very readable discussion of the many ways we try to influence other people. The book is based both on empirical research and on the author's experiences with salespeople, public relations agents, fund-raisers, and others whose livelihood depends on successfully influencing people.

MILGRAM, S. (1974). *Obedience to authority: An experimental view*. New York: Harper and Row. A complete description of Milgram's research program and the many variations he conducted plus Milgram's own theoretical analysis of his finding.

MILLER, A. G. (1986). *The obedience experiments: A case study of controversy in social science*. New York: Praeger. A thoughtful review of Milgram's original studies and later replication studies by other researchers. The book discusses both ethical and methodological critiques of Milgram's work, and considers the applicability of these laboratory studies to understanding the Holocaust and other cases of genocide.

MOSCOVICI, S. (1985). Social influence and conformity. In G. Lindzey & E. Aronson (Eds.), *Handbook of social psychology*, 3rd ed., Vol. 2. New York: Random House, pp. 347–412. A comprehensive and somewhat technical review of conformity research and theory, with special attention to the influence of minorities.

13 BEHAVIOR IN GROUPS

We are all members of groups that have enormous influence on our lives. Most of us are born into a family group and spend much of our childhood interacting with parents and siblings. As we venture into the larger social world, we encounter new groups—perhaps a neighborhood play group, a kindergarten class, Cub Scouts or Brownies, or a group at a church or synagogue. As we grow up, we begin to join clubs, sports teams, work groups, political parties, and other organizations.

In this chapter, we begin by defining a group and examining some of the basic processes of group interaction including communication and competition versus cooperation. We then investigate the nature of leadership in groups, and explore group productivity and decision-making. We conclude with a brief look at some of the potentially negative aspects of group life—deindividuation and social contagion.

BASIC FEATURES OF GROUPS

Defining a Group

We spend time in many different kinds of *social aggregates*, which is the general term for any collection of people (McGrath, 1984). Here are some examples of the different types:

- *A statistical aggregate*: For research purposes, it is sometimes useful to group together for analysis all members of a particular social category, such as all redheads, all women, all unemployed heads of household, or everyone over 65. Members of a statistical aggregate all have some common characteristic, although they are not likely to know each other or to interact.

- *An audience*: All the people watching the 6 o'clock news on Channel 4 in New York City are part of the same audience, even though they are not necessarily aware of one another and do not interact.

- *A crowd*: When people are in physical proximity and responding to a common situation or stimulus, we call them a crowd. Examples would be fans gathered outside a rock star's dressing room, people lining up outside a department store waiting for a special sale to begin, or people gathering to watch a street brawl.

- *A team*: A set of people who interact regularly for some particular purpose or activity, such as a work group, sports team, or bridge club, is a team.

- *A family*: Although there are many types, families usually consist of a set of people who are related by birth or legal arrangements and who usually share a common residence.

- *Formal organization*: Larger aggregates of people often work together in some clearly structured way to accomplish a joint goal. Examples would be a school system, a church or synagogue, a national political party, the Sierra Club, or the National Rifle Association.

In everyday language we might speak of all these aggregates as "groups." But social scientists use the term *group* in a narrower, more technical way.

Groups are social aggregates in which members are *interdependent* and have at least the potential for mutual *interaction*. In most groups, members have regular face-to-face contact. This definition of a group is an extension of the basic definition of an interpersonal relationship given in Chapter 9. The definition emphasizes that the essential feature of a group is that members influence one another in some way.

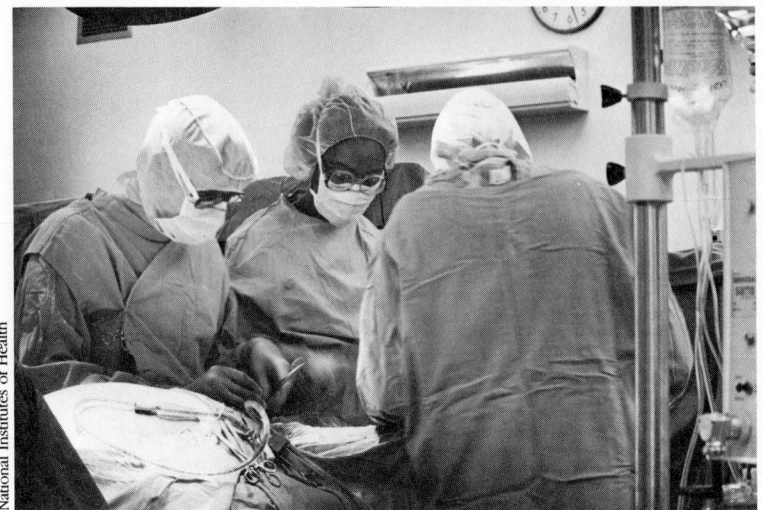

Members of an operating room team work closely together to perform delicate surgery. Because their actions are interdependent, they constitute a true social group.

Based on this definition, a statistical aggregate such as football players in general is not a group, since the people in this category do not know one another, have face-to-face contact, or influence one another. The members of the Dallas Cowboys football team are a group because they interact regularly and their actions affect one another. Similarly, all the children who watch "Sesame Street" on TV are part of a common audience, but they are not a group. However, all the children in Mrs. Garcia's second-grade class who listen to their teacher reading a story are part of a group.

Groups vary in many ways: size, duration, values and goals, and scope. One of the most important dimensions is size. The smallest group is the dyad or couple. Most research on groups has focused on small groups ranging from about 3 to 20 people. As social aggregates get much larger, they tend to become formal organizations and may no longer involve knowledge and interaction among all members. To emphasize the distinction between groups and formal organizations, some researchers prefer the term "small group" for social units in which members have face-to-face interaction.

Groups vary in duration, how long the group stays together. Families may continue to exist for many generations, with new members joining the group through birth or marriage and others leaving

through death or divorce. Members of a jury might work together for a few days on a particular case, and then be disbanded at the end of the trial.

Groups also differ widely in values and goals. Consider for a moment the differences among a chess club, the local Young Republicans group, the Gay and Lesbian Student Association, and a religious education class. Which, if any, of these groups you might consider joining depends a great deal on your personal values, interests, and goals.

The breadth or scope of activities performed by a group is another important dimension. Some groups focus on a single issue. For instance, in response to a threatened tuition increase, a group of college students might form a task force to formulate alternatives and present them to the University administration. Here, a group is created for one specific purpose. In contrast, groups such as families engage in a great many different activities.

Research on small groups has sometimes studied naturally occurring groups such as families, teammates, or work groups. But there is also a long tradition of studying "concocted groups" (McGrath, 1984), groups deliberately created by a researcher. In a typical study, groups of strangers (usually college students) are brought together in a lab to spend a few hours working on a group decision-making task. We'll discuss the results of experimen-

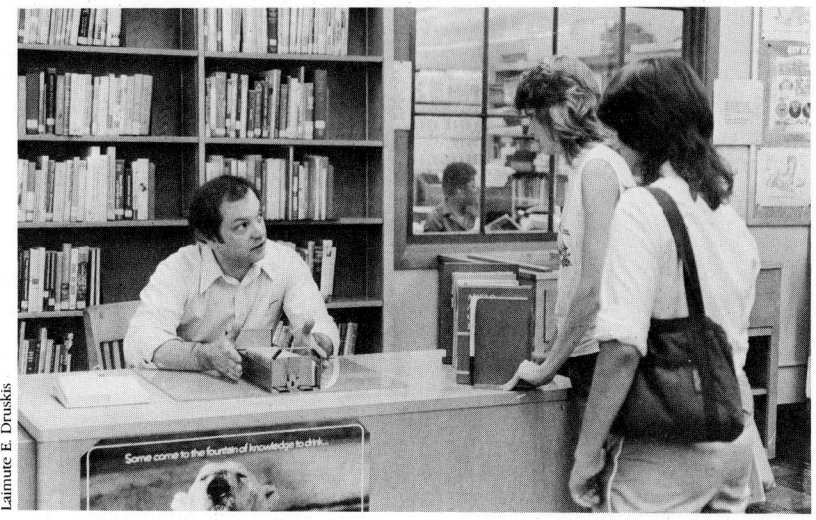

Two students talk to a reference librarian. Roles define the activities of both parties: students have a right to ask questions about books (but not about the weather at the beach or the answers to their upcoming calculus exam) and librarians are expected to provide bibliographic information (but not to report their taste in books to their parents or write term papers for them).

tal studies on groups later in this chapter. For the moment, it is useful to note that whereas naturally occurring groups are often relatively enduring and broad in scope, most experimental groups are short-lived and relatively narrow in focus.

Social Roles

When a number of people are brought together in a group, they do not remain entirely undifferentiated. They develop patterns of behavior, divide tasks, adopt different roles, and so on. For example, Merei (1949) observed that after three or more meetings, groups of young children formed traditions: They decided where each child would sit in the room, who would play with which toy, what sequence of activities would be followed, and so on. In informal groups such as this one, differentiated behavior patterns emerge over time as a result of group interaction.

Often, however, the basic structure of a group is predetermined. The student entering school, the worker taking a new job, the person joining a bridge club are all confronted with a preexisting social structure. For example, in a small computer software business, there may be four distinct *positions*: the owner who created the business, the programmers who develop new software packages, a sales representative, and a secretary. The positions in nearly any social system differ in *social status* (prestige or ranking). In the software company, the owner probably has the highest status and the largest salary; the secretary probably has the lowest status and salary.

Associated with each position is a particular **social role,** a set of rules and understandings about what the person in that position is expected to do, what the responsibilities are, and so on. Roles define the division of labor in the group. In some groups, such as the software company, positions, roles, and status are explicit and may even be described in a formal organizational chart. Individuals must adapt to the requirements of their position in the group, although they may try to redefine or renegotiate existing patterns.

Cohesiveness

In some groups, the bonds between members are strong and enduring. In other groups, members are loosely linked, lack a sense of "groupness," and tend to drift apart over time. As we noted in Chapter 12, **cohesiveness** refers to the forces, both positive and negative, that cause members to remain in a group (Festinger, 1950). Cohesiveness is a characteristic of a group as a whole. It depends on the individual level of commitment each person has to the group.

A key positive force increasing cohesiveness is the interpersonal attraction that exists among group members (Ridgeway, 1983). When group members like each other and are connected by bonds of friendship, cohesiveness is high. Indeed, researchers have often measured cohesiveness by assessing the amount of mutual liking among group members.

Second, people's motivation to remain in a group is also influenced by the instrumental goals of the group. We often participate in groups as a means to an end—a way to earn a salary, to play a sport we enjoy, to work for a worthy cause. Our attraction to a group depends on the match between our goals and those of the group, and also on how successfully the group accomplishes its objectives. This point was illustrated in a recent study. Snyder, Lassegard, and Ford (1986) investigated how individuals react when they belong to a group (even one artificially constructed by researchers) that fails in performing a group task. Compared to people in successful groups, members of unsuccessful groups did more to "distance" themselves from the group, for example, by not wearing their team badge. Individuals apparently wanted to avoid identification with an unsuccessful group.

A third positive factor is the extent to which a group interacts effectively and harmoniously. We would undoubtedly prefer to be on a team that works efficiently, rather than on one that wastes our time and misuses our skills. More generally, anything that increases group satisfaction and morale should enhance cohesiveness.

Group cohesiveness is also affected by negative forces that discourage members from leaving, even if they are dissatisfied. Sometimes people stay in groups because the costs of leaving are high or because they have no available alternatives. We may despise our co-workers at the factory, but stay because there are no other job openings in town. We may dislike our teachers, but stay in their classes because we have no choice in the matter.

Communication

Communication is essential to group activities, whether it be the endless talking at a committee meeting, the shared intimacies of a late-night con-

FIGURE 13–1 The amount of communication by members of a group follows a logarithmic or exponential curve. Regardless of the size of the group, the most talkative members do about 40 percent of the communicating and the amount of the other members' communication drops off sharply. (Adapted from Stephan & Mishler 1952.)

versation between friends, or a family conference to make plans for a vacation.

A feature of most groups is that some people talk a great deal and others say very little. In a seminar, for example, there usually seem to be one or two people who monopolize the discussion, regardless of the topic. They do most of the talking, and the rest say only an occasional word or two.

Perhaps the most striking aspect of this phenomenon is that it occurs no matter what the size of the group. Regardless of how many members there are, communication follows a fairly regular pattern that can be represented by a logarithmic function. Figure 13–1 illustrates this pattern for groups of four, six, and eight. Note that in all cases, one person does a great deal of talking, the next most talkative person talks considerably less, and so on. In an eight-member group, two people contribute 60 percent of the conversation, one contributes 14 percent, and the other five contribute only 26 percent among them. Clearly, the exact percentage contributed by each person will vary from group to group. There are even some groups in which all members make equal contributions. But by and large, a pattern roughly similar to the one illustrated appears in most groups.

COMMUNICATION NETWORKS We have been discussing groups as though every member were free to communicate with every other member. This is true in a discussion group, but there are many groups in which communication is limited. Several studies have investigated the effects of a variety of so-called **communication networks.**

The typical study in this area consists of forming a group to work on some problem and imposing limits on the communication permitted among the members. This is done by putting the subjects in separate rooms or booths and allowing them to communicate only by written messages or an intercom system. The experimenters are then able to control who can talk with whom, and a large number of different communication patterns can be imposed.

Some of these patterns are represented for groups of five people in Figure 13–2: There you

FIGURE 13–2 Examples of different types of communication networks.

Circle

Chain

Y–pattern

Wheel

In this football huddle, the quarterback gives teammates instructions for the next play. This illustrates a wheel communication network in which messages are channeled through one person.

can see that the structures determine freedom of communication. In the circle, all members are equal—each can talk to two neighbors and to no one else. In the chain, two of the members can each talk to only one person. Obviously, in terms of communication it is worse to be at the end of a chain. The three other members are equal in terms of the number of persons they can talk to, but the person in the middle is more central. The two intermediate people are somewhat isolated from the opposite ends. This progression is carried a step further in the Y-shaped structure. With three end members, only one of the others is able to talk to two people, and the fifth member is able to talk to three. In the wheel, one member can talk to everyone else, but all the other members can talk only to the central one.

COMMUNICATION NETWORKS, MORALE, AND EFFICIENCY
Research shows that communication patterns such as these affect many aspects of group life (Ridgeway, 1983; Shaw, 1981). Communication networks influence group *morale*. Leavitt (1951) found that the more freedom group members had to talk, the more satisfied they were. The person who could talk to everyone was the most content, whereas those on the end of a chain, who could talk to only one other person, were the least content. Since the total morale of a group depends on the satisfaction of all group members, not just those in key positions, overall group satisfaction is highest in patterns such as the circle, where everyone has an equal opportunity to communicate.

Communication networks can also affect the *efficiency* of group problem-solving. Although the evidence on how different kinds of networks affect group performance is not entirely consistent, most of the data suggest that centralized groups are more effective when they work on simple problems, and decentralized groups are more effective with complex problems. Imagine, for example, that each member of a group is given a card with a different symbol on it and the group task is to make a list of all the symbols. This kind of simple task is ideal for groups with highly centralized communication networks: The leader can easily collect the information from each individual and compile the final list. But complex problems are usually accomplished more effectively by groups with decentralized communication patterns, where freer interaction among members is possible.

TASK PERFORMANCE IN GROUPS

Do people do their best work alone or with others present? Are two heads better than one? Are groups usually more successful in getting a task done than individuals alone would be? Social psychologists have studied these issues in depth.

Social Facilitation versus Inhibition

How does the presence of other people influence an individual's performance on a task? Consider two examples. John is an outstanding high school runner who hopes one day to try out for the Olympics. He trains very hard, and notices that he runs better with a training partner than by himself. His best performances have been during actual track meets when he was running against tough competitors. Susan is taking her first class in acting. At home in the privacy of her bedroom, she delivers her lines with accuracy and self-confidence. In front of her classmates, she stumbles over her part. As these examples suggest, the presence of others sometimes enhances and sometimes impairs an individual's performance.

Everyday experience suggests that people sometimes perform better in the presence of others than when they are alone. This is called **social facilitation.** Social psychologists have long been fascinated by this phenomenon. Indeed, experimentation in social psychology is often traced to an experiment in social facilitation conducted by Triplett in 1898. Noting that cyclists raced faster when they were in competition than when alone, Triplett devised an experiment to see whether children would work faster on a task in the presence of others. As he predicted, children worked harder pulling in a fishing reel in a group setting than alone.

Many studies have demonstrated this effect (see review by Guerin, 1986). In the 1920s, for example, Allport (1920, 1924) had subjects work on such tasks as crossing out all the vowels in a newspaper column, doing easy multiplication problems, or writing refutations of a logical argument. Even though participants always worked individually on the task, they were more productive when there were five other people in the room than when they were alone. Social facilitation has been found when the others who are present are actually performing the same task (are "co-actors") and when the other person is an observer or experimenter. Facilitation can also occur in the "mere presence" of another so long as there is some uncertainty

A top-ranked gymnast competes in a national competition, watched by a panel of judges and many spectators. For trained athletes who have learned their routines well, the presence of an audience is likely to improve performance. This is known as social facilitation.

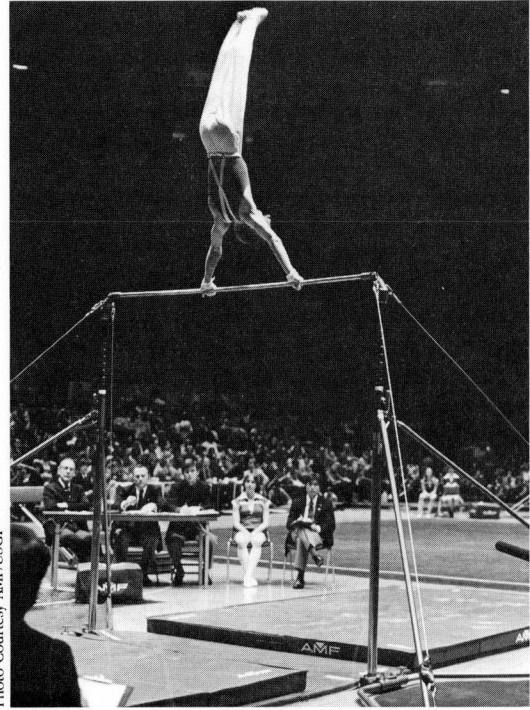

Photo Courtesy AMF/USGF

about the other person's behavior or intentions (Guerin, 1986).

Social facilitation is not limited to humans. It has also been demonstrated in rats, cockroaches, and parakeets. For instance, Chen (1937) found that individual ants dug three times more sand when they were in groups than when they were alone.

On the other hand, the presence of others sometimes inhibits individual performance, a phenomenon called *social inhibition* of performance. In Allport's early studies (1924), people in a group setting wrote more refutations of a logical argument, but the quality of the work was lower than when they worked alone. Another study (Pessin, 1933) found that the presence of a spectator reduced individual performance on a memory task. Why does this happen?

A major answer was offered by Robert Zajonc (1965). He suggested that being in the presence of others increases an individual's drive or motivation. Whether this increased drive facilitates or interferes with performance depends on the task. When a task requires a response that is well-learned or innate, called a *dominant response*, increased motivation is helpful. The presence of others will facilitate performance on relatively simple tasks, such as crossing out vowels or doing easy arithmetic. For a highly trained athlete, the presence of others is likely to improve performance. But when a task requires a behavior that is not well-learned, the increased motivation impairs performance. Examples would be solving difficult arithmetic problems, memorizing new material, or writing complex logical deductions. For Susan, struggling to remember her lines, an audience may simply increase stage fright and inhibit a good performance. If she were more experienced and had performed the part every night for months, the audience might help her overcome boredom and improve her performance.

Research has generally supported the basic idea that the effect of the presence of others depends on the kind of task. A recent study (Michaels et al., 1982) provides an interesting illustration in a field setting. These researchers observed the behavior of people playing pool in a college student union building. They identified pairs of players who were either above or below average in their play, and secretly made records of their scores. Then,

teams of four confederates approached the players and watched them closely during several more rounds of play. Zajonc's theory predicts that good players will benefit from an audience, but poor players will not. The results provided clear support for this prediction. When good players were being watched by four others, their accuracy rose from 71 to 80 percent. When poor players were observed, their accuracy dropped from 36 to 25 percent.

Although there is general agreement that the presence of others increases individual drive or motivation, there is considerable controversy about the nature of the drive (Baron, 1986; Guerin, 1986; Sanders, 1984). Some suggest there is an innate tendency to become aroused by the mere presence of other people. Another view is that others motivate us because we have learned to be concerned about how they may evaluate us or about looking good in front of others. A third view is that the presence of others is distracting. On easy tasks that do not require full attention, we may compensate for the distraction by trying harder and may actually perform better. But distractions created by other people work in reverse on complex tasks. A recent extension of this idea is the *distraction-conflict model* (Baron, 1986; Sanders, Baron, & Moore, 1978), which suggests that the presence of others is arousing because it creates a conflict between two basic tendencies—(1) to pay attention to the audience or co-actors and (2) to pay attention to the task. This conflict increases arousal, which then either helps or hinders task performance, depending on whether the dominant response is correct. These explanations are not necessarily contradictory: It is possible that all these processes can occur, depending on the situation.

Social Impact Theory

Our discussion so far has concerned the question of when the presence of others has positive or negative effects on individual performance. **Social impact theory** addresses the more general issue of how strong an influence (either positive or negative) these others have. As developed by Latané (1981), this theory suggests that the total impact of other people on an individual depends on their number, strength, and immediacy. This is shown

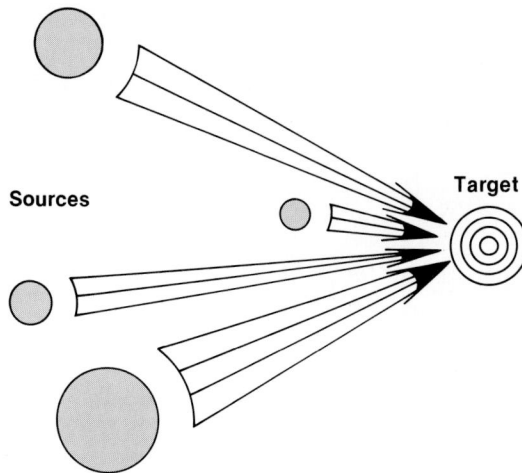

Sources

Target

FIGURE 13–3 The impact of an audience on a target depends on the number of people present (number of circles), the immediacy of the people (nearness of the circles), and the strength or importance of the people (size of the circles). (Adapted from Latané, 1981, p. 344.)

schematically in Figure 13-3. The impact of other people increases as the *number* of observers increases. Thus Susan should experience more stage fright performing in front of 50 people than 5.

Another factor is the *strength* of the social forces, that is, the importance or power of the people present. Strength might be determined by such things as status, age, and the relationship between the individual and those others. Susan might feel significantly worse about performing in front of her teacher or a casting director than in front of her peers.

The third factor is the *immediacy* of the audience, their closeness to the individual in time or space. Susan's reactions should be stronger if she has a live audience than if she is being watched on a video monitor located in another room (Borden, 1980). Latané suggests that social impact theory can be compared to light falling on a surface: The total amount of light depends on the number of light bulbs, the wattage of the bulbs, and their closeness to the surface.

Social impact theory is still relatively new and controversial (Jackson, 1986; Mullen, 1985, 1986). To date, empirical evidence has supported predic-

tions about the impact of group size: The larger the group or audience, the more impact it has on an individual's performance. However, evidence about the importance of strength and immediacy is not clear at this point.

SOCIAL LOAFING   Social impact theory has sparked renewed interest in an intriguing aspect of social life, the observation that individuals work less hard as members of a group than they would alone. This effect, known as **social loafing,** was first discussed in the late 1880s by a French agricultural engineer named Max Ringelmann (Kravitz & Martin, 1986). As part of a study of work efficiency in horses, oxen and men, Ringelmann asked student volunteers to pull as hard as they could on a rope. He measured their effort in kilograms of pressure using a strain gauge. Sometimes the participants worked alone and sometimes in groups of 7 or 14 people. Common sense and research on social facilitation might predict that the men would work harder when they were part of a team than when they were alone. Just the opposite happened. When pulling alone, individuals averaged about 85 kg per person. In groups of seven, the total group force was only 65 kg per person and in the largest groups, each individual's contribution fell to 61 kg.

More recent studies by Latané and his colleagues (Latané, Williams, & Harkins, 1979) have provided further evidence about social loafing. In one study, undergraduate men were asked to make as much noise as they could by cheering or by clapping. Each person performed alone, in pairs, in groups of four, and in groups of six. The results, presented in Figure 13–4, clearly show that the noise produced by each individual decreased as the size of the group increased. This is the same pattern Ringelmann found. The social loafing effect is similar to the bystander effect discussed in Chapter 11: As the number of witnesses to an emergency increases, the likelihood that any one person will intervene often decreases.

How can we explain the fact that the presence of others sometimes leads to social facilitation and sometimes causes social loafing? Latané proposes that these patterns occur in different situations. In facilitation situations, the individual is the sole target of influence from an audience or from co-workers (as shown in Figure 13–3). The social impact of

As the number of workers in a group increases, so does the tendency toward loafing on the job.

Tom McHugh, Photo Researchers, Inc.

FIGURE 13–4 A comparison of the intensity of noise an individual makes alone and in groups. (Adapted from Latané, Williams & Harkins, 1979, p. 825.)

the others is all directed at the individual; as the number of people present increases, their social impact on the individual also increases. Social loafing situations occur when group members work together on a task assigned by an outsider. As shown in Figure 13–5, each individual is only one of several targets of the outsider's influence. When others stand with the individual as targets of forces coming from outside the group, the social impact of the outsider is divided among group members. As the size of the group increases, the pressure felt by each individual decreases.

Latané suggests that cognitive processes may contribute to social loafing. People may believe that others in the group are not working as hard as they could. Not wanting to do more than their own fair share, these people may do less work to insure that the situation is equitable (Jackson & Harkins, 1985). Further, individuals may feel that in a collective activity, their own contribution will be less recognizable, leading to a diffusion of responsibility. Social loafing decreases when the task is difficult or challenging, and when individuals believe they can make a unique contribution to the group effort (Jackson & Williams, 1985). As researchers learn more about the causes of social loafing, we will be better able to counteract it by

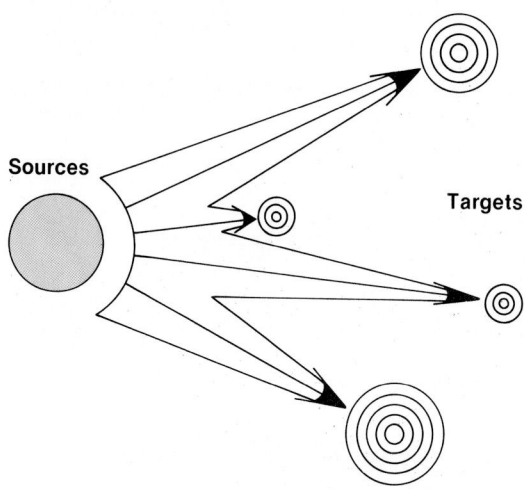

FIGURE 13–5 When each individual is only one of several targets of social influence, the impact of the audience on the individual is lessened. (Adapted from Latané, 1981, p. 349.)

giving individuals a greater sense of personal responsibility and involvement.

Type of Task

When are two (or more) heads better than one at solving a problem? To answer this question, we first need to consider the variety of tasks that groups can perform (Steiner, 1972).

An *additive task* is one in which group productivity is the sum of individual efforts. When a group of friends works together to push a pickup truck with a dead battery out of a busy intersection, the group effort is the sum of how hard each person works. A crucial factor in additive tasks is whether group members are able to coordinate their efforts effectively. In the truck example, it would be important for everyone to push at the same time, and in the same direction. The rope pulling task used by Ringelmann was an additive task—the total effort exerted was the sum of the effort of each individual. Although social loafing may diminish the contribution of each individual to an additive task, the total contribution still usually exceeds what any one person could do alone. (Try pushing a stalled truck by yourself if you doubt this generalization.) On additive tasks, group productivity is generally superior to the efforts of any one person.

Neighbors struggle together to free a car trapped in a snowdrift. In an additive task such as this, the success of the group depends on the combined efforts of all individuals.

Lynn McLaren, Photo Researchers, Inc.

BOX 13–1

BRAINSTORMING: A CLASSIC METHOD FOR GROUP

PROBLEM-SOLVING

If an advertising executive must develop catchy slogans for a campaign to encourage drivers to use seat belts, should she have her staff members work on the problem individually, or should she bring them together as a group to work jointly on the task? Much of the early work on group problem-solving involved an activity called brainstorming that was devised by an advertising executive (Osborn, 1957).

Brainstorming is a technique for coming up with new or creative solutions to problems. A group is given a specific problem to discuss, such as advertising slogans for a new brand of toothpaste. Members are instructed to think of as many different suggestions as they can in a short time period.

The rules of brainstorming, as outlined by Osborn, included these:

1. Criticism is ruled out. Adverse judgment of ideas must be withheld until later.
2. Freewheeling is welcomed. The wilder an idea, the better. It is easier to tame down than to perk up.
3. Quantity is wanted. The greater the number of ideas, the more likelihood of winners.
4. Combination and improvement are sought. In addition to contributing ideas of your own, you should suggest how ideas of others can be turned into better ideas or how two or more ideas can be joined into still another one.

In a classic study on brainstorming (Taylor, Berry & Block, 1958), subjects were assigned at random to five-person groups or to an individual condition. The people in both conditions were then given five problems and 12 minutes to work on each one. One problem was stated as follows: "Each year a great many American tourists visit Europe, but now suppose that our country wished to get many more European tourists to visit America during their vacations. What steps can you suggest that would get more European tourists to come to this country?" The subjects were told their task was to consider the problems and to offer as many and as creative solutions as they could. There were obviously no "correct" solutions.

Subjects in the alone condition were divided at random into five-person aggregates. That is, although each worked alone, for purposes of the analysis they were considered a unit, and their total production was compared to the production of the actual groups. Taylor et al. compared 5 hours of work done by a five-person group with 5 hours done by five individuals working alone.

The results, presented in Table 13–1, can be considered in terms of the quantity of ideas produced and also in terms of their originality. Quantity consisted of the number of different ideas produced by the real groups and the aggregates. If two people in an aggregate produced the same idea, it was counted as only one. As the table shows, individuals

TABLE 13–1

Comparing the Brainstorming Productivity of Groups and Individuals

Condition	Mean Number of Different Ideas	Mean Number of Unique Ideas
Real five-person groups	37.5	10.8
Five individuals working alone (aggregates)	68.1	19.8

Source: Taylor, Berry & Block (1958).

working alone (the aggregates) scored higher than the actual groups. Five individuals working alone produced almost twice as many solutions and unique ideas as five people working together. Someone working alone can concentrate better and also does not worry about competing with others in order to express his or her own ideas. This and other studies have generally found that whatever stimulation a brainstorming group may produce is apparently more than offset by the interfering and distracting effects of other people (Lamm & Trommsdorf, 1973).

A *conjunctive task* is one in which all group members must succeed for the group to succeed. For a spy team to slip successfully across enemy lines, it is essential that every member remain undetected. A false move by any one person endangers the whole mission. For conjunctive tasks, group productivity is only as good as the *least* competent group member, the "weakest link."

In a *disjunctive task*, only one person needs to solve a problem for the entire group to succeed. If a research group is trying to solve a complex mathematical equation, any one person with the right answer can ensure the group's effectiveness.

Group performance on disjunctive tasks depends on the skill of the *most* competent member. In tasks of this sort, groups usually have an advantage over individuals.

An even more complex situation occurs when a group has a task that can be subdivided among group members. In a football game, for example, teammates specialize in particular types of activities. Group productivity depends not only on the effort and skill of the best or worst player, but also on the group's ability to coordinate individual activities, often under time pressure (Kelly & McGrath, 1985) or other situational constraints.

GROUP DECISION-MAKING

The Dean of a major law school has to make an important and controversial decision about the school's policy on the admission of ethnic minority students. Should she make the decision alone, or consult with a group of advisors? Common sense suggests that groups are likely to make better decisions than individuals. After all, a group is likely to have more information than a single individual, a group may be better able to examine all sides of an issue, and group discussion should help to prevent a rash or extreme decision. However, social psychological research indicates that groups do not necessarily make wiser or more moderate decisions. Groups are vulnerable to special social forces that can affect decision-making. We will consider two group processes—polarization and "groupthink."

Group Polarization

In 1961 James Stoner observed that group decisions are riskier than the individual views held by the members before discussion. This finding, called the **risky shift,** sparked considerable interest, in part because it seemed to contradict the popular belief that groups are relatively conservative and stodgy about decision-making.

In a typical risky-shift study, subjects read about a number of complex situations, such as the one

President Ronald Reagan meets with his top advisors. How might group processes affect decision-making in this type of group?

TABLE 13–2

An Example of the Situations Used to Study Group Polarization

---

Mr. E is president of a metals corporation in the United States. The corporation is quite prosperous and Mr. E has considered the possibility of expansion by building an additional plant in a new location. His choice is between building another plant in the United States, where there would be a moderate return on the initial investment, or building a plant in a foreign country, where lower labor costs and easy access to raw materials would mean a much higher return on the initial investment. However, there is a history of political instability and revolution in the foreign country under consideration. In fact, the leader of a small minority party is committed to nationalizing, that is, taking over all foreign investments.

Imagine that you are advising Mr. E. Listed below are several probabilities of continued political stability in the foreign country under consideration. Please check the lowest probability that you would consider acceptable in order for Mr. E's corporation to build in that country.

- The chances are 1 in 10 that the foreign country will remain politically stable.
- The chances are 3 in 10 that the foreign country will remain politically stable.
- The chances are 5 in 10 that the foreign country will remain politically stable.
- The chances are 7 in 10 that the foreign country will remain politically stable.
- The chances are 9 in 10 that the foreign country will remain politically stable.
- Place a check here if you think Mr. E's corporation should not build a plant in the foreign country, no matter what the probabilities.

Source: Kogan and Wallach (1967), pp. 234–235.

described in Table 13–2. In each situation, several choices, ranging from very high risk to very low risk, were available. Subjects were asked to consider each situation carefully and to decide what recommendation they would make or which choice they would prefer. Subjects made their decisions individually and did not know they were going to discuss them later. Then subjects were brought into a group and asked to discuss each problem and to reach a unanimous group decision. Under these conditions, there was a strong tendency for the group decision to involve greater risk than the average of the decisions made by the individuals.

Many studies conducted in the United States, Canada, and Europe replicated this basic finding

of a group shift toward greater risk, but some began to find exceptions. In particular, some groups actually made more conservative decisions (see Fraser, Gouge, & Billig, 1971). Today, research has shown that when the initial opinions of group members are conservative, group discussion results in a shift toward more extreme conservatism. When the initial opinions tend toward risk, group discussion results in a shift toward greater risk. This basic finding that group discussion leads to more extreme decisions is called **group polarization.**

Several explanations for group polarization have been offered (Myers & Lamm, 1976). In a recent review of published research, Isenberg (1986) found support for two main explanations.

The *persuasive arguments* perspective emphasizes that people gain new information as a result of listening to pro and con arguments in the group discussion (Burnstein & Vinokur, 1975). The more numerous and persuasive the arguments in favor of a position, the more likely group members are to adopt that decision. However, group discussions do not usually examine all conceivable pro and con arguments, nor do they present all positions with equal conviction (Stasser & Titus, 1985). Often, the majority of arguments tend to support the members' initial position, so that people usually hear more reasons in favor of their own opinion than against it. Group discussion may also encourage members to think about various arguments and to commit themselves more actively to a particular position. The information presented during the discussion may thus convince people of the correctness of their original views, and so lead to more extreme opinions.

A second major explanation emphasizes *social comparison* and self-presentational processes (Goethals & Zanna, 1979; Sanders & Baron, 1977). The idea is that group members are concerned with how their own opinions compare to those of others in the group. During discussion, individuals may learn that others share their attitudes and indeed that some people even have stronger (more extreme) views than they do. A desire to be seen positively, as confident or bold, may therefore lead individuals to shift toward even more extreme positions than those of fellow group members. This is essentially a form of one-upmanship, in which individuals try to be "better" than average. As Brown explained, "To be virtuous . . . is to be different from the mean—in the right direction and to the right degree" (1974, p. 469). Current research provides support for both persuasive arguments and social comparison processes, and suggests that both processes sometimes occur simultaneously.

Other possible explanations have also been proposed (Fraser & Foster, 1984). It has been suggested that people may feel freer to make risky decisions in a group because of a diffusion of responsibility for their actions. Another possibility is that social identification processes are at work (Turner, 1985; Mackie, 1986). The idea is that discussion causes individuals to focus on their group membership.

This in turn leads to a more stereotyped perception of the group's opinions; members come to perceive the group's position as more extreme than it really is. As a result, individuals feel pressure to shift their own views to conform with this perceived norm.

Groupthink

Sometimes a seemingly reasonable and intelligent group of people comes to a decision that in retrospect is obviously a disaster. Irving Janis (1982) says this may be the result of a process he calls **groupthink.** As outlined in Figure 13–6, the pro-

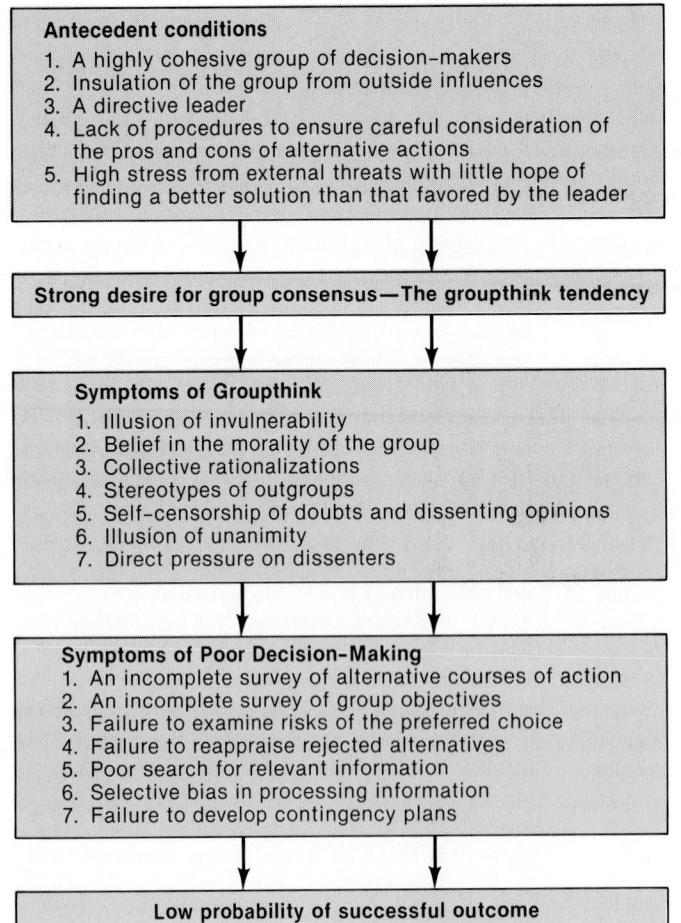

FIGURE 13–6   An analysis of groupthink. (Adapted from Janis, 1982, p. 244.)

cess begins with the group feeling invulnerable and excessively optimistic. The group comes to a decision without allowing any member to express doubts about it. Members shield themselves from any outside information that might undermine this decision. Finally, the group believes its decision is unanimous, even with considerable unexpressed dissent.

Under these circumstances, the group maintains extremely high morale because of the mutual support for the decision. But since disagreements both inside and outside the group are prevented, the decisions can sometimes be disastrous.

Janis suggests that groupthink occurs most often in highly cohesive groups that are able to seal themselves off from outside opinions and that have very strong, dynamic leaders. These leaders propose a particular solution to a problem and argue strongly for it. Group members do not disagree partly because they are afraid of being rejected and partly because they do not want to lower morale. According to Janis, skeptical members do not just go along with the group; they actually convince themselves that their own doubts are trivial and not worth expressing.

Janis claims that groupthink contributed to several disastrous episodes in United States foreign policy. He cites the lack of preparation for the Japanese "surprise" attack on Pearl Harbor in 1941, the Bay of Pigs invasion of Cuba in the 1960s, the escalation of the Vietnam war during the same decade, and Nixon's attempted Watergate coverup in the early 1970s. In all these cases, a small group of powerful politicians, generally led by the president, made a decision in isolation from dissenting voices or from information that would have changed the eventual decision.

Here is how Janis describes the Bay of Pigs fiasco: President John Kennedy and his advisors hatched a plan to land anti-Castro agents, mostly Cubans living in exile in the United States, on Cuban territory. Their ultimate goal was to overthrow the Communist Castro government. The plan called for the invaders to land at the Bay of Pigs. If the initial landing was unsuccessful, the invaders were to retreat into the Escambray Mountains. The planners apparently thought this escape route was a good one, since there were anti-Castro guerrillas in these mountains. Incredibly, no one in the planning group bothered to look at a detailed map of the area. If they had, they would have realized that the mountains were separated from the landing area by 80 miles of swamps and marsh that no army could have gotten through. As it happened, the rest of the plan was also so badly conceived that the invading force was virtually wiped out before it could even consider a retreat.

Janis has offered various suggestions for combatting groupthink and enhancing the effectiveness of group decision-making. These include:

1. The leader should encourage each group member to air objections and doubts about proposed decisions. For this to be effective, the leader must be willing to accept criticism of his or her ideas.
2. The leader should initially remain impartial in discussions, stating preferences and expectations only after group members have expressed their own views.
3. The group should divide into subcommittees to discuss issues independently and then come together to hammer out differences.
4. Outside experts should be invited to participate occasionally in group discussions and should be encouraged to challenge the views of the group members.
5. At each meeting, at least one person should be assigned the role of critic or devil's advocate to challenge group ideas.

These suggestions are designed to force the group to consider many alternatives, to avoid a false illusion of consensus, and to consider all relevant information.

Empirical support for the notion of groupthink comes from two sources. First, at least some of Janis's ideas are based on and supported by basic research on group processes (Janis, 1982). Second, there have been a few direct tests of specific predictions from the model (Longley & Pruitt, 1980). In one laboratory study (Flowers, 1977), for example, teams of students met to discuss a hypothetical problem. Some group leaders were trained to use a "closed" style that should increase groupthink; others were trained to use an "open" style. As predicted, groups with open leaders made more use of the information available to them and came up with more possible solutions to the problem. Contrary to prediction, however, there was no difference in the amount of groupthink in high-cohesion groups (made up of acquaintances) and low-cohesion groups (made up of strangers).

The group processes Janis calls groupthink are apparently quite complex (see Longley & Pruitt, 1980). Many cohesive groups with strong leaders make excellent decisions. Indeed, the various groups involved in the disasters studied by Janis often made reasonable decisions on other occasions. Both the Roosevelt and Kennedy administrations are thought by many to have been extremely effective in dealing with other crisis situations. More research will be needed to clarify the conditions under which decision-makers engage in groupthink.

COMPETITION VERSUS COOPERATION

In some groups, people interact cooperatively: They help each other, share information, and work together for mutual benefit. In other groups, people compete: They put their own goals first and strive to outperform the rest. What determines whether group behavior is competitive or cooperative?

An important factor is the reward structure of the situation—the way in which rewards and desired outcomes are allocated. A *competitive reward structure* exists when one person's gain is another's loss. If you win a pot in poker, the other players must lose. In an Olympic swimming match, only one person can get the gold medal. If a course is graded on a curve, only a few students can get A grades. In these situations, the outcomes of group members are negatively linked; an individual does best when others do poorly.

In other situations, there is a *cooperative reward structure*. In order for a football team to win games, teammates must work together. People's rewards are positively linked, so that what happens to one affects all the others. The better each player does, the more likely it is that the entire team will be victorious.

An *individualistic reward structure* exists when the outcomes of individuals are independent of each other. Here, what happens to one has no impact on the others. If a teacher gives an A to everyone who gets 90 percent correct on a test, it is possible for all students to get As, or for none to get As. Each person's grade is independent of how classmates perform.

Often, the reward structure in a situation is mixed or unclear. People have choices about whether to cooperate or to compete. How do people behave when the situation permits either competition or cooperation?

Laboratory Studies

Much of the research on competition and cooperation has used laboratory games that simulate key features of everyday interaction. We will discuss research using two of the most popular games, the trucking game and the prisoner's dilemma. A common finding from these studies is that subjects (usually middle-class, white college students) tend to compete, even when cooperation would be a more rewarding strategy.

THE TRUCKING GAME In a classic experiment on this topic, Deutsch and Krauss (1960) used a simple two-person game called the *trucking game*. Subjects were each asked to imagine that they were running a trucking company (either the Acme or the Bolt Company) and had to get a truck from one point to another as quickly as possible. The two trucks were not in competition; they had different starting points and different destinations. There was, however, one hitch—the fastest route for both converged at one point to a one-lane road, and they had to go in opposite directions (see Figure 13–7 on page 396). The only way both could use

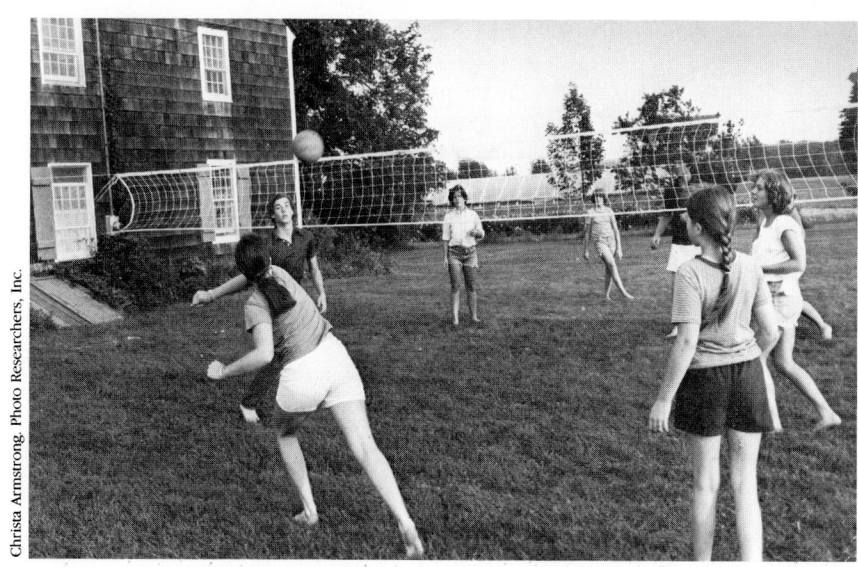

Christa Armstrong. Photo Researchers, Inc.

Whether people compete or cooperate depends on the reward structure in the situation. The Olympics are fiercely competitive because only one person can get the gold medal in each event. Here Eric Heiden (below) displays the five gold medals he won in the 1980 Olympics. In a game of volleyball (above), interaction among members of each team is cooperative. A great shot by one player helps all the teammates.

UPI/Bettmann Newsphotos

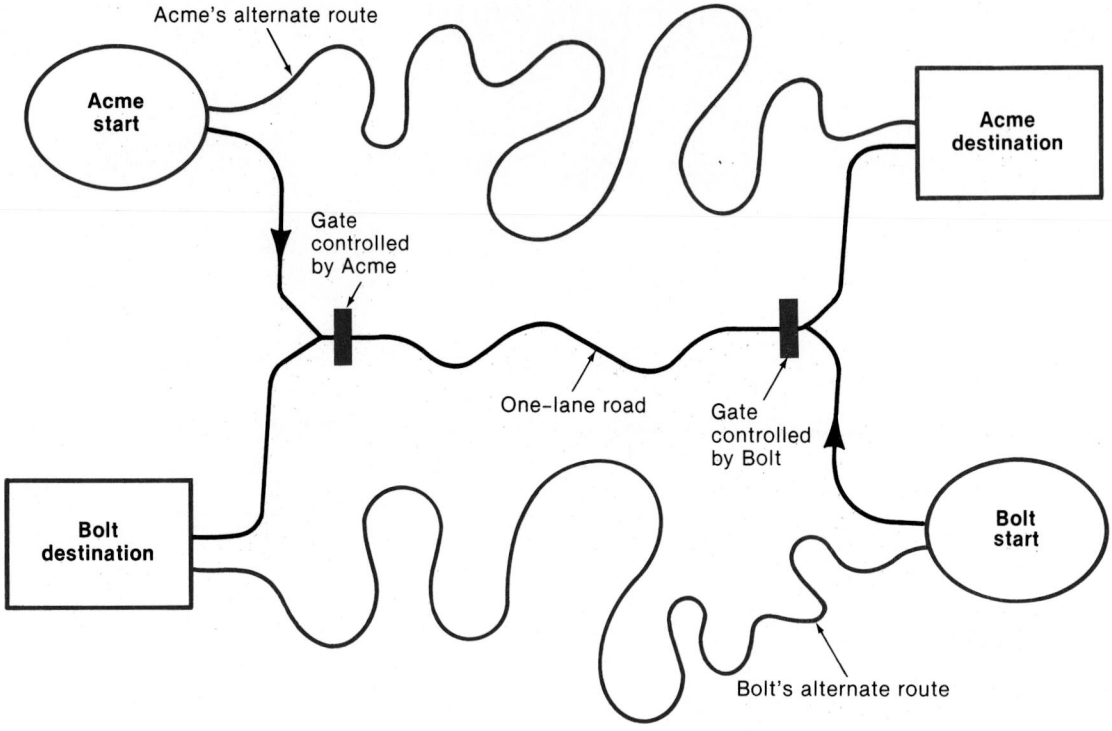

FIGURE 13–7 Road map of the trucking game. The players must get their truck to its destination as quickly as possible. Although they can do this efficiently only by cooperating and sharing the one-lane road, they often compete, particularly when gates are provided. (Adapted from Deutsch & Krauss, 1960, p. 183.)

the road would be for one of them to wait until the other had passed through. If either truck entered the road, the other could not use it; and if they both entered the road, neither of them could move at all until one had backed up. In addition, each player had a gate across the direct route that could be raised by pressing a button. The gate prevented the road from being used.

Each truck was provided with an alternative route that did not conflict with the other's, but was much longer. In fact, the game was set up so that taking the alternative route was guaranteed to lose points, whereas taking the direct route would gain points for both sides, even if they alternated at the one-lane section of the road. The players were told that their goal was to earn as many points as possible for themselves. Nothing was said about earning more points than the other player.

The results of this experiment were striking. It was clear to the participants that the optimal strategy was to cooperate by alternating in using the one-lane road. In this way, they could both use the direct route and one would be delayed only a few seconds while the other was getting through. Despite this, there was little cooperation between the players. Instead of allowing each other to use the one-lane road, they fought for its use, raised their gates, and both of them ended up losing points.

In a typical trial, both sides would try to use the road and would meet in the middle, head on. They would stubbornly stay there for a while, each refusing to retreat. The players might laugh nervously or make nasty comments. Finally, one of them would back up, erect the barrier, and use the alternate route. On the next trial, they would do the same thing, and so it went. An occasional

Prisoner A

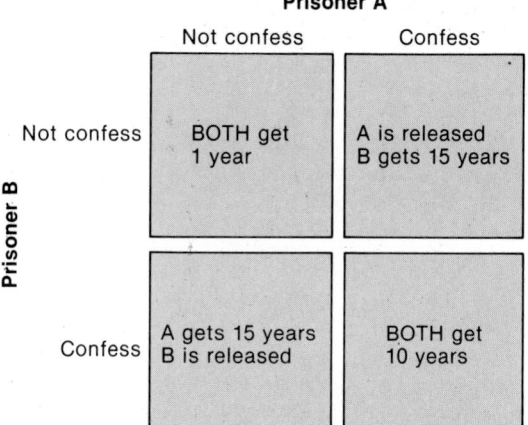

	Not confess	Confess
Not confess	BOTH get 1 year	A is released B gets 15 years
Confess	A gets 15 years B is released	BOTH get 10 years

FIGURE 13–8 Prototype of prisoner's dilemma game. Two prisoners have the choice of confessing or not confessing. If they trust and support each other by not confessing, each receives a light sentence; if they both confess, they receive relatively heavy sentences; and if one confesses and the other does not, the former is released while the latter gets a very heavy sentence. The dilemma is that if either one has complete trust in the other, he would do best by being untrustworthy himself and confessing.

cooperative trial might occur, but most trials were competitive.

THE PRISONER'S DILEMMA The tendency to compete is not due to unique characteristics of the trucking game. It also occurs in many other games, such as the *prisoner's dilemma*, so-called because it is based on a problem faced by two suspects at a police station. The district attorney thinks the suspects have committed a major crime together but has no proof against either one. The prisoners are put into separate rooms, and each is told that he has two alternatives—to confess or not to confess. If neither confesses, they cannot be convicted of a major crime. But the district attorney tells them he can get them convicted of minor crimes and that they will both receive minor punishments. If they both confess, they will be convicted of the major crime. But the district attorney says he will ask for leniency. If one of them confesses and the other does not, the confessor will be freed for

helping the state, and the other suspect will get the maximum penalty. The situation is shown in Figure 13–8.

Obviously, there is a conflict. If one suspect thinks his partner is going to confess, it is essential for him to confess also; on the other hand, the best joint outcome is for neither to confess and then for both to take the minor sentences. Thus, if the suspects trust each other, they should not confess. However, if one suspect trusts his partner and is convinced he will not confess, the first would do even better to confess and in that way be freed.

We do not know what real prisoners would do under these circumstances. In research on the problem, much of the drama is removed but the game is basically similar. Instead of playing for their freedom, subjects play for points or money. They play in pairs but usually are not allowed to talk to each other. Each player has a choice of two strategies, and each player's payoff depends both on what he does and on what his partner does.

The exact pattern of payoffs varies; a typical one is shown in Figure 13–9 for two players, Pete and

FIGURE 13–9 Typical prisoner's dilemma game matrix. The top figure in each square cell indicates A's payoff; the bottom indicates B's payoff. X is a cooperative choice, because it allows both members to win. The choice of Y is competitive, because only the one who chooses it has a chance of winning and both may lose. With this matrix there is a great deal of competition.

Pete

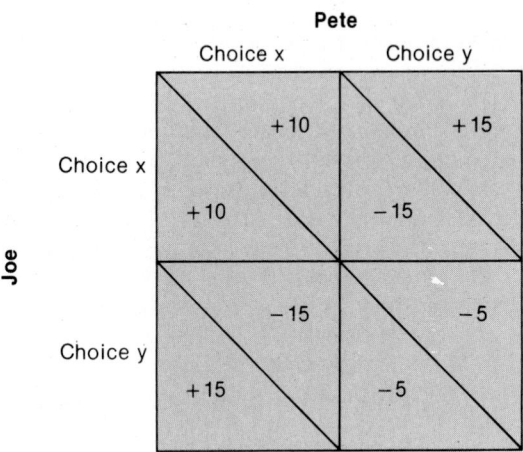

	Choice x	Choice y
Choice x	+10 / +10	+15 / −15
Choice y	−15 / +15	−5 / −5

Joe. If both choose option X, each gets 10 points. If Pete chooses X and Joe chooses Y, Pete loses 15 and Joe wins 15. If both choose Y, they both lose 5 points. In other words, they can cooperate (choose X) and both win, or they can compete (one or both choosing Y) and try to win a lot but risk losing.

The players are told that the goal is to score as many points as they can. It is clear to virtually all of them that the way to have the highest score is for both to select X (the cooperative choice) on every trial. But just as with the trucking game, there is a strong tendency to compete. In a typical game, only about a third of the choices are cooperative. Moreover, as the game progresses (and the players have usually won fairly few points), the number of cooperative choices actually goes down. The players choose the competitive strategy more and more, despite the fact that they know they can win more by cooperating.

One factor in this competitive behavior is that for any single play, the competitive choice has a short-run advantage. Let us analyze the game shown in Figure 13–9 more closely. If Pete selects the cooperative strategy, his payoff depends on what Joe does. If Joe chooses the cooperative strategy, Pete wins 10 points; if Joe chooses competitively, Pete loses 15 points. If Pete chooses the competitive strategy, once again his payoff depends on Joe. If Joe chooses the cooperative strategy, Pete wins 15 points; if Joe chooses competitively, Pete loses 5. In either case, Pete would do better by choosing the competitive strategy than he would by selecting the cooperative one. If Joe picks cooperatively, Pete wins 15 instead of 10; if Joe chooses competitively, Pete loses 5 instead of 15.

The dilemma is that over a long series of trials, Pete would be much better off if both he and Joe agreed to cooperate. They would both win on all trials rather than winning on some and losing on others. This would clearly maximize their individual gains, and so it would be the most rational strategy.

The only advantage of the competitive choice is that one player can score more than the other, even though he always scores less than he would have if both had picked the cooperative choice. When subjects in these studies were questioned about their reasons for behaving as they did, many

of them reported that they wanted to "beat" the other player. This occurred despite the fact that the experimenter had told them the aim of the game was to get as high a score as possible.

Determinants of Competition versus Cooperation

Many factors determine whether people interact cooperatively or competitively. Experimental game studies show that when the reward structure of a situation is mixed or ambiguous, college students often adopt a competitive strategy that prevents them from maximizing their rewards. But in situations where the reward structure is more explicit and where the rewards themselves are more important than in simulation games, rewards can enhance cooperation. The same students who strive to "beat" their partner in the trucking game may behave very cooperatively in their families or with their roommates—in settings where cooperation is expected and rewarded. Researchers have identified several other situational and personal factors that influence competition.

It has been suggested that Americans are some of the most competitive people on earth, and cross-cultural studies of children would seem to support this view (see review by Werner, 1979). A program of research by Millard Madsen (1971) and his colleagues has investigated the development of competitive behavior in children from around the world. In these studies, children are asked to play games with peers, and the extent to which they select cooperative versus competitive strategies is assessed. Children from Western technological societies are consistently more competitive than children from developing countries in Latin America, Africa, and the Middle East. In one study (Madsen, 1971), for example, 8-year-old Mexican children cooperated on about 7 of 10 trials, whereas 8-year-old Americans cooperated on less than 1 trial in 10.

Within a given society, children from urban areas are more competitive than children from rural areas. And children from middle-class homes compete more than children from lower-class homes. It appears that one of the correlates of industrialization and affluence is greater competitiveness. These differences are usually explained in terms of the rewards and values particular social environments provide for growing children.

Individual differences have also been observed. Kuhlman and Wimberley (1976) recorded people's behavior in several games, including the prisoner's dilemma. They were able to classify individuals into three types, based on how they responded in the game situations. *Cooperators* were concerned with maximizing the joint rewards received by both self and the partner. *Competitors* were oriented toward maximizing their own gains relative to those of the partner—they wanted to do better than the partner. *Individualists* were oriented toward maximizing their own gains, with no concern for the gains or losses of the partner. The researchers found that each type of person tended to assume that the partner had a similar orientation: For example, cooperators tended to expect a partner to behave cooperatively toward them. The main point is that people may vary in their predispositions to compete or cooperate.

Communication among partners is another important factor. In general, more communication leads to more cooperation. In the Deutsch and Krauss trucking game study, three different communication conditions were included. Some subjects were required to communicate; others were given the opportunity to talk if they wanted to; a third group was not allowed to communicate. Cooperation was greatest when communication was required, and least when communication was impossible.

Similar results have been found using the prisoner's dilemma game. Wichman (1970) found that competition was greatest when no communication was possible, somewhat less when partners could talk but not see each other, and least when partners could both see and talk to each other. Wichman found that when there was no communication, about 40 percent of responses were cooperative; when verbal communication was permitted, cooperation increased to more than 70 percent of trials. Communication enables partners to urge each other to cooperate, to discuss their plans, to make promises, to convince each other that they are trustworthy, to learn about each other and so on. Assum-ing that partners have any tendency to cooperate, knowledge about each other should facilitate it.

The size of a group also influences cooperation. In several studies, researchers have adapted the general prisoner's dilemma situation so that groups of three or more people can play. Studies (such as Komorita & Lapworth, 1982) have found that as the size of the group increases, cooperation decreases. The specific reasons for greater competition in larger groups have not been determined. It seems likely that as groups increase in size, there will more often be at least one person who adopts an exploitative, selfish orientation. Further, larger groups may feel less pressure to cooperate because of a general diffusion of responsibility among group members.

A final factor is reciprocity. We have seen throughout this book that there is a general norm of reciprocity: People often feel obligated to return both favors and insults. There is some evidence that in the course of interaction, initial competition provokes more competition, and cooperation sometimes (but not always) encourages further cooperation. One strategy that seems especially successful in fostering cooperation is reciprocal concessions. The players take turns giving up a little. This is the traditional compromise solution to most conflicts: Each side starts with an extreme position and then retreats gradually until a common meeting ground is found.

If one player makes a small concession and then waits for the other to do the same, there is indeed greater eventual cooperation (Esser & Komorita, 1975). However, a crucial element of this strategy is timing. A person who gives in too much at once may appear weak and the other will not reciprocate. The concessions must be gradual and sequential. In fact, according to Wall (1977) the most effective technique is to make reciprocal concessions slightly larger than those made by the other person. This reinforces the other's cooperation and results in large concessions and quick agreement. Obviously this does not work unless both sides are willing to cooperate to some extent. If one is totally competitive, the one who tries cooperating will only be taken advantage of and end up with a weaker position than before.

LEADERSHIP

Some form of leadership exists in all groups (Hollander, 1985). The central attribute of leadership is social influence. The leader is the person who has the most impact on group behavior and beliefs. He or she is the one who initiates action, gives orders, makes decisions, settles disputes between group members, offers encouragement, serves as a model, and is in the forefront of group activity. These examples illustrate some of the ways a leader might influence a group; any particular leader may not do all of them.

Leadership Structure

Social scientists refer to a group's unique pattern of leadership as the leadership structure of the group. In some groups, this is relatively simple. The committee responsible for planning a New Year's party at the office may consist of one enthusiastic leader and several followers. In other groups, the pattern of leadership is more complex. Who are the leaders in a professional football team? Possible leaders might include the owners, the general manager, the head coach, the captains of the various team units, the quarterback who calls the plays, or individual team members who serve as informal spokesmen for the team. In this case, various individuals are in charge of different aspects of team functioning, and each exerts influence in specific types of group activities. So whereas some groups have only one leader, other groups have two or more. In general, groups are more likely to have several leaders when they face diverse and complex tasks requiring many types of skills. Then it makes sense to have multiple leaders, each a specialist in some particular aspect of the group's activities (Ridgeway, 1983).

FORMAL AND INFORMAL LEADERS Groups differ in the extent to which their leadership structure is formal or informal. Large organizations such as a business or a school have formal organization charts indicating the official chain of command and giving guidelines about patterns of decision-making and supervision. Even in smaller groups, such as clubs and fraternities, there may be elected officers with specified responsibilities. At the other extreme, some groups have no formal leaders at all. Friendship groups are one example.

What is important to recognize, however, is that groups without formal leaders still have patterns of informal leadership. One person may be more articulate and persuasive than others in group discussions, and so have more influence on decisions. Someone else may emerge as the person to whom others turn to smooth over conflicts within the group. All groups, even those that say they are leaderless, have some leadership structure. And even in groups with formal leaders, there is often a pattern of informal leadership that can be very different from the official structure. The president of the student council may be the official head of the group, but unofficially it may be another officer who actually has the greatest influence in decision-making.

PATHS TO LEADERSHIP Individuals can become group leaders in several ways. One way to become a leader is to be appointed by someone outside the group. An army lieutenant is the official leader of the company, and is appointed by people higher up in the military organization. Because of this position, the lieutenant can give orders to everyone else in the company, but none of them can give the lieutenant orders. In other situations, such as clubs or student government, a leader is elected by group members. In a third process, a group member emerges over time as a leader. When people interact repeatedly, as in a group of friends or classmates, some individuals typically emerge as informal leaders. These leaders do not have official titles, but most group members would generally agree that a particular person or set of people are

All groups have some form of leadership structure. When friends get together, leadership is informal—the person who is most talkative and persuasive emerges as the leader. At a business meeting, the formal leader directs group activities.

Ken Karp

the leaders. Outside observers can also spot emergent leaders by watching such things as who talks most in group discussions and whose opinions are most likely to prevail in group decisionmaking.

TYPES OF LEADERSHIP ACTIVITIES   In general, the leaders of any group must perform two types of activities. **Task leadership** concerns accomplishing the goals of the group—getting the work of the group done successfully. The task leader gives suggestions, offers opinions, and provides information for the group. He or she controls, shapes, directs, and organizes the group in carrying out a specific task. **Social leadership** focuses on the social and emotional aspects of group interaction. The social leader concentrates on keeping the group running smoothly and happily, is concerned about people's feelings, uses humor to relieve tension, and tries to encourage group cohesiveness.

Extensive research (see Bales, 1970; Burke, 1971) has shown that both task and social leadership are important to effective group functioning. The qualities necessary for the two types of leadership are somewhat different. A social leader must be friendly, agreeable, conciliatory, concerned about feelings, and socially oriented. A task leader must be efficient, directive, and knowledgeable about the particular task at hand. In some groups, one person will be the task leader and a different person will be the social leader. But in other situations, one person will combine the functions of both.

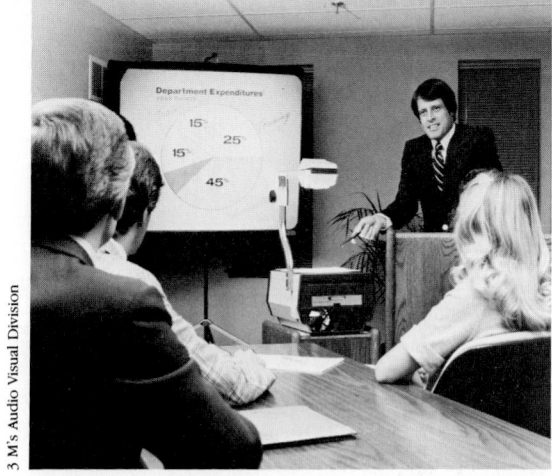
3 M's Audio Visual Division

Who Becomes a Leader?

The search for factors that cause some people and not others to become leaders is an old one. Two contrasting views have emerged: One emphasizes the unique personal characteristics of the leader, and the other the situational forces acting on the group.

CHARACTERISTICS OF THE PERSON   The "great person" theory of leadership suggests that some people, because of personality or other unique characteristics, are destined to lead. To test this idea, many empirical studies have compared the characteristics

Laima Druskis

Irene Springer

A.T. & T. Co. Photo Center

Irene Springer

Which of these four jurors is most likely to be selected as jury foreman? How might age, race, gender, or other personal characteristics influence the jury's choice of their leader?

of leaders and followers (Yukl, 1981). Surprisingly few qualities have been found that consistently separate leaders from followers. In a general way, however, three factors are associated with leadership (Ridgeway, 1983).

First, leaders tend to excel in those abilities that help the group to accomplish its goals. In some situations, intelligence correlates with leadership (Fiedler, 1986). In other situations, leadership might be linked to political expertise, physical strength, or skills relevant to the activities and goals of the group. A great quarterback like Joe Montana or the star of a basketball team like Larry Bird almost automatically becomes a task leader of the team.

Second, leaders tend to have interpersonal skills that contribute to successful interaction. In general, being cooperative, organized, articulate, and interpersonally sensitive would be an asset. Such characteristics enhance a person's functioning as a social leader.

A third factor is motivation. Leaders usually desire recognition and prominence; they are more ambitious, achievement-oriented, and willing to assume responsibility. We emphasize, however, that although these qualities enhance a person's leadership potential, none is a sure guarantee of actually becoming a leader.

CHARACTERISTICS OF THE SITUATION   Another approach to leadership emphasizes situational factors. A striking demonstration of situational forces comes from the research on communication networks described earlier in this chapter. The basic idea is that communication is essential for leadership, so the person who can communicate most freely tends to become the leader. In situations such as a wheel network, where all communications are channeled through one person, that individual should become the leader.

A study by Leavitt (1951) showed how the predetermined communication patterns in a situation affect the emergence of a leader. After working in one type of group for a while, group members were asked if there was a group leader and to name that leader. There was a clear progression from the wheel to the circle in terms of who became the leader. The number shown at each position in Figure 13–10 (see p. 404) is the number of times the person in that position was named leader. For wheel groups, virtually everyone named the central

person as the leader. For the circle groups, only half the members named a leader at all, and there was little agreement about who the leader was. The other groups fell in between. It appears that simply being in a position to control communication can make a person a leader.

Today, most researchers believe that who becomes a leader depends in large part on the *match* between the characteristics of the person and the needs of the situation confronting the group. It should be obvious that different situations require different qualities in a leader. Take the case of expertise. The particular types of knowledge or ability that are relevant vary dramatically from one situation to another. Being able to pitch well may be a real asset in becoming captain of the fraternity softball team, but it would not contribute much to heading the debate team. Further, expertise is a relative matter. A first-year law student might be the "legal expert" in her family, but would not necessarily become a leader among her law school classmates or professors.

TRANSACTIONAL APPROACHES   Neither the "great person" nor the situational approach pay much attention to the role of *followers* in determining who becomes the leader. The transactional approach serves to remedy this gap (Hollander, 1985). The central point of this approach is that the interaction between leader and followers works both ways. The perceptions and attitudes of followers partly determine who becomes leader. Leaders, in turn, usually pay close attention to the views of followers and may modify their leadership behavior in response to the actions of their followers. In small groups, the willingness of group members to accept the leader's influence depends on processes of social exchange. Leaders who fail to provide rewards or to move the group toward its goals, who are perceived as unfair, and who are unresponsive to group needs will be disliked, and may jeopardize their leadership position. On a larger scale, voters select candidates they perceive as sharing their values and goals. Elected officials who ignore the wishes of their constituents may not win re-election.

Leadership Style

Think back to your high school teachers and the different ways they led a class. One may have been a dictator who insisted on discipline and obedience.

FIGURE 13–10 Communication networks and choice of leaders. The positions connected by a line can communicate directly to each other. The networks range in centrality of communication from the circle (least central, least restricted) to the wheel. The number at each position indicates the number of times the member at that position was considered the leader of the group. (Adapted from Leavitt, 1951.)

Another may have been a "nice guy" who emphasized student participation and created a relaxed classroom atmosphere. Researchers have tried to classify styles of leadership and to determine how they affect group functioning. Box 13–2 describes a classic study of "democratic" and "authoritarian" leaders. A more recent analysis of leadership style is Fiedler's contingency model.

FIEDLER'S CONTINGENCY MODEL Researchers generally agree that group performance is affected by the match between the style of the leader and the circumstances of the group. The consequences of a particular style depend on (are contingent on) various characteristics of the group itself. One prominent version of this approach is Fiedler's **contingency model of leadership effectiveness.**

Fiedler (1978, 1981) identifies two styles of leadership, corresponding roughly to the distinction between task and social leadership that we made earlier. Those leaders who give highest priority to getting the work of the group done successfully and who deemphasize relations among group members are called *task-oriented leaders*. The coach who says that "winning is the only thing" and ignores the feelings of team members is an example. In Fiedler's model, those leaders who reverse these priorities by putting group relations first and task accomplishment second are called *relationship-oriented leaders*. This sort of coach would say that it doesn't matter whether you win or lose, so long as you get along with your teammates.

Fiedler also classifies group situations along a continuum from those that are highly favorable to control by the leader to those that are unfavorable. At one extreme are high-control situations in which a leader has high legitimate power, is well liked and respected by the group, and in which the group's task is structured and clear-cut. An example would be a popular Scout leader showing a group of preteens how to set up a tent. At the

BOX 13–2

DEMOCRATIC AND AUTHORITARIAN LEADERS

At the end of World War II, a classic series of studies on leadership was conducted by Lewin, Lippitt, and White (1939). Kurt Lewin, a refugee from Nazi Germany, and his colleagues investigated the differences between "democratic" and "authoritarian" leaders. They formed several clubs for boys, each with an adult male leader trained to adopt a different style of leadership. In the *authoritarian style*, all decisions were made by the leader. He was very directive and controlling, gave few explanations, and remained rather aloof from the group. In the *democratic style*, boys were encouraged to discuss group policies and to make their own decisions with the assistance of the leader. Members could select their own partners and decide how to divide up the work. All clubs met for several months. To study group reactions, the researchers staged various events, such as the leader leaving the group for a while or coming late to a group meeting. The boys' behavior was observed during club meetings, and follow-up interviews were conducted outside the group.

Clear differences emerged in the behavior of members in democratic and authoritarian groups. First, the groups differed in emotional tone. The democratic groups were friendlier and more relaxed; members were more group-minded and used the word "we" (instead of "I") with greater frequency. The atmosphere in the authoritarian groups was tense. Boys showed more hostility and aggression, sometimes toward the leader and sometimes toward a group member who became the scapegoat. Boys seemed to form weaker group ties.

A second major difference was that democratic groups encouraged boys to take more initiative. If an authoritarian leader left the room, the boys stopped working on their assigned project. If a democratic leader left, the boys kept on working. Boys in authoritarian groups seemed more dependent on the leader and less capable of working on their own. Apparently, boys in democratic groups participated more, got to know other boys better, identified more with the group, and consequently were more satisfied with the group activities (Ridgeway, 1983).

It is important to note, however, that these results favoring democratic groups occurred in the context of American society. In cultures where people do not expect or value participatory democracy, results might be very different. For instance, in a society where elders are supposed to instruct the young, a democratic leader could be perceived as irresponsible, lazy, and inept, and so group morale might be lower.

Lewin, Lippitt, and White also examined the effect of democratic and authoritarian leadership styles on group productivity. They found that authoritarian groups actually spent somewhat more time working on their projects and completed slightly more projects. The researchers argued, however, that democratic groups made products of higher quality and that members took a more personal interest in their projects. Unfortunately for champions of participatory democracy, subsequent research has not supported this view (Ridgeway, 1983). Although members of democratic groups are generally happier than members of authoritarian groups, they are not necessarily any more productive.

FIGURE 13–11 Fiedler's model of how group performance is determined by the leader's style and situational control. When control is either very low or very high, task-oriented leaders are more effective in encouraging productivity. When situational control is moderate, relationship-oriented leaders are more effective. (Adapted from Fiedler, 1981, p. 625.)

other extreme are low-control situations in which the leader has little legitimate authority, has poor relations with group members, and is confronted with a task that may require creative or complex solutions. An example would be an inexperienced and unpopular student teacher who is asked to lead a group discussion with high school seniors about ways to improve school spirit.

A main goal of Fiedler's research has been to determine which types of leaders are most effective in which situations. His results, replicated in a number of different studies, are shown in Figure 13–11. Task-oriented leaders are more effective in increasing group productivity in *both* extremely high and extremely low control situations. In other words, both the Scout leader and the student teacher would be advised to give priority to the task. Relationship-oriented leaders are most effective in situations where the leader has moderate

control—where the leader gets along well with group members but has a complex task, or when the leader is disliked but the task is clear.

One conclusion we can draw from Fiedler's model is that the effectiveness of either type of leader will change if there is a change in control. For example, one study of army infantry squads (Bons & Fiedler, 1976) found that a squad leader's situational control increased from moderate to high as he gained experience and on-the-job training. In accord with Fiedler's theory, task-oriented squad leaders were at first less effective than relationship-oriented leaders. But as the situation changed, task leaders increased and relationship leaders decreased in effectiveness. The key point is that no one style of leadership is effective in all situations. Ultimately, the most effective leader may be the person who can adapt his or her leadership style to match the situation.

SOCIAL CONTAGION AND DEINDIVIDUATION

Most often, behavior in groups is fairly routine: High school students go through their lessons at school, workers make decisions and perform their jobs at the factory, and so on. But occasionally, people in groups act in extreme and irrational ways.

In 1931, a young black man, accused of raping a white woman, was being held in a southern jail. There was no evidence against him except that he was in the general vicinity of the crime. A crowd gathered outside the jail, built up, and got more

When the anonymity of being in a group causes people to lose a sense of their personal identity, antisocial behavior becomes more likely. During a massive power blackout in New York City, these looters, young and old, ransacked a grocery store and carried off merchandise.

UPI/Bettmann Archives

and more excited and enraged. Members of the crowd talked of lynching, and before long the crowd had turned into an angry mob. It rushed the jail, broke down the doors, and dragged the prisoner from his cell. He was tortured and killed in a sadistic orgy of violence.

That groups sometimes become disorganized is hardly surprising. The more interesting phenomenon is that people in groups will behave in ways they would not by themselves. In 1896 Le Bon suggested that people in a mob tend to feel and behave the same way because the emotions of one person spread through the group. When one person does something, even if it would ordinarily be unacceptable to most of the others, everyone else tends to do it also. He called this *social contagion*: Mob behavior is infectious, like a cold spreading through members of a school classroom.

As noted in our discussion of aggression (Chapter 10), Le Bon explained social contagion in terms of a breakdown of normal control mechanisms. Our actions are usually controlled by our moral sense, our value system, and the social rules we have learned. In groups, we sometimes lose a sense of responsibility for our own actions; we feel that the group is responsible. Our own control system is weakened or breaks down. Once an individual's control mechanism is weakened, primitive, aggressive, and sexual impulses are free to be expressed, and this results in violent, immoral acts.

Social psychologists (see Festinger, Pepitone, & Newcomb, 1952; Zimbardo, 1970) have translated these ideas into more modern terms. They propose that people in groups sometimes experience **deindividuation.** Personal identity is replaced by an identity with the goals and actions of the group. The individual becomes less aware of his or her own values and behavior, and instead focuses on the group and the situation (Diener, 1980). Deindividuation involves a loss of personal responsibility, as well as heightened sensitivity to what the group is doing. In a sense, each person in the group thinks of his or her own actions as being part of the *group's* behavior. This causes people to feel less responsible for their own actions and less concerned about the consequences. And it can set the stage for antisocial acts. But deindividuation can also lead an individual to act in prosocial ways—if the group favors such actions.

A key factor is anonymity. Anything that makes members of a group less personally identifiable should increase the effect. The more anonymous the group members are, the less they feel they have an identity of their own, the more irresponsibly they may behave. In a mob, most of the people do not stand out as individuals. They blend together and, in a sense, do not have an identity of their own. Conversely, to the extent that they are identifiable and feel they are, they retain their feelings of individuality and are less likely to act irresponsibly.

BOX 13–3

MASS HYSTERIA: SOCIAL CONTAGION
AND PHYSICAL ILLNESS

One early spring, most of the 35 workers in a university computer center keypunch room were mysteriously taken ill (Stahl, 1982). They complained of a "strange and burning odor" and suffered from headaches, nausea, vomiting, hyperventilation, and tearing eyes. So serious was the problem that 10 workers were taken to the local emergency room. Many suspected that a "mystery gas" had caused the outbreak. The university called in a physician and a professor of environmental studies to investigate. The epidemic soon subsided, and the experts told workers that the problem may have been caused by an atmospheric inversion due to smoke from a local power plant. What the experts did not tell the workers was that there was absolutely no evidence from lab tests that any atmospheric inversion had actually caused the illness.

In 1983, during a time of great tension in the Israeli-occupied West Bank of the Jordan, a mass illness broke out among Arab residents. On one day alone, over 300 school girls were hospitalized, triggering violence that wounded two Israeli soldiers and a Palestinian youth. The victims, mostly teenage girls, complained of nausea, dizziness, blurred vision, and stomach aches. Many Palestinians in the area suspected that the Israelis were somehow poisoning them. Israeli officials reported that extensive investigations had found no evidence of foul play.

Both these true stories illustrate a phenomenon popularly called "mass hysteria." In a typical case, symptoms such as fainting and nausea break out among a group of people, perhaps co-workers or classmates. Victims are often young, poorly paid, and female. The symptoms spread rapidly to other group members and are blamed on some mysterious source, such as a poison gas or an insect. Experts find no physical or organic explanation for the illness, which subsides in several days. This phenomenon, technically called "mass psychogenic illness," is believed to be caused by group processes rather than physical pathogens (see the review by Colligan, Pennebaker, & Murphy, 1982).

Mass psychogenic illness generally occurs as a group reaction to severe stress. In the case of the computer center workers, the daily stress of a monotonous, low-paying job with rigid rules was compounded by heavy construction going on next door. For a two-week period, workers were exposed to frequent but unexpected dynamite blasts throughout the day. In the case of the Arab schoolgirls, stress resulted from the recent warfare and constant Arab-Israeli tensions on the West Bank.

The first victims of mass psychogenic illness are often social isolates, who may have few friends and may have had previous fainting spells. Soon, however, the illness spreads through friendship and communication networks to other group members. It is important to emphasize that the symptoms experienced in such cases are real and often quite painful and distressing. Stricken individuals are not faking illness; their suffering is genuine. What is fascinating about this fairly rare occurrence is that the cause of the illness is social-psychological rather than physiological.

Explanations for mass psychogenic illness are still preliminary. It appears that many symptoms such as hyperventilation and fainting are related to stress, and may be further heightened as rumors about "mystery gases" or other "poisons" spread. Group processes may cause the victims to define their symptoms as more serious than they might otherwise, and lead people to attribute their illness to mysterious external threats rather than to stress and anxiety.

In an experiment by Singer, Brush, and Lublin (1965) to test this notion, some subjects were made easily identifiable and others were made more difficult to identify. In the former condition, everyone dressed in normal clothes, which meant that each was dressed differently from the others. In addition, the subjects were called by name, and everything was done to make each one stand out as an individual. In the latter condition, all the subjects put on identical lab coats. The experimenter avoided using their names and, in general, tried to give the impression that their individual identities did not matter much. The group then discussed a variety of topics, including one that required the use of obscene language.

Groups in the low-identifiable condition showed much more freedom in all the discussions and particularly in the one involving obscene words. There were fewer pauses in the conversation, a more lively discussion, and a greater willingness to use obscene language than was necessary for a good discussion of the topic. Subjects who were more easily identified were much more constrained and appeared quite reluctant to use the taboo words.

A more dramatic illustration of deindividuation was provided in an experiment by Zimbardo (1970). Groups of four young women were recruited to take part in a study supposedly involving empathic responses to strangers. In one condition, participants were greeted by name, wore name tags, and were easily identifiable. In another condition, subjects wore oversized white lab coats and hoods, were never called by name, and were difficult to identify. All the groups were given an opportunity to deliver electric shocks to a person not in the group. The subjects who were not identifiable gave almost twice as many shocks as the others. Apparently being less identifiable produced a marked increase in aggression, supporting the idea that

loss of individuality is one cause of the violent, antisocial behavior sometimes exhibited by groups.

A clever demonstration of the deindividuation effect involved children who were trick-or-treating on Halloween. In this study (Diener et al., 1976), some of the children were asked their names by the adults in the homes, and others were not. Then they were given the opportunity to steal extra candy when the adult was not present. Those who had been asked their names were less likely to steal, even though the chances of getting caught were virtually zero in all cases.

Johnson and Downing (1979) have pointed out that in almost all the research, subjects have worn disguises or masks that have negative implications. Zimbardo used Ku Klux Klan outfits; most Halloween masks are of monsters or ghosts. Perhaps it is not the anonymity that increases the violation of norms, but the kind of disguise. To test this, anonymity was produced by having people wear Ku Klux Klan outfits or nurses' outfits consisting of white hats and coats. Those wearing outfits were compared to others wearing normal clothing. It was found that the Ku Klux Klan outfit had only a slight effect on the level of shock subjects gave (thus not replicating Zimbardo's results). Perhaps more important, the nurses' uniforms actually reduced the number of shocks given. Although anonymity sometimes produces increased aggression, these results indicate that people are influenced by social context—in this case by the uniforms they wore. If the uniform implies positive, prosocial behavior, the wearer may behave accordingly.

The critical factor in deindividuation is not membership in a group, but anonymity. Research (reviewed by Diener, 1980) has shown the importance of anonymity and reduced self-awareness in creating the effect. There is no evidence that simply being in a group produces deindividuation or increases antisocial behavior. For example, Diener (1976) observed young adults in a situation in which they were free to act aggressively toward someone who would not harm them in any way. In all conditions, the subjects first observed someone else acting aggressively toward the "victim" and thus had a model to imitate. Yet subjects who were alone with the victim were actually more aggressive than those who were in a group. In this case, being in a group *decreased* aggressiveness. Being in a group leads to deindividuation only when the group provides anonymity and directs the individual's focus away from the self and toward the social setting.

KEY TERMS IN CHAPTER 13

brainstorming	deindividuation	risky shift	social loafing
cohesiveness	groups	social facilitation	social role
communication networks	groupthink	social impact theory	task leader
contingency model of leadership effectiveness	group polarization	social leader	

SUMMARY

1. A group is a social aggregate in which people are interdependent: what happens to one person affects the outcomes for other group members. Social roles are rules and understandings about how various group members should behave; roles define the rights and responsibilities of group members. Cohesiveness refers to both the negative and positive forces that cause members to stay in a group.

2. Communication is essential to group activities. In most groups, some people talk more than others. Limits imposed on communication create various communication networks. Centralized networks (one person is allowed to talk to everyone, but the other people can talk only to the central person) are efficient for solving simple problems. Decentralized networks produce higher morale and are probably superior for solving complex problems.

3. Whether people perform a task better alone or in a group depends on the particular activity. The presence of others usually improves performance on a well-learned behavior (social facilitation effect) but impairs performance on a new or poorly-learned behavior (social inhibition effect).

4. Social impact theory proposes that the influence of an audience on an individual depends on the number of observers, the strength (importance) of the audience, and the immediacy of the audience. Social loafing refers to a situation in which individuals work less hard as members of a group than they would alone.

5. There is a tendency for groups to make more extreme decisions than individuals alone. This group polarization effect sometimes leads to riskier decisions, and sometimes to more conservative decisions. Two main explanations for polar-

ization emphasize the importance of persuasive arguments and social comparison processes.

6. Highly cohesive groups with a directive leader may be vulnerable to groupthink. This is a decision-making process that discourages criticism and can lead to poor decisions.

7. Much research on competition and cooperation has used laboratory games such as the trucking game and prisoner's dilemma. In these studies, Americans often tend to compete, even when they would obtain greater external rewards from cooperation. Situational factors affecting competition include the reward structure of the situation, the amount of communication among partners, and the size of the group. One strategy for reducing competition is reciprocal concessions.

8. Group leaders are those who have the most impact on group behavior and beliefs. A task leader focuses on accomplishing group goals successfully. A social leader strives to maintain harmony and high morale. People who become leaders tend to excel in abilities that help the group achieve its goals, to be socially-skilled, or to be highly motivated to be a leader. According to Fiedler's contingency model, the success of a leader depends on the match between the leader's style (task-oriented versus relationship-oriented) and the nature of the situation.

9. People in groups sometimes behave in unusual or antisocial ways that individuals alone would not. This has been called social contagion. Social psychologists explain this effect in terms of deindividuation. The anonymity of groups can reduce an individual's feelings of personal responsibility, leading the individual to act more impulsively.

SUGGESTED READINGS

FIEDLER, F. E., & GARCIA, J. E. (1987). *Leadership: Cognitive resources and performance*. New York: Wiley. A comprehensive review of Fiedler's theory and research with attention to the impact of intelligence and other "cognitive resources" on leadership.

FORSYTH, D. R. (1983). *An introduction to group dynamics*. Monterey, CA: Brooks/Cole. A readable textbook that discusses such group processes as leadership, problem-solving, and deindividuation.

HOLLANDER, E. P. (1985). Leadership and power. In G. Lindzey & E. Aronson (Eds.), *Handbook of social psychology*, 3rd ed. vol. 2. New York: Random House, pp. 485–538. A professional level review and analysis of recent research and theory on leadership.

JANIS, I. L. (1982). *Groupthink: Psychological studies of policy decisions and fiascoes*, 2nd ed. Boston: Houghton Mifflin. Presents Janis's theory and reviews some of the research testing hypotheses about groupthink.

PAULUS, P. B. (Ed.) (1980). *The psychology of group influence*. Hillsdale, NJ: Erlbaum. An excellent collection of articles on group behavior written by leading experts. Contains detailed discussions of such topics as social facilitation, group polarization, and deindividuation.

McGRATH, J. E. (1984). *Groups: Interaction and performance*. Englewood Cliffs, NJ: Prentice-Hall. A comprehensive textbook covering most aspects of group functioning.

WRIGHT, G. (Ed.) (1985). *Behavioral decision making*. New York: Plenum. A multidisciplinary collection of papers on various aspects of decision making by groups.

14 PREJUDICE

People's prejudices concern their perceptions of other individuals and groups, and their attitudes and behavior toward them. Why does a friend's father refuse to hire Mexicans as clerks in the bank? Why did millions of Germans support the Nazi Party with its explicitly anti-Semitic proposals? How easy is it to change these perceptions and attitudes? How can it be done? All these questions are essentially applications of the principles discussed in earlier chapters. And they are not minor matters: Prejudice is one of the most important areas of applied social psychology.

Prejudices can determine who gets hired and who gets fired, whether it is the arbitrary judgment of a casting director in a large movie studio or the vote of a faculty meeting on a tenure decision, or the decision made by a civil service grievance panel. In court, prejudices can determine who goes to jail and who goes free. Prejudice can have a chilling effect on members of minority groups who are attempting to exercise their rights. However courageous they may be, they may sometimes want to retreat from a place where "they are not wanted." In all these cases, prejudice has a major impact on other lives—sometimes on thousands or millions of other lives.

PREJUDICE: WHAT IS IT?

Antagonism toward members of a social group has proved to be perhaps the most socially destructive type of attitude. Over six million European Jews were murdered by the Nazis in the 1940s, under the guise of "purifying" the European racial stock. Today only a fraction of that number of Jews remain in Europe. The number of North American Indians dropped from an estimated three million in the seventeenth century to 600,000 today. The Spanish genocide of Indians in Latin America is even more appalling.

In the United States, racial prejudice against blacks by whites has been a tenacious social problem. It has resulted in an enormous catalog of social ills, ranging from the deterioration and near-bankruptcy of large cities to poverty, shorter life expectancy, high levels of crime and drug abuse, and human misery of all kinds among blacks themselves. Racism dates back at least as far as the earliest contact between English travelers and Africans in the sixteenth century. The memoirs of the English show them to have been fascinated by the strangeness of the Africans. They were especially struck by the Africans' blackness, a color with overwhelm-ingly bad connotations for the Englishmen of the day. They perceived the Africans as looking like apes; as engaging in savage and uncivilized behavior; and as having "heathen" religions (Jordan, 1968). These earliest white impressions about black Africans contain most of the anti-black stereotypes still common in the twentieth century.

The importation of Africans into America as slaves codified these negative reactions. The Africans were treated as property, and often as subhuman beings. Although the slave trade was abolished in 1808, almost 90 percent of all blacks in the United States were still slaves in 1860, just before the outbreak of the Civil War. And emancipation did not noticeably improve their lot. At the beginning of World War II, the average black man in his twenties had not gone past the sixth grade in school. In the half-century before World War II, thousands of individual blacks were lynched by mobs of whites, usually on some suspicion (often unjustified, or at least uninvestigated) of their involvement in a crime against whites. Most blacks lived in the South, where they still were largely segregated by law. Restaurants, movie houses, and buses had sepa-

Public Sale of Negroes,

By RICHARD CLAGETT.

On Tuesday, March 5th, 1833 at 1:00 P. M. the following Slaves will be sold at Potters Mart, in Charleston, S. C.

Miscellaneous Lots of Negroes, mostly house servants, some for field work.

Conditions: ½ cash, balance by bond, bearing interest from date of sale. Payable in one to two years to be secured by a mortgage of the *Negroes,* and appraised personal security. *Auctioneer will pay for the papers.*

A valuable Negro woman, accustomed to all kinds of house work. Is a good plain cook, and excellent dairy maid, washes and irons. She has four children, one a girl about 13 years of age, another 7, a boy about 5, and an infant 11 months old. 2 of the children will be sold with mother, the others separately, if it best suits the purchaser.

A very valuable Blacksmith, wife and daughters; the Smith is in the prime of life, and a perfect master at his trade. His wife about 27 years old, and his daughters 12 and 10 years old have been brought up as house servants, and as such are very valuable. Also for sale 2 likely young negro wenches, one of whom is 16 the other 15, both of whom have been taught and accustomed to the duties of house servants. The 16 year old wench has one eye.

A likely yellow girl about 17 or 18 years old, has been accustomed to all kinds of house and garden work. She is sold for no fault. Sound as a dollar.

House servants: The owner of a family described herein, would sell them for a good price only, they are offered for no fault whatever, but because they can be done without, and money is needed. He has been offered $1250. They consist of a man 30 to 33 years old, who has been raised in a genteel Virginia family as house servant, Carriage driver etc., in all which he excels. His wife a likely wench of 25 to 30 raised in like manner, as chamber maid, seamstress, nurse etc., their two children, girls of 12 and 4 or 5. They are bright mulattoes, of mild tractable dispositions, unassuming manners, and of genteel appearance and well worthy the notice of a gentleman of fortune needing such.

Also 14 Negro Wenches ranging from 16 to 25 years of age, all sound and capable of doing a good days work in the house or field.

Almost all blacks in the United States are descendents of slaves forcibly imported from Africa, whereas almost all other Americans are descended from people who immigrated by choice. What kinds of behaviors might have been adaptive for people trapped in this "peculiar institution" with almost no hope for escape? What traces of those behaviors might exist today?

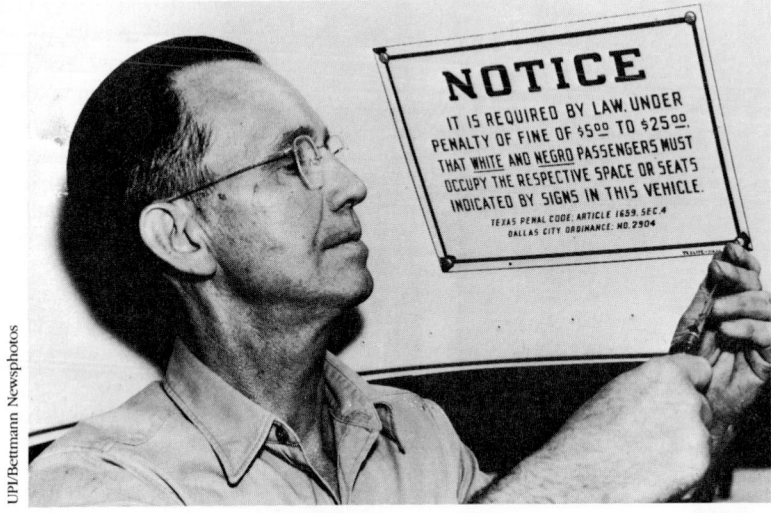

Until 1964, Southern cities such as Dallas required blacks to sit in the back of the bus, while whites sat in the front.

UPI/Bettmann Newsphotos

rate sections for blacks and whites. This formal, legalized segregation was not outlawed until 1964.

Prejudice and discrimination toward a wide variety of minority groups have been common throughout the history of the United States. However, the "peculiar institution" of slavery, and the legalized system of segregation that followed it, were unique to the black population. As a result, achieving equality has been much more difficult for blacks than for any other minority group.

Prejudice against blacks has been more difficult to eradicate. To be sure, whites today are much more accepting of formal equality than they were even twenty years ago; they strongly support blacks' rights to equal public accommodations, public office, fair housing, and so on. And violence by whites against blacks has dropped greatly. After World War II, lynching came to a nearly complete halt. Still, violent incidents continue on occasion. Much publicity was given to the death of a young black man in 1986, who with two friends was attacked by a mob of white youths outside a pizza parlor in an all-white neighborhood in Howard Beach, N.Y.

And there is still strong resistance to programs that would help blacks reach full equality—for example, school integration and affirmative action (Campbell, 1971; Taylor, Sheatsley, & Greeley, 1978). This white resistance is rooted in considerable measure in what we call group antagonism. Because antagonism by whites toward Afro-Ameri-

cans has been such a difficult and important problem in the United States, much of our discussion of prejudice will focus on it as an example.

Its Components

Social psychologists generally distinguish three different components of group antagonism. These roughly correspond to the three components of any attitude presented in Chapter 6: cognitive, affective, and behavioral.

THE COGNITIVE COMPONENT   **Stereotypes,** the cognitive component of group antagonism, are beliefs about the personal attributes shared by people in a particular group or social category. Those applied to Jews and blacks in years gone by are shown in Table 14–1. In this study, college students were given a long list of trait adjectives, and then asked to check which ones applied to each of several groups, such as Jews, blacks (or Negroes, as they were then called), and other groups. The same procedure was repeated in 1933, 1951, 1967, and 1982. Note the persistence of the core themes over a long period of time: the shrewd and ambitious Jews, the ignorant and fun-loving blacks.

Stereotypes can be thought of as cognitive schemas about a particular social group. Like any schema, stereotypes distort reality to achieve order

TABLE 14-1

Stereotypes of Blacks and Jews in Four Generations of College Students

Trait	STEREOTYPES OF JEWS (% CHECKING TRAIT)			
	1933	1951	1967	1982
Shrewd	79%	47%	30%	—
Grasping	34	17	17	—
Sly	20	14	7	—
Mercenary	49	28	15	—
Materialistic	—	—	46	—
Industrious	48	29	33	—
Ambitious	21	28	48	—
Aggressive	12	—	23	—
Persistent	13	—	9	—
Talkative	13	—	3	—
Intelligent	29	37	37	—
Practical	—	—	19	—
Loyal to family ties	15	19	19	—
Very religious	12	—	7	—

Trait	STEREOTYPES OF BLACKS (% CHECKING TRAIT)			
	1933	1951	1967	1982
Superstitious	84%	41%	13%	6%
Very religious	24	17	8	23
Ignorant	38	24	11	10
Stupid	22	10	4	1
Naive	14	—	4	4
Lazy	75	31	26	13
Physically dirty	17	—	3	0
Slovenly	13	—	5	2
Unreliable	12	—	6	2
Happy-go-lucky	38	17	27	15
Pleasure-loving	—	19	26	20
Musical	26	33	47	29
Ostentatious	26	11	25	5
Sensitive	—	—	17	13
Gregarious	—	—	17	4
Talkative	—	—	14	5
Imitative	—	—	13	9

Note: Some traits were not asked at all time points.
Source: These data come from Karlins et al. (1969) and from Dovidio & Gaertner (1986), p. 7.

and simplicity. In that sense, they are not necesarily bizarre, deviant, or pathological. They become destructive when they ignore the evidence of reality and are generalized to all group members.

THE AFFECTIVE COMPONENT **Prejudice** is the affective or evaluative component of group antagonism. It is an evaluation of a group or of a single individual based mainly on the person's group membership. Usually it is a negative evaluation; we say someone is prejudiced against members of a particular group. But sometimes people are prejudiced in favor of a group (usually their own!). As a result, prejudice has the same like–dislike quality of the affective or evaluative dimensions discussed earlier regarding impressions (Chapter 3) and attitudes (Chapter 6). But prejudice has the additional quality of prejudgment. The perceiver evaluates other people on the basis of their social or racial category rather than on the basis of information or facts about them as individuals. In this sense prejudice is not very reasonable, and perhaps even illogical or irrational.

One variant on prejudice bears mentioning: **ethnocentrism.** This refers to the belief that one's own group (called the **ingroup**) is the center of everything, and is superior to all other groups (which are called **outgroups**). Thus the ingroup is perceived as most virtuous, superior, and holding the best values; the outgroup is contemptible, immoral, inferior, weak, distrusted, and criminal (Brewer, 1986).

THE BEHAVIORAL COMPONENT **Discrimination** is the behavioral component of group antagonism. This is the behavioral acceptance or rejection of a person based on (or at least influenced by) his or her group membership. For many years, Southern restaurants refused to seat Chinese and black customers in restaurants that catered to whites. That is an example of discriminatory behavior. Quotas for the hiring, admission, or promotion of workers and students based on their group membership are another example. In recent years, the occasional use of quotas to aid minorities has been described as "reverse discrimination" because it favors a minority group at the expense of the majority.

CONSISTENCY AMONG COMPONENTS The three components of group antagonism are related but are not identical. Certainly unflattering stereotypes, prejudice, and discrimination usually go together. Some people will engage in all three more often than others. And some minority groups will bear the brunt of all three more than others.

But to some extent, the components are independent. Stereotypes of different groups can differ quite a bit in cognitive content, but yield equally strong negative prejudices. Historically, the majority of Americans have had quite different stereotypes about blacks and Jews, as Table 14–1 shows, but until recent years the level of prejudice against the two groups was quite similar. Nor are prejudice and discrimination always identical, as is true for any combination of attitudes and behavior. A great deal of prejudice can exist with very little discrimination, particularly if there are firm legal prohibitions against discriminatory behavior.

Effects of prejudice

ON PERCEPTIONS Prejudice and stereotypes influence attitudes and behavior in almost every conceivable way. First of all, they influence perceptions about individual members of the target group. Sagar and Schofield (1980) presented sixth-graders with brief verbal descriptions and artist's drawings of interactions between two children, such as one asking another for cake or one bumping the other in the hallway. The races of the two children were systemically varied in the drawings. Other children were then asked to tell a story about what had happened. Both black and white children described the behavior as more mean and threatening when blacks were involved than when whites were. Presumably this is due to the stereotype that such interactions are likely to be more hostile than friendly if blacks are involved.

Another example illustrates class stereotyping. Darley and Gross (1983) showed subjects a brief film of a child in a working-class urban neighborhood or a posh suburban park. Subjects were then shown a videotape of the same child in school responding to achievement test problems. When the subjects were asked to evaluate the child's test performance, they rated it as significantly better if they had seen her in the upper-class neighborhood, presumably because the stereotype is that such upper-class children do better in school. In both cases, stereotypes colored subjects' perceptions of social interactions.

ON EVALUATION Psychological pressures toward psychological consistency (discussed in Chapter 6) frequently lead us to form attitudes that are consistent with our prejudices. The impact of racial prejudice in a mock jury situation was the focus of one study (Ugwuegbu, 1979). White college students at a Midwestern university were asked to participate as jurors in a study of jury behavior. They read a description of an alleged rape of a 19-year-old woman by a 21-year-old man on the campus. The race of both victim and defendant were varied. Then the subjects were asked how much harm the defendant intended, how responsible he was for the rape, whether or not he was guilty, and what penalty he deserved. The responses were graded to form an index of perceived culpability.

As Table 14–2 shows, a black defendant was seen as more culpable than a white. This was especially true with a white victim. The strength of the evidence against the defendant was also varied: In a strong evidence condition, both the victim and an eyewitness could identify the assailant; in a weak evidence condition, neither was sure. A middle or "marginal" condition pitted the victim's identification against the defendant's denials, with ambiguous reports by witnesses and police. The biggest effects

TABLE 14–2

Perceived Culpability of Male Defendant as a Function of His Race and Strength of Evidence

	STRENGTH OF EVIDENCE			
	Near Zero	Marginal	Strong	Total
Race of Defendant				
Black	7.2	17.1	24.4	15.9
White	6.5	12.9	21.7	13.8

Source: Adapted from Ugwuegbu (1979), p. 140. Entries are ratings of culpability on a 36 point scale where high values indicate greater perceived culpability.

of defendant race occurred when the evidence was marginal, as shown in Table 14–2. Then the black defendant was perceived as considerably more guilty than the white defendant. But when there was little evidence of guilt, neither was thought culpable; when there was strong evidence, both were. The need for consistency, therefore, induced people to bias their perceptions of the defendant in line with prejudice against blacks primarily when there was some ambiguity about the real situation.

Prejudice also influences people's political responses to minority groups. For example, in elections that pit a black candidate against a white candidate, a white voter's prejudice is often the best predictor of which candidate he or she will support. This was true in Massachusetts when a black, Edward Brooke, ran his first victorious race for the United States Senate (Becker & Heaton, 1967). And it was true in Los Angeles when a black city councilman, Tom Bradley, twice challenged the incumbent white mayor, Sam Yorty (Kinder & Sears, 1981). Bradley lost the first time and won the second. In all these elections, the overall level of whites' prejudice was low enough that Brooke and Bradley attracted many white votes. But the best predictor of which whites voted against them was prejudice.

Prejudice is also the best predictor of how white people feel about busing schoolchildren for racial integration. The most prejudiced people are almost unanimously opposed to it, even if they are liberal in other respects. Conversely, less prejudiced whites are more favorable toward busing (Sears, Hensler, & Speer, 1979). In short, prejudice strongly influences people's political attitudes and behavior, whether it is their preferences about public policy or their voting behavior.

BOX 14–1

ANGLOPHILIA AND RUSSOPHOBIA

Another application of the consistency idea is that "similarity breeds liking," as described in Chapter 8. We like a new person or group on the basis of the consistency of their attitudes or values with our own.

Why do we like some countries and dislike others? Nincic and Russett (1979) tested a simple theory about countries that corresponds to the reasons we like some people and dislike others: we like countries that are *similar* to ours and that share *interests* (economic or security) with us. They coded a large number of countries for similarity in terms of racial composition, language, religion, political system, and economic activity. Shared interests were indexed in terms of direct American capital investment, trade, military bases, and American military personnel stationed there.

Liking for foreign countries by American citizens was strongly affected by both factors independently. Canada was high on both and liked very much, North Vietnam low on both and much disliked. Japan was seen as dissimilar but having shared interests and was liked somewhat. The Scandinavian countries were seen as similar, but having few shared interests, and were also liked somewhat. Mexico fell about in the middle on all three dimensions.

ON BEHAVIOR Prejudiced attitudes can also produce discriminatory behavior in more subtle, indirect ways. For example, parents' prejudice can affect their children's behavior. In one study, white children of prejudiced parents were less likely to engage in interracial social contact in integrated schools than were children of less prejudiced parents. The consequence was that the opportunity for contact with children of another race did not increase their own racial tolerance as much as it did for children of less prejudiced parents who engaged in more interaction with minority children (Stephan and Rosenfeld, 1978). So our prejudices can influence not only our own attitudes and behavior, but those of our children as well, and therefore can restrict their opportunities to grow up as racially tolerant persons.

Basis in Reality

We will discuss formal theories about the origins of these group antagonisms later on in the chapter. But for now, it is important to note that the major debate has been over whether group antagonisms are based in reality or not. Most people probably feel that their attitudes toward various social groups simply reflect the realities of the group's shared characteristics. And most of us probably feel that we acquire these perceptions through our experience with group members, whether it is direct face-to-face experience or some other less direct kind.

Indeed, stereotypes do stem to some extent from the real differences among people, due to the categorization process we described in Chapter 3. Groupings are partly based on real differences between people—old people are plainly different from young people, and Hindus are plainly different from Irish Catholics, just as blacks are from whites.

Even so, much of the stereotype-generating categorization into groups is based on little more than arbitrary social norms. We categorize on the basis of salient attributes. Salience depends to a large degree on where our attention is directed, and that usually depends on the norms we have learned. In the United States, for example, race is extremely salient, primarily because of our history of having placed Afro-American slaves in a lower caste. By

---

BOX 14–2

HOW MUCH BLACK DOES IT TAKE TO MAKE A "BLACK"?

The arbitrariness of this categorization process is perhaps illustrated most vividly by the famous "separate-but-equal" Supreme Court decision in 1896, *Plessy* v. *Ferguson*. In the racially segregated South during the century following emancipation, the definition of who was black and who was white varied considerably. In some states a single drop of Negro blood classified a person as a Negro. *Plessy* v. *Ferguson* defined a Louisiana pupil with one black great-grandparent and seven white ones as colored, and assigned the pupil to an all-Negro segregated school. The Chinese who settled in Mississippi after the Civil War were designated as colored and were subject to the same restrictions as blacks. But this categorization gradually changed, and by World War II Chinese were largely treated as if they were white. The point is that although these classifications were quite arbitrary, they had serious consequences for the people involved.

contrast, in Cuba or Brazil, race is not as salient; people's skin colors span the full range, and categorization by race is less common. And in Lebanon or Northern Ireland, religious preference is the major basis for categorization; people are either Muslim or Christian, or Catholic or Protestant. Race is hardly important at all.

A second problem with the idea of reality-based stereotypes is that the stereotype holders very often have little personal experience with the stereotyped group, and therefore cannot have acquired the stereotype by generalizing about people they have known. For example, the students who participated in the study in Table 14–1 had had very little personal contact with members of either stereotyped group. Especially in the earlier years, very few blacks and Jews were permitted to attend Princeton, the college these students attended.

What is most impressive therefore is that the college students surveyed shared the same standard stereotypes of these two groups, having had almost no direct contact with them. This suggests that stereotypes are largely a matter of social tradition. Gender stereotypes will be discussed in some detail in the next chapter. In that regard, of course, we all share a great deal of personal experience with the group in question—but as we will see, the reigning stereotypes have much more to do with social norms than with real sex differences.

People tend to experience their own antagonisms toward other social groups as rooted in the characteristics of the groups themselves. As in other cases of the actor-observer bias in attributions discussed in Chapter 5, they attribute their own perceptions of other people to the internal dispositions of those people. These perceptions may have some "grain of truth" to them, but they are generally not fully plausible. Personal experience with the group is often quite fragmentary, and the perceptual basis for the stereotype too arbitrary, for "reality" to be an adequate explanation for the antagonisms. As we will see, learned social norms are usually the most powerful factor.

THEORETICAL APPROACHES

There are five main theories of prejudice. *Social learning* theories deal with a particular individual's prejudice, and locate the causes in the prejudiced person's learning experiences with parents, friends, teachers, and so on. *Cognitive* theories emphasize how cognitive processes such as categorization, salience, and schemas contribute to prejudice. *Motivational* theories look for the origins of prejudice in the prejudiced person's personality. *Social identity theory* analyzes how people categorize the social world into ingroups and outgroups, and gain self-esteem based on the status of their own ingroup relative to the status of relevant outgroups. It therefore combines the cognitive and motivational approaches. *Group conflict* theories examine when and how prejudice develops in a particular society, culture, or group. They generally focus on groups instead of individuals; they try to explain how Americans in general feel about Japan and the Japanese instead of being concerned with the attitudes of any particular individual. They tend to explain prejudice as resulting from the real conflicts of interest that exist between groups.

Social Learning

Perhaps the simplest of the theoretical approaches, social learning theory, views prejudice as being learned the same way people learn other values. The prejudice is a social norm in the person's culture or subculture. It is acquired by the child in the process of socialization. It is transmitted interpersonally as part of a large package of norms. The child acquires such prejudiced attitudes to gain acceptance by others. This continued transmission and expression of the prejudice reinforce its role as a cultural norm (Ashmore & DelBoca, 1981).

It is easy to document the existence of norms of ethnic and racial prejudice all over the world. For example, white North Americans' prejudice toward various national and ethnic groups has been very stable through much of the twentieth century. The peoples of the British Isles have been liked the most, and those from Asia and Africa the least. Prejudice against Germans, Italians, and Japanese, increased at the time of World War II, and against the Russians during the Cold War. Otherwise, white North Americans' prejudices have changed little. If comparable data were available from other societies, they would doubtless show the same historic enmities—for example, between Vietnamese and Cambodians, or toward untouchables in India, or tribal hatreds in Africa.

These prejudices are acquired quite early in life. The most salient ones, like racial prejudice in this country, are acquired well before adolescence. White children learn that blacks are socially inferior in a variety of ways, simply by being told and by observing the society in which they live. To show this, Goodman (1952) observed 103 black and white children intensively for a full year. She concluded that racial awareness was already present in many children at ages 3 and 4, and that 25 percent of the 4-year-olds were already expressing strongly entrenched race-related values. No white child ever expressed a wish to be like a black child, while the black children expressed much more conflict about their color.

Certainly by the early grade school years, most American children are aware of racial differences in our society and of the prevailing norms about the races, at least in some form. As children move through grade school, they increasingly perceive differences between the races, but often do not become sensitive to differences among members of other races (Katz, 1976). The experiences children have during the grade school years are crucial, because by early adolescence racial prejudice has crystallized and is much more difficult to break down. The consequence is that prejudice is considerably stronger in some areas of the society than in others. For example, it is stronger in the South than in other regions, it is stronger in the working class than in the middle class, it is stronger among older whites (who were brought up in a more segregationist period) than among younger whites, and so on (see Maykovich, 1975; Middleton, 1976).

Parents play a particularly important role in the child's acquisition of prejudice. There are consistent correlations between parents' and children's racial and ethnic attitudes (Ashmore & DelBoca, 1976). Parents often transmit these attitudes without directly instructing their children, since attitudes can be learned by association or by imitation as well as by direct reinforcement. Children observe their parents' attitudes and behavior and pick up many nonverbal cues in their reactions to people of other races. But parents frequently are reluctant to express prejudice openly and freely. One result is that children are not perfectly accurate in the attitudes they attribute to their parents, particularly about matters not currently in the news or in the middle of controversy (Niemi, 1973).

As children grow older, peer groups become increasingly important. Normally peer groups mostly reinforce parents' views, because of the similarities in social background and values of people sharing a common community environment. But occasionally the parents' attitudes conflict with those in the child's environment. Children probably acquire prejudice from a broad range of cues from their parents and a broad range of other people as well.

The media represent another potential source of social learning, especially for children. As indicated earlier, minorities have historically been given relatively little attention in the media. For example, before television, magazines such as *Life* and *The Saturday Evening Post* reached very large national audiences. As of 1949–50, blacks were in only 0.5 percent of all ads and in 2.5 percent of all nonadvertising material, despite the fact that they comprised about 10 percent of the population. Even in 1967, only 4 percent of all TV commercials included blacks (Greenberg & Mazingo, 1976). In a content analysis of Los Angeles newspapers from the late nineteenth century to the late 1960s, Johnson et al. (1971) found almost no references to blacks until the Supreme Court's school desegregation case in 1954. So far as the media were concerned, blacks were simply invisible. Skimpy as this coverage was, it tended to be highly stereotyped; 80 percent of the blacks in ads were maids, cooks, or servants for whites. The newspaper coverage that did appear was largely focused on sensational events, entertainment, and crime (Johnson et al., 1971).

This has changed considerably. On prime time television, blacks appear much more often than they used to. By 1973, 14 percent of TV commercials were using blacks. Weigel, Loomis, and Soja (1980) conducted a careful content analysis of prime time television broadcasting from the 1977 and 1978 seasons. Blacks appeared in 20 percent of the product commercials, 52 percent of the situation comedies, and 59 percent of the drama shows. In situation comedies, at least one black character was visible 22 percent of the time.

Moreover, the black-white interactions shown on television tend now to be more egalitarian. The old days of showing blacks in subordinate roles seem to have vanished. Over 70 percent of the cross-racial interactions "occurred within institutional settings in which at least some black characters appeared to hold positions of authority or positions requiring technical sophistication" (Weigel et al., 1980, p. 889). Blacks and whites were about equally likely to have the higher-status roles in these interactions (see Table 14–3).

But—and this seems to mirror the actual state of interracial relations in the United States today—the cross-racial interactions tended to be infrequent, distant, formal, and centered on the workplace. Blacks are still given small parts; and they are still depicted quite differently from whites. Table 14–3 shows that blacks' appearances on television tended to be quite brief; some whites were almost always in view, whereas only rarely were one or more blacks in view. Further, blacks' appearances

remain quite segregated. Very little of the time were blacks and whites shown as interacting with each other (less than 4 percent of the time even in comedies), and they were scarcely ever on the screen at the same time (less than 8 percent of the time even in comedies). Only 10 percent of the cross-racial interactions occurred outside the workplace, whereas 47 percent of the white-white interactions did. Black-white interactions were less intimate and involved much less shared decision-making than white-white interactions.

Cross-racial interaction is particularly distant when it is between males and females. Whereas the majority of male-female interactions involving whites had some element of flirtation or sexual involvement, 93 percent of those involving blacks and whites were rated as "ritualized greetings or situationally dictated exchanges" (p. 891). So if children were to take their cue from television today, they would assume that relations between the races were somewhat rare, distant, formal, and occur primarily at work. Cross-racial romances would be seen as quite deviant. Of course, all this is still a great improvement over the invisibility and the stereotyped behavior presented earlier in this century.

Motivational Theories

Some intrapersonal theories of prejudice analyze it as an outgrowth of motivational tensions within the individual. These are sometimes called psychodynamic theories because they emphasize the particular dynamics of the specific individual's personality.

One such theory treats prejudice as displaced

TABLE 14–3

Prime Time Commercials and Programming: Relative Frequencies of White and Black Appearances, and Cross-Racial Appearances and Interactions

Timing Category	PERCENT OF HUMAN APPEARANCE TIME			
	Drama	Comedy	Total	Commercials
White appearances	99.5%	86.0%	95.8%	96.6%
Black appearances	3.3	22.0	8.3	8.5
Cross-racial appearances	2.8	7.9	4.1	5.1
Cross-racial interactions	1.5	3.6	2.0	1.7

Source: Weigel et al. (1980), p. 888.

aggression. Displacement occurs when the source of frustration or annoyance cannot be attacked because of fear or simple unavailability. If there is an economic depression and a man loses his job, he feels angry and aggressive, but there is no obvious person at fault. Under these circumstances, people look for a **scapegoat**—someone whom they can blame for their difficulties and whom they can attack.

Another psychodynamic theory treats prejudice as a personality disorder, just like a phobia about snakes or a neurotic need for approval. The best-known example of this theory is found in work on the **authoritarian personality** (Adorno et al., 1950). This impressive program of research was sponsored by the American Jewish Committee to try to understand the rise of anti-Semitism in the 1930s and the compliant behavior of Germans toward Hitler. Their conclusion was that anti-Semitism developed from a particular personality syndrome called the authoritarian personality. It is characterized by (1) rigid adherence to (and harsh punishment for deviation from) conventional values and patterns of behavior; (2) an exaggerated need to submit to, and identify with, strong authority; (3) generalized hostility; and (4) a mystical, superstitious cast of mind.

The authoritarian personality was thought to stem from early rearing by a domineering father and punitive mother. As an adult, the individual repeats the experience, but now he or she is in the driver's seat, bullying and punishing those who are deviant or disobedient. People of other races and religions, the handicapped or weak of all kinds, those with unconventional life styles all fall under the authoritarian's iron boot. The authoritarian thinks his or her group is wonderful, and all other groups are disreputable and disgusting.

Research on authoritarianism quickly got caught up in technical disputes about the data (see Christie & Jahoda, 1954; Kirscht & Dillehay, 1967). The psychological analysis just presented also became somewhat controversial. A central problem was that researchers failed to distinguish adequately between sociocultural learning and personality factors in its explanation of anti-Semitism.

For example, it was found that working-class whites were disproportionately anti-Semitic. Was this because a disproportionate number of them had authoritarian personalities? It was easy to show that working-class parents demanded more submission from their children and dealt more harsh punishment than did middle-class parents (Lipset, 1960), so the conditions for producing authoritarian personalities were certainly present. Alternatively, perhaps their anti-Semitism was a historical norm that had been passed down from generation to generation. Many working-class families were only a generation or two removed from areas of Europe where extreme anti-Semitism had reigned for centuries. So anti-Semitism could have stemmed from learning a traditional norm, and not from a personality obsessed with authority and domination. As a result of these complexities, motivational theories are not as popular in social psychology as they were some years back.

Cognitive Processes

Earlier we analyzed extensively the cognitive processes that produce impression formation. Chapters 3 and 4 present explanations for the impressions one person has of another. Extending such theories about cognitive processes to impressions of groups and of group members has been one of the most active research areas on prejudice in recent years. The central idea is that certain systematic cognitive biases naturally accompany impression formation. Perceivers try to develop a structured impression of another person, which necessarily breeds distortions. And they overrespond to the most salient stimuli. Such efforts can, all by themselves, produce prejudice and stereotyping.

CATEGORIZATION Perceivers naturally categorize other people into groups, the most common being gender, racial, and age groups. We immediately identify a stranger as a man or woman, black or white, child or grownup or old person. Beyond that, we quickly pigeonhole the person into such other social categories as class and nationality. Then we use subtler categories, such as tall ones, pretty ones, jocks, obnoxious ones, or whatever. This **categorization** process has a number of important consequences (Hamilton & Trolier, 1986; Linville et al., 1986; Wilder, 1986). It helps the perceiver process information about a lot of individuals in an efficient way. But it can blur the distinctions among the members of a particular group. For example, observers of group discussions including equal numbers of blacks and whites were more likely to confuse the contributions of people within a race than to confuse their contributions across race, as we indicated in Chapter 3 (Taylor et al., 1978). The implication is that information is stored in terms of social category, not in terms of the specific people. Observers remember that something was said by a black person or a white person, not which person said it.

There are other examples of this same phenomenon of perceptual blurring among people who have been categorized as being in a social group. Observers perceive members of a group as being similar to each other, and dissimilar to members of other groups, even when group members have been arbitrarily or randomly assigned to the group (Wilder, 1981). People who are in a group, as opposed to being independent individuals, are perceived as more influenced by the other people; the fact of their group membership leads to more situational attributions, again even though they may have been assigned to a group on wholly arbitrary grounds (Wilder, 1978).

SALIENCE   Categorization into groups is often based simply on some very prominent, salient cues. Skin color differentiates blacks and whites; body type, hair length, clothing, and voice differentiate men and women; accent differentiates foreigners from natives, and so on.

This kind of salience has a number of predictable effects, as we saw in Chapter 3. We pay more attention to salient stimuli, so these differences tend to be on our mind when we encounter members of other groups, especially when they stand out in the environment. A white researcher in a ghetto school stands out; so did Jackie Robinson when he was the first black major league baseball player.

The problem is that perceivers make more extreme evaluations of and more dispositional attributions about salient people. For example, the only female in a law firm is highly salient. If she is out of work because of illness, dispositional attributions are likely. Others may say she is "sickly," self-indulgent, or maybe even malingering. If a male is out for the same reason, we make more situational attributions; we attribute his absence to an illness over which he has no control, perhaps extend more sympathy, and cover his workload.

SCHEMAS   If stereotypes are cognitive structures that consist of a set of expectations regarding a social group, they can be thought of as **schemas,** with the same consequences we have already discussed in Chapter 3. New information inconsistent with schemas tends to be rejected. Therefore it influences observers' interpretations of their actual behavior. This was illustrated in the Sagar and Schofield (1980) study cited earlier, in which children interpreted a black child's behavior in a drawing as more mean and threatening than a white child's.

Attributions about the person are also affected. If someone's behavior is inconsistent with our stereotype of that person, we explain it as due to the situation, not the person. If we are forced to make an internal attribution, it probably will be to some temporary, unstable cause. A good example concerns whites' explanations for racial differences in socioeconomic status. Blacks, on the average, have always been lower in income, employment, educational level, and occupational status than whites. How do whites explain this? Years ago the main attribution for this relative lack of success was stable and internal; blacks were innately inferior in a variety of ways. Whites have gradually surrendered this notion, however. But the racial difference in status remains. So how do whites explain it now? The tendency is to invoke such unstable internal causes as lack of effort and low aspirations (Ashmore & DelBoca, 1976).

SELF-FULFILLING PROPHECIES   Such schemas about a group's behavior can, in turn, produce stereotype-confirming behavior on the part of the minority group member. That is, our stereotypes influence not only our own thinking, but also the behavior of the *victims* of stereotyping when we interact with them. In this sense, a stereotype can be a **self-fulfilling prophecy.** This further step in the process is in some ways even more damaging. Members of the victimized group begin to live up to the stereotype, to exhibit the very characteristics the stereotype says they have. If we think all Poles are bumblers, we are likely to interact with them as if we expected them to bumble at any opportu-

BOX 14–3

THE PERCEIVED POWER OF THE "SOLO"

Some of the most salient people in our society are the "solos"—the one black astronaut in a news conference, the only woman engineer in an office, the one white starting in a professional basketball game, and so on. If mere perceptual salience is responsible for biasing observers' perceptions of causal importance, one would think these "solo" individuals would be perceived as having an exaggerated causal role in their social settings. The effects of the salience created by being a solo member of a minority group in a context dominated by majority group members are illustrated in a series of studies conducted by Taylor and her colleagues (1977; see Taylor, 1981b). They varied the distinctiveness of a minority person in a discussion group by setting up discussions by groups that were all white, had one black, or were evenly divided in race. The discussion was presented via tape recording, and exactly the same tape was used in all cases. However, each speaker was identified with a still slide as he spoke, and in this way the race of the speakers was varied. Observers of this mixed-media discussion rated the speakers for amount of contribution to the discussion. The "solo" black stood out as talking more and being more influential than did the same speaker in either of the other contexts, where his race did not make him so salient because he was portrayed as just one black in a group that was racially evenly divided, or as a white in an all-white group. The token's contributions were also remembered better than those of the minorities in the integrated group. Interestingly enough, these tokens may themselves suffer cognitive deficits as a result of their token status; in one study (Lord & Saenz, 1985), tokens remembered less of the discussion in which they had participated (and supposedly dominated!) than did other participants or observers.

nity. And, interestingly enough, this will increase the likelihood that they will behave in a stereotype-confirming way.

Much research shows that people behave in a way that confirms others' expectations. In the classroom, children conform to teachers' expectations about their competence; research subjects live up to researchers' expectations; and in therapy the client's progress may be a function of the therapist's expectations. In all these cases, one person's expectations can influence the other person's behavior, even when those expectations are based on false information about the target person. The expectation acts as a self-fulfilling prophecy, because the

expectation produces the behavior in the target person (see Rosenthal & Rubin, 1978).

When applied to stereotypes, the chain of self-fulfilling prophecy involves four steps: (1) a stereotype (expectation) about how the other person will behave; (2) a change in the stereotype holder's own behavior; which (3) produces a change in the target person's behavior; and finally (4) the perception of the target person's behavior as confirming the stereotype rather than as a response to the holder's own behavior. Snyder and Swann (1978) showed this in an ingenious way. They told each subject (the "perceiver") he was going to interact with another subject (the "target") who was described as hostile, liking contact sports, cruel, and insensitive, or as nonhostile, liking poetry and sailing, kind, and cooperative. This description set up the perceiver's stereotype of the target. Then the perceiver and target (who was also a naive subject) engaged in a series of reaction time tests that allowed both to behave in a hostile way (by administering loud, painful, distracting noises to each other).

Not surprisingly, it turned out that expecting a hostile partner led perceivers to administer more high-intensity noises. But the targets, completely ignorant of how they had been described to the other person, also administered more noise if they had been described as hostile, as shown in the top line of Table 14–4. Remember, the targets had been described as hostile or nonhostile at random, so this higher level of hostile behavior had to be caused by the perceiver's expectations. And the perceivers, reasonably enough, saw the "hostile" target as more hostile than the "nonhostile" target, in view of the behavioral confirmation of their expectations. This is shown in the second line of the table.

The most interesting aspect of this experiment then followed. The target was put through the same task with a new, completely naive subject. Neither knew about the "hostile" or "nonhostile" description randomly assigned earlier to the target. Nevertheless, the target continued to live up to expectations. The third row shows he gave more noise, and the fourth row, that he was regarded as more hostile in this new interaction.

So this experiment demonstrates that expecta-tions affect the stereotyper's own behavior toward the person, whose behavior in return confirms the stereotype. Not only that, but the victim later behaves in a stereotype-confirming manner in other situations, even toward people who are completely ignorant of the stereotype. So even in neutral environments, with people who do not share the stereotype, the victim of prejudice still tends to exhibit stereotype-confirming behavior.

Perhaps the most destructive result is that the target person will come to believe the stereotype accurately applies to him or her. In a similar study by Fazio and his colleagues (1981), the subjects exhibited behavior in the experiment itself that confirmed the expectations of their partners. But they were then placed in a completely different social situation, where they interacted with a new confederate. The subject still lived up to the original expectations in interacting with this new person. And the subject's own self-ratings also lived up to the original partner's expectations. Through the self-perception process described earlier (Chapter 5), the subjects took their own behavior as genuinely reflecting their own personalities, even though it had been induced by the other person's expectations. In short, not only was the stereotype holder's behavior influenced by these arbitrary expectations, but the victims' behavior and self-perceptions also came to reflect the stereotype.

INGROUP VS. OUTGROUP   Another aspect of the cognitive approach is that one's perspective is altered by virtue of being a member of one group rather than another. In particular, members of the *ingroup*

TABLE 14–4

Effects of Perceivers' Expectations on Target Person's Behavior

	Hostile Label	Nonhostile Label
First Interaction, with Informed Perceiver		
Hostile behavior	4.12[a]	3.17
Perceiver's impression of target's hostility	3.83	3.64
Second Interaction, with Naive Perceiver		
Hostile behavior	4.30	2.70
Perceiver's impression of target's hostility	3.66	2.75

[a] The higher the number, the greater the hostility exhibited or perceived.
Source: Snyder and Swann (1978), p. 155.

have quite different perceptions about their group than they do about *outgroups*, and different from those held by outgroup members. Americans are likely to perceive Japanese very differently than a Japanese person would. And they will perceive Americans quite differently. The ingroup constitutes "us" and outgroups are "them" (Brewer, 1986). Being in an ingroup places one in a unique perspective.

Specifically, we often simply categorize members of an outgroup as just another anonymous group member rather than perceiving them as individuals. We see the person as "an Asian" rather than as Stanley Wong. This has important consequences. For one thing, people in an ingroup are likely to assume similarity among outgroup members, even on dimensions irrelevant to the categorization. To illustrate this, Allen and Wilder (1979) created two groups of subjects, supposedly on the basis of artistic preferences. The subjects assumed people within each group shared beliefs, even on topics quite irrelevant to art, and differed from members of the other group. In particular, we tend to perceive greater group homogeneity in the outgroup than in the ingroup: people see the outgroup as more homogeneous than the ingroup in terms of traits, personality, and even number of subtypes "*They* are all alike, whereas *we* are quite diverse!" (Hamilton & Trolier, 1986; Linville et al., 1986).

Social Identity Theory

Social identity theory, developed by Henri Tajfel (1982), has come to some prominence recently as a blend of the motivational and cognitive approaches. It involves three basic assumptions. First, people categorize the social world into ingroups and outgroups, as we have seen. Second is a motivational assumption, that people strive for a positive self-concept, and they derive a sense of self-esteem from their social identity in the ingroup. Third, their self-concept is partly dependent on how they evaluate their ingroup relative to other groups. Therefore they engage in behavior that both distinguishes their group from other groups, and benefits their group and fellow ingroup members relative to outgroup members (Tajfel & Turner, 1986). This process produces a kind of social competition be-

tween groups, in which people try to boost the status of their own group as a way of boosting their own self-esteem.

Numerous studies show that the mere act of categorization can produce discrimination when it involves categorizing people into "us" (an ingroup) and "them" (an outgroup). Even a completely arbitrary categorization of people as being in one group as opposed to another leads to discriminatory behavior. This has been called the *minimal intergroup discrimination* effect, based on a series of studies by Henri Tajfel and his colleagues (1971). Once people feel they belong to a group, they tend to favor other group members at the expense of nonmembers (or members of other groups). This tendency can be seen in more favorable evaluations of ingroup members than outgroup members, or in more favorable allocation of rewards to ingroup members. Favoritism can be observed even when the basis for group membership is purely arbitrary and even when the person gets little or nothing tangible from the group.

The simplest demonstrations of such effects are in Tajfel's studies, using the so-called **minimal intergroup situation.** In these studies, students were brought into a laboratory and divided into two groups on the basis of some arbitrary procedure. In one typical study, they were divided into two groups supposedly on the basis of their preferences between the two modern painters Klee and Kandinsky (though in fact they were assigned randomly to the two groups). They had no actual interaction with fellow group members (the ingroup) or members of the other group (the outgroup), but they were asked to evaluate all individuals in the experiment and distribute some rewards to them.

The general finding has been that participants evaluated ingroup members more positively, and rewarded them more than outgroup members (Brewer, 1979). This ingroup favoritism occurs even when the subjects cannot themselves get any direct benefit from their behavior, other than the vicarious one of rewarding the self via the investment of social identity in the group. Furthermore people act not only to reward the ingroup in absolute terms, but to benefit it relative to the outgroup. So they will try to maximize the *difference* between rewards given to the ingroup and those given the outgroup. And they will try to provide relatively more benefits to the ingroup even when it means the ingroup gets less in absolute terms (Wilder, 1986).

Ingroup favoritism shows up in a number of other indicators as well. Other ingroup members' traits are described more favorably than those of outgroup members (Allen & Wilder, 1975). People expect more favorable treatment from the ingroup than from the outgroup (Howard & Rothbart, 1980). And there is a vast literature indicating a group variant of the self-serving attributional biases we discussed in Chapter 5; generally people make more favorable attributions about fellow ingroup members than about outgroup members (Hamilton & Trolier, 1986, p. 132).

You might think that the subjects would feel some special liking for ingroup members because they were supposedly selected for their similar tastes in art, and similarity is a strong determinant of liking, as we saw in Chapter 8. But later experiments made it clear to the subjects that their assignments to groups were completely random, and they shared no common characteristics with other ingroup members. Locksley et al. (1980) assigned subjects to be a Phi or a Gamma by having them pull a lottery ticket out of a can, with the same results: Subjects allocated significantly more rewards to ingroup than to outgroup members.

The intriguing thing about these findings is that they occur so consistently despite the fact that the ingroup–outgroup distinction in these experiments is in reality almost completely meaningless. Mere categorization, on whatever basis, seems to trigger ingroup favoritism. So, merely making the group distinction salient produces judgments more favorable to the ingroup. Indeed, in one experiment, simply printing the task materials on the same color paper as that on which the group were distinguished—"blues" or "greens"—produced ingroup favorites (Wilder & Shapiro, 1984).

The point is that mere categorization leads to ingroup favoritism and discrimination against the outgroup, even when there are no selfish gains to be made or any especially pleasurable interaction with the ingroup, or any especially unpleasant interaction with the outgroup. These subjects were not allowed to reward themselves, and they could not be rewarded by other ingroup members. They had no interaction with members from either group. The purely cognitive act of categorization, apart from any other factors, was enough to promote different responses to ingroup and outgroup.

It is important to note that the social identity theory links cognitive and motivational approaches. It is the mere cognitive categorization of people into ingroup and outgroup that has consequences for the individual's self-esteem. This is nicely illustrated in a study that shows people had higher self-esteem if they were both categorized into groups *and* could discriminate against the outgroup than if they were not categorized and could discriminate, or were categorized and could not discriminate. People like to be part of a group that is superior (Lemyre & Smith, 1985).

Group Conflict Theories

Prejudice is defined as the affect felt by one individual toward a group and its members, and all of the foregoing theories locate its origins in the psychological functioning of that individual. But a number of other theories trace prejudice instead to conflicts between two groups—the group to which the prejudiced person belongs (the ingroup) and the group that is the target of prejudice (the outgroup). There are several versions of such group conflict theories.

REALISTIC GROUP CONFLICT   The theory of **realistic group conflict** argues that when two groups are in competition for scarce resources, they threaten each other. This creates hostility between them and thus produces mutually negative evaluations. So prejudice is an inevitable consequence of a reality conflict. Perhaps it can be minimized, but it cannot be eliminated altogether because it is created by unavoidable realities. This is a form of the incentive theories we presented in Chapter 6. Attitudes are determined by the real costs and benefits posed by the group in question.

This theory would lead us to expect antagonism between the Palestinians and Israelis: Because they claim the same territory, they fight each other. Whites will be angry at blacks if blacks are hired on affirmative action programs and whites are excluded from those jobs. In recent years, increasing

Two days of rioting in 1982 followed the shooting of a black youth by police in Miami. Were blacks' reactions based on realistic group conflict?

UPI/Bettmann Newsphotos

numbers of Asian-Americans have been excelling in academic work. If they are to be admitted to prestigious universities, correspondingly fewer students from other backgrounds will be admitted. So it would not be surprising, according to realistic group conflict theory, for prejudice against Asian-Americans to rise. Some historical analyses suggest that Chinese and Japanese immigrants to the United States were well received as long as they did menial work no one else wanted to do. Only later, when they began to compete with Caucasians for jobs, did prejudice mount.

If prejudice arises because one group really threatens the other, then the most threatened individuals ought also to be the most prejudiced. The whites who most perceive their neighborhoods as being threatened with racial integration, or with crime by blacks, or with influxes of black children into the schools, ought to be the most prejudiced (Rothbart, 1976).

However, a number of studies have shown that threats posed by blacks to whites' own lives have surprisingly little impact on their levels of prejudice or on their preferences regarding government racial policies (Sears, 1987). For example, whites'

opposition to busing for racial integration is generally not based on concern about their own children. Parents of white children in school districts with busing (or threatened with busing) have about the same attitudes about busing as do nonparents or those who live in areas remote from any possibility of busing (McConahay, 1982; Sears & Allen, 1984). In another study, whites' fears that blacks might harm them in the areas of neighborhood desegregation, economic competition, busing, and crime had no effect on their general racial attitudes. Nor did they influence whites' voting behavior in hotly contested local (Los Angeles) mayoralty elections pitting a black candidate against an incumbent white who was openly hostile toward civil rights (Kinder & Sears, 1981).

Despite the obvious appeal of realistic group conflict theories, then, considerable evidence indicates that racial prejudice in the United States is not strongly based in such realities. This is not to say that realistic group conflict is never an important factor. Studies of ethnic conflicts in South Africa, Belgium, and Northern Ireland do trace them to real competition in such areas as labor and housing markets. A breakdown in ethnic segregation is particularly likely to bring ethnic groups into such direct conflicts (Olzak & Nagel, 1986).

RELATIVE DEPRIVATION   Another version is **relative deprivation** theory. This refers to discontent that arises not necessarily from objective conditions, but from the subjective feeling of being deprived relatively more than some other person or group. When people feel deprived relative to another group, they may express their resentment in the form of group antagonism. For example, in a fast-growing economy, the economic situations of all groups may be improving quite impressively. But if one group is doing better than another, this would create feelings of relative deprivation among members of the less well-off group. This in turn might lead to antagonism against the favored group. This was one explanation for the ghetto riots of the 1960s. Although everyone was doing better, blacks felt that their situations were not improving as much as those of whites, and the result was antiwhite violence (Sears & McConahay, 1973). According to Bernstein and Crosby (1980), relative deprivation is also likely to produce such antagonism when people feel entitled to a particular valued object they do not have, feel they once could have attained it but no longer can, and compare themselves to some group that has it.

GROUP INTEREST   These versions of realistic group conflict theory view the key mechanism as being group members' belief that their *own* lives are being or will be harmed by the target group. This is therefore an *egoistic* process of self-interest. But this assumption, that people operate out of a selfish concern for their own well-being, has been challenged in two ways.

First, as indicated above, Kinder & Sears (1981) found that personal racial threats had very little impact on whites' political preferences between black and white candidates. Instead, antagonism toward blacks that focused on racial symbols had a much stronger impact. Whites in the United States now overwhelmingly endorse the general principle of equal opportunity and oppose overt racial discrimination. But they are often quite opposed to racial progress at an abstract, symbolic level, when

it violates their other values. Most do not like symbols such as "forced busing," "reverse discrimination," or "welfare." And this opposition is not based on self-interest or how these racial issues might affect them personally. It seems to be a blend of primitive antiblack feeling and traditional sociopolitical values. These investigators (Sears and McConahay, 1973, and Kinder and Sears, 1981) coined the term **symbolic racism** to describe the phenomenon.

Other research suggests that the key fear might be that one's group will be harmed, irrespective of whether or not the individual group ·member is personally harmed (Bobo, 1983; Sears & Kinder, 1985). The threat may be to "us," not to "me." Even whites who live in towns with no blacks at all, or who have no children, can be upset about busing because it signals a displacement of whites by blacks. Hence the key factor may not be self-interest but group interest—the group may have a stake in a particular outcome. Therefore people may experience relative deprivation, but as **fraternal deprivation** rather than egoistic deprivation— the feeling that the group is deprived relative to some other group, whether or not the individual is.

For example, Vanneman and Pettigrew (1972) found that working-class whites' hostility toward blacks resulted from feelings that they were not gaining as fast as blacks were; the resentment was of the gains being made by blacks as a group. Guimond and Dubé-Simard (1983) conducted a similar analysis of French-speaking residents of Quebec, a province in which English-speaking residents had for many years enjoyed many economic advantages. They found that feelings of fraternal deprivation among French-speaking residents were strongly related to their desire for political autonomy—for separation from the rest of Canada.

The egoistic versions of realistic group conflict theory usually do not have the impact on either prejudice or political preferences that group-centered versions do. The teams of Guimond and Dubé-Simard (1983) and Vanneman and Pettigrew (1972) both report that fraternal deprivation had a much stronger effect on group antagonism, nationalism, and voting behavior than did egoistic deprivation. Evidently people are more sensitive to the

Having a black mayor of Chicago or any other major American city would have been inconceivable as recently as the 1950s. But change does not come without conflict, as in the case of the late Mayor Harold Washington of Chicago.

symbols of how their group is doing than they are to how they themselves are doing.

Part of the reason for the small impact of egoistic discontent is that people tend to separate their attitudes about their own situations from their attitudes about society. And prejudice is first and foremost a set of attitudes about how groups should be treated in society, not about how one's own life should be going. Prejudices against particular groups focus more on how different groups should be treated and how institutions and government should be organized, and less on how the prejudiced person should be treated.

Comparison

Each of the foregoing broad theoretical approaches points to different factors as causes of prejudice. There is some truth in all of them. For example, normal cognitive processes of categorization and of special attention to salient stimuli can increase stereotypes and discriminatory behavior. It is doubtful that such cognitive processes are sufficient to produce a consistent pattern of bias all by themselves, however. They require learning that produces prejudice against particular groups, and specific stereotypical content. Blacks are stereotypically

thought to be lazy and musical, and Chinese hardworking, though both are perceptually quite different from whites. But the perceptual distinctiveness of these minority groups may be necessary to get a pattern of group discrimination started, and it certainly helps to maintain it.

In general, social learning plays a major role in defining what is "appropriate" prejudice, what the "correct" stereotypes are, and what is acceptable behavior toward other groups and what is not. The wide variations in the treatment of any given group around the globe and across history testify to that, as do the major differences in the treatment of different groups within a society. In 1850, blacks could be bought and sold like cattle; today elaborate legal machinery protects their right to be treated like other people. Slavery hardly existed for other groups in this country, nor for blacks in most other societies. In most Muslim countries women must wear veils, may not engage in premarital or extramarital sexual relations, and do not compete with men for jobs. American women are not so restricted today, though in the nineteenth century they were much less free. Personality tensions and cognitive biases therefore operate within a cultural framework that determines how much prejudice exists, when it can be expressed, and toward whom. This cultural framework is transmitted through learning.

REDUCING PREJUDICE

Studies of attitude change, as summarized in Chapter 7, would make it appear that people's attitudes are susceptible to change. Similarly, studies of conformity and obedience suggest that people's behavior can be influenced rather readily. Well-known techniques of social influence (or other forms of power) can produce behavior wholly contradictory to the person's attitudes, or even to the person's perceptions of reality. Subjects freely administer shock to inoffensive people when they are told to, or express beliefs that go against their sense perceptions. So it might seem that prejudice might be easily changed, as well.

But things turn out not to be so easy. As Hovland (1959) pointed out, the success of persuasion depends in part on whether it is attempted in an experimental laboratory or in the real world. In the controlled environment of a laboratory, it is generally easy to change attitudes. Even a simple written essay can produce changes in attitudes toward foreign aid, atomic submarines, tuition rates in college, brushing teeth, cancer and cigarettes, the quality of a poem, and so on. Subjects read or hear their communication, are asked to state their own beliefs, and tend to agree with the communication more after reading or hearing it than they did before (or than does a control group that did not read or hear it). Attempts to change people's attitudes in the world outside the laboratory tend to be much less successful. It is well to contrast the ease of attitude or behavior change in the laboratory with the difficulty of similar change in real life, at least of such attitudes as racial prejudices.

The main approach to prejudice reduction has been direct intergroup contact. The belief has been that contact would help break down stereotypes, and that proximity and interaction would increase liking, as it normally does in other situations (see Chapter 8). International student exchanges, the Olympic Games, international conferences—all are predicated on this assumption. Does contact really work?

Early Field Studies

Since World War II, for a variety of reasons, America's major institutions have gradually become less segregated. The military, schools, professional sports, and most work situations are no longer fully segregated. This development has given social scientists opportunities to test the effects of contact. Racial prejudice and antagonisms decreased in World War II when black and white soldiers fought together (Stouffer et al., 1949). At the start of the war, military policy was to avoid racially mixed units. However, as time went by and white infantry replacements came to be in short supply, the Army allowed black volunteers to join previously all-white units. Surveys before this desegregation showed most white soldiers opposed it, but afterward there was much less opposition. The greatest support came from those white soldiers who were most closely associated with the blacks. No realistic conflicts arose between the groups because instead of competing, they were fighting a common enemy. Unrealistic stereotypes decreased markedly because of the greater knowledge gained by familiarity.

Some other early research also indicated that increased contact reduced antagonism, prejudice, and stereotypes. Studies on public housing have found less antagonism in both blacks and whites in integrated than in segregated areas. Deutsch and Collins (1951) compared two housing projects in which tenants were assigned to apartments without regard to race with two projects in which blacks and whites were kept in different buildings. White homemakers in the integrated projects were less prejudiced and more likely to have a black as a

The armed services were among the first public institutions to be racially desegregated, but for the most part not until after World War II. The descendents of these troops in an all-black unit could march in racially integrated units in the 1980s.

U.S. Army Photograph

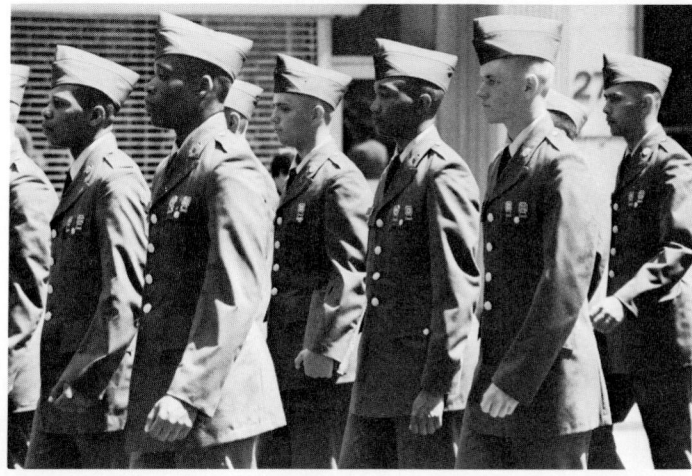

Marc Armstrong

"best friend." Similar results have been reported in studies on integrated working conditions. When blacks were hired to work in department stores in New York City, white clerks became progressively more accepting of them. White customers had similar positive reactions. Comparable results have been found among police officers and government workers.

The best recent reviews suggest, however, that contact, by itself, is not always beneficial. For example, school desegregation by itself has not been shown to reduce prejudice in all cases. What research there is does not show a strong pattern one way or the other (see Amir, 1976; Stephan & Rosenfield, 1978).

Contact Theory

Most experts have concluded that the specific *type* of interracial contact is the crucial factor. The most widely shared theory among social psychologists has been Allport's (1954) **contact theory,** which holds that intergroup contact decreases hostility between the races only when the contact meets three necessary conditions:

1. Close contact—it is not enough for people to coexist in the same geographical space; they must be brought together in close interaction. Some forms of school or work desegregation do not promote very close contact, such as when white and black students are in different "tracks" in a high school and attend quite different classes, or when the executives of a firm are all white and the clerical workers are black, and they have little close interaction.

2. Cooperative interdependence—whites and blacks need to be working together for common goals and to depend upon each others' efforts, as in World War II.

3. The contact must be of equal status—resentments build up if the traditional status imbalance is maintained, and stereotypes cannot easily be broken down. Contact occurs, for example, when a black clean-up man works for a Jewish businessman, but situations of this kind simply perpetuate traditional stereotypes.

As subsequently elaborated by Cook (1978; also see Brewer & Miller, 1984, p. 291), close contact is important for two rather different reasons. First of all, it provides opportunities to disconfirm pre-

vailing stereotypes about outgroup characteristics. We have earlier seen numerous examples of the difficulties people have in overcoming their own schemas, stereotypes, and expectations. Such simplifying cognitive structures greatly ease the task of processing the great complexities of the social world. As a result, a great deal of new evidence is often required to produce change, especially when these structures have been in place for many years, and are constantly reinforced by others. Very close contact with individual minority members may be required, therefore, if such stereotypes are to be disconfirmed.

Second, very close contact may also be necessary to promote intimate interpersonal associations. We have seen in earlier chapters how important proximity and familiarity are in producing liking. Mere occasional, superficial contact is not likely to produce the close relationships that break down the distance between races.

4. The presence of egalitarian social norms is also emphasized in later versions of contact theory (Cook, 1978; Brewer & Miller, 1984). When intergroup contact is forced upon a situation in which everyone opposes the contact—as for instance in a school district in which the school board, superintendent, teachers, and parents all want continued racial segregation—it will be hard for the contact between children to have beneficial effects.

Professional football has provided numerous opportunities for the optimal kinds of intergroup contact. Here Joe Namath and O. J. Simpson are inducted into the Pro Football Hall of Fame.

AP/Wide World Photos

Recent Research

Much research has been done in recent years to test these hypotheses from contact theory. For example, Clore and co-workers (1978) ran an interracial summer camp in which campers, administrative staff, and counselors were all evenly divided between blacks and whites. The researchers tried to maximize: (1) close contact, by mixing the living arrangements by race; (2) cooperative interdependence, by creating primitive conditions that demanded cooperation such as fire building, cooking, and planning activities; and (3) equal status, by selecting campers from similar backgrounds. The one-week experience was successful in increasing the percentage of interracial choices campers made for partners in playing games.

Another program of research has been conducted by Stuart Cook (1984). This has involved long-term interaction either in school or in work situations. They systematically varied most of the factors specified above as theoretically central to the contact hypothesis. The findings of these and other studies show much support for the contact

hypothesis. Cooperation within groups increases interpersonal attraction, whereas competition between groups lessens it. Equal status between individuals is vital, as are shared values and beliefs, and similar levels of competence. Contact must be continuing and of long duration, it should continue outside the immediate situation, and it must be of some nonsuperficial quality. And it is important that it occur in a context of institutional and normative support for the contact (Stephan, 1985, p. 643).

APPLICATION Social psychologists have been quite active in trying to introduce such procedures into desegregated schools, with the idea that desegregation can reduce prejudice only if these conditions prevail. Standard educational procedures have been compared with new procedures introducing interdependent "teams" that cooperate to complete classroom assignments. For example, Eliot Aronson and his colleagues have used what they call a *jigsaw technique*. Children are placed in small learning groups, usually consisting of five or six participants. They meet in the group for about an hour a day to focus on one particular lesson. Each person is assigned one portion of the day's lesson, and is

What are the elements of this situation that meet, or fail to meet, the appropriate conditions for intergroup contact?

Ken Karp

responsible for teaching that material to the rest of the group. Since no one can put together the whole picture without the information contributed by others, the students are interdependent.

Ultimately, each student's learning is evaluated separately, but unless all cooperate in contributing their unique pieces of knowledge, none can do very well. Through this technique, the children get to know each other very well, and in addition they come to appreciate the abilities and contributions of all the other children. Aronson and his co-workers report good success with this technique in increasing peer liking across ethnic and racial groups, and in increasing the self-esteem of minority children (see Aronson & Osherow, 1980).

COMPLICATIONS Brewer and Miller (1984) point out some complications with implementation of the contact hypothesis. One is with equal status. The school or work situation may seem to provide equal status, such as giving two employees the same job title or a teacher treating two children equally. But pre-existing differences in group status may carry over into the situation. The new immigrant child who can barely speak English and who has only one dress to wear to school will not be of equal status to a doctor's daughter whose great grandparents settled in the area, despite the teacher's best efforts.

Another is with the amount of contact required to make a difference. We have seen, in the discussion of cognitive factors, how difficult it is to disconfirm stereotypes. They are like schemas, and people resist or ignore or reinterpret disconfirming information. A single integrated experience, or contact with a "token" member of a minority group, is usually not enough. Disconfirmation requires repeated exposure to multiple instances, not just one "exception to the rule" (Weber & Crocker, 1983).

Cooperative interdependence is important, and works—but only if it is successful. If people are cooperating and they fail, it is too easy to blame the minority member. If people work together in wars, or games, or classroom jobs and things go badly, they may resent each other and become even more hostile. For this reason, Cook (1984) reports that the competence of the group member, rather than the person's race, is the critical factor in determining respect and attraction from others. On the other hand, Cook also reports that group success boosts respect for less-competent teammates.

Finally the norms of the surrounding community are very important. Even if the interracial experience is successful within one limited site, people will go back into their normal lives. If they are then surrounded by prejudiced people, they may quickly revert. This is one of the difficulties in trying to prevent prejudice in the children of prejudiced parents. The children may begin to develop more tolerant attitudes, but if their parents do not support the tolerance at home, it will weaken the effects of the school experience.

THE FUTURE

The human race has had a long history of one group's abusing another. Strong and powerful majorities often subject weak minorities to deprivation and disadvantages of many kinds. What can we expect from the future?

New Forms of Racism

College students' negative stereotypes of Jews and blacks have plainly declined over time, as we saw earlier in Table 14.1. But there is debate about whether or not the historical stereotypes of Jews as clannish, unethical, power-hungry, pushy, and intrusive have changed dramatically over time. Some say yes (Stember, 1966); others say no (Selznick & Steinberg, 1969). Similarly, there is debate about the meaning of this decrease in students' negative stereotypes of blacks. The traditional forms of racism against blacks involved stereotypes of their lack of intelligence, laziness, and so on, along with opposition to racial integration in a variety of arenas such as housing, schools, jobs, and marriage. This has been called "old-fashioned" or "redneck" racism (McConahay, 1986). But others have argued that only the form of racism has changed; its strength remains unchanged.

In many respects, whites' racial attitudes have indeed changed quite markedly over time. In 1942, only a minority of whites believed that white and black children should go to the same schools (2 percent in the South, and 40 percent in the North). But by 1970, most had come around to supporting integration (45 percent in the South, 83 percent in the North (see Dovidio & Gaertner, 1986). Similarly, negative racial stereotypes have been declining in the general public as well as among students. As indicated earlier, in the mass media, blacks are portrayed more often, and in less stereotypical roles, than they once were. In the late 1940s, magazine ads rarely showed blacks, and only then in low-skilled labor categories such as maids or servants to whites. Now they are shown more often, and rarely in such low-skilled labor categories. Similarly, in the early days of television, blacks were rarely shown, and when they were, they usually took orders from whites. Now they appear more frequently, on about half the shows, and in a wide variety of roles (Dovidio & Gaertner, 1986; Greenberg, 1986).

Nevertheless, substantial levels of racial prejudice continue to exist. Large minorities of whites continue to hold the ancient stereotypes of blacks, and to wish to maintain distance from them (e.g. half continue to disapprove of interracial marriage, about one-third do not want black neighbors, and about 20 percent continue not to want integrated schools; Dovidio & Gaertner, 1986). Many of the gains in media coverage have come about from pressure by black groups, such as the NAACP, rather than from more liberal values among media producers. And many blacks appear as mere tokens rather than as central or dominating figures in television shows or movies.

Moreover, while racism has declined according to most indicators, white support for the principal mechanisms for promoting racial equality has not kept pace. Support for affirmative action, open housing laws, busing for integration, or government spending for other programs benefiting blacks has remained weak, and is not visibly increasing (Schuman et al., 1985). A lively set of controversies has arisen about the possible interpretation of this contrast between gradually liberalized racial attitudes, and resistance to further change. Five general possibilities have been offered.

One is that the new liberalism in whites' support for integration is just *lip-service*; that whites just mouth the socially desirable responses to such

Whites strongly opposed busing in the 1970s. Here 2000 opponents of busing from Louisville, Ky., many of them members of pro-busing labor unions, march on the Capitol in 1975. How would you interpret their acting contrary to their unions?

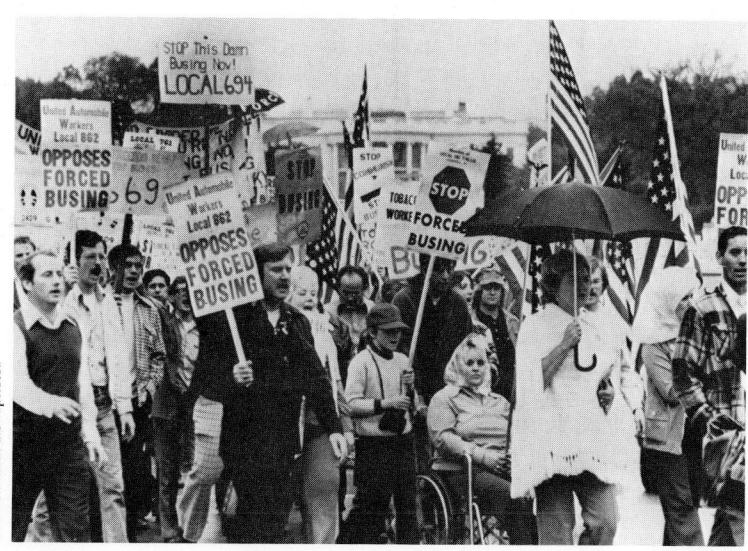

UPI/Bettmann Newsphotos

questions, but underneath retain the same old racism. According to this reasoning, social norms have changed—whites know they are supposed to support equality—but their basic attitudes have not. So when they are asked questions about racial stereotypes, prejudice, or discrimination, they know they are supposed to support equality, and they give the socially desirable liberal answer: They say, yes, black children are as intelligent as white children, and yes, they should have the right to go to the same schools. But on questions that pose issues of racial equality more indirectly, where opposition to equality is less likely to be regarded as racist—for example, on busing—they allow their true racism to come through, and they resist (McConahay, 1986).

A related interpretation assumes that the support for general principles of equality is genuine but *superficial*. It is easy to support equality in the abstract, but supporting actual implementation has real and costly implications, so whites resist that. Jackman (1978), for example, argues that those who endorse abstract principles of racial equality lack any real commitment to it, as shown by the fact that they fail to back it up with support for its implementation. The highly educated, in particular, fall into this category, since they are the ones who have been taught most thoroughly to support equality in the abstract, and who in fact express the greatest support for it. But they show no more support for implementing it than do the less educated.

Another contention is that the contrast reflects genuine *ambivalence* on the part of individual whites. Most white Americans, it is said, do feel some special sympathy for blacks, out of a recognition that they have been handicapped by slavery, prejudice, and discrimination, and their consequences, such as poverty and unemployment. But they also perceive blacks' faults as contributing to this plight, particularly their lack of ambition and failure to take advantage of opportunities, criminal behavior, drug and alcohol abuse, promiscuity, and so on. This leaves the white person with "conflicting sentiments, consisting of friendliness and sympathy on one side and disdain and aversion on the other" (I. Katz et al., 1986, p. 42).

Others have suggested that old-fashioned racism has been replaced by a new form called **aversive racism** (Kovel, 1970; Gaertner & Dovidio, 1986). This form describes whites as conflicted between their genuinely egalitarian value systems and their negative feelings toward blacks. Ashamed of their negative feelings, these whites do not want to acknowledge them, and consequently they avoid blacks so as not to act in a way contrary to their true egalitarian values. This allows them to avoid confrontation with their true prejudices, and thus protect their images of themselves as unprejudiced persons. Their primary affects toward blacks, then, are discomfort, uneasiness, and fear, rather than hostility or hate, as in old-fashioned racism. Behaviorally, they simply want to avoid blacks.

Finally, as indicated earlier, still others suggest that old-fashioned racism has been replaced by another more modern version called *symbolic racism* (Kinder & Sears, 1981; McConahay & Hough, 1976; Sears & McConahay, 1973). This is defined as a blend of antiblack affect and traditional American values such as those embodied in the Protestant ethic. It is characterized by feelings that blacks are pushing too hard and making unfair demands, and that they therefore are getting undeserved special attention and undeserved gains, such as jobs or college admissions (McConahay, 1986). Data supporting this view show that whites' opposition to busing or affirmative action or to black political candidates such as Jesse Jackson, is strongly influenced by both antiblack affect and nonracial values (Sears, 1987).

Prospects of Tolerance

Using the principles of appropriate contact laid out above, what are the prospects for prejudice reduction? Specifically, what kinds of situations would be likely to reduce prejudice, and what kinds would not? Mere desegregation would not be enough. That is, mere contact is not enough; real interaction is required. And it would have to be done in such a way as to promote equal-status relationships between the races. Being teammates on a professional football team would. Being fellow conspirators in a prison break would. Having a black janitor in an office building, or a black maid in a middle-class household, would not. Having both races in a lecture class would not. Pitting a black basketball team against a white team would not. But having interracial teams to solve homework problems in a statistics class would.

Are the most helpful kinds of intergroup situations common in our society? Unfortunately, through most of our history they have not been. Prior to the 1950s, American society was organized in a way that afforded almost no opportunities for equal-status, cooperative, interdependent contact between blacks and whites. Almost all American institutions were segregated. There were white colleges and there were black colleges. Only whites were permitted to play professional sports in the major leagues. Black athletes had to play on all-black teams in black leagues. Military units were either all-black or all-white. Most blacks lived in the South, and of course in the South segregation was the law in public accommodations, schools, transportation, politics, and every other social institution. There were such gross differences between blacks and whites in income, education, and occupational status that the chance of widespread equal-status contact was minimal.

Today, contact of this type does occur in the armed forces, where blacks and whites work and fight together with more or less equal rank (at least among enlisted soldiers), and in factories and stores in which members of the two races hold comparable jobs. But in many businesses, professions, and schools, interracial contact is often between people of different status. Integration frequently occurs by bringing blacks in at the bottom of the ladder, whether as students or apprentices, or in the least desirable jobs. They then have to interact with whites who outrank them. Under these circumstances, increased contact seems less likely to have a positive effect and may even have a negative effect on relations between blacks and whites.

One of the trickiest things to ensure is continued intimate contact. There are many obstacles to it. People strongly prefer to associate with those like themselves. Every study of voluntary contacts between children in the schools has shown a strong tendency for them to associate more with their own race than any other. This is true both before and after desegregation (Schofield, 1978). It varies a great deal across settings: In some cases, there is considerable interracial mixing; in others, almost total segregation. But it shows how far we are from being a truly multiracial "melting pot." Both majority and minority have a tendency to avoid cross-racial interaction. This makes it especially difficult to get the most prejudiced people in contact with minorities. The phenomenon of "white flight," whereby white children leave desegregated schools, illustrates how hard it is to ensure any interracial contact at all, much less ensuring that the circumstances of the contact will be helpful. This is why one of the touchiest aspects of desegregation is the relative proportions of each group. If the minority proportion is too high, the majority will flee, thereby diminishing the opportunity for contact.

Furthermore, desegregation requires the full support of political and judicial authorities. People have to be willing to overcome the temporary discomforts of association with unfamiliar people, and they are less likely to do so if they know they can easily escape. The practical difficulties of desegregation do not mean it should be abandoned, because there are important moral and legal reasons for it. However, it is not a magic remedy for racial prejudice.

Indeed no one approach is going to solve the problem. Intergroup antagonism seems to be a fundamental aspect of the human condition. Every society in the world takes group membership into consideration when determining how it will treat any individual. In a sense, the United States has set a higher standard for itself than most countries and has embarked on an ambitious program of group equality. The Bill of Rights and the later constitutional amendments (especially the Fourteenth) set up extremely idealistic guidelines. At the same time, the United States has tried to accommodate a bewildering variety of groups from all parts of the world, including Africans, Vietnamese, Hungarians, Hispanics, Russian Jews, and British Puritans. It is not surprising, therefore, that it should have failed to some degree. We cannot be complacent, because all too much suffering in our society is caused by racial prejudice. But it is also well to remember the very considerable harmony and group tolerance that has allowed such a Noah's ark of humanity to coexist and cooperate for so many years.

KEY TERMS IN CHAPTER 14

authoritarian personality	ethnocentrism	prejudice	self-fulfilling prophecy
aversive racism	fraternal deprivation	realistic group conflict	social identity theory
categorization	ingroup	relative deprivation	stereotype
contact theory	minimal intergroup situation	scapegoat	symbolic racism
discrimination	outgroup	schema	

SUMMARY

1. Prejudice, stereotypes, and discrimination correspond to the affective, cognitive, and behavioral components of intergroup antagonism.

2. Stereotypes and prejudice strongly influence the individual's attitudes and behavior in a variety of areas.

3. Social learning is probably the strongest determinant of stereotypes and prejudices against minority groups. Prejudices frequently develop in childhood and adolescence. Although parents have an important part in the development of prejudice, they are by no means the only, or even necessarily the most important, source of its acquisition.

4. Cognitive approaches view stereotyping and prejudices as arising from such normal cognitive processes as categorization, over-attention to salient cues, schematic processing, as well as getting self-esteem from one's own social identity.

5. Group conflict theories view prejudice as stemming from the realities of intergroup competition; and psychodynamic theories, from the individual's particular personality dynamics.

6. The various theories tend to focus on somewhat different phenomena rather than providing competing explanations for the same events.

7. Interracial contact is probably the most effective technique for reducing prejudice. But by itself, it is not extremely effective; it is more likely to be successful if it involves close contact, cooperative interdependence, and equal status.

8. Although some forms of racial prejudice have diminished in recent years, others have come along to take their place.

9. Our society is not organized very well to provide the kinds of interracial contact that will best break down racial prejudices. For that reason, special efforts need to be made if prejudice is to be reduced substantially.

SUGGESTED READINGS

BREWER, M. B., & KRAMER, R. M. (1985). The psychology of intergroup attitudes and behavior. *Annual Review of Psychology*, 36, 219–243. A thorough review of recent research.

DOVIDIO, J. F., & GAERTNER, S. L. (Eds). (1986). *Prejudice, discrimination, and racism*. New York: Academic Press. An excellent collection of essays on race relations, summarizing the most current and recent research.

KATZ, P., & TAYLOR, D. (Eds.). (1987). *Towards the elimination of racism: Profile in controversy*. New York: Plenum. A stimulating collection of essays on the major controversies in race relations research, presenting one pro and one con on each controversy.

MILLER, N., & BREWER, M. B. (Eds.). (1984). *Groups in contact: The psychology of desegregation*. New York: Academic Press. An up-to-date collection of research articles on the contact hypothesis.

STEPHAN, W. G. (1985). Intergroup relations. In G. Lindzey and E. Aronson (Eds.), *Handbook of social psychology*, 3rd ed., Vol. 2, New York: Random House, pp. 599–658. Another thorough review of recent research, from the cognitive perspective.

TAJFEL, H. (1981). *Human groups and social categories*. Cambridge, MA: Cambridge University Press. A thorough account of social identity theory.

WORCHEL S. & AUSTIN, W. G. (Eds.). (1986). *Psychology of intergroup relations*, 2nd ed. Chicago: Nelson-Hall. An up-to-date collection of essays on the major topics of research in the social psychology of intergroup relations.

15 GENDER IN SOCIAL LIFE

On a radio talk show, the host is discussing teenage sexuality with a medical expert. The second caller, Chris, asks a question about the birth control pill. The researcher begins his answer by asking Chris if she herself is considering using the pill. After a pause, Chris blurts out, "I'm a boy." Everyone seems embarrassed, the researcher apologizes, and the host rephrases the question. I, like other listeners, think about Chris's high-pitched voice and gentle manner. Would I have made the same mistake?

A noted psychologist begins a study of the behavior of young children. Concerned that knowledge of a child's gender might influence the way observers interpret the child's activities, the researcher asks parents to bring their children to the study dressed in overalls and T shirts. To the researcher's surprise, her effort to conceal the toddlers' gender backfires. Although all children arrive in denims, many of the little girls wear overalls with ruffles or bows.

You glance casually at the driver of the sports car stopped at a traffic light. Noting a gray sweatshirt and prominent chin, you assume the person is a man. But something about the face makes you look again. You quickly study the person's physique. The smooth cheeks give no hint of stubble. The shoulders are a bit broad for a woman, but perhaps she's a swimmer. The arm resting on the car door conceals the person's chest, but reveals slender, delicate fingers. Neither rings nor earrings are visible. Then the light changes and the car moves off, leaving you puzzling about the driver's sex.

As these examples indicate, gender is one of the basic categories in social life. In meeting new people, we inevitably try to identify them as male or female. There are many reasons for this tendency. One is that the English language has gender-linked pronouns such as "he" and "she," "his" and "hers."

Gender categorization usually occurs automatically, without our giving it much thought. Most of the time, cues about gender are readily available from physical characteristics such as facial hair or breasts and from style of dress. People commonly display their gender as a prominent part of their self-presentation. Research also finds that parents usually dress their children in a way that readily identifies the child's sex. A recent study of infants observed in suburban shopping malls found that 90 percent of the infants were dressed in clothes that were sex-typed in color or style. For instance, whereas 75 percent of the girls wore or carried something pink, none of the boys did. In contrast, 79 percent of the boys wore or carried something blue, while only 8 percent of girls did (Shakin, Shakin & Sternglanz, 1985). Unusual situations where we cannot be certain of a person's gender call attention to the categorization process, and typically lead us to seek information to resolve the matter.

Our tendency to divide the world into masculine

These children practice traditional male-female roles—she as the well-dressed and caring mommy, and he as the expert physician. Childrens' toys and games teach lessons about what males and females can and should do.

Ewing Galloway

BOX 15-1

GENDER BIAS IN LANGUAGE

In English, the words "he" and "man" have had to serve two functions. They refer both to specific males and to human beings in general (Martyna, 1980). Many adults learned in high school that it is grammatically correct to say "each person took *his* turn," even when most of the people involved are female. Similarly, we were taught that "mankind" includes both sexes, just as a "chairman" can be a woman. When "he" and "man" are used to refer to both sexes, they are said to be *generic* terms. Grammarians have justified the use of the generic masculine as a convenient shorthand. However, feminists have criticized this linguistic practice, arguing that it subtly reaffirms male dominance and contributes to the "invisibility" of women in society.

Psychological research shows that the so-called generic masculine is *not* necessarily perceived as including both sexes (see review by Henley, 1986). For example, Martyna (1980) asked a large sample of students from kindergarten through college to complete sentence fragments such as "When a police officer leaves the station," "When a secretary first arrives at the office," or "When a teenager finishes high school." Martyna found that when the sentences contained a traditionally masculine role word such as "police officer," 96 percent of subjects used "he" in completing the sentence. When the sentences contained a traditionally feminine role word such as "secretary," none of the students used "he"

and feminine categories is not limited to person perception; many objects and activities are also commonly defined as masculine and feminine. At an early age, children learn that dolls and cooking utensils are for girls, and that toy trucks and guns are for boys (Robinson & Morris, 1986). Most 4-year-olds believe that doctor, police officer, and construction worker are male jobs, and that secretary, teacher, and librarian are female jobs (Gettys & Cann, 1981).

This process of **gender typing** continues in adulthood. One study found that college students identified icepicks, barbells, wrenches, and chest strengtheners as masculine objects, and eggbeaters, thimbles, rolling pins, and laundry baskets as feminine. Some objects, such as headphones, electric outlets, and corkscrews, were seen as gender-neutral (Reis & Jackson, 1981). Married couples often distinguish between "men's work," such as mowing the lawn, taking out the garbage, or barbecuing

and "women's work," such as housecleaning or childcare. Although a few occupations such as psychologist and personnel officer are seen by adults as gender-neutral, most jobs are perceived as gender-typed (Shinar, 1975). You should have no trouble guessing how most people categorize the following jobs: secretary, brain surgeon, truck driver, elementary school teacher, nurse, and judge.

This distinction between male and female is a universal organizing principle in all human societies. As children, boys and girls are expected to learn different skills and to develop different personalities. As adults, men and women typically assume distinctive gender-linked roles as husband or wife, mother or father. Cultures vary in exactly what is defined as masculine or feminine and in the degree to which they accentuate gender differences or similarities. But the use of gender to structure at least some elements of social life has been basic.

and 87 percent used "she." In gender-neutral sentences such as that about a teenager, 65 percent of subjects used "he," 5 percent used "she," and 30 percent used alternatives such as "they." Clearly, students did not always use "he" to refer to both sexes.

Given that people do not always use the generic masculine, do they nonetheless understand it when they encounter it? MacKay and Fulkerson (1979) designed a study to find out. College students listened to a series of sentences read aloud on a tape recording. Examples included "A lawyer must frequently argue his case out of court," and "A nurse must frequently help his patients get out of bed." These sentences used the word "he" generically and so could logically refer to both males and females. Some students were asked whether each of these sentences could refer to a man, and 99 percent responded correctly that each could. In contrast, other students were asked if each sentence could refer to a woman. This time, 87 percent of responses were wrong: Students said that the sentences could not refer to a woman, when logically they could. This and other studies indicate that the use of pronouns such as "he" can bias interpretations.

We do not always use the generic masculine the way grammarians say we should. When we hear a discussion of the "best man for the job," we often conjure up a mental image of a male. When we read about the "chairman of an important committee," we assume the person is a man. If we were asked to think carefully about these terms, we would most likely acknowledge that "he" can refer to a female, but this is not our first reaction. The use of the so-called generic masculine simplifies communication at the expense of accuracy.

One consequence of these findings is that many organizations, including the American Psychological Association and most textbook publishers, have developed new guidelines for writing that explicitly discourage the use of the generic masculine. Instead, authors are urged to substitute terms that will be understood accurately, such as "chairperson" (for "chairman"), "human nature" (for "the nature of man"), or "firefighter" (for "fireman"). Alternatives to the use of the generic "he" include using the plural, alternating the use of "he" and "she" throughout the text, or using a phrase such as "he or she."

GENDER IN THE EYE OF THE BEHOLDER

We begin with a seemingly simple question: How does the gender of other people influence our perception and evaluation of them and their behavior? The emphasis here is on gender as a characteristic of the *target* of impression formation. Research shows that our beliefs about what typical men and women are like can color our perceptions of individuals and bias our evaluations of their performance.

Gender Stereotypes

How do you think men and women differ? Do you believe that one sex is usually more aggressive or more nurturant than the other? How do the sexes typically compare on such qualities as being courageous, neat, logical, gentle, squeamish, dominant, or gullible? Beliefs about the personal attributes of women and men are **gender stereotypes.** All stereotypes, whether based on gender, race, ethnicity, or other groupings, refer to an image of what the typical member of a particular social category is like. But a useful distinction can be made between cultural and personal stereotypes (Ashmore, Del Boca, & Wohlers, 1986).

CULTURAL STEREOTYPES   We are all exposed to images of the sexes presented by our culture. Movies, pop music, television, and other mass media convey messages about the nature of masculinity and femininity. So do religious teachings, educational materials, art, and literature. The societal-level images of the sexes conveyed in these places are **cultural stereotypes.** You probably know these stereotypes quite well, although you may not have thought about them very much.

On TV, for example, we can see anxious housewives desperately trying to avoid tell-tale spots on the family's clothes or pondering the best food for a finicky cat. Young women appear obsessed with staying thin or competing for men's attention by wearing the right pantyhose or jeans. Off camera, the voices of male experts solemnly offer advice. On screen, men in impressive offices extol the virtues of razor blades or copying machines. Systematic research has found that the most common TV commercial depicts a male expert instructing a female consumer about a particular product. In a typical study (McArthur & Resko, 1975), 70 percent of men were shown as experts, whereas 86 percent of women were product users. Female experts and male consumers were the exception.

A trip to an art museum would also find men and women portrayed in traditional gender-typed activities. A study of highly acclaimed paintings and sculptures found that men were often shown in professional work or warfare, whereas women usually did housework or childcare (O'Kelly, 1980). Significantly more women than men were portrayed as passively "doing nothing." Nearly a quarter of women but only 2 percent of men were depicted as "objects" who were not engaged in any identifiable activity.

These studies and other analyses of newspaper articles, award-winning children's books, university textbooks, and other diverse elements of culture have found several general themes in the portrayal of the sexes. Whereas men are shown in a wide variety of social roles and activities, women are more often restricted to domestic and family roles. Men are commonly portrayed as experts and leaders, women as subordinates. Men are usually depicted as more active, assertive, and influential than women. And although females are slightly more than half the population, they are often under represented in the media. In recent years there have been efforts to change these media images so they portray men and women in less rigidly gender-typed ways. We are slowly beginning to see a few women in the business world and a few men in the kitchen.

Do these cultural portraits of the sexes actually have an effect on people's daily lives? Evidence suggests that they can. An example is provided by research on TV commercials. Television now reaches 95 percent of American homes, and some social critics claim that Americans may have a TV set on as many as four or five hours a day. An experimental study of women college students demonstrated the potential influence of TV (Jennings, Gies, & Brown, 1980). Participants were randomly assigned to one of two conditions. Half the participants saw four commercials depicting the sexes in traditional roles. Men were portrayed as the authorities and were the center of attention; women were shown as sex objects or in domestic roles. The experimental commercials were closely modeled after real ones. In one, for example, a tiny woman serves her large, hungry husband a packaged dinner. The implicit message is that the wife's role is to cater to and please her husband. In another, an attractive man authoritatively extols the virtues of an alcoholic beverage. At the close of the commercial, a seductive woman slithers up and coyly says that she would also choose the same drink. Here the woman is presented as a sex object who follows the man's advice. In the second experimental condition, women participants saw reversed-role versions of the same commercials in which the females were the central figures and the males were shown in the homemaking and seductive roles.

Results indicated that exposure to TV commercials had a significant effect on subsequent behavior. After watching the films, participants engaged in one of two tasks. Some performed a test designed to measure their conformity, while others were rated on self-confidence as they gave a short, extemporaneous speech. Women who watched traditional commercials conformed more and showed less self-confidence than women who watched the nontraditional commercials. The researchers concluded that regardless of whether people buy the product advertised in commercials, they may buy the implicit images of femininity and masculinity conveyed.

PERSONAL STEREOTYPES As individuals, we may or may not agree with cultural depictions of the sexes. **Personal stereotypes** are our own unique beliefs about the attributes of groups of people such as women and men. Individuals construct personal stereotypes in at least two different ways.

One way individuals think about gender is in terms of general personality traits that characterize each sex. Most of us have beliefs about the global features that distinguish males and females. To get some idea of your own views on this matter read the list of adjectives in Table 15–1. Decide whether you personally think each trait is more characteristic of men or of women, or equally true of both sexes.

TABLE 15–1

Common Gender Stereotypes

More Characteristic of Men	More Characteristic of Women
Aggressive	Gentle
Independent	Tactful
Unemotional	Talkative
Objective	Religious
Dominant	Aware of feelings of others
Like math and science	Neat in habits
Active	Interested in own appearance
Competitive	Quiet
Logical	Express tender feelings
Worldly	Enjoy art and literature
Self-confident	Cry easily
Act as leader	Dependent
Adventurous	Do not use harsh language
Ambitious	Strong need for security

College students rated the "typical man" and the "typical woman" on a long list of adjectives. Traits that at least 75 percent of students thought were more characteristic of men are shown in the left column. Traits that 75 percent of students thought were more characteristic of women are shown in the right column.
Source: Adapted from Rosenkrantz, Vogel, Bee, Broverman, & Broverman (1968), p. 291.

You probably found this a fairly easy task. People usually develop broad generalizations about the traits shared by men and women and about the traits that distinguish the sexes. As Table 15-1 shows, most respondents in one study (Rosenkrantz et al., 1968) rated men higher on traits associated with competence, such as leadership, objectivity, and independence. In contrast, most people rated women higher on traits associated with warmth and expressiveness, such as gentleness and awareness of the feelings of others.

Some psychologists believe that instead of calling these sets of traits "masculine" and "feminine," we should use terms that are not inherently linked to gender. Thus, traditional masculine traits are often described as instrumental or "agentic," meaning that they focus on accomplishing tasks and acting independently. Traditional feminine traits are described as expressive or "communal," because they emphasize the expression of feelings and a sense of caring for others.

A second way in which people think about gender is to develop images of different types of males and females (Ashmore et al., 1986; Clifton, McGrath, & Wick, 1976; Taylor, 1981). Instead of thinking about females "in general," we may think of more specific categories of women, such as mothers, career women, beauty queens, tomboys, or spinsters. Similarly, instead of having a single, uniform image of males, we may distinguish such types as fathers, businessmen, hardhats, sissies, jocks, chauvinists, or nerds (Holland & Skinner, 1987). In other words, we may form *schemas* about specific types of males and females who embody distinctive clusters of traits. Thus one person might believe that mothers are nurturant and self-sacrificing, that beauty queens are gorgeous but emptyheaded, or that tomboys are youthful, athletic, and adventurous. An important point is that social types often incorporate some attributes typically associated with the other sex: A career woman may be seen as assertive and independent (masculine traits) as well as attractive and tactful (feminine traits).

Activating Stereotypes

What determines whether we relate to another person largely on the basis of stereotypes or as a unique individual? In other words, what situations increase

These three women suggest quite different images of femininity—a beauty queen, a "tomboy" baseball player, and a kindly grandmother rocking on her front porch. We combine information about gender and other characteristics to form stereotypes about distinct types of males and females. What might you infer about the personality and life aspirations of each of these women?

or decrease the influence of stereotypes? Social psychologists are just beginning to answer this question. Two important factors are the amount of information we have about the person and the salience of the person's group membership.

AMOUNT OF INFORMATION The less information available about a person, the more likely we are to perceive and react to him or her on the basis of stereotypes. For example, when adults know nothing about a baby except its sex, they tend to react to the child in stereotyped ways. In one study (Condry & Condry, 1976), adults watched a videotape of a baby. Although everyone watched the same videotape, half were told they were watching a boy and half were told they were watching a girl. People who thought the child was a boy rated the child as significantly more active and forceful than people who thought the child was a girl. The child's response to a jack-in-the-box toy was rated as showing more "fear" if the child was a girl, and more "anger" if the child was a boy.

In another study (Sidorowicz & Lunney, 1980), college students actually interacted with a baby described either as a boy or a girl. Both boy and girl babies were used. Half the time the gender label was correct; half the time it was not. The dependent variable of interest was which of three toys the adult selected to use in playing with the child. Among those who thought they were playing with a boy, 65 percent selected the football, 20 percent selected the doll, and 15 percent selected the gender-neutral teething ring. In contrast, among adults who thought the child was a girl, 80 percent selected the doll, 15 percent the football, and 5 percent the teething ring. In this situation, since the adults knew nothing about the preferences of the individual child, they apparently made guesses based on gender stereotypes.

When we have more information about the unique attributes of a particular person, we rely less on stereotypes (Locksley, et al., 1980). For instance, we may believe that most males are highly assertive, and so assume when we meet a new man that he too will be assertive. But we may also have learned from past experience that our friend Leon is shy and unassuming. The effect of gender stereotypes can be eliminated when we have relevant information about a specific person.

The Supreme Court Historical Society

If you saw this woman in a supermarket, you might assume her to be a suburban homemaker or school teacher. In reality, Sandra Day O'Connor is the first woman to serve on the U.S. Supreme Court. The less information we have about a person, the more we fall back on gender stereotypes.

SALIENCE OF GENDER A second factor that can activate the use of stereotypes is the salience of the person's group membership, in this case gender (Taylor, 1981). For example, a person's gender is more salient when he or she is in a numerical minority, such as being the only woman in an all-male work group. "Token integration" often creates groups with just one minority person. Token or "solo" status calls attention to the person's distinctive social category and makes solos especially vulnerable to stereotyping. A study by Taylor (1981) illustrates this point. Students evaluated the members of a six-person tape-recorded discussion group. Some groups had just a 'solo" man or just a "solo" woman; others were evenly divided between men and women.

After listening to the tape, subjects rated the group's members. In actuality, the solo's contribution to the discussion was identical to that of one of the members of the gender-balanced group. But Taylor found that the solos were perceived as talking more and making a stronger impression than members of the more gender-balanced groups. In addition, solos tended to be perceived as playing gender-stereotyped roles. Solo women were seen as "motherly, nurturant types, bitches, or as the group secretary." Solo men were perceived as "father figures, leaders, or macho types." Group composition accentuated the solo's gender and fostered stereotyped perceptions of the solo's behavior.

The Dangers of Stereotypes

As Chapter 4 on social cognition indicated, it is quite natural for us to try to simplify complex life experiences by categorizing and generalizing. Personal stereotypes, like other social schemas, are one way in which we try to make sense of life. But like other mental crutches, stereotypes have certain inherent problems.

One problem is that stereotypes always oversimplify and sometimes are dead wrong, as we'll see later in the chapter. For example, the belief that men are more intelligent than women has been disproved by scientific research. Unfortunately, people seldom examine the accuracy of their stereotypes. If we encounter someone who does not fit a stereotype, we often simply decide the person

---

BOX 15-2

MAKING STEREOTYPES COME TRUE

A young man goes on a blind date with a woman he has never met before. Based on hearsay, he believes her to be a rather traditional "Southern belle" type. Accordingly, he dresses rather formally, puts on his most gentlemanly manners, and treats her in a somewhat old-fashioned way. Just as he expected, she defers to his suggestions, waits for him to open doors, and acts in what he considers a very "ladylike" way. Only later does he learn that his advance information was wrong; she is, in fact, usually a fairly assertive nonconformist. This story shows how expectations can become self-fulfilling prophecies. The man's beliefs about his date shaped his own behavior toward her. The woman, wanting to spend a pleasant evening, responded by acting in a conventionally "ladylike" way herself. The result was that the man's expectations set in motion an interpersonal process that appeared to confirm his prior beliefs.

Gender stereotypes often become self-fulfilling prophecies. This point was cleverly demonstrated in a study by Berna J. Skrypnek and Mark Snyder (1982). A male college student is led to believe that his partner for an experiment is either a stereotypic man (independent, assertive, ambitious, and masculine), or a stereotypic woman (shy, gullible, soft-spoken, and feminine). In reality, the partner is always a woman, a naive subject who has been randomly assigned the label of "man" or "woman." Since the two partners communicate from separate rooms by a system of lights, the partner's real gender is never revealed. The woman is told nothing about her partner, how she has been described to him, or the is "the exception that proves the rule." We do nothing to change our stereotype. Further, as Box 15–2 indicates, we sometimes act in ways that turn stereotypes into self-fulfilling prophecies.

A second problem is that stereotypes exaggerate differences *between* groups and minimize differences *within* groups. Gender stereotypes can make it seem that all men are alike, when in fact there are enormous individual differences among men. The same is true about differences among women. And gender stereotypes can also make it seem that men and women are utterly different, when in fact similarities are usually much greater than differences. For example, there is great variation among men in aggressiveness: individuals range from nonassertive males who wouldn't hurt a fly to mass murderers. In contrast, the average difference between males and females in aggressiveness, while

real, is much smaller in magnitude. Gender stereotypes can create a very distorted view of human nature.

A final danger of stereotypes is that they are often used to justify prejudice and discrimination against members of certain groups. Historically, the false belief that women were not as smart as men and that women lacked ambition was used to deny women an education and to keep them at home.

Stereotypes that have a basis in fact can also be misused in a discriminating way. There are, for example, small but consistent sex differences in math ability (favoring men) and in verbal ability (favoring women). Yet if we were recruiting applicants for a job such as newspaper writer that requires verbal skills, it would be foolish to exclude all male candidates, since some men are likely to be verbally gifted and some women may not be.

goals of the study. In this way the researchers systematically manipulate the gender expectations of the male subject.

In the first phase of the study, the partners must negotiate how to divide work on 12 hypothetical tasks. Some tasks are traditionally masculine (fixing a light switch or baiting a fish hook), some are feminine (icing a birthday cake or ironing a shirt), and some are neutral (coding test results, washing windows). The rules set by the experimenter give the man greater initiative in the bargaining process. As predicted, the man's expectations about his partner shape his own actions significantly. If he thinks his partner is a conventional woman, the male subject is more likely to select masculine tasks for himself and to refuse to switch tasks than if he thinks his partner is a man. As a result, the female subject winds up being assigned more of the feminine tasks if she is arbitrarily labeled a "female" than if she is believed to be a "male."

In the second phase, the researchers investigate whether this initial behavior pattern would continue over time. Accordingly, they change the rules of the interaction so that the woman now has greater control over the bargaining. Nonetheless, a woman who is labeled as "female" continues to select more feminine tasks than does a woman labeled as a "male." The woman actually comes to initiate behavior consistent with the gender to which she has been randomly assigned!

This study provides a powerful demonstration that in dyadic interactions, one person's beliefs and stereotypes about another can channel their interaction so that the other person engages in stereotype-confirming behavior. Our actions are shaped not only by our own interests and preferences, but also by the expectations of those with whom we interact. When others expect us to act in gender-typed ways and communicate these expectations through their behaviors, we may put aside personal preferences and instead act out the others' stereotypes.

Recruitment and hiring practices that categorically reject one sex are not only discriminatory but unwise. A sounder policy is to use a task-relevant selection procedure, such as giving all applicants a skill test and then selecting the high performers regardless of sex.

Evaluating Performance

Do we typically give women and men equal credit for equal work? Or do gender stereotypes distort judgments of performance? In the world of work, stereotypes often depict men as more competent than women. In one national survey (Rosen & Jerdee, 1978), for example, male managers generally perceived women workers as lower than men in skill, motivation, and work habits. Women were believed to be less employable and promotable, and to have less ability to make decisions and to cope with stress. Research shows that general stereotypes such as these can bias evaluations of the performance of individuals (see review by Nieva & Gutek, 1981). This evaluation bias can cut both ways, however; sometimes it favors men, and occasionally it favors women.

One of the first demonstrations of gender bias in evaluation was provided by Philip Goldberg in 1968. He investigated whether women were biased in evaluations of other women. Goldberg selected six professional articles from such fields as law, elementary education, and art history. The articles were edited to about 1,500 words each and combined in test booklets. The experimental manipulation concerned the gender of the authors. The same article bore a male name (such as John T. McKay) in one booklet and a female name (such as Joan T. McKay) in another. Each booklet contained three articles by "men" and three by "women." College women read the six articles and then rated each on persuasiveness, style, and competence.

Results indicated that the same article was judged more favorably when it had a male author than when it had a female author. Goldberg's results appeared to show that women are indeed prejudiced against women. But before leaping to a hasty conclusion, it is important to know that Goldberg's findings sparked a rash of research. The results of over a hundred studies indicate that a pro-male bias is common, but by no means universal. The challenge today is to understand when and how gender bias occurs.

One important factor influencing evaluation is the gender typing of the task or job. In general, men have an advantage in masculine jobs and women have an advantage in feminine jobs. In one study (Cash, Gillen, & Burns, 1977), professional personnel consultants rated applicants' résumés for masculine jobs (automobile salesperson), feminine jobs (office receptionist), and gender-neutral jobs (motel desk clerk). For masculine jobs, men were perceived as better qualified, were expected to be more successful, and were given stronger recommendations. For feminine jobs, women were rated more favorably. For gender-neutral jobs, men and women were given similar ratings. In all cases, however, the résumés of the men and women were actually identical.

In another study (Levinson, 1975), students responded by phone to job ads that had appeared in the newspaper. Some of the jobs were traditionally masculine (bus driver, management trainee, security guard) and some were feminine (receptionist, housekeeper, dental assistant). None required advanced training. A male and female applicant with identical qualifications called about each job.

Gender bias was said to occur when the "sex-appropriate" caller was encouraged to apply, but the "sex-inappropriate" caller was not. In one case, for example, a female caller for a restaurant management training program was told that her having only two years of college and no prior management experience disqualified her. A male with the identical background was scheduled for an interview. In all, 28 percent of the women asking about masculine jobs and 44 percent of the men asking about feminine jobs were discouraged. This suggests considerable gender bias linked to the gender typing of occupations.

A second factor influencing evaluation bias is the amount of relevant information available about the person. Gender bias in evaluations is most common when little information is provided about the individual's ability. This is consistent with our earlier finding that people rely more on stereotypes when they know little about an individual. One study of evaluation bias (Frank & Drucker, 1977) provided extensive information about a male or female manager, including copies of letters, memos, and other materials allegedly written by the person. Subjects used this material as a basis for evaluating the manager's sensitivity, organizing and decision-making ability, and communication effectiveness. The experimental manipulation was whether the materials were written by "John Griffin" or "Joan Griffin." Given all this information about the specific individuals, no evaluation bias occurred; John and Joan were rated identically.

Finally, there is some evidence that stereotype-breaking behavior can occasionally win a person "extra" credit. In particular, when a woman excels in a traditionally masculine job, she may be perceived more favorably than an equally successful man. Abramson et al. (1977) found that a highly successful female attorney was rated more vocationally competent than an identically successful male attorney. Similarly, Taynor and Deaux (1973) presented students with descriptions of a person whose quick thinking in an armed robbery helped the police capture a criminal. When the person was a woman, she received more positive evaluations than a man in the identical situation. The unusualness of a woman's successful performance in masculine situations appears to win her a more favorable evaluation than her male counterpart. Whether something comparable occurs for men who excel in traditionally feminine activities is an interesting but unanswered question.

So far, we have considered evaluations of the quality of women's and men's performance. Another way in which gender bias can occur is in the attributions people make to explain success or failure. Research has found that men's success is more often seen as resulting from ability. In contrast, women's success is more often attributed to the ease of the task (Feather & Simon, 1975), to extreme effort (Taynor & Deaux, 1975), or to luck (Deaux & Emswiller, 1974). Ability attributions usually produce more favorable evaluations of successful performance. Differences in attributions for men's and women's performance may create a subtle bias that diminishes recognition of women's

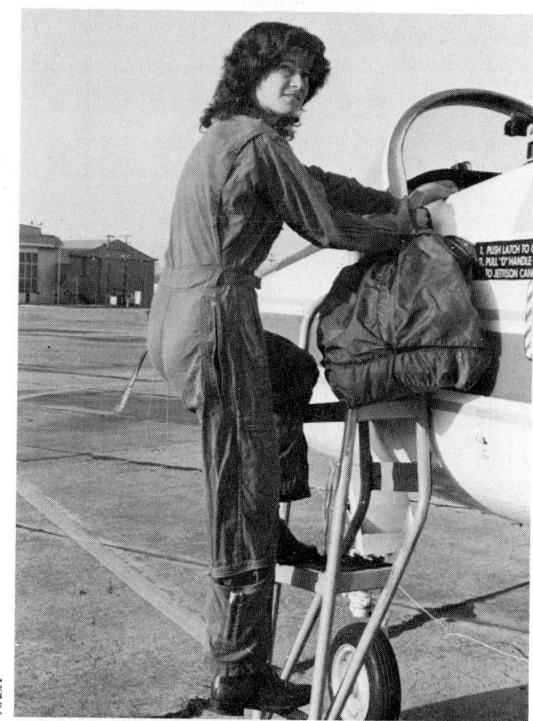

Sally Ride is the first woman to become a U.S. astronaut. As a woman in a largely male profession, Dr. Ride's solo status makes her gender especially salient.

skills and instead explains female success as due to situational or chance factors.

In summary, a person's gender can influence the way we evaluate the person and explain his or her performance. Evaluation bias often favors men, especially in masculine situations. However, women may have an advantage in feminine situations and when they excel in masculine activities. When substantial information is available about the stimulus person, evaluation bias often disappears. Finally, it appears that female and male evaluators are equally prone to engage in evaluative bias based on the performer's gender.

Having seen how the perceptions of other people are affected by whether they are female or male, we turn now to the question of how gender influences our self-perception.

GENDER AND THE SELF

Gender is a basic element in our self-concept. Knowing that "I am a woman" or "I am a man" is a core part of our personal identity. Further, many people perceive themselves as having gender-typed interests and personalities.

Gender Identity

Knowledge that we are a male or female, our sense of **gender identity,** is acquired early in life. By age 2 or 3, children are aware of their own gender and can tell us whether they are a girl or a boy. By age 4 or 5, children can correctly label others by gender. However, this understanding of gender differs from that of adults. Research by Kohlberg (1966) and other developmental psychologists has documented the surprising fact that young children think they can change gender if they want to.

In one study, Kohlberg showed children a picture of a girl and asked whether she could be a boy if she wanted to or if she played boys' games or if she wore a boy's haircut and clothes. Most of the 4-year-olds said that she *could.* By age 6 or 7, however, children insisted that such a gender transformation would be impossible. Kohlberg believes this shift in children's conception of gender is part of a more general pattern of cognitive development. The same 4-year-old who says she could change gender might also say the family cat could become a dog by cutting off its whiskers. Adults know that if you pour a pint of water from a tall skinny glass into a short fat one, the volume of water stays the same. But the 4-year-old would probably disagree, perhaps arguing that the short glass had less.

Young children do not see the physical world as constant. As children get older, a combination of experience and maturation enables them to reach a more advanced stage of mental development in which they understand that gender, water volume, and other physical properties remain the same despite changes in external appearance. An important developmental milestone occurs when children understand that gender is fixed and unchanging: Once a boy (or a girl), always a boy (or girl).

Knowing that we are male or female does not mean we think about our gender identity all the time. In one study (McGuire & Padawer-Singer, 1976), for example, only about 20 percent of sixth-graders spontaneously mentioned their gender when asked to "tell us about yourself" and to "describe what you look like." For many children, other characteristics were more salient, as for a girl who answered: "I am twelve years old. I was born in South Carolina. I have two sisters and a dog. I have a babysitting job every day after school. . . . I hate arithmetic but I like our teacher" (pp. 746–747). The salience of gender identity depends on many factors, including the proportion of males and females in our environment. The study described above found that boys and girls were twice as likely to mention their own gender if their classroom at school had an excess of children of the other sex. We are apparently more aware of our own gender when we are in a numerical minority. This is like the token or solo effect discussed earlier for gender stereotypes, where the gender of a lone man or woman in a group is more salient to observers than it would be in a gender-balanced group.

For most of us, the acquisition of gender identity is a smooth and trouble-free process. We are classified as male or female at birth, treated as a boy or girl by our parents, and easily learn our own gender as we grow up. For a few people, however, developing gender identity is a problem. Transsexuals are a case in point. Such individuals are biologically members of one gender, but develop the belief that they are really members of the other. In the most common case, a person is to all outward appearances a male, but that person's psychological reality is being a woman trapped in a male body.

The causes of transsexualism are still a mystery. Most often, transsexuals show no signs of biological abnormality. Genetically, hormonally, and physiologically, they are "normal" members of their gender. Yet at a very early age they develop a self-concept at odds with their physical characteristics. This puzzling situation is profoundly disturbing to the individuals involved. Efforts to help transsexuals by psychotherapy have had very little success; it is not easy to change a deeply rooted sense of gender identity. As a result, some have advocated sex-change surgery as one way to reconcile this mind-body problem.

Psychological Masculinity, Femininity, and Androgyny

Gender identity is an either-or matter; people believe they are either a male or a female. However, individuals differ markedly in the degree to which they perceive themselves as having all the different masculine or feminine characteristics that make up conventional gender stereotypes. In terms of their **gender self-concept,** highly "masculine" people would believe they possess the attributes, interests, preferences, and skills society typically associates with maleness. Highly "feminine" people would believe they possess the attributes, interests, preferences, and skills associated with femaleness. Psychologists have long been interested in measuring individual differences in self-perceptions of psychological masculinity and femininity.

A typical masculinity-femininity test might ask such questions as whether a person prefers showers (masculine) or tub baths (feminine), whether the person would rather work as a building contractor (masculine) or librarian (feminine), whether the person is active (masculine) or passive (feminine). An important feature of these tests is that they view masculinity and femininity as mutually exclusive polar opposites. People get a single score on the test: High scores indicate masculinity (many masculine choices) and low scores indicate femininity (few masculine choices).

In more recent times, social psychologists have challenged this one-dimensional view of psychological masculinity and femininity (see Spence & Helmreich, 1978, 1980). Sandra Bem (1974, 1981), for example, proposed that some people might see themselves as having both masculine and feminine characteristics. Such a person might enjoy both carpentry and cooking, might be very assertive (a masculine trait) at work but very nurturant (a feminine trait) at home, and so on. Bem called these people psychologically **androgynous,** borrowing from the Greek terms for male (andro) and female (gyne). Bem emphasized that the androgynous person is not a moderate who falls halfway between extreme masculinity and femininity. Rather, the androgynous person views himself or herself as combining strong masculine and strong feminine attributes. This two-dimensional model is shown in Figure 15–1 (see next page).

To investigate this idea, Bem constructed a new test with separate dimensions for masculinity and for femininity, making it possible for a person to score high on both. In the Bem Sex Role Inventory, people rate their personal qualities using 60 adjectives: 20 masculine (assertive, independent), 20 feminine (affectionate, understanding), and 20 gender-neutral (sincere, friendly). When Bem administered her test to samples of college students, she found some traditionally gender-typed individuals, both masculine men (who scored high on M and low on F) and feminine women (who scored high on F and low on M). More interesting, however, was the fact that some people rated themselves high on both masculine and feminine characteristics, showing the androgynous pattern Bem predicted.

The exact percentages of gender-typed and androgynous people vary somewhat from study to study. Typical are results from a study of California college students (Bernard, 1980). Roughly 40 percent of students perceived themselves as traditionally gender-typed, and 25 percent were androgynous. An "undifferentiated" subgroup included 20 percent of men and 21 percent of women who scored low on both masculine and feminine traits. Finally, a few people showed a pattern of reverse gender typing—specifically feminine men (5 percent) and masculine women (12 percent). The important point is that although traditional gender typing is the most common pattern, a sizable minority of people perceive themselves as combining both masculine and feminine qualities.

Research on androgyny has raised basic ques-

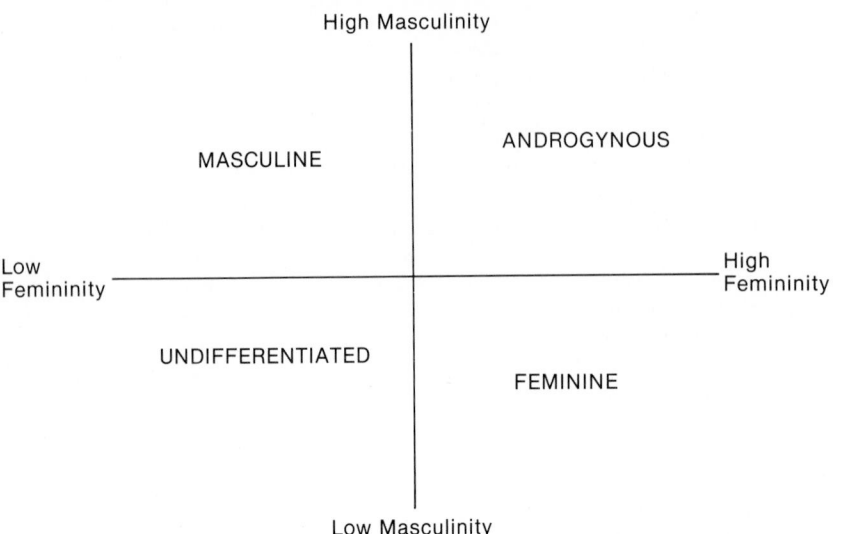

High Masculinity

MASCULINE

ANDROGYNOUS

Low Femininity

High Femininity

UNDIFFERENTIATED

FEMININE

Low Masculinity

FIGURE 15–1 A two-dimensional model of psychological masculinity and femininity.

tions about how psychological masculinity and femininity affect well-being. One long-standing view has been that to ensure mental health, boys and men should be masculine in their interests and attributes, whereas girls and women should be feminine. This *congruence model* (Whitley, 1983) proposes that adjustment is enhanced when there is an "appropriate" match between gender and self-concept. In contrast, the newer *androgyny model* of well-being argues that it is better for people to have both masculine and feminine traits. In particular, it has been proposed that androgynous individuals surpass traditionally sex-typed individuals in having greater behavioral flexibility and higher self-esteem.

BEHAVIORAL FLEXIBILITY Bem hypothesized that masculine people will perform well in situations calling for task competence or assertiveness; feminine people will do well in situations requiring nurturance or emotional expressivity; and androgynous people will do well in both types of situations. Some empirical support for this prediction has been found. In one study (Bem, 1975), masculine and androgynous individuals did better than feminine individuals on a test of ability to resist group pressure for conformity. In another study (Bem, Mar-

tyna, & Watson, 1976), feminine and androgynous individuals did better on tasks requiring nurturance, including playing with a baby and responding to a transfer student who was having problems adjusting to a new college.

At this point, research on the behavior of androgynous people is still relatively new, and definitive conclusions must await further evidence. It seems safe to say, however, that existing findings challenge the congruence model and suggest that androgynous people may be at least as effective as gender-typed people in social interactions (Pleck, 1981).

SELF-ESTEEM Feeling good about oneself is a key ingredient in mental health. The congruence model predicts that self-esteem should be highest for masculine men and feminine women—people with "appropriate" gender self-concepts. In contrast, the androgyny model asserts that androgynous individuals who perceive themselves as having both positive masculine and positive feminine attributes should have higher self-esteem than gender-typed individuals. A large number of studies have investigated this topic (Whitley, 1983), and they suggest an unexpected conclusion.

Basically, research once again provides no support for the congruence model. And results offer only weak support for the androgyny model. Instead, the biggest factor influencing self-esteem seems to be how a person scores on psychological masculinity. Both masculine and androgynous individuals usually have high self-esteem. The added benefit for androgynous people of being feminine as well as masculine is statistically significant, but very small in size. Researchers are still puzzling about why masculinity appears to be so central to self-esteem. One possibility is that in this culture, self-esteem is closely linked to the kinds of traits traditionally labeled as masculine, such as independence, assertiveness, and competence. Another possibility is that self-esteem scales are biased and do not adequately assess elements of self-esteem that are associated with femininity; in other words, the pattern of results is due to a methodological weakness in the tests being used (Whitley, 1986).

SOME CAUTIONS Research on the behavioral flexibility and self-esteem of gender-typed and androgynous individuals challenges the model that "appropriate" gender typing is essential to mental health. Masculine men and feminine women do not seem to have an advantage over androgynous individuals. But although the concept of androgyny has provided a useful correction to earlier work on masculinity and femininity, we should be cautious about accepting it uncritically.

First, androgyny measures are very limited in scope; they focus on self-perceptions of task competence and emotional expressiveness. In actuality, most people probably view masculinity and femininity much more broadly as including appearance, sexual behavior, and social roles as well as personality (Myers & Gonda, 1982). Further, these different components of masculinity and femininity are probably not part of a single, consistent dimension (Spence & Helmreich, 1980). One woman might, for instance, think of herself as masculine in personality (assertive, ambitious, and independent), feminine in appearance (short and voluptuous), and androgynous in social roles (both a wife-mother and a career woman). Existing androgyny instruments do not capture this complexity.

Second, androgyny is possible only in some areas such as personality; a person could perceive

himself or herself as warmly nurturant in some situations and coldly competitive in others. But in different domains, masculinity and femininity actually are mutually exclusive. In reproduction, for example, insemination and childbearing are each exclusive to one sex.

Third, current work on androgyny tells us little about how salient masculinity and femininity actually are in people's thinking about themselves. The Bem Sex Role Inventory and other tests ask people to rate themselves on traits society labels as masculine or feminine (Spence & Helmreich, 1980). But responses to these tests do not tell us whether people spontaneously label their own actions this way. If gender typing is really important, a person might think: "Gee, it makes me feel feminine to have prepared such a fine meal for my family," or "I feel more masculine for having stood up to my boss today." But if gender typing is not so vital, people might recognize their own nurturance or assertiveness, but identify these as human traits unrelated to gender. We do not know how prominent masculine and feminine labels actually are in people's self-concepts.

Finally, discussions of masculinity and femininity often touch on personal values and ideals. For those who endorse more traditional views about the sexes, the preservation of clear-cut distinctions between masculinity and femininity is an important goal. For those who want to expand the options available to both sexes, the blurring of distinctions is seen as desirable. Indeed, some feminists have rejected androgyny as an ideal because it preserves the notion that there are distinct masculine and feminine qualities even as it gives permission to people to have both types of attributes. Instead, some (such as Garnets & Pleck, 1979) have argued that we should move toward "sex-role transcendence." Personal attributes and preferences should no longer be associated with gender. Psychological research can clarify how gender affects our self-concept and can identify the consequences of various patterns, but it cannot tell people what ideals to adopt for their own lives.

So far, our discussion of gender has focused on perception—impressions of others and of ourselves. Now we turn to the topic of actual differences in the behavior of women and men.

GENDER DIFFERENCES IN BEHAVIOR: THEORETICAL APPROACHES

People debated about sex differences long before the invention of social psychology. For centuries, personal experience and intuition were the basis for such discussions. Today, scientific theories and research are providing a more balanced and comprehensive understanding of gender differences in behavior.

Early discussions often asked whether gender differences were caused by "nature or nurture," by biology or learning. We now know that such simple dichotomies are misleading. A full explanation of gender differences must consider both the biological capacities of the sexes and the social environment in which males and females live. It has also become clear that there is no single, general explanation for *all* differences between males and females. Rather, the causes of gender differences in math ability may be quite distinct from the causes of gender differences in self-disclosure, and so on. Four broad perspectives on the causes of gender differences emphasize the influence of biology, of childhood socialization, of social roles, and of social situations.

The Influence of Biology

Gender differences are undoubtedly affected by biology. Physical differences in height, in the ability to bear children and to breastfeed them, and so on, are obvious. The impact of sex hormones, both on the unborn fetus and on adults, is a lively topic of investigation, as are possible sex differences in the brain. Some sociobiologists are even suggesting that genetic evolution contributes to gender differences in human behavior (see Box 15–3).

The point social psychologists emphasize is that basic biological differences can be greatly increased or reduced by social forces. For example, sex differ-

ences in physical size and strength may once have given males a clear-cut advantage over females in warfare. But with modern aircraft and push-button weapons, brute force is less important for soldiers of either sex. Childbirth provides another illustration of the interplay of biology and society. Women are physically capable of having a dozen or more babies during a lifetime, but because of contemporary social attitudes and contraceptive technology, the typical American woman has only two or three children. Today, American wives typically outlive their husbands by several years. But in colonial days, when women had many children and childbirth was hazardous, the situation was reversed— men usually lived longer than women. The impact of biological gender differences can vary dramatically depending on the social environment.

Childhood Socialization

This perspective emphasizes the ways in which people learn about gender and acquire "sex-appropriate" behavior during childhood. An important idea is that society has different expectations and standards for the behavior of males and females. Imagine a father whose young daughter enters the living room dressed in Mommy's earrings, silk robe, and high heels, and climbs on Daddy's knee. The father is likely to smile at his daughter, give her a big hug, and compliment her on being such a pretty little girl. Now imagine that a 5-year-old boy were to do exactly the same thing. Although a modern Daddy might not punish his son, it is likely he would communicate firmly that feminine clothes are not appropriate for boys.

Through such experiences and the processes of reinforcement and modeling described in Chapter 1, children learn what society expects for boys

BOX 15–3

THE EVOLUTION OF GENDER DIFFERENCES

In his book, *The Evolution of Human Sexuality* (1979), Donald Symons outlines a sociobiological analysis of gender differences. Like other sociobiologists, he looks to genetic inheritance and the process of evolution for the causes of many gender differences.

Symons argues that humans have evolved in ways that maximize the likelihood of their individual genes being passed on to offspring and thus "surviving" in future generations. Whereas men produce many sperm, women typically produce only one egg per month and then must invest time and energy in pregnancy and nursing a baby. As a result, the most effective reproductive strategies for the two sexes differ. For men, the survival of one's own genes ("reproductive success") is enhanced by impregnating as many women as possible and investing little time and energy in the rearing of any one child. Hence men are biologically disposed to have many sexual partners and limited contact with infants. In contrast, for women reproductive success depends on maximizing the chances that the few children a woman can produce will survive to maturity. Women are disposed to be involved in the care of infants and to seek a long-term relationship with a man who can also contribute to the development of their children.

Symons and other sociobiologists believe that males and females have distinctive genetically based dispositions. They recognize, however, that whether such dispositions are translated into gender differences in actual behavior depends a good deal on the environment. The sociobiological perspective is still quite controversial, but it provides an interesting example of how biological factors might influence gender differences in attitudes and behavior.

and girls. The different social experiences of boys and girls lead to relatively enduring sex differences in attitudes, interests, skills and personality traits that continue into adulthood.

Social Roles

A third perspective emphasizes that a person's behavior is strongly influenced by social roles (Eagly, 1987). The lives of adults are structured by their various roles as family members and workers. A key idea is that many important social roles are defined differently for the two sexes. Within the family, people often have quite different expectations for mothers and fathers, for husbands and wives, for sons and daughters. In the world of work, occupational roles are often sex-typed. Consider your own images of nurses versus truck drivers, kindergarten teachers and business tycoons. Further, women's work roles are often lower in social status, prestige and power than those of men: he's the "boss" and she's the secretary.

Traditional social roles affect the behavior of males and females in several ways. They perpetuate a division of labor by gender, with women as home-

Traditional rules about what males and females should do are breaking down. Here, a twelve-year-old girl earns money delivering newspapers and a first grade boy gets a sewing lesson at school.

makers and childcare providers, and men as bread-winners. They influence the skills and interests people first develop in childhood and later refine as adults. Little girls often play with cooking sets and dolls in preparation for adult roles as wives and mothers. In addition, the effects of gender-linked roles may "spill over" into new situations. We may learn from experiences in the family and at work that men have higher status and are more authoritative than women. When we meet a new person, we may use their sex as a cue, inferring, for example, that a man is likely to be a confident leader and that a woman is likely to be a supportive follower (Eagly, 1987). As we saw earlier in this chapter, such expectations can become self-fulfilling prophecies.

Social Situations

Another major influence on behavior is the social setting. A man might talk about football and cars with his male buddies, peppering his speech with four-letter words, but "clean up his act" and change the topic of conversation with a new girlfriend. The gender of the person we are with is one powerful situational determinant of behavior.

This effect was illustrated in a study of who interrupts whom in casual conversations. The researchers unobtrusively tape-recorded the conversations of male-male, female-female, and male-female pairs as they chatted spontaneously in coffee shops, drugstores, and other public places (Zimmerman & West, 1975). Interruptions were ten times more frequent in the male-female conversations than in the same-sex ones. More striking, in same-sex pairs, men and women were equally likely to initiate an interruption; but in mixed-sex dyads, men initiated 96 percent of all interruptions. A laboratory study of conversations in mixed-sex groups (McMillan, Clifton, McGrath, & Gale, 1977) found similar but less extreme results. As shown in Table 15-2, men and women were equally likely to interrupt another person of the same sex. But when cross-sex inter-

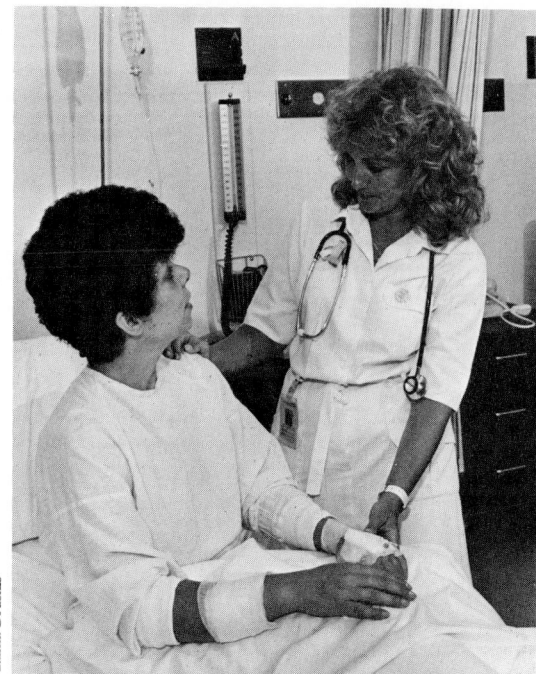

Is the woman talking to this patient a nurse or a physician? In our society, many jobs have traditionally been segregated by sex. Although changes are occuring, nurses are still typically women and doctors are usually men.

Laima Druskis

TABLE 15–2

Mean Number of Interruptions per Half-Hour in Mixed-Gender Discussion Groups

Gender of Person Who Is Interrupted	GENDER OF INTERRUPTER	
	Male	Female
Male	2.36	0.93
Female	5.24	2.50

Source: Adapted from McMillan, Clifton, McGrath, & Gale (1977).

tudes about women's roles, and half believed that he rejected traditional roles. As predicted, the women applicants tried to impress the interviewer. Women who thought the interviewer preferred traditional women wore more makeup and jewelry, talked less during the interview, described themselves in a more stereotypically feminine way, and were evaluated as more "attractive" by male raters than women who thought the interviewer preferred nontraditional women. The desire to be liked and accepted by others can lead us to act in more or less gender-typed ways, depending on the situation.

Situational constraints can prevent people from acting in accord with their own preferences and beliefs about gender. For example, many parents believe mothers should have greater responsibility for child care than fathers, and mothers usually do spend more time with children, even when the mother has a full-time job. However, an exception occurs when a wife's work schedule literally prevents her from doing all the childcare. One study (Berk & Berk, 1979) found that when wives worked an evening shift so that they had to leave home before dinner, fathers wound up, of necessity, giving the kids dinner and putting them to bed. The more general point is that a variety of situational factors, such as the gender composition of a group, the expectations of other people, or the constraints of a work schedule, can have great impact on how men and women behave.

ruptions occurred, it was five times more likely for a man to interrupt a woman as vice versa. For another illustration of the impact of group gender composition, this time in the society as a whole, see Box 15–4 on the next page.

Our desire to be liked by other people often leads us to conform to their expectations about how males and females should behave, regardless of our own personal beliefs. In one experiment (von Baeyer, Sherk, & Zanna, 1981), college women participated in a simulated job interview. By random assignment, half the women were led to believe that the male interviewer had quite traditional atti-

BOX 15–4

TOO MANY WOMEN: SEX RATIOS AND SOCIAL LIFE

In their book, *Too Many Women: The Sex Ratio Question* (1982), Marcia Guttentag and Paul Secord investigate the social effects of the ratio of males to females in society. Although approximately equal numbers of males and females are born each year, the ratio of male-to-female adults of marriageable age is quite variable cross-culturally. It is affected by wars, migration, the hazards of childbearing, the quality of prenatal care, infanticide of girl children, and so on. On the American frontier, for example, men outnumbered women, often by substantial proportions. By contrast, in 1980 in the United States the situation was reversed. For every 100 females, there were only 95 males. Ethnic differences in sex ratios have also been noted. Among black Americans, the current sex ratio imbalance is even more extreme, with an average of only 89.6 males per 100 females (Tucker, 1986). What are the social and personal consequences of variations in sex ratios between the sexes?

Guttentag and Secord begin by arguing that in all societies, men have relatively greater structural power than women. That is, men control the economy, religion, government, and so on. However, through the principles of social exchange (discussed in Chapter 9), sex ratios influence patterns of dominance in the personal relations of men and women in courtship and marriage. When there is an undersupply of women, as in America before World War II, young women are highly valued and protected. Men are eager to form a committed relationship through marriage. Women gain status through marriage, and are able to achieve economic mobility by "marrying up." Husband and wife roles are highly differentiated—there are clear-cut definitions of "men's work" and "women's work." Both sexes stress sexual monogamy, although a double standard may permit greater sexual freedom for men.

In contrast, Guttentag and Secord propose that when women are in oversupply, as in the 1970s and 1980s in America, the relations between the sexes are quite different. Specifically, marriage and commitment are deemphasized. A high proportion of women are never-married or divorced, and single-parent families headed by women increase. For example, 1980 census data for Los Angeles county in California showed that 14 percent of all white women were divorced and 24 percent of white women aged 25 to 34 had never been married (Tucker, 1986). For black women, confronted with a more severe shortage of black men, the overall rate of divorce was 23 percent, and the proportion of black women aged 25 to 34 who have never married was 31 percent. Under such conditions, Guttentag and Secord propose, women may feel personally devalued and powerless, and feminist movements are likely to arise.

The basic argument of Guttentag and Secord—that sex ratios in society have a profound impact on heterosexual relationships—is provocative. The researchers support their arguments with examples of societies ranging from ancient Greece to medieval Europe to contemporary Africa. Their views must still be considered controversial. But they are likely to spark a lively scientific debate. Work on sex ratios provides a fascinating illustration of a way in which societal-level factors may influence the daily lives of women and men.

THE SOCIAL BEHAVIOR OF WOMEN AND MEN

American psychologists have long been interested in sex differences. A great deal of research has compared the behavior of males and females, especially that of children and college students.

CLASSIC WORK BY MACCOBY AND JACKLIN   In 1974, Eleanor Maccoby and Carol Jacklin published a landmark book called *The Psychology of Sex Differences*. They reviewed hundreds of studies of sex differences in many psychological characteristics, such as verbal ability, intelligence and aggressiveness. Maccoby and Jacklin attempted to evaluate this research carefully, excluding studies with methodological weaknesses and accepting as true only those findings replicated in several studies by different investigators. They concluded that sex differences had been firmly established in only four areas. On average:

1. Females score higher than males in verbal ability, such as reading and vocabulary.
2. Males score higher than females in mathematical ability.
3. Males score higher than females on visual-spatial ability.
4. Males are more aggressive than females.

Equally important, Maccoby and Jacklin concluded that some stereotypes about sex differences were clearly wrong. The sexes do not differ in overall intelligence, nor in general level of achievement motivation or striving for excellence. The authors also debunked the idea that girls are better at rote learning and simple repetitive tasks, whereas boys are better at tasks requiring higher-level cognitive processing.

Maccoby and Jacklin emphasized individual intellectual abilities in their review. As social psychologists, we are more concerned with social skills and behavior. We have already described some of these differences earlier in this book. In Chapter 9, for example, we considered sex differences in self-disclosure and love. Here, we will take a closer look at male-female differences in aggression, helping, conformity, and nonverbal communication. Before beginning our review, however, we need to introduce a new innovation in sex difference research, the use of meta-analysis.

META-ANALYSES OF SEX DIFFERENCES   As the number of studies of sex differences has increased, it has become more difficult for investigators to read and synthesize research to arrive at general conclusions. Traditionally, reviews of research literature have relied heavily on the judgment of the reviewers to select a balanced sample of studies and to eliminate methodologically flawed research. A persistent problem for reviewers has been inconsistency across studies. What can we conclude if 20 studies find men are better at Skill X, but 10 studies find women are better, and 10 studies find no differences? Often, researchers have used a "vote-counting" approach to resolving these discrepancies, assuming, for example, that a sex difference "exists" if it occurs in the majority of studies.

In an effort to develop more systematic ways to review and synthesize empirical findings, researchers have begun to use new techniques called **meta-analysis** (Eagly, 1987; Hyde & Linn, 1986). This approach uses statistical methods to pool information from many studies in order to arrive at an overall estimate of the size of sex differences. We might find, for instance, that the average sex difference on Skill X is less than one-tenth of a standard deviation—quite a small effect that may not be of much practical importance.

Statistics are also used to test for the consistency (homogeneity) of findings across studies. When results from different studies are found to be highly inconsistent, the reviewer looks for factors other than gender that may be important in explaining the inconsistency. Perhaps men are better at Skill X only when tested by a male experimenter, or only in group testing situations, or only if they come from working class backgrounds. Instead of merely noting that findings are inconsistent, the goal is to try to explain the reasons for the inconsistency. Meta-analyses also encourage reviewers to consider very carefully how they select a sample of studies to review. It has been suggested, for instance, that reviews should include not only published studies, but also unpublished doctoral dissertations. The reasoning here is that studies which find no sex differences may be less likely to be accepted for publication, thus biasing published research toward overestimating sex differences. In the following sections, we present some of the findings of recent analyses of sex differences.

Aggression

One of the most consistent sex differences is the greater frequency of aggressive behavior by males (Eagly & Steffen, 1986; Hyde, 1986). Around the world, it is men who are the warriors. Violent crime is also largely a male domain. Whether it be the activities of teenage gangs, underworld crime figures, or a lone assassin, it is usually men who use physical force in illegal pursuits. According to FBI statistics, 87 percent of those arrested for murder in 1981 were men (see Table 15–3 for other statistics). During childhood, boys are usually rated as more aggressive than girls by teachers, parents, and peers. So whether it be socially approved aggression in wartime, illegal violence, or children's play, males take the lead in aggressive behavior.

Two recent meta-analyses review more than a hundred studies of aggression (Eagly & Steffen, 1986; Hyde, 1986). They found that males are more aggressive than females in both verbal and physical aggression, although the gender gap is bigger for physical aggression. Larger sex differences are found in naturalistic settings (e.g., hitting and kick-

Football provides a socially-approved context for male aggression. But theorists disagree about whether aggressive sports provide a wholesome outlet for innate male aggressive drives, or rather teach men to become even more aggressive.

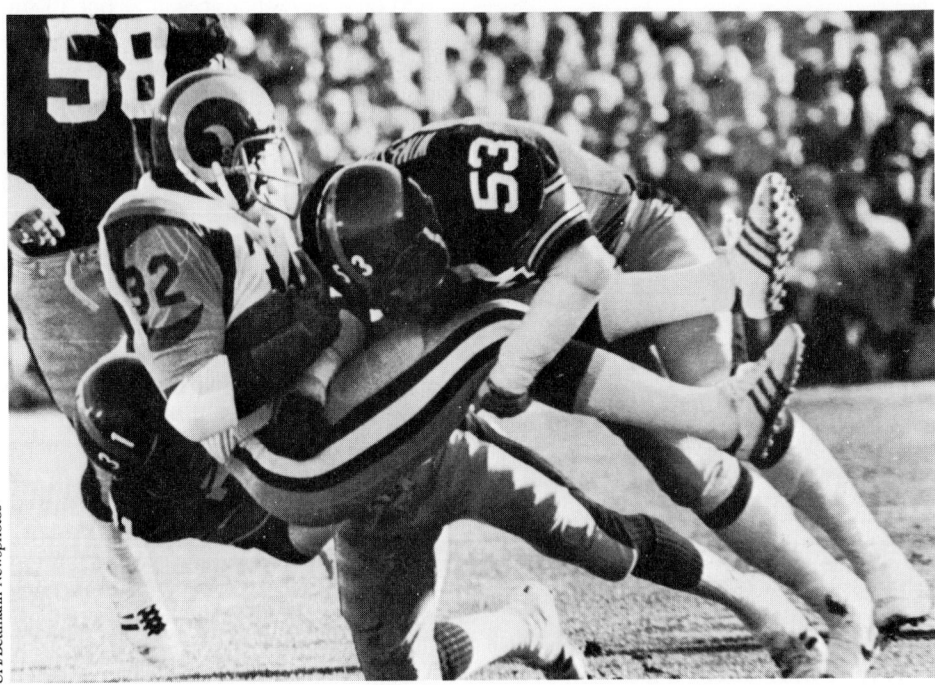

UPI/Bettmann Newsphotos

TABLE 15–3

FBI Statistics Comparing Arrests for Violent Crimes by Men and Women

Type of Offense	1972			1981		
	Total Number	Men (%)	Women (%)	Total Number	Men (%)	Women (%)
Murder and nonnegligent manslaughter	12,312	84	16	16,082	87	13
Forcible rape	15,455	100	0	24,713	99	1
Robbery	90,245	94	6	124,737	93	7
Aggravated assault	125,798	87	13	220,194	87	13
All violent crime	243,810	90	10	385,726	90	10

Source: Adapted from *Uniform Crime Reports: Crime in the United States, 1981.* Federal Bureau of Investigation, U.S. Department of Justice, August 26, 1982.

ing on a playground) than for more controlled laboratory settings (e.g., hitting a plastic bobo doll in a research room). Hyde (1986) suggests that males may be more likely than females to engage in spontaneous aggression, but that males and females respond more similarly in controlled lab conditions. In addition, Eagly and Steffen (1986) found evidence that women feel more guilt and anxiety about behaving aggressively. Women were also more concerned about the harm their aggression may cause the victim and about the danger of retaliation that their aggression might bring to themselves.

Helping Behavior

In a meta-analytic review of 172 studies of prosocial behavior, Eagly and Crowley (1986) found a significant sex difference: Men were more likely than women to offer assistance. However, the researchers noted several important qualifications to this general conclusion. First and foremost, they emphasized that most social-psychological studies of helping have investigated bystander intervention, that is, offering aid to a stranger in distress. This is a very narrow way to conceptualize prosocial behavior because it excludes a wide range of helpful acts such as caring for children, comforting a friend, or taking an elderly relative to a clinic.

Using a social roles perspective, Eagly and Crowley propose that whereas female roles foster helping that is nurturant and caring, male roles foster helping that is heroic and chivalrous. Bystander

intervention research documents men's greater chivalry. Men are more likely than women to help strangers in distress, and the average size of the sex difference is about one third of a standard deviation. Sex differences are most likely to occur when the victim or requester is female, when there is an audience, and in situations that women perceive as dangerous. Unfortunately, existing research tells us little about helping that occurs in private relations among friends and relatives. Eagly and Crowley identified five studies showing that women were more likely than men to do personal favors for friends and to provide advice about personal problems. Clearly, a more complete understanding of sex differences in helping will require studies that go beyond bystander intervention to investigate helping in a wide variety of settings.

Conformity

Stereotypes portray women as more yielding, gullible, and conformist than men. According to Eagly (1987), traditional social roles dictate that men should be less easily influenced than women. Social-psychological studies have typically investigated conformity and compliance in laboratory settings where an individual interacts with strangers.

Two early reviews of the empirical research on social influence (Eagly, 1978, 1983) reported that significant sex differences occurred in only a minority of studies. Eagly found 62 studies that investigated sex differences in persuasion—that is, the extent to which a person is influenced by hearing arguments in favor of or against an issue. Only 16 percent of these studies found that women were more easily persuaded; the vast majority found no differences. Similarly, Eagly found 61 studies of responses to group pressures for conformity, as in the Asch experiment described in Chapter 12. Here again, only 34 percent of studies found that women conformed significantly more. In those cases where sex differences did occur, they were usually small in magnitude (Eagly & Carli, 1981).

A recent meta-analysis by Becker (1986) took another look at this research area. She found much inconsistency across studies, with the results varying by the type of social influence involved, the nationality of subjects, and other factors. Nonetheless, she did find evidence that in both persuasion and group pressure studies, there was a small but significant tendency for women to be influenced more than men. At present, it is difficult to reach a solid conclusion about this research area. Further, since virtually all of the studies have been done in laboratory settings with strangers, it would be unwise to make generalizations to everyday interactions at work, school or home.

Nonverbal Communication

Stereotypes about female "intuition" suggest that women may be better than men at decoding or "reading" nonverbal behavior. Thus it might be speculated that mothers are more expert than fa-

thers at telling whether a crying baby is hungry, wet, or suffering gas pains. Similarly, the stereotype would suggest that women may be better able to sense whether another person is feeling depressed or embarrassed or tired. Many studies have addressed this question by comparing men's and women's accuracy at decoding another person's emotions from facial cues, body language, or tone of voice.

In a typical study, subjects watch a videotape of a person expressing a series of emotions, such as happiness, disgust, or fear. After viewing each segment of the film, subjects indicate which of several emotions they think is being expressed. In other studies, subjects listen to voices that have been "content filtered"—altered so that the words are garbled and only the tone is distinct. Judith Hall (1978) reviewed 75 such studies that permitted gender comparisons. In 68 percent, women were better decoders than men; in 13 percent, men were better than women; and in 19 percent no gender differences occurred.

This tendency for females to excel at nonverbal decoding has been found in schoolchildren, teenagers, and adults. Several possible explanations have been offered. One is that females have a genetically "programmed" sensitivity to nonverbal cues because of their role in caring for preverbal infants. Another suggestion is that women are trained to be experts in emotional matters, and so learn to be more skillful in nonverbal communication.

GENDER DIFFERENCES IN PERSPECTIVE: CHANGING ROLES

Aside from the biological facts of life, just how different are males and females? Psychological research offers no simple conclusion. At the level of basic abilities and personal dispositions, gender differences are often small in magnitude, no more than a few points on a standardized test. For example, Eagly (1983) estimated that gender explains only about 1 percent of all the variability between

people in conformity and persuasibility. Similarly, Hall (1978) estimated that gender accounts for only 4 percent of variation in decoding nonverbal messages. Hyde (1981) reported that gender explains only 1 percent of individual differences in verbal ability, 1 percent in math ability, and 4.5 percent in visual-spatial ability. For these types of behaviors, the range of human variation is great and the average differences between the sexes are small. Such gender differences may be "statistically significant," yet essentially trivial. Other alleged gender differences, such as in general intelligence or achievement motivation, have been disproved.

At the same time, our everyday experiences repeatedly show that men and women often use their basic talents and drives in different ways. A man with high achievement strivings may channel his energies into starting his own business; a traditional woman with equally great desire for achievement may take up gourmet cooking or become a "super mom." Clear-cut differences do exist between the activities that are usually "men's work" and those that are "women's work."

But newspapers today are filled with stories about the changing roles of men and women. Whether a writer heralds these changes as a "stride toward equality" or laments the collapse of "traditional values," few would deny that the lives of men and women are not what they used to be. One way to assess these changes is to compare contemporary gender roles with the older, traditional patterns. Traditional gender roles were organized around two basic principles. The first idea was that men and women should perform distinctive activities, that there should be a division of labor by gender. The second idea was that men should be the dominant sex, both at home and in society at large.

Division of Labor

There is much evidence that rigid distinctions between what men should do and what women should do are breaking down. During this century, women have increasingly come to do things formerly considered "for men only." In particular, women's participation in paid work has increased dramatically, decreasing men's exclusive role as the family breadwinner. In 1940, only 15 percent of married women worked for pay, but by 1975 the figure had risen to 44 percent (Bane, 1976). Today, more than half of all married women have paying jobs. Even more remarkable is the fact that in 1985, 54 percent of women with children under age 6 were working for pay.

Women have begun to enter occupations such as law, medicine, and engineering that were once the near exclusive domain of men. Women have also made major gains in higher education. In 1978, for the first time in United States history, more women than men entered college. These are changes of great personal and social significance.

Yet women are far from equal partners in the world of work. Women continue to be concentrated in lower-status "female jobs" such as secretary, nurse, and teacher. Partly as a result, the average woman worker earns only about 57 cents for every dollar earned by a man. Even when women make it into high-status jobs, they often experience bias not encountered by their male peers.

Are men today doing more things formerly considered "for women only"? Everyday examples of such changes are easy to find. It is not unusual these days to see a father in the delivery room assisting in the birth of his child or taking his toddler to the supermarket. In public schools, many home economics classes have gone "coed"; more boys are learning to cook and to babysit. However, men's participation in housework and childcare—*family work* as some call it—is still relatively small. One study (Robinson et al., 1977) found that husbands' total family work averaged only 11.2 hours per week.

A surprising finding from research by Robinson and others is that the amount of time a husband spends on housework and childcare is *not* related to whether or not his wife has a paid job. A husband whose wife has a 40-hour a week job spends no more time on household chores than a husband whose wife is home full time. Women perform most homemaking and childcare activities, regardless of whether they have a paid job or not. The only difference is that employed wives spend less time on family work (about 28 hours per week) than do fulltime homemakers (about 53 hours per week).

Recent studies (Pleck, 1981) show some signs that men in dual-worker marriages may be doing a little more at home, but the change is quite small. Baruch and Barnett (1986) found that married men with children spent about 29 hours per week interacting with their children compared to 44 hours spent by the wife. As in earlier studies, the total amount of time the husband spent with his children was *not* affected by whether or not the wife had

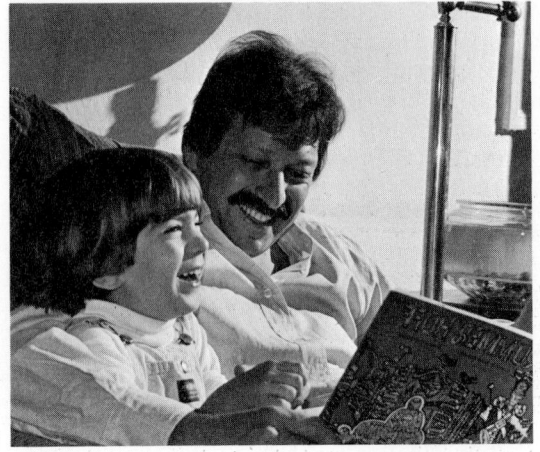

Many couples today reject rigid rules about "men's work" and "women's work." It is much more common to find men cooking and caring for children, activities traditionally delegated to women.

a fulltime paid job or was a fulltime homemaker. However, fathers in dual-worker families did differ from fathers with homemaker wives in two ways: They spent about 10 percent more "solo" time (when the wife was absent) with their children and performed 5 percent more of the homemaking chores. For most families, homemaking and childcare continue to be largely "women's work."

Male Dominance

The second basic idea in traditional gender roles is that males should be the leaders both at home and in society at large. Changes are clearly occurring in both arenas. In the public section, laws denying women the vote, forbidding women to own property, and in general defining women as second-class citizens are largely a thing of the past. In recent years we've seen the first woman elected governor and the first woman appointed to the U.S. Supreme Court. Nonetheless, the numbers of women in the power circles of society are still small. In 1980, women were only 2 percent of U.S. senators and 4 percent of members of the House of Representatives. For an example closer to home, consider the college you attend. Chances are that there are many women secretaries and a few women professors, but that the chairperson of your

department, most of the deans and top-level administrators, and the president are male. Women are still very far from being equal partners in public affairs.

In the family, the extent of male dominance is harder to assess. As we discussed in Chapter 9, marriages in which the husband is the all-powerful patriarch are uncommon today. Nonetheless, proponents of the traditional pattern of greater male power are easy to find. A striking example is the bestseller *Fascinating Womanhood,* by Helen Andelin (1963). She advocates a benevolent form of male dominance, arguing that women should defer to their husbands and take pleasure in being cared for. The man, she writes, should be the "undisputed head of the family." The wife "must accept him as her leader, support and obey him" (pp. 134–135). But although male dominance has vocal supporters, many people today reject this view.

In 1981, when Lady Diana married Prince Charles, the future king of England, she broke with tradition in her wedding vows: She did not promise to obey her husband. A Westminster Abbey clergyman explained: "Marriage is the kind of relationship where there should be two equal partners, and if there is to be a dominant partner it won't be settled by this oath" (*Los Angeles Times*, July 2, 1981, 18). Many other young couples share this view (Peplau, 1984), and it seems likely that male dominance is less pronounced than it used to be (Scanzoni & Scanzoni, 1981).

In contemporary society, multiple definitions of gender roles co-exist. The options available to peo- ple today, both at work and in personal relation- ships, are much less limited by gender than in the past.

KEY TERMS FOR CHAPTER 15

androgynous	gender identity	gender stereotypes	meta-analysis
cultural stereotypes	gender self-concept	gender typing	personal stereotypes

SUMMARY

1. Gender is one of the most basic categories in social life. The process of labeling people, things, and activities as "masculine" and "feminine" is called gender typing.

2. Gender stereotypes are beliefs about the typical personal attributes of males and females. Cultural stereotypes are societal-level images of the sexes found in the media, art, and literature. Personal stereotypes are the unique beliefs held by an individual about the typical attributes of men and women.

3. Stereotypes are most likely to influence our per- ception of other people when we have little infor- mation available and when a person's gender is especially salient. One problem with gender ster- eotypes is that they can bias evaluations of the performance of individual men and women.

4. Gender identity, knowledge that we are female or male, is acquired early in childhood. An impor- tant developmental milestone occurs when chil- dren come to understand that gender is constant and unchanging. Transsexuals have a severe gen- der identity problem: They believe their true psy- chological gender is different from their biologi- cal gender.

5. Beliefs about masculinity and femininity are im- portant elements in our self-concept. Androgy- nous people rate themselves high in both mascu- line (instrumental) and feminine (expressive) qualities. Recent research has challenged the con- gruence model assertion that psychological well- being is greatest for traditionally "masculine" men and "feminine" women.

6. There are four major theoretical perspectives on the causes of gender differences. A biological ap- proach emphasizes the impact of physical differ- ences, sex hormones, and genetics. A childhood socialization approach emphasizes ways in which we acquire relatively stable gender-typed charac- teristics through social learning processes. A so- cial roles perspective emphasizes that people tend to conform to the expectations of gender-linked social roles such as husband or nurse. A final approach emphasizes that people's behavior var- ies from situation to situation, depending on such factors as the sex composition of the group, the nature of the task or activity, and the social expec- tations of others.

7. Much research has investigated sex differences in abilities and social behaviors. A new technique

called meta-analysis provides a quantitative approach to integrating findings from many different studies. Research, mostly with American children and college students, finds that on average males are better at math, score higher on visual-spatial ability, are more aggressive, and are more likely to help a stranger (especially a female) in distress. In contrast, females are better in verbal ability, in nonverbal communication, and may be more helpful in personal relations. Research on sex differences in conformity is inconsistent and hard to evaluate.

8. In daily life, women and men often use their basic talents and drives in distinctive, gender-linked ways. Traditional gender roles prescribed a division of labor by sex and conferred greater power on men. Despite social change, both these traditional patterns continue. In general, however, people today are less constrained by gender than in the past.

SUGGESTED READINGS

ASHMORE, R. D., & DEL BOCA, F. K. (Eds.). (1987). *The social psychology of female-male relations*. New York: Academic Press. An excellent collection of review articles by experts in the field. Topics include gender stereotypes, sex-role attitudes, and the nature of male-female relations at work and in personal life.

FAUSTO-STERLING, A. (1985). *Myths of gender: Biological theories about women and men*. New York: Basic Books. A feminist critique of biological analyses of sex differences including sociobiology, sex differences in genes, hormones, and the brain. A readable book that assumes little prior scientific knowledge.

HENLEY, N. M. (1977). *Body politics: Power, sex, and nonverbal communication*. Englewood Cliffs, NJ: Prentice Hall. A classic analysis of gender differences in the use of touch, space, time, and other aspects of nonverbal communication. Written for students and available in paperback.

MATLIN, M. W. (1987). *The psychology of women*. New York: Holt, Rinehart and Winston. An up-to-date and comprehensive text on the psychology of gender. Available in paperback.

O'LEARY, V., UNGER, R. K., & WALLSTON, B. S. (Eds.). (1985). *Women, gender, and social psychology*. Hillsdale, NJ: Erlbaum. Leading social psychologists discuss new research on gender and such topics as achievement motivation, equity, helping behavior, close relationships, groups, and masculinity/femininity.

PLECK, J. H. (1981). *The myth of masculinity*. Cambridge, MA: MIT Press. A detailed analysis of research and theories on masculinity; somewhat technical, but well worth the effort.

TAVRIS, C., & WADE, C. (1984). *The longest war: Sex differences in perspective, 2nd ed.* New York: Harcourt Brace Jovanovich. A delightful introduction to research and theories about gender differences, including cross-cultural studies. A very readable paperback.

16 ENVIRONMENTAL PSYCHOLOGY

Recently, people have become more and more concerned about the environment. The environmental movement has focused attention on the quality of the air we breathe and the water we drink, on how new dam construction harms wildlife, and how strip mining devastates the landscape and causes floods. We are beginning to realize that virtually all aspects of the world around us can have profound and potentially negative effects on our health and well-being.

Social scientists, including psychologists, have also become concerned about how the environment affects us. Just as toxic chemicals in the air and the ground can damage physical health, so other characteristics of the environment can damage mental and social health. Noise, crowding, building design, and community structure all determine the quality of our lives and our day-to-day functioning. **Environmental psychology** is a relatively new branch of psychology that focuses on the relationships between the physical environment and human behavior and well-being (Stokols & Altman, 1987). We will examine some of the main findings of environmental psychologists.

HUMAN SPATIAL BEHAVIOR

How do people use the space around them to regulate their social interactions? This is one of the questions asked by environmental researchers, who use the term **proxemics** to refer to the study of human spatial behavior (Hall, 1959). We will consider two aspects of how humans use space: personal space and territoriality.

Personal Space

Suppose you are standing by yourself in a physician's waiting room, and the nurse walks up to you. How close does she actually come? Three inches? Ten inches? Two feet? Suppose you are sitting on a park bench and a well-dressed man sits down immediately next to you. How does that make you feel? Would you feel differently if he sat down five feet away? How close to other people do you usually stand? Does it make any difference if they are friends, strangers, or members of your family? Does it make any difference if you are standing at a cocktail party, on a bus, or on line at the Post Office?

As these examples suggest, people have pre-ferred distances for social interaction, depending on who they are with and the activity. People treat the physical space immediately around them as though it were a part of themselves; this zone has been called their **personal space.** According to Sommer (1969):

> Personal space refers to an area with an invisible boundary surrounding the person's body into which intruders may not come. Like [porcupines], people like to be close enough to obtain warmth and comradeship but far enough away to avoid pricking one another. (p. 26)

In social interactions, people try to maintain an acceptable balance between being too close for comfort or awkwardly distant.

Personal space is often measured by the physical distance a person maintains from others. But personal space involves much more than physical distance. At very close distances, we can touch and smell another person, talk in hushed whispers, and see their features very clearly. At far distances, we may need to talk loudly and have quite different possibilities for social contact.

Edward Hall (1959), an anthropologist, sug-

Charles Gatewood

J. Latta

Laimute Druskis

According to Edward Hall, there are distinct zones of interpersonal interaction. Lovers maintain "intimate distance" of less than 18 inches. A friendly conversation takes place at a "personal distance" of 18 inches to 4 feet. We use "social distance" of 4 to 7 feet for a formal business meeting.

gested four basic zones for interpersonal interaction:

- *Intimate distance*, from 0 to 18 inches, is illustrated by a couple making love, by a mother nursing an infant, by wrestlers locked in a tight hold.
- *Personal distance*, from 18 inches to 4 feet, is the distance for friendly conversation.
- *Social distance*, from 4 to 7 feet, is the distance for a formal business meeting.
- *Public distance*, from 12 to 25 feet, requires a loud voice and is illustrated by someone giving a lecture.

According to Hall, the social situation determines which of these zones people prefer to use. Intimate and personal distance are typically used for informal interactions with friends, family, or close associates. Social and public distances are used for more formal interactions among casual acquaintances or strangers.

Research has generally supported Hall's basic idea (Aiello, 1987). For instance, friends prefer to stand closer together than do strangers (Ashton, Shaw & Worsham, 1980), and people who want to seem friendly choose smaller distances (Patterson & Sechrest, 1970). People who are sexually attracted to each other also stand close (Allgeier & Byrne, 1973). Although most people do not think much about personal space, we are nonetheless aware of the unwritten rules about space use in our culture. For example, we know that standing close together is usually a sign of friendship or interest. It may be one of the most important and easiest ways of telling someone you have just met that you like him or her. The other person is immediately aware of your interest, and if the person is not interested, he or she will generally move away to make that clear.

Group Differences in Spatial Behavior

Many factors affect our use of space. As an anthropologist, Hall was especially interested in cross-cultural differences in spatial behavior. If you have traveled much outside the United States, you have no doubt noticed that people in other countries differ in how close they stand while talking. People in some cultures stand closer together than you are accustomed to, whereas people in other cultures maintain a greater distance. Research in this area has found that cultural norms determine typical personal space preferences. White North Americans, the English, and the Swedes stand the farthest apart; Southern Europeans stand closer; and Latin Americans and Arabs stand the closest (Little, 1968; Sommer, 1969). Although much observation remains to be done in Africa, Eastern Europe, and Asia, it is clear that consistent differences exist all over the world.

These cultural differences might be considered a piece of interesting but trivial information if it were not for the fact that preferences in personal distance can sometimes have important social consequences. People from cultures with different preferences may misinterpret one another's actions. For example, an American and a Pakistani have a problem when they stand near to each other to talk. The American likes to stand about three or four feet away, whereas the Pakistani would ordinarily stand much closer. Obviously, they cannot both have their way. If they are unaware of the cultural difference, they may execute a little dance around the room. The Pakistani feels uncomfortably far away and moves closer. The American feels uncomfortable and retreats, which in turn causes the Pakistani to move closer again. Moreover, as this is going on, the Pakistani may feel that the American is being cold and unfriendly, while the American thinks the other is being overly intimate and pushy.

In addition to cross-cultural variations, personal space may also vary within a culture. As you may have guessed, men and women tend to use personal space somewhat differently. Pairs of women stand closer together than do pairs of men (Horowitz et al., 1970), and women often tend to stand closer to whomever they are with (Hartnett et al., 1970; Leibman, 1970). Violent prisoners prefer greater distances than do nonviolent prisoners (Gilmour & Walkey, 1981).

Territorial Behavior

You arrive at the library to study for your midterm exam in social psychology. To your distress, every seat is taken. Most seats are physically occupied by someone, and the rest are "staked out" with coats, books, briefcases, and other markers. You consider whether or not to move someone's belongings and take the chair, but think better of it, not wanting to face an argument.

People often lay claim to a particular place as "theirs." A **territory** is an area controlled by a specific individual or group. Territorial behavior includes actions designed to stake out or mark a territory and to claim ownership. Whereas personal space is physically connected to a person—a distance from the person's body to that of other people—territories do not necessarily require physical presence. As the library example suggests, people often try to guard their territory from intrusion while they are absent.

Territorial behavior is a way that people regulate social interaction, and it can serve many specific functions. Territorial rules can simplify and bring order to daily interactions. For instance, when family members share bedrooms, they usually designate some areas for personal use. Each person has his or her own part of the closet, dresser, or side of a shared bed (Altman, Nelson, & Lett, 1972). Family members tend to have fixed places at the dinner table, places that are changed only when people are eating alone or when guests are present. Territoriality also contributes to the maintenance of privacy—control over the information others have about us and the extent to which social contact occurs. The goal of territorial behavior is not necessarily to be alone, but rather to control access to oneself and one's property. Finally, territorial behavior provides a way to communicate information about our self and our interests. The rose-covered white picket fence surrounding a suburban house marks the property line, but it also conveys an image of the owners.

TYPES OF TERRITORIES   Altman (1975) has distinguished three main types of human territories:

A *primary territory* is owned and used exclusively by an individual or group. A house, for example, is clearly owned by a person or family, controlled on a relatively permanent basis, and important in their daily lives. Unwelcome intrusions into a primary territory are a serious matter.

A *secondary territory* is a space that is used regularly, but shared with others. You may always take the same seat in your chemistry lab and get annoyed if someone else sits in it before you arrive, but you know that the space is not exclusively yours. Secondary territories are semi-public, and so there is more ambiguity of ownership and control.

Public territories are places like a park or airport waiting lounge where everyone presumably has an equal right of access. We may stake out a spot on the beach with a beach chair and blanket, but we know that our claim is temporary; getting a choice spot depends on getting there ahead of the other beachgoers.

TERRITORIAL MARKERS   One interesting research focus has been the way people mark and personalize their territories (Brown, 1987). **Territorial markers** often serve a preventive function. They let others know that a particular area is claimed. In a study of behavior in the library, Becker (1973) found that people were least likely to select a table that was physically occupied by another person. Not surprisingly, physical presence is a strong marker. But people were also discouraged by the presence of books and personal belongings on a table; the more markers present, the greater the avoidance. Quite subtle gestures can also serve as territorial markers.

A study in a game arcade (Werner, Brown & Damron, 1981) found that body gestures were territorial markers. A confederate stood by an electronic game called Space Invaders. The researchers varied how far the confederate stood from the machine, and whether or not the confederate placed a hand on the edge of the machine. The confederate never touched the actual controls. New players were significantly less likely to approach the machine when the confederate stood close and when he touched the machine. In public settings where it is not possible to use permanent markers, touch and physical

We use territorial markers to claim a particular space and prevent unwanted intrusions. This woman has used her sandals, bookbag, and newspaper to indicate her control of the area.

News and Information Service, University of Texas at Austin

THE HOME FIELD ADVANTAGE IN SPORTS

In competitive sports, teams usually do better when playing at home than "on the road." A study of professional basketball, baseball, and football teams found that all teams won a greater percentage of their home games than games played elsewhere (Hirt & Kimble, 1981). The home field advantage was most striking for basketball, where professional teams won about 65 percent of home games but only 35 percent of away games. An analysis of the 1976–77 National Basketball Association season found that even teams who finished last in their division won nearly 60 percent of their home games (Watkins, 1978). And even the most powerful division champions performed relatively poorly on the road. Schwartz and Barsky (1977) have concluded that playing at home is as strong a factor in a team's performance as the quality of the players.

Why is it better to play on your home territory? Greater familiarity with the home field and the fatigue of travel may contribute, but they are not the whole answer (Schwartz & Barsky, 1977). Psychological factors are also important. Territorial dominance may be one explanation. Home teams may do better because they are on their own turf. Visitors may feel wary and inhibited because they are not on their home ground. An even more important factor may be the behavior of the spectators. A team usually has more fans on hand for home games. According to Schwartz and Barsky, the social support provided by the home audience is a crucial factor. They also suggested that encouragement from an audience is most effective when it is sustained for some time and when the audience is most compact (high in social density). This may explain why the home team advantage is most pronounced for indoor sports such as basketball, where spectators are in a small enclosed space, rather than for outdoor games such as football, which are played in large arenas.

proximity may be subtle signs of temporary "ownership."

Territorial markers also serve to display aspects of an individual's personality or interests. In one study (Vinsel, Brown, Altman, & Foss, 1980), photographs were taken of the wall decorations in dorm rooms of newly entering first-year university students. Virtually all students hung at least one object, such as a poster or photograph, on the wall by the bed. Women were more likely than men to use relationship items, such as personal photos; men were more likely to use impersonal items, such as a sports poster. Differences were also found between the markers of students who later dropped out of the university and those who remained in

school. The decorations of continuing students showed more identification with the new school and community, such as school posters and maps of the local area. The displays of dropouts suggested a greater commitment to past life and families.

Defending and Sharing Space

Personal space and territorial behavior are used to control social interaction. On the one hand, we want to defend ourselves and our territory from unwanted "invasions." But equally important, we often want to share ourselves and our space with friends and loved ones. Thus, our reaction to some-

Audience encouragement may influence sports performance through the process of social facilitation, discussed in Chapter 13. In this view, supportive audiences increase an athlete's arousal or motivation. When someone performs a well-learned task, increased arousal usually improves performance. Thus highly skilled athletes should benefit from heightened arousal.

In an extension of this work, Greer (1983) looked at negative behavior by fans, such as booing and hissing. Researchers observed the behavior of home and visiting men's college basketball teams over a two-year period. The researchers noted every instance of sustained crowd protest that lasted for at least 15 seconds, and then recorded the behavior of both teams during the next five minutes. Performance measures included scoring, violations, and turnovers.

Greer found that very short crowd protests occurred in virtually every game, but sustained outbursts happened only about half the time, for a total of 15 games. Ten of these booing incidents were directed at the referees for calls made against the home team. In four cases, the protest expressed displeasure with referees who failed to call violations on visiting players. One protest was directed at the players on the visiting team. All protests were in support of the home team. Following these episodes, there was a consistent improvement in home team performance and a decline in visitor performance. Greer suggested that protests by home fans may interfere with the concentration of visiting players and reduce their effectiveness.

Recently, an interesting reversal of the home field advantage has been documented by Baumeister and Steinhilber (1984). They proposed that when a team is on the brink of winning a championship, playing before a supportive audience may lead to increased self-attention that can impair performance. In a final, decisive game, playing at home may cause players to "choke." To support their claim, the researchers examined records for baseball World Series games and for national basketball championships. Consistent with previous research, they found that playing at home was an advantage for games early in the season. But at the end of the season, teams did worse when they played at home. For example, home baseball teams won 60 percent of the first two games in the World Series, but lost 59 percent of the final games. Although playing at home is often an advantage, it may become a disadvantage when the pressure to win is greatest.

one who enters our space can vary greatly, depending on the way we define the situation.

Our attributions about the other person's motives—whether we interpret the actions as friendly, rude, or possibly even dangerous—are important. A study by Koneci and his associates (1975) involved having a confederate stand very close to a person who was waiting on a corner to cross the street. In this situation, people apparently interpreted the stranger's behavior as an unwelcome invasion, and crossed the street much faster than usual to escape from the stranger's presence.

Another experiment (Sundstrom & Sundstrom, 1977) investigated the effect of having a stranger ask permission to sit next to a person. Confederates approached a same-sex stranger sitting on a public bench. Before sitting down, half the confederates asked permission—they asked whether it was OK if they sat down on the bench. The other half of the time, the confederates sat down without asking permission. It appears that women and men interpreted this situation quite differently.

Women seem to have interpreted the request for permission as the beginning of an unwanted social contact. They left sooner when the confederate asked permission than when the confederate did not. In contrast, men seemed to have interpreted the request for permission as a sign of politeness. Men who were asked permission stayed on the bench longer than men who were not asked.

The point is that our reactions to others who enter our space depend on how we interpret the situation and the person's motives.

When physical space is limited and we are forced to share it with others, we may feel crowded. The misery of squeezing into a packed bus on a hot summer day is one example. The experience of crowding has been an important research topic in environmental psychology.

CROWDING

One hundred million people every year, one billion people every ten years—that is the rate at which the population of the world is increasing. As you can see in Figure 16–1, it took tens of thousands of years for the world population to reach half a billion. Two hundred years passed before the population doubled and reached 1 billion. But the next doubling to 2 billion took only eighty years, and the doubling to 4 billion only forty-five years. At the present rate of growth, the number of people on earth will double again and reach 8 billion in only thirty-five years.

Fortunately, we are beginning to see the first signs that the population explosion may be slowing down. The government of China, which has almost a quarter of the population of the world, is making a determined effort to reduce the birth rate. Other governments, including some in South America and Africa, which have traditionally had extremely high birth rates, are also beginning to encourage people to limit family size. Probably the most promising sign is that people all over the world now seem to desire smaller families more than they did in the past. Families in which women typically would have had seven or eight children twenty years ago now have only four or five. Nonetheless, there is

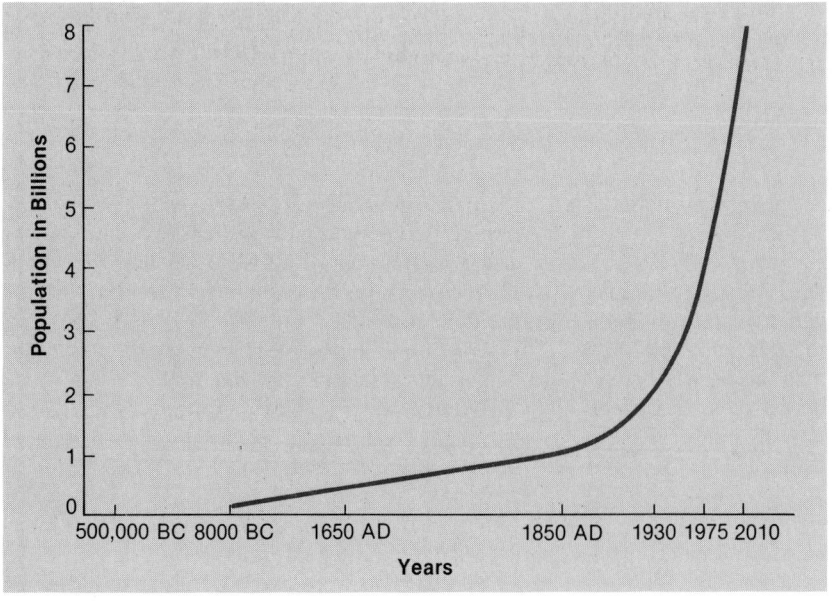

FIGURE 16–1 Growth of world population.

no question that, barring some catastrophe, the population of the world will continue to increase well into the twenty-first century and perhaps beyond that.

This population explosion has serious consequences for practically every aspect of our lives. It strains the economic resources of the world, exhausts natural resources, pushes up the cost of fuel, food, and every other necessary item, and leads to pollution. As populations increase, resources must be shared by more and more people. There is just so much good land, so much oil, so much wood for houses, and so on. In the United States, for example, the national parks are so crowded that it is practically "standing room only" in the more popular ones. They are still beautiful, but they are no longer a place to enjoy in solitude.

One of the consequences of the population explosion is that the concentration of people in and around cities is increasing steadily. Most of the populations of the United States, Canada, and the other industrialized countries have become increasingly concentrated in and around urban centers. Even though the central cities have actually lost population over the past 20 or 30 years, the larger metropolitan areas have grown enormously because suburbs have become so large. Therefore, the question of how crowding affects us is of more and more concern (Baum & Paulus, 1987). For a look at the effects of crowding in animals other than humans, see Box 16–2 on page 480.

Definitions

Researchers who study the effects of crowding find it essential to distinguish between objective measures of population density and subjective feelings of being crowded. **Social density** refers to the objective number of people in a given space. Density might be measured in terms of the number of people per square foot. **Crowding** refers to the subjective experience of feeling cramped and not having enough space. Density may or may not be unpleasant, but crowding is always unpleasant and negative, by definition. When we say we feel "crowded," we are usually complaining.

Moreover, this feeling of being crowded can occur regardless of the amount of space we actually have. It is more likely to be aroused when we are cramped, but we sometimes feel crowded even when we have plenty of space around us. There are times when three is a crowd no matter how much space is available. If you like to swim at deserted beaches, the presence of a few other people may make you feel that the beach is overcrowded, whereas you might not feel crowded at a party even if there were fifty other people in a fairly small room. Crowding refers to the psychological state of discomfort and stress associated with wanting more space than is available.

Theories of Human Crowding

When do people experience the presence of others as crowding? A number of explanations have been given that emphasize cognitive processes—the way people perceive, interpret, and react to their social environment.

SENSORY OVERLOAD   Stanley Milgram (1970) proposed that whenever people are exposed to too much stimulation, they experience sensory overload and can no longer deal with all the stimulation. Social density is one source of stimulation that can sometimes produce overstimulation and feelings of being crowded. Milgram believes that sensory overload is always unpleasant and interferes with a person's ability to function properly. People deal with overload by screening out some of the stimulation and attending only to what is most important.

Individual differences in reactions to social density may reflect differences in preferred level of stimulation. Some people may like high levels of stimulation—they like the radio blaring all the time, study in busy rooms, and watch television while carrying on a conversation or doing a crossword puzzle. Others like low levels of stimulation. When they work, it has to be quiet; if they watch television, they do not want any distractions. For high-stimulation people, high social density may be the right level of stimulation and so be perceived as pleasant and exciting. In contrast, for low-stimulation people, high social density may be disruptive and so be perceived as crowding.

DENSITY-INTENSITY   Jonathan Freedman (1975) proposed a different explanation, that high density in-

BOX 16-2

CROWDING IN ANIMALS

Biologists and ethologists have done a great deal of research on how nonhuman animals react to high-density experiences. Although animals do not complain of subjective feelings of crowding, they do sometimes display signs of distress when population density is high.

In many studies, small groups of animals, usually rats or mice, have been put in an enclosed space, provided with food, water, and other necessities, and otherwise left alone (Snyder, 1968; Southwick, 1955; Terman, 1974). Under these circumstances, a dramatic phenomenon occurs. The group behaves normally for a while, and the population grows. Then, at some point, the population peaks and either stops growing or declines sharply. Instead of continuing to produce more offspring that survive, the animals sometimes cease reproducing or produce offspring that die very soon. In other words, normal reproductive functions are severely disrupted merely because the animals are enclosed in a limited area.

In addition, there is substantial evidence that animals living under conditions of high density, or simply being enclosed, suffer physiological damage. Their adrenal glands become enlarged (Christian, 1975; To & Tamarin, 1977). Their reproductive organs decrease in size or in activity (Davis & Meyer, 1973; Snyder, 1968).

Finally, there is some evidence that social behavior is also affected. In a famous series of studies, Calhoun (1962) placed rats in cages specifically designed to produce very high densities in certain areas. The animals in these cages exhibited a wide range of abnormal behavior. They fought violently, mated indiscriminately, trampled nests and the young who were in them, and failed to build adequate nests in the first place. Calhoun called this phenomenon of antisocial and disruptive behavior a **behavioral sink.** Although other work (Terman, 1974) has failed to find these effects on aggressiveness, there is little doubt that under some circumstances high density does cause a breakdown in normal social behavior.

The rats in Calhoun's behavioral sink were simultaneously exposed to very small physical spaces and to many other animals. Subsequent research has tried to examine separately the effects of these two factors. Results suggest that the sheer amount of space available is not the crucial element. Animals alone in small cages do not show these effects. Rather, the harmful effects are linked to being enclosed *in groups.* Animals in groups suffer negative effects, regardless of the physical size of their cages (Terman, 1974). In many situations, social density seems to be more important than physical space (Freedman, 1979).

In any case, humans are not rats. We have much more complex social systems, higher levels of cognitive functioning, all sorts of rules and laws and customs with which to deal with the environment, and a flexible system of communication with other people. Generalizing from work on other animals to humans is always both difficult and questionable. This is particularly true when complicated social factors and interpersonal relations are involved. Thus, although this work on other animals is suggestive, we must look at research on humans to discover how they respond to crowding.

These spectators are tightly packed in a stadium. But high social density is not always unpleasant. At an exciting sports match, it may be exhilarating to be part of a crowd of loyal fans cheering the home team to victory.

Ken Karp

tensifies usual reactions to a social situation. Just as turning up the volume on a stereo magnifies our reaction to music, so increasing density magnifies our reaction to other people. If we dislike the music, we will dislike it more when it is loud than when it is soft; if we like it, we will like it more when it is loud. Similarly, whatever our response to other people who are near us, increasing density intensifies that response. If we like them, we will like them more; if we dislike them, we will dislike them more. If we are afraid, nervous, angry, aggressive, friendly, or anything else in low-density situations, we will feel more of it in high-density situations.

Some direct support for this view is provided by a series of studies by Freedman and his colleagues (Freedman, 1975). In this research, situations were deliberately made pleasant or unpleasant. Increasing density should intensify responses, making the pleasant situation more pleasant and the unpleasant more unpleasant. That is what these studies show.

This explanation of crowding seems to fit quite nicely into many of our everyday experiences. Sometimes the presence of many people is unpleasant and sometimes it is pleasant, but generally it does appear to intensify the social situation. Riding a bus is not always pleasant. If the bus is crowded, it can become really unpleasant. Or consider a party. If there are only 20 people in a huge room, the party tends to be flat, unexciting, dull. In fact, under these circumstances people will usually collect in the kitchen or at one end of the room. The same 20 people in a small room will make a much better party, assuming of course that they are pleasant people. If they are unpleasant, the small room will produce a less pleasant experience than the large room. In other words, basically positive situations usually become more positive when density is increased; negative ones become more negative.

LOSS OF CONTROL   High density can make people feel they have less control over their actions, and so create feelings of being crowded (Baron & Rodin, 1978). The idea is that with so many people in a small space, each individual is less able to control the situation, to move around freely, to avoid undesired contact.

This loss of control can have several negative features. Since people usually want as much control as possible over their lives, simply feeling powerless or helpless is, in itself, negative. Further, high density may prevent people from maintaining a desired degree of privacy (Altman, 1975). High density may also lead to problems in the coordination of activities. When three people share a small dorm room, they may literally bump into each other, make it difficult for individuals to study or sleep when they want, and so on. Under high-density conditions, people are more likely to interfere with each other's activities, leading to feelings of frustration and anger (Schopler & Stockdale, 1977).

Research has begun to provide evidence that a lack of perceived control produces the feeling of being crowded. For example, Sherrod (1974) had students work under high-density conditions and provided some with a button that, if pushed, would signal the experimenter to remove them from the situation. Although no one actually used the button, students who were given this sense of control over their environment were less negatively affected by the high density.

Closely related to control may be the ability to predict what a situation will be like. Kline and Harris (1979) told subjects to anticipate a high- or low-density room, and then confirmed or did not confirm their expectation. The results were that the objective number of people in the room by itself had no effect. Instead, subjects did better when their expectations were confirmed than when their expectations were not confirmed. In other words, there were no negative effects of being in a high-density room so long as it was anticipated.

ATTRIBUTIONS A final explanation for crowding emphasizes causal attributions. According to Stephen Worchel and his colleagues, we feel crowded when we experience physiological arousal and attribute it to the excessive closeness of other people (Worchel & Teddie, 1976). In this view, the subjective experience of crowding requires two elements—a physiological state of arousal and a cognitive label attributing the arousal to the presence of too many people.

According to the attribution perspective, if people in a high-density situation can be induced to attribute their arousal to something other than the people present, they should feel less crowded. This point was demonstrated by Worchel and Yohai (1979). In their study, subjects sat very close together in 5-person groups. Subjects who were falsely told that they were being exposed to stressful "inaudible noise" reported feeling significantly less crowded than did subjects in the identical situation who were given no alternate attribution for the source of their arousal.

In general, Worchel and his colleagues argue, when people can be distracted away from focusing on the people present in a situation, they should feel less crowded (Webb, et al., 1986). For example, when subjects in high-density conditions were exposed to arousing (humorous, sexual, or violent) television shows, they experienced significantly less crowding than people watching a non-arousing program under the same conditions. Indeed, people in cramped quarters rated the humorous movie as funnier and the violent movie as more violent, and tended to enjoy the arousing movies more.

It is likely that sensory overload, density-intensification, loss of control and causal attributions can all play a part in producing the experience of crowding. With these general principles in mind, we now turn to empirical studies of crowding.

Researchers have used many approaches to study the effects of human crowding. We will consider three types of research. One approach examines the impact of population density in cities on such social ills as crime and suicide. Another investigates the effects of crowded living conditions in families, schools, and prisons. A third approach has used laboratory studies to conduct controlled experiments on exposure to high-density situations.

Population Density in Cities

Several studies have concentrated on the effects of population density in the largest metropolitan areas of the United States. The measure of density is the number of people per square mile. In other words, this type of study is concerned simply with how many people live within the boundaries of the city relative to the size of the city. How does this measure of density affect the quality of life? For example, does density correlate with the amount of crime in a city? It has been found (Freedman, Heshka, & Levy, 1973) that there is a small but significant correlation between density and crime when only those two factors are considered (r = about .35).

Of course, density tends to be highly correlated with other factors such as income, and income in turn is also highly correlated with crime rate. It is therefore impossible to tell from the simple correlation whether density causes crime or whether some other factor, such as income, leads to both higher

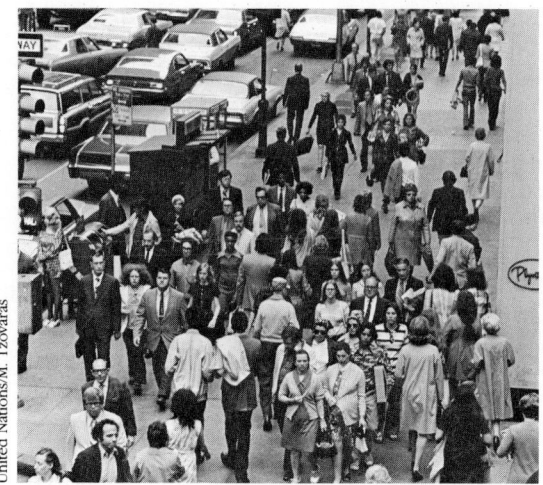

People in large cities are confronted daily with crowded sidewalks and congested streets. But the psychological consequences of urban crowding are not generally as bad as people think.

density and higher crime rates. This is the "third-variable" problem discussed in Chapter 2. When researchers have used statistical procedures to control for the effect of income and other social factors, the relationship between population density and crime disappears. Across the major U.S. metropolitan areas, once income is controlled, there seems to be little relationship between density and crime rates. For example, Los Angeles has one of the lowest densities but one of the highest crime rates in the United States. So density is not responsible for crime.

This result may seem surprising, given our stereotype of urban life as crowded and crime-ridden. Yet studies show that most people in major cities function well psychologically (Fischer, 1984). The incidence of mental disturbance is no higher in large cities than in smaller communities (Srole, 1972). People in cities are no more likely to commit suicide than people in smaller communities (Gibbs, 1971). In fact, urban dwellers say they are just as happy as people who live in suburbs, small towns, or rural areas (Shaver & Freedman, 1976). In a book on the urban experience, Fischer (1984) con-

cludes that the belief that urbanites are more stressed, disordered, alienated, or unhappy than ruralites is false. Population density in cities is not the generally harmful factor it is often thought to be.

Residential Density

Several studies have examined the effects of social density in households on well-being. Probably the most impressive research of this type was conducted by Mitchell (1971), who went into a vast number of homes in Hong Kong, one of the most crowded cities in the world. He measured the exact size of each family's living space, computed the density of people in the home, and took measures of anxiety, nervousness, and other symptoms of mental strain. In this study, a typical person shared a space of about 400 square feet with ten or more people. Yet despite these cramped conditions, Mitchell found no appreciable relationship between density and pathology. Similar results were found in a study in Toronto (Booth, 1976).

Another opportunity to study residential crowding is provided by young adults living in dormitory settings. Studies at Rutgers University (Karlin, Epstein, & Aiello, 1978) compared students living two to a room versus three to a room, all in rooms designed to hold two students. Tripled students reported significantly more stress and disappointment than doubled students. These effects were more severe for women students, who attempted to make their cramped quarters into a homelike environment, than for men, who spent more time away from their rooms. Tripled students of both sexes got significantly lower grades. However, in later years, when students were no longer living in high-density environments, their grades improved. In another study, students in triple rooms reported feeling less control over their environments (Baron, Mandel, Adams & Griffen, 1976), suggesting that this may be one reason for the negative effects of tripled dorms.

The effects of limited living quarters can be quite variable, however. One dramatic demonstration comes from a case study of Peace Corps volunteers (MacDonald & Oden, 1973). In this study, five married couples agreed voluntarily to share an unpartitioned 30- by 30-foot room during the twelve-week training program. The volunteers agreed to this experience in order to gain some insight into the hardships they might encounter once overseas. They were compared to other Peace Corps couples living in more spacious hotel rooms.

Despite their very dense living conditions, the couples living communally showed no adverse effects and saw their experience as a positive challenge. They apparently developed high morale and a spirit of cooperation. Clearly, those who volunteered for the communal living arrangement may have had different personalities than the nonvolunteers, and they knew that the situation was only temporary. The point of the example, however, is that very high density living can be a positive experience under certain circumstances.

Studies of prison inmates also provide evidence about the effects of residential density. Prisoners housed in single cells have been found to have lower blood pressure than inmates living in dormitory-type cells (D'Atri, 1975; McCain, Cox, & Paulus, 1976). Research based on archival data has also linked high-density living quarters in prison to higher death rates and to psychiatric problems (McCain et al., 1976).

In reviewing these mixed findings, Epstein (1981) proposed that the negative effects of residential density are least likely when residents have a cooperative attitude and some degree of perceived control. Families seem to suffer least from crowded homes, presumably because they have control over their homes and have established patterns of interacting that minimize the problems of high-density living. At the other extreme, prisoners, who have little control over their environment and may have little motivation to cooperate, show negative effects from high density living.

Laboratory Studies

To further clarify the complex effects of density, researchers have turned to carefully controlled laboratory experiments. Participants in these studies are typically exposed to very high density conditions for a short period of time. In some ways, this is quite like many real-world encounters with crowding that are also fairly short in duration. For example, a New Yorker may find herself in a crowded elevator or subway for a few minutes, on a crowded sidewalk while going to work, or in a packed department store. Experiments dealing with short-term crowding may be helpful in telling us how such crowding in the real world affects us.

The standard procedure for most of this experimental work is to put some people in a small room, the same number of people in a large room, and look for any differences on a wide variety of measures. The general pattern of results is clear: High density is not generally harmful to people. As we will see, this does not mean that high density is good for people, nor that it never has bad effects. What it means is that the effects are complicated. We will consider laboratory studies of the impact of density on task performance and social behavior, and then consider gender differences in reactions to crowding.

TASK PERFORMANCE   Quite a few studies have investigated task performance under crowded and uncrowded conditions. There are two reasons why this is an important issue. The first is a practical one: People often work under high-density conditions, and we would like to know how this affects performance. If it turned out that high density interfered with their work, presumably managers in factories, offices, and other workplaces would try to reduce density. The second reason for studying this is theoretical: It is well established that when people are under stress or are aroused for any reason, they tend to do less well on difficult and complex tasks, though they often perform better on easy, familiar tasks. If people perform less well on complex tasks when they are crowded, this would indicate that high density is stressful or arousing. Most of the research indicates that high density has little or no effect on task performance.

Freedman, Klevansky, and Ehrlich (1971) had hundreds of subjects of various ages and backgrounds work on many different tasks. Some subjects worked under very cramped conditions (as little as 3 to 4 square feet per person), whereas others had lots of space. There were no consistent differences of any kind. This finding has been repeated in many other experiments (Griffitt & Veitch, 1971; Stokols et al., 1973; Nogami, 1976). Further evidence that density does not necessarily impair task performance comes from studies of people working and living in such cramped environments as submarines, space ships, or air raid shelters. Not everyone who participates in such experiences enjoys them, but most people do just fine and perform quite competently (Smith & Haythorn, 1972).

Although research on task performance generally shows little negative impact from high density, there are some exceptions to this general pattern. A few studies (Paulus, 1980b) have found that density impairs task performance. Sometimes both sexes are negatively affected by high density (Evans, 1979), but sometimes only men perform less well under high density, whereas women perform slightly better (Paulus et al., 1976). The results of these studies are at odds with the majority of other research. Nevertheless, they suggest that for some people high density may impair performance. In addition, these studies raise the possibility that there may be important sex differences in response to density.

Finally, whenever a particular job requires a lot of room or moving around, and whenever the presence of other individuals in a small space directly interferes with doing the task, performance will suffer (Heller, Groff, & Solomon, 1977). McCallum and associates (1979) showed that when the resources available were inadequate for the number of people, performance suffered. Obviously, other people can get in the way if there is not enough space. You cannot play a good game of tennis if there are 40 people on the court; 9 people cannot play the same piano simultaneously (or at least they will not play it very well); and even reading a newspaper on a bus is difficult if you are so cramped that you cannot turn the pages. This is not a psychological effect in the usual sense of the word. Rather, it is a purely physical consequence of not having adequate space to perform a particular task.

SOCIAL BEHAVIOR   It seems that crowding might be more likely to affect social behavior than task perfor-

mance. After all, when people are in close proximity, their social relationships may change in response to the situation. Actually, research on this issue has found no consistent overall effects of density on social behavior. People in crowded conditions are not in general more aggressive, more friendly, more nervous, or less happy than people under less crowded conditions. Studies of adults (Freedman, 1975; Nogami, 1976) have found no consistent differences between high- and low-density conditions.

The findings regarding children's reactions to variations in density are somewhat less consistent. Several studies have observed children in playgrounds or school playrooms. Ginsberg and associates (1977) found that boys engaged in more fighting in smaller playgrounds, although the fights did not last as long as they did in larger areas. In contrast, a series of careful observations by Smith and Connelly (1972) indicated no effect of density on the amount of fighting. Rohe and Patterson (1974) suggest that as long as there are adequate facilities and toys, the amount of space makes little difference. This seems to have been supported by two studies (Loo & Smetana, 1978) that found little overall effect of density on aggressiveness, anger, happiness, or positive group interactions among preschoolers and 10-year-old boys.

Thus, with a few exceptions, this work generally indicates few overall effects of variations in density on social behavior or mood. But when less space is combined with reduced facilities, the effect may be negative. And we should remember that this often occurs in the real world. People who have less space in their homes, for example, typically have fewer facilities as well. Children who are provided a tiny playroom in a poorly equipped school are probably also given relatively few toys to play with. But the negative consequences then are due mainly to the poor facilities, not to the lack of space. On the other hand, to return to a point made earlier, some games cannot be played in too small a space. Basketball and running games require a large play area. In these instances, high density will interfere with the games and may accordingly reduce the fun.

ENVIRONMENTAL STRESS: NOISE

It's Monday morning and Charlie begins his day driving to work. As he pulls onto the already congested freeway, he closes the car windows to keep out the noise and pollution of the city. Later, driving through a particularly narrow and dangerous stretch of highway, he feels his muscles tensing and notices that he is gripping the steering wheel. The summer day has begun to heat up, and Charlie feels a trickle of perspiration forming on his back. The urban landscape of highways, factories, and dreary tenements does little to improve his mood. Charlie fondly remembers the weekend he just spent in the mountains, where the air was crisp and clean. The country sounds of birds and crickets were a welcome relief from the din of the city. The lovely mountains and woods had created an atmosphere of calm and relaxation.

The physical environment has strong effects on our feelings and social interactions. One important factor is the extent to which the physical environment is stressful (Evans & Cohen, 1987). Some environmental stressors, such as earthquakes or floods, are sudden and powerful; they dramatically alter people's lives. Also important, however, are the daily hassles created by environments that expose us to noise, heat, air pollution, and other irritants. Much research on stress in the physical environment has studied the effects of noise, and we will focus our discussion on that topic.

Unless you are in a specially constructed soundproof chamber, you are always exposed to noise. For those with normal hearing, sound is one of the most important means of knowing about and experiencing the world. A silent world is virtually impossible to imagine. However, psychologists are especially concerned about the effects of noise be-

The quiet serenity of the country is becoming a rare experience. In industrialized societies, most people live and work in cities where they are exposed to high levels of noise.

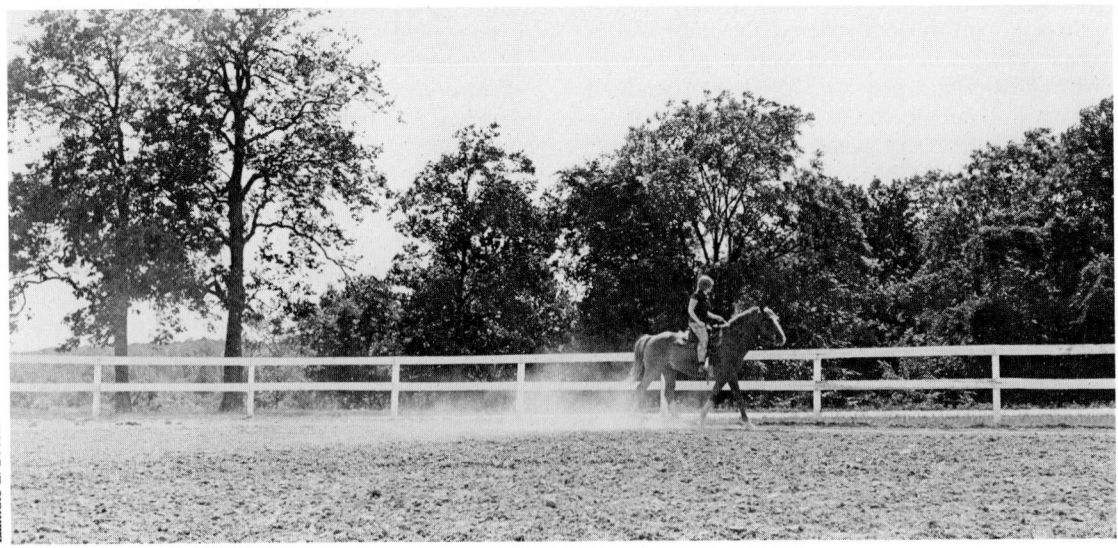

Laimute E. Druskis

cause so much of modern industrial life involves the production of noise, and because the amount of noise to which people are exposed in cities is often extremely high.

Not only do traffic, construction, machinery of all kinds, and powerful stereo equipment produce noise of great intensity, but millions of people in a relatively small area create high noise levels. In fact, one of the most striking aspects of cities is their constant high noise levels, as compared to suburbs and rural areas. According to the U.S. Bureau of the Census (1973), excessive noise is the most common neighborhood complaint of community residents. Just what effect does noise have on us?

Short-Term Noise

Sometimes we are exposed to short bursts of very loud noise—sounds of a dynamite blast from the construction site next door or the shrill barking of a neighbor's dog. Our initial reaction to a burst of very loud noise is strong. Everyone is familiar with one typical response—the so-called startle reflex. An unexpected loud noise causes us to jump, flex our stomach muscles, blink, and generally react physically. Even if we are expecting the noise, we respond physiologically with increased blood pressure, sweating, and other signs of arousal. In addition, loud noise interferes with our ability to perform tasks. We do less well on both simple and complex tasks. Clearly, loud noise is upsetting, causes physiological arousal, and prevents us from functioning at our usual level.

ADAPTATION However, these disruptive effects generally last only a short while. The most important finding from studies of short-term noise is that people adapt very quickly. It takes only a few minutes for physiological reactions to disappear and for performance to return to normal. After 10 minutes or less, people who are subjected to short bursts of extremely loud noise behave very much like people who hear moderate or low noise. This is true even for noise levels over 100 decibels, which is roughly equivalent to a big jet coming in low over your head or a huge truck rumbling by right next to you. As long as the noise is not so loud

that it actually produces pain or physical damage, people adapt to it very quickly (Glass & Singer, 1972).

You can see this effect in a study by Glass and Singer in which people were exposed to background noise (no noise condition) or to a meaningless jumble of noise at 108 decibels in short bursts for 23 minutes. As shown in Figure 16–2, the loud noise did cause physiological arousal, but the arousal lasted only a few minutes. Moreover, after 4 minutes, all subjects did equally well on a variety of tasks, including simple arithmetic, matching sets of numbers (deciding whether 68134 and 68243 are identical), scrambled words, and higher-level mathematics. Once they get used to the noise, people perform almost any task as well with loud noise as they do in quieter environments.

There are a few important exceptions to this finding, however. In particular, noise does seem to affect performance on some kinds of tasks, especially complex ones. Donald Broadbent (1957) and others have shown that certain kinds of monitoring tasks are more difficult to do with loud noise. For example, if someone is required to watch three dials to be sure none of them goes over a certain point, high levels of noise interfere with performance. Similarly, it is apparently harder to do two tasks at the same time in a noisy environment. In one study (Finkelman & Glass, 1970), subjects had

FIGURE 16–2 **Physiological response (GSR) to loud noise. After a strong initial response, subjects adapt quickly. (Adapted from Glass & Singer, 1972.)**

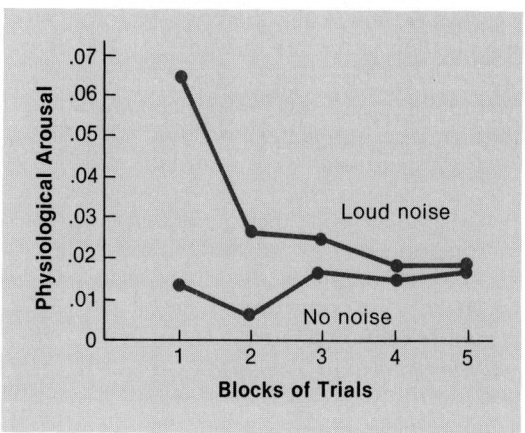

to repeat digits they heard over headphones while at the same time turning a steering wheel to track a moving line. Noise level did not affect the primary task, which was the tracking, but it made the subjects less accurate at repeating the digits. Presumably, noise is distracting and interferes with the performance of complex tasks that already strain our capacity to concentrate.

Most of the time we are only doing one thing at a time, so the effects of noise are probably quite limited. On the other hand, it is well to remember that some sensitive jobs do involve exactly the kinds of complex monitoring tasks that seem to be affected by loud noise. The pilot of a plane must watch many different dials while operating a variety of instruments; flight controllers have similar problems; and even the typical driver of a car has many things to attend to at once. (It is a little frightening to realize that these critical jobs, especially those of pilot and flight controller, are performed under conditions of considerable noise.) With this potentially important exception, short-term exposure to loud noise appears to have little detrimental effect.

THE IMPORTANCE OF PREDICTABILITY AND CONTROL However, this is not the whole story about short-term noise. We have seen throughout this book that our reactions to situations are influenced by our ability to predict what will happen and to control it. A series of experiments by Glass and Singer (1972) demonstrated that loud noise may have negative aftereffects if the noise is not under the control of the individual. In particular, if the noise is predictable (occurring every 60 seconds or only when there is a warning) or if the person can turn off the noise, no bad effects occur. But if the noise seems to be totally out of the control of the person, certain kinds of performance may suffer once the noise ceases.

The experiments were straightforward but ingenious. Subjects heard bursts of noise for a set period of time while they performed tasks. Then they performed other tasks with no noise. The crucial variation was that the circumstances under which the noise occurred gave the person a sense of control or did not. In one study, people heard short bursts of loud or soft noise. The major variation was that the noise bursts came either exactly 1 minute apart (and were therefore predictable) or at random intervals. Even though subjects heard just as much noise in the two conditions, the effects were entirely different.

During the noise section of the study, all groups performed equally well regardless of how loud the noise was or whether it was predictable. But afterward, as shown in Table 16–1, those who had heard the predictable noise performed better than those who had heard random noise. In fact, unpredictable soft noise caused more errors than predictable loud noise. This was true despite the fact that subjects reported finding the predictable and unpredictable noise equally annoying.

In other studies, subjects were given a feeling of control by telling them they could stop the noise whenever they wanted to by pressing a button or by signaling their partner, who would then stop it. Even though subjects never did actually stop the noise, this feeling of control was apparently enough to eliminate the negative effects. There was no decline in performance either during or after the noise.

A later study (Sherrod, Hage, Halpern & Moore, 1977) replicated and extended these results. Subjects were allowed to start the noise, stop it, both start or stop it, or allowed no control whatever. As in the earlier work, control reduced the negative effects of the noise. Moreover, the more control they had, the better the people performed. In this study, unlike any previous work, the presence of uncontrollable noise actually caused subjects to do less well on a proofreading task while the noise was present. In line with the earlier work, the main result was that those exposed to controllable noise performed better on problems *after* the noise ended.

TABLE 16–1

Aftereffects of Predictable and Unpredictable Noise on Proofreading

Condition	Number of Errors
No noise	26.4
Soft predictable	27.4
Soft unpredictable	36.7
Loud predictable	31.8
Loud unpredictable	40.1

Source: Adapted from Glass & Singer (1972).

The importance of control may help us understand the effects of noise in the real world. Most of the noise in a city is fairly constant or predictable. There is the continuous noise of cars and trucks on the streets, periodic noise of trains in some communities, and the general din caused by many people. On the other hand, some noise is both unpredictable and uncontrollable. Jackhammers, firecrackers, backfiring cars, planes, and sudden loud music from radios fill the air with noise at random intervals and are therefore probably much more annoying than the usual background noise. It seems likely that the absolute level of the noise is less important than this unpredictability. Indeed, it is unpredictable kinds of noises that most people complain about.

Long-Term Exposure to Noise

Some research suggests that long-term exposure to noise can have detrimental effects. A large apartment house in New York City is built over a highway, and because of the design of the building, the noise levels inside are quite high. Lower floors are almost always noisier than higher ones, and this situation provides an ideal natural experiment on the effects

of long-term noise. Cohen, Glass, and Singer (1973) measured reading achievement and ability to make auditory discriminations of children who had lived in the building for at least four years.

As you can see in Figure 16–3, those who lived on lower floors did worse on both measures. The louder the noise on their floor, the less well they read and the poorer their auditory discriminations. More recent studies (such as Cohen, Evans, Krantz, Stokols & Kelly, 1981) have also found that noisy environments can impair children's intellectual performance. Studies further suggest that although people are able to adapt to short-term noise, they may not adapt to long-term noise, such as that experienced by those who live near a busy airport (Cohen & Weinstein, 1981).

How Noise Affects Social Behavior

In recent years, researchers have begun to investigate the impact of noise on social behaviors (Cohen & Weinstein, 1981). One finding is that noise appears to reduce attention to social cues. In one study (Cohen & Lezak, 1977), students watched slides while learning lists of nonsense syllables in a noisy or a quiet room. The slides showed people

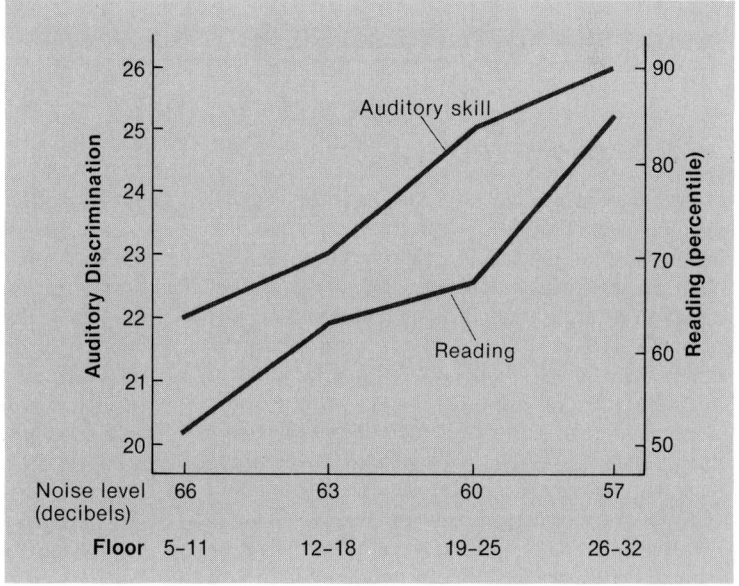

FIGURE 16–3 Noise level in apartment and children's reading and auditory skills. The lower the noise level, the better the children performed. (Adapted from Cohen, Glass, & Singer, 1973.)

in common daily activities and in dangerous situations. For example, one slide showed two men shaking hands in front of a house; another showed one man threatening another with a knife in front of a house. After seeing the slides, students were unexpectedly asked questions about them. Those exposed to noise remembered significantly fewer of the social situations than did those in the quiet condition.

Similarly, in a field study (Korte & Grant, 1980) pedestrians on noisy streets were less likely to notice unusual objects on the sidewalk (such as a woman holding a large teddy bear) than were pedestrians on a quiet street. In other words, loud noise may cause people to narrow the focus of their attention and so miss social cues in the environment.

In the chapter on prosocial behavior, we reviewed several studies showing that people are less helpful in noisy situations than in quiet ones. There is also some evidence that noise can increase aggressiveness (Geen & O'Neal, 1969). In one study (Donnerstein & Wilson, 1976), students were either angered or treated in a neutral manner, and then were given an opportunity to give electric "shocks" to another person as part of a learning experiment.

Angered students in a noisy room gave significantly more shocks than did nonangered students or angered students in a quiet room.

A second experiment (Donnerstein & Wilson, 1976) demonstrated that perceived control can alter the noise-agression link. In this study, students first worked on math problems in a high-noise or no-noise condition. Later, students were able to give electric "shocks" to another person as part of a learning experiment. Some students had been angered by a confederate of the researcher; some had not. Students who had been exposed to loud noise and angered gave more shocks than those who had not been angered or who had not been exposed to the noise. However, angered students who had been able to control the loud noise (to turn it off if they wanted to) were no more aggressive than those not exposed to the noise, even when they did not actually use their control.

These and other studies suggest that noise can sometimes increase aggressive behavior, but that this may only occur when people perceive no control over the noise and when they have an independent reason to be angry. In other words, noise may not be a direct cause of aggression, but rather may intensify preexisting aggressive tendencies.

ARCHITECTURAL DESIGN

One of the most fascinating questions facing environmental psychologists is how the design of buildings, roads, and shopping centers affects us. Certainly the structures we produce, the so-called **built environment,** are an extremely important part of our world. And some of them seem to "work" better than others. Some houses are pleasant to be in and function smoothly, others are not. Some stores minimize congestion and generally make the shopping experience relatively positive; others have the reverse effect. And the same is true about virtually every other structure we build.

Architects are deeply concerned with making their designs work well, but by and large they have

to rely entirely on their own intuition and experience. Until very recently there was no systematic research on how design affects people, and even now psychologists and sociologists are only beginning to study the problem seriously. But at least they are beginning to understand some of the ways in which design influences people, and perhaps soon they will be able to give some guidance to architects based on solid research. For the moment, most of the research done by psychologists has been on the structure of dormitories (obviously of interest to many people at universities) and high-rise versus low-rise housing.

Dormitory Design

College dormitories are generally built according to two different designs. One type has single or double rooms located along a long corridor, with social areas and bathrooms shared by all corridor residents. A second type has suites of rooms consisting of several bedrooms located around a common living room, usually with the residents of just these bedrooms sharing bathroom facilities. The amount of space available to each resident is approximately the same for both designs. Yet the two designs seem to have different effects on the residents.

A series of studies (Baum & Valins, 1977; Baum et al., 1978) compared corridor and suite arrangements. The research indicates that students who live in suite-type dormitories are more sociable and friendlier. At first glance, this seems obvious. Clearly, if you share a living room with, say, nine other people (five bedrooms with two people each), you will get to know these nine other students. In a sense, you have a "family" living situation. If you share a room with only one person, it takes greater effort to get to know other people on the floor.

As we noted in Chapter 8, proximity is one of the major factors in liking and friendship. The suite arrangement puts more people in close proximity and therefore should lead to more friendships. Thus far, this follows directly from our knowledge of the effects of proximity and certainly would be expected. The striking aspect of Baum's and Valins's work is that these sociability differences seem to carry over into the world outside the dormitory. When the students are observed in the psychology laboratory, the suite residents are friendlier than the corridor residents. For example, in one study a student arrived at the laboratory and was shown into a room in which another student (actually a confederate) was sitting. There were several chairs in the room, and the question was how close to the other student the subject would sit. Suite residents tended to sit closer than corridor residents, and to initiate more conversations.

One problem with this research is that students are not always randomly assigned to rooms. Perhaps more sociable people request assignment to suites. Another problem is that suites are sometimes newer

than corridor dorms, and the two types of housing are sometimes located on different parts of the campus. To overcome these problems, Baum and Davis (1980) conducted an intervention experiment. They obtained permission to assign first-year women students randomly to living conditions. To further control the environment, the researchers devised the architectural intervention shown in Figure 16–4 (p. 494).

Baum and Davis selected two identical long-corridor floors in the same building, each housing about 40 students. On the intervention floors, they converted several bedrooms in the middle of the corridor into lounges and installed doors to divide the corridor into two smaller units, each housing about 20 students. As a further comparison, they studied a "short" corridor in another building that also housed about 20 students. In all settings, students had about the same amount of physical space, and the density was relatively high. The researchers gave questionnaires to dorm residents at the beginning of the school year and at several times during the year. They made systematic observations of social interactions in the dorm and of behavior in a laboratory situation.

The results of this experiment were very consistent with earlier findings. After living in the dorm for several weeks, residents on the short corridors reported feeling less crowded, having fewer problems regulating social contacts in the dorm, and having a greater sense of control over life in the dorm than did students on the long corridor. Short-corridor residents also reported that they were more successful in forming friends in the dorm, and they were observed to have more social interactions in lounges and corridors. In the laboratory, students who had been randomly assigned to short corridors showed greater friendliness toward a research confederate and expected to have more control over the experiment than did long-corridor residents. These results provide strong evidence that an architectural design feature—in this case the size of the residential living group—can significantly affect feelings and social interactions.

Two main factors appear to be at work in these dormitory settings. First, smaller residential units (suites and short corridors) are more conducive to group formation and friendship than are larger units. Since it is usually more pleasant to interact with friends than with strangers, dorm designs that encourage friendships are experienced as more positive. Second, smaller residential units increase students' sense of personal control over the environment. In long-corridor dorms, students are constantly being required to meet and interact with many others on the floor. When they walk to the bathroom or common lounge areas, they necessarily share the corridor and facilities with many others, most of whom are not friends and with whom they might prefer not to interact.

Thus, they are overloaded with social contacts and have difficulty avoiding them. In contrast, those who live in suites or short corridors have a self-contained living unit they share only with people they get to know quite well. They therefore have much more control over their social interactions, which presumably increases satisfaction with their term in the control room and half in the "friendly" room. Students were not told they were being studied; the switch in rooms was explained as occurring because the original room was needed for videotaping.

The most striking finding from this study is that students performed significantly better on regular course exams when they were in the friendly rather than the sterile classroom. It thus appears that the physical environment can affect the amount of learning that occurs, at least as measured by scores on tests. In addition, students were asked to evaluate their instructor halfway through the term and again at the end of the term. The instructors were rated significantly more positively during the time the class met in the attractive classroom. In the experimental room instructors were evaluated as more knowledgeable, more interesting, and better organized than they were in the control room. So our evaluations of other people are at least partly influenced by the physical setting in which we interact with them.

residence and their general sense of control over their lives.

High-Rise and Low-Rise Housing

Although students are naturally quite concerned about dormitory design, a much more serious problem for our society is how high-rise housing affects people. Since the 1950s, vast numbers of high-rise buildings have been constructed for our rapidly expanding population. Some of these buildings are huge—thirty or forty stories, with hundreds or even thousands of individual apartments. Others are smaller. But all contrast sharply with the private homes or four- or five-story apartment houses characteristic of previous housing. It has become a matter of great social importance to determine whether

BR = Bedroom
 B = Bathroom
 L = Lounge

Long-corridor floor

Intervention floor

Short-corridor floor

FIGURE 16–4 Floor plans of the dormitory floors. The intervention floor was originally identical to the long-corridor floor but was remodeled to form two short corridors separated by doors and lounges. The short-corridor floor was in another building. (Adapted from Baum & Davis, 1980, p. 475.)

high-rise housing of this sort is a good environment in which to live.

THE FAILURES: PRUITT IGOE Some high-rise buildings have been failures. They have gotten run down, the halls have been defaced, the apartments have been allowed to deteriorate, crime and vandalism have made the buildings unsafe, and people have moved out whenever they were able. The most dramatic example of this kind of failure is the Pruitt Igoe project built in the 1950s in St. Louis. Designed by a leading architect, the complex had 33 high-rise buildings with 2,800 modern apartments. Built with public funds for low- and middle-income families, this "showcase" project became a disaster.

Located in the midst of an urban slum, the project never attracted middle-income families who could afford to live in better neighborhoods, and so rental revenues were less than anticipated. Teenage gangs invaded the halls and elevators to rob and terrorize residents. Walls were covered with graffiti, and physical conditions deteriorated as needed maintenance and repairs were not made. Tenants who could find other housing moved out. Ultimately, conditions deteriorated to such a point that the buildings were condemned and torn down. This multimillion-dollar housing project was a total loss.

PSYCHOLOGICAL EFFECTS: SOME IMPORTANT FACTORS On the one hand, we know that most high-rise buildings, both public and private, have been successful at least to the extent that people continue to live in them and function reasonably well. In cities such as Toronto, San Francisco, and Boston, high-rise apartments and condominiums in fashionable neighborhoods are considered very desirable. The central question addressed by environmental psychologists is whether high-rise and low-rise buildings have different psychological effects on residents, and in particular, whether high-rise housing is typically harmful.

In general, research does not find major differences between the health or general well-being of those who live in high-rise versus low-rise housing. A few studies (Holahan & Wilcox, 1978; McCarthy & Saegert, 1978) have found that high-rise residents are less happy with their social relations, more concerned about safety, and feel more crowded. But other studies (Friedman, 1979; Michelson, 1977) have found the opposite: High-rise residents reported feeling more content with their buildings and more satisfied with their social relations. Overall, few consistent differences have been found.

In understanding these results, it is important to keep in mind that the experience of high-rise living can vary considerably: Living in the penthouse of a beautiful high-security apartment building is quite different from living at the top of a poorly maintained public housing project in a rundown area. Further, it is likely that high-rise housing (or for that matter any kind of housing) may not be suitable for everyone. Although none of the research produced consistent differences between high- and low-rise housing, there is no question that some people prefer one or the other.

Parents with young children often complain that high-rise housing presents great difficulties in supervising the children (Michelson, 1970). Someone who lives on the twentieth floor cannot watch a child in the playground on the street floor. Many parents are reluctant to let their young children ride elevators alone, so that even if they can play on the street, it is inconvenient to get them there. Perhaps because of this, residents of high-rise housing are often less satisfied with their housing than are people who live in their own homes. Moreover, high-rise residents do not value the friendliness of their neighborhood as much (Wellman & Whitaker, 1974). None of these differences is large or related to any noticeable differences in health or general satisfaction, but the differences do exist. In other words, people complain more about high-

rise housing, even though research has not shown any actual negative effects.

As with the dormitory design studies, research on high-rise housing faces enormous difficulty in equating the residents of the various kinds of buildings. People are not randomly assigned to housing in our society, so that residents of different buildings almost always differ in potentially important ways. In cities like New York, which has many high-rise apartments, upper-, middle-, and working-class families all live in high-rise buildings. Many people who can afford to live anywhere choose to live in a high-rise building in the middle of New York City. In other words, high-rise buildings are not only for low-income families. But middle- and upper-class families do generally have a choice, whereas poorer families often are forced to live in a high-rise because it is the only housing available.

This lack of choice may itself cause problems, and it should therefore probably be a matter of public policy to provide choice for all people. That is, if we continue to build high-rise apartments for low-income people, we should also provide the alternative of low-rise buildings for these same people. Although high-rise buildings may not have any negative effects, being forced to live in one (or to live anywhere with no choice) may be psychologically harmful.

LIFE IN THE CITY

The United States and Canada are largely urban societies, with more than 70 percent of the population living in or around cities. So it becomes important to ask how living in cities differs from living elsewhere. This question is especially relevant today. In addition to financial problems, our cities are beset by high crime rates, rundown schools, heavy welfare rolls, and high unemployment. In recent years, public opinion about cities has become increasingly negative. In a 1978 Gallup poll

asking Americans whether they would prefer to live in a city, a suburb, a small town or on a farm, only 13 percent chose the city. Of those who actually lived in cities, only 21 percent said they preferred city living.

City dwellers are more likely than others to criticize their community, and to complain about schools, housing, taxes, and lack of safety (Fischer, 1984). On the other hand, people continue to move to metropolitan areas, suggesting that cities must also hold positive attractions. In fact, as we will see, research indicates that city life does not have negative psychological effects on people. The city may not be to everyone's liking, but it is not inherently harmful to mental health or personal relationships.

PHYSICAL AND SOCIAL ENVIRONMENT   The experience of living in cities is affected by both the physical and the social environment (Fischer, 1984). Physically, big cities are typically noisier, dirtier, and more polluted than small towns. Urban population density often necessitates high-rise apartments rather than single-family homes. In the city, trees and grass give way to concrete and asphalt. But although such factors as noise and high-rise buildings may be unpleasant, they do not necessarily have negative consequences. Further, cities offer many advantages that may compensate for the difficulties of urban life. It is in cities that we find major art museums, theaters, and concert halls; the latest medical technology; financial and political centers; specialized stores and services.

The social context of city living also differs from that of towns and rural areas. High social density is the hallmark of the city, and urbanites are more often exposed to crowds. Cities also have people from many ethnic, racial, and religious backgrounds. The social composition of cities differs from that of small towns. Cities tend to attract people who are younger, less likely to be married, have fewer children, and are higher in socioeconomic status. New immigrants are also likely to gravitate to urban centers. Do these differences in the physical and social environment of cities harm city dwellers?

PHYSICAL AND MENTAL HEALTH   In terms of physical and mental health, living in a town versus living in a city is not an important factor (Fischer, 1984). Whatever advantages people in small communities may have in terms of lower stress and a more healthful environment are apparently offset by the urbanite's greater access to health care services. Rates of mental disturbance and psychosis are about the same for those who live in cities, small towns, and even rural communities (Srole, 1972). Nor do city

people feel any more anxious or unhappy than other people.

In a survey of a large number of Americans (Shaver & Freedman, 1976), those who lived in cities said that they were just as happy and calm as those who lived in small towns or rural areas. These findings are all the more striking since city dwellers do report less satisfaction with their living environment than those who live outside of cities. Apparently dissatisfaction with facets of city living does not affect people's personal feelings of happiness and overall life satisfaction.

A study (Franck, 1980) of people who had recently moved to New York City or to a small town in upstate New York sheds light on this finding. The newcomers in this research were all beginning graduate students who were interviewed during the first year in their new environment. Newcomers to New York City were more likely than those in the small town to report that the move increased their fears about crime and safety, and made them more distrustful of other people. City residents were more likely to report being stressed by exposure to panhandlers, drunks, addicts, and "crazies."

However, the big city people also reported many compensating positive features of the urban experience. They came to enjoy the variety of people they saw in the city and felt that they had become more broadminded. In other words, city life has not only unique problems, but unique pleasures as well.

SOCIAL RELATIONS   It has been suggested that one of the most pernicious effects of urban life may be to weaken social relationships. Sociologist George Simmel (1903) thought that city residents would be so overloaded by superficial contacts that they would have fewer intimate friends than those who live in smaller communities. However, despite the common belief that life in the big city leads to alienation and social isolation, empirical research seriously challenges this view.

In a recent survey study, Claude Fischer (1982) obtained detailed information about the social relations of more than 1,000 people living in large cities, suburbs, small towns, and semi-rural areas in northern California. Overall, no differences were found between city dwellers and others in the number of their social ties or the quality of their social relations. For example, city dwellers were as likely as townspeople to report having someone they could talk to about personal matters; the overall level of social support available to an individual was not related to community size.

Fischer did find, however, that people in cities differed somewhat in the types of relationships they had. Urbanites reported fewer ties to relatives, neighbors, or church groups, and more ties to friends, co-workers, and others with similar interests or hobbies. Fischer explains this pattern largely in terms of self-selection. For instance, city dwellers are more likely to be young, unmarried, or foreign-born—all factors that would reduce relations with relatives, and increase ties to friends and associates. The important point is that those who live in big cities report just as much "social connectedness" as those who live in smaller communities.

The newcomer study adds further to this portrait of city life. Franck (1980) found that newcomers to New York City and to a smaller town were equally successful in making friends, but it took the city dwellers somewhat longer to do so. Shortly after arriving, city dwellers reported having fewer friends than those in the small town, but several months later this difference had disappeared. City dwellers said they found it harder to make friends, but ultimately they had just as many friends as people in the smaller community.

The one aspect of social relations that is affected by community size is interaction with strangers (Korte, 1980). We have already seen that city dwellers are more fearful of crime, more concerned about their personal safety, and more distrustful of others. Perhaps not surprisingly, people in cities are less likely to help a stranger in distress than are people in smaller communities (see Chapter 11). Research (Korte, 1980) has found that in urban environments people are usually less likely to help someone who dials a wrong telephone number, to return a "lost" letter, to do small favors, to help a lost child, or to let a stranger use a phone.

DIVERSITY OF LIFE STYLE   Although city dwellers are less helpful to strangers, they are also more accepting of others whose life styles differ from their own. The populations of small towns tend to be more homogeneous than those of cities with respect to race, religion, ethnic background, political views, and just about anything else you can think of. People who do not fit comfortably in a small town often seek like-minded companions in the big city. Cities tend to attract people who are "different" from the average, and to treat these groups better. It is not surprising, for example, that the largest and most visible homosexual communities are found in major metropolitan areas. It is not that cities produce alternate life styles, but rather that city dwellers are more accepting of individual differences.

In fact, one study (Hansson & Slade, 1977) found that city people were actually more helpful toward an extremist group, in this case the Communist Party, than were people in small towns. In this study, the experimenters dropped letters that were addressed to an individual, to someone who was apparently performing at the "Pink Panther Lounge," or to the Communist Party headquarters. The researchers counted how many of each "lost" letter were returned. The townspeople returned somewhat more letters to the individual and the Pink Panther Lounge, but many fewer to the Communist Party. The authors concluded that people in small towns may be somewhat more helpful as long as the person in need belongs to an acceptable category; the city people were much more helpful toward nonconformists.

By this point, it should be clear that reactions to the city depend on the particular individual. Just as some people like high levels of stimulation and others do not, so some people are city lovers and some are not. Individuals have optimal levels of stimulation, which may actually change as they live in one type of environment or another (Geller, 1980). If you like a high level of stimulation, you may enjoy cities, find them exciting and invigorating, and dislike small towns as dull and uninteresting. The key issue is the match between the person's characteristics and the community. Indeed, research (Shaver & Freedman, 1976) indicates that people who do not like their community (whatever it is) tend to be less happy and healthy. Although the size of the community does not affect happiness, an individual's satisfaction with the community does.

KEY TERMS IN CHAPTER 11

behavioral sink

built environment

crowding

environmental psychology

personal space

proxemics

social density

territorial markers

territory

SUMMARY

1. Environmental psychology considers how the physical environment affects people's behavior and well-being. The field has concentrated on such topics as how humans use space, crowding, noise, the design of buildings, and life in the city.

2. Proxemics is a general term for the study of how people use space. Personal space refers to the physical space immediately around a person that the person treats as an extension of the self. The distance we prefer to stand from other people depends on our ethnic background, our gender, and our relation to the people. Hall has distinguished four basic zones for interpersonal interaction: intimate, personal, social, and public distance.

3. A territory is an area controlled by a person or group. Altman has distinguished primary, secondary, and public territories. People use various markers to identify and lay claim to their territory. Our reaction to someone who enters our territory depends on how we interpret the act—as friendly, rude, hostile, and so on.

4. Crowding is the subjective experience of feeling cramped and not having enough space. In contrast, social density refers to the objective number of people in a given area. According to the sensory overload theory of crowding, high social density creates an unpleasantly high level of stimulation.

According to the density-intensity theory, high social density intensifies usual reactions to a social situation, making bad situations worse and good ones better. A third view is that high density may cause people to experience a distressing loss of personal control. A final perspective is that we feel crowded when we attribute our physiological arousal to the presence of too many people.

5. Research shows that crowding does not necessarily have harmful consequences. High population density in cities is not a cause of crime or mental illness. In laboratory studies, even very high density conditions do not usually impair task performance or lead to antisocial behavior. In some situations, however, high density can be harmful. For example, students living in tripled dorm rooms and prisoners sharing cramped cells may show signs of distress. High density is probably most harmful when it interferes with accomplishing specific goals and when it is associated with a perceived loss of control.

6. Noise affects us less than we might think. As long as noise is not so loud that it causes physical damage, people adapt to short exposure to loud noise and perform most tasks at their normal level. Only complex tasks seem to be impaired by short-term loud noise. Prolonged exposure to loud noise can have negative effects on hearing and intellectual performance.

7. Architectural design can influence people's behavior. College students who live in suite-type dormitories and in small living units are more sociable and friendlier than those who live on long corridors. Smaller residential units may make it easier to form friendships and may increase a sense of personal control. However, high-rise housing is not necessarily worse than low-rise housing.

8. Urban living is not generally less healthy than living in other kinds of communities. People often find that the difficulties of city life are offset by the advantages of being in a cultural and business center. The effect of community size depends on the preferences and characteristics of the individual.

SUGGESTED READINGS

COHEN, S., EVANS, G. W., STOKOLS, D., & KRANTZ, D. S. (1986). *Behavior, health and environmental stress*. New York: Plenum. Considers the impact of environmental stress on human behavior and well-being.

FISCHER, C. S. (1984). *The urban experience*, 2nd ed. New York: Harcourt Brace Jovanovich. A readable textbook that reviews research and theories about life in cities.

FISHER, J. D., BELL, P. A., & BAUM, A. (Eds.). (1984). *Environmental psychology*, 2nd ed. New York: Holt, Rinehart & Winston. A comprehensive survey of the field of environmental psychology.

JONES, D. M., & CHAPMAN, A. J. (Eds.). (1984). *Noise and society*. New York: Wiley. A detailed look at the effects of noise.

SOMMER, R. (1969). *Personal space: The behavioral basis for design*. Englewood Cliffs, NJ: Prentice-Hall. A classic discussion of the topic.

STOKOLS, D., & ALTMAN, I. (Eds.). (1987). *Handbook of environmental psychology*. New York: Wiley. A very recent collection of chapters by leading experts provides a professional-level overview of research and theory in the field.

17 SOCIAL PSYCHOLOGY AND HEALTH

ost of us think about our health in physical terms. Either we are sick or we are healthy, and we know which state we are in on the basis of the cues we get from our body. However, as the following anecdotes suggest, health is a psychological issue as well as a physical one.

Bob, a 22-year-old member of the tennis team, has been told to stop smoking because it is sapping his energy during matches. He wants to stop, but so far, he has been unable to do so.

Lisa broke up with her boyfriend last week, and she faces a major test in her chemistry course next week. She has just come down with the flu.

Ellen recently went to see a physician about her headaches. The doctor was cold, aloof, and seemed to dismiss her complaints as trivial. She has decided not to follow the doctor's advice, but instead to go to a relaxation training course to see if it can help her.

Mark, who is currently 19, has suffered from diabetes since he was 12 years old. Although he knows he should inject himself with insulin twice a day, he sometimes "forgets" and has ended up in the hospital as an emergency case four times in the last six months.

The realization that health is a psychological as well as physical issue has given rise to an exciting new field, health psychology. The psychological study of health considers four main areas:

1. Promoting and maintaining health
2. Preventing and treating illness
3. Identifying the causes and correlates of health, illness, or other dysfunctions
4. Improving the health care system and the formation of health policy. (Matarazzo, 1980)

An important lesson of health psychology is that health is not a purely physical matter, but rather a *biopsychosocial state*. According to the **biopsychosocial model**, a person's state of health is a complex interaction among several factors: biological factors such as a genetic predisposition to a particular disease or exposure to a flu virus; psychological factors such as the experience of stress; and social factors such as the amount of social support one receives from one's friends and family. Once we recognize that psychological and social factors as well as biological ones are involved in health and illness, it is clear that good health is something that everyone achieves by engaging in a healthy lifestyle, rather than something merely to be taken for granted.

The field of health psychology draws on many sources: clinical psychology, developmental psychology, physiological psychology, learning and behavior, as well as social psychology. In this chapter, we will examine the social-psychological processes that affect how we stay healthy and how we behave when we are ill. First, we consider health behaviors—such actions as using seatbelts, eating an adequate diet, not smoking, and drinking only in moderation. Health behaviors are important because they are directly responsible for the major health problems in our society. Next, we examine the impact of stress on the development of illness, and the growing evidence that people who experience a high degree of stress in their lives are more vulnerable to diseases of all kinds. In the third section, we consider how people recognize when they are ill, including how they determine that particular physical sensations are illness symptoms and how they decide that those symptoms require treatment. We will also discuss problems that people often or sometimes have communicating with physicians and other health caregivers, and how these problems can influence a patient's illness-related behaviors and recovery. Finally, we will look at social-psychological processes involved in adjustment to chronic diseases. These diseases—such as heart disease, cancer, and diabetes—now account for the major causes of death in our country, yet people suffering from these illnesses often live 20 years or longer. Consequently, psychological and social adjustment to the altered lifestyles such diseases create is an issue of major importance.

HEALTH BEHAVIORS

At one time, our major health problems involved infectious diseases such as influenza, pneumonia, and tuberculosis. Now, however, these problems have been largely brought under control due to improvements in public health (such as sewage control) and improved medical care (such as the availability of immunizations). Currently, the major health problems faced by citizens of industrialized nations are "preventable" disorders. These include such chronic diseases as heart disease, cancer, and diabetes, as well as lifestyle-related problems such as drug and alcohol abuse and traffic accidents (Matarazzo, 1982). These problems are called preventable because they result at least in part from health behaviors which people can control. For example, annual cancer deaths in the United States could be reduced by 25 percent to 30 percent if everyone stopped smoking (American Cancer Society, 1982). Deaths due to heart disease would decline substantially if people lowered the cholesterol in their diet, stopped smoking, and reacted more effectively to stress (American Heart Association, 1984). Deaths due to vehicular accidents could be reduced by 50 percent if drinking-and-driving were eliminated (DHHS, 1981). An examination of the nation's health goals for 1990 (see Table 17–1), developed by the Department of Health and Human Services, clearly shows that the majority of these goals are related to lifestyle factors. If most of us practiced good health behaviors, our current national health problems would decline substantially and average life expectancy would increase.

What Is a Health Behavior?

Health behaviors are actions undertaken by people who are healthy to enhance or maintain their good health. The importance of basic health habits was illustrated in a classic study conducted by Belloc and Breslow (1972). These scientists began by defin-

ing seven health habits: sleeping 7 to 8 hours a night, not smoking, eating breakfast each day, having no more than one or two alcoholic drinks each day, getting regular exercise, not eating between meals, and being no more than 10 percent overweight. They then interviewed 6,000 residents of

TABLE 17–1

Fifteen Specific Ways to Improve Health for Americans by the Year 1990

In the 1970s the U.S. Department of Health and Human Services, under Patricia Harris, developed a set of goals to improve the health of the American populace. These goals served as targets for intervening in local health services. The important point to note in this list is how many of them involve lifestyle changes and behavior modification.

A. *Preventive Health Services*
  1. Teaching people how to control high blood pressure
  2. Implementing programs of effective family planning
  3. Establishing programs to improve health care for pregnant women and infants
  4. Establishing effective immunization programs for children and at-risk adults
  5. Educating adolescents and adults regarding the control of sexually transmitted diseases

B. *Health Protection*
  6. Managing toxic chemicals and wastes
  7. Developing and implementing effective occupational safety and health standards
  8. Developing procedures to reduce accidents (especially vehicular accidents) and injuries
  9. Fluoridating water and improving preventive dental health care
  10. Surveillance and control of infectious diseases

C. *Health Promotion*
  11. Reducing smoking
  12. Reducing the misuse of alcohol and drugs
  13. Developing programs for effective nutrition
  14. Improving physical fitness and increasing exercise
  15. Developing effective techniques for the control of stress and violent behavior

Source: Based on Matarazzo (1983) and Harris (1980).

Poor health habits such as smoking are responsible for the major causes of death in this country. Unfortunately, they often begin early in life before people realize the damage their actions will produce.

as much as we should. Some of the worst offenders in terms of health behaviors are college students (e.g., Leventhal & Cleary, 1980). Why is this the case? Recall the disorders we identified earlier as the major health problems facing the nation, including heart disease, diabetes, and cancer. Most of these disorders usually strike older people and are uncommon among college students. Therefore, these diseases often seem very remote to a student. It may seem almost impossible that the health habits developed in adolescence and young adulthood could possibly influence health so many years away. Yet this is clearly the case.

Many chronic diseases develop slowly, taking as long as 20 or 30 years for the damage to be done. Accordingly, the health habits a college student practices now have a direct effect on whether or not that person develops a chronic illness. Moreover, health behaviors often become habits. If you have become used to skipping breakfast every day, it may be difficult when you get older to remember that you should eat breakfast. Or if you begin smoking as an adolescent, you may find yourself with a stubborn habit that is very difficult to break as an adult. The health habits of teenagers and young adults are significant, then, for two reasons: first, they lay the groundwork for diseases that may occur later in life; second, patterns established in youth can become habits that are difficult to modify years later.

Health Attitudes and Health Behaviors

Since health behaviors are so essential to good health, it is important to understand what leads people to practice good health behaviors. Social psychologists have actively explored the determinants of effective health behaviors and have pursued several different approaches. Most of these approaches have been based on attitude theories like those discussed in Chapter 6. These theories make the assumption that if people can be persuaded that their current habits are risky, they will be motivated to change those habits.

FEAR APPEALS One of the earliest attitude approaches to changing health behaviors relied on increasing people's fear, a topic we discussed in

Alameda County, California, and asked them to indicate which of these behaviors they regularly practiced. The residents were also asked to indicate how many illnesses they had had, which illnesses they had had, how much energy they had, and how disabled they had been (for example, how many days of work they had missed) over the previous 6 to 12 months. The results of this study indicated that the more health behaviors people practiced, the fewer illnesses of all kinds they reported having, and the more energy they said they had.

Unfortunately, few people follow all these good health behaviors. Although most of us practice some health behaviors such as not smoking or keeping our weight down, most of us violate at least a few others such as not getting enough sleep, having too much to drink on occasion, and not exercising

Chapter 6. Approaches to health-behavior modification that rely on fear appeals hypothesize that if people become afraid that a particular health habit is hurting their health, they will change their behavior so as to reduce their fear. For example, in a classic study we examined earlier, Janis and Feshbach (1953) exposed three groups of college student subjects to messages designed to create a low, medium, or high level of fear about the relationship between the failure to brush teeth and the extent of tooth and gum decay. Contrary to expectation, high fear was not the most effective message. Apparently, the high fear message scared people so much that it made them defensive. Instead, a moderate fear appeal, coupled with instructions about toothbrushing, was actually the most effective in increasing tooth brushing within this group of students (Janis, 1967).

Despite the early promise of fear appeals, subsequent research showed that fear alone may not have any consistent effect on behavior change. If people only feel scared or vulnerable but do not think they can do anything positive to improve the situation, their fear may actually inhibit the practice of a health behavior rather than promote it.

PARALLEL RESPONSE MODEL Howard Leventhal (1970), a psychologist who explored the effectiveness of fear appeals early in his career, became increasingly dismayed that fear appeals were off target for understanding health behaviors. He suggested that when people become fearful about a particular health problem, two parallel processes are engaged: fear control and danger control. This perspective is called the parallel response model. Fear control involves managing the emotional reaction to the threat. For example, to control the fear produced by a frightening message about tooth and gum decay, a student may just tune out the message. The other response is danger control. Danger control involves taking action to reduce the danger. A student who began regular toothbrushing in response to the message would be responding to danger control with effective action.

The point of Leventhal's approach is that fear alone will not change a health behavior. Information about effective actions an individual can take is needed to help change health behaviors. For example, Leventhal, Watts, and Pagano (1967) exposed subjects to a high or low fear message about the need to stop smoking. In addition, half the subjects in each group received specific instructions on how to change their smoking habit. The fear-arousing message alone increased the desire to stop smoking, but it had no effect on smoking behavior. However, the students exposed to the specific instructions on how to reduce their smoking showed a significantly lower level of smoking over a 3-month period.

The important point of parallel response theory is that, to be effective, health messages must not merely alert people to the dangers they face. These messages must provide specific information about the health habit people need to adopt in order to reduce the threat to their health.

THE HEALTH BELIEF MODEL An approach to health behaviors that integrates these important points is the **health belief model** (Hochbaum, 1958; Rosenstock, 1966). This theory states that whether or not a person practices a particular health behavior is affected by two factors: the degree to which the person perceives a personal health threat and the perception that a particular health practice will be effective in reducing that threat.

The perception of a personal health threat is itself influenced by at least three factors: (1) general health values (including interest in health and concern about health); (2) specific beliefs about vulnerability to a particular disorder; and (3) beliefs about the consequences of the disorder (that is, whether or not they are serious). For example, a person may decide he should stop smoking if he values his health, feels threatened by the possibility of heart disease due to smoking, and perceives the threat of heart disease to be serious.

The belief that a specific health habit can reduce threat also breaks down into several subcomponents: whether or not the individual thinks a particular health practice will be effective against the disorder in question, and whether or not the costs of undertaking that measure exceed the benefits of the measure (Rosenstock, 1974b). For example, the man who feels vulnerable to a heart attack and is considering giving up smoking may believe that stopping smoking alone will not reduce his health risk. He might also feel that stopping smoking would simply interfere with his enjoyment of life too much to justify the action. Thus, although he may see his health as threatened by the habit of smoking, he might not stop smoking unless he also believes that stopping smoking would be sufficient to reduce the threat and that the benefits of stopping smoking would exceed the costs. Figure 17–1 illustrates the health belief model and its components.

The health belief model not only helps predict who might practice a particular health behavior, it also explains the conditions under which people might change their health behaviors. For example, if something occurs in an individual's life to increase the perception of a health threat or the perception that a specific health behavior could reduce that threat, the health behavior itself might change. An example of these points comes from the experience of one of our students a few years ago.

This student (call him Bob) was the only person in the class who smoked, and he was the object of some pressure from the instructor and the students to quit. He was familiar with the Surgeon General's report (USPHS, 1964) indicating that smoking is a risky behavior. Although he acknowledged that smoking is linked to both lung cancer and heart disease, he believed that the links are fairly weak. Moreover, because he was in good health and played a number of sports, he felt relatively invulnerable to these diseases. However, over Thanksgiving vacation, Bob went home as he always did to a large family gathering and discovered to his shock that his favorite uncle, a chain smoker all his adult life, had lung cancer and was not expected to live more than a few months. Suddenly, health became a more salient value for Bob. Bob's feelings of susceptibility to lung cancer changed dramatically because a member of his own family had been struck down and because the link between smoking and cancer had been graphically illustrated. Bob's perceptions of the value of stopping smoking changed as well. He concluded that this step might be sufficient to ward off the threat of the disease, and that the cost of quitting smoking was not as great as he had originally thought. When Bob returned from Thanksgiving vacation, he had stopped smoking.

Generally, the health belief model has done a good job of predicting health behaviors as varied as participation in tuberculosis-screening programs (Hochbaum, 1958), polio vaccinations (Rosenstock, Derryberry, & Carriger, 1959), flu immunizations (Cummings, Jette, & Rosenstock, 1978), preventive

FIGURE 17–1 The health belief model applied to the health behavior of stopping smoking.

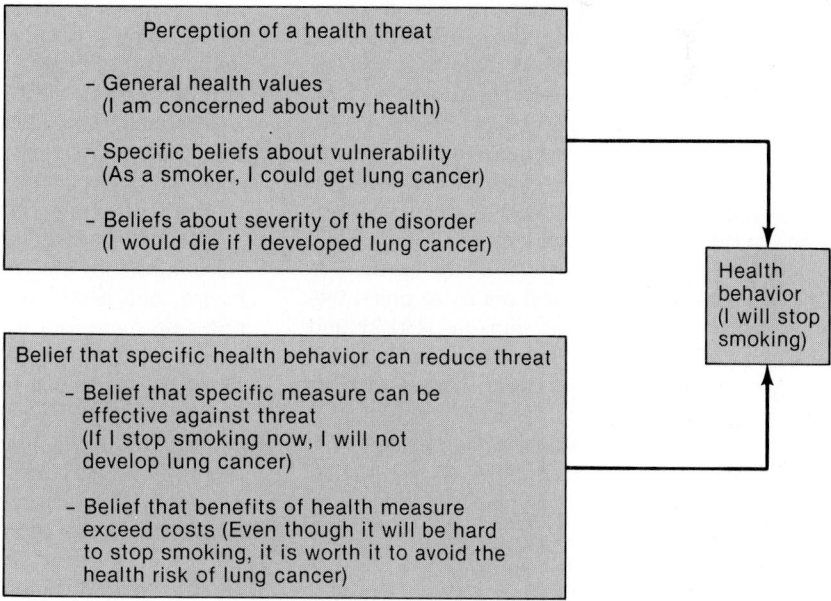

dental care (Kegeles, 1963), smoking reduction/cessation (Kaufert, et al., 1986), medical checkups (Haefner & Kirscht, 1970), genetic screening (Becker, et al., 1975), breast self-examination (Calnan & Moss, 1984), and dieting for obesity (Becker et al., 1977) (see Janz & Becker, 1984 for a review). Clearly, our beliefs about our vulnerability and the efficacy of specific health behaviors do indeed affect our health behaviors.

PERSONAL CONTROL AND HEALTH BEHAVIORS The two models we have just reviewed, namely the parallel response model and the health belief model, emphasize perceptions of vulnerability and beliefs about the importance of particular health behaviors. But undertaking many health behaviors also requires a sense of personal control—a belief that one can actually perform the health behavior. In Chapter 5, we saw how important feelings of personal control can be in adjusting to such distressing experiences as crowding and cancer. People who feel they have some control over their actions and their environment seem to respond better to those stressful events than do people who feel they lack personal control. For example, cancer patients who believed they could take action to reduce the likelihood that the cancer would return were better adjusted psychologically than patients who lacked these feelings of control (Taylor, Lichtman, & Wood, 1984). This is also true with respect to health behaviors. The impact of personal control on health behaviors has been most clearly demonstrated in the research of Albert Bandura (1986a, 1986b).

Bandura reasoned that an important determinant of the practice of health behaviors is a sense of self-efficacy: the belief that one is able to control one's practice of a particular behavior. For example, a smoker who believes she will not be able to break her habit probably will not try to quit, however much she thinks that smoking is risky and that stopping smoking is desirable. Similarly, an overweight man may have more success with his diet if he is convinced that he has the self-control to restrict his eating. Research has shown that self-efficacy affects health behaviors as varied as smoking, dietary changes, and the use of condoms by gay men to avoid exposure to the AIDS virus (Coates, Morin, & McKusick, 1986).

In summary, then, whether or not a person practices a particular health behavior depends upon several beliefs and attitudes:

1. The perceived threat to one's health
2. The perceived effectiveness, ease, and desirability of a particular health practice
3. A sense of self-efficacy that one can actually undertake the health practice.

PROTECTION MOTIVATION MODEL A more recent approach to understanding health behaviors developed by Rogers (1984) integrates all of these factors. The protection motivation model maintains that the motivation to protect one's self from a health threat is based on four beliefs:

1. The threat is severe (magnitude of threat).
2. One is personally vulnerable to the threat (i.e., its occurence is likely).
3. One is able to perform the response needed to reduce the threat (self-efficacy).
4. The response will be effective in overcoming the threat (response efficacy).

According to the model, when beliefs about these four factors are strong, then protection motivation is aroused, and an individual is more likely to change his or her attitudes toward a health behavior and to adopt that health behavior. An important point in Roger's protection motivation theory is the assumption that fear is not an essential element in this process. That is, it is not necessary to frighten people to get them to change their health beliefs and practices. One must instead direct communications toward changing their attitudes about the severity of the threat, personal vulnerability, self-efficacy, and response efficacy.

To apply the protection motivation model toward improving a person's health attitudes and behavior, one needs to identify an individual's attitudes on these four variables, determine which if any need to be changed, and direct communications to the individual that will alter the relevant beliefs. Thus, for example, if a smoker believes that smoking produces serious consequences such as cancer or heart disease, perceives himself as personally vulnerable to it, believes that stopping smoking will be effective in overcoming this threat, but doubts his or her ability to stop smoking, then a relevant attitude-change communication would be to increase perceptions of self-efficacy for stopping smoking (e.g., Maddux & Rogers, 1983).

In summary, recent approaches to understanding and modifying health behaviors have examined four factors now thought to be important in the practice of health behavior: perception of a health threat, perception of personal vulnerability to that health threat, the belief that a particular health behavior will reduce that threat, and a sense of self-efficacy that one can undertake the behavior.

Through understanding the determinants of health behaviors, it may be easier to see why so few people actually practice good health behaviors overall. The smoker may decide that it is too hard to change (low self-efficacy). The nonexerciser may believe that exercise alone would not reduce the risk of a particular disease. The obese individual may not perceive that being overweight is actually a threat to her health. For a health behavior to occur, all four of these factors must fall into place, and there are any number of beliefs or rationalizations a given person may have for not undertaking a particular health behavior.

Health Attitudes and the Mass Media

Approaches to attitude change such as the protection motivation model are potentially of great social importance. One of the goals of preventive health education is to reach as many people as possible. Principles derived from attitude-change approaches can be used to create health messages for mass audiences. A good mass media communication that can be used on TV or radio has the potential to change the health practices of large numbers of people simultaneously. We have all seen televised messages urging us to increase the fiber in our diet, reduce our cholesterol, or stop smoking. How successful are these messages?

Unfortunately, evaluation of these efforts suggest fairly limited success (Atkin, 1979; Lau et al., 1980). Mass media communications seem to bring about modest changes in health attitudes and even more modest changes in behavior. Why is this the case? Consider the following example. A few years ago, the American Cancer Society aired an antismoking TV ad made by the actor Yul Brynner, before he died of lung cancer. The ad begins, "By the time you see this, I will be dead." Most people agree that the message is a powerful and sobering reminder of the importance of not smoking. However, does the message itself do anything to change smoking behavior? The answer is no. The ad may make a smoker worry more that he should stop smoking, but smoking is a deeply ingrained behavior, difficult to alter, and the message alone does little to combat this problem.

A classic study conducted by the Stanford Heart Disease Prevention Program (Meyer, et al., 1980) illustrates this point graphically. These researchers developed a mass media intervention designed to get people to change their health habits and reduce their risk of heart disease. Three communities of similar size and social composition were identified and evaluated concerning risk factors associated with heart disease both before and after the study. The risk factors examined included smoking, diet, and exercise.

One town served as a control group and received no campaign. The second and third towns were both exposed to a mass media campaign concerning smoking, diet, and exercise over a 2-year period via television, radio, newspapers, advertising posters, billboards, and printed materials. In the third town, the media campaign was supplemented by face-to-face instruction in the modification of risk factors directed at residents at highest risk for heart disease.

The results indicated modest attitude change and behavior change in the community exposed only to the mass media campaign. As a consequence of the campaign, the residents were more knowledgeable about risk factors, and they reported that they had reduced their consumption of dietary cholesterol and fats somewhat. There was also some evidence that blood pressure and blood cholesterol levels had been reduced. However, much more dramatic and lasting effects were found when the media campaign was coupled with behavioral instruction for individuals at highest risk (Leventhal, Nerenz, & Strauss, 1980). The media campaign alone appears to have been somewhat effective in informing individuals about their risks but not necessarily in modifying behavior.

Before we conclude that the mass media are ineffective for changing health behaviors, some benefits should be underscored. First, media communi-

Mass media messages designed to change health behaviors can be effective in inducing the motivation to change, but alone they produce very little behavior change.

cations can alert people to health risks they might otherwise not know about (Lau et al., 1980). That is, they may help people to feel more vulnerable to a health threat. For example, antismoking messages like the one involving Yul Brynner may not change smoking, but they successfully raise the consciousness of the American public about the dangers of smoking (Leventhal & Cleary, 1980; see also Mogielnicki et al., 1986). Perhaps more important, the media can have cumulative effects over time by changing the values associated with a particular health practice. For example, the widespread attention given the dangers of smoking may be largely responsible for turning the majority of the American public against smoking as a habit (Leventhal & Cleary, 1980).

Overall, however, attitudinal approaches to the modification of health behaviors have had fairly modest effects. The main reason is that, as we saw in Chapter 6, behavior is under the control of many factors, and attitudes are only one factor. In the case of smoking or overeating, for example, there are many cues in the environment that lead people to perform these behaviors even when they know they should change their habits and even when they want to change. Consequently, recent efforts to modify health behavior have expanded their approach. Whereas attitudinal approaches are still important for raising people's consciousness about the need to practice good health behaviors, approaches have been developed that also focus on the behaviors themselves and on the situational cues that maintain such behaviors independent of attitudes. Because the factors associated with any individual's health behaviors are largely unique to that individual, this approach tailors a behavior change program specifically to each individual. This approach, called cognitive-behavior modification, is described in the next section.

Cognitive Behavioral Approaches to Health Behavior Modification

Increasingly, those who want to alter stubborn health behaviors have begun to focus on the specifics of each individual's unique habits, health cognitions, and environment that may promote a faulty health behavior or undermine the practice of a desirable new one. This approach, which comes out of social learning theory (Chapter 1), is called cognitive-behavior therapy. This perspective maintains that in order to change a health habit, one needs to understand the stimuli in the environment and the individual's cognitions that control that habit and modify them so as to encourage the development of a new health habit (Lazarus, 1971; Thoresen & Mahoney, 1974).

Consider, for example, the case of a woman who is 40 pounds overweight and at risk for heart disease. To get her to reduce her weight, first one needs to understand her eating behavior, the factors that give rise to her eating when it occurs, and the stimuli that are associated with her eating. To address these issues, a psychologist might begin an intervention for weight reduction by having her systematically observe her eating. She would be trained to take notes about her eating behavior and the circumstances under which it occurred. The psychologist might then initiate an effort to alter the stimuli that are associated with eating. For example, if this woman eats while she is watching television, she might be retrained only to eat at the kitchen table with the television off. By removing the association of television with food, one of the enjoyable factors associated with overeating would thereby be removed. Similarly, the presence of desirable and fattening foods like cookies and ice cream might also act as stimuli for eating, and so this woman might be urged to clear her refrigerator and shelves of these foods. Next she might be taught to reward herself for changing her eating behavior. For example, she might be encouraged to set up a schedule of projected weight goals, and then be told to reinforce herself with some pleasurable activity such as going to a movie each time she met a particular weight-loss goal. She might also be encouraged to use techniques of self-punishment. For example, if she failed to bring her eating under control and ate forbidden foods, she might punish herself by unplugging her television for a day or two.

The cognitions people have about their health habits also influence the practice of those health habits. In particular, cognitions about one's sense of self-efficacy are especially important (Bandura, 1986b; Thoresen & Mahoney, 1974). For example, an individual can undermine a diet by thinking such thoughts as "I'll never be able to do this" or "I've tried to diet many times before and always been unsuccessful." In contrast, cognitions that support one's ability to accomplish the health behavior change ("I'm going to be successful at this") can help promote health habit change. Accordingly, the woman who is trying to lose 40 pounds may be encouraged to recognize the self-statements that she usually makes about her eating habits and taught to modify those so that they will support, rather than undermine, her resolve to lose weight.

Psychologists recognize that many health behaviors are related to social factors (Chaney, O'Leary, & Marlatt, 1978). For example, some behaviors such as smoking or overeating may occur primarily in social settings to control anxiety. Accordingly, psychologists may encourage smokers or overeaters to join social-skills training programs or assertiveness training programs so that they can develop effective new social skills to substitute for their old faulty health behaviors. Our overweight woman might be taught effective social skills to prevent overeating at parties.

The kind of cognitive behavioral change program described here is called broad-spectrum cognitive-behavioral therapy because it draws on a wide variety of behavior change techniques (Lazarus, 1971). This kind of program has shown at least modest effectiveness in modifying problems of alcohol abuse (DHHS, 1981), smoking (Leventhal & Cleary, 1980), and obesity (Brownell, 1982; Lovibond, Birrell, & Langeluddecke, 1986). Most of the professionals who actually conduct these kinds of interventions are clinical psychologists rather than social psychologists. However, social psychological research has helped us to understand the behavior change process by making several factors clear. First, strong motivation to change a health behavior is an essential first step in the behavior change process, and this can often be fostered by effective attitude change techniques. Second, social-psychological research on the attitude-behavior relationship has shown why attitude change programs alone are relatively unsuccessful in modifying health behaviors. Finally, social-psychological research has highlighted the importance of the social environment for the occurrence of health behaviors, and has helped in designing specific programs of behavioral modification.

Health habits alone are not sufficient to ward off the threats of chronic illness, although they help substantially. Stressful life experiences and the ways people cope with those stressful events also have an impact on health and illness. We examine these issues in the next section.

BOX 17–1

SMOKING PREVENTION PROGRAMS

Some health habits, like smoking, are so difficult to change once they are in place that researchers attempt to prevent these behaviors before they ever have a chance to take root. One such example is smoking among young adolescents. Smoking is clearly a social behavior acquired at least in part by modeling the behavior of others. When a youngster of age 10 or 11 observes others such as parents or older peers smoking, he is likely to perceive the behavior as pleasurable and unthreatening. Observing a positive role model who is enjoying the risky behavior lowers the belief that negative consequences will occur and raises the expectation of positive consequences.

Social psychologist Richard Evans and his colleagues at the University of Houston drew on these ideas to create a smoking prevention program in the Houston school system (Evans, 1976; Evans et al., 1978). The program was implemented primarily through posters and films. These materials highlighted this disadvantages of smoking for the adolescent. Although most adolescents know that smoking is a bad habit, they believe that health consequences lie far in the dim future. Consequently, Evans's antismoking materials highlighted the negative effects on immediate health: the financial cost of smoking, and the negative social consequences of smoking (such as rejection by others), rather than the long-term health risks.

Because previous research had shown smoking among young adolescents to be tied to desires to be independent and to cultivate a strong self-image, this image was directly addressed in the intervention. The films and posters conveyed such messages as, "You can decide for yourself" and "Here are the facts so you can make a decision." The materials also showed how cigarette advertisers use subtle techniques to try to manipulate people into smoking. Consequently, Evans's materials attempted to convey the image of the smoker as someone vulnerable to advertising gimmicks, rather than someone who is independent.

The importance of the peer group for smoking behavior was addressed in several ways. First, high-status, slightly older peer leaders were featured in the films and posters as the primary agents delivering the interventions. They demonstrated through role-playing how to resist peer pressure to smoke and how to maintain the decision not to smoke. The films illustrated techniques young adolescents could use to resist peer pressure, such as stalling for time or putting counterpressure on the smoker (telling her she is a fool for ruining her health). In some of Evans's research, these messages were later reinforced by actual contact with an older peer in a small group after exposure to the filmed materials.

These kinds of smoking prevention programs are now widely implemented in school systems, and results suggest that they have been at least somewhat successful in reducing the onset of adolescent smoking. Their long-term effectiveness remains to be addressed (McAlister, 1975; Evans & Jacobs, 1981; Telch et al., 1982; Vartianen et al., 1983; Luepker, Johnson, Murray, & Pechacek, 1983; Best et al., 1984; Leventhal & Cleary, 1980; Johnson, Hansen, Collins, & Graham, 1986).

STRESS AND ILLNESS

Most of us have more experience with stress than we care to remember. Stress is discovering that your alarm clock did not go off the morning of a major test or finding out that your car won't start when you need to drive to a job interview. The experience is fundamentally a physiological one. Your body moves into a state of heightened arousal, your mouth goes dry, your heart beats faster, your hands may shake a little, and you may perspire more heavily.

Most of us think of these experiences as unnerving but temporary, not producing any lasting damage. However, researchers now believe that the experience of stress is important because, over time, stress can wear down the body, making it more vulnerable to illness. Repeated exposure to stressful events and repeated engagement of the physiological changes that accompany stress (increased blood pressure, blood sugar level, respiration, and the like) exert wear and tear on the physiological system. This, in turn, may lay the groundwork for a variety of disorders including heart disease, hypertension, and even cancer (e.g., Selye, 1956, 1976; Jemmott & Locke, 1984; Friedman & Rosenman, 1974).

But what is **stress**? Most of us think of stress as intrinsic to particular events such as being stuck in traffic, getting a poor grade on a test, being late for an appointment, or losing a notebook. Yet despite some commonalities in the experience of stress, not everyone perceives the same events as stressful. For example, one person may experience a job interview as threatening, while another may welcome it as a challenge. Similarly, your next-door neighbor might find your radio tuned to the latest rock music to be highly stressful, whereas for you it may be pleasurable. Because of these individual differences in the experience of stress, most definitions consider stress to involve a relationship between an individual and an environment (Lazarus & Launier, 1978).

The fact that stress is, to some degree, in the eye of the beholder makes it clearly a psychological process. That is, events are stressful when they are appraised as stressful and not otherwise. This viewpoint has been most clearly developed by Richard Lazarus (Lazarus, 1966; Lazarus & Folkman, 1984). Lazarus argues that when a person confronts a new or changing environment, he or she scans the environment to identify its meaning. This process is called *primary appraisal*. A new event may be perceived as beneficial, as neutral, or as negative. Beneficial and neutral events may prompt no additional effort on the part of the perceiver. An event perceived as negative, however, may be further appraised for any possible harm, threat, or challenge it may hold.

Harm is the assessment of damage that has already been done by the event. Thus, for example, if your alarm clock failed to go off and you subsequently missed a test, you may face serious consequences such as a failing grade. *Threat* is the assessment of possible future damage that may be brought about by the event. For example, missing a test may lower the instructor's opinion of you and lower your final grade at the end of the year. *Challenge* is the potential for a person ultimately to overcome and profit from an event. For example, a student who uses missing the test as an opportunity to become acquainted with the professor personally may actually benefit from what initially seemed to be a hopelessly bad situation.

The important idea is that psychological appraisal determines whether or not an event is experienced as stressful. A classic study by Speisman, Lazarus, Mordkoff, and Davidson (1964) illustrated this point. College student subjects viewed a gruesome anthropology film in which the young men of a particular tribe were initiated into the tribe by undergoing rites that included mutilation of their genitals. Before viewing this film, the students were exposed to one of four experimental conditions designed to influence how they would perceive the film. One group heard a description that emphasized the pain and trauma these initiates were undergoing. A second group listened to an intellectually oriented anthropological description of the tribal rites. A third group heard a lecture that deemphasized the pain the initiates experienced, emphasizing instead their excitement over their entry into the tribe. A control group heard no narrative but only viewed the film.

After the film had ended, measures of arousal (skin conductance and heart rate) and self-reports of emotionality by the subjects were collected as indicators of the degree of stress the four groups of students had experienced. The results indicated that the groups that had witnessed these bloody events in the context of the lecture or the anthropological description experienced considerably less stress than did the group whose attention was focused on the pain and trauma. This study, then, illustrates that whether or not one experiences stress is heavily dependent upon how one views an event.

Once an individual has assessed an event for its harm, threat, and challenge, a process known as *secondary appraisal* begins. Secondary appraisal is the assessment of one's ability to deal with the threat. It is called secondary because it follows primary appraisal and depends upon the degree to which the event has been assessed as harmful, threatening, or challenging. Secondary appraisal involves looking over one's resources and abilities (such as time or money) and determining whether or not they will be sufficient to overcome the problems posed by the stressful event. For example, if you miss the test but learn that a makeup will be given three days later, the amount of stress you will experience may be low. Since you have already studied for the test and you have an additional three days to prepare for it, your ability to meet this challenging situation (i.e., the test) should be very high. However, if you learn instead that the professor expects you to make up the missed test by writing an additional paper for the course, you may look over your obligations and the time remaining in the semester and wonder how you will ever be able to take on this additional requirement. In this case, your secondary appraisal of your resources for meeting this demand on your time and energies suggests that you have very little to expend on this task; consequently, your experience of stress may be high. Thus, the experience of stress is a balance between primary and secondary appraisal. When harm and threat are high and resources (like time and attention) are minimal, a lot of stress may result. When resources are plentiful and threat is low, stress may be minimal.

What Makes Events Stressful?

As we have seen, events are stressful only to the degree that they are perceived as stressful. However, some types of events are more likely to be perceived as stressful than others. Any event that requires a person to adjust, make changes, or expend resources has the potential to be stressful. For example, although Christmas is usually viewed as a positive event, it may also be highly stressful, since it can involve last-minute shopping, extensive travel, social occasions with relatives, excessive consumption of alcohol and rich food, and little sleep.

Negative or unpleasant events are more likely to be perceived as stressful than are positive ones. For example, a $20 parking ticket typically causes a person more distress than spending twenty dollars to go to a noisy crowded rock concert, even though the latter experience may actually be more physiologically arousing. Unpleasant events cause people more psychological distress and produce more physical symptoms than do more positive stressful events (e.g., Myers, Lindenthal, & Pepper, 1972; Sarason, Johnson, & Siegel, 1978; McFarlane et al., 1980).

Uncontrollable or unpredictable events are more stressful than controllable or predictable ones (McFarlane et al., 1980; Vinokur & Selzer, 1975). This is because an event that is uncontrollable or unpredictable does not enable the person going through the stress to make a plan or develop ways of coping with the problem. For example, the sound of static on your own radio may be less distressing than static from a neighbor's radio, because you can always turn off your own radio or change the station whereas you may not have the same degree of control over your neighbor's radio.

Ambiguous events are often perceived as more stressful than clear-cut events. For example, if you

Even positive events, such as Christmas, can be stressful because they produce change and frenzy in people's lives.

Eric Kroll/Taurus Photos

have been attracted to a fellow student in a class, and one day this person treats you in a cold, aloof manner, you may ruminate over why this is the case. Did you do something to offend this person? Is he or she simply having a bad day? Presumably if you knew what was wrong you could correct it quickly, but not knowing means you are stuck trying to figure out what has gone wrong. Clear stressors let people get on with finding solutions and do not leave them stuck at the problem-solving stage. The ability to take assertive action vis-à-vis a stressful event is usually associated with less distress and better coping (Gal & Lazarus, 1975). However, when a stressful event is ambiguous, a person has little opportunity to take action. He or she instead must devote energy to understanding the event, which can be a time-consuming, resource-sapping task.

How Stress Can Cause Illness

The experience of stress is a problem for people not only because it produces emotional distress and physiological arousal, but because over time it may lay the groundwork for illness.

MAJOR STRESSFUL LIFE EVENTS   The earliest research to demonstrate this point examined the role of

major **stressful life events** in the onset of illness. Newspapers and magazines often highlight dramatic cases in which individuals who have experienced a major stressful event suddenly develop a serious illness or even die:

> A dramatic example is the death of the 27-year-old army captain who had commanded the ceremonial troops at the funeral of President Kennedy. He died 10 days after the president of a "cardiac irregularity and acute congestion," according to the newspaper report of medical findings. (Engel, 1971, p. 774)

> A 39-year-old pair of twins who had been inseparable died within a week of each other; no cause of death was mentioned. (Engel, 1971, p. 774)

Much of the research designed to show the importance of major life events in the onset of illness has used a questionnaire called the Social Readjustment Rating Scale. As can be seen in Table 17–2, the Social Readjustment Rating Scale lists a variety of potentially stressful events that require people to make changes in their lives. Through extensive testing, the events selected for the scale were determined to be the ones that, on the average, force people to make the greatest change in their lives. The points reflect the relative amount of change that must be made. Thus, for example, if one's

TABLE 17-2

The Social Readjustment Rating Scale

Rank	Life Event	Mean Value
1. Death of spouse		100
2. Divorce		73
3. Marital separation from mate		65
4. Detention in jail or other institution		63
5. Death of a close family member		63
6. Major personal injury or illness		53
7. Marriage		50
8. Being fired from work		47
9. Marital reconciliation with mate		45
10. Retirement from work		45
11. Major change in the health or behavior of a family member		44
12. Pregnancy		40
13. Sexual difficulties		39
14. Gaining a new family member (e.g., through birth, adoption, oldster moving in, etc.)		39
15. Major business readjustment (e.g., merger, reorganization, bankruptcy, etc.)		39
16. Major change in financial state (e.g., a lot worse off or a lot better off than usual)		38
17. Death of a close friend		37
18. Changing to a different line of work		36
19. Major change in the number of arguments with spouse (e.g., either a lot more or a lot less than usual regarding childrearing, personal habits, etc.)		35
20. Taking out a mortgage or loan for a major purchase (e.g., for a home, business, etc.)		31
21. Foreclosure on a mortgage or loan		30
22. Major change in responsibilities at work (e.g., promotion, demotion, lateral transfer)		29
23. Son or daughter leaving home (e.g., marriage, attending college, etc.)		29
24. Trouble with in-laws		29
25. Outstanding personal achievement		28
26. Wife beginning or ceasing work outside the home		26
27. Beginning or ceasing formal schooling		26
28. Major change in living conditions (e.g., building a new home, remodeling, deterioration of home or neighborhood)		25
29. Revision of personal habits (dress, manners, associations, etc.)		24
30. Trouble with the boss		23
31. Major change in working hours or conditions		20
32. Change in residence		20
33. Changing to a new school		20
34. Major change in usual type and/or amount of recreation		19
35. Major change in church activities (e.g., a lot more or a lot less than usual)		19
36. Major change in social activities (e.g., clubs, dancing, movies, visiting, etc.)		18
37. Taking out a mortgage or loan for a lesser purchase (e.g., for a car, TV, freezer, etc.)		17
38. Major change in sleeping habits (a lot more or a lot less sleep, or change in part of day when asleep)		16
39. Major change in number of family get-togethers (e.g., a lot more or a lot less than usual)		15
40. Major change in eating habits (a lot more or a lot less food intake, or very different meal hours or surroundings)		15
41. Vacation		13
42. Christmas		12
43. Minor violations of the law (e.g., traffic tickets, jaywalking, disturbing the peace, etc.)		11

Source: Holmes & Rahe (1967).

spouse dies, virtually every aspect of life is disrupted, and so this event has the highest number of "life change units" assigned to it. On the other hand, getting a traffic ticket may be annoying but, in and of itself, it is unlikely to produce much change in one's life.

To obtain a score on the Social Readjustment Rating Scale, one simply checks the events that have occurred within the past year and totals up the point values associated with those events. Although all people will have experienced at least some stressful events during the year, some will have experienced a lot, and it is this group, according to Holmes and Rahe, that is most vulnerable to illness. In one study, Rahe, Mahan, and Arthur (1970) obtained scores on the SRRS from sailors who were about to depart on a 6-month cruise. They selected this group because during the 6 months that the men would be on board ship, they would be subjected to the same rather dull and unchanging environment. Therefore, if life events have an impact on the likelihood of illness, one should be able to see differences in the rates of illness of the sailors who had highly stressful lives just before departure, relative to those with less stress in their lives just before departure. In fact, the predictions were borne out. Sailors who had experienced more major stressful life events were most likely to get sick and to be sick longer than those who had experienced few stressful life events.

DAILY HASSLES   More recently, psychologists have begun to suspect that the more minor stressful events or the daily hassles of life may also have a cumulative and negative impact on health. Such hassles include being stuck in a traffic jam, waiting in line, doing household chores, or having difficulty making a small decision. Most of us think of these as just an annoying part of life, yet they may turn out to be bad for our health. Although research is not yet conclusive, it may ultimately emerge that the wear and tear of daily life predicts illness and psychological stress better than the more major but relatively rare stressful events (Kanner, Coyne, Schaeffer, & Lazarus, 1981; Monroe, 1983; DeLongis et al., 1982). Now you have a really good reason not to let anyone hassle you!

In short, then, research suggests that both major stressful events and more minor stressors are problematic not only because they produce psychological distress but because they can also increase the likelihood of physical illness.

COPING WITH STRESSFUL EVENTS

Once a person experiences an event as stressful, he or she usually begins to make efforts to cope with that event. **Coping** is the process of attempting to manage demands that are viewed as taxing or exceeding one's resources (Lazarus & Launier, 1978; Lazarus & Folkman, 1984). It is the process of trying to manage and master stressful events.

Coping with a stressful event is a dynamic process. For example, the impending breakup of a romantic relationship can produce a variety of reactions, ranging from emotional responses such as sadness or indignation to actions such as efforts at reconciliation or attempts to find engrossing, distracting activities. These coping efforts will in turn be influenced by the way the partner in the relationship responds. With encouragement from the partner, one may make renewed efforts at reconciliation, whereas anger or rejection may drive one further away.

Generally, researchers distinguish between two types of coping efforts: problem-solving efforts and efforts at emotional regulation (Pearlin & Schooler, 1978; Lazarus & Folkman, 1984; Leventhal & Nerenz, 1982). *Problem-solving efforts* are attempts to do something constructive to change the stressful circumstances. *Emotion-focused coping* involves efforts to regulate the emotional reactions to the stressful event. Both types of efforts can occur simultaneously. For example, if the romantic partners break up, each person may try to cope with the loss by mulling over the events and may also take constructive action by meeting new people.

What Is Successful Coping?

Ultimately, what constitutes successful coping? This is not an easy question to answer, and researchers differ in the criteria they use to measure successful coping. Some emphasize the effects of coping on measures of physiological and biochemical functioning. Coping efforts are generally considered to be more successful if they reduce arousal and its indicators such as heart rate, pulse, and skin conductivity. A second criterion of successful coping is whether or not and how quickly people can return to their previous life activities. Many stressful events disrupt ongoing daily life activities such as work or leisure. To the extent that a person's coping efforts enable him or her to resume activities, coping may be judged to be successful. Finally, and most commonly, researchers judge coping according to its effectiveness in reducing psychological distress. If negative emotions such as anxiety and depression are reduced by a coping effort, the coping effort is judged to be successful (Lazarus & Folkman, 1984).

The ways in which a person copes with a stressful event and whether or not that coping will ultimately be successful in reducing stress depend upon a

FIGURE 17–2   The coping process.

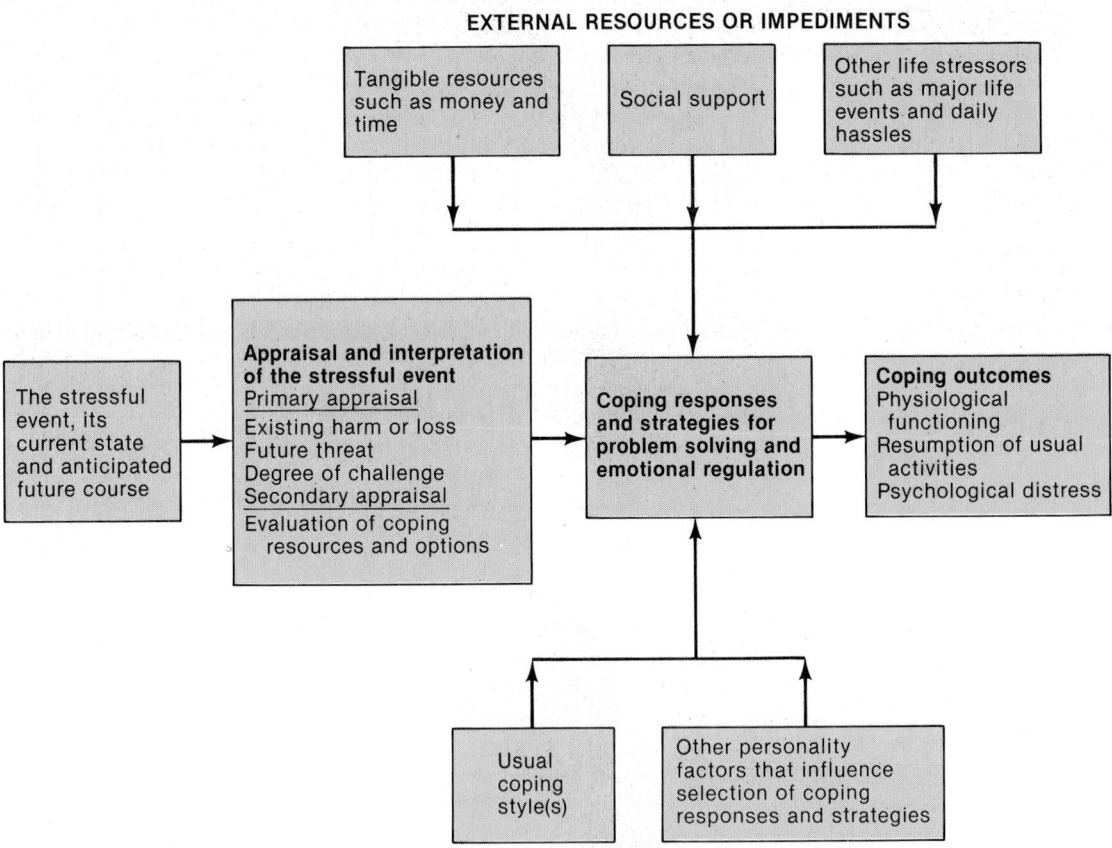

variety of coping resources. Internal resources consist of coping styles and personality attributes. External resources include money, time, social support, and other life stressors that may be occurring at the same time. All of these factors interact with each other to determine coping processes, (e.g., Wiebe & McCallum, 1986). A model of the coping process is presented in Figure 17–2. In the next section, we consider a few of these coping resources in detail.

Coping Style

Coping style is one internal coping resource. It consists of a general propensity for a person to deal with a stressful event in a particular way.

AVOIDANCE VERSUS CONFRONTATION All of us know people who meet stressful events head on and seem to tackle problems directly, whereas we may also know other people who are more likely to avoid stressful events by minimizing their significance or withdrawing from them through alcohol, drugs, or television. In fact, researchers have extensively compared individuals who cope with threatening events by minimizing or avoiding them versus people who are more likely to confront trouble directly.

Neither coping style is necessarily more effective than the other in managing stress. Each seems to have its own advantages and liabilities. People who cope with stress by minimizing or avoiding it appear to cope effectively with short-term threats. However, if the threat is repeated or persists over time, a strategy of avoidance may not be so successful. People who cope by using avoidance may be unable to deal with the possibility of future threat and may not make enough efforts to anticipate and manage subsequent problems (Taylor & Clark, 1986; Suls & Fletcher, 1985).

In contrast, individuals who cope with threatening events through confrontation or vigilance may engage in the cognitive and emotional efforts that are helpful for dealing with long-term threats, but in the short run, they may be more anxious as they deal with the stressor directly (e.g., Miller & Mangan, 1983). For example, the avoider may cope well with a trip to the dentist because he puts the event out of his mind until just before it happens. However, the avoider may cope poorly with ongoing job stress because this is not an event that can easily be put out of mind; the stress recurs daily despite efforts to avoid it. In contrast, the vigilant coper may fret over a visit to the dentist and cause internal distress. However, he or she may make constructive efforts to reduce stress on the job, and thereby ameliorate the situation.

TYPE A BEHAVIOR Some coping styles may succeed in dealing with the psychological distress of stressful events but may nonetheless have an adverse effect on health. Perhaps the best example is the "Type A behavior" syndrome that has been associated with heart disease. The Type A syndrome is a behavioral and emotional style marked by an aggressive, unceasing struggle to achieve more and more in less time, often in competition with other individuals or forces. Type A behavior is marked by three components: easily aroused hostility, a sense of time urgency, and competitive achievement striving (Rosenman, 1978). So-called Type B's, with whom Type A's are usually compared, are less driven individuals who do not show these behavior patterns in response to stressful events. There are several measures of Type A behavior, items from one of which are given in Table 17–3.

Type A individuals lead fast-paced lives. They work longer weeks and put in more overtime than do Type B's. They are impatient with what they perceive as people's slow behavior and may complete people's sentences for them or show other signs of impatience. They often concentrate on several activities simultaneously. Despite the fact that Type A's often achieve substantial accomplishments, they may evaluate their achievements in terms of quantity instead of quality and be dissatisfied with their output. They are likely to challenge and compete with others, especially in moderately competitive situations (Rosenman, 1978).

Differences in behavior and performance of Type A's and Type B's do not show up in all circumstances. Rather, these differences are most likely to appear in particular situations. First, in situations that are moderately competitive, Type A's are more likely than Type B's to work harder and to try to achieve more. Thus, for example, while both Type A's and Type B's may work hard on a graded test, a Type A person is more likely than the Type B to push hard on a practice exam as well. Type A's

TABLE 17–3

The Jenkins Activity Survey: A Measure of Type A Behavior

The Jenkins Activity Survey measures Type A behavior by asking people about their typical responses to frustrating, difficult, and competitive situations. The following are a few examples of items that appear on that survey:

1. When you listen to someone talking and this person takes too long to come to the point, how often do you feel like hurrying the person along?
    Frequently
    Occasionally
    Never
2. Do you ever set deadlines or quotas for yourself at work or at home?
    No
    Yes, but only occasionally
    Yes, once a week or more
3. Would people you know well agree that you tend to get irritated easily?
    Definitely yes
    Probably yes
    Definitely no
    Probably no
4. Would people who know you well agree that you tend to do most things in a hurry?
    Definitely yes
    Probably yes
    Definitely no
    Probably no

Note: If you answered these questions by giving the high-frequency answers, you show at least some characteristics of the Type A individual.
Source: From Jenkins, Zyzanski, & Rosenman (1979).

also work harder on situations that are difficult to control. Thus, for example, if a particular professor is impossible to please, the Type A student may persist longer than the Type B student in trying to win the professor's approval. Type A's outperform Type B's in difficult situations that call for endurance. For example, if Type A and Type B students were both given lengthy essay exams to take home, the Type A might work longer than the Type B. In contrast, Type B's outperform Type A's on tasks that require slow, careful work or a broad focus of attention. The Type A individual tends to get impatient on tasks that must be done slowly or that require full attention because he or she usually wants to get on with the next task and usually has at least a portion of his or her attention devoted to what will come next. So, for example, the Type A might finish an essay exam before the Type B because the Type A could work

at his or her own pace. The Type B might outperform the Type A on an assembly line task that requires the slow, careful assemblage of complex machine parts.

Type A behavior is important because it has been reliably related to the development of coronary artery disease (Haynes, Feinlieb, & Kannell, 1980). The excessive arousal in response to stressful events that Type A's experience, followed by dramatic decreases in arousal, may be the mechanism that produces damage to the arteries, although this issue is still under debate (Glass, 1976). Recently, investigators have suggested that hostility may be a more strongly implicated component of Type A behavior for heart disease than the other attributes (Matthews, 1982; Carver & Humphries, 1982).

Research will no doubt continue to uncover the personality attributes and coping styles that arise in response to stressful events, ones which may reduce or augment the likelihood that stressful events will ultimately have a negative effect on health.

Social Support

In Chapters 8 and 9, we saw how important social relationships are to people for satisfying their social needs. Recent work by health psychologists clearly indicates that these socially supportive relationships may also mute the effects of stress, help people cope with stress, and enhance health. The social support provided by others may even reduce the likelihood of illness and help people recover more quickly from illness (House, 1981; see also Schaeffer, Coyne, & Lazarus, 1981).

Social support is an interpersonal exchange in which one person gives help to another. Social support may be provided in any of several ways. First, *emotional concern* expressed through liking, love, or empathy can be supportive. For example, if you are going through an awkward breakup with a romantic partner, expressions of caring from friends can be very welcomed. Second, *instrumental aid*, such as the provision of goods or services during stressful times, can be an act of social support. For example, if you are having difficulty getting to your classes on time because your car is unreliable, a friend's offer to fix your car would be very supportive. Third, *providing information* about a stressful situation can be helpful. For example, if

Socially supportive relationships can help keep people well and help them to recover quickly from illness.

United Nations/John Isaac

you feel poorly prepared for an exam and someone who took the course last year gives you information about types of questions on the midterm and final, this may be very useful in helping you study. Finally, information may be supportive when it is relevant to *self-appraisal* or self-evaluation. For example, if you are uncertain whether you have made the right decision in breaking up with your boyfriend or girlfriend, information from your friends telling you that you did the right thing for the right reasons can be very comforting. Social support can come from a spouse or partner, family members, friends, or social and community contacts such as clubs and churches or temples.

Research demonstrates that social support effectively reduces psychological distress during stressful times. For example, a study of residents' reactions following the nuclear reactor accident at Three Mile Island, Pennsylvania, revealed the importance of social support (Fleming, Baum, Gisriel, & Gatchel, 1982). Following the accident, residents were interviewed by a team of researchers about their reactions to the events and the presence of supportive family and friends. Those who reported having family and friends they felt close to showed lower levels of psychological distress in response to the accident than those who reported lower levels of social support.

Social support also appears to lower the likelihood of illness and to speed recovery from illness when it does occur (Wallston, Algana, DeVellis, & DeVellis, 1983). Some impressive evidence for the importance of social support in combating the threat of illness comes from a survey of adults in Alameda County, California (Berkman & Syme, 1979). Almost 7000 people were interviewed regarding their personal, social, and community ties, and their death rate was tracked over a 9-year period. The results showed that people who had few social and community ties were more likely to die during this period than were people who had more such ties.

Research has tried to identify exactly how social support affects stress, and two possibilities have been extensively explored. One hypothesis, called the *direct effects hypothesis*, maintains that social support is always beneficial, during nonstressful times as well as during stressful times. The other hypothesis, termed the *buffering hypothesis*, maintains that the physical and mental health benefits of social support are chiefly evident during periods of high stress: When there is little stress, social support may have few physical or mental health benefits. According to the buffering hypothesis, social support acts as a resource that blunts the effects of stress or enables the individual to cope with high levels of stress more effectively. Extensive research now suggests that social support can have both direct effects and buffering effects (Wills, 1984; Cohen & Hoberman, 1983; Wortman, 1984).

The beneficial effects of social support are not necessarily cumulative. That is, it is not always the case that people who have more friends and family are better supported than people who have fewer friends or family members. Having at least one close companion may be the most important factor in predicting whether or not an individual is socially supported (see, for example, House, Robbins, & Metzner, 1982). In fact, having too much or overly intrusive social support may actually make a stressful event more stressful (Lieberman, 1982; Suls, 1982). For example, a person who belongs to a "dense" social network (friendship groups in which everyone interacts a lot and knows each other well) may find himself or herself besieged by contradictory advice and interference when undergoing a stressful event. If you are deciding which of several graduate schools to attend and every one of your relatives has a different bit of advice, they might not be very supportive to you during this stressful time. Similarly, if you are breaking up with a boyfriend or girlfriend and your friends have divided into two camps, those who think you should stick it out and those who think you should get rid of the creep, you might find that it would have been easier to have made the decision without the advice of your friends. Nonetheless, despite potential adverse affects, it is evident that the social relationships that many of us take for granted actually contribute to our mental and physical health.

Stress Management

Some individuals have difficulty coping with stressful events on their own. Stress management programs have developed to help people deal with these events more effectively (e.g., Ganster et al., 1982; Roskies, 1980; Chesney, Eagleston, & Rosenman, 1981). Such programs may train people generally in stress management techniques that can be used for a wide variety of stressful events or they may focus on coping with a particular stressful event such as the demands of college. Stress management programs typically include three phases. In the first phase, participants learn what stress is and how to identify the stressful events in their own lives.

In the second phase, they acquire and practice skills in coping with stress. And in the final phase, they practice these stress management techniques in targeted stressful situations and then monitor their effectiveness (e.g., Meichenbaum & Jaremko, 1983).

As an example, college can be a stressful experience for many students. For some, it is the first time they are away from home, and they must cope with the problems of living in a dormitory surrounded by strangers. They may have to share a room with a person of very different background and habits. High noise levels, communal bathrooms, institutional food, and difficult academic schedules may all be very trying. In addition, the fledgling college student may discover that academic life is more rigorous than he or she had expected. Whereas each student may have been a star in high school, there is more competition in college. Consequently, course loads are heavier and grades typically lower. Coping with the first C, D, or F can be a deflating and anxiety-arousing experience.

Some colleges and universities have instituted programs to help students cope with these stressful events by learning stress management techniques. Commonly, in the first phase of such programs, the student learns what stress is and how it creates wear and tear on the system. Students learn that stress is in the eye of the beholder rather than inherent in events themselves. That is, they learn that college life is not inherently stressful but can become stressful depending on how a student perceives it. Through these messages, students begin to see that if they acquire appropriate stress management techniques, they may come to experience currently stressful events as less stressful. In sharing their experiences of stress, many students find reassurance in the fact that other students have experiences similar to their own.

In the next phase, students are trained to observe their own behavior closely and to record the circumstances they find most stressful. They also typically record their physiological, emotional, and behavioral reactions to the stressful events. They may write down any maladaptive efforts they made to cope with the stressful events such as sleeping too much, eating, watching television, or taking drugs.

Once they learn to chart stressful responses, students are encouraged to examine what causes those experiences. For example, one student may feel overwhelmed with academic life only when she must deal with speaking out in class, whereas another student may experience stress primarily when he thinks about having to use the computer in a particularly demanding course. By pinpointing precisely the circumstances that initiate a student's feelings of stress, that student can more precisely identify his or her own trouble spots.

Students are next trained to recognize the negative self-talk they may go through when they face stressful events. Thus, for example, the student who fears speaking out in class may come to recognize how her own self-statements contribute to the stress she feels, ("I hate asking questions," and "I always get tongue-tied"). Such negative self-talk undermines feelings of self-efficacy and will become a target for modification later in the intervention.

Typically, a student will next set specific goals that he or she wants to meet to reduce the experience of college stress. For example, one student's goal may be to learn to speak in class without suffering overwhelming anxiety. For another, the goal may be to go see a particular professor about a problem. Once the goals have been set, the student next identifies some behaviors that can help meet those goals. For example, the student who fears speaking out in class may decide that she will begin to raise her hand whenever she knows the answer to factual questions that will require only a one- or two-word response. By beginning with relatively little speaking out in class, she may then be able to train herself to give longer answers that can ultimately enable her to speak more effectively.

Once the student has set some realistic goals and identified some target behaviors, he or she will learn how to engage in positive self-talk. For example, the student desiring to overcome a fear of oral presentations might remind herself of the occasions when she has spoken successfully in public. Once some success in speaking publicly has been achieved, the same student might encourage herself by highlighting the positive aspects of the experience (for example, holding the attention of the audience or making some good points). As she becomes more effective, she might try to create opportunities to speak publicly and reward herself each time she does to by engaging in some desirable activity such as going to a movie.

Typically, students also learn some ways of modifying the physiological reactions associated with stress. Usually, these methods involve relaxation-training techniques and may include deep breathing, muscle relaxation, guided imagery, meditation, and similar techniques (English & Baker, 1983; Benson, Greenwood, & Klemchuk, 1975). Such methods can help reduce heart rate, muscle tension, and blood pressure. Then, if a student finds that the stress of college life is becoming overwhelming, he or she can take a 5- or 10-minute break, breathe deeply and relax completely, and then return to tasks more free of previous tensions.

As may be evident, most stress management programs include a wide array of cognitive behavioral techniques that an individual can use to combat stress. Some will work better for some students, and others will work better for other students. By presenting a broad array of coping techniques, students have a broad set of skills from which to choose ones that work for them individually.

RECOGNIZING, INTERPRETING, AND SEEKING TREATMENT FOR SYMPTOMS

The effective management of stress and the practice of good health behaviors cannot always prevent the onset of symptoms and illness, and the recognition that one is sick and should seek professional treatment. When and how does a person decide that he or she is sick? The answer to this question depends heavily on social and psychological factors. Psychological factors influence how people recognize symptoms and interpret them, whether or not they believe those symptoms indicate illness, and whether or not they think the health care system is the best place to obtain treatment.

The Recognition of Symptoms

In order to label yourself as sick, you first have to notice that you are sick. Noticing symptoms is, in part, a psychological process that seems to depend heavily on one's focus of attention. When your focus of attention is directed inward, symptoms are detected more quickly than when your focus of attention is directed externally toward the environment. People who are focused on themselves (their bodies, their emotions, and their reactions in general) notice their symptoms more quickly than do people who are externally focused on their environment and activities (Pennebaker, 1983). People who hold boring jobs, who are social isolates, who keep house, or who live alone typically report more symptoms than do people who have interesting jobs, who have more active social lives, who work outside of their home, or who live with others (Pennebaker, 1983). A possible reason for these differences is that people whose lives are more active experience more distractions, and therefore they attend to themselves less than do people who have relatively little activity in their lives (Pennebaker, 1983).

Situational factors also influence whether or not a person recognizes a particular symptom. Boring situations make people more attentive to symptoms than interesting situations. For example, people are more likely to notice itchiness or tickling in their throats and to cough in response to these sensations during boring parts of movies than during the interesting parts (Pennebaker, 1980). Joggers are more likely to experience fatigue and to be aware of their running-related symptoms if they are running on a boring course than if they are running on a course that is more interesting and varied (Pennebaker & Lightner, 1980). In fact, any experience that causes a person to direct his or her attention outward decreases the likelihood that a symptom will be perceived, whereas any factor that directs attention inward will increase the chances that symptoms will be perceived (Scheier, Carver, & Gibbons, 1979; Pennebaker & Lightner, 1980; Pennebaker, 1983; Fillingim & Fine, 1986).

You may have noticed that more students seem to get sick during exam time than at other times during the school year. Of course, there are many possible reasons for this fact. Some people may feign illness to avoid taking exams, and others may wear themselves down in a frenzied last-minute effort to study. However, some of the individuals who become ill during exam time do so primarily because spending hours and hours with nothing to do but study gives them plenty of time to notice any symptom they might have such as coughing, sneezing, or discomfort. Therefore, they may be more likely to recognize the symptom, label it as illness, and seek treatment during these times than when their lives are fuller and more distracting.

In summary, then, attentional factors are significant determinants of whether or not a symptom is noticed. The evidence for this point has come largely from studies of college students who have experienced such minor symptoms as coughing or nasal congestion. However, the argument can also be applied to more serious and meaningful symptoms. Thus, for example, a woman whose life is full of distracting activities may be less likely to notice a lump growing in her breast than a woman with a less active life and so be less likely to seek early treatment. Similarly, a man who is developing chest pains indicative of heart disease may not be aware of it if his attention is usually directed outward, away from his body.

The Interpretation of Symptoms

As we have seen, the recognition of symptoms can be influenced by psychological factors. The interpretation of those symptoms can also be affected by psychological factors. As we saw in Chapter 4, people's schemas about the events in their lives can guide the gathering and interpretation of information. So it is with symptom interpretation as well. Previous experience with a particular symptom may lead a person to a particular interpretation based on the schema developed for that symptom. For example, a person with a long history of recurrent sore throats may dismiss a particular sore throat as yet another instance of this pattern, failing to recognize that he has a more serious disorder such as a strep infection. A person who has never had swollen glands in conjunction with a cold may conclude that swollen glands are serious and merit treatment, even though someone else with a long history of swollen glands would not reach that conclusion (Safer, Tharps, Jackson, & Leventhal, 1979; Leventhal, Nerenz, & Strauss, 1980).

Expectations about symptoms influence their interpretation. People often ignore symptoms they are not expecting and amplify ones they do expect (Leventhal, Nerenz, & Strauss, 1980). For example, women who believe they are close to their menstrual periods may interpret vague sources of discomfort as premenstrual symptoms, whereas women who believe that their periods are several days away may ignore these same bodily sensations (Ruble, 1977).

The interpretation of symptoms also depends upon which part of the body is affected. When symptoms affect a part of the body that is highly valued such as the face, they may prompt attention more quickly than when a symptom involves another part of the body. Or, if a symptom limits mobility, as in the case of swollen ankles, it may lead a person to seek treatment more quickly than if mobility is not limited. An example of the social-psychological interpretation of symptoms is presented in Box 17–2 on the next page.

Social interaction also affects how people interpret symptoms. Try to recall the last time you experienced some ambiguous symptom and were uncertain of its meaning. You may have consulted some of your friends or neighbors to find out if they had experienced similar symptoms and to get their opinions on what the symptoms might mean. Perhaps you were reassured that the symptoms meant nothing and that you should simply leave them alone. Alternatively, you might have been warned that the symptom was possibly indicative of a major problem for which you should seek treatment. This casual and informal exploration of possible diagnoses of symptoms has been termed the *lay referral network* and refers to the fact that people often exchange information with family and friends about the interpretation of symptoms well before any medical treatment is sought (Freidson, 1960).

Seeking Treatment for Symptoms

Social-psychological factors are also involved in seeking formal treatment for symptoms from medical caregivers. For example, the health belief model that we considered earlier predicts that a person will seek treatment for symptoms under particular conditions: when he or she believes that the symptoms may be severe and that medical treatments could overcome the threat. A woman who believes that her sore throat is due to a viral infection may not seek treatment, since there are no effective remedies to combat viruses. However, a person who believes that his sore throat is due to a bacterial infection for which penicillin would be effective might be more likely to seek treatment.

The degree to which a person is integrated into a community also influences whether or not he or she will use health services in that community. That is, a person who has friends in a community, ties to the community, and involvement in community activities may be more likely to learn about health services and to use them in response to symptoms than a person who is less involved in a community (Suchman, 1964).

In conclusion, then, the processes of recognizing and interpreting symptoms and of seeking treatment are heavily influenced by social-psychological factors. Attentional factors and the demands of one's social and physical environment often conspire to call attention to or reduce attention to symptoms. In addition, prior experience and social communication help people to interpret the meaning of otherwise ambiguous sensations. The use of health services also depends on such social-psychological factors as attitudes toward the symptoms and the possible treatments and interactions with others in one's environment. As we shall now see, social-psychological processes extend into the practitioner's office as well.

Patient-Practitioner Interaction

Interacting with a physician or nurse regarding medical treatment is a social process involving interpersonal communication, person perception, social judgments, and social influence. One of the earliest judgments that most patients make is whether or

Box 17–2

THE JUNE BUG EPIDEMIC: A CASE OF HYSTERICAL

CONTAGION

In Chapter 13, we examined mass hysteria—a group response to collective stress. In that context, we noted that group processes can help people develop explanations for the vague physical symptoms they may experience as a result of stress. Often, such explanations center around physical illness. One of the most famous examples of this point is the so-called June Bug epidemic.

In June of 1962, a mysterious disease broke out in the dressmaking department of a southern United States textile plant. Sixty-two workers were affected by such symptoms as nausea, numbness, dizziness, and occasional vomiting. Almost all of the affected workers reported that they had been bitten by some kind of bug immediately prior to experiencing the symptoms. However, health officials who investigated the incident could obtain no reliable description of the suspected insect, and an examination of the factory turned up no bug that could have produced the disease.

Public health experts began to suspect that the epidemic might be a case of mass hysteria, and accordingly they looked for certain common patterns that distinguished the "victims" from unaffected workers. Most of the workers were married women with children and were attempting to combine full-time work with marriage and motherhood—an often exhausting situation. The epidemic occurred during the busiest month of the year, when there was pressure on workers to put in overtime and to speed up production. Many of the workers had been feeling anxious and nervous both about their work situation and about trying to combine their work pace with family obligations.

The workers who had been "bitten" by the June Bug, then, were workers who had the most stress in their lives—married women with children who were simultaneously trying to cope with the further demands of increased productivity and overtime. Job anxieties coupled with physical manifestations of fatigue (such as dizziness) created symptoms that could be labeled as "illness," given appropriate circumstances. The rumor of a suspicious bug and the presence of ill co-workers apparently provided these circumstances leading to the epidemic that resulted (Kerckhoff & Back, 1968).

not they think their physician is technically competent. Most patients conclude that their physician is, although the standards used for making such a judgment are not always appropriate (Ben-Sira, 1976; Ware, Davies-Avery, & Stewart, 1978). Most of us know little about medicine and standards of practice and so we evaluate medical care using the only information we have: whether or not we like the practitioner and whether or not he or she is warm and friendly or cool and uncommunicative. When people are asked what is important to them in their medical care, they rate the manner in which the care is delivered at least as high as the technical quality of care (Ware et al., 1978; Feletti, Firman, & Sanson-Fisher, 1986).

One of the problems that arises in patient-physician interaction, even when patients and physicians have some basic confidence in each other, is faulty communication (e.g., Samora, Saunders, & Larson, 1961; McKinley, 1975). Practitioners often use jargon and technical language that patients do not understand, and they may inadvertently depersonalize the patient by referring to the patient's symptoms rather than the patient as a person (Kaufman, 1970; Chafetz, 1970).

> Recently, when I was being given emergency treatment for an eye laceration, the resident surgeon abruptly terminated his conversation with me as soon as I lay down on the operating table. Although I had had no sedative or anesthesia, he acted as if I were no longer conscious, directing all his questions to a friend of mine—questions such as, "What's his name?" "What occupation is he in?" "Is he a real doctor?" etc. As I lay there, these two men were speaking about me as if I were not there at all. The moment I got off the table and was no longer a cut to be stitched, the surgeon resumed his conversation with me, and existence was conferred upon me again. (Zimbardo, 1970)

Patients, too, contribute to faulty communication by failing to pay attention to what they are being told, and by responding to false cues in the situation and reading too much into a physician's comments (Golden & Johnston, 1970; Greer, 1974; DiMatteo & DiNicola, 1982). For example, a patient may be so distressed by swollen glands that he fails to hear the physician's instructions about taking penicillin. Instead, he may incorrectly interpret the physician's sober manner as confirmation of his private fear that he has cancer, when in fact he has only a treatable case of strep infection.

The treatment setting itself often contributes to undermining effective communication. The physician may have a backlog of patients in the waiting room, and accordingly he or she is under pressure to see each patient for as little time as possible. The patient is being asked to communicate symptoms efficiently and effectively to a physician when he or she may be in a poor state to do so. It is difficult to be coherent when one is in pain, running a fever, or simply anxious about the meaning of a

Laimute Druskis

Communication between patient and practitioner can be improved by training physicians in effective communication techniques.

particular problem. In summary, then, a variety of factors can inadvertently conspire to impede communication.

Adherence to Medical Treatment

Faulty communications between patient and practitioner are problematic for several reasons. First, they may undermine the use of health services in the future. Patients whose emotional needs are not met in their interactions with physicians are less likely to return to that physician in the future, and may instead turn to alternative medical services (Ware, Davies-Avery, & Stewart, 1978). Even more important, patients may not adopt the behaviors and treatments recommended by their practitioners, resulting in failure to adhere to treatment. It is currently estimated that about one-third of patients typically fail to follow treatment recommendations. Depending upon the disorder and recommendation, noncompliance may vary from a low of 15 percent for such recommendations as tablets or ointments to a staggering high of 93 percent for lifestyle advice such as to stop smoking or lose weight (Davis, 1968a; DiNicola & DiMatteo, 1984).

These problematic rates of nonadherence can be traced to several factors. First, patients who are dissatisfied with the quality of their care may decide consciously not to follow a treatment and thereby undermine their health. Second, in order to follow through on a treatment regimen, a patient must understand it, and often, understanding is not achieved. Adherence is high when a patient receives a clear, jargon-free explanation of the origin, diagnosis, and treatment recommendations associated with the disorder. Adherence is also increased if the instructions are written down, if the patient has repeated back the instructions, if any unclear sections are clarified, and if the instructions are repeated more than once (DiMatteo & DiNicola, 1982; DiNicola & DiMatteo, 1984). Unfortunately, these seemingly simple steps are often not taken during brief and rushed visits with a physician.

The qualities of the treatment also influence whether or not a patient will adhere to it. Treatments that are complex, involving several medications or measures, are less likely to be adhered to completely than treatments that are simple, involving perhaps one medication. Treatments that must be implemented on a long-term basis such as over several months show lower rates of adherence than treatments that are short term over just a few days; over time adherence simply falls off. Treatments that interfere with regular life activities produce lower rates of adherence than those that can be implemented relatively easily (Kirscht & Rosenstock, 1979). For example, a patient who is required to rest in the middle of a busy working day might find it nearly impossible to do so.

Adherence is higher with treatments that seem "medical." For example, if a patient is given a set of foul-tasting pills and told to take one every 3 hours for three days, he or she is more likely to adhere to that recommendation than if he or she

is told to get rest, avoid stressful experiences, stop smoking, or lose weight. The reason is that patients may not see lifestyle recommendations as truly medical, and therefore may not follow through. They may believe that their social activities, the stressful nature of their work life, and whether or not they smoke are their own business and that the physician's tasks are restricted to providing "medical" treatments for diagnosable conditions.

Another reason why physicians' recommendations to alter lifestyle behaviors often show low rates of compliance is because these aspects of life are difficult to modify. As we noted earlier in the chapter, such stubborn health habits as overeating, smoking, or drinking to excess may have become habitual and may be tied to certain cues and stimuli in the social environment. These cues alone can maintain a habit, even when the motivation to change the behavior is there.

In Chapter 11 we were introduced to the concept of *reactance*, a psychological state that results when people feel their freedoms have been arbitrarily restricted (Brehm, 1966; Brehm & Brehm, 1981). The withdrawal of freedom can be very threatening, especially when highly valued activities are involved. Many illnesses and treatments have precisely these effects. For example, being put on bed rest by a physician may seem like an arbitrary and useless step to you. It may also cause you to miss a midterm and several weekend parties. Adherence under such circumstances is very low, both because the treatment recommendations threaten freedoms and because personal frustration can result when one is unable to do what one wishes.

Improving Patient-Practitioner Communication

How can we improve patient-practitioner communication? One method that has recently been implemented by social psychologists in medical schools is to train fledgling physicians in effective techniques of communication (DiMatteo & DiNicola, 1982). For example, physicians are trained how to provide information to patients in a manner that is comprehensible and jargon-free without being simple-minded. Such programs also stress the importance of communicating treatment information clearly and testing for recall to be certain that the patient has understood the treatment regimen. Methods of communicating warmth and friendliness to a patient, even through such simple nonverbal behaviors as smiling, leaning forward, or shaking hands can also help improve the communication process (DiMatteo, Friedman, & Taranta, 1979; DiMatteo, Hays, & Prince, 1986).

Training physicians in the effective use of techniques of social influence identified in Chapter 12 can also improve the communication process and ultimately increase adherence to treatment (Rodin & Janis, 1979). Physicians are high-status people, and have a high degree of authority by virtue of their medical expertise. This type of power is termed *legitimate authority*. But practitioners can also draw on their "referent" power by becoming significant individuals in their patients' lives. If the patient feels that the practitioner's approval and acceptance are rewarding, then the practitioner will be able to influence the attitudes and decisions of the patient that are relevant to treatment. When the practitioner is able to use both referent power and legitimate power, adherence is increased (Rodin & Janis, 1979; Janis, 1983a).

Physicians are also in a unique position to influence a patient's behavior because they interact on a one-to-one basis. Health recommendations can be tailored to the individual needs and vulnerabilities of that particular patient. These conditions maximize attitude and behavior change. The face-to-face interaction provides an effective setting for holding the patient's attention, repeating and clarifying instructions, extracting commitments from the patient to adhere to the treatment, and assessing any possible sources of resistance to compliance. Thus, for example, the patient for whom bed rest was recommended can explain to the physician about the importance of midterms and missing social activities, and the patient and physician together may be able to work out a compromise. The face-to-face setting also provides an opportunity for the practitioner to stress unique aspects of the patient's situation. For example, patients who are told by their physicians that they are particularly vulnerable to lung cancer by virtue of their smoking are more likely to stop than in response to other health communications about smoking (Pederson, 1982). Finally, because of the face-to-face situation and the likelihood of additional visits, the physician has the patient under surveillance at least to some degree and can monitor progress during subsequent visits.

In summary, then, the processes of diagnosis, treatment recommendations, and following through on treatment are clearly social-psychological ones. Information must be effectively communicated in order for a patient to adhere, and effective techniques of social influence can help instill the desire to follow through on treatment.

Psychological Effects of the Health Care Setting

A mere two or three decades ago, many patients saw a family physician for virtually every ailment. In seeing the same physician month after month and year after year, they came to know the physician as a person and to trust his or her judgment. Increasingly, however, health care is dispensed in a clinic or a hospital setting from strangers with whom the patient has no personal relationship. These kinds of settings do not provide the warm and satisfying bonds that a long-term relationship can. Consequently, patients can feel alienated from these health care settings. Often a patient must wait a long time to see the physician, and when it is finally the patient's turn, the visit may be short and perhaps unsatisfying. Communications may be brief, and the patient may be referred to one or more additional specialists. The patient may come away from the treatment setting feeling that he or she has been depersonalized and passed around from physician to physician.

Social psychologists have not yet fully explored the social-psychological impacts of health care institutions on patients. However, it is evident, even from this cursory look, that health settings can often influence a patient's behavior substantially. There is evidence that when patients feel alienated from the setting in which their health care was dispensed, they are less likely to return for follow-up visits and less likely to follow through on treatment recommendations (Freidson, 1961; Ware, Davies-Avery, & Stewart, 1978; Mechanic, 1975; Barr, 1983). Moreover, these experiences can lead an individual to feel out of control and unable to exert effort

The crowding, long waits, and short visits experienced by many patients in clinics and hospitals can produce high dissatisfaction with medical care.

in his or her own behalf. As one dissatisfied hospital patient put it:

> When you are really sick, you are at the mercy of the hospital staff. In my opinion, you've got to have luck on your side. You've got to be lucky enough to get key people in the hospital who are really alert and who wish to do a job; and have someone on the shift at the time you need them who wants to give the service or you are just out of luck. I think you could die in one of these hospitals of a heart attack before anyone came to help you. (quoted in Tagliacozzo & Mauksch, 1972, p. 169)

Threats to freedom engendered by the treatment environment, including hospitals and clinics, may lead some patients to lash out against authority and deliberately undertake behaviors that sabotage their own treatment. Other patients may become passive and helpless, but feel unable to express their anxiety and depression to others because they want to be considered good patients (Taylor, 1979,

1981c). It is likely that social psychologists will become increasingly involved in the effort to understand the adverse effects of health institutions upon patients and their behavior in the future and to be involved in the redesign of such services.

Psychological Control and Adjustment to Treatment

As has already been noted, feelings of control over one's health and treatment regimen appear to be important for health behaviors as varied as preventive health practices and adherence to treatment. So important have these feelings of control been found to be, that many social psychologists have drawn upon the concept of psychological control in designing interventions with medical patients. The idea behind these interventions is that if patients are given a sense of control during a noxious medical procedure, it will enable them to adjust to that procedure more successfully than if they do not have such feelings of control (Averill, 1973; Miller, 1979; Thompson, 1981; Fiske & Taylor, 1984).

Consider, for example, the patient who must undergo an endoscopic examination in which a tube is swallowed so that it can take pictures of the stomach. This is a very unpleasant procedure for most patients. Feelings of control might be instilled in several different ways: Patients can be given a specific *behavior* they can undertake to control the event, such as instruction in swallowing the tube. Patients can be given *information* about the procedures involved in the examination to enhance feelings of prediction and control. Alternatively, they may be given a *cognitive control* technique, whereby they learn to think about the aversive sensations in a way that makes them seem less unpleasant. Generally speaking, psychologists have found that control-based interventions, whether they draw on behavioral interventions, cognitive interventions, or simply the provision of information, are successful in helping patients adapt to unpleasant medical procedures (Johnson, 1984; Fiske & Taylor, 1984).

For example, in one study, Johnson and Leventhal (1974) developed two interventions for patients awaiting an endoscopic examination. The first was designed to reduce adverse emotional reactions by providing patients with specific information about the sensations they could expect during the procedure (*information control*). The second intervention was designed to provide a sense of *behavior control* by teaching patients how to breathe deeply and to swallow the tube effectively to minimize gagging. One-fourth of the patients awaiting the examination received the first treatment, one-fourth received the second treatment, one-fourth received both treatments, and the remainder of the patients received no intervention other than cursory, preparatory instructions. The behavior control manipulation significantly reduced anxiety when it was combined with the sensory description information. The sensory information alone or in combination with the behavioral instructions significantly reduced patients' reports of anxiety and nurses' ratings of patients' anxiety. Thus, both the information manipulation and the behavior information had an impact on adjustment to this medical procedure.

Feelings of psychological control appear to affect not only adjustment to specific unpleasant medical procedures, but also health more generally. This point was dramatically illustrated in a study of nursing home residents by Langer and Rodin (1976). The purpose of their study was to see if the introduction of an element of control into a nursing home environment could improve the morale and health of these institutionalized elderly people. Patients on one floor were given small plants to care for (behavior control); they were also asked to choose when they wished to participate in some of the nursing home activities (decision control). Patients on a comparison floor were also given plants, but they were told that the staff would care for them. They participated in the same activities as the first group of patients, but they were assigned to times rather than being able to choose those times.

Several weeks later, nurses rated the mood and activity level of the patients, patients reported their own mood, and behavioral measures of patients' activity levels were collected. The results revealed that the patients who had been given some control were more active and had a greater sense of well-being than those on the comparison floor. A year later, those patients were still psychologically and physically healthier than the patients who had not received the interventions designed to enhance feelings of control (Rodin & Langer, 1977). The importance of feelings of control is well illustrated by this study, because the control-enhancing manipulations were actually quite modest. Thus, this study illustrates how powerful and helpful the variable of psychological control can be, and how it can have a long-term effect on major health outcomes.

SOCIAL-PSYCHOLOGICAL PERSPECTIVES ON CHRONIC ILLNESS

At any given time, 50 percent of the population has some chronic condition that requires medical management (Cole, 1974). This includes major conditions such as cancer or heart disease, as well as relatively minor ones such as a partial hearing loss or recurrent episodes of herpes. Perhaps a more startling statistic is that most of us will eventually develop at least one chronic disability or disease that may alter our daily lives for many years and ultimately be the cause of our death. As we noted at the beginning of this chapter, chronic illness now accounts for the major health problems in this country, and these are conditions with which people may often live for many years.

Precisely because chronic diseases are chronic, they often have a major impact on the social and psychological lives of these patients. Some patients may have to curtail their work or social lives extensively, and others find that their time is dominated by repeated trips to the physician and tests designed to chart the course of the disease. The impact of chronic illness is a relatively new area of investigation for social psychologists, and consequently there is much work to be done in understanding exactly what the psychosocial effects of the various chronic diseases are. A beginning effort toward such understanding has been undertaken in several specific areas.

Cognitions about Illness and Treatment

As we saw in Chapter 4, cognitive theories or schemas about events often strongly affect how those events are perceived and interpreted. Recently, social psychologists have examined whether the cognitions people have about their chronic illness, such as their attributions regarding its causes or the beliefs about its controllability, influence their psychological adjustment to illness and the course of treatment. Beginning research suggests that such beliefs can be important.

Some researchers have suggested that patients form an organized, cognitive picture of their illness that influences their adjustment (e.g., Nerenz & Leventhal, 1983; Lau & Hartman, 1983; Turk, Rudy, & Salovey, 1986; Bishop & Converse, 1986). In essence, these are illness schemas. They include such factors as the name of the illness and its symptoms (i.e., its identity), its cause, duration, and consequences. Patients have at least three models of illness (Nerenz & Leventhal, 1983). *Acute* illness is short in duration with no long-term consequences and is believed to be caused by specific viral or bacterial agents. An example is flu. *Chronic* illness is caused by many factors, including faulty health habits, and is long in duration with often severe consequences. Cancer is an example. *Cyclic* illness is marked by alternating periods when there may be no symptoms and others when there are many. Recurrent episodes of herpes is an example.

One of the problems that may arise in adjustment to chronic illness is that patients may adopt an inappropriate model for their disorder, particularly the acute model. For example, patients suffering from hypertension (high blood pressure) may believe that if they feel well, their blood pressure must be under control, and therefore they need no longer take their medication (Meyer, Leventhal,

& Gutmann, 1985). In fact, hypertension is called the silent killer precisely because patients often experience no symptoms and conclude erroneously that they no longer need treatment. Consequently, it is important for practitioners and others involved in health care to explore patients' understanding of their illness to see if they are using an appropriate illness model in understanding their disorder and its treatment.

Perceptions of the cause of illness may also be important. Researchers have noted that most people suffering from chronic illness develop theories about where their illnesses came from (e.g., Schain, 1976; Meyerowitz, 1980). Such theories about the origins of chronic illness include stress, physical injury, disease-causing bacteria, and God's will. Of perhaps greater interest is where patients ultimately place the blame for illness. Do they blame themselves, another person, the environment, or a quirk of fate?

Self-blame for illness is widespread. Patients frequently perceive themselves as having brought on their own illnesses. What are the consequences of self-blame? Unfortunately, a definitive answer to this question is not yet available. Some researchers have suggested that self-blame can lead to guilt and self-recrimination, and that self-blaming patients may adjust poorly to their illness because they focus on things they could have done or should have done to prevent it (see Krantz & Deckel, 1983). On the other hand, some researchers have suggested that self-blame can be adaptive under some circumstances. One study (Bulman & Wortman, 1977) found that patients who had suffered spinal cord injuries (paraplegics and quadriplegics) and who took responsibility for the circumstances that produced their injuries were better adjusted than patients who blamed other people or circumstances for their disorders. Perceiving the cause as self-generated may have represented an effort to assume control over the disorder (Bulman & Wortman, 1977). However, other research suggests that self-blame may be neither maladaptive nor adaptive (e.g., Silver, 1982; Taylor, Lichtman, & Wood, 1984; Miller & Porter, 1983). It may be that self-blame is adaptive for some disorders and not others.

It does appear, however, that individuals who blame other people for their disorders often adjust more poorly (Taylor et al., 1984; Bulman & Wortman, 1977). Perhaps poorly adjusted people single out others to blame for their illness, or it may be that by blaming other people, these patients adjust less well to their illness because of the unresolved anger and hostility they experience toward those who they believe are responsible for their illness.

Researchers have also examined whether patients who believe they can control their illnesses are better adjusted than those who do not see their illnesses as under personal control. Patients develop a number of control-related beliefs with respect to chronic illness. They may believe, as do many cancer patients, that they can prevent a recurrence of the disease through good habits or even sheer force of will (Taylor et al., 1984). Heart patients or patients suffering from multiple sclerosis may believe that by avoiding stressful situations, they will avoid exacerbating their disorder. Other patients such as diabetics may believe that by complying with treatment and physician recommendations, they achieve some personal control over their illness. We have already noted that feelings of personal control appear to be important in the practice of preventive health behavior, illness-related behaviors, and adjustment to medical procedures. What evidence there is suggests that belief in control is also adaptive for chronically ill patients. For example, breast cancer patients who believed that they had some control over their illness were better adjusted to their cancer than were patients without such beliefs (Taylor, Lichtman, & Wood, 1984; see also Affleck, et al., &, 1986).

In summary, then, patients' beliefs regarding their illnesses represent an exciting but puzzling new avenue for social-psychological investigation. Health cognitions can lead to better health behavior, high rates of compliance, and ultimately better quality of life. However, as yet, the exact effects of some health cognitions are unknown, and so their exploration clearly merits continued investigation.

Chronic Disease and Patients' Changing Lives

A chronic disease like cancer or diabetes often has an impact on all aspects of a patient's life. Work may be threatened or terminated by the need for extensive treatments or by the debilitating side ef-

fects of the disorder. The patient's psychological state is almost certainly affected in that the diagnosis of a chronic illness can produce extreme fear and anxiety or depression, as the patient realizes that his or her life activities may be permanently curtailed by the disorder (Burish & Bradley, 1983). Because of physical changes that occur, loss of income due to job restriction, or the need for help from others, the entire family and even friends are often affected by one individual's experience of chronic illness (Turk & Kerns, 1985). A patient's spouse may suddenly have to take on additional responsibilities that once fell to the partner who is now ill. Young children are sometimes forced

A chronic illness affects not only the patient's life, but the lives of family and often friends as well.

Irene Springer

into taking on more responsibilities than would normally be expected for their age group. Often, then, it is not just the patient who may experience psychosocial difficulties, but the spouse, children, and others who must adjust to these changes (Burish & Bradley, 1983).

Problems in social communication and social support can also arise. For example, Wortman and Dunkel-Schetter (1979) have suggested that cancer patients are sometimes inadvertently victimized by their family members and friends. Cancer can create two conflicting reactions in family and friends. Feelings of fear and aversion to cancer develop, because the disease is so frightening to most people. But most people also believe appropriate behavior toward cancer patients requires a cheerful, optimistic front, so the patient will feel better. The conflict between these reactions may produce ambivalence toward the patient and anxiety about interacting with him or her. Consequently, family and friends may physically avoid the cancer patient or may avoid open communication about the disease. These discrepancies in behavior (i.e., positive verbal but negative nonverbal behavior) can create confusion and upset, as we saw in Chapter 3, and can lead the patient to feel rejected or abandoned by loved ones.

Certain communication barriers may also arise between patients and family members over chronic illness. For example, research shows that cancer patients, like other victims of chronic illness, often need to talk about their illness and their feelings about their disease, but that family members may prematurely terminate such conversations in the mistaken belief that patients' needs to air their fears are counterproductive. In some cases, family members believe that such discussions would actually aggravate the illness. In other cases, such efforts reflect family members' and friends' beliefs that the patient must come to terms with the illness and not dwell on it (Lichtman & Taylor, 1986). Silver and Wortman (1980) have suggested that these misunderstandings may arise in part because family members and friends believe unrealistically that victims of misfortunes should begin to adjust successfully to the disorder within a short time. In fact, many victims of misfortune, including those suffering from chronic illness, need many months or even years to overcome the problems created by their circumstances.

To summarize, then, because people often live with chronic illnesses for long periods of time, these illnesses may pervade all aspects of their lives. Until relatively recently, the health care community largely ignored the changes in self-concept, personal relationships, and work that can result from chronic disease. However, health psychologists are now beginning to examine the social and psychological factors that not only give rise to these chronic conditions but also those that follow from it. Through such efforts, there is hope that the health of the American population can be improved by keeping those who are currently healthy in good health and by ameliorating the life circumstances of those who have developed illnesses.

KEY TERMS IN CHAPTER 17

biopsychosocial model	health belief model	stressful life event
coping	stress	

SUMMARY

1. Health psychology examines the role of psychological factors in the promotion and maintenance of health; the prevention and treatment of illness; the identification of causes and correlates of health, illness, or other dysfunctions; and the improvement of the health care system and health policy formation.

2. The major health problems of our country involve lifestyle disorders—including cancer, diabetes, heart disease, drug and alcohol abuse, and vehicular accidents. Lifestyle disorders are preventable and can potentially be influenced by psychological interventions.

3. Attitude change techniques have been applied to understanding the practice of health behaviors. Whether or not a person practices a health behavior depends upon: the perceived threat that a particular health hazard poses to an individual; the perceived severity of that hazard; the perceived effectiveness of the particular health practice in question; and a sense of self-efficacy that one can undertake the recommended health practice. Overall, however, attitudinal approaches to the modification of health behaviors have had fairly modest effects.

4. Increasingly, psychologists have drawn upon cognitive behavioral analyses of health habits to understand the specific stimuli in an environment and the health cognitions that control health habits. By modifying these stimuli and cognitions, one may encourage the development of more healthy behaviors.

5. Stress is a major health issue, because it causes psychological distress and because it can have an adverse effect on health. Stress, however, is not intrinsic to situations but is rather the consequence of a person's appraisal processes. When people perceive events as harmful, threatening, or challenging and are uncertain whether their coping resources will be sufficient to deal with the events, they experience stress. Negative, uncontrollable, and ambiguous events are most likely to be perceived as stressful.

6. Coping consists of problem-solving efforts and efforts at emotional regulation that attempt to reduce the stress of stressful events. Coping resources and liabilities include coping style, social support, time, money, and the presence of other stressful events in one's life. Stress management programs help people make more effective use of their coping resources in dealing with stressful events.

7. The recognition and interpretation of symptoms are influenced by social-psychological factors. When attention is directed outward, people are less likely to notice symptoms than when attention is directed inward. The interpretation of symptoms is influenced by prior experience, expectations about the meaning of symptoms, and which part of the body is involved. Communications with others are influential in whether or not people seek treatment for symptoms.

8. Adherence to treatment is often very low, in part because of communication difficulties between patient and practitioner. Practitioners often provide jargon-filled and simplistic explanations, whereas patients are guilty of not learning or following through on treatment recommendations. Interventions that draw on principles of social influence can help improve this situation.

9. Interventions that utilize the principle of psychological control with patients awaiting noxious medical procedures have been very successful in helping patients adjust to these procedures.

10. Adjustment to chronic illness depends in part on the cognitions people have about their illness such as its cause and whether or not they feel they can control it.

11. Communication problems between the chronically ill patient and their family members often occur. Friends and family members may not understand or may be unable to meet the communication needs of chronically ill patients who have to work through the impact that the illness is having upon their lives.

SUGGESTED READINGS

BURISH, T. G., & BRADLEY, L. A. (Eds.) (1983). *Coping with chronic disease: Research and applications.* New York: Academic Press. This edited collection describes the difficulties and issues confronted by patients facing a variety of specific chronic diseases.

GATCHEL, R. J. & BAUM, A. (1983). *An introduction to health psychology.* Reading, MA: Addison-Wesley. A readable overview of the field of health psychology.

MATARAZZO, J. D., WEISS, S. M., HERD, J. A., MILLER, N. E., & WEISS, S. M. (Eds.) (1984). *Behavioral health.* New York: John Wiley. An edited collection concerning the psychological issues involved in maintaining and achieving good health.

TAYLOR, S. E. (1986). *Health psychology.* New York: Random House. A readable and comprehensive introduction to the field of health psychology.

18 POLITICAL PSYCHOLOGY

From 1939 to 1945, virtually the entire globe was enveloped in the most destructive war in history, which pitted Germany, Italy, and Japan against the allied nations led by the United States, England, and the Soviet Union. Today, only a few decades since the end of World War II, the United States and England are closely allied with West Germany, Italy, and Japan in a power struggle (fortunately, still peaceful) against their former ally, the Soviet Union. Most of the postwar years all nations have been living under the threat of a nuclear annihilation of all civilization, which could be initiated by little more than a verbal command from one person in Washington or Moscow.

How are the leaders of these countries able to mobilize vast numbers of their populations to wage war? How do they accomplish such marked changes in national sentiment and outlook? Is their behavior rational or irrational? Are people really so changeable, gullible, indeed fickle, as this implies? Are people oblivious to the nuclear threat? ignorant of it? denying it?

Such questions are the stuff of political psychology in its most consequential form. Political psychology represents the application of psychology to political processes ranging from summit conferences and declarations of war to decisions about who should be members of the local school board.

In the past two decades, political psychology has become a self-conscious, if small, academic specialty in its own right. Primarily an interdisciplinary field, it has mainly attracted psychologists (social, personality, and clinical), political scientists (in politics and international relations), historians, and psychiatrists, with a smattering of sociologists, anthropologists, lawyers, and educators.

Political psychology has been stimulated very much by the urgent political problems of the day, especially those with actually or potentially devastating human consequences. Before World War II, this meant studying the rise of totalitarianism and anti-Semitism. In the 1950s, Communism, the radical right, the Cold War, the Arab-Israeli conflict, and the specter of nuclear war became key issues. Later it was terrorism, maniacs in high office, and the transitional problems of post-colonial nations. Many of the concerns of political psychology are, therefore, those of its political era. These concerns have also resulted in basic research on a wide variety of political processes, such as political recruitment, decision making by political leaders, voting behavior and political participation by the general public, political socialization, the impact of the media in politics, and international conflict. These are the basic topics we will discuss in this chapter.

PERSONALITY AND POLITICS

Perhaps the first major work in the field was *Human Nature in Politics* by Graham Wallas (1921). Consistent with the prevailing views of the day, this work was characterized by a strong Darwinian emphasis on instinct and natural selection. Unconscious motivation and habit, rather than rational thought, guided political decisions. Thus mob rule and irrationality were the staples of political life (Stone & Smith, 1983).

The dominant influence over political psychology in the next three decades was **psychoanalytic theory.** The fundamental data base of psychoanalytic research is the intensive study of an individual person, just as psychoanalytic therapy is based on the lengthy treatment of an individual patient. Not surprisingly, then, its main legacy became **psychobiography:** the psychoanalytic analysis of a specific individual. This began with Freud's study of the

Renaissance artist Leonardo da Vinci, and resulted later, as we will see, in numerous psychobiographies of political leaders.

As a consequence of these beginnings, a "psychological" approach to politics came to mean, to many people, studying the effects of personality in politics. While this defines the field too narrowly, the topic has remained a central one in political psychology (Greenstein, 1975; Elms, 1976; Hermann, 1977). Most psychologists would define personality as a set of generalized predispositions to behave in a particular way, regardless of the person's situation or role. In recent years the focus on such personality predispositions has come under attack on the grounds that personality dispositions are not so consistent with behavior across varying situations as personality theorists had claimed (Mischel, 1969). As a result, political psychologists have more recently looked at a wider variety of personal predispositions, including attitudes, motives, decision style, modes of interpersonal interaction, stress responses, and expertise (Greenstein, 1975).

Recruitment

A major substantive interest has been in political recruitment: Who becomes a political leader? Lasswell (1930), a major early psychoanalytic theorist, asserted that people went into political life to satisfy private motives, but then disguised them in political rhetoric. In his terms, private conflicts become displaced onto public objects, and then are rationalized in the name of the public good. For example, a young man might have a strong unconscious conflict about authority, manifested in anti-authority rebellion. He might then take up revolutionary causes on behalf of the underprivileged, cloaking his neurotic conflict about authority in the noble rhetoric of the public interest. By this account, people are recruited to political life for neurotic personal reasons. Lasswell later (1948) argued that one particularly strong such neurotic motive was the need for power in people with low self-esteem. To such people the exercise of power provides compensation for feelings of inadequacy by demonstrating their great importance to themselves and to others. The "power-hungry" politician is there-

fore seen as motivated by feelings of inadequacy. And indeed case studies of political leaders frequently turn up pervasive feelings of insecurity, low self-esteem, early deprivation, ungratified social and personal needs, and the like (see Burns, 1978, Ch. 3; Barber, 1985; Mazlish, 1972; Lasswell, 1948; Wolfenstein, 1967; Elms, 1976; Glad, 1973). These findings have supported Lasswell's view that political participation compensates for personal feelings of inadequacy in at least these cases.

In contrast, Lane (1959) argued that a successful democratic politician requires a healthy, well-balanced personality. And indeed most data show that political participation among ordinary citizens is associated with healthy personalities. The most active citizens have high self-esteem and a strong sense of personal efficacy, and their basic physical, safety, and social needs are satisfied (Knutson, 1973; Renshon, 1974; Lane, 1959; Sniderman, 1975). Such disagreement concerning the mental health of those recruited to politics recurs throughout the personality-and-politics literature.

Psychobiographical studies of political leaders are, of course, vulnerable to criticism in terms of the availability of data and intrusion of the biographers' own motives (Falk, 1985; Glad, 1973). Usually biographers must infer these important and hidden aspects of the person's personality from quite indirect sources of evidence, such as letters, speeches, or the comments of friends and associates. Very often the person is either dead or unavailable for interview. Moreover, political biographers often have their own political biases.

The conflicts between these two sets of findings are also partly due to the fact that these analyses of the inner lives of the political elite focus especially on their particular conflicts and anxieties. This has been the case, for example, in studies of Lenin, Woodrow Wilson, Eleanor Roosevelt, Lyndon Johnson, and Richard Nixon. But surely, according to standardized personality tests these individuals would, relative to humanity at large, be shown to be strikingly strong, confident, effective human beings. Current research tends, therefore, to focus on how particular disabilities might produce difficulties in certain specific political tasks or roles, rather than to attempt to gauge the overall level of mental health among the politically active.

Richard Nixon, making his first public speech after releasing White House transcripts of Watergate conversations.

Elite Decision Making

A second major area of interest is the impact of personality upon the behavior of the political elite. Rogow's (1963) biography of James Forrestal, the first U.S. Secretary of Defense, argues that his suicide was brought on by progressive paranoia, surely a potentially dangerous condition for someone in charge of the armed services of the United States! The Georges' (1956) excellent biography of Woodrow Wilson depicts his identification with, and repressed hostility toward, a stern and demanding father. When Wilson became frustrated, this conflict could be expressed by rage and rigidity. The Georges suggest that this aspect of Wilson's personality was partly responsible for his stubborn refusal to compromise with the U.S. Senate about the League of Nations, which ultimately resulted in the United States not joining that predecessor of the U.N. Mazlish's (1972) biography of Richard Nixon describes his need to create crises in order to cope with his fear of death, along with such potentially hazardous traits as suspiciousness, social isolation, difficulty in decision making, and a need for an emotional enemy.

Such studies of individual leaders have limited capacity for generalizing beyond the person in question. As a result, various more general typologies of political leaders have been proposed to capture major differences in political orientation. Barber's (1985) typology of American presidents is perhaps the best known. He classifies leaders in terms of two cross-cutting dimensions: (1) whether they are active or passive, and (2) whether their dominant affect is positive, such that they enjoy their work, or negative, so they are always fighting it (see Table 18–1). In his scheme, the most dangerous are the "active negatives," such as Wilson, Johnson, and Nixon. This type is characterized by unusual self-concern, perfectionism, an all-or-nothing quality in self-perception, denial of self-gratification, and great concern with control of one's aggression. When threatened, the active-negative type has a tendency to rigidify. One consequence is that he may focus anger on a personal enemy; another is that he may cling tightly to a failing policy, stand and fight, and even order others to die for him.

TABLE 18–1

Types of Presidents

	Positive	Negative
Active	Franklin D. Roosevelt	Woodrow Wilson
	Harry S. Truman	Lyndon Johnson
	John F. Kennedy	Richard M. Nixon
Passive	Warren Harding	Calvin Coolidge
	Ronald Reagan	Dwight D. Eisenhower

Source: Barber (1985).

Personality or Situation?

Another question pits the situation against personality dispositions. This is the same question that attribution theorists assume preoccupies ordinary people in their efforts to understand themselves and others: Is an action caused by the person's disposition or by the situation? When applied to politics, this becomes "the 'man' versus the times" question of leadership. Are "great men" in politics great

---

BOX 18–1

RIGIDITY OF THE RIGHT?

One longstanding hypothesis is that extremely conservative attitudes develop as a means of coping with psychodynamic conflicts that can be traced back to childhood. These attitudes are accompanied by oversimplified, black-and-white, rigid cognitive styles, because ambiguity is ego-threatening (Adorno et al, 1950; Tetlock et al., 1984). As a result, conservatives are said to be more intolerant of ambiguity, dogmatic, and prone to think in rigid, black-and-white terms. In a number of studies, Tetlock and colleagues have tested this hypothesis by doing content analyses of the public statements of public figures that yield a measure of **integrative complexity.** This is defined in terms of two dimensions: differentiation, which measures the number of dimensions of the problem or issue that the person takes into account in his thinking, and integration, the development of complex connections among these dimensions (1984). Tetlock finds, for example, that conservative senators have regularly thought in less complex, more simplified ways than liberal senators. And the same holds for Supreme Court justices: The conservatives have shown less integrative complexity in their decisions (Tetlock et al., 1985). Even when conservatives were in control of the Senate, and presumably responsible for dealing with the complexities and tradeoffs of practical legislation, they displayed less complex thinking than did liberals—though the difference was much less marked; responsibility for formulating legislation did force more complex thinking (Tetlock et al., 1984). In a final study, he showed that the most integratively complex members of the British House of Commons were the moderate socialists, with the least complex being both the extreme socialists and extreme conservatives (Tetlock, 1984). In short, these studies provide considerable support for the rigidity-of-the-right hypothesis, with some qualifications: The extreme left is also quite intolerant of ambiguity, and even conservatives become more complex when forced to cope with the practical realities of exercising power.

because of unusual personal qualities, or because they just happened to have been in power during good times?

A number of studies have been done testing various predictors of political leaders' effectiveness. For example, Simonton (1986a) has attempted to determine what factors are associated with historians' evaluations of the greatness of American presidents. He found five significant factors: length of time in office, length of time in war, lack of scandal, being a war hero (like Washington, Jackson, Grant, and Eisenhower), and being assassinated in office. Of course none of these is a personality trait, though it is possible that some might be effects of personality (e.g., a power motive might lead a president to go to war, or to become so controversial he would be more likely to be assassinated). But Simonton, in the same study, tested for the effects of a number of personality dimensions, such as power or affiliation motives, dominance and extroversion orientations, and dogmatism, and these predicted neither greatness nor the above-mentioned predictors of greatness. The one exception proves to be judgments of intellectual brilliance, which he does find to add significantly to the prediction of greatness (Simonton, 1986b). These data would suggest it is the president's situation, rather than his personality, that is the key to his success.

In a related effort, Simonton (1981) found that "accidental" presidents—vice presidents who assumed the presidency because of the death or resignation of the president—are not regarded as having performed as well as the presidents elected in their own right. Again, the question is whether this is due to the situation—they were not elected—or to their lesser abilities. He first analyzes the personal characteristics of both presidents and vice-presidents, such as age, education, and political or electoral experience. Finding they do not differ, he concludes that difference in performance is unlikely to be on the basis of personal characteristics (Simonton, 1985). The same study finds that accidental presidents do not differ from others with regard to these same characteristics, but that accidental presidents' terms are marked by such evidence of ineffectiveness as cabinet resignations, Senate rejections of cabinet and Supreme Court nominees, and congressional overrides of presidential vetoes. Simonton therefore concludes that it is the situation—how accidental presidents take office—that is responsible, not their personalities. Presumably, accidental presidents are regarded as less legitimate than presidents elected in their own rights. While such investigations cannot ultimately resolve "the 'man' versus the times" question, they do begin to specify the factors that are important in our judgments of greatness, and link them to basic processes of person perception as discussed in earlier chapters.

PUBLIC OPINION AND VOTING

A second major influence on political psychology has been survey research on publilc opinion and voting behavior. Sociologists introduced it in the 1940s with studies of voters in small communities. Lazarsfeld, Berelson, and Gaudet (1948) at first emphasized the origins of the vote in large social groupings. Catholics, the working class, and city dwellers were more likely to vote Democratic, while Protestants, the middle class, and those living in rural areas were more likely to vote Republican.

Later these same authors analyzed these differences as resulting from the direct interpersonal influence of family members: parents passing their partisan preferences on to children, and husbands and wives and co-workers influencing each other, especially making sure that each other did not stray from the "right" vote for their social category (Berelson, Lazarsfeld, & McPhee, 1954). The dominant causal factors were groups and social influence (as opposed, say, to media influence or personality).

Later it became feasible to do truly national studies of voting behavior. This resulted (beginning in 1952) in a long series of voting studies that have been conducted by the Survey Research Center at the University of Michigan, which are now called the American National Election Studies. These studies led to an individual decision-making analysis best developed in *The American Voter* (Campbell et al, 1960).

Party Identification

In this pivotal book, Campbell and others argued that voters are largely nonideological and minimally informed. The central variable in the voting decision is **party identification,** a standing preference for one political party or the other, typically developed early in preadults' lives on the basis of family socialization. By a simple process of cognitive consistency (much like that outlined earlier in Chapter 6), party identification in turn determines partisan attitudes toward the various major elements of an election campaign. These would include evaluations of the candidates, perceptions of which candidates were closer to the voter on a given issue, and perceptions of benefits to various social groups. A lifelong Republican might therefore evaluate Ronald Reagan very favorably and his Democratic opponent unfavorably, approve of Reagan's opposition to tax increases and support for "star wars" and the contras in Nicaragua, and perceive Reagan's election as good for middle-class businessmen like himself. This collection of partisan attitudes toward the candidates and issues of the campaign, shaped by a longstanding, underlying party identification, proved to predict quite accurately the individual's vote.

The American Voter has been challenged from a number of other perspectives in the years since it was published. Much of the criticism has contended that the key factors are current political and economic realities rather than such longstanding psychological dispositions as party identification. The underlying question is one that runs through the political psychological approach: Is *homo politicus* uninformed, inconsistent, irrational, operating from anachronistic preferences and prejudices out of touch with current reality—or is he/she informed, consistent, sensible, and rational, operating from a set of stable preferences and values, and responsive to external reality?

Not surprisingly, specialists in political psychology often arrive at different answers to this question from those who are more influenced by economic approaches. The former tend to emphasize the power of early learning, myths, and symbols (Converse, 1975; Edelman, 1971; Sears & Citrin, 1985). Longstanding predispositions such as party identification, nationalism, or racial prejudice determine voters' responses to the symbols of the current political world. The role of party identification has been of particular importance. The authors of *The American Voter* contended that voters are ill-informed and thus vote on the basis of party because it is a simplifying cue. When it comes to voting for members of Congress, these researchers observed that most people do not even know the candidates, and therefore vote on the basis of party identification, with some bias toward favoring the incumbent, who is usually better known (Stokes & Miller, 1962).

Those with a less psychological orientation emphasize the voter's consistency, rationality, and responsiveness to current economic and political realities. For example, some argue that voters do not just ritualistically vote for the same party year after year, but make sensible judgments about the past performance of the president, and then vote to support or oppose his continuing in office accordingly (Fiorina, 1981). Other researchers suggest that voters with deteriorating personal economic situations will vote against incumbent administrations (Lewis-Beck, 1985). In congressional voting, this viewpoint suggests that the incumbents' service to their constituents is a key factor; some members of Congress are quite visible and effective in dealing with their constituents' problems with the federal government, while others are not. The key factor is the reality of whether that constituent service is done effectively or not (Mann & Wolfinger, 1980). Still others suggest that voters vote on the basis of reasonable judgments of the incumbent's performance in office, and that party identification is itself influenced by incumbent performance (Kinder & Kiewiet, 1979; Fiorina, 1981). Similarly, the voter's policy preferences affect the vote and even party identification when the parties and candidates differ unmistakably in policy positions (Markus, 1979). Thus when the two parties began to diverge sharply on civil rights policy in the 1960s, conservative voters moved toward the Republicans, and liberals to the Democrats. All of these are cases in which voters are said to respond in a sensible, informed manner to the current positions and performance of political leaders in office, rather than adhering to blind loyalties acquired early in life.

Economic Realities

SOCIOTROPIC VERSUS SELF-INTEREST   A major area of contention is the role of current economic realities. Kramer (1971) observed that macroeconomic conditions, such as the health of the general economy, play a major role in determining the outcomes of elections. Hence the party of the president tended to lose congressional seats in elections held when the economy had turned bad. This finding had more than one possible interpretation at the individual level, however. It is possible that individuals whose own economic situation deteriorates are the ones who then vote against candidates of the president's party. That is the **self-interest** hypothesis. On the other hand, voters may respond to economic news more generally, and vote against the president's party when the news about the national economy is bad, even if they themselves are not particularly badly hurt. That is termed the **sociotropic** hypothesis: People vote on the basis of what is good for the society as a whole, rather than on the basis of what is good for them in particular.

Considerable careful research has been done to test these hypotheses by determining which of two kinds of items are more closely related to individuals' votes: their judgments about whether their own family's finances have deteriorated or not, and about whether the nation's economy has. The clear finding is that voters' "sociotropic" judgments of the incumbent's management of the economy are the deciding factor rather than more egocentric, self-interested judgments about their own financial situations; sociotropic voting is more common than self-interested voting (Kinder & Kiewiet, 1979).

This finding mirrors the more general psychological point discussed in Chapter 14, that material

self-interest plays a relatively minor role in the individual's vote. Self-interest proves to have minimal effects on policy preferences on such issues as busing (Kinder & Sears, 1981; Sears & Allen, 1984), national health insurance (Sears et al., 1980), and taxes and spending (Sears & Citrin, 1985). Even unemployment has surprisingly few direct effects on the individual's political attitudes (Schlozman & Verba, 1979). More generally, longstanding predispositions such as party identification and racial intolerance seem to play a much stronger role.

ATTRIBUTIONS   Why is self-interested voting comparatively rare? Several investigators have pursued an attributional explanation. The idea is that most people normally do not attribute changes in their own personal well-being to the political situation (such as the government, the president, the president's party, or its congressional candidates) or even to larger social conditions. This is consistent with our observation in Chapter 5 that Americans are biased toward internal attributions for their own situation. However, people are likely to attribute responsibility for the nation's economy as a whole to the president. Herbert Hoover found that out, to his great regret; he was personally blamed for the Great Depression of the 1930s! People might tend, then, to vote on the basis of conditions for which the president is plausibly responsible—the state of the general economy—but not on the basis of conditions for which he is not likely responsible—the voter's own pocketbook. The minority who do hold the president or society responsible for their personal situations might use them as a basis for voting, however.

To test this, Feldman (1982), using a national survey, coded voters' explanations for changes in their personal finances as "personally located" (wage increases, promotions, more members of the family working, increased expenses, lay-offs) or "societally located" (inflation, taxes, etc.). The hypothesis was that self-interested voting should be greater among those who gave societally located explanations for their own poor finances. There was evidence for that conclusion. Only about 20 percent gave societally located attributions. And slipping personal finances did have little impact on voting except among those making societal attri-

BOX 18-2

WONDERFUL WINNERS AND VICTIMIZED LOSERS

Consistent with the self-serving attributional bias discussed in Chapter 5, Feldman (1982) found that only 1% of those who felt their own finances were getting better gave societal attributions, against 46% of those whose well-being worsened; people take credit for success, and blame others for failure! Political candidates are also subject to the self-serving attributional bias. Interviews were conducted by Kingdon (1967) with the winning and losing candidate in each of 33 races in Wisconsin for the U.S. Senate, House, state senate, state assembly, and five statewide offices. The candidates were asked a series of questions about why they thought they had won or lost. The winners thought the most important factor was the characteristics of the candidates. The losers downplayed that factor and blamed the outcome on party label ("the voters just voted a party line against my side"). Some of the results are shown in the table below. In addition, the losers blamed their loss on the voters' ignorance: 70 percent of the losers said the voters were "not informed," compared to 32 percent of the winners.

For "wins" throughout their careers, 75 percent of the respondents emphasized matters within their control: "their hard work, personal service to constituents, matters of campaign strategy, building a reputation, and publicizing themselves." For their "defeats," 90 percent of the respondents emphasized matters beyond their control: "the party makeup of the district, the familiar name or other unbeatable characteristics of the opponent, national and state trends, lack of money, or other uncontrollable circumstances" (p. 141).

Comparison of Winners and Losers on Perceived
Causes of Election Outcomes

Most Important Causes	Winners	Losers
Characteristics of the candidates	62%	35%
Election issues	17	7
Party label	21	59
	100%	100%[a]

[a] Rounding error.
Source: Kingdon (1967).

butions, among whom they had significant effects on both presidential and congressional voting (also see Lau & Sears, 1981).

In turn, personal economic well-being had a significant political effect only among those who rejected the "ethic of self-reliance." These people rejected both the Protestant work ethic—the idea that success is dependent on one's own hard work—and the idea of equal opportunity—the idea that anyone who wants to work can get a job, and that everyone in our society gets an equal chance. That is, only the 18 percent who rejected both ideas—who believed that opportunity was blocked and that hard work did not matter—would so externalize their explanations of economic factors that they would vote against the incumbent on that basis. In short, the "ethic of self-reliance," expressed in internal attributions for one's own success, means that few people blame their own problems on the president or even the government, and so few people cast their votes against the president for that reason.

Consistency and Ideology

Another question that has drawn much attention is the degree of consistency and ideological thinking in public opinion. This again raises the fundamental question of whether the general public thinks politically in an informed, sensible, coherent, and sophisticated manner, or simply uses such superficial cues as party identification without greater thought. At first researchers asked whether or not the public mirrored the standard abstract ideological categories used by political elites to organize political life cognitively (Converse, 1964; Campbell et al., 1960). That is, do most members of the general public think about politics in terms of a general personal political ideology such as liberalism or conservatism? Early research suggested they do not; very few people seem to possess such abstract political ideologies. Similarly, Converse (1964) found that the low level of "constraint" (i.e., interdependence among elements as indexed by correlations across attitudes on issues) existed in the average individual's belief system. People did not seem to

have strong, consistent views across many issues, so this too indicated a low level of ideological thinking in the mass public. Finally, people might have quite firm and meaningful, but idiosyncratic, belief systems, so their attitudes might not fit together in the same way, but be quite stable over time. However, Converse (1970; 1975) also found their attitudes toward many political issues are quite unstable over time.

A number of key areas of public opinion have also been marked by logical inconsistencies. For example, inconsistencies have frequently been noted on such civil liberties issues as freedom of speech and on racial integration (Sears & Allen, 1984; Sullivan, Pierson, & Marcus, 1982), as indicated in Chapter 14. Most people are tolerant in the abstract but intolerant in more concrete situations. Most people believe in free speech for all, but far fewer would grant it to such unpopular groups as Communists or the Ku Klux Klan. Similarly, most whites believe in racial integration in the abstract, but far fewer support such concrete methods of implementing it as busing. And most people resist higher taxes and want smaller government (in the abstract), but also want to maintain or even expand government social programs (Sears & Citrin, 1985).

This view of the public as inconsistent and illogical has been extensively challenged. Much of the argument again concerns whether or not citizens are responding in a rational way to political realities. On the reality-oriented side, it is argued that the public will think ideologically only when political elites offer genuinely different ideological alternatives, as they generally do not, but did in the mid-1960s and early 1970s (Nie et al., 1979); that freedom of speech for national enemies such as Communists is denied only when they are perceived as being dangerous, as in the early 1950s (Stouffer, 1955; Sullivan et al, 1982); that the white public supports integration, but not busing, which is perceived to be ineffective; and that it supports radical tax cuts, but not cuts in essential government services because of high levels of waste in government, the many "frills" in these services, or a willingness to pay user fees. Nevertheless, this "irrational" inconsistency is a prominent feature of public opinion.

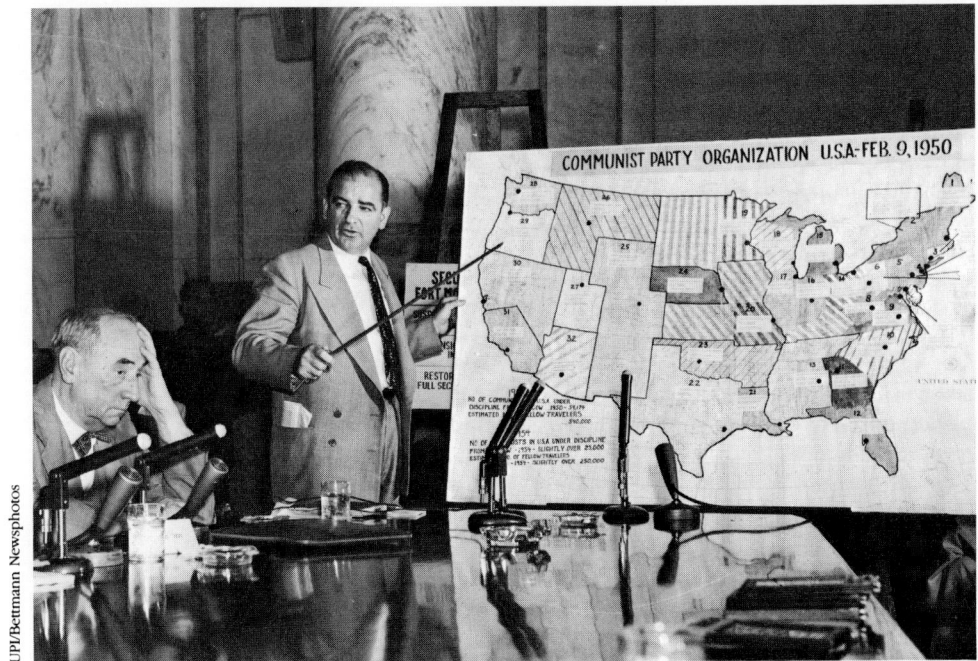

Senator Joseph McCarthy making his case for widespread penetration of the Communist Party into American life. Support for free speech for political dissidents was at a low ebb during the "McCarthyite" era in the early 1950s.

UPI/Bettmann Newsphotos

Political Participation

Political participation differs widely in its form—from such mainstream behavior as voting, the main activity of ordinary citizens, to engaging in protest or revolutionary behavior, or serving as an official in a legitimate government. Social psychologists have analyzed voting turnout principally in terms of citizenship norms (especially "citizen duty," the norm of an obligation to vote, and "political efficacy," the sense that one's vote counts), attitudes about the election itself (whether or not the contenders differ very much), interpersonal pressures (such as being contacted by a party worker, interviewed in a survey, or driven to vote by a neighbor), and the political context (e.g., how easy it is to register to vote) (see Kinder & Sears, 1985).

Early analyses of participation in mass movements were inspired by Freud's analysis of group psychology, and his followers, perhaps most notably Fromm's *Escape from Freedom* (1941). More socio-

logical treatments focused particularly on the rootlessness or alienation produced by migration and the disintegration of primary group ties (Kornhauser, 1959), the consequences of working class life (Lipset, 1981), or the costs associated with an open, mobile society (Bettelheim & Janowitz, 1964).

Protest and revolutionary activity have been analyzed recently in more socio-psychological terms. One is that political discontent arises not from outcomes judged as poor in absolute terms but from **relative deprivation,** as discussed in Chapter 14. This hypothesis has taken several forms. One is the "J-curve" (Davies, 1962) hypothesis, that argues that discontent results from rising expectations that are unfulfilled. When a disadvantaged group begins to get more favorable treatment, it builds up its expectations; if, as inevitably happens, the situation stops improving at some point, the group becomes discontented, and revolts. This was used by Davies (1969) to explain why blacks rioted so extensively in the 1960s, just when the civil rights movement and the "war on poverty" gave them unprecedented gains.

A related idea is that resentment stems not from appraisals of objective reality but from insidious social comparisons. In World War II, servicemen in units with speedy promotion procedures, such as the airforce, frequently had worse morale than those in units with slower promotion, such as the MP's; presumably the former more often saw their peers promoted more speedily (Stouffer et al., 1949). In recent years, it has seemed that the key ingredient is **fraternal deprivation,** the sense that one's group is disadvantaged relative to other groups, rather than egoistic deprivation, the sense that one is disadvantaged relative to other individuals (Vanneman & Pettigrew, 1972).

Finally, recent analyses of black, feminist, student, and antiwar protest movements in the United States have emphasized the role of political socialization, or resocialization, particularly of social and political values, and have in turn traced outbreaks of protest to prior changes in social and economic conditions. Black protest is partly linked to rising expectations stemming from the widespread migration by blacks from the rural South to Northern and Western metropolises (Sears & McConahay, 1973); feminism is associated with a rising resentment of discrimination against women among the better-educated working women of recent decades who are less burdened by child care or economic dependency on a male (Klein, 1984); and youth or student protest has been linked to the early family learning of liberal values in an affluent society (Flacks, 1967; Inglehart, 1981).

In this area, too, such psychological theories conflict with economic approaches. The simplest economic approaches suggest that poor outcomes produce political discontent. Thus the poor and disadvantaged should engage in the most protest. Psychologists have challenged this view in several ways. Tyler and his colleagues (1986) have argued that the perception of **procedural justice** is the key factor in understanding discontent. That is, if people feel that fair procedures have been adopted, and are applied even-handedly, they will accept without great protest even such undesirable outcomes as being poor, or going to jail if convicted for a crime, or having the candidate they opposed be elected president. Tyler et al. have supported this view in a number of studies on courtroom defendents' satisfaction with police and courts, and on voters' satisfaction with political outcomes: The perception of fairness, rather than necessarily the pleasantness of one's own fate, is the key determinant of satisfaction with the outcome.

Group Conflict

Early voting studies emphasized social and political groups as key determinants of political behavior. As indicated earlier, Catholics, working class, and urban residents voted Democratic; Protestants, middle-class, and rural residents voted Republican (Lazarsfeld et al., 1948). Today there is renewed interest in racial and gender conflict in politics.

RACE IN POLITICS   A major new theoretical approach to racial conflict has grown out of various cognitive theories. Kluegel and Smith (1986) have developed attributional models of the theories people have about racial differences. They describe a "dominant ideology" held by whites that attributes blacks' disadvantage to their lack of effort (i.e., to controllable internal causes). Second, racial attitudes clearly play an important role in determining policy preferences on racial issues such as busing and affirmative action, evaluations of black political candidates, and even such nonracial policies as property tax (and government spending) reduction (Kinder & Sears, 1981; Sears & Citrin, 1985). As we saw in Chapter 14, some argue that the key racial attitude is **symbolic racism,** a blend of antiblack affect and traditional values (Kinder & Sears, 1981; McConahay, 1982). Others disagree and see personal racial threats or realistic group conflict at work (Bobo, 1983). Realistic racial threats generally have a much weaker effect than does symbolic racism, but the role of group conflict is less clear (Sears & Kinder, 1985).

The self-serving attributional biases discussed in Chapter 5 are often applied to groups with which one is identified. Sears and McConahay (1973) reported on interviews with people in Los Angeles done shortly after the massive rioting by blacks in Watts in 1965. People tended to give explanations that exonerated their own group from blame. As Table 18–2 shows, blacks who were arrested over-

TABLE 18-2

What Do You Think Caused the Watts Riots?

Perceived Causes	BLACKS		WHITES
	Arrestees	Community Sample	Community Sample
Stable external (grievances about society, pent-up hostility)	85%	64%	34%
Unstable external (weather, accident, chance happening)	8	11	28
Stable internal (Communists, criminals, agitators)	2	9	29
Don't know, no answer	6	17	10
	101%[a]	101%[a]	101%[a]

[a] Rounding error.
Source: Adapted from Sears & McConahay (1973), p. 160.

whelmingly blamed the rioting on the miserable situation blacks found themselves in, and on the justifiable hostility and desire for revenge those conditions produced. Most blacks in the community who were neither arrested nor for the most part involved in the rioting came to the same conclusion—the causes lay in a stable, bad, external situation. Whites, on the other hand, were more likely to blame chance external factors or bad individual rioters.

This difference in attributions for the rioting had great political significance, of course. If the real causes lay in bad local conditions, as the blacks said, then those conditions should be changed. This would indicate a need to develop governmental programs that would help blacks in terms of housing, health, jobs, education, and so on. If the true causes lay in some fluke, such as hot weather, nothing need be done. If malicious agitators or criminals were reponsible, a harsh "law and order" policy might be appropriate. Stable external attributions supported liberal policies; unstable external or stable internal attributions gave ammunition to political conservatives.

GENDER IN POLITICS The women's movement and the many postwar changes in women's roles in society have prompted renewed attention to women's roles in politics. As recently as the 1950s, women had lower levels of political involvement than men, which was reflected in fewer political opinions, and lower levels of political interest, sense of efficacy, and voting turnout. The conventional explanation was that the female sex role made women dependent on men, uninterested in power, and distasteful of conflict (Lane, 1959; Campbell et al., 1960; Shapiro & Mahajan, 1986; Sears, 1969). Presumably, few gender differences in attitudes existed except in matters of morality, such as sex and prohibition.

Today, registration and turnout now seem to be quite similar for men and women (Wolfinger & Rosenstone, 1980; Poole & Zeigler, 1985), and women are nearly as likely as men to have opinions on political issues (Shapiro & Mahajan, 1986). There is the well-heralded evidence of a recent "gender gap" in the general public's attitudes, especially in women's greater opposition to Ronald Reagan and the Republican Party since 1980 (Frankovic, 1982). This mirrors the fact that the Democratic and Republican parties clearly polarized in the 1980s on women's issues.

An interesting line of research has begun to look for the effects of changes in women's social roles upon their group consciousness, and thus upon their political attitudes (Klein, 1984; Gurin, 1985). Women today, compared to thirty years ago, are more likely to be working, highly educated, unmarried, and free of caretaking for small children. This new reality has the potential for increasing sensitivity to discrimination against women, and in turn, converting those perceptions into potent partisan instruments.

It certainly has increased their sensitivity. But

whether it has done so through a sense of self-interest, group consciousness, or through conversion to feminist ideology as a result of the women's movement is less clear. Young, single women are clearly the most liberal (Frankovic, 1982). But the circumstances of women's private lives have rather little spillover into their political lives (Sapiro, 1983). It is not clear that women vote more on the basis of how candidates stand on women's issues than male voters do (Mansbridge, 1985). Women's sense of group consciousness is relatively weak, though increasing, so it is not evident that it is strong enough to explain the political effects (Gurin, 1985). Rather, the best evidence is that the "gender gap" is mostly due to women's longstanding greater aversion to the use of force, such as war, capital punishment, or other harsh responses to crime (Smith, 1984). It does not seem to be due to such gender issues as ERA or affirmative action for women (Frankovic, 1982; Mansbridge, 1985). Despite the polarization of the parties on women's issues, then, the "gender gap" seems not to be very strongly a matter of self- or group-interest. Rather, the equally substantive polarization of the parties over issues relating to the international use of force, such as war, defense spending, and arms control, seems to have been more important.

POLITICAL SOCIALIZATION

The central assertion made by *The American Voter* was that persisting divisions within the electorate based on party were the most powerful factors in voting behavior (Campbell et al., 1960). Attitudes toward them seemed to be acquired early in life, at the hands of the family (Campbell et al., 1960; Hyman, 1959), pointing to the political socialization process. This view contained several propositions that lent themselves to more detailed test. One is the issue of parental socialization.

Parental Socialization

As mentioned earlier, attitudes are assumed to be learned in the same way as any other disposition, through the basic processes of association, reinforcement, and imitation. Children are exposed to certain things about the world. They are also reinforced for expressing some attitudes. In addition, imitation or identification is important in the learning process. Children spend a great deal of time with their parents, and after a while begin to believe as they do even when there is no deliberate attempt at influence. The same process works with peer groups, teachers, or any important figures in a child's life.

Children tend therefore to adopt the dominant attitudes of their environment. This means the parents may have a great deal of influence on some issues. For example, as shown in Table 18–3, a high percentage of high school seniors favored a given political party when both parents agreed on that party, with only about 10 percent having the opposite preference (Jennings & Niemi, 1974). The same national survey of high school seniors and their parents revealed that 83 percent agreed on a presidential candidate, and that there were similarly high levels of agreement regarding other partisan preferences.

However, parent-offspring agreement was much less in many other areas. The extent of parent influence over offspring's attitudes seems to depend most of all on the clarity and frequency of communication between them. Obviously, parents are much more likely to communicate clearly and repeatedly their presidential preference in the heat of an election campaign than some subtle, relatively abstract aspect of their philosophy of life. In the same study, 92 percent of the students were able to report accu-

TABLE 18–3

Relationship between Party Preferences of Parents and Children

Parent	HIGH SCHOOL SENIORS (N = 1852)			
	Democratic	Independent	Republican	Total
Democratic	32.6%	13.2%	3.6%	49.4%
Independent	7.0	12.8	4.1	23.9
Republican	3.4	9.7	13.6	26.7
Total	43.0	35.7	21.3	100.0

Source: Adapted from Jennings & Niemi (1974).

rately which candidate their parents favored, but on other issues such as granting free speech to Communists, they were strikingly inaccurate—indeed, it often appeared they were simply guessing about their parents' beliefs (Niemi, 1974).

Within the family, this lack of communication leads to some predictable biases and misperceptions about one another's attitudes. One might be called a *generosity bias*. When they are ignorant of the truth, children tend to attribute a socially desirable characteristic to the parent, such as having voted for the winning rather than the losing candidate. Another is the *false consensus bias*, in which a child falsely attributes the same atttitude to the parent as he himself holds. On more diffuse and

obscure issues, children and husbands and wives all seem to exaggerate terribly the extent to which they all agree (Niemi, 1974). These biases, and the considerable gaps in communication they attempt to fill, limit the degree of influence parents have over children's attitudes (Tedin, 1974).

More generally, friends are the dominant influence over adolescent attitudes in a large number of areas that do not lend themselves to early, simple, repetitive, accurate communication of parental attitudes. One example is marijuana use. In the study shown in Table 18–4, adolescent use of marijuana was highly correlated with friends' use, and hardly at all with parents' drug use. The table shows, for example, that of all the students whose parent used

These children are being socialized to anti-busing attitudes. What is their cognitive understanding of the issues? What about their affective reactions?

UPI/Bettmann Newsphotos

TABLE 18–4

Adolescent Marijuana Use Related to Best-Friend Use and Parental Drug Use

Parent Used Psychoactive Drug?	BEST SCHOOL FRIEND USED MARIJUANA?	
	Yes	No
Yes	67%	17%
No	56	13

Note: Entry is percent in each category that use marijuana. Use patterns for each group are self-reported.
Source: Adapted from Kandel (1974).

drugs and whose best friend had used marijuana, 67 percent had themselves used marijuana. However, only 17 percent had if their best friend had not, even if a parent had.

So parents' influence tends to be more limited than many early observers originally thought (Jennings & Niemi, 1974). In general, parents have maximum influence on simple, concrete, recurrent issues like partisan choice, religious denomination, or prejudices against minority groups. They have relatively little influence on more diffuse, subjective, occasional issues, where communication is likely to be sporadic and fuzzy, such as religious philosophy, political cynicism, interpersonal trust, or civil liberties.

Higher Education

One important determinant of the effects of higher education is exposure to new peer group norms. Students who have spent most of their years living in their parents' home and surrounded by childhood friends are introduced to an environment containing many different kinds of people with many different beliefs. Not surprisingly, this exposure has a profound effect on many of them. They change many attitudes held since childhood; they reevaluate other attitudes in the light of the new information. In general, much of their belief system may undergo considerable reorganization.

A classic demonstration of such change was provided by Newcomb's (1943) study of alumnae of Bennington College. At the time, this was a small, exclusive women's college in Vermont that first opened, with a very liberal faculty, in the early 1930s. Newcomb traced the changes in attitudes

"They sent her to Bennington to lose her Southern accent, and then she turned her back on everything."

some students experienced during their college years. Most of the students came from affluent, conservative families, yet there were large and marked changes toward liberalism as the women progressed through the school. Newcomb's careful analysis of these attitude changes shows that they were most common among women who identified with Bennington, and who had the closest social relationships with other students and faculty. In other words, for these students, Bennington served as an important reference group, and their attitudes changed through the influence of their peer group.

Another interesting finding concerned the students' attitudes after they left school. Did their liberalism persist, or did they regress to their parents' conservatism? Newcomb and his associates (1967) studied the women twenty years later and found that their political views had remained remarkably stable. Those who left college as liberals were still liberals, and the conservatives were still conservatives. More precisely, the women's senior-year attitudes were better predictors of their attitudes twenty years later than were their freshman attitudes.

Newcomb attributed this stability to the social environments the women entered after college. He found almost perfect political agreement between the graduates and their husbands; these affluent-but-liberal women had found affluent-but-liberal husbands. The occasional regressions could be attributed to the fact that some liberal women had married husbands in occupations such as banking or corporation law, and could be expected to move in a conservative world.

This study emphasized the importance of environment as a determinant of possible attitude change. However, it is a rare college that shows the political homogeneity of the small, exclusive, isolated, and highly liberal Bennington campus (Newcomb's follow-up revealed that today even Bennington does not show the same degree of liberalism). The most important conclusion of the Bennington study, and indeed of this chapter, is that mere exposure to information will not be sufficient to change high-commitment attitudes. Intense, interpersonal contact such as that in the Bennington experience is necessary, and indeed may be necessary for years afterward if the change is to be maintained.

Persistence of Early Socialization

Another question raised by *The American Voter* is the persistence of early-socialized predispositions across the life span. Do people in fact maintain the same party identification throughout their lives? This has been investigated in several ways, each of which has its strengths and weaknesses (see Kinder & Sears, 1985). Persistence clearly is quite high for party identification (Converse, 1975; Converse & Markus, 1978; Jennings & Markus, 1984). But it is not completely invariant; party identification does change somewhat in response to events, especially in early adulthood (Glenn, 1980). Political events such as the Vietnam War or racial conflict can disrupt it early in adulthood (Markus, 1979). When people make major geographical moves, es-

This young girl is witnessing a peace march with her parents. What do you think the lasting impact of such socializing experiences will be on her later life?

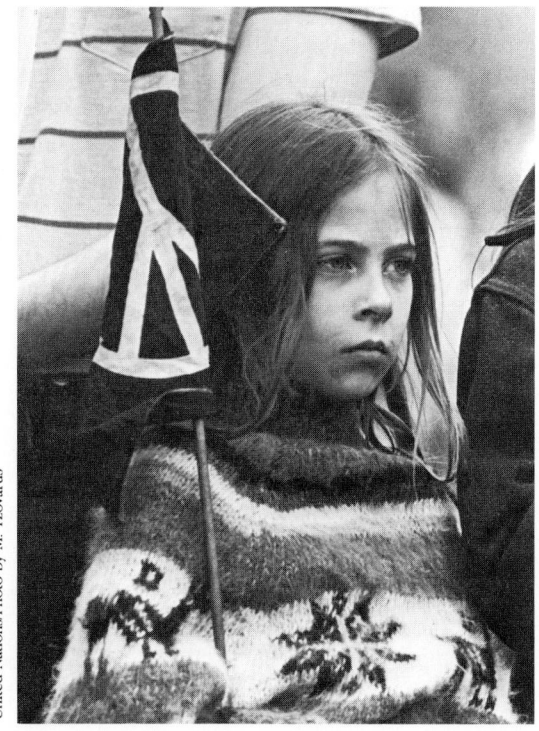

United Nations/Photo by M. Tzovarus

pecially in early adulthood, it is disrupted (Brown, 1987). Poor performance by one's party when in power can weaken one's party identification (Fiorina, 1981). And of course times change; party identification has not been socialized as strongly in early life in the late 1970s and 1980s as it was in the 1940s and 1950s; today's young people do not have the strong party loyalties their parents and grandparents did (Wattenberg, 1984). Overall,

the emphasis among researchers has probably shifted away from believing that party identification is acquired in permanent form in early adolescence, toward believing that early adulthood is a formative period with lasting effects (see Jennings & Markus, 1984). And there is greater appreciation for how people adjust their preferences (even if only modestly) later in life to accommodate changed realities.

THE MEDIA AND POLITICS

Another major area of research focuses on the role of the media in politics. Everyone is familiar with seeing the President speak on television, and watching the news at night, and it sometimes seems that nothing of any importance occurs in politics that is not due to television. We live in a mass media era, in which people are said to spend more time with the media than they do with one another. But as we discovered in Chapter 10 in examining the effects of media violence on real-life behavior, the media may not dominate people's lives as much as this would imply.

Three Eras

THE FIRST PHASE: GREAT POWER   Research on the effects of the media in politics has gone through three phases (Sears & Whitney, 1973). The first began in the 1920s and 1930s when radio became widely available throughout the Western world, and talking movies, with accompanying newsreels, became a source of mass entertainment. For the first time, political leaders could reach huge masses of people not merely through the printed word but through radio and visual channels.

Simultaneously came the rise of charismatic political leaders who were extremely effective mass communicators, such as Hitler, Mussolini, Churchill, and Franklin Roosevelt. Among the most

frightening spectacles were the great public rallies held by the Nazi party, with hundreds of thousands of followers chanting and singing and marching, all seeming to be puppets in Nazi hands. Social scientists greeted such herdlike behavior with horror. Though in general they conducted little empirical analysis, they assumed that this kind of propaganda was extremely persuasive. Why? Because, they assumed, the audience was captive, attentive, and wholly gullible (Institute for Propaganda Analysis, 1939).

THE SECOND PHASE: MINIMAL EFFECTS   These speculations highlighted the need for more systematic test of media impact. A second phase therefore consisted of systematic empirical research on the impact of the mass media, using the new method of public opinion polling. An influential early product was *The People's Choice* (Lazarsfeld, Berelson, & Gaudet, 1948), the careful analysis of voter decision-making during the 1940 campaign already discussed. It reported two main findings: (1) Relatively few respondents changed their preferences throughout the whole campaign, contrary to the fears of the earlier analysts. True, many voters had been undecided and subsequently made up their minds, but even these people decided according to their predispositions. (2) Those changes that did occur were not closely linked to mass media exposure. Rather, how people ultimately voted was strongly related to preexisting social background, as indicated earlier. In fact, the audiences for each candidate's campaign communications generally had been his supporters even before they heard his propaganda. They exposed themselves to the side they already preferred. This was called **selective exposure.** Finally, personal contacts were more important than media propaganda. The authors concluded that the voting decision was "a social experience."

The major implication was that the media simply reinforced prior predispositions, rather than creating large numbers of converts. A good deal of such media research was done in the 1940s and 1950s, and was usually summarized with a viewpoint that might be called the **minimal effects model** (see Klapper, 1960). It asserts that mass communication ordinarily does not serve as a necessary and sufficient cause of audience effects, and more often reinforces existing attitudes.

THE THIRD PHASE: RENEWED RESPECT   The last two decades have ushered in still a third era, this of renewed respect for the power of the media in politics. Partly this was due to television and the seeming devotion of the American public to it. Partly it was due to changes in the content of television: Presidents were increasingly able to reach mass audiences through "command performances" on prime time television; "media experts" became increasingly prominent in political campaigns and spent large amounts of campaign money; and the Vietnam War became "the first television war." Critiques were published of "presidential television" decrying the president's overly easy access to the public (Minow, Martin, & Mitchell, 1973); of the clever tricks used by media consultants in the "selling of the president" (McGinniss, 1969); and of the tendency of television news to criticize every institution in America, and create cynical and negative attitudes throughout the citizenry (Robinson, 1976).

The idea behind this "new look" in media research is that the media, and television in particular, do in fact have powerful persuasive effects, and so the pre-television "minimal effects model" is just outdated. Selective exposure should be overcome by big events, such as the political parties'

Bill Fitz-Patrick, The White House

As President, Ronald Reagan has been known as "the Great Communicator." Although he has had expert media consultants, he has personal qualities that make him especially appealing on television. What do you think they have been?

nominating conventions, election-day coverage, or televised debates, or by prime time political programming that attracts the viewing public for other reasons, such as brief political commercials, television news, and information about poll results. Similarly, strong political predispositions such as party identification, that promote the reinforcement of prior preferences, should be neutralized under many circumstances, such as nonpartisan elections, primary elections, or voting on ballot propositions. And in general, television should be more potent now because of the long-term decline in strength of party loyalties.

Let us take a closer look at the role of the media—first assessing media impact in politics, and then looking at some areas in which the media play their most substantial role.

Limited Impact

Are the media in fact as effective as this "new look" suggests? In general, campaigns conducted through the mass media are not as successful in producing massive changes in attitudes as one might think. Occasionally, a person who is virtually unknown at the beginning of a political campaign can win election by virtue of intensive advertising and face-to-face contacts. "Jimmy Who?" became President-Elect Carter in 1976. But it is usually extremely difficult in a short period of time to produce any sizable change in people's attitudes about something they really care about and are involved in. Many apparent cases of mass persuasion turn out, on close study, to have produced remarkably little real change.

Among the big media events in recent years have been televised debates between the major presidential candidates. In 1960 there were four televised debates between John F. Kennedy and Richard M. Nixon, each covered live, and whole, by all three major networks. Audience studies revealed that 55 percent of the adult population watched all four debates, and 80 percent watched at least one. Journalists widely ascribed Kennedy's narrow victory in the election to his success in these debates. Yet careful survey research revealed that there were no substantial changes in voter preference following the debates (Katz & Feldman, 1962).

Similarly, the single 1980 Carter-Reagan debate, held a week before election day and often regarded as a major influence in Reagan's last-minute victorious surge, brought only 7 percent of Carter's previous supporters to Reagan's side and cost him 1 percent of his previous supporters, according to a CBS News poll done immediately after the debate. In a close race such changes were important, but they cannot be said to have been massive or even decisive.

Research has also examined the effects of regular media programming on political attitudes. Some television series have dealt explicitly with problems of racism and prejudice, and have been enormously popular. The television series "Roots," depicting the history of Afro-Americans from pre-slavery life in Africa to the present, played to record-breaking audiences in 1976. However, exposure to the series had no significant effect on whites' perceptions of the hardships of slavery or on racial egalitarianism. Viewers' reactions to the series were most strongly determined by their preexisting racial attitudes (Hur & Robinson, 1978; Ball-Rokeach et al., 1981). Similarly, reactions to Archie Bunker, the bigoted working-class white man who was the lead character in the series "All in the Family," were strongly determined by the viewer's prior level of racial prejudice (Brigham & Giesbrecht, 1976). In both cases, reinforcement of prior predispositions, rather than attitude change, seemed to be the major effect. Why are the media generally so ineffective in producing major changes of political attitudes? That is, what are the major obstacles they face in political life?

Low Levels of Exposure

People in the business of affecting public attitudes know that their most critical and difficult problem is reaching the people that want to influence. The average newspaper editorial is only read by 25 percent of the newspaper's readers (Becker, McCombs, & McLeod, 1975). Television news is very often thought to be much more influential because so many people watch it. But do they? One typical study found only 23 percent of the adult (age 18 and above) population watch the nightly national news programs on CBS, NBC, or ABC on an average weeknight, and most adults (53 percent) never watched even one such program in a two-week span (J. Robinson, 1971).

Even these relatively few watchers seem not to have been watching very carefully. In a telephone survey in the San Francisco Bay area of people who had watched one of the TV news shows earlier in the evening, Neuman (1976) found that people could recall, on the average, only 6 percent of the stories covered in an average half-hour show. Memory improved when the interviewer ran down the list of headlines: Another 22 percent were remembered with supporting details, and 21 percent without any details. But half the stories were completely forgotten. With so many people not in the audience, and such poor attention among those who are, massive attitude change would seem to be unlikely.

THE RATINGS GAME VS. REAL AUDIENCES

How can we reconcile these modest audiences with the network claims of vast audiences? The networks generally rely on Nielsen ratings, which are based mainly on whether a household's television set is on or off, though they also make some use of viewer diaries. The Nielsen ratings showed, for example, that in 1976 the average household had a TV set on 6.82 hours per day (Comstock et al., 1978, p. 89).

This figure overestimates actual viewing in several obvious ways. First of all, the Nielsen sample probably includes an excessive number of regular television viewers, since the family must contract with Nielsen to be included in the study. Second, it does not tell us if anyone is watching the set. It could be just sitting there in the living room playing to nobody. Movies taken of living rooms indicate that the TV set is on, but no human being is even in the room part of the time (19 percent in one study), and some of the time people are in the room and the set is on, but no one is watching (an additional 21 percent; see Comstock et al., 1978, p. 142). So 40 percent of the time the set is on, but no one is watching. And, finally, even when they are supposed to be watching, the viewers may be doing something else and not paying close attention. Another study videotaped people watching TV and found an amazing variety of other activities going on, including pacing, ironing, playing Monopoly, answering the phone, conversing, wrestling, dancing, and undressing (ibid., p. 144). The mother often fills out the viewing diaries for all family members for the whole week on Saturday, when she finally has some spare time, but cannot remember their viewing in great detail.

In 1987, Neilsen switched to a new system of electronic monitoring in which each individual in the sample is required to press a button when starting or stopping viewing. The reliability of this system remains to be seen. (For a careful analysis of television ratings, see Beville, 1985; Webster & Wakshlag, 1985).

Major political events, like presidential debates, would seem to have been remarkable exceptions. For example, in 1976, eighty million people were said to have watched at least one of the debates. But more careful analysis found that only a minority watched more than one debate, and that only about a quarter of the public watched even one debate all the way through (Sears & Chaffee, 1979). Many would not be watching television at all, and most others would be watching other shows. Most viewers consider a football game or a good movie more interesting than a political speech. Thus, in politics and public affairs, the percentage of the potential audience reached by any message is quite small.

SELECTIVE EXPOSURE   As difficult as the low level of exposure makes life for propagandists, they have other problems. When a message does get through, the person it reaches is likely already to agree with it. As indicated earlier, this phenomenon is called selective exposure. People tend to be exposed relatively less to information that disagrees with what

Reaching an audience is one of the problems people face when trying to change attitudes. Not everyone can attract this kind of a crowd just to hear a speech.

they believe. Democrats hear talks mostly by other Democrats; religious people hear talks favoring religion; and farmers tend to read articles in favor of farmers. Similar selective processes can bias processing at the perceptual, learning, or memory stages.

What evidence is there that such selective processes pose major obstacles to political communicators? There is considerable evidence that real audiences are in fact biased toward initial agreement with the propagandist. This has been called *de facto selective exposure*. When the Republicans put on

a television special; mostly Republicans watch. When Democrats put on a special, mostly Democrats watch (Sears & Freedman, 1967). Why does this de facto selective exposure occur?

Some assume that individuals actively seek out supportive information and avoid nonsupportive as a way of maintaining the consistency of their own attitudes. This has been called *motivated selective exposure*. This is certainly a plausible idea, but there are just about as many studies producing a preference for supportive information as there are producing a preference for nonsupportive informa-

BOX 18–4

THE COMPLIANT COMMUNICATORS

Another possible reason for de facto selectivity is that communicators tailor their messages to their audiences. Since similarity in attitudes increases liking (see Chapter 8), speakers should be evaluated more positively if they modified their messages to agree with their audience. This would make the audience *look* as if they were being selective, even though in reality the communicator is just trying to be ingratiating (Sears, 1968). To test this idea, Newtson and Czerlinsky (1974) had moderates on the Vietnam War communicate their positions to hawks and to doves. In every case, the speakers significantly displaced their messages toward the positions they expected the audience to hold; they communicated a more hawkish position to the hawks and a more dovish position to the doves than they actually held. To see if the same process works outside the laboratory, Miller and Sigelman (1978) content-analyzed Lyndon Johnson's speeches on the Vietnam War from mid-1967 to the end of his presidency in early 1969. They also coded the audiences either as hawkish (the Veterans of Foreign Wars or First Cavalry Division) or as "other" (Congress, American Milk Producers, Young Democrats). They found a substantial correlation ($r = .501$); more hawkish audiences attracted more hawkish speeches from President Johnson.

tion, and a large number show no difference at all (Sears, 1968). The most likely conclusion from the research is that motivated selectivity is not a strong force in most situations (though see Zillman & Bryant, 1985, for a summary of contrary views). The same tends to be true of selective learning and retention. A number of careful studies show that people do not learn supportive information more quickly than nonsupportive information, nor do they retain it longer or more completely (Smith & Jamieson, 1972).

The major exception to this lack of selectivity in information acquisition is **selective attention.** A number of clever experiments have been done in which the subject is given the opportunity to press a button to eliminate static masking a persuasive communication. Brock and Balloun (1967) found that subjects would be more likely to tune in to a supportive than to a nonsupportive message.

Kleinhesselink and Edwards (1975) took it a step further, finding that people would block out nonsupportive messages as long as they were hard to refute, but would happily listen to those that were easy to refute. So the work on selective exposure and selective attention indicates that, for a variety of reasons, it is hard to get the message through to people who already disagree with it.

Even a communicator who has been successful in getting the message to the target is a long way from changing the target's opinion. For example, both Democrats and Republicans watched the Reagan-Carter TV debate in 1980, but they differed enormously in their evaluation of them. The overwhelming journalistic consensus was that Reagan had "won" the debate. Yet, as you can see in Table 18–5, only 10 percent of pro-Carter viewers thought Reagan had won. New information is interpreted in terms of existing attitudes. This seems to be a typical response to most such mass communications.

New information seems to be incorporated into existing attitudes without changing them very much. Why is this so? So much resistance to attitude change suggests that the attitudes in question must reflect fairly strong commitments. In fact, this is a major problem in achieving change in real situations. The communications that attract enough attention to get past all the barriers happen also to encounter strong, highly committed attitudes in a great many people. The result is that people use modes of resolution other than attitude change to restore cognitive consistency when it is upset by a discrepant persuasive communication.

All the modes of resolution discussed in Chapter 7 are relevant here. For one thing, people are likely simply to reject outright arguments that are discrepant from their own previous attitude. Pressures toward cognitive consistency cause the beliefs and values that fit into the already existing structure to be more easily accepted than those that do not fit in. For example, if people consider themselves conservatives they will be more likely to believe positive things about conservatives and negative things about liberals. They are also more likely to favor ideas proposed by conservative politicians than to favor those proposed by liberals.

Source derogation also takes place. When politicians take a position on the unpopular side of a hotly contested issue, their own reputations suffer. Walter Mondale, in 1984, was on the "wrong" side of the question of raising taxes to balance the federal budget. Ronald Reagan, like most voters, opposed any raises in taxes. As a consequence, voters did not change attitudes on taxation very much; rather, they derogated Mondale. Perceptual distortions follow the same pattern.

Voters distort the positions on issues taken by candidates to make them more consistent with their own preferences. A voter might feel we should get tough with the USSR, yet for other reasons be strongly committed to a candidate who favors expanded arms control agreements with the Soviets. The voter may well then distort his or her perception of the candidate's position, to increase consistency. The result of using all these modes of resolution is that people can expose themselves to discrepant information in the media and not show any real attitude change.

Greater Impact

SOME EXAMPLES   Occasionally, some media events or the political events they describe break through these barriers and produce considerable attitude change all by themselves. Following the assassination of President John F. Kennedy, at about 12:30 P.M. (CST) Friday, November 22, 1963, the three television networks covered the story virtually nonstop for four days. They covered the assassination of Lee Harvey Oswald, the alleged assassin. They also covered the religious service, the cortege to Arlington Cemetery, the burial there, several processions through the streets of Washington, and countless retrospectives and interviews with prominent people. The total coverage ranged from 60

TABLE 18–5

Voter Judgment of Who Won the Carter-Reagan Debate, 1980

Predebate Preference	Who Won?			Total (Percent)
	Carter	No Choice	Reagan	
Carter	69%	21%	10%	100%
Anderson	31	28	41	100
Undecided	27	43	30	100
Reagan	5	13	82	100

Note: Data from a nationwide CBS News/*New York Times* telephone survey of Americans of voting age.
Source: Adapted from CBS News release, October 29, 1980.

This famous photo shows Lyndon Johnson being sworn in as president on Air Force 1, alongside his wife and Jacqueline Kennedy, shortly after the death of John F. Kennedy.

AP/Wide World Photos

to 71 hours across the three networks (Rubin, 1967). Public exposure was massive, with the median American adult watching almost half of this programming.

The emotional and attitudinal effects of this experience were extraordinary. Before the assassination, Kennedy had not been thought nearly so exceptional. He had run behind his party and barely won election, was rated by the public as doing no better a job than most presidents (Mueller, 1973), and indeed has subsequently been judged by historians to be a little above average among American presidents. But, according to a survey completed the following week (Sheatsley & Feldman, 1965), 53 percent said they cried, 30 percent said they felt *more* upset than *most* people (and only 8 percent, less). Only 19 percent of the public said they had carried on "pretty much as usual." The attitudinal effects were no less impressive: Half the population called Kennedy one of the best two or three presidents in history, and only 2 percent called him "somewhat below average." It is impossible to separate the effects of the assassination itself from those of its television coverage in producing

these changes. But it is widely agreed that the television coverage was instrumental in making the events among the most memorable in American history.

Another dramatic series of events were the Watergate revelations. At the height of his political fortunes, immediately after a smashing re-election victory in 1972, President Richard M. Nixon slowly but surely was revealed as having participated in covering up a burglary of Democratic party headquarters carried out by some of his campaign workers. Most of his top aides were sooner or later implicated in the scandal and were imprisoned, and Nixon himself ultimately became the first American president to resign, in disgrace.

The events came to a head when a crucial tape recording was made public, producing, in a period of just three days, a sharp increase of 15 percent in those desiring Nixon's forceful removal from office (Laing & Stevenson, 1976). The strong change in public attitude forced the President to resign.

As we have seen, presidential debates have not themselves proved to be overwhelming persuasive instruments. But the media frequently make postdebate judgments about who "won" or "lost" the debate, and these may be quite influential. The Langs (1979) found that the immediate postviewing judgment of "who won" the first Carter-Ford debate in 1976 yielded a Carter edge of 18 percent. But media commentators quickly came to a consensus that Ford had done better than expected, and concluded that he had therefore "won" the debate. The Langs found a Ford margin of 21 percent among those interviewed several days later, after all the media commentary.

A fourth example concerns the potential influence on voting turnout of election-night broadcasts of exit polls, computer projections, concession speeches, and other premature communications about election outcomes. The concern arises because the polls are generally not yet all closed (especially on the West Coast) when results are announced. It is feared that voter turnout will be reduced if it appears that the outcome has already been settled.

Recent careful studies have begun to reveal some definite dampening effects of such projections on turnout. The 1972 election featured early projections of a Nixon landslide over George McGovern. One careful analysis concluded that the projections had resulted in a cut in turnout in the Pacific states of about 2.7 percent (Wolfinger & Linquiti, 1981). Similarly, on election day 1980, network projections began appearing even before the polls closed in many Eastern states. President Carter publicly conceded over an hour before the polls closed in California. And several prominent Democratic senators and representatives later attributed their narrow defeats to the reduced Democratic turnout caused by these media announcements. A postelection survey found that 47 percent were aware of projections of the outcome before local poll-closing time (Jackson, 1983). Turnout was cut more than 20 percent among those who heard the projections or concession speeches and had not already voted by 6 P.M. EST. Clearly, the Democratic candidates seemed to have something real to complain about. And the media, something to think about.

OVERCOMING OBSTACLES TO CHANGE   What do these positive instances of media impact on political orientations have in common? Most notably, they rank among the relatively few political events that have attracted very high levels of media exposure in the general public. The average person watched the Kennedy assassination events almost nonstop for four days. Watergate was in the headlines and dominating all news reports for about two years. Very large numbers of people prove to have learned of the media's "verdict" on presidential debates. And the election-night media projections of who has won a presidential election prove also to reach a great many people, one way or another. So part of the key to overcoming the obstacles to change is massive exposure.

Second, not all attitudes are emotionally laden and deeply held. The media may have a major persuasive impact when members of the audience are not especially committed to their attitudes. Also, attitudes toward new attitude objects, such as the Ayatollah Khomeini or acid rain or the Sandinistas in Nicaragua, may depend on media coverage. And the media may be more decisive in primary and nonpartisan elections than in general elections, because these elections involve fewer standing predispositions. The meteoric rise in 1976 of the nearly unknown Jimmy Carter is a good example (Patterson, 1980).

CONVEYING INFORMATION   Nevertheless, the media are much more successful in providing information than in changing deeply held attitudes. Presidential debates increase voters' familiarity with the candidates' positions on campaign issues (Sears & Chaffee, 1979). Children learn a great deal from television, ranging from Sesame Street to weather forecasts (Comstock et al., 1978).

One of the earliest demonstrations of this information gain from mass communication is found in the wartime research by Hovland, Lumsdaine, and Sheffield (1949). The Army commissioned them to evaluate the effectiveness of orientation films shown to draftees and volunteers. These films were intended to explain the reasons for World War II, make new soldiers more sympathetic to the war effort, and turn them into enthusiastic fighters.

The researchers did find markedly increased levels of information about the war as a result of viewing the films. For example, the films clearly communicated factual details about the Battle of Britain, such as the relative sizes of the German and British air forces, the focusing of German bombings on ports and ships, and the fact that the Germans would have physically invaded England except for the resistance of the British air force. But attitudes toward the British and the war— such as whether the British were going all out, whether or not they would have given up with more bombing, or whether they would hold out to the end, along with attitudes toward the Germans and Japanese—were largely unaffected.

But even here it would be a mistake to expect too much from the media. We already mentioned Neuman's (1976) study indicating viewers could recall only 6 percent of the stories they had seen and heard on the national news earlier that evening. In another national survey, J. Robinson (1972) found that people who watched TV news frequently were not significantly more familiar with the names of such public personalities as Ralph Nader and Bob Dylan than people who never watched TV news

at all. Part of the problem is that people do not usually pay close attention to television news. And part of the problem is that TV news tends to emphasize the more entertaining features of the day's events, rather than the more serious side. For example, when it comes to elections, TV news emphasizes the "horserace" or "hoopla" aspect of the campaign, not the issues. Broadcasts focus on who is ahead, what the campaign strategies are, who made the latest mistake, and pictures of motorcades or people in funny hats, not complex policy positions (Patterson & McClure, 1976). So regular viewers hardly knew any more about candidates' policies than nonviewers.

Newspaper reading, on the other hand, does seem to contribute consistently to the public's information level. On the average, regular newspaper readers increased in their issue awareness during the 1972 campaign twice as much as did nonregular readers (Patterson & McClure, 1976, p. 52). National

Hoopla at the 1984 Republican Convention. President Reagan was unopposed, so the trick was to attract television coverage in the absence of any real suspense about the outcome.

Stan Wakefield

samples show newspaper and newsmagazine reading associated with greater familiarity with news personalities, even with controls for demographic factors and other forms of media exposure (J. Robinson, 1972). Comparable tests show much weaker effects of television news.

AGENDA SETTING   In recent years, much attention has been paid to the media's role in **agenda setting.** That is, events given a great deal of media coverage tend to become foci of public attention (Comstock et al., 1978). One important early study (Funkhouser, 1973) showed that the public's sense of priorities during the 1960s (as reflected in the Gallup poll question, "What is the most important problem facing the nation?") was determined by the volume of news coverage given various issues (as indexed by the number of articles in newsmagazines). The public's priorities bore more relationship to media coverage than to such indicators of "reality" as the number of troops actually involved in Vietnam, the crime rate, and so on. Thus media coverage of Watergate, the Vietnam War, the campus unrest of the late 1960s, and the ghetto riots and assassinations of the 1960s all made them the number one problems of the day (also see MacKuen, 1981).

Several recent experiments have indicated that greater television news coverage induces higher issue salience in laboratory situations. In one, adults viewed television newscasts in which the amount of coverage given particular issues was varied experimentally. This manipulation significantly influenced the perceived importance of these issues, even on a questionnaire given 24 hours later. In a second, this salience manipulation influenced the basis for the respondents' evaluations of the president. They tended to base their approval of his performance on his handling of the particular issue made salient in the experiment (Iyengar, Peters, & Kinder, 1982; Iyengar, Kinder, Peters, & Krosnick, 1984).

The experiments, some conducted with ordinary citizens rather than college students, using real network news segments, providing a week's worth of news, and conducted under rather realistic circumstances, indicate that television news can, under the right circumstances, have an agenda-setting effect.

LONG-TERM CHANGE   Most studies have dealt with relatively brief or short-term mass communications—single programs or short series on TV, or newspaper endorsements in a particular campaign.

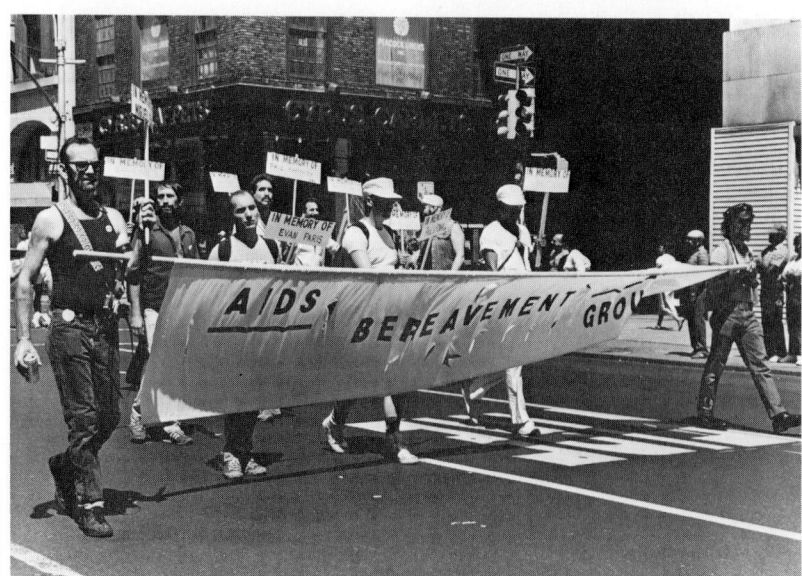

The AIDS epidemic is a classic case of media agenda-setting. From being an unknown disease it quickly became regarded as a major national problem. What is the distinctive role of the media, as opposed to the reality of the disease, in producing this outcome?

Laima Druskis

But many important changes of attitude may occur over extended periods of time—attitudes toward the enemy in wartime, or value changes over many years on matters such as religion or sexuality. These more gradual changes may be responsive to equally long-term patterns of media communication.

One example is Mueller's (1973) finding that the patterns of American casualties were associated with long-term reductions in support for wars in Korea and Vietnam. The earliest casualties caused big declines in public support; later casualties made less difference, as if the public had become "hardened" to the fighting. This study provides no direct information on the media's role, but that was surely the main vehicle by which the public as a whole learned about the casualties.

A somewhat more direct test of long-term impact treats campaign expenditures as a determinant of election outcomes. Presumably the more money a candidate spends on a campaign, and the more media expenditure and exposure, the more votes he or she should receive. Wattenberg (1982) has shown that media expenditures in the 1978 congressional general elections were reasonably strongly related to the intensity and salience of voters' attitudes toward candidates. This was particularly true in districts where the party organizations were not very important, and where expenditures were mainly targeted for the mass media rather than for posters, billboards, and so on.

The amount of campaign expenditures ought to be most decisive when little is known about the candidates and the choice is moderately confusing. Thus campaign expenditures should most affect the vote when (1) three or more candidates are running, (2) they are all relatively unknown, and (3) only moderate levels of expenditure are involved. Indeed, Grush et al. (1978) found that in House and Senate primary elections, campaign expenditures were strongly related to the vote when no incumbent or "notorious" candidate (past incumbent, famous person, or past governor or attorney general) was running.

Similarly, in presidential primaries campaign expenditures were strongly related to voting success in the early phase of the primary season, particularly for the less successful candidates (Grush, 1980). During the later primaries, earlier successes became more important predictors than campaign expenditures. Again, the media are primarily important with massive exposure about candidates the public has only weak attitudes about. Heavy media expenditures can boost an unknown candidate up from deep in the pack, given that there is no overwhelmingly better known candidate. But there is little evidence of that effect against a very well-known single opponent.

These studies remain rather indirect tests of media impact, however, since they do not use media content as the independent variable. Nevertheless, there is some evidence of relatively greater media impact providing information, agenda-setting, and longer-term effects. But we should not overestimate the magnitude of effects even here. As with media violence, it is much easier to document effects in the laboratory than in real life.

INTERNATIONAL CONFLICT

Another major influence on political psychology has been international conflict. During the 1950s the Cold War inspired much psychological work on international conflict, just as today work is focused on international tensions in and around the Middle East. A comprehensive psychological approach to international conflict would require consideration of many factors, including mutual perceptions of contending parties, attitudes toward each (such as nationalism and outgroup antagonisms), economics, social roles, organizational behavior and group dynamics within decision-making groups, and bargaining and negotiation (e.g., Stagner, 1967). We can discuss only a small portion of this terrain here.

Images and Misperception

A convenient starting point is the images that contending adversaries hold about themselves and each other. These can focus on nations, political leaders, or populaces. And we might be interested in the images held by either elite decision-makers or the general public. For example, we might be interested in whether or not the American public views the Russian people as fundamentally hostile to the United States, and whether or not the Russian people are seen as supporting the Soviet government. Similarly, we might be interested in the images that officials in the U.S. State Department have of the Soviet government's intentions in Central America, and in the images that the Soviet decision-makers have, in turn, of American leaders' intentions.

The first priority for psychologists has been to identify patterns of misperception. Finlay et al. (1967) feel that people delight in having a foreign enemy, and so tend to distort their perceptions to create enemy figures. White (1970) describes a number of other common misperceptions, such as "the diabolical enemy," "the moral self," and "the virile self." He describes a pattern of distortion that is mutually engaged in by two opposing nations, terming it **mirror image.** Each side believes *it* has peaceful intentions, and is afraid of the other side; the other side is perceived as aggressive and threatening, so one's own militarism is justified as self-defense. He has carefully shown how these general biases might be applied to the cases of Soviet-American relations and the Vietnam conflict.

Jervis (1976) contrasts the "deterrence" and "spiral" models of international relations. The deterrence model holds that a powerful nation must be firm in its resolve, and not give potential aggressors concessions; indeed it must be willing to go to war to defend its interests: Firmness can check aggression. The idea is that if you give them an inch, they will take a mile. A classic example is British Prime Minister Neville Chamberlain's capitulation to Adolf Hitler at Munich in 1938, an act which is widely believed to have unleashed Hitler's aggressive aspirations. The spiral model, instead, holds that other nations are likely to develop aggressive intentions sooner or later, so to protect one's security it is necessary at all times to be the aggressor. This viewpoint, not surprisingly, tends to bias the perceiver toward seeing danger everywhere. In a similar vein, Herrmann (1985) contrasts three images of Soviet-American relations: "communist expansionism," "real politik expansionism," and "real politik defensive."

In the basic cognitive terms we introduced earlier (especially in Chapters 4 and 5), these misperceptions are analyzed as black-and-white, oversimplified thinking, and egocentric perceptions that satisfy self-serving motives. Jervis (1976) particularly emphasizes overestimations of the unity and planfulness of behavior, wishful thinking, egocentricity, and the dissonance-reducing defense of prior commitments.

Another line of analysis has focused on personality, rather than misperception based on standard cognitive variables, as determinants of international images. Personal insecurity is presumed to be especially important in producing excessive loyalty to one's own nation and conformity to its norms, adherence to conventional social roles (e.g., the military), unconsciously expressed hostility, and oversimplification and intolerance of ambiguity (White, 1970). Etheredge (1978) has particularly emphasized the role of the male *machismo* or "male narcissism syndrome" in producing leaders that like to "play hardball" or threaten force; they perceive international relations in excessively competitive, coercive, combative, adversarial terms.

Public Opinion

In dealing with international relations it is even more important than usual to distinguish leaders' perceptions from those of the mass public. The general public is considerably less likely to be informed and have clear opinions on foreign policy than on matters closer to home. As a result, public opinion proves particularly responsive to bold acts by national leaders, demonstrated most dramatically by Mueller (1973) in the support given American presidents when they attacked the enemy in the Vietnam and Korean wars. There is a similar "rally 'round the flag" effect when some disaster befalls, such as the Bay of Pigs invasion of 1961, in which the C.I.A. was routed trying to overthrow the Castro government in Cuba, or the surprise Tet offensive in 1968, in which the Viet Cong took over many areas of South Vietnam and placed the Americans on the defensive. This seems to reflect a more general tendency to support presidents in foreign policy (Sears, 1969). Mueller (1973) goes further and surprisingly enough identifies the well-educated and the young as the "followers" who follow most. Why they are the quickest to rush to the president's support is less clear; perhaps it is because the well-educated are most attuned to the media, and thus to the president's reasoning, and the young have the fewest strong predispositions to help resist his appeals.

Foreign Policy Elites

Political psychologists, like many other social scientists, have tried their hands at comprehensive theories of elite decision making. One major effort is Janis and Mann's (1977) conflict theory of decision making. This centers upon emotion-laden decisional conflicts, the various patterns of coping behavior common in such conflicts, the antecedents of such coping patterns, and their various consequences for decisional rationality. This is an effort to develop a unique but comprehensive theory of decision making, and it draws examples (or evidence) from a wide variety of arenas.

Most important, it develops some insights that are unique to the psychological approach. One point is that decisional conflicts are inherently emotional and thus stressful. Such stress can have a number of negative effects, such as reducing the complexity of information processing, and it can lead to defensive avoidance and wishful thinking. Janis and Mann offer various techniques for coping constructively with stress, primarily relying on vigilance. Decision makers need to inform themselves adequately beforehand about the decision, but particularly about the emotions likely to accompany the decision and its aftermath, and come to grips with them.

Some personality characteristics may be particularly relevant to and dangerous in foreign policy decision-making. The *machismo* syndrome cited earlier is an example. Even birth order may have considerable consequence. Stewart (1977) presents some evidence that first-borns and only children tend to lead us into crisis, war, and civil conflict, presumably because as children they inherited responsibility for the family. "Machiavellian" personalities (Christie & Geis, 1970) demonstrate a lack of interpersonal affect, ideological commitment, and concern with conventional morality. They may therefore be highly appropriate for foreign minister positions (such as those held with great effect by Bismarck and Henry Kissinger), who can be held in check by heads of state. But they would be utterly unsuited for the head of state position itself, which requires behavior more conventionally approved of (Elms, 1976).

Cognitive consistency theories generate numerous examples of decision-makers' biases in favor of decisions consistent with their predispositions and images. For example, enemies are believed to have bad intentions, poor morals, and indeed, bad traits in general (Finlay, Holsti, & Fagan, 1967). An especially important notion is that of a leader's *operational code* (Leites, 1951; George, 1969); his beliefs about the nature of politics and political conflict, historical developments, and strategy and tactics. This is similar to the schema notion discussed earlier. Leites suggests that the operational codes of the Bolshevik leaders who led the Russian Revolution, and led the Soviet Union for many years, were quite different from those of contemporary American leaders. The Bolsheviks were willing to engage in high-risk activities as long as subsequent events could be controlled, so that the sequence could be aborted in the event of failure; American leaders, with their sensitivity to public opinion and concern about the next election, abhor the idea of public failure, and thus poorly understand Soviet leadership.

Recent information-processing theories in psychology offer similar insights. Most of these fall generally under the rubric of social cognition (Fischer & Johnson, 1986; Lau & Sears, 1986). One central tenet is that information-processing tends to be "theory-driven" rather than "data-driven." Some of the most interesting implications involve elite decision-makers' "learning from history" (Jervis, 1976); too often those lessons are learned too early in life, and hence are anachronistic when applied later in life, or give too much weight to firsthand or vivid experiences, or to efforts that were successful even if for accidental reasons.

Most foreign policy decisions are made with extensive small group deliberation, so it is perhaps not surprising that one of the most influential efforts by a political psychologist involves **groupthink,** factors inherent in highly cohesive small groups that can produce terrible foreign policy fiascoes (Janis, 1982). High group cohesiveness produces pressures toward conformity and thus suppression of dissent, and of one's own doubts, and illusions of unanimity and invulnerability. Janis persuasively argues for the critical role of groupthink in generating such American fiascoes as the Bay of Pigs, Pearl Harbor, Watergate, and Vietnam (for critiques, see Longley & Pruitt, 1980; Tetlock, 1983a).

DEATH AND HORROR

All historical eras must confront the horrible acts committed in the quest for political power. Our era is no exception. It lives under the nuclear cloud as well, which we think of as a new ingredient, though the plagues and pestilences and scorched earths of the past may have hardly seemed less total. Psychologists have seemed most comfortable in exploring these matters. Economists are obviously uncomfortable with the irrational, and political scientists, with the disorderly and impractical. Many psychologists, on the other hand, seek out the extremes, the irrational, the deep, the mysterious, the sense of horror and despair—and even, from another perspective, the astonishing ability of the human being to weather, adapt to, and even come to enjoy, many quite unpleasant situations.

As indicated earlier, Americans' responses to the assassination of President Kennedy were examined in great detail (Greenberg & Parker, 1965; Wolfenstein & Kliman, 1965) in terms of their great emotionality, grieving, over-idealization of the dead president, and especially its impact on children. Reactions to the Nazi Holocaust have become a matter of great interest, among other things for the questions it raised about the apparent passivity of so many Jews (e.g., Zuckerman, 1984). The apparent mass suicide of residents of Jonestown has raised questions both about individual charisma (of Jones himself) and collective action, perhaps in terms of collective regression (Ulman & Abse, 1983). Terrorism has provoked much analysis of the personalities and motives of terrorists themselves, of course, but also of its effects on the population it attempts to influence. Some research suggests it does indeed inspire fear and anxiety (among Israelis), but a hardening of attitude against the terrorists' causes (see Friedland & Merari, 1985).

Perhaps the lack of antinuclear activism is like the generally low level of activism in the United States on almost any political issue, and the apparent minimal impact of antinuclear media presentations, like the minimal impact of the political media more generally (Fiske, 1987). The nuclear stalemate has inspired considerable research as well. In some sense the relative lack of public concern over it, despite some realistic estimates of nuclear effects, has been a source of puzzlement (Fiske, Fischoff, & Milburn, 1983).

As an identifiable specialty, political psychology has drawn together a variety of intellectual strands previously located solely in the traditional social science disciplines. It has done so partly because it does offer a unique perspective on politics, one emphasizing such familiar psychological concerns as emotion and stress, mechanisms of information processing, interpersonal relationships, and the irrational, among others. The coalescence of these strands is particularly valuable at this time because of the great popularity of economic explanations of political behavior, which offer a strikingly different account. One of the necessary consequences of this focus upon individuals and their irrationali-

Despite the awesome threat of nuclear war (or perhaps because of it), there has been relatively little popular protest or political action about it.

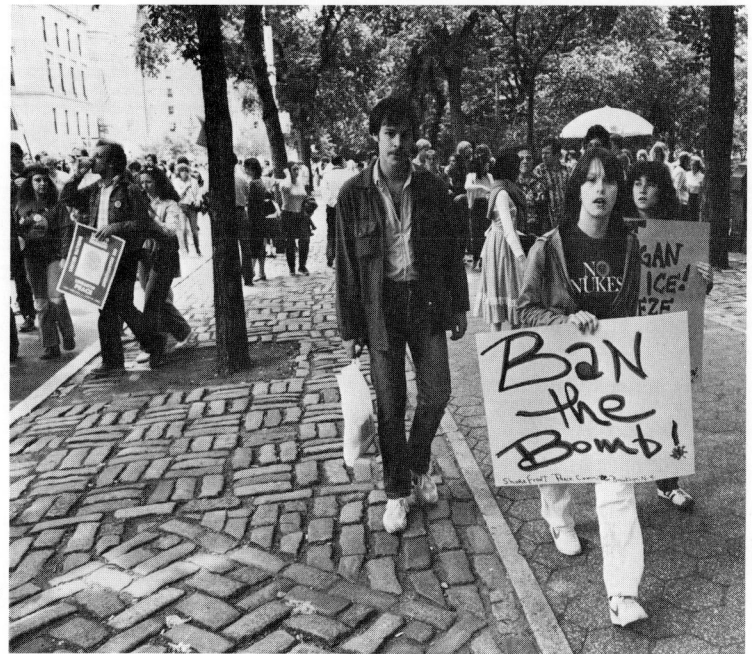

Ken Karp

ties is a strong normative undercurrent that usually leads to a caring, understanding, good-hearted empathy for them. A political reformist impulse follows close behind, and that can produce less rigorous research than social psychologists are accustomed to. The tension between this reformist impulse and the scientific tough-mindedness emphasized elsewhere in this book is but one of the several that make political psychology lively and provocative.

KEY TERMS IN CHAPTER 18

agenda-setting	minimal effects model	psychoanalytic theory	selective exposure
fraternal deprivation	mirror image	psychobiography	self-interest
groupthink	party identification	relative deprivation	sociotropic
integrative complexity	procedural justice	selective attention	symbolic racism

SUMMARY

1. One major debate in political psychology is whether people recruited to political leadership tend to be fulfilling neurotic needs or are among the most healthy and effective human beings.

2. The dominant theory of voting behavior views a longstanding party identification, acquired early in life, as the major influence on the vote. Voters are thought to be generally ill-informed, nonideological, and to have rather weak attitudes on issues.

3. This dominant theory has been challenged in recent years by the view that voters do respond in a moderately informed manner to the realities of life, in terms of their economic situations, issue differences between candidates, presidential performance, and congressional constituency service.

4. Racial and gender issues are receiving much current attention, especially the bases of whites' negative political responses to racial issues and black candidates, and of women's political mobilization.

5. Party identification is quite stable through the life span, though it probably remains open to significant influence through early adulthood. It is influenced to some extent by one's parents, although not as exclusively as once thought. Today's young voters have weaker party identifications than did their predecessors.

6. Social scientists have gone through three markedly different phases in assessing the impact of the media in politics. In the 1930s it was thought to be an awesomely powerful new weapon, and in the 1940s and 1950s to have minimal effects. Today there is renewed respect for its role. Nevertheless, far-ranging attitude changes are rarely produced by the media.

7. A major obstacle is lack of exposure to discrepant information. Political propaganda also is often ineffective because it encounters highly committed attitudes, so any new information is selectively interpreted by members of the audience to reinforce their prior attitudes.

8. The media can produce massive changes in political attitudes, but usually only in those rare cases in which there is a high level of exposure. The media can be effective, however, in agenda setting, providing information, or changing low-commitment attitudes, or in producing change through repeated exposure over long time periods.

9. A number of common misperceptions in international relations have been identified, including the need to identify an enemy, the mirror images that contending powers have of each other, and the tendency to overuse the "lessons of history." These fit social cognition theory and research.

10. Elite decision-making in international relations is also subject to bias due to the stress and emotionality inevitably associated with it, and to the group dynamics of decision-making elites.

SUGGESTED READINGS

Janis, I. L. (1982). *Victims of groupthink*, 2nd ed. Boston: Houghton-Mifflin. A series of case studies analyzing foreign policy "fiascoes" (and some successes) as a result of "groupthink." Includes chapters on Pearl Harbor, the Bay of Pigs, Watergate, among others.

JERVIS, R. (1976). *Perception and misperception in international politics*. New Jersey: Princeton University Press. The best application of social cognition theory and research to government decision-makers' perceptions of international relations; many fascinating case studies.

KINDER, D. R., & SEARS, D. O. (1985). Public opinion and political action. In G. Lindzey and E. Aronson (Eds.), *Handbook of social psychology,* 3rd ed., Vol. 2. New York: Random House. A comprehensive account of research on public opinion concerning politics in the United States. Relates that research to the social-psychological principles discussed in this chapter.

KRAUS, S., & PERLOFF, R. M. (Eds.). (1985). *Mass media and political thought: An information-processing approach*. The best of the contemporary socio-psychological approaches to mass media effects, including nonverbal communication, schemas, and agenda-setting.

LAU, R. R., & SEARS, D. O. (1986). *Political Cognition: The 19th Annual Carnegie Symposium on Cognition*. Hillsdale, NJ: Erlbaum. A recent collection of papers that apply social cognition research and theory to politics. The "schema" concept appears most often.

McGUIRE, W. J. (1986). The myth of massive media impact: Savagings and salvagings. In G. Comstock, (Ed.), *Public Communication and Behavior, Vol. 1*. Orlando: Academic Press. A thorough but surprisingly brief review of the empirical evidence on the twelve principal areas of hypothesized media impact: "The demonstrated impacts are surprisingly slight."

Political Psychology. A quarterly journal that publishes a wide variety of research, ranging from psychobiography and peace research to voting behavior.

WHITE, R. K. (Ed.) (1986). *Psychology and the prevention of nuclear war*. New York: New York University Press. A broad collection of the best of psychologists' thinking about international conflict in the nuclear era.

GLOSSARY

Actor-observer bias The tendency for observers to overestimate the importance of the actor's dispositions, and for the actor to overestimate the importance of the situation, in explaining the actor's behavior.

Affective component That part of an *attitude* consisting of a person's emotional feelings associated with beliefs about an attitude object; consists mainly of the evaluation of the object (like–dislike, pro–con).

Agenda-setting Mass communications that focus the public's attention on certain issues, and therefore determine what issues the public is concerned about. If the media focus intensively on inflation, the public becomes concerned with inflation; if they focus on Central America, so will the public.

Aggression Any action intended to hurt others; may also refer to the internal state of wanting to hurt others (aggressive feelings).

Aggression anxiety Anxiety about expressing overt aggression, usually with respect to a particular target.

Altruism An act performed voluntarily to help another person when there is no expectation of receiving a reward in any form. See also *prosocial behavior.*

Androgynous In psychology, the term used to refer to people who believe they possess both traditionally feminine and masculine characteristics. An androgynous person's self-concept includes both masculine/instrumental qualities (e.g., being independent and strong) and feminine/expressive qualities (e.g., being nurturant and gentle).

Anger Aggressive feelings.

Antisocial aggression Aggressive acts such as murder that violate commonly accepted social norms.

Applied research Research designed to answer questions about specific, real-world issues, usually without concern for any general theoretical or scientific issues.

Archival research Techniques based on the analysis of data already available in archives or published records.

Assimilation In the study of attitude change, this is the tendency to perceive a communication of low discrepancy as being even less discrepant than it is in fact. That is, the target overestimates agreement with a communicator who disagrees only moderately with him or her.

Association A link in memory between different stimuli that occur together in time and place. Through pairing, reactions to one stimulus become associated with the other. This is one of the basic processes by which learning occurs.

Attachment The emotional bonds that form between people in a close relationship. In infancy, attachment is seen when a child responds positively to one special person, wants to be with that person, seeks the person out when frightened, etc. Ainsworth has identified three styles of infant attachment: secure, avoidant, and anxious/ambivalent.

Attitude Enduring response disposition with a *cognitive component,* an *affective component,* and a *behavioral component.* We develop and hold attitudes towards persons, objects, and ideas.

Attitude-discrepant behavior Acts inconsistent with a person's attitudes. When an individual behaves in a way inconsistent with a belief, *cognitive dissonance* is produced and there is a tendency for the attitude to change.

Attribution The process by which people make inferences about the causes of behavior or attitudes.

Attribution theory The principles that determine how attributions are made and what effects these causal attributions have.

Authoritarian personality A personality type who is overly deferential to authority and hostile to minority groups.

Averaging principle In impression formation, this is the idea that various informational inputs about a person or other attitude object are processed solely in terms of their evaluation of the object, and then averaged together to form an overall attitude.

Aversive racism Attitudes toward members of a racial group that embody both egalitarian social values and negative affects, resulting in avoidance of that racial group. For example, whites' avoidance of blacks might result from attitudes that combine values of equality and negative feelings.

Balance theory Heider proposed that we strive to maintain consistency among our sentiment and unit relationships. We are motivated to like people we are connected to by physical proximity or other links, to like people we agree with, and to dislike those we disagree with.

Basic research Research designed to examine general relationships among phenomena rather than specific questions about particular issues.

Behavioral component That part of an attitude consisting of the person's tendencies to act toward the attitude object. A child's attitude toward a pet cat may include the tendencies to pet and cuddle the animal.

Behavioral sink The term used by Calhoun to describe the findings that rats placed in very high-density cages showed antisocial and disruptive behavior.

Behaviorism The influential analysis of learning associated with Watson, Pavlov, and Skinner, which investigates only overt behavior, not subjective states such as thoughts, feelings, or attitudes. Behaviorism identifies association and reinforcement as the key determinants of learning.

Biopsychosocial model The view that a person's state of health is jointly determined by biological factors (such as exposure to a virus), psychological factors (such as stress), and social factors (such as degree of social support).

Body language Information transmitted about attitudes, emotions, and so on by nonverbal bodily movements and features, such as posture, stance, touch, and so on.

Brainstorming A technique for coming up with new and creative solutions for problems. Members of a group discuss a problem and generate as many different solutions as they can, withholding criticism until all possibilities have been presented.

Breakpoints The starting or ending points of a behavioral act, as perceived by an observer.

Built environment Buildings, roads, shopping centers, and other structures built by humans.

Bystander effect When other people are present, it is less likely that any one person will offer help to a stranger in distress. The diffusion of responsibility created by the presence of other people is one explanation of the bystander effect.

Bystander intervention Coming to the aid of a stranger in distress.

Categorization The process by which we perceive stimuli in groups or categories rather than perceiving each individual stimulus in isolation from the others.

Catharsis Freud's idea that by expressing *aggression,* a person's aggressive drive can be reduced.

Causal attribution See *attribution.*

Central traits A trait is central to the extent that it is associated with many of the stimulus person's other characteristics. Traits such as warm or cold are considered central because they are important in determining overall impressions.

Close relationship A personal relationship involving much interdependence. Partners in close relationships usually interact frequently, have relatively strong influence on each other, and engage in a variety of activities together.

Cognitive component That part of an attitude consisting of the person's beliefs, knowledge, and facts about the attitude object.

Cognitive consistency Tendency for people to seek consistency among their attitudes; regarded as a major determinant of attitude formation and change.

Cognitive dissonance Theory developed by Festinger according to which inconsistency (dissonance) between two cognitive elements produces pressure to make these elements consonant. It has been applied to a wide range of phenomena, including decisions and attitude-discrepant behavior.

Cognitive miser Description of people as having limited information-processing capabilities, and therefore adopting various cognitive shortcuts. For example, we cannot perceive all stimuli in our perceptual field at once, so we focus on the most salient ones.

Cognitive response theory The theory that attitude change following receipt of communication depends on the cognitive responses it evokes. If it produces negative thoughts, it will be rejected; if it evokes positive thoughts, it will be accepted. Counterarguing is a crucial mechanism for resisting persuasion, according to this theory.

Cohesiveness In group dynamics, the forces, both positive and negative, that cause members to remain in a group. Cohesiveness is a characteristic of a group as a whole, and results from the degree of *commitment* of each individual to the group.

Commitment to an attitude The extent to which a person is tied to, involved in, or for any reason finds it difficult to give up an attitude, judgment, or other kind of position.

Commitment to a relationship All the forces that act to keep a person in a relationship or group. Positive forces include interpersonal attraction and satisfaction with a relationship; negative forces include such barriers to ending a relationship as the lack of alternatives or having made large investments in the relationship.

Communication networks In some groups there are constraints on the channels of communication available to members. Four types of communication networks are the circle, chain, wheel, and Y-pattern.

Companionate love A somewhat practical type of love that emphasizes trust, caring, and tolerance of the partner's flaws. Companionate love may develop slowly in a relationship as partners become more interdependent. Sometimes contrasted with *passionate love.*

Comparison level One standard we use to evaluate the quality of our social relationships. Our comparison level refers to the level of benefits we expect or believe we deserve based on our past experience in relationships.

Comparison level for alternatives A second standard we use to evaluate the quality of our social relationships. Our comparison level for alternatives refers to evaluating one particular relationship against other relationships that are currently available to us.

Compliance Performance of an act at another's request.

Conformity Voluntary performance of an act because others also do it. Conformity often results from a person's desire to be right (informational influence) and/or desire to be liked (normative influence.)

Contact theory The theory that prejudice against a social group can be reduced by appropriate kinds of contact with individual members of that group.

Contagious violence Spreading of the aggressive feelings or behavior of a small number of people throughout the entire group, as described by LeBon

and others. Most frequently used to describe mob violence.

Contingency model of leadership effectiveness Fiedler's model distinguishing between task-oriented and relationship-oriented leaders. When the group situation is either highly favorable or highly unfavorable to control by the leader, task-oriented leaders are more effective. In intermediate situations where the leader has moderate control, relationship-oriented leaders are more successful.

Contrast In the study of attitude change, the tendency to perceive a communicator's position as being farther away from the individual's own position than it actually is.

Coping The process of managing internal or environmental demands that are appraised as taxing or exceeding one's resources. Coping may involve active problem solving efforts and also efforts at emotional control.

Correlational design Passively measuring two variables and determining whether or not they are associated with each other. Studies relating smoking to lung cancer are correlational: They measure the amount of smoking each person has done and whether or not he or she gets lung cancer in order to determine if the two are related. The major problem with correlational designs is determining whether or not a correlation reflects a cause-and-effect relationship.

Covariation Judgments of covariation involve determining how strongly two things are related such as the time of day and frequency of crime, or the ingestion of caffeine and alertness. When social perceivers expect two things to go together, they tend to overestimate the actual degree of covariation.

Credibility In attitude change, how expert a communicator is perceived to be about the topic of communication and how much he or she is trusted by the individual receiving the communication.

Crowding The subjective experience of feeling cramped or not having enough space.

Cultural stereotypes Societal-level images of members of a social group such as those found in art, literature, religious teachings, and the mass media. See *personal stereotypes.*

Deindividuation Loss of a sense of personal identity and responsibility in a group, which can lead people to do things they would normally not do when alone. Anonymity is a key factor in deindividuation.

Demand characteristics Aspects of a study that make subjects more aware of their participation in research and thus bias their behavior, by avoiding negative evaluations from the experimenter, cooperating with the experimenter to verify the hypothesis, etc.

Dependent variable   In an experiment, the responses to the independent variable being manipulated or measured.

Discounting cue   A cue associated with a communication that reduces its persuasive influence, such as a low-prestige source. If, over time, the association between communication and the cue erodes, the influence of the communication may increase.

Discounting principle   In making attributions, the tendency to reduce reliance on one particular cause to the extent that other plausible causes exist. If, for example, a judge gives the death penalty to a criminal, we might conclude that she was generally a tough judge, but we would be less likely to do so if we also discovered that the law demanded the death penalty for the crime that was committed.

Discrepancy   In the study of attitude change, the distance between the communicator's and the target's position on the issue discussed in the communication. A communicator may argue that tuition should be doubled; that position will be highly discrepant to a student who believes it should not change, but only moderately discrepant to a student who thinks a modest increase is reasonable.

Discrimination   The behavioral component of group antagonism. People discriminate against a disliked group by refusing its members access to desired jobs, educational opportunities, country clubs, restaurants, places of entertainment, and so on.

Disinhibition   General loosening of the tight control over anger when it has once been released under socially approved conditions; that is, once a person has committed a socially approved aggressive act, he or she has fewer inhibitions about aggression under other conditions.

Displacement   Expression of *aggression* toward a target other than the source of frustration or annoyance. Typically, it occurs because the original source is not available or because there are reasons for restraining aggression against the original target.

Dispositional attribution   Perceiving the cause of a person's action as being in the person's dispositions, such as personality, ability, or attitudes.

Distraction   Stimulus that draws attention away from a persuasive message. It sometimes increases attitude change by making it harder for people to defend a position against the arguments in the message.

Door-in-the-face technique   A technique for gaining compliance with a request by first asking for a much larger request. After the larger request is refused, the person is more likely to agree to the second, smaller request.

Egocentric bias   In *attribution theory,* perceiving an exaggerated causal role for oneself in determining events.

Elaboration-likelihood model   A theory of persuasion and attitude change in which the key variable is the amount of careful thought given to the arguments (elaboration likelihood). With more careful processing, attitude change will depend more on the real strength of the arguments, and less on peripheral cues.

Emotional loneliness   A type of loneliness that results from the absence of an intimate attachment relationship, such as might be provided for children by their parents or for adults by a spouse or close friend. See also *loneliness; social loneliness.*

Empathic concern   Feelings of sympathy and caring for others—in particular, sharing vicariously or indirectly in the suffering of other people. Strong feelings of empathic concern would motivate a person to help someone in need.

Environmental psychology   The branch of psychology that studies the relationships between the physical environment and human behavior and well-being.

Equity theory   An offshoot of *social exchange theory* that focuses on fairness in relationships. A relationship is equitable when the ratio of a person's profits to contributions is the same for everyone. The theory postulates that when individuals perceive inequity, both underbenefited and overbenefited partners feel distress and take steps to restore equity.

Ethnocentrism   The belief that the ingroup is the center of the social world, and superior to all outgroups.

Evaluation   Most important basic dimension underlying impression formation and attitudes; the goodness or badness of another person, object, or concept. See also *affective component.*

Exchange theory   See *social exchange theory.*

Expectancy-value theory   This theory predicts that decisions are based on the combination of two factors: (1) the value of the various possible outcomes of the decision and (2) the likelihood or probability that each outcome will actually occur.

Experimental design   Type of research in which the researcher randomly assigns people to two or more conditions, varies in a controlled manner the treatment each condition is given, and then measures the effects on the subjects' responses. Though experiments are often difficult to arrange, they have the advantage of yielding clear information about cause and effect. Any differences between groups in the outcome of the experiment must of necessity be due to the variables that were experimentally manipulated.

Experimenter bias   Biases introduced into the results of an experiment, usually in the direction of falsely confirming the hypothesis, as a result of unintended biases in the experimenter's favor.

External attributions   Attributions of causality for a person's behavior or attitudes to factors external to the individual, such as luck, other people, or the weather.

External validity   Extent to which the results of a study are generalizable to other populations and settings.

False consensus   Bias in perceptions of others such that one exaggerates how common one's own opinions or behaviors are.

Fantasy aggression   An imagined act of aggression. It may tend to reduce direct aggression.

Field experiment   Study in which variables are systematically manipulated and measured in real-life, nonlaboratory settings.

Figure-ground principle   In social perception, the basic principle that attention is drawn to stimuli that stand out against a background. Figural stimuli are those that stand out; the background is called the ground. This principle has generated much of the research on salience in social perception.

Foot-in-the-door technique   A technique for gaining compliance with a request by first getting the person to comply with a smaller request. After agreeing to a small request, the person is more likely to comply with the larger request.

Forewarning   Warning an individual that a communicator intends to influence him or her, or of the specific position the communicator will take.

Fraternal deprivation   The perception that one's group is disadvantaged relative to other groups.

Frustration   The blocking or thwarting of goal-directed behavior. A child is frustrated when a parent refuses to let the child color the bathroom wallpaper with crayons or smear ice cream on the dining room table.

Fundamental attribution error   The tendency for observers to overestimate the causal importance of a person's dispositions and underestimate the importance of the situation when they explain the person's actions.

Gender identity   The knowledge that we are male or female. Gender identity is acquired early in life.

Gender self-concept   The degree to which a person perceives that he or she possesses traditionally masculine and feminine characteristics.

Gender stereotypes   Beliefs about the typical personal attributes of males and females. According to traditional gender stereotypes, women are believed to have expressive or communal qualities, such as being nurturant and gentle. Men are believed to have instrumental or agentic qualities such as being independent, assertive, and competent.

Gender typing   The process of labeling things, activities, and people as "masculine" or "feminine." For example, many people consider dolls, ruffles, and housecleaning to be feminine.

Gestalt   The theory that people form coherent and meaningful perceptions based on the entire perceptual field, so that the whole is different from the sum of its parts.

Group   A social aggregate in which members are interdependent (have mutual influence on each other) and have at least the potential for mutual interaction.

Group norms   See *social norms.*

Groupthink   Term used by Janis to describe an impairment in decision making and sound judgment that can occur in highly cohesive groups with a strong, dynamic leader. Group members isolate themselves from outside information, try to please the group leader, and agree on a decision even if it is irrational.

Group polarization   When a group discusses an issue, people often come to support more extreme positions than they did initially. This sometimes leads to a *risky shift*, and sometimes to a cautious shift, depending on the initial views of group members.

Halo effect   A liked person is assumed to have good qualities of many kinds, whether or not the observer has any information about those qualities.

Health belief model   According to this model, whether or not a person practices a particular health behavior depends on whether or not the person (1) perceives a personal health threat and (2) believes that a particular health practice will be effective in reducing that threat.

Heuristic   A shortcut for problem solving that reduces complex or ambiguous information to more simple judgmental operations.

Illusion of control   A bias in causal attribution whereby we perceive ourselves as being able to control our lives and the events around us more than is probably the case in fact.

Illusory correlation   The belief that two things are related to each other because prior expectations dictate that they ought to go together, when in fact the two things bear little or no relationship to each other.

Imitation   See *observational learning.*

Implicit personality theory   The ordinary person's theory about which personality traits go with which other traits, such as "weak" going with "cowardly," or "calm" going with "decisive."

Incentive theory　An attitude theory that predicts people will hold whichever attitude position offers the most positive incentives and the fewest negative incentives.

Independent variable　The variable in a study that is interpreted as the cause of changes in the dependent variable. The independent variable is systematically manipulated by the researcher in an experiment, and passively measured in a correlational study.

Informed consent　The requirement that research subjects must freely choose to participate, after being informed about the study, the procedures that will be used, and the costs and benefits of the study.

Ingroup　A group to which the individual belongs and which forms part of his or her social identity.

Inoculation　McGuire's notion that people are more resistant to the effects of persuasive communications when they are exposed to weak counterarguments.

Instrumental aggression　Aggression committed as a means to some goal other than harming the target. The goal of war is usually not to hurt soldiers (although this often happens), but rather to gain political power, land, wealth, prestige, or resources.

Integrative complexity　An index of the complexity of a person's thinking about a particular issue: How many dimensions are taken into consideration and how complex are the connections among these dimensions?

Interdependence　The condition in which two or more people have some degree of mutual influence on each other's feelings, thoughts, or behaviors.

Internal attributions　Attributions of causality to factors internal to the individual, such as his or her attitudes, personality, ability, emotions, race, or effort.

Internal validity　The extent to which cause and effect conclusions can validly be drawn from the research.

Just world　The belief that people get what they deserve. If good things happen to people, it is because they have worked hard, been honest, or been foresighted; if bad things happen to them, it is because they were lazy, careless, stupid, or dishonest. One consequence is that victims are blamed for their misfortunes, even if in reality they are not to blame.

Learned helplessness　A generalized belief, based on repeated experiences in one situation, that an individual has no control over his or her outcomes, even in other situations where control would be possible. This can lead to feelings of loss of control and depression.

Loneliness　The psychological discomfort we feel when our social relations lack some essential feature. This deficit may be quantitative (too few relationships) or qualitative (unsatisfying relationships).

Low-ball technique　A technique for gaining compliance in which the influencer obtains a commitment from the person before revealing hidden costs of the request.

Matching principle　In dating and marriage, people tend to have partners who are similar to themselves in attitudes, values, ethnic background, religion, social class, education, and many other personal characteristics.

Membership group　A group of which the individual is a member.

Mere exposure effect　Simply being exposed frequently to a person or object tends to increase our liking for that person or object. Repeated exposure most often enhances liking when our initial reactions to the person are neutral or positive, when no conflict of interests exists, and when the repetition is not so great that it causes satiation.

Meta-analysis　A quantitative approach to summarizing and synthesizing the results of many empirical studies on a topic, such as sex differences in aggression. Statistics are used to estimate the overall size of the "effect" or sex difference, and also to test for the consistency (homogeneity) of a finding across studies.

Middle-range theories　Theories that attempt to account for major categories of behavior, but do not attempt to cover all human behavior in general. These theories might attempt to explain attitude change, *or* attribution *or* aggression, but not all three.

Minimal effects model　The description of mass communications as mainly reinforcing the recipient's prior attitudes, rather than as creating widespread attitude change.

Minimal intergroup situation　The basic research situation for social identity theory: People are arbitrarily classified into groups, and then allowed to allocate rewards to each other.

Minimal risk　The idea that the risk anticipated in any research project must be no greater than the risk encountered in daily life.

Minority influence　Influence that members of a minority have over the larger majority in a group.

Mirror image　Images held by members of two conflicting nations, each of which feels their own nation is peace-loving and afraid of the other nation, which is regarded as hostile and threatening.

Misattribution　Assigning the cause of a particular behavior or emotional state to a stimulus other than the actual cause, such as thinking a lecture is exciting when actually you are stimulated by having drunk ten cups of coffee.

Naive psychology The ordinary person's informal theories about what determines human behavior.

Negativity effect Tendency for impressions to be influenced more by negative traits than by positive traits. Hence positive impressions are more vulnerable to change than negative impressions.

Nontheoretical question A research question that is motivated by a desire to understand a particular phenomenon without linking it to any more general theories.

Nonverbal leakage The communication of true emotions through nonverbal channels even when the person's verbal communication tries to cover them up.

Norm See *social norms*.

Norm of reciprocity The social norm that we are expected to reward those who reward us. For example, if someone helps us, we feel obligated to help that person in return.

Norm of social justice Human groups develop norms about fairness and the just distribution of resources. Norms of social justice may contribute to prosocial behavior.

Norm of social responsibility A social norm dictating that we should help others who depend on us. This may contribute to prosocial behavior.

Observational learning Learning by watching what others do and doing the same; also applies to forming attitudes by modeling those of others, such as parents or teachers.

Outgroup Any group other than the *ingroup*.

Overjustification Giving people high rewards for performing a task can undermine their intrinsic interest in the task, presumably because they attribute their liking for the task to the reward rather than to their own intrinsic interest in the task.

Paralanguage Information conveyed by variations in speech other than actual words and syntax, such as pitch, loudness, hesitations, and so on.

Party identification A person's underlying, stable preference for one political party over its rivals.

Passionate love The emotionally charged type of love that sometimes characterizes the early stages of romantic relationships. Often contrasted with *companionate love*.

Person perception Process of forming impressions of others, making judgments about their personalities, and adopting hypotheses about the kind of persons they are.

Personal distress An individual's reactions to the suffering of others, including horror, shock, helplessness, and concern. Since personal distress focuses on the self, it can motivate people to ignore or avoid the suffering of others, rather than offering assistance.

Personal space The physical space immediately around their bodies that people treat as though it were a part of themselves. Hall has suggested four basic zones for interpersonal interaction: intimate, personal, social, and public.

Personal stereotypes An individual's own beliefs about the attributes of members of a particular group. Personal stereotypes may be similar to or different from *cultural stereotypes*.

Positivity bias General tendency to express positive evaluations of people more often than negative evaluations. Also called the "leniency effect" or "person positivity bias."

Power See *social power*.

Prejudice The affective component of group antagonisms; disliking a group or members of a group.

Priming effect The tendency for recently used or thought-about material to influence the interpretation of subsequent information.

Principle of least interest According to social exchange theory, the balance of power in a relationship is affected by the relative dependency of the two partners. According to the principle of least interest, the partner who is less interested (less dependent) will tend to have greater power.

Procedural justice Satisfaction with one's outcomes, because of a perception that the procedures generating them were fair.

Prosocial aggression Aggressive acts that support commonly accepted social norms, such as a soldier shooting an enemy sniper during combat.

Prosocial behavior An act that helps or is intended to help others, regardless of the helper's motives. Prosocial behavior is a broader category than *altruism*.

Prototype A schema defined by the specific features of a particular type of person, such as librarian or effete snob.

Proxemics The term used by Hall to describe the study of how people use space.

Psychoanalytic theory Theory of human behavior based originally on Freud's work. It emphasizes instincts, unconscious motivation, and the ego defenses people construct to protect themselves against their own irrational drives.

Psychobiography Biographies of prominent political leaders, usually written from the perspective of psychoanalytic theory.

Random assignment Placement of subjects into experimental conditions in a way that guarantees that the assignment is made entirely by chance, such as by using a random number table. This is an essential characteristic of an experiment.

Random sample A group of people participating in a study who are selected from the broad population by a random process, and who therefore are representative of that broad population.

Rational model of inference A model assuming a logical, correct way to put information together to reach a judgment.

Reactance Brehm's concept that people attempt to maintain their freedom of action. When this freedom is threatened, they do whatever they can to restore it, for instance, refusing to comply with a request.

Realistic group conflict The theory that antagonism between groups arises from real conflicts of interest and the frustrations those conflicts produce. Two groups in conflict over the fishing rights in a certain segment of the ocean may start to hold prejudices and act aggressively toward each other as a result of the reality-based intergroup conflict.

Reference group A group to which a person belongs or uses as a basis of comparison. The group serves as a standard for the person's own behavior and attitudes. Group norms can act as a persuasive force leading to attitude change, or prevent change by supporting the individual's position when it is attacked.

Reinforcement The process by which a person or animal learns to perform a particular response by being rewarded when it is performed.

Relative deprivation The theory that the amount of social discontent a person or group experiences depends on the level of deprivation relative to what other people or groups have, or what the deprived person or group had in the past, rather than on the absolute amount of deprivation. Poverty should therefore produce the most discontent when the poor people previously had more money, or when others around them have more, regardless of how much or how little money they have in absolute terms.

Reverse-causality problem The problem that arises in correlational research when the presumed cause might in fact be the actual effect. Children who watch a lot of television do most poorly in school. But does their television viewing cause poor grades? Or does their poor school performance cause them to escape from schoolwork by watching TV?

Risk-benefit analysis Assessing the ethics of a research project by comparing the risks posed to the subjects with its benefits to the subjects and to society at large.

Risky shift After taking part in a group discussion of an issue, people are sometimes willing to support riskier decisions than they were before the group discussion. This is part of a more general process of *group polarization*, which can lead either to riskier or more cautious decisions, depending on the initial views of group members.

Role See *social role.*

Salience The quality that makes a particular stimulus stand out and be noticed. Bright, noisy, colorful, unusual, and novel stimuli are usually the most salient.

Sanctioned aggression Aggression that is permissible (though not necessarily encouraged) according to the norms of the individual's social groups.

Scapegoat A person who, because he or she is weak, different, and easily distinguishable, tends to be selected as a target of displaced aggression.

Schema An organized system or structure of cognitions about some stimulus or type of stimulus, such as a person, personality type, group, role, or event.

Selective attention Tendency for people to pay more attention to a supportive message than to a non-supportive message.

Selective exposure Tendency for persuasive communications not to reach the intended audience because audience members tend to be exposed mostly to sources they agree with. Should be distinguished from "motivated selectivity," a presumed psychological tendency to avoid nonsupportive information.

Self-fulfilling prophecy The tendency for an individual's expectations about the future to influence that future. Prejudice can serve as a self-fulfilling prophecy by determining how the prejudiced person acts toward the victim, which may in turn influence the victim to act in a way that confirms the first person's prejudices.

Self-handicapping Engaging in actions that produce insurmountable obstacles to success, so the inevitable failure can later be attributed to the obstacle rather than one's own lack of ability.

Self-interest The hypothesis that the individual's political behavior is motivated by what is best for his or her short-term material well-being.

Self-reference effect The improved memory for others' characteristics that results from perceivers linking them to their own characteristics.

Self-serving bias Attributional bias that is motivated by a need to raise or protect the perceiver's self-esteem. People explain their successes as internally caused, thus boosting their self-esteem. People also tend to deny blame for their failures, thus avoiding a loss of self-esteem.

Sexual arousal State of sexual excitement.

Sexual violence Violent physical attacks that have a sexual component; for example, rape.

Shift of meaning Tendency for the connotations of a trait to change when placed in a different context. This is the explanation for context effects given by cognitive theories of impression formation.

Situational attribution Perceiving the cause of a person's action as lying in the situational forces acting upon the person, such as social influence or economic incentives.

Sleeper effect Delayed attitude changes that are not apparent immediately after exposure to the communication.

Social cognition The field of social psychology concerned with how people think about themselves, about other people, and about the social environment.

Social comparison theory Festinger proposed that people have a drive to evaluate themselves. In the absence of objective nonsocial criteria, people evaluate themselves by comparison with other people. In an uncertain or ambiguous situation, people may want to affiliate with others in order to make social comparisons.

Social density The objective number of people in a given space, such as the number of people living per square mile in a major city.

Social exchange theory An analysis of interpersonal interaction in terms of the costs and benefits each person gives and receives. Because people in a relationship or group are interdependent (that is, the outcomes one person receives depend on what others do, and vice versa), individuals must coordinate their behavior to maximize their joint benefits. This is one of the motivational theories of social interaction.

Social facilitation The tendency for people (and other kinds of animals) to perform better on simple, well-learned tasks when others are present than when they are alone.

Social identity theory A theory that people spontaneously categorize the social world into ingroups and outgroups, and experience high self-esteem to the extent that their ingroups have more status than the outgroups.

Social impact theory According to Latané, the influence (either positive or negative) of an audience on a target individual depends on three factors: the number of observers, the strength of the audience (e.g., their importance), and the immediacy of the audience in time or space.

Social leadership Refers to activities designed to promote group harmony and *cohesiveness*. The social leader focuses on the social and emotional aspects of interaction in order to keep a group running smoothly and happily. Sometimes contrasted with *task leadership*.

Social learning theory A modern derivative of behaviorism that places primary emphasis on how people learn social behaviors from one another, especially through social reinforcement and imitation.

Social loafing Individuals sometimes work less hard as members of a group than they would if they worked alone. Individuals may feel that their own efforts will be less recognizable in a group, which leads to a diffusion of responsibility and diminished effort by individuals.

Social loneliness Type of loneliness that results when a person lacks a sense of social integration or community that might be provided by a network of friends, co-workers, or neighbors.

Social norms Rules and expectations about what members of a social group should do or be like. The standards of behavior that determine whether specific actions, attitudes, or beliefs are approved or disapproved by the individual's social group. Also called "group norms."

Social penetration Altman and Taylor's theory about the process by which people gradually attain closeness and intimacy in a relationship. The theory emphasizes that as relationships develop, self-disclosure increases in both breadth (range of topics) and depth (intimacy).

Social power This refers to one person's ability to influence deliberately the behavior, thoughts, or feelings of another person.

Social role A set of social norms (rules and understandings) about how a person in a particular social position (such as mother or professor) is expected to behave. Roles define the rights and responsibilities of members of couples, groups, and other social units.

Sociobiology A relatively new field in biology that uses evolutionary theory to explain the social behavior of humans and other animals.

Sociotropic In political psychology, the idea that political behavior is motivated by perceptions of what is best for the collectivity (the nation, the society), not the self.

Source derogation Reducing inconsistency by derogating the source of a discrepant communication rather than changing one's attitudes.

Stereotype Beliefs about the characteristics of members of a group or social category. This is the cognitive component of group antagonism.

Stress A process of appraising environmental events as harmful, threatening, or challenging, and of responding to that appraisal with physiological, emotional, cognitive, and behavioral changes.

Stress occurs when people perceive that their personal resources are not sufficient to meet the demands of the environment.

Stressful life event An event in a person's life that requires him or her to make changes; believed to contribute to the likelihood of illness.

Supportive defense In attitude change, positive arguments for an individual's own position, provided in advance of a persuasive attack to help protect that attitude.

Symbolic racism Antagonism toward a social group based on symbols and values rather than self-interest. For example, opposition to the progress of blacks, or to policies promoting that progress, that is based both in antagonism toward blacks and in support for traditional values.

Task leadership Activities designed to accomplish the goals of a group and to get the work of the group done successfully. The task leader directs and organizes the group in carrying out a specific task. Sometimes contrasted with *social leadership*.

Territorial markers Objects and nonverbal gestures that people use to mark and personalize their territories. For example, a person may stake out a seat in the library using a bookbag, sunglasses, and notebook.

Territory An area controlled by a specific individual or group. Altman has distinguished primary, secondary, and public territories.

Theoretical question A research question stemming from a theory.

Third-variable problem A problem with interpreting correlational research. When two variables are correlated with each other, is one the cause of the other? Or is some third variable the cause of both? Couples' satisfaction with their sex life is correlated with how long they remain a couple. But is sexual compatibility the cause of long-lasting relationships? Or are both caused by a more general level of trust and understanding?

Transfer of affect The theory that attitude change takes place by transferring the affect associated with one attitude object to another. Watching a goodlooking model use a particular brand of soap in the shower transfers the positive affect associated with the model to the brand of soap, supposedly compelling the viewer to buy that brand.

Violent erotica Films, books, or magazines that combine sexual themes, such as nudity or sexual encounters, with violence, usually against women.

REFERENCES

ABEL, E. L. (1977). The relationship between cannabis and violence: A review. *Psychological Bulletin, 84,* 193–211.

ABELSON, R. P. (1959). Modes of resolution of belief dilemmas. *Journal of Conflict Resolution, 3,* 343–352.

ABELSON, R. P. (1976). Script processing in attitude formation and decision making. In J. S. Carroll & J. W. Payne (Eds.), *Cognition and social behavior.* Hillsdale, NJ: Erlbaum.

ABRAMSON, L. Y., SELIGMAN, M. E. P., & TEASDALE, J. D. (1978). Learned helplessness in humans: Critique and reformulation. *Journal of Abnormal Psychology, 87,* 49–74.

ABRAMSON, P. E., GOLDBERG, P. A., GREENBERG, J. H., & ABRAMSON, U. M. (1977). The talking platypus phenomenon: Competency ratings as a function of sex and professional status. *Psychology of Women Quarterly, 2,* 114–124.

ADORNO, T. W., FRENKEL-BRUNSWIK, E., LEVINSON, D. J., & SANFORD, R. N. (1950). *The authoritarian personality.* New York: Harper & Row.

AFFLECK, G., TENNEN, H., PFEIFFER, C., & FIFIELD, J. (1986). *Appraisals of control and predictability in adapting to a chronic disease.* Unpublished manuscript. Hartford: University of Connecticut School of Nursing.

AGETON, S. S. (1983). *Sexual assault among adolescents.* Lexington, MA: Lexington Books.

AHAMMER, I. M., & MURRAY, J. P. (1979). Kindness in the kindergarten: The relative influence of role playing and prosocial television in facilitating altruism. *International Journal of Behavioral Development, 2,* 133–157.

AHMED, S. M. S. (1979). Helping behavior as predicted by diffusion of responsibility, exchange theory, and traditional sex norms. *Journal of Social Psychology, 109,* 153–154.

AIELLO, J. (1987). Human spatial behavior. In D. Stokols & I. Altman (Eds.), *Handbook of environmental psychology.* New York: Wiley.

AIELLO, J. R., & COOPER, R. E. (1972). The use of personal space as a function of social affect. *Proceedings of the 80th Annual Convention of the American Psychology Association, 7,* 207–208.

AINSWORTH, M. D. S. (1973). The development of infant-mother attachment. In B. M. Caldwell & H. N. Ricciuti (Eds.), *Review of child development research* (Vol. 3). Chicago: University of Chicago Press.

AINSWORTH, M. D. S., BLEHAR, M. C., WATERS, E., & WALL, S. (1978). *Patterns of attachment: A psychological study of the strange situation.* Hillsdale, NJ: Erlbaum.

AJZEN, I., & FISHBEIN, M. (1980). *Understanding attitudes and predicting social behavior.* Englewood Cliffs, NJ: Prentice-Hall.

AJZEN, I., & MADDEN, T. J. (1986). Prediction of goal-directed behavior: Attitudes, intentions, and perceived behavioral control. *Journal of Experimental Social Psychology, 22,* 453–474.

ALDER, C. (1985). An exploration of self-reported sexually aggressive behavior. *Crime and Delinquency, 31,* 306–331.

ALICKE, M. D., SMITH, R. H., & KLOTZ, M. L. (1986). Judgments of physical attractiveness: The role of faces and bodies. *Personality and Social Psychology Bulletin, 12*(4), 381–389.

ALLEN, V. L., & LEVIN, J. M. (1971). Social support and conformity: The role of independent assessment of reality. *Journal of Experimental Social Psychology, 7,* 48–58.

ALLEN, V. L., & WILDER, D. A. (1975). Categorization, belief similarity, and intergroup discrimination.

Journal of Personality and Social Psychology, 32, 971–977.

ALLEN, V. L., & WILDER, D. A. (1979). Group categorization and attribution of belief similarity. *Small Group Behavior, 10,* 73–80.

ALLGEIER, E. R., & BYRNE, D. (1973). Attraction toward the opposite sex as a determinant of physical proximity. *Journal of Social Psychology, 90,* 213–219.

ALLPORT, F. H. (1920). The influence of the group upon association and thought. *Journal of Experimental Psychology, 3,* 159–182.

ALLPORT, F. H. (1924). *Social psychology.* Boston: Riverside Editions, Houghton Mifflin.

ALLPORT, G. W. (1935). Attitudes. In C. Murchison (Ed.), *A handbook of social psychology.* Worcester, MA: Clark University Press.

ALLPORT, G. W. (1954). *The nature of prejudice.* Garden City, NY: Doubleday.

ALTMAN, I. (1975). *The environment and social behavior.* Monterey, CA: Brooks/Cole.

ALTMAN, I., & HAYTHORN, W. W. (1965). Interpersonal exchange in isolation. *Sociometry, 23,* 411–426.

ALTMAN, I., NELSON, P. A., & LETT, E. E. (1972). The ecology of home environments. *Catalog of Selected Documents in Psychology.* Washington, DC: American Psychological Association.

ALTMAN, I., & TAYLOR, D. A. (1973). *Social penetration: The development of interpersonal relationships.* New York: Holt, Rinehart & Winston.

AMABILE, T. M., HENNESSEY, B. A., & GROSSMAN, B. S. (1986). Social influences on creativity: The effects of contracted-for reward. *Journal of Personality and Social Psychology, 50,* 14–23.

AMATO, P. R. (1983). Helping behavior in urban and rural environments: Field studies based on a taxonomic organization of helping episodes. *Journal of Personality and Social Psychology, 45*(3), 571–586.

AMERICAN CANCER SOCIETY (1982). *Cancer facts and figures, 1983.* New York: American Cancer Society.

AMERICAN HEART ASSOCIATION (1984). *Heart facts, 1984.* Dallas: American Heart Association.

AMIR, Y. (1976). The role of intergroup contact in change of prejudice and ethnic relations. In P. A. Katz (Ed.), *Towards the elimination of racism* (pp. 245–308). Elmsford, NY: Pergamon Press.

ANDELIN, H. B. (1963). *Fascinating womanhood.* New York: Bantam.

ANDERSON, C. A., & FORD, C. M. (1986). Affect of the game player: Short-term effects of highly and mildly aggressive video games. *Personality and Social Psychology Bulletin, 12,* 390–402.

ANDERSON, N. H. (1959). Test of a model for opinion change. *Journal of Abnormal and Social Psychology, 59,* 371–381.

ANDERSON, N. H. (1965). Averaging vs. adding as a stimulus-combination rule in impression formation. *Journal of Experimental Psychology, 70,* 394–400.

ANDERSON, N. H. (1966). Component ratings in impression formation. *Psychonomic Science, 6,* 279–280.

ANDERSON, N. H. (1968a). A simple model for information integration. In R. P. Abelson et al. (Eds.), *Theories of cognitive consistency: A sourcebook.* Chicago: Rand McNally.

ANDERSON, N. H. (1968b). Likableness ratings of 555 personality-trait words. *Journal of Personality and Social Psychology, 9,* 272–279.

ANDERSON, N. H., & HUBERT, S. (1963). Effects of concomitant verbal recall on order effects in personality impression formation. *Journal of Verbal Learning and Verbal Behavior, 2,* 379–391.

ANDREWS, K. H., & KANDEL, D. B. (1979). Attitude and behavior. *American Sociological Review, 44,* 298–310.

APPLE, W., & HECHT, K. (1982). Speaking emotionally: The relation between verbal and vocal communication of affect. *Journal of Personality and Social Psychology, 42,* 864–875.

APPLE, W., STREETER, L. A., & KRAUSS, R. M. (1979). Effects of pitch and speech rate on personal attributions. *Journal of Personality and Social Psychology, 37,* 715–727.

APSLER, R., & SEARS, D. O. (1968). Warning, personal involvement, and attitude change. *Journal of Personality and Social Psychology, 9,* 162–166.

ARCHER, R. L., & BERG, J. H. (1978). Disclosure reciprocity and its limits: A reactance model. *Journal of Experimental Social Psychology, 14,* 527–540.

ARKIN, R. M., & BAUMGARDNER, A. H. (1985). Self-handicapping. In J. H. Harvey & G. Weary (Eds.), *Basic issues in attribution theory and research* (pp. 169–202). New York: Academic Press.

ARMS, R. L., RUSSELL, G. W., & SANDILANDS, M. L. (1979). Effects on the hostility of spectators of viewing aggressive sports. *Sociometry, 42,* 275–79.

ARMSTRONG, E. A. (1965). *Bird display and behavior: An introduction to the study of bird psychology,* 2nd ed. New York: Dover.

ARNDT, W. B., JR., FOEHL, J. C., & GOOD, F. E. (1985). Specific sexual fantasy themes: A multidimensional study. *Journal of Personality and Social Psychology, 48,* 472–480.

ARONSON, E. (1984). *The social animal,* 4th ed. New York: W. H. Freeman.

ARONSON, E., & CARLSMITH, J. M. (1963). The effect of the severity of threat on the devaluation of forbidden behavior. *Journal of Abnormal and Social Psychology*, 66, 584–588.

ARONSON, E., & LINDER, D. (1965). Gain and loss of esteem as determinants of interpersonal attractiveness. *Journal of Experimental Social Psychology*, 1, 156–171.

ARONSON, E., & OSHEROW, N. (1980). Cooperation, social behavior, and academic performance: Experiments in the desegregated classroom. In L. Bickman (Ed.), *Applied social psychology annual* (Vol. 1). Beverly Hills, CA: Sage Publications.

ARONSON, E., TURNER, J. A. & CARLSMITH, J. M. (1963). Communicator credibility and communication discrepancy as determinants of opinion change. *Journal of Abnormal and Social Psychology*, 67, 31–36.

ARONSON, E., WILLERMAN, B., & FLOYD, J. (1966). The effect of a pratfall on increasing interpersonal attractiveness. *Psychonomic Science*, 4, 227–228.

ASCH, S. E. (1946). Forming impressions of personality. *Journal of Abnormal and Social Psychology*, 41, 258–290.

ASCH, S. E. (1951). Effects of group pressure upon the modification and distortion of judgments. In H. Guetzkow (Ed.), *Groups, leadership and men*. Pittsburgh, PA: Carnegie Press.

ASHMORE, R. D., & DEL BOCA, F. K. (1976). Psychological approaches to understanding intergroup conflict. In P. A. Katz (Ed.), *Towards the elimination of racism* (pp. 73–124). Elmsford, NY: Pergamon Press.

ASHMORE, R. D., DEL BOCA, F. K., & WOHLERS, A. J. (1986). Gender stereotypes. In R. D. Ashmore & F. K. Del Boca (Eds.), *The social psychology of female-male relations* (pp. 69–119). New York: Academic Press.

ASHTON, N. L., SHAW, M. E., & WORSHAM, A. P. (1980). Affective reactions to interpersonal distances by friends and strangers. *Bulletin of the Psychonomic Society*, 15, 306–308.

ATKIN, C. (1979). Research evidence on mass mediated health communication campaigns. In D. Nimmo (Ed.), *Communication yearbook 3*. New Brunswick, NJ: Transaction Books.

ATTORNEY GENERAL'S COMMISSION ON PORNOGRAPHY. (1986). Final Report. Washington, D.C.: U.S. Department of Justice.

AUSTIN, W. (1980). Friendship and fairness: Effects of type of relationship and task performance on choice distribution rules. *Personality and Social Psychology Bulletin*, 6, 402–408.

AVERILL, J. R. (1973). Personal control over aversive stimuli and its relationship to stress. *Psychological Bulletin*, 80, 286–303.

AVERILL, J. R. (1983). Studies on anger and aggression: Implications for theories of emotion. *American Psychologist*, 38, 1145–1160.

AVERILL, J. R., & BOOTHROYD, P. (1977). On falling in love in conformance with the romantic ideal. *Motivation and Emotion*, 1(3), 235–247.

BALES, R. F. (1970). *Personality and interpersonal behavior*. New York: Holt, Rinehart & Winston.

BALL-ROKEACH, S. J., GRUBE, J. W., & ROKEACH, M. (1981). Roots: The next generation—Who watched and with what effect? *Public Opinion Quarterly*, 45, 58–68.

BANDURA, A. (1986a). Self-efficacy mechanism in physiological activation and health-promoting behavior. In J. Madden IV., S. Matthysse, & J. Barchas (Eds.), *Adaptation, learning and affect*. New York: Raven Press.

BANDURA, A. (1986b). *Social foundations of thought and action: A social cognitive theory*. Englewood Cliffs, NJ: Prentice-Hall.

BANDURA, A., ROSS, D., & ROSS, S. A. (1961). Transmission of aggression through imitation of aggressive models. *Journal of Abnormal and Social Psychology*, 63(3), 575–582.

BANDURA, A., ROSS, D., & ROSS, S. A. (1963). Imitation of film-mediated aggressive models. *Journal of Abnormal and Social Psychology*, 66, 3–11.

BANE, M. J. (1976). *Here to stay: American families in the twentieth century*. New York: Basic Books.

BARASH, D. P. (1977). *Sociobiology and behavior*. New York: Elsevier.

BARBER, J. D. (1985). *The presidential character: Predicting performance in the White House*, 3rd. ed. Englewood Cliffs, NJ: Prentice-Hall.

BARGH, J. A. (1984). Automatic and conscious processing of social information. In R. S. Wyer & T. K. Srull (Eds.), *Handbook of social cognition* (Vol. 3, pp. 1–43). Hillsdale, NJ: Erlbaum.

BAR-HILLEL, M., & FISCHHOFF, B. (1981). When do base rates affect predictions? *Journal of Personality and Social Psychology*, 41, 671–680.

BARKER, R. G., DEMBO, T., & LEWIN, K. (1941). Frustration and regression: An experiment with young children. *University of Iowa Studies in Child Welfare*, 18 (1).

BARON, J. N., & REISS, P. C. (1985). Same time, next year: Aggregate analyses of the mass media on violent behavior. *American Sociological Review*, 50, 347–363.

BARON, R. A. (1971a). Magnitude of victim's pain cues and level of prior anger arousal as determinants of adult aggressive behavior. *Journal of Personality and Social Psychology*, 17, 236–243.

BARON, R. A. (1971b). Aggression as a function of magnitude of victim's pain cues, level of prior anger arousal, and aggressor-victim similarity. *Journal of Personality and Social Psychology*, 18, 48–54.

BARON, R. A. (1974). Aggression as a function of victim's pain cues, level of prior anger arousal, and exposure to an aggressive model. *Journal of Personality and Social Psychology, 29,* 117–124.

BARON, R. A. (1977). *Human aggression.* New York: Plenum Press.

BARON, R. A., & BALL, R. L. (1974). The aggression-inhibiting influence of nonhostile humor. *Journal of Experimental Social Psychology, 10,* 23–33.

BARON, R. A., & BELL, P. A. (1975). Aggression and heat: Mediating effects of prior provocation and exposure to an aggressive model. *Journal of Personality and Social Psychology, 31,* 825–832.

BARON, R. A., & BELL, P. A. (1976). Aggression and heat: The influence of ambient temperature, negative affect, and a cooling drink on physical aggression. *Journal of Personality and Social Psychology, 33,* 245–255.

BARON, R. A., & BELL, P. A. (1977). Sexual arousal and aggression by males: Effects of type of erotic stimuli and prior provocation. *Journal of Personality and Social Psychology, 35,* 79–87.

BARON, R. M., MANDEL, D. G., ADAMS, C. A., & GRIFFEN, L. M. (1976). Effects of social density in university residential environments. *Journal of Personality and Social Psychology, 34,* 434–446.

BARON, R. M., & RODIN, J. (1978). Perceived control and crowding stress: Processes mediating the impact of spatial and social density. In A. Baum & Y. Epstein (Eds.), *Human response to crowding.* Hillsdale, NJ: Erlbaum.

BARON, R. S. (1986). Distraction-conflict theory: Progress and problems. In L. Berkowitz (Ed.), *Advances in experimental social psychology* (Vol. 20). New York: Academic Press.

BARR, J. K. (1983). Physicians' views of patients in prepaid group practice: Reasons for visits to HMOs. *Journal of Health and Social Behavior, 24,* 244–255.

BAR-TAL, D., BAR-ZOHAR, Y., GREENBERG, M. S., & HERMON, M. (1977). Reciprocity behavior in the relationship between donor and recipient and between harmdoer and victim. *Sociometry, 40*(3), 293–298.

BARUCH, G. K., & BARNETT, R. C. (1986). Consequences of fathers' participation in family work: Parents' role strain and well-being. *Journal of Personality and Social Psychology, 51*(5), 983–992.

BATSON, C. D., COCHRAN, P. J., BIEDERMAN, M. F., BLOSSER, J. L., RYAN, M. J., & VOGT, B. (1978). Failure to help when in a hurry: Callousness or conflict? *Personality and Social Psychology Bulletin, 4*(1), 97–101.

BAUM, A., AIELLO, J. R., & CALESNICK, L. E. (1978). Crowding and personal control: Social density and the development of learned helplessness. *Journal of Personality and Social Psychology, 36,* 1000–1011.

BAUM, A., & DAVIS, G. E. (1980). Reducing the stress of high-density living: An architectural intervention. *Journal of Personality and Social Psychology, 38*(3), 471–481.

BAUM, A., & PAULUS, P. (1987). Crowding. In D. Stokols & I. Altman (Eds.), *Handbook of environmental psychology.* New York: Wiley.

BAUM, A., & VALINS, S. (1977). *Architecture and social behavior: Psychological studies of social density.* Hillsdale, NJ: Erlbaum.

BAUMEISTER, R. F. (1982). A self-presentational view of social phenomena. *Psychological Bulletin, 91,* 3–26.

BAUMEISTER, R. F., & STEINHILBER, A. (1984). Paradoxical effects of supportive audiences on performance under pressure: The home field disadvantage in sports championships. *Journal of Personality and Social Psychology, 47*(1), 85–93.

BAVELAS, J. B., BLACK, A., LEMERY, C. R., & MULLETT, J. (1986). "I *show* how you feel": Motor mimicry as a communicative act. *Journal of Personality and Social Psychology, 50,* 322–329.

BEATTIE, A. E., & MITCHELL, A. A. (1985). The relationship between advertising recall and persuasion: An experimental investigation. In L. F. Alwitt & A. A. Mitchell (Eds.), *Psychological processes and advertising effects: Theory, research, and applications* (pp. 129–155). Hillsdale, NJ: Erlbaum.

BECKER, B. J. (1986). Influence again: An examination of reviews and studies of gender differences in social influence. In J. S. Hyde & M. C. Linn (Eds.), *The psychology of gender: Advances through meta-analysis* (pp. 178–209). Baltimore: Johns Hopkins University Press.

BECKER, F. D. (1973). Study of spatial markers. *Journal of Personality and Social Psychology, 26*(3), 439–445.

BECKER, J. F., & HEATON, E. E., JR. (1967). The election of Senator Edward W. Brooke. *Public Opinion Quarterly, 31,* 346–358.

BECKER, L. B., McCOMBS, M. E., & McLEOD, M. M. (1975). The development of political cognitions. In S. H. Chaffee (Ed.). *Political communication: Issues and strategies for research* (pp. 21–63). Beverly Hills, CA: Sage.

BECKER, M. H., KABACK, M., ROSENSTOCK, I., & RUTH, M. (1975). Some influences on public participation in a genetic screening program. *Journal of Community Health, 1,* 3–14.

BECKER, M. H., MAIMAN, L., KIRSCHT, J., HAEFNER, D., & DRACHMAN, R. (1977). The health belief model and dietary compliance: A field experiment. *Journal of Health and Social Behavior, 18,* 348–366.

BELL, R. (1968). A reinterpretation of the direction of effects in studies of socialization. *Psychological Review, 75,* 81–85.

BELLEZZA, F. S. (1984). The self as a mnemonic device:

The role of internal cues. *Journal of Personality and Social Psychology, 47*, 506–516.

BELLOC, N. D., & BRESLOW, L. (1972). Relationship of physical health status and family practices. *Preventive Medicine, 1*, 409–421.

BEM, D. J. (1967). Self-perception: An alternative interpretation of cognitive dissonance phenomena. *Psychological Review, 74*, 183–200.

BEM, S. L. (1974). The measurement of psychological androgyny. *Journal of Consulting and Clinical Psychology, 42*, 155–162.

BEM, S. L. (1975). Sex role adaptability: One consequence of psychological androgyny. *Journal of Personality and Social Psychology, 31*, 634–643.

BEM, S. L. (1981). Gender schema theory: A cognitive account of sex typing. *Psychological Review, 88*, 354–364.

BEM, S. L., MARTYNA, W., & WATSON, C. (1976). Sex typing and androgyny: Further explorations of the expressive domain. *Journal of Personality and Social Psychology, 43*, 1016–1023.

BEN-SIRA, Z. (1976). The function of the professional's affective behavior in client satisfaction: A revised approach to social interaction theory. *Journal of Health and Social Behavior, 17*, 3–11.

BENSON, H., GREENWOOD, M. M., & KLEMCHUCK, H. (1975). The relaxation response: Psychophysiological aspects and clinical applications. *International Journal of Psychiatry in Medicine, 6*, 87–98.

BENSON, P. L., KARABENICK, S. A., & LERNER, R. M. (1976). Pretty pleases: The effects of physical attractiveness, race, and sex on receiving help. *Journal of Experimental Social Psychology, 12*, 409–415.

BENTLER, P. M., & SPECKART, G. (1981). Attitudes "cause" behaviors: A structural equation analysis. *Journal of Personality and Social Psychology, 40*, 226–238.

BERELSON, B. R., LAZARSFELD, P. F., & MCPHEE, W. N. (1954). *Voting: A study of opinion formation in a presidential campaign.* Chicago: University of Chicago Press.

BERGLAS, S., & JONES, E. E. (1978). Drug choice as a self-handicapping strategy in response to noncontingent success. *Journal of Personality and Social Psychology, 36*, 405–417.

BERK, R. A., & BERK, S. F. (1979). *Labor and leisure at home: Content and organization of the household day.* Beverly Hills, CA: Sage Publications.

BERKMAN, L. F., & SYME, S. L. (1979). Social networks, host resistance, and mortality. A nine-year followup study of Alameda County residents. *American Journal of Epidemiology, 109*, 186–204.

BERKOWITZ, L. (1965). Some aspects of observed aggression. *Journal of Personality and Social Psychology, 2*, 359–369.

BERKOWITZ, L. (1968). Responsibility, reciprocity, and social distance in help-giving: An experimental investigation of English social class differences. *Journal of Experimental Social Psychology, 4*, 46–63.

BERKOWITZ, L. (1970). The contagion of violence. In W. J. Arnold & M. M. Page (Eds.), *Nebraska symposium on motivation.* Lincoln: University of Nebraska Press.

BERKOWITZ, L. (1972). Social norms, feelings, and other factors affecting helping and altruism. In L. Berkowitz (Ed.), *Advances in experimental social psychology* (Vol. 6). New York: Academic Press.

BERKOWITZ, L. (1983). Aversively stimulated aggression: Some parallels and differences in research with animals and humans. *American Psychologist, 38*, 1135–1144.

BERKOWITZ, L., & FRODI, A. (1979). Reactions to a child's mistakes as affected by her/his looks and speech. *Social Psychology Quarterly, 42*, 420–425.

BERKOWITZ, L., & GEEN, R. G. (1966). Film violence and the cue properties of available targets. *Journal of Personality and Social Psychology, 3*, 525–530.

BERKOWITZ, L., & GEEN, R. G. (1967). Stimulus qualities of the target of aggression: A further study. *Journal of Personality and Social Psychology, 5*, 364–368.

BERKOWITZ, L., & RAWLINGS, E. (1963). Effects of film violence on inhibitions against subsequent aggression. *Journal of Abnormal and Social Psychology, 66*, 405–412.

BERNARD, J. (1972). *The future of marriage.* New York: Bantam.

BERNARD, L. C. (1980). Multivariate analysis of new sex role formulations and personality. *Journal of Personality and Social Psychology, 38*, 323–336.

BERNSTEIN, M., & CROSBY, F. (1980). An empirical examination of relative deprivation theory. *Journal of Experimental Social Psychology, 16*, 442–456.

BERNSTEIN, W. M., STEPHAN, W. G., & DAVIS, M. H. (1979). Explaining attributions for achievement: A path analytic approach. *Journal of Personality and Social Psychology, 37*, 1810–1821.

BERRY, D. S., & MCARTHUR, L. Z. (1985). Some components and consequences of a babyface. *Journal of Personality and Social Psychology, 48*, 312–323.

BERSCHEID, E. (1983). Emotion. In H. H. Kelley et al., *Close relationships* (pp. 110–168). New York: Freeman.

BERSCHEID, E., GRAZIANO, W., MONSON, T., & DERMER, M. (1976). Outcome dependency: Attention, attribution, and attraction. *Journal of Personality and Social Psychology, 34*, 978–989.

BERSCHEID, E., & WALSTER, E. (1967). When does a

harm-doer compensate a victim? *Journal of Personality and Social Psychology, 6,* 435–441.

BERSCHEID, E., & WALSTER, E. H. (1978). *Interpersonal attraction,* 2nd ed. Reading, MA: Addison-Wesley.

BEST, J. A., FLAY, B. R. TOWSON, S., RYAN, M. J., PERRY, C. L., BROWN, K. S., KERSELL, M. W., & D'AVERNAS, J. R. (1984). Smoking prevention and the concept of risk. *Journal of Applied Social Psychology, 14,* 257–273.

BETTELHEIM, B., & JANOWITZ, M. (1964). *Social change and prejudice.* Glencoe, NY: Free Press.

BEVILLE, H. M., JR. (1985). *Audience ratings: Radio, television, and cable.* Hillsdale, NJ: Erlbaum.

BICKMAN, L. (1971). The effect of another bystander's ability to help on bystander intervention in an emergency. *Journal of Experimental Social Psychology, 7,* 367–379.

BICKMAN, L., & KAMZAN, M. (1973). The effect of race and need on helping. *Journal of Social Psychology, 89,* 73–77.

BIRDWHISTELL, R. I. (1970). *Kinesics and context: Essays on body motion communication.* Philadelphia: University of Pennsylvania Press.

BISHOP, G. D., & CONVERSE, S. A. (1986). Illness representations: A prototype approach. *Health Psychology, 5,* 95–114.

BLAU, P. M. (1964). *Exchange and power in social life.* New York: Wiley.

BLUMENTHAL, M. D., KAHN, R. L., ANDREWS, F. M., & HEAD, K. B. (1972). *Justifying violence: Attitudes of American men.* Ann Arbor, MI: Institute for Social Research.

BOBO, L. (1983). Whites' opposition to busing: Symbolic racism or realistic group conflict? *Journal of Personality and Social Psychology, 45,* 1196–1210.

BOCHNER, S., & INSKO, C. A. (1966). Communicator discrepancy, source credibility, and opinion change. *Journal of Personality and Social Psychology, 4,* 614–621.

BOND, M. H., & DUTTON, D. G. (1975). The effect of interaction anticipation and experience as a victim on aggressive behavior. *Journal of Personality, 43*(3), 515–527.

BONS, P. M., & FIEDLER, F. E. (1976). Changes in organizational leadership and the behavior of relationship- and task-motivated leaders. *Administrative Science Quarterly, 21,* 433–472.

BOOTH, A. (1976). *Urban crowding and its consequences.* New York: Praeger.

BORDEN, R. J. (1980). Audience influence. In P. B. Paulus (Ed.), *Psychology of group influence* (pp. 99–132). Hillsdale, NJ: Erlbaum.

BORGIDA, E., & CAMPBELL, B. (1982). Belief relevance and attitude-behavior consistency: The moderating role of personal experience. *Journal of Personality and Social Psychology, 42,* 239–247.

BORGIDA, E., & HOWARD-PITNEY, B. (1983). Personal involvement and the robustness of perceptual salience effects. *Journal of Personality and Social Psychology, 45,* 560–570.

BOUCHER, J., & OSGOOD, E. E. (1969). The pollyanna hypothesis. *Journal of Verbal Learning and Verbal Behavior, 8,* 1–8.

BOWER, G. H., & GILLIGAN, S. G. (1979). Remembering information related to one's self. *Journal of Research in Personality, 13,* 420–432.

BOWLBY, J. (1969). *Attachment and loss: Vol. 1. Attachment.* New York: Basic Books.

BRADLEY, G. W. (1978). Self-serving biases in the attribution process: A reexamination of the fact or fiction question. *Journal of Personality and Social Psychology, 36,* 56–71.

BRAIKER, H. B., & KELLEY, H. H. (1979). Conflict in the development of close relationships. In R. L. Burgess & T. L. Huston (Eds.), *Social exchange in developing relationships.* New York: Academic Press.

BRAMEL, D., TAUB, B., & BLUM, B. (1968). An observer's reaction to the suffering of his enemy. *Journal of Personality and Social Psychology, 8,* 384–392.

BRECKLER, S. J. (1984). Empirical validation of affect, behavior, and cognition as distinct components of attitude. *Journal of Personality and Social Psychology, 47,* 1191–1205.

BREHM, J. W. (1956). Post-decision changes in desirability of alternatives. *Journal of Abnormal and Social Psychology, 52,* 384–389.

BREHM, J. W. (1966). *A theory of psychological reactance.* New York: Academic Press.

BREHM, S. S., & BREHM, J. W. (1981). *Psychological reactance: A theory of freedom and control.* New York: Academic Press.

BREWER, M. B. (1979). In-group bias in the minimal intergroup situation: A cognitive-motivational analysis. *Psychological Bulletin, 86,* 307–324.

BREWER, M. B. (1986). The role of ethnocentrism in intergroup conflict. In S. Worchel & W. G. Austin (Eds.), *Psychology of intergroup relations* (pp. 88–102). Chicago: Nelson-Hall Publishers.

BREWER, M. B., DULL, V., & LUI, L. (1981). Perceptions of the elderly: Stereotypes as prototypes, *Journal of Personality and Social Psychology, 41*(4), 656–670.

BREWER, M. B., & MILLER, N. (1984). Beyond the contact hypothesis: Theoretical perspectives on desegregation. In N. Miller & M. B. Brewer (Eds.), *Groups in contact: The psychology of desegregation* (pp. 281–302). New York: Academic Press.

BRIAR, S. (1966). Welfare from below: Recipients' view

of the public welfare system. In J. Brock (Ed.), *The law of the poor*. San Francisco: Chandler.

BRIGHAM, J. C., & GIESBRECHT, L. W. (1976). All in the family: Racial attitudes. *Journal of Communication*, *26*, 75–84.

BROADBENT, D. E. (1957). Effects of noise on behavior. In C. M. Harris (Ed.), *Handbook of noise control*. New York: McGraw-Hill.

BROCK, T. C. (1965). Communicator-recipient similarity and decision change. *Journal of Personality and Social Psychology*, *1*, 650–654.

BROCK, T. C., & BALLOUN, J. L. (1967). Behavioral receptivity to dissonant information. *Journal of Personality and Social Psychology*, *6*, 413–428.

BROWN, B. B. (1987). Territoriality. In D. Stokols & I. Altman (Eds.), *Handbook of environmental psychology*. New York: Wiley.

BROWN, P., KEENAN, J. M., & POTTS, G. R. (1986). The self-reference effect with imagery encoding. *Journal of Personality and Social Psychology*, *51*, 897–906.

BROWN, R. (1974). Further comment on the risky shift. *American Psychologist*, *29*, 468–470.

BROWN, T. A. (1986). *Migration and politics in America*. Chapel Hill: University of North Carolina Press.

BROWNELL, A. (1982). Obesity: Understanding and treating a serious, prevalent and refractory disorder. *Journal of Consulting and Clinical Psychology*, *50*, 820–840.

BRYAN, J. H., & TEST, N. A. (1967). Models and helping: Naturalistic studies in aiding behavior. *Journal of Personality and Social Psychology*, *6*, 400–407.

BULMAN, R. J., & WORTMAN, C. B. (1977). Attributions of blame and coping in the "real world": Severe accident victims react to their lot. *Journal of Personality and Social Psychology*, *35*, 351–363.

BURGER, J. M. (1986). Increasing compliance by improving the deal: The that's-not-all technique. *Journal of Personality and Social Psychology*, *51*(2), 277–283.

BURGER, J. M., & PETTY, R. E. (1981). The low-ball compliance technique: Task or person commitment? *Journal of Personality and Social Psychology*, *40*, 492–500.

BURGESS, E. W., & WALLIN, P. (1953). *Engagement and marriage*. Philadelphia: Lippincott.

BURGESS, R. L., & HUSTON, T. L. (Eds.). (1979). *Social exchange in developing relationships*. New York: Academic Press.

BURISH, T. C., & BRADLEY, L. A. (1983). *Coping with chronic disease: Research and applications*. New York: Academic Press.

BURKE, P. J. (1971). Task and social-emotional leadership role performance. *Sociometry*, *34*, 22–40.

BURNKRANT, R. E., & HOWARD, D. J. (1984). Effects of the use of introductory rhetorical questions versus statements on information processing. *Journal of Personality and Social Psychology*, *47*, 1218–1230.

BURNS, J. M. 1978. *Leadership*. New York: Harper & Row.

BURNSTEIN, E., & VINOKUR, A. (1975). What a person thinks upon learning he has chosen differently from others: Nice evidence for the persuasive-arguments explanation of choice shifts. *Journal of Experimental Social Psychology*, *11*, 412–426.

BUUNK, B., & BRINGLE, R. G. (1987). Jealousy in love relationships. In D. Perlman & S. Duck (Eds.), *Intimate relationships: Development, dynamics, and deterioration* (pp. 123–147). Beverly Hills: Sage.

BYRNE, D. (1971). *The attraction paradigm*. New York: Academic Press.

BYRNE, D., CLORE, G. L., & SMEATON, G. (1986). The attraction hypothesis: Do similar attitudes affect anything? *Journal of Personality and Social Psychology*, *51*(6), 1167–1170.

CACIOPPO, J. T., & PETTY, R. E. (1979). Effects of message repetition and position on cognitive response, recall, and persuasion. *Journal of Personality and Social Psychology*, *37*, 97–109.

CACIOPPO, J. T., & PETTY, R. E. (1985). Central and peripheral routes to persuasion: The role of message repetition. In L. F. Alwitt & A. A. Mitchell (Eds.), *Psychological processes and advertising effects: Theory, research, and applications* (pp. 91–111). Hillsdale, NJ: Erlbaum.

CACIOPPO, J. T., PETTY, R. E., KAO, C. F., & RODRIGUEZ, R. (1986). Central and peripheral routes to persuasion: An individual difference perspective. *Journal of Personality and Social Psychology*, *51*, 1032–1043.

CALDWELL, M. A., & PEPLAU, L. A. (1982). Sex differences in same-sex friendship. *Sex Roles*, *8*(7), 721–732.

CALHOUN, J. B. (1962). Population density and social pathology. *Scientific American*, *206*, 139–148.

CALNAN, M. W., & MOSS, S. (1984). The health belief model and compliance with education given at a class in breast self-examination. *Journal of Health and Social Behavior*, *25*, 198–210.

CAMPBELL, A. (1971). *White attitudes toward black people*. Ann Arbor, MI: Institute for Social Research.

CAMPBELL, A., CONVERSE, P. E., MILLER, W. E., & STOKES, D. E. (1960). *The American voter*. New York: Wiley.

CAMPBELL, D. T. (1975). On the conflicts between biological and social evolution and between psychology and moral tradition. *American Psychologist*, *30*(12), 1103–1126.

CAMPBELL, D. T., & STANLEY, J. C. (1963). *Experimental and quasi-experimental designs for research*. Chicago: Rand McNally.

CAMPBELL, J. D., TESSER, A., & FAIREY, P. J. (1986). Conformity and attention to the stimulus: Some temporal and contextual dynamics. *Journal of Personality and Social Psychology*, *51*(2), 315–324.

CANTOR, J. R., ZILLMANN, D., & BRYANT, J. (1975). Enhancement of experiences of sexual arousal in response to erotic stimuli through misattribution of unrelated residual excitation. *Journal of Personality and Social Psychology, 32,* 69–75.

CANTOR, N., & MISCHEL, W. (1977). Traits as prototypes: Effects on recognition memory. *Journal of Personality and Social Psychology, 35,* 38–48.

CANTOR, N., & MISCHEL, W. (1979). Prototypes in person perception. In L. Berkowitz (Ed.), *Advances in experimental social psychology* (Vol. 12). New York: Academic Press.

CARLSMITH, J. M., & ANDERSON, C. A. (1979). Ambient temperature and the occurrence of collective violence: A new analysis. *Journal of Personality and Social Psychology, 37,* 337–344.

CARLSTON, D. E., & SHOVAR, N. (1983). Effects of performance attributions on others' perceptions of the attributor, *Journal of Personality and Social Psychology, 44*(3), 515–525.

CARVER, C. S., & GLASS, D. C. (1978). Coronary-prone behavior pattern and interpersonal aggression. *Journal of Personality and Social Psychology, 36,* 361–366.

CARVER, C. S., & HUMPRIES, C. (1982). Social psychology of the Type A coronary-prone behavior pattern. In G. S. Saunders & J. Suls (Eds.), *Social psychology of health and illness.* Hillsdale (pp. 33–58). NJ: Erlbaum.

CASH, T. F., GILLEN, B., & BURNS, D. S. (1977). Sexism and "beautyism" in personnel consultant decision making. *Journal of Applied Psychology, 62,* 301–310.

CATER, D., & STRICKLAND, D. (1975). *TV violence and the child.* New York: Russell Sage.

CERVONE, D., & PEAKE, P. K. (1986). Anchoring, efficacy, and action: The influence of judgmental heuristics on self-efficacy judgments and behavior. *Journal of Personality and Social Psychology, 50,* 492–501.

CHAFETZ, M. E. (1970). No patient deserves to be patronized. *Medical Insight, 2,* 68–75.

CHAIKEN, S. (1979). Communicator physical attractiveness and persuasion. *Journal of Personality and Social Psychology, 37,* 1387–1397.

CHAIKEN, S. (1980). Heuristic versus systematic information processing and the use of source versus message cues in persuasion. *Journal of Personality and Social Psychology, 39,* 752–766.

CHAIKEN, S., & BALDWIN, M. W. (1981). Affective-cognitive consistency and the effect of salient behavioral information on the self-perception of attitudes. *Journal of Personality and Social Psychology, 41,* 1–12.

CHAIKEN, S., & EAGLY, A. H. (1976). Communication modality as a determinant of message persuasiveness and message comprehensibility. *Journal of Personality and Social Psychology, 34,* 605–614.

CHAIKEN, S., & EAGLY, A. H. (1983). Communication modality as a determinant of persuasion: The role of communicator salience. *Journal of Personality and Social Psychology, 45,* 241–256.

CHAIKEN, S., & YATES, S. (1985). Affective-cognitive consistency and thought-induced attitude polarization. *Journal of Personality and Social Psychology, 49,* 1470–1481.

CHAIKIN, A. L., & DERLEGA, V. J. (1974). Liking for the norm-breaker in self-disclosure. *Journal of Personality, 42,* 117–129.

CHANEY, E. F., O'LEARY, M. R., & MARLATT, G. A. (1978). Skill training with alcoholics. *Journal of Consulting and Clinical Psychology, 46,* 1092–1104.

CHEN, S. C. (1937). Social modification of the activity of ants in nest-building. *Physiological Zoology, 10,* 420–436.

CHESNEY, M. A., EAGLESTON, J. R., & ROSENMAN, R. H. (1981). Type A behavior: Assessment and intervention. In C. K. Prokop & L. A. Bradley (Eds.), *Medical psychology: Contributions to behavioral medicine* (pp. 20–34). New York: Academic Press.

CHRISTIAN, J. J. (1975). Hormonal control of population growth. In B. E. Elefheriou & R. L. Sprott (Eds.), *Hormonal correlates of behavior* (Vol. 1). New York: Plenum Press.

CHRISTIE, R., & GEIS, F. L. (1970). *Studies in Machiavellianism.* New York: Academic Press.

CHRISTIE, R., & JAHODA, M. (Eds.). (1954). *Studies in the scope and method of "the authoritarian personality": Continuities in social research.* Glencoe, IL.: The Free Press.

CIALDINI, R. B. (1985). *Influence: Science and practice.* Glenview, IL: Scott, Foresman.

CIALDINI, R. B., BAUMANN, D. J. & KENRICK, D. T. (1981). Insights from sadness: A three-step model of the development of altruism as hedonism. *Developmental Review, 1,* 207–223.

CIALDINI, R. B., CACIOPPO, J. T., BASSETT, R., & MILLER, J. A. (1978). Low-ball procedure for producing compliance: Commitment then cost. *Journal of Personality and Social Psychology, 36,* 463–476.

CIALDINI, R. B., SCHALLER, M., HOULIHAN, D., ARPS, K., FULTZ, J., & BEAMAN, A. (1987). Empathy-based helping: Is it selflessly or selfishly motivated? *Journal of Personality and Social Psychology, 52*(4), 749–758.

CIALDINI, R. B., VINCENT, J. E., LEWIS, S. K., CATALAN, J., WHEELER, D., & DARBY, B. L. (1975). Reciprocal consessions procedure for inducing compliance: The door-in-the-face technique. *Journal of Personality and Social Psychology, 31,* 206–215.

CLARK, M. S. (1984). Record keeping in two types of relationships. *Journal of Personality and Social Psychology, 47,* 549–557.

CLARK, M. S., & MILLS, J. (1979). Interpersonal attraction in exchange and communal relationships. *Journal of Personality and Social Psychology*, *37*, 12–24.

CLARK, M. S., MILLS, J., & POWELL, M. C. (1986). Keeping track of needs in communal and exchange relationships. *Journal of Personality and Social Psychology*, *51*(2), 333–338.

CLARK, R. D., & WORD, L. E. (1972). Why don't bystanders help? Because of ambiguity? *Journal of Personality and Social Psychology*, *24*, 392–400.

CLARK, R. D., & WORD, L. E. (1974). Where is the apathetic bystander? Situational characteristics of the emergency. *Journal of Personality and Social Psychology*, *29*, 279–287.

CLIFTON, A. K., McGRATH, D., & WICK, B. (1976). Stereotypes of woman: A single category? *Sex Roles*, *2*, 135–148.

CLINE, V. H., CROFT, R. G., & COURRIER, S. (1973). Desensitization of children to television violence. *Journal of Personality and Social Psychology*, *27*, 360–365.

CLORE, G. L., BRAY, R. B., ITKIN, S. M., & MURPHY, P. (1978). Interracial attitudes and behavior at a summer camp. *Journal of Personality and Social Psychology*, *36*, 107–116.

CLORE, G. L., & BYRNE, D. (1974). A reinforcement-affect model of attraction. In T. L. Huston (Ed.), *Foundations of interpersonal attraction* (pp. 143–165). New York: Academic Press.

COATES, T. J., MORIN, S. F., & McKUSICK, L. (1986). *Consequences of AIDS antibody testing among gay men: The AIDS behavioral research project.* Unpublished manuscript, University of California, San Francisco.

COCHRAN, S. D., & HAMMEN, C. L. (1985). Perceptions of stressful life events and depression: A test of attributional models. *Journal of Personality and Social Psychology*, *48*, 1562–1571.

COHEN, C. E. (1981). Person categories and social perception: Testing some boundaries of the processing effects of prior knowledge. *Journal of Personality and Social Psychology*, *40*, 441–452.

COHEN, F., & LAZARUS, R. (1979). Coping with the stresses of illness. In G. C. Stone, F. Cohen, & N. E. Adler (Eds.), *Health psychology—A handbook* (pp. 217–254). San Francisco: Jossey-Bass.

COHEN, S., EVANS, G. W., KRANTZ, D. S., STOKOLS, D., & KELLY, S. (1981). Aircraft noise and children: Longitudinal and cross-sectional evidence on adaptation to noise and the effectiveness of noise abatement. *Journal of Personality and Social Psychology*, *40*, 331–345.

COHEN, S., GLASS, D. C., & SINGER, J. E. (1973). Apartment noise, auditory discrimination, and reading ability in children. *Journal of Experimental Social Psychology*, *9*, 407–422.

COHEN, S., & HOBERMAN, H. M. (1983). Positive events and social supports as buffers of life change stress. *Journal of Applied Social Psychology*, *13*, 99–125.

COHEN, S., & LEZAK, A. (1977). Noise and attentiveness to social cues. *Environment and Behavior*, *9*, 559–572.

COHEN, S., & WEINSTEIN, N. (1981). Nonauditory effects of noise on behavior and health. *Journal of Social Issues*, *37*(1), 36–70.

COLE, P. (1974). Morbidity in the U.S. In C. L. Erhardt & J. Berlin (Eds.), *Mortality and morbidity in the U.S.* Cambridge, MA: Harvard University Press.

COLEMAN, J. F., BLAKE, R. R., & MOUTON, J. S. (1958). Task difficulty and conformity pressures. *Journal of Abnormal and Social Psychology*, *57*, 120–122.

COLLIGAN, M. J., PENNEBAKER, J. W., & MURPHY, L. R. (1982). *Mass psychogenic illness: A social psychological analysis.* Hillsdale, NJ: Erlbaum.

COMMISSION ON OBSCENITY AND PORNOGRAPHY. (1970). *Report of the commission on obscenity and pornography.* New York: Bantam.

COMSTOCK, G. (1975). *Television and human behavior: The key studies.* Santa Monica, CA: The Rand Corporation.

COMSTOCK, G. (1982). Violence in television content: An overview. In D. Pearl, L. Bouthilet, & J. Lazar (Eds.), *Television and behavior: Ten years of scientific progress and implications for the eighties: Vol. II: Technical reviews.* Rockville, MD: National Institute of Mental Health.

COMSTOCK, G., CHAFFEE, S., KATZMAN, N., McCOMBS, M., & ROBERTS, D. (1978). *Television and human behavior.* New York: Columbia University Press.

CONDRY, J., & CONDRY, S. (1976). Sex differences: A study in the eye of the beholder. *Child Development*, *47*, 812–819.

CONVERSE, P. E. (1964). The nature of belief systems in mass publics. In D. E. Apter (Ed.), *Ideology and discontent* (pp. 206–261). New York: Free Press.

CONVERSE, P. E. (1970). Attitudes and non-attitudes: Continuation of a dialogue. In E. R. Tufte (Ed.), *The quantitative analysis of social problems* (pp. 168–189). Reading, MA: Addison-Wesley.

CONVERSE, P. E. (1975). Public opinion and voting behavior. In F. I. Greenstein & N. W. Polsby (Eds.), *Handbook of political science* (Vol. 4, pp. 75–170). Reading, MA: Addison-Wesley.

CONVERSE, P. E., & CAMPBELL, A. (1960). Political standards in secondary groups. In D. Cartwright & A. Zander (Eds.), *Group dynamics*, 2nd ed. (pp. 300–318). Evanston, IL: Row, Peterson.

CONVERSE, P. E., & MARKUS, G. B. (1979). Plus ça change . . .: The new CPS election study panel. *American Political Science Review*, *73*, 32–49.

COOK, S. W. (1978). Interpersonal and attitudinal outcomes in cooperating interracial groups. *Journal of Research and Development in Education, 12,* 97–113.

COOK, S. W. (1984). Cooperative interaction in multi-ethnic contexts. In N. Miller & M. Brewer (Eds.), *Groups in contact: The psychology of desegregation* (pp. 156–186). New York: Academic Press.

COOK, S. W., & PELFREY, M. (1985). Reactions to being helped in cooperating interracial groups: A context effect. *Journal of Personality and Social Psychology, 49*(5), 1231–1245.

COOK, T. D., & FLAY, B. R. (1978). The persistence of experimentally induced attitude change. In L. Berkowitz (Ed.), *Advances in experimental social psychology* (Vol. 11, pp. 2–59). New York: Academic Press.

COOPER, J., & JONES, R. A. (1970). Self-esteem and consistency as determinants of anticipatory opinion change. *Journal of Personality and Social Psychology, 14,* 312–320.

CRAIG, K. D., & PATRICK, C. J. (1985). Facial expression during induced pain. *Journal of Personality and Social Psychology, 48,* 1080–1091.

CRAIK, F. I. M., & TULVING, E. (1975). Depth of processing and the retention of words in episodic memory. *Journal of Experimental Psychology: General, 194,* 268–294.

CRAMER, R. E., WEISS, R. F., STEIGLEDER, M. K., & BALLING, S. S. (1985). Attraction in context: Acquisition and blocking of person-directed action. *Journal of Personality and Social Psychology, 49,* 1221–1230.

CRANO, W. D. (1983). Assumed consensus of attitudes: The effect of vested interest. *Personality and Social Psychology Bulletin, 9,* 597–608.

CROCKER, J. (1981). Judgment of covariation by social perceivers. *Psychological Bulletin, 90,* 272–292.

CROCKER, J., HANNAH, D. B., & WEBER, R. (1983). Person memory and causal attributions. *Journal of Personality and Social Psychology, 44*(1), 55–66.

CUMMINGS, K. M., JETTE, A. M., & ROSENSTOCK, I. M. (1978). Construct validation of the health belief model. *Health Education Monographs, 6,* 394–405.

CUNNINGHAM, M. R. (1979). Weather, mood, and helping behavior: Quasi-experiments with the sunshine Samaritan. *Journal of Personality and Social Psychology, 37*(11), 1947–1956.

CUNNINGHAM, M. R. (1981). Sociobiology as a supplementary paradigm for social psychological research. In L. Wheeler (Ed.), *Review of personality and social psychology* (Vol. 2, pp. 69–101). Beverly Hills: Sage.

CUNNINGHAM, M. R. (1986). Measuring the physical in physical attractiveness: Quasi-experiments on the sociobiology of female facial beauty. *Journal of Personality and Social Psychology, 50*(5), 925–935.

CURTIS, R. C., & MILLER, K. (1986). Believing another likes or dislikes you: Behaviors making the beliefs come true. *Journal of Personality and Social Psychology, 51,* 284–290.

CUTRONA, C. E. (1982). Transition to college: Loneliness and the process of social adjustment. In L. A. Peplau & D. Perlman (Eds.), *Loneliness: A sourcebook of current theory, research and therapy* (pp. 291–309). New York: Wiley-Interscience.

CUTRONA, C. E., & RUSSELL, D. (in press). The provisions of social relationships and adaptation to stress. In W. H. Jones & D. Perlman (Eds.), *Advances in personal relationships* (Vol. 1). Greenwich, CT: JAI Press.

DABBS, J. M., JR., & LEVENTHAL, H. (1966). Effects of varying the recommendations in a fear-arousing communication. *Journal of Personality and Social Psychology, 4,* 525–531.

DARLEY, J. M., & BATSON, C. D. (1973). "From Jerusalem to Jericho": A study of situational and dispositional variables in helping behavior. *Journal of Personality and Social Psychology, 27,* 100–108.

DARLEY, J. M., & FAZIO, R. H. (1980). Expectancy confirmation processes arising in the social interaction sequence. *American Psychologist, 35,* 867–881.

DARLEY, J. M., & GROSS, P. H. (1983). A hypothesis-confirming bias in labeling effects. *Journal of Personality and Social Psychology, 44*(1), 20–33.

DARLEY, J. M., & LATANÉ, B. (1968). Bystander intervention in emergencies: Diffusion of responsibility. *Journal of Personality and Social Psychology, 8,* 377–383.

DARWIN, C. (1871). *The descent of man.* London: Murray.

DARWIN, C. (1872). *The expression of the emotions in man and animals.* London: Murray.

D'ATRI, D. A. (1975). Psychophysiological responses to crowding. *Environment and Behavior, 7,* 237–250.

DAVIDSON, A. R., & JACCARD, J. J. (1979). Variables that moderate the attitude-behavior relation: Results of a longitudinal survey. *Journal of Personality and Social Psychology, 37,* 1364–1376.

DAVIDSON, A. R., YANTIS, S., NORWOOD, M., & MONTANO, D. E. (1985). Amount of information about the attitude object and attitude-behavior consistency. *Journal of Personality and Social Psychology, 49,* 1184–1198.

DAVIES, J. C. (1962). Toward a theory of revolution. *American Sociological Review, 27,* 5–19.

DAVIES, J. C. (1969). The J-curve of rising and declining satisfactions as a cause of some great revolutions and a contained rebellion. In H. D. Graham & T. R. Gurr (Eds.), *The history of violence in America* (pp. 547–576). New York: Bantam.

DAVIS, G. J., & MEYER, R. K. (1973). FSH and LH in the snowshoe hare during the increasing phase of the 10-year cycle. *General Comparative Endocrinology, 20*, 53–60.

DAVIS, J. D. (1976). Self-disclosure in an acquaintance exercise: Responsibility for level of intimacy. *Journal of Personality and Social Psychology, 33*, 787–792.

DAVIS, J. D. (1977). Effects of communication about interpersonal process on the evolution of self-disclosure in dyads. *Journal of Personality and Social Psychology, 35*, 31–37.

DAVIS, M. S. (1968). Variation in patients' compliance with doctors' advice: An empirical analysis of patterns of communication. *American Journal of Public Health, 58*, 274–288.

DEAUX, K., & EMSWILLER, T. (1974). Explanations of successful performance on sex-linked tasks: What is skill for the male is luck for the female. *Journal of Personality and Social Psychology, 29*, 80–85.

DECI, E. L., & RYAN, R. M. (1985). *Intrinsic motivation and self-determination in human behavior.* New York: Plenum.

DEGREE, C. E., & SNYDER, C. R. (1985). Adler's psychology (of use) today: Personal history of traumatic life events as a self-handicapping strategy. *Journal of Personality and Social Psychology, 48*, 1512–1519.

DELONGIS, A., COYNE, J. C., DAKOF, G., FOLKMAN, S., & LAZARUS, R. S. (1982). Relationship of daily hassles, uplifts, and major life events to health status. *Health Psychology, 1*, 119–136.

DENGERINK, H. A., SCHNEDLER, R. W., & COVEY, M. K. (1978). Role of avoidance in aggressive responses to attack and no attack. *Journal of Personality and Social Psychology, 36*, 1044–1053.

DEPARTMENT OF HEALTH AND HUMAN SERVICES. (1981). *Alcohol and health.* Rockville, Md.: Secretary of Health and Human Services, National Institute of Alcohol Abuse and Alcoholism.

DEPAULO, B. M., ROSENTHAL, R., EISENSTAT, R. A., ROGERS, P. L., & FINKELSTEIN, S. (1978). Decoding discrepant nonverbal cues. *Journal of Personality and Social Psychology, 36*, 313–323.

DEPAULO, B. M., ROSENTHAL, R., GREEN, C. R., & ROSENKRANTZ, J. (1982). Diagnosing deceptive and mixed messages from verbal and nonverbal cues. *Journal of Personality and Social Psychology, 18*, 433–446.

DEPAULO, B. M., STONE, J. I., & LASSITER, G. D. (1985). Telling ingratiating lies: Effects of target sex and target attractiveness on verbal and nonverbal deceptive success. *Journal of Personality and Social Psychology, 48*, 1191–1203.

DERLEGA, V. J. (1984). Self-disclosure and intimate relationships. In V. J. Derlega (Ed.), *Communication, intimacy, and close relationships* (pp. 1–10). New York: Academic Press.

DERLEGA, V. J., & CHAIKIN, A. L. (1975). *Sharing intimacy: What we reveal to others and why.* Englewood Cliffs, NJ: Prentice-Hall.

DERLEGA, V. J., DURHAM, B., GOCKEL, B., & SHOLIS, D. (1981). Sex differences in self-disclosure: Effects of topic content, friendship, and partner's sex. *Sex Roles, 7*(4), 433–447.

DERLEGA, V. J., & GRZELAK, A. L. (1979). Appropriate self-disclosure. In G. J. Chelune (Ed.), *Self-disclosure: Origins, patterns, and implications of openness in interpersonal relationships.* San Francisco: Jossey-Bass.

DEUTSCH, F. M., & LAMBERTI, D. M. (1986). Does social approval increase helping? *Personality and Social Psychology Bulletin, 12*(2), 149–157.

DEUTSCH, M. (1985). *Distributive justice: A social psychological perspective.* New Haven, CT: Yale University Press.

DEUTSCH, M., & COLLINS, M. E. (1951). *Interracial housing: A psychological evaluation of a social experiment.* Minneapolis: University of Minnesota Press.

DEUTSCH, M., & KRAUSS, R. M. (1960). The effect of threat on interpersonal bargaining. *Journal of Abnormal and Social Psychology, 61*, 181–189.

DEVINE, P. G., & OSTROM, T. M. (1985). Cognitive mediation of inconsistency discounting. *Journal of Personality and Social Psychology, 49*, 5–21.

DIAMOND, I. (1980). Pornography and repression: A reconsideration. *Signs: Journal of Women in Culture and Society, 5*, 686–701.

DIENER, E., & DEFOUR, D. (1978). Does television violence enhance program popularity? *Journal of Personality and Social Psychology, 36*, 333–341.

DIENER, F. (1980). Deindividuation: The absence of self-awareness and self-regulation in group members. In P. B. Paulus (Ed.), *Psychology of group influence.* Hillsdale, NJ: Erlbaum.

DIENER, F., FRASER, S. C., BEAMAN, A. L., & KELEM, Z. R. T. (1976). Effects of deindividuation variables on stealing among Halloween trick-or-treaters. *Journal of Personality and Social Psychology, 33*, 178–183.

DILLARD, J. P., HUNTER, J. E., & BURGOON, M. (1984). Sequential-request persuasive strategies: Meta-analysis of foot-in-the-door and door-in-the-face. *Human Communication Research, 10*, 461–488.

DIMATTEO, M. R., & DINICOLA, D. D. (1982). *Achieving patient compliance: The psychology of the medical practitioner's role.* New York: Pergamon Press.

DIMATTEO, M. R., FRIEDMAN, H. S., & TARANTA, A. (1979). Sensitivity to bodily nonverbal communications as a factor in practitioner-patient rapport. *Journal of Nonverbal Behavior, 4,* 18–26.

DiMATTEO, M. R., HAYS, R. D., & PRINCE, L. M. (1986). Relationship of physicians' nonverbal communication skill to patient satisfaction, appointment noncompliance, and physician workload. *Health Psychology, 5,* 581–594.

DiNicola, D. D. & DiMATTEO, M. R. (1984). Practitioners, patients, and compliance with medical regimens: A social psychological perspective. In A. Baum, S. E. Taylor, & J. E. Singer (Eds.), *Handbook of Psychology and Health* (Vol. 4). Hillsdale, NJ: Erlbaum.

DION, K. K. (1972). Physical attractiveness and evaluations of children's transgressions. *Journal of Personality and Social Psychology, 24,* 285–290.

DION, K. K., BERSCHEID, E., & WALSTER, E. (1972). What is beautiful is good. *Journal of Personality and Social Psychology, 24,* 285–290.

DION, K. L., & DION, K. K. (1973). Correlates of romantic love. *Journal of Consulting and Clinical Psychology, 41,* 51–56.

DOLLARD, J., DOOB, L., MILLER, N. E., MOWRER, O. H., & SEARS, R. (1939). *Frustration and aggression.* New Haven, CT: Yale University Press.

DONNERSTEIN, E. (1980). Aggressive erotica and violence against women. *Journal of Personality and Social Psychology, 39,* 269–277.

DONNERSTEIN, E. (1983). Erotica and human aggression. In R. Geen & E. Donnerstein (Eds.), *Aggression: Theoretical and empirical reviews.* New York: Academic Press.

DONNERSTEIN, E., & BARRETT, G. (1978). Effects of erotic stimuli on male aggression toward females. *Journal of Personality and Social Psychology, 36,* 180–188.

DONNERSTEIN, E., & BERKOWITZ, L. (1981). Victim reactions in aggressive erotic films as a factor in violence against women. *Journal of Personality and Social Psychology, 41,* 710–724.

DONNERSTEIN, E., & DONNERSTEIN, M. (1972). White rewarding behavior as a function of potential for black retaliation. *Journal of Personality and Social Psychology, 24,* 327–333.

DONNERSTEIN, E., & DONNERSTEIN, M. (1975). The effects of attitudinal similarity on interracial aggression. *Journal of Personality, 43,* 485–502.

DONNERSTEIN, E., DONNERSTEIN, M., & EVANS, R. (1975). Erotic stimuli and aggression: Facilitation or inhibition. *Journal of Personality and Social Psychology, 32,* 237–244.

DONNERSTEIN, E., DONNERSTEIN, M., SIMON, S., & DITTRICHS, R. (1972). Variables in interracial aggression: Anonymity, expected retaliation, and a riot. *Journal of Personality and Social Psychology, 22,* 236–245.

DONNERSTEIN, E., & HALLAM, J. (1978). Facilitating effects of erotica on aggression against women. *Journal of Personality and Social Psychology, 36,* 1270–1277.

DONNERSTEIN, E., & WILSON, D. W. (1976). Effects of noise and perceived control on ongoing and subsequent aggressive behavior. *Journal of Personality and Social Psychology, 34,* 774–781.

DOOB, A. N., & WOOD, L. (1972). Catharsis and aggression: The effects of annoyance and retaliation on aggressive behavior. *Journal of Personality and Social Psychology, 22,* 156–162.

DORNBUSCH, S. M., HASTORF, A. H., RICHARDSON, S. A., MUZZY, R. E., & VREELAND, R. S. (1965). The perceiver and the perceived: Their relative influence on the categories of interpersonal cognition. *Journal of Personality and Social Psychology, 1,* 434–440.

DOSSER, D. A., BALSWICK, J. O., & HALVERSON, C. F. (1986). Male inexpressiveness and relationships. *Journal of Social and Personal Relationships, 3(2),* 241–258.

DOVIDIO, J. F., & GAERTNER, S. L. (Eds.). (1986). *Prejudice, Discrimination, and Racism.* New York: Academic Press.

DWECK, C. S. (1975). The role of expectations and attributions in the alleviation of learned helplessness. *Journal of Personality and Social Psychology, 31,* 674–685.

DYCK, R. J., & RULE, B. G. (1978). Effect on retaliation of causal attributions concerning attack. *Journal of Personality and Social Psychology, 36,* 521–529.

EAGLY, A. H. (1978). Sex differences in influenceability. *Psychological Bulletin, 85,* 86–116.

EAGLY, A. H. (1983). Gender and social influence: A social psychological analysis. *American Psychologist, 38(9),* 971–981.

EAGLY, A. H. (1987). *Sex differences in social behavior: A social-role interpretation.* Hillsdale, NJ: Erlbaum.

EAGLY, A. H., & CARLI, L. L. (1981). Sex of researchers and sex-typed communications as determinants of sex differences in influenceability: A meta-analysis of social influence studies. *Psychological Bulletin, 90(1),* 1–20.

EAGLY, A. H., & CROWLEY, M. (1986). Gender and helping behavior: A meta-analytic review of the social psychological literature. *Psychological Bulletin, 100(3),* 283–308.

EAGLY, A. H., & STEFFEN, V. J. (1986). Gender and aggressive behavior: A meta-analytic review of the social psychological literature. *Psychological Bulletin, 100(3),* 309–330.

EAGLY, A. H., & TELAAK, K. (1972). Width of the latitude of acceptance as a determinant of attitude change.

Journal of Personality and Social Psychology, 23, 388–397.

EAGLY, A. H., & WARREN, R. (1976). Intelligence, comprehension, and opinion change. Journal of Personality, 44, 226–242.

EAGLY, A. H., WOOD, W., & CHAIKEN, S. (1978). Causal inferences about communicators and their effect on opinion change. Journal of Personality and Social Psychology, 36, 424–435.

EDELMAN, M. (1971). Politics as symbolic action: Mass arousal and quiescence. Chicago: Markham Publishing.

EDWARDS, W. (1954). The theory of decision-making. Psychological Bulletin, 51, 380–417.

EINHORN, H. J. (1980). Overconfidence in judgment. In R. A. Shweder (Ed.), New directions for methodology of social and behavioral science (Vol. 4). San Francisco: Jossey-Bass.

EINHORN, H. J., & HOGARTH, R. M. (1981). Behavioral decision theory: Processes of judgment and choice. Annual Review of Psychology, 32, 53–88.

EKMAN, P. (1982). Emotion in the human face, 2nd ed. Cambridge, Eng.: Cambridge University Press.

EKMAN, P., & FRIESEN, W. V. (1971). Constants across cultures in the face and emotion. Journal of Personality and Social Psychology, 17, 124–129.

EKMAN, P., & FRIESEN, W. V. (1974). Detecting deception from the body or face. Journal of Personality and Social Psychology, 29, 288–298.

EKMAN, P., FRIESEN, W. V., & SCHERER, K. (1976). Body movements and voice pitch in deceptive interaction. Semiotica, 16, 23–27.

ELKIN, R. A., & LEIPPE, M. R. (1986). Physiological arousal, dissonance, and attitude change: Evidence for a dissonance-arousal link and a "Don't Remind Me" effect. Journal of Personality and Social Psychology, 51, 55–65.

ELLSWORTH, P. C., & CARLSMITH, J. M. (1973). Eye contact and gaze aversion in an aggressive encounter. Journal of Personality and Social Psychology, 28, 280–292.

ELLSWORTH, P. C., FRIEDMAN, H. S., PERLICK, D., & HOYT, M. E. (1978). Some effects of gaze on subjects motivated to seek or to avoid social comparison. Journal of Personality and Social Psychology, 14, 69–87.

ELMS, A. C. (1976). Personality in politics. New York: Harcourt Brace Jovanovich.

EMSWILLER, T., DEAUX, K., & WILLITS, J. E. (1971). Similarity, sex, and requests for small favors. Journal of Applied Social Psychology, 1(3), 284–291.

ENGEL, G. L. (1971). Sudden and rapid death during psychological stress. Annals of Internal Medicine, 74, 771–782.

ENGLISH, E. H., & BAKER, T. B. (1983). Relaxation training and cardiovascular response to experimental stressors. Health Psychology, 2, 239–259.

EPSTEIN, Y. M. (1981). Crowding stress and human behavior. Journal of Social Issues, 37(1), 126–144.

ERBER, R., & FISKE, S. T. (1984). Outcome dependency and attention to inconsistent information. Journal of Personality and Social Psychology, 47, 709–726.

ERON, L. D. (1982). Parent-child interaction, television violence and aggression of children. American Psychologist, 37, 197–211.

ERON, L. D., HUESMANN, L. R., LEFKOWITZ, M. M., & WALDER, L. O. (1972). Does television violence cause aggression? American Psychologist, 27, 253–263.

ESSER, J. K., & KOMORITA, S. S. (1975). Reciprocity and concession making in bargaining. Journal of Personality and Social Psychology, 31, 864–872.

ETHEREDGE, L. (1978). A world of men: The private sources of American foreign policy. Cambridge, MA: MIT Press.

EVANS, G. W. (1979). Behavioral and physiological consequences of crowding in humans. Journal of Applied Social Psychology, 9, 27–46.

EVANS, G. W., & COHEN, S. (1987). Environmental stress. In D. Stokols & I. Altman (Eds.), Handbook of environmental psychology. New York: Wiley.

EVANS, G. W., & JACOBS, S. V. (1981). Air pollution and human behavior. Journal of Social Issues, 37, 95–125.

EVANS, R. I. (1976). Smoking in children: Developing a social-psychological strategy of deterrence. Journal of Preventive Medicine, 5, 122–127.

EVANS, R. I., ROZELLE, R. M., MITTELMARK, M. B., HANSEN, W. B., BANE, A. L., & HAVIS, J. (1978). Deterring the onset of smoking in children: Knowledge of immediate physiological effects and coping with peer pressure, media pressure, and parent modeling. Journal of Applied Social Psychology, 8, 126–135.

FALK, A. (1985). Aspects of political psychobiography. Political Psychology, 6, 605–619.

FARRENKOPF, T. (1974). Man-environment interaction: An academic department moves into a new building. Unpublished doctoral dissertation, University of Massachusetts.

FAZIO, R. H. (1981). On the self-perception explanation of the overjustification effect: The role of the salience of initial attitude. Journal of Experimental Social Psychology, 17, 417–426.

FAZIO, R. H., CHEN, J., MCDONEL, E. C., & SHERMAN, S. J. (1982). Attitude accessibility, attitude-behavior consistency, and the strength of the object-evaluation association. Journal of Experimental Social Psychology, 18, 339–357.

FAZIO, R. H., EFFREIN, E. A., & FALENDER, V. J. (1981). Self-perceptions following social interaction. Journal of Personality and Social Psychology, 41, 232–242.

FAZIO, R. H., POWELL, M. C., & HERR, P. M. (1983). Toward a process model of the attitude-behavior relation: Accessing one's attitude upon mere observation of the attitude object. *Journal of Personality and Social Psychology, 44,* 723–735.

FAZIO, R. H., SANBONMATSU, D. M., POWELL, M. C., & KARDES, F. R. (1986). On the automatic activation of attitudes. *Journal of Personality and Social Psychology, 50,* 229–238.

FEATHER, N. T., & SIMON, J. G. (1975). Reactions to male and female success and failure in sex-linked occupations: Impressions of personality, causal attributions, and perceived likelihood of different consequences. *Journal of Personality and Social Psychology, 31*(1), 20–31.

FELDMAN, N. S., HIGGINS, E. T., KARLOVAC, M., & RUBLE, D. N. (1976). Use of consensus information in causal attributions as a function of temporal presentation and availability of direct information. *Journal of Personality and Social Psychology, 34,* 694–698.

FELDMAN, R. E. (1968). Response to compatriot and foreigner who seek assistance. *Journal of Personality and Social Psychology, 10*(3), 202–214.

FELDMAN, S. (1982). Economic self-interest and political behavior. *American Journal of Political Science, 26,* 446–466.

FELDMAN, S. (1983). Economic individualism and American public opinion. *American Politics Quarterly, 11,* 3–30.

FELETTI, G., FIRMAN, D., & SANSON-FISHER, R. (1986). Patient satisfaction with primary-care consultations. *Journal of Behavioral Medicine, 9,* 389–399.

FENIGSTEIN, A. (1979). Does aggression cause a preference for viewing media violence? *Journal of Personality and Social Psychology, 37,* 2307–2317.

FESHBACH, S. (1955). The drive-reducing function of fantasy behavior. *Journal of Abnormal and Social Psychology, 50,* 3–12.

FESHBACH, S. (1961). The stimulating versus cathartic effects of a vicarious aggressive activity. *Journal of Abnormal and Social Psychology, 63,* 381–385.

FESHBACH, S. (1970). Aggression. In P. Mussen (Ed.), *Carmichael's Manual of Child Psychology* (Vol. 2). New York: Wiley.

FESHBACH, S., & SINGER, R. D. (1971). *Television and aggression.* San Francisco: Jossey-Bass.

FESTINGER, L. (1950). Informal social communication. *Psychological Review, 57,* 271–282.

FESTINGER, L. (1954). A theory of social comparison processes. *Human Relations, 7,* 117–140.

FESTINGER, L. (1957). *A theory of cognitive dissonance.* Evanston, IL: Row, Peterson.

FESTINGER, L., & CARLSMITH, J. M. (1959). Cognitive consequences of forced compliance. *Journal of Abnormal and Social Psychology, 58,* 203–210.

FESTINGER, L., & MACCOBY, N. (1964). On resistance to persuasive communications. *Journal of Abnormal and Social Psychology, 68,* 359–366.

FESTINGER, L., PEPITONE, A., & NEWCOMB, T. (1952). Some consequences of deindividuation in a group. *Journal of Abnormal and Social Psychology, 47,* 383–389.

FESTINGER, L., RIECKEN, H. W., & SCHACHTER, S. (1956). *When prophecy fails.* Minneapolis: University of Minnesota Press.

FESTINGER, L., SCHACHTER, S., & BACK, K. (1950). *Social pressures in informal groups: A study of human factors in housing.* Stanford University Press.

FIEDLER, F. E. (1978). Recent developments in research on the contingency model. In L. Berkowitz (Ed.), *Group processes* (pp. 209–225). New York: Academic Press.

FIEDLER, F. E. (1981). Leadership effectiveness. *American Behaviorial Scientist, 24*(5), 619–632.

FIEDLER, F. E. (1986). The contribution of cognitive resources and behavior to leadership performance. In C. F. Graumann & S. Moscovici (Eds.), *Changing conceptions of leadership* (pp. 101–114). New York: Springer-Verlag.

FIELDS, J. M., & SCHUMAN, H. (1976). Public beliefs about the beliefs of the public. *Public Opinion Quarterly, 40,* 427–448.

FILLINGIM, R. B., & FINE, M. A. (1986). The effects of internal versus external information processing on symptom perception in an exercise setting. *Health Psychology, 5,* 115–123.

FINKELMAN, J. M., & GLASS, D. C. (1970). Reappraisal of the relationship between noise and human performance by means of a subsidiary task measure. *Journal of Applied Psychology, 54,* 211–213.

FINLAY, D. J., HOLSTI, O. R., & FAGEN, R. R. (1967). *Enemies in politics.* Chicago: Rand-McNally.

FIORINA, M. P. (1981). *Retrospective voting in American national elections.* New Haven, CT: Yale University Press.

FISCHER, C. S. (1982). *To dwell among friends: Personal networks in town and city.* Chicago: University of Chicago Press.

FISCHER, C. S. (1984). *The urban experience,* 2nd ed. New York: Harcourt Brace Jovanovich.

FISCHER, G. W., & JOHNSON, E. J. (1986). Behavioral decision theory and political decision making. In R. R. Lau & D. O. Sears (Eds.), *Political cognition: The 19th annual Carnegie Symposium on Cognition* (pp. 55–65). Hillsdale, NJ: Erlbaum.

FISCHER, W. F. (1963). Sharing in pre-school children as a function of amount and type of reinforcement. *Genetic Psychology Monographs, 68,* 215–245.

FISHBEIN, M., & AJZEN, I. (1975). *Belief, attitude, intention and behavior: An introduction to theory and research.* Reading, MA: Addison-Wesley.

FISHER, J. D., NADLER, A., & WHITCHER-ALAGNA, S. (1982). Recipient reactions to aid. *Psychological Bulletin, 91,* 33–54.

FISKE, S. T. (1980). Attention and weight in person perception: The impact of negative and extreme behavior. *Journal of Personality and Social Psychology, 38*, 889–906.

FISKE, S. T. (1981). Social cognition and affect. In J. Harvey (Ed.), *Cognition, social behavior, and the environment*. Hillsdale, NJ: Erlbaum.

FISKE, S. T. (1982). Schema-triggered affect: Applications to social perception. In M. S. Clark & S. T. Fiske (Eds.), *Affect and cognition: The 17th annual Carnegie Symposium on Cognition*. Hillsdale, NJ: Erlbaum.

FISKE, S. T. (1987). People's reactions to nuclear war: Implications for psychologists. *American Psychologist, 42*, 207–217.

FISKE, S. T., FISCHHOFF, B., & MILBURN, M. A. (Eds.). (1983). Images of nuclear war. *Journal of Social Issues, 39*(Whole issue No. 1).

FISKE, S. T., & TAYLOR, S. (1984). *Social cognition*. Reading, MA: Addison-Wesley.

FLACKS, R. (1967). The liberated generation: An exploration of the roots of student protest. *Journal of Social Issues, 23*, 53–75.

FLEMING, R., BAUM, A., GISRIEL, M. M. & GATCHEL, R. J. (1982, September). Mediating influences of social support on stress at Three Mile Island. *Journal of Human Stress*, pp. 14–22.

FOA, U. G. (1971). Interpersonal and economic resources. *Science, 71*, 345–351.

FOA, U. G., & FOA, E. B. (1974). *Societal structures of the mind*. Springfield, IL: Charles C Thomas.

FOLKES, V. S. (1982). Forming relationships and the matching hypothesis. *Personality and Social Psychology Bulletin, 8*(4), 631–636.

FOLKES, V. S., & SEARS, D. O. (1977). Does everybody like a liker? *Journal of Experimental Social Psychology, 13*(6), 505–519.

FORSYTH, D. R. (1983). *An introduction to group dynamics*. Monterey, CA: Brooks/Cole.

FORSYTH, D. R., & POPE, W. R. (1984). Ethical ideology and judgments of social psychological research: Multidimensional analysis. *Journal of Personality and Social Psychology, 46*, 1365–1375.

FRANCK, K. A. (1980). Friends and strangers: The experience of living in urban and nonurban settings. *Journal of Social Issues, 36*(3), 52–71.

FRANK, F. D., & DRUCKER, J. (1977). The influence of evaluatee's sex on evaluation of a response on a managerial selection instrument. *Sex Roles, 3*, 59–64.

FRANKOVIC, K. A. (1982). Sex and politics—new alignments, old issues. *PS, 15*, 439–448.

FRASER, C., & FOSTER, D. (1984). Social groups, nonsense groups and group polarization. In H. Tajfel (Ed.), *The social dimension: European developments in social psychology* (Vol 2, pp. 473–497). London: Cambridge University Press.

FRASER, C., GOUGE, C., & BILLIG, M. (1971). Risky shifts, cautious shifts, and group polarization. *European Journal of Social Psychology, 1*, 7–30.

FREEDMAN, J. L. (1963). Attitudinal effects of inadequate justification. *Journal of Personality, 31*, 371–385.

FREEDMAN, J. L. (1964). Involvement, discrepancy, and change. *Journal of Abnormal and Social Psychology, 69*, 290–295.

FREEDMAN, J. L. (1965). Long-term behavioral effects of cognitive dissonance. *Journal of Experimental Social Psychology, 1*, 145–155.

FREEDMAN, J. L. (1975). *Crowding and behavior*. New York: Viking Press.

FREEDMAN, J. L. (1984). Effect of television violence on aggressiveness. *Psychological Bulletin, 96*, 227–246.

FREEDMAN, J. L., & FRASER, S. C. (1966). Compliance without pressure: The foot-in-the-door technique. *Journal of Personality and Social Psychology, 4*, 195–202.

FREEDMAN, J. L., HESHKA, S., & LEVY, A. (1973). Population density and pathology: Is there a relationship? *Journal of Experimental Social Psychology, 11*, 539–552.

FREEDMAN, J. L., KLEVANSKY, S., & EHRLICH, P. (1971). The effect of crowding on human task performance. *Journal of Applied Social Psychology, 1*, 7–25.

FREEDMAN, J. L., & SEARS, D. O. (1965). Warning, distraction, and resistance to influence. *Journal of Personality and Social Psychology, 1*, 262–266.

FREEDMAN, J. L., & STEINBRUNER, J. D. (1964). Perceived choice and resistance to persuasion. *Journal of Abnormal and Social Psychology, 68*, 678–681.

FREIDSON, E. (1960). Client control and medical practice. *American Journal of Sociology, 65*, 374–382.

FRENCH, J. (1944). Organized and unorganized groups under fear and frustration. *University of Iowa studies in child welfare*. Iowa City: University of Iowa.

FRENCH, J., & RAVEN, B. (1959). The bases of social power. In D. Cartwright (Ed.), *Studies in social power* (pp. 150–167). Ann Arbor, MI: Institute for Social Research.

FRIED, R., & BERKOWITZ, L. (1979). Music hath charms . . . and can influence helpfulness. *Journal of Applied Social Psychology, 9*, 199–208.

FRIEDLAND, N., & MERARI, A. (1985). The psychological impact of terrorism: A double-edged sword. *Political Psychology, 6*, 591–604.

FRIEDMAN, L. (1979). *The relationship of some architectural variables to the social behavior of building residents*. Unpublished doctoral dissertation, Columbia University.

FRIEDMAN, M., & ROSENMAN, R. H. (1974). *Type A behavior and your heart*. New York: Knopf.

FRIEDRICH, L. K., & STEIN, A. H. (1973). Aggressive and prosocial television programs and the natural behavior of preschool children. *Monographs of the Society for Research in Child Development, 38* (4, Serial No. 151).

FROMM, E. (1941). *Escape from freedom*. New York: Holt.

FULTZ, J., BATSON, C. D., FORTENBACH, V. A., McCARTHY, P. M., & VARNEY, L. L. (1986). Social evaluation and the empathy-altruism hypothesis. *Journal of Social and Personality Psychology, 50*(4), 761–769.

FUNKHOUSER, G. R. (1973). The issues of the sixties: An exploratory study in the dynamics of public opinion. *Public Opinion Quarterly, 37*, 62–75.

GAL, R., & LAZARUS, R. S. (1975). The role of activity in anticipating and confronting stressful situations. *Journal of Human Stress, 1*, 4–20.

GANSTER, D. C., MAYES, B. T., SIME, W. E., & THARP, G. D. (1982). Managing organizational stress: A field experiment. *Journal of Applied Psychology, 67*, 533–542.

GARNETS, L., & PLECK, J. (1979). Sex role identity, androgyny, and sex role transcendence: A sex role strain analysis. *Psychology of Women Quarterly, 3*, 270–283.

GEEN, R. G., & O'NEAL, E. C. (1969). Activation of cue-eliciting aggression by general arousal. *Journal of Personality and Social Psychology, 11*, 289–292.

GEEN, R. G., & PIGG, R. (1970). Acquisition of an aggressive response and its generalization to verbal behavior. *Journal of Personality and Social Psychology, 15*, 165–170.

GEEN, R. G., & QUANTY, M. B. (1977). The catharsis of aggression: An evaluation of a hypothesis. In L. Berkowitz (Ed.), *Advances in experimental social psychology* (Vol. 10, pp. 2–39). New York: Academic Press.

GEISELMAN, R. E., HAIGHT, N. A., & KIMATA, L. G. (1984). Context effects on the perceived physical attractiveness of faces. *Journal of Experimental Social Psychology, 20*, 409–424.

GELLER, D. M. (1980). Responses to urban stimuli: A balanced approach. *Journal of Social Issues, 36*(3), 86–100.

GEORGE, A. L. (1969). The "operational code": A neglected approach to the study of political leaders and decision making. *International Studies Quarterly, 13*, 190–222.

GEORGE, A. L., & GEORGE, J. L. (1956). *Woodrow Wilson and Colonel House: A personality study*. New York: The John Day Co.

GERGEN, K. J., ELLSWORTH, P., MASLACH, C., & SEIPEL, M. (1975). Obligation, donor resources, and reactions to aid in three cultures. *Journal of Personality and Social Psychology, 31*, 390–400.

GERGEN, K. J., GERGEN, M. M., & METER, K. (1972). Individual orientations to prosocial behavior. *Journal of Social Issues, 8*, 105–130.

GETTYS, L. D., & CANN, A. (1981). Children's perceptions of occupational sex stereotypes. *Sex Roles, 7*(3), 301–308.

GIBBS, J. P. (1971). Suicide. In R. K. Merton & R. A. Nisbet (Eds.), *Contemporary social problems*, 3rd ed. (pp. 271–312). New York: Harcourt Brace Jovanovich.

GILBERT, D. T., & JONES, E. E. (1986). Perceiver-induced constraint: Interpretations of self-generated reality. *Journal of Personality and Social Psychology, 50*, 269–280.

GILMOUR, D. R., & WALKEY, F. H. (1981). Identifying violent offenders using a video measure of interpersonal distance. *Journal of Consulting and Clinical Psychology, 49*, 287–291.

GILOVICH, T., JENNINGS, D. L., & JENNINGS, S. (1983). Causal focus and estimates of consensus: An examination of the false-consensus effect. *Journal of Personality and Social Psychology, 45*, 550–559.

GINSBURG, H. J., POLMAN, V. A., YANSON, M. S., & HOPE, M. L. (1977). Variation of aggressive interaction among male elementary school children as a function of changes in spatial density. *Environmental Psychology and Non-verbal Behavior, 2*, 67–75.

GLAD, B. (1973). Contributions of psychobiography. In J. N. Knutson (Ed.), *Handbook of political psychology* (pp. 296–321). San Francisco: Jossey-Bass.

GLASS, D. C. (1977). *Behavior patterns, stress, and coronary disease*. Hillsdale, NJ: Erlbaum.

GLASS, D. C., & SINGER, J. E. (1972). *Urban stress*. New York: Academic Press.

GLENN, N. D. (1980). Values, attitudes, and beliefs. In O. G. Brim, Jr. & J. Kagan, (Eds.), *Constancy and change in human development* (pp. 596–640). Cambridge, MA: Harvard University Press.

GOETHALS, G., & KLOS, D. S. (Eds.). (1970). *Experiencing youth: First-person accounts*. Boston: Little, Brown.

GOETHALS, G. R., COOPER, J., & NAFICY, A. (1979). Role of foreseen, foreseeable, and unforeseeable behavioral consequences in the arousal of cognitive dissonance. *Journal of Personality and Social Psychology, 37*, 1179–1185.

GOETHALS, G. R., & ZANNA, M. P. (1979). The role of

social comparison in choice shifts. *Journal of Personality and Social Psychology*, 37, 1179–1185.

GOFFMAN, E. (1952). On cooling the mark out: Some aspects of adaptation to failure. *Psychiatry*, *15*, 451–463.

GOLDBERG, P. (1968). Are women prejudiced against women? *TransAction*, 5(5), 28–30.

GOLDEN, J. S., & JOHNSTON, G. D. (1970). Problems of distortion in doctor-patient communications. *Psychiatry in Medicine*, *1*, 127–149.

GOLDMAN, W., & LEWIS, P. (1977). Beautiful is good: Evidence that the physically attractive are more socially skillful. *Journal of Experimental Social Psychology*, *13*, 125–130.

GOLDSTEIN, J. H., & ARMS, R. L. (1971). Effects of observing athletic contests on hostility. *Sociometry*, *34*, 83–90.

GOLDSTEIN, J. H., DAVIS, R. W., & HERMAN, D. (1975). Escalation of aggression: Experimental studies. *Journal of Personality and Social Psychology*, *31*, 162–170.

GOODMAN, M. E. (1952). *Race awareness in young children*. Reading, MA: Addison-Wesley.

GORANSON, R. E., & BERKOWITZ, L. (1966). Reciprocity and responsibility reactions to prior help. *Journal of Personality and Social Psychology*, *3*, 227–232.

GORDON, S. L. (1981). The sociology of sentiments and emotions. In M. Rosenberg & R. H. Turner (Eds.), *Social psychology: Sociological perspectives* (pp. 562–592). New York: Basic Books.

GORN, G. (1982). The effects of music in advertising on choice behavior: A classical conditioning approach. *Journal of Marketing Research*, *46*, 94–101.

GORN, G. J., & GOLDBERG, M. E. (1980). Children's responses to repetitive TV commercials. *Journal of Consumer Research*, *6*, 421–425.

GOTTMAN, J. M. (1979). *Marital interaction: Experimental investigations*. New York: Academic Press.

GOULD, R., & SIGALL, H. (1977). The effects of empathy and outcome on attribution: An examination of the divergent-perspectives hypothesis. *Journal of Experimental Social Psychology*, *13*, 480–491.

GOULDNER, A. W. (1960). The norm of reciprocity: A preliminary statement. *American Sociological Review*, *25*, 161–179.

GRAMZA, A. F. (1967). Responses of brooding nighthawks to disturbance stimulus. *Auk*, *84*(1), 72–86.

GRANBERG, D. (1984). Attributing attitudes to members of groups. In J. R. Eiser (Ed.), *Attitudinal judgment*. New York: Springer-Verlag.

GREEN, S. K., BUCHANAN, D. R., & HEUER, S. K. (1984). Winners, losers, and choosers: A field investigation of dating initiation. *Personality and Social Psychology Bulletin*, *10*(4), 502–511.

GREENBERG, B. S. (1986). Minorities and the mass media. In J. Bryant & D. Zillmann (Eds.), *Perspectives on media effects* (pp. 165–188). Hillsdale, NJ: Erlbaum.

GREENBERG, B. S., & MAZINGO, S. L. (1976). Racial issues in mass media institutions. In P. A. Katz, (Ed.), *Towards the elimination of racism* (pp. 309–340). Elmsford, NY: Pergamon Press.

GREENBERG, B. S., & PARKER, E. B. (1965). Summary: Social research on the assassination. In B. S. Greenberg & E. B. Parker (Eds.), *The Kennedy assassination and the American public* (pp. 361–382). Stanford, CA: Stanford University Press.

GREENBERG, J., & COHEN, R. L. (Eds.), (1982). *Equity and justice in social behavior*. New York: Academic Press.

GREENBERG, J., PYSZCZYNSKI, T., & SOLOMON, S. (1982). The self-serving attributional bias: Beyond self-presentation. *Journal of Experimental Social Psychology*, *18*, 56–67.

GREENBERG, M. S., & FRISCH, D. M. (1972). Effects of intentionality on willingness to reciprocate a favor. *Journal of Experimental Social Psychology*, *8*, 99–111.

GREENSTEIN, F. I. (1975). Personality and politics. In F. I. Greenstein & N. W. Polsby (Eds.), *Handbook of political science*, 2nd ed. (Vol. 2, pp. 1–92). Reading, MA: Addison-Wesley.

GREENWALD, A. G. (1968). Cognitive learning, cognitive response to persuasion, and attitude change. In A. G. Greenwald, T. C. Brock, & T. M. Ostrom, (Eds.), *Psychological foundations of attitudes* (pp. 147–170). New York: Academic Press.

GREENWELL, J., & DENGERINK, H. A. (1973). The role of perceived versus actual attack in human physical aggression. *Journal of Personality and Social Psychology*, *26*, 66–71.

GREER, D. L. (1983). Spectator booing and the home advantage: A study of social influence in the basketball arena. *Social Psychology Quarterly*, *46*(3), 252–261.

GREER, S. (1974). Psychological aspects: Delay in the treatment of breast cancer. *Proceedings of the Royal Society of Medicine*, *64*, 470–473.

GRIFFIT, W., & VEITCH, R. (1971). Hot and crowded: Influences of population density and temperature on interpersonal affective behavior. *Journal of Personality and Social Psychology*, *17*, 92–98.

GROSS, A. E., & LATANÉ, J. G. (1974). Receiving help, reciprocation, and interpersonal attraction. *Journal of Applied Social Psychology*, *4*(3), 210–223.

GROSS, A. E., WALLSTON, B. S., & PILIAVIN, I. M. (1979). Reactance, attribution, equity, and the help recipient. *Journal of Applied Social Psychology*, *9*(4), 297–313.

GRUDER, C. L., ROMER, D., & KORTH, B. (1978). Dependency and fault as determinants of helping.

Journal of Experimental Social Psychology, 14, 227–235.

GRUSH, J. E. (1980). Impact of candidate expenditures, regionality, and prior outcomes on the 1976 Democratic presidential primaries. *Journal of Personality and Social Psychology, 38,* 337–347.

GRUSH, J. E., MCKEOGH, K. L., & AHLERING, R. G. (1978). Extrapolating laboratory exposure research to actual political elections. *Journal of Personality and Social Psychology, 36,* 257–70.

GUERIN, B. (1986). Mere presence effects in humans: A review. *Journal of Experimental Social Psychology, 22,* 38–77.

GUIDUBALDI, J., PERRY, J. D., & NATASI, B. K. (1987). Growing up in a divorced family: Initial and long-term perspectives on children's adjustment. In S. Oskamp (Ed.), *Family processes and problems: Social psychological aspects. (Applied Social Psychology Annual 7,* pp. 202–237). Beverly Hills, CA: Sage.

GUIMOND, S., & DUBÉ-SIMARD, L. (1983). Relative deprivation theory and the Quebec nationalist movement: The cognition-emotion distinction and the personal-group deprivation issue. *Journal of Personality and Social Psychology, 44,* 526–535.

GURIN, G., VEROFF, J., & FELD, S. (1960). *Americans view their mental health: A nationwide survey.* New York: Basic Books.

GURIN, P. (1985). Women's gender consciousness. *Public Opinion Quarterly, 49,* 142–163.

GUTTENTAG, M., & SECORD, P. F. (1982). *Too many women: The sex ratio question.* Beverly Hills, CA: Sage.

HACKER, H. M. (1981). Blabbermouths and clams: Sex differences in self-disclosure in same-sex and cross-sex friendship dyads. *Psychology of Women Quarterly, 5*(3), 385–401.

HAEFNER, D., & KIRSCHT, J. (1970). Motivational and behavioral effects of modifying health beliefs. *Public Health Reports, 85,* 478–484.

HALL, E. T. (1959). *The silent language.* Garden City, NY: Doubleday.

HALL, J. A. (1978). Gender effects in decoding nonverbal cues. *Psychological Bulletin, 85*(4), 845–857.

HALL, K. R. L. (1960). Social vigilance behavior of the chacuma baboon (Papio ursinus). *Behavior, 16*(3,4), 261–294.

HAMBURG, D. A., & ADAMS, J. E. (1967). A perspective on coping behavior: Seeking and utilizing information in major transitions. *Archives of General Psychiatry, 19,* 277–284.

HAMILL, R., WILSON, T. D., & NISBETT, R. E. (1980). Insensitivity to sample bias: Generalizing from atypical cases. *Journal of Personality and Social Psychology, 39,* 578–589.

HAMILTON, D. L. (1981). Cognitive representations of persons. In E. T. Higgins, C. P. Herman, & M. P. Zanna (Eds.), *Social cognition: The Ontario symposium* (Vol. 1). Hillsdale, NJ: Erlbaum.

HAMILTON, D. L., & GIFFORD, R. K. (1976). Illusory correlation in interpersonal perception: A cognitive basis of stereotypic judgments. *Journal of Experimental Social Psychology, 12,* 392–407.

HAMILTON, D. L., & TROLIER, T. K. (1986). Stereotypes and stereotyping: An overview of the cognitive approach. In J. F. Dovidio & S. L. Gaertner (Eds.), *Prejudice, discrimination, and racism* (pp. 127–164). New York: Academic Press.

HAMILTON, D. L., & ZANNA, M. P. (1972). Differential weighting of favorable and unfavorable attributions in impressions of personality. *Journal of Experimental Research in Personality, 6,* 204–212.

HAMILTON, D. L., & ZANNA, M. P. (1974). Context effects in impression formation: Changes in connotative meaning. *Journal of Personality and Social Psychology, 29,* 649–654.

HAMILTON, V. L. (1978). Obedience and responsibility: A jury simulation. *Journal of Personality and Social Psychology, 36,* 126–146.

HAMPSON, S. E., & DAWSON, W. J. M. (1985). Whatever happened to pollyanna? *Personality and Social Psychology Bulletin, 11,* 106–117.

HANSEN, G. L. (1985). Perceived threats and marital jealousy. *Social Psychology Quarterly, 48*(3), 262–268.

HANSSON, R. O., & SLADE, K. M. (1977). Altruism toward a deviant in city and small town. *Journal of Applied Social Psychology, 7,* 272–279.

HARKNESS, A. R., DEBONO, K. G., & BORGIDA, E. (1985). Personal involvement and strategies for making contingency judgments: A stake in the dating game makes a difference. *Journal of Personality and Social Psychology, 49,* 22–32.

HARRIS, P. R. (1980). *Promoting health—preventing disease: Objectives for the nation.* Washington, D.C.: U.S. Government Printing Office.

HARTMANN, D. P. (1969). Influence of symbolically modeled instrumental aggression and pain cues on aggressive behavior. *Journal of Personality and Social Psychology, 11,* 280–288.

HARTNETT, J. J., BAILEY, K. G., & GIBSON, F. W., JR. (1970). Personal space as influenced by sex and type of movement. *Journal of Psychology, 76,* 139–144.

HARVEY, J. H., WEARY, G., & HARRIS, B. (1981). *Perspectives on attributional processes.* Dubuque, IA: Wm. C. Brown.

HASTIE, R., & KUMAR, P. A. (1979). Person memory: Personality traits as organizing principles in memory for behavior. *Journal of Personality and Social Psychology, 37,* 25–38.

HATFIELD, E., & SPRECHER, S. (1986). *Mirror, mirror*

. . . *The importance of looks in everyday life.* Albany, NY: State University of New York Press.

HATKOFF, S., & LASSWELL, T. E. (1979). Male-female similarities and differences in conceptualizing love. In M. Cook & G. Wilson (Eds.), *Love and attraction.* Oxford, Eng.: Pergamon Press.

HAYNES, S. G., FEINLEIB, M., & KANNEL, W. B. (1980). The relationship of psychosocial factors to coronary heart disease in the Framingham Study, III: Eight-year incidence of coronary heart disease. *American Journal of Epidemiology, 111,* 37–58.

HAZAN, C., & SHAVER, P. (1987). Romantic love conceptualized as an attachment process. *Journal of Personality and Social Psychology, 52,* 511–524.

HEIDER, F. (1958). *The psychology of interpersonal relations.* New York: Wiley.

HELLER, J. R., GROFF, B. D., & SOLOMON, S. H. (1977). Toward an understanding of crowding: The role of physical interaction. *Journal of Personality and Social Psychology, 35,* 183–190.

HENDRICK, C., HENDRICK, S., FOOTE, F. H., & SLAPION-FOOTE, M. J. (1984). Do men and women love differently? *Journal of Social and Personal Relationships, 1,* 177–195.

HENLEY, N. M. (1986, April). *Sex bias in language: What we know and don't know.* Invited address presented at the Eastern Psychological Association, New York.

HENNIGAN, K. M., HEATH, L., WHARTON, J. D., DEL ROSARIO, M. L., COOK, T. D., & CALDER, B. J. (1982). Impact of the introduction of television on crime in the United States: Empirical findings and theoretical implications. *Journal of Personality and Social Psychology, 42,* 461–477.

HERMANN, M. G. (Ed.) (1977). *A psychological examination of political leaders.* New York: Free Press.

HERRMANN, R. K. (1985). American perceptions of Soviet foreign policy: Reconsidering three competing perspectives. *Political Psychology, 6,* 375–411.

HIGBEE, K. L. (1969). Fifteen years of fear arousal: Research on threat appeals, 1953–1968. *Psychological Bulletin, 72,* 426–444.

HIGGINS, E. T., & BARGH, J. A. (1987). Social cognition and social perception. *Annual Review of Psychology, 38,* 369–425.

HIGGINS, E. T., & BRYANT, S. L. (1982). Consensus information and the fundamental attribution error: The role of development and in-group versus out-group knowledge. *Journal of Personality and Social Psychology, 43,* 889–900.

HIGGINS, E. T., RHODEWALT, F., & ZANNA, M. P. (1979). Dissonance motivation: Its nature, persistence, and reinstatement. *Journal of Experimental Social Psychology, 15,* 16–34.

HIGGINS, E. T., RHOLES, W. S., & JONES, C. R. (1977). Category accessibility and impression formation. *Journal of Experimental Social Psychology, 13,* 141–154.

HILL, C. T., RUBIN, Z., & PEPLAU, L. A. (1976). Breakups before marriage: The end of 103 affairs. *Journal of Social Issues, 32*(1), 147–168.

HILTON, J. L., & DARLEY, J. M. (1985). Constructing other persons: A limit on the effect. *Journal of Experimental Social Psychology, 21,* 1–18.

HIRT, E., & KIMBLE, C. E. (1981, May). *The home-field advantage in sports: Differences and correlates.* Paper presented at the annual meeting of the Midwestern Psychological Association, Detroit.

HOCHBAUM, G. (1958). *Public participation in medical screening programs* (DHEW Publication No. 572, Public Health Service). Washington, D.C.: U.S. Government Printing Office.

HODGES, B. H. (1974). Effect of valence on relative weighting in impression formation. *Journal of Personality and Social Psychology, 30,* 378–381.

HOFFMAN, C., MISCHEL, W., & BAER, J. S. (1984). Language and person cognition: Effects of communicative set on trait attribution. *Journal of Personality and Social Psychology, 46,* 1029–1043.

HOFFMAN, C., MISCHEL, W., & MAZZE, K. (1981). The role of purpose in the organization of information about behavior: Trait-based versus goal-based categories in person cognition. *Journal of Personality and Social Psychology, 40,* 211–225.

HOFFMAN, M. L. (1981). Is altruism part of human nature? *Journal of Personality and Social Psychology, 40*(1), 121–137.

HOGARTH, R. M. (1980). *Judgment and choice: The psychology of decision.* New York: Wiley.

HOKANSON, J. E. (1961). Vascular and psychogalvanic effects of experimentally aroused anger. *Journal of Personality, 29,* 30–39.

HOKANSON, J. E., & BURGESS, M. (1962). The effects of three types of aggression on vascular processes. *Journal of Abnormal and Social Psychology, 64,* 446–449.

HOLAHAN, C. J., & WILCOX, B. L. (1978). Residential satisfaction and friendship formation in high- and low-rise student housing: An interactional analysis. *Journal of Educational Psychology, 70*(2), 237–241.

HOLLAND, D., & SKINNER, D. (1987). Prestige and intimacy: The cultural models behind Americans' talk about gender types. In D. Holland & N. Quinn (Eds.), *Cultural models in language and thought* (pp. 78–111). New York: Cambridge University Press.

HOLLANDER, E. P. (1985). Leadership and power. In G. Lindzey & E. Aronson (Eds.), *Handbook of social psychology,* 3rd ed. (Vol. 2, pp. 485–538). New York: Random House.

HOLMES, T. H., & RAHE, R. H. (1967). The social readjustment rating scale. *Journal of Psychosomatic Research, 11,* 213–218.

HOLTZ, R., & MILLER, N. (1985). Assumed similarity and opinion certainty. *Journal of Personality and Social Psychology, 48,* 890–898.

HOLTZWORTH-MUNROE, A., & JACOBSON, N. S. (1985). Causal attributions of married couples: When do they search for causes? What do they conclude when they do? *Journal of Personality and Social Psychology, 48,* 1398–1412.

HOMANS, G. C. (1965). Group factors in worker productivity. In H. Proshansky & L. Seidenberg (Eds.), *Basic studies in social psychology.* New York: Holt, Rinehart & Winston.

HOOK, J. G., & COOK, T. D. (1979). Equity theory and the cognitive ability of children. *Psychological Bulletin, 86,* 429–445.

HORNSTEIN, H. A., FISCH, E., & HOLMES, M. (1968). Influence of a model's feeling about his behavior and his relevance as a comparison other on observers' helping behavior. *Journal of Personality and Social Psychology, 10*(3), 222–226.

HOROWITZ, M. J., DUFF, D. F., & STRATTON, L. O. (1970). Personal space and the body buffer zone. In H. Proshansky, W. Ittelson, & L. Rivlin (Eds.), *Environmental psychology: Man and his physical setting.* New York: Holt, Rinehart & Winston.

HOUSE, J. A. (1981). *Work stress and social support.* Reading, MA: Addison-Wesley.

HOUSE, J. A., ROBBINS, C., & METZNER, H. L. (1982). The association of social relationships and activities with mortality: Prospective evidence from the Tecumseh Community Health Study. *American Journal of Epidemiology, 116,* 123–140.

HOUSE, J. S., & WOLF, S. (1978). Effects of urban residence on interpersonal trust and helping behavior. *Journal of Personality and Social Psychology, 36,* 1029–1043.

HOVLAND, C. I. (1959). Reconciling conflicting results derived from experimental and survey studies of attitude change. *American Psychologist, 14,* 8–17.

HOVLAND, C. I., HARVEY, O. J., & SHERIF, M. (1957). Assimilation and contrast effects in reactions to communication and attitude change. *Journal of Abnormal and Social Psychology, 55,* 244–252.

HOVLAND, C. I., & JANIS, I. L. (1959). Summary and implications for further research. In C. I. Hovland & I. L. Janis (Eds.), *Personality and persuasibility.* New Haven, CT: Yale University Press.

HOVLAND, C. I., JANIS, I. L, & KELLEY, H. H. (1953). *Communication and persuasion.* New Haven: Yale University Press.

HOVLAND, C. I., LUMSDAINE, A. A., & SHEFFIELD, F. D. (1949). *Experiments on mass communication.* Princeton, NJ: Princeton University Press.

HOVLAND, C. I., & PRITZKER, H. A. (1957). Extent of opinion change as a function of amount of change advocated. *Journal of Abnormal and Social Psychology, 54,* 257–261.

HOVLAND, C. I., & SEARS, R. R. (1940). Minor studies of aggression: Correlation of lynchings with economic indices. *Journal of Psychology, 9,* 301–310.

HOVLAND, C. I., & WEISS, W. (1952). The influence of source credibility on communication effectiveness. *Public Opinion Quarterly, 15,* 635–650.

HOWARD, J. A. (1984). Societal influences on attribution: Blaming some victims more than others. *Journal of Personality and Social Psychology, 47,* 494–505.

HOWARD, J., & ROTHBART, M. (1980). Social categorization and memory for in-group and out-group behavior. *Journal of Personality and Social Psychology, 38,* 301–310.

HUESMANN, L. R. (1982). Television violence and aggressive behavior. In D. Pearl, L. Bouthilet, & J. Lazar (Eds.), *Television and behavior: Ten years of scientific progress and implications for the eighties: Vol. II: Technical reviews.* Rockville, MD: National Institute of Mental Health.

HUESMANN, L. R., & ERON, L. D. (1986). The development of aggression in American children as a consequence of television violence viewing. In L. R. Huesmann & L. D. Eron (Eds.), *Television and the aggressive child: A cross-national comparison* (pp. 45–80). Hillsdale, NJ: Erlbaum.

HUESMANN, L. R., ERON, L. D., & YARMEL, P. W. (1987). Intellectual functioning and aggression. *Journal of Personality and Social Psychology, 52,* 232–240.

HUESMANN, L. R., & MALAMUTH, N. M. (1986). Media violence and antisocial behavior: An overview. *Journal of Social Issues, 42,* 1–6.

HUNT, M. M. (1959). *The natural history of love.* New York: Knopf.

HUR, K. K., & ROBINSON, J. P. (1978). The social impact of "Roots." *Journalism Quarterly, 55,* 19–24.

HUSTON, T. L. (1983). Power. In H. H. Kelley et al., *Close relationships* (pp. 169–219). New York: Freeman.

HUSTON, T. L., RUGGIERO, M., CONNER, R., & GEIS, G. (1981). Bystander intervention into crime: A study based on naturally-occurring episodes. *Social Psychology Quarterly, 44*(1), 14–23.

HYDE, J. S. (1981). How large are cognitive gender differences? A meta-analysis using w^2 and d. *American Psychologist, 36,* 892–901.

HYDE, J. S. (1986). Gender differences in aggression. In J. S. Hyde & M. C. Linn (Eds.), *The psychology of gender: Advances through meta-analysis* (pp. 51–66). Baltimore: Johns Hopkins University Press.

HYDE, J. S., & LINN, M. C. (1986). *The psychology of gender: Advances through meta-analysis.* Baltimore: Johns Hopkins University Press.

HYMAN, H. H. (1959). *Political socialization*. Glencoe, NY: Free Press.

INGLEHART, R. (1981). Post-materialism in an environment of insecurity. *American Political Science Review*, 75, 880–900.

INKELES, A. (1983). *The third century*. Stanford, CA: Hoover Institution Press.

INSKO, C. A., SMITH, R. H., ALICKE, M. D., WADE, J., & TAYLOR, S. (1985). Conformity and group size: The concern with being right and the concern with being liked. *Personality and Social Psychology Bulletin*, 11(1), 41–50.

INSTITUTE FOR PROPAGANDA ANALYSIS. (1939). *The fine art of propaganda: A study of Father Coughlin's speeches*. New York: Harcourt and Brace.

ISEN, A. M. (1970). Success, failure, attention, and reaction to others: The warm glow of success. *Journal of Personality and Social Psychology*, 15, 294–301.

ISEN, A. M., CLARK, M., & SCHWARTZ, M. F. (1976). Duration of the effect of good mood on helping: Footprints on the sands of time. *Journal of Personality and Social Psychology*, 34, 385–393.

ISEN, A. M., & LEVIN, P. F. (1972). Effects of feeling good on helping: Cookies and kindness. *Journal of Personality and Social Psychology*, 21, 384–388.

ISEN, A. M., & SIMMONDS, S. F. (1978). The effect of feeling good on a helping task that is incompatible with good mood. *Social Psychology Quarterly*, 41, 346–349.

ISENBERG, D. J. (1986). Group polarization: A critical review and meta-analysis. *Journal of Personality and Social Psychology*, 50(6), 1141–1151.

IYENGAR, S., KINDER, D. R., PETERS, M. D., & KROSNICK, J. A. (1984). The evening news and presidential evaluations. *Journal of Personality and Social Psychology*, 46, 778–787.

IYENGAR, S., PETERS, M. D., & KINDER, D. R. (1982). Experimental demonstrations of the "not-so-minimal" consequences of TV news programs. *The American Political Science Review*, 76(4), 848–858.

JACKMAN, M. R. (1978). General and applied tolerance: Does education increase commitment to racial integration? *American Journal of Political Science*, 22, 302–324.

JACKSON, J. E. (1983). Election night reporting and voter turnout. *American Journal of Political Science*, 27, 615–635.

JACKSON, J. M. (1986). In defense of social impact theory: Comment on Mullen. *Journal of Personality and Social Psychology*, 50(3), 511–513.

JACKSON, J. M., & HARKINS, S. G. (1985). Equity in effort: An explanation of the social loafing effect. *Journal of Personality and Social Psychology*, 49(5), 1199–1206.

JACKSON, J. M., & WILLIAMS, K. D. (1985). Social loafing on difficult tasks: Working collectively can improve performance. *Journal of Personality and Social Psychology*, 49(4), 937–942.

JAFFE, Y., MALAMUTH, N., FEINGOLD, J., & FESHBACH, S. (1974). Sexual arousal and behavioral aggression. *Journal of Personality and Social Psychology*, 30, 759–764.

JANIS, I. L. (1967). Effects of fear arousal on attitude change: Recent developments in theory and experimental research. In L. Berkowitz (Ed.), *Advances in Experimental Social Psychology* (Vol. 3, pp. 166–224). New York: Academic Press.

JANIS, I. L. (1982). *Groupthink: Psychological studies of policy decisions and fiascoes*, 2nd ed., Boston: Houghton Mifflin.

JANIS, I. L. (1983). Improving adherence to medical recommendations: Prescriptive hypotheses derived from recent research in social psychology. In A. Baum, S. E. Taylor & J. Singer (Eds.), *Handbook of psychology and health* (Vol. 4, pp. 113–148). Hillsdale, NJ: Erlbaum.

JANIS, I. L., & FESHBACH, S. (1953). Effects of fear-arousing communications. *Journal of Abnormal and Social Psychology*, 48, 78–92.

JANIS, I. L., & GILMORE, J. B. (1965). The influence of incentive conditions on the success of role playing in modifying attitudes. *Journal of Personality and Social Psychology*, 1, 17–27.

JANIS, I. L., KAYE, D., & KIRSCHNER, P. (1965). Facilitating effects of "eating-while-reading" on responsiveness to persuasive communications. *Journal of Personality and Social Psychology*, 1, 181–185.

JANIS, I. L., & MANN, L. (1965). Effectiveness of emotional role-playing in modifying smoking habits and attitudes. *Journal of Experimental Research in Personality*, 1, 84–90.

JANIS, I. L., & MANN, L. (1977). *Decision making*. New York: Free Press.

JANOFF-BULMAN, R. (1979). Characterological versus behavioral self-blame: Inquiries into depression and rape. *Journal of Personality and Social Psychology*, 37, 1798–1809.

JANZ, N. K. & BECKER, M. H. (1984). The health belief model: A decade later. *Health Education Quarterly*, 11, 1–47.

JELLISON, J. M., & GREEN, J. (1981). A self-presentation approach to the fundamental attribution error: The norm of internality. *Journal of Personality and Social Psychology*, 40, 643–649.

JEMMOTT, J. B. III, & LOCKE, S. E. (1984). Psychosocial factors, immunologic mediation, and human susceptibility to infectious diseases: How much do we know? *Psychological Bulletin, 95*, 78–108.

JENKINS, C. D., ZYZANSKI, S. J., & ROSENMAN, R. H. (1979). *Jenkins Activity Survey*. Cleveland: Psychological Corp.

JENNINGS, J., GEIS, F. L., & BROWN, V. (1980). Influence of television commercials on women's self-confidence and independent judgment. *Journal of Personality and Social Psychology, 38*(2), 203–210.

JENNINGS, M. K., & MARKUS, G. B. (1984). Partisan orientations over the long haul: Results from the three-wave political socialization panel study. *American Political Science Review, 78*, 1000–1018.

JENNINGS, M. K., & NIEMI, R. G. (1974). *The political character of adolescence*. Princeton, NJ: Princeton University Press.

JERVIS, R. (1976). *Perception and misperception in international politics*. Princeton, NJ: Princeton University Press.

JOHNSON, C. A., HANSEN, W. B., COLLINS, L. M., & GRAHAM, J. W. (1986). High-school smoking prevention: Results of a three-year longitudinal study. *Journal of Behavioral Medicine, 9*, 439–452.

JOHNSON, J. E. (1984). Psychological interventions and coping with surgery. In A. Baum, S. E. Taylor, & J. E. Singer (Eds.), *Handbook of psychology and health* (Vol. IV, pp. 167–185). Hillsdale, NJ: Erlbaum.

JOHNSON, J. E., & LEVENTHAL, H. (1974). Effects of accurate expectations and behavioral instructions on reactions during a noxious medical examination. *Journal of Personality and Social Psychology, 29*, 710–718.

JOHNSON, J. T., & DROBNY, J. (1985). Proximity biases in the attribution of civil liability. *Journal of Personality and Social Psychology, 48*, 283–296.

JOHNSON, P. B., SEARS, D. O., & MCCONAHAY, J. B. (1971). Black invisibility, the press, and the Los Angeles riot. *American Journal of Sociology, 76*(4), 698–721.

JOHNSON, R. D., & DOWNING, L. L. (1979). Deindividuation and valence of cues: Effects of prosocial and antisocial behavior. *Journal of Personality and Social Psychology, 37*, 1532–1538.

JOHNSON, T. E., & RULE, B. G. (1986). Mitigating circumstance information, censure, and aggression. *Journal of Personality and Social Psychology, 50*, 537–542.

JONES, E. E. (1979). The rocky road from acts to dispositions. *American Psychologist, 34*, 107–117.

JONES, E. E., & BERGLAS, S. (1978). Control of attributions about the self through self-handicapping strategies: The appeal of alcohol and the role of underachievement. *Personality and Social Psychology Bulletin, 4*, 200–206.

JONES, E. E., & HARRIS, V. A. (1967). The attribution of attitudes. *Journal of Experimental Social Psychology, 3*, 1–24.

JONES, E. E., & NISBETT, R. E. (1972). The actor and the observer: Divergent perceptions of the causes of behavior. In E. E. Jones et al., *Attribution: Perceiving the causes of behavior*. Morristown, NJ: General Learning Press.

JONES, E. E., & SIGALL, H. (1971). The bogus pipeline: A new paradigm for measuring affect and attitude. *Psychological Bulletin, 76*, 349–364.

JONES, E. E., WORCHEL, S., GOETHALS, G. R., & GRUMET, J. F. (1971). Prior expectancy and behavioral extremity as determinants of attitude attribution. *Journal of Experimental Social Psychology, 7*, 59–80.

JONES, W. H. (1982). Loneliness and social behavior. In L. A. Peplau & D. Perlman (Eds.), *Loneliness: A sourcebook of current theory, research and therapy* (pp. 238–254). New York: Wiley-Interscience.

JONES, W. H., BRIGGS, S. R., & SMITH, T. G. (1986). Shyness: Conceptualization and measurement. *Journal of Personality and Social Psychology, 51*(3), 629–639.

JONES, W. H., CARPENTER, B. N., & QUITANA, D. (1985). Personality and interpersonal predictors of loneliness in two cultures. *Journal of Personality and Social Psychology, 48*(6), 1503–1511.

JORDAN, W. D. (1968). *White over black: American attitudes toward the Negro, 1550–1812*. Chapel Hill: University of North Carolina Press.

KAHNEMAN, D., & TVERSKY, A. (1982). The simulation heuristic. In D. Kahneman, P. Slovic, & A. Tversky (Eds.), *Judgment under uncertainty: Heuristics and biases* (pp. 201–209). New York: Cambridge University Press.

KALICK, S. M., & HAMILTON, T. E. (1986). The matching hypothesis reexamined. *Journal of Personality and Social Psychology, 51*(4), 673–682.

KALLGREN, C. A., & WOOD, W. (1986). Access to attitude-relevant information in memory as a determinant of attitude-behavior consistency. *Journal of Experimental Social Psychology, 22*, 328–338.

KANDEL, D. (1974). Inter- and intragenerational influences on adolescent marijuana use. *Journal of Social Issues, 30*, 107–135.

KANDEL, D. (1978). Similarity in real-life adolescent friendship pairs. *Journal of Personality and Social Psychology, 36*, 306–312.

KANIN, E. J., DAVIDSON, K. R., & SCHECK, S. R. (1970). A research note on male-female differentials in the experience of heterosexual love. *Journal of Sex Research, 6*(1), 64–72.

KANNER, A. D., COYNE, J. C., SCHAEFFER, C., & LAZARUS, R. S. (1981). Comparison of two modes of stress measurement: Daily hassles and uplifts versus major life events. *Journal of Behavioral Medicine, 4*, 1–39.

KAPLAN, K. J., FIRESTONE, I. J., DEGNORE, R., & MORRE, M. (1974). Gradients of attraction as a function of disclosure probe intimacy and setting formality: On distinguishing attitude oscillation from attitude change—Study one. *Journal of Personality and Social Psychology, 30*, 638–646.

KAPLAN, R. M., & SINGER, R. D. (1976). Television violence and viewer aggression: A reexamination of the evidence. *Journal of Social Issues, 32*, 35–70.

KARLIN, R. A., EPSTEIN, Y. M., & AIELLO, J. R. (1978). Strategies for the investigation of crowding. In A. Esser & B. Greenbie (Eds.), *Design for community and privacy*. New York: Plenum Press.

KARLINS, M., COFFMAN, T. L., & WALTERS, G. (1969). On the fading of social stereotypes: Studies in three generations of college students. *Journal of Personality and Social Psychology, 13*, 1–16.

KASSIN, S. M. (1985). Eyewitness identification: Retrospective self-awareness and the accuracy-confidence correlation. *Journal of Personality and Social Psychology, 49*, 878–893.

KATZ, D., & BRALY, K. W. (1933). Racial stereotypes of 100 college students. *Journal of Abnormal and Social Psychology, 28*, 280–290.

KATZ, E., & FELDMAN, J. J. (1962). The debates in the light of research: A survey of surveys. In S. Kraus (Ed.), *The great debates* (pp. 173–223). Bloomington: Indiana University Press.

KATZ, I., WACKENHUT, J., & HASS, R. G. (1986). Racial ambivalence, value duality, and behavior. In J. F. Dovidio & S. L. Gaertner (Eds.), *Prejudice, discrimination, and racism* (pp. 35–60). New York: Academic Press.

KAUFERT, J. M., RABKIN, S. W., SYROTUIK, J., BOYKO, E., & SHANE, F. (1986). Health beliefs as predictors of success of alternate modalities of smoking cessation: Results of a controlled trial. *Journal of Behavioral Medicine, 9*, 475–489.

KAUFMAN, M. R. (1970). Practicing good manners and compassion. *Medical Insight, 2*, 56–61.

KEATING, C. F., MAZUR, A., SEGALL, M. H., CYSNEIROS, P. G., DIVALE, W. T., KILBRIDE, J. E., KOMIN, S., LEAHY, P., THURMAN, B., & WIRSING, R. (1981). Culture and the perception of social dominance from facial expression. *Journal of Personality and Social Psychology, 40*, 601–614.

KEEFER, R., GOLDSTEIN, J. H., & KASIARZ, D. (1983). Olympic games participation and warfare. In J. H. Goldstein (Ed.), *Sports violence*. New York: Springer-Verlag.

KEGELES, S. (1963). Why people seek dental care: A test of a conceptual formulation. *Journal of Health and Human Behavior, 4*, 166–173.

KELLEY, H. H. (1950). The warm-cold variable in first impressions of persons. *Journal of Personality, 18*, 431–439.

KELLEY, H. H. (1967). Attribution theory in social psychology. In D. Levine (Ed.), *Nebraska Symposium on Motivation* (pp. 192–238). Lincoln: University of Nebraska Press.

KELLEY, H. H. (1972). Attribution in social interaction. In E. E. Jones, et al. (Eds.), *Attribution: Perceiving the causes of behavior*. Morristown, NJ: General Learning Press.

KELLEY, H. H. (1979). *Personal relationships: Their structures and processes*. Hillsdale, NJ: Erlbaum.

KELLEY, H. H. (1983). Love and commitment. In H. H. Kelley et al., *Close relationships* (pp. 265–314). New York: Freeman.

KELLEY, H. H., BERSCHEID, E., CHRISTENSEN, A., HARVEY, J. H., HUSTON, T. L., LEVINGER, G., McCLINTOCK, E., PEPLAU, L. A., & PETERSON, D. R. (1983). *Close relationships*. New York: Freeman.

KELLEY, H. H., & THIBAUT, J. W. (1978). *Interpersonal relations: A theory of interdependence*. New York: Wiley-Interscience.

KELLEY, H. H., & VOLKART, E. H. (1952). The resistance to change of group-anchored attitudes. *American Sociological Review, 17*, 453–465.

KELLEY, H. H., & WOODRUFF, L. (1956). Members' reactions to apparent group approval of a counternorm communication. *Journal of Abnormal and Social Psychology, 52*, 67–74.

KELLEY, S., JR., & MIRER, T. W. (1974). The simple act of voting. *American Political Science Review, 68*, 572–591.

KELLY, J. R., & McGRATH, J. E. (1985). Effect of time limits and task types on task performance and interaction of four-person groups. *Journal of Personality and Social Psychology, 49*(2), 395–407.

KELMAN, H. C., & HOVLAND, C. I. (1953). "Reinstatement" of the communicator in delayed measurement of opinion change. *Journal of Abnormal and Social Psychology, 48*, 327–335.

KENRICK, D. T., & GUTIERRES, S. E. (1980). Contrast effects and judgments of physical attractiveness: When beauty becomes a social problem. *Journal of Personality and Social Psychology, 38*, 131–140.

KENRICK, D. T., & JOHNSON, G. A. (1979). Interpersonal attraction in aversive environments: A problem for the classical conditioning paradigm? *Journal of Personality and Social Psychology, 37*, 572–579.

KERCKHOFF, A. C., & BACK, K. W. (1968). *The June bug: A study of hysterical contagion*. New York: Appleton-Century-Crofts.

KERNIS, M. H., & WHEELER, L. (1981). Beautiful friends and ugly strangers: Radiation and contrast effects in perception of same-sex pairs. *Personality and Social Psychology Bulletin, 7*, 617–620.

KIDDER, L. H., FAGAN, M. A., & COHN, E. S. (1981). Giving and receiving: Social justice in close relationships. In M. J. Lerner & S. C. Lerner (Eds.), *The justice motive in social behavior: Adapting to times of scarcity and change* (pp. 235–259). New York: Plenum Press.

KINDER, D. R., & KIEWIET, D. R. (1979). Economic discontent and political behavior: The role of personal grievances and collective economic judgments in congressional voting. *American Journal of Political Science, 23*, 495–527.

KINDER, D. R., & SEARS, D. O. (1981). Prejudice and politics: Symbolic racism versus racial threats to the good life. *Journal of Personality and Social Psychology, 40*, 414–431.

KINDER, D. R., & SEARS, D. O. (1985). Public opinion and political action. In G. Lindzey & E. Aronson (Eds.), *Handbook of social psychology*, 3rd ed., (pp. 659–741). Reading, MA: Addison-Wesley.

KING, C. E., & CHRISTENSEN, A. (1983). The relationship events scale: A Guttman scale of progress in courtship. *Journal of Marriage and the Family, 45*, 671–678.

KINGDON, J. W. (1967). Politicians' beliefs about voters. *The American Political Science Review, 61*, 137–145.

KIPNIS, D. (1984). The use of power in organizations and in interpersonal settings. In S. Oskamp (Ed.), *Applied social psychology annual 5* (pp. 179–210). Beverly Hills, CA: Sage.

KIRSCHT, J. P., & DILLEHAY, R. C. (1967). *Dimensions of authoritarianism*. Lexington: University of Kentucky Press.

KIRSCHT, J. P., & ROSENSTOCK, I. M. (1979). Patients' problems in following recommendations of health experts. In G. C. Stone, F. Cohen, & E. Adler (Eds.). *Health psychology—A handbook* (pp. 189–216). San Francisco: Jossey-Bass.

KLAPPER, J. T. (1960). *The effects of mass communications*. Glencoe, IL: Free Press.

KLEIN, E. (1984). *Gender politics: From consciousness to mass politics*. Cambridge, MA: Harvard University Press.

KLEIN, K., & HARRIS, B. (1979). Disruptive effects of disconfirmed expectancies about crowding. *Journal of Personality and Social Psychology, 37*, 769–777.

KLEINHESSELINK, R. R., & EDWARDS, R. W. (1975). Seeking and avoiding belief-discrepant information as a function of its perceived refutability. *Journal of Personality and Social Psychology, 31*, 787–790.

KLINNERT, M. D. (1981, April). *Infants' use of mothers' facial expressions for regulating their own behavior*. Paper presented at the annual meeting of the Society for Research in Child Development, Boston.

KLUEGEL, J. R., & SMITH, E. R. (1986). *Beliefs about inequality*. Hawthorne, NY: Aldine.

KNOX, R. E., & INKSTER, J. A. (1968). Postdecision dissonance at post time. *Journal of Personality and Social Psychology, 8*, 319–323.

KNUTSON, J. N. (1973). *The human basis of the polity: A psychological study of political man*. Hawthorne, NY: Aldine.

KOGAN, N., & WALLACH, M. A. (1967). Risk taking as a function of the situation, the person, and the group. In G. Mandler (Ed.), *New directions in psychology* (Vol. III). New York: Holt, Rinehart & Winston.

KOHLBERG, L. (1966). A cognitive-developmental analysis of children's sex-role concepts and attitudes. In E. E. Maccoby (Ed.), *The development of sex differences*. Stanford, CA: Stanford University Press.

KOMAROVSKY, M. (1967). *Blue-collar marriage*. New York: Vintage.

KOMORITA, S. S., & LAPWORTH, C. W. (1982). Cooperative choice among individuals versus groups in an *N*-person dilemma situation. *Journal of Personality and Social Psychology, 42*, 487–496.

KONECNI, V. J. (1975). Annoyance, type and duration of post-annoyance activity, and aggression: The "cathartic" effect. *Journal of Experimental Psychology: General, 104*, 76–102.

KONECNI, V. J., & DOOB, A. N. (1972). Catharsis through displacement of aggression. *Journal of Personality and Social Psychology, 23*, 379–387.

KONECNI, V. J., & EBBESEN, E. B. (1976). Disinhibition versus the cathartic effect: Artifact and substance. *Journal of Personality and Social Psychology, 34*, 352–365.

KONECNI, V. J., LIBUSER, L., MORTON, H., & EBBESEN, E. B. (1975). Effects of a violation of personal space on escape and helping responses. *Journal of Experimental Social Psychology, 11*, 288–299.

KORNHAUSER, W. (1959). *The politics of mass society*. Glencoe, NY: Free Press.

KORTE, C. (1971). Effects of individual responsibility and group communication on help-giving in an emergency. *Human Relations, 24*, 149–159.

KORTE, C. (1980). Urban-nonurban differences in social behavior and social psychological models of urban impact. *Journal of Social Issues, 36*(3), 29–51.

KORTE, C. (1981). Constraints on helping in an urban environment. In J. P. Rushton & R. M. Sorrentino (Eds.), *Altruism and helping behavior*. Hillsdale, NJ: Erlbaum.

KORTE, C., & GRANT, R. (1980). Traffic noise, environmental awareness, and pedestrian behavior. *Environment and Behavior, 12*, 996–1003.

KOVEL, J. (1970). *White racism: A psychohistory*. New York: Pantheon.

KRAFKA, C., & PENROD, S. (1985). Reinstatement of context in a field experiment on eyewitness identification. *Journal of Personality and Social Psychology, 49*, 58–69.

KRAMER, G. H. (1971). Short-term fluctuations in U.S. voting behavior, 1896–1964. *American Political Science Review, 65*, 131–143.

KRANTZ, D. S., & DECKEL, A. W. (1983). Coping with coronary heart disease and stroke. In T. G. Burish & L. A. Bradley (Eds.), *Coping with chronic disease: Research and applications* (pp. 85–107). New York: Academic Press.

KRAUSS, R. M., APPLE, W., MORENCY, N., WENZEL, C., & WINTON, W. (1981). Verbal, vocal, and visible factors in judgments of another's affect. *Journal of Personality and Social Psychology, 40*, 312–320.

KRAUSS, R. M., GELLER, V., & OLSON, C. (1976, September). *Modalities and cues in the detection of deception*. Paper presented at the annual meeting of the American Psychological Association.

KRAUT, R. E. (1978). Verbal and nonverbal cues in the perception of lying. *Journal of Personality and Social Psychology, 36*, 380–391.

KRAUT, R. E., & JOHNSTON, R. E. (1979). Social and emotional messages of smiling: An ethological approach. *Journal of Personality and Social Psychology, 37*, 1539–1554.

KRAUT, R. E., & POE, D. (1980). Behavioral roots of person perception: The deception judgments of customs inspectors and laymen. *Journal of Personality and Social Psychology, 39*, 784–798.

KRAVITZ, D. A., & MARTIN, B. (1986). Ringlemann rediscovered: The original article. *Journal of Personality and Social Psychology, 50*(5), 936–941.

KREBS, D. L., & MILLER, D. T. (1985). Altruism and aggression. In G. Lindzey & E. Aronson (Eds.), *Handbook of social psychology*, 3rd ed. (Vol. 2, pp. 1–71). New York: Random House.

KRECH, D., & CRUTCHFIELD, R. A. (1948). *Theory and problems of social psychology*. New York: McGraw-Hill.

KUHLMAN, D. M., & WIMBERLEY, D. L. (1976). Expectations of choice behavior held by cooperators, competitors, and individualists across four classes of experimental game. *Journal of Personality and Social Psychology, 34*, 69–81.

KUIPER, N. A., & ROGERS, T. B. (1979). Encoding of personal information: Self-other differences. *Journal of Personality and Social Psychology, 37*, 499–514.

KULIK, J. A. (1983). Confirmatory attribution and the perpetuation of social beliefs. *Journal of Personality and Social Psychology, 44*(6), 1171–1181.

KUNDA, Z., & SCHWARTZ, S. H. (1983). Undermining intrinsic moral motivation: External reward and self-presentation. *Journal of Personality and Social Psychology, 44*, 763–771.

KUTNER, B., WILKINS, C., YARROW, P. R. (1952). Verbal attitudes and overt behavior involving racial prejudice. *Journal of Abnormal and Social Psychology, 47*, 649–652.

LAING, R. D., & STEVENSON, R. (1976). Public opinion trends in the last days of the Nixon administration. *Journalism Quarterly, 53*, 294–302.

LAMM, H., & TROMMSDORF, G. (1973). Group versus individual performance on tasks requiring ideational proficiency (brainstorming): A review. *European Journal of Social Psychology, 3*, 361–388.

LANDY, D., & ARONSON, E. (1969). The influence of the character of the criminal and his victim on the decisions of simulated jurors. *Journal of Experimental Social Psychology, 5*, 141–152.

LANDY, D., & SIGALL, H. (1974). Beauty is talent: Task evaluation as a function of the performer's physical attractiveness. *Journal of Personality and Social Psychology, 29*, 299–304.

LANE, R. E. (1959). *Political life: Why people get involved in politics*. Glencoe, NY: Free Press.

LANG, G. E., & LANG, K. (1979). Immediate and mediated responses: First debate. In S. Kraus (Ed.), *The great debates: Carter vs. Ford 1976* (pp. 298–313). Bloomington: Indiana University Press.

LANGER, E. J. (1975). The illusion of control. *Journal of Personality and Social Psychology, 32*, 311–328.

LANGER, E. J., BLANK, A., & CHANOWITZ, B. (1978). The mindlessness of ostensibly thoughtful action. *Journal of Personality and Social Psychology, 36*, 635–642.

LANGER, E. J., & RODIN, J. (1976). The effects of choice and enhanced personal responsibility for the aged: A field experiment in an institutional setting. *Journal of Personality and Social Psychology, 34*, 191–198.

LAPIERE, R. T. (1934). Attitudes vs. actions. *Social Forces, 13*, 230–237.

LARSON, R., CSIKSZENTMIHALYI, M., & GRAEF, R. (1982). Time alone in daily experience: Loneliness or renewal? In L. A. Peplau & D. Perlman (Eds.), *Loneliness: A sourcebook of current theory, research and therapy* (pp. 40–53). New York: Wiley-Interscience.

LASSWELL, H. D. (1930). *Psychopathology and politics*. New York: The Viking Press.

LASSWELL, H. D. (1948). *Power and personality*. New York: W. W. Norton.

LASSWELL, M., & LOBSENZ, N. M. (1980). *Styles of loving*. New York: Ballantine Books.

LASSWELL, T. E., & LASSWELL, M. (1976). I love you but I'm not in love with you. *Journal of Marriage and Family Counseling, 2*(3), 211–224.

LATANÉ, B. (1981). The psychology of social impact. *American Psychologist, 36*, 343–356.

LATANÉ, B., & DARLEY, J. M. (1968). Group inhibition of bystander intervention in emergencies. *Journal of Personality and Social Psychology, 10*, 215–221.

LATANÉ, B., & DARLEY, J. M. (1970). *The unresponsive bystander: Why doesn't he help?* New York: Appleton-Century-Crofts.

LATANÉ, B., & NIDA, S. (1981). Ten years of research on group size and helping. *Psychological Bulletin, 89*(2), 308–324.

LATANÉ, B., WILLIAMS, K., & HARKINS, S. (1979). Many hands make light the work: The causes and consequences of social loafing. *Journal of Personality and Social Psychology, 37*, 822–832.

LATANÉ, B., & WOLF, S. (1981). The social impact of majorities and minorities. *Psychological Review, 88*, 438–453.

LAU, R. R. (1982). Negativity in political perception. *Political Behavior, 4*, 353–378.

LAU, R. R. (1985). Two explanations for negativity effects in political behavior. *American Journal of Political Science, 29*, 119–138.

LAU, R. R., & HARTMAN, K. A. (1983). Common-sense representations of common illnesses. *Health Psychology, 2*, 167–185.

LAU, R. R., KANE, R., BERRY, S., WARE, J., & ROY, D. (1980). Channeling health: A review of televised health campaigns. *Health Education Quarterly, 7*, 56–89.

LAU, R. R., & RUSSELL, D. (1980). Attributions in the sports pages. *Journal of Personality and Social Psychology, 39*, 29–38.

LAU, R. R., & SEARS, D. O. (1981). Cognitive links between economic grievances and political responses. *Political Behavior, 3*, 279–302.

LAU, R. R., & SEARS, D. O. (Eds.). (1986). *Political cognition: The 19th annual Carnegie Symposium on Cognition.* Hillsdale, NJ: Erlbaum.

LAZARSFELD, P. F., BERELSON, B., & GAUDET, H. (1948). *The people's choice*, 2nd ed. New York: Columbia University Press.

LAZARUS, A. A. (1971). *Behavior therapy and beyond.* New York: McGraw-Hill.

LAZARUS, R. S. (1966). *Psychological stress and the coping process.* New York: McGraw-Hill.

LAZARUS, R. S. (1984). On the primacy of cognition. *American Psychologist, 39*, 124–129.

LAZARUS, R. S., & FOLKMAN, S. (1984). *Stress, appraisal, and coping.* New York: Springer-Verlag.

LAZARUS, R. S., & LAUNIER, R. (1978). Stress-related transactions between person and environment. In

L. A. Pervin & M. Lewis (Eds.), *Internal and external determinants of behavior.* New York: Plenum.

LEARY, M. R., ROGERS, P. A., CANFIELD, R. W., & COE, C. (1986). Boredom in interpersonal encounters: Antecedents and social implications. *Journal of Personality and Social Psychology, 51*(5), 968–975.

LEARY, M. R., & SHEPPERD, J. A. (1986). Behavioral self-handicaps versus self-reported handicaps: A conceptual note. *Journal of Personality and Social Psychology, 51*, 1265–1268.

LEAVITT, H. J. (1951). Some effects of certain communication patterns on group performance. *Journal of Abnormal and Social Psychology, 46*, 38–50.

LeBON, G. (1896). *The crowd: A study of the popular mind.* London: Ernest Benn.

LEDERER, L. (ED.). (1980). *Take back the night: Women on pornography.* New York: Morrow, 1980..

LEE, J. A. (1973). *The colors of love.* New York: Bantam Books.

LEE, J. A. (1977). A typology of styles of loving. *Personality and Social Psychology Bulletin, 3*, 173–182.

LEIBMAN, M. (1970). The effects of sex and race norms on personal space. *Dissertation Abstracts International, 31*, 3038–3039.

LEITES, N. (1951). *The operational code of the politburo.* New York: McGraw-Hill.

LEMYRE, L., & SMITH, P. M. (1985). Intergroup discrimination and self-esteem in the minimal group paradigm. *Journal of Personality and Social Psychology, 49*, 660–670.

LEPPER, M., GREENE, D., & NISBETT, R. (1973). Undermining children's interest with extrinsic rewards: A test of the "overjustification hypothesis." *Journal of Personality and Social Psychology, 28*, 129–137.

LERNER, M. J. (1965). The effect of responsibility and choice on a partner's attractiveness following failure. *Journal of Personality, 33*, 178–187.

LERNER, M. J. (1980). *The belief in a just world: A fundamental delusion.* New York: Plenum Books.

LEVENTHAL, H. (1970). Findings and theory in the study of fear communications. In L. Berkowitz (Ed.), *Advances in experimental social psychology* (Vol. 5, pp. 120–186). New York: Academic Press.

LEVENTHAL, H., & CLEARY, P. D. (1980). The smoking problem: A review of the research and theory in behavioral risk modification. *Psychological Bulletin, 88*, 370–405.

LEVENTHAL, H., & NERENZ, D. R. (1982). A model for stress research and some implications for the control of stress disorders. In D. Meichenbaum & M. Jaremko (Eds.), *Stress prevention and management: A cognitive behavioral approach.* New York: Plenum.

LEVENTHAL, H., NERENZ, D., & STRAUSS, A. (1980). Self-regulation and the mechanisms for symptom appraisal. In D. Mechanic (Ed.), *Psychosocial epidemiology*. New York: Watson.

LEVENTHAL, H., WATTS, J. C., & PAGANO, F. (1967). Effects of fear and instructions on how to cope with danger. *Journal of Personality and Social Psychology, 6,* 313–321.

LEVINE, R. A., & CAMPBELL, D. T. (1972). *Ethnocentrism: Theories of conflict, ethnic attitudes, and group behavior.* New York: Wiley.

LEVINGER, G. (1979). A social psychological perspective on marital dissolution. In G. Levinger & O. C. Moles (Eds.), *Divorce and separation: Context, causes, and consequences.* New York: Basic Books.

LEVINGER, G., & SNOEK, J. G. (1972). *Attraction in relationship: A new look at interpersonal attraction.* Morristown, NJ: General Learning Press.

LEVINSON, R. M. (1975). Sex discrimination and employment practices: An experiment with unconventional job inquiries. *Social Problems, 22,* 533–543.

LEWIN, K., LIPPITT, R., & WHITE, R. K. (1939). Patterns of aggressive behavior in experimentally created social climates. *Journal of Social Psychology, 10,* 271–299.

LEWIS-BECK, M. S. (1985). Pocketbook voting in U.S. national election studies: Fact or artifact? *American Journal of Political Science, 29,* 348–356.

LEYENS, J. P., CAMINO, L., PARKE, R. D., & BERKOWITZ, L. (1975). Effects of movie violence on aggression in a field setting as a function of group dominance and cohesion. *Journal of Personality and Social Psychology, 32,* 346–360.

LICHTENSTEIN, M., & SRULL, T. K. (1985). Conceptual and methodological issues in examining the relationship between consumer memory and judgment. In L. F. Alwitt & A. A. Mitchell (Eds.), *Psychological processes and advertising effects: Theory, research, and applications* (pp. 113–128). Hillsdale, NJ: Erlbaum.

LICHTMAN, R. R., & TAYLOR, S. E. (1986). Close relationships and the female cancer patient. In B. L. Andersen (Ed.), *Women with cancer: Psychological perspectives* (pp. 233–249). New York: Springer-Verlag.

LIEBERMAN, M. A. (1982). The effects of social supports on responses to stress. In L. Goldberger & L. Breznitz (Eds.), *Handbook of stress* (pp. 764–783). New York: Free Press.

LINDER, D. E., COOPER, J., & JONES, E. E. (1967). Decision freedom as a determinant of the role of incentive magnitude in attitude change. *Journal of Personality and Social Psychology, 6,* 245–254.

LINVILLE, P. W. (1982). The complexity-extremity effect and age-based stereotyping. *Journal of Personality and Social Psychology, 42,* 193–211.

LINVILLE, P. W., & JONES, E. E. (1980). Polarized appraisals of outgroup members. *Journal of Personality and Social Psychology, 38,* 689–703.

LINVILLE, P. W., SALOVEY, P., & FISCHER, G. W. (1986). Stereotyping and perceived distributions of social characteristics: An application to ingroup-outgroup perception. In J. F. Dovidio & S. L. Gaertner (Eds.), *Prejudice, discrimination, and racism* (pp. 165–208). New York: Academic Press.

LINZ, D., PENROD, S., & DONNERSTEIN, E. (1986). Issues bearing on the legal regulation of violent and sexually violent media. *Journal of Social Issues, 42,* 171–194.

LIPSET, S. M. (1960). *Political man.* Garden City, NY: Doubleday.

LIPSET, S. M. (1981). *Political man: The social bases of politics,* (expanded ed.). Baltimore: Johns Hopkins University Press.

LITTLE, K. B. (1968). Cultural variations in social schemata. *Journal of Personality and Social Psychology, 10,* 1–7.

LLOYD, S., CATE, R., & HENTON, J. (1982). Equity and rewards as predictors of satisfaction in casual and intimate relationships. *Journal of Psychology, 110,* 43–48.

LOBDELL, J., & PERLMAN, D. (1986). The intergenerational transmission of loneliness: A study of college females and their parents. *Journal of Marriage and the Family, 48,* 589–595.

LOCKSLEY, A., BORGIDA, E., BREKKE, N., & HEPBURN, C. (1980). Sex stereotypes and social judgment. *Journal of Personality and Social Psychology, 39*(5), 821–831.

LOCKSLEY, A., ORTIZ, V., & HEPBURN, C. (1980). Social categorization and discriminatory behavior: Extinguishing the minimal intergroup discrimination effect. *Journal of Personality and Social Psychology, 39,* 773–783.

LONDON, P. (1970). The rescuers: Motivational hypotheses about Christians who saved Jews from the Nazis. In J. Macaulay & L. Berkowitz (Eds.), *Altruism and helping behavior* (pp. 241–250). New York: Academic Press.

LONGLEY, J., & PRUITT, D. G. (1980). Groupthink: A critique of Janis's theory. In L. Wheeler (Ed.), *Review of personal and social psychology* (Vol. 1). Beverly Hills, CA: Sage Publications.

LOO, C., & SMETANA, J. (1978). The effects of crowding on the behavior and perception of 10-year-old boys. *Environmental Psychology and Nonverbal Behavior, 2,* 226–249.

LORD, C. G. (1980). Schemas and images as memory aids: Two modes of processing social information. *Journal of Personality and Social Psychology, 38,* 257–269.

LORD, C. G., LEPPER, M. R., & MACKIE, D. (1984). Attitude prototypes as determinants of attitude-behavior consistency. *Journal of Personality and Social Psychology, 46,* 1254–1266.

LORD, C. G., LEPPER, M. R., & PRESTON, E. (1984). Considering the opposite: A corrective strategy for social judgment. *Journal of Personality and Social Psychology, 47,* 1231–1243.

LORD, C. G., & SAENZ, D. S. (1985). Memory deficits and memory surfeits: Differential cognitive consequences of tokenism for tokens and observers. *Journal of Personality and Social Psychology, 49,* 918–926.

LORGE, I. (1936). Prestige, suggestion, and attitudes. *Journal of Social Psychology, 7,* 386–402.

LOVIBOND, S. H., BIRRELL, P. C., & LANGELUDDECKE, P. (1986). Changing coronary heart disease risk-factor status: The effects of three behavioral programs. *Journal of Behavioral Medicine, 9,* 415–437.

LUDWIG, D., FRANCO, J. N., & MALLOY, T. E. (1986). Effects of reciprocity and self-monitoring on self-disclosure with a new acquaintance. *Journal of Personality and Social Psychology, 50,* 1077–1082.

LUEPKER, R. V., JOHNSON, C. A., MURRAY, D. M., & PECHACEK, T. F. (1983). Prevention of cigarette smoking: Three-year follow-up of an educational program for youth. *Journal of Behavioral Medicine, 6,* 53–61.

LURIGIO, A. J., & CARROLL, J. S. (1985). Probation officers' schemata of offenders: Content, development, and impact on treatment decisions. *Journal of Personality and Social Psychology, 48,* 1112–1126.

LYNCH, J. G., JR., & COHEN, J. L. (1978). The use of subjective expected utility theory as an aid to understanding variables that influence helping behavior. *Journal of Personality and Social Psychology, 36,* 1138–1151.

MAASS, A., & CLARK, R. D. (1984). Hidden impact of minorities: Fifteen years of minority influence research. *Psychological Bulletin, 95*(3), 428–450.

MAASS, A., CLARK, R. D., & HABERKORN, G. (1982). The effects of differential ascribed category membership and norms on minority influence. *European Journal of Social Psychology, 12,* 89–104.

MACCOBY, E. E., & JACKLIN, C. N. (1974). *The psychology of sex differences.* Stanford, CA: Stanford University Press.

MACDONALD, W. S., & ODEN, C. W. (1973). Effects of extreme crowding on the performance of five married couples during twelve weeks of intensive training. *Proceedings of 81st Annual Convention of the American Psychological Association, 8,* 209–210.

MACKAY, D. G., & FULKERSON, D. G. (1979). On the comprehension and production of pronouns. *Journal of Verbal Learning and Verbal Behavior, 18,* 661–673.

MACKIE, D. M. (1986). Social identification effects in group polarization. *Journal of Personality and Social Psychology, 50*(4), 720–728.

MACKUEN, M. B. (1981). Social communication and the mass policy agenda. In M. B. MacKuen & S. L. Coombs (Eds.), *More than news: Media power in public affairs* (pp. 19–144). Beverly Hills, CA: Sage.

MADDUX, J. E., & ROGERS, R. W. (1983). Protection motivation and self-efficacy: A revised theory of fear appeals and attitude change. *Journal of Experimental Social Psychology, 19,* 469–479.

MADSEN, M. C. (1971). Developmental and cross-cultural differences in the cooperative and competitive behavior of young children. *Journal of Cross-Cultural Psychology, 2,* 365–371.

MAJOR, B., MUELLER, P., & HILDEBRANDT, K. (1985). Attributions, expectations, and coping with abortion. *Journal of Personality and Social Psychology, 48,* 585–599.

MALAMUTH, N. M. (1981). Rape fantasies as a function of exposure to violent sexual stimuli. *Archives of Sexual Behavior, 10,* 33–47.

MALAMUTH, N. M. (1983). Factors associated with rape as predictors of laboratory aggression against women. *Journal of Personality and Social Psychology, 45,* 432–442.

MALAMUTH, N. M. (1986a). Do sexually violent media indirectly contribute to antisocial behavior? Unpublished manuscript, University of California, Los Angeles.

MALAMUTH, N. M. (1986b). Predictors of naturalistic sexual aggression. *Journal of Personality and Social Psychology, 50,* 953–962.

MALAMUTH, N. M., & BRIERE, J. (1986). Sexual violence in the media: Indirect effects on aggression against women. *Journal of Social Issues, 42,* 75–92.

MALAMUTH, N. M., & CHECK, J. V. P. (1981). The effects of mass media exposure on acceptance of violence against women: A field experiment. *Journal of Research in Personality, 15,* 436–446.

MALAMUTH, N. M., CHECK, J. V. P., & BRIERE, J. (1986). Sexual arousal in response to aggression: Ideological, aggressive, and sexual correlates. *Journal of Personality and Social Psychology, 50,* 330–340.

MALAMUTH, N. M., & DONNERSTEIN, E. (1982). The effects of aggressive-pornographic mass media stimuli. In L. Berkowitz (Ed.), *Advances in experimental social psychology* (Vol. 15, pp. 103–136). New York: Academic Press.

MANIS, M., AVIS, N. E., & CARDOZE, S. (1981). Reply to Bar-Hillel and Fischhoff. *Journal of Personality and Social Psychology, 41,* 681–683.

MANN, L. (1977). The effect of stimulus queues on queue-joining behavior. *Journal of Personality and Social Psychology, 35,* 437–442.

MANN, L., & JANIS, I. L. (1968). A follow-up study on the long-term effects of emotional role playing. *Journal of Personality and Social Psychology, 8,* 339–342.

MANN, T. E., & WOLFINGER, R. E. (1980). Candidates and parties in congressional elections. *The American Political Science Review, 74,* 617–632.

MANSBRIDGE, J. J. (1985). Myth and reality: The ERA and the gender gap in the 1980 election. *Public Opinion Quarterly, 49,* 164–178.

MANSTEAD, A. S. R., PROFFITT, C., & SMART, J. L. (1983). Predicting and understanding mothers' infant-feeding intentions and behavior: Testing the theory of reasoned action. *Journal of Personality and Social Psychology, 44,* 657–671.

MARKUS, G. B. (1979). The political environment and the dynamics of public attitudes: A panel study. *American Journal of Political Science, 23,* 338–359.

MARKUS, H. (1977). Self-schemata and processing information about the self. *Journal of Personality and Social Psychology, 35,* 63–78.

MARKUS, H., & NURIUS, P. (1986). Possible selves. *American Psychologist, 41,* 954–969.

MARKUS, H., & SMITH, J. (1981). The influence of self-schemata on the perception of others. In N. Cantor & J. Kihlstrom (Eds.), *Personality, cognition, and social interaction.* Hillsdale, NJ: Erlbaum.

MARKUS, H., SMITH, J., & MORELAND, R. L. (1985). Role of the self-concept in the perception of others. *Journal of Personality and Social Psychology, 49,* 1494–1512.

MARKUS, H., SMITH, J., & MORELAND, R. L. (in press). The role of the self in social perception: A cognitive analysis. *Psychological Review.*

MARKUS, H., & ZAJONC, R. B. (1986). The cognitive perspective in social psychology. In G. Lindzey & E. Aronson (Eds.), *Handbook of social psychology* 3rd ed. (Vol. 1, pp. 137–230). New York: Random House.

MARTYNA, W. (1980). The psychology of the generic masculine. In S. McConnell-Ginet, R. Borker, & N. Furman (Eds.), *Women and language in literature and society* (pp. 69–78). New York: Praeger.

MARUYAMA, G., FRASER, S. C., & MILLER, N. (1982). Personal responsibility and altruism in children. *Journal of Personality and Social Psychology, 42*(4), 658–664.

MATARAZZO, J. D. (1980). Behavioral health and behavioral medicine: Frontiers for a new health psychology. *American Psychologist, 35,* 807–817.

MATARAZZO, J. D. (1982). Behavioral health's challenge to academic, scientific, and professional psychology. *American Psychologist, 37,* 1–14.

MATARAZZO, J. D. (1983). Behavioral health: A 1990 challenge for the health sciences professions. In J. D. Matarazzo, N. E. Miller, S. M. Weiss, J. A. Herd, & S. M. Weiss (Eds.), *Behavioral health: A handbook of health enhancement and disease prevention* (pp. 3–40). New York: Wiley.

MATHES, E. W., ADAMS, H. E., & DAVIES, R. M. (1985). Jealousy: Loss of relationship rewards, loss of self-esteem, depression, anxiety and anger. *Journal of Personality and Social Psychology, 48,* 1552–1561.

MATHEWS, K. E., & CANON, L. K. (1975). Environmental noise level as a determinant of helping behavior. *Journal of Personality and Social Psychology, 32*(4), 571–577.

MATLIN, M., & STANG, D. (1978). *The Pollyanna principle: Selectivity in language, memory, and thought.* Cambridge, MA: Schenkman.

MATTHEWS, K. A. (1982). Psychological perspectives on the Type A behavior pattern. *Psychological Bulletin, 91,* 293–323.

MAY, J. L., & HAMILTON, P. A. (1980). Effects of musically evoked affect on women's interpersonal attraction toward and perceptual judgements of physical attractiveness of men. *Motivation and Emotion, 4,* 217–228.

MAYKOVICH, M. K. (1975). Correlates of racial prejudice. *Journal of Personality and Social Psychology, 32,* 1014–1020.

MAZLISH, B. (1972). *In search of Nixon: A psychohistorical inquiry.* New York: Basic Books.

MCALISTER, A. (1975). Helping people to quit smoking: Current progress. In A. J. Enelow & J. B. Henderson (Eds.), *Applying behavioral science to cardiovascular risk: Proceedings of a conference* (pp. 147–165). Seattle: American Heart Association.

MCARTHUR, L. A. (1972). The how and what of why: Some determinants and consequences of causal attribution. *Journal of Personality and Social Psychology, 22,* 171–193.

MCARTHUR, L. Z. (1981). What grabs you? The role of attention in impression formation and causal attribution. In E. T. Higgins, C. P. Herman, & M. P. Zanna (Eds.), *Social cognition: The Ontario symposium* (Vol. 1). Hillsdale, NJ: Erlbaum.

MCARTHUR, L. Z., & FRIEDMAN, S. A. (1980). Illusory correlation in impression formation: Variations in the shared distinctiveness effect as a function of the distinctive person's age, race and sex. *Journal of Personality and Social Psychology, 39,* 615–624.

MCARTHUR, L. Z., & POST, D. L. (1977). Figural emphasis and person perception. *Journal of Experimental Social Psychology, 13,* 520–535.

MCARTHUR, L. Z., & RESKO, B. G. (1975). The portrayal of men and women in American TV commercials. *Journal of Social Psychology, 97,* 209–220.

MCCAIN, G., COX, V. C., & PAULUS, P. B. (1976). The relationship between illness, complaints and degree of crowding in a prison environment. *Environment and Behavior, 8,* 283–290.

MCCALLUM, P., RUSBULT, C. E., HONG, G. K., WALDEN, T. A., & Schopler, J. (1979). Effects of resource availability and importance of behavior on the experience of crowding. *Journal of Personality and Social Psychology, 37*, 1304–1313.

McCARTHY, D., & SAEGERT, S. (1978). Residential density, social overload, and social withdrawal. *Human Ecology, 6*, 253–272.

McCLELLAND, D. C. (1976). *The achieving society*. New York: Irvington.

McCONAHAY, J. B. (1982). Self-interest versus racial attitudes as correlates of anti-busing attitudes in Louisville: Is it the buses or the blacks? *Journal of Politics, 44*, 692–720.

McCONAHAY, J. B. (1986). Modern racism, ambivalence, and the modern racism scale. In J. F. Dovidio & S. L. Gaertner (Eds.), *Prejudice, discrimination, and racism* (pp. 91–126). New York: Academic Press.

McCONAHAY, J. B., & HOUGH, J. C., Jr. (1976). Symbolic racism. *Journal of Social Issues, 32*(2), 23–45.

McCORMICK, N. B. (1979). Come-ons and put-offs: Unmarried students' strategies for having and avoiding sexual intercourse. *Psychology of Women Quarterly, 4*, 194–211.

McCORMICK, N. B., & JESSER, C. J. (1983). The courtship game: Power in the sexual encounter. In E. R. Allgeier & N. B. McCormick (Eds.), *Changing boundaries: Gender roles and sexual behavior* (pp. 64–86). Palo Alto, CA: Mayfield.

McFARLAND, C., & ROSS, M. (1982). Impact of causal attributions on affective reactions to success and failure. *Journal of Personality and Social Psychology, 43*, 937–946.

McFARLANE, A. H., NORMAN, G. R., STREINER, D. L., ROY, R., & SCOTT, D. J. (1980). A longitudinal study of the influence of the psychosocial environment on health status: A preliminary report. *Journal of Health and Social Behavior, 21*, 124–133.

McGINNISS, J. (1969). *The selling of the president, 1968*. New York: Trident Press.

McGRATH, J. E. (1984). *Groups: Interaction and performance*. Englewood Cliffs, NJ: Prentice-Hall.

McGUIRE, W. J. (1960). A syllogistic analysis of cognitive relationships. In C. I. Hovland & M. J. Rosenberg (Eds.), *Attitude organization and change*. New Haven, CT: Yale University Press.

McGUIRE, W. J. (1964). Inducing resistance to persuasion: Some contemporary approaches. In L. Berkowitz (Ed.), *Advances in experimental social psychology* (Vol. 1, pp. 192–229). New York: Academic Press.

McGUIRE, W. J. (1969). The nature of attitudes and attitude change. In G. Lindzey & E. Aronson (Eds.), *The handbook of social psychology*, 2nd ed. (Vol. 3, pp. 136–314). Reading, MA: Addison-Wesley.

McGUIRE, W. J. (1981). The probabilogical model of cognitive structure and attitude change. In R. E.

Petty, T. M. Ostrom, & T. C. Brock (Eds.), *Cognitive responses in persuasion*. Hillsdale, NJ: Erlbaum.

McGUIRE, W. J. (1985). Attitudes and attitude change. In G. Lindzey & E. Aronson (Eds.), *Handbook of Social Psychology*, 3rd ed. (Vol. 2, pp. 223–346). New York: Random House.

McGUIRE, W. J., & PADAWER-SINGER, A. (1976). Trait salience in the spontaneous self-concept. *Journal of Personality and Social Psychology, 33*(6), 743–754.

McGUIRE, W. J., & PAPAGEORGIS, D. (1961). The relative efficacy of various types of prior belief defense in producing immunity against persuasion. *Journal of Abnormal and Social Psychology, 62*, 327–337.

McKINLEY, J. B. (1975). Who is really ignorant—physician or patient? *Journal of Health and Social Behavior, 16*, 3–11.

McMILLAN, J. R. CLIFTON, A. K., McGRATH, D., & GALE, W. S. (1977). Women's language: Uncertainty or interpersonal sensitivity and emotionality? *Sex Roles, 3*(6), 545–559.

MECHANIC, D. (1975). The organization of medical practice and practice orientation among physicians in prepaid and nonprepaid primary care settings. *Medical Care, 13*, 189–204.

MEEHL, P. E. (1954). *Clinical versus statistical prediction: A theoretical analysis and review of the literature*. Minneapolis: University of Minnesota Press.

MEHLMAN, R. C., & SNYDER, C. R. (1985). Excuse theory: A test of the self-protective role of attributions. *Journal of Personality and Social Psychology, 49*, 994–1001.

MEHRABIAN, A. (1972). *Nonverbal communication*. Chicago: Aldine-Atherton.

MEICHENBAUM, D. H., & JAREMKO, M. E., (Eds.). (1983). *Stress reduction and prevention*. New York: Plenum.

MEREI, F. (1949). Group leadership and institutionalization. *Human Relations, 2*, 23–29.

METALSKY, G. I., ABRAMSON, L. Y., SELIGMAN, M. E. P., SEMMEL, A., & PETERSON, C. (1982). Attributional styles and life events in the classroom: Vulnerability and invulnerability to depressive mood reactions. *Journal of Personality and Social Psychology, 43*, 612–617.

MEYER, A. J., NASH, J. D., McALISTER, A. L., MACCOBY, N., & FARQUHAR, J. W. (1980). Skills in training in cardiovascular health education campaign. *Journal of Consulting and Clinical Psychology, 48*, 129–142.

MEYER, C. B., & TAYLOR, S. E. (1986). Adjustment to rape. *Journal of Personality and Social Psychology, 50*, 1226–1234.

MEYER, D., LEVENTHAL, H., & GUTMANN, M. (1985). *Symptoms in hypertension*. Unpublished manuscript, Department of Psychology, University of Wisconsin, Madison.

MEYER, J. P. (1980). Causal attribution for success and failure: A multivariate investigation of dimensionality, formation, and consequences. *Journal of Personality and Social Psychology, 38,* 704–718.

MEYER, J. P., & KOELBL, S. L. M. (1982). Students' test performances: Dimensionality of causal attributions. *Personality and Social Psychology Bulletin, 8*(1), 31–36.

MEYER, J. P., & MULHERIN, A. (1980). From attribution to helping: An analysis of the mediating effects of affect and expectancy. *Journal of Personality and Social Psychology, 39*(2), 201–210.

MEYEROWITZ, B. E. (1980). Psychosocial correlates of breast cancer and its treatments. *Psychological Bulletin, 87,* 108–131.

MICHAELS, J. W., ACOCK, A. C., & EDWARDS, J. N. (1986). Social exchange and equity determinants of relationship commitment. *Journal of Social and Personal Relationships, 3*(2), 161–175.

MICHAELS, J. W., BLOMMEL, J. M., BROCATO, R. M., LINKOUS, R. A., & ROWE, J. S. (1982). Social facilitation and inhibition in a natural setting. *Replications in Social Psychology, 2,* 21–24.

MICHELSON, W. (1970). *Man and his urban environment: A sociological approach.* Reading, MA: Addison-Wesley.

MICHELSON, W. (1977). *Environmental choice, human behavior, and residential satisfaction.* New York: Oxford University Press.

MIDDLETON, R. (1976). Regional differences in prejudice. *American Sociological Review, 41,* 94–117.

MIDLARSKY, E., BRYAN, J. H., & BRICKMAN, P. (1973). Aversive approval: Interactive effects of modeling and reinforcement on altruistic behavior. *Child Development, 44,* 321–328.

MILAVSKY, J. R., KESSLER, R., STIPP, H., & RUBENS, W. S. (1982). Television and aggression: Results of a panel study. In D. Pearl, L. Bouthilet, & J. Lazar (Eds.), *Television and behavior: Ten years of scientific progress and implications for the eighties: Vol. II. Technical reviews.* Rockville, MD: National Institute of Mental Health.

MILGRAM, S. (1963). Behavioral study of obedience. *Journal of Abnormal and Social Psychology, 67,* 371–378.

MILGRAM, S. (1965). Some conditions of obedience and disobedience to authority. *Human Relations, 18,* 57–75.

MILGRAM, S. (1970). The experience of living in cities. *Science, 167,* 1461–1468.

MILGRAM, S. (1974). *Obedience to authority: An experimental view.* New York: Harper & Row.

MILGRAM, S., BICKMAN, L., & BERKOWITZ, L. (1969). Note on the drawing power of crowds of different size. *Journal of Personality and Social Psychology, 13,* 79–82.

MILGRAM, S., & SHOTLAND, R. L. (1973). *Television and antisocial behavior: Field experiments.* New York: Academic Press.

MILLAR, M. G., & TESSER, A. (1986). Thought-induced attitude change: The effects of schema structure and commitment. *Journal of Personality and Social Psychology, 51,* 259–269.

MILLER, A. G. (1975). Actor and observer perceptions of the learning of a task. *Journal of Experimental Social Psychology, 11,* 95–111.

MILLER, A. G. (1976). Constraint and target effects in the attribution of attitudes. *Journal of Experimental Social Psychology, 12,* 325–339.

MILLER, A. G. (1986). *The obedience experiments: A case study of controversy in social science.* New York: Praeger.

MILLER, A. G., JONES, E. E., & HINKLE, S. (1981). A robust attribution error in the personality domain. *Journal of Experimental Social Psychology, 17,* 587–600.

MILLER, D. T., & PORTER, C. A. (1983). Self-blame in victims of violence. *Journal of Social Issues, 39*(2), 139–152.

MILLER, D. T., & ROSS, M. (1975). Self-serving biases in the attribution of causality: Fact or fiction? *Psychological Bulletin, 82,* 213–225.

MILLER, D. T., & TURNBULL, W. (1986). Expectancies and interpersonal processes. *Annual Review of Psychology, 37,* 233–256.

MILLER, J. G. (1984). Culture and the development of everyday social explanation. *Journal of Personality and Social Psychology, 46,* 961–978.

MILLER, L. C., & KENNY, D. A. (1986). Reciprocity of self-disclosure at the individual and dyadic levels: A social relations analysis. *Journal of Personality and Social Psychology, 50,* 713–719.

MILLER, L. W., & SIGELMAN, L. (1978). Is the audience the message? A note on LBJ's Vietnam statements. *Public Opinion Quarterly, 42,* 71–80.

MILLER, M. G., & TESSER, A. (1986). Thought-induced attitude change: The effects of schema structure and commitment. *Journal of Personality and Social Psychology, 51,* 259–269.

MILLER, S. M. (1979). Controllability and human stress: Method, evidence, and theory. *Behaviour Research and Therapy, 17,* 287–304.

MILLER, S. M., & MANGAN, C. E. (1983). Interacting effects of information and coping style in adapting to gynecologic stress: Should the doctor tell all? *Journal of Personality and Social Psychology, 45,* 223–236.

MINOW, N. N., MARTIN, J. B., & MITCHELL, L. M. (1973). *Presidential television.* New York: Basic Books.

MINTZ, A. (1946). A reexamination of correlations between lynchings and economic indices. *Journal* of *Abnormal and Social Psychology, 41*, 154–160.

MISCHEL, W. (1969). Continuity and change in personality. *American Psychologist, 24*, 1012–1018.

MISCHEL, W. (1979). On the interface of cognition and personality: Beyond the person-situation debate. *American Psychologist, 34*, 740–754.

MITA, T. H., DERMER, M., & KNIGHT, J. (1977). Reversed facial images and the mere-exposure hypothesis. *Journal of Personality and Social Psychology, 35*, 597–601.

MITCHELL, R. E. (1971). Some social implications of high-density housing. *American Sociological Review, 36*, 18–29.

MOGIELNICKI, R. P., NESLIN, S., DULAC, J., BALESTRA, D., GILLIE, E., & CORSON, J. (1986). Tailored media can enhance the success of smoking cessation clinics. *Journal of Behavioral Medicine, 9*, 141–161.

MOLM, L. D. (1985). Relative effects of individual dependencies: Further tests of the relation between power imbalance and power use. *Social Forces, 63*(3), 810–837.

MONROE, S. (1983). Major and minor life events as predictors of psychological distress: Further issues and findings. *Journal of Behavioral Medicine, 6*, 189–205.

MONSON, T. C., & SNYDER, M. (1977). Actors, observers, and the attribution process: Toward a reconceptualization. *Journal of Experimental Social Psychology, 13*, 89–111.

MORELAND, R. L., & ZAJONC, R. B. (1982). Exposure effects in person perception: Familiarity, similarity and attraction. *Journal of Experimental Social Psychology, 18*, 395–415.

MORGAN, C. J. (1978). Bystander intervention: Experimental test of a formal model. *Journal of Personality and Social Psychology, 36*, 43–55.

MORGAN, C. J., & LEIK, R. K. (1979). Simulation theory development: The bystander intervention case. In R. B. Smith & B. Anderson (Eds.), *Social science methods: Vol. 3: Theory construction*. Halstead Press.

MORIARTY, T. (1975). Crime, commitment, and the responsive bystander. Two field experiments. *Journal of Personality and Social Psychology, 31*, 370–376.

MORRIS, W. N., & MILLER, R. S. (1975). The effects of consensus-breaking and consensus-preempting partners on reduction in conformity. *Journal of Experimental Social Psychology, 11*, 215–223.

MORTON, T. L. (1978). Intimacy and reciprocity of exchange: A comparison of spouses and strangers. *Journal of Personality and Social Psychology, 36*, 72–81.

MOSCOVICI, S. (1985). Social influence and conformity. In G. Lindzey & E. Aronson (Eds.), *Handbook of social psychology*, 3rd ed. (Vol. 2, pp. 347–412). New York: Random House.

MOSCOVICI, S., LAGE, E., & NAFFRECHOUX, M. (1969). Influence of a consistent minority on the responses of a majority in a color perception task. *Sociometry, 32*, 365–379.

MOSS, M. K., & PAGE, R. A. (1972). Reinforcement and helping behavior. *Journal of Applied Social Psychology, 2*, 360–371.

MUELLER, C., & DONNERSTEIN, E. (1977). The effects of humor-induced arousal upon aggressive behavior. *Journal of Research in Personality, 11*, 73–82.

MUELLER, J. E. (1973). *War, presidents, and public opinion*. New York: Wiley.

MULLEN, B. (1985). Strength and immediacy of sources: A meta-analytic evaluation of the forgotten elements of social impact theory. *Journal of Personality and Social Psychology, 48*, 1458–1466.

MULLEN, B. (1986). Effects of strength and immediacy in group contexts: Reply to Jackson. *Journal of Personality and Social Psychology, 50*(3), 514–516.

MULLEN, B. (1986). Atrocity as a function of lynch mob composition. *Personality and Social Psychology Bulletin, 12*, 187–198.

MYERS, A. M., & GONDA, G. (1982). Utility of the masculinity-femininity construct: Comparison of traditional and androgyny approaches. *Journal of Personality and Social Psychology, 43*(3), 514–523.

MYERS, D. G., & LAMM, H. (1976). The group polarization phenomenon. *Psychological Bulletin, 83*, 602–627.

MYERS, J. K., LINDENTHAL, J. J., & PEPPER, M. P. (1972). Life events and mental status: A longitudinal study. *Journal of Health and Social Behavior, 13*, 398–406.

MYERSCOUGH, R., & TAYLOR, S. (1985). The effects of marijuana on human physical aggression. *Journal of Personality and Social Psychology, 49*, 1541–1546.

NATIONAL INSTITUTE OF MENTAL HEALTH (1982). *Television and behavior: Ten years of scientific progress and implications for the eighties: Vol. I: Summary report*. Rockville, MD: National Institute of Mental Health.

NEMETH, C. J. (1986). Differential contributions of majority and minority influence. *Psychological Review, 93*(1), 23–32.

NERENZ, D. R., & LEVENTHAL, H. (1983). Self-regulation theory in chronic illness. In T. G. Burish & L. A. Bradley (Eds.), *Coping with chronic disease: Research and applications* (pp. 13–35). New York: Academic Press.

NEUMAN, W. R. (1976). Patterns of recall among television news viewers. *Public Opinion Quarterly*, 115–123.

NEWCOMB, T. M. (1943). *Personality and social change*. New York: Dryden Press.

NEWCOMB, T. M. (1961). *The acquaintance process*. New York: Holt.

NEWCOMB, T. M. (1963). Persistence and regression of changed attitudes: Long-range studies. *Journal of Social Issues, 19*, 3–14.

NEWCOMB, T. M. (1968). Interpersonal balance. In R. P. Abelson et al. (Eds.), *Theories of cognitive consistency: A sourcebook*. Chicago: Rand-McNally.

NEWCOMB, T. M., KOENIG, K. E., FLACKS, R., & WARWICK, D. P. (1967). *Persistence and change: Bennington College and its students after 25 years*. New York: Wiley.

NEWTSON, D. (1976). Foundations of attribution: The perception of ongoing behavior. In J. H. Harvey, W. J. Ickes, & R. F. Kidd (Eds.), *New directions in attribution research* (Vol. 1). Hillsdale, NJ: Erlbaum.

NEWTSON, D., & CZERLINSKY, T. (1974). Adjustment of attitude communications for contrasts by extreme audiences. *Journal of Personality and Social Psychology, 30*, 829–837.

NEWTSON, D., ENGQUIST, G., & BOIS, J. (1977). The objective basis of behavior units. *Journal of Personality and Social Psychology, 35*, 847–862.

NIE, N. H., VERBA, S., & PETROCIK, J. R. (1979). *The changing American voter* (enlarged ed.). Cambridge, MA: Harvard University Press.

NIEMI, R. G. (1973). Political socialization. In J. Knutson (Ed.), *Handbook of political psychology*. San Francisco: Jossey-Bass.

NIEMI, R. G. (1974). *How family members perceive each other*. New Haven, CT: Yale University Press.

NIEVA, V., & GUTEK, B. (1981). *Women and work: A psychological perspective*. New York: Praeger.

NINCIC, M., & RUSSETT, B. (1979). The effect of similarity and interest on attitudes toward foreign countries. *Public Opinion Quarterly, 43*, 68–78.

NISBETT, R. E., & BORGIDA, E. (1975). Attribution and the psychology of prediction. *Journal of Personality and Social Psychology, 32*, 932–943.

NISBETT, R. E., CAPUTO, C., LEGANT, P., & MARECEK, J. (1973). Behavior as seen by the actor and as seen by the observer. *Journal of Personality and Social Psychology, 27*, 154–164.

NISBETT, R. E., KRANTZ, D. H., JEPSON, C., & FONG, G. T. (1982). Improving inductive inference. In D. Kahneman, P. Slovic, & A. Tversky (Eds.), *Judgment under uncertainty: Heuristics and biases* (pp. 445–462). New York: Cambridge University Press.

NISBETT, R. E., KRANTZ, D. H., JEPSON, C., & KUNDA, Z. (1983). The use of statistical heuristics in everyday inductive reasoning. *Psychological Review, 90*, 339–363.

NISBETT, R. E., & KUNDA, Z. (1985). Perception of social distributions. *Journal of Personality and Social Psychology, 48*, 297–311.

NISBETT, R. E., & ROSS, L. (1980). *Human inference: Strategies and shortcomings of social judgment*. Englewood Cliffs, NJ: Prentice-Hall.

NISBETT, R. E., & SCHACHTER, S. (1966). Cognitive manipulation of pain. *Journal of Experimental Social Psychology, 2*, 227–236.

NOGAMI, G. Y. (1976). Crowding: Effects of group size, room size, or density? *Journal of Applied Social Psychology, 6*, 105–125.

NOLEN-HOEKSEMA, S., GIRGUS, J. S., & SELIGMAN, M. E. P. (1986). Learned helplessness in children: A longitudinal study of depression, achievement, and explanatory style. *Journal of Personality and Social Psychology, 51*, 435–442.

NORMAN, R. (1975). Affective-cognitive consistency, attitudes, conformity, and behavior. *Journal of Personality and Social Psychology, 32*, 83–91.

NORMAN, R. (1976). When what is said is important: A comparison of expert and attractive sources. *Journal of Experimental Social Psychology, 12*, 294–300.

NOVAK, D. W., & LERNER, M. J. (1968). Rejection as a consequence of perceived similarity. *Journal of Personality and Social Psychology, 9*, 147–152.

O'KELLY, C. (1980). Sex-role imagery in modern art: An empirical examination. *Sex Roles, 6*(1), 99–112.

OLZAK, S., & NAGEL, J. (1986). *Competitive ethnic relations*. New York: Academic Press.

ORVIS, B. R. (1977). *The bases, nature, and affective significance of attributional conflict in young couples*. Unpublished doctoral dissertation, University of California, Los Angeles.

ORVIS, B. R., KELLEY, H. H., & BUTLER, D. (1976). Attributional conflict in young couples. In J. H. Harvey, W. Ickes, & R. F. Kidd (Eds.), *New directions in attribution research* (Vol. 1, pp. 353–386). Hillsdale, NJ: Erlbaum.

OSBORN, A. F. (1957). *Applied imagination*. New York: Scribners.

OSGOOD, C. E., SUCI, G. J., & TANNENBAUM, P. H. (1957). *The measurement of meaning*. Urbana: University of Illinois Press.

OWENS, J., BOWER, G. H., & BLACK, J. B. (1979). The "soap-opera" effect in story recall. *Memory and Cognition, 7*, 185–191.

PAGEL, M. D., & DAVIDSON, A. R. (1984). A comparison of three social-psychological models of attitude and behavioral plan: Prediction of contraceptive behavior. *Journal of Personality and Social Psychology, 47*, 517–33.

PALLAK, M. S., SOGIN, S. R., & VAN ZANTE, A. (1974). Bad

decisions: Effect of volition, locus of causality, and negative consequences on attitude change. *Journal of Personality and Social Psychology, 30*, 217–227.

PARK, B. (1986). A method for studying the development of impressions of real people. *Journal of Personality and Social Psychology, 51*, 907–917.

PARKE, R. D., BERKOWITZ, L., LEYENS, J. P., WEST, S. G., & SEBASTIAN, R. J. (1977). Some effects of violent and nonviolent movies on the behavior of juvenile delinquents. In L. Berkowitz (Ed.), *Advances in experimental social psychology* (Vol. 10, pp. 136–173). New York: Academic Press.

PARLEE, M. B. (1979, OCTOBER). The friendship bond. *Psychology Today*, pp. 43–54, 113.

PATTERSON, M. L., & SECHREST, L. B. (1970). Interpersonal distance and impression formation. *Journal of Personality, 38*, 161–166.

PATTERSON, T. E. (1980). *The mass media election: How Americans choose their president*. New York: Praeger.

PATTERSON, T. E., & McCLURE, R. D. (1976). *The unseeing eye*. New York: Putnam.

PAULUS, P. B., ANNIS, A. B., SETA, J. J., SCHKADE, J. K., & MATTHEWS, R. W. (1976). Density does affect task performance. *Journal of Personality and Social Psychology, 34*, 248–253.

PEARLIN, L. I., & SCHOOLER, C. (1978). The structure of coping. *Journal of Health and Social Behavior, 19*, 2–21.

PEDERSON, L. L. (1982). Compliance with physician advice to quit smoking: A review of the literature. *Preventive Medicine, 11*, 71–84.

PENNEBAKER, J. W. (1980). Perceptual and environmental determinants of coughing. *Basic and Applied Social Psychology, 1*, 83–91.

PENNEBAKER, J. W. (1983). Accuracy of symptom perception. In A. Baum, S. E. Taylor, & J. Singer (Eds.), *Handbook of psychology and health* (Vol. 4, pp. 189–217). Hillsdale, NJ: Erlbaum.

PENNEBAKER, J. W., & LIGHTNER, J. M., (1980). Competition of internal and external information in an exercise setting. *Journal of Personality and Social Psychology, 39*, 165–174.

PENNINGTON, N., & HASTIE, R. (1986). Evidence evaluation in complex decision making. *Journal of Personality and Social Psychology, 51*, 242–258.

PENROD, S., LOFTUS, E., & WINKLER, J. (1982). The reliability of eyewitness testimony: A psychological perspective. In N. L. Kerr & R. M. Bray (Eds.), *The psychology of the courtroom* (pp. 119–168). New York: Academic Press.

PEPLAU, L. A. (1984). Power in dating relationships. In J. Freeman (Ed.), *Women: A feminist perspective*, 3rd ed. Palo Alto, CA: Mayfield.

PEPLAU, L. A., & GORDON, S. L. (1985). Women and men in love: Gender differences in close heterosexual relationships. In V. E. O'Leary, R. K. Unger, & B. S. Wallston (Eds.), *Women, gender and social psychology* (pp. 257–292). Hillsdale, NJ: Erlbaum.

PEPLAU, L. A., & PERLMAN, D. (1982). *Loneliness: A sourcebook of current theory, research and therapy*. New York: Wiley-Interscience.

PERLMAN, D., & OSKAMP, S. (1971). The effects of picture content and exposure frequency on evaluations of Negroes and whites. *Journal of Experimental Social Psychology, 7*, 503–514.

PERLMAN, D., & PEPLAU, L. A. (1984). Loneliness research: A survey of empirical findings. In L. A. Peplau & S. Goldston (Eds.), *Preventing the harmful consequences of severe and persistent loneliness* (pp. 13–46). (DHHS Publication No. ADM 84–1312). Washington, DC: U.S. Government Printing Office.

PESSIN, J. (1933). The comparative effects of social and mechanical stimulation on memorizing. *American Journal of Psychology, 45*, 263–270.

PETERSON, C., SCHWARTZ, S. M., & SELIGMAN, M. E. P. (1981). Self-blame and depressive symptoms. *Journal of Personality and Social Psychology, 41*, 253–259.

PETERSON, D. R. (1983). Conflict. In H. H. Kelley et al., *Close relationships* (pp. 360–396). New York: Freeman.

PETTY, R. E., & BROCK, T. C. (1981). Thought disruption and persuasion: Assessing the validity of attitude change experiments. In R. E. Petty, T. M. Ostrom, & T. C. Brock (Eds.), *Cognitive responses in persuasion*. Hillsdale, NJ: Erlbaum.

PETTY, R. E., & CACIOPPO, J. T. (1977). Forewarning, cognitive responding, and resistance to persuasion. *Journal of Personality and Social Psychology, 35*, 645–656.

PETTY, R. E., & CACIOPPO, J. T. (1979). Issue involvement can increase or decrease persuasion by enhancing message-relevant cognitive responses. *Journal of Personality and Social Psychology, 37*, 1915–1926.

PETTY, R. E., & CACIOPPO, J. T. (1981). *Attitudes and persuasion: Classic and contemporary approaches*. Dubuque, IA: Wm. C. Brown.

PETTY, R. E., & CACIOPPO, J. T. (1984). The effects of involvement on responses to argument quantity and quality: Central and peripheral routes to persuasion. *Journal of Personality and Social Psychology, 46*, 69–81.

PETTY, R. E., & CACIOPPO, J. T. (1986). *Communication and persuasion: Central and peripheral routes to attitude change*. New York: Springer-Verlag.

PETTY, R. E., CACIOPPO, J. T., & SCHUMANN, D. (1983).

Central and peripheral routes to advertising effectiveness: The moderating role of involvement. *Journal of Consumer Research, 10*, 135–146.

PETTY, R. E., OSTROM, T. M., & BROCK, T. C. (1981). Historical foundation of the cognitive response approach to attitudes and persuasion. In R. E. Petty, T. M. Ostrom, & T. C. Brock (Eds.), *Cognitive responses in persuasion*. Hillsdale, NJ: Erlbaum.

PETTY, R. E., WELLS, G. L., & BROCK, T. C. (1976). Distraction can enhance or reduce yielding to propaganda: Thought disruption versus effort justification. *Journal of Personality and Social Psychology, 34*, 874–884.

PHILLIPS, D. P. (1986). The found experiment: A new technique for assessing the impact of mass media violence on real-world aggressive behavior. In G. Comstock (Ed.), *Public Communication and Behavior* (Vol. 1, pp. 259–307). New York: Academic Press.

PILIAVIN, I. M., PILIAVIN, J. A., & RODIN, J. (1975). Costs, diffusion, and the stigmatized victim. *Journal of Personality and Social Psychology, 32*(3), 429–438.

PILIAVIN, I. M., RODIN, J., & PILIAVIN, J. A. (1969). Good Samaritanism: An underground phenomenon? *Journal of Personality and Social Psychology, 13*(4), 289–299.

PILIAVIN, J. A., DOVIDIO, J. F., GAERTNER, S. L., & CLARK, R. D. (1981). *Emergency intervention*. New York: Academic Press.

PINES, A., & ARONSON, E. (1983). Antecedents, correlates, and consequences of sexual jealousy. *Journal of Personality 51*(1), 108–136.

PLECK, J. H. (1981). *The myth of masculinity*. Cambridge, MA: The MIT Press.

POOLE, K. T., & ZEIGLER, L. H. (1985). *Women, public opinion and politics: The changing political attitudes of American women*. New York: Longman.

PRATKANIS, A. R., GREENWALD, A. G., LEIPPE, M. R., & BAUMGARDNER, M. H. (In press). In search of reliable persuasion effects: III. The sleeper effect is dead. Long live the sleeper effect. *Journal of Personality and Social Psychology*.

PRENTICE-DUNN, S., & ROGERS, R. W. (1980). Effects of deindividuating situational cues and aggressive models on subjective deindividuation and aggression. *Journal of Personality and Social Psychology, 39*, 104–113.

PRENTICE-DUNN, S., & SPIVEY, C. B. (1986). Extreme deindividuation in the laboratory: Its magnitude and subjective components. *Personality and Social Psychology Bulletin, 12*, 206–215.

RAHE, R. H., MAHAN, J. L., & ARTHUR, R. J. (1970). Prediction of near-future health change from subjects' preceding life changes. *Journal of Psychosomatic Research, 14*, 401–406.

RANDS, M., & LEVINGER, G. (1979). Implicit theories of relationship: An intergenerational study. *Journal of Personality and Social Psychology, 37*, 649–661.

RAVEN, B. H., & RUBIN, J. Z. (1983). *Social psychology*, 2nd ed. New York: Wiley.

REGAN, D. T. (1968). *The effects of a favor and liking on compliance*. Unpublished doctoral dissertation, Stanford University.

REGAN, D. T., & FAZIO, R. (1977). On the consistency between attitudes and behavior: Look to the method of attitude formation. *Journal of Experimental Social Psychology, 13*, 28–45.

REGAN, D. T., & TOTTEN, J. (1975). Empathy and attribution: Turning observers into actors. *Journal of Personality and Social Psychology, 32*, 850–856.

REINISCH, J. M., & SANDERS, S. A. (1986). A test of sex differences in aggressive response to hypothetical conflict situations. *Journal of Personality and Social Psychology, 50*, 1045–1049.

REIS, H. T., & JACKSON, L. A. (1981). Sex differences in reward allocation: Subjects, partners and tasks. *Journal of Personality and Social Psychology, 40*(3), 465–478.

REIS, H. T., SENCHAK, M., & SOLOMON, B. (1985). Sex differences in the intimacy of social interaction: Further examination of potential explanations. *Journal of Personality and Social Psychology, 48*, 1204–1217.

RENSHON, S. A. (1974). *Psychological needs and political behavior: A theory of personality and political efficacy*. New York: Free Press.

RHINE, R. J., & SEVERANCE, L. J. (1970). Ego-involvement, discrepancy, source credibility, and attitude change. *Journal of Personality and Social Psychology, 16*, 175–190.

RIDGEWAY, C. L. (1983). *The dynamics of small groups*. New York: St. Martin's Press.

RIESS, M., ROSENFELD, P., MELBURG, V., & TEDESCHI, J. T. (1981). Self-serving attributions: Based private perceptions and distorted public descriptions. *Journal of Personality and Social Psychology, 41*, 224–231.

RIESS, M., & TAYLOR, J. (1984). Ego-involvement and attributions for success and failure in a field setting. *Personality and Social Psychology Bulletin, 10*, 536–543.

ROBINSON, C. C., & MORRIS, J. T. (1986). The gender-stereotyped nature of Christmas toys received by 36-, 48-, and 60-month-old children. *Sex Roles, 15*(1/2), 21–32.

ROBINSON, J., & MCARTHUR, L. Z. (1982). Impact of salient vocal qualities on causal attribution for a speaker's behavior. *Journal of Personality and Social Psychology, 43*, 236–247.

ROBINSON, J. P. (1971). The audience for national TV news programs. *Public Opinion Quarterly*, *35*, 403–405.

ROBINSON, J. P. (1972). Mass communication and information diffusion. In F. G. Kline & P. J. Tichenor (Eds.), *Current perspectives in mass communication research* (pp. 71–93). Beverly Hills, CA: Sage Publications.

ROBINSON, J. P., YERBY, J., FIEWEGER, M., & SOMERICK, N. (1977). Sex-role differences in time use. *Sex Roles*, *3*, 443–458.

ROBINSON, M. J., (1976). Public affairs television and the growth of political malaise: The case of "the selling of the Pentagon." *American Political Science Review*, *70*, 409–432.

ROCHA, R. F., & ROGERS, R. W. (1976). Ares and Babbitt in the classroom: Effects of competition and reward on children's aggression. *Journal of Personality and Social Psychology*, *33*, 588–593.

RODIN, J., & JANIS, I. L. (1979). The social power of health-care practitioners as agents of change. *Journal of Social Issues*, *35*, 60–81.

RODIN, J., & LANGER, E. J. (1977). Long-term effects of a control-relevant intervention with the institutionalized aged. *Journal of Personality and Social Psychology*, *35*, 897–902.

ROGERS, R. W. (1984). Changing health-related attitudes and behavior: The role of preventive health psychology. In J. H. Harvey, J. E. Maddux, R. P. McGlynn, & C. D. Stoltenberg (Eds.), *Social perception in clinical and counseling psychology* (Vol. 2, pp. 91–112). Lubbock: Texas Tech University Press.

ROGERS, R. W., & MEWBORN, C. R. (1976). Fear appeals and attitude change: Effects of a threat's noxiousness, probability of occurrence, and the efficacy of coping responses. *Journal of Personality and Social Psychology*, *34*, 54–61.

ROGERS, R. W., & PRENTICE-DUNN, S. (1981). Deindividuation and anger-mediated interracial aggression: Unmasking regressive racism. *Journal of Personality and Social Psychology*, *41*, 63–73.

ROGERS, T. B., KUIPER, N. A., & KIRKER, W. S. (1977). Self-reference and the encoding of personal information. *Journal of Personality and Social Psychology*, *35*, 677–688.

ROGOW, A. A. (1963). *James Forrestal: A study of personality, politics, and policy*. New York: Macmillan.

ROHE, W., & PATTERSON, A. (1974). The effects of varied levels of resources and density on behavior in a day care center. In D. Carson (Ed.), *EDRA V*, pp. 161–171.

ROMER, D., GRUDER, C. L., & LIZZADRO, T. (1986). A person-situation approach to altruistic behavior.

Journal of Personality and Social Psychology, *51(5)*, 1001–1012.

ROSEN, B., & JERDEE, T. H. (1978). Perceived sex differences in managerially relevant characteristics. *Sex Roles*, *4*, 837–843.

ROSENBAUM, M. E. (1986). The repulsion hypothesis: On the nondevelopment of relationships. *Journal of Personality and Social Psychology*, *51(6)*, 1156–1166.

ROSENBERG, M. J. (1960). An analysis of affective-cognitive consistency. In C. I. Hovland & M. J. Rosenberg (Eds.), *Attitude organization and change*. New Haven, CT: Yale University Press.

ROSENBERG, S., NELSON, C., & VIVEKANANTHAN, P. S. (1968). A multidimensional approach to the structure of personality impressions. *Journal of Personality and Social Psychology*, *9*, 283–294.

ROSENFELD, L. B. (1979). Self-disclosure avoidance: Why I am afraid to tell you who I am. *Communication Monographs*, *46*, 63–74.

ROSENFELD, P., GIACALONE, R. A., & TEDESCHI, J. T. (1984). Cognitive dissonance and impression management explanations for effort justification. *Personality and Social Psychology Bulletin*, *10*, 394–401.

ROSENKRANTZ, P., VOGEL, S., BEE, H., BROVERMAN, I., & BROVERMAN, D. M. (1968). Sex-role stereotypes and self-concepts in college students. *Journal of Consulting and Clinical Psychology*, *32*, 287–295.

ROSENMAN, R. (1978). The interview method of assessment of the coronary-prone behavior pattern. In T. Dembroski, S. Weiss, J. Shields, S. Haynes, & M. Feinleib (Eds.), *Coronary-prone behavior* (pp. 55–70). New York: Springer-Verlag.

ROSENSTOCK, I. M. (1966). Why people use health services. *Milbank Memorial Fund Quarterly*, *44*, 94ff.

ROSENSTOCK, I. M. (1974). Historical origins of the health belief model. *Health Education Monographs*, *2*, 328–335.

ROSENSTOCK, I. M., DERRYBERRY, M., & CARRIGER, B. (1959). Why people fail to seek poliomyelitis vaccination. *Public Health Reports*, *74*, 98–103.

ROSENTHAL, R. (1986). Media violence, antisocial behavior, and the social consequences of small effects. *Journal of Social Issues*, *42*, 141–154.

ROSENTHAL, R., & ROSNOW, R. L. (1975). *The volunteer subject*. New York: Wiley.

ROSENTHAL, R., & RUBIN, D. B. (1978). Interpersonal expectancy effects: The first 345 studies. *The Behavioral and Brain Sciences*, *3*, 377–415.

ROSKIES, E. (1980). Considerations in developing a treatment program for the coronary-prone (Type A) behavior pattern. In P. O. Davidson & S. M. Davidson (Eds.), *Behavior medicine: Changing health lifestyles* (pp. 38–69). New York: Brunner/Mazel.

Ross, A. S. (1971). Effect of increased responsibility on bystander intervention: The presence of children. *Journal of Personality and Social Psychology, 19(3),* 306–310.

Ross, L. (1977). The intuitive psychologist and his shortcomings: Distortions in the attribution process. In L. Berkowitz (Ed.), *Advances in experimental social psychology* (Vol. 10). New York: Academic Press.

Ross, L., Amabile, T. M., & Steinmetz, J. L. (1977). Social roles, social control, and biases in social-perception processes, *Journal of Personality and Social Psychology, 35,* 485–494.

Ross, L., Greene, D., & House, P. (1977). The "false consensus effect": An egocentric bias in social perception and attribution processes. *Journal of Experimental Social Psychology, 13,* 279–301.

Ross, M. (1975). Salience of reward and intrinsic motivation. *Journal of Personality and Social Psychology, 32,* 245–254.

Ross, M., & Sicoly, F. (1979). Egocentric biases in availability and attribution. *Journal of Personality and Social Psychology, 37,* 322–336.

Rothbart, M. (1976). Achieving racial equality: An analysis of resistance to social reform. In P. A. Katz (Ed.), *Towards the elimination of racism* (pp. 341–375). Elmsford, NY: Pergamon Press.

Rothbart, M., Fulero, S., Jensen, C., Howard, J., & Birrell, B. (1978). From individual to group impressions: Availability heuristics in stereotype formation. *Journal of Experimental Social Psychology, 14,* 237–255.

Rotton, J., & Frey, J. (1985). Air pollution, weather, and violent crimes: Concomitant time-series analysis of archival data. *Journal of Personality and Social Psychology, 49,* 1207–1220.

Rowland, W. D. (1983). *The politics of TV violence: Policy uses of communications research.* Beverly Hills, CA: Sage.

Rubenstein, C. M., & Shaver, P. (1982). The experience of loneliness. In L. A. Peplau & D. Perlman (Eds.), *Loneliness: A sourcebook of current theory, research and therapy* (pp. 206–223). New York: Wiley-Interscience.

Rubin, B. (1967). *Political television.* Belmont, CA: Wadsworth.

Rubin, L. (1976). *Worlds of pain.* New York: Basic Books.

Rubin, Z. (1970). Measurement of romantic love. *Journal of Personality and Social Psychology, 16,* 265–273.

Rubin, Z. (1973). *Liking and loving: An invitation to social psychology.* New York: Holt, Rinehart & Winston.

Rubin, Z. (1975). Disclosing oneself to a stranger: Reciprocity and its limits. *Journal of Experimental Social Psychology, 11,* 233–260.

Rubin, Z., Hill, C. T., Peplau, L. A., & Dunkel-Schetter, C. (1980). Self-disclosure in dating couples: Sex roles and the ethic of openness. *Journal of Marriage and the Family, 42,* 305–317.

Rubin, Z., Peplau, L. A., & Hill, C. T. (1981). Loving and leaving: Sex differences in romantic attachments. *Sex roles, 7(9),* 821–835.

Ruble, D. N. (1977). Premenstrual symptoms: A reinterpretation. *Science, 197,* 291–292.

Ruble, D. N., & Feldman, N. S. (1976). Order of consensus, distinctiveness, and consistency information and causal attributions. *Journal of Personality and Social Psychology, 34,* 930–937.

Rusbult, C. E. (1980). Commitment and satisfaction in romantic associations: A test of the investment model. *Journal of Experimental Social Psychology, 16,* 172–186.

Rusbult, C. E. (1983). A longitudinal test of the investment model: The development (and deterioration) of satisfaction and commitment in heterosexual involvements. *Journal of Personality and Social Psychology, 45,* 101–117.

Rusbult, C. E. (1987). Responses to dissatisfaction in close relationships: The exit-voice-loyalty-neglect model. In D. Perlman & S. Duck (Eds.), *Intimate relationships: Development, dynamics and deterioration* (pp. 209–237). Beverly Hills, CA: Sage.

Rusbult, C. E., Johnson, D. J., & Morrow, G. D. (1986a). Impact of couple patterns of problem solving on distress and nondistress in dating relationships. *Journal of Personality and Social Psychology, 50,* 744–753.

Rusbult, C. E., Johnson, D. J., & Morrow, G. D. (1986b). Predicting satisfaction and commitment in adult romantic involvements: An assessment of the generalizability of the investment model. *Social Psychology Quarterly, 49(1),* 81–89.

Rusbult, C. E., Zembrodt, I. M., & Gunn, L. K. (1982). Exit, voice, loyalty, and neglect: Responses to dissatisfaction in romantic involvements. *Journal of Personality and Social Psychology, 43,* 1230–1242.

Rushton, J. P. (1980). *Altruism, socialization and society.* Englewood Cliffs, NJ: Prentice-Hall.

Rushton, J. P., & Campbell, A. C. (1977). Modeling, vicarious reinforcement and extraversion on blood donating in adults: Immediate and long-term effects. *European Journal of Social Psychology, 7,* 297–306.

Rushton, J. P., Fulker, D. W., Neale, M. C., Nias, D. K. B., & Eysenck, H. J. (1986). Altruism and aggression: The heritability of individual differences. *Journal of Personality and Social Psychology, 50*(6), 1192–1198.

RUSHTON, J. P., & TEACHMAN, G. (1978). The effects of positive reinforcement, attributions, and punishment on model-induced altruism in children. *Personality and Social Psychology Bulletin, 4*(2), 322–325.

RUSSELL, J. A., & BULLOCK, M. (1985). Multidimensional scaling of emotional facial expressions: Similarity from preschoolers to adults. *Journal of Personality and Social Psychology, 48,* 1290–1298.

RYAN, W. (1971). *Blaming the victim.* New York: Vintage.

SAEGERT, S., SWAP, W., & ZAJONC, R. B. (1973). Exposure, context, and interpersonal attraction. *Journal of Personality and Social Psychology, 25,* 234–252.

SAFER, M. A., THARPS, Q. J., JACKSON, T. C., & LEVENTHAL, H. (1979). Determinants of three stages of delay in seeking care at a medical care clinic. *Medical Care, 17,* 11–29.

SAGAR, H., & SCHOFIELD, J. W. (1980). Racial and behavioral cues in black and white children's perceptions of ambiguously aggressive acts. *Journal of Personality and Social Psychology, 39,* 590–598.

SALANCIK, G. R., & CONWAY, M. (1975). Attitude inferences from salient and relevant cognitive content about behavior. *Journal of Personality and Social Psychology, 32,* 829–840.

SAMORA, J., SAUNDERS, L., & LARSON, R. F. (1961). Medical vocabulary knowledge among hospital patients. *Journal of Health and Social Behavior, 2,* 83–89.

SAMPSON, E. E. (1977). Psychology and the American ideal. *Journal of Personality and Social Psychology, 35,* 767–782.

SANDE, G. N., ELLARD, J. H., & ROSS, M. (1986). Effect of arbitrarily assigned status labels on self-perceptions and social perceptions: The mere position effect. *Journal of Personality and Social Psychology, 50,* 684–689.

SANDERS, G. S. (1984). Self-preservation and drive in social facilitation. *Journal of Experimental Social Psychology, 20,* 312–322.

SANDERS, G. S., & BARON, R. S. (1977). Is social comparison irrelevant for producing choice shifts? *Journal of Experimental Social Psychology, 13,* 303–314.

SANDERS, G. S., BARON, R. S., & MOORE, D. L. (1978). Distraction and social comparison as mediators of social facilitation effects. *Journal of Experimental Social Psychology, 14,* 291–303.

SAPIRO, V. (1983). *The political integration of women.* Urbana: University of Illinois Press.

SARASON, I. G., JOHNSON, J. H., & SIEGEL, J. M. (1978). Assessing the impact of life changes: Development of the Life Experience Survey. *Journal of Consulting and Clinical Psychology, 46,* 932–946.

SARNOFF, I., & ZIMBARDO, P. G. (1961). Anxiety, fear and social affiliation. *Journal of Abnormal and Social Psychology, 62,* 356–363.

SATOW, K. L. (1975). Social approval and helping. *Journal of Experimental Social Psychology, 11,* 501–509.

SAUNDERS, D. M., FISHER, W. A., HEWITT, E. C., & CLAYTON, J. P. (1985). A method for empirically assessing volunteer selection effects: Recruitment procedures and responses to erotica. *Journal of Personality and Social Psychology, 49,* 1703–1712.

SAWYER, J. (1966). Measurement and prediction, clinical and statistical. *Psychology Bulletin, 66,* 178–200.

SCANZONI, L. D., & SCANZONI, J. (1981). *Men, women and change,* 2nd ed. New York: McGraw-Hill.

SCHACHTER, S. (1951). Deviation, rejection, and communication. *Journal of Abnormal and Social Psychology, 46,* 190–207.

SCHACHTER, S. (1959). *The psychology of affiliation.* Stanford, CA: Stanford University Press.

SCHACHTER, S. (1964). The interaction of cognitive and physiological determinants of emotional state. In L. Berkowitz (Ed.), *Advances in Experimental Social Psychology* (pp. 49–80). New York: Academic Press.

SCHACHTER, S., & SINGER, J. E. (1962). Cognitive, social and physiological determinants of emotional state. *Psychological Review, 69,* 379–399.

SCHAEFER, C., COYNE, J. C., & LAZARUS, R. S. (1981). The health-related functions of social support. *Journal of Behavioral Medicine, 4,* 381–406.

SCHAIN, W. S. (1976). Psychological issues in counseling mastectomy patients. *Counseling Psychologist, 6,* 45–49.

SCHEIER, M. F., CARVER, C. S., & GIBBONS, F. X. (1979). Self-directed attention, awareness of bodily states, and suggestibility. *Journal of Personality and Social Psychology, 37,* 1576–1588.

SCHIFTER, D. E., & AJZEN, I. (1985). Intention, perceived control, and weight loss: An application of the theory of planned behavior. *Journal of Personality and Social Psychology, 49,* 843–851.

SCHLEGEL, R. P., CRAWFORD, C. A., & SANBORN, M. D. (1977). Correspondence and mediational properties of the Fishbein model: An application to adolescent alcohol use. *Journal of Experimental Social Psychology, 13,* 421–430.

SCHLENKER, B. R., HALLAM, J. R., & McCOWN, N. E. (1983). Motives and social evaluation: Actor-observer differences in the delineation of motives for a beneficial act. *Journal of Experimental Social Psychology, 19,* 254–273.

SCHLOZMAN, K. L., & VERBA, S. (1979). *Injury to insult*:

Unemployment, class, and political response. Cambridge, MA: Harvard University Press.

SCHMITT, D. R., & MARWELL, G. (1972). Withdrawal and reward reallocation as responses to inequity. *Journal of Experimental Social Psychology, 8,* 207–221.

SCHNEIDER, D. J. (1973). Implicit personality theory: A review. *Psychological Bulletin, 79,* 294–309.

SCHNEIDER, D. J., & MILLER, R. S. (1975). The effects of enthusiasm and quality of arguments on attitude attribution. *Journal of Personality, 43,* 693–708.

SCHOENRADE, P. A., BATSON, C. D., BRANDT, J. R., & LOUD, R. E. (1986). Attachment, accountability, and motivation to benefit another not in distress. *Journal of Personality and Social Psychology, 51(3),* 557–563.

SCHOFIELD, J. (1978). School desegregation and intergroup relations. In D. Bar-Tal & L. Saxe (Eds.), *Social psychology of education: Theory and research.* New York: Wiley.

SCHOPLER, J., & STOCKDALE, J. E. (1977). An interference analysis of crowding. *Journal of Environmental Psychology and Nonverbal Behavior, 1,* 81–88.

SCHUMAN, H., & JOHNSON, M. P. (1976). Attitudes and behavior, *Annual Review of Sociology, 2,* 161–207.

SCHUMAN, H., STEEH, C., & BOBO, L. (1985). *Racial attitudes in America: Trends and interpretation.* Cambridge, MA: Harvard University Press.

SCHWARTZ, B., & BARSKY, S. (1977). The home advantage. *Social Forces, 55,* 641–661.

SCHWARTZ, J. C., & SHAVER, P. (In press). Emotions and emotion knowledge in interpersonal relations. In W. Jones & D. Perlman (Eds.), *Perspectives in interpersonal behavior and relationships* (Vol. 1). Greenwich, CT: JAI Press.

SCHWARTZ, S. H. (1977). Normative influences on altruism. In L. Berkowitz (Ed.), *Advances in experimental social psychology* (Vol. 10). New York: Academic Press.

SCHWARTZ, S. H. (1978). Temporal instability as a moderator of the attitude-behavior relationship. *Journal of Personality and Social Psychology, 36,* 715–724.

SCHWARTZ, S. H., & GOTTLIEB, A. (1980). Bystander anonymity and reactions to emergencies. *Journal of Personality and Social Psychology, 39(3),* 418–430.

SCHWARZ, N., & CLORE, G. L. (1983). Mood, misattribution, and judgments of well-being: Informative and directive functions of affective states. *Journal of Personality and Social Psychology, 45(3),* 513–523.

SEARS, D. O. (1968). The paradox of de facto selective exposure without preferences for supportive information. In R. P. Abelson, E. Aronson, W. J. McGuire, T. M. Newcomb, M. J. Rosenberg, & P. H. Tannenbaum (Eds.), *Theories of cognitive consistency: A sourcebook* (pp. 777–787). Chicago: Rand-McNally.

SEARS, D. O. (1969). Political behavior. In G. Lindzey & E. Aronson (Eds.), *Handbook of social psychology,* 2nd ed. (Vol. 5, pp. 315–458). Reading, MA: Addison-Wesley.

SEARS, D. O. (1982). *Positivity bias in evaluation of public figures.* Paper presented at the annual meeting of the American Political Science Association, Denver.

SEARS, D. O. (1983). The person-positivity bias. *Journal of Personality and Social Psychology, 44,* 233–250.

SEARS, D. O. (1986). College sophomores in the laboratory: Influences of a narrow database on social psychology's view of human nature. *Journal of Personality and Social Psychology, 51,* 515–530.

SEARS, D. O. (In press). Symbolic racism. In P. Katz & D. Taylor (Eds.), *Towards the elimination of racism: Profile in controversy* (pp. 53–84). New York: Plenum.

SEARS, D. O., & ALLEN, H. M., JR. (1984). The trajectory of local desegregation controversies and whites' opposition to busing. In N. Miller & M. Brewer (Eds.), *Groups in contact: The psychology of desegregation* (pp. 123–151). New York: Academic Press.

SEARS, D. O., & CHAFFEE, S. H. (1979). Uses and effects of the 1976 debates: An overview of empirical studies. In S. Kraus (Ed.), *The great debates, 1976: Ford vs. Carter* (pp. 223–261). Bloomington: Indiana University Press.

SEARS, D. O., & CITRIN, J. (1985). *Tax revolt: Something for nothing in California* (enlarged ed.). Cambridge, MA: Harvard University Press.

SEARS, D. O., & FREEDMAN, J. L. (1967). Selective exposure to information: A critical review. *Public Opinion Quarterly, 31,* 194–213.

SEARS, D. O., FREEDMAN, J. L., & O'CONNOR, E. F., JR. (1964). The effects of anticipated debate and commitment on the polarization of audience opinion. *Public Opinion Quarterly, 28,* 615–627.

SEARS, D. O., HENSLER, C. P., & SPEER, L. K. (1979). Whites' opposition to "busing": Self-interest or symbolic politics? *American Political Science Review, 73,* 369–384.

SEARS, D. O., & KINDER, D. R. (1985). Whites' opposition to busing: On conceptualizing and operationalizing group conflict. *Journal of Personality and Social Psychology, 48,* 1141–1147.

SEARS, D. O., LAU, R. R., TYLER, T. R., & ALLEN, H. M., JR. (1980). Self-interest vs. symbolic politics in policy attitudes and presidential voting. *American Political Science Review, 74,* 670–684.

SEARS, D. O., & MCCONAHAY, J. B. (1973). *The politics of violence: The new urban blacks and the Watts riot*. Boston: Houghton Mifflin. Reprinted by University Press of America, 1981.

SEARS, D. O., & WHITNEY, R. E. (1973). Political persuasion. In I. deS. Pool, W. Schramm, F. W. Frey, N. Maccoby, & E. B. Parker (Eds.), *Handbook of communication* (pp. 253–289). Chicago: Rand-McNally.

SEARS, R. R., MACCOBY, E., & LEVIN, H. (1957). *Patterns of child rearing*. Evanston, IL: Row, Peterson.

SEARS, R. R., WHITING, J. W. M., NOWLIS, V., & SEARS, P. S. (1953). Some child-rearing antecedents of aggression and dependency in young children. *Genetic Psychological Monographs, 47*, 135–236.

SEGAL, M. W. (1974). Alphabet and attraction: An unobtrusive measure of the effect of propinquity in a field setting. *Journal of Personality and Social Psychology, 30*(5), 654–657.

SELIGMAN, C., BUSH, M., & KIRSCH, K. (1975). Relationship between compliance in the foot-in-the-door paradigm and size of first request. *Journal of Personality and Social Psychology, 33*, 517–520.

SELYE, H. (1956). *The stress of life*. McGraw-Hill.

SELYE, H. (1976). *Stress in health and disease*. Woburn, MA: Butterworth.

SELZNICK, G. J., & STEINBERG, S. (1969). *The tenacity of prejudice: Anti-semitism in contemporary America*. New York: Harper & Row.

SHAKIN, M., SHAKIN, D., & STERNGLANZ, S. H. (1985). Infant clothing: Sex labeling for strangers. *Sex Roles, 12*(9/10), 955–964.

SHANTEAU, J., & NAGY, G. F. (1979). Probability of acceptance in dating choice. *Journal of Personality and Social Psychology, 37*, 522–533.

SHAPIRO, R. Y., & MAHAJAN, H. (1986). Gender differences in policy preferences: A summary of trends from the 1960s to the 1980s. *Public Opinion Quarterly, 50*, 42–61.

SHAVER, P. (1986, August 26). Being lonely, falling in love: Perspectives from attachment theory. Invited address presented at the annual meeting of the American Psychological Association, Washington, D.C.

SHAVER, P., & FREEDMAN, J. L. (1976, August). Happiness. *Psychology Today*.

SHAVER, P., HAZAN, C., & BRADSHAW, D. (In press). Love as attachment: The integration of three behavioral systems. In R. J. Sternberg & M. Barnes (Eds.), *Anatomy of love*. New Haven, CT: Yale University Press.

SHAVER, P., & KLINNERT, M. D. (1982). Schachter's theories of affiliation and emotion: Implications of developmental research. In L. Wheeler (Ed.), *Review of personality and social psychology* (Vol. 3). Beverly Hills, CA: Sage.

SHAVER, P., & RUBENSTEIN, C. (1980). Childhood attachment experience and adult loneliness. In L. Wheeler (Ed.), *Review of personality and social psychology* (Vol. 1, pp. 42–73). Beverly Hills, CA: Sage.

SHAVER, P., SCHWARTZ, J. C., KIRSON, D., & O'CONNOR, C. (In press). Emotion knowledge: Further exploration of a prototype approach. *Journal of Personality and Social Psychology*.

SHAW, M. E. (1981). *Group dynamics: The psychology of small group behavior*, 3rd ed. New York: McGraw-Hill.

SHEA, J. D. C. (1981). Changes in interpersonal distances and categories of play behavior in the early weeks of preschool. *Developmental Psychology, 17*, 417–425.

SHEATSLEY, P. B., & FELDMAN, J. J. (1965). A national survey of public reactions and behavior. In B. S. Greenberg & E. B. Parker (Eds.), *The Kennedy assassination and the American public* (pp. 149–177). Stanford, CA: Stanford University Press.

SHERIF, M. (1935). An experimental study of stereotypes. *Journal of Abnormal and Social Psychology, 29*, 371–375.

SHERMAN, S. J., CHASSIN, L., PRESSON, C. C., & AGOSTINELLI, G. (1984). The role of the evaluation and similarity principles in the false consensus effect. *Journal of Personality and Social Psychology, 47*, 1244–1262.

SHERMAN, S. J., PRESSON, C. C., & CHASSIN, L. (1984). Mechanisms underlying the false consensus effect: The special role of threats to the self. *Personality and Social Psychology Bulletin, 10*, 127–138.

SHERMAN, S. J., PRESSON, C. C., CHASSIN, L., BESENBERG, M., CORTY, E., & OLSHAVSKY, R. W. (1982). Smoking intentions in adolescents: Direct experience and predictability. *Personality and Social Psychology Bulletin, 8*, 376–383.

SHERMAN, S. J., PRESSON, C. C., CHASSIN, L., CORTY, E., & OLSHAVSKY, R. (1983). The false consensus effect in estimates of smoking prevalence: Underlying mechanisms. *Personality and Social Psychology Bulletin, 9*, 197–208.

SHERROD, D. R. (1974). Crowding, perceived control and behavioral aftereffects. *Journal of Applied Social Psychology, 4*, 171–186.

SHERROD, D. R., & DOWNS, R. (1974). Environmental determinants of altruism: The effects of stimulus overload and perceived control on helping. *Journal of Experimental Social Psychology, 10*, 468–479.

SHERROD, D. R., HAGE, J. N., HALPERN, P. L., & MOORE, B. S. (1977). Effects of personal causation and perceived control on responses to an aversive environment: The more control, the better. *Journal of Experimental Social Psychology, 13,* 14–27.

SHIFFRIN, R. M., & SCHNEIDER, W. (1977). Controlled and automatic human information processing: II. Perceptual learning, automatic attending, and a general theory. *Psychological Review, 84,* 127–190.

SHINAR, E. H. (1975). Sexual stereotypes of occupations. *Journal of Vocational Behavior, 7,* 99–110.

SHOTLAND, R. L., & HEINOLD, W. D. (1985). Bystander response to arterial bleeding: Helping skills, the decision-making process, and differentiating the helping response. *Journal of Personality and Social Psychology, 49(2),* 347–356.

SHOTLAND, R. L., & HUSTON, T. L. (1979). Emergencies: What are they and do they influence bystanders to intervene? *Journal of Personality and Social Psychology, 37(10),* 1822–1834.

SHOTLAND, R. L., & STRAW, M. K. (1976). Bystander response to an assault: When a man attacks a woman. *Journal of Personality and Social Psychology, 34,* 990–999.

SHWEDER, R. A. (Ed.). (1980). Fallible judgement in behavioral research. In *New directions for methodology of social and behavioral science* (Vol. 4). San Francisco: Jossey-Bass.

SIDOROWICZ, L. S., & LUNNEY, G. S. (1980). Baby X revisited. *Sex Roles, 6(1),* 67–74.

SIEBENALER, J. B., & CALDWELL, D. K. (1956). Cooperation among adult dolphins. *Journal of Mammology, 37,* 126–128.

SIEGEL, J. M. (1986). The multidimensional anger inventory. *Journal of Personality and Social Psychology, 51,* 191–200.

SIGALL, H., & OSTROVE, N. (1975). Beautiful but dangerous: Effects of offender attractiveness and nature of the crime on juridic judgment. *Journal of Personality and Social Psychology, 31,* 410–414.

SILVER, R. L. (1982). *Coping with an undesirable life event: A study of early reactions to physical disability.* Unpublished doctoral dissertation. Northwestern University, Evanston, IL.

SILVER, R. L., & WORTMAN, C. B. (1980). Coping with undesirable life events. In J. Garber & M. E. P. Seligman (Eds.), *Human helplessness: Theory and applications.* New York: Academic Press.

SILVERMAN, I. (1971, September). Physical attractiveness and courtship. *Sexual Behavior,* 22–25.

SIMMEL, G. (1903). *Sociology of Georg Simmel.* New York: Macmillan, 1950. Translation of German edition.

SIMONTON, D. K. (1981). Presidential greatness and performance: Can we predict leadership in the White House? *Journal of Personality, 49,* 306–323.

SIMONTON, D. K. (1985). The vice-presidential succes-

sion effect: Individual or situational basis? *Political Behavior, 7,* 79–99.

SIMONTON, D. K. (1986a). Presidential greatness: The historical consensus and its psychological significance. *Political Psychology, 7,* 259–284.

SIMONTON, D. K. (1986b). Presidential personality: Biographical use of the Gough adjective check list. *Journal of Personality and Social Psychology, 51,* 149–160.

SIMPSON, J. A., CAMPBELL, B., & BERSCHEID, E. (1986). The association between romantic love and marriage: Kephart (1967) twice revisited. *Personality and Social Psychology Bulletin, 12(3),* 363–372.

SINGER, J. E., BRUSH, C., & LUBLIN, S. D. (1965). Some aspects of deindividuation: Identification and conformity. *Journal of Experimental Social Psychology, 1,* 356–378.

SINGER, J. L., SINGER, D. G., & RAPACZYNSKI, W. (1984). Family patterns and television viewing as predictors of children's beliefs and aggression. *Journal of Communication, 34,* 73–89.

SIVACEK, J., & CRANO, W. D. (1982). Vested interest as a moderator of attitude-behavior consistency. *Journal of Personality and Social Psychology, 43,* 210–221.

SKOLNICK, P. (1977). Helping as a function of time of day, location, and sex of victim. *Journal of Social Psychology, 102,* 61–62.

SKRYPNEK, B. J., & SNYDER, M. (1982). On the self-perpetuating nature of stereotypes about women and men. *Journal of Experimental Social Psychology, 18,* 277–291.

SLIVKEN, K. E., & BUSS, A. H. (1984). Misattribution and speech anxiety. *Journal of Personality and Social Psychology, 47,* 396–402.

SLOCHOWER, J., WEIN, L., WHITE, J., FIRSTENBERG, S., & DIGUILIO, J. (1980). Severe physical handicaps and helping behavior. *Journal of Social Psychology, 112,* 313–314.

SMITH, E. R., & LERNER, M. (1986). Development of automatism of social judgments. *Journal of Personality and Social Psychology, 50,* 246–259.

SMITH, P. K., & CONNELLY, K. (1972). Patterns of play and social interaction in preschool children. In N. B. Jones (Ed.), *Ethological studies of child behavior.* Cambridge, Eng.: Cambridge University Press.

SMITH, S., & HAYTHORN, W. H. (1972). Effects of compatibility, crowding, group size, and leadership seniority on stress, anxiety, hostility and annoyance in isolated groups. *Journal of Personality and Social Psychology, 22,* 67–79.

SMITH, S., & JAMIESON, B. D. (1972). Effects of attitude and ego involvement on the learning and retention of controversial material. *Journal of Personality and Social Psychology, 22*, 303–310.

SMITH, S. S., & RICHARDSON, D. (1983). Amelioration of deception and harm in psychological research: The important role of debriefing. *Journal of Personality and Social Psychology, 44*, 1075–1082.

SMITH, T. W. (1984). The polls: Gender and attitudes toward violence. *Public Opinion Quarterly, 48*, 384–396.

SNIDERMAN, P. M. (1975). *Personality and democratic politics*. Berkeley: University of California Press.

SNIDERMAN, P. M., & BRODY, R. A. (1977). Coping: The ethic of self-reliance. *American Journal of Political Science, 21*, 501–522.

SNYDER, C. R., LASSEGARD, M. A., & FORD, C. E. (1986). Distancing after group success and failure: Basking in reflected glory and cutting off reflected failure. *Journal of Personality and Social Psychology, 51*(2), 382–388.

SNYDER, C. R., SMITH, T. W., AUGELLI, R. W., & INGRAM, R. E. (1985). On the self-serving function of social anxiety: Shyness as a self-handicapping strategy. *Journal of Personality and Social Psychology, 48*, 970–980.

SNYDER, M., BERSCHEID, E., & GLICK, P. (1985). Focusing on the exterior and the interior: Two investigations of the initiation of personal relationships. *Journal of Personality and Social Psychology, 48*(6), 1427–1439.

SNYDER, M., & SWANN, W. B., JR. (1976). When actions reflect attitudes: The politics of impression management. *Journal of Personality and Social Psychology, 34*, 1034–1042.

SNYDER, M., & SWANN, W. B., JR. (1978). Hypothesis-testing processes in social interaction. *Journal of Personality and Social Psychology, 36*, 1202–1212.

SNYDER, M., TANKE, E. D., & BERSCHEID, E. (1977). Social perception and interpersonal behavior: On the self-fulfilling nature of social stereotypes. *Journal of Personality and Social Psychology, 35*, 656–666.

SNYDER, M. L., & JONES, E. E. (1974). Attitude attribution when behavior is constrained. *Journal of Experimental Social Psychology, 10*, 585–600.

SNYDER, M. L., STEPHAN, W. G., & ROSENFIELD, D. (1976). Egotism and attribution. *Journal of Personality and Social Psychology, 33*, 435–441.

SNYDER, R. L. (1968). Reproduction and population pressures. In E. Steller & J. M. Sprague (Eds.), *Progress in physiological psychology*. New York: Academic Press.

SOGIN, S. R., & PALLAK, M. S. (1976). Bad decisions, responsibility, and attitude change: Effects of volition, foreseeability, and locus of causality of negative consequences. *Journal of Personality and Social Psychology, 33*, 300–306.

SOLANO, C. H., BATTEN, P. G., & PARISH, E. A. (1982). Loneliness and patterns of self-disclosure. *Journal of Personality and Social Psychology, 43*, 524–531.

SOLOMON, L. Z., SOLOMON, H., & STONE, R. (1978). Helping as a function of number of bystanders and ambiguity of emergency. *Personality and Social Psychology Bulletin, 4*(2), 318–321.

SOMMER, R. (1969). *Personal space: The behavioral basis of design*. Englewood Cliffs, NJ: Prentice-Hall.

SOMMER, R., & OLSEN, H. (1980). The soft classroom. *Environment and Behavior, 12*(1), 3–16.

SORRELS, J. P., & KELLEY, J. (1984). Conformity by omission. *Personality and Social Psychology Bulletin, 10*(2), 302–305.

SOUTHWICK, C. H. (1955). The population dynamics of confined house mice supplied with unlimited food. *Ecology, 36*, 212–215.

SPEARS, R., VAN DER PLIGHT, J., & EISER, J. R. (1985). Illusory correlation in the perception of group attitudes. *Journal of Personality and Social Psychology, 48*, 863–875.

SPEISMAN, J., LAZARUS, R. S., MORDKOFF, A., & DAVIDSON, L. (1964). Experimental reduction of stress based on ego defense theory. *Journal of Abnormal and Social Psychology, 68*, 367–380.

SPENCE, J. T., & HELMREICH, R. L. (1978). *Masculinity and femininity: The psychological dimensions, correlates, and antecedents*. Austin: University of Texas Press.

SPENCE, J. T., & HELMREICH, R. L. (1980). Masculine instrumentality and feminine expressiveness: Their relationships with sex role attitudes and behaviors. *Psychology of Women Quarterly, 5*(2), 147–163.

SPRAFKIN, J. N., LIEBERT, R. M., & POULOS, R. W. (1975). Effects of a prosocial televised example on children's helping. *Journal of Experimental Child Psychology, 20*, 119–126.

SROLE, L. (1972). Urbanization and mental health: Some reformulations. *American Scientist, 60*, 576–583.

SRULL, T. K., & WYER, R. S., JR. (1979). The role of category accessibility in the interpretation of information about persons: Some determinants and implications. *Journal of Personality and Social Psychology, 37*, 1660–1672.

STAGNER, R. (1967). *Psychological aspects of international conflict*. Belmont, CA: Brooks/Cole Publishing Co.

STAHL, S. M. (1982). Illness as an emergent norm or doing what comes naturally. In M. J. Colligan, J. W. Pennebaker, & L. R. Murphy (Eds.), *Mass psycho-*

genic illness: *A social psychological analysis* (pp. 183–198). Hillsdale, NJ: Erlbaum.

STASSER, G., & TITUS, W. (1985). Pooling of unshared information in group decision making: Biased information sampling during discussion. *Journal of Personality and Social Psychology, 48*(6), 1467–1478.

STECK, L., LEVITAN, D., MCLANE, D., & KELLEY, H. H. (1982). Care, need, and conceptions of love. *Journal of Personality and Social Psychology, 43*, 481–491.

STEELE, C. M., & SOUTHWICK, L. (1985). Alcohol and social behavior I: The psychology of drunken excess. *Journal of Personality and Social Psychology, 48*, 18–34.

STEIN, A. H., & FRIEDRICH, L. K. (1972). Television content and young children's behavior. In J. P. Murray, E. A. Rubinstein, & G. A. Comstock (Eds.), *Television and social behavior: Vol. 2. Television and social learning*. Washington, DC: U.S. Government Printing Office.

STEINEM, G. (1980). Erotica and pornography: A clear and present difference. In L. Lederer (Ed.), *Take back the night: Women on pornography*. New York: Morrow.

STEINER, I. D. (1972). *Group process and productivity*. New York: Academic Press.

STEMBER, C. H. (1966). The recent history of public attitudes. In C. H. Stember et al. (Eds.), *Jews in the mind of America*. New York: Basic Books.

STEPHAN, F. F., & MISHLER, E. G. (1952). The distribution of participation in small groups: An exponential approximation. *American Sociological Review, 17*, 598–608.

STEPHAN, W. G. (1985). Intergroup relations. In G. Lindzey & E. Aronson (Eds.), *Handbook of social psychology*, 3rd ed. (Vol. 2, pp. 599–658). New York: Random House.

STEPHAN, W. G., & ROSENFIELD, D. (1978). Effects of desegregation on racial attitudes. *Journal of Personality and Social Psychology, 36*, 795–804.

STERNBERG, R. J. (1986). A triangular theory of love. *Psychological Review, 93*, 119–135.

STERNBERG, R. J., CONWAY, B. E., KETRON, J. L., & BERNSTEIN, M. (1981). People's conceptions of intelligence. *Journal of Personality and Social Psychology, 41*, 37–55.

STEWART, L. H. (1977). Birth order and political leadership. In M. G. Hermann (Ed.), *A psychological examination of political leaders* (pp. 205–236). New York: Free Press.

STOKES, D. E., & MILLER, W. E. (1962). Party government and the saliency of Congress. *Public Opinion Quarterly, 26*, 531–546.

STOKOLS, D. & ALTMAN, I. (Eds.). (1987). *Handbook of environmental psychology*. New York: Wiley.

STOKOLS, D., RALL, M., PINNER, B., & SCHOPLER, J. (1973). Physical, social, and personal determinants of the perception of crowding. *Environment and Behavior, 5*, 87–115.

STONE, W. F., & SMITH, D. C. (1983). Human nature in politics: Graham Wallas and the Fabians. *Political Psychology, 4*, 693–712.

STORMS, M. D. (1973). Videotape and the attribution process: Reversing actors' and observers' points of view. *Journal of Personality and Social Psychology, 27*, 165–175.

STORMS, M. D., & NISBETT, R. E. (1970). Insomnia and the attribution process. *Journal of Personality and Social Psychology, 16*, 319–328.

STOUFFER, S. A. (1955). *Communism, conformity, and civil liberties*. New York: Doubleday.

STOUFFER, S. A., SUCHMAN, E. A., DeVINNEY, L. C., STAR, S. A., & Williams, R. M., Jr. (1949). *The American soldier: Adjustment during army life*. New York: Wiley.

Straus, M. A., Gelles, R. J., & Steinmetz, S. K. (1981). *Behind closed doors: Violence in the American family*. Garden City, NY: Doubleday Anchor Books.

STRAYER, F. F., WAREING, S., & RUSHTON, J. P. (1979). Social constraints on naturally occurring preschool altruism. *Ethology and Sociobiology, 1*, 3–11.

STRUBE, M. J., TURNER, C. W., CERRO, D., STEVENS, J., & HINCHEY, F. (1984). Interpersonal aggression and the type A coronary-prone behavior pattern: A theoretical distinction and practical implications. *Journal of Personality and Social Psychology, 47*, 839–847.

STRYKER, S., & STATHAM, A. (1985). Symbolic interaction and role theory. In G. Lindzey & E. Aronson (Eds.), *Handbook of social psychology*, 3rd ed. (Vol. 1, pp. 311–378). New York: Random House.

SUCHMAN, E. (1964). Sociomedical variations among ethnic groups. *American Journal of Sociology, 70*, 319–331.

SUEDFELD, P. (1982). Aloneness as a healing experience. In L. A. Peplau & D. Perlman (Eds.), *Loneliness: A sourcebook of current theory, research and therapy* (pp. 54–69). New York: Wiley-Interscience.

SUINN, R. M., & BLOOM, L. J. (1978). Anxiety management training for pattern A behavior. *Journal of Behavioral Medicine, 1*, 25–36.

SULLIVAN, J. L., PIERESON, J. E., & MARCUS, G. E. (1978). Ideological constraint in the mass public: A methodological critique and some new findings. *American Journal of Political Science, 22*, 233–249.

SULS, J. (1982). Social support, interpersonal relations, and health: Benefits and liabilities. In G. S.

Sanders & J. Suls (Eds.), *Social psychology of health and illness* (pp. 255–273). Hillsdale, NJ: Erlbaum.

SULS, J., & FLETCHER, B. (1985). The relative efficacy of avoidant and nonavoidant coping strategies: A Meta-analysis. *Health Psychology, 4,* 249–288.

SUNDSTROM, E., & SUNDSTROM, M. G. (1977). Personal space invasions: What happens when the invader asks permission? *Environmental Psychology and Nonverbal Behavior, 2,* 76–82.

SURGEON GENERAL'S SCIENTIFIC ADVISORY COMMITTEE. (1972). *Television and growing up: The impact of televised violence: Report to the Surgeon General.* U.S. Public Health Service, Dept. of Health, Education, and Welfare Publication N. HSM 72–9090. Rockville, MD: National Institute of Mental Health.

SWANN, W. B., JR., & ELY, R. J. (1984). A battle of wills: Self-verification versus behavioral confirmation. *Journal of Personality and Social Psychology, 46,* 1287–1302.

SWANN, W. B., JR., & STEPHENSON, B. (1981). Curiosity and control: On the determinants of the search for social knowledge. *Journal of Personality and Social Psychology, 40,* 635–642.

SWEENEY, P. D., ANDERSON, K., & BAILEY, S. (1986). Attributional style in depression: A meta-analytic review. *Journal of Personality and Social Psychology, 50,* 974–991.

SWENSON, C. H. (1972). The behavior of love. In H. A. Otto (Ed.), *Love today* (pp. 86–101). New York: Dell.

SYMONS, D. (1979). *The evolution of human sexuality.* New York: Oxford University Press.

TAGLIACOZZO, D. L., & MAUKSCH, H. O. (1972). The patient's view of the patient's role. In E. G. Jaco (Ed.), *Patients, physicians, and illness,* 2nd ed. (pp. 185–201). New York: Free Press.

TAJFEL, H. (Ed.). (1982). *Social identity and intergroup relations.* Cambridge, MA: Cambridge University Press.

TAJFEL, H., BILLIG, M. G., BUNDY, R. P., & FLAMENT, C. (1971). Social categorization and intergroup behavior. *European Journal of Social Psychology, 1,* 149–178.

TAJFEL, H., & TURNER, J. C. (1986). The social identity theory of intergroup behavior. In S. Worchel & W. G. Austin (Eds.), *Psychology of Intergroup Relations* (pp. 7–24). Chicago: Nelson-Hall Publishers.

TANFORD, S., & PENROD, S. (1984). Social influence model: A formal integration of research on majority and minority influence processes. *Psychological Bulletin, 95,* 189–225.

TARDE, G. (1903). *The laws of imitation.* New York: Holt, Rinehart & Winston.

TAYLOR, D. G., SHEATSLEY, P. B., & GREELEY, A. M. (1978). Attitudes toward racial integration. *Scientific American, 238,* 42–49.

TAYLOR, D. W., BERRY, P. C., & BLOCK, C. H. (1958). Does group participation when using brainstorming facilitate or inhibit creative thinking? *Administrative Science Quarterly, 2,* 23–47.

TAYLOR, S., VARDARIS, R., RAWITCH, A., GAMMON, C., CRANSTON, J., & LUBETKIN, A. (1976). The effects of alcohol and delta-9-tetrahydrocannabinol on human physical aggression. *Aggressive Behavior, 2,* 153–161.

TAYLOR, S. E. (1975). On inferring one's attitudes from one's behavior: Some delimiting conditions. *Journal of Personality and Social Psychology, 31,* 126–131.

TAYLOR, S. E. (1979). Hospital patient behavior: Reactance, helplessness, or control? *Journal of Social Issues, 35*(1) 156–184.

TAYLOR, S. E. (1981a). The interface of cognitive and social psychology. In J. H. Harvey (Ed.), *Cognition, social behavior, and the environment* (pp. 189–212). Hillsdale, NJ: Erlbaum.

TAYLOR, S. E. (1981b). A categorization approach to stereotyping. In D. L. Hamilton (Ed.), *Cognitive processes in stereotyping and intergroup behavior* (pp. 83–114). Hillsdale, NJ: Erlbaum.

TAYLOR, S. E. (1981c). The impact of health institutions on recipients of services. In A. Johnson, O. Grusky, & B. Raven (Eds.), *Contemporary health services: A social science perspective.* Boston: Auburn House.

TAYLOR, S. E. (1982). Social cognition and health. *Personality and Social Psychology Bulletin, 8*(3), 549–562.

TAYLOR, S. E. (1983). Adjustment to threatening events: A theory of cognitive adaptation. *American Psychologist, 38,* 1161–1173.

TAYLOR, S. E., & CLARK, L. F. (1986). Does information improve adjustment to noxious events? In M. J. Saks & L. Saxe (Eds.), *Advances in applied social psychology* (Vol. 3, pp. 1–28). Hillsdale, NJ: Erlbaum.

TAYLOR, S. E., & CROCKER, J. (1981). Schematic bases of social information processing. In E. T. Higgins, C. P. Herman, & M. P. Zanna (Eds.), *Social cognition: The Ontario symposium* (Vol. 1). Hillsdale, NJ: Erlbaum.

TAYLOR, S. E., CROCKER, J., FISKE, S. T., SPRINZEN, M., & WINKLER, J. D. (1979). The generalizability of salience effects. *Journal of Personality and Social Psychology, 37,* 357–368.

TAYLOR, S. E., & FISKE, S. T. (1975). Point of view and perceptions of causality. *Journal of Personality and Social Psychology, 32,* 439–445.

TAYLOR, S. E., & FISKE, S. T. (1978). Salience, attention, and attribution: Top of the head phenomena. In L. Berkowitz (Ed.), *Advances in experimental social psychology* (Vol 11, pp. 249–288). New York: Academic Press.

TAYLOR, S. E., FISKE, S. T., CLOSE, M., ANDERSON, C., & RUDERMAN, A. (1977). *Solo status as a psychological variable: The power of being distinctive.* Unpublished manuscript, Harvard University.

TAYLOR, S. E., FISKE, S. T., ETCOFF, N. L., & RUDERMAN, A. J. (1978). Categorical and contextual bases of person memory and stereotyping. *Journal of Personality and Social Psychology, 36,* 778–793.

TAYLOR, S. E., LICHTMAN, R. R., & WOOD, J. V. (1984). Attributions, beliefs about control, and adjustment to breast cancer. *Journal of Personality and Social Psychology, 46,* 489–502.

TAYLOR, S. E., & THOMPSON, S. C. (1982). Stalking the elusive "vividness" effect. *Psychological Review, 89,* 155–181.

TAYLOR, S. P., & GAMMON, C. B. (1975). Effects of type and dose of alcohol on human physical aggression. *Journal of Personality and Social Psychology, 32,* 169–175.

TAYNOR, J., & DEAUX, K. (1973). When women are more deserving than men: Equity, attribution and perceived sex difference. *Journal of Personality and Social Psychology, 28,* 360–367.

TAYNOR, J., & DEAUX, K. (1975). Equity and perceived sex differences: Role of behavior as defined by the task, the mode and the action. *Journal of Personality and Social Psychology, 32,* 381–390.

TEDIN, K. L. (1974). The influence of parents on the political attitudes of adolescents. *American Political Science Review, 68,* 1579–1592.

TELCH, M. J., KILLEN, J. D., McALISTER, A. L., PERRY, C. L., & MACCOBY, N. (1982). Long-term follow-up of a pilot project on smoking prevention with adolescents. *Journal of Behavioral Medicine, 5,* 1–8.

TENNEN, H., AFFLECK, G., & GERSHAM, K. (1986). Self-blame among parents of infants with perinatal complications: The role of self-protective motives. *Journal of Personality and Social Psychology, 50,* 690–696.

TERMAN, C. R. (1974). Behavioral factors associated with cessation of growth of laboratory populations of prairie deermice. *Research in Population Ecology, 15,* 138–147.

TESSER, A., & CONLEE, M. C. (1975). Some effects of time and thought on attitude polarization. *Journal of Personality and Social Psychology, 31,* 262–270.

TESSLER, R. C., & SCHWARTZ, S. H. (1972). Help-seeking, self-esteem, and achievement motivation: An attributional analysis. *Journal of Personality and Social Psychology, 27,* 318–326.

TESSOR, A. (1978). Self-generated attitude change. In L. Berkowitz (Ed.), *Advances in experimental social psychology* (Vol. 11). New York: Academic Press.

TETLOCK, P. E. (1983). Policymakers' images of international conflict. *Journal of Social Issues, 39,* 67–86.

TETLOCK, P. E. (1984). Cognitive style and political belief systems in the British House of Commons. *Journal of Personality and Social Psychology, 46,* 365–375.

TETLOCK, P. E., BERNZWEIG, J., & GALLANT, J. L. (1985). Supreme court decision making: Cognitive style as a predictor of ideological consistency of voting. *Journal of Personality and Social Psychology, 48,* 1227–1239.

TETLOCK, P. E., HANNUM, K. A., & MICHELETTI, P. M. (1984). Stability and change in the complexity of senatorial debate: Testing the cognitive versus rhetorical style hypotheses. *Journal of Personality and Social Psychology, 46,* 979–990.

THIBAUT, J. W., & KELLEY, H. H. (1959). *The social psychology of groups.* New York: Wiley.

THOMAS, M. H., HORTON, R. W., LIPPINCOTT, E. C., & DRABMAN, R. S. (1977). Desensitization of portrayals of real-life aggression as a function of exposure to television violence. *Journal of Personality and Social Psychology, 35,* 450–458.

THOMPSON, S. C. (1981). Will it hurt less if I can control it? A complex answer to a simple question. *Psychological Bulletin, 90,* 89–101.

THOMPSON, S. C., & KELLEY, H. H. (1981). Judgments of responsibility for activities in close relationships. *Journal of Personality and Social Psychology, 41,* 469–477.

THOMPSON, W. C., COWAN, C. L., & ROSENHAN, D. L. (1980). Focus of attention mediates the impact of negative affect on altruism. *Journal of Personality and Social Psychology, 38,* 291–300.

THORESEN, C. E., & MAHONEY, M. J. (1974). *Behavioral self-control.* New York: Holt.

TILKER, H. A. (1970). Socially responsible behavior as a function of observer responsibility and victim feedback. *Journal of Personality and Social Psychology, 14,* 95–100.

TO, L. P., & TAMARIN, R. H. (1977). The relation of population density and adrenal gland weight in cycling and noncycling voles (Microtus). *Ecology, 58,* 928–934.

TOI, M., & BATSON, C. D. (1982). More evidence that empathy is a source of altruistic motivation. *Journal of Personality and Social Psychology, 43,* 281–292.

TORIS, C., & DePAULO, B. M. (1984). Effects of actual deception and suspiciousness of deception on interpersonal perceptions. *Journal of Personality and Social Psychology, 47,* 1063–1073.

TRIVERS, R. L. (1971). The evolution of reciprocal altruism. *Quarterly Review of Biology, 46,* 35–57.

TRZEBINSKI, J., McGLYNN, R. P., GRAY, G., & TUBBS, D.

(1985). The role of categories of an actor's goals in organizing inferences about a person. *Journal of Personality and Social Psychology, 48,* 1387–1397.

TUCKER, L., HORNSTEIN, H. A., HOLLOWAY, S., & SOLE K. (1977). The effects of temptation and information about a stranger on helping. *Personality and Social Psychology Bulletin, 3*(3), 416–421.

TUCKER, M. B. (1986). Sex ratio imbalance among Los Angeles Afro-Americans. *ISSR Working Papers in the Social Sciences, 2*(4). Los Angeles: Institute for Social Science Research, University of California.

TURK, D. C., & KERNS, R. D. (1985). *Health, illness, and families: A life-span perspective.* New York: Wiley.

TURK, D. C., RUDY, T. E., & SALOVEY, P. (1986). Implicit models of illness. *Journal of Behavioral Medicine, 9,* 453–474.

TURNER, C. W., HESSE, B. W., & PETERSON-LEWIS, S. (1986). Naturalistic studies of the long-term effects of television violence. *Journal of Social Issues, 42,* 51–74.

TURNER, J. C. (1985). Social categorization and the self-concept: A social cognitive theory of group behavior. In J. E. Lawler (Ed.), *Advances in group processes* (Vol. 2, pp. 77–122). Greenwich, CT: JAI Press.

TURNER, R. H. (1962). Role-taking: Process versus conformity. In A. H. Rose (Ed.), *Human behavior and social processes: An interactionist approach.* Boston: Houghton Mifflin.

TVERSKY, A., & KAHNEMAN, D. (1973). Availability: A heuristic for judging frequency and probability. *Cognitive Psychology, 5,* 207–232.

TVERSKY, A., & KAHNEMAN, D. (1974). Judgment under uncertainty: Heuristics and biases. *Science, 185,* 1124–1131.

TYBOUT, A. M. & SCOTT, C. A. (1983). Availability of well-defined internal knowledge and the attitude formation process: Information aggregation versus self-perception. *Journal of Personality and Social Psychology, 44*(3), 474–91.

TYLER, T. R., & DEVINTZ, V. (1981). Self-serving bias in the attribution of responsibility: Cognitive versus motivational explanations. *Journal of Experimental Social Psychology, 17,* 408–416.

TYLER, T. R., RASINSKI, K. A., & GRIFFIN, E. (1986). Alternative images of the citizen: Implications for public policy. *American Psychologist, 41,* 970–978.

TYLER, T. R., & SEARS, D. O. (1977). Coming to like obnoxious people when we must live with them. *Journal of Personality and Social Psychology, 35,* 200–211.

UGWUEGBU, D. C. E. (1979). Racial and evidential factors in juror attribution of legal responsibility. *Journal of Experimental Social Psychology, 15,* 133–146.

ULMAN, R. B., ABSE, D. W. (1983). The group psychology of mass madness: Jonestown. *Political Psychology, 4,* 637–661.

U.S. BUREAU OF THE CENSUS. (1973). *Annual housing survey: 1973 U.S. and regions: Part B, indicators of housing and neighborhood quality.* Current Housing Report Series H-150–73-B. Washington, DC: U.S. Government Printing Office.

U.S. DEPARTMENT OF HEALTH, EDUCATION AND WELFARE, PUBLIC HEALTH SERVICE, CENTER FOR DISEASE CONTROL (1964). *Smoking and health: Report of the advisory committee to the Surgeon General of the Public Health Service.* (Publication No. PHS1103.) Washington, D.C.: U.S. Government Printing Office.

VALINS, S. (1966). Cognitive effects of false heart-rate feedback. *Journal of Personality and Social Psychology, 4,* 400–408.

VALINS, S., & RAY, A. A. (1967). Effects of cognitive desensitization on avoidance behavior. *Journal of Personality and Social Psychology, 7,* 345–350.

VANNEMAN, R. D., & PETTIGREW, T. F. (1972). Race and relative deprivation in the urban United States. *Race, 13,* 461–486.

VARTIANEN, E., PALLONEN, U., MCALISTER, A., KOSKELA, K., & PUSKA, P. (1983). Effect of two years of educational intervention on adolescent smoking (The North Karelia project). *Bulletin of the World Health Organization, 61,* 529–532.

VINOKUR, A., & SELZER, M. (1975). Desirable versus undesirable life events: Their relationship to stress and mental distress. *Journal of Personality and Social Psychology, 32,* 329–337.

VINSEL, A., BROWN, B. B., ALTMAN, I., & FOSS, C. (1980). Privacy regulation, territorial displays, and effective individual functioning. *Journal of Personality and Social Psychology, 39*(6), 1104–1115.

VON BAEYER, C. L., SHERK, D. L., & ZANNA, M. P. (1981). Impression management in the job interview: When the female applicant meets the male (chauvinist) interviewer. *Personality and Social Psychology Bulletin, 7*(1), 45–52.

WAGNER, E. (1984). Recognition of own and others' utterances in a natural conversation. *Personality and Social Psychology Bulletin, 10,* 596–604.

WAGNER, H. L., MacDONALD, C. J., & MANSTEAD, A. S. R. (1986). Communication of individual emotions by spontaneous facial expressions. *Journal of Personality and Social Psychology, 50,* 737–743.

WALL, J. A., JR. (1977). Operantly conditioning a negotiator's concession making. *Journal of Experimental Social Psychology, 13,* 431–440.

WALLAS, G. (1921). *Human nature in politics.* New York: Knopf. Originally published in 1908.

WALLBOTT, H. G., & SCHERER, K. R. (1986). Cues and channels in emotion recognition. *Journal of Personality and Social Psychology, 51*, 690–699.

WALLER, W. (1938). *The family: A dynamic interpretation*. New York: Dryden Press.

WALLERSTEIN, J. S., & KELLY, J. B. (1975). The effects of parental divorce: Experiences of the preschool child. *Journal of the America Academy of Child Psychiatry, 14*, 600–616.

WALLSTON, B. S., ALGANA, S. W., DEVELLIS, B. McE., & DEVELLIS, R. F. (1983). Social support and physical health. *Health Psychology, 2*, 367–391.

WALSH, J. (1983). ABC objections to linkage of aggression to TV violence in NIMH report brings social scientists into contention in novel public skirmish. *Science, 220*, 804–805.

WALSTER, E., ARONSON, E., & ABRAHAMS, D. (1966). On increasing the persuasiveness of a low-prestige communicator. *Journal of Experimental Social Psychology, 2*, 325–343.

WALSTER, E., ARONSON, E., ABRAHAMS, D., & ROTTMAN, L. (1966). Importance of physical attractiveness in dating behavior. *Journal of Personality and Social Psychology, 4*, 508–516.

WALSTER, E., & WALSTER, G. W. (1963). Effects of expecting to be liked on choice of associates. *Journal of Abnormal and Social Psychology, 67*, 402–404.

WALSTER, E., & WALSTER, G. W. (1978). *A new look at love*. Reading, MA: Addison-Wesley.

WALSTER, E., & WALSTER, G. W., & BERSCHEID, E. (1978). *Equity: Theory and research*. Boston: Allyn & Bacon.

WALSTER, E., & WALSTER, G. W., & TRAUPMANN, J. (1978). Equity and premarital sex. *Journal of Personality and Social Psychology, 36*, 82–92.

WARE, J. E., JR., DAVIES-AVERY, A., & STEWART, A. L. (1978). The measurement and meaning of patient satisfaction: A review of the literature. *The Health and Medical Care Services Review, 1*, 1–15.

WATKINS, M. (1978, January 9). Why N.B.A. teams succeed at home. *The New York Times*, p. C23.

WATSON, D. (1982). The actor and the observer: How are their perceptions of causality different? *Psychological Bulletin, 92*, 682–700.

WATSON, R. I., JR. (1973). Investigation into deindividuation using a cross-cultural survey technique. *Journal of Personality and Social Psychology, 25*, 342–345.

WATTENBERG, M. P. (1982). From parties to candidates: Examining the role of the media. *Public Opinion Quarterly, 46*, 216–227.

WATTENBERG, M. P. (1984). *The decline of American political parties, 1952–1980*. Cambridge, MA: Harvard University Press.

WATTS, W. A., & HOLT, L. E. (1979). Persistence of opinion change induced under conditions of forewarning and distraction. *Journal of Personality and Social Psychology, 37*, 778–789.

WEARY, G., JORDAN, J. S., & HILL, M. G. (1985). The attributional norm of internality and depressive sensitivity to social information. *Journal of Personality and Social Psychology, 49*, 1283–1293.

WEBB, B., WORCHEL, S., RIECHERS, L., & WAYNE, W. (1986). The influence of categorization on perceptions of crowding. *Personality and Social Psychology Bulletin, 12*(4), 539–546.

WEBER, R., & CROCKER, J. (1983). Cognitive process in the revision of stereotypic beliefs. *Journal of Personality and Social Psychology, 45*, 961–977.

WEBER, S. J., & COOK, T. D. (1972). Subject effects in laboratory research: An examination of subject roles, demand characteristics, and valid inferences. *Psychological Bulletin, 77*, 273–295.

WEBSTER, J. G., & WAKSHLAG, J. (1985). Measuring exposure to television. In D. Zillmann & J. Bryant (Eds.), *Selective exposure to communication* (pp. 35–62). Hillsdale, NJ: Erlbaum.

WEIGEL, R. H., LOOMIS, J. W., & SOJA, M. J. (1980). Race relations on prime time television. *Journal of Personality and Social Psychology, 39*, 884–893.

WEIGEL, R. H., VERNON, D. T. A., & TOGNACCI, L. N. (1974). Specificity of the attitude of a determinant of attitude-behavior congruence. *Journal of Personality and Social Psychology, 30*, 724–728.

WEINER, B. (1979). A theory of motivation for some classroom experiences. *Journal of Educational Psychology, 71*, 3–25.

WEINER, B. (1980). A cognitive (attribution)-emotion-action model of motivated behavior: An analysis of judgments of help-giving. *Journal of Personality and Social Psychology, 39*(2), 186–200.

WEINER, B. (1982). The emotional consequences of causal attributions. In M. S. Clark & S. T. Fiske (Eds.), *Affect and cognition: The 17th annual Carnegie Symposium on Cognition*. Hillsdale, NJ: Erlbaum.

WEINER, B. (1986). *An attributional theory of motivation and emotion*. New York: Springer-Verlag.

WEINER, B., RUSSELL, D., & LERMAN, D. (1979). The cognition-emotion process in achievement-related contexts. *Journal of Personality and Social Psychology, 37*, 1211–1220.

WEISS, R. S. (1973). *Loneliness: The experience of emotional and social isolation*. Cambridge, MA: MIT Press.

WEISS, R. S. (1974). The provisions of social relationships. In Z. Rubin (Ed.), *Doing unto others*. Englewood Cliffs, NJ: Prentice-Hall.

WEISS, W., & FINE, B. J. (1956). The effect of induced

aggressiveness on opinion change. *Journal of Abnormal and Social Psychology*, *52*, 109–114.

WELLMAN, B., & WHITAKER, M. (1974). *High-rise, low-rise: The effects of high-density living*. Toronto: Ministry of State, Urban Affairs, Canada, B.74.29.

WELLS, G. L., & HARVEY, J. H. (1977). Do people use consensus information in making causal attributions? *Journal of Personality and Social Psychology*, *35*, 279–293.

WELLS, G. L., & MURRAY, D. M. (1984). Eyewitness confidence. In G. Wells & E. Loftus (Eds.), *Eyewitness testimony: Psychological perspectives* (pp. 155–170). New York: Cambridge University Press.

WELLS, W. D. (1973). *Television and aggression: Replication of an experimental field study*. Unpublished manuscript, Graduate School of Business, University of Chicago.

WERNER, C. M., BROWN, B. B., & DAMRON, G. (1981). Territorial marking in a game arcade. *Journal of Personality and Social Psychology*, *41*(6), 1094–1104.

WERNER, E. E. (1979). *Cross-cultural child development*. Monterey, CA: Brooks/Cole.

WETZEL, C. G., & WALTON, M. D. (1985). Developing biased social judgments: The false-consensus effect. *Journal of Personality and Social Psychology*, *49*, 1352–1359.

WHITE, G. L. (1976). *The social psychology of romantic jealousy*. Doctoral dissertation, University of California, Los Angeles, University Microfilms No. 77–7700.

WHITE, G. L. (1980). Physical attractiveness and courtship progress. *Journal of Personality and Social Psychology*, *39*, 660–668.

WHITE, G. L. (1981). Jealousy and partner's perceived motive for attraction to a rival. *Social Psychology Quarterly*, *44*(1), 24–30.

WHITE, L. A. (1979). Erotica and aggression: The influence of sexual arousal, positive affect, and negative affect on aggression behavior. *Journal of Personality and Social Psychology*, *37*, 591–601.

WHITE, R. K. (1970). *Nobody wanted war: Misperception in Vietnam and other wars*. Garden City, NY: Doubleday.

WHITLEY, B. E. (1983). Sex role orientation and self-esteem: A critical meta-analytic review. *Journal of Personality and Social Psychology*, *44*, 765–778.

WHITLEY, B. E., JR. (1986). *Masculinity, femininity, and self-esteem: A mutlitrait-multimethod analysis*. Paper presented at the annual meeting of the American Psychological Association, Washington, D.C.

WHYTE, W. H., JR. (1956). *The organization man*. New York: Simon and Schuster.

WICHMAN, H. (1970). Effects of isolation and communication on cooperation in a two-person game. *Journal of Personality and Social Psychology*, *16*, 114–120.

WICKER, A. W. (1969). Attitudes versus action: The relationship of verbal and overt behavior responses to attitude objects. *Journal of Social Issues*, *25*(4), 41–78.

WICKER, A. W. (1971). An examination of the "other variables" explanation of attitude-behavior inconsistency. *Journal of Personality and Social Psychology*, *19*, 18–30.

WIEBE, D. J., & McCALLUM, D. M. (1986). Health practices and hardiness as mediators in the stress-illness relationship. *Health Psychology*, *5*, 425–438.

WIESENTHAL, D. L., ENDLER, N. S., COWARD, T. R., & EDWARDS, J. (1976). Reversibility of relative competence as a determinant of conformity across different perceptual tasks. *Representative Research in Social Psychology*, *7*, 319–342.

WILDER, D. A. (1977). Perception of groups, size of opposition, and social influence. *Journal of Experimental Social Psychology*, *13*, 253–258.

WILDER, D. A. (1978). Perceiving persons as a group: Effects on attributions of causality and beliefs. *Social Psychology*, *1*, 13–23.

WILDER, D. A. (1981). Perceiving persons as a group: Categorization and intergroup relations. In D. L. Hamilton (Ed.), *Cognitive processes in stereotyping and intergroup behavior* (pp. 213–257). Hillsdale, NJ: Erlbaum.

WILDER, D. A. (1986). Social categorization: Implications for creation and reduction of intergroup bias. In L. Berkowitz (Ed.), *Advances in Experimental Social Psychology* (Vol. 19, pp. 291–355). New York: Academic Press.

WILDER, D. A., & SHAPIRO, P. N. (1984). Role of outgroup cues in determining social identity. *Journal of Personality and Social Psychology*, *47*, 342–348.

WILKE, H., & LANZETTA, J. T. (1970). The obligation to help: The effects of amount of prior help on subsequent helping behavior. *Journal of Experimental Social Psychology*, *6*, 488–493.

WILLIAMSON, J. B. (1974). The stigma of public dependency: A comparison of alternative forms of public aid to the poor. *Social Problems*, *22*, 213–238.

WILLS, T. A. (1984). Supportive functions of interpersonal relationships. In S. Cohen & L. Syme (Eds.), *Social support and health* (pp. 61–82). New York: Academic Press.

WILSON, E. O. (1971). *The insect societies*. Cambridge, MA: Belknap Press of Harvard University Press.

WILSON, E. O. (1975). *Sociobiology, the new synthesis*. Cambridge, MA: Harvard University Press.

WILSON, L., & ROGERS, R. W. (1975). The fire this time:

Effects of race of target, insult, and potential retaliation on black aggression. *Journal of Personality and Social Psychology*, *32*, 857–864.

WILSON, T. D., & LASSITER, G. D. (1982). Increasing intrinsic interest with superfluous extrinsic constraints. *Journal of Personality and Social Psychology*, *42*, 811–819.

WOLF, S. (1985). Manifest and latent influence of majorities and minorities. *Journal of Personality and Social Psychology*, *48*(4), 899–908.

WOLFENSTEIN, E. V. (1967). *The revolutionary personality*. Princeton, NJ: Princeton University Press.

WOLFENSTEIN, M., & KLIMAN, G. (Eds.). (1965). *Children and the death of a president*. Garden City, NY: Doubleday.

WOLFINGER, R., & LINQUITI, P. (1981). Tuning in and turning out. *Public Opinion*, *4*, 56–60.

WOLFINGER, R. E., & ROSENSTONE, S. J. (1980). *Who votes?* New Haven, CT: Yale University Press.

WOLFSON, M. R., & SALANCIK, G. R. (1977). Observer orientation and actor-observer differences in attributions for failure. *Journal of Experimental Social Psychology*, *13*, 441–451.

WOLL, S. (1986). So many to choose from: Decision strategies in videodating. *Journal of Social and Personal Relationships*, *3*(1), 43–52.

WOLLIN, D. D., & MONTAGNE, M. (1981). College classroom environment. *Environment and Behavior*, *13*(6), 707–716.

WOOD, W. (1982). Retrieval of attitude-relevant information from memory: Effects on susceptibility to persuasion and on intrinsic motivation. *Journal of Personality and Social Psychology*, *42*, 798–810.

WOOD, W., & EAGLY, W. H. (1981). Stages in the analysis of persuasive messages: The role of causal attributions and message comprehension. *Journal of Personality and Social Psychology*, *40*, 246–259.

WOOD, W., KALLGREN, C., & PRIESLER, R. (1985). Access to attitude relevant information in memory as a determinant of persuasion. *Journal of Experimental Social Psychology*, *21*, 73–85.

WOODWORTH, R. D. (1938). *Experimental psychology*. New York: Holt.

WORCHEL, S. (1984). The darker side of helping: The social dynamics of helping and cooperation. In E. Staub et al. (Eds.), *Development and maintenance of prosocial behavior: International perspectives on positive morality*. New York: Plenum.

WORCHEL, S., & BROWN, E. H. (1984). The role of plausibility in influencing environmental attributions. *Journal of Experimental Social Psychology*, *20*, 86–96.

WORCHEL, S., & TEDDIE, C. (1976). The experience of crowding: A two-factor theory. *Journal of Personality and Social Psychology*, *34*, 30–40.

WORCHEL, S., & YOHAI, S. (1979). The role of attribution in the experience of crowding. *Journal of Experimental Social Psychology*, *15*, 91–104.

WORTMAN, C. B. (1975). Some determinants of perceived control. *Journal of Personality and Social Psychology*, *31*, 282–294.

WORTMAN, C. B. (1976). Causal attributions and personal control. In J. H. Harvey, W. Ickes, & R. F. Kidd (Eds.), *New directions in attribution research* (Vol. 1, pp. 23–52). Hillsdale, NJ: Erlbaum.

WORTMAN, C. B. (1984). Social support and the cancer patient: Conceptual and methodologic issues. *Cancer*, *53*, 2339–2360.

WORTMAN, C. B., & DUNKEL-SCHETTER, C. (1979). Interpersonal relationships and cancer: A theoretical analysis. *Journal of Social Issues*, *35*(1), 120–155.

WYER, R. S., JR. (1974). Changes in meaning and halo effects in personality impression formation. *Journal of Personality and Social Psychology*, *29*, 829–835.

WYER, R. S., JR. (1976). An investigation of relations among probability estimates. *Organizational behavior and human performance*, *15*, 1–18.

WYER, R. S., JR., & SRULL, T. K. (1980). The processing of social stimulus information: A conceptual integration. In R. Hastie, et al. (Eds.), *Person memory: The cognitive basis of social perception*. Hillsdale, NJ: Erlbaum.

WYER, R. S., JR., & SRULL, T. K. (1981). Category accessibility: Some theoretical and empirical issues concerning the processing of social stimulus information. In E. T. Higgins, C. P. Herman, & M. P. Zanna (Eds.), *Social cognition: The Ontario symposium*, (Vol. 1, pp. 161–198). Hillsdale, NJ: Erlbaum.

YUKL, G. A. (1981). *Leadership in organizations*. Englewood Cliffs, NJ: Prentice-Hall.

ZAJONC, R. B. (1965). Social facilitation. *Science*, *149*, 269–274.

ZAJONC, R. B. (1968). Attitudinal effects of mere exposure. *Journal of Personality and Social Psychology*, (Monograph Suppl., Pt. 2), 1–29.

ZAJONC, R. B. (1980). Feeling and thinking: Preferences need no inferences. *American Psychologist*, *35*, 151–175.

ZANNA, M. P., & COOPER, J. (1974). Dissonance and the pill: An attribution approach to studying the arousal properties of dissonance. *Journal of Personality and Social Psychology*, *29*, 703–709.

ZANNA, M. P., & HAMILTON, D. L. (1977). Further evidence for meaning change in impression formation. *Journal of Experimental Social Psychology*, *13*, 224–238.

ZEICHNER, A., & PIHL, R. O. (1979). Effects of alcohol and behavior contingencies on human aggression. *Journal of Abnormal Psychology*, *88*, 153–160.

ZILLMANN, D., & BRYANT, J. (1974). Effect of residual

excitation on the emotional response to provocation and delayed aggressive behavior. *Journal of Personality and Social Psychology, 30,* 782–791.

ZILLMANN, D., & SAPOLSKY, B. S. (1977). What mediates the effect of mild erotica on annoyance and hostile behavior in males? *Journal of Personality and Social Psychology, 35,* 587–596.

ZIMBARDO, P. G. (1970). The human choice: Individuation, reason and order versus deindividuation, impulse and chaos. In N. J. Arnold & D. Levine (Eds.), *Nebraska symposium on motivation, 1969.* Lincoln: University of Nebraska Press.

ZIMBARDO, P. G., WEISENBERG, M., FIRESTONE, I., & LEVY, B. (1965). Communicator effectiveness in producing pubic conformity and private attitude change. *Journal of Personality, 33,* 233–256.

ZIMMERMAN, D. H., & WEST, C. (1975). Sex roles, interruptions and silences in conversation. In B. Thorne & N. Henley (Eds.), *Language and sex: Difference and dominance* (pp. 105–129). Rowley, MA: Newbury House.

ZUCKERMAN, A. S. (1984). The limits of political behavior: Individual calculations and survival during the Holocaust. *Political Psychology, 5,* 37–52.

ZUCKERMAN, M. (1979). Attribution of success and failure revisited, or: The motivational bias is alive and well in attribution theory. *Journal of Personality, 47,* 245–287.

ZUCKERMAN, M., AMIDON, M. D., BISHOP, S. E., & POMERANTZ, S. D. (1982). Face and tone of voice in the communication of deception. *Journal of Personality and Social Psychology, 43,* 347–357.

ZUCKERMAN, M., DEPAULO, B. M., & ROSENTHAL, R. (1981). Verbal and nonverbal communication of deception. In L. Berkowitz (Ed.), *Advances in experimental social psychology* (Vol. 14). New York: Academic Press.

ZUCKERMAN, M., LARRANCE, D. T., SPIEGEL, N. H. & KLORMAN, R. (1981). Controlling nonverbal displays: Facial expressions and tone of voice. *Journal of Experimental Social Psychology, 17,* 506–524.

NAME INDEX

SUBJECT INDEX

Discounting cue, 220–21
Discounting principle, 122, 125
Discrepancy, and attitude change, 193–94, 196, 203–4, 213, 215–18
Discrimination, 416, 417, 419, 427–28
Disgust, 76, 77, 79
Disinhibition, 312
Disjunctive task, 388
Displaced aggression, 308–10, 313, 422–23
Dispositional attribution, 124, 126
  and interpersonal conflict, 262
  and judgments of trustworthiness, 200
  overuse of, 136–37
  about salient people, 424
Dissimilarity, 245
Dissonance, postdecisional, 176–78
Dissonance, theory, 167
Distance. *See* Personal space
Distraction, and attitude change, 218–19
Distraction-conflict model, 384
Distinctiveness information, 123, 140
Distressing events
  and illness, 512–13
  need for causal attribution, 121
Divorce
  effect on children, 235
  and sex ratios, 462
Domestic violence. *See* Family violence
Dominance, and facial expression, 77–78
Dominant response, 384
Domino theory of communism, 104–6
Door-in-the-face technique, 370
Dormitory design, 491–93
Double minorities, 364
Drives
  dissonance as, 176, 187–88
  social facilitation and inhibition, 384
Drugs, and aggression, 309

Ebbinghaus forgetting curve, 220
Economic conditions
  and aggression, 291–92
  effect on voting behavior, 542–44
Efficiency, of communication networks, 382
Egocentric bias, 144
Eichmann defense, 5–6
Elaboration-likelihood model, 164–65, 197, 207, 214–15, 217, 218–19, 222
Elites, decision making by, 538, 565–66
Emergencies, 25–26, 348
Emotional concern, 518
Emotional loneliness, 234
Emotion-focused coping, 515–16
Emotions. *See also* Affect; Feelings
  and attributions, 129–34
  nonverbal communication of, 80–85, 86
  in passionate love, 279
  in personal relationships, 257, 274–75
  recognition of, 75–77
  in romantic love, 281–82
  universal expression of, 77–79
Empathetic concern, 339–40
Environment
  in gestalt theory, 12
  and helping behavior, 335–36
  in learning theory, 11

Environment (*cont.*)
  primary and secondary appraisal, 511–12
Environmental psychology, 472–97
  architectural design, 490–95
  crowding, 478–85
  human spatial behavior, 472–78
  life in the city, 495–97
  stress due to noise, 486–90
Equality rule, 260
Equity, actual vs. psychological, 261
Equity theory, 260–61, 344–45
Escalation phenomenon, 312
Escape from Freedom (Fromm), 545
Ethics, in research, 45–50
Ethnocentrism, 416
Evaluation. *See also* Person perception
  averaging principle, 54–55, 60
  of communicator, 198–203
  consistency in, 56–57
  dimensions of, 53–54
  gender bias in, 452–53
  of ingroup vs. outgroup members, 427
  positivity bias, 58–59
  and prejudice, 417–18
  and salience, 64
Evaluation apprehension, 334
Evaluative (affective) component of attitudes, 156, 158–59, 176–77
Evolutionary theory, 19
  facial expression of emotion, 77
  gender differences, 458, 459
  prosocial behavior, 342
Evolution of Human Sexuality (Symons), 459
Exchange relationship, 268
Exchange theory, 352
Expectancy-value theory, 14–15
  attitude formation, 164
  fear and attitude change, 206–7
  interpersonal attraction, 244
Expectations. *See also* Schemas
  and attributions, 117–18, 125–26, 146
  and information gathering, 94–95, 99
  and interpretation of symptoms, 523
  and judgments of covariation, 98
  and judgments of trustworthiness, 200
  and schemas, 102, 103
  self-fulfilling prophecies, 112, 425–26
Experience. *See* Past experience
Experimental research design, 28–29, 30–31, 32 (*table*)
Experimenter bias, 42–43
Expertise
  basis of power, 367
  of communicator, 198–99, 201
  and leadership, 403
External attribution, 119
  overemphasis by actors, 137–40
  reasons for making, 125
  self-serving, 142
  tests of, 123
  and willingness to help, 341
External validity, 34, 36
  of media violence studies, 317–18
Eyebrows, emotional expressiveness, 77–78
Eye contact, 81–83, 277
Eye-of-the-beholder effect, 72–75
Eyewitness identification, 76

Facial expressions
  and deception, 86, 88
  judging emotions by, 75–79
  in nonverbal communication, 83
  smiling, 77–78, 228–29
Facilitation, social, 383–84
Facts, vs. attitudes, 159
Failure, attribution of, 118, 119, 133, 142, 143–44, 146
Fair exchange, 260–61, 265
False consensus, 144–46, 549
Familiarity, 245–47, 251
Family, as a group, 377
Family violence
  escalation of, 291
  incidence, 287–88
  social heredity, 305
  and verbal aggression, 313
Fantasy aggression, 313
Fascinating Womanhood (Andelin), 468
Favoritism, to ingroup, 427
Fear
  affiliating to reduce, 229–31
  arousal of, and attitude change, 205–7
  arousal of, and health behaviors, 503–4
  identifying emotion, 76, 77, 78, 79
  and personal relationships, 275
  of violent crime, 3
Federal Communications Commission, 315
Federal government research guidelines, 45–50
Feelings. *See also* Affect; Emotions
  aggressive, 290
  effect of attributions on, 117
  effect of schemas on, 104
  of romantic love, 279
Field research, 32, 34–35
  on media violence, 319–20, 323–24, 327
Figure/ground perception, 12–13
  and causal attribution, 137
  and negativity effect, 65
  and salience, 63
First impressions. *See* Impression formation
Foot-in-the-door technique, 369, 370
Foreign policy
  effect of schemas on, 104–6
  elite decision making, 565–66
Forewarning, effect of, 215–18
Formal organization, 377, 378
Fraternal deprivation, 430–31, 546
Freedom, loss of, in receiving help, 351–52
Frequency judgments, 107
Freudian psychology, 14
Frustration
  and aggression, 8, 29, 30, 38, 291–92, 303
  reducing, 306
Functional distance, 250
Fundamental attribution error, 136–37, 138, 139, 140, 151

Game-playing love, 281
Games, studies using, 394–98, 399
Generalized halo effect, 61
General Social Survey, 38

Interdependence (*cont.*)
  of pairs, 255–57
  and reduction of prejudice, 434, 436
Interest
  and eye contact, 81–82
  intrinsic, 127–29
  principle of least, 262
Internal attribution, 119
  anger produced by, 292
  overuse of, 136–37
  and responsibility for consequences,
    184–85
  self-serving, 142–45
  tests of, 123
Internal control, 151–53
Internal states, 72, 126–34. *See also*
    Attributions; Emotions
Internal validity, 33
International conflict, 536–66
Interpersonal attraction, 226–52
  attachment in childhood, 227–29
  basic principles, 237–38
  and cohesiveness of group, 380
  and commitment, 265
  and familiarity, 245–48
  laboratory studies, 229–31
  and loneliness, 232–36
  and personal characteristics, 238–41
  and proximity, 249–52
  and similarity, 242–45
  and social needs, 229–31
Interpersonal level of analysis, 6–7, 8
Interuniversity Consortium for Political
    and Social Research (ICPSR), 38
Interview techniques, 37
Intimacy
  component of love, 282–83
  and self-disclosure, 269–74
Intimate distance, 473
Introspection, 126–27
Investment, in relationship, 266, 267

Jealousy, 282
Jews
  Nazi persecution, 5–6, 46, 289, 339,
    413, 566
  stereotypes about, 415, 416 (*table*), 436
Jigsaw technique, 435–36
Jonestown, 566
Joy, 275
Judgment. *See* Social judgment
June Bug epidemic, 534
Just world, illusion of, 147–49

Kerner Commission, 306
Knowledge bias, 200
Korean War, 213, 563, 564

Labeling
  of arousal as anger, 294
  of emotions, 129–33
  and self-perceived attitudes, 186
Labor, division of, 467–68
Laboratory research, 32–34
  on affiliation, 229–31
  on competition vs. cooperation,
    394–98

Laboratory research (*cont.*)
  on media violence and aggressive
    behavior, 316–17, 324–26, 327
  on social density, 484–85
Language, gender bias in, 444–45. *See also*
    Communication
Lay referral network, 523
Leadership, 400–406
  and groupthink, 393
  operational codes, 565
  political, 537–40
  structure, 400
  style, 403–6
League of Nations, 538
Learned helplessness, 149–50
Learned inhibition, 306–8
Learning
  of aggression, 294–301
  and classroom design, 492–93
  to help, 345–46
  of message, and attitude change,
    194–95
Learning mechanisms, 10–11
Learning theories, 10–11
  attachment in childhood, 228–29
  arousal and attitude change, 205, 207
  attitude formation, 161–63
  effect of media violence, 316
  impression formation, 55, 60
  reinforcement and interpersonal
    attraction, 237–38
Least effort principle, 166
Least interest principle, 262
Legitimate authority, 368
  Milgram studies, 376–77
  of physician, 521
Likability, 74, 208
Liking
  and attitude change, 201, 202, 209
  components, 238–41
  and familiarity, 245–47
  and group cohesiveness, 380
  and helping, 340–41
  vs. love, 276–77
  postdecisional changes, 176–77
  principle of, 237–38
  and proximity, 249–52
  and self-disclosure, 270–72
  and similarity, 242–45, 418
Locus of causality, 118–19
Logical error, 104
Loneliness, 232–36
  among college students, 41–42
Looking glass self, 17
Love, 274–84
Low-ball technique, 370
Loyalty, and problem solving, 264–65
Lying. *See* Deception
Lynchings, 291, 301–2, 406–7, 413, 415

Machismo syndrome, 564, 565
Mail surveys, 37
Male dominance, 468–69
Marijuana, 308
Marital conflict
  causal attribution, 121, 142–43, 144
  incidence, 263
  and jealousy, 282
  violent, 287, 305, 313

Marriage
  balance of power in, 262–63
  changing social norms, 261–62
  and interpersonal attraction, 244
  loneliness in, 236
  and love, 275
  role making in, 18
  and sex ratios, 462
Mass hysteria, 408, 524
Mass psychogenic illness, 408, 524
Matching principle, 244
Meaning
  seeking, in impression formation, 60,
    61–63
  shared, in symbolic interaction, 16, 17
  shift of, 62
Media
  effect on health behaviors, 507–8
  portrayal of women, 446–47
  role in politics, 552–63
  source of social learning of prejudice,
    421–22
  violence, 3–4, 313, 314–27
Medical treatment, 523–29
Membership group, 202
Memory, social, 13. *See also* Recall
Mental shortcuts, 106–8
Mere exposure effect, 246–47, 248
Message. *See also* Communication
  distortion of, 193–94
  learning, 194–95
Meta-analysis, 463–64
Middle-range theories, 20, 26
Mimicry, 83
Mindlessness, and compliance, 365
Minimal effects model, 553
Minimal intergroup discrimination effect,
    427
Minimal intergroup situation, 427
Minimal risk, in research, 46, 48–50
Minorities
  influence in groups, 363–65
  influence of prejudice on political
    response to, 418
Mirror image, international misperception,
    564
Misattribution, of one's own emotional
    state, 131–32, 187
Misperception
  due to categorization, 67
  and international conflict, 564
  of message, 193–94, 204
Mob behavior, 301–2, 406–7
Modeling, and learning to help, 345–46
Mood, and prosocial behavior, 339
Morale, and communication network, 382
Motivated selective exposure, 556–57
Motivation
  and deception, 86–88, 89
  and leadership, 403
  for prosocial behavior, 339–40
  self-perception of, 127–29
  and social facilitation and inhibition of
    performance, 384
Motivational biases, 142–47
Motivational theories, 14–16
  of attitudes, 161, 163–65
  of prejudice, 420, 422–23, 428
Multiple channels, 84–85
Murder, 4, 5–6, 287